MORMON CINEMA
Origins to 1952

Mormon Arts Center
P. O. Box 230465
New York, NY 10023-0008
mormonartscenter.org

ISBN-13: 978-0-692-13709-3

cover images courtesty of the L. Tom Perry Special Collections,
Harold B. Lee Library, Brigham Young University, Provo, Utah

Designed by Connor King and Cameron King
Printed in U.S.A.

Mormon Cinema was published on the occasion of the Mormon Arts
Center Festival, June 28-30, 2018. The Center gratefully acknowledges
the contributions of donors who made this publication possible.

MORMON CINEMA

Origins to 1952

RANDY ASTLE

MORMON ARTS CENTER
NEW YORK CITY

CONTENTS

Preface   i

Introduction   1

    Mormonism and the Movies   1

    Five Waves of Mormon Film   7

01 Origins   13

    A History of the Church   13

    Early Artistic Roots and Parallels   22

    Proto-Cinema: Modernization in Painting and Art   40

    Early Mormonism and the Magic Lantern View   50

    The Great Accommodation and Arrival of Cinema   61

02 The First Wave: The New Frontier (July 1898-23 October 1929)   71

    Mormons and the Mainstream Industry   73

       Mormons at the Movies: Commercial Exhibition and Distribution   73

       "Preaching the Gospel of Better Recreation": The Ward Movie and Private Church Film Exhibition   97

       Mormons Go to Hollywood   110

       Hollywood Comes to the Mormons   129

    Mainstream Depictions of Mormons   141

       The First Films: 1898-1904   141

       A Trip to Salt Lake City: The Anti-Mormon Film Begins   144

       The Roots of Anti-Mormon Cinema   149

       The First Assault: 1911-1912   160

Contents

Waxing and Waning: Anti-Mormon Films 1914-1922   172

Institutional and Independent Films   190

The Mormons' First Movies   190

The First Features: *One Hundred Years of Mormonism* and
The Story of the Book of Mormon   195

The Clawson Brothers   207

Institutional Broadcasting Begins   219

All Faces West   222

The End of an Era   229

03 The Second Wave: Home Cinema   233

Mainstream Depictions of Mormons   238

The Production Code: A Kinder Hollywood   238

Newsreels and Nonfiction   248

The Major Features: 1940-1950   256

Mormons and the Mainstream Industry   283

At Home in the Industry   283

Independent Mormon Films   313

Corianton and Commerical Production in the 1930s   313

Home Movies as Home Cinema   329

Institutional Films   345

The Church Centennial and *The Message of the Ages*   345

Home Media: Filmstrips and Missionary Media   353

Home Distribution and Exhibition   374

Postwar: Deseret Film Productions and the 1947 Utah Centennial   392

Home Broadcasting: From Radio to Television   411

The Welfare Films   424

Contents

A Sacred Film: The Temple Endowment   428

Creating the BYU Motion Picture Department   436

Notes   443

Preface   443

Introduction   443

1 - Origins   448

2- The First Wave: The New Frontier   476

3 - The Second Wave: Home Cinema   558

Index   607

PREFACE

In writing a study of Mormon cinema I have hopefully interested two otherwise unaffiliated groups: students of Mormonism and of film. While there are happily occasional overlaps in these groups, I have tried to write with the knowledge that for the most part those familiar with Mormon history and terminology might be ignorant of cinematic theory and history, and vice versa. I have therefore attempted to address a dual audience, explaining the details of Mormonism for the benefit of cinephiles and those of cinema for the benefit of Latter-day Saints and pupils of Mormon studies. I hope that this will not alienate either group by over-explaining the already familiar but will rather allow for greater inclusion and understanding for both types of reader. In either case I have tried to keep such contextual distractions to a minimum and place longer explanations in the footnotes.

There is at the outset, however, a need to explain some basic Mormon terminology for those who might not be familiar with it. The official name of the Church is The Church of Jesus Christ of Latter-day Saints. The common nickname of *Mormon* comes of course from the Book of Mormon, a work of scripture published by Church founder Joseph Smith in 1830 that is peculiar to the Church and its offshoots. Members of the Church, however, just as often refer to themselves as Latter-day Saints with the abbreviation *LDS* serving a modifier, as in *LDS Church*. Modern Church leaders periodically advise adherents to avoid the term *Mormon* and instead use the Church's full name and refer to themselves as members of the Church of Jesus Christ. For instance, in 2011 Apostle M. Russell Ballard said, "We do not need to stop using the name *Mormon* when appropriate, but we should continue to give emphasis to the full and correct name of the Church itself. In other words, we should avoid and discourage the term 'Mormon Church.'"[1] Therefore, there has been some mild disagreement over whether to call films relating to this movement *Mormon cinema* or *LDS cinema*. Some have informally argued that *LDS cinema* refers exclusively to institutionally produced films, those made by the Church itself, with *Mormon cinema* implying independent productions. However, given each term's broad usage—for instance, the

very popular *LDS Film* Festival exclusively features independent, not institutional, films—I don't believe that to be the case. In fact, while each possibly
connotes distinct characteristics, I find the difference largely immaterial and,
to adhere to the dominant usage in Mormon studies and journals like *Dialogue,
Sunstone, BYU Studies,* the *Journal of Mormon History,* and *Mormon Historical
Studies*—and, indeed, the name of the Mormon Arts Center which is publishing
this book—I generally use the terms *Mormon, Mormon Church,* and *Mormon
cinema* throughout. Although fundamentalist Mormons—that is, contemporary
polygamists such as members of the Fundamentalist Church of Jesus Christ
of Latter-day Saints—are not members of the LDS Church, they are frequently pertinent to discussions of film and the Mormon movement, and using the
broader term Mormon allows me to include them when appropriate along with
mainstream Latter-day Saints. I recognize that even the term *fundamentalist
Mormon* is problematic, and I hope that my use of these terms is not offensive to
either LDS or FLDS readers, and that all readers can recognize the doctrinal and
organizational differences between different branches of the Latter-day Saint
movement while recognizing their similar treatment in many films and television programs. Other Mormon groups, particularly the Community of Christ—
formerly the Reorganized Church of Jesus Christ of Latter-day Saints—have
featured in fewer films and hence receive minimal attention in these pages.

I am also aware of the awkwardness of such idiosyncratic and potentially alien-
ating terms as *non-Mormon* and *nonmember*, ubiquitous in Mormon parlance,
to indicate those not of the faith; again, Church leaders like Elder Ballard have
rightly counseled against their use.[2] Despite these difficulties I have nonethe-
less resorted to these terms rather extensively to indicate individuals, primarily filmmakers, who are not Latter-day Saints. I have done so as a convenient
shorthand without any intent of oversimplifying complex social and theological
issues, including the actual religious or sociological views of these people.
Likewise, it is for reasons of clarity alone that I use the capitalized *Church* to
indicate the LDS or Mormon Church, to which I refer much more frequently than
others, and the lower-case *church* for other denominations or the Christian
movement in general.

This work is a history of what is in many respects an ethnic cinema. Unlike
purely racial or national cinemas, however, Mormon cinema also includes a
devotional component, one that can in other contexts, such as theological or
ecumenical discussions, prove contentious. I have therefore not written with
an agenda to prove Mormonism true or false, but have merely attempted to

Preface

confine myself to the historical narrative and cultural artifacts. I do, however, occasionally use language that assumes Mormon doctrines are true and Church members' spiritual experiences real. I have done this for semantic reasons, to avoid the repeated use of phrases such as "a *supposed* revelation," "a *reputed* inspiration," or "an *alleged* translation of an ancient text." Like historian Richard Bushman says at the outset of his seminal biography *Joseph Smith: Rough Stone Rolling*, I believe that in evaluating a religious people it is more fulfilling to accept the legitimacy that their beliefs have for them and focus attention on how those impulses have affected their culture and, in this case, cinema and aesthetics.[3] I believe this would be a profitable approach in a work treating any culture of faith and I hope it does not alienate those who disagree with Mormon theology.

Finally, I would like to thank all the historians, scholars, filmmakers, librarians, archivists, editors, and friends who contributed to this book. My gratitude goes to the Mormon Arts Center, Richard Bushman, and especially Glen Nelson for sponsoring and publishing this work and seeing it through its final stages of development. It would not have seen fruition without their confidence and assistance.

A version of this book first appeared as a portion of an article in a 2007 issue of *BYU Studies* (46:2) co-edited by Gideon Burton and myself. Burton, a true friend and mentor—and Assistant Professor of English at Brigham Young University—received co-authorial credit on that article due to his extensive editorial involvement in its progression over five years and two continents. While the present work is entirely my own effort, his imprint on my thinking endures and I remain extremely grateful for his guidance and input and the opportunity he gave me to be involved with that issue; though he was already a prolific and respected Mormon literary critic, his advocacy has been a driving force behind my own work and that of many others interested in Mormon film. I am also grateful for all those at *BYU Studies* for their assistance with that earlier article—and others I have written for them since—and in allowing the work's enlargement and publication outside the Brigham Young University aegis. I am particularly grateful to John W. Welch, Roger Terry, and Jennifer Hurlbut. I'm also grateful to J. Michael Hunter, BYU's Mormon Studies Librarian and Chair of the Religion/Family History Department at the Harold B. Lee Library, who invited me to revise and update that article for Praeger's broad-reaching two-volume *Mormons and Popular Culture* in 2012. The current work represents half of that article expanded to a book-length treatise.

Thanks to the many people who assisted with my publications and presentations on other areas of Mormon cinema: the late Laraine Wilkins, Angela Hallstrom, the late Valerie Holladay, Scott Hatch, Kristine Haglund, Lavina Fielding Anderson, Sherry Baker, Joel Campbell, Lane Williams, Stephen Carter, Micah Nickolaisen, Lindsay Hansen Park, Jim Murphy, and Mary Ellen Robertson. Appreciation also goes to the superb video collections of Mormon films at the Orem (Utah) Public Library and the Media Center of BYU's Harold B. Lee Library, through which I was able to access the majority of the nearly 1,600 films viewed for my study of Mormon film; special thanks go to Julie Williamsen, then the HBLL's Theatre & Media Arts and Communications Librarian, and the library's Mormon Media Committee for their generous assistance in purchasing dozens of DVDs of otherwise unavailable titles entirely for my research purposes. Williamsen also devoted precious funds to allow me to work for six months as the library's Mormon Film Specialist, an opportunity through which I was able to complete much of my research while hopefully providing useful bibliographical material to the library in return. Trevor Alvord, Cyndee Frazier, Cindy Brightenburg, John Murphy, Norm Gillespie, James Dearden, and James V. D'arc, all at the HBLL, also helped with this effort, procuring and creating VHS tapes and DVDs and screening film prints not available on video. Richard Dutcher, in addition to answering many questions, also showed me film and video versions of his films that aren't publicly available. Also special thanks go to D'arc, Peter G. Czerny, Tom Lefler, Richard Alan Nelson, and Roger Terry for reviewing large portions of the manuscript and giving in-depth notes, comments, and corrections. My friend and neighbor Kent S. Larsen II, a scholar and publisher of Mormon literature, provided invaluable assistance and encouragement over many years while the manuscript proceeded slowly forward, keeping it alive and progressing toward publication.

Others who merit mention for their personal help include Mary Christenson Aagard, Joyce Anderson, Travis Anderson, Xan Aranda, Michael Austin, Lex de Azevedo, Thomas Baggaley, Amy Barrington, Chris Beheim, Karen Bolzendahl, Nathan Botts, Barrett Burgin, Brian Cannon, Jared Cardon, Kjerste Christensen, T. C. Christensen, Nick Dawson, Lisa DeLong, John-Charles Duffy, Dean Duncan, Travis Eberhard, Joyce and Charles Farnsworth, Tim Fowers, Terryl Givens, Don Godfrey, Kurt Hale, Robert Hall, Carolyn Hanson, John Hatch, Eric Hawkins, Michael Hicks, Preston Hunter, David Kent Jacobs, Matt Jennejohn, Peter N. Johnson, John Madsen, April Chabries Makgoeng, Brandt Malone, Robert Nelson, Ardis Parshall, Marvin Payne, Josh Probert, Jorge Ramirez Rivera, Cindy Reid, John Reim, Tod Robbins, Alyssa Rock, Eric Samuelsen, Michael Schaertl,

Preface

Mike Sellers, Vicki Dawn Nordgren Shields, Reed Smoot, Chantelle Squires, Robert Starling, Sharon Swenson, Ben Unguren, Michael Van Wagenen, Ken Verdoia, Christian Vuissa, Greg Whiteley, John Williams, Dan Wotherspoon, and many others who I'm surely neglecting to mention here. The twelve students in my LDS Cinema class at BYU winter semester 2006 offered additional insights and helped me refine many of my ideas, and thanks go to Sharon Swenson and Tom Lefler for allowing me that teaching opportunity.

A general thanks must go to the professors who have most influenced my thoughts concerning film history and theory: James Felt at Olympus High School in Salt Lake City for first interesting me in film, unbeknownst to him; Dean Duncan, Darl Larsen, April Chabries Makgoeng (also my first and best employer in a production setting), Eric Samuelsen, and Sharon Swenson at BYU, for introducing me to film history and theory proper through core courses and wonderful excursions into areas like film music and Asian cinema; and Alan Bernstein—who taught me to be precise, profound, and generous in my film work—Barry Salt— who personified scientific exactness coupled with unbounded enthusiasm in film analysis—and the rest of the faculty at the London Film School, who consistently worked theoretical underpinnings into our practical production work.

I'm equally grateful to the pioneers of Mormon film history for their work that serves as the foundation without which this book would have been impossible: James V. D'arc, David Kent Jacobs, Richard Alan Nelson, and Wetzel O. Whitaker, who not only created many of the films in question but had the foresight to record his experiences as well.

Particular thanks to my parents Lynn and Marian Astle for their logistical support and research while I have lived geographically far from the center of Mormon cinema, and for housing me—and watching their grandchildren far beyond the call of duty—when I visited Utah and spent too many hours at the library or watching DVDs. My mother did not live to see the finished product, but I hope she would be pleased. Finally, immeasurable love and gratitude go to my wife Carol for her unshakable support, her inexhaustible patience, and other reasons far too innumerable to list. Carol, you are my light and my rock and by far the most important thing in my life. I love you more than I can say or show and don't know what I would be without you. This book is for you.

INTRODUCTION

What is a church and what is a theatre? Are they two and not one? Can they exist sepa-rate?— William Blake, ca. 1810 [1]

Mormons and the Movies

Yoda is not President Kimball, to begin with.

But as a member of the Church of Jesus Christ of Latter-day Saints, I spent the 1980s and '90s firmly believing that he was. Indeed, in my experience it seems most American Mormons believe that the diminutive Jedi master was based physically, mentally, and emotionally on Spencer Woolley Kimball, the President of the LDS or Mormon Church at the time Yoda first appeared in *The Empire Strikes Back* in 1980. Indeed, the evidences were—and remain—compelling: President Kimball was the presiding High Priest over the entire Church; Yoda was the master Jedi, the most revered and powerful in the entire galaxy. President Kimball was famously short and, like Yoda, was thus seen as a spiritual giant in a small, frail, and ill body. President Kimball's face seemed quite similar to Yoda's and his ears, though smaller, pointed slightly out in the same way. His wispy hair was an exact match. And his most distinctive feature, his voice, raspy and low after throat surgery in 1957, was uncannily similar to puppeteer Frank Oz's vocalization for the *Star Wars* films. President Kimball was a man who often walked with a cane but, like Yoda with Luke, urged Church members to lengthen their stride, try harder, go faster, and reach improbable heights. Yoda's instruction from the middle of *The Empire Strikes Back*—"No, try not. Do or do not. There is no try"—seemed simply an embellished version of President Kimball's famously oft-repeated maxim: "Do it." [2]

Now, years later, I am unable to uncover any evidence that Yoda's designers had President Kimball in mind [3]—despite the involvement of producer Gary Kurtz, who was raised as a Mormon, on the first two *Star Wars* films [4]—but the fact that this belief remains part of Mormon folklore today illustrates how perva-sively cinema permeates Mormon life and how complexly it relates to Mormons' beliefs and culture. Indeed, the *Star Wars* franchise is an apt example, as its

Introduction

cultural resonance extends far beyond Yoda to include alleged plot similarities between the films and the Book of Mormon and the rather pervasive belief that the Force—and essentially all of *Star Wars* cosmology—is based on Mormon theology, primarily principles such as the priesthood, Light of Christ, and Holy Ghost, which together Mormons believe comprise divine gifts, authority, and enabling agents that may give the power to discern thoughts, receive divine guidance, or even perform miracles; hence young Mormon women and especially men are frequently likened to young Padawan Jedi-in-training, learning to use these powers and resist the allure of the Dark Side. Personally I have heard such comparisons preached many times in Mormon worship services, and not long ago I saw a speaker show (illegally) a lengthy clip from Genndy Tartakovsky's animated *Star Wars: Clone Wars* (2003) television series to a group of teenage Mormon boys to draw exactly these parallels. Even as early as 1978, a year after the original *Star Wars'* release, Benjamin Urrutia wrote in the Mormon literary journal *Dialogue* that other cultures had possibly influenced the film before asserting that "the strongest similarities . . . in basic themes, ideology, and philosophy, can be found in the Book of Mormon and other scriptures of the Church."[5] And speaking in 1992, prominent Mormon historian Richard L. Bushman observed that "Latter-day Saints equate Force with Holy Ghost and consider it a religious achievement when Luke does trust the Force." Thinking phenomenologically about how audiences view the films, he mused that non-Mormon spectators might just come to unwittingly share some Mormon beliefs, such as a desire to listen to the Holy Spirit, while watching.[6] Even if George Lucas had never even heard of the Book of Mormon, the permeation of *Star Wars* into Mormon thought is astounding, including through the most recent Disney-produced films.[7] It speaks volumes that, in my case, I do not recall how the association between Yoda and President Kimball filtered down to me: it was simply part of my Mormon culture.

To many, this close symbiosis between Mormonism and cinema may be surprising. It certainly doesn't conform to the perhaps common image of Mormons as modern Puritans, political and cultural conservatives who avoid "lurid" popular culture and would at best produce ascetic art, if any. But this view misses the depth to which performance, art, drama, literature, and kitsch are infused into popular Mormonism, at least in North America where Mormons are in fact some of the most—not least—eager consumers of popular culture. In a 2008 interview the five-time Oscar-nominated actress Amy Adams, who was raised in the Church until she was a teenager, was asked if her family's faith stood in the way of her desire to act. Her simple response: "Are you kidding? Mormons are the most performing group of people you've ever met!"[8] Anyone who's heard of the Osmonds would most likely agree.

And they would be right: for a culturally conservative group that even today numbers at best less than 16 million people worldwide, Mormonism has given rise to an astonishing number of writers, filmmakers, technicians, and businesspeople who have contributed immensely to the motion picture industry—and they're not all Donnys and Maries. Mormons have helped lead companies like Disney, CBS, and Kodak and contributed to the development of television, stereophonic sound, IMAX, color video, the NTSC video standard, video games, the Sundance Film Festival, 3D computer animation, and motion picture franchises as diverse as *Battlestar Galactica, Toy Story, Despicable Me,* and *Twilight,* as well as thousands of individual films ranging thematically from *Natural Born Killers* (1994) to *Napoleon Dynamite* (2004). Without Mormons there would be no Buzz Lightyear, no Minions, no flubber, no "When You Wish Upon a Star," not even *Fifty Shades of Grey* (2015). When James Barrie needed an American performer to originate the role of Peter Pan in 1904, he turned to "America's best loved actress," the Mormon-born Maude Adams.[9] And nearly thirty years later when King Kong carried his love to the top of the Empire State Building, he chose Fay Wray, also from a Mormon family.[10] In 1929 the first televised photographic image was of Mormon Pem Farnsworth and in 1940 the first public performance of stereophonic sound, at Carnegie Hall, featured the Mormon Tabernacle Choir, a feat the choir replicated in the world's first intercontinental satellite video broadcast a generation later in 1962. Today Amy Adams, Aaron Eckhart, Ryan Gosling, Keri Russell, Katherine Heigl, Yuki Saito, and the late Paul Walker, who were all born into or passed through the Church, are instantly recognizable to millions of viewers worldwide—not to mention the work of similarly affiliated directors like Hal Ashby, James Cruze, Colin Low, Neil LaBute, Lino Brocka, Don Bluth, Trent Harris, and Dustin Lance Black. When I served as a full-time missionary and people asked me if Mormons could watch television, I used to delight in answering, "Watch it? We invented it!"

Mormon subject matter is also appealing. In 1887 Sir Arthur Conan Doyle's original Sherlock Holmes novella *A Study in Scarlet* was simply another of many Victorian tales featuring Mormonism as a lurid backdrop. More recently, with nine Tony's and a legion of other awards *The Book of Mormon* became one of the most acclaimed plays on the stage, consistently selling out the most expensive tickets in Broadway history to that point and breaking records in London's West End and everywhere else it toured.[11] Among the hundreds of actors who have

Introduction

portrayed mainstream or fundamentalist Mormon characters on screen are John Wayne, Charlton Heston, Anne Hathaway, Tyrone Power, Jeanne Tripplehorn, Aaron Paul, Joseph Gordon-Levitt, Katie Holmes, Vincent Price, Helen Hunt, Amanda Seyfried, Fred Willard, Margaret O'Brien, Rodney Dangerfield, Harry Dean Stanton, Trey Parker, Meryl Streep, Paul Rudd, Chloë Sevigny, Philip Seymour Hoffman, Mary Astor, Yeardley Smith, Ben Lyon, Frank Borzage, Ward Bond, Casey Affleck, Dean Jagger, Mary-Louise Parker, Ed Harris, Jessica Lange, Jon Voight, Andrew Dice Clay, Calista Flockhart, Jean Seberg, Bill Paxton, Patrick Wilson, Julia Garner, Kathy Bates, Kevin Sorbo, Christopher Gorham (twice), Jane Darwell (twice), and character actor Russell Simpson (three times); those who have played fictionalized versions of real-life Mormons include Dustin Hoffman, Crispin Glover, Jane Seymour, Sean Penn, Kate Winslet, Paul Newman, and even Stephen Colbert—in Hoffman's case winning an Oscar for Best Actor in *Rain Man* (1988). Furthermore, directors as diverse as Alfred Hitchcock, John Ford, Danny Boyle, Edgar Reitz, Errol Morris, Henry Hathaway, Garry Marshall, Peter Greenaway, James Benning, Otto Preminger, Mike Nichols, Ross McElwee, Jonathan Demme, Paul Thomas Anderson, Matthew Barney, and Steven Soderbergh (twice) and have all explored Mormon storylines. When Homer Simpson opens his door to see Kang and Kodos—two green, slobbering, one-eyed, tentacled aliens—on his doorstep his obvious response is to roll his eyes and exclaim, "Oh great—Mormons!"

But this conviviality with cinema doesn't just apply to its production. Mormons consume movies voraciously, even inside their own chapels; indeed, for the majority of the twentieth century one of the most common social events in the Church was the "ward movie night," in which Mormon meetinghouses would be transformed into makeshift movie theaters to show "wholesome" Hollywood fare. Gideon Burton, a Brigham Young University English professor and scholar of Mormon literature and film, describes this from his own adolescence:

> For decades the ward movie was a cultural institution in the church. I personally learned the rudiments of movie capitalism as the Teacher's Quorum President in the Butler Twentieth Ward in Salt Lake City in the 70s. From the local library I checked out 16mm prints of *Snowball Express* or *The Apple Dumpling Gang* and then helped my quorum make money for camping trips by selling popcorn and charging admission to my ward neighbors. In those many years before ubiquitous VCRs, the ward movie was a principal means for Mormons to get acquainted with the film medium.[12]

Such memories are familiar for American Church members who lived between the 1920s and 1980s, but while this was the great Mormon fundraiser of the twentieth century, such film screenings were cultural as much as commercial ventures. Travis Anderson, another BYU professor and former head of the school's robust International Cinema program, recalled that his baptism at eight years of age—a traditional Mormon rite of passage—proved memorable not because of the ordinance but because it was followed by a screening of *The Three Stooges Meet Hercules* (1962), shown as part of his congregation's monthly matinee series: "I remember those films with great clarity and affection, even though they weren't always cinematic masterpieces: *Doctor Dolittle, Ice Station Zebra,* and scores of old Disney films . . . Being baptized and watching *The Three Stooges Meet Hercules.* Film and faith. The two are fused together in my mind so solidly I almost can't separate them."[13]

For decades the halls of Mormon meetinghouses have morphed naturally into makeshift movie palaces as actual worship services, not just their postludes, have become cinematic events. In 1949 Church-employed filmmaker Frank Wise explained in the Church's official magazine how future architects could incorporate projection booths into chapel designs, with angled mirrors inside the booth saving space and allowing for projection onto a screen built right into the wall. At that point "very little use of these modern teaching aids [was] in evidence in the wards of the Church,"[14] but when he revisited the subject thirteen years later in 1962 he could note that "since facilities for the use of motion picture films are now a regular requirement by the General Authorities and boards of the Church, the wards and stakes will want to provide an adequate [projection] screen just as they are already required to provide an adequate projector and operator for these occasions."[15] The occasions in question were large semiannual meetings known as stake conferences—a stake being a group of about five to twelve geographically contiguous congregations, or wards—when hundreds to even thousands of Church members would sit for at least two hours to sing hymns, pray, listen to visiting Church leaders, and, of course, watch a film.

Today many meetinghouses have a retractable screen built into the ceiling of the chapel right above the pulpit, but typical Mormon frugality and pioneer ingenuity often find a homelier solution to classroom film exhibition. Author, scholar, and memoirist Joanna Brooks recalls from growing up in Los Angeles in the 1980s that, if she and her classmates "begged hard enough, we could convince our teachers to put down their Salt Lake City–printed lesson manuals and show" Church-produced movies and filmstrips right "against the church's cool white cinder-block walls."[16]

Introduction

A favorite was Man's Search for Happiness, a seminal short film from 1964 which never failed to whisk her mind off to matters of life, death, and eternity.

> Every time I saw *Man's Search for Happiness* I promised myself: I would be different. For what were they to me, the passing pleasures of this life—profanity, face cards, and Coca-Cola, even my favorite birthday zip-up vinyl boots—the hollow pleasure of the spooky carnival of earthlife? What were any of these next to the knowledge of who I was, where I came from, and where I was going? In the cool safety of the darkened Sunday School room, I hugged my knees and felt the pull of a great, deep longing through the center of my chest.[17]

The ward movie night as fundraiser has fallen victim to changes in fundraising policies, increased attention to copyright law, and access to home video, but the Mormon cinematic tradition lives on in continued experiences like Burton's, Anderson's, and Brooks's as well as in other social events, youth class video projects, recreational filmmaking activities, thousands of Mormon-themed online videos,[18] and other components of a robust cinematic culture. As just one example, for several years unwed adult Mormons in both Manhattan and Los Angeles/Santa Monica have each held annual amateur film festivals that are as much social event as artistic enterprise.[19] Additionally, virtually all Mormons have seen, if not *Man's Search for Happiness*, innumerable other examples of the many hundreds of didactic films that the Church itself has produced since the 1910s and that continue to be shown in Sunday School classes, evening "fireside" meetings, missionary lessons, general conferences and other fetes, leadership training meetings, weekday youth instruction, and daily across the airwaves, cable television, and Internet. Mormon cinema is simply an omnipresent component of Mormon life.

There have been several partial histories of Mormon film written in the past, looking a specific periods or areas of emphasis. These have come in the form of scholarly articles, personal memoirs, master's theses, and now even the occasional documentary film. In this volume I attempt to draw upon all of these, synthesize them, augment them with my own thoughts and research, and complete them through the end of the Second Wave in 1952. As I have studies the history of Mormon film for nearly two decades I've seen how integral it is to Mormon thought, creating cultural touchstones, influencing societal norms, forming adherents' self-perception, and even shaping doctrine. I've therefore come to see the history that you now hold in your hand as a cultural study no just of films that deal with Mormonism, but of Mormonism itself through the lens of cinema.

Five Waves of Mormon Film

While no history can ever be exhaustive, such a history does require a broad purview. My purpose therefore is to survey the historical relationship between movies and Mormonism, including the people, events, and cultural forces both within the faith and without that have shaped the evolution of Mormon filmmaking, the role of film in Mormon life, and the way Mormons have been depicted on film by others. These stories are intertwined: Mormon-themed films made outside of—and in opposition to—the faith were the initial catalyst that caused the Church to enter filmmaking in earnest in the 1910s; in turn, the production and widespread use of films by the Church over the last century showed the faithful that film was a respectable and even exciting field, thus encouraging many of them to enter filmmaking and create their own independent productions. Eventually, some Mormon filmmakers like Richard Dutcher reacted against both outside and institutional films, creating movies that eschew what they saw as the flat-out cultural mistakes made by non-Mormons on the one hand and idealistic characterizations and pat storylines in Church-sponsored productions on the other. Even those Mormon filmmakers whose work never deals with religious subjects but who have participated in the entertainment industry as actors, technicians, executives, and creative personnel fit into the story, as they are also part of the Mormon film movement—and their direct skills and indirect influence have occasionally come back to shape Mormon-themed productions as well.

While the current volume deals with Mormon film from its prehistory to the end of 1952, to properly situate it it's important at the outset to have a bird's eye view of Mormon cinema up to the present. The history of Mormon film divides naturally into five distinct chronological periods beginning in 1898 and averaging roughly twenty-four years each (with the first period slightly longer due to a gradual start in the first years after the advent of cinema), with subsequent waves beginning in 1929, 1953, 1974, and 2000, placing us as of this writing in the midst of the fifth, though a sixth period may be emerging in the 2010s with the advent of digital online cinema. Because it's also important to understand Mormon cinema's prehistory I begin in Chapter 1 by examining the nineteenth-century precedents for film and its parallels in other branches of Mormon art; I then devote the remaining two chapters of this work to the First and Second Waves, with the rest of the history and an expansive critical analysis to follow in subsequent works. Before examining them in detail, however, an overview might be in order:

Introduction

The First Wave (1898–1929): The New Frontier

This period coincides roughly with cinema's silent era, before the introduction of synchronous sound arrived in 1927. Films in this period divide fairly distinctly between sensationalist pictures aimed at exploiting Mormonism's history and somewhat propagandistic films made in response by the Church itself and those sympathetic to it. All of the films from this period were shot on 35mm black and white stock and were generally released to a paying public in commercial cinemas.

The Second Wave (1929–1953): Home Cinema

This period has sometimes been considered a hiatus in Mormon filmmaking, though this is increasingly apparent as a misinterpretation. Pioneering work in filmstrips, radio, and hitherto unheralded motion pictures was laying the groundwork for all future Mormon filmmaking efforts. Depictions from outside the Church became much fewer and kinder in their representations. On a technical level, both sound and cheaper 16mm film stock were introduced, with the occasional use of color. The Church created a tremendous private film distribution network that sidestepped commercial theaters, allowing filmmakers to create works that otherwise would not have existed and creating a culture of cinematic awareness among all practicing Mormons.

The Third Wave (1953–1974): Judge Whitaker and the Classical Era

The Third Wave marks the beginning of the BYU Motion Picture Department and the production of Church-sponsored films that continues unbroken to the present. Hundreds of films were made, generally on color 16mm stock, and distributed privately throughout the Church and to other viewers. More Mormon filmmakers undertook production of religiously themed films on their own, with varying results, and as Hollywood's self-censorship relaxed depictions of Mormons as objects of curiosity reemerged in mainstream films.

The Fourth Wave (1974–2000): The Mass Media Era

In this period the advent of video both reduced costs and provided additional distribution outlets, particularly television and sales of VHS tapes, that allowed many more Mormons to place films within the marketplace, causing the total quantity of independent work to increase dramatically. The Church also enlarged the scope of its efforts by creating other production entities beyond BYU, often shooting on 35mm or even 70mm stock, and distributing its work through a variety of channels including satellite broadcasts, television, VHS cassettes, and destination cinemas at Church-owned visitors' centers. Depictions of Mormons in mainstream film returned to occasional sensationalist representations but included many thought-provoking portrayals as well, while large numbers of Mormons were working in the entertainment industry.

The Fifth Wave (2000–present): Mainstream Realism

The Fifth Wave began by returning to the First: Mormon cinema once again featured Mormon filmmakers releasing their Mormon-themed films on 35mm film in commercial theaters to a paying public, but this time creating a much larger niche market within American Mormonism. DVD distribution of institutional and independent Mormon film constituted a major market, while more recently the Internet and digital cinema suggest new formats and modes of distribution. Perhaps most importantly, the Fifth Wave is a post-classical era in which independent, mainstream, and even institutional depictions of the faith have all begun treating Mormonism with more complexity than ever before. Church members are starting to sense the emergence and importance of their own film tradition, suggesting the legitimacy of a culturally identifiable but institutionally independent Mormon cinema.

Running through all of these periods are four distinct sub-currents that help to organize the chronological discussion; though there is obvious overlap between categories, I use these labels in the following chapters for clarity and consistency. Each is more or less prominent in a given period, but all occur in each of the five waves and together they constitute the larger field of Mormon cinema:

Depictions of Mormons in Mainstream Films

Institutional (Church-Produced) Films

Independent Mormon Films

Mormons Working in the Mainstream Industry

Mormon literary scholars have used similar categories in their construction of the Mormon Literature & Creative Arts Database, which in addition to literary works by and about Mormons includes books by non-Mormons important for

Introduction

their depiction of the Church, like Zane Grey's *Riders of the Purple Sage* (1912), and mainstream work by Mormon writers with no discernible Mormon content, such as contemporary author Anne Perry's Victorian detective novels.[20] Even though only half the history is treated here, it's my hope that a broad survey—including all aspects of cinema as a social phenomenon—will help create connections and continuity for the reader and expand the concept of what we can rightfully consider the domain of Mormon cinema.

Dividing the history into periods in this way can be useful in characterizing extended moments in the course of Mormon film, and similar constructs can be found in other fields as well. In Mormon literature and some national cinemas such as China's such periods are named *generations*; Mormon literati are well aware of the term "Lost Generation," for instance, to indicate a group of Mormon writers who gained national recognition in the 1930s and '40s, and observers of Chinese film easily identify the "Fifth Generation" with directors like Chen Kaige, Zhang Yimou, and Tian Zhuangzhuang. With Mormon film, however, I have chosen to call these periods *waves* rather than generations because not only has the brevity of the periods allowed many individuals to work in multiple eras, something not implied in a generational label, but a *new wave*, a popular term in film history, indicates not just a personnel or chronological difference but a fundamental artistic one between the new and the old it is replacing. The most famous cinematic new waves, such as those that occurred across Europe and the Americas in the 1950s and '60s, all materialized as conscious reactions against preceding norms, using innovative stylistic techniques to emphasize their originality: the authentic locations, non-actors, and plebeian storylines of Italian neorealism, rejecting the staid upper-class "white telephone" films of the prewar era; the use of jump cuts, freeze frames, antiheroes, and disjointed narratives in the French *Nouvelle Vague,* in contrast with France's overwrought and literary "tradition of quality" of the 1930s and '40s; the use of non-actors and improvisation, humor, eroticism, and political satire in the Czechoslovak New Wave to undermine the Stalinist state-approved films produced after the 1948 coup; and so on with the New Hollywood films of the 1960s, Brazil's Cinema Novo of the '60s and '70s, the Hong Kong New Wave of the '80s, the Chinese Fifth Generation of the '90s, and other examples. Eventually all these new modes are absorbed into mainstream practice, making way for another wave to replace them. Although Mormon film has generally not been so self-aware as these movements—with the exception of the Fifth Wave, whose initial filmmakers actively promoted the originality of their work—it has adhered remarkably closely to this pattern.

I am aware that such broad stylistic labels may, of course, oversimplify complex historical trends and may often misrepresent the actuality of filmmaking practice, such as the prominence of professional actors in "actor-less" Italian neorealist films; for similar reasons Mormon literary critics have sometimes challenged the use of the generational model for Mormon literature. In all cases we should at minimum understand both the utility and limitations of a "wave" model; such limitations can be seen in Thomas Elsaesser's caution about overly simplistic classifications of the rapid events in West German cinema from the 1960s to '80s:

> The impression of successive waves, amplifying and building on each other, is almost inescapable. Hence the tendency for critics to construct a classic rise-and-decline story: after the groundswell of the 1960s, the crest of the wave carried the individual geniuses of the star directors to the top in the 1970s. The death in 1982 of the most prolific and gifted among them, [Rainer Werner] Fassbinder, soon followed by the end of the political era of Helmut Schmidt, symbolically broke the wave, dispersing the creative energies and scattering the remaining talents.
>
> This account, attractive though it may be as a narrative, is too metaphorical by far. It seriously misrepresents the structural features and different historical forces at work. One may agree that by the mid-1980s the New German Cinema was no longer new, and possibly no longer either German or cinema (happening mostly on television), but to know what exactly determined these shifts requires a look at underlying factors and a knowledge of its pre-history.[21]

None of this invalidates the utility of discussing Young German Film or New German Cinema; indeed, it actually shows the care with which we should proceed in a way that usually fails to happen in Germany's case when those two distinct movements are conflated into one. And it's also good advice to remember while considering the waves of Mormon film, which—like in Italy, France, Czechoslovakia, West Germany, and essentially any other case—have occurred in a complex historical framework and amidst the high-pressure daily grind and financial stakes inherent in film production. The five waves can be useful, but I agree that to understand Mormon cinema we too must look at underlying factors and a broad view of history, not just a simplistic idea of what each twenty-four-year period entailed.

Introduction

But with these caveats in mind, I still feel that introducing the construct of waves into the history of Mormon film may be immensely useful by providing a common language and reference points. It provides a convenient shorthand, for instance, allowing for labels such as "a Third Wave film," but more importantly it reveals large trends and historical patterns present in each period. One example is that the mainstream depiction of Mormons in the Second Wave was wildly different—more compassionate, more nuanced—than in the either First or Third, just as the release of Mormon-made films in theaters starkly differentiated the Fifth Wave from the home video outlets of the Fourth. And to illustrate the value of identifying repetitive patterns, we can see that in the years after 2004 theatrical Mormon feature films had increasing difficulty at the box office, causing some to prognosticate the demise of the entire movement. Within the five-wave framework, however, we see that the beginning of each wave—the Third and Fifth especially—have caused an eruption of activity which has often appeared like the advent of Mormon cinema itself; the Fifth Wave is simply the most recent and visible such phenomenon. After this initial activity has saturated the market there is in each case a longer period in which a smaller group of truly committed filmmakers gradually increases quality until a critical mass is reached and the next wave emerges. Thus the post-2004 slowdown of theatrical Mormon films can be seen not as the end of an era but the beginning of the Fifth Wave's winnowing period, with sporadic but high-quality films like *The Saratov Approach, Hawaiian Punch* (both 2013), *Once I Was a Beehive* (2015), and *Saturday's Warrior* (2016) now indicating the period's maturation. I expect the Fifth Wave to continue with this process until a Sixth Wave emerges sometime around 2024.

I hope that being aware of the waves can assist in assessing issues like these, and that the labels, which are always limited, won't take precedence over the actual events and films in question; it is, in the end, simply an organizational tool. Other critics are certainly encouraged to amend, challenge, or replace the five-wave structure, but it is my hope that from this point forward at least some model will be in place to contextualize discussions of Mormon film.

1 ORGINS

[Tolstoy] thought two thirds of their religion deception, but said that on the whole he pre-ferred a religion which professed to have dug its sacred books out of the earth to one which pretended that they were let down from heaven. — Andrew D. White, 1901 [1]

A History of the Church

Understanding Mormon history is essential to understand Mormon film history, beginning not in 1898 with the First Wave but much earlier with the religious, cultural, and artistic climate that caused the First Wave to emerge as it did. There are many reasons for this, foremost among them because it situates Mormon film within a broader cultural context—the forces and society that gave rise to Mormon films just as they gave rise to all other aspects of Mormon art and society. Second, many events in Church history have served as subject matter for the films themselves, especially those set in the nineteenth century, so knowing the history sheds light on the films. In this chapter, therefore, I out-line the history of the Church, touch upon other forms of Mormon art that relate to Mormon film, and look at artistic, technological, and societal trends among Mormons in the years directly leading up to the invention of cinema that led them to engage with moving pictures in the way that they did.[2]

Orthodox Latter-day Saints believe that all humankind are children of God, a Heavenly Father and Mother, and that this earth was provided us by them as a testing ground on which to learn and progress in preparation for a celestial eternal existence; we lived as spirits before the world was created and we each individually accepted the opportunity to receive physical bodies and enter mortality with its attendant pains, sorrows, and joys. Jesus Christ offered the perfect example of mortal deportment and, through his atoning suffering, death, and resurrection, provided the way for all mankind to receive forgiveness of sins and exaltation in a godlike state akin to our heavenly parents. This pattern of progression through premortality, mortality, and postmortal glory—which is variably called the plan of salvation, plan of happiness, or other titles—and its

associated truths relating to faith, repentance, sacrifice, and other principles
have always been the same and have always been taught, with divinely given
priesthood authority, whenever a righteous people has existed on the earth.
Thus the modern Church is a latter-day equivalent of covenant communities
in former eras or dispensations and the essence of the gospel taught today is
the same as was preached by Adam, Enoch, Noah, Abraham, Moses, Elijah, and
Christ himself. Soon after the deaths of Christ's early apostles the Church fell
into a state of apostasy in which important doctrines were altered and priesthood, revelation, and other key characteristics of the true Church were lost.
This condition lasted until the nineteenth century when Christ appeared to and
called a new prophet, Joseph Smith, Jr.

Smith was born on December 23, 1805 in Vermont and when he was a boy his
family moved to upstate New York, eventually settling near the town of Palmyra
on the new Erie Canal north of the Finger Lakes. At that time the western region
of the state became known as the burned-over district of the Second Great
Awakening, a major religious revival involving Methodists, Baptists, Presbyterians, Shakers, and other faiths that lasted from the 1790s to around the 1840s.
The religious excitement influenced the Smith family, including young Joseph,
and in the spring of 1820, when he was fourteen, he felt prompted to ask God in
prayer which church he should join. He walked to a small glen just west of his
family farm and prayed for guidance. After overcoming what he described as the
destructive "power of some actual being from the unseen world" (Pearl of Great
Price: Joseph Smith—History 16),[3] he saw the heavens open and God the Father
and Jesus Christ appear. They forgave his sins and instructed Smith to join no
church, as all were corrupt, and said that Smith himself would be an instrument
in restoring the true Church to the earth. This theophany has become known to
Mormons as the First Vision and its location as the Sacred Grove.

Three years passed before Smith's next celestial visitation. During the fall equi-
nox on September 21 and 22, 1823 he was visited four times by a resurrected
person named Moroni who instructed him about the kingdom of God and told
him of a set of ancient plates of gold in book form buried in a nearby hillside,
which gave a record of a lost American civilization. Moroni, who in life had been
the last prophet of this people, gave Smith annual instruction at the site—which
later Mormons would dub the Hill Cumorah after a Book of Mormon name—until 1827, when Smith obtained the plates and eventually began translating them
into English through revelation. While engaged in this work he and his scribe
Oliver Cowdery received more revelations and the priesthood authority under

the resurrected hands of John the Baptist and Peter, James, and John. Having received this authority, been baptized, and published the record as the Book of Mormon—Mormon was Moroni's father and the chief author and compiler of the record—Smith organized the Church of Christ on April 6, 1830 in the nearby village of Fayette.

What followed was a fourteen-year period of both growth and opposition. Converts joined the new Church in great numbers while those against it frequently organized and strove to push "the Mormonites" out of their communities, often eventually with the use of force. Rather than leaving new Church members scattered across the country, Smith advocated a policy of gathering: all converts were to leave their homes and come to the center of the Church. In 1831 this became the town of Kirtland, Ohio, located just east of Cleveland. There the Mormons built their first temple and, upon its completion in 1836, Smith and Cowdery received additional priesthood keys from Moses, Elias (sometimes thought to be Noah), and Elijah. But in 1831 Smith had also learned through revelation that a city of Zion, a New Jerusalem equivalent to the Biblical city of Enoch, was to be built on the western border of Missouri, then the edge of the United States (D&C 57);[4] thus a series of colonies was established there. By late 1837 external opposition, financial trouble, and intense internal dissension in Ohio made Kirtland untenable, causing those who remained faithful to abandon their temple and flee to Missouri, but in the meantime the opposition there had increased dramatically as well. The Mormons were driven from Zion in Jackson County to Clay County and then to Far West in Caldwell County, all around present-day Kansas City (then essentially nonexistent). In 1838 violence on both sides escalated in the "Mormon War" and Governor Lilburn Boggs issued an executive "Extermination Order" ordering that the Mormons be driven from the state or, ostensibly, killed. That winter Smith and several associates were imprisoned in a dungeon in the town of Liberty.

Under the direction of Brigham Young, then the acting leader of the Quorum of the Twelve Apostles, the Church's second highest governing body, the Mormons fled east of the Mississippi to Illinois. When Smith was allowed to escape and joined them the next spring he healed the sick, ordered a riverside swamp drained for settlement, and renamed the hamlet of Commerce, where many of the Mormons were gathering, Nauvoo. With the Church's first influx of European converts, within a few years Nauvoo had expanded into a picturesque antebellum riverside city that at 12,000 people was one of the state's largest. Prosperity allowed Smith to introduce some of his most advanced theological concepts, such as temple worship, vicarious ordinance work for the deceased, mankind's potential to become gods, and, secretly, plural marriage between one man and multiple women. Opposition returned, however, as old grudges from Missouri combined with new rumors of clandestine polygamy to fuel animosity toward the Mormons. Smith spent much time avoiding re-arrest from Missourian officials, but when disaffected Mormons in Nauvoo published a newspaper exposing polygamy, Smith, acting as mayor under the authority of the generous city charter, ordered the printing press destroyed as a public menace and was soon imprisoned in nearby Carthage, Illinois for inciting a riot. On June 27, 1844, while awaiting a second trial, he and his brother Hyrum were shot and killed by a black-faced mob, presumably under Governor Thomas Ford's blind eye.

A succession crisis followed, but soon Brigham Young emerged as the next leader of most of Smith's followers, later becoming President of the Church. He managed to complete a temple in Nauvoo while ironically making preparations to leave the United States entirely and journey west to the Rocky Mountains in what was then northern Mexico, though probably with an eye toward filibustering it for the U.S. This trek began in February 1846. After a terrible year spent entirely in crossing Iowa, the Mormons wintered in eastern Nebraska just north of present-day Omaha then pushed across the Great Plains in 1847, with the last of the vanguard company, including Young, reaching the Great Salt Lake Valley in present-day Utah on July 24, 1847. The next June 4,000 settlers were in the valley when hordes of shield-backed katydids, now known as the Mormon cricket, threatened to eat all their crops. The Mormons were saved by flocks of seagulls that devoured the insects over a two-week span; this "miracle of the gulls" entered Mormon lore as a sign of God's grace for his beleaguered people.

Then began arguably the greatest organized migration and colonization effort in American history, with thousands of converts coming from the eastern United States and Europe by covered wagon and either remaining in Great Salt Lake City or dispersing under Young's direction to additional settlements far and wide. Over four hundred of these were founded during his lifetime, primarily small towns in present-day Utah, Idaho, Arizona, and Nevada, but also including the large modern cities of Las Vegas and San Bernardino; Mormons also constituted the first complete non-native families in what became San Francisco, and it was a Mormon-owned printing press that sparked the California Gold Rush. For a few years in the 1850s Young experimented with having immigrants from the east avoid costly wagons and teams and instead pull their own possessions in large wheelbarrows called handcarts. This was largely successful but a disastrous experience with two groups, the Martin and Willie companies, caught in the early winter of 1856-57, in which over 200 died, helped lead to the experiment's end by 1860. Besides, travel on the trail became faster as it became more used, allowing wagons from Salt Lake to head east and return with immigrants multiple times in one season, and the 1869 completion of the transcontinental railroad outside Ogden, north of Salt Lake City, transformed the immigrant experience for the remainder of the century.

The late 1800s was also the period of the Church's greatest opposition, this time not from vigilante mobs but the United States government. Many among the first pioneers intended to leave the country entirely for Mexico, but soon after they reached the Salt Lake Valley the Mexican-American War—in which a large battalion of Mormon soldiers participated—extended the national boundaries to include their new home. After 1852, when Church leaders publicly announced polygamy, the Mormons were involved in an escalating series of confrontations with the federal government. Though the extent to which polygamy was practiced will always be debated, it can be safely claimed that a vast majority Church members at the time supported the practice as doctrine while less of them actually lived in polygamous households.[5] In the 1850s the infant Republican Party saw the issue as an inroad in its campaign against slavery: if individual territories could decide on plural marriage then they could also in regards to human bondage. Their 1856 platform essentially claimed Democrats supported these "twin relics of barbarism," helping prompt Democratic President James Buchanan to send troops to Utah to suppress an alleged rebellion. This 1857 Utah War narrowly avoided open hostilities but displaced Brigham Young as territorial governor, stationed a permanent body of American troops outside Salt Lake City, and greatly disrupted Mormon colonizing and missionary efforts. One tremendous act of violence resulting from the Mormons' hysteria was the Mountain Meadows Massacre in southern Utah: that fall a group of over 140 California-bound immigrants from Arkansas was besieged then tricked to relinquish their firearms and slaughtered by Mormons with coerced Paiute assistance. Years later local bishop John D. Lee was convicted and executed as the chief organizer of the massacre, but although he was involved he was essentially a scapegoat for many others who had also participated, and though there is no firm evidence to support it critics continue to claim his orders came from as high up as Brigham Young; more likely, however, is that Young was most likely innocent of planning the affair but certainly complicit in condoning and covering it up afterwards.

Origins

Following the Civil War—in which the Mormons, including some slaveholders, by and large supported the Confederacy[6]—and the initial acts of Reconstruction, the federal government returned attention to "the Mormon problem" with action coming primarily in the form of legislation and court rulings in a period the Mormons quickly came to call "the Raid." The 1862 Morrill Act, which made bigamy a crime, was upheld in 1879 with the Supreme Court decision Reynolds v. United States, which distinguished between religious beliefs and religious practices in their Constitutional protection. The 1882 Edmunds Act and the 1887 Edmunds-Tucker Act took harsher measures, imprisoning hundreds of Mormons, officially disincorporating the Church, barring polygamists from jury duty and voting, and escheating all Church property valued in excess of $50,000 to the federal government; it took the Church nearly fifty years to recover from this financial blow. Utah women, the first in the nation to vote, were disfranchised and Utah Territory was repeatedly denied statehood.[7] Mormons responded by forming polygamous colonies in Canada and Mexico and creating an underground network for hiding polygamists; the Church's third President, British-born John Taylor, who had been severely wounded during Joseph Smith's assassination, died in hiding in 1887. Facing the threat of further persecution including loss of all Church property, his successor Wilford Woodruff issued a Manifesto on October 6, 1890 that officially ended the troublesome practice. A practical discontinuance was more difficult to achieve, however, with the formation of several splinter groups—some still extant, including the Fundamentalist Church of Jesus Christ of Latter-day Saints—and even the covert continuance of the practice within the main body of the Church for many years. Hence, the stigma of polygamy has in various ways stayed with Mormonism up to the present, particularly in film and literature.

With the discontinuance of polygamy and the adoption of other accommodations, Utah gained statehood in 1896. Immigration of converts to the state faded as an institutional practice and the Mormons, now thoroughly connected to the rest of the world, began to turn outward. In the early 1900s an unorganized diaspora began which accelerated after World War II. The first temple—which implies a large Mormon population—outside North America was dedicated in Laie in the Territory of Hawaii, near the northern tip of Oahu, on November 27, 1919 and the first outside the United States soon followed in the Mormon enclave of Cardston, Alberta, Canada on August 26, 1923. This began a major trend of building temples—and thus symbolically Zion, which now carried a metaphorical rather than geographical meaning—wherever Church membership warranted throughout the world; after Salt Lake City's in 1893 another temple would not be built in Utah until 1972, a time span in which nine others were built throughout North America, Europe, and the Pacific.

Utah was hard hit during the Great Depression, and the Church, which had always cared for its poor, responded to this and the New Deal by creating a welfare program that provided material assistance and work opportunities for its members and others; this core program has expanded to include today a vast global humanitarian and disaster relief capability. World War II involved Mormons on both sides of the conflict and the Church strove to alleviate suffering in its aftermath, most visibly in a European reconstruction tour by apostle Ezra Taft Benson and subsequent efforts to care for members behind the Iron Curtain. Convert rates continued to grow slowly but steadily through the 1950s and '60s, but by the 1970s—despite often unpopular political positions such as openly opposing the Equal Rights Amendment and tacitly supporting the Vietnam War—there proved to be a fulcrum in the exponential growth of Church membership. At this time, Church President Spencer W. Kimball emphasized missionary work and strove to gain official recognition for the Church in numerous nations like Portugal and Poland that hitherto had not allowed Mormon proselytizing.

In conjunction with this emphasis, in June 1978 Kimball received a revelation extending priesthood ordination and temple entrance to worthy Mormons of black African descent from whom these had previously been withheld, ending years of open controversy—though the issue is still controversial—and opening doors for Church growth in Africa, , and other regions. Since then the growth rate in Sub-Saharan Africa has been high but, lacking a large base population, the Church there is still relatively small, reaching 250,000 members across 27 countries by 2009.[8] Larger total Mormon populations have emerged in Latin America and parts of Asia and the Pacific; Mexico, for instance, has the second-largest Mormon population after the United States, surpassing the one million mark in 2004. Today Mexico has 226 stakes, Brazil even more at 246, Peru 98, the Philippines 85, Chile 74, Argentina 72, the United Kingdom 45, and even the small Pacific nations of Tonga and Samoa 18 each.[9] With the 2016 dedication of the Provo City Center Temple the Church had constructed 150 temples around the world with another 27 in some stage of development, placing the buildings in such unlikely yet typical places as French Polynesia, Ukraine, the Democratic Republic of the Congo, Rome, Taiwan, and Hong Kong in mainland China. Major portions of the Book of Mormon have been translated into over 100 languages, with the entire book available in 82, representing a major effort to reach isolated and indigenous language groups like Chamorro, Quichua, Pohnpeian, Zulu, and

Origins

Guaraní;[10] in early 2011 the Church printed its 150 millionth copy of the book.[11] Less than two years later Church President Thomas S. Monson lowered the age requirements for full-time missionary service by one year for men and two years for women (making them eighteen and nineteen years old, respectively) and by 2013 the resulting influx of new missionaries pushed the total past 60,000 for the first time in years, on up to its peak at a record high of over 85,000 in 2014, and created 58 new geographic mission areas in addition to the pre-existing 347; of these new missions 26 were in Latin America, 5 in Africa, and 4 in the Philippines alone, reflecting the significant Church growth in each of these areas.[12]

Citizens of such countries have increasingly been called as Area or General Authorities in the Church's high ranking Quorums of the Seventy,[13] and in 2008 the German-born Dieter F. Uchtdorf became the first European in the Church's First Presidency since 1931 and only the second ever to not speak English as a first language. In 2014 the Church's Young Women's organization for adolescent girls expanded its governing board outside Utah to include women living in Africa, Brazil, Japan, Peru, and New York City, reflecting Salt Lake City's increasing remoteness from many Latter-day Saints.[14] Today there are far more Mormons outside the United States than within it as congregations meet in nearly every country in the world, with communist and Middle Eastern countries represented mainly by congregations of expatriate Americans, although immigrant Cubans, Chinese, Iranians, Vietnamese, Pakistanis, and others have joined the Church abroad. In 2016, however, congregations of local people formed in both Iraq and war-torn Syria, with new stakes opening in Liberia, Benin, and the Czech Republic for the first time.[15] Mormons have served in the legislatures of Tonga, New Zealand, Britain, Scotland, Canada, Uruguay, Mexico, Denmark, Brazil, and Japan,[16] and in 2013 Niankoro Yeah Samaké, the mayor of Ouelessebougou, ran a serious third-party campaign for the presidency of conflict-ridden Mali where non-Muslims, let alone Mormons, make up just 5% of the population. Then in 2017 Jacinda Ardern, who left the Church in her twenties over concerns about LGBTQ rights, became the Prime Minister of New Zealand and the first head of state raised in the Church.[17]

As of 2017 total global Church membership was an estimated 15.8 million.[18] This is still miniscule compared to Roman and Orthodox Catholicism or many Protestant denominations, but it does indicate impressive growth stemming from Mormonism's strong emphases on missionary work and large families. Presently there are nearly 5.7 million Mormons in the United States, which makes their numbers roughly comparable to the estimated 6.5 million Jews in America and 13.3 million Jews worldwide.[19] The Church is often reported as one of the fastest growing religions in either the United States or the world, while other statistics describe it, at 1.89% of the population, as between the fourth and eighth largest denomination in the country. In recent years, however, societal shifts and new ways of accessing information have destabled the previous trajectory of growth.

Mormonism, then, is facing a transitional moment as it grapples with the Information Age, but even taking these struggles into account it remains a vibrant and increasingly complex phenomenon. It is also certainly true that the Church's growth since the 1970s has been nothing less than essential for the commercial viability and narrative diversity of Mormon films in recent years. Whatever its growth potential, Mormonism also seems to generate a large amount of activity and attention compared to its actual membership numbers. Mormons have been overrepresented in the U.S. Congress for years, for instance, and in 2013 the 113th Congress continued the trend with seventeen Church members, comprising 3% of the Congress, nearly double Mormonism's 1.89% national penetration.[20] In terms of public attention, especially in the U.S., the Church in general received a great deal of scrutiny in 1997 when it celebrated the sesquicentennial of the pioneers' founding of Salt Lake City, in 2002 when Salt Lake City hosted the Winter Olympics, and especially in 2011 and '12 when a number of factors—including *The Book of Mormon* on Broadway and the prominence of Mormons like Glenn Beck, Harry Reid, and Stephenie Meyer—convened around Mitt Romney's presidential campaign to create a flurry of interest in the Church. Romney, a Republican from a prominent family in the Church, was the first Mormon to be nominated for President by a major national party, and even before he obtained the nomination journals like the *New York Times* and *Newsweek* proclaimed the period as "the Mormon Moment."[21] While many Mormons of both parties surely wanted to step back out of the spotlight by the time Romney lost the election to President Obama in November 2012, it was debatable whether that signaled the end of the Mormon moment itself.[22] But even as it faded, the year-and-a-half exposure had an effect on public perception: on February 6, 2013 television satirist Stephen Colbert concluded a *Colbert Report* segment on Scientology by asking, "The question remains, what is Scientology? A respectable modern religion like Mormonism, or a weird creepy cult like Mormonism two years ago?" The fact this earned laughs from his audience illustrates the public's recognition of the Mormon moment and the faith's emerging acceptance in American society.[23]

Origins
Early Artistic Roots and Parallels

Because motion pictures didn't arise in a vacuum—and don't exist in one today—we must also look at Mormonism's engagement with the other arts to gain a complete perspective of its use of cinema. As Terry Lindvall says of the entire Christian film movement, "for more comparative social histories aiming to uncover marginal influences on film history [and] to more fully contemplate audiences and their reception of media, we must focus on the ways in which the advent of the moving picture was understood within the context of previous types of art."[24] Nineteenth-century Mormon art was either a direct ancestor of Mormon film—as in the cases of photography and drama—or anticipated it in style, themes, and content. Such similarities have continued, of course, up to the present, with evolving trends in twentieth- and twenty-first-century arts mirroring similar shifts in film. Thus even a cursory discussion of Mormon music, dance, architecture, sculpture, literature, drama, photography, and painting will enhance the extended analysis of Mormon film that follows and will help concretely illustrate how and why early Mormon film emerged as it did.

Perhaps the most surprising things about Mormon art are its combined breadth, variety, and richness, and the alacrity with which Mormon artists in all ages have embraced new aesthetic trends and sought to reinterpret them in the context of their own worldview. Indeed, there was little indolence at all in Mormonism's initial engagement with the arts. Just a month after the Church was organized in 1830, Joseph Smith received a revelation instructing his wife Emma to compile "a selection of sacred hymns" because the Lord considered "the song of the righteous [to be] a prayer unto me" (D&C 25:11-12). Within eighteen months an initial compilation was complete and the singing of hymns such as John Newton's "Zion" inaugurated a rich and varied musical tradition.[25] Engaging in other arts was difficult on the frontier and later in the arid Great Basin, and certainly not every Mormon could be called an artist or aesthete, but love of art still ran deep through the hearts of many early converts from New England, Britain, and Scandinavia; in 1842 in Nauvoo—where Mormonism had its first engagement with drama, painting, photography, and fiction—Smith wrote that his people sought after "anything virtuous, lovely, or of good report or praiseworthy" (Pearl of Great Price—Articles of Faith 13),[26] an attitude applicable to aesthetics as much as to theology. Many 1847 pioneers considered Shakespeare essential luggage,[27] and, like the builders of medieval cathedrals, early Mormon artisans deemed any art or craft they struggled to produce as contributing to the physical—and hence spiritual—beauty of Zion; a common refrain was that even the bells on the horses—and eventually the Salt Lake Temple doorknobs—would be engraved with "Holiness to the Lord." A pragmatic belief, born from the lean years in early pioneer Utah, that art should be utilitarian and socially uplifting remains central to Mormon art today, yet eventually amateur domestic arts became supplemented by fine art as professionals moved their practice into the studio and the gallery. Still, the breadth of Mormon creative expression—including all folk and fine art—is impressively vast, ranging from a legion of homemade quilts and samplers to Mount Rushmore by Gutzon Borglum.

Because Mormon art has always been surprisingly quick to adopt the latest secular trends and incorporate them into devotional work much of it closely resembles other art of its period. This pattern helped prepare Mormons to engage with movies quickly and wholeheartedly after 1895, as well as later electronic media like radio, television, video, the Internet, and virtual reality. It also means that, even though Utah has always been behind Paris and New York as a hub of new artistic activity, those who would expect Mormon art to be consistently ascetic or primitive would be incredibly mistaken.

The road has not always been smooth, of course. The peculiarities of the Mormon worldview have created a number of dynamic conflicts within the faith's cultural expression. In his 2007 book *People of Paradox* Terryl Givens identifies four of these, describing them as "especially rich and fertile tensions, or thematic pairings . . . which have inspired recurrent and sustained engagement on the part of writers, artists, and thinkers in the Mormon community."[28] These include the tension between authoritarianism and radical populism in a highly hierarchical church that simultaneously encourages individual agency and revelation; the tension between intellectual certainty and searching that comes from Mormons' belief that their doctrines contain the fullness of the gospel but that many great truths remain yet to be revealed from heaven; the tension between the sacred and the banal resulting from Joseph Smith's vision of a contiguous and often overlapping heavenly and earthly sphere; and the tension from Mormons' perception of themselves as a called and elect people who are nevertheless cast out from and disdained by mainstream society. Such trends can be traced across the arts throughout the Church's eighteen decades and will surface again throughout this book in regards to film.

In addition to these, Mormon art is continually situated between conservatism and modernity or the avant-garde. Throughout its artistic history those people and organizations within the Church who have been eager to embrace the new have had to deal with the reactionary and conservative voices found in any bureaucratic institution, in this case coming both from leaders in positions of authority and the grassroots Church membership. In a sense, a conservative-radical dichotomy reflects Givens's paradox of authority versus populism, inasmuch as authoritative institutions frequently encourage conservative aesthetics in order to maintain control over their populations' self-expression and perception. But this tension is distinctive enough—and can be seen in the work of independently employed artists frequently enough—to warrant specific mention. Often it can be seen in the work of one individual, such as fashion designer Rose Marie Reid, who revolutionized the women's swimsuit industry in the mid-twentieth century with provocatively forward-thinking designs, fabrics, and even bust treatments that included strapless bras, but who refused to design the new bikinis that eventually represented the cutting-edge of her field because she felt they violated her conservative moral (Mormon) values.[29] And as often as Mormon artists navigate such personal decisions and moments of self-censorship for moral or social reasons, there are just as many cases where disparate voices within as large a community as Mormonism are in conflict about the accepted role of new or provocative aesthetic developments. One well-known example was a 1997 exhibit of around fifty Rodin sculptures at Brigham Young University's Museum of Art in which four large statues—the *Prodigal Son, Monument to Balzac, Saint John the Baptist Preaching*, and most famously *The Kiss*—were "requested, authorized, and paid for by BYU"[30] eighteen months prior to the exhibit but then deemed obscene by university administrators and left in their shipping crates throughout the show. Similarly, in 2009 a performance of Euripedes' *The Bacchae* by a visiting University of Utah company was cancelled a few hours before opening due, supposedly, to the play's frequent references to wine and the conflict between God (Dionysus) and man, and the production's use of phallic symbols and visible female cleavage. The last-minute nature of these decisions and, in the case of Rodin, the fact that no other religious institution had censored the touring exhibition brought generally unfavorable national attention to the university. A two-hundred-student protest in front of the school's administration building, which neighbors the museum's permanent sculpture garden, had no affect on the decision about the statues but illustrates the diversity of opinion even among Mormons at the Church's highly conservative flagship university.[31]

Throughout the arts we can see Mormons reacting against what they perceive as Other, foreign, or threatening. But this should not overshadow the speed with which other Church members have taken to new forms or the world's great art, a fact doubly remarkable considering many early converts' New England Puritan roots. Emma Smith's initial foray into devotional music set the precedent for this in at least two ways that were controversial at the time but which modern-day Mormons generally know nothing about. First, nineteenth-century religionists were divided over the nature of hymn singing, whether it should be a spontaneous expression of devotion based in an oral call-and-response pattern called line singing, the dominant American tradition up to that time (if singing was allowed at all; in some churches it wasn't), or whether music should be more grounded in a printed text. Smith's interpretation of her assignment to compile a set of hymns as justifying her *printing* it in book form put her and her husband firmly in the latter—more innovative—camp. This was still uncharted territory, however: even though her initial compilation was completed by 1831 it did not come off the press until 1836, and musical notation was only gradually introduced to accompany lyrics over subsequent decades.[32]

Second, while she included several "hymns of the restoration," that is new Mormon poetry from the likes of Parley P. Pratt, Eliza R. Snow, Edward Partridge, William W. Phelps, and possibly even herself,[33] Smith also firmly demonstrated the propriety of borrowing from Protestantism with her inclusion of forty-two Protestant hymns already known by Mormon converts; as Michael Hicks has pointed out, the original 1830 revelation said nothing about composition or publication of hymns at all, but merely a "selection" from the traditions of other churches.[34] Thus Smith's divinely sanctioned search outside the Mormon community set the standard for later Mormon artists of all stripes to seek their inspiration from Isaac Watts, Claude Monet, Flannery O'Connor, or Andy Warhol, an article of faith made more concrete in Joseph's omnivorous 1842 pronouncement cited above about seeking for anything good or praiseworthy. What is good in theory can prove difficult in practice, however, and conservative voices called to oversee Mormon hymnody have consistently opposed the adoption of doctrinally vague "gospel songs" brought in from Protestant Sunday schools. Such efforts have only had limited success as new titles have been admitted to each edition of the Mormon hymnbook; some highly controversial songs like "Nearer, My God, to Thee" and "How Great Thou Art" are now among Mormonism's most popular.[35]

From this beginning, Mormon music has flourished perhaps more than any other art form. The nineteenth-century Church fostered a multitude of amateur choirs, and today four-part congregational singing remains the most common component of Mormon music, with most congregations also featuring a volunteer choir for special numbers. The Church's most conspicuous musical organization is of course the Mormon Tabernacle Choir, begun in its initial form under John Parry in 1849 from an influx of musically inclined Welsh converts to the Salt Lake Valley. In fact, the vast majority of the Church's nineteenth-century musical leaders came from Europe—William Pitt, Charles J. Thomas, John Tullidge, Domenico Ballo, David Calder, Ebenezer Beesley, George Careless, Evan Stephens, and Joseph J. Daynes, the first Tabernacle organist—and they, along with a few Americans, second-generation Utahns, and composers of art music helped develop Utah's early musical culture.[36] This culture specifically prepared Utah for the arrival of motion picture theaters and their need for pianists and other musicians during the silent era; typical of Church organists of the 1910s and '20s was J. J. McClellan, who accompanied the Tabernacle Choir on Sundays and spent the rest of the week playing the organ and leading the sixteen-piece orchestra at the American Theatre to accompany the images on the silver screen.[37]

This close relationship between sacred and secular musicianship may have most visibly crystallized during the days of silent cinema, but it existed long before and since. The Nauvoo Brass Band, for instance, played a processional while marching in front of Joseph and Hyrum's bodies in June 1844 and performed in general conference in Utah in October 1848, but spent most their time in the intervening years playing at Iowan dancehalls and at campfire dances and worship services across the prairie. Such versatility has occasionally led to stylistic conflicts. Hicks has said that tensions in Mormon music "fall into two main categories, the cross-cultural and the cross-generational."[38] The hegemony of Western religious music is forced upon congregations throughout the world, in the first case, and, in the second, Mormon youth have always been quick to adopt each generation's popular music while older leaders have remained consistently conservative, if occasionally accommodating, toward new sounds. In the 1800s leaders advocated square dances over round dances like the waltz, but successive generations supported the waltz and similar forms of ballroom over newer trends associated with jazz, then jazz over rock and roll, then even soft rock over rap, hard rock, and hip-hop.[39] Despite this frequent hesitancy, this shows that since the beginning Mormons, including those in charge, have made at least some space for popular music. Brigham Young, for instance, outspokenly criticized widespread Protestant characterizations of fiddling as the devil's music: "Every decent fiddler," he said, "will go into a decent kingdom."[40] Under such auspices it was not surprising for fiddles to augment the burgeoning bands, orchestras, and other musical groups in pioneer Utah—besides the Nauvoo Brass Band including the Salt Lake City Band, the Deseret Dramatic Association orchestra, and multiple bands of the Nauvoo Legion[41]—and this atmosphere later allowed for young Mormons like Spencer Kimball and Howard

Hunter, both future Church presidents, to feel perfectly at ease earning a living playing piano and alto saxophone, respectively, in jazz and ragtime dance bands in the 1920s; in 1925 Paul Whiteman's jazz orchestra even played in the Salt Lake Tabernacle.[42] By the 1970s the new subgenre of Christian soft rock found ready acceptance among Mormons, as evidenced by the work of composer Lex de Azevedo and the enormous popularity of his stage musicals *Saturday's Warrior* and *My Turn on Earth,* although apostle Ezra Taft Benson had earlier denounced similar music as "sacrilegious, apostate deception."[43] Still, Mormon musicians have continued to proliferate in popular genres, and while many have adhered to "wholesome" soft rock or easy listening styles like the King Sisters, the Lettermen, and the Osmonds, others have pushed boundaries, from jazz musicians like early big band leader Red Nichols and later guitarist Alvino Rey, one of the chief architects of the steel pedal guitar, to rock musicians like Randy Bachman of the Guess Who/Bachman-Turner Overdrive and Dan Reynolds and Wayne Sermon of Imagine Dragons. Gladys Knight converted to the faith after her heyday with the Pips, and other rock bands with Mormon musicians include the Killers, Maroon 5, Neon Trees, Arcade Fire, Pearl and the Beard, The Moth and the Flame, and Low; genres like folk, classical, jazz, opera, and country—such as with the trio SHeDAISY—have similar Mormon representation.

Dance followed an essentially identical pattern. Virtually taboo among many nineteenth-century sects, dance was accepted by Joseph Smith and embraced by Brigham Young and his followers. Smith reportedly felt some antipathy towards dancing, yet it became popular in Nauvoo, Smith himself was described as an able dancer, and on the journey west Young received a revelation which commanded the pioneers, like King David's ancient Israelites, to "praise the Lord with singing, with music, [and] with dancing" (D&C 136:28); in fact, soon after this was recorded at the pioneers' 1846 Winter Quarters in Nebraska the departure of the Mormon Battalion was marked with a farewell ball one outside observer described by saying, "A more merry dancing rout I have never seen;"[44] smaller but no less festive dances followed along the trail.[45] Dance remained a major pastime in early Utah—in 1849 the *Frontier Guardian* noted that "among the Saints, it is regarded not only as a civil recreation, but a religious exercise when conducted by the sanction and under the government of the Church"[46]— and, while huge dance meets for young people, held in large venues like football stadiums, rose and largely faded in the twentieth century, social dances, generally held in "cultural halls"—that is, basketball courts—literally contiguous to Mormon chapels, are still a major activity for Mormon adolescents and single adults, although chaperones still frequently seek to maintain control by intoning against sexually suggestive movements or too-close contact between partners.[47] It's generally a social expectation for teens to deride such rules, at times proclaiming their independence from adults' standards while generally adhering to them all the same, thus embodying a hormonally charged version of the tension between conservative conformity and progressive self-expression in a single dancing couple.

Meanwhile, performance dance has flourished at the Church's schools and its Polynesian Cultural Center, a tourist attraction in Hawaii where the hula and other Polynesian and Pasifika dances have been part of the entertainment since 1963. Dance was introduced at BYU nearly a century earlier, the very year it was founded as a Church academy in 1875, and since then ballet, modern, ballroom, jazz, tap, and folk dance have garnered international recognition for the school and its performing groups like the Cougarettes, Young Ambassadors, and Ballroom Dance Company. Professionals have run their own dance companies, generally modern—Odyssey Dance Theatre in Salt Lake City, M.E.L.D. Danceworks in New York, CONDER/dance in Tempe, and Howe Danceworks in Los Angeles, among many others—and danced in myriad groups from Carolyn Dorfman Dance Company to the Houston Ballet. Gaining even more national exposure, in recent years Mormon dancers have appeared frequently on television programs like *So You Think You Can Dance* and *Dancing with the Stars*. It was not without reason that in 1959 *Time* magazine described the Church as "the dancingest denomination in America," a title that seems to hold quite true today.[48]

Like dance, Mormon architecture has undergone tremendous changes since 1830. Joseph Smith's earliest—and most enduring—contribution to Mormon building projects came in the form of city planning. Taking a lead from eastern and midwestern cities of the seventeenth and eighteenth centuries—most notably realized in DeWitt Clinton's 1811 plan for Manhattan—Smith's grid pattern for the unrealized city of Zion in western Missouri featured broad straight streets running in cardinal directions spreading from a central temple plot; this was replicated in Nauvoo, Salt Lake City, and hundreds of smaller municipalities throughout the mountain west, with Mormon villages frequently placing all buildings within this grid and farmland outside the periphery.[49] The buildings that lined these streets generally mirrored architectural styles common throughout America—or from British and Scandinavian immigrants' homelands—particularly the homes, stores, and workshops typical of daily nineteenth-century life.[50] Domestic buildings constituted the vast majority of the Mormon built environment, but interestingly Smith received repeated revelations about architectural specifics for ecclesiastical structures; though remarkable, this may be expected given his fascination with the Old Testament and the degree of specificity there on the Tabernacle and Solomon's temple. Thus, the design of the Church's first temple in Kirtland (built between 1833 and 1836) was originally seen in vision by Smith and his two counselors and subsequently laid out in a printed revelation (D&C 95:13-17) and the inspired designs of a newly formed Church building committee headed by Joseph's brother Hyrum (D&C 94:13-15; 95:14). The dimensions of secular buildings were also occasionally given by inspiration and even direct revelation—D&C 94:3-12 describes an office building and printing shop, for instance—illustrating the conflation of the sacred and mundane in Smith's theology.

Still, even divinely guided architecture borrowed from the world just as heavily as Emma Smith's hymns and Mormons' dance steps. The Kirtland Temple featured a combination of Federalist, Georgian, and Gothic Revival styles, and a few years later William Weeks's plan for the Nauvoo Temple (constructed 1841-46) exhibited a firm understanding of Greek Revivalism,[51] one of the Church's more popular styles. After the pioneer exodus a knowledge of the world's sacred buildings was deemed sufficiently important that architect Truman Angell journeyed across Europe to study the works of Christopher Wren and others before designing the Gothic Revival Salt Lake Temple (1853-1893).[52] Indeed, Gothic Revivalism was a popular form that can be noticed in the three other temples—St. George (1877), Logan (1884), and Manti (1888)—that were completed while the Salt Lake structure was underway. But these also looked to more contemporary trends, particularly the use of Second Empire and Colonial Revival styles in Manti. And some buildings were completely unprecedented: the Church's most remarkable structure was the Salt Lake Tabernacle (1863-67), proximate to the temple and built with an oval dome and no internal columns. Worked on by Angell, Henry Grow, William H. Folsom, and others, it reflected a monumental style all the Mormons' own. Frank Lloyd Wright later described it as "one of the architectural masterpieces of the country and perhaps the world."[53]

A similar mixture of originality and borrowing continued in smaller tabernacles and meetinghouses until Mormon architecture shifted from pioneer pragmatism into a golden age sometimes called "Mormon Moderne" that lasted through the first half of the twentieth century. Despite the limitations imposed by meetinghouse needs—a bishop's office, a cultural hall, a Relief Society room for women, a kitchen, classrooms, etc.—architects showed great creativity while expanding into completely modern styles, particularly in meetinghouses but also, for instance, in the use of Frank Lloyd Wright's Prairie Style in Hyrum Pope and Harold Burton's 1912 design for the Alberta, Canada Temple. Art Deco and other styles were used by Pope, Burton, Edward Anderson, Georgius Young Cannon, Joseph Don Carlos Young, and numerous other forward-thinking architects, and in 1966 the *Church News* boasted that meetinghouses outside the U.S. "range in architectural style from modern tile and stucco structures in Managua, Nicaragua, to the native-built 'Choza' made from palm trunks, limbs and coconut fronds."[54] But by the 1960s growth of Church membership and inhibitive construction expenses, especially after a decade of deficit-funded overbuilding from 1955 to 1965,[55] as well as an increased emphasis on conformity under a new correlation program, caused the Church to create a new building committee and adopt a plan of standardized architecture that allowed the Church to efficiently expand across the globe while unfortunately generally limiting originality and local influence in construction projects, particularly outside the U.S. in regions like the Far East, Russia, and Africa where traditional architecture is far different from suburban Utah.[56] Still, visually recognizable Mormon architecture is now a global phenomenon, and it remains the costliest and, arguably, most omnipresent form of art in Mormon worship.[57]

Contemporary Mormon architects, for their part, have not been confined to religious structures. Especially since the beginning of the twentieth century noted architects in Utah, like Taylor Woolley and R. Lloyd Snedaker, were matched by others outside the state, like Georgius Cannon and William S. Lewis in California and Neil L. Astle in Nebraska. Top architects working today include Tony Yamada, who took over Walter Gropius's group and now works primarily in Salt Lake, and Jeff Stebar of Perkins+Will in Atlanta; Stebar's selection to design the new Philadelphia Temple, inspired by that city's historic buildings like Independence Hall, shows the continued fluidity of Mormon architects moving between secular and Church-commissioned work.[58]

Mormon sculpture is often connected with architecture, starting with Mormonism's first major statuary executed for the Nauvoo Temple: it was in Nauvoo that Joseph Smith first introduced the concept of vicarious baptisms for the deceased, and hence William Weeks designed twelve life-sized oxen, one for each tribe of Israel, to hold the basement baptismal font;[59] these were carved in wood by Elijah Fordham in 1841 and replaced with a limestone version, executed by a team of stone-carvers under William W. Player, in 1845. The exterior walls also featured extensive relief carving, the most famous being the moonstones and sunstones that formed the base and capital, respectively, of the thirty pilasters.

Finally, the bell tower was capped with a wooden weathervane in the shape of a flying winged angel, leafed in gold by the Nauvoo Tinners Association under the direction of Dustin Amy. This representation of the postmortal Moroni, though altered, would later appear on nearly all temples; all versions feature a trumpet symbolizing the proclamation of the gospel to all the earth as implied in Revelation 14:6. Unfortunately nearly all of the Nauvoo Temple statuary was destroyed with the building, which burned in an 1848 arson and was largely toppled by a tornado two years later; three original sunstones survive, including one in the Smithsonian's National Museum of American History.[60]

In Utah sculpture flourished. Much of it evinced existing folk tradition, such as the myriad pioneer tombstones done in the style of New England gravestone art[61] and the furniture and children's toys made from wood, generally pine.[62] Most professional sculptors, however, studied in New York or Paris—an emerging trend with all Mormon visual artists in the late nineteenth century—and emulated contemporary styles like Impressionism and masters like Rodin and Aristide Maillol. Many artists' work existed somewhere between these progressive styles and the more traditional Neo-Classicism, which had passed its peak by the mid-1800s. Ralph Ramsay, born and trained in England, is perhaps the best-remembered fine artist who worked with wood; his case for the Salt Lake Tabernacle organ, though never completed to its full design, embodies a much "more stylistic and less ornate" version of the Boston Music Hall's Walcker organ case,[63] and his 1859 *Eagle Gate*, though later replaced by a bronze version, remains a landmark in downtown Salt Lake City today. Fellow Briton David Hughes is remembered for his ship figureheads as well as his ornate pioneer cabinets.[64]

Artists working in stone and bronze are perhaps better known, including Cyrus Dallin, whose parents appear to have left the Church before he could be baptized (Mormon children are not baptized, and hence are not officially Church members, until age eight)[65] and who worked in Utah and, primarily, Boston, and whose works include portraits of Paul Revere at the Old North Church and Massasoit at Plymouth Rock, as well as the equestrian *Appeal to the Great Spirit* outside the Museum of Fine Arts, Boston; brothers Solon and Gutzon Borglum— who also supposedly were never baptized despite their Mormon childhoods— the latter of whom began the Stone Mountain relief sculpture outside Atlanta as well as Mount Rushmore;[66] Mahonri Young, who studied in Paris and created Mormon monuments such as *The Prophet* and *The Patriarch* (both 1911), the *Seagull Monument* (1913), the enormous *This Is the Place Monument* at the mouth of Salt Lake City's Emigration Canyon (1947), and a 1949 marble statue of his grandfather Brigham for the Statuary Hall in the U.S. Capitol building that shows his "ability to carve vigorously textured surfaces into believable human figures";[67] and Norwegian-born Torlief Knaphus, whose fundamentally classical nine-foot *Angel Moroni Monument* at the Hill Cumorah (1935) vigorously reimagines the Moroni figure, while his bronze *Handcart Monument* at Temple Square, done in 1947 from a smaller 1927 work, has the rougher texture and feel of a Degas. Other sculptors like brothers J. Leo and Avard T. Fairbanks, who both studied in Paris, continued to push Mormon sculpture out of any predefined school into eclectic originality well into the late twentieth century; Avard, a vigorous supporter of the classical academic tradition, may be the most prolific creator of identifiably Mormon sculpture, with work on the grounds of the Hawaii Temple, Winter Quarters cemetery, Temple Square, Manti Temple, Provo City Hall, Brigham Young University, Susquehanna River side, and elsewhere.[68] Since the 1970s sculptors like Dennis Smith (quite likely Mormonism's most prolific sculptor today), Franz Johansen, Frank Riggs, Neil Hadlock, Trevor Southey, Peter Myer, and Niki Covington have carried on this tradition,[69] while other often younger artists like Valerie Atkisson de Moura, Pat Bowman, Laura Erekson Atkinson, Karl Hale, and Smith's son Andrew have pushed into the areas of hanging mobiles, kinetic sculpture, and multimedia work.

Mormon literature, when seen in its entirety, is the broadest ranging of Mormon arts. If we consider it to include not just fiction and poetry but any component of the written or even formal spoken word then the category expands to include scripture, pamphlets, history and criticism, journalism, family histories and genealogies, theology and apologetics, personal essays and memoir, sermons and speeches, diaries and journals—even scrapbooks—and oral folklore. It should, in fact, be remembered, as Eugene England and others have pointed out, that Mormonism itself began with the publication of a book.[70] Throughout his life Joseph Smith was intricately involved with translating, writing, and publishing the written word. During Mormon literature's foundational period, which lasted from 1830 until roughly 1880,[71] much of the writing consisted of sermons and histories, though, as mentioned earlier, the Church also gave a platform to gifted poets like Parley Pratt, Eliza Snow, and William Phelps. Some flirted with fiction—Pratt's 1844 short story "A Dialogue between Joseph Smith and the Devil" is generally considered the first such effort—but for the most part fiction was avoided, even as a pastime for readers, and Church leaders frequently intoned against its demoralizing effect, primarily on the grounds that it was untrue. In 1862 Brigham Young preached that those who read novels will go to hell[72] and in 1881 George Q. Cannon, a newspaper editor and counselor to four Church

Presidents, advised, "Do not spend your time in reading novels or any works of fiction,"[73] an admonition that was not always heeded even by the faithful.

In fact, by the 1880s a new generation of Utahns was feeling more amenable to novels, so in order to fight "the fiction problem" Church leaders took a cue from the "Home Industry" movement of the previous few decades—a program of domestic manufacture designed to promote self-sufficiency, especially after the railroad arrived in 1869—and sought to foster indigenous, isolationist fiction in a movement that came to be known as Home Literature. An 1888 speech (cited in the Introduction) by writer and future apostle Orson F. Whitney became its manifesto and soon writers like Nephi Anderson, Susa Young Gates, and Emmeline B. Wells were producing didactic fiction that celebrated Mormon thought and life.[74] The mentality of the Home Literature movement, which lasted at least until the 1930s and hence overlapped with much film production, has had tremendous ramifications for Mormon filmmaking up to the present.

But by the '30s pioneer Utah was firmly ensconced in the modern Union, and many new authors chafed at Home Literature's provincialism. Receiving their name from Hemingway's term for American authors, including several expatriates, who came of age during the First World War, members of this Lost Generation—Maurine Whipple, Virginia Sorensen, Vardis Fisher, and nearly a dozen others—generally left the state—and often their faith—to find success with national presses and readers, often through writing about their Mormon roots, as in Whipple's novel *The Giant Joshua* (1942), Sorensen's short story collection *Where Nothing Is Long Ago* (1963), and Fisher's fictionalized Church history *Children of God* (1939). Some, like Samuel W. Taylor, flirted with screenwriting, and a few of their prose stories would be adapted to film, such as his *The Man with My Face*, filmed in 1951, and *The Absent-Minded Professor* from a decade later.[75]

By the 1960s Mormonism had grown and matured sufficiently that another generation of writers combined the faithfulness of the Home Literature authors—though displaying more heterodoxy in their work and lives—with the artistic excellence of the Lost Generation to create a movement of "Faithful Realism" that continues in some form up to today. Led initially by Clinton F. Larson, this group includes novelists, poets, and essayists like Douglas Thayer, Levi S. Peterson, Susan Howe, Lance Larsen, Donald R. Marshall, Linda Sillitoe, Orson Scott Card, Louise Plummer, Margaret Blair Young, and a host of others, on up to the present with emerging authors like Angela Hallstrom, Brady Udall, and Stephenie Meyer. Like with Meyer, author of the *Twilight* series, Mormons have made a strong contribution to young adult fiction and children's books—such as with Rick Walton, a picture book author and mentor to many others. Publishers and editors, such as Anne Sowards at Penguin Group and Stacy Whitman at Tu Books, are just as influential as many authors. On a broader scale, throughout the twentieth century the progression of Mormon literature interestingly parallels and presages—generally by about twenty years—events in Mormon cinema, and dozens of films have been adapted from the page, from *One Hundred Years of Mormonism* in 1913 to *Love, Kennedy* (2017) over a century later.[76]

As mentioned, genres and forms generally termed as sub-literary—diaries, hymns, sermons, and histories, for instance—have prospered within the Mormon tradition. For a long time these were critically ignored, but in recent years, as Eugene England points out, "poststructuralism and various forms of ethical criticism have helped us see beyond such distinctions" and fully appreciate this literature.[77] England himself was the foremost advocate for the personal essay/memoir as the quintessential Mormon literary form,[78] and as an author he has been joined by P. A. Christensen, Edward Geary, Terry Tempest Williams, Phyllis Barber, Elna Baker, Nicole Hardy, Jana Riess, and Joanna Brooks as some of the best practitioners of the form. But not all such writing is happening in books and journals, as the Internet has expanded creative Mormon nonfiction in ways previously unimaginable. Blogs explicitly about Mormon subjects are often grouped under the rubric of "the Bloggernacle" and may be written by individuals or, more commonly, coalitions of authors; the best-known are frequently quite erudite and focus on cultural, historical, and doctrinal issues, as with *By Common Consent, Times and Seasons, A Motley Vision, Rational Faiths, Feminist Mormon Housewives, Modern Mormon Men,* and *Juvenile Instructor*.[79] There are many more individual Church members blogging about general topics, including an enormous cadre of skilled, candid, and incredibly popular "Mormon mommy bloggers" who write about their families and daily lives, exposing thousands of readers to Mormon belief in the process.[80] This plethora of online nonfiction—along with an equal number of audio podcasts—lends credence to England's claim that the personal essay is the area of Mormon literature that has "the greatest potential for making a uniquely valuable Mormon contribution both to Mormon cultural and religious life and to that of others";[81] this also reflects the fact that Mormons have always gone to great efforts to utilize the latest publishing technology—including sites like Tumblr and Pinterest and, since about 2005, online video—to communicate with the world.

While they distrusted fiction, early Mormon leaders were remarkably well disposed toward drama, once again bucking the national trend wherein "the theater was undoubtedly the most hated of all the fine arts in eighteenth-century America."[82] Amateur dramatic performances began during the Nauvoo period and have arguably remained the dominant form of Mormon theatrical expression, with thousands of large-scale pageants and more intimate "road shows" performed throughout the twentieth century. Perhaps the first recorded instance of amateur theater was an ad hoc troupe that performed at least twice during the winter of 1841,[83] followed by a staging of scenes from *Richard III* in Philadelphia the next year. This latter venture was produced by Thomas A. Lyne, a recent convert and professional actor who journeyed to Nauvoo and induced Joseph Smith to form the Nauvoo Dramatic Company. Their first full play was *Pizarro, or Virgins of the Sun*, wherein not only did women play the female roles considered scandalous elsewhere, but Brigham Young played the pagan High Priest—in later years Lyne feigned remorse, joking that Young had "been playing the character with great success ever since."[84] Just a month before his death Joseph Smith took time out from caring for his sick and pregnant wife to attend performances of both *Damon and Pythias* and *Idiot Witness*.[85] In Utah Young became the chief patron of the theater, encouraging small dramatic groups and forming the volunteer Deseret Dramatic Association on October 6, 1849, quite early in Salt Lake City's history. This group performed plays in the Old Bowery on Temple Square until March 1852 when it moved into the Social Hall on 100 East; when this was formally dedicated on January 1, 1853, with performances commencing two weeks later, it became not only Salt Lake's "first prominent building to be commissioned, constructed, dedicated, and used,"[86] but also the first playhouse west of the Missouri. The immense Salt Lake Theatre opened on March 8, 1862 with the play *The Pride of the Market,* and a Home Dramatic Club was formed in 1880. While the Social Hall gradually transferred to other uses, the Theatre, under Hiram B. Clawson, John T. Caine, and others, flourished as one of America's great stages and lasted until 1929, by which time other houses like the Capitol Theatre were available. It became a required stop for any traveling thespians, hosting the likes of "Maude Adams, Lillian Russell, P. T. Barnum, the Barrymores, Eddie Foy, and Al Jolson" over its sixty-seven-year career.[87] Hiram Clawson's sons Chet and Shirl, raised by their actress mother on these boards, would become a defining force of early Mormon cinema, and the Theatre itself became a prime location for prestige film exhibition in the silent era.[88]

Although this early dramatic enthusiasm initially set Mormons apart from other American religionists, the view of Brigham Young and his associates that the theater could have a moralizing effect on its audience—as well as its performers[89]—came to be increasingly shared as melodrama spread its influence across the nation. While Ibsen, Strindberg, and Chekhov were pioneering realism on the stages of Europe, the Salt Lake Theatre's first hit was the 1773 British comedy *She Stoops to Conquer* and its most popular plays were Augustin Dalys's *Under the Gaslight*, James Sheridan Knowles's *The Hunchback*, Douglas Jerrold's *Black Ey'd Susan*, and E. L. Blanchard's pantomime *Aladdin*—along with *Hamlet, Othello,* and *Macbeth*.[90] In melodrama, Mormons and similar Americans found a way to endorse a clear delineation between good and evil with just rewards and consequences for each; and the Mormons additionally transformed the playhouse into a physical space that could cohere their isolated community and reflect their social structure through performance and even audience seating arrangements.[91] Young's most famous statement on drama intimates its moralizing potential rather than its aesthetic value: "If I were on a cannibal island and had the task of civilizing it, I would straightway build a theatre for that very purpose."[92] His counselor Heber C. Kimball said he felt the same sensations at the Salt Lake Theatre's dedication as in the Tabernacle,[93] and Young added, "We do expect the people to come to [the Theatre] praying, and their whole souls devoted to God, and to their religion";[94] three years later he expanded, "With our efforts to instruct, please and amuse one another by means of the stage . . . though we may not conform to the standard of the world, it is our privilege nevertheless to have that Spirit with us that will cause light and peace and joy and a feeling of satisfaction to fill our bosoms."[95] This ethos of isolated devotion and self-improvement was of course at the heart of the Home Literature movement—although no plays were written locally—and carried into Mormon cinema in the 1900s. Indeed, as Mormon filmmaking came to gain prominence over Mormon theater, the melodrama and moralizing apparent in hundreds of films can be traced back directly to the nineteenth-century stage.

Despite a few stray efforts, it wasn't until the twentieth century and especially the 1960s that indigenous Mormon playwriting emerged as a distinct form. Many Mormon plays throughout this period retained a morally simplistic melodramatic flair, but as with literature and film other playwrights have reached for more realistic and complicated material. Some have written for a general audience, beginning with Edward William Tullidge in the 1800s and including more recent writers like the husband-wife team of Nathan and Ruth Hale, Tim Slover, Julie Jensen, Erik Orton, and Neil LaBute, the most celebrated playwright to ever emerge from the faith. As with literature, Clinton Larson's influence in the 1960s catalyzed a new generation of Mormon playwrights who have frequently gravitated toward Mormon themes; this includes Doug Stewart, Eric Samuelsen, Carol Lynn Pearson, Thomas F. Rogers, James Arrington, J. Scott Bronson, Louise

Hansen, Susan Howe, Robert Lauer, and many others. Recently Melissa Leilani Larson, Mahonri Stewart, LeeAnne Hill Adams, and Matthew Greene, among others, have picked up the gauntlet for a new generation of playwrights—as well as directors, producers, stage managers, and actors. In recent years, for instance, Scott Reynolds's Handcart Ensemble and Andrea and Adam Daveline's MOD Theatre Company have both produced excellent adaptations of classical texts Off-Broadway in New York, and a small contingency of dramatic companies such as Salt Lake's Plan-B Theatre Company are committed to producing regular Mormon theater in Utah and beyond.[96] With all of this activity, dozens of plays have moved from the stage to the screen over the years, including Orestes U. Bean's *Corianton* (filmed in 1931), Scott S. Anderson's *The Best Two Years* (2003), Eric Samuelsen's *Peculiarities* (2006), and Carol Lynn Pearson's forthcoming *Facing East*.

If drama was the dominant aesthetic progenitor of Mormon film, then photography was its technological parent. Infant photographic equipment was unavailable during Mormonism's founding years but Louis Daguerre perfected his technique in the winter of 1838-39 while the Mormons were fleeing Missouri, and within five years recent convert Lucian R. Foster was making daguerreotypes in Nauvoo.[97] Joseph Smith possibly sat for a daguerreotype shortly before his death in 1844—a great deal of modern discussion has centered around possible photographic images of the prophet[98]—and others like Wilford Woodruff and Willard Richards verifiably had daguerreotype portraits taken during this time, in addition to photographers taking landscape shots such as of the Nauvoo Temple.[99] Foster did not go west with the pioneers, but once in Salt Lake City several other photographers, mostly British immigrants, took up the infant medium, and photography expanded in Utah while Matthew Brady and others in the east were popularizing the form. The first of these men was Marsena Cannon, who brought his daguerreotypy equipment to the valley in 1850 and soon moved into ambrotype, tintype, and other wet plate techniques. He was joined by Charles W. Carter in 1859, Charles R. Savage in 1860, Edward Martin in 1865, Charles W. Symons in 1867—who merged his studio with Alexander Fox in 1874—and James Fennemore in 1870. In their varied speeds of adoption of the newest photographic technology these men demonstrated the tension between progressivism and conservatism; Carter, for instance, learned the new wet plate collodion technique while serving in the Crimean War in the 1850s but kept using it long after dry plate technology had surpassed it thirty years later.[100]

After these pioneering efforts George Edward Anderson became perhaps the best-known Mormon photographer who carried his work into the 1900s. Prominent photographers since the 1890s have included Charles Ellis Johnson, Elfie Huntington, James Crockwell, James Shipler, J. George Midgley, Harold Allen, Russell Lee, the painter George Beard, Craig J. Law, and John Telford,[101] as well as hundreds of others working with film cameras and, later, digital images, while photographers from outside the faith such as Ansel Adams and Dorothea Lange have also found Mormons to be profitable subject matter.[102] Because Anderson's professional life, which lasted from the 1880s until his death in 1928, overlapped the advent of moving pictures it particularly illustrates the link between Mormon photography and cinematography: his work documenting Mormons' quotidian and spiritual lives carried the tradition of the earlier pioneer photographers into the twentieth century, forming a link between them and the work of Chet and Shirl Clawson, who began making similar documentary motion pictures in the 1910s and 20s. Furthermore, Anderson's work documenting the Church's important historical sites, published primarily in his 1909 booklet *The Birth of Mormonism in Picture*—along with the photographs of other early travelers like John B. Fairbanks, primarily a painter, on Benjamin Cluff's 1900-02 expedition to find Book of Mormon lands in Mexico—anticipated events of Mormon film's Second Wave in which cheap and portable 16mm cameras allowed many amateur filmmakers to record documentary scenes far outside the Mormon heartland. This surge in Mormon documentaries in the 1930s coincided with general increased interest in amateur photography as Mormons also began taking still cameras on their travels, such as Thomas Farrar Whitley's remarkably well-documented three-year mission to Tonga starting in 1935 and George Lofstrom Strebel's trip with the BYU Art Caravan to Nauvoo over the old Mormon Trail in 1936.[103] Also, while Utah filmmakers in cinema's early years still had to import motion picture cameras from New Jersey or Los Angeles, a robust photographic industry in the 1800s meant that an infrastructure was in place for film development and postproduction in the early 1900s, allowing motion pictures to be fully developed, edited, and exhibited locally. Today Mormon photographers shoot weddings and events, fashion, advertising, photojournalism, portraiture, landscapes, and carefully composed art pieces; thanks to the advent of digital tools like DSLR cameras with high megapixel video many, like Mark Hedengren, Josh Maready, and Zack Taylor, now move fluidly between creating still and moving pictures.

Finally, painting and other graphic arts are neither a true narrative art form like fiction and drama nor a technological cinematic predecessor like photography, but they nevertheless had a tremendous influence on Mormon film, particularly as the tradition of narrative tableau created in early Mormon paintings continued into the fiction films of the twentieth century. The first Mormon painting partook of the popular interest in self-taught domestic art, particularly portraiture, in early nineteenth-century America. In the 1830s various Church members commissioned personal portraits, but Mormon portraiture didn't emerge as a distinctive genre until the relative stability of Nauvoo in the 1840s. British convert Sutcliffe Maudsley is the best-known painter of Joseph Smith and his family, and he was soon joined by fellow Britons William Warner Major, Robert Campbell, Thomas Ward, and others. In Utah the continual influx of British and Scandinavian converts served to diversify style and content matter, and as in architecture traditions from their homelands remained strongly evident: the work of painters trained at Copenhagen's Royal Academy of Art, for instance, showed how at that school "genre painting and local and regional historical painting were strongly encouraged as a cultural bulwark against advancing German cultural and military aggression."[104] Even after decades of living in America's Great Basin these traits were merely transferred to Mormon, rather than Scandinavian, life and history. Principle Scandinavian painters were C. C. A. Christensen, Samuel Hans Jepperson, and Jacob Johannes Martinus Bohn from Denmark and Danquart A. Weggeland from Norway, while notable Britons included Major, William Armitage, Alfred Lambourne, John Tullidge, Henry Lavender Adolphus Culmer, Reuben Kirkham, and George Beard, nearly all of whom carried on the landscape tradition—depicting "nature as a symbol of purity and religious power"[105]—of English Romanticism in their new desert home. Essentially only one native-born American, George M. Ottinger from Pennsylvania, gained prominence during Utah's founding period.[106]

Before the turn of the century Mormon painters, like sculptors, were seeking education outside the area, and throughout the last hundred years a multitude of artists found success with both devotional and commercial work. The latter was initially aided by affordable lithography and new outlets like Western-themed magazines, but by the 1950s Mormon artists working in San Francisco, Chicago, New York, and elsewhere—Minerva Teichert, one of Mormonism's best-known painters, operated out of her Wyoming ranch house—could not be distinguished from their non-Mormon peers.[107] It could be argued that in recent years Mormonism has given rise to its own distinct schools of painting, as shown in the similarity of style in religious work of painters like Liz Lemon Swindle, Simon Dewey, Greg Olsen, Del Parson, Joseph Brickey, and others generally concentrated around Utah. But since 1987 a triennial competition of visual art held by the Church History Museum (formerly known, more appropriately, as the Church Museum of History and Art) at Temple Square has shown strong traditions in other styles and techniques. Former curator Richard Oman in particular has been an indefatigable advocate for Mormon artwork coming from international and indigenous traditions such as Native American basket, pottery, and textile work in the southwestern United States and Indonesian batik textiles from the Pacific. Today Mormon painters explore religious themes across an incredibly broad range of styles: from Jon McNaughton in Utah, who creates primitive but popular portraits and group scenes promoting political and social ultraconservatism, to American expatriate Lisa DeLong in London, whose profound, beautiful, and frequently abstract work is based in ancient Islamic traditions of sacred geometry and the medieval *Book of Nature*.

Proto-Cinema: Modernization in Painting and Art

The term *proto-cinema* generally refers to any devices that foreshadowed the cinematic experience—tools that predated 1895 while resembling the act of watching a moving image projected onto a two-dimensional screen. It's a broad term that can include projection equipment like magic lanterns, small mechanical devices like the zoetrope, or even more primitive media like the camera obscura or, in the broadest sense, Paleolithic cave paintings. Nineteenth-century Mormons utilized a great many of these, starting with the least technologically advanced: monumental paintings depicting the Mormon story.

Around 1983 "Judge" Wetzel Whitaker, for three decades the Church's most influential filmmaker, began his memoirs by describing the well-known *Mormon Panorama* of C. C. A. Christensen from a century earlier. Whitaker essentially describes Christensen as a prototypical filmmaker, saying he

> was inspired with the idea of painting important events that had transpired in the Church on canvas strips, ten feet by seven feet, and then sewing them together. They were then rolled on an aspen pole and, with the aid of a crank-like mechanical device, the pictures could advance from one scene to another as he would explain each picture audibly from a written script.[108]

Christensen completed his monumental project in the early 1890s, and film, Whitaker surmised, must not have been far behind. But while he was right about the cinematic impulse in Christensen's work (about which he had directed a documentary), Whitaker perhaps underestimated the prevalence of its ethos in nineteenth-century Mormonism, where panoramic pictures had been seen as an essential tool in evangelizing for years. As Christensen himself wrote in 1892, "Pictures and decoration have now become such a necessity in our enlightened age that the art of drawing is considered equal to the art of writing." He followed this claim by discussing "the advantages and necessity of joining in the mighty progress of our age in the area of art and science,"[109] a statement that clearly seems to portend the invention of cinema three years later. But Mormons had more than an enthusiasm for modern progress: they were also compelled to tell what they saw as their sacred history: as Christensen also stated, "history will preserve much, but art alone can make the narration of the suffering of the Saints comprehensible for the following generation."[110]

It was with this didactic project in mind that Mormons had begun panoramic painting nearly fifty years earlier in Nauvoo. In the 1840s St. Louis, just two hundred miles downriver, was both a major transportation center for Mormon immigrants—with between three and seven hundred living there at any time—and the center of panorama exhibition in the United States.[111] One could argue that panoramic painting had existed in China and Japan for centuries, but the pertinent Western form had emerged in Britain in the 1790s, eventually becoming an enormously popular entertainment throughout Europe and North America before being replaced by motion pictures and other activities. The term *panorama* implies a wide net encompassing distinct forms: sometimes paintings would be a static 360° view of famous sites like the Gardens of Versailles and sometimes they would be lengthy canvases like Christensen's that would scroll laterally—hence the later cinematic term *to pan* a shot. These works would tour from city to city, generally accompanied by an orator, nearly exactly how film prints would eventually be shown. It was in this way that the river port of St. Louis became a hub for panorama exhibition, with important titles shown there in the 1840s including *Panoramic View of the Hudson River, Grand Historical Panorama of the Antediluvian World, The Bombardment of Vera Cruz,* and an incomparably immense "grand Panorama of St. Louis" by the genre's most successful artist John Banvard,[112] as well as at least four pieces—by the artists John Rowson Smith, Samuel B. Stockwell, Leon de Pomarede, and Henry Lewis—of views of the Mississippi that included Nauvoo and its prominent hilltop temple.[113] Later, in 1852 after the Mormons had gone west, painter John Wesley Jones exhibited his *Pantoscope of California, Nebraska, Utah, and the Mormons* on the east coast, promoting it as the largest painting in the world, produced for the astronomical sum of $40,000.[114]

Origins

It was in this milieu that Church member Philo Dibble, a businessman and body-guard of Joseph Smith who had survived a serious wound in the 1833 Battle of the Big Blue River during Mormonism's Missouri conflicts, became the first to attempt panoramic painting of the Mormon story soon after the prophet's death in 1844. "I dreamed I was standing under a large tree in company with others," he wrote of a decisive night not long after the martyrdom. "I looked and saw Brother Joseph coming with a sheet of paper in his hand. The paper was rolled up. Joseph threw the roll into the top of the tree. The roll came tumbling down through the limbs, and all under the tree watched the roll to catch it, and I caught it."[115] This was his heavenly commission, and, as he was more entrepreneur than artist, he enlisted William Major and other painters and worked on his panorama throughout the decade, producing two canvasses reportedly of a staggering 128 feet each, with images of Joseph Smith addressing the Nauvoo Legion three days before his death and Joseph and his brother Hyrum being murdered in Carthage Jail. The first canvas premiered on April 4, 1845, less than a year after Smith's death, with admission costing twelve and a half cents.[116] Work continued on the paintings throughout the time of the Mormon exodus and the problem of transporting them west actually delayed Dibble's emigration a few years—he exhibited them in Winter Quarters while en route—but once in Utah he and others amplified the first paintings with others of the pioneer story, displaying the full work at least by 1857 in the town of Spanish Fork. There are records of him giving various exhibitions throughout the 1860s, but by 1878 the aged Dibble was using the much lighter and more practical magic lantern to display his art; this small machine (to which I'll return shortly) projected the image from a glass slide onto a screen in a process close to modern cinema. In Dibble's case

> a heavy curtain was hung across the stage on which he showed slides
> of painted canvases depicting church history . . . The most unique
> attraction was pictures of the trip of the Mormon Battalion to Mexico,
> among which was one showing the stampeding buffalo when they
> attacked the long train of wagons. The spectators were held breathless
> as he showed the narrow escape of Levi Hancock as he was attacked
> by a bull but came off none the worse . . . All these pictures were
> accompanied by a dramatic recital of the story which Mr. Dibble gave
> in his nasal voice. Another picture showed a frightened buffalo goring
> several horses as they dropped in their harnesses.[117]

Dibble continued to travel with his images and various physical artifacts related to Joseph Smith—including one of his seer stones, the death masks Dibble made of Joseph and Hyrum (now at the Church History Museum), and a diagram/map Joseph had allegedly drawn showing the locations of the Lost Ten Tribes—until at least 1885, giving him ample time to interest many other artists in the potential of the panorama.[118] Such a burden did not entirely rest upon his shoulders, of course, as the panorama craze followed the Mormons and the railroad west: in November 1881, for instance, the Salt Lake Theatre hosted Dan Sullivan's Irish comedy company for the original play *A Trip Through the Emerald Isle* and "a grand Panorama of Ireland" featuring "One Hundred Beautiful Paintings."[119] Similar exhibitions must have followed suit.

Perhaps the next locally produced panorama was an 1876 collaboration between Reuben Kirkham and Alfred Lambourne, whose primary employment was painting scenery for the Salt Lake Theatre, when they created a series of over sixty canvases entitled *Across the Continent; or, From the Atlantic to the Pacific*. Though this was a national scene ranging from coast to coast, Salt Lake City received special attention, as one contemporary reviewer described: "[T]he pictures . . . are twelve feet, six inches long, and of proportionate height, save one, a view of Salt Lake City, which is twenty-five feet long."[120] By this time magic lantern lectures featured cross-dissolves and other lighting effects, and Lambourne and Kirkham responded by supplementing their canvases "with moving-water effects and a fully rigged ship."[121] Kirkham displayed *Across the Continent* for at least ten years,[122] and it was possibly in response to this that Christensen began his *Mormon Panorama* in 1878.

This newer piece became the Church's best-remembered panorama for its rugged but simple depictions of handcart pioneers and other Mormon stalwarts. It eventually spanned twenty-three tempera paintings of six-by-ten-feet each, covering Church history from the First Vision to frontier Utah. As Terryl Givens has said, Christensen's "paintings, in their homespun, quasi-primitive style, powerfully document the harrowing, the heroic, and the quotidian episodes of Mormonism's early history. Widely reproduced, they are the most influential face of early Mormon art and Mormon experience."[123] Richard Oman summarizes this by saying that Christensen "was easily the most important early LDS historical painter."[124] It would be a small step from the *Mormon Panorama*'s traveling lecture of the 1890s to the traveling lecture accompanying the silent film *One Hundred Years of Mormonism* in 1913, one year after Christensen's death.

Though the Mormon panorama reached its apex with Christensen, he was far from the Church's last panoramic painter. Some kept to secular subjects, like

Origins

Robert Smith of Payson, Utah who in 1887 toured the state with his paintings of the pyramids and other wonders and "great events."[125] But others followed Christensen's lead in depicting the Mormon story: in 1892 Frank Pickering of the Payson *Enterprise* hired scenic artist Samuel Jefferson to paint "a panorama of Utah scenes which are to be taken to New York City and put upon exhibition";[126] how this project fared is unknown. And though he did not paint panoramas per se, William Armitage did create the two largest easel paintings of the period, *Joseph Smith Preaching to the Indians* and *Christ's Appearance to the Nephites*,[127] a pair of commissions for the Salt Lake Temple in 1890. The paintings' scope at 10x16 feet each and narrative tableau fed directly into the panoramic tradition.[128]

Similarly, in 1888 George Reynolds, best remembered as the voluntary test subject of the Supreme Court's 1878 Reynolds v. United States case, though not an artist himself, edited and published *The Story of the Book of Mormon*, the first book of art illustrating that book of scripture. Creating a printed collection of paintings, while innovative, followed precedents such as the printmaking firm Currier & Ives, launched in 1857, and artists like George Caleb Bingham, whose lithographs, distributed through the American Art-Union and the Parisian publisher Goupil & Cie from roughly 1846 to '52, made him one of the most recognizable artists in America: 9,500 subscribers received a copy of his *The Jolly Boatman* in 1848. With this type of encouraging precedent, Reynolds's Book of Mormon project included two components: the actual paintings themselves by many of Utah's best artists, and their black and white mechanical reproduction and compilation in a bound form that was easily sold, bought, and transported. Scriptural paintings were a surprisingly rare genre among Mormons up to this point, and thanks to its use of mass lithography this book established the category, becoming far more publicly available than any panorama paintings with around 3,000 copies sold in its first year. It was also used widely in Church instruction—as films and videos would later be—and quickly inspired a second series of Book of Mormon paintings.[129] This series, called *Lessons from the Life of Nephi*, was commissioned by Reynolds, painted by Christensen, engraved by the Chicago printer Vandercook & Co., and published in the Church periodical the *Juvenile Instructor* in 1891, marking another milestone in the creation of mass-produced illustrations and making Christensen a pioneer in both panoramic and printed Mormon art.[130] It's also quite likely that both these scriptural series helped inspire the first major attempt to film the Book of Mormon in 1913.

Despite the quality of their artwork and the aggressive use of the best available printing technology, *The Story of the Book of Mormon* and *Lessons from the Life of Nephi* are nearly forgotten today, but another innovation apparently occasioned by panorama painting remains one of the best-known aspects of Mormon art: the painting of landscape murals on the interior walls of temples. Although this did not involve mechanical reproducibility or immense scrolling canvases, it brought the concept of large-scale narrative painting into the Church's most sacred precincts and thus made it germane to the highest levels of Mormon worship. In Nauvoo this worship took on the form of the endowment ceremony, a processional liturgy that depicts the creation of the world, events in the Garden of Eden, and Adam and Eve's progression through degrees of devotion culminating in a return to a celestial kingdom; different spaces in the temple represented the locations of the story, ending in a "Celestial Room" where patrons congregated after completing the rite, which could take up to five hours. The temples in Kirtland and Nauvoo did not have individual rooms for the Creation, Garden, etc., like later temples, although in Nauvoo cordoned-off sections of the large central hall, created by an adjustable hung curtain, reportedly featured potted plants and other decorations to visually imply scenery for the newly developed ceremony. According to William Clayton, Joseph Smith's clerk and one of Nauvoo's chief historians, the Celestial Room, which the Nauvoo Temple did have, was "adorned with a number of splendid mirrors, paintings and portraits,"[131] including at least twenty-two individual and family portraits that had been borrowed from prominent members of the community, as well as one large standing portrait of Brigham Young commissioned from artist Selah Van Sickle. Thus the besieged community saw itself reflected in the room; the west wall even displayed a map of the city.[132]

Despite the popularity of panoramas, including Dibble and Major's prominent work—and the fact that Major himself was, with Van Sickle, one of the two artists who created most of the Nauvoo Temple portraits—the Nauvoo Temple featured only this framed art and no wall murals. This might have been due to the building's imminent abandonment or to Young's desire to foster solidarity and inculcate loyalty in the community by featuring portraits of Church leaders who had not fomented dissent and apostasy after Smith's death—portraits, and reminders, that could be taken west with the people.[133] But while temple officiators in Nauvoo performed their tasks unaided by anything more than these paintings and some greenery, the Saints' permanence in Utah as well as the presence of multiple landscape artists there must have made the possibility of permanent murals alluring. Thus the Endowment House, a semi-permanent facility in Salt Lake where temple ordinances were administered while the actual temple remained under construction, featured both interior greenery and painted murals. The original St. George Temple in 1877 repeated the large unadorned interior assembly hall of the Nauvoo and Kirtland Temples, but when it was modified into individual endowment rooms in 1881 murals were included. And the Logan and Manti Temples, completed in 1884 and 1888, included murals in their designs from the beginning.[134] By the time the Salt Lake Temple was completed eight years after Manti murals were an unquestionable part of temple décor, and a plant conservatory outside the Garden Room initially continued the tradition of live foliage as well.[135] Years later, murals' position as a movie-like narrative tool was tacitly emphasized when they were discontinued with the Bern, Switzerland Temple in 1955, which instead featured blank walls and a filmed presentation of the endowment complete with elaborate onscreen scenery, a pattern followed in nearly every temple since.

These plants and pictures were not intended as static art; rather, they were integral parts of a lively costume drama more in the tradition of medieval workman guilds' festive miracle and morality plays than the Masonic rites from which Joseph Smith initially derived the endowment. The "script" of the endowment was originally an oral tradition, leaving great room for individual interpretation and variability with each new rendition. Performances were also reportedly energetic, with an actor like William Phelps, a printer and Church leader mentioned earlier for his poetic contribution to Mormonism, imbuing the role of Satan with the vigor of a jester, even hissing and slithering around the floor after Brigham Young—in the role of God—cursed him to go on his belly as a serpent. Contemporary commentaries "reveal Phelps as a great comic actor and the endowment as a lively drama with costumes, sets, and props" including raisins tied to an evergreen shrub to represent the fruit of the tree of knowledge of good and evil that Phelps tried to entice worshippers to eat. His costume, which varied, at times included "a tight-fitting suit of black, slashed with pink, pointed shoes, helmet, and a hideous mask." Still, Young complained that "it requires some imagination to invest this place with all the beauty that is supposed to have belonged to the original garden," and thus no efforts were spared in either performance or décor to achieve the effect. In its interactive participatory nature, the nineteenth-century Mormon temple endowment created a type of communal art difficult to find elsewhere in America—or in the hushed and staid style of Mormon temple worship today.[136]

Thus the temple, particularly in Salt Lake City, is a prime site where we can see the modernization of Mormon art in the 1890s, especially in the progression from panorama to play to film, an evolution all the more striking given the sacred nature of the building and the traditionally commercial—even profane—reputation of pastimes like the panorama, theater, and, later, motion pictures. This juxtaposition, however, merely serves to reiterate Mormons' comfort with utilizing the world's artistic trends to advance their religious program, a tendency that received a striking affirmation throughout the Salt Lake Temple in other ways as well.

For half a century Mormons in and around Utah Territory had done their best to create art under adverse environmental, economic, and, with the anti-polygamy raid, legal circumstances. In this time Mormon art had become integral to its religious culture, as the temple murals in Logan, Manti, and St. George proved. But this probably also made the limitations of Mormon artists like C. C. A. Christensen more evident, with his panoramas reaching the height of their popularity precisely as Church leaders were planning the interior decoration of the Salt Lake Temple. Thus George Q. Cannon of the First Presidency must have been intrigued in March 1890 when a young painter named John Hafen proposed that the Church fund him and two associates to study fine art in Paris for one year. Hafen gave a careful financial estimate in his initial proposal, but his most passionate words were about the "necessity of cultivating any talent God has bestowed upon His children." Obliquely referring to the current murals, panoramas, and paintings that Cannon was no doubt familiar with, he asked boldly

> What are we going to do, brother Cannon, when one beautifull [sic] Temple in Salt Lake City is ready to receive inside decoration? Who is there amongst all our people capable to do anything near like justice to art work that should be executed therein? I must confess that it is impossible for me to see any other or more consistent course to pursue in this matter than to give two or three young men who possess talent in this direction a chance to develop in [this] way...[137]

The plan was not unprecedented: Parisian study was becoming increasingly popular with Utah artists like James T. Harwood and Harriet Richards (who married there in 1891), John Clawson, Cyrus Dallin, and, in 1899, Mary Teasdel.[138] But the proposal to have the Church foot the bill was forward, to say the least. After two months Cannon, Church President Wilford Woodruff, and his other counselor Joseph F. Smith demonstrated their enthusiastic approval of the plan by not only agreeing to donate $2,160 to the artists' cause—at a time when all the Church's property was in escheatment to the federal government and its other assets were under very real threat of loss—but by officially calling them as missionaries as well, giving them a priesthood commission specifically to study art rather than proselytize. Thus Hafen, Lorus Pratt, and John Fairbanks—they would later be joined in France by Edwin Evans and Herman Haag—were set apart by three apostles on June 3 and soon after set out on what would eventually be called the Paris Art Mission, arriving there on July 24—Pioneer Day. They enrolled at the Académie Julian, then the premiere art school in the world, and began training. They "focused their formal education on academic figure drawing, sketching the male and female nude," but gradually migrated toward the Barbizon School of plein-air landscape painting under the tutelage of Albert-Gabriel Rigolot.[139]

Indeed, it was outside school as much as in it that they gained their education as they encountered Impressionism, then starting to wane, and the more burgeoning schools of Post-Impressionism, Symbolism, Pointillism, and Art Nouveau. They would have seen not just Whistler, Manet, Monet, Degas, Gauguin, Moreau, and Renoir, but also the perhaps more extreme styles typical of Pissarro, Cézanne, Toulouse-Lautrec, Seurat, Signac, and Van Gogh (who shot himself outside the city three days after the missionaries' arrival there); while setting them apart and perhaps thinking of the previous year's Exposition Universelle in Paris, apostle Heber J. Grant advised, "See everything on earth that you can,"[140] and the missionaries' journals indicate they were anxious to comply. After years of Mormon isolationism, including the xenophobic Home Industry movement of the 1850s-70s and the call of Orson Whitney just two years earlier in 1888 for Mormon writers to abandon worldly muses like Milton and Shakespeare in favor of homespun inspiration, this open engagement with the most advanced schools and museums in the artistic capital of the Western world—approaching its period of energetic fin de siècle bohemian revolution, at that—was nothing short of audacious, especially given the Church's dire straits in the months before the Manifesto. Terryl Givens describes it thus: "The use of church funds for artists to practice drawing nude models in *fin-de-siècle* Paris in preparation for adorning the sacred inner precincts of a Mormon temple is surely one of the great ironies of Mormon religious history."[141] But it worked, pushing Mormon art out of its pioneer past: the decidedly modern murals of the Salt Lake Temple that these men executed upon their return bear much more in common with the French avant-garde than with Christensen's stark panoramas.[142]

For someone walking through the temple's rooms, then or now, such modernism would not seem out of place. Though its initial design in the 1850s was based in the fading style of Gothic Revivalism, with granite blocks hauled to the site by oxcart, to think of the temple entirely as a pioneer edifice in a conservative style is incomplete: by the time it was dedicated in 1893 the world was much closer chronologically to the completion of the Empire State Building than the death of Joseph Smith. Over a century into the Industrial Revolution, the temple's finishers had no qualms making their building as modern as possible. They commissioned a twelve-foot stained glass window of the First Vision from Tiffany and Company, demonstrating their willingness to install a work from New York City's leading Art Nouveau designer in the temple's Holy of Holies.[143] Similarly, initial plans for gas lighting shifted to wired electricity in the final seven years of construction—an electric power plant had been operational in Salt Lake since 1881—with wires and plumbing routed inside the thick granite walls.[144] Elevator shafts were added to the interior plans by 1887 and the elevator lifts were constructed, reportedly at great expense, by the New York firm Otis Brothers and Company using the same hydraulic process of grooved wheels situated in a pulley arrangement that the company had used in the new Eiffel Tower four years earlier.[145]

Finally, crowning the temple's highest spire was the statue of the *Angel Moroni*. This image, which has become perhaps the most recognizable symbol of the Church, was conceived and created by Cyrus Dallin. He too had studied at the Académie Julian where he met Rodin and studied under Henri Chapu, and his affinity for the French tradition is evident in this, one of his best-known works. No temple since Nauvoo had featured a figure on the spire, and Dallin, with just this distant precedent, made sweeping changes, removing the angel's wings, placing it upright in a forward stride, and draping it in a realistically flowing robe. His classical Beaux-Arts design, in fact, is completely reminiscent of the most famous statue, Beaux-Arts or otherwise, in the world: Frédéric Bartholdi's *Statue of Liberty,* which was completed in New York Harbor just five years before Dallin made his initial Moroni model in October 1891. The raised right arm holding a beacon—either torch or trumpet— to the world, the uplifted clean-shaven face and flowing hair, the left arm held by the side (later versions of *Moroni* would hold the golden plates or a scroll), the foot marching forward from under the robes, the welcoming stance facing the east, all indicate an affinity that though unnoted today probably did not escape many observers, a great many of them European immigrants, at the *Angel Moroni*'s installation atop the temple in 1892. These stylistic similarities also made thematic sense: *Moroni* is, after all, Mormonism's ensign to beckon the world's huddled masses to a new home.[146]

Early Mormonism and the Magic Lantern View

All of this demonstrates the degree to which Mormon artists and artisans were willing to embrace the new, including the cinema that would arrive two and a half years after the temple's dedication. But there were also other devices more commonly seen as proto-cinematic that Mormons began to use in the years leading up to 1895. A family of handheld or tabletop optical toys that presaged cinema was immensely popular in the Victorian age, beginning with the thaumatrope in the 1820s and including the praxinoscope, phenakistoscope, stereoscope, zoetrope, and stroboscope. With the exception of the stereoscope, which produced a static three-dimensional effect, each was based on the twin principles of intermittent motion and persistence of vision: when images are presented rapidly but distinctly the human eye and brain merge them together or perceive them as one continual "moving" image; this is how film and video still operate today. The early toys generally featured a variation of a spinning disc with multiple drawn images and some kind of slot or viewing device to provide the necessary visual break to cause the images to appear to move rather than blur together. As private entertainments, devices like these did not warrant mention in the press or even necessarily personal journals, thus making it difficult to gauge how extensively they were had among the Mormons in the west, let alone those who lived in the eastern states or Europe. It could be assumed, though, that Mormons were just as eager as others of this era for new visual and narrative amusements, and as with all eastern merchandise their usage in Utah almost certainly increased after the arrival of the railroad.

With that said, it seems extremely unlikely that there would be many optical devices created with Mormon subject matter, and to our knowledge there was only one, released in 1904, nearly a decade after the advent of cinema, when the New York firm of Underwood & Underwood produced the stereo view of "The Latter Day Saints' Tour from Palmyra, New York to Salt Lake City, Utah through the Stereoscope." Like a modern children's 3D viewfinder, the stereoscope, stereograph, or stereo view was basically a binocular eyepiece with each lens focused on one of two slightly offset images of the same picture; these combined to create a three-dimensional effect. At the turn of the century Underwood & Underwood was one of the largest creators of stereoscopes and stereoscopic photographs in the world, creating popular boxed sets of exotic locations in their "Travel System" series. "The Latter Day Saints' Tour" featured thirty-eight views by photographer James Ricalton of everything from the Smith family farm in Palmyra to swimmers in the Great Salt Lake, all taken three years before George Edward Anderson's better-known photographic tour of historic Church sites. Sales were apparently sufficient to prompt Underwood & Underwood to commission Seventy and Assistant Church Historian B. H. Roberts to adapt one of his recent books into a 132-page booklet to accompany their images. Through its choice of subjects, its depiction of Mormons as typical middle-class Americans, and the inclusion of the well-respected Roberts' writing, "The Latter Day Saints' Tour" represented a major softening of the public portrayal of the Mormon story—indeed, with it the Mormons became "the only religious group . . . to have a pictorial history in stereo"[147]—and it was certainly the first instance of Mormon media produced at such an expansive scale.[148]

Although we know little about the Mormons' use of small optical toys, there is more information about larger proto-cinematic technologies. The camera obscura, for instance, is a darkened space with a pinhole opening in the wall or ceiling, with or without a glass lens, which projects a view from outside onto a wall or the floor; the camera, which is Italian for *chamber*, could be a small box or, perhaps more commonly, an entire room capable of holding a group of spectators along with the projected moving image. It became popular as an entertainment after the 1500s, though its invention arguably dates back to ancient Greece and China. There is no known camera obscura in the Mormon settlements prior to the 1880s, but it seems likely Church members would have encountered them in Europe or east of the Mississippi, and it is also possible that unknown temporary structures in Utah were assembled and dismantled in a single carnival season. The first known camera obscura in the state, however, was an apparently permanent one at Fuller's Hill Pleasure Gardens, a Salt Lake City fairground just west of the present-day campus of the University of Utah.

The park was opened by William Fuller, a British convert to the Church, in 1875, and while he might have constructed the camera obscura in that decade we know for certain that he was advertising it for the Independence Day celebrations of 1880. An 1887 illustration of the resort seems to show the camera obscura standing near the eastern edge of the grounds, somewhere close to the present day 1300 East and 200 South. Though patrons could enter the structure we don't know its exact scale or dimensions or the object of its view, although it seems from the illustration to have a used a periscope-like turret common in more advanced camera obscuras that would have projected straight down onto the floor or a table in the center of the room. Various holes in the turret could have pointed in different directions, making it possible to have multiple views of the fairgrounds and the nearby city streets down the hillside. The camera obscura was mentioned in the press again when the park opened in May of 1881 and 1882, and improvements made in 1882—a "New and More Powerful Lens" and "New Power Fan . . . to Reduce the Heat"—imply that Fuller hoped it would remain at least for the imminent future, so it probably lasted until the federal government took over the property in the 1890s as part of the negotiations to achieve Utah statehood. Still, for over a decade the attraction was situated squarely in the world of the carnival: the park's ten-cent admission price provided entrance to the camera obscura and the 400 views of the stereopticon—if the patron didn't opt for the shooting gallery or four tries at the carnival game "Aunt Sally" instead.[149]

This double bill of the camera obscura with the stereopticon, in fact, points to the most common type of proto-cinema among the Mormons: the magic lantern. Dating back at least to the 1600s, magic lanterns were akin to twentieth-century slide projectors: painted images on glass slides were illuminated by flame, gaslight, or electric bulb onto a screen while a narrator told a story or expounded on a factual topic. By the mid-1800s a dual-lens system known as the stereopticon allowed for easier effects like dissolves and superimpositions between two slides. Lanterns bore an obvious resemblance to the earlier painted panoramas but, as mentioned in Philo Dibble's case, reduced cost for presenters and allowed for greater mobility, as well as mechanical reproducibility and the option to display photographs as the technology to print photos on the glass slides improved.

Religionists took strongly to the format as lanterns gained popularity in the 1800s, and Terry Lindvall identifies several points of synchronicity between this brand of proto-cinema and nineteenth-century Protestantism. As mentioned in the Introduction, John Fallon's work as a traveling exhibitor of panoramas and stereopticon lectures was funded by the Central Congregational Sunday School in Massachusetts; others like John Stoddard, Burton Holmes, Joseph Boggs Beale, and Lyman H. Howe followed in his footsteps, and by the time magic lanterns hit the peak of their popularity innumerable presentations featured religious content, including productions of *Quo Vadis, The Pilgrim's Progress,* and *Ben-Hur.*[150] In Utah, Mormons weren't the only ones exploiting the medium: Presbyterians, Unitarians, and others all presented regular lantern lectures on religious and secular topics, sometimes in bi-weekly series.[151] But the most enthusiastic adopters of the technology were Utah's Congregationalists, as described—and contextualized—by the Mormon-operated Provo *Evening Dispatch* in 1894:

> The stereopticon has come to be a recognized adjunct of religious work. In some of the largest churches east it is used with success, in both regular and other services. Beautiful pictures, reproductions of the finest works of art in existence, can thus be made to lend a charm and power to genuine gospel work which would not be possible by other means. Such use of the instrument is yet a novelty in many places but it is none the less wise and effective for that, if properly done. In the services now being held nightly at the Congregational church, Rev. John D. Nutting of Salt Lake, makes use of the stereopticon in varied ways for both pictures and hymns. Tonight at 7:30 there will be an illustrated service of song for half an hour followed by the sermon and other parts of the service. A most hearty invitation is extended to all.[152]

It appears that Reverend Nutting's lectures were the tip of an iceberg. The Salt Lake papers of the 1890s are replete with notices of Congregationalist magic lantern events, including frequent lectures at their school building Hammond Hall and main church building at Independence Hall, with secular topics—astronomy, geology, and a trip through Yellowstone, for instance—receiving as much attention as the sacred.[153] It seems from the *Evening Dispatch*'s language that the Mormons in Utah observed the Congregationalists' actions with admiration if not jealousy, and this surely helped increase the frequency of their own lectures, although they had tentatively begun first using the medium much earlier.

Once again, we have no way of knowing when the first magic lantern presentation was given by a Church member or to a Mormon audience. It seems reasonable, however, that as with panoramas and camera obscuras Mormons would have been quite familiar with the format long before producing their own slides—and that they nearly certainly first encountered it in the east. Dibble's 1878 use of the magic lantern, not long after the stereopticon's invention, is perhaps the first recorded instance of the medium in the Church, but its popularity in the mountain west probably increased gradually with the modernizing effect of the completed railroad in 1869. What we do know with complete certainty is how enamored Mormons became with the medium. Magic lanterns were apparently ubiquitous enough that in March 1887, less than a week after the Edmunds-Tucker Act required prospective Mormon jurors, voters, and public officials to take an oath denouncing polygamy, the populace adopted the term

Origins

"swallowing the rat" from "The Ratcatcher," a popular lantern show, to describe the act of taking the oath.[154] That magic lanterns could so permeate the culture as to influence Mormon vernacular during the anti-polygamy raid is fascinating.

This begins to show lanterns' influence among Mormons in the years immediately preceding cinema, but Mormon interest in the medium remarkably lasted for another hundred years. Though in the twentieth century the magic lantern itself would be replaced by machines that projected images from rolls or individual frames of 35mm film rather than glass slides, the act of showing still images with a spoken or prerecorded narration became a wildly popular medium within the Church, especially for proselytizing and teaching in the Church Educational System, with hundreds of different lectures prepared and innumerable thousands of public and private presentations given throughout the world. In fact, Mormons continued using slide shows, sometimes presented on videocassette, through the 1980s, nearly a century after moving pictures had made the form essentially obsolete everywhere else on the globe.

Whatever individual presentations from the 1870s remain lost to history, magic lantern and especially stereopticon shows gained traction among the Mormons in the next decade. As with the camera obscura at Fuller's Hill Pleasure Gardens, fairgrounds were a popular early venue; the Fuller's Hill stereopticon featured between 300 and 400 views, as the slides were called, of sites throughout the United States and Europe, and it's probable that stereopticons were featured at resorts like Eden Park in Bountiful, Sylvan Glen in Ogden, Geneva, Saratoga, and Murdock Resort on Utah Lake, Lagoon in Farmington, and the Salt Palace, Majestic Park, Calder's Park, and other resorts in Salt Lake City.[155] But these were not the only venues: another coalition of exhibitors—a company "of well-known parties in this city"—gave nightly outdoor shows in February 1884 in the street opposite the Salt Lake post office, evenings which were reportedly well attended despite occurring in the dead of winter. Original photographs of Salt Lake City were included along with France, Italy, and London, and the entire event, which was apparently free to the public, was paid for by showing "advertisements of the leading business houses of the city." Scenes were projected "upon an immense canvas, which occupies the entire space between the buildings. The light used is intensely bright, and the effect is very pretty."[156] Children's shows were also popular, with lanterns used in matinees at theaters, private birthday parties, and even an 1888 Electric Clock Exhibition two blocks from Temple Square that besides clocks and the stereopticon included a Punch and Judy show, miniature glass works, a three-headed songstress, and a floating head illusion.[157]

Of course theater stages, ideally suited for magic lanterns, became the primary venue for their exhibition, the Salt Lake Theatre foremost among them. For
instance, in February 1881 the traveling British astronomer Richard A. Proctor
gave two illustrated lectures there about planetary evolution to a large audience.[158] That such lectures were a regular event is shown in the description of an
1884 presentation by one J. A. MacKnight, a traveling lecturer and former U.S.
consul to Saint Helena, showing slides of the island and the life of Napoleon:
"Mr. MacKnight has secured the use of the Novelty Advertising Company's admirable stereopticon, which is incomparably finer than any other ever seen here.
The views, too, which will be reflected over a space of thirty feet in diameter,
are very far ahead of the best ever exhibited in Salt Lake City."[159] While this was
impressive, by May 1890 the Theatre was advertising its use of a 1,000-square-
foot canvas and "dissolving views" projected by "a powerful oxy-hydrogen stereopticon"; admission had also increased to twenty-five cents.[160] Lantern lecturers
also traveled to regional theaters. In 1888 Wadsworth, Glass & Co. sponsored
a "magic lantern entertainment" at the town theater in American Fork, "a rare
treat for the citizens of that vicinity."[161] Throughout rural Utah Mormons began
their integration into the larger American society through such shows.

The abundance of historical, medical, and scientific lectures meant that magic
lanterns also found a welcome home in the academy. In August 1893 Brigham
Young Academy, the predecessor of BYU, had its first publicized lecture, given by
Zonia Baber, who was thus also the first recorded female magic lantern lecturer
in Utah, though she was hopefully preceded by others of whom we're unaware.[162]
Prominent educators used the medium, like Cyrus Dallin who gave at least two
illustrated lectures, including one at the newly rechristened University of Utah,
while in the area to work on his *Moroni* statue.[163]

But apparently the most prolific and popular lecturer was Dr. James E. Talmage,
a native Briton, polymathic geologist, impressive orator, prolific author, and university president who would be called to the apostleship in 1911. In the 1880s,
though, he was in his mid-twenties and split his energies between pursuing his
education at Johns Hopkins University in Baltimore and supporting academic
and social causes in Provo, Utah. In this latter role he began giving fundraising
lectures for institutions like the Provo Free Reading Room, forerunner of the
public library, and his reputation grew so that when he moved to Salt Lake City
in 1888 "he was besieged with requests to speak before various Church, civic,
and social groups throughout the area. He had an innate dislike of refusing such
requests and there is no doubt that he honestly enjoyed the role of lecturer.

Consequently, he tried to fill as many as possible of these assignments although the strain grew steadily heavier."[164] Many of his lectures were given without visual aids, but he apparently took to using magic lanterns quite early in his oratorical career, with illustrated lectures including titles like "The Earth's Formation" (February 1885), "A History of the Earth" (April 1887), "An Hour with the Insects" (November 1890), "Fragments of Earth-lore" (February 1894), "Pompeii, a City of the Past," (November 1894), and the volubly titled "Geology, Historical Sketch of the Sciences: In the Beginning, the Geological Record; Development and Progress Declared by the Rocks: Unity of Design Apparent; illustrated by stereopticon views" (March 1895); he continued with even greater frequency into 1896 and beyond.[165] As a scientist, Talmage also frequently included physical specimens and live experiments in his lectures, and he would have been as interested in the preparation of his full-color lantern slides as in his oral presentation and physical materials. His slides probably included photographs along with drawings and diagrams, and in the early 1890s he moved more fully into the role of a prototypical nonfiction filmmaker when he documented his visits to Rome, Pompeii, Finland, Russia, and other European locales with his own photography. The resulting lectures "The Eternal City" and "Sights and Scenes In Russia" coincided chronologically with early Lumière actualities of exotic locations and anticipated silent-era ethnographic documentaries like *Nanook of the North* (1922) and *Grass* (1925). *The Salt Lake Herald* reported Talmage's photographs of Rome were "very fine and numerous," with shots of "the catacombs, ruins, the cathedrals and other objects of interest, [which] lent a vividness and reality to the word paintings"[166] while "Sights and Scenes In Russia" "was illustrated by vivid stereopticon views from photographs taken by Dr. Talmage."[167]

"The Eternal City" was presented at the 1,400-seat Assembly Hall on Temple Square and "Sights and Scenes In Russia" before an estimated 6,000 auditors inside the much larger Tabernacle, illustrating the trend through the 1880s and '90s for the Church to allow the use of its buildings for stereopticon lectures. Talmage himself gave his 1887 "History of the Earth" in the Fourteenth Ward Assembly Rooms in Salt Lake, a mixing of the scientific and religious that might seem incongruous today.[168] Other lecturers to use Church-owned facilities included an afternoon Sunday School party for children of Salt Lake's Twentieth Ward that may have been presented by photographer Charles Savage in January 1882; a presentation of scenic views from around the world by the traveling lecturer H. L. Rogers at the Fifteenth Ward meetinghouse in January 1886; a lecture on American history in the same ward's music hall in February 1887; a "vivid" and "graphic" historical lecture, apparently on ancient civilizations, by Elder J. H.

Ward in the Sixteenth Ward Assembly Rooms in July 1890; a lecture on ancient Egypt in the Burlington chapel on H. and Third Streets in June 1894; a presentation of "historical, temperance, religious and comic views" at the Seventeenth Ward meetinghouse then, the next day, Twenty-second Ward meetinghouse in January 1897; and a subsequent "entertainment" at the Twenty-second Ward meetinghouse featuring "stereopticon views, gramophone selections and other amusing specialties" in February 1898, by which point the magic lantern was being displaced by newer technologies, as "those present enjoyed themselves thoroughly, being especially interested in the work of the gramophone, Edison's latest invention."[169]

Such lectures for adults apparently always charged admission, usually ten but sometimes fifteen cents per head, with proceeds generally going to the ward Sunday School or youth program, which at that time had autonomous treasuries from the general Church or ward funds; this set the precedent for many decades of showing motion pictures to fill congregational coffers. In 1896 the Young Ladies Mutual Improvement Association of Lehi, Utah held a fair at Garff's opera house that featured a lecture by C. K. Sarave, not to raise funds for the young ladies themselves but for missionaries leaving to preach abroad.[170] Talmage's Roman and Russian lectures were among the largest such events as they raised funds, respectively, for local kindergartens and the Church's Young Men's Mutual Improvement League for teen boys, the latter fetching a cool $500. When he delivered a subsequent lecture on Russia—a sequel, essentially—a few months later in 1898, the *Salt Lake Herald* anticipated that "a crowd like that which Professor Talmage attracted before should be drawn out" and therefore "the tabernacle will without doubt be thronged."[171] A few weeks earlier he had used the Assembly Hall for a second lecture on Pompeii—another sequel or revision—and the building had evidently proven too small for his popularity.[172] Thus the *Deseret News* used the same language—"the Tabernacle should be thronged tonight"—a year later when he presented a new lecture called "Scandinavia and Her People" for the benefit of the Deseret Museum, where he was the chief curator.[173] The Tabernacle was, all in all, the best venue for the types of crowds Talmage generated.

It was also, of course, the largest venue in the entire state, and it's not entirely clear how these events were accommodated. The building had seats for the crowds, of course, but making sure they could see the images must have taken effort, including a large enough screen and lantern bulb with sufficient throw to illuminate it and make the image clear from the balcony and back pews. To do so, a "big canvas," recorded at four hundred square feet in 1898, was stretched in front of the pulpit. While less than half the size of the Salt Lake Theatre's 1,000-foot screen, it presumably was visible all the way to the back, especially since the stereopticon was lit with electricity rather than gaslight.[174] Larger screens could have been used on other occasions, but even at this size the Tabernacle proved very popular and the Church began either renting it out or allowing its use for traditional traveling lecturers not of the faith, following the precedent since at least 1884 of the building's frequent rental by traveling musicians like John Philip Sousa.[175] In 1898 Miss Helen Kelleher held the podium, showing two hundred views of sites in California that were "said to be second only to a personal visit." This was held "under the auspices of the Mutual Improvement associations," but what percentage of the proceeds the professional Miss Kelleher took home is unknown.[176] A year later the actor David C. Bangs delivered a version of *Ben-Hur* in the Assembly Hall with over one hundred views,[177] and two months after this a Catholic priest named Father Younan gave a lecture on India that proved so popular that "the crowds that have been flocking to hear him have outgrown the Assembly hall" and he was moved into the Tabernacle, thus creating the interesting phenomenon of a Catholic priest speaking to a primarily Mormon audience in the Salt Lake Tabernacle on the subject of Hindu and Muslim India—with two hundred stereopticon views, of course.[178]

If meetinghouses, ward music halls, and even the two most prominent public buildings on Temple Square could be used for lantern lectures while well-known Church members like James Talmage were lending credence to the populist medium, then it was a matter of little time before Church members and others began producing lantern slides and scripts on overtly Mormon-themed topics. Some dealt simply with the wonders of Utah, its geography and especially the industry and happiness of its people. These included a scioptico series from the 1870s, produced by a Philadelphia company, centered around the Union and Central Pacific Railroad that included a "Salt Lake City Panorama" and interior and exterior views of the Tabernacle, and Brigham Young's home, and a broader course of lectures on Utah and Salt Lake City by a professional lecturer from New England who received assistance from local Mormons in August 1890.[179] Most lectures, though, dealt more specifically with Mormon history or belief, Philo Dibble's Church history series being perhaps the first and most prominent example. In February 1897 Salt Lake City's Fourth Ward presented a lecture that included "the leading events in Mormon history" along with the life of George Washington.[180] That summer a special stereopticon exhibition by the Pioneer Jubilee commission honored Utah's first founders, many of whom were present, on the city's fiftieth anniversary.[181] In June 1898, during a musical soirée in the home of Lizzie Thomas Edward and Sadie Benedict, members of the Tabernacle Choir privately showed slides of the group's recent tour to California.[182] And in 1899 the Twentieth Ward assembly hall hosted a stereopticon presentation of the life of Christ, featuring over fifty views, "giving a most interesting panorama of the Holy Land, and picturing famous periods in the life and ministry of our Savior," presented by William A. Morton assisted by J. A. Christensen.[183] Morton was a popular author of doctrinal books and leader in the Church-wide administration of the Sunday School, a capacity in which he would later be influential in establishing private Church film distribution. Equally importantly, in 1915 he would be one of the driving forces behind the film *The Story of the Book of Mormon*. His experience in creating or even just presenting these narrative pictures of Christ for the magic lantern probably bolstered his belief in the power of images, still or moving, in teaching gospel principles, as well as giving him the confidence and experience to help push a scriptural film, on which he served as a producer and screenwriter, through to completion.

But perhaps the most portentous use of the stereopticon in the Church came not at home in Utah but abroad. In preparing for an eleven-week tour of Norway and his native Britain in 1898, James Talmage, at the invitation of the British mission presidency and the Church's First Presidency, "took with him from home an extensive series of stereopticon photographs, illustrative of our towns and cities, humble dwellings . . . schools, academies . . . irrigation processes, mines and mining operations . . . the unsurpassed scenery of our lakes, canyons, and mountains . . . and numerous other items of interest." Missionaries in Britain arranged for him to rapidly tour through Glasgow, Belfast, and nine English cities, and despite fears of small crowds in the hot summer months, which were "not lecture months" with their late sunsets and August bank holiday, the results were reportedly positive beyond expectation.

> In no single instance, we are told, was an unsatisfactory audience present: and on most occasions vast congregations assembled to hear the lecture on "Utah and its People." It is needless to say that the audiences were enthusiastic in their commendation of the subject and praise of the lecturer. Many people in Utah have heard lectures by Dr. Talmage, and his illustrated talks aided by stereopticon views have been enjoyed by thousands. His popularity abroad, where he is at all known, is evidently no less than that which attends his work at home.[184]

The British press responded favorably and the audiences were both large and generous, with, for example, a reported 800 people attending in Norwich and 700 turned away after a 1,600-seat hall was filled in Oldham outside Manchester. But the significance of this stereopticon tour comes not from Talmage's lectures themselves but from the precedent they set. Within fifteen years illustrated lectures were considered the most effective way missionaries could spend their time, and by the period of the Second Wave England, where Talmage would return as mission president from 1924 to 1928, was at the center of a whirlwind of activity that would revolutionize how the Church has used media ever since. Furthermore, one David O. McKay organized the black tie lecture in Glasgow and was thoroughly impressed with the results; he would remain interested in Church audiovisual work after being called as an apostle in 1906 and assuming responsibility for the Sunday School, where he worked with Morton to encourage film exhibition. He was President of the Church in 1953 when BYU built its Motion Picture Studio and he remained staunchly devoted to it until his death in 1970. Dr. Talmage's 1898 presentations might not have been the first illustrated lectures by a Mormon abroad, but they planted seeds that would bear fruit for over a century.[185]

Along with the stereopticon, camera obscura, temple murals, and mass-produced art monographs, there were other events around this time indicating the Church was artistically moving toward its engagement with cinema. There was the calculated public relations success of the first trip the Tabernacle Choir ever took outside Utah, to the 1893 World's Columbian Exposition in Chicago, First Presidency in tow, where they not only met with great acclaim but placed second in the formal competition—with widespread belief that only the judges' prejudice kept them from winning first. Using the Choir in a public relations gambit was a new concept for Church leaders, and when it paid off tremendously they became convinced this type of endeavor was worth the effort. "Members of the Tabernacle Choir," the First Presidency wrote to choir members in 1895, "are really acting as missionaries, called for their special work." Though this attitude may seem obvious today, at the time it was a groundbreaking reconceptualization of the choir's purpose.[186] There was also Wilford Woodruff's use of a phonograph to record his memory of Joseph Smith and testimony of the gospel in March 1897, the first use of recording technology by a Church President.[187] And finally there was the encouraging local success of authors like Nephi Anderson as well as Mormon drama in the 1902 play *Corianton*, which had a subsequent run at Broadway and a 1931 film adaptation. All of this, from the Paris art missionaries' study of nude figure drawing to the Salt Lake Temple's "five unique and costly drinking fountains of variegated onyx,"[188] as unrelated to cinema as they may seem, were emblematic of how the Mormons were preparing to engage with the foreign provenance, advanced technology, developing aesthetics, and unchurched morals of the moving image. As Terryl Givens has said,

> even as Mormon choirs prepared to display their talents in Chicago—not to reveal to an amused public the ethnologically interesting tunes of an isolated cultural curiosity, but to compete successfully on equal terms with America's finest choirs—Mormon leaders were preparing to assimilate into the décor of their most sacred edifice the cutting-edge influences of the European art establishment. Into the world and into the temple—henceforth, Mormon culture and the secular cultural mainstream would flow more freely into each other.[189]

Which is exactly what would be needed for Mormon cinema to be born.

The Great Accommodation and Arrival of Cinema

Thus the Church was prepared aesthetically, artistically, and even technologically for motion pictures, and a final overview of the larger social, political, and philosophical views among the Mormons in the 1890s—the decade that gave birth to cinema—will assist in understanding their initial reception of film and their attitude toward it all the way up to the present. This is because the changes in Mormon art in this decade were essentially symptomatic of greater shifts in Mormon society. Historians have called this period the Great Accommodation as it represents the moment when Church members consciously cast away their isolationism and end-times millennialism in favor of ever-increasing rapport with the nation and world. As early as 1922 Mormon sociologist Ephraim Edward Ericksen noted this shift in Mormon thought from kingdom building to national conformity in his book The Psychological and Ethical Aspects of Mormon Group Life. Modern historian Thomas Alexander appropriately named his comprehensive history of the Church from 1890 to 1930 Mormonism in Transition, his primary thesis being that the Great Accommodation shaped modern Mormonism at least as much as—if not more than—any events in the Church's founding or pioneer periods. And in his landmark work The Angel and the Beehive, Mormon sociologist Armand Mauss traces Mormonism's official and grassroots efforts at achieving conformity with mainstream American society that began in this decade all the way through their peak in the 1960s, after which American Mormons, perhaps feeling too similar to the rest of the country, began pushing to reintroduce cultural and political differentiations into their niche society. Although the 1890s must be understood as a response to the events surrounding polygamy in the 1880s,[190] it could be persuasively argued that the 1890s were the most influential decade in Mormon history in terms of the lives and thoughts of Church members for generations to come; in sum, it set the stage for larger engagement with the United States and world in the twentieth and twenty-first centuries.

The greatest change, which set the wheels in motion for everything that followed, was of course the nominal cessation of polygamy on October 6, 1890.[191] President Woodruff's Manifesto announcing the end of the practice came not as overt revelation but in the form of a fiat—stating the change in light of all the political and financial reasons polygamy could no longer be maintained in the face of federal opposition—a distinction that caused many of the faithful, including some apostles, to disregard it and continue the practice semi-covertly within the Church or more or less openly in breakaway sects founded in subsequent decades.[192] Still, this doctrinal concession began the slow process for moralists and government officials in America and Europe to warily ease pressure and allow the Mormons to live and preach unmolested, although it would take at least a generation for the issue of polygamy to reach a degree of closure—and it still remains in essence an open wound today.

The Church also made many other concessions, both willingly and, as with polygamy, begrudgingly, in the following years. Polygamy, highly visible, was *the* moral issue at stake for Protestant reformers who opposed the Church, much in the same way the abolition and temperance movements found their strength in Christian fervor, but for Washington the issue was much more about the Church's political control, as President Rutherford B. Hayes noted in his personal journal in January 1880: "Now the territory is virtually under the theocratic government of the Mormon Church . . . To destroy the temporal power of the Mormon Church is the end in view."[193] One 1885 editorial in a Massachusetts newspaper elaborated on the relationship between polygamy and politics:

> When the antislavery agitation was at its hight [sic] popular feeling at the North was exercised chiefly with the immoral quality of slavery as an institution. Yet the war of the Rebellion, by which slavery was overthrown[,] turned on an altogether different issue, the question namely of political sovereignty . . . Popular judgment is today repeating the

same blunder in the matter of Mormonism . . . It will be discovered all at once that the essential principle of Mormonism is not polygamy at all but the ambition of an ecclesiastical hierarchy to wield sovereignty.[194]

Every state and territory, not just in the South, agitated for their own strong local autonomy in the years surrounding the Civil War; the difference with Utah came in the perceived strength of the Church organization and Mormons' common, though perhaps waning, belief that they were preparing a political as well as spiritual kingdom to receive Christ at his Second Coming. Thus when Reconstruction shifted emphasis from the South to the West, the federal government demanded that the Mormons guarantee their national allegiance, demonstrating it through their actions, before the Territory of Utah could be admitted as a state—beyond the state constitutional provision banning plural marriage.

Accordingly, seeking to court additional sympathy in Washington, on June 10, 1891 the Church dissolved the local People's Party, which it had sponsored since 1870 in opposition to the anti-Mormon Liberal Party. Church leaders not only encouraged members to affiliate with the national parties but sought to overcome most Mormons' distrust of Republicanism, which had spearheaded the national movement against Mormonism for half a century, by literally assigning many Church leaders and lay members to join each party, anecdotally sometimes dividing entire congregations right down the middle. Absolute parity was not the ultimate goal, however, as the Church hierarchy—in contrast with the general membership, which leaned Democratic—had begun working with outside Republicans a few years earlier in hopes that the GOP would help the Church enter national politics and protect its commercial interests "in banking, railroads, mining, sugar, and other industries."[195] Indeed, it was due to a quid pro quo promise of Republican support for Utah statehood that Woodruff decided to issue his Manifesto, without consultation with the Quorum of the Twelve Apostles, twelve days after meeting with party leaders in San Francisco. Once the public polygamy ban was in place Church leaders remained convinced that "Republicans would support Utah's statehood, amnesty for polygamists, and the return of the church's confiscated property."[196] Hence, Church leaders like future president Joseph F. Smith—who would become something of a political boss in Utah's Republican machine—openly crusaded for years for members to join the party, sometimes using more than simple persuasion. The overall strategy worked, with Republican Church members gaining roughly equal numbers with Democrats for several decades, setting the stage for a more complete transition beginning in the 1960s when a large majority of American Mormons began moving toward political conservatism; today "Mormons are the most heavily Republican-leaning religious group in the U.S."[197]

Simultaneously, the Church also shut down most of its private academies that it had essentially run since soon after the pioneers' arrival in 1847 and in earnest since the founding of Brigham Young Academy in 1875. Government-run schools had been deemed untrustworthy to teach Mormon children but in 1890 the Territorial Legislature passed Utah's first Free Public School Act, creating compulsory secondary schools throughout the territory. Church members began tentatively accepting these institutions—establishing weekday religious classes to supplement public school students' secular education—before the Panic of 1893 put an additional strain on private academies and promoted the use of public education. The divestment of Church academies continued so that by 1934 only a handful remained: Brigham Young University—rechristened from an academy in 1903—LDS Business College in Salt Lake City, Ricks College in northeast Idaho (today Brigham Young University–Idaho), and Juarez Academy in Mexico; some schools changed ownership, such as present-day Weber State University and Eastern Arizona College, and others simply closed. In the early twentieth century the Church strengthened its nascent system of weekday religious classes, the Church Educational System, that worked in tandem with public high schools and universities; as mentioned, this would later become a major client of and exhibition venue for Church-produced filmstrips and videos.[198]

Finally and perhaps most importantly, by the 1890s the Church was abandoning its communal economic projects in favor of assimilation into mainstream capitalism. Joseph Smith's revelations are replete with commands and instructions regarding economic egalitarianism and redistribution of wealth—88 out of 112 of his canonized revelations touch on economic matters[199]—and in Utah these principles were put to the test in communal industries, banks, commerce, and entire towns. This communal idealism was not too out of place in Jacksonian America, but, decades later, it even more than polygamy situated Mormons in unacceptable opposition to the laissez-faire attitudes of the industrialized robber baron era. One by one, internal difficulties and external pressures caused the communal efforts to die out, and though the Church has retained numerous business interests up to the present it has done so in a much more corporate guise than the worker-owned joint-stock companies of the 1860s and '70s. As Leonard Arrington summarizes in *Great Basin Kingdom,* his landmark work of nineteenth-century Mormon economic history,

> Tie-ups had been made with eastern capital; the corporate form had

replaced the theocratic and cooperative forms of a generation earlier; Mormons were joining Chambers of Commerce, civic clubs, and working closely with Gentiles [non-Mormons] in Utah in many business ventures; and the church no longer insisted that members "ask counsel" and "take counsel" in regard to economic affairs. Most of the goals of the pioneer church—the gathering, the Mormon village, unique property institutions, economic independence, the theocratic Kingdom—were abandoned, or well on their way toward abandonment, at the end of the century.[200]

A few pages later he adds that with the 1908 decision that tithing could henceforth only be paid in cash rather than in kind such as produce or livestock, "the church no longer offered a geographic and institutional alternative to Babylon . . . Individualism, speculation, and inequality—once thought to be characteristics of Babylon—were woven into the fabric of Mormon life."[201]

Other perhaps less noticeable changes of the time included the complete dissolution of the already weak Council of Fifty, which had once functioned as the main political arm of the Church; the transfer of a monthly fast day and accompanying testimony meeting from Thursday to Sunday to allow employers to remain open during the week; and the gradual disappearance of charismatic gifts of the spirit such as interpreting dreams and speaking in tongues. Glossolalia had arisen in Mormonism's earliest days and individuals had even occasionally been called and set apart by priesthood authority to exercise it, but ultimately it faded with the deaths of those who had practiced it in the 1800s.[202]

The people involved in all these decisions probably saw the changes in politics, education, business, and worship style as positive steps toward rapprochement with the rest of the nation, and the Mormons' conciliatory efforts were rewarded when Utah gained its long-awaited statehood on January 4, 1896. The Great Accommodation was crucial in achieving this, but it also helped that Grover Cleveland was in his second nonconsecutive term as President. His predecessor the Republican Benjamin Harrison was in office from 1889-1893, when the Mormons made most of their concessions including the Manifesto, but even though his administration and the Republican Congress admitted North and South Dakota, Wyoming, Montana, Idaho, and Washington to the Union—the most under any President since Washington—and even though he pardoned all polygamists and Republicans had been working locally with the Mormons to reshape their religion, Utah was denied statehood during his administration because of its well-known tendency to lean Democratic, a concern Cleveland and the newly elected Democratic Congress did not share. They passed an Enabling Act in 1894 that allowed Utah to apply for statehood, which was granted two years later after extensive lobbying by Hiram Clawson, Isaac Trumbo, and others.[203]

The end of the pioneer era was marked by at least three other events that involved significantly less outside coercion and had no direct effect on Utah's statehood or Mormons' national acceptance. The first was the dedication of the Salt Lake Temple on April 6, 1893. After forty years of labor by hundreds of workmen, including many who didn't live to see its completion, the temple became a concrete symbol of the Church's permanence in the west as well as of global Mormonism in its entirety. But ironically, as its modern trappings implied, it simultaneously signaled the end of the fading pioneer era as well. The next temple would not be completed until 1919 and from this point on they would be built not just in the faith's heartland but wherever Church membership warranted.

Similarly, by the 1890s Church leaders cautiously ceased admonishing converts to immigrate to Utah, instead advising them to stay where they lived and "establish Zion" in their homelands. This effectively marked the end of the gathering begun under Joseph Smith in the 1830s. After this, Zion became a spiritual metaphor rather than geographic location and the influx of religious immigrants to Utah trickled off, although it would take several years for it to completely cease; my own grandmother emigrated from the Netherlands to Utah in 1915 after her family joined the faith, but such instances were now anomalous rather than the norm, and the pioneer era was over. The Church, shifting focus from inward isolation to outward accommodation, was now ready to exist throughout the world.

The third event was not related to the Church specifically but was still necessary for the establishment of cinema among the Mormons. Motion pictures required electricity, and Mormon country was electrifying as quickly as anywhere else in the U.S. As mentioned, the Salt Lake area opened its first power plant—the proprietors of which claimed it was the fifth in the world[204]—in 1881; portentously for film, one of the first buildings to be crudely outfitted was the Walker Brothers' Grand Opera House, a multipurpose theater, and in 1893 the area's first major building to incorporate incandescent lights and become truly electrically functional was the Murray Opera House just south of Salt Lake City.[205] Power quickly spread throughout the city and to rural regions: by the 1920 census "Utah [had] a higher percentage of farm homes served with electricity than ... any other State."[206] Over 34% of Utah farms were electrified, compared with the national average of 7%, implying the potential for rural motion picture projection as well.

While all this was going on in Utah, motion pictures were being invented in Europe and the eastern United States. Cinematic technology began with photographic technology, of course, but required a strip of pliable film, rather than earlier forms of plate-based photography and paper film, that could rapidly pass through a camera. The first modern motion film stock—with a semi-transparent celluloid base, a layer of adhesive gelatin substrate, and another of light-sensitive emulsion—was invented in 1889 by Henry M. Reichenbach, working for George Eastman and basing his work on that of brothers J. W. and I. S. Hyatt from 1865 and Hannibal Goodwin from 1888. In 1891 William K. L. Dickson, working for Thomas Edison, cut this type of film into a strip 35mm wide for use in his kinetoscope, a one-person viewing apparatus that ran the film in a continuous loop; as with the mutoscope, Herman Casler's competing device, Dickson and Edison used rotating cylinders for recording their images. But this continual motion would need to be replaced by an intermittent mechanism for greater stability in the camera and the ability to project onto a screen during exhibition. Robert W. Paul and Birt Acres worked together on such a system in England and created a 35mm film camera in the spring of 1895; additional work into the 1900s eventually yielded reliable systems like the hammer-and-claw system or Maltese cross whereby film rolls' continual movement could be transformed into intermittent motion near a camera's or projector's gate. Even before such mechanisms were perfected, the French brothers Louis and Auguste Lumière succeeded in projecting an image and on December 28, 1895 they premiered their cinématographe—a projector/camera-in-one that had been functional since at least February when they applied for a patent—to an audience at the Grand Café in Paris; because this featured a projected image and a paying public this is the date usually cited as the advent of cinema, although the German Maximillian Skladanowsky had done the same thing with his invention the Bioskop in Berlin on November 1; he couldn't compete with the Lumières' superior technology and capital, however, and hence remains largely forgotten by history. The cinématographe dominated the industry for several years, eventually giving it its name, but new breakthroughs in recording and projection systems continued apace in England, the United States, France, and Germany.[207]

The fact that these events occurred at the same time Mormonism was transforming itself to engage more fully and fluidly with the world may not seem coincidental to many Latter-day Saint observers. It is common for devout Church members to believe in a sort of "salvation" or "faithful history," in which "divine intervention has played an important role in the restoration and establishment of the LDS Church."[208] This includes events like the guarantee of religious freedom in the infant United States and Joseph Smith's family being led to live near where the golden plates were deposited, but it also includes more abstract beliefs about how all advances in communication, medicine, engineering, and science are revealed to man from deity and that the rapid proliferation of scientific knowledge in the last two hundred years is due to the fact that God is again communicating with mankind, creating a modern Renaissance to allow his Saints to prepare the world for Christ's Second Coming. Though fanciful, this belief is not without empirical merit—perhaps by way of confirmation bias—to those already predisposed to believe it. Evidence abounds: Religious historian Nathan Hatch has pointed out that the Second Great Awakening itself, which gave rise to Mormonism, was essentially a "revolution in communications, preaching, print, and song; and these measures were instrumental in building mass popular movements"[209] like Mormonism, which could not have thrived as it did without the printing press.[210] More recent technologies helped as well, and the Mormons accepted them also as heavenly gifts: the transcontinental telegraph line, for instance, reached Salt Lake City in 1861 and after the Civil War Mormons worked assiduously, primarily donating "tithing labor," to create a north-south line to link their settlements. Brigham Young offered a dedicatory prayer to consecrate the line

> to the Lord God of Israel, whom we serve, for the building up of His Kingdom, praying that this and all other improvements may contribute to our benefit, and the glory of our God; until we can waft ourselves by the power of the Almighty from world to world to our fullest satisfaction.[211]

Blessing the telegraph was more than rhetorical flourish: Young and his followers truly believed the Lord had provided it for their use in building the kingdom—just as he would give them trans-planetary locomotive powers after the Resurrection. Young put this belief succinctly when he told those southern Utah settlers who the telegraph would serve that "all the great discoveries and appliances in the arts and sciences are expressly designed by the Lord for the benefit of Zion in the last days."[212] Since its invention cinema has often been included in pronouncements like this: as mentioned in the Introduction, in the February 1913 issue of the *Young Woman's Journal* Levi Edgar Young published an article entitled "'Mormonism' in Picture" in which he makes a list of recent inventions, identifying how each one "added to the means of promulgating the gospel," before stating that "the moving picture together with all the other modern inventions is to help us carry the Mission of Christ to all the world, and to bring humanity home to the true principles of salvation."[213] Twenty years later apostle and scientist John A. Widtsoe echoed this by saying "the radio, the phonograph, the motion picture have come to benefit humanity . . . As we move over the earth with our message, we need more and more to use all of these devices, as they come along . . . These things no doubt will come, for the Church of Christ is always progressing without violating the fundamentals of our faith."[214] In 1980 M. Russell Ballard of the Twelve said of technologies such as satellites and computers, "I happen to believe these things have been inspired and created for the building of the kingdom of God. If others use them, that's fine, but their basic purpose is to help spread the gospel."[215] And in 2014 apostle David Bednar even asserted that the social media platforms Facebook, YouTube, Instagram, Pinterest, and Twitter, all of which he cited by name, are "inspired tools" provided by heaven to help proclaim the gospel "and to accomplish the Lord's work."[216]

By the 1910s, then, many Mormons saw film as just the most recent manifestation of God providing the technological means to spread the gospel, and the apparent inspiration of so many isolated individuals like Dickson, Paul and Acres, and the Lumières, combined with their process of piecemeal *bricolage* that reassembled component parts of bicycles, firearms, and traditional cameras—as well as new concepts like the Latham loop in America and Maltese cross in Britain—into the new apparatus of cinematography, could all serve to further cement Mormons' belief that full-motion filmmaking was a divine gift—how else could such an unlikely process have been orchestrated? What is perhaps the first mention of motion pictures in a Church-owned publication, the July 2, 1891 edition of the *Deseret News*, makes this view abundantly clear:

> It is no trouble at all to believe in miracles when we have them every day before our eyes in plain sight. Surely a miracle equal to any related of old time is the kinetograph, Edison's latest. The name comes from two Greek words, meaning to write motion. This is exactly what the kinetograph does. By means of electricity and photography this truly scientific miracle is accomplished. That is the kind the Nineteenth century miracles are—scientific.[217]

Views like this were part salvation history and part intimations of Progressive Era enthusiasm, but they influenced profoundly how Mormons—and other Christian groups[218]—would envision their use of film even up to the present, especially, as we'll see, in the production of propagandistic films by the Church itself. As Christ's parable of the talents shows, a divine investiture eventually requires a divine accounting of the use of the gift: filmmaking, then, became a stewardship.

Origins

Whether we accept a view of cinematic intelligent design or not, the timing of cinema's invention in the 1890s could not have been more propitious for Mormonism. Motion pictures matured as a storytelling medium precisely at the time Mormonism matured into a movement willing and able to interact with the wider nation and world. By the 1900s both were perfectly prepared for each other, and Mormonism's engagement with cinema began in earnest.

2 THE FIRST WAVE: THE NEW FRONTIER (JULY 1898—23 OCTOBER 1929)

The Church that is not equipped to show motion pictures is as incomplete as a church without an organ. — Reverend Leslie Willis Sprague, 1921 [1]

In calling this era a new frontier there is some danger of making too broad of comparisons between nineteenth-century settlers and twentieth-century businessmen. The latter were products of the Industrial Revolution, the very event that, as films from *Union Pacific* (1939) to *Butch Cassidy and the Sundance Kid* (1969) have shown, erased the American frontier with railroads and corporations. Kristin Thompson for one has pointed out how the pervasive myth of "the Hollywood pioneers" of the early 1900s is somewhat exaggerated and disassociates these filmmakers from the large industrial entities that supported them.[2] From Edison and the Lumières onward, developments in cinematic style and technology have been backed by immense amounts of capital and industrial assets, and Mormon cinema is no different. But despite this caveat, the pioneer analogy in this case still holds merit and provides a useful lens through which to view early Mormon filmmaking.

There are at least three reasons for this. First, most of the earliest films dealing with Mormonism—whether apparently for or against it—set their stories in the Church's then recent pioneer past. Second, Mormon filmmakers like brothers Shirl and Chet Clawson were only a generation removed from Utah's true pioneers: the short twenty-six-year span between the 1869 coming of the railroad to Utah and the 1895 advent of cinema in Paris meant that many who actually walked the plains also watched the movies. The Clawsons' father Hiram, for example, journeyed to Salt Lake City in 1848 then lived there until his death in 1912, possibly long enough to see his sons begin their filmmaking work and certainly long enough to have attended other moving picture shows, something that, as a long-time manager of the Salt Lake Theatre, he was likely to have done. At least two younger 1847 pioneers lived until 1940, the year when *His Girl Friday, The Philadelphia Story, The Grapes of Wrath,* and *Pinocchio*—as well as Fox's pioneer epic *Brigham Young*—were released, and Hilda Anderson Erickson,

The First Wave: The New Frontier

the last living person to journey to Utah before the railroad, died on January 1, 1968, just days after *Valley of the Dolls, Doctor Dolittle,* and *The Graduate* came out for the Christmas holiday.[3] Joseph F. Smith, President of the Church during most of the First Wave, was born while his father Hyrum was held in Liberty Jail in November 1838 and also crossed the plains in 1848, but lived to oversee the Church's first official filmmaking efforts, even appearing in many of the Clawsons' short pictures.

The third reason is more thematic than these but is also arguably more important: it is the fact that the majority of early Mormon filmmakers were forced to assume a proud isolationist stance in response to what they saw as the mainstream industry's attacks on their religion. The First Wave has also been called the "Anti-Mormon Film Era"[4] because of the slew of films that portrayed the Church sensationally. Mormons who tried to defend their faith—including ecclesiastical leaders, politicians, and businessmen—were largely without recourse to political redress or allies outside the Church, leaving the filmmakers among them to their own devices to broaden the public conversation and depict what they saw as the glories of their scriptures, forebears, and contemporary leaders on film, thus at least providing an alternate narrative to that depicted in movies like *A Victim of the Mormons* (1911). The Church members who worked on films like *One Hundred Years of Mormonism* (1913) and *The Story of the Book of Mormon* (1915) must have felt like their nineteenth-century parents and grandparents on the pioneer trail: facing overwhelming odds with no worldly assistance but with a divine commission which would eventually allow them to prevail. Well insulated from the filmmaking centers around New York and Los Angeles, their films were a matter of pride, proclaiming to the world that Zion flourished in the tops of the mountains. In telling their story on film they had guides—modern Jim Bridgers like Thomas Ince and D. W. Griffith—but they still must have felt as though they were blazing ahead where none had gone before yet where God wanted them to go. And then, like the original pioneers once in the valley, they too sought to establish long-term roots in the field, not haphazardly but with great planning and control, often under Church direction.

A possible fourth reason for the First Wave's title lies in its films' aesthetic qualities. What remains of the work today appears to have a stark, rough-hewn primitivism akin to Christensen's pioneer panoramas, especially in fiction films. This is, of course, largely due to the development of cinematic language and style that was still occurring in the world at large, but even in the 1920s, long after classical and avant-garde styles had matured in Europe and the American coasts, Mormon filmmakers such as the Clawsons were still operating in an artisanal system akin to the 1890s, completely disassociating themselves technically and artistically from the mature industry, whether it be represented by *Battleship Potemkin* (1925) or the Keystone Kops.

It is possible, however, to overstate this point. The bulk of the Clawsons' work was documentary footage, and in this respect what survives does not appear too different from the most notable titles of early documentary feature films like *Nanook of the North* (1922) or *Moana* (1926)—although it bears little in common with more formally constructed films like *Drifters* or *Man with a Movie Camera* (both 1929). Much of our interpretation of the Clawsons' nonfiction films—and early Mormon narrative films—would depend on the original editing, and unfortunately precious little of that remains. The most readily available version of the Clawsons' work, the film *Latter-day Saint Leaders: Past and Present*, was compiled in 1948 from fragments of footage, making the editing unrepresentative of how they intended it to be displayed, and the bulk of their material held in the Church's archive is essentially raw footage that hasn't been edited at all beyond the stringing of one entire shot after another. Any observation about the pioneer aesthetic of the Clawsons and by extension other Mormon filmmakers, therefore, has as much or more to do with their two-man working method—in contrast with Hollywood's industrial model with specialized labor in place by 1916—as with the style of their films. In this sense they were indeed the pioneers of Mormon cinema, forging a new frontier.

Mormons and the Mainstream Industry

Mormons at the Movies: Commercial Exhibition and Distribution

But before any Mormon ever picked up a camera, their first and arguably most lasting contribution to cinema was patronage. It has remained a consistent and powerful force ever since, influencing not just Mormon filmmakers but millions more who have never considered a career in the film industry. We don't know when the first Mormons viewed a moving picture, though once again it's probable it occurred outside Utah rather than in it. We do know that Utah newspapers started noticing moving picture technology the same time as their national peers. Two months before the *Deseret News* described "the magician" Edison's kinetograph as a nineteenth-century miracle in July 1891, the *Salt Lake*

The First Wave: The New Frontier

Herald ran a front-page story detailing how the device would work in tandem with the phonograph to create what we today know as synchronized sound films.[5] Three years later in 1894 when Edison's newer kinetoscope entered the market the *Herald* first posted its own notice that the device was completed and the strongman Sandow chosen as its first subject, then a few months later reprinted the *Boston Herald*'s lengthier glowing testimonial of the new device in action.[6]

The original kinetoscope, which predates projected cinema, was a medium-sized cabinet containing a loop of 35mm film, zigzagged inside to allow for the maximum possible running time, which at forty to fifty feet was less than a minute. A standing viewer peered through a peephole on the top of the box to see the film running between a light and shutter; there was no sound and the image repeated as long as the machine ran. Competitors and copycats followed Edison into the field, raising general interest in the science and potential of motion pictures, even among the general populace: at a January 1898 meeting of the Nineteenth Century Club in Provo, for instance, a Mrs. De Moisy presented a paper about "the process by which pictures of objects in motion are produced, and the method of showing them by means of the kinetoscope, phantascope, vitascope and other machines"; within two years the Church's *Improvement Era* followed suit, reprinting a notice from *Popular Science* about time-lapsed kinetoscope films, evidently the first mention of motion pictures in a Church publication.[7]

Accordingly, the first motion pictures in Utah were shown on the kinetoscope and its chief competitor the mutoscope. The first kinetoscope in the area was apparently installed at Peeble's drug store in Ogden in February 1895.[8] That was a single machine; the first parlor devoted exclusively to displaying multiple kinetoscopes—along with phonograph records—was operating in Salt Lake City at least by May 1896 when it moved from 263 to 134 South Main Street, less than two blocks from the three-year-old temple. This venue was managed by a woman named S. Adella Tuttle who, at around age twenty, may have become Utah's first professional motion picture exhibitor. She advertised new songs every week, but we don't know how quickly she rotated her moving picture program. "LADIES," one ad proclaims, "step into the phonograph and kinetoscope parlors while up town and rest. Visitors always welcome."[9] This was apparently a success, and other halls followed. One quite popular attraction was a mutoscope parlor that was installed in the Union Pacific office on Main Street on April 12, 1900. The mutoscope—patented by Herman Casler in 1894, the same year Edison's team perfected the kinetoscope—utilized a sequence of images printed on card stock, like a flipbook, to create the illusion of motion. This parlor, which was free and open to the public—most other machines cost one penny per use—had six mutoscopes exhibiting pictures, fittingly, from the railroad's "Overland route," resulting, according to one grandiloquent reporter, in a scene in which normally

> staid professional men and timed maidens one and all craned their necks to get a glimpse of the latest novelty. During the process, owing to the fact that but two persons could obtain a comfortable view at one time, several spring creations of the milliner's art were placed considerably out of plumb. H. M. Clay trembles to think what will occur when the existence of the gratis show becomes generally known.
>
> The most popular series is that of the overland express, which is seen approaching in the dim distance and finally comes apparently racing out of the mutoscope to annihilate Francis B. Choate in the back office. So impressed was a tardy conference visitor with the illusion yesterday that he nearly succeeded in rendering the pedal extremity of a placid old gentleman into pulp in his hasty endeavor to jump the track.[10]

It is possible that this parlor remained in use until the office was moved to the new Union Pacific Depot west of downtown in 1909, though its appeal much longer than that is doubtful. But by the turn of the century kinetoscopes and mutoscopes evidently proliferated across the area, as a 1902 *Herald* article on the rapid growth of the "penny in the slot business"—including vending machines providing tests of strength and fortune tellers as well as dispensers of peanuts, candy, gum, and caramels—described them as common and accepted among the religious class: "Some of the pictures are rather risqué, but it may be said in extenuation that they are not half so bad as the announcements on the machines would lead the investigator to believe." [11]

It's a little difficult to determine precisely when projected cinema gained ubiquity in Utah, in part because of the continued use of the popular term *kinetoscope* for several years to refer to motion pictures that were now projected onto a screen. This was partly due to the familiarity of the term—as how in recent years we still use the term *film* for movies that were neither originated nor distributed on cellulose acetate—and partly due to branding among competing motion picture projectors; hence the (usually capitalized) Biograph, Vitascope, Phantoscope, and other devices. Edison himself knew that projected cinema for group audiences would quickly make his single-customer kinetoscopes economically obsolete, so he pushed his moving picture personnel to create the Projecting Kinetoscope, which obtained a sizeable portion of the market before the end of the century. Thus it's occasionally impossible to tell whether some journalistic references to the *kinetoscope* are to the projected or self-contained variety.

With that said, the first-known record of a movie screening in Utah actually implies projected film exhibition may have already occurred: the March 17, 1897 *Deseret News* states that the "Edison Viorescope, the latest of the motion picture machines," would be exhibited at the Lyceum Theatre, a variety hall that existed from 1896-98 at 35 West 200 South, again a mere two blocks from the now nearly four-year-old temple (and today a multilevel parking lot). The "Viorescope," which the next day's paper calls the "Vivescope," is most likely the Vitascope, a projector developed by Thomas Armat and Charles Francis Jenkins and marketed under Edison's name starting in April 1896 while the projecting kinetoscope was underway. But the article's nondescript headline and location in the paper, its phrase calling it "the latest of the motion picture machines," and that term's placement after a long list of other attractions that the Eunice Goodrich Vaudeville Company would be presenting all imply that a motion picture machine was not a complete novelty to the area; otherwise savvy promoters would have publicized it more vigorously. But what this article does indicate with certainty is that Utah had a public motion picture show by at least March 19, 1897, if not earlier.[12]

This and subsequent presentations illustrate that in Utah vaudeville was film's primary initial distribution method, taking the medium not just to Salt Lake, Ogden, and Provo, but many of the smaller towns in the Mormon Corridor extending from southern Idaho to northern Arizona. For instance, in November 1902 the Kickapoos vaudeville company and medicine salesmen entered a weeklong engagement in Coalville, Utah, a minute community halfway between Salt Lake City and the Wyoming border. The next January the company was playing in Diamondville, Wyoming, where one very young audience member noted that "they show moving pictures and pictures that don't move," presumably a magic lantern, and related how he had attended six nights of the company's seven-night stay.[13] The trend continued for several years: in 1906 one A. B. Jensen brought a lyric soprano, a posing dog, "educated pets," and other acts along with "Life Motion Pictures" to an unnamed venue in rural Logan, not far south of Idaho. And by 1905 or '06 a "Pop" Young controlled a chain of small theaters throughout northern Utah and southern Idaho that included short film exhibitions along with "'variety' bills and repertoire performances."[14] It seems that this popular and itinerant art form was ideal for disseminating the first moving pictures to the Mormons and their neighbors.

Film's first more permanent exhibition sites in Utah were possibly the amusement resorts that had long boasted camera obscuras and magic lanterns: in 1902 Ogden's Glenwood Park purchased a "kinetoscope of the latest pattern," though whether this meant it projected the image or not is unclear. This was duplicated in Salt Lake City, where the Saltair Pavilion, the most famous resort in Utah, was showing moving pictures at least by 1905 if not earlier. Saltair was built largely by the Church on the water of the Great Salt Lake in 1893, where it became an incredibly popular spot, even among Mormons, for its picnics, aquatics, roller coaster, and free-flowing alcohol. In noting Saltair's film showings in 1905, the *Salt Lake Tribune* spent much more effort describing its refurbished theater, a melodrama, a strongman, and a woman who could lift an entire piano and performing pianist with her teeth than on the moving pictures, once again implying that they were not the greatest novelty on offer.[15]

These early associations of vaudeville, carnivals, and ribaldry sometimes became cemented in the minds of Church members and their leaders. One of Salt Lake City's first film reviews, in 1906, described a series of films as "very demoralizing to any audience, especially to a Salt Lake [e.g. principally Mormon] audience at this particular time." The protagonist's exploits were "not the most edifying spectacle in the world, and it would not be amiss to prohibit the picturing of such 'heroes.'"[16] And in 1910 Joseph F. Smith, in the first known pronouncement of a Mormon Church President on motion pictures, decried the morals of modern drama and "other entertainment houses," saying that, "the drama of the day and the prevailing moving picture and vaudeville shows, it may be added, are as untrue to life as they are indecent."[17] Indeed, Richard Nelson, the foremost historian of this period, has indicated that as motion pictures became more common, "editorials in Utah as elsewhere echoed the concern, particularly of churchmen, that the unparalleled impact of the moving picture image would harmfully influence susceptible minds."[18] Though conceited and quite likely sexist, this worry for others was sincere within the conservative faith. President Smith exhibited true if patriarchal interest in 1912 when he discussed the daughters of over-indulgent parents:

> To be out at night, to be off to pleasure resorts, with strangers, perhaps; associating with men they do not know and never saw before; being free and unsuspecting in their natures, willing to accept the offers of

courtesy and kindness of perfect strangers—in a ball-room, or dance-hall, at a theatre, or any other place where they may happen to be; and the first thing they know, they are entrapped and ruined.[19]

If this was the attitude Church leaders took toward film's introductory milieu, we can also hear more than a tinge of jealousy in the rhetoric of Mormon missionaries in the British Isles, who lamented "those pleasure-hungry multitudes who prefer a silly 'moving picture,' in an atmosphere laden with nauseating tobacco fumes, to the finest sermon in the stateliest church ever erected in Christendom."[20] Some Mormons, however, welcomed vaudeville and motion pictures, as the Church's management of Saltair shows. In 1912 the Church leased the Salt Lake Theatre to one John Cort, who immediately organized a season of "'pop' vaudeville" under the management of prominent Mormon George D. Pyper, and in 1910 the Harry Lauder and Julian Eltinge vaudeville troupe was scheduled to appear in the Tabernacle itself. For many this went one step too far: *Variety* reported that "non-Mormons say the Tabernacle is the proper place for vaudeville [but] many Mormons believe that entertainment amounts to desecration of the Tabernacle and object strenuously to it." In the end conservative voices won out and no show occurred, in effect affirming the Church's official disapproval on the form.[21] Church members who perceived movies as frivolous at best or sinful at worst derived their attitude largely from these associations—with vaudeville, carnies, sexual predators, tobacco, and the generally misguided masses—of early film exhibition in Utah and abroad.

Itinerant film exhibitors toured with their wares for several years into the twentieth century,[22] but by the early 1900s cinema was moving into more permanent venues, and legitimate stage theaters became an ideal location; for many it was an easy switch from their already established magic lantern shows. The Salt Lake Theatre was showing kinetoscope pictures by 1902: that October the Beaty Brothers showed fiction films, actualities, and historical reproductions including the McKinley assassination, Carrie Nation smashing a saloon, Prince Henry of Prussia's U.S. visit, a man with four heads, and the traditional train scenes, battle scenes, and haunted hotel trick shots. The theater maintained regular film showings throughout the remainder of its existence, becoming a venue for prestige pictures; in 1916, for instance, it was the city's prime location for showing D. W. Griffith's Civil War epic *The Birth of a Nation*.[23]

Another early theater to convert to film was the Grand Opera House at 121 East 200 South. Opened in 1894 and operating under a series of owners and names, the Grand was showing films before October 1904 when the *Lehi Banner* announced that its current offerings from the International Bioscope Company "must not be confounded with the many picture shows seen here before [as] the English Bioscope is the most perfect instrument in existence for the projection of life motion pictures." In addition to significant locally made films that will be discussed later, these screenings on October 24 and 25 included George Méliès's 1902 *A Trip to the Moon* and Edwin S. Porter's 1903 *The Great Train Robbery* and *Life of an American Fireman*, as well as films of *Uncle Tom's Cabin*, *Rip Van Winkle*, *Robinson Crusoe*, *Gulliver's Travels*, *Little Red Riding Hood*, and scenes of the St. Louis World's Fair, the Russo-Japanese War, and other events. Admission ranged between 25 and 50 cents for adults and 10 cents for children.[24] Also, the Salt Palace, a theater and recreation center built in 1899 on 900 South, added film exhibition to its dance hall, bicycle races, and scenic railway during the period between its renovation in 1906 and its destruction by fire in 1910. Later, the Capitol Theatre, a traditional theatrical venue built in 1913, became one of the last converted but longest lasting motion picture halls in a 1927 renovation: it functioned exclusively as a movie theater until a restoration in the mid-1970s; today it is the city's home for opera and ballet.[25]

With films shown everywhere from amusement parks to opera houses, by 1905 they were popular enough to warrant their own devoted viewing spaces. Thus that June 19 when a Pittsburgh storefront was converted into a permanent film exhibition hall and dubbed a *nickelodeon*—denoting its five-cent admission fee—it set off a boom of similar theaters throughout the United States, including in Mormon cities. According to Nelson, even at the turn of the century the shops on Salt Lake City's Main Street, where Adella Tuttle and other kinetoscope exhibitors had operated, were being equipped to show projected films, and with the nickelodeon boom Salt Lake reportedly had as many exhibition facilities as any comparable city in the nation.[26] Most of these were clustered around Temple Square, particularly on Main and State Streets just south of the temple in an area that became known as Film Row. One nickelodeon was operated by Mrs. J. H. Young at 131 South Main, essentially next door to Tuttle's old parlor; though we don't know how long it operated, it was in the news in October 1907 when a young mother attempted suicide there by swallowing laudanum during a children's matinee. The week before, a less horrifying act occurred at another nickelodeon when one C. F. Schneider attempted to steal a candy slot machine from the lobby; while he was, perhaps not surprisingly, caught, this does indicate the very early sale of concessions in Utah film theaters.[27]

The First Wave: The New Frontier

The nickelodeon boom provided permanent exhibition venues across the country, but larger and statelier facilities would be needed both to attract the upper classes who saw films as a plebeian entertainment and, conversely, to support the longer and costlier "feature" presentations that the maturing industry was producing by the 1910s. Thus, in addition to converted stage theaters, many new houses included film projection in their initial design: probably the first—certainly the most aggressively advertised before 1910— was the Orpheum Theater at 132 South State Street that opened on Christmas Day 1905 with permanent film exhibition along with live vaudeville. The general manager Martin Beck and local manager W. L. Jennings promoted their films under the name of the "Kinodrome," a theater that featured a fifteen-piece orchestra and cost between 15 and 75 cents a show, or a dollar for box seats; 1,000-foot reels of film were generally procured from a distributor in Chicago, and by late 1906 a 2,000-foot production of *Kathleen Mavoureen* was shown. More standard offerings included news items, panoramas, and popular fictional pieces like Edwin Porter's trick film *The Dream of a Rarebit Fiend* in 1906. The Orpheum's Second Empire structure by architect Carl M. Neuhausen was often seen nationally as a model for other theaters that would handle both cinematic and live performances, yet it too underwent a conversion in 1918 to make it exclusively a movie house. It operated under various names and, with the Villa Theatre in the Holladay area, was one of the city's first theaters to show widescreen films in 1953, until the Church purchased it in 1972 and restored it into a dramatic venue called the Promised Valley Playhouse where it showed religious and popular plays until its demolition in 2002-03.[28]

The Orpheum was soon joined by many others. The New Grand Theatre under manager R. J. Riddell was showing films by April 1906, when singer Violet McCoy appeared "in new songs and motion pictures," meaning probably that she sang on her own and perhaps along with illustrated lyrics. Conversely, the play *A Parisian Princess*, presented that May, was interpolated with films during the scene changes, and in a bid to increase film attendance on Mondays one lady patron could get in free for every purchased ticket.[29] Also in 1906 the Lyric Theatre under a Mr. Sullivan and Mr. Considine opened its "Lyricscope," offering three showings a day until it was renamed the Shubert Theatre in 1908.[30] Indeed, by February 1906 the city had enough theaters that the *Deseret Evening News* said motion pictures had become "a fad in Salt Lake," and in October 1907 *Variety* reported that "the Nickelodeon, Red Theatorium, Gem Theatre, Family Theatre and Electric Theatre are all doing a great business with their moving pictures."[31] At this point new theaters were arriving quickly: in 1907

the partnership of Trent & Wilson opened the Electric Theater with manager
Harry A. Sims in the Brooks Arcade building on State Street and, just a few days
later, Max Florence, a Lithuanian Jew and saloon operator who claimed to be
a member of the Church, opened the Red Theatorium on Main Street near 300
South; in 1908 the Isis Theater Company was operating its namesake theater in
Ogden while in Salt Lake brothers William and Charles Minor opened the Empire
Theater less than a block south of the Orpheum at 156 South State Street; and
in 1909 Florence opened the Elite Theater and a family business known as the
Midgleys, who later ran several other houses, opened the Casino theater, their
first. In 1910 when they opened the Liberty Theater it was, with 1,900 seats,
"then the finest house in the West." There were many more venues in the early
1910s, including the Photoplay theater, a 250-seat house built by ranchers
and owned and run, uniquely, by a woman, a Mrs. McGrath; the Princess, which
due to its location in the Sugar House area was the first "neighborhood house"
outside the city center; the Mehesy theater; and others.[32]

The community of theater owners, though competitors, were also business
associates, frequently interacting to ensure the common growth of film
exhibition in Utah or to buy or sell individual theaters with other members of the
group. They formed a business association of film exhibitors and distributors
in 1916, corresponding with the growth of labor unions among their employees
that resulted in at least one general strike, in 1920.[33] These formal and informal
associations were critical to fostering a community and robust industry, and
as the movie business grew many individuals owned and operated multiple
theaters, although unlike in the days of the kinetoscope and nickelodeon, when
many proprietors were women, these were apparently all men.

One notable example was Harry R. Rand, a Congregationalist who found great
success among the Mormons. He had owned a chain of hotels in the west until
being nearly ruined by the 1906 San Francisco earthquake. He subsequently
reinvented himself with movie theaters by running his own distribution
exchange, opening twenty-six theaters across the country, and dubbing himself
"the Nickle King" or "Nickle Rand" [sic] with five-cent halls before moving
into more expensive fare, including several theaters in Salt Lake and Denver.
He purchased and renovated the struggling Empire Theater in 1909, billing
it, improbably, as Utah's first exclusive film exhibition space (although he
employed a Miss Eva Johnson as a soloist to perform while the film reels were
being changed). Under the management of R. H. Klappkir the Empire rotated
its selection of primarily Biograph shorts daily; with 300 seats the auditorium

represented a significant leap past the old nickelodeons and storefront facilities. Rand turned the theater over to W. E. Shipley in 1916, who then ran it until 1950. Physically unable to convert to that decade's widescreen formats because of its long narrow auditorium, the venue closed five years later.[34]

Though the Empire didn't compare in size with the 900-seat Orpheum or 1,900-seat Liberty, in December 1910 Rand renovated and reopened the Daniels Theater, which had been damaged in a fire, in partnership with his son Walter. At 2,000 seats it was billed as "the largest life motion picture house in America," and it also featured electric signs, enamel and gold decorations, damask draperies, a ladies' waiting room, and "a new ventilating system . . . which changes the entire atmosphere every sixty seconds."[35] By 1912 he was planning a 3,000-seat theater, saying, "This form of entertainment is inmensely [sic] popular here and there is every reason to believe that a large, elegant picture theater would pay."[36] Though this site didn't materialize, his holdings eventually included venues such as the Photoplay and his eponymic Rand theaters, the first of which opened on Main Street before 1910. He acquired the Isis Theatre on 300 South around 1919, and continued to operate it personally until his retirement in 1933; he passed away two years later.[37]

Max Florence, already mentioned, was the previous owner of the Isis. He began as an employee for others but soon purchased not only the Isis but the Shubert, Luna, Bungalow—which he converted from a stage theater after it was damaged in a fire—and other theaters to his portfolio, allegedly owning fifty-four houses between Salt Lake, Ogden, and Provo. He also branched into film distribution, all of which caused him to be described as "practically controll[ing] everything in the film and picture show line in the city" before bad business eventually forced him to sell off all but these latter two properties.[38]

William H. Swanson, known to friends as Billy, also owned and operated several theaters in the region, even buying the Bungalow from Florence after another fire, renaming it the Rex and making it a fireproof and respectable theater. Swanson was a non-Mormon who worked in different areas but centered much of his initial energy in northern Utah. Though perhaps best remembered as one of the founders of what became Universal Studios—while he was still in Utah—Swanson was also very influential in early Utah film distribution and proved a well-placed advocate for the Church in its campaign against the anti-Mormon films of the 1910s. He began as a theater owner in Chicago around 1906, reportedly erecting that city's first high-class theater devoted entirely to films, before eventually moving west to acquire several Utah venues by the early

1910s. When he acquired the Rex, Liberty, and American theaters (the latter discussed below) in 1916, it was the largest film-related deal in Utah history and gave the Swanson Circuit, as his properties were known, the largest theater holdings in the state. Swanson leased out the Liberty, operated the Rex himself, and ran the American as "his pet—the apple of his eye." He eventually moved on to other ventures, but his affection for the Mormon public who helped make him successful was evidenced not only in his advocacy against antagonistic films but in an annual holiday tradition he instituted in 1916 when he invited all the city's orphans and "Old Folks," members of the Church's then-organization for the elderly, to a free organ recital and film screening at the American Theater.[39]

Until 1916 the director, secretary, and manager of the Swanson Circuit was Harry Sims, who had entered film exhibition at least with the Trent & Wilson firm in 1907 if not earlier and by 1913 was known as "the oldest picture man, in point of proprietorship, in the state of Utah."[40] In May 1916 he left Swanson to manage his own properties throughout the state, and that September he announced that his new firm, the Deseret Theater Company, would build a new structure known as the Deseret Theater where the Isis then stood; although this never happened, the use of the Book of Mormon term and old territorial name "Deseret" harkened back strongly to Utah's pioneer past, showing either a shrewd desire to market to the Mormon populace or Sims's own religiosity as he attempted to marry his LDS faith with his profession, a decision that could have been catalyzed by the excitement surrounding the pro-Mormon films *One Hundred Years of Mormonism* and *The Story of the Book of Mormon* in 1913 and 1915. While Sims continued to work in the industry it is unfortunate that nothing more apparently came of this particular company.[41]

Though his holdings were not nearly as extensive as any of these men's, D. Lester Park is today perhaps Mormonism's best remembered early film exhibitor, due primarily to his later film production work, the fact that we are certain of his Church membership, and also possibly because of his prominent grandson author Orson Scott Card. Born in the Millcreek area of south Salt Lake in 1888, Park laid claim to being "the first man to show a motion picture in the state."[42] Though this was obviously showman's bravado—he would have been nine years old when projected films reached Utah—it is true that by 1905, at age seventeen, he had gained prominence in the local industry, presumably with nickelodeons. He worked frequently with his brothers Byron and Allen, making theirs another family enterprise. In the summer of 1907 Lester was badly burned in a fire while operating a projector at a theater on Salt Lake's Main

The First Wave: The New Frontier

Street, and Byron, also working the projector, escaped injury in a similar fire at a theater on State Street the following February. Such events were not uncommon in the early days of highly flammable nitrate-based film (the frequency of film-related fires caused nitrocellulose stock to be replaced by nonflammable cellulose acetate in the 1930s), but in this case it indicates that both brothers were working in theaters, either their own or someone else's, as young men. In the summer of 1908 they took over the Grand Theater in Salt Lake City with partner A. M. Cox and manager Howard S. Mills. Receiving their film prints from the Laemmle Film Service of Chicago, the proprieters held a daily matinee and evening performance, charging ten cents for adults and a nickel for children. The Parks remained at least intermittently involved with film exhibition for some time, eventually becoming associated with Ogden rather than Salt Lake, and by 1917 they had changed their sights from showing to creating motion pictures.[43]

Nationally, the steady progression from nickelodeons to theaters with 1,000 seats to 2,000 seats or more continued—and some would say peaked—with the creation of the famously opulent and enormous movie palaces around 1914, the year the Mark Strand Theatre opened in Times Square. New York and Los Angeles perhaps had the most famous such theaters, but they proliferated throughout the 1910s and Roaring Twenties in cities like Oakland, Detroit, Jersey City, and, of course, Salt Lake. In fact, when the American Theater opened on 241 South Main Street—less than a block from Rand's Empire Theater—on July 8, 1913, it was on the cusp of the craze, anticipating New York's Strand, often considered the first picture palace, by eight months. With 3,000 seats, it also accommodated 250 more patrons, though its cost of $150,000 was well below the Strand's million-dollar price tag. Still, at the time it was touted as the largest movie theater in the world, and it certainly proved a force to be reckoned with locally—more than tripling the size of the Orpheum and including a 165-foot marble and onyx lobby, ventilation, an electric sign, and a huge $30,000 concert organ. Opened by the Midgleys and sold after a few months to Albert Scowcroft's Liberty Theater Company of Ogden, it was then managed and part-owned by Harry Sims. A few years later it was sold to Swanson—perhaps how Sims and Swanson began working together—who eventually brought in manager Homer E. Ellison from Denver but retained ownership of the theater until it passed to Fred Dahnken in 1923 and then to a corporation of local businessmen in 1927; it closed two years later. Throughout its early years the American ran a five-reel program every night with seats ranging from five to twenty cents, and its prominence allowed it to secure an exclusive local exhibition deal with Fox and possibly other studios. Opening exactly twenty years after the Salt Lake temple dedication, it was certainly one of the most opulent buildings the city had ever seen, and it must have prodded local residents, Mormon and otherwise, toward their belief that bigger means better.[44]

Other large theaters followed throughout the state; as with elsewhere in the nation, many were among their cities' most notable structures. In 1912 Joe Goss, previously a manager at the Orpheum in Ogden, took over the Rex in that city, "considered by all who have seen it to be the prettiest moving picture house west of Chicago."[45] Provo's Princess Theater was built in 1913, G. H. Wilson's Alhambra Theater in Ogden by 1916, and various others—including the Oracle, Utah, Lyceum, and Cozy—followed, through to Ogden's enormous Egyptian Theater in 1924.[46] Today Salt Lake's oldest operating cinema is the Tower Theater from 1926; at 900 East and 900 South it helped lead the spread of theaters outside the city center. It was, however, highly renovated in 1950, losing its titular medieval-towered façade.[47] Today the Tower, an arthouse cinema operated by the Salt Lake Film Society, is the last vestige of the city's early exuberant film culture. Essentially all the others have been demolished or renovated beyond recognition.

In big cities the movie palaces flourished, but by the 1920s smaller cinemas stretched from Pocatello, Idaho to Flagstaff, Arizona, thus joining the telegraph and railroad in connecting much of small-town Mormon country with the rest of the nation for the first time: "They brought the larger world into Provo and Panguitch and Parowan, and in the process bound them ever more tightly into the fabric of American culture."[48] Rural theaters were smaller and simpler, of course, and often served other community purposes, with vaudeville continuing its connection with small town film exhibition long after its importance had faded in the larger cities.[49] March 1912, for instance, a typical month in Logan, saw films playing along with vaudeville acts at the Liberty Theater, swapping nights with musical theater at the Opera House, and playing autonomously at the Oak and Lyric theaters. The Liberty at this time had just come under the management of Guy Gilbert, a veteran vaudeville showman, thus making it natural "that the little playhouse [would] have all the latest good things in the vaudeville and motion picture line."[50] Some small theaters were the most notable buildings in their communities. In Brigham City, a town halfway between Logan and Ogden, the Opera House, an old pioneer theater from 1862, was converted to a combined vaudeville and movie theater in 1914; the Venice Theater in Nephi, just south of Utah Valley, was a two-story, 500-seat affair that was cooled by a subterranean creek running under its flooring, often over-chilling patrons during hot desert summers; and when the Midgleys' Casino theater in Salt Lake closed in the 1910s, its "ornate copper and brass façade, with the name of the house carried out in big electric letters on a framework arch" was transferred to a theater in the hamlet of Gunnison in the middle of the central Utah desert, making that movie theater "the most striking thing about the town."[51] Other houses included the Jewel Theatre in Santaquin, the eponymous Delta Theatre in Delta, the Lyric and Star theaters in Price, the Star Theatre in Jerome, Idaho, and the Orpheum, Egyptian, and American theaters in the old mining town of Park City, future home of the Sundance Film Festival. There was even a solution, based on the old itinerant vaudeville model, for areas too sparsely populated for a permanent film exhibition site: in 1931 "Bishop" Alma Flanagan (Alma is the name of a male Book of Mormon prophet) began touring old pioneer towns in southern Utah with his own portable film projecting apparatus, bringing the joys of the silent classics to communities like Springdale, Rockville, New Harmony, La Verkin, and Kanarraville, and accepting payment in everything from cash to cabbages.[52]

But even with the best of movie houses, rural viewers still didn't enjoy the variety of programming available in cities. Trips to town became occasions for entertainment as well as shopping and dining, a national phenomenon that was given a unique local spin thanks to Utah's predominant religion. Every April and October Mormons from across the region journeyed to Salt Lake City for the Church's semiannual general conference, resulting in a windfall for local hotels, retailers, restaurants, and, now, film exhibitors as theaters were packed with patrons who couldn't see the pictures on offer any other time of the year; the Utah State Fair was scheduled each October to take advantage of the same crowds. The practice started early—the aforementioned mutoscope parlor at the Union Pacific railroad office strategically opened during the April 1900 conference—and continued into at least the 1930s. In April 1906 the *Salt Lake Herald* described the variety of worldly entertainments offered to religious pilgrims at the Orpheum Kinodrome:

> The Orpheum management promises one of the best bills yet at the State street house for conference week, and in order that none of the visitors shall be disappointed daily matinees will be in order on and after Thursday until the following Thursday, with the excption of Sunday, and Monday, when there will be a change of bill. This week's offering will embrace some comedy turns, singing specialties and spectacular novelties.[53]

The spoils could be significant. *Variety* reported that this same April 1906 conference brought 10,000 people into the city and "all of the houses enjoyed a flourishing business"; in October 1907 the same reporter noted that "the great Mormon conference began Oct. 4, and brought several thousand visitors to the city, which crowded all places of amusement."[54] Trade journals gave similar accounts in 1907, 1917, 1925, 1926, 1927, and into the '30s. At that point the Depression and the conference's availability via radio began to reduce the number of visitors: in April 1931 they were estimated at 12,000, in October 8,000, and in 1932 a mere 3,600. Still, conference week remained a significant—and sometimes the only—way for rural viewers to see the pictures they wanted, as one "wistful" inhabitant of the tiny farming community of Malta, Idaho showed when he asked a Salt Lake City theater manager if *The Girl of the Golden West* would be showing during the April 1938 conference—and the manager obliged. Obviously the most attractive films were reserved for these crowds, with *The Birth of a Nation* a typical example for a prestige picture: after finishing its initial three-week run at the Salt Lake Theatre in early 1916, it returned for an additional week during the April conference.[55]

So many patrons during conference week meant competition between theaters was fierce, occasionally resulting in impressive feats of advertising gimmickery. Sometimes this was circumspect, such as a phonograph company's window displays of records of popular Mormon hymns, but at times the salesmanship became much more brazen. In 1919 three airplanes dropped leaflets and free tickets to the American Theater's showing of the film *Sahara* on the downtown area, and in spring 1920 two other theaters, the Paramount-Empress and the Kinema, each staged more audacious stunts to promote their conference films. First the Paramount-Empress, managed by former reporter and publicist George E. Carpenter, sent a veiled dancing girl around the city to give unannounced performances at an auto show, a hotel cabaret, a Main Street store window, and a Rotary Club dinner before it was revealed as a promotion for the film *On with the Dance*. We're told that the entire city became curious—some of it was scandalized—and that the financial reward for the theater was great.[56] The dancer's performances apparently came just before conference when the film itself opened, but the Kinema launched a strikingly similar campaign for *The Virgin of Stamboul* right "when it counted big; during the Mormon Conference" itself. In this case a mysterious Turkish girl, also veiled, paraded through the city on horseback, steering her "gaily caparisoned steed" through the throngs of worshippers literally leaving services at Temple Square. Meanwhile several newspaper articles described her engagement to a shiek and, later, her mysterious disappearance from her hotel room—along with the appearance of the shiek smoking a water pipe in a downtown store front—before the ultimate reveal that it was all an advertisement resulted in "long lines of people . . . waiting for the show to open each day."[57] Such stunts apparently continued to be successful; during the October 1922 conference the Paramount-Empress advertised *Her Gilded Age* with a window display "in which a pretty young girl bared her legs and had them painted by a Japanese artist in full view of a gaping throng" at fifteen-minute intervals throughout the day. It was not the bare legs but the interracial contact that was most scandalous, so the papers assured the public that the "Japanese" artist was actually a made-up Caucasian woman.[58] It's likely that exhibitors staged many similar promotions in the 1910s and early '20s, but with the decline in attendance from outlying cities today's conference goers no longer get to witness such corporeal spectacles.

Of course such promotions evince P. T. Barnum-style showmanship, making them difficult to execute and ineffective if done too frequently. During the rest of the year, then, theater owners relied on more conventional advertising methods like marquees and newspaper notices. In 1914 the Liberty Theatre Company, having just acquired both the American and Liberty theaters in Salt Lake City, began weekly publication of *American Photoplay Weekly*, promoting it as the world's first weekly film fan magazine published by a theater. The specificity of this claim means it very well might have been true, even though nationally distributed fan magazines like *Motion Picture Story* (later shortened to just *Motion Picture*) and *Photoplay* had begun publication elsewhere in the country as early as 1911.[59] *American Photoplay Weekly* was still apparently Utah's first such publication and a major undertaking for any company or film market: "as many as five thousand copies were distributed without charge throughout the city each week."[60] To compete, Louis Marcus's Notable Feature Film Company, also of Salt Lake, began a semi-monthly house organ called *Real Reels*, edited by George Carpenter, by mid-1915.[61] Competing film fan magazines indicates Salt Lakers were often awash in movie culture even when not at the theater. The magazines seem to have contained a hybrid of fiction and plot summaries, celebrity gossip, and legitimate industry news, thus keeping their predominantly Mormon readers abreast of everything from Pola Negri's latest romance to how Harold Lloyd performed his own stunts.

With movies a permanent component of most Mormons' lives, the many theaters in their region became, as noted in Chapter 1, one of the chief employers of Mormon musicians during the silent era. Very early in film history, exhibitors realized the benefit of using music to mask the silent images' uncanny effect and cover up the noise of projectors and audience babble; that music could relay emotional information relevant to a film narrative was an added bonus that soon became its primary justification. There is no mention of musicians playing in Utah's earliest kinetoscope parlors, which also often featured phonographs as well, but they must have been regular features of film theaters, especially music halls that also showed vaudeville, by the turn of the century. Performers would have been primarily pianists, followed by various string, wind, and even percussion players who filled out the largest venues, particularly by the 1910s. The Orpheum, as mentioned, featured a fifteen-piece orchestra under the direction of the Norwegian-born Mormon convert and violinist Willard Weihe, an incredible feat in the very early year of 1905, and it even seems that it was not the first such ensemble as "a number of the members of the Theater orchestra," an earlier venue, "joined that at the new house."[62] Weihe's orchestra provided concert music along with their film accompaniments, such as a performance of Mendelssohn's *A Midsummer Night's Dream* overture at a double feature of the short comedies *Post No Bills* and *The Dream of a Racetrack Fiend* in 1906, an interesting mix of ostensibly high and low art.[63] When the Park brothers opened the Grand Theater in 1908 Morris C. Stephenson led a small orchestra there, and, like Eva Johnson at the Orpheum, a tenor named Mellwood Wilson sang ballads with illustrated still images while the film reels were being changed.[64] In Ogden the first venue with multiple musicians was the Electric Theatre on 2500 South just east of Washington Boulevard. It was led by violinist Roy Wilkins and included George Warner on the traps (that is, drums) and, remarkably, a female pianist named Maude Strong. As the city paper recalled in 1923,

> In the days when Wilkins and his gang tremaloed and G stringed the heroine to her long-drawn out death or hurried on the chase which was the feature of so many films in that day, the big features were one reel in length and the name Pathé, Essanay, Edison, Vitagraph and Lubin were the most popular. The shows lasted one hour and sandwiched in between the reels were the famous illustrated songs.[65]

Soon organs became staples at all the large and many of the smaller houses. The Midgleys' 1910 Liberty Theater in Salt Lake was noted as possibly the first to have a pipe organ installed, making it "the wonder of the city."[66] And as movie theaters grew in size in the early 1910s they became as noted for their immense organs as for their films: the Rex in Ogden in 1912 featured "a $20,000 pipe organ that [was] played three times a day by [Edward] Kimball, one of the Mormon Tabernacle artists."[67] When the Paramount-Empress opened in Salt Lake in 1916, Weihe became its musical director and Kimball its organist, with Franz Rath at the piano. Kimball was still there after the organ was enlarged during the influenza quarantine of 1918 when all the city's theaters were closed. Management made it clear they did not want the new organ to "replace the orchestra; it will alternate with the orchestra during the shows and special recitals will be rendered from time to time."[68] Kimball and Weihe were not alone in creating a musical connection between the Tabernacle and nearby film theaters, as they were joined by many other prominent instrumentalists who played for both the theaters and the Church.

The best known of these was John Jasper McClellan, Jr., known popularly by his initials J. J. Having studied in Michigan and Germany, McClellan became the chief Tabernacle organist in 1900, where he initiated the free weekly concerts that became the precursor for the *Music and the Spoken Word* broadcasts (for which Kimball, the assistant organist under McClellan, was the original performer); additional Tabernacle performances included free VIP concerts for the likes of Buffalo Bill and his rodeo players.[69] Just as he had simultaneously taught at Brigham Young Academy and played piano for the Salt Lake Opera Company in the 1890s, McClellan now found time to see to his Tabernacle duties and perform in multiple concerts and cinematic venues. In 1910 he signed with Samuel Newhouse to lead the orchestra of the just-opened Newhouse Theatre, a $250,000 music hall-cum-movie theater, patterned after New York's New Theatre, that was part of the nationwide William Morris Circuit.[70] From there he moved to the American Theater at its opening in 1913 where he conducted the seventeen-man orchestra and operated its enormous Kimball organ, using its multiple voicings to achieve a net effect, he said, equivalent to thirty-five performers. Silent film musicians often took their cues from popular and classical music, and a sample of the American's sources—from Wagner, Puccini, Mendelssohn, Schubert, Strauss, and others—reveals the theater's high-art ambitions. It was also one of the first theaters in the country to put accomplished classical musicians in its permanent employ, and two years after it opened the trade journal *Moving Picture World* reported that the quality of its music helped it remain among the best "of the show places of Mormonopolis."[71] When Maurice Tobin took over the theater and expanded its organ in 1916—making it now the second largest in the state, after the Tabernacle's—McClellan's dedicatory concert had 3,500 attendees, "the

largest ever assembled at a motion picture theater in this city,"[72] including the
governor, mayor, and Joseph F. Smith and other Church leaders. At that point
the orchestra was expanded to twenty performers, including Weihe as assistant
director and occasional concertmaster. McClellan gave performances at
theaters besides the American, touring as far as Spokane, and by 1916 he was
so well known on the motion picture circuit that he was able to promote Bendix
brand sheet music for film accompaniment, proclaiming "it gives me much
satisfaction and pleasure to interpret the work of such artists" as those who
produced the Bendix arrangements.[73]

Even in the late 1920s, as talking pictures were poised to make live music
obsolete in movie theaters, Mormon musicians, like others, continued to
pursue their careers in film work. Alexander Schreiner, the German-born
son of Mormon converts, represents the generation of Mormon musicians
after Kimball, Weihe, and McClellan. Born in 1901, he was involved with the
Tabernacle Choir from the 1920s until the '70s, but he began his career at age
sixteen by playing for McClellan at the American. He followed that with a stint
at a theater in Butte, Montana, then, after a Church mission and study in Paris,
he played at Grauman's Metropolitan Theatre in California and then Salt Lake's
Capitol Theatre when Louis Marcus bought it for $300,000 and converted it for
film exhibition. This last position, begun in 1927, must have been short-lived as
synchronized sound began making its way into theaters that same year, and
Schreiner spent the rest of his life as a concert organist, educator, composer,
and, most famously, accompanist in the Tabernacle.[74]

Publicity and exhibition, including musical performance, are only half of the
equation in getting motion pictures in front of viewers, and Mormons and their
fellow Utahns were equally involved in the nascent film distribution business.
Soon after motion picture production became a viable commercial endeavor,
small companies sprang up to act as middlemen between film producers and
local exhibitors. They handled the logistical process of shipping film prints from
production companies to exhibitors and dealt with finances as the distribution
of money back up the production chain became just as complex as shipping
film canisters to the world's scattered theaters. Often called film exchanges
in cinema's early years, these firms were frequently focused in key cities like
Chicago but also spread throughout the country, including in Utah.

One of the earliest, even prototypical, examples was Charles P. Madsen—a
common surname of Scandinavian Mormon families—the general manager
of Charles P. Madsen & Co. at 115 East 100 South, literally feet from Temple

Square. He held numerous patents for devices like gramophones and curling irons in the very early twentieth century, so getting involved with motion picture distribution would have been a similar business venture involving new technology. In the November 2, 1902 *Salt Lake Herald* the firm advertised: "If you want to make big money, start an electric theatre and show life motion pictures of all the latest events. We furnish you complete outfit, including pictures, at very small cost, and instruct you thoroughly how to operate same free. This is a splendid opportunity for men of small means."[75] He also sold both internally viewed and projecting kinetoscopes. It's unknown how many exhibitors engaged with Madsen, but by 1910 he appears to have relocated to Chicago where he worked on further electric devices like the combination sad-iron and cooker; in 1917 he was listed as a research engineer at the Driver Harris Wire Company in Harrison, New Jersey. Despite what little we know of his early film venture and whether he was even a Church member himself, Madsen remains among the first film distributors in Mormonism.[76]

There were others involved exclusively in distribution, but many suppliers were also theater owners who, in order to maximize profit, opened their own distribution exchanges. This combination of distribution and exhibition is an example not only of slight vertical integration (omitting the production portion of the filmmaking mechanism) but of the not terribly efficient regional distribution model of the early film industry. In Utah, the Trent & Wilson firm may have been the first company to venture into both businesses with its Trent & Wilson Film Exchange, operating before 1910. The Rands, the Midgleys, Max Florence, William Swanson, and the Isis Theater Company all became as involved in distribution as they were with exhibition. The Isis, for instance, "besides owning different moving picture houses conducts an extensive film exchange, supplying numerous houses in the intermountain region, the Northwest and on the coast."[77] Swanson ran the Rex Film Exchange, and the Max Florence Film Exchange functioned not only as the nucleus for his own theaters but also served two other distributors, the General Film Company and the Progressive Film Exchange. In 1915 Universal made Salt Lake its distribution headquarters for the entire western United States, indicating the city's importance, and other national companies like the Triangle Film Corporation and the DeLuxe Feature Film Exchanges maintained offices there as well. In 1917 Harmon W. Peery, manager of the Ogden Theatre, hosted representatives from three west coast production studios, including Fox, to discuss the necessity of establishing another local film exchange; such enterprises continued until regional exchanges were by and large superseded by organizations with a national network, though this too had its roots in Utah.[78]

It is, in fact, because of his vision of a national network that William W. Hodkinson, one of the most influential distributors in the history of cinema, eclipsed all these initial efforts. Born in Independence, Kansas in 1881 and not a Mormon himself, Hodkinson began by working in the communications industry as a telegrapher, signal operator, and in other positions for Western Union and similar firms. He was drawn west to Utah and by 1907 opened "a nickel-store show"[79] in Ogden, the city which would remain his base for many years. His initial associates included apparent Church members Harry Sims, Walter Richey, and, at the Liberty Theatre Company, Albert Scowcroft and Charles Ziemer. By 1909 he launched the Progressive Film Exchange out of Oregon, which soon merged with Max Florence and was distributing films in Utah, where he began aggressively expanding his theater holdings and raising his admission fees. His local exchange with Florence was purchased by the General Film Company, making Hodkinson its manager and Florence's associate Louis Marcus his assistant. He then left Marcus to run the Utah interests and branched into San Francisco and Los Angeles, where he rented films for lengthier runs and concentrated on the longer multiple-reel pictures that were starting to come out of Hollywood. As he had attempted with the General Film Company, he decided to sidestep the traditional system of states rights film sales and create instead a national rather than regional network. Starting with his interests in the western states, he merged with other distribution companies in New York, Boston, Philadelphia, and Pittsburgh and on May 8, 1914 incorporated as the Paramount Pictures Corporation; the *Ogden Standard*, in announcing the new company, noted that Hodkinson "first saw the vision of this powerful combination seven years ago when, as an employee of the General Film company in Salt Lake, he used to discuss problems on the solution of giving moving picture fans the best." These discussions were probably with Marcus, who at this point was hired as the Manager of Paramount's Intermountain territory.[80] The name Paramount reportedly came from a New York City apartment building, and Hodkinson himself created the logo of stars surrounding a mountain peak based on Ogden's Ben Lomond Mountain. In order to have a premiere theater in Utah, in February 1916 he bought the Empress, an old vaudeville hall at 53 South Main Street in Salt Lake City, and rechristened it the Paramount-Empress; it was managed first by Homer E. Ellison, then later by Marcus followed, as mentioned, by George Carpenter.[81]

But it was with distribution that Hodkinson proved most innovative and influential. The state-by-state method of selling film distribution rights limited distributors' power and film producers' potential income. But Hodkinson saw a way around that. Within days of incorporating Paramount he contracted to distribute the films of two new production companies—Adolph Zukor's Famous Players Film Company and the Jesse Lasky Feature Play Company—throughout the entire country.

> By combining nationally, advances could be guaranteed for future productions that would be much higher than what might have been raised in separate states rights contracts, thus encouraging the production of more ambitious films. In exchange for exclusive distribution rights and 35 percent of the rentals, Paramount agreed to advance $20-$25,000 for each five-reel film and pay for the cost of prints and trade advertising.[82]

The "Hodkinson" or "Paramount system" has caused Hodkinson to be described as the man "who had the deepest influence on the development of the movie industry," or, more simply, "the man who invented Hollywood."[83] Though similar (and similarly hyperbolic) epithets have been applied to others, in Hodkinson's case it does acknowledge the fact that his national distribution system catalyzed the shift in power from the East Coast trust companies, centered under the conglomerate Motion Picture Patents Company,[84] to the West Coast independent studios, as well as increasing the amount of capital available for more lavish and hence lucrative films—an impressive accomplishment for a man who started by selling five-cent movie tickets in Ogden, Utah.

Aligning with Zukor, however, proved personally disastrous for Hodkinson, as his ambitious associate quickly set about obtaining complete control of the company. Zukor "was uncomfortable about being, technically, a cog in the Paramount wheel" and, as the president of a fledgling production studio, disagreed with Hodkinson's hesitancy to "turn Paramount into a producing organization." Thus he and Lasky bought out enough of Paramount's original shareholders that by June 1916 they held majority ownership and forced Hodkinson to resign. They then merged their studios into the Famous Players-Lasky Corporation and transformed Paramount into not just a full-fledged studio but "the world's most impressive producing concern, as the *Film Daily* put it, 'the United States Steel Corp. of the motion picture industry.'"[85] Today Paramount is the oldest film studio in America, having made innumerable film and television productions, though few viewers of its contemporary animated logo guess at the company's origins in Utah's Wasatch Mountain range. It also continued to have immense influence in theaters in the Mormon Corridor for many years: one 1920 ad lists a bevy of theaters besides the Paramount-

Empress—in Utah, Nevada, and Idaho towns like Clifton, Elko, Hyde Park, Hyrum, Malad, Morgan, Pocatello, Preston, Randolph, and Smithfield—that exclusively showed Paramount pictures.[86]

Louis Marcus, for his part, proved more than a footnote in Hodkinson's story. A Brooklyn native, Marcus came to Utah in 1907 and found success there and in Idaho primarily as a theater owner and manager but also as a distributor. He managed both the Max Florence Exchange and the Notable Feature Film Company early in his career, and in the 1920s his Louis Marcus Enterprises ran several locations, giving him significant local prominence along with his association with Paramount. In 1931 he parlayed this into a successful run at the mayor's office, becoming the only Jew to ever serve in that position in Salt Lake City's history. Despite a partial retirement from the film business in 1929, while mayor he continued to have an active interest in his theaters, for example supervising a potential local merger between Paramount and Fanchon & Marco, Inc., which now owned the Orpheum. He died in office in 1936. That the primarily Mormon populace would elect a Jewish New York motion picture man during the depths of the Great Depression must reflect at least in part the esteem in which they held that industry.[87]

Obviously many of Utah's early film distributors were not Mormon themselves, although the majority of their clientele was. But there were several Latter-day Saints involved in this aspect of the business, with a few well outside of Utah. David P. Howells of Los Angeles was a pioneer in the distribution of American films to Asia and the Pacific, first by purchasing the Far Eastern rights of the World Film Corp., then by establishing the distribution program for Metro Pictures Corporation, a forerunner of Metro-Goldwyn-Mayer, for the Far East, Australia, and New Zealand, and finally by contracting on his own for First National's pictures, making his firm one of "the most extensive of the independent international distributors" until he dissolved it and moved to Salt Lake in 1925. He spent his last years in both cities, including serving as a Mormon bishop in Los Angeles. Slightly later, Gus Harms took a different tack, becoming the number-two man at the National Theatre Supply Company in Omaha, supplying theaters throughout the Plain States with projectors, organs, and any other equipment they needed.[88]

All of this—the presence of multiple theaters, established film distributors, film magazines, and even nascent film production—led to a vibrant cinematic culture among the Mormons in the 1910s and '20s. In 1914 one paper described the optimistic assessment of H. T. Nolan, an associate of William Swanson, that "Salt Lake has the best motion picture development in this country ... As for motion picture houses, Mr. Nolan said, Salt Lake is ahead of Denver, which itself surpasses any other city in the United States."[89] In 1917 F. H. Richardson, a noted expert in film projection techniques, described Salt Lake City as having "so many excellent examples of the photoplay theater that any attempt to adequately describe them would of necessity fail, from lack of space."[90] And in 1921 it was estimated that 30,000 people attended the movies in the greater Salt Lake area every day, representing roughly a quarter of the city's population of 118,000.[91] Mormons were demonstrably devoted to their movies, but the situation still allowed for detractors. Richardson for one found much to lament in the management of the theaters and their cavalier choices in projectors, bulbs, screens, and auditoria layouts. A few years earlier George Carpenter had called Salt Lake the "Dead Head City of America," scathingly describing how exhibitors' promotions—primarily the giving away of 40,000 free tickets a week—had transformed the city from "the best show town for its size anywhere" to, bluntly, the worst, a condition which he feared could never be fully repaired; other writers echoed the sentiment, with *Variety* calling the city "one large den of dead-heads" in 1915.[92] At that time "legitimate [stage] productions shunned Salt Lake City as a pestilence, as they had no desire to perform before audiences who had entered the theatres free,"[93] but through the negotiations of labor unions, theater owners, and, presumably, newspaper managers such promotions eventually diminished and Salt Lake and Ogden theaters recovered much of their business while selling full-priced fares. In the 1920s even the Church's organ the *Improvement Era* noted that Utah's tens of thousands of daily film patrons translated into enormous amounts of tax revenue for the state from movie ticket sales.[94]

The Church periodical, in fact, was not too hesitant to get in on the act. In the decades when Church publications ran advertisements—a practice stopped in 1970—new film releases were occasionally as good as any other advertisers. In 1918 the *Era* ran a full-page photograph of Douglas Fairbanks leaping over the Grand Canyon, and though this was actually a government ad to encourage the purchase of war bonds, the equivalent for Mormons today would be like seeing George Clooney splashed across the pages of the *Ensign*.[95]

This ad is indicative of greater issues than just where the *Era* procured its advertising revenue. It shows that Hollywood recognized Salt Lake City—and, indeed, all of Mormon country—as a respectable market worthy of attention. The photo of Fairbanks was in fact in conjunction with a cross-country tour he was taking with fellow stars Mary Pickford and Charlie Chaplin that, significantly, included Salt Lake City on its itinerary. Just as the Salt Lake Theatre had attracted top talent like Sarah Bernhardt and E. .L. Davenport to come play on its stage a generation earlier, now film producers accounted for the city in the publicity and distribution of their pictures. Though technically to promote war bond sales, this particular trip's greatest legacies would be the romantic affair it augmented between Fairbanks and Pickford as well as the formation of United Artists by all three of the stars, along with D. W. Griffith, in 1919. As for Chaplin, he had performed vaudeville in the city before and now found it either so delightful or so remote that he returned incognito in 1920 to edit *The Kid*, one of his best films, in his hotel room while essentially hiding out to protect the print from his estranged wife and her agents. 400,000 feet of film from 500 canisters littered every inch of his room—quite illegally, due to its flammability—until he and two assistants finished the edit and previewed the film, unannounced, in a local theater, where the enthusiastic response convinced him he had a hit on his hands that he could safely take east to New York.[96]

By the time the Depression approached, the cities and towns of the Great Basin were firmly on the film exhibiton map and members of the Mormon Church throughout the world thoroughly engrained into cinema's popular culture, often to their ecclesiastical leaders' chagrin. Despite this occasional disdain from Church leadership, however, the high levels of film patronage combined with national attitudes of the Progressive Era actually catalyzed a non-commercial force in film exhibition that would arguably have a greater influence on Mormon culture than the commercial theaters. In 1923 *Variety* reported that "Salt Lake City has more amusement places for its population than any city in America. In addition, the Mormon church has an amusement hall in every ecclesiastical division throughout the city, and there are about 50 of them."[97]

The new player was none other than the Church itself.

"Preaching the Gospel of Better Recreation": The Ward Movie and Private Church Film Exhibition

The growth of cinema in Utah couldn't help but prompt a response from Church leaders, who quickly grasped film's educational and socializing promise as well as its demoralizing potential. Hence, by the 1910s they taught that strict control must be exercised over film screenings. Corresponding with a larger reformation movement in America, the Church created programs and institutions that would permanently reshape its social climate, including Mormons' engagement with the movies.

The roots of this, of course, long predate cinema and have their basis not so much in moral censorship as in the Church's efforts to shape the social conditions of its members, growing not only out of the panoramas and magic lantern presentations of the 1800s but also other nineteenth-century amusements and more expansive social practices. In the early Church, entertainment was typical of antebellum America, focusing around events like dances, concerts, and impromptu athletic contests, none of which was necessarily overseen by ecclesiastical authority. But after the journey west the Church's organizational hierarchy expanded far more than under Joseph Smith, and so did the minutiae of its interests, so that in early Utah Church authorities often controlled innumerable aspects of Mormons' lives: where they settled, what they did for a living, and even when and to how many people they married. Social and recreational activities fell well within the hierarchy's purview, governing areas like dress, music, theater, social dance, and courtship rituals, so that "the role of the hierarchy in providing social control was pervasive until the mid-1880s,"[98] or, as one scholar summarized it, "the Mormons . . . spiritualized recreation."[99] Later, Church members' penchant to follow top-down directives in personal and otherwise non-religious affairs was enhanced by the threatening incursion of modernism and other outside influences that had threatened in 1856 then begun in earnest after 1869; this was repeated when the Church entered the more optimistic Progressive Era of the 1890s-1920s; both these forces deserve brief attention.

Modernism in this context connotes societal changes that "challenge the existing social order and ideals" of a community; in the nineteenth century this included "such things as the development of cities, occupational specialization and industrialization, the adoption of secular and rational norms, an increased democratization of the political process, a decline in agrarianism, and an increased diversity of ideas and life-styles."[100] For Mormons it essentially stemmed from increased contact with the rest of the United States. The threat that modernization presented to Brigham Young's Church is often remembered in terms of commerce: in 1869 Mormons responded to the transcontinental railroad by enhancing their Home Industry movement, striving for economic self-sufficiency and reinvigorated moral principles in the face of potentially corrupting Gentile merchandise and lifestyles. Many began to mobilize to protect their presumably most impressionable members—women and girls—

from outside contamination. Reformation among adult women had a profound influence on their lives during the thirty-five years that the Senior and Junior Cooperative Retrenchment Association operated,[101] and the Young Ladies Retrenchment Organization has lasted from 1869 to the present—today it's known as the Young Women program—giving birth to a similar organization for adolescent boys in 1875.[102]

Movements like these, while an attempt to retain the Mormons' individuality, ironically often made them more similar to their Protestant counterparts who they so distrusted. That is exactly what had happened a few years earlier in the late 1850s when the Mormons first felt besieged by the U.S. government, prompting a reformation movement that swept through Utah Territory. Apostles toured through Mormon settlements "warning of hellfire and judgment, and invoking sacrifice and obedience"; many Mormons were rebaptized or entered into plural marriage as a sign of their recommitment to their faith. One unintended result was the emergence of wards as the center of Mormon life, something that would be crucial for ward-centered film screenings after 1900.

> Before the Reformation most Mormons within a fair distance would travel to the center of Salt Lake City on Sundays to hear Brigham Young and the apostles preach in the Tabernacle . . . On weeknights they would attend small prayer meetings or meetings of the Relief Society and the priesthood quorum. But the Reformation emphasized the importance of the wards. During the settlement of Utah, wards were primarily understood as social and economic organizations; the bishops had custody over aid to the poor, directed settlement efforts, and resolved disputes. They would meet to woship irregularly. The apostles who preached the Reformation, however, gathered the Mormons by wards and emphasized the importance of ward meetings. By the end of the Reformation many wards were building meetinghouses and holding regular Sunday meetings there—and looking more and more like the congregations of other American faiths.[103]

Such reformations recurred periodically; just before his death in 1877 Brigham Young once again overhauled all priesthood quorums to better organize them and, fittingly, place them under ward supervision. In short, "by the late nineteenth century to be a Mormon increasingly meant meeting a set of standards in personal behavior, and as the nineteenth century wore on, the religious culture of Mormonism shifted to reflect priorities of socialization."[104]

The First Wave: The New Frontier

Today the central dilemma of this entire era is best remembered through the film *Pioneers in Petticoats*, which the Church made in 1969 to commemorate the centennial of the girls' organization. The film shows how a Church-sponsored dance, though initially seen as boring, is wholesome and enjoyable, while the entertainment at the public tavern is lewd and openly dangerous, ending in an attempted rape. The film also promotes proper speech and avoidance of American slang ("Fiddle-dee-dee!"), the female characters' homemade clothes, and romantic attachment to Mormon boys faithfully away serving proselytizing missions. But even more than its historical depiction, which is only partially accurate, Pioneers in Petticoats feels immediate: it projects the concerns of Church leaders in 1969 onto events from 1869, demonstrating through its very production how the use of controlled social events as a reaction against modernism is a perpetual endeavor in the Church; its creators wanted to persuade teen viewers to participate in social activities sponsored by their local wards rather than striking out on their own, something which Church leaders thought could prove morally disastrous in the wake of the Summer of Love. Indeed, supervision yields safety and autonomy danger in Church films across generations, including *How Near to the Angels* (1956), *Measure of a Man* (1962), *Morality for Youth* (1982), *On the Way Home* (1992), and *195 Dresses* (2011). The moral is consistently the same: recreation properly supervised by ward-level Church authorities and in compliance with Church standards is vastly superior to seeking entertainment on one's own where worldly influences may overpower the unsuspecting. This mindset took firm hold among Mormons for the first time in the newly unisolated decade of the 1870s when Church leaders quickly decided they could save their youth in large part by controlling their social activities.

While Mormons' initial attitude towards modernization embodied a pessimistic view of assault from the outside world, their engagement with the Progressive Era a generation later was expansive and optimistic. From Joseph Smith's first pronouncement about establishing a city of Zion, utopianism has run through much Mormon thought and hence prepared the Church well for the turn of the century when educators like John Dewey and politicians like Theodore Roosevelt embodied a new national spirit of optimism and belief in the virtues of bureaucracy to reform society and lift up its least advantaged members. Progressives "believed that effective organization and the promotion of virtue went hand in hand; they are two manifestations of a single commitment, and the former can indeed promote the latter." On a national level they "created the Federal Reserve, the eight-hour workday, the NAACP, the women's suffrage movement, Prohibition, and dozens of other laws and organizations designed to solve social ills and instill American society with middle-class values of democracy, industry, and education."[105] Many Protestants were active participants in this fervor, as the Social Christian movement sought to redeem entire populations from ills like poverty to prepare the world for Christ's Second Coming.[106]

Within the Church, the rapid changes of the Great Accommodation provoked a similar response, permanently reshaping it with a more ecumenical view of the outside world. We have already seen this faith in the world's knowledge and institutions in the work of James Talmage. Not only did his lectures cover a vast array of historical, geographical, and scientific knowledge, he devoted his life to various schools, libraries, museums, and social causes before eventually entering full-time Church service, where he remained among the most prolific educators in the upper hierarchy. He was joined in his Progressive ideals by fellow authors and General Authorities B. H. Roberts and John A. Widtsoe. "All three men regularly booked speaking engagements across the nation and represented their church at various conferences and gatherings . . . [They] were in many ways typical of the Progressive era. Their education bequeathed to them a very Progressive faith in the capacities of human reason, education, and effort along with their particular subjects of study."[107] The Church programs that formed under leaders like these sought to instill these same values, and did so at a time Church leaders may have acutely felt the need to reassert their influence in members' lives. With the Great Accommodation the Church had lost not just polygamy but control over schooling, politics, and business. Thus, leaders now worked through their bureaucracy to regain influence in more secular areas like recreation, employing an ideology that coincided with the era's national confidence in communal social programs. Thus, for example, for decades the names of the youth organizations were the Young Women's and Young Men's *Mutual Improvement Associations*, as their entire purpose was to improve young people through institutional effort.[108] This same spirit fostered the advent of several other distinct yet associated innovations within the Church besides film exhibition. While many of these are still present today, Mormons rarely realize their common origin.

First to follow in the wake of the new youth programs were publications to instruct teens and other segments of the Mormon populace. The young men's group began publishing the *Improvement Era* in November 1897, and this was followed by the Deseret Sunday School Union's *The Juvenile Instructor* in 1901, the Primary's *Children's Friend* in 1902, and the Genealogical Society of Utah's *Utah Genealogical and Historical Magazine* in 1910, with genealogical research itself becoming a permanent fixture of Mormonism during these years.[109] Church leaders also worked to create weekday instruction for youth through seminary programs affiliated with public high schools. The first of these was an initiative of the Granite Stake in connection with Granite High School in Salt Lake City in September 1912, followed by a program in Mt. Pleasant, Utah in 1916 and then spreading throughout the region.[110] Similarly, in the 1850s the Church had created a program for teenage boys to learn outdoor skills like camping and hunting; it was subsumed into the YMMIA by the 1880s, thus priming that organization to quickly adopt the Boy Scouts of America program after its founding in 1910. Individual wards began affiliating that year, the Church created an independent MIA Scouts program in 1911, and then it fully adopted the BSA program Church-wide in May 1913.[111] Some Church units had built social or amusement halls since the 1870s, but the national emphasis on educational and recreational space—seen in the growth of the YMCA movement—now spurred Church leaders to build libraries and gymnasiums en masse. The largest of these was the Deseret Gymnasium, a Church-owned public facility completed in downtown Salt Lake in 1910, but more typical were the scores of ward libraries and gyms or basketball courts built adjacent to chapels that became known as cultural halls and today still serve for all types of Scouting, athletic, social, and artistic events.[112] Their construction indicates a high level of interest in sports: Salt Lake City formed an outdoor athletic league in 1904, the Church began training ward leaders in sports like vaulting, wrestling, fencing, and gymnastics in 1911, and by the end of the decade official programs in baseball, volleyball, and basketball had spread throughout the Church, for years centering around national tournaments and remaining firmly in place throughout the century; the phenomenon of "ward basketball" even inspired the 2006 film *Church Ball*.[113] Cultural halls also frequently included stages that could be used for dramatic presentations. By 1910 the MIA had begun publishing lists of approved plays and sponsoring stake dramatic clubs through its new Committee on Music and Drama, and in the summer of 1911 the Granite Stake held its first "road show" or "merry-go-round" in which each ward's youth traveled to different meetinghouses to present a one-act play. In June 1914 drama was added to the list of annual MIA contests, and amateur road shows would arguably remain the dominant form of Mormon drama to the end of the century.[114] A third Granite Stake innovation that was soon adopted throughout the Church was a weekly "Family Home Evening," in which families spent Tuesday nights together discussing gospel topics and socializing together.

The Granite Stake began this in late 1909 and the First Presidency adopted the program Church-wide in a circular letter dated April 27, 1915.[115] Finally, the informal nineteenth-century program of "block teachers," pairs of lay members who visited other families in their homes, was adapted into the bureaucracy as "acting teachers" in 1909. Renamed "ward teaching" in 1912 and then "home teaching" in 1963, until 2018 it remained a fundamental component of contemporary Mormon society—featuring in films like *It's the Ward Teachers* (1956), *In the Service of God* (2003), and *The Home Teachers* (2004)—and the new approach to ministry still reflects the way in which Progressive Era attitudes successfully subsumed something as common as neighborliness into the Church's bureaucratic system.[116]

Less formally, Church groups like the MIA began overseeing other recreational practices. In December 1903, for instance, the *Era* published a list of amusements that were sanctioned by the MIA General Board: dancing, amateur theatricals, picnics, concerts, and home socials. By 1910 there were myriad editorials and sermons against saloons, vagrancy, vaudeville, and other demoralizers, with later statements warning against "evil" activities such as automobiling and smoking. Often local "amusement committees" were formed and many stakes began building and operating a new generation of amusement halls. In June 1911, the MIA organizations held a conference in the Tabernacle devoted entirely to recreation and social affairs, with speakers like Bryant Hinckley and the Granite Stake's Zina Cannon discussing issues such as chaperonage, how to create attractive events, and Sabbath day observance.[117]

The common theme among all of these innovations is the reinvention of the Church, and especially the ward, as the center of Mormon social life and an organizational institution capable of sponsoring well-supervised activities for youth and others. It was in this milieu that institutional film exhibition found a welcome home. The first recorded screening sponsored by a ward—or the Church in any capacity—was on Thursday, November 21, 1901. The Salt Lake City Eighteenth Ward held a fundraiser in its meetinghouse for its associated Sunday School and Mutual Improvement Associations, featuring a magic lantern lecture on the history of the Church by Ephraim H. Nye, who had just returned from overseeing the California Mission. The kinetoscope, however, and not the magic lantern, reportedly illustrated some of the events discussed, and while this could have been misreported it also possibly indicates that some local Church members had filmed rough reenactments of moments in Church history for this occasion. The song "The Holy City" was then sung along to magic lantern illustrations, and the remainder of the evening was devoted to traditional motion pictures—of unknown subjects—followed by more nationalistic lantern views like the inaugural parade of President McKinley, who had been assassinated just two months earlier.[118]

It is more than likely that similar ward-sponsored film screenings followed, or even preceded, this.[119] Throughout the subsequent decade members of other faiths in the Mormon heartland, partaking of the same Progressive spirit, added films to their offerings as well. For instance the Methodist Reverend B. F. Short used three short films to illustrate his sermon on June 25, 1911, with the Mormon-run *Salt Lake Herald-Republican* describing it as an innovation for the city and delight for the congregation: "The idea has never before been put into practice in Salt Lake, although it has been employed with great success in many of the larger eastern cities."[120] As Reverend Short openly planned to make the use of film a permanent endeavor, some Mormon observers must have begun considering showing films themselves. The most important of these was George D. Pyper, the General Secretary of the Sunday School and longtime manager of the Salt Lake Theatre. He was responsible for first showing films there, and he evidently had no fear of utilizing it in his ecclesiastical duties as well. He probably watched the monumental Biblical picture *From the Manger to the Cross* during its initial Salt Lake release in 1912 and evidently saw in it the means to outdo the Methodists. Acting in behalf of the Deseret Sunday School Union board he began negotiating with the Kalem Film Company and by August 1913 had secured the rights for the film's regional distribution: beginning on September 8 it ran for a week at the Salt Lake Theatre then was exhibited through December in wards in Utah, Idaho, and Wyoming. The *Salt Lake Tribune* reported, "Some of the higher Sunday School officials have in the past disapproved of the use of motion pictures in the study of the Scriptures, but it has been decided that they can be used successfully and with effect,"[121] and the Church-owned *Deseret News* simply added, "The motion picture is a wonderful invention. It may just as well be employed in the service of religion."[122]

Though this effort was apparently successful, the general Sunday School did not directly follow it with any other attempts, despite the establishment of an educational film exchange, Education Film and Service Corporation, in Salt Lake in 1913—with several prominent Mormons, including Church leaders Levi Edgar Young and Rudger Clawson, on the board of advisors—which would have made more titles available. Individual wards began purchasing projectors and holding screenings, though, and in 1916 an educator in Spokane claimed that the

Church had spent $60,000 on film exhibition just that year, but this is dubious and regular Church-wide attempts to exhibit films would have to wait for two additional events: the creation in 1916 of a Church Social Advisory Committee, with Stephen L Richards as chair and Pyper as assistant chair, and the end of World War I in 1918.[123]

The Social Advisory Committee embodied a confluence of Church leaders' concerns, particularly their interest in youth recreation and their Progressive belief that it could be properly regulated through organizational effort. The Committee's specific catalyst was a September 1916 letter from the First Presidency to the leaders of the children's Primary organization, asking them "to cooperate with the Young Ladies' Mutual Improvement Association and the Relief Society in promoting modesty of dress among young women."[124] Female leaders of these three auxiliary groups met in November and designed a long-range campaign against not only modern fashion but modern music—jazz—as well. The Young Men and Sunday School joined the efforts, and by the end of the year all Church auxiliaries were represented and had settled on the name of the Social Advisory Committee. Richards, who was soon ordained an apostle, and his associates set about trying to influence the broader society as well as oversee the recreation of Mormon youth. Workshops, conferences, and published instructions on everything from proper dance steps to the dangers of tobacco followed, and soon the Committee branched out from recreation to start engaging in serious social work, gaining professional training for some of its members that could then be relayed down to volunteer workers at the ward level. Driven by an enthusiasm that their social gospel was the Lord's work, the Committee soon got involved in politics and expanded its focus to cover nearly every aspect of society. As representatives of the always active Granite Stake viewed it when attending an eight-week course in recreation at the Deseret Gym in 1923, they were "preaching the gospel of better recreation" and were "determined to know what constitutes [a] successful recreational endeavor" so that they could pass it along to their fellow stake members.[125]

In their initial meeting the women of the Committee proposed censoring movies depicting crime, but nothing came of this suggestion.[126] Still, although it had a slow start with film, the Committee eventually involved itself with movies in several ways. The horrors of World War I and the influenza epidemic may have crushed the optimism of the Progressive Era, but when they were over it ironically paved the way for increased national interest in film as an educational tool, including outspoken support by men like Thomas Edison. This interest touched Utah and the Mormons as well: a new state-of-the-art film library at the University of Utah began serving churches of all denominations, among other clients, in 1920.[127] At the same time, in 1919 the Mormons, like all other churches in the U.S., were astounded by the success of the Methodist Episcopal Centenary in Columbus, Ohio. The event featured an eight-story outdoor movie screen before a seating space for an estimated four million viewers, including film pioneers Adolph Zukor and D. W. Griffith. A specially produced film cost a reported $300,000; Griffith and others raised an additional $120 million to outfit all 21,000 Methodist congregations in the world with projection equipment and send the film abroad.[128] The success of the fete and the film sparked an increased interest in film exhibition and production among all other denominations, including Presbyterians with their program known as New Era Films, as well as Baptists, Lutherans, Congregationalists[129]—and Mormons. The Social Advisory Committee quickly assessed the challenge, and just days after the Methodist event they were reportedly "considering the advisability of arranging for a regular series of films to be shown in the amusement halls throughout the Church."[130]

After this initial discussion it was, perhaps predictably, George Pyper and William Morton, who had helped create both magic lantern series and a motion picture, who at a general Social Advisory Committee meeting on December 16 proposed regularizing Church-sponsored "motion picture evenings" at ward amusement halls.[131] The concept was accepted and promoted—Richards gave the program official endorsement at the October 1920 general conference[132]— making film exhibition a Church-wide, if initially uncoordinated, endeavor; the acquisition of projection equipment and film prints, primarily through the University of Utah, was still overseen at the local level. Thus regular Mormon film exhibition was born as a mix of grassroots and hierarchical effort, a combination that did not seem incongruous at all at the time, and though the Social Advisory Committee was disbanded in 1922 film exhibition—and most of its other programs—continued under the MIA and other auxiliary organizations.

So what were these early screenings like? For one thing, they were not just an occasional event but, rather, a major and frequent way in which most Mormons regularly consumed films, despite the plethora of commercial theaters that surrounded them. Movies shown in meetinghouse chapels could have been accompanied by an organ or piano, while those shown in amusement halls might have featured combinations of string instruments, depending on the local community's talents; such accompaniments depended on the community's talentpool, of course, so it's also possible that many screenings were simply shown silently. Also, the majority of screenings were held just for amusement and education rather than as fundraisers, with admission fees simply covering costs. There was certainly a belief throughout the faith that no Church-sponsored social activity should earn a profit. As early as 1911 Edward Anderson taught that any social function designed as a moneymaker would be by default a social failure.[133] Thus in a *Ford International Weekly* article ten years later James Talmage described the new movie nights' purpose from both a social and economic perspective:

> The motion picture is a feature of ward recreation; and an effective censorship of subjects is exercised, whereby the films exhibited in the social centers are such as conform as nearly as possible to the Church standard of morals. It should be added that the Church engages in no recreational work for profit, its sole purpose being to provide wholesome entertainment at cost; though "benefit" performances or exhibitions are allowed, the proceeds from which are applied to some local need, such as additional equipment, renovation of the amusement hall, beautifying the grounds, and the like.[134]

In 1924 the First Presidency reiterated that "the making of money is not the primary object" of film exhibition and Melvin Ballard, an apostle and the Assistant Secretary of the YMMIA, asserted that while "recreation must carry its own burdens, it should not . . . be burdened with the responsibility of financing wards or stakes in their financial programs."[135] Still, this open back door—to provide cash for local needs—would very much become the rule in the ensuing decades.

As for which films were shown, we can ascertain a great deal by looking at the *Improvement Era*, which began publishing annotated lists of films approved by the Joint Committee of Recreation of the MIA's General Board in January 1924, with an apparent predilection for Mary Pickford and Douglas Fairbanks: titles featuring either of these two actors included *The Three Musketeers, Little Lord Fauntleroy* (both 1921), *When the Clouds Roll By* (1919), *Pollyanna* (1920), *Tess of the Storm Country,* and *Robin Hood* (both 1922), along with a few others like *Disraeli* (1921) with George Arliss and *The Headless Horseman* (1922) with Will Rogers; all the films were available from the University of Utah. Documentary film as we know it today was in its infancy in the early 1920s, but it's possible that newsreels and other "educational" material—perhaps even locally made films by the Clawson brothers or others—made it into the lineups, although a historical biopic like *Disraeli* or a literary adaptation like *The Three Musketeers* would have been considered educational. But most importantly these films were fun, made by Hollywood for entertainment, and that remained the heart of ward movie nights throughout their entire existence. The *Era* in the 1920s frequently featured similar articles with recommended films, commentary, and even one set of lesson plans in basic media literacy, with the types of recommended titles varying little from this initial list.[136]

There were, however, some who still saw film primarily as a moral threat rather than a social good, such as in a 1922 attack against the movies by Ogden Stake President Thomas E. McKay that drew cautious responses in cinema's defense from Levi Edgar Young and McKay's older brother David. In 1925 the *Exhibitors Trade Review* reported that some Mormons were trying to "exclude all but clean pictures from" Utah, and in 1927 Judge George Parker banned all films on Sundays in Provo.[137] Nevertheless, this seems much more the exception than the rule in the 1920s, and with private film exhibition this well established, and with a forty-year history of ward-owned amusement halls, it wasn't hard for a few Mormons to combine these concepts and build their own proper cinemas. The Fountain Green Theatre, opened in 1918 by the local ward in a small sheep-farming town in north central Utah, was apparently that community's only film theater. Half the space was devoted to a dance hall, which became the primary social center of the town, while the theater showed dramatics like children's plays and silent films: John Oldroyd operated the hand-cranked projector while vaudeville musician Deniece Blackham accompanied screenings on a piano. The ward ran the theater until 1944, and it eventually entered other uses and laid vacant for thirty years before being restored as a community center in 2004. Also in 1918 local Church trustees in Cowley, Wyoming purchased the Hub Theatre, which ran at least until 1930, and it's likely that other wards and stakes, especially in underserved small towns like these, did the same.[138]

One final way in which this enthusiasm for Progressive ideals and educational spaces manifested itself was in the creation of exhibits and what today we would call visitors' centers to explain Church history and doctrine to outsiders. After the success of the Mormon delegation at the World's Columbian Exposition in 1893, such efforts seemed like an obvious step in fostering public relations and innovating proselytizing efforts. Although the Church prepared exhibits for events like the 1909 Alaska-Yukon-Pacific Exposition at Seattle, the first and most important result of this effort was at the geographic center of the Church: the Bureau of Information, which opened at Temple Square—then still known as the Temple Block—in June 1902. Within three years 200,000 people had visited—one record indicates there were about 3,000 daily—and 100,000 printed tracts had been given away. Although no film screenings were held here in these early years, by the 1940s the Bureau was overseeing film exhibition at Temple Square, and in subsequent years films, videos, and now interactive digital displays have been the defining hallmark of Church visitors' centers around the globe.[139]

The rise of these exhibitions and bureaus relates to the fact that, even while Mormons were taking so enthusiastically to the use of motion pictures in their heartland, they were also increasing their use of magic lantern lectures and even phonographs among missionaries serving abroad. It seems likely that other presentations followed in the decade after the success of James Talmage's 1898 lecture tour of the United Kingdom, but lanterns came into prominent missionary use in early 1911 through the work of Andrew Jenson. A native Dane and prolific Church historian and lecturer, Jenson now presided over the Danish-Norwegian Mission, where he presented over fifty illustrated lectures—one known title was "Utah and her People"—throughout Denmark and Norway. That August he became the first Scandinavian mission president to visit Iceland, and while en route he and his traveling companions gave presentations aboard the ship and in Scotland and the Faroe Islands. Once in Iceland Jenson lectured (in Danish) in Reykjavik, where attendance was poor but the missionaries remained optimistic.[140] Gustive O. Larson, who oversaw Church Sunday Schools in Nevada, was equally active in that state, California, and Arizona in the early 1920s, repeatedly giving the lectures "The History of Mormonism" with 140 slides, "Ancient American Civilization" with 100 slides, and "The History of Temples and Temple Work" with slightly fewer. In 1923 it was estimated that 30,000 people had heard "Ancient American Civilization" alone, and after his release in 1924 lecturing was continued by Joseph Jeppson and a Sister Hogan.[141] Similar reports came from the eastern states, Great Britain, Oregon, Texas, Hawaii, France, and Germany as stereopticons spread throughout the Church's missions. By 1924 the Church in Utah was producing slides that missionaries could purchase before departing for their labors, meaning that somewhat standardized illustrated lectures would have been present in essentially every mission in the world.[142]

Film and visual media use had revolutionized Mormonism, helping move it out of its pioneer past and into the twentieth century. By 1925 Mormon film screenings became so frequent that Church leaders, represented by apostle

The First Wave: The New Frontier

Reed Smoot's private secretary Parlay Eccles, entered negotiations with professional distributors to organize their "exhibition halls and gathering places ... into a circuit, operating along recognized theatrical lines."[143] Several hundred such halls would show films one or two nights a week, and, while this agreement apparently never happened, it does indicate the voracious appetite for content that such an extensive network of amusement halls had—and how frequently Mormons were watching films together in their own private venues.[144] In fact, Mormon exhibition affected commercial cinemas in the western U.S. so strongly that professional film men occasionally organized against them. In 1918 the Intermountain Theatres Association began a series of unfair competition complaints with a government grievance board. The resolution, which did not come until 1934, stated that the Mormon wards could continue charging the below-market rate of ten cents per screening—or one dollar for a family for a month of attendance—but each ward could now only hold one screening per week—implying that they previously held more—and films shown had to have completed their commercial run at least ninety days earlier.[145]

Film was now so integral a component of Mormon life that *Improvement Era* editorials confidently prophesied the day when they would be able to breach the next frontier of exhibition and send moving pictures directly into people's homes, perhaps via the new technology of radio.[146] Little did they know that one of their own was already creating the technology to do just that, and the invention of television would be the greatest but by no means only contribution that Mormons would make to the mainstream film industry during the First Wave.

Mormons Go to Hollywood

While this film exhibition apparatus grew primarily within Mormonism's central enclave around Utah, other Church members were abandoning that region to establish a periphery of communities elsewhere in the United States. The foremost of these was in Los Angeles, where in January 1923 the Church organized its first stake outside the Rocky Mountains—and its first in a major metropolitan area. Continued growth from immigration and local conversions caused this stake to be divided in 1927, creating the aptly named Hollywood Stake. By that year California was home to over 20,000 Mormons; growth in other filmmaking centers was only slightly behind, with the first stake formed in New York City in 1934. As the Mormon population grew alongside the maturing film industry in areas like southern California, many Church members began working in a variety of motion picture-related capacities, many of which we may never know about.[147]

It may be asked what Mormons working on mainstream secular movies have to do with more traditional—e.g. religious—Mormon cinema, particularly when a great many filmmakers born into the Church do not affiliate with it as adults. I believe this moves beyond a mere curiosity factor in a number of ways. First, most if not all Mormon filmmakers who have made religiously oriented films have also spent a large portion of their careers on secular work, and this experience necessarily influences their filmmaking practice when they turn to devotional subjects. Second and conversely, their Mormon beliefs or roots in the culture often influence all of their filmmaking, either in practice or content—even when they move away from their childhood faith. Third, taking a narrower view there are multiple instances of Mormons who have not evinced much religious belief—incidentally a tremendously difficult thing for an outsider to judge—who nevertheless contributed directly or indirectly to institutional and independent Mormon-themed films. Fourth, the accumulation of Mormon professionals, even completely irreligious ones, in the mainstream industry has led to a critical mass of talent that has allowed Mormon cinema to emerge as a distinguishable ethnic entity. Though this is an oversimplification, other niche cinemas—Jewish, queer, African-American, Asian-American—have followed a similar pattern, with many members of those groups working in mainstream films before some of them gained the cultural confidence to make pictures about their own group. Although there are nuances and exceptions in all of these cases, it is safe to say that there would be no Mormon cinema, institutional or independent, in Utah today if not for generations of LDS filmmakers working in California over the past century: Los Angeles has been just as important to Mormon film as Salt Lake City or Provo. Fifth, those members by birth who abandon the Church are just as intriguing as those who remain faithful as they represent an important aspect of Mormon history—the great many individuals who have chosen to leave the Church—in the twentieth and twenty-first centuries. Without telling their stories we cannot understand the full mosaic of Mormon life. Sixth and finally, although Mormons were relatively sparse in early Hollywood, some did perform important roles that influenced the course of the entire industry.

The most significant director to come out of Mormonism in the silent era was James Cruze. He enjoyed spinning yarns about his childhood, making the truth somewhat difficult to ascertain, but he was born Jens Vera Cruz Bosen in 1884, apparently the son of convert immigrants from Denmark. He also claimed to have Ute Indian ancestry and to have been born on a reservation near Vernal in eastern Utah, but more prevalent reports have him born outside

Ogden in the north of the state. He was raised in a religious home but began distancing himself from the faith in his adolescence, although in one 1914 interview he described himself as a modern Mormon—meaning one more interested in Christian Science than in acquiring a harem.[148] He began as a child performer in a touring Indian medicine company before forming his own stock ensemble to perform Shakespeare and contemporary melodramas. He reportedly fled home and the monotony of farm life around age fifteen, then in 1906 he moved to the east coast and began acting in films; eventually he became attached to the Lubin Manufacturing Company and then, in 1912, the Thanhouser Film Corporation, becoming one of its leading men for the rest of the decade in films like *Joseph in the Land of Egypt* and the serials *The Million Dollar Mystery* and *Zudora* (all 1914), although he claimed to prefer character roles like Dr. Jekyll and Mr. Hyde. He performed for various other companies as well then in 1915 made his directorial debut for the Palo Alto Company in California, steadily increasing his directing work along with his acting. Settled in California permanently, he contracted with Paramount, becoming one of the most prominent directors of the 1920s, with a remarkable output varying from satirical comedies to genre thrillers to huge epics. His work with Wallace Reid capped the actor's career as a matinee idol and he helped Fatty Arbuckle transition from shorts to features, but he is best remembered today for his epic dramas, primarily westerns, with films like *The Covered Wagon* (1923), *The Pony Express* (1925), *Old Ironsides* (1926), *I Cover the Waterfront* (1933), *Sutter's Gold* (1936), and *Gangs of New York* (1938).

The Covered Wagon in particular is often cited as his masterpiece, and it also revived the struggling genre of the western by staging it on an epic canvas for the first time; its success briefly made Cruze, at $7,000 a week, the highest-paid director in the world. Although the film depicted a non-Mormon wagon train on the Oregon Trail, parts of it were filmed in Cruze's native Utah—particularly a bison stampede staged on Antelope Island in the Great Salt Lake—and it included a trail marker left by Brigham Young and a comical reference to his many wives. *The Pony Express* and *Old Ironsides* were also partially filmed in Utah, and the original 9,949-foot version of *The Pony Express* included an appearance by Brigham Young that was cut from the 9,801-foot release version. Despite well-praised films like *I Cover the Waterfront* Cruze continually struggled with alcoholism, his domestic disputes with his second wife actress Betty Compson (probably also LDS), financial mismanagement and lawsuits, and, ultimately, the waning quality of his films. He died virtually penniless in 1942, his contributions to cinema outshone, whether justifiably or not, by contemporaries like John Ford (with westerns) and Ernst Lubitsch (with melodramas).[149]

A lesser-known Mormon director was F. Harmon Weight. Born in Salt Lake City in 1887, he began his career as a teenage trapeze acrobat for the Barnum & Bailey circus. He then became serious about acting, performing first in dramatic stage productions of the Church's Mutual Improvement Association and then around 1906 in his own amateur dramatic club, graduating to professional productions, including his own stock company, by the 1910s. He headed additional companies in Portland, Seattle, and Tacoma before moving to California, where by 1916 he was a "chief scenario editor" for Universal. His writing credits are unknown, but that same year he began working as an assistant director—with the 1921 version of *Disraeli* the most prominent film he worked on in that capacity—and a year later he had his directorial debut with *The Ruling Passion* with Doris Kenyon and *Disraeli*'s star George Arliss, who also appeared in Weight's second film, *The Man Who Played God* (also 1922). He directed at least fourteen more films in that decade, such as the modern *The Taming of the Shrew* adaptation *Midnight Madness (1928)* and the Rin Tin Tin film *Frozen River* (1929). After that he apparently phased out of filmmaking, assistant directing two other films in the early '30s, and he died in Los Angeles in 1978 at the age of ninety-one.[150]

Weight's work writing scenarios is telling, as notable Mormon screenwriters were more plentiful than directors, with a few others occasionally trying their hands at directing as well, though not as consistently as Weight did. Jack Jevne had a successful career that spanned decades. A native of Provo, he served in World War I before moving to L.A. to start his film career, which included writing the scripts for at least fifty-eight pictures between 1919 and 1955. He directed two movies in 1935, but remains best known for writing films like *Eve's Leaves* (1926), the Laurel and Hardy farce *Way Out West* (1937), the Constance Bennett-Cary Grant horror-comedy *Topper* (1937), and another ghost story called *Wonder Man* (1945); he was, incidentally, also the third-billed writer on Cruze's *I Cover the Waterfront*. In 1956 his last-billed film, *Autumn Leaves*, was not his work at all: Jevne leant his name to the blacklisted writer Jean Rouverol Butler so that she could continue to work during the House Un-American Activities Committee's Hollywood purge. He then retired and passed away in 1972.[151]

Elliot J. Clawson was a nephew of Hiram Clawson and cousin of the filmmaker brothers Shirl and Chet Clawson and apostle Rudger Clawson. He began working in 1913 and spent his career almost entirely within the silent era, penning eighty-one produced screenplays, only a fraction of them shorts, by his retirement in 1929. Best remembered today is the 1925 *The Phantom of the Opera* with Lon Chaney, but his work ranged from westerns (*The Man from Red Gulch*, 1925) to adventures (*West of Zanzibar*, 1928) to literary adaptations, besides Gaston Leroux including films like *The Flame of Life* (1923) from Frances Hodgson Burnett's *That Lass o' Lowrie's*. In 1930 he received four separate nominations for the Best Adapted Screenplay Academy Award for *The Cop, Sal of Singapore, Skyscraper*, and the war drama *The Leatherneck*; the award went to Lubitsch's historical drama *The Patriot*, but Clawson's quadruple nomination remains an unrepeated feat.[152]

Another screenwriter from a notable Mormon family was Waldemar Young. Born in 1878, a year after both the death of his grandfather Brigham and birth of his brother Mahonri, whose career as a sculptor was mentioned in Chapter 1, Waldemar arrived at screenwriting via stints at the *Salt Lake Herald, San Francisco Chronicle,* and *San Francisco Examiner*, as well as incomplete studies in English at Stanford. He moved into writing stage comedy routines and publicity copy before signing with Universal in 1919; he subsequently wrote for Famous Players-Lasky, MGM, and Paramount, authoring eighty-one screenplays by the time he died from pneumonia in 1938. He contributed to two of Cecil B. DeMille's period epics—*The Sign of the Cross* in 1932 and *Cleopatra* in 1934—as well as some of Gary Cooper's most successful films, such as *The Plainsman* in 1936 and *The Lives of a Bengal Lancer* in 1935, for which he received an Oscar nomination.[153]

Harvey H. Gates contributed to well over 200 screenplays between 1913 and his death in 1948. His mother was Susa Young Gates, Brigham Young's daughter, an author and editor of fiction and nonfiction, and one of Mormonism's most prominent feminist activists. Born in Oahu in 1889 while Susa and her husband Jacob were serving there as missionaries, Harvey grew up in Salt Lake City's Twenty-fourth Ward. After serving a mission of his own in the northwestern states he returned to Utah and worked as a journalist for various Salt Lake City papers before moving to New York where he studied playwriting, edited the *Universal Weekly*, and served as a film critic for the *New York Dramatic Mirror*. He then transitioned into screenwriting, initially being associated with actor and director Romaine Fielding in Arizona before moving to Universal's story staff in Los Angeles; he later became a chief story editor for the Mormon-born producer Oliver Morosco and for Famous Players-Lasky, turning out dozens of short scenarios in the 1910s and moving into features in the 1920s. He worked steadily throughout the '30s and '40s, though never on prestige pictures, and some of his best-known works come from this time, such as *Black Dragons* (1942) and the wartime East Side Kids series of features about a group of young friends in New York City solving murders and taking on Japanese spies. His last film, the western *Racing Luck*, came out two weeks after he passed away.[154]

But the most unique—and prominent—screenwriter of the First Wave also had the most questionable relationship with Mormonism. June Mathis was born June Beulah Hughes in Colorado in 1887 but raised in Salt Lake City, which she always proudly claimed as her true hometown. There is a chance that as a child she joined or otherwise associated with the Church—perhaps through her step-father, a Utah native—although she never spoke of any such connection and, as an adult, professed devotion to the Bible while also being well-known for her Spiritualist, nearly occult, beliefs. Despite the lack of documentary evidence many Mormons claimed her as one of their own; a 1927 *Improvement Era* article proudly lists Mathis along with others as evidence of Utah's refinement, the implication being that Mormonism helped make these filmmakers into ambassadors of the state's civility.[155]

If we can't determine her childhood religious affiliation, we do know that Mathis was one of the most powerful women in early Hollywood. She became the head of Metro Pictures Corporation's scenario department and soon was essentially producing many of her pictures, which allowed her to pull both director Rex Ingram and actor Rudolph Valentino out of obscurity for her adaptation of the anti-war novel *The Four Horsemen of the Apocalypse* in 1921. She thus is credited with making Valentino a star and they were lifelong friends; today their remains lay side by side in her family vault. But she was also a major force at four different studios, at one point overseeing the final edit of Erich von Stroheim's *Greed* (1924) from six hours to two and a half, and when she died suddenly in 1927 she was in the process of helping form the Academy of Motion Picture Arts and Sciences. If her relationship with Mormonism was questionable, her influence on the American film industry was not.[156]

Mathis was not the only woman in Valentino's life with Mormon connections. His second wife Natacha Rambova, who feuded with Mathis over the film *The Young Rajah* (1922), was born as Winifred Shaughnessy in Salt Lake City in 1897. Her father was Catholic but through her Mormon mother she was a great-granddaughter of Heber C. Kimball, Brigham Young's longtime counselor. After her parents divorced Rambova moved with her mother to San Francisco where they entered the social elite; she then attended boarding school in Surrey, southeast of London, and danced in New York City with the Imperial Russian

The First Wave: The New Frontier

Ballet Company where she assumed her pseudonym. Her dancing career didn't last, but it gave her a taste for design that soon translated into work as a Hollywood art director and costume designer. She began by working for the actress Alla Nazimova, which pulled her into Mathis's and Valentino's circle. Having been introduced to Spiritualism, she once memorably held a séance in the Salt Lake Tabernacle, which her cousin Edward Kimball serenaded on the organ, in which she and a medium made contact with Joseph Smith, Brigham Young, Heber Kimball, and a flying Angel Moroni dressed in a blue robe. She designed for Cecil DeMille and other directors, then after marrying Valentino continued with several of his films—including some arguably scandalous designs—and other titles throughout the early 1920s, eventually working as a writer and producer and even occasional actress as well. Put off by films' plebeian nature, she moved into fashion and became increasingly important in the Spiritualist community, living in Europe—where she fled from fascism in both Spain and France—and New York for the rest of her life. Despite her preference for Spiritualism over her mother's faith, one could say Rambova unwittingly played the role of the nineteenth-century Mormon woman quite well: when she married Valentino in Mexico in 1922 his divorce from his first wife, actress Jean Acker, was not yet finalized, resulting, technically, in Rambova becoming Valentino's plural wife—and he being jailed for bigamy and put on probation by Metro. It was Mathis, of course, who steered the couple through this, and they later wed again, legally, though their union lasted only three years.[157]

The most prominent early film producer unquestionably born into the Church was Oliver Morosco, although like Rambova he apparently moved away from the faith while young. He was born Oliver Mitchell in Logan in 1875 then also went with his mother to San Francisco when his parents divorced, possibly as a result of his father's polygamy. There, a circus and theater impresario named Walter Morosco adopted Oliver and his brother, though their mother had by then remarried someone else, and trained them in the family business. In 1899 Oliver moved to Los Angeles where he eventually owned several theaters, and by 1906 he was producing plays in New York as well, where he ran over forty productions on Broadway and opened the Morosco Theatre in 1917. Though he remains best known for his plays and theaters, around 1913 he began an ambitious, though short-lived, venture as a producer and writer of motion pictures. Information is scant on the full range of the Oliver Morosco Photoplay Company's productions, but he adapted several stage plays and Jack London novels and was best known for boosting the careers of stage actors on the screen; titles included

The Yankee Girl, Peer Gynt, The Tongues of Men (all 1915), *The House of Lies,*
and *Madame La Presidente* (both 1916). In 1913 Morosco planned a string
of film theaters throughout the northwest, but by 1915 he was releasing his
films through Paramount, and as this company grew it eventually subsumed
Morosco's filmmaking interests. He stopped producing movies around 1917 and
lost his fortune in a speculative real estate investment in 1926; he was struck
and killed by a street tram in Hollywood in 1945. His son Walter, named after
Oliver's adopted father, also became a successful producer, writer, director, and
actor in the 1920s through '40s, though he had no connection with the Church
beyond his ancestry.[158]

At least one other producer was apparently a believing Mormon who,
interestingly, had no connection with Utah at all. Ralph J. Pugh converted to
the Church as an adult in his native Britain, where he originally worked for the
London-based First National Film Company, evidently a different firm than
the better-known American studio of that name. Because of his position in the
industry he proved important in helping his friend U.S. Senator Reed Smoot
oppose anti-Mormon films in the 1920s, particularly the British *Trapped by
the Mormons* and *Married to a Mormon* (both 1922). Later in the decade the
government required quotas of domestic films to match the influx of foreign
productions, causing British producers to rush to build new studio space in
which to create the mandated "quota quickies"; thus in March 1927 Pugh
created British Incorporated Pictures. Backed financially by a Lancashire
businessman named Rupert Mason and ostensibly backed morally by luminary
Britons like Conan Doyle, Pugh planned to convert the Palace of Engineering
from the recent British Empire Exhibition at Wembley in northwest London into
a massive film production complex. He created Wembley Central Film Studios
with thirty-five acres and 277,200 square feet of potential studio floor space, for
a price tag of £147,500, but backing fell through within a year and Pugh had to
sell his properties to Wembley National Studios, a less ambitious and thus more
risk-averse firm. He continued to work in the industry for at least a few years,
producing the forty-three-minute comedy *Above Rubies* in 1932, but nothing
else of his subsequent career is known.[159]

Given their long theatrical history, it is unsurprising that more Mormons entered
the nascent film industry as performers than in any other capacity. As the
Deseret News reported in 1916, some "natives of the Bee-Hive state went from
the stage to the studios; others went directly to the studios, though most of
them had had experience in amateur theatricals and were interested in the

work."[160] The prevalence of Mormon theater allowed a whole generation of actors to transfer easily to the screen.

Perhaps the most prominent was John Gilbert, billed after Valentino's death as the greatest lover of the screen. His maternal great-grandparents joined the Church in England and emigrated to Logan, Utah. His mother Ida Adair Apperly thus was born into the faith, but in 1898 she married the producer of a stock company as it came through town and left Utah for a life in the theater, where she earned little but performed well as a leading lady. In 1899 the marriage, short-lived, produced one child, born John Cecil Pringle, who accompanied his mother on the road and also spent several years in Logan with his more devout relatives, though there is no record of his baptism into the Church—"almost a Mormon," he quipped in a 1920 interview (and he was, in fact, baptized as an infant in the Church of England at the request of his father). As a youth he took the surname of his stepfather, a comic actor named Walter Gilbert, and he began appearing on stage in child's roles in whatever company his mother was with at the time. After her death in 1913 he managed to translate his acting experience into a contract with Thomas Ince. He moved from there to Fox, where he appeared in cheap melodramas and became an established actor. A switch to MGM in 1924 helped make him a star, especially with his appearances in *His Hour* and *He Who Gets Slapped* in 1924 and *The Merry Widow* and King Vidor's World War I epic *The Big Parade* in 1925. This last title, in which Gilbert movingly depicts an amputee decades before the introduction of digital effects, was America's top-grossing film until *Gone with the Wind* (1939), allowing Gilbert to reportedly become the first actor to negotiate a contract over one million dollars as he appeared in films like *Flesh and the Devil* (1926) with Greta Garbo. These two also appeared together in *Love* (1927), *Woman of Affairs* (1928), and *Queen Christina* (1933), and a rocky off-screen relationship ensued, almost but never quite ever reaching matrimony—most poignantly when she left him at the altar in 1926. Gilbert's fame did not last long after the advent of talkies, when he increasingly became a victim of poor roles and, reportedly, the personal animosity of MGM head Louis Mayer over Garbo. Still, by the time of his death in 1936 he had appeared in nearly one hundred pictures and helped create the image of a Hollywood star.[161]

Betty Compson, born Eleanor Luicime Compson in 1897, grew up in the village of Beaver, Utah. Though she occasionally disavowed any Mormon roots, most contemporary sources identified her as a member of the Church, making it probable that she was somehow affiliated with it as a youth, especially since she grew up in a small pioneer town rather than the more cosmopolitan Salt Lake City or Ogden. Her father died when she was young so she dropped out of school and helped earn a living for the family by playing her violin in vaudeville acts in Salt Lake City. After she joined a touring company she was spotted by moving picture casting agents and made her first appearance on screen in 1915, acting with Universal but primarily with Al Christie's company, appearing in forty-one short comedies for him in 1916 alone, often paired with Fatty Arbuckle. In 1918 she was fired over disagreements with Christie, but by then she was moving into feature films, a transition bolstered by her success in Paramount's *The Miracle Man* with Lon Chaney in 1919, and she actually founded her own production company in 1920 and began producing—and starring in—pictures like *Prisoners of Love* (1921). She continued working for others throughout the decade as well, and in 1928 she starred in two of her most famous pictures, Josef von Sternberg's *The Docks of New York* and the partial-talkie *The Barker*, for which she received an Oscar nomination. Her success with speaking parts led to a busy career in the 1930s, but the quality of her roles began to diminish and her career declined until her last picture, *Here Comes Trouble*, in 1948. She was also beset by personal problems: she wed James Cruze in 1924, a marriage that only lasted six years and left Compson responsible for hundreds of thousands of dollars of Cruze's outstanding debts and back taxes. This affected her for years, and when she retired from pictures it was to help her third husband run an ashtray manufacturing business. But by that point she had appeared in over 200 films and earned a star on the Hollywood Walk of Fame. She died of a heart attack in 1974.[162]

Like John Gilbert, actress Fay Wray's family had a complicated history with Mormonism. Her grandfather joined the Church when Mormons cared for his injuries after the Mexican-American War, but he and his wife resisted polygamy and their daughter, Wray's mother, abandoned her Mormon husband and eloped to Canada in 1900 with another man. Despite this initial evasion from the Church, they settled in the Mormon ranching colony of Cardston, where Wray was born in 1907, and then relocated to the Mormon settlement of Mesa, Arizona before returning to Salt Lake City—with a short stay in the town of Lark—from around 1912 to 1919, the years when young Fay would have become eligible for baptism, an ordinance she may or may not have received. Around 1918 she won a contest through the *Salt Lake Telegraph* to have a screen test. Nothing became of the project, but she was hooked and soon moved to Los Aneles and started appearing as an extra before moving up with westerns and other pictures at Universal. Her fame as an ingénue grew throughout the

The First Wave: The New Frontier

'20s until she was leading in presitigious pictures such as von Stroheim's *The Wedding March* (1928). She continued to work steadily with the coming of sound and played her most memorable role in 1933 as the female lead in Merian Cooper's *King Kong*, gaining fame for her capacity to scream throughout much of the picture; after the early '30s, in fact, she frequently appeared in horror films such as *Dr. X, The Most Dangerous Game* (both 1932), *The Mystery of the Wax Museum*, and *The Vampire Bat* (both 1933). She nominally retired in 1942 but continued to work through the '60s, ultimately appearing in over 120 productions, and she became a playwright in her later years. Thrice married, including to screenwriters John Monk Saunders and Robert Riskin, she died in New York in 2004.[163]

Interestingly, *King Kong* had one more brush with Mormonism: Brigham Young University's Motion Picture Archive now houses the Merian C. Cooper collection—including over seventy boxes of papers, seventy-five reels of film, and at least one Kong armature—and curator James D'arc was instrumental in the 2005 restoration of the film.[164]

A similar career was followed by Margaret Livingston, who never achieved the level of stardom she desired but nevertheless worked steadily throughout the silent era. She was born in Salt Lake City in 1900 and ran away from home to enter pictures in 1916; she was briefly followed in the 1920s by her sister Ivy, who earned only a handful of acting credits. Margaret made dozens of low-budget "quickies" in the 1910s and moved into higher-quality pictures by the '20s, being best remembered for playing the urban temptress in F. W. Murnau's masterpiece *Sunrise* (1927). Other notable films included *Through the Breakers* (1928) and the early talkie *Smart Money* with James Cagney and Edward Robinson (1931). She was generally considered director Thomas Ince's mistress and was with him when he either fell ill or was shot on William Randolph Hearst's yacht in 1924, dying a few days later; she was depicted as his lover in Peter Bogdanovich's 2001 film *The Cat's Meow*. A few years after marrying bandleader Paul Whiteman in 1931 she retired from the screen; the two remained married until his death in 1967, and Livingston passed away in 1984.[165]

At least three Mormons worked for the great comedy director Mack Sennett at Keystone Studios. Mary Thurman, née Christiansen, was raised in Richfield, Utah and after completing a degree at the University of Utah began a teaching career before being discovered by Sennett while vacationing in Los Angeles. In 1915 she became one of his most prominent Bathing Beauties—her obituary claimed she "had the most beautiful figure of all the old Mack Sennett girls."[166]

She performed in numerous light Keystone films before moving on to dramatic pictures, primarily for Pathé, and in 1923 she became a free agent. From 1916 to '19 she was married to Victor Thurman, a prominent Utah businessman, and by 1925 she had appeared in nearly sixty pictures. While filming in a Florida swamp, however, she contracted malaria, which led to her death from pneumonia that December. Her funeral was held in her childhood church in Richfield.[167]

Another Bathing Beauty was Ora Carew. She was born, as Ora Whytock, in 1896 and raised in the former home of apostle and Salt Lake City mayor Daniel H. Wells. At age fourteen she began a touring vaudeville act with her sister, traveling to San Francisco and, for a year and a half, Mexico. Returning to the U.S., she started her film career with director Christy Cabanne and the Fine Arts branch of the Triangle studio before being cast by Sennett in February 1916. His films helped make her famous, although when transitioning to dramatic roles in 1919 she said, "I would have forged ahead much more quickly if I'd stuck to the drama . . . If it hadn't been for comedy stunts, probably I'd have been a dramatic star by this time."[168] She did become a minor star, however, with pictures like *Go West, Young Man* with Tom Moore (1918), but by the 1920s her work was suffering and, after making forty pictures, she retired in 1928. She married twice—both during her professional peak—and had her only daughter when she was sixteen years old; she died in Los Angeles in 1955.[169]

But the best-known Mormon to work with Sennett was Mack Swain. Born in Salt Lake City in 1876, he was named Moroni by his father, a stone layer who worked throughout most the boy's childhood on the Salt Lake Temple. "Mack" attended the Eleventh Ward school and began his career there, performing in amateur Church productions before entering vaudeville at age fifteen, followed by minstrel shows and other stock companies. With his wife Cora King Swain he founded the Mack Swain Theatre Company in the early 1910s, but though he always retained an interest in live theater he joined Keystone in 1913 and quickly found his footing as a slapstick film star, aided by his huge six-foot two-inch 280-pound frame, oversized moustache, and a spit curl down the middle of his forehead. He was most frequently paired with Chester Conklin in twenty-six Ambrose and Walrus comedies, but he also became good friends with his fellow trouper Charlie Chaplin, who helped revive his career at First National after Swain left Sennett's service. He appeared opposite the Tramp in *The Idle Class* (1921), *Pay Day* (1922), *The Pilgrim* (1923), and, most famously, *The Gold Rush* (1925). As the Klondike prospector Big Jim McKay, Swain held his own with

The First Wave: The New Frontier

Chaplin in some of the most iconic scenes of silent comedy, such as when the starving duo delicately eats Charlie's shoe or slides around the wobbling cabin floor as it teeters on the edge of a cliff. He worked into the sound era—such as in *Soup to Nuts* (1930), the Three Stooges' first film—and died of heart failure shortly after retiring in 1935.[170]

Many other Mormon performers with notable careers deserve mention. Art Acord, known as "the Mormon cowboy," gained fame in rodeos before moving into pictures, first as a stuntman then actor, eventually appearing in over one hundred films, mostly westerns; he also occasionally wrote scenarios. He was decorated for his service in France in World War I, married thrice, and died of an apparent suicide in Mexico in 1931 at age forty, perhaps brought on by shell shock from his wartime service. Charles Meakin reportedly appeared in over 3,000 films between the early 1920s and his death in 1961, the vast majority of which were bit parts and often uncredited. Best remembered for his short comedies from the late 1920s, including *The Stunt Man* (1927), *When George Hops* (1928), and *Reckless Rosie* (1929), Meakin represents a brand of workingclass actor who never became a star but had a long and consistent career nevertheless. Lee (Leonard) Shumway, a grandson of early Church leader L. John Nuttall, was born in the old Cannon family home on South Temple Street. A stage actor before turning to film in 1909, he initially specialized as a heavy for Universal and other studios before moving into venerable roles such as lawmen in his later years. He appeared in 458 films, including many serials and westerns, before his retirement in 1953. Hazel Dawn was born as Hazel Tout in Ogden in 1891 but accompanied her father on a mission to his native Wales when she was eight. Consequently, she studied theater and music in Europe and earned her reputation on the stage in London rather than America. In 1911 the play *The Pink Lady* brought her to New York—where she was also in the original Ziegfeld Follies—and to the attention of the Famous Players Film Company. She starred in a dozen films between 1914 and 1920, but her main career was always on the stage and she retired altogether after marrying a mining tycoon in 1927. After his death she worked in an advertising firm casting department, and she appeared on film at least once more, in 1943, and on several television programs in the '50s. Frank Jonasson's father had been a prominent lawyer in pioneer Utah, and he was born in 1878 in the Avenues north of Temple Square. He too began his career on the stage, starting his own stock company in 1904 and playing Shiblon in a 1910 revival of the Book of Mormon play Corianton at the Colonial Theatre. He joined the New York-based Kalem Company around 1914. This firm specialized in shorts and serials, and he played in at least 115 pictures—such as *The Man on Watch* (1915), *The Midnight Man* (1919), and Cruze's *Old Ironsides*—by his retirement in 1930. He died twelve years later near Los Angeles. Mae Bosen, who was known both as May Cruze and Mae Bosen Cruze, joined her older brother James at Thanhouser in New Rochelle in 1912, appearing in a handful of shorts over the next four years. She did not stay in the business as long as her brother, however: she made her last film in 1916 then probably lived either in Utah or California; she reportedly passed away in Los Angeles in 1965 and was buried in her native Ogden.[171]

But perhaps the most unlikely Mormon actress to enter motion pictures at this time was Sarah Alexander. Born in western Virginia in 1836, she joined the Church and by the 1860s was a dancing soubrette in Brigham Young's Salt Lake City Stock Company. She played both in Utah and in touring companies for years, before eventually taking her niece Lisle Leigh east to New York where, retired from the stage, she raised the girl and trained her as an actress. Then in 1916 both women, at ages eighty and thirty-seven, were contracted by William Fox to appear in the film *Caprice of the Mountains*; they each continued to work for Fox, Alexander appearing in four more films and Leigh three. Given her age, Alexander's debut was quite newsworthy, garnering repeat attention in the trade journal *Motion Picture News*, and the *Deseret News* reported that she "was distinguished as the eldest actress who had ever been filmed."[172]

There is another group of actors who, like June Mathis, were raised primarily in Utah but whose biographies give no firm evidence of Mormon parentage or of their joining the Church as youths themselves. The possibility remains that these performers were indeed LDS, however, and even if not they did emerge from the strong dramatic culture that existed in Mormon Utah at the time, often beginning their acting careers with Church-sponsored troupes. Arthur Morse Moon is a good example of this: born in Garden City, Kansas in 1889, Moon was brought to Utah as a child by his actor father and he began appearing on stage in 1906. He became a well-liked comic actor with various stock companies in Utah before touring the eastern states, and in 1914 he began appearing in comedies from Universal and then a small production company named Vogue. Within four years he acted in over seventy short films. His wife Donna Drew, a Salt Lake City native, was a stage actress who only appeared in five films before the couple died within days of each other—apparently victims of the 1918 influenza epidemic—while performing on stage in Helena after just three years of marriage. Vera Sisson was born in Salt Lake City in 1895 and raised there and in Denver. She found fame in westerns opposite J. Warren Kerrigan and was a top star in Universal and Biograph melodramas in the late 1910s. Her star then faded and she permanently retired in 1926; she was married to director Richard Rosson and tragically overdosed on barbiturates in 1954, a year after his own suicide. Marguerite Clayton, an Ogden native who attended Catholic school in Salt Lake, was spotted by an Essanay Film Manufacturing Company representative while on stage at the Salt Lake Theatre. She appeared in over sixty Essanay westerns, playing opposite Broncho Billy Anderson, before transferring to their Chicago studio to act primarily in melodramas until her retirement in 1928. Julia Dean, born in St. Paul in 1878, lived in Salt Lake from age six to sixteen. She was primarily a stage actress but appeared on screen in the 1910s and then, after a lengthy stage career, again from 1944's *The Curse of the Cat People* until her death in 1952. Alfred W. Wertz, born in 1893, grew up in Ogden and went to Salt Lake High School. He trained as a civil engineer before being cast on sight for a picture, and he began playing juvenile leads for Universal. Most of his credits were under the pseudonym Willard Wayne, with at least one performance credited to Ed Wertz, making it hard to gauge his complete output, but he appeared in at least seventeen pictures between 1916 and 1922 before, probably, returning to his main career; he passed away in Riverside, California in 1966. DeWitt C. Jennings, while born in Missouri in 1879, spent his youth in Utah and performed extensively with Salt Lake City's various dramatic organizations. He had a successful stage career underway when he was cast in Cecil DeMille's *The Warrens of Virginia* in 1915. He worked steadily, mainly as a heavy or in paternal roles, and transitioned well into talkies, with six films in 1929 alone. His best-remembered roles came in the 1930s, perhaps most prominently as sailing master Fryer in *Mutiny on the Bounty* in 1935. He died in Hollywood two years later, with over 150 films to his credit. Finally, Charles "Buddy" Post was born in Salt Lake City in 1897; his first appearance was a bit part in the 1918 Mary Pickford picture *M'Liss* and he worked regularly until 1933 in films like the short 1919 Fatty Arbuckle-Buster Keaton vehicle *Back Stage* and King Vidor's 1924 adventure melodrama *Wild Oranges*.[173]

Post also spent 1930 and '31 working as a production manager on westerns, a career shift illustrative of the fact that, although we know the most about Mormon actors, many Church members, like production designer Natacha Rambova, found work in other technical positions in the early industry. One 1916 *Deseret News* article stated that "in addition to those who play parts in the photoplays, the technical departments of the various producing concerns give employment to several Utahns, some of whom have risen to enviable positions in their specialties."[174] Shirl Clawson worked briefly for Universal's camera department in the early 1910s, for instance, and in all likelihood there were many Mormons working as electricians, carpenters, costume designers, hairdressers, truck drivers, and other positions but who received less attention from the press than their onscreen counterparts.

One of these was cinematographer Lawrence Dallin Clawson, known as Dal (presumably after Cyrus Dallin, whose surname became a popular male first name among Mormons). He was a grandson of Hiram Clawson and his second wife Margaret, the son of prominent Salt Lake City physician Stanley Clawson, the nephew of Stanley's younger brother apostle Rudger Clawson, and the half-nephew—through a different plural wife of Hiram—of Church filmmakers Shirl and Chet, although he was only a few years younger than them. Born in 1885, Clawson studied mechanical engineering at the University of Utah and was living in Los Angeles by 1912, with his first recorded production credit—Lois Weber's adaptation of *The Merchant of Venice*—in 1914. He continued to work prolifically for Weber on films like *Hypocrites* (1915) as well as for Universal, Morosco, the American Film Company, and others, quickly advancing to high-profile projects like Thomas Ince's epic pacifist film *Civilization* (1916). In 1919 he was a founding member of the American Society of Cinematographers, now the oldest and one of the most important associations of filmmakers in the world. His career in the 1920s began strongly—he was the preferred cameraman for star Anita Stewart at Louis B. Mayer's studio—and included the early musical *Syncopation* and the Duke Ellington short *Black and Tan* (both 1929), but he began to increasingly shoot second unit work and B movies. His last films, shot on the east coast, were from 1932, and he died there, in Englewood, New Jersey, on July 18, 1937, within an hour of his mother's death in Salt Lake City.[175]

Grant Whytock, actress Ora Carew's brother, worked as an editor from 1917 until his retirement in 1970. Born in Salt Lake City in 1894, Whytock spent his career in Los Angeles where he was initially associated with the director Rex Ingram; he later cut for the likes of Rowland V. Lee, Jacques Tourneur, and Erich von Stroheim, including the eighteen-reel version of *Greed*; he was often a free agent but worked contractually for Metro/MGM in the 1920s and United Artists in the '30s and again in the '60s. Notable works included *The Devil's Passkey* (1920), *The Four Horsemen of the Apocalypse*, *Scaramouche* (1923), *The Emperor Jones* (1933), *The Count of Monte Cristo* (1934), *Timbuktu* (1959), and *Jack the Giant Killer* (1962). In the 1940s he assistant produced eight films, and through the '50s and '60s he produced eleven others, with an emphasis on westerns.[176]

The First Wave: The New Frontier

But despite the surprising abundance of Mormons who worked throughout the early film industry, the two Church members who had the greatest impact on the course of world cinema—and in one case, arguably, world history—were not filmmakers at all but scientists, who both began their work during this period, although the effects of what they accomplished wouldn't be felt until later. Harvey Fletcher was born in Provo on September 11, 1884 of pioneer parents. He enrolled in what was then Brigham Young Academy and upon failing his first physics course he re-enrolled, earned an A+, and gradually shifted his interest from a career in business to one in science. In 1908 he entered the University of Chicago where he earned his doctorate under Robert Millikan, collaborating with him on the oil drop experiment to measure the precise charge of electrons that subsequently earned Millikan the Nobel Prize in Physics; although it was Fletcher's idea to use oil rather than water, he allowed Millikan to take sole credit in return for credit for himself on another related experiment that would count towards his degree. This research led to the development of vacuum tubes and all related electronic devices. While at school he took extra courses, taught high school, and operated magic lanterns for lectures before graduating summa cum laude in 1911. In 1916, after a few years as head of BYU's physics department, he moved to New York to join the Western Electric Company's Research Division, eventually working as Director of the Acoustical Research Division of the Bell Telephone Laboratories, where he stayed until 1949. He then taught at Columbia for three years—devout throughout his life, while on the east coast he also served as a bishop and, later, president of the Church's New York, New York Stake—before returning to BYU to be Director of Research and the creator and first dean of the College of Physics and Engineering Sciences, where he remained until his retirement in 1958. He passed away from a stroke in 1981, just a few years shy of one hundred.

Fletcher's work at Bell Labs is the most germane to a history of cinema. While there he undertook a groundbreaking study of the phonemes and acoustics of human speech, and his technical work "led directly to high-fidelity recording, sound motion pictures, the first accurate clinical audiometers to measure hearing, the first electronic hearing aid (he was pleased that Thomas A. Edison wore one of his hearing aids), the development of the artificial larynx, improved telephone transmission, sonar, and stereophonic recording and transmission."[177] His work influencing sound films involved not the synchronization process but the quality of the sound reproduced, as his research into acoustics led to improved frequency ranges for recording and reproductive equipment, allowing for the full range of sounds necessary for a successful talking picture. In the late

'20s and early '30s Fletcher received numerous offers from Hollywood studios to develop their initial sound departments, all of which he declined, although in a 1930 interview he did claim that his greatest personal satisfaction was in the "guidance of a group that has done the fundamental research work which has made possible the present good quality of speech and music reproduction from the radio, talking pictures, and the phonograph."[178]

After this, his work with stereophonics, which he initially called auditory perspective and which was much more attributable to his individual efforts than sound film, had the largest effect on the film industry. He began this work in earnest around 1931, creating events featuring live transmissions such as a demonstration using binaural earphones at the 1932 Chicago World's Fair and a transmission of the Philadelphia Orchestra from that city's Academy of Music to a select audience of government officials at Constitution Hall in Washington, D.C. This latter effort was undertaken with Arthur C. Keller and the orchestra's conductor, composer Leopold Stokowski, and in December 1931 this trio succeeded in making the first stereophonic recording. A few months later they created Stokowski's first stereo disc for public sale—Alexander Scriabin's "Poem of Fire"—by switching from shellac to vinyl, an important change in the history of the record industry. Fletcher continued making advances in the field, increasing the number and accuracy of different channels, including an April 1940 Carnegie Hall concert, again with Stokowski, which among other sounds included a three-track stereo recording of the Mormon Tabernacle Choir. He repeated this performance at the Eastman School of Music in Rochester and in a theater in Hollywood. These recordings with the Tabernacle Choir were on magnetic film stock, rather than tape or disks, indicating the way for stereo to be introduced to motion pictures, while Fletcher himself turned to other areas of interest. Stereophonic sound made its first major appearance in the movies in *The Robe* in 1953 and became common after 1975 with the Dolby system. Its effect on the film and music industries is incalculable and most historians of audio technology deem Harvey Fletcher its primary creator; he was highly lauded in life and received a posthumous Grammy specifically for his work with stereo in 2016.[179]

Even the importance of stereo, however, pales in comparison with the most celebrated invention of Philo T. Farnsworth: television. Born of pioneer stock near Beaver in south central Utah on August 19, 1906, Farnsworth soon moved—via covered wagon—with his family to the farming towns of Blackfoot and then Rigby near Idaho Falls. While attending high school there in 1920-23 he proved a prodigious scientist and avid reader, especially on the pioneering television experiments of John Logie Baird and Charles Francis Jenkins; he also began working with electricity, maintaining the farm's generator and building an electronic washing machine for his mother. Family legend goes that fourteen-year-old Philo observed the rows he was plowing in his uncle's field and struck upon the concept of video scanning by sending individual electrons in a series of similar straight lines. Previous designs had all utilized moving mechanical parts, and the concept of making television entirely electronic opened the door for its actual creation. He received encouragement from his high school chemistry teacher and determined to make television a reality. After high school Farnsworth began attending BYU but his desire for a college degree was thwarted by its cost and his father's death. Instead he briefly attended the U.S. Naval Academy in Annapolis, helped with his family's boarding house in Provo, and ran a short-lived radio repair company in Salt Lake City. His partner there, also Mormon, was named B. Clifford Gardiner, and he would become both Philo's assistant in his television experiments and his brother-in-law when Philo married his sister Elma, known as Pem. After their marriage in 1926, she became an integral part of his work, so much that he frequently described her as his equal partner.

In Salt Lake City Farnsworth came to the attention of George Everson, an investor who paid for Phil, Pem, and Cliff to relocate to Los Angeles then San Francisco. They converted a loft at 202 Green Street, between Telegraph Hill and the bay, into a makeshift laboratory where, on September 7, 1927, the trio achieved the first all-electronic television transmission. The first static image of a single horizontal line was soon replaced by moving images of cigarette smoke and, as mentioned in the Introduction, Pem and then Cliff themselves. Their first public demonstration was given on July 2, 1929, the day in which "for the first time in television history an all-electric television system was operating" with no moving parts of any kind.[180] This was improved upon and repeated for a multiple-day demonstration at the Benjamin Franklin Institute in Philadelphia in August 1934, followed by limited broadcast of the 1936 Summer Olympics in Berlin.

Despite this early success—and Farnsworth's willingness to share credit with everyone who had contributed to television—in the 1930s he was brought into lengthy patent disputes with RCA, which claimed its employee Vladimir Zworykin to be the primary inventor of television and the 1939 New York World's Fair the device's first public demonstration. Friction with RCA and its head David Sarnoff actually began when the company's representatives visited Farnsworth in San Francisco in 1932, then it escalated when he moved to Philadelphia. The U.S. Patent Office eventually ruled in Farnsworth's favor, legally establishing him as the sole inventor of electronic television, but the struggle took a severe toll on his health and financial wellbeing. His career peaked with the establishment of the Farnsworth Television and Radio Corporation in 1938. In later years he continued to live modestly, further developing television technology and turning his attention to other issues, including the electron microscope, the infant incubator, and nuclear fusion, which occupied his final years at his own private company and at BYU; his work also contributed to electronic newspaper printing, star tracking for astronomy, and navigation of the space shuttle. He died of pneumonia, like his father, in Salt Lake City in 1971.

Farnsworth envisioned television as a means to unite and educate humanity, as with the 1969 moon landing (which used a version of his own original camera), and reportedly felt angry and remorseful when it was used differently; he often wouldn't allow his own children to watch it. Today, BYU Broadcasting's Philo T. Farnsworth Society advocates for television programming of which he would have approved. Despite struggles with alcohol, tobacco, and depression throughout his life—including alcoholism's contribution to his death—he was a deeply spiritual man and always maintained some degree of affiliation with the Church. Mormon leaders, including Church President Heber Grant and his counselor J. Reuben Clark, toured Farnsworth's San Francisco facility in 1935—and had their images broadcast by his camera—and in the October 1969 general conference Church President David McKay called him "one of our own eminent scientists . . . who testified to me that he knows that he was directed by a higher source in gaining his scientific knowledge." The next year, not long before his death, Farnsworth reiterated, "I am a deeply religious man, I know that God exists. I know that I never invented anything. I have been a medium by which these things were given to the culture as fast as culture could earn them. I give the credit to God."[181]

Hollywood Comes to the Mormons

In addition to Mormons going to Hollywood, it did not take long for the film industry to discover Mormon country. The arid desert so prized by Brigham Young because it would not attract Gentile interlopers into his Great Basin kingdom quickly came to be seen by the new Los Angeles studios as a prime spot for location filming. By the 1920s Hollywood crews began to place Utah on the global map, perhaps the first time the state was known as anything other than the isolated enclave of polygamous Mormons. Again, the production of

major studio films in the state may seem tangential to Mormon cinema, but
it too has enhanced a reciprocal relationship between Latter-day Saints and
the industry. This was particularly obvious when early religious productions
like *One Hundred Years of Mormonism* generated interest in establishing
permanent studios in Salt Lake City (discussed below), but the majority of
Hollywood filming took place in the open deserts and canyons of the south, an
area previously known for little else besides the Mountain Meadows Massacre.
This didn't occur by happenstance: generally, enterprising local Mormons,
working-class farmers and businessmen, courted Hollywood studios to bring
the lucrative new film industry to their small communities, an important but
usually unremarked way in which Mormons influenced early mainstream film
production. The result today is that major films are continually produced in
Utah—over 700 since the 1920s—bringing, for example, over $144 million to
the state's economy in 2004 alone.[182]

James D'arc, the foremost historian of filmmaking in Utah, sees the appearance
of the studios in the 1920s as the fourth major influx of outsiders since the
arrival of the Mormon colonists in 1847. Like the three previous waves—
California-bound gold prospectors in 1849, federal troops in 1857, and
merchants and businessmen brought by the railroad in 1869 (plus, it could be
argued, miners and related capitalists after 1862)—film production brought
some problems and cultural clashes but also "much-needed hard currency to
the struggling settlement[s] through commerce with outsiders."[183] The fact that
Utah, particularly southern Utah, has been used so extensively by the studios
suggests how beneficial the relationship has been for both parties: filmmakers
get convenient and remarkable settings for their productions and residents get
an influx of cash—as one Moab-area rancher put it: "They don't take anything
but pictures and don't leave anything except money."[184]

There is also no small degree of pride for locals at seeing their home on the
screen, even though, with the versatility of the landscape proving one of the
state's top draws, it has generally stood in for somewhere else. Occasionally
Utah has been identified as itself, as in *127 Hours* (2010), *The World's Fastest
Indian* (2005), and the opening sequence of *Indiana Jones and the Last
Crusade* (1989), but much more commonly it has represented other states or
an unidentified locale in the broader American west, whether in westerns—
including *Butch Cassidy and the Sundance Kid*, *The Plainsman* (1966), *How the
West Was Won* (1963), *Pony Express* (1953), *Warlock* (1959), *Once Upon a Time
in the West* (1968), *Back to the Future Part III* (1990), *Maverick* (1994), and *The*

Lone Ranger (2013)—or contemporary films—such as *Easy Rider* (1969), *Broken Arrow* (1996), *Mission: Impossible II* (2000), *Forrest Gump* (1994), *Hulk* (2003), *Austin Powers in Gold Member* (2002), and *Thelma and Louise* (1991), with its memorable climax filmed near Dead Horse Point northeast of Canyonlands National Park. Utah has also substituted for more exotic locales, such as the Palestinian desert in *The Greatest Story Ever Told* (1965), prehistoric earth in *2001: A Space Odyssey* (1968), the Mongol Steppe in *The Conqueror* (1956), Kafiristan in *The Man Who Would Be King* (1975), and even extraterrestrial planets in *Star Trek* (2009), *John Carter* (2012), *Galaxy Quest* (1999), and, perhaps to best effect, the original *Planet of the Apes* (1968) as well as its 2001 remake. Though Salt Lake City and northern Utah came to Hollywood's attention later, there is now a vibrant filmmaking culture there as well, with productions like the television show *Touched by an Angel* (1994-2003) and the *High School Musical* film series (2006-2008) frequently giving work to local film crews, including many Church members; individual titles that have filmed in northern Utah include *The Sandlot* (1993), *Dumb and Dumber* (1994), *Independence Day* (1996), *Footloose* (1984), and *Legally Blonde 2* (2003). All in all, the state has proven a cost-effective and visually striking substitute for "Egypt, Germany, Iraq, Ireland, Israel, Italy, Mexico, Scotland, Timbuktu, and Beijing, as well as the states of Massachusetts, Oklahoma, Nevada, Wyoming, New York, Missouri, Arizona, Colorado, South Dakota, California, Iowa, Nebraska, North Carolina, Illinois, and Texas."[185]

The first and most important Mormons to entice Hollywood to southern Utah were the Parry brothers—Gronway, Chauncey, and Caleb, who went by his middle name Whitney—in Cedar City, without whom "the Hollywood movie studio crews might never have come to Utah, or at least not as early—nor as often—as they did . . ."[186] The brothers were born in Salt Lake City in the late 1800s but their pioneer grandparents lived in Pine Valley—roughly halfway between Cedar City and St. George—and it was while visiting there that Gronway, the oldest sibling, fell in love with the vistas of "Utah's Dixie." Both Gronway and Chauncey studied the area's geology while at the University of Utah, and Gronway worked on a road survey crew in Kane, Garfield, and Iron counties in 1913. He moved permanently to Cedar City in Iron County in 1915 to teach animal husbandry at a branch of Utah State Agricultural College (today Utah State University), and he soon took up the dream of many nineteenth-century explorers and current residents of transforming southern Utah into a tourist destination, a reality made likely by President Roosevelt's inauguration of the first national monuments, including Zion Canyon, in the early 1900s.

The First Wave: The New Frontier

Gronway and Chauncey were soon managing a hotel, selling cars, running an automobile stage line for passengers without their own transportation, and serving as the official liaisons for the Department of the Interior. With experienced camp operator William W. Wylie they incorporated the National Park Transportation and Camping Company in 1917, a year after Congress created the National Park Service; thanks in large part to lobbying by the Parrys Zion Canyon became a national park two years later. After the war, in which both brothers served, they discovered that Wylie had voted them out of their own firm; thus they started from scratch with the Utah-Grand Canyon Transportation Company. In the early 1920s they helped entice Union Pacific to build a rail line closer to Zion and the north rim of the Grand Canyon. The spur allowed the brothers to host President Harding in 1923, along with an entourage of government and Mormon officials including Herbert Hoover and Church President Heber Grant; Harding died later on this trip. The next year the Utah Parks Company began the process of buying out the Parrys' company, which allowed them to open lodges at Bryce Canyon and other sites as well as turn their attention to moving pictures.

Cedar City, named for the local juniper trees, sits on a semi-arid plateau just northeast of the Mojave Desert, giving it a diverse local environment including not just deserts but forests, prairies, and striking rock formations and canyons in Cedar Breaks National Monument and Bryce Canyon and Zion Nation Parks. Chauncey saw the potential these diverse regions held for film production and began a letter-writing campaign to California studios, offering to host them in a visit to Utah. Western actor Tom Mix, one of the biggest stars of the 1920s, was the first to accept: he toured Zion and Bryce Canyons with the Parrys in June 1924, his frequent director Lynn Reynolds returned in July, and an entire crew arrived in August to shoot the film *The Deadwood Coach* for Fox. Cedar City held a parade in Mix's honor but residents were dismayed that he failed to compete in the local rodeo as he had promised. Still, production, which included DeWitt Jennings as a character actor, went smoothly with good weather, boding well for future films. In his written apology for having to miss the rodeo, Mix waxed prophetic: "We have pioneered the picture production business in your section much to our satisfaction and that of the director, and we feel that our reports on the possibilities of your country will induce many other companies to follow."[187]

This would take some time to be fulfilled, however. In 1926—the year the buyout of the brothers' company was completed—two productions, *The Shepherd of the Hills* and *Ramona*, filmed in the area. The former was a First National

Pictures production set in the Missouri Ozarks that Chauncey convinced director Albert Rogell could be profitably filmed in Utah, and the latter was an Inspiration Pictures title directed by Edwin Carewe and starring a young Dolores del Rio on the cusp of her stardom. Ironically, both crews arrived to film at the exact same spot in Cedar Breaks National Monument on the same day, and a much-publicized peace conference had to be held in the Utah Parks Company's El Escalante Hotel; though some locals dismissed this "coincidence" as a publicity stunt, it worked, helping advertise Cedar City as a filming location to readers in Chicago and Los Angeles.[188]

Subsequently, both Chauncey and Gronway spent months photographing locations for a portfolio Chauncey repeatedly took to Hollywood beginning in 1928. "With his good humor and vibrant leadership, Chauncey charmed MGM, 20th Century Fox and Paramount studios into serious consideration of Southern Utah as a movie location."[189] Along the way, however, he had learned that this would take more than enticing scenery: film crews required greater infrastructure than tourists and he wanted to give it to them. Thus, while the Parrys remained involved with the Utah Parks Company around Cedar City, they also came to see Kanab, a miniscule settlement fifty miles southeast on the Arizona border, as a virgin territory where they could dominate the field. The town, named from a Paiute word for the willows surrounding the nearby creek, was dedicated by Brigham Young in 1870, nineteen years after Cedar City. Its population in 1930 was a mere 1,300 residents—today it is only 4,500, compared with Cedar City's 29,000—but it was and remains well situated, with good access to most of the same national parks and monuments as Cedar City as well as the Grand Staircase-Escalante National Monument to the east and the north rim of the Grand Canyon to the south. Chauncey and Gronway thus invested $90,000 on a fourteen-acre lot and motel there, dubbed it the Parry Lodge, and began working to build up its amenities and reputation in Los Angeles. With this they "could now offer movie companies train transportation into Cedar City, accommodations at the newly completed El Escalante Hotel across from the depot, UPC busses and limos to transport the cast and crew to and from the locations, and if more convenient, his new lodge and restaurant in Kanab."[190] They provided catering, electricity, livestock, improved roads, authentic covered wagons and props, and even extras for the cast.

This took some time, of course, during which Cedar City saw its heyday as a filmmaking center. John Waters, a Paramount-contracted director, filmed more productions there than anyone else, including the 1927 film *Nevada* with Gary

The First Wave: The New Frontier

Cooper and Thelma Todd which inaugurated Bryce Canyon to filmmaking. Cecil B. DeMille filmed much of *Union Pacific* near Iron Springs west of the town in 1938. The next summer Henry Hathaway appropriately filmed most of the wagon train sequences for Fox's *Brigham Young* near the Parowan Gap, with the climactic scene of the seagulls and the crickets filmed near Provo in northern Utah. Dozens of other films, primarily westerns, were made in the area during this prolific period, which concluded with Universal's Technicolor musical *Can't Help Singing* with Deanna Durbin in 1944, though it was also used for the Olivia de Havilland vehicle *The Proud Rebel* in 1958 and other film and television productions up to the present.[191] Interestingly, the area has recently become known for its theater, including the Tony Award-winning Utah Shakespeare Festival, held annually at Cedar City since 1962, and the Tuacahn Center for the Arts northwest of St. George, a venue opened in 1995 which features concerts, dance, straight and musical theater, an arts-oriented high school, and an erstwhile Mormon Arts Festival.

Business in Kanab took slightly longer to establish, with *The Bad Man of Brimstone* (1937) possibly the first major production, but after 1938, when Chauncey and Gronway invested their own money in the film *Feud on the Range* (1939) to help grease the wheels, film work there began to increase rapidly while that in Cedar City declined.[192] This film, originally known by the working title *The Kanab Kid*, was soon followed by *El Diablo Rides*—which was also partially financed by the Parrys and produced by the small studio Metropolitan Pictures—*Westbound Stage*, and *Lure of the Wasteland* (all 1939), the area's first color picture. At that point a former producer named Denver Dixon, who had appeared onscreen in both *Feud on the Range* and *El Diablo Rides*, announced that he was establishing a permanent production company in the town: he incorporated Security National Pictures in December 1938 with local businessman Guy Chamberlain as vice president and between fourteen and twenty other Kanab residents as stockholders and investors. The firm built a small studio with a forty-by-sixty-foot stage and outdoor western street set; upon its completion this was christened "Utah's Hollywood," a title quickly adopted by Kanab in its entirety as the local government and businesses sought to promote the town with larger Hollywood studios. Dixon's first film effort was a local story, *The Mormon Conquest* (1935), which will be discussed in Chapter 3. This failed to meet expectations, and though Dixon rented his facility to Monogram for the production of two films in 1939, it was soon back to the Parrys to bring in Hollywood talent.[193]

At this they succeeded spectacularly, starting with the serials *The Great Adventures of Wild Bill Hickok* and *Overland with Kit Carson* in 1939. Fritz Lang's $1.3 million film *Western Union* in 1940 proved the area could handle a major production and within a few years Kanab became America's "most-often-used filming location outside California,"[194] and the sobriquet of "Utah's Hollywood" became simply "Little Hollywood." High-profile films like *Arabian Nights* (1942), *The Desperadoes* (1943), *My Friend Flicka* (1943) and its sequels, *Smoky* (1946), *Green Grass of Wyoming* (1948), *Red Canyon*, and *Calamity Jane* and *Sam Bass* (both 1949) filled out the decade, with the 1950s, with the arrival of television, initially just as busy. Although productions began to diminish late in that decade, many notable films—*The Planet of the Apes*, for instance—continued to made around Kanab throughout the '60s.[195] As Chauncey's daughter Louise recalled of Kanab's heyday:

> . . . Everybody in Kanab at one time or another was probably in more movies than most of the stars. They were Indians; they would decorate them all up, put them on a horse, and then in groups they would run down across in front of the camera, and do all these chasings and whatever else they had to do. But all of those horses came from the local people, except for their stars which they brought with them which they had specially trained to do that. Everything else came right out of Kanab area, and Fay Hamblin was their wrangler.[196]

Essentially, throughout this entire period a host of local Mormons found themselves, thanks to the Parrys, in the movie business, working as extras, stand-ins, horse wranglers, drivers, launderers, and other positions, including the numerous housewives who, in their own kitchens, prepared each evening's catering under Whit Parry's direction. The wranglers Merle "Cowhide" Adams and Fay Hamblin deserve special mention. Adams worked from *The Dude Rancher* in 1934 to the 1970s, handling the horses, often appearing onscreen and delivering dialogue, and teaching actors like Roddy McDowall and Fred MacMurray how to ride their mounts. Hamblin, most likely a relation of the area's early settler and Church leader Jacob Hamblin, also filled multiple positions for just as many years. He worked as a riding instructor, technical consultant, and as onscreen talent, from *The Dude Rancher* to his only speaking role in *The Outlaw Josey Wales* with Clint Eastwood in 1976, the year of his death. In later years he increasingly handled managerial roles including overseeing entire productions, including their finances, and in 1968 he was chosen to represent Utah Governor Calvin Rampton in meetings with studios in

The First Wave: The New Frontier

California. Howard W. Koch, a production chief at Paramount who had frequently filmed in southern Utah, spoke at Hamblin's funeral, and Hamblin's wife Ina had the words "WORKED WITH MOVIE IND 37 YRS" inscribed on their tombstone.[197]

Whit Parry estimated that filmmaking represented fifty percent of Kanab's economy in the 1940s, and it perhaps slightly increased after an airport was built in 1949. The town was featured heavily in the national press, not just film industry trade journals but general readership periodicals like *Coronet* magazine, the *Saturday Evening Post*—which called it "Hollywood's No. 1 branch production center"—*Life* magazine—which repeated the "Utah's Hollywood" nickname—and even *National Geographic*, which dedicated thirty-five pages of photographs and text to Kanab's best filming locations. Such attention could bring new problems. In a community where "there were perhaps twelve people in the whole town who weren't Mormon" there was significant concern about the decadent lifestyles of visiting Hollywood stars; thus Whit built a bar, the Black Cat, on the Parry Lodge property that was open only to visiting filmmakers: the only local allowed inside was the bar tender, who had never tasted alcohol in his life. With accommodations like these the celebrities and the Mormons got along fine.[198]

In fact, the locals and visitors frequently enjoyed rubbing shoulders, as when Burl Ives repeatedly dined at the Adams home in 1946, favoring the family with impromptu a capella performances. All three of the Parry brothers developed personal friendships with the casts and crews, including stars like Will Rogers, who frequently had the Parrys as guests at his Santa Monica ranch, and Spencer Tracy and Clark Gable, who both occasionally spent their vacations in Utah cougar hunting with Chauncey and Gronway.[199] As far as the work, Chauncey was in charge of the operation. He tended to focus on forging connections with the studios and overseeing productions; Gronway assisted with this but also liaised with local businesses that became involved with filmmaking; Whit, who had studied law at Stanford and graduated in business from the University of Utah, ran the lodge and oversaw catering. The brothers' faith filtered through their salty cowboy lifestyle: Whit served a mission in Weimar Germany before joining his brothers' company, but could reportedly cuss with impressive alacrity. And Chauncey, "although a highly religious man ... could blister the paint on buses and melt a camera lens while expressing his displeasure at the performance of a horse."[200] The devotion of all three brothers to their business and to filmmaking was unquestionable. Unfortunately, Chauncey was killed in a car accident in 1943, a tragedy mourned throughout

Kanab. "Gronway, Whitney, and Fay Hamblin continued providing for the movie and television companies into the 1960s." After a personal financial setback Whit sold the Parry Lodge to his former partner Bernell Lewis in 1966, and he struggled with ulcers, cancer, and a new restaurant across the street from his old lodge, dying in mid-1967. Gronway, the oldest brother who in his later years had increasingly focused on transportation and restoring vintage wagons, passed away the next year.[201]

Though Kanab produced the lion's share of Utah-filmed titles during Hollywood's classical era, Monument Valley is probably the state's best-known location. This is due essentially to the remarkable work of just one director: John Ford. He first filmed in Utah for *Drums Along the Mohawk*, the first prestigious color film shot in the state, in the summer of 1939. This was made in the Dixie National Forest outside Cedar City with assistance from the Parrys along with a Los Angeles supply company. Ford was struck with the beauty of the scenery, the clarity of the sky for lighting the Technicolor camera, and ease of the production; star Henry Fonda speculated that there was "something in the air up here that makes for good fellowship . . . I don't believe that any of us ever enjoyed a location more than this."[202] Ford was sufficiently pleased to return that very same year for the film *Stagecoach*, choosing this time to work over a hundred miles to the southeast in an area that previously had not seen much filming.

Monument Valley straddles the Utah-Arizona border midway between present-day Lake Powell and the Four Corners. Though it covers a mere five square miles, under John Ford's eye its sandstone buttes "have defined what decades of moviegoers think of when they imagine the American West."[203] It had actually attracted filmmaking as early as 1923 when author Zane Grey insisted that Paramount use it for the adaptation of his book *The Vanishing American* (1925), even taking Jesse Lasky on a ten-day horseback trip to close the sale. Lasky was so smitten that he insisted on using Monument Valley and Rainbow Bridge for all of Paramount's subsequent Zane Grey films. However it was *Stagecoach*, made by Ford for United Artists, that made the area famous, even though it was only onscreen for about ninety seconds with the rest of the picture shot in California. Ford was enticed there by newly arrived local resident Harry Goulding who, like the Parrys, promoted his area's scenic value and helped provide for the film crew's needs. Though Goulding, a scion of Colorado sheep ranchers, was apparently not LDS, much of the supporting personnel that he and Ford used over the years most likely were. The director returned again and again, showing off the valley's jagged skyline and crimson rocks in *My Darling Clementine*

The First Wave: The New Frontier

(1946), *Fort Apache* (1948), *She Wore a Yellow Ribbon* (1949; these three films, all based on James Warner Bellah stories, are now known as Ford's *Cavalry Trilogy*), *The Searchers* (1956; occasionally described as both Ford's masterpiece and the greatest western ever made), and his last epic western, *Cheyenne Autumn* in 1964. It became known as "John Ford Country," "virtually . . . his private filming preserve"[204] and a major boon for the local tourism industry. It was here that utilizing the landscape truly became part of "Ford's technique in translating the Western into legend," with "the eroded crimson and scarlet buttes and bluffs, the gigantic sculptures of time and weather which make the efforts of mankind appear irrelevant and vain. By setting the wheels of transport and the uniforms of an official army against these prehistoric masses, Ford reduces the image of human progress to a few insects crawling beneath the indifferent stone faces of the ages."[205] A contrasting perspective holds that Ford's "stagecoaches, cavalry troops, ranchers, and gunfighters . . . traveled among mesas and stone spires soaring toward the heavens, which bestowed on the narrative a mythological weight and epic proportion, as in a cathedral where songs and prayers rise to the great space above."[206] Through any interpretation, Monument Valley created the atmosphere that made these films such masterpieces.

Although he created the brand, Ford of course did not hold a monopoly on the area. *The Vanishing American*'s director George B. Seitz returned to Monument Valley to film *Kit Carson* in 1940, and David Miller filmed a brief segment of *Billy the Kid* there in 1941. It wasn't until the 1960s and '70s that it became well-trafficked by other directors, most notably Sergio Leone for *Once Upon a Time in the West* with Henry Fonda, and Dennis Hopper for *Easy Rider* with Fonda's son Peter; other films include *The Trial of Billy Jack* (1974), *White Line Fever, The Eiger Sanction* (both 1975), *National Lampoon's Vacation* (1983), on up to recent films like *A Million Ways to Die in the West* and *Transformers: Age of Extinction* (both 2014). Godfrey Reggio included it in his poetic documentary *Koyaanisqatsi* (1982), and it was even animated in both *Cars* (2006) and *The Lego Movie* (2014) as well as in a dozen video games.[207] Interestingly, in 1964 Church filmmakers Scott and Judge Whitaker set part of their film *Man's Search for Happiness* there, with the main characters walking onto an outcrop known as John Ford's Point—thanks to the frequency with which it has been filmed—and surveying the view as a narrator testifies that life is "part of a glorious everlasting plan." With a perhaps conscious nod to Ford, these filmmakers present the vista of Monument Valley—equated through a dissolve to the spires of the Salt Lake Temple—as a stone testament of the majesty of God.

Ford was also influential in introducing filmmaking to the Biblically named town of Moab in Grand County, 150 miles north of Monument Valley near the Colorado border and the Arches and Canyonlands National Parks. This happened in 1949 when he filmed *Wagon Master* (1950), his picture about the Mormon pioneers who settled southern Utah (discussed in Chapter 3). Once again a local resident enticed him to the area; this time it was George White, a local cattle rancher and state highway superintendent, who, along with his wife Essie, apparently was of Mormon stock. Other histories say local photographer Harry Reed first introduced Ford to images of Moab's vistas, but in either case it was White who, in 1949, created the Moab Movie Committee and began coordinating logistics and liaising with the Utah Department of Publicity & Industrial Development. When Ford and his Argosy Pictures Corporation associates arrived they were greeted by the Publicity Department's chair J. A. Theobald, who may have been Mormon, and former Salt Lake City mayor Ab Jenkins, who definitely was; these men oversaw Argosy's relationship with the state throughout filming, which, given *Wagon Master*'s subject matter, involved many other Mormons in its production.

Ford immediately returned to make *Rio Grande* (1950) and under White's direction—with ample support from the local Mormon population, augmented by others following a boom in uranium mining—Moab and its surrounding parks began to flourish as a filmmaking center at the same time Kanab's importance diminished. Westerns made there include *The Battle at Apache Pass* (1952), *Border River, Taza, The Son of Cochise* (both 1954), *Smoke Signal* (1955), Edward Dmytryk's *Warlock, Ten Who Dared* (1960), *The Comancheros* (1961; director Michael Curtiz's last film), *Rio Conchos* (1964), *Blue* (1968), and the Disney television film *Run, Cougar, Run* (1972); it was also used for portions of *The Greatest Story Ever Told*. Production slowed in the 1970s, but it continued to be used for projects as varied as the *MacGyver* television pilot (1985), comedies like *Larger Than Life* (1996) and *City Slickers II: The Search for Curly's Gold* (1993), and major films like Ridley Scott's *Thelma and Louise*, Walter Hill's *Geronimo: An American Legend* (1993), and recent films—not always successful—like *127 Hours, John Carter, After Earth* (2013), and *The Lone Ranger*.[208]

George White's influence was at least as great as the Parrys', particularly in his far-sighted vision that would lead to fostering film production through the local and state government rather than exclusively through private enterprise. When he created the Moab Movie Committee as an offshoot of the Moab Chamber of Commerce in 1949 it was the first such entity in the world. He worked as head of this organization for decades, courting studios and coordinating shoots—including housing filmmakers with local residents—and thus ensuring Moab's filmmaking primacy during the 1950s and '60s. Under the new name of the Moab Film Commission, the organization was so successful throughout these decades that in the 1960s Kanab created the Kanab Area Motion Picture Association to woo back wandering Hollywood studios; in late 1967 this informal group incorporated as Kanab Movieland, Inc., though it met with only limited success and dissolved by the late 1970s. Moab's efforts were more fruitful, prompting the Utah state government to investigate film promotion on a statewide level in the mid-'70s. Governor Cal Rampton, a Mormon Democrat with a longstanding interest in procuring Hollywood money for his state, began a concerted effort to court the industry, leading in 1977 to the creation of a statewide Film Development Office under John Earle, which in turn led directly to the creation of the Sundance Film Festival. Potentially increased competition with other regions of the state prompted Moab to create an organization known as the Moab Film Promotion, and simultaneously Bette L. Stanton—a descendent of handcart pioneers and southern Utah's early settlers who had grown up in Kanab during its "Little Hollywood" era—led the Moab Film Commission (and the Grand County Economic and Community Development department) to great success in tandem with the Utah Film Commission's executive director Leigh von der Esch. One major coup, for instance, was procuring part of Steven Spielberg's *Indiana Jones and the Last Crusade* with a last-minute location change from Colorado. In 1993 the Moab commission assumed responsibility for San Juan County, becoming the Moab to Monument Valley Film Commission, and in that year southeastern Utah took in $11 million in revenue from Hollywood film crews.[209]

But the effect of George White's concept of film commissions—partly-to-fully governmental, nonprofit, public organizations—has stretched far beyond Utah and the Mormons. The model quickly spread throughout the country, enough so that in 1975 the nonprofit Association of Film Commissioners International formed in Los Angeles to facilitate communication between these groups. Today a similar organization, the European Film Commissions Network, operates out of Brussells, and over 1,000 commissions exist in over 100 countries, ranging from the mammoth Mayor's Office of Film, Theatre & Broadcasting in New York City to those in developing industries like the Rwanda Film Commission in Kigali. The Moab to Monument Valley Film Commission remains, of course, the oldest of all these, and the spread of its model across the globe represents the largest contribution a tiny Mormon hamlet could possibly make to the development of world cinema.[210]

Mainstream Depictions of Mormons

The First Films: 1898-1904

Given the artistic, political, and social context of Mormon assimilation into national norms in the 1890s, it is particularly fitting that the Church's first recorded brush with film production came in 1898, outside Utah in a situation consciously designed to demonstrate Mormons' similarity to other Americans. The Spanish-American War was the United States' first conflict after Utah's admission to the union, and despite some prominent pacifists like senior apostle Brigham Young Jr. the majority of Mormons in the state, Church President Wilford Woodruff included, viewed the war as an opportunity to display their patriotism and similarity to other Americans; this conflict was, after all, steeped in nationalistic press coverage and it would be advantageous for the Mormons to be associated with it. We can situate their perspective towards the war in Matthew Bowman's description of the Church's entry into the American body politic after Utah statehood:

> ...It is perhaps surprising that the Mormons did not enter the Union more grudgingly. Despite their long standoff with the federal government, they began the new century with tremendous confidence that the stuff of early twentieth-century American life—its values, ideas, habits—was eminently suited to the pursuit of their religion. Their task became assimilation, finding ways to translate the things America demanded of them into the language and imperatives of their own faith. If Joseph Smith's Zion community had faded, its values were not destroyed, and the Mormons were confident that other paths to them must lay open.[211]

This is exactly what Woodruff saw in the jingoistic rallying cries for war with Spain in early 1898. On April 28, two months after the sinking of the Maine in Havana Harbor and three days after Congress's declaration of war, Woodruff's First Presidency announced that Mormons should support the government and if needed volunteer for war service. While this ended decades of "selective pacifism" in which all Mormons deferred to Church leaders about matters of military service, it was also a fairly open position of support as the United States prepared for conflict.[212]

Hence, when federal legislation passed allowing Colonel Jay L. Torrey to form three companies of elite cavalry—the Rough Riders—Utahns reacted with some of the strongest enthusiasm and highest volunteer rates in the country, in addition to the many volunteer infantrymen and two artillery batteries that had already come from the state. Today Theodore Roosevelt's Rough Rider unit is the best remembered, but Col. Torrey himself commanded a regiment known informally as the Rocky Mountain Riders (or Cavalry). He appointed John Q. Cannon, the volatile pro-war editor of the *Deseret News* and son of George Q. Cannon, President Woodruff's First Counselor, captain of the Utah Company, which consisted of eighty-six men, mostly Mormon. The group was mustered into service on or soon after May 15, 1898 at Fort Russell, Wyoming[213] and traveled by rail to Jacksonville, Florida; a train accident en route injured Torrey and placed Cannon, a lieutenant colonel, in temporary command of the entire unit; his influence was such that even his paper's rival, the *Salt Lake Tribune*, acknowledged him as the "father of the regiment."[214]

Despite their zeal to serve in combat the Rocky Mountain Riders remained in Jacksonville throughout the summer, thus missing the famous charge up San Juan Hill on July 1, although they would be stationed in Havana that fall after hostilities had ended. But their stay in Florida allowed them to be on hand in July when the New York-based American Mutoscope Company sent a crew to film short actualities or prototypical newsreels of the popular cavalry units. Among many other titles is one called *Salt Lake City Company of Rocky Mountain Riders*, a remarkably lengthy 154-ft. piece—approximately two and a half minutes—that apparently included portraits, group shots, and of course equestrian demonstrations. Another film alternatively called *Rocky Mountain Riders Rough Riding* and *Rocky Mountain Riders Jacksonville* almost certainly featured the Utah volunteers as well, and other titles that these men may have appeared in include *Rough Riders and Army Mules, Col. Torrey's "Rough Riders"* (or *Rough Riders on Parade*), and *Rough Riding* (or *Rough Riders Jacksonville*).[215] As news pieces, these films were produced and distributed very quickly and, given the national enthusiasm for the war, were certainly distributed as widely as possible. There were screenings of *Rough Rider* films in early August in Los Angeles, on August 21 in San Francisco, and on September 5 in Paris, Kentucky, for example, and at least one print was still playing a full year later on November 19, 1899 in Washington, D.C. Along with footage of the Rough Riders, the filmmakers—now renamed the American Mutoscope and Biograph Company and soon simply to be known as Biograph—presented footage of the conflict in Cuba itself, including battleships, Havana's Morro Castle, and various war heroes and groups of servicemen, all of which "won enthusiastic applause from an appreciative audience."[216] Teddy Roosevelt, however, was unquestionably the star of the hour; often the films, whatever the individual titles may have been, were all grouped together and booked as *Roosevelt's Rough Riders*.[217]

Thus, while the Utah Company was disappointed to not engage the Spanish, Cannon and his men *did* become the first Latter-day Saints to be filmed, and the nation's celebration of them along with other Rough Riders from around the country represents a successful leap forward in the Church's image eight years after the Manifesto and five after the World's Columbian Exposition where, despite the Tabernacle Choir's musical success, Mormon speakers like James Talmage had been denied the opportunity to present. Indeed, the nation's laudatory treatment of Utah's volunteers in the press and the cinema proved President Woodruff, who died that September, correct about the war's possible public relations benefit for the Church. This cinematic approval would not last for long, but it was an auspicious beginning less than three years after motion pictures were invented.[218]

After this national debut, the Mormons' next cinematic appearance may have been more provincial. In addition to possible films made by members of the Church in 1901, in October 1904 the American Mutoscope and Biograph Company once again filmed a group of Mormons, this time the crowds leaving the Tabernacle during general conference, along with members of the Provo and Ogden fire departments and possibly other scenes—all presented "in natural colors," which possibly meant hand tinting of the filmstrip. The event was probably deemed newsworthy because the controversy over seating Senator-elect Reed Smoot had raised national interest in Mormonism, and in fact this was the conference at which Joseph F. Smith issued the Second Manifesto, banning polygamy with much more forceful language than had ever been used before. Sessions were held on Thursday October 6, Friday the 7th, and Sunday the 9th, making one of these days the second confirmed instance of a professional film crew recording a Mormon subject—and the first professional filmmaking within Utah. It's quite interesting that despite the sensationalistic interest in polygamy throughout the country Biograph chose to shoot a placid general conference and then exhibited its footage to the Mormons themselves, implying, as with their *Rocky Mountain Rider* films, a more compassionate or at least journalistic approach than Mormons would generally receive over the next few years. The film's first recorded local screening, mentioned previously, was on October 24 at the Grand Opera House in downtown Salt Lake. These early Biograph shorts, which are all lost today, boded a positive role for Mormons as cinematic subject matter, but it would be the next film that set a precedent, opening a new chapter in how Mormons would be depicted on film.[219]

The First Wave: The New Frontier

"A Trip to Salt Lake City": The Anti-Mormon Film Begins

The Smoot hearings, as the series of Senate sessions was known, prompted a surge in many types of media portrayals of Mormonism, including at least one film: *A Trip to Salt Lake City* in 1905. Most examples were highly critical of the faith and polygamy, prompting many historians to use the term "anti-Mormon" to describe them; I have opted to use the same terminology despite recognizing its problematic nature, which I discuss in the next section.

Actually, given the sensationalistic depictions of Mormonism in Victorian literature it is amazing that a critical film about Mormons did not come earlier or that there were not initially more of them. We do know of some possible cinematic precursors in the short British film *Personal* (1904), directed by Wallace McCutcheon, and the remake by the comic French star Max Linder, *Ten Women for One Husband* (1905), which both created comedy from quasi-polygamous situations in which multiple women vie to wed a single man. These European films were incidental, however, with the characters apparently having no direct connection with Mormonism.

At issue now was the election of Reed Smoot to the U.S. Senate. Having been ordained an apostle in 1900 and gained new Church President Joseph F. Smith's permission, he ran as a Republican in 1903 and won. Smoot was not the first member of the upper Mormon hierarchy to seek national office: in 1898 B. H. Roberts, a Seventy, had been elected to the House of Representatives but public disdain for polygamy prevented him from taking his seat. Smoot, unlike Roberts, was never a polygamist; thus the state senators who elected him— this was previous to the 17th Amendment which allows for the direct election of senators—must have presumed that he would be more palatable to the American public. This hope proved ill founded, however, as "his position as an apostle made up the difference between him and Roberts"[220] and many of the Americans who signed the 3,100 petitions against him were concerned not just about polygamy but about whether a Mormon apostle would put loyalty to country over church or whether he would be beholden to President Smith in his political decisions. Thus a Senate hearing over Smoot's seating commenced in March 1903 and continued until 1907.

Questions about polygamy were not baseless and would be fueled in the mass media for years following the trial. The Woodruff Manifesto of 1890 was incredibly—and probably deliberately—ambiguous. Rather than announcing a cessation of polygamy and the specific terms this would entail, it merely indicated President Woodruff's intention to submit to the Edmunds and Edmunds-Tucker Acts and influence members of the Church to do the same. This ambiguity resulted in a great deal of social anomie amongst the Saints, with some believing a restriction only applied within the United States, others continuing to contract secret plural marriages in the U.S., and many more continuing to cohabit with their plural families well into the twentieth century. In order to protect the Church Woodruff and others issued occasional "statements that the church was no longer sanctioning plural marriages"[221] or encouraging cohabitation, but polygamous families, though down from 2,451 in 1890 to around 900 by 1902,[222] continued to be a fact of life well into the twentieth century, with over 200 Mormon men entering polygamy between 1890 and 1904, generally with the First Presidency's approval; my own grandfather, for instance, was born of a plural wife on January 3, 1903, just days before Smoot was elected on January 20.[223]

When the questioning in the Senate began it quickly became evident that the entire Church, not just Reed Smoot, was on trial in Washington, a place Mormons quickly dubbed "the seat of war."[224] President Smith, who had fathered eleven children with his wives since 1890 and authorized new plural marriages as recently as 1900,[225] became a central figure of the hearings as he and other Church leaders were repeatedly subpoenaed to testify. The questions themselves were grueling, particularly for Smith, but the pressure went well beyond the Capitol Building into the court of public opinion: hence the October 1904 Second Manifesto to convince the country that polygamy was in fact completely forbidden. Subsequently, apostles John W. Taylor and Matthias Cowley refused to either abide by this new document or testify in Washington and thus were removed from the Quorum of the Twelve in 1905; Taylor was later excommunicated and Cowley had his priesthood revoked. Events like these and Smith's admission in the congressional record that he had not received any revelations as President of the Church transferred into sardonic headlines, newspaper cartoons, and jingles like the popular "The Mormon Coon" and "Scoot, Smoot, Scoot," which includes the lyrics: "Can't you get wise to the fact that you're not wanted? / Don't you see that you wouldn't fit? / Back, pack your old carpet sack, / and spank your feet on the homeward track, / Scoot – Smoot – Scoot."[226] Political cartoons were particularly acerbic, nationally but especially locally in Utah with both the *Salt Lake Tribune* and *Salt Lake Herald* frequently publishing cartoons on the trial. Michael Harold Paulos describes how

Smith was furious with the *Salt Lake Tribune*, in part because over a four-year period (1903-1907), the daily newspaper published more than 300 cartoons lampooning most aspects of his public life, including his polygamous family life and his position as president of the LDS Church vis-à-vis with Utah politics and Utah business interests. . . . *Tribune* cartoons frequently portrayed a balding Smith, with a long scraggily beard, wearing plaid pants, a large black trench coat, and sunglasses. One such cartoon depicted a macabre Smith as "The King of Utah," sitting on a throne.[227]

Smith was understandably frustrated with this treatment in the press, complaining to Smoot in April 1904, one year into the hearings, "I have been horribly caricatured and made hideous in cartoons, and slandered and lied about most outrageously."[228] *A Trip to Salt Lake City*, copywrited on June 5, 1905 and released that year while the hearings were still in full swing, did not depict Smith personally but followed the same pattern as these cartoons. The American Mutoscope and Biograph Company, after having produced the two previous Mormon-themed films, had by now vastly improved its technology and risen to become the Edison Company's chief competitor in the United States.[229] Around 1903 the firm began a shift away from nonfiction reporting towards dramatic productions, and *A Trip to Salt Lake City* was most likely shot in the company's Manhattan studio at Broadway and 13th Street, just south of Union Square in what is today known as the Roosevelt Building. It was probably filmed in their original sunlit rooftop studio, essentially a glass-roofed enclosure that could rotate 360 degrees to follow the light, although one historian asserts that "by 1904, Biograph was using a completely enclosed studio entirely lit with many racks of Cooper-Hewitts suspended from the ceiling and on vertical floor stands; indeed so many that the effect was quite like the overall diffuse daylight illumination in the large glass studios Pathé and Méliès were using."[230] Whether cast by the sun or tubes of mercury vapor, the film's light is relatively diffuse, cast essentially from overhead with sharp drop-off near the floor and on the drapery framing the action. No production information survives, so the writer, director, cast, and crew remain anonymous, but remarkably the film was preserved by the Library of Congress—an extreme rarity for this period—making it the oldest extant Mormon film.[231]

A single shot lasting roughly two-and-a-half minutes and featuring no intertitles, the pantomimed story is simple enough: Inside a traveling Pullman railway car six women in succession each lead a young child into their respective sleeping berths. A single father then arrives struggling to carry three more children; the first six youngsters emerge and the man attempts to give them all a piggyback ride but is overwhelmed by his boisterous progeny then henpecked by his formidable spouses. He leaves for an unknown reason—in his absence there is a clever moment when one portly wife steals his hat, hanging outside another wife's bunk, and places it outside her own—then returns with a large industrial milk canister. Hoses are supplied to each bunk, thus meeting the drinking needs of his large family, with the visual connection between a Mormon brood and an industrialized dairy farm made clear. Still, the job is done in remarkable fashion and an impressed railroad porter enthusiastically congratulates the polygamist on his ingenuity.

Given the overall atmosphere of the Smoot hearings, it's unsurprising that we find no mention of *A Trip to Salt Lake City* in Church or Utah records, as it would have been just one additional annoyance during a much larger controversy. Perhaps the film failed to gain any response from Church leaders, as later pictures would, because it was so mild-mannered compared with the more personal attacks in newspaper editorials and cartoons, perhaps because they thought it more astute to ignore it, or perhaps because it never even came to their attention. It remains unknown, for instance, if *A Trip to Salt Lake City* ever actually played in the city of its title, though non-Mormon Utahns, such as those who regularly enjoyed the *Tribune*'s scathing cartoons, would probably have appreciated it. It is also unknown whether any news footage beyond the footage of the October 1904 general conference were made about the Smoot hearings.

While critical in tone, *A Trip to Salt Lake City* differs remarkably from most later anti-Mormon films simply by being funny. It uses humor to make its point about the absurdity of polygamy in a way that films like *A Victim of the Mormons* and *A Mormon Maid* (1917) never attempt. But from the context of 1905 we can also deduce something about the film that is not evident when viewing it today, which is that it was not just the innocuous comedy we may see it as now but a strident piece of timely political satire directed squarely against elite Utah Mormons like Smoot and Smith, even if the film did not depict them directly. Several cartoons that appeared in the *New York World* illustrate this in their similarity to *A Trip to Salt Lake City*'s storyline: one

> depicts a ghoulish patriarch ... bringing an Easter gift to one of his eight incarcerated wives while exclaiming "Wifey!" ... Another ... presents a chorus of 41 wailing children calling out "Papa!" to a bearded figure, representing Smith, reading from the Book of Mormon. On his right is a cabinet with separate drawers for the five wives (and a provocatively

unnumbered one, suggesting that Smith might marry again), while a huge bottom drawer holds "General Household Accounts." A poster above spoofs the popular Victorian slogan: "What is Home without a [crossed out] Some Mothers."[232]

The similarities to the film are obvious, and it is easy to see both how these cartoons would have translated easily into cinema and how viewers in 1905 would have been predisposed to see *A Trip to Salt Lake City*'s beleaguered polygamist patriarch, perhaps returning from a laborious official visit to Washington D.C., as a representation of all Mormonism or stand-in for its current prophet or even Smoot, who at forty-eight bore some resemblance to the film's clean shaven polygamist. *A Trip to Salt Lake City* was a firm nationalistic statement that Mormons as late as 1905 had flouted U.S. law and their own supposed revelations in continuing to live polygamy, that they therefore had no place in the public sphere, and that Smoot should be denied his seat and sent packing back to Salt Lake. It is, in other words, a perfect record of at least one strand of popular opinion about the Church at the beginning of the twentieth century. In summarizing the editorial cartoons of those years, Paulos cites two historians' evaluation of satirical cartoons in general that perfectly summarizes *A Trip to Salt Lake City* as well: "'Cartoons vibrantly reflect their moment in time: the costumes and conversations, the prejudices and fear,' and even though its 'popularity may prove ephemeral,' cartoons serve as a potent historical artifact, giving clues to subsequent generations what were previous time period's interests, beliefs, and values."[233] Through this film we see what the American public in 1905 found interesting about the Mormons and how they saw Mormonism in opposition to their progressive beliefs and values.

Still, with the Senate's 42-28 vote on February 20, 1907 to allow Smoot to retain his seat—after the popular President Roosevelt, who tended to like the Mormons, had thrown his weight behind the Senator—Mormonism and polygamy again receded somewhat from the public eye. Soon Reed Smoot was a powerful and respected statesman, serving on the Appropriations Committee and chairing the Finance Committee for ten years, where he remains best known for co-sponsoring the unfortunate 1930 Smoot-Hawley Tariff that exacerbated the Great Depression.[234] Despite this late misstep he was a nationally prominent politician and, more importantly for the Church, helped convey an image of a contemporary, pragmatic, and nearly corporate Mormonism that reflected how the Church would strive to be seen from that point on. Although anti-Mormon cinema would not resurface in force until 1911,

A Trip to Salt Lake City showed the enduring appeal polygamy held as cinematic subject matter. It had, in fact, been a subject of literary fascination for decades, and for a proper understanding of First Wave films that depict Mormonism as a closed-off, violent, and misogynistic society, we must situate them within this literary tradition that had been making roughly the same arguments since the 1840s.[235]

The Roots of Anti-Mormon Cinema

On October 16, 1847 the last of the year's pioneer companies—Mormon Battalion veterans coming from service in southern California—walked into the Salt Lake Valley. The final companies from the east, under future apostles Charles C. Rich and Jedediah Grant, had arrived just two weeks earlier and, despite the prominence of July 24 in Mormon culture today, the vast majority of immigrants had been in the valley less than a month. On the day that Battalion members were trudging into their new mountain home, halfway around the world in London an aspiring thirty-one-year-old writer named Charlotte Brontë published her first novel, *Jane Eyre*. Combining equal parts Gothic romance and documentary realism, *Jane Eyre* tells the story of a talented orphan who is able to find happiness despite years of disadvantage and cruel mistreatment; it remains largely unparalleled in its lucid depiction of the inner psychology of a strongwilled female protagonist. The central crucible of Jane's story is the revelation at her wedding that her fiancé and employer Edward Rochester is actually trying to lure her into a bigamous marriage, as his lawful wife Bertha is still alive and hidden away in Rochester's manor. Jane deliberates the circumstances—that his first wife was unchaste and is dark-skinned, violent, and irretrievably insane—but still cannot accept such a match and flees across the moor, nearly starving to death in her desperation to get away. Rochester is left to not only grieve Jane's loss, but to physically suffer for his intended sin as Bertha burns down his manor, destroying his fortune, scorching his eyes, and rendering his arm impotent in the process.

> Although Bertha dies, she is not consumed by the fire; she crashes down to a gory, very physical end, whilst the flames claim Rochester as their victim, enacting on his body the very mutilation Jane had wished, figuratively, to impose on herself. On deciding to leave Rochester, Jane had called on the language of the Bible to define the mental torture to which she should subject herself: 'you shall, yourself, pluck out your right eye; yourself cut off your right hand.' . . . Christ's prescription for

would-be adulterers is enacted literally, however, on Rochester by the hand of Bertha. Metaphor is instantiated in his sightless eyes, and useless arm.[236]

Many commentators have seen this act, brought to pass on Rochester by his first, slighted wife, as a feminist requital against his brutal chauvinism, a position argued further in Jean Rhys's revision of Bertha's story in *Wide Sargasso Sea*. Visible throughout Brontë's entire novel is her unmitigated opprobrium for any person or institution that would oppress, belittle, or especially enslave women—a brand of misogyny that is epitomized by the proposition of a plural marriage. It is only once he has paid for his crimes that Rochester is free to marry Jane—monogamously—as a contrite and born-again man, with Jane supporting him, financially and physically, and literally guiding him by the hand until, forgiven, he regains his sight.

Jane Eyre never mentions Mormonism, but it remains the finest novel to ever treat the subject of polygamy, masterfully showing it to be a concept morally repugnant to God and oppressive to women that only male chauvinists and autocrats would pursue. These assertions would reverberate for decades on the page, stage, and screen, and in making them the book set the standard for all less-skilled writers who would deal with Mormon polygamy specifically— except that most Mormon characters, far more villainous than Rochester, never share in his opportunity for absolution. But even he had to first pass through a penance that, through its extreme physical brutality, illustrates the gravity with which Victorian society viewed plural marriage. And because polygamy was not only sinful but also deviant we shouldn't be surprised at how popular it became as a sensationalist literary subject matter on both sides of the Atlantic, especially after the Church's public announcement of the practice in August 1852. The image of the sex-obsessed Mormon Elder became such common cultural currency that it entered the lexicon as a synonym for lechery and from 1884 until 1931 the American patent medicine industry used images of virile Mormon men to sell aphrodisiacs to what they must have assumed were envious gentlemen.[237] Many works, including films on the 1910s and '20s, accused Mormon missionaries of converting young women with the intention of bringing them into polygamous relationships. Mormons vehemently denied such accusations, but we must admit that at least before the Manifesto some missionaries did precisely that. Apostle Parley P. Pratt, for instance, brought two girls, Martha Monks and Ann Agatha Walker, home from his brief 1846- 47 mission to England, and married both as they began the trek west.[238] But even though polygamy was the defining characteristic of nineteenth-century Mormonism's public image, it was not its only point of interest. Perceived tendencies towards deceitfulness, unfailing obedience to ecclesiastical authority, internal solidarity and separation from outsiders, and physical violence all made for formidable villains and gripping reading.

I should point out that the term "anti-Mormon" is problematic on many fronts, not least because it groups all works concerned with Mormonism into two myopic camps—"pro" and "anti"—when in fact there is a whole universe of positions available, including no position at all. It's also simply an "intellectually lazy thing to do," substituting "an adjective for an argument and avoid[ing] the responsibility of actually responding to things" on their own terms. Perhaps most importantly, "the promiscuous use of terms like 'anti-Mormon' makes it difficult to talk about the literature that really was anti-Mormon—the vicious, mean-spirited stuff that was used to raise mobs in Nauvoo and armies a generation later." Many of the nineteenth century's "anti-Mormon" books, especially those by humorists like Artemus Ward and Mark Twain, simply don't meet that standard of malevolence; some even defend the Mormons against their attackers in Missouri and Illinois, while others "use Mormon characters as heroes or set interesting romantic or adventure stories against the backdrop of Mormon polygamy."[239] In the Fourth and especially Fifth Waves films that are often labeled anti-Mormon actually portray nuanced views of the Church that simply don't conform with faithful dogma, therefore begging the question whether they should be called anti-Mormon at all; we should be equally open to the possibility that some books of the 1800s and films of the 1910s that were universally accepted at the time as attacks against the Church, from a less impassioned perspective appear more romantic or titillating than aggressive. In other words, as Mormon literary critic Richard Cracroft put it, these authors were not necessarily attacking the Church so much as "distorting polygamy for fun and profit."[240]

This is certainly true of the First Wave itself: during the so-called "Anti-Mormon film era" a full quarter of the pictures produced by outsiders about Mormons— possibly eight out of thirty-two films—were comedies. Some of these aimed a satirical lens at Mormonism and polygamy in particular, but many did not; they simply invoked Mormonism for a laugh. It seems that the anti-Mormon film era, like the anti-Mormon literary era that preceded it, was just as interested in entertainment and profit as any moral crusade.

If that can be our position with the equanimity of hindsight, we must also recognize that in the context of vigilante mobs in Illinois or broken families under the Edmunds-Tucker Act, books like these certainly *felt* like direct attacks, and even in the 1910s events like missionaries' expulsion from Germany and Sweden and debates in the British Parliament about allowing them to continue preaching gave Mormons cause to believe that cinematic distortions of their faith were part of a larger coordinated assault. If "not everything—and not even *most* things—written about Mormonism fits into either the 'anti-' or 'apologetic' pigeonholes . . . the stark opposition of these categories [still] brings into focus the polarizing quality of Joseph Smith's claims to modern revelation."[241] We should also recognize that Mormons were not alone in being misrepresented onscreen, as Jews, Muslims, African Americans, non-European immigrants, and especially Native Americans all received similar or, frequently, worse treatment.

The earliest anti-Mormon books did indeed hope to inflict harm and stop Joseph Smith's movement before it could get started. Initial critics like Ezra Booth, Philastus Hurlbut, John C. Bennett, Thomas Sharp, and Eber Howe used the same power of the press that had so empowered Smith to charge him with general "untrustworthiness, laziness, and craftiness," along with plagiarism and fraud in the composition of the Book of Mormon. Howe codified these complaints in his 1834 book *Mormonism Unvailed*, which "became a prototype, the opening (book-length, at least) volley in a protracted struggle over religious ideas that would surround the church"[242] up to the present day. Within a few years of this, however, a new component of Mormonism emerged that made for perhaps even more exciting reading—violence. During the Missouri conflict of 1838 some Mormons openly fought against their opponents in skirmishes like the Battle of Crooked River, while at the same time Church member Sampson Avard, probably with the tacit approval of Smith's First Counselor Sidney Rigdon and maybe even Smith himself, organized a clandestine society of perhaps eighty men known most commonly as the Danites—after prophecies in the Book of Daniel about the Saints taking over "the kingdom" forever (e.g. Daniel 7:18)—to operate against prominent apostates like Oliver Cowdery, William Phelps, Lyman Johnson, and David and John Whitmer. When these men fled the Mormon settlements, Avard turned his attention to attacks and plunder against Missourians, actions which figured prominently into Church leaders' trial and incarceration in Liberty Jail that winter. Court documents first revealed the Danites' existence to the world, and even though by that point they had supposedly been disbanded—their leaders would soon be excommunicated as well—the possibility of a secret body tasked with enforcing the prophet's will through violence proved an irresistible literary trope. When author Frederick

Marryat presented the Danites to a much broader audience with his 1843 book *Monsieur Violet: His Travels and Adventures among the Snake Indians*, he ensured that the possibility of violence would surround Mormonism from that point on.[243]

The Danites themselves apparently had just a brief initial existence in the summer of 1838, and most Mormon literary historians claim that it was only on the pages of novels that they lived on in the early Utah years. Indeed, some have argued that, despite the monstrous aberration of the Mountain Meadows Massacre, "incidents of violence on the Utah frontier were rare considering the expanse of the Mormon settlement." While this is true in this context, to be accurate we must acknowledge that a variation of the Danite organization existed in various forms in the 1850s and for a time afterward. These men—who in 1858 included Orrin Porter Rockwell, Howard Egan, Ephraim Hanks, and William (Bill) Hickman, among others[245]—were known by different names over the years: the Brothers of Gideon, the Avenging Angels, the Sons of Dan, the Destroying Angels, Brigham's boys, or, perhaps most commonly, simply the be'hoys or b'hoys, a common slang term for a thug or gang member (originating in New York, it is an approximation of an Irish pronunciation of "boys"). In Utah they functioned surprisingly closely to how Marryat described them in Missouri, assaulting and murdering occasional outsiders, preventing dissenting Mormons from leaving the territory, and castrating, killing, and even apparently decapitating perceived apostates who had fallen outside the proscribed norms of Mormon society.[246] These men felt justified in this thanks to the importance of obedience to prophetic authority in Mormon life and the strange new doctrine of blood atonement that rose to prominence in these years.

This belief, apparently invented by Brigham Young in Nauvoo and proclaimed widely throughout the 1856 reformation and for years afterwards, taught that certain sins were so heinous they could be forgiven only by shedding the sinner's blood, resulting in his or her death. This allowed perpetrators to view a murder as the taking of a life in order to save a soul—a righteous act. Young, his counselors Heber Kimball and Jedediah Grant, other apostles, and many local-level Church leaders all advocated the doctrine: in 1854, for example, Kimball taught that adulterers should be decapitated and that "unclean" women should be wiped "out of existence," while the *Deseret News* published Grant's statement that it was Mormons' "right to kill a sinner to save him, when he commits those crimes that can only be atoned for by shedding his blood."[247] Young occasionally advocated practices such as murders, decapitations, and castrations, framing the doctrine in terms of brotherly kindness: "Will you love your brothers or sisters likewise, when they have committed a sin that cannot be atoned for without the shed[d]ing of their blood?" he asked in 1857. "Will you love that man or woman enough to shed their blood?"[248]

For a time, such teachings gave many Mormons certainty of the theological necessity of occasional violence, which in turn gave expression to their anger at the violence that had been perpetrated against *them* in Missouri and Illinois. Still, they recognized the unusual nature of this belief and the immense interest they had in downplaying to the American public any inherent violence in their faith; thus they maintained secrecy around violent actions and decried as scurrilous any books or articles that mentioned Danites or blood atonement. And it is true, as Terryl Givens has said, that, "quickly distorted and sensationalized, the doctrine of 'blood atonement' loomed far larger in popular fiction than in Mormon theology."[249] But, as Mountain Meadows showed, there was genuine substance to the claims that in some ways Mormonism encouraged violence—it was not as aberrant as many Mormons, then or now, would like to believe.[250] Thus the fictional and cinematic Mormons who descended upon unsuspecting wagon trains, who tracked the movements of suspected dissenters, or who prevented them from leaving the territory without permission remain widely dismissed by Mormon literary scholar but nevertheless were based on more than a grain of historical fact.[251]

None of this, however, could have anticipated the extent to which these themes would thrive in the realm of fiction, drama, and cinema. With *Monsieur Violet* Marryat "succeeded in creating a myth that would define Mormonism in popular fiction long after his own books had faded into obscurity."[252] Literary Danites soon took on mammoth proportions, with many socially crusading authors aspiring to treat Mormonism in the same way *Uncle Tom's Cabin* treated slavery. By the end of the 1800s fifty-six books with Danites had been published in England and the United States, with twenty-one in the 1880s alone, the decade of the greatest U.S. governmental opposition to Mormonism. The best known is Sir Arthur Conan Doyle's *A Study in Scarlet* (1887) because it gave us the character of Sherlock Holmes, but other titles included *The Mormoness: The Trials of Mary Maverick* (1853), *Boadicea: The Mormon Wife* (1855), *Mormon Wives* (1856), *The Wild Huntress* (1861), *Eagle Plume, the White Avenger: A Tale of the Mormon Trail* (1870), *Bessie Baine; or, The Mormon's Victim* (1876), *The Doomed Dozen; or, Dolores, the Danite's Daughter* (1881), *The Danite Chief* (1887), and *The Bradys Among the Mormons; or, Secret Work in Salt Lake City* (1903). Cincinnatus Heine (or "Joaquin") Miller's 1876 book *First Fam'lies of the*

Sierras was so popular that within a year of its publication he adapted into a play called *Danites in the High Sierras*, a production that played for decades; in 1880 it reportedly became the first "completely American company to tour . . . Britain,"[253] and it has been described as "the height of the literary portrayal of the Danites."[254] There were even autobiographical exposés like Bill Hickman's *Brigham's Destroying Angel* (1872) and Ann Elza Young's *Wife No. 19, or The Story of a Life in Bondage* (1875), which described her experience as Brigham Young's plural wife. Overall these books were well-enough known that in 1858 the term Danite was used as a derisive name for the National Democrats, a group of Illinois Democrats who allied with Republicans and opposed Stephen Douglas in his re-election campaign against Abraham Lincoln. Soon Danites and Mormons were being satirized—a sure sign of cultural saturation—in works like *Artemus Ward: His Panorama* (1869), Mark Twain's *Roughing It* (1872), Max Adler's *The Tragedy of Thompson Dunbar, A Tale of Salt Lake City* (1879), and Fanny and Robert Louis Stevenson's *The Dynamiter* (1883).[255]

Nineteenth-century anti-Mormon literature arguably peaked with *Danites in the High Sierras*, and after the Manifesto and patriotic acts like participating in the Spanish-American War Mormons must have hoped these stories would fade away. But if public interest was dwindling, the Smoot hearings reignited it. In the four years after the trial fifteen Mormon-themed cartoons appeared in the American satirical magazine *Puck*, and while they assumed a generally "tolerant, if condescending, mood," one showed "the Senator being wound up with a key by the larger, bearded Mormon hierarchy lurking behind the scenes and draped with Polygamy, Mountain Meadows Massacre, Resistance to Federal Authority, Murder of Apostates, Mormon Rebellion, and Blood Atonement."[256] The old accusations remained intact. In fact, religion scholar Martin E. Marty has said "that Mormons were 'safely describable as the most despised large group' in America at the end of the nineteenth century,"[257] and it would take many years for that to change.

One reason was that the Mormons themselves had not entirely changed. The Smoot hearings revealed just how entrenched polygamy remained, and, while Brigham's boys may have disappeared and increasing numbers of Mormons dismissed blood atonement as a frontier relic, in other quarters it was still endorsed well into the twentieth century. Since it took so many years for Mormons to extricate blood atonement from their theology, it is unsurprising that violence should feature in films about Mormons in the 1910s, when such doctrines were still relatively fresh.

The First Wave: The New Frontier

The early 1900s saw continued publications critical of the Church. The century was inaugurated with Lily Dougall's 1899 *The Mormon Prophet*, an attempt at a serious biographical novel on Joseph Smith that B. H. Roberts praised in the *New York Times*, and particularly with the resurgeance of anti-Mormon animus in the early 1910s it again proved profitable for a authors to publish any type of anti-Mormon fiction: roughly forty-four such books were published between 1900 and 1920.[258] At the same time, books like these began to be outshined by the rise of anti-Mormon drama. This transition from the written page to live performance indicates a shift in audience preferences and presages the progression to anti-Mormon films of the 1910s.

Nineteenth-century anti-Mormon drama expanded beyond *Danites in the High Sierras*. Public interest in Mountain Meadows reawakened with the execution of John D. Lee in March 1877. Even during his 1876 trial one dramatic troupe in Colorado performed stagings of the massacre, and Buffalo Bill Cody may have been the first after Lee's death to capitalize on the theme with his 1878 melodrama *May Cody, or Lost and Won*. The play was a hit, touring the country for over two years and saving Cody's faltering career with its tale of a young woman abducted from a wagon train before its annihilation and nearly forced into a polygamous marriage with Brigham Young when her brother—Buffalo Bill—arrives and saves her from the clutches of the Mormons. *One Hundred Wives*, a similar thriller starring Ada Gilman as the distressed damsel, toured for two seasons in 1880, and *Danites in the High Sierras* played throughout the decade and beyond.[259]

As in other areas, the Reed Smoot embroglio revived interest in putting Mormons onstage. A spate of new plays, all essentially lifted wholesale from the plots of anti-Mormon literature, began with Smoot's election in 1903 and continued even after films started taking their place in 1911. Producer Charles E. Blaney had briefly premiered *The Mormon Wife* on Broadway in 1901, and the renewed interest in Mormonism allowed him to stage it in Buffalo and New Orleans in 1903 and '04, then to promote it to other markets for at least another year.[260] In December 1903 the burlesque *The Mormon* opened in Baltimore and in 1904 Cliff W. Grant changed the title of a burlesque he was already developing to *The Mormon Queen*. While the term burlesque did not yet connote variety acts or striptease and instead referred to a comedy or satire, this show did include a chorus of singing and dancing girls, an appropriate context for a Mormon. It played in Atlantic City and included a young Al Jolson in a supporting role. Also in late 1904 Charles Logan of Dallas produced *Richard Loraine*, a drama set in

Salt Lake City that included a Mormon Elder as the villain. That October Sam T. Jack's Theatre in Chicago premiered the lighter *The Mormon's Troubles*. A few months later in January 1905 *The Mormons*, about another coerced bride, played at Watson's Cozy Corner in Brooklyn—it was revived in Chicago in 1906 and '07—and so on with the comic operetta *The Wanderer* in Philadelphia in May 1905, the four-act comedy *Utah* which toured Maine, New Brunswick, and Nova Scotia in May 1906, the burlesque *The Mormon Senator* in Peoria, Illinois in July 1907, and a second play entitled *The Mormon* in Chicago in May 1910. Stock characters of Mormons, especially long-bearded lascivious men, remained a common theme in burlesque throughout the 1910s, as did Mormon-themed songs interspersed among other unrelated numbers.[261]

The two biggest stage hits that blended into the era of anti-Mormon films were Joseph Le Brandt's thriller *Through Death Valley, or the Mormon Peril*, which premiered on Broadway in October 1907, and *The Girl from Utah*, which opened in London in 1913. *Through Death Valley* played at the American Theater at Times Square before touring the country and playing in London in 1911. The story is about a Mormon family, of course including an eligible young woman, being pursued by Danites as they flee across the desert and into the Grand Canyon to affect their escape. Olive Harper adapted it as a novel in 1907, and in both its literary and dramatic guise it anticipated Zane Grey's 1912 book *Riders of the Purple Sage*, which featured a similar chase.[262] *The Girl from Utah* portrayed a young American woman who flees to London to escape a bigamous marriage and who, with the help of her British beau, manages to elude her Mormon suitor. Opening in October 1913, it ran for 195 shows on the West End and played another 140 on Broadway in 1914, with a brief revival there the next summer; it also toured South Africa, Australia, and New Zealand. Music was by Paul Rubens and Sidney Jones, but the American version included five additional songs by a young Jerome Kern. His "They Didn't Believe Me" became a standard and "established a pattern for musical comedy love songs that lasted through the 1960s."[263] With the success of these productions and moving pictures like *A Mormon Maid*, Mormon plays continued to be staged into the 1920s, when public interest finally moved on from the vices of plural marriage and coordinated Danite murders.[264]

From drama to journalism to the halls of Congress, the events of 1903-07 vividly showed that the Mormon image had not progressed far beyond the days of Brigham Young. Some of the repercussions of the Smoot hearings weren't obvious for a few years, but by 1910 a new wave of anti-Mormon sentiment emerged in the United States and especially in Europe. In September 1911 film distributor Max Florence surprised Church leaders by announcing that he had secretly taken photographs of the interior of the Salt Lake Temple and demanding a large payment or else he would distribute them publicly. When they refused to be blackmailed he sold them as gaudy postcards. Simultaneously, a series of critical articles appeared in muckraking magazines like *Cosmopolitan, McClure's, Pearson's,* and *Everybody's Magazine,* charging that the Church was "attacking the American family, education and government,"[265] and new nonfiction books included a biography of Joseph Smith by I. Woodbridge Riley, *Story of the Mormons* by William Alexander Linn, and *The Birth of Mormonism* by John Quincy Adams of the Auburn Theological Seminary. The message of these books and articles—such as that Mormons were still practicing clandestine polygamy—made its way to Europe, and in England, Germany, the Netherlands, and Scandinavia Protestant ministers railed against the Mormon menace and local and national governments started paying attention. Magic lantern lectures about the evils of the Church became popular in the United States and Europe, and a surge of novelists like the American Zane Grey, who was more concerned with a good story than Mormon doctrine, and the British Winifred Graham, who actually did hate the Church and who became a major anti-Mormon crusader for the next fifteen years, helped recast public opinion against the faith. In 1911 in a period known as the "Mormon Scare," Graham helped formulate an organized crusade of English activists against Mormonism, and although the government after deliberating took no action against the Church or its missionaries—thanks in large part to the efforts of the young Home Secretary Winston Churchill—there were a few cases of mob violence. Much of the anti-Mormon activity took shape in the form of propagandistic fiction like Graham's *Ezra the Mormon* (1907) and *The Love Story of a Mormon* (1911), and using the cinema as a new tool in this campaign was a logical tactic—for profiteers as well as crusaders. We shouldn't be at all surprised that films criticizing Mormonism were produced in England and Denmark before America caught on.[266]

Given this historical overview of media that led to the rise of the anti-Mormon film, we can ask what influenced the authors, publishers, playwrights, and producers involved to create "anti-Mormon" art at all. Why such a great interest in Mormonism in general and polygamy and blood atoning Danites in particular? First, some authors like Philastus Hurlbut and John C. Bennett felt genuinely deceived during their time within the Church and wanted to protect others from what they saw as its threat, a sincere moral sentiment that extended to

Christian activists like Winifred Graham as well. This animus toward Mormon doctrine has motivated sincere critics for generations and has been the force behind many truly anti-Mormon works which have sought to discredit the Church, usually on doctrinal grounds. Certainly a belief that polygamy exploited women motivated a great many activists, including authors and playwrights, in the years that plural marriage was still accepted and practiced in the Church.

Second, it served as an activity of self-definition for American and European societies, as Mormonism proved an excellent foil against which to to contrast broad conservative values. Terryl Givens has quoted Edward Said in this regard, that "'self-confirmation' in general is 'based on a constantly practiced differentiation of itself from what it believes to be not itself. And this differentiation is frequently performed by setting the valorized culture over the Other.'"[267] In the young United States, then, "Mormonism was perceived as representing values and practices antithetical to the evolving image of America. Exaggerating these conflicts—emphasizing or inventing Mormonism's alien character, strange beliefs, and hostile intents toward American institutions—could only facilitate the self-definition of a people who chose to see themselves as theologically Protestant, morally Puritan, and politically Jacksonian."[268] In England, those who wished to maintain Victorian virtues into the Edwardian era similarly saw Mormonism as a foreign embodiment of all that opposed the values of centuries of British civilization. Although the most important elements in "these [anti-Mormon works]—Danites, blood atonement, secret polygamy, Church security, and elaborate conspiracies against gentiles . . . would not even be recognized by twentieth-century Mormons as part of their religion,"[269] they have remained central to recent literary depictions of the faith and were particularly visible in anti-Mormon films of the Fourth Wave. This is because in the 1980s as much as the 1880s, these artworks showed Americans what they were by simply showing them what they were not.

Third, though Christian zeal and self-definition might have been the underlying psychological motivation behind these works, of much more immediate interest was profit. The Church lent itself to sensationalism, as "the evil fact of polygamy made credible almost any fiction about Mormonism"; it was, in other words, easy to distort Mormonism and thus accommodate the Victorian

> affinity for 'phantasmagorias' of all kinds seen through contrast,
> exaggeration, simplification, and generalization. . . . More to the point,
> these authors [like Marryat and Conan Doyle] wrote their 'Mormon'
> books during financially difficult phases of their careers. A lucrative

> market existed for Mormon stories, which appealed both to the reform-
> minded and the curious, the pious and the prurient.... Victorian
> novelists dwelt on myths about the Mormons because the facts were
> simply too mundane.[270]

The audience was buying, and by the 1910s the ambitius new film studios
wanted in on the act.

The First Assault: 1911-1912

After weathering the Smoot hearings and negative publicity like *A Trip to Salt
Lake City* Utah Mormons may have been pleased to see various films that
treated their state without any negative reference to its dominant religion. In
1907 the Kansas City-based Hale's Tours and Scenes of the World company, a
firm specializing in travelogues and "phantom rides," films shot from moving
trains and often exhibited in theaters built like railroad cars, produced the short
A Trip to Utah, which probably featured vistas of the state's mountains and
deserts and possibly views near the Salt Lake City depot as well.[271] At least
two films with Utah themes—*The Uprising of the Utes* (1910) and *A Perilous
Ride* (1911)—focused on the Ute Indians rather than the Mormons. And in
November 1912 the Edison Company also produced a travelogue, this one
entitled *Salt Lake City, Utah, and its Surroundings*; its stance may be detected
by its advertising material, which described the city as "beautifully located at
the base of the high mountains" and the temple as a "masterpiece of Western
architecture."[272] It was quickly embraced by Church members and was soon
being shown in the infant Church Education program.[273]

But in 1911 a slew of anti-Mormon productions began with a vehemence that
shocked Church members: at least eight films critical of Mormonism would be
released in 1911 and '12, and of the seven of these that played in the United
States six premiered within the three-month span of December 1911 to
February 1912, a tremendous burst of cinematic activity that made its effect
felt throughout the remainder of that year. The three features of the silent era
still available today—*A Victim of the Mormons, A Mormon Maid,* and *Trapped
by the Mormons*—are generally viewed as camp and are watched with great
bemusement, but within the milieu of rising anti-Mormon sentiment, Latter-
day Saints appropriately considered them serious assaults. The threat to the
Church, especially with the onslaught that arrived in 1912, was palpable.[274]

The first of these films, one of the era's comedies, belied the serious nature of what was about to come. In August 1911 the Hepworth Manufacturing Company, a pioneering British studio, released *Tilly and the Mormon Missionary*, a farcical chase film that, at 550 feet, probably ran around six minutes. This was part of a series of roughly twenty shorts released between 1910 and 1915 about two cockney sisters Tilly and Sally—played respectively by Alma Taylor, fast on her way to becoming "England's Mary Pickford," the country's first major star, and Chrissie White—whose mischievous and anarchic tendencies got them into constant trouble: in *Tilly and the Fire Engines* the girls borrow a horse-drawn engine for a joy ride, dousing their pursuers with water, and in *Tilly's Party* they crash a celebration, wreak havoc in the kitchen and rollerskate through the house before a successful getaway via bicycle (both these films were also from 1911). *Tilly and the Mormon Missionary*, directed by Lewin Fitzhamon, was certainly a burlesque of the entire 1911 "Mormon scare," although all we know of the plot is that the girls pose as gypsies and then are chased by a Mormon and their uncle, a recurring character. Innocuous enough, but the pairing of Mormons with gypsies was indicative of how both were seen as exotic, foreign, and mystical, a common association that recurred in *Trapped by the Mormons* eleven years later. Plus, it should be safe to assume that the Mormon chasing Tilly and Sally had matrimony in mind, although these girls surely proved in less need of a male rescuer than later victims of the Mormons would be. Other groups like suffragists would also fall prey to the *Tilly* films' satire, but Mormonism was such a hot topic that in Denmark two feature-length productions, *A Victim of the Mormons* and *The Flower of the Mormon City* (1911), were underway while *Tilly and the Mormon Missionary* was playing in British cinemas.[275]

At this time Germanic churches were decrying all foreign bodies that they saw as threats to their congregations. When European Mission President Rudger Clawson came to Germany in the summer of 1910 to investigate anti-Mormon agitation he was arrested and held overnight and received a banishment decree; that December German Mission President Thomas McKay and twenty other missionaries were deported. This atmosphere permeated the region— in November 1911 a similar attempt to ban missionaries from Sweden was partially successful. And in Denmark in 1908 Hans Peter Freece, an American and former Mormon, published a book criticizing the faith; in 1911 he was employed by the Interdenominational Council of Women to tour Ireland, England, and Denmark speaking against the Church, while several Lutheran ministers toured Scandinavia with magic lantern lectures "for the purpose of 'unveiling' 'Mormonism.'"[276] Plus there were reports throughout Europe of

The First Wave: The New Frontier

Mormons seducing or kidnapping girls to whisk them off to Utah, baseless accusations that nevertheless provided fertile soil for several films. Mormonism was very much in the public discourse, making it a topical subject for a motion picture.[277]

Executives at Nordisk Films Company, *A Victim of the Mormon*'s production company, were certainly aware of these events, but that alone doesn't account for their decision to make one of their longest and most prestigious productions to date about a minor American religion. This was the "Golden Age" of Danish cinema, when Denmark's film industry dominated all other European competitors, and Nordisk Films was one of its top studios, well established in Europe and North America, the latter through their distribution subsidiary Great Northern Films. Nordisk's founder Ole Olsen oversaw this empire and wanted to make it grow, so he himself conceived of *Victim* as a way to do that, first by exploiting the developing star system with celebrities like Vlademar Psilander, perhaps Denmark's most popular actor, who would play the Mormon role, and second by using all this talk about Mormons trying to abduct young women as a way to add a unique new angle to the already existing genre of the white slave trade film. For the past decade the Danish film industry had been pushing the state of the art of cinema in both length and quality—longer films allowed for more elaborate plots—and it also began producing erotic dramas, films that "tended to specialize in sensationalist narratives concerned with private intrigues that intersected with dangers to the general public, in particular involving criminality and sexuality."[278] In 1907 Nordisk produced a short film called *The White Slave Girl* that added the social element of organized crime gangs that kidnap girls and sell them into prostitution, but it was with *The White Slave Trade* (1910) that the genre took off; this film by the studio A/S Fotorama was incredibly popular and, at forty minutes, was Denmark's longest film to that point. Nordisk actually copied it shot for shot, and the company used their extensive distribution network to make their version of *The White Slave Trade* a hit throughout Europe. A flurry of films followed in 1910 and into 1911 and studios began looking for ways to make their films stand out, such as the 1912 film *Shanghaied*, about a man who is kidnapped and impressed into service as a sailor. But in 1911, with all the agitation in Denmark and elsewhere about Mormonism it was natural to substitute abducting women for prostitution with abducting them for polygamy, and both Nordisk and Fotorama began working on a film on that theme. In other words, Olsen intended *Victim* as the latest film in an already popular genre, not as the inauguration of a new genre of Mormon pictures.[279]

A Victim of the Mormons (Mormonens Offer) tells the story of Nina Gram (Clara Pontoppidan), a young woman whose brother Olaf introduces her to an old friend named Reverend Andrew Larsson (Psilander), a Mormon missionary who quickly woos her away from her fiancé Sven and absconds with her to the mission home (in English-language prints the names were changed to Florence, George, Andrew Larson, and Leslie, respectively). Olaf and Sven set off in pursuit, but with the help of other Mormon agents Larsson evades them at the mission home and then again at the dock as he boards a ship sailing for the United States. By now Nina has changed her mind and Larsson detains her forcibly, preventing her escape and suicide. While following on the next ship Olaf and Sven call ahead to have Larsson apprehended in New York, but he disembarks successfully and soon reaches Salt Lake City. Here Nina meets Larsson's first wife, eventually becoming essentially imprisoned with her in Larsson's home. Larsson attends a baptismal service of four women in the the Mormon temple, a sequence which adds little to the plot but much to the film's exoticism, as they wear white robes and perform strange hand gestures, and there is a strange pipe organ above the baptismal font. When he leaves, there is a car chase as Olaf and Sven pursue him home, where he falls through a trapdoor into Nina's basement cell. In the ensuing fight Larsson attempts to shoot Nina, but Sven deflects the shot and the bullet kills Larsson instead. Both women are saved and Nina and Sven are reunited. The plot is sensationalist and melodramatic, not to mention hardly realistic; contemporary critics pointed out the absurdity of the Mormons having an entrenched network of cunning enablers abroad but nothing but their own dull wits that prove unable to protect them at home in Salt Lake City.[280] Nevertheless, it remains a thrilling chase film even today, and imagining how audiences would have felt in 1911, when very little had been attempted at this scale before, we can see how it would have proven a popular spectacle.

A Victim of the Mormons was subtitled *A Drama of Love and Sectarian Fanaticism* but was also known simply as *Et Offer*, or just *The Victim*. It was directed by August Blom, a veteran of Nordisk and star director at the height of his popularity who had directed both their remake of *The White Slave Trade* and *The White Slave Trade's Final Victim* earlier in 1911. Victim was purposely set in an indistinct Danish city, but Blom primarily shot around Copenhagen, substituting that city for Salt Lake as well; the seaside scenes were filmed on the northeastern coast of Zealand, and the Salt Lake Temple was a building at Copenhagen's Zoological Gardens. This technique was not just due to budgetary issues, but also reveals Nordisk's intention to primarily target an international audience that wouldn't necessarily know what Salt Lake City looks like. At one point the climactic car chase crosses over a bridge, for instance, something common enough to Europeans but completely out of place in Salt Lake, not to mention the absence of mountains surrounding the city. One American missionary who saw the film in Chesterfield, England complained bitterly about the "ignorant" substitution of English locations for Utah, all the while apparently unaware of the fact that the vistas onscreen were in fact Danish. The film is also an excellent example of a confident director working in the years just as cinematic language was solidifying into its classical form: Blom uses extensive axial cuts—cuts along the camera's view—and cross-cutting between locations as the two men pursue Larsson and Nina across two continents. In the end he produced a film of 3,200 feet broken across three reels; projection speeds varied at this point, but the Danish Film Institute's video of *Victim* runs just over fifty-one minutes, making it not just the longest film of 1911 but one of the longest films ever released at that point. Mormon film distributor Lester Park claimed that it was "'possibly the seventh three-reel' film ever produced."[281]

The film premiered at Copenhagen's Panoptikon Theater on Monday October 2, 1911, and opened in London nine days later, quickly spreading throughout the United Kingdom, Norway, France, where it was known as *Le Sacrifice du Mormon*, and other continental markets. As with the white slave trade films, *Victim* was positioned as a socially crusading work: the Danish program to accompany the film announced, "He who sees this film and reads this text booklet is warned against the deception of Mormonism."[282] Coincidentally the play *Through Death Valley* reached England at roughly the same time, and by November they were joined by Fotorama's film *The Flower of the Mormon City*. The combination of these three works presented a direct assault on the Church and its missionary efforts throughout Europe. Rudger Clawson, who then led the Church there, at first thought it might blow over, but by December the film was still performing well enough that Clawson spearheaded a campaign to discredit it—"A living picture is, after all, quite a live thing," he wrote the First Presidency, "and often times makes a lasting impression on the mind. *A Victim of the Mormons and Through Death Valley, or The Mormon Peril* are plays that are in every sense lurid and sensational."[283] As early as October, missionaries in Denmark, Norway, and England had standardized their response by standing outside any cinema showing these pictures and selling or distributing pamphlets, initially a tract coincidentally written just before the films' release called "£200 Reward," offering money to anyone able to prove female abduction to Utah, but now Clawson wrote a new essay called "The Anti-'Mormon' Moving

Pictures and Play" which directly addressed *Victim*'s claims and was reportedly well received. When *Victim* played in Bristol in May, the theater manager allowed the missionaries to distribute "£200 Reward" inside the lobby and expressed his hope that this would help them in their work, which they reported it did, with an increased number of investigators at their Sunday meeting. Not all reported responses were as civil, though: one theater owner in Liverpool claimed that he had been threatened by the "Mormon Brotherhood" and Mormon-led riots were reported at screenings there and elsewhere, although the *Millennial Star*, the Church's periodical in London, dismissed such reports as publicity hoaxes. By February 173,000 copies of "£200 Reward" had been distributed in the UK, and Clawson regained his confidence. Although they might have been putting a positive spin on their discouragement, missionaries in Hull, Norwich, York, and various other English, Norwegian, and Danish cities reported that the two films were actually helping their work more than hurting it. And by that April an Elder in Norwich wrote that "the wind that blew so strongly from the thousands of ministers and religious bigots and office seekers, over this isle, a few months ago, for the purpose of freeing themselves from 'Mormonism,' has terminated in our favor."[284]

Fotorama's film *The Flower of the Mormon City (Mormonbyens Blomst)* grew out of the same Danish white slave trade genre as *Victim* and, although we don't know its exact premiere date, it evidently was playing in England by November 1911, touring extensively throughout Great Britain through 1912. It also played in Scandinavia and the Netherlands, where it was also known as *The Pearl of Utah*. Although in November 1912 one missionary in Amsterdam announced that *Victim* and *Flower* only served to "stir up curiosity and bring many to an investigation of the gospel,"[285] in August the films played as a double feature in Birmingham, complete with an anti-Mormon lecture given between the two screenings. This resulted in small mobs forming over the course of several days, breaking the windows in the new mission offices and causing a safety concern for missionaries there. That month mob violence threatened the city of Sunderland as well, and a short while later a missionary in Norwich was actually tarred—as had been a sixty-year-old Briton Mormon that spring— then in January 1913 a mob of 500 people violently broke up a Sunday School meeting in Ipswich. Whatever confidence Clawson, Andrew Jenson, or other missionaries displayed early in 1912, incidents like these show that general anti-Mormon sentiment, spurred by the Danish films, would continue to haunt them essentially until the war brought more pressing matters.[286]

The First Wave: The New Frontier

Nordisk and Fotorama were in head-to-head competition, and *The Flower of the Mormon City*, though less known today, was no second-tier effort. It had nearly the same running time as *Victim*; different sources list it as 2,800 or 3,000 feet, compared with *Victim*'s 3,200, so it would have run around forty-five to fifty minutes over the course of three reels, which advertisers boasted included fifty "exciting and effective parts."[287] In fact, *Flower* actually had much more in common with the majority of anti-Mormon films that would follow: unlike *Victim* it was a period piece, a western set in the pre-Manifesto era, which allowed for more violent storylines and the Danites to make their cinematic debut. The narrative follows Kristine, a Danish girl who as a child moves with her father to Utah. Years later she is wanted for the harem of an apostle's son, and is only narrowly rescued from Mormon concupiscence by her beau Tom, an American cowboy who returns to Denmark with her. The director and writer(s) are unknown, but it starred Jenny Roelsgaard as Kristine, Gunnar Helsengreen as John the lecherous Mormon, and Aage Schmidt as Tom.

While things appeared to be calming down for Mormons in Europe by the beginning of 1912, that is exactly when Nordisk and Fotorama launched the global distribution of these pictures in earnest, as well as when other production companies began putting out their own Mormon pictures. *A Victim of the Mormons* was sent to markets like Australia and Brazil, where it opened on February 2. But the big prize was the United States. Foreseeing a hit, Nordisk used the release of *Victim*, along with three other prestige pictures, to announce the reorganization of their North American distribution arm, which would now be known as the Great Northern Special Feature Film Company. Aiming for a February release, they began advertising to film exchanges in December, which is how distributor Lester Park learned about it. On January 6 he alerted the First Presidency—Joseph F. Smith, Anthon Lund (who was Danish), and Charles Penrose—and began protesting the film himself in the trade journal *Moving Picture World*. Thanks to Park's notice Church leaders in Utah thought they might have enough time to stop the film's American release, but then they learned that another film, *The Mountain Meadows Massacre*, had opened in California just days earlier, and *An Episode of Early Mormon Days* had been playing even longer. There would be no quick or easy solution to what was quickly becoming a flood of films.[288]

From December to February the movies seemed to come faster than Mormons could keep track. *An Episode of Early Mormon Days* opened on December 14, followed by *The Mountain Meadows Massacre* in early January, *The Mormon* on

January 25, *A Victim of the Mormons* on February 3, *The Danites* on February 19, and *Marriage or Death* on February 22; although *The Flower of the Mormon City* was opening in other countries as early as February, it might not have reached the United States until spring. With this many films coming all at once, Mormon Church leaders, politicians, and businessmen had to work together, and quickly, to block, censor, and otherwise discredit the wave of pictures. In doing so they had some mitigated successes and many more failures, often simply boosting the films' publicity through their opposition.

The Mountain Meadows Massacre is an excellent example of this. Both it and *An Episode of Early Mormon Days* were produced by the French studio Pathé Frères, which at that time was the largest film company in the world, owning film exchanges and hundreds of theaters, manufacturing the majority of film cameras and projectors used throughout the world, and producing a sizeable number of their own pictures each year, including inventing the newsreel format in 1908. Given the company's size there's a slight possibility that either or both films were produced by its American branch, but it appears that these and Pathé's third Mormon picture, *Marriage or Death*, were all shot in France— making that country, through this one studio, the top producer of anti-Mormon films in 1911-12.[289] While not as long as the two Danish films—*Episode* was only 820 feet—these first two French offerings are important as the first films to deal explicitly with Mountain Meadows as a historical incident rather than just depict a fictitious wagon train as later films would do, although *An Episode of Early Mormon Days*, which was released a month earlier, might have fictionalized its storyline more; interestingly, the Mormons in this film were not motivated by polygamy but by sheer bloodlust alone. Whatever their differences, both films depicted Joseph Smith assisting Brigham Young in plotting the massacre, apparently the first times these men were depicted on screen.

Pathé's first two films films apparently began their theatrical runs on the west coast. *An Episode of Early Mormon Days* didn't receive as much attention from Church members as *The Mountain Meadows Massacre*, but on January 24 a fight between Mormon and non-Mormon patrons nearly broke out at one San Francisco screening.[290] But since *Mountain Meadows* through its very title was seen as a direct affront to the state of Utah, the Salt Lake Commercial Club and other local business interests spearheaded a campaign to suppress it. They petitioned Pathé to remove it from circulation entirely, writing to the New Jersey headquarters themselves and enlisting associates in the Los Angeles Chamber of Commerce to lobby the company's subsidiary there. William Spry, Utah's

The First Wave: The New Frontier

Mormon governor, got involved, as did the Alhambra theater chain, threatening to boycott all Pathé films in their theaters in Utah, Idaho, and Wyoming. Meanwhile, Eastern States Mission President Ben E. Rich found himself, like Clawson in England, on the front line against the movie studios. He went to the National Board of Review of Motion Pictures in New York City to try to persuade it to not approve the film, only to learn that it had already given approval in November. A Progressive Era institution, the National Board had been formed as a branch of the People's Institute settlement house in 1908 to view and identify all films suitable for public consumption. As a moral authority only it had no power to actually censor or ban a film, but its approval was seen as important and Mormons hoped that by blocking it for works like *The Mountain Meadows Massacre* and *A Victim of the Mormons* they could keep theaters from showing them. Mormons like Rich appealed to the Progressive impulse to censor public entertainment for the greatest social benefit, but another Progressive ideal actually worked against them as polygamy, like prostitution, was deemed a social ill and therefore films treating it in a constructive manner would be seen as desireable by the National Board members.[291]

Rebuffed by the board, Mormons now turned to the court of public opinion. *The Deseret News* editorialized against the film and the connection it would create in viewers' minds between the bloodshed and "odium of long ago" and the Church and state of today.[292] While such an argument would have carried little water outside of Utah—the massacre had occurred just fifty-five years previously—the Salt Lake Commercial Club successfully entered into a dialogue with Pathé: the studio pointed out the amount of money already spent on production, prints, and advertising, and offered to withdraw the film if they were compensated for this, a not uncommon offer at the time. However, the Utah businessmen equated this with blackmail and refused, and in the end *Mountain Meadows* ran unaltered and presumably had its effect. In June a viewer in Canada decried the shocking realism of the onscreen slaughter, saying it "brought back much to the minds of the older ones [in the theater] and put a never-to-be-forgotten impression upon the minds of the younger ones."[293] Mormonism was again successfully paired with bloodshed in the public mind.

The campaign against *A Victim of the Mormons*, in which the Church took a more active part, was only slightly more successful. Anticipating the film's February 3 release, Ben Rich and William Spry were now joined by Reed Smoot in the Senate and William Swanson in the Utah film industry—at this time a board member of the Motion Picture Distributing and Sales Company (MPDSC), which handled all the Great Northern Film Company's releases—to try to convince the National Board of Review to disapprove it, or, failing that, to otherwise stop Great Northern from releasing it. Even though *Victim* was not being distributed through the MPDSC, Swanson was able to negotiate with Great Northern's agent to buy up all the states' rights for the film for $6,750. Spry, however, was furious at the offer and threatened to ban all Mormon-related films in his state. Instead the Mormons and an increasing number of non-Mormon Utahns like Swanson intensified their efforts to have the film censured by the National Board of Review. Ben Rich's nephew Isaac Russell, a New York City journalist, met with individual members of the board and learned that the votes already cast in the film's favor might be reversed if he could prove *Victim* was part of a propagandistic campaign against the Church. Russell argued that four politically motivated anti-Mormon magazine articles of 1910 arrived in Denmark at the same time as Hans Freece, which inspired "filmmakers in Denmark to portray the Mormons as kidnappers of young women"[294] as part of slanderous campaign. Rich gathered stories about how missionaries had been put in physical danger by anti-Mormon films, and this, along with protests from Smoot, Spry, and the Salt Lake Commercial Club finally convinced the National Board's top officers to review the film. On January 24 they announced Great Northern would have to remove all references to Mormonism to receive approval, a proposition which the company rejected. Thus the board rescinded its approval of *Victim* days before its intended release. This seemed a great victory for the Mormons, who thought the film would now never be seen, but, undeterred, Great Northern went ahead with the release as planned. The resulting controversy primarily centered around what critics claimed was the National Board of Review's attempt at film censorship thanks to special interest lobbying, and many people were drawn to the film simply by the fact that it was now deemed even more salacious than before—plus to see what the "Mormon racket" was trying to suppress. As one trade journal reported, "One thing that has tended to rouse interest in this picture is the antagonistic attitude of the so-called Mormon church, which has given the subject the widest publicity and tended to rouse great public interest in the picture."[295] Great Northern and individual exhibitors even highlighted this opposition in their advertising, as in a sign outside a California theater that proclaimed: "A Picture That Has Startled Two Hemispheres. Fortune Spent by Mormons to Prohibit Pictures. We are Showing Just the Same."[296] The Mormons concurred, admitting defeat: as Rich complained in a letter to Smoot, the Church had "accomplish[ed] little except to advertise the [film] and thus increase [its] circulation."[297] Just three weeks after *Victim*'s premiere in New York the company advertised that only a few states remained to purchase distribution rights; it was selling well. Before the month was out it was showing not just in major metropolises but small markets like Amarillo, Texas and Ardmore, Oklahoma. Mormon missionaries had no choice but to mimic their European counterparts and distribute literature outside the theater.[298]

While protesting *A Victim of the Mormons* to the National Board of Review, Swanson, Rich, and their allies made a concurrent case against *The Mormon*. This film, sometimes called *The Mormons,* was a 1000-foot picture about a young scout searching for wagon trains in order to kill the men and kidnap the women. Complications ensue when he spots a lone wagon belonging to a family with two daughters. He falls in love with one of the young women and deserts the Church to save her from his father and the apostles. In the ensuing battle her father is killed, but the scout gets away with his new bride and her family, leaving his old Mormon father to mourn the loss of his apostate son. Produced by the small independent American Film Manufacturing Company, better known as Flying A, it starred the well-known J. Warren Kerrigan and Pauline Bush and was one of the first directorial efforts of Allan Dwan, later a prominent director. Through the Motion Picture Distributing and Sales Company William Swanson was able to persuade the studio to change the name of the picture, but it was nevertheless released in New York under the original title on January 25. Even called *The Mormon*, it didn't represent too great of a relative threat to the Church: as one reviewer said, "The picture has no special strength, nor any noticeable weakness except the result of the battle. It will serve as a filler."[299]

As their similar plots reveal, these films were all heavily indebted to the old anti-Mormon books and plays, so we should not be surprised that one firm, the Chicago-based Selig Polyscope Company, actually adapted one of these to film directly. The 1877 play *Danites in the High Sierras* had made a star of actor McKee Rankin, who exploited it as a personal vehicle for over twenty years. Thus in 1911, although he was too old to perform in it, he wrote the screenplay for an adaptation called simply *The Danites* himself, which Francis Boggs then directed, making this the first Mormon film adapted from preexisting material. It was released in two parts on February 19 and 20. Given the popularity of the play, industry attention was extremely high, with a large advertising campaign and positive reviews. Because the plot served as the prototype for films like *The Flower of the Mormon City* and *An Episode of Early Mormon Days*, its story seems fairly typical, and as with *An Episode* the Danites' pure bloodlust is a much more important issue than polygamy. Nancy Williams and her younger brother Georgie survive a Danite attack on her westward-bound wagon train, although the Danites Hickman and Carter receive an order to kill these two survivors. When they dispatch Georgie Nancy briefly pursues them, but failing to catch them she disguises herself as a boy and assumes the name Billy Piper. As Billy, she befriends the only woman—called "the widow"—in the town where she now lives, eventually revealing her true identity only to her. Time passes and Hickman and Carter are still trying to find Nancy, and when they suspect Billy is actually their prey they move toward a final showdown at the widow's cabin where her new husband pulls his gun on the Danites to secure Nancy's escape but she, upon seeing them, is struck by terror and has a fatal heart attack. The Danites thus have fulfilled their mission and ride off to terrorize more settlers.

Some reviewers noted that references to Mormonism were minimal: the villains are referred to exclusively as Danites, not Mormons, and the reason for their villainy is never explained. Mormons certainly saw it as another undesireable film, but they gave it little attention amidst greater threats like *A Victim of the Mormons*, and without any Mormon references the film was easily approved by the National Board of Review. The Selig company specialized in location production of Westerns, and the film was praised for its scope and vistas, but releasing it in two parts rather than as a single film hurt its reception. Still, it faired well in the United States and toured as far as Brazil in January 1912 and even Beira, Mozambique in June 1913, demonstrating the progress of its international distribution. In October 1912 the President of the Church's mission in South Africa complained that *The Danites, The Flower of the Mormon City,* and *A Victim of the Mormons* were all playing there simultaneously, although like nearly all missionaries he claimed the films were actually beneficial to the work.[300]

Finally, just two days after *The Danites'* release, Pathé premiered their third Mormon film in two months, the one-reel *Marriage or Death*. Once again, it featured an outsider girl in Utah being forced into a loathsome marriage, a chase in which, this time, the Mormons are assisted by Indians—an oblique reference to Mountain Meadows—a capture, and a near-wedding rescue by a band of cowboys from a local ranch. News about this film reached Joseph F. Smith on February 17, thus instigating yet another rapid campaign to stop the film's release on February 21. Ben Rich again petitioned the National Board of Review to censure the film and at one point actually believed that he had achieved this, but, perhaps stung by the blow to their legitimacy that stemmed from *A Victim of the Mormons'* controversy, board members declined to take any action to reverse the approval they had given *Marriage or Death* the previous November.[301]

The onslaught of these seven films was apparently the most pressing matter in Mormons' minds in the early months of 1912, eclipsing the Titanic disaster and all other issues in their recorded speeches and publications. And some of the films continued to be shown in anti-Mormon lectures for years to come.[302] While they were insulting to all Mormons, they probably had little effect on the everyday lives of Church members in the Mormon Corridor. But for those laboring as missionaries or hoping to improve Utah's standing on the national stage they were a constant concern and actually prompted public relations work on a scale that had never been done in the Church before. At the time, though, there was little success to be seen. Tellingly, the steady flow of missionary correspondence insisting that the films were actually helping their proselytizing was not accompanied by increases in convert baptisms, tithing receipts, or the return of disaffected members; rather, the Church growth rate plummeted from 5.62% in 1910 to 2.52% in 1912.[303] In the face of such overwhelming opposition, Church leaders took a defiant tone, but even though there would never be an onslaught as intense as 1912 they were far from seeing the end of the anti-Mormon film.

Waxing and Waning: Anti-Mormon Films 1914-1922

With so many similar pictures saturating the market throughout 1912, it's not surprising this was followed by a sharp dropoff in anti-Mormon films; the cycle had run its course and there were no more profits to be had. In fact, interest in the Mormon problem in general dissipated; in 1915 one missionary wrote from Sheffield, England that "we are practically free from persecution at present, as the people are so absorbed in the war that the 'Mormon' elders are almost lost sight of. In fact, the greatest obstacle that we have to meet is indifference."[304] This represents a significant change from just two years earlier.

There were no anti-Mormon films released in 1913. In fact, in this year not only did Mormons begin releasing their own positive features, discussed below, but Bison Life Motion Pictures, a west coast subsidiary of the New York Motion Picture Company, released a two-reel film called *The Romance of the Utah Pioneers*. A film that displayed rare sympathy not only for Mormons but also for Native Americans, it depicted Edward Martin and his new bride Alice as he leads a company of handcart pioneers west. Counterposed with this is the story of a young Indian couple; the girl is abducted by Mexican bandits, causing the braves to attack the Mexicans and free her. Enraged against all outsiders, the Indian warriors determine to annihilate the handcart pioneers as well. But when the young woman sees that the pioneers are starving and dying of exposure she convinces the men to assist them rather than attack them, and they lead them to water and give them life-saving supplies. We don't know who wrote or directed the picture, but it starred Louise Fazenda in what might have been her first role and Bison was under the general direction of Thomas Ince, who was already on his way to becoming one of the most influential directors and producers of early American cinema. The studio's sympathetic depiction of Mormons was a surprising choice, contrasting as it did with the wave of critical films from the previous year, and *The Romance of the Utah Pioneers* constitutes the first cinematic portrayal, and the only silent one, of the handcart pioneers. Unfortunately nothing is known of its distribution and there is no record of Mormons' reaction to it.[305]

From 1914 to 1922 there were roughly a dozen anti-Mormon films, the majority clustered into three groups: three adaptations of *A Study in Scarlet*—one British, one American, and one French—released in 1914-15, three prestigious American films in 1917-18, which represent the high point of the anti-Mormon film movement, and two more British films in 1922, which were part of another less successful anti-Mormon crusade and which signaled the demise of the genre until roughly the 1970s. At the same time there was a surprising number of films that, like *Tilly and the Mormon Missionary*, mined Mormonism for comedy, with most of them centered around 1915. This burst of humor into the middle of the "anti-Mormon film era" illustrates two things: first, that this name for the period is only marginally appropriate, as not all films from the First Wave had an agenda against the Church—and with some lost films like *A Study in Scarlet* (1914) and *The Mormon Uncle* (1920) we have no way of knowing certainly how much Mormon content there was or how it was handled—second, that by 1915, when five humorous or adventurous films about Mormonism came out in the United States and England, Mormons were no longer seen as a threat to mainstream society and hence could now simply be laughed at. The humor could still be caustic, to be sure, but it didn't function like in *A Trip to Salt Lake City*, which focused its satire on a pressing political issue. Instead, films like *A Puritan Conscience* (1915) merely treated Mormons as anachronistic kooks, not to be taken seriously in any sense.

Indeed, with the exception of *Trapped by the Mormons* and *Married to a Mormon* in 1922, even the supposedly anti-Mormon films of these years were motivated by other factors—usually profit—rather than actual animus against the Church, as the *Study in Scarlet* films illustrate. The British version, produced by George B. Samuelson, written by Harry Engholm, and directed by George Pearson, was probably at least partially prompted by rising patriotism as the country was engulfed in the Great War. Sherlock Holmes was the embodiment of British intellect and reserve, and an adaptation of his first adventure—although it wasn't the first Holmes film—would boost the country's spirit. In France and the USA this patriotic component was missing, but it appears much more appropriate to see these films as part of a small cycle of Holmes pictures rather than a resurgence of deliberately anti-Mormon filmmaking. There is also considerable confusion about them: we have no information at all about the French production except that it was released in 1915, close on the heels of the British release and just before the parody *A Study in Skarlit*, one of the many Mormon comedies of that year. And the two English-language versions have, until recently, often been confused by historians as the same picture; both are lost, which has made their study rather difficult.

All three films, of course, featured essentially the same plot. A murder in London is explained by the cab driver culprit via a long flashback to pioneer Utah: a man and girl, the last survivors of an ill-fated wagon train, are rescued by Brigham Young and the Mormon pioneers. The man adopts the girl, Lucy, and they live among the Mormons, but when she grows up she is, of course, commanded to enter plural marriage. At the same time she falls in love with a young non-Mormon, and the three of them attempt to escape the Avenging Angels. They fail, however, as the older man is killed and Lucy forced into polygamy after all, resulting in her death from grief. The young man who survives vows vengeance on his sweetheart's murderers. He trails them to London and kills them there, and that is the case that Holmes is called upon to solve. In Samuelson and Pearson's version, Holmes only appears in the last two reels, with the first four taking place entirely in Utah.

The only thing that set Conan Doyle's story apart from other anti-Mormon literature was its addition of the British detective, but this was a stroke of genius, as Holmes of course proved much more memorable than any other element of any story dealing with Mormonism. Conan Doyle actually wrote a stage version of *Scarlet* in 1890 called *Angels of Darkness*, but Holmes and Watson don't appear in it at all, and the play was never staged. Thus it was left to George Samuelson to create the first major dramatic incarnation of the tale, with the blessing of the author. Samuelson had begun his career as a film distributor before opening a studio at Worton Hall, Isleworth near Hounslow in west London. Scarlet was his first production; he had Pearson shoot the majority of it there but they used the beaches of Southport, north of Liverpool, and Cheddar Gorge in Somerset to stand in for exterior locations in Utah's desert and mountains. Holmes was played by Samuelson's accountant James Braginton because of his resemblance to illustrations in the books, while other performers were popular actors like Fred Paul, Agnes Glynne, Harry Paulo, and Winifred Pearson.

The result was a 5,800-foot, ninety-minute film that was reasonably popular with critics: one said the film, "though not quite one of the best of Holmes' exploits, is decidedly one of the best of his creator's novels, and the producers have, without question, made the best of it . . . Every scene is interesting for itself and holds the attention enthralled." Most striking was the location footage, and the reviewer's description reveals the lingering prejudice from the 1911 crusade:

> The religious ritual and social tyranny of these people are presented
> in a series of original and memorable scenes. Sir Arthur himself
> made much of this part of the book, and it is only the barest justice
> to say that his adaptors have succeeded admirably, not merely in the
> "property" and photographic elements, but also in suggesting the close,
> stuffy atmosphere of the Mormons' creed combined with its flagrant
> freedom in another sense.[306]

The film was probably released on December 28, 1914 and was a success for Samuelson's studio, which operated under various owners until the early 1950s. It's likely that the success of this *A Study in Scarlet* is what inspired the French version as well as the British parody. Today Samuelson's film is seen as a milestone in British cinema and remains on the British Film Institute's "Most Wanted" list of missing productions.[307]

The American version was only two reels, or approximately 2,000 feet or twenty minutes, long. It was an early effort by the two-year-old Universal Film Manufacturing Company, later better known simply as Universal, and was directed by Francis Ford, a prolific actor who sometimes directed and who therefore cast himself as the famed detective. Ford was the elder brother of the future director John Ford, who had just moved to California that summer, and John actually played Dr. Watson in the film as well as working as a general assistant. Written by Grace Cunard, the film was evidently released on December 29, one day after the British version, and received similar reviews:

The First Wave: The New Frontier

"The characterizations are none too strong, but the story is well put on and holds the interest firmly . . . The cabby's story is well-pictured, the American scenes being elaborately staged."[308] There was apparently little to no response by Mormon Church authorities to any of these productions as there had been in 1912 and would be again in 1917-18. Some Mormons must have wanted to curtail the films' influence, but in an apparent case of picking their battles Church leaders may have decided that trying to censor Sherlock Holmes simply wasn't going to be worth the effort. Probably the most important reason none of the *Study in Scarlet* films received a robust response from the Church was that they simply didn't represent enough of a threat; in Europe in particular it would be hard to drum up another anti-Mormon crusade while bombs were falling from the sky.

The war was not a big enough deterrent in the United States, however, although it was getting more difficult to bring a Mormon film to fruition. In 1915 the historian Ruth Kauffman was contracted to adapt her Marxist history of the Church *The Latter-day Saints: A Study of the Mormons in the Light of Economic Conditions* to the screen for the Humanology Film Producing Company, a socially conscious studio in Medford, Massachusetts, but this never materialized. Similarly, Equitable Motion Pictures Corporation attempted to film the play *Polygamy*, a successful production by Harriet Ford and Harvery O'Higgins that was just closing on Broadway, about a woman escaping an unwanted plural marriage; the actress Margarita Fischer was contracted for the lead, but the project never made it to the screen.[309]

In 1917, however, anti-Mormon films reached their zenith with a most successful film, *A Mormon Maid*. Though told on a more epic scale than any anti-Mormon film before or since, the plot was essentially traditional. John and Nancy Hogue and their beautiful daughter Dora live alone in the American west, but after Mormons save them from an Indian attack they decide it will be safer to live among the Mormons than on their own, which they do for two years. Dora falls in love with a young innocent Mormon named Tom Rigdon but also catches the lustful eye of apostle Darius Burr, the driving force behind the puppet leader Brigham Young. Doubting Hogue's loyalty, Burr and his band of hooded Danites force him into a second marriage in return for Dora's freedom, but when Nancy finds out she commits suicide. This prompts Hogue, Tom, and Dora to attempt an escape, but they are intercepted by the Avenging Angels who guard the city's perimeter. In the ensuing scuffle Hogue is killed and Dora captured and sentenced to marry Burr. She is taken to the temple and dressed in white robes, but, having discovered the doctrine that plural wives must be virgins, she lies about her maidenhood to avoid the ceremony. Enraged, Burr kidnaps her again, and Tom enlists the help of a renegade Danite to free her one final time. The two intercept Burr and Dora outside the city, where a fight ensues and Dora shoots Burr. The helpful Danite unmasks to reveal he is actually Dora's wounded but living father in disguise, and the happy trio rides off into the night, safe from the Mormon menace.

Although anti-Mormon sentiment was not what it once was, salacious Mormon storylines could still succeed, as *The Girl from Utah* showed on Broadway in 1914. The 1916 merger between Famous Players, the Lasky Company, and Paramount Pictures into Famous Players-Lasky made Adolph Zukor and Jesse Lasky eager to find a major property to establish them as a studio to be reckoned with. Production for the studio was overseen by Lasky, his brother-in-law Samuel Goldwyn, and Cecil B. DeMille, who was named the company's Director General, and these men found in Mormonism an opportunity in capitalize on the success of D. W. Griffith's mammoth *The Birth of a Nation* from the previous year. That film, generally considered the first great American feature, depicts the creation of the Ku Klux Klan in the Reconstruction South and their heroic resistance against mulattos and Yankee carpetbaggers. The film's racism was controversial even in 1915, but its financial and artistic success were indisputable. By the end of 1917 it reportedly earned the unheard-of sum of $60 million, and Famous Players-Lasky wanted to exceed it.

Their concept was to link *A Mormon Maid*'s Avenging Angels with the Klan, and the importance of that connection cannot be overemphasized. Most significantly, the Danites were dressed as Klansmen, with white pointed hoods veiling their faces, the only difference being the Mormon "All-Seeing Eye" painted on their chests. One intertitle even diverts from the plot to editorialize that historically these costumes were the direct predecessor of the Klan's, a complete fabrication. There had been a few graphic representations of capped or even hooded Danites in anti-Mormon literature, apparently deriving from Mormon temple apparel, and of course on a practical level having the Danites cover their faces allowed for the plot device of John Hogue's disguise, but the motivation for this costuming choice went back no further than Griffith's film, something that was obvious to audiences: in its review *Variety* said the film occupied "the same relative position to Mormonism that *The Birth of a Nation* does to the negro question, polygamy, of course, being subject to legislative control at the present time."[310] There were two major differences between the two films, however: unlike the noble Klansmen in *The Birth of a Nation*, the Mormons here are clearly portrayed as villains. More importantly, *The Birth of a Nation* has received resistant and revisionist readings ever since its release that *A Mormon Maid* simply has not. And while it wasn't as important a milestone in film history as *The Birth of a Nation*, *A Mormon Maid* was still a landmark film and remains available today, so its neglect by historians who would deconstruct its messaging is surprising.[311]

The film was written by Paul West with assistance from Charles Sarver and directed by Robert Z. Leonard, an actor who had recently found success behind the camera; we don't know the extent of DeMille's involvement, but during this period he frequently helped write scenarios and assisted directors under his supervision.[312] Fully exploiting Hollywood's developing star system, the producers cast Mae Murray as Dora, Hobart Bosworth, a veteran actor who had once worked in the mines of Park City, Utah, as John Hogue, and a rising star named Frank Borzage, a Catholic Utahn who would later become a prominent director, as Tom. *A Mormon Maid*'s technical merits were higher than previous anti-Mormon films, due to its immense budget, scenic vistas shot at the Lasky Ranch in southern California, the excellent work of cinematographer Charles Rosher, and the maturation of classical filmmaking itself, which crystallized around 1916. All of this makes the film feel familiar to modern eyes; as historian Richard Nelson says, "Artistically, the film is an excellent example of much of the best in early Hollywood filmmaking."[313] It originally ran eight reels but was cut down to five, with the 5,000 remaining feet running about seventy minutes. Murray, who married Robert Leonard in 1918, reportedly felt uneasy about the story's prejudice and its stark narrative filled with "constant confusion and sorrow," and strongly regretted the film throughout her life.[314]

A Mormon Maid previewed on January 11, 1917, then showed to distributors at a Valentine's Day matinee at New York's Strand Theatre, with sales beginning in the lobby immediately after the screening. On April 22 it opened to the public at the Park Theatre at Columbus Circle—where the play *Polygamy* had run from December 1914 to April 1915—and soon it was showing to the public in New York state, New Jersey, and other markets. Critics praised the film, while generally recognizing that it was no *Birth of a Nation*. *Motography* raved about its "thrills, suspense, action, forceful portrayal, good production, and so on," adding, "If one is not thrilled all the way to the core after witnessing this production he is of a different make-up than the average spectator ... It ranks among the most powerful releases of the year."[315] And the *Motion Picture*

News forecast great profits: "Commercially worthy its artistic merit is no less prominent. The story . . . contains a wonderfully strong plot that possesses several moments of the greatest dramatic power."[316] Not all were so entranced, however: *Photoplay*'s critic wrote, "I doubt the propriety of a play attacking an existing sect...." Despite being a "well-told, convincingly written story" it remained "a morbidly unnecessary rehash of a certain phase of American history."[317]

Newspaper critics also wryly noted the opposition *A Mormon Maid* would surely arouse in Salt Lake City. And they were right: the Church could not ignore such an important production, but once again it found itself at an extreme disadvantage in opposing it. Mormons first learned of the film from a *New York Times* article in December 1916. Eastern States Mission President Walter Monson began the campaign against it, writing to the *Times*, "Why must this wholesale slandering of a people go so merrily on?"[318] The paper didn't even print his letter, and once again Mormons' efforts did nothing but heighten interest, although this time, at least, members of the National Board of Review were more amenable to their concerns, flagging the film for the General Committee's review before the Church even contacted them. Committee members debated about whether offending a "religious sect" was grounds to withhold approval, but they ultimately sanctioned the film while recommending the insertion of a disclaimer at the beginning. This may have been done with certain prints, but with others exhibitors inserted intertitles quoting from the Smoot hearings to verify that all the information in the film was essentially factual. And even in Utah an attempt to establish a state censorship board to block the film failed, although individual theaters there and in Idaho united in refusing to play it. The sales agents Hiller & Wilk publicly toyed with holding a grand screening in the Tabernacle, but obviously no such event would ever take place and this appears to simply be a ploy to increase publicity. When the film finally opened, on its first night in New York one Norman Crowther, probably a full-time missionary, and several associates disrupted the screening with their protests. The lights were thrown up and the entire audience engaged in a yelling match before police ejected the Mormons. Before the screening resumed one former Mormon vouched for the film's accuracy and a representative of the National Anti-Mormon League briefly spoke, saying "that in reality not half [about the Mormons] had been told."[319] Similar disruptions repeated the next two nights but then ceased—it played at the Park until May 6, earning over $7,000 in its first week—and there are no other reports of attempts by Mormons to disrupt screenings throughout its entire run.[320]

The First Wave: The New Frontier

Despite having access to Paramount's nationwide distribution system, the company decided on states' rights distribution—Richard Nelson has speculated they may have wanted to avoid attaching any controversy to the Paramount name—which was overseen by a new distributor named Friedman Enterprises, Inc., which in turn contracted the aforementioned sales agency of Hiller & Wilk to do the majority of the legwork for selling each state. They allegedly launched the most extensive and costly advertising campaign in film history to that point—with "one million post cards, one thousand 24-sheet posters, a nationwide newspaper campaign"[321] and other publicity activities—and within a few weeks claimed to have received 896 inquiries from buyers, bookers, and exhibitors. Company President Benjamin Friedman reported: "I never saw anything like it in my experiences . . . Our returns show an increase of almost one thousand per cent, some blocks of territory showing an increase as high as eight hundred, and others as high as fourteen hundred. Maybe it's the 'different' subject; maybe there are more Mormons and anti-Mormons than most of us know. Why, even from Utah, Colorado and Idaho, Mormon states, in essence, the bidders have been startlingly large."[322] Friedman was, of course, acting as a salesman, but it is true that sales to exhibitors—and their ticket sales to viewers—were high, as *A Mormon Maid* became a standard by which other states' rights films would be measured. After beginning its run on the east coast and Detroit it had long engagements in eastern cities like Cleveland and Buffalo—where hooded actors rode horseback through the streets to advertise the film—before sales spread westward and southward by the summer, followed by regional sales in the Pacific Northwest, New England, California, and other regions in the fall. It was not universally acclaimed; a California critic dismissed it, "Cannot be termed a good picture but it gets over," and one viewer in Chicago simply called it "a crazy picture." The Chicago Board of Censors actually cut some dialogue offensive to Mormons, and audience turnout there was so tepid that at least one theater pulled the film early, although it was still playing at other Windy City venues a full year later.[323] This was much more the exception than the rule, though, as overall *A Mormon Maid* proved incredibly popular. By June Friedman reported that U.S. rights were essentially all sold, and available foreign markets would sell out within a few weeks as well.[324] The film also proved extremely popular with anti-Mormon organizations like the National Reform Association and the National Anti-Mormon League, which used it in traveling lectures for many years; in 1918 they had a successful tour around Syracuse and Rochester, near Mormonism's birthplace, but some critics asserted that the entire campaign, which involved people with a financial interest in *A Mormon Maid*, was a front to increase profits for the film. Still, lectures and screenings were popular events, and even purely profit-motivated exhibitors continued to show the film as long as the crusaders.[325]

Hiller & Wilk headed up international sales as well, beginning by June with Scandinavia, which remained neutral in the European conflict, South America, and the Philippines, followed by Mexico. In May the distribution rights for Australia and New Zealand were sold for a record price, and, despite its release being held up by a petition from Utah governor Simon Bamberger to block the film from showing there, by August three prints proved insufficient so a record number of five separate prints were touring Australia, breaking revenue records in Melbourne and Sydney and provoking such an enthusiastic response that it prompted potential buyers in London to seek the British rights despite the war; it was showing there by July 1918. It opened in Canada in November, and other nonbelligerent territories in 1917 and '18. The end of hostilities in Europe probably gave *A Mormon Maid* new life there as well, and some prints continued to play domestically and abroad for several years. There are records of screenings in South Africa in 1919 and Ohio as late as 1922, and 16mm prints could still be rented in the 1940s. Although often largely forgotten today, *A Mormon Maid* was unquestionably the climax of the silent anti-Mormon films.[326]

Though perhaps nothing could match this in force or scope, other productions followed. On September 1 and October 27, 1918 the Fox Film Corporation, predecessor of Twentieth Century-Fox, released *Riders of the Purple Sage* and its sequel *The Rainbow Trail*, two films based on recent novels by the popular western writer Zane Grey. The plot offered some innovations along with a great deal of routine: in *Riders*, a Mormon girl named Jane Withersteen falls in love with former Texas Ranger Jim Lassiter, who is searching for his sister who was abducted by Mormons. He discovers she's dead but helps his niece to escape and rescues a young orphan named Fay. In the process he kills the Mormons' leader and flees with Jane and Fay to a nearly impenetrable valley. They are about to be caught when Lassiter pushes a boulder down on the Mormons in the valley's only entrance, thus safely sealing the trio inside to live in peace. In *The Rainbow Trail* many years have passed and a relative of Lassiter's named Shefford is searching for him. However, irate Mormons beat him to the closed valley, force an entrance, and kidnap Fay, now a young adult. A raid by U.S. marshals to enforce anti-polygamy laws fails when the women won't testify against their husbands, but Shefford falls in love with Fay at the trial and is able to help her escape. There is a chase and battle in which all four heroes are saved by the arrival of the marshals.

The First Wave: The New Frontier

Both films were directed by the Scottish Frank Lloyd, who had recently directed *Les Misérables* and *A Tale of Two Cities* (both 1917) for Fox, and starred Mary Mersch as Jane, but it was William Farnum as both Lassiter and Shefford who was the production's greatest star. A close friend of Grey, Farnum was on a hunting trip with him when he first struck upon the story, and the two men worked out Lassiter's character together. William Fox personally purchased the film rights to the books in the spring of 1918 for a total of $5,000, and production took place that summer. Location shooting for *Riders* lasted about a month in Arizona, mostly around the Grand Canyon, with the climax filmed at the mouth of a small canyon near Flagstaff, followed by indoor and studio lot filming back in Los Angeles; Grey himself was on set the entire time. The filmmakers enlisted 150 Civil War veterans from a government retirement center to play the band of maurading Mormons, reportedly achieving a spectacular effect, while a group of plural wives was reportedly portrayed by stage mothers and their children who were unaware of why they were being filmed. Production continued straight into *The Rainbow Trail* in L.A., and completed back in Arizona in late summer; *Riders* ran for seven reels at 6,470 feet, *Rainbow* for six at 5,500. Besides the striking locations, the stunts, camerawork, and acting were all reportedly strong, and both films were released as part of Fox's new Standard Pictures brand of prestige productions to somewhat mixed but generally positive reviews. One said the second film featured plenty of "routine Western riding, battles between the Mormons and U.S. Marshals, with considerable footage devoted to the secret Mormon village where the plural wives were kept," although not as much as he would have liked.[327] Though not as heavily promoted as *A Mormon Maid*, these were still films to be reckoned with; as another critic said, "Bill Farnum's name and the fact that this is a Mormon story ought to pull considerable at the box office."[328]

During the films' initial release in 1918 the Church found itself typically impotent, although all its efforts with *A Mormon Maid* may have influenced how these films were marketed: the *Motion Picture News* advised theater owners "if you work the Mormon angle refer to those in the picture as outlaws from their own religious cult and then you won't be damning people that are today perfectly law-abiding."[329] The films performed well enough that Fox decided to re-release them in 1921. Mormons once again took up the effort to suppress them, and this time, for once, they were, surprisingly, successful. The crusade was led by Reed Smoot, in close communication with Church President Heber Grant and assisted by other prominent Mormons like F. C. Schramm, Salt Lake Mayor Clarence Neslen, and Utah Governor Charles R. Mabey. Grant strongly considered litigation to gain a publicity platform or actually win damages, but all their efforts appeared doomed until two representatives from Fox approached Smoot seeking his support in eliminating a 30% excise tax on motion pictures; the quid pro quo dealmaking evidently took all of five minutes, with William Fox later personally apologizing and promising the films' complete elimination from the market—a major coup for the Mormons—although it took a reminder from the Senator to have them pulled from Europe as well, and missionaries reported they were still showing in South Africa in 1922, although there they had "done more good than harm."[330] Mr. Fox even proposed doing a positive picture on Mormonism, a possibility Grant embraced heartily, calling it the only offer to "picturize certain historical events that have occurred in the history of the Church . . . that has had any appeal to me in it."[331] It appears, however, that Fox never had any intention of making good; in fact, the entire arrangement was rather astute: by this point the pictures had probably made their profits— although Fox claimed he was taking a $300,000 loss—making their removal a nominal gesture, and it also gave Fox valuable assistance in eliminating the objectionable tax. Smoot and Grant undoubtedly realized this but rightly felt that by finally suppressing an anti-Mormon picture the Church achieved a major public relations victory and possibly discouraged future filmmakers, which may have proven true. The most unfortunate result of the entire affair was that the studio was so successful at destroying the films that they are completely lost today.

The ramifications of this victory reverberated for years. It's possible, for instance, that there's a connection between William Fox's promise in 1921 and his studio's production of *Brigham Young*, essentially the film he had proposed, in 1940. But even in 1924, Tom Mix, Fox's biggest star, announced that he would be starring in a remake of *Riders* but with all of the Mormon elements removed; he was visiting southern Utah to film *The Deadwood Coach* at the time and, while plans for this remake may have already been underway, it seems Mix's time spent with Chauncey and Gronway Parry and their Mormon neighbors influenced the decision. This version came out in 1925, with Senator Smoot approving the films beforehand, and additional remakes in 1931, 1941, and 1996 all avoided any references to the faith. Mormonism became such a taboo subject that in 1924 a film based on a Zane Grey novel with a *positive* stance on the Church, *The Heritage of the Desert*, also had its Mormon elements removed.[332]

It is, however, unlikely that producers now saw the Church as having much political muscle. The disappearance of the American anti-Mormon film was most likely due to its loss of sensationalism and the increasing moral regulation of the industry. There was, however, still some activity. In 1920 the Louis B. Mayer film *The Fighting Shepherdess*, about a single woman battling to maintain her ranch against encroachers, featured a supporting character called Mormon Joe; this role was played by Noah Beery, whose brother Wallace would star in the Mormon pioneer film *Bad Bascomb* in 1946. In April 1920 author Charles Felton Pidgin advertised the scenario *The House of Shame*, "a melodramatic story of Mormon life in Salt Lake City,"[333] but it was never made into a film, implying a lack of interest among American producers. Even the Fidelity Picture Plays Syndicate, a blatantly anti-Mormon organization organized by Hans Freece, who had toured Scandinavia in 1911, and other activists, failed to complete an exposé potentially titled either *The Mormon* or *The Power of the Mormons*, which they tried to produce between 1919 and 1921. A script was written by Frank J. Cannon, Utah's first senator, the son of former First Presidency member George Q. Cannon, and now an active advocate against the Church, and the company incorporated in Ohio but was never able to raise the funds for the film. In some finished productions that presumably would call for Mormonism the Church was simply omitted: in 1920 screenwriter C. A. Short and director Elliott Howe saw fit to name a two-reel western after *The Mormon Trail* while not including any actual Mormons onscreen; instead it featured a young man wrongly accused of holding up his own wagon train. This was repeated one year later when the serial *The Exploits of Battling Dick Hatton* included an episode entitled, again, "The Mormon Trail," and then in 1926 with the western *Salt Lake Trail*.[334]

The anti-Mormon film would be given one last gasp in Europe, however, where Mormonism once again became a hot topic after the postwar return of American missionaries. English activists like Winifred Graham, fresh back from a successful postwar visit to a conference in Pittsburgh where she succeeded in getting James Talmage booed offstage, attempted to revive public antipathy against the Church and polygamy, and between early 1919 and May 1920 the United Kingdom denied missionaries visas, with similar events in Sweden and as far afield as South Africa. Numerous plays were staged throughout the country,[335] while Winifred Graham published another book, *Sealed Women*, and helped convince the fledgling Master Films studio at Teddington southwest of London to simultaneously undertake not one but two anti-Mormon films, *Trapped by the Mormons* and *Married to a Mormon*. The first of these was based on her own book *The Love Story of a Mormon* from the 1911 campaign; the back-to-back films were written by Frank Miller and produced and directed by Harry B. Parkinson.

Trapped by the Mormons was a seventy-two-minute effort depicting a girl named Nora Prescott (American actress Evelyn Brent) who is, characteristically, wooed away from her fiancé by a mesmeric Mormon missionary named Isoldi Keene (Louis Willoughby). They abscond from her home in northern England to London but are pursued and observed by Nora's beau and a police inspector. Keene's "sister" is condemned to death when she tells Nora she is actually his wife; the other Elders agree to kill Nora as well to save Keene face. Nora signals for help with a handkerchief the inspector had given her, and he arrives with her fiancé in time to save both women. The Mormons are hauled off to prison and the happy couple reunited. In its basic outline *Trapped* is thus very similar to other anti-Mormon stories about girls rescued from polygamy before they are sealed into it, but in contrast *Married to a Mormon* begins with the titular marriage followed by the revelation of the husband's foul religion. He plots to take his wife (again played by Brent) to Utah but she is—once again—saved by her former lover. This time the Mormon is actually killed by the boyfriend of a prospective second wife, a dramatic necessity given that divorce was presumably not an option. But what is the same is that once again the polygamous Mormons are defeated and monogamous bliss confirmed.

Perhaps because of *Trapped by the Mormons*' continual availability on film and video, extensive missionary correspondence from the time, a fair amount of recent scholarship on it, and even a 2005 remake, it is probably the best-known of the anti-Mormon films and is usually treated as the most important and lethal of them, although both descriptions better apply to *A Mormon Maid*. *Trapped* and *Married* premiered in the West End in March and April 1922 then toured throughout England, where they seem to have been met with critical disdain but a fair degree of public popularity. One reviewer wrote of *Trapped*: "There is no room for propaganda on the screen ... It is inartistic and usually dull if not boring; this picture is no exception...." And another of *Married*: "Unfortunately, it is not only propaganda but very rubbishy melodrama, made worse by the continual hinting at dreadful immoralities which are never shown."[336] The *Variety* reviewer recognized that *Trapped* stemmed from "the present crusade against Mormon missionaries" but added that "the picture is very crude melodrama and is more likely to raise hearty laughter than any feeling of fear or repugnance."[337] Even when announcing the production of *Married to a Mormon*, *Variety* pointed out the limited appeal of the topic so many years after the official end of polygamy: "It promises to be as crudely melodramatic as the first, but as the Mormon boom will probably be over before it is finished it will not have the same pull."[338]

The First Wave: The New Frontier

The missionary apparatus was by now well equipped to respond to such pictures. In Hull one theater manager reportedly thought the film poor and the returns disappointing, allowing missionaries to distribute nearly 3,000 pamphlets outside his doors. This caused George Osmond Hyde to write home that the film "was the best stroke of advertising that we have put forth since coming over here. In three evenings we let more people know that we are here than we could have done in three months at ordinary tracting from door to door."[339] Similar reports came from cities like Leeds and Birmingham and countries such as South Africa; in Australia future Church leader Marion G. Romney saw *Trapped*, happily distributing tracts afterward. In England the upsurge in activity led to the re-establishment of a congregation in York that had been closed for three years, and the April 1922 Church conference at Grimsby had double the attendance over the previous October. Nevertheless, the agitation didn't prove an entire boon. Future Church President Ezra Taft Benson wrote in his diary: "Winnifred Graham on our track again."[340] He was kicked out of homes and hounded by crowds to the point of calling on police protection. Apostle Orson Whitney served as the European Mission President at the time, and the stress caused by the anti-Mormon campaign aggravated his ill health as he struggled with a failing kidney and prostate. He was replaced in November by his younger colleague David McKay, who by the spring of 1923 saw that the agitation was severe enough that, out of concern for missionaries' safety, he curtailed door-to-door proselytizing and street meetings in many areas, as well as re-emphasizing the strict rule that no missionaries were to teach or even be seen with young women; this rule in an updated form remains one of the standards of missionary conduct today. With full-time missionaries thus curtailed in how they could search for new contacts, McKay struck upon the idea of making "every member a missionary," that is, local members of the Church could help find and teach their friends and neighbors, giving the missionaries teaching opportunities without exposing them to charges of lechery. When he became President of the Church in 1951 McKay made this motto a centerpiece of his administration, and it revolutionized how missionary work has been conducted ever since.[341]

Although a much reduced strand of anti-Mormon sentiment remained for several years, the height of Graham's 1922 English crusade was short-lived, as even other anti-Mormon activists pointed out that polygamy was now a moot issue. By July 1923 an elder in Norwich reported: "The anti-'Mormon' movement of a year ago has died down to almost nothing. The enemy played himself out, and the old polygamy stories were rehashed to such an extent that the public became tired of them."[342] In North America, however, Church leaders were less willing to rely on public goodwill; fresh off their success with *Riders of the Purple Sage* and *The Rainbow Trail*, they wanted to keep the films from ever screening at all. Attempts to suppress them in Canada in 1924 failed, but Senator Smoot was again successful in blocking their initial release in the United States; though *Trapped* was re-released in England in 1928 as *The Mormon Peril*, it apparently never saw an American screen until decades later, when it was seen as an arthouse or historical novelty rather than a direct threat to the Church. The anti-Mormon film was not extinct, but the lackluster success of these two projects certainly helped put it in remission. By the 1930s, Mormonism had outlived its sensationalism, and lurid depictions virtually disappeared from the page, stage, and screen.[343]

In the midst of this wave of anti-Mormon films—indeed, in the year that *The Birth of a Nation* was inspiring Famous Players-Lasky to produce *A Mormon Maid*—a plethora of Mormon comedies burst forth. *A Puritan Conscience*, a three-reel comedy from the New York-based Flamingo Film Company in January 1915, poked fun at Mormons without actually having any Mormon characters in it at all. An adult brother and sister who have both abandoned the Puritanism of their youth are reunited after a long separation and try to fool each other into thinking they are still religious. The brother buys a country house and puts on old-fashioned Puritan robes, causing his new neighbors to assume he's a Mormon. Additional cases of mistaken identity ensue, with every female visitor being judged a new plural wife and the village parson calling the polygamist to repentance. When an African-American maid arrives and the locals think the Mormon is indulging in miscegenation, however, it's too much and everyone in the house is arrested; the brother and sister happily confess their deceit to each other in jail.[344]

Subsequent films in 1915 illustrate how fuzzy the definition "anti-Mormon" actually is. After the three serious adaptations of *A Study in Scarlet* were released in England, the U.S., and France, the British comedy duo Fred and Will Evans wrote, directed, and starred in a parody called *A Study in Skarlit*, where they played Sherlokz Homz and Professor Moratorium. The film is lost and we don't know any other cast members, but it's likely that the entire Mormon element of the original was jettisoned entirely in favor of a pure send-up of Sherlock Holmes and his most famous rival, who did not figure into the original *Study in Scarlet* in any way. If this is true then it hardly counts as a Mormon film at all, although the exclusion of Mormonism in 1915 might be just as telling as if it had been included.[345]

The First Wave: The New Frontier

Two other British films that year definitely included Mormon characters, but again it's difficult to evaluate whether they were shown using the old stereotypes from 1912 or in a more humorous mode. *Deadwood Dick and the Mormons* and *Deadwood Dick Spoils Brigham Young* were part of England's first serial *The Adventures of Deadwood Dick*, and produced by Samuelson Films and starring Fred Paul, the producer and star of the recent *A Study in Scarlet*. The Deadwood Dick character harked back to the penny dreadful novels of the nineteenth century, the Victorian equivalent of American dime novels that told their stories in weekly installments. Deadwood Dick was an Englishman who found adventure in the American west, and he remained a popular character through many books and films; there was also an American *Deadwood Dick* feature filmed in Utah in 1922 and a 1940 serial from Columbia; the name was even so popular that it was assumed by several real cowboys associated with the town of Deadwood in South Dakota. The episodes of *The Adventures of Deadwood Dick* were unique for a serial in that they ran two full reels and told a rather self-contained story, although there was continuity from one installment to the next, rather than one story broken up into multiple short chapters as was normally done. The Mormon episodes were parts three and four of a six-part series, and while we don't know anything of their content—what are Dick's adventures among the Mormons and how exactly does he spoil Brigham Young?—it seems that these films, which have previously been classified as anti-Mormon works, leaned more toward high adventure than any serious social criticism. One suspects, however, that polygamy and Danites played more than a small role, for if there was any sure way to spoil Brigham Young in 1915 it would have been by freeing Dick's recurring love interest (Joan Ferry) from a forced marriage despite all the efforts of Brigham's agents. As to *why* Samuelson Films made a full third of this series about Mormons, it probably stemmed directly from *A Study in Scarlet*: Mormons were already on their minds and entire sets, props, and actors might very well have been recycled from that film into these.[346]

Finally that year, in December 1915 Pathé's American branch released *Excuse Me* through their Gold Rooster line of prestige films. A five-reel comedy of errors set aboard a westward-bound express train, the film features one engaged couple and numerous other people in various states of matrimonial satisfaction, with plenty of ribaldry and miscommunications over the course of the journey. When the train stops in Utah, however, and a Mormon minister boards, the young reverend who had been fleeing his religious career quickly re-dons his robes and marries the young couple before the Mormon can make off with the bride. This is the climax of the film, for after the Mormon threat is defeated all the romantic entanglements are easily worked out.[347]

After this profusion of activity in 1915 there was a reduction in the number of comic mentions of Mormonism, just as with waning anti-Mormon films, with only four more known titles produced through the remainder of the silent era. The first of these was *My Sister-in-Law from America (Min Svigerinde fra Amerika)*, a seven-minute short from Nordisk Films that was released in Denmark on New Year's Day 1917. Written by Valdemar Hansen and directed by the prolific Lau Lauritzen, Sr., the film depicts a man whose wife catches him with his mistress, so he lies and introduces her as the visiting wife of his brother who has emigrated to America. Things get complicated when the brother returns for an unexpected visit and is forced to play along. Then when the actual wife arrives the hero maintains the charade by declaring she is also his sister-in-law, exclaiming, "My brother's a Mormon, the happy beast!" That the protagonist's wife merely shrugs and shows this "plural wife" to her room shows how far Danish sentiment had shifted since 1912. There is very little of substance to *My Sister-in-Law from America*, but along with *A Trip to Salt Lake City* it is the only extant short film from this period, having been preserved and even posted online by the Danish Film Institute.[348]

Germany released *The Mormon Uncle (Der Mormonenonkel)*, its only known Mormon-related film of the First Wave, in 1920; this was made by the production company Martin Dentler GmbH and shot by the Austrian cinematographer Heinrich Gärtner early in his career, but nothing else is known about it, including how sardonic or earnest its position on the Church was. Then in 1922 Denmark released its final offering, *He Is a Mormon (Han er Mormon)*. A thirteen-minute (1,160-foot) short alternately known as *Nalle's Engagement (Nalles Forlovelse)*, this was again directed by Lauritzen and starred Frederik Buch in his last collaboration with the director. Though the film is lost the DFI has preserved Valdemar Andersen's handwritten script, and a remaining still photograph shows the middle-aged Buch enticing nine young women with some sort of conversation.[349]

The climactic wedding of *Excuse Me* was inverted in the final comedic take on Mormonism in the silent era. This was *Hands Up!* from Famous-Players Lasky in January 1926, nine years after it had produced *A Mormon Maid*. Directed by Clarence Badger and starring Keystone veteran Raymond Griffith, this was a Civil War farce about Jack, a Confederate spy trying to stop the Yankees from obtaining a trove of gold. There are escapades with Indians and of course the war itself, but Jack also gets romantically entangled with the two daughters of the gold miner, played by none other than Mack Swain. At the climax Jack's about to be lynched as a bigamist when news of General Lee's surrender at Appomattox Court House distracts the mob. The three lovers still don't know what to do, however, until Brigham Young (Charles French) fortuitously arrives and announces he's happily married to nineteen women! The trio hops into the back of his wagon, with the gold, and the film ends on a close-up of a sign reading, "To Salt Lake City"; even this was tamed down from the originally shot version, deemed too provocative, in which Jack actually marries both women onscreen under Brother Brigham's patron hand, but in either case it was a fitting benediction for silent-era depictions of polygamy, which reached their zenith with *A Mormon Maid* and gradually faded to this comic coda before disappearing for decades. The film was a hit, with critics raving about its "ingenuity, imaginativeness and originality" and how Griffith was "flying in the face of movie tradition and getting away with it beautifully."[350] In this and other comic films, condoning polygamy, even humorously, was indeed a break from the past, but it was one that the world was ready for, and in films from *Brigham Young* to *They Call Me Trinity* (1970) to *Big Love* (2006-11) polygamy would never again be the monolithic monstrosity that it was in the First Wave.

A third type of film should be mentioned as well: the newsreel. We know of quite a few that featured the Church in these decades. Both before and after its anti-Mormon films of 1912 Pathé Frères released a number of newsreels on Mormon topics. These were likely shot by Shirl and Chet Clawson and will be discussed in connection with their work. In addition, in July 1916 Selig-Tribune released a newsreel profiling Lem Spilsbury, a Mormon scout and interpreter who served under John J. Pershing in his expedition to capture Pancho Villa. In 1920 the Paramount-Empress theater in Salt Lake sent a production crew to film Utah's delegates and other representatives at the Republican National Convention, including Reed Smoot and other prominent state Republicans. And in 1922 Vitagraph released *Towering Wonders of Utah*, a one-reel news piece on "the strange rock formations in the Mormon state."[351]

Institutional and Independent Films

The Mormons' First Movies

Ironically, the greatest legacy of the silent anti-Mormon films was to transform the Church into a dedicated creator of motion pictures and visual media. The general conference in April 1912, when the first wave of anti-Mormon pictures had just hit, is illuminating in this regard. President Joseph F. Smith devoted his entire opening address to the recent onslaught of antagonistic sentiment, emphasizing the hollowness of the claims against the Church and closing with an oblique reference to moving pictures as "the most keen subtle and cunning processes that ever were known to man."[352] His counselor Charles Penrose expressed a desire to present Church doctrines and practices on an equal footing with those who were now attacking them,[353] and two future Church Presidents who would be vital to the growth of institutional Church filmmaking—Heber J. Grant and David O. McKay—spoke more specifically and optimistically than any others. Grant described the current pictures as vile, wicked, and libelous, and offered hope for a time when truth would be able to circumvent the globe as quickly as these films,[354] and McKay said, "A stronger means of disseminating knowledge, even than the press, has been brought to bear against us. I refer to the motion picture show." He quoted a letter from a missionary in New England describing *A Victim of the Mormons* as "quite offensive" and decrying the censors for failing to reject it. But he also intimated at the potential benefit films could have for the Church, saying that while literature depends on readers' mental images, with films, "when you may sit and see it acted, see it portrayed as naturally as though it were being enacted in the every-day life, then the mental pictures are given as definitely and as rapidly as the motions of the actors can portray them."[355] Within just a few months the Mormon hierarchy had determined that film could convey a message much more powerfully, swiftly, and widely than any written tract or spoken sermon, and thus they were already working to harness its power and gain a level platform with their critics by telling the Mormon story as they saw it on film. The results of this experiment—which included feature films, short documentaries, and the exhibition of films like *From the Manger to the Cross* discussed earlier— would deeply impress McKay, a professional educator: eleven years later as he oversaw the British response to *Trapped by the Mormons* and *Married to a Mormon* he wrote that "the cinema, or 'moving picture show,' is to-day one of the greatest educational forces, if not the greatest educational force in the world... Second only to travel, or seeing life itself, is the cinema!"[356]

These would not be the first Mormon-made motion pictures, however. As mentioned, the earliest known film by and about Mormons came in 1901 when the Salt Lake City Eighteenth Ward exhibited locally produced pictures on topics of Church history; this is the second-known instance of Mormons appearing on film anywhere, after the *Rocky Mountain Rider* pictures of 1898. This was an amateur effort for ward fundraising, but Mormons' first commercial use of cinema came on July 26, 1908 with the formation of the Rocky Mountain Moving Picture Company, Utah's first native film production firm, in Salt Lake City, with O. T. Sampson as president and Walter Park (sometimes Parks, and evidently no relation to brothers Lester, Byron, and Allen Park), an experienced camera operator, overseeing production. It's unknown which of the firm's principal personnel were Mormon, but it's likely that at least some if not most of them were, and much of their subject matter dealt with the Church. Specializing in "taking views of the different points of interest in Utah and the West in general,"[357] the film included a 3,000-foot panoramic shot of Salt Lake's "principal buildings, street scenes, the Mormon temple, tabernacle, [and] temple grounds" among their first 20,000 feet of footage, which included other sites of Church and state historical interest.[358] These were showing in Utah in October 1908, and the company desired to distribute them to theaters further afield to promote tourism, but we don't know how extensively they traveled. In the weekly meeting of the First Presidency and Quorum of the Twelve on June 30, 1910, President Smith reported that Governor William Spry had introduced him to "a man named Hutchinson who proposed the idea of illustrating the chief points in the history of the Church by means of moving pictures...." This was most likely S. W. Hutchinson, one of the Rocky Mountain Moving Picture Company's directors; the firm was evidently now prepared to branch into larger fictional productions and offered to contribute $15,000 to the project, which would mainly focus on the journey west from Nauvoo. The General Authorities agreed to pursue it, but evidently nothing came of it as we have no further record of the venture.[359]

The company's idea of using scenic films to promote the state caught on, however. At the first monthly banquet of the Utah Manufacturers' Association in February 1910 both Governor Spry and the Church's Presiding Bishop Charles Nibley spoke about the need to advertise Utah's industries to other states, and the publicity committee outlined a motion picture campaign that could be carried out to that effect; to what extent the association executed this plan is unknown. Additionally, in December 1912 the Utah Motion Picture Company shot between 700 and 800 feet of footage of Salt Lake City landmarks, and it's probable that the Clawsons and other filmmakers continued the trend throughout the 1910s and '20s. Before this, though, Utah's second production company was the Revier Motion Picture Company, founded by Harry Revier in 1910. A Philadelphia native and probably not Mormon himself, Revier was among the many filmmakers who sought to escape the attention of Thomas

Edison's Motion Picture Patents Company in New Jersey by building studios in far-flung cities with clear skies and a variety of outdoor locations. Before the industry consolidated in Hollywood it seemed equally probable that it might coalesce in Fort Lauderdale, Augusta, Ithaca, or even Ogden, and filmmakers like Revier wanted to be in at the ground floor of that growth.[360] He built a multi-building studio in Salt Lake City's Sugar House area, claiming it was the largest in the west, to capture the "natural scenery of the Mormon State."[361] He also branched into fiction production, announcing the western *Love's Sorrow* in 1910. His studio, however, only lasted a few years before he moved on to Los Angeles. He would later return to collaborate with Church members, so it's quite possible he employed some in this earlier endeavor as well.[362]

In January 1912, when anti-Mormon films were arriving en masse in the United States, William H. Harbeck, an apparently non-Mormon filmmaker for the Canadian Pacific Railway, announced, through his own production company, a 15-18,000-foot film entitled *The Romance of Mormonism* that would tell the story of the Church from its founding to the present. A prolific director and producer, he hired Revier and Walter Park to shoot footage of contemporary Salt Lake City while he was away on other projects, and on January 24 they began by filming the temple, Tabernacle, and nearby Hotel Utah. Harbeck meanwhile traveled to Seattle to prepare a film on Alaska and the Yukon, and then journeyed to Europe to film scenic shots there and study outdoor production techniques with Léon Gaumont in Paris, knowledge that would have applied to both his upcoming major projects. After a few weeks he set out to return to the States to begin his Mormon and Yukon films in earnest, but he booked his passage on the Titanic—he probably filmed onboard during the journey and was contracted to disembark early and film its arrival in New York—and was among its victims on April 15. Without their producer Park and Revier abandoned the project, and thus the sinking of the Titanic aborted what would have been the first great Mormon film. To the extent that it was executed, it may have had Mormon involvement—we don't know Park's religious affiliation, for instance—but along with *The Romance of the Utah Pioneers* from the following year it indicates a changing perspective from the mainstream industry in the midst of many much more anti-Mormon films.[363]

Around the same time, James Cruze had begun a career as an actor in California and was eager to move behind the camera, and he reportedly envisioned a film about the Mormon migration as a perfect vehicle to do so. At some point in the early 1910s he spent at least four weeks in Utah attempting to raise funds and assistance among prominent Church members. "He said he'd weave a love story thru it and make it a big picture and we'd all make a lot of money," one acquaintance recalled. But he hadn't yet directed anything and his potential investors, who all knew him from his youth, "didn't think he'd make good," so no one put up the money. Cruze returned to acting and eventually began directing with other projects. He most likely remembered his Mormon pioneer concept when Jesse Lasky hired him to make *The Covered Wagon* in 1923, but back in Utah the seed Cruze planted in Mormons' minds reportedly became one major impetus behind the 1913 film *One Hundred Years of Mormonism*.[364]

While they may have been hesitant with Cruze, Church leaders were becoming increasingly amenable to the idea of using media such as motion pictures to represent themselves, as shown by the 1912 general conference and simultaneous events in the field of still photography. As mentioned, on September 16, 1911 Max Florence announced in the *Salt Lake Tribune* that sometime in July a disaffected Mormon named Gisbert Bossard had smuggled a camera inside the Salt Lake Temple while it was closed for cleaning. Florence attempted to blackmail Church leaders by asking for $100,000 to suppress the resulting photographs' publication. Joseph F. Smith ignored Florence's demand, but James Talmage, probably drawing on his years of experience with illustrated lectures, went one step further and proposed the Church publish its own photographs of the temple interior, professional images of sufficient quality to make Florence's work irrelevant, and which they could frame in the context of a book that explains the sanctity and purpose of temples. This was an audacious concept—the Church had never published images of the sacred precincts of a temple before—but Smith approved it immediately and commissioned Talmage to write *The House of the Lord*, one of the major theological works for which he is best remembered; he also called him to the Quorum of the Twelve Apostles when a vacancy occurred that December. Talmage and Ralph Savage, son of pioneer photographer Charles Savage, were photographing in the temple by September 26, and by the end of the month they had submitted their work to the U.S. copyright office in an attempt to block Florence from owning the rights to all images of the temple interior. President Smith publicly offered to make the photographs available "to magazines and moving picture people"[365] before the book was complete, and by October 21 the Levi Company of New York City was selling the images as magic lantern slides for general commercial release; forty slides could be purchased for $40 or rented for a week for $20. Meanwhile Talmage spent several months writing his text, and *The House of the Lord*, published on September 30, 1912, was a landmark not just of Mormon doctrinal writing but of Mormon photography. It included thirty-one black and white plates of the Salt Lake Temple and another fifteen of the Kirtland, Nauvoo, St. George, Logan, and Manti buildings. This, along with other photographic efforts like the 1909 publication of George Edward Anderson's *The Birth of Mormonism in Picture* by the Church's general Sunday School board and the 1913 novel *Kawich's Gold Mine*, which was illustrated with photos of the St. George Temple and Mormon underground sites from the 1880s, showed the power of the still image in telling the Mormon story. When coupled with the obvious influence of films like *A Victim of the Mormons*, it begged the question why the Church was not producing its own moving images as well.[366]

The First Features: "One Hundred Years of Mormonism" and "The Story of the Book of Mormon"

Beset by anti-Mormon motion pictures, in June 1912 Church leaders decided to do exactly that. That month the General Authorities struck a deal with the local Ellaye Motion Picture Company to make a huge film telling the Church's full history; although it was based in Utah, some writers have seen the company's name as a homophone for the "L.A." Motion Picture Company, perhaps in a bid to connect it with the growing film industry there. The idea to produce the picture probably came from many quarters simultaneously, but who functioned on behalf of the Church in the specific negotiations with Ellaye is unknown. The company was formed expressly for the purpose of creating this film, and though it is unclear what percentage of its $50,000 backing came from the Church, Ellaye's president and general manager Harry A. Kelly gave Church leaders final cut approval in return for logistical assistance and endorsement of the finished product. They chose the title *One Hundred Years of Mormonism*, taking it from a popular Church textbook by John Henry Evans published for the 1905 centennial of Joseph Smith's birth. The film was apparently not a direct adaptation, but the subject matter was obviously extremely similar.

Church leaders soon learned how difficult narrative filmmaking can be. They reportedly disapproved of how Kelly's team was spending its funds—there is some speculation that they ran through the entire $50,000 without completing the picture—and the filmmakers, in turn, found the Church too invasive and controlling, possibly of the film's content as well as the firm's management. Although they advertised it would be complete by September, by October it was only three-fifths of the way through production. Kelly broke the contract and the Church retained control of the film and immediately sought out another new company, the California-based Utah Moving Picture Company, to finish it.

The First Wave: The New Frontier

This new firm purchased the Ellaye company and assumed its contract. It was capitalized at $100,000 with a $30,000 production budget, in addition to the money Ellaye had already spent. On November 27 Norval MacGregor, a non-Mormon near the beginning of his career, was announced as the new director; he was to receive assistance from Hobart Bosworth, who of course went on to star in *A Mormon Maid* four years later. In December another non-Mormon, the rising Hollywood scriptwriter Nell Shipman, was brought in to revise the screenplay; she received $2,500 for her work, reportedly a new pay scale for a screenwriter, especially a female one. This is important in the history of the burgeoning Hollywood film industry, but it also indicates the film's importance to its backers and the degree of care that went into creating the most engaging and accurate story.

For once the cast was literally in the thousands, including many actual pioneers who reenacted their journey, although there were forty principal characters and 150 main extras. Brigham Young was played by his grandson Frank Young, who went on to star in more than thirty films in the 1920s; he is the only performer in the film whose name we know. In addition to shooting in authentic locations in Utah, the production included large-scale recreations in Los Angeles of Independence, Nauvoo, and other historic sites—some reportedly up to a half mile in scope, and all faithfully recreated from historical photographs. Some complicated scenes such as the Haun's Mill massacre, an incident of the 1838 Missouri conflict, necessitated simultaneous shooting with four cameras to capture the burning houses, one of the first times multi-camera production was used in fiction filmmaking; the Russian film *Defence of Sevastopol* from 1911, just one year earlier, is often credited as the first to use the technique. Most importantly, at six reels running for roughly ninety minutes—later a seventh reel would reach two hours—it was truly gigantic for its time, dwarfing prestige productions like *A Victim of the Mormons*. It has occasionally been described as one of the first "feature films" in cinema history, and although this is a problematic term which had an evolving meaning in the early twentieth century, it is true that *One Hundred Years of Mormonism* was one of the longest films ever made at that point, particularly in the United States.[367]

By the time the project switched from the Ellaye Motion Picture Company to the Utah Moving Picture Company, nearly 5,000 feet had been shot. Exactly what this consisted of is not entirely known, but Kelly had overseen production of pioneers descending Emigration Canyon and a possible river crossing at the Jordan River near Murray. It remained for MacGregor and his crew to shoot "Joseph Smith's start from the East, and the journey to the Mormon stronghold,"[368] which was predicted to consist of only the rather small amount of 1,000 feet. In fact the film went from Ellaye's anticipated five reels to six before MacGregor was finished with his month of production. This evidently took place entirely in Los Angeles, something particularly important given Utah's cold winters, although he may have shot another river crossing scene in Utah, during which the lead wagon was nearly swept away. In the end the film started with Joseph Smith's birth, omitted his First Vision but focused on receiving the Book of Mormon, persecution through to his death and then the journey of the pioneers, with some culminating shots of modern Utah; other events since 1847 and all references to polygamy were completely omitted.[369] After completing 225 feet of retakes, a 9,000-foot version was edited down to 5,000 feet by January 1913. Three prints were struck and dyed with a four-tint process; the emulsion of entire scenes was colored, blue to represent night, for instance, or possibly yellow, rose, or amber for other moods.[370]

On the morning of February 3, 1913 Joseph F. Smith and about forty other Church leaders attended a preview at the Salt Lake Theatre as part of a meeting of the Church's Sunday School board, and it opened to the public later that day in the largest premiere in the city's history, grossing $1,800 in its first two days, a state record. Newspaper ads declared its spectacle: "Historically correct. Burning of Mormon village. Hundreds of horsemen, oxen, Indians, militia, mobs, PIONEERS" and tickets ran from fifteen to seventy-five cents.[371] The Salt Lake Theatre was reportedly so crowded that up to 400 people had to sit on the stage behind the screen and have the intertitles, which they saw in reverse, read to them by William T. Nuttall, the advance manager for the film. At the end of these two days of screenings Nuttall also convinced Smith and his counselors to rescind their approval of the film; paradoxically, this action demonstrated their goodwill toward it and the belief that it would fare better with the general public if it weren't directly endorsed by the Church. While one print traveled through northern Utah and Idaho, where it was "met with the unqualified approval of all the people who have seen it, both members of the 'Mormon' faith, and others,"[372] the other two prints opened in San Francisco and Los Angeles on the 9th; in March one print was showing in Mesa and Safford, Arizona to overflowing houses. Each screening was accompanied by a lecture, originally given by William G. Colvin in San Francisco, Levi Edgar Young of the Seventy in Salt Lake, and MacGregor himself in Los Angeles; this was delivered while the film played, as the speaker explained "many interesting incidents that otherwise would not be understood."[373] Drawing from the tradition of panorama and magic lantern lectures, this practice was fairly common in these years. After receiving feedback from months of screenings, the filmmakers decided to add some cuts and reshoots. Among these was footage of the April 1913 general conference, which President Smith allowed them to record to "enliven the picture by making a record of one of our tabernacle services."[374]

Reports on the film's artistic merits were mixed. In Salt Lake screenings were reportedly accompanied by frequent spontaneous applause, as when the Angel Moroni gives Joseph Smith the Urim and Thummim to translate the plates or the pioneers first survey the Salt Lake Valley. Young wrote an article called "'Mormonism' in Picture" in the February 1913 *Young Woman's Journal*, wherein he extolled every aspect of the film and averred "it will appeal to all Latter-day Saints, and will serve as a potent factor in showing the world something of the dramatic and tragic side of the rise and growth of 'Mormonism.'" He went on to claim that "the moving picture . . . is to do much to inculcate a knowledge of the world and art . . . The moving picture with all the other modern inventions is to help us carry the Mission of Christ to all the world, and to bring humanity home to the true principles of salvation."[375] Others were more cautious with their praise. President Smith's statement after the preview screening seems formal and vague at best: "On the whole the film is commendable. It shows an effort to tell as it occurred the story of the movements of the Church from its organization until the arrival of the pioneers here. The makers evidently tried to be perfectly fair in its presentation, and the general trend is worthy of much commendation."[376] James Talmage was freer to be candid in his personal journal, stating it was "not a complete success" and contained "many crudities and historical inaccuracies," although in the end he thought "the general effect will be good."[377] Professional critics seemed to agree with President Smith that the second half depicting the pioneers was more engaging than the first portion on the pre-1847 Church, a frequent complaint being the age of the actor portraying young Joseph Smith. The *Deseret News* correspondent called the pioneer sequences "very impressive, especially to those who know by experience, or have heard from their parents, of the thrilling stories of the trials and hardships of the early days of Utah," but overall suggested several changes "in order to make the film still more interesting."[378]

All of the screenings thus far had been handled directly by the Church or the Utah Moving Picture Company, but in June 1913 the firm was ready to start selling states' rights to local distribution circuits, a traditional distribution strategy in the early 1910s, and the film, which was now also sometimes known, perhaps more appropriately, as *The Rise and Growth of Mormonism*, also had a weeklong encore run in Salt Lake City's Colonial Theatre in July to allow Utah audiences to see its revisions. At this point, however, the Los Angeles-based Golden State Moving Picture Company apparently purchased all distribution rights to the film. The company's general manager was Ernest Shipman, and he had a personal interest in seeing that his wife Nell's film had as wide a distribution as possible, so he oversaw much of its domestic release himself. He spent two summer months in Salt Lake City overseeing a second set of reshoots, up to 3,000 additional feet, which now put the picture at seven reels and nearly two hours' length. New footage included the Pioneer Day celebrations on July 24, including the parade in downtown Salt Lake and a phalanx of 8,000 marching children, and additional celebrations in the Tabernacle. With the film now in its third and final form, the Golden State Moving Picture Company put an end to sales to state exchanges and instead opted to maintain control of the picture and continue touring it throughout the country themselves. Particular emphasis remained around the Mormon Corridor, but it did open in Chicago on June 3, and in 1914 the revised version briefly played in Utah yet again, because the version screened there in 1913 hadn't included the reshoots of that summer.

There was still the possibility of international sales, of course. In February 1913 Levi Young gave the most optimistic account of these prospects by claiming that orders had been placed in "London, St. Petersburg, Rome, Buenos Ayres [sic], Montreal, Paris, Berlin, New York, and Pekin[g],"[379] cities that the Ellaye Motion Picture Company had merely claimed they would target when the film was complete. But trade journals report a more realistic distribution strategy that centered largely on the domestic market. Before the Golden State company's involvement, international rights were purchased by the Five Continents Exchange and Sales Company, and its officers in New York and London were negotiating with different foreign territories when the London representative died unexpectedly, leaving foreign distribution afloat. After the transfer to Golden State Shipman traveled to New York to sell the film in the eastern states and investigate the "European, Asiatic and Australian fields."[380] When he continued on to London a few weeks later, however, he decided not to include *One Hundred Years* in his portfolio, but rather to focus on other films the company represented. This seems to have been the end of the film's foreign distribution aspirations, although some historians have noted that it might have screened in London. In August, perhaps while Shipman was still in New York, Reed Smoot recorded in his journal that apostle George Albert Smith was enroute to Manhattan to screen the film and ensure it "was alright before presenting it to the public in moving pictures,"[381] but the results of his work there are also unknown. The only distribution outside the western states that we are certain about was a campaign begun by local Church leaders in Alberta in December 1913 to screen the film at Cardston and then across Canada. Again, their success outside the Mormon enclaves in southern Alberta is unknown.

Still, within the United States, the film reportedly earned $25,000 in 1913, a decent sum for such a narrowly targeted picture but short of its production budget—which, though initially $30,000, was advertised in December 1912 as exceeding $50,000—besides marketing and distribution costs. At least $22,000 of this revenue came from its initial release primarily in Utah and Idaho, where promoters claimed it had a "tremendous run."[382] This means *One Hundred Years of Mormonism* was financially a flop, but it appears Church members were focused primarily on the film's public relations merits. One full-page advertisement in the *Moving Picture World* encapsulated the proselytizing ethos behind the film, saying it included an "accurate representation of [the Church's] tragedies, persecutions, massacres, and terrible hardships endured during their winter pilgrimage to the Great Salt Lake Valley."[383] The general public was aware of this purpose, and perhaps the film couldn't overcome the taint of propaganda. One film industry reporter conjectured how it could be used in proselytizing then summarized: "It is the plan of the leaders of the church by showing films to offset other motion pictures which portray Mormonism and its leaders from Brigham Young down in an unfavorable light."[384] In this sense it was a success, but it was an approach that quickly showed its limitations: just a decade later one Mormon who had been involved with it recalled, "I guess it's no good. We're ashamed to show it to anyone now."[385] Wanting to both make a quality dramatic film and portray their faith in a positive light, the Mormon creators behind *One Hundred Years* were caught on a razor's edge that has plagued Mormon filmmakers ever since; the problem of how to make films that don't become "preachy" has never been resolved. Since it's lost we unfortunately cannot judge *One Hundred Years* on its own merits, but we can surmise that, while it did not stem all criticism of the Church or future anti-Mormon films like *A Mormon Maid*, after the barrage of antagonistic pictures in 1912 most Church members must have been relieved and even proud to see their history treated with such respect.[386]

In fact, despite any artistic faults *One Hundred Years of Mormonism* is unquestionably the most important Mormon film of the silent era. Various of its "promoters (with only slight overstatement) claimed it was the longest picture ever completed devoting itself to a single story."[387] While this is less than true, the fact that it predates *The Birth of a Nation* by two years is remarkable in American film history. From a Mormon perspective, it is pivotally important, as David Jacobs has pointed out, for at least three reasons: it is "the *only* silent movie sanctioned by the Church as essentially authentic, the *only* film utilizing genuine relics from the pioneer trek, and the *only* picture drawing on the experience of still-living pioneers," both as actors and otherwise.[388] In fact, in March 1913 over one thousand pioneers, including at least one who had journeyed to Utah in 1847, viewed the film in a special screening; the *Salt Lake Tribune* noted: "One by one the early pioneers are passing into the valley of silence, and it is not considered likely that so many of the first builders of the city will ever gather together again on a similar occasion."[389] The film has also been lost, one of the great tragedies of the First Wave, but in the late 1990s Robert Starling, who was working as a producer for the Church's Audiovisual Department, discovered a few minutes of *One Hundred Years* footage catalogued incorrectly in the Church History Library in Salt Lake City. Though not a complete copy, this find constitutes one of the most important discoveries in recent Mormon film history.[390]

Initially after completing production the Utah Moving Picture Company planned to create more pictures. Nell Shipman was contracted to write several short films on Mormon and other themes, and in January 1913 Norval MacGregor began shooting her adaptation of a short story about a get-rich-quick scheme, which was being funded by Mormon producer Oliver Morosco, one of his first investments in actual film production. It's unclear that this film was ever completed, but soon both Shipman and MacGregor were working for other studios and the Utah Moving Picture Company closed.[391]

Despite this company's disappearance in Los Angeles, *One Hundred Years of Mormonism*, like *God's Army* eighty-seven years later, galvanized Mormon filmmakers to build up the industry right in their heartland and use the medium to tell more of their stories. Its most important progeny was the three-reel *The Story of the Book of Mormon*, produced by William A. Morton and Anton Johan Theodor Sorensen, acquaintances from time served together as missionaries in Scandanavia, in 1915. It may be recalled that in 1899 Morton presented and perhaps helped create a magic lantern lecture about the life of Jesus, and in 1920 he would be instrumental in establishing film exhibition in the Church's Sunday School. At this point, in 1913, he was best known for his Church work and as an author of missionary pamphlets and popular doctrinal and historical books, many for children, such as *The Gospel Primer* (1897), *A Child's Life of Our Savior* (1900), *Mother Stories from the Book of Mormon* (1911), and *From Plowboy to Prophet: Being a Short History of Joseph Smith, for Children* (1912).

The idea for *The Story of the Book of Mormon* didn't originally come from either of these men, however. Rather, an enthusiastic young cinematographer named Shirl Clawson struck upon it after seeing *One Hundred Years of Mormonism* in its theatrical run in Utah; the name may have been intentionally drawn from George Reynold's 1888 book mentioned in the previous chapter, or may have been coincidentally the same. Clawson wanted to tell the story of the entire Book of Mormon, a task which would take several films totaling many hours, and it's unlikely he would have found the ambition to undertake such a project without the example of the two-hour pioneer film before him. It's even less likely that he could have found any willing collaborators, but with the apparent disappearance of anti-Mormon films and success of *One Hundred Years* in 1913 anything may have seemed possible.

Clawson reached out to Morton, whose writing he probably knew, at some point in the spring or summer of 1913 to ask him to write a scenario adapting the entire 500-page book to film. They contracted for a payment of $400 once the screenplay was complete and approved by the First Presidency. Morton spent six months writing three drafts, his story ranging from the beginning of First Nephi to the end of the Book of Moroni, a thousand-year history, and late in the year he submitted it to a committee President Smith had specially appointed consisting of James Talmage, Levi Young, Morton's Sunday School supervisor Horace H. Cummings, and Shirl Clawson's half-brother apostle Rudger Clawson. They approved Morton's work and he passed the screenplay on to Clawson. Unfortunately he had thus far been unable to raise the money to produce the film, so he apparently withheld payment from Morton and hired his brother Chet, who had a business background, to help with the production. The brothers renewed Morton's contract and on December 20 Chet announced the project in the *Deseret Evening News* with a plan to begin shooting the following spring: "The remarkable history of the Nephite and Lamanite peoples will be produced at enormous expense, and with the grandeur which will make it one of the greatest motion pictures in existence."[392] Despite their optimism, however, the project floundered. In 1914 they were forced to renew Morton's contract two additional times, and the funds for production never materialized. At first they wanted to incorporate a company at $100,000, but Morton managed to talk them down to a more reasonable $50,000. Still, when they did at some point incorporate it was probably for an even lower sum than that, but by the end of the year the entire enterprise had fizzled out, and any money that had been raised was lost.

That was the situation on May 2, 1915, when Morton attended a reunion for missionaries and immigrants from Scandinavia in the town of Malone. The screenplay evidently came up while he was speaking with Sorensen, and the possibility of a new collaboration without the Clawsons began to emerge. The very next day Morton wrote from Salt Lake to Sorensen, who ran an undertaking business in Milford in southwestern Utah, saying that he thought they could make the film on their own and that President Smith would even let them exhibit it in the Tabernacle for at least one night. He later sent a copy of his script for the first part of the Book of Mormon—later portions of the narrative would have to wait for additional films—and Sorensen was sold: "No doubt it came from the Lord to spur me on in the production of pictures of these sacred records," he said.[393] Meanwhile Morton called on Chet but found that the Clawsons had made no progress. "There is not a dollar in the treasury towards the producing of the picture," he wrote Sorensen on July 15, "neither is there a dollar in sight. Indeed, the Clawson Brothers are in no better position today to produce the film than they were two and a half years ago. I feel that I have just been wasting time with them, so I have decided to break off all negotiations with them, and to start out on my own account in an effort to produce the first part of the Story of the Book of Mormon." He reached out to three film producers in Los Angeles and received an estimate that the budget for a 2,000-foot film would be roughly $2,000, one dollar per foot. Aiming for a release during the October 1915 general conference, he estimated that 20,000 people would watch it for ten cents apiece, "which would almost pay for the film. I also feel that, besides the good that the picture would do, large profits could be realized from it. Indeed, I know of no business in which so much good, clean money could be made."[394] Sorensen apparently agreed, responding that he could raise a $2,500 production budget if Morton would give him control and title. Morton notified the Clawsons that he was breaking their contract and turned over the rights to Sorensen in return for 10% of net profits.

At this point Sorensen sold his business and brought in local bishop William J. Burns as a business partner, but even with the profit from his undertaking company it proved difficult to raise the funds. Anthon Lund and Charles Penrose, Smith's counselors in the First Presidency, and Andrew Jenson, the Assistant Church Historian and former Scandinavian mission president, became involved in helping Sorensen look for other sources. He apparently got briefly carried away, also hoping for a $100,000 capitalization, but as Morton's plans began to materialize this was brought down to as low as $10,000, which would include the production budget. First Morton moved the proposed production from Los Angeles to Salt Lake City, then he hired one Bryant S. Young to direct. In addition to adding scenes such as Nephi's vision of Mary and Jesus Young suggested publishing the script as a fundraising method; using images from the film to illustrate charts, maps, and actual copies of the Book of Mormon was also considered. Many people volunteered their time to keep expenses low. The department store ZCMI gave Sorensen a wholesale account for fabric and other materials, and the entire Relief Society of the Forest Dale Ward, under Anna Danieldsen, made all the costumes for free. To aid in designing these and the sets Sorensen purchased two books from the Deseret Book store, one of which was William Hole's book of paintings *The Life of Jesus of Nazareth Portrayed in Colours*. They based the character of Lehi on a picture of Nicodemus, his wife Sariah on a painting of a faithless murmurer, and Nephi, the young prophet, on Jesus Christ himself. Some scenes would be shot in the nearby canyons, but the majority of production would take place at a clubhouse and open-air stage on the corner of 2600 South and 700 East; the clubhouse would also be used for dressing rooms and a dark room. While the sets and costumes were being constructed Morton cast all the principle roles, primarily from Salt Lake Temple workers accustomed to acting out the endowment ceremony. Anthon Lund's son and Jenson's fellow Assistant Church Historian A. William Lund played Nephi, but the other actors are unknown.

Production took place in the early fall of 1915 under Morton and Young's supervision, with a professional cameraman hired from California for $10 a day. The planned two-reel film grew into three, so the finished production probably ran around half an hour. The story follows Lehi's family as they leave Jerusalem in 600 B.C. and journey across the desert to the ocean; while Morton's surviving scenario ends there, we know from surviving images and text in the *Juvenile Instructor* magazine that the heroes build a ship, journey to the Americas, and separate into the two groups that will become the Nephites and Lamanites. Lehi's elder sons Laman and Lemuel constantly rebel while the younger siblings Nephi and Sam remain faithful throughout the journey. The script, which is still intact in the Church History Library, includes large portions of text lifted directly from the Book of Mormon itself, along with notes and images from Hole's book. Morton also wrote intertitles explaining doctrinal issues like how the characters came from both the tribes of Ephraim and Manasseh.[395]

Though the producers sometimes used *The Life of Nephi* as a working title, it was released under the name *The Story of the Book of Mormon*. The filmmakers missed their target of the October general conference, which was held October 3-6, but it premiered soon afterwards, on October 25, at the Utah Theatre in Salt Lake City. They probably only struck one print, and Sorensen personally delivered it to theaters all over northern Utah throughout that fall and winter; screenings were accompanied by a lecture, so he also likely gave this as well, although it's unclear whether this was given before or after screenings or, as with *One Hundred Years*, while the film actually played. In November it screened in American Fork, indicating a Utah Valley circuit after the initial Salt Lake City run, and on February 2 and 3 it showed at the Oak Theater in Logan, implying that Sorensen was traveling north toward Idaho in early 1916. The film was particularly popular as a didactic tool for youth: on February 2 sixty-five children from the Logan Primaries traveled on sleigh to the theater to watch the matinee performance. However, financial returns were apparently insufficient to continue with the next installment of the project, and this narrative from First Nephi is all of The *Story of the Book of Mormon* that was ever produced. Sorensen left no record of how long he toured with the film or what he did with the print and negative afterwards, but like most First Wave films it was soon lost.[396]

In fact, it appears that he soon decided showing an entire moving picture was less worthwhile than simply giving a magic lantern lecture; traveling with and exhibiting slides was less cumbersome and in his mind probably achieved the same effect. During production he had rented a still camera from the Charles R. Savage Company, and photographs were taken and developed of each scene so that the footage could be evaluated immediately without developing and projecting entire camera reels of 35mm motion picture film. These photographs were also intended to be the images used in any merchandising efforts such as illustrated books and though no books emerged from the project, Morton used his Church position to publish twelve of the images, with one to two pages of explanatory text, in each issue of the Sunday School's *Juvenile Instructor* throughout 1917. Sorensen also had forty-four photographs transferred to multiple sets of 3.5 x 4-inch glass slides that were then painted by hand. With these he was able to reach a much wider audience at meetinghouses and other small venues, claiming years later that he had shown them to "tens of thousands of people in the Rocky Mountain States as well as in the east."[397] Since the film print is lost, today these slides are our only connection to the original film. A leather suitcase containing three incomplete sets of slides—with just thirty-four images each—was donated to the Church Historical Department, where they sat in obscurity for over forty years until they were rediscovered by Brian Sokolowsky in 2002. Like Robert Starling's discovery of fractions of *One Hundred Years of Mormonism*, Sokolowsky's work cataloguing and digitizing these slides is one of the landmark achievements of recent Mormon film archiving.[398]

Other Utah movie studios and projects arose in the wake of these two films, including the Utah Theatre Company in 1913, carnival worker James J. Ford's unnamed production company in Salt Lake in 1914, the Satchwa General Amusement Enterprises Company, which also produced live outdoor entertainments, in 1914-15, the Arrowhead Motion Picture Company in 1914-15, the Overland Feature Film Company in 1915, the Ogden Feature Film Company in 1917, and Albert Scowcroft and Lester Park's Ogden Pictures Corporation in 1917-19. It's probable that Mormonism's worldview influenced the content of many films, such as the sympathetic portrayal of Native Americans, another minority group beleaguered in the cinema, in Satchwa's *Big Heart* (1914), or the pro-Prohibition stance of *The Child and the Beast* (1915) by an unknown producer. Park and Scowcroft, both veterans of Ogden's film exhibition industry, avowed they were motivated by civic pride in their city and state, but it appears from his later production of *Corianton* that Park also desired to create films about Mormonism. Ogden Pictures completed two nationally distributed five reelers, the melodramas *The Lust of the Ages* (1917), in which Lillian Walker starred and for which they enticed Harry Revier back to the state to direct and appear onscreen, and *The Grain of Dust* (1918). They also advertised that they were applying for patents on 3D stereoscopy methods that they evidently never implemented. In the late 1920s a company known as Utah Productions released *Winds of the Pampas* (1928) with Arthur Varney directing and local actor Ralph Cloninger in the lead role, and they may have released a Henry Otto picture called *The Urge Within* and other pictures as well.[399]

It's possible that one more attempt was made to create a Mormon-themed feature film in the 1910s. As mentioned, around 1918 a twelve-year-old Fay Wray, who was living in Salt Lake City, procured enough new subscriptions for the *Salt Lake Telegraph* to win a screen test to star in a film about the state's early Mormon settlers. She was filmed on the grounds of the county courthouse in Salt Lake, holding roses to her face on a park bench and then, subsequently, at Fort Douglas outside the city, where she wore a period costume and rode a horse along with several U.S. soldiers from the fort, presumably also in costume. She was told she had got the lead role but she never heard anything else about it. In her autobiography Wray speculates that the director traveled to another city to run a similar scam raising subscriptions for another paper. Both Wray and another girl who had been promised a character part, Katherine Wright, had to move to California to launch their acting careers. But the episode remains intriguing: either another pioneer film was planned and fell through in the development process, or *One Hundred Years of Mormonism* was sufficiently memorable that five years later the *Telegraph* could dupe Salt Lake's Mormon inhabitants by pretending to promote a similar production. In either case, it shows that Mormon subject matter was now viable for all sorts of motion pictures—and Utah's film industry was sufficiently robust to plausibly support them.[400]

Even some members of the Church hierarchy were eager to re-enter the film business. In 1916 General Authorities offered Arthur Powelson, a cameraman who may have collaborated with Talmage and Savage on the *House of the Lord* photographs, a contract to create a series of motion pictures for the Church. He declined the offer, but it gives a tantalizing glimpse into how the Mormon hierarchy still wanted to harness cinema's potential in the middle of the 1910s. And this desire spread to the lay membership as well. In the early 1920s at least one missionary in the Eastern States Mission procured a camera and filmed his fellow missionaries in New York City and Washington, D.C. On September 21-23, 1923 when mission president and seventy B. H. Roberts presided over a conference at Palmyra celebrating the centennial of the Angel Moroni's appearance to Joseph Smith, footage was shot at the Smith family farmhouse and the Hill Cumorah, where a meeting was held including visiting Church leaders and 160 missionaries. Footage of this event was later assembled into an amateur newsreel and shown at a mission reunion in 1934, shortly after Elder Roberts' death. Miraculously, five minutes of this footage has survived and is held at the Church History Library. Such amateur cinematography blossomed in the 1930s, becoming a defining characteristic of the Second Wave, but even at this point it shows how eager Mormons were to express their faith through film. If features like *One Hundred Years of Mormonism* and the entire *Story of the Book of Mormon* were prohibitively difficult to replicate, then mobile cameramen shooting simple nonfiction footage might be able to tell the Mormon story in a different way. And despite their initial failure working with William Morton in 1914, this is exactly what Shirl and Chet Clawson did, thus becoming the most prolific and important filmmakers of the First Wave.[401]

The Clawson Brothers

Shirl was born Shirley Young Clawson in Salt Lake City on November 15, 1881, and Chet—whose full name was Chester, perhaps after Chester, South Carolina where the family had some roots—followed two years later on December 5, 1883. They were two of ten children of Hiram B. and Emily Clawson. Hiram joined the Church in 1838 and rose to prominence through his close association with Brigham Young, who employed him as his personal business manager for many years. The variety of his activities in early Utah exemplifies the range of his interests and his indefatigable energy: he was a supervising mason on the Council House, Salt Lake Theatre, and other buildings; he served as acting architect on the Salt Lake Temple while Truman Angell was away; he designed the original *Eagle Gate*; he was an adjutant general of the Nauvoo Legion and fought in local Indian wars; he was the first general superintendent of ZCMI as well as owning and running various other mercantile businesses; he lobbied Congress for Utah's statehood; and of course he owned and operated the Salt Lake Theatre. His religious devotion matched his business and civic activities: he served as the bishop of the Salt Lake City Twelfth Ward from 1882 until 1904 and married four wives, fathering forty-two children among them, the most prominent being Rudger Clawson who served twenty-two years as President of the Quorum of the Twelve. Shirl and Chet's mother was Hiram's fourth wife Emily Augusta Young, the second of Brigham Young's daughters he married. She was born in 1849, making her twenty-three years Hiram's junior. Her mother was Emily Partridge, daughter of the Church's first bishop Edward Partridge and a plural wife of Joseph Smith; she married Young after Smith's martyrdom in 1844 and gave birth to her namesake daughter, their second child, after reaching the Salt Lake Valley. In fact she lived, not far from the Clawsons, until 1899, often traveling or staying with them, so although Shirl and Chet never met their grandfather Brigham Young they did know their widowed grandmother intimately. Hiram's many business successes made him one of Salt Lake City's more affluent citizens, and Shirl's children recalled years later that unlike other children their father and uncle were given luxury items like a pony and cart and never had to worry about finding work or money as they grew up.[402]

Interest in theater ran strong in the family. Hiram had been a protégé of dramatist Thomas Lyne in Nauvoo and actually assisted as a stagehand in the first play put on there, *Pizarro*, in 1844, throwing "fire from heaven" onstage; he also performed monologues at the city's Masonic Hall and other venues. He's rumored to have staged *The Taming of the Shrew* and *The Merchant of Venice* while actually crossing the plains in 1848, and he helped organize the Deseret Dramatic Association and performed in the old Bowery on Temple Square while essentially overseeing construction of the Salt Lake Theatre. Upon its completion in 1868 Brigham Young appointed him its first manager, and both of Young's daughters who he married became celebrated actresses there. In 1873 the Church actually sold the Theatre to Hiram and some associates, and he continued managing it for several years. While Shirl studied drafting at Brigham Young Academy and briefly worked on his sister's farm in Alberta and as a conductor on the Oregon Short Line Railroad, he picked up the acting bug from his parents and appeared in everything from minstrel shows at Church fairs to prestige productions at the Salt Lake Theatre, such as when he played Melek, the leader of some hedonistic Zoramite revelers, in the original 1902 production of Orestes Bean's Book of Mormon play *Corianton*. This production toured as far east as Kansas City before succumbing to unreceptive audiences and financial pressures, but it still might have partly inspired Shirl to create *The Story of the Book of Mormon* in 1913.[403]

It's possible that he also became interested in the new medium of motion pictures in the early 1900s. He was in his late teens when projected movies started appearing in Utah, and twenty-three years old when the 1905 nickelodeon boom hit. At that time, in November 1905, he was called on a mission to England, and when he returned home in February 1908 he lost no time in returning to theatrical pursuits, joining a choir under J. J. McClellan for a Salt Lake Theatre production that summer and acting again at least by January 1910, when he appeared in the musical comedy *The Terrible Frost*. He met his wife Gertrude Romney, a daughter of another prominent Mormon family, in an opera chorus in the Theatre—he playing a priest and she a nun—and they were married on February 8, 1911. But while Shirl picked up his parents' love of the theater, Chet's interests tended more towards his father's businesses. In 1909 he was selling real estate and fire insurance out of the Utah Savings and Trust Building, in 1910 he became president of his own Annex Cafeteria company, and in 1911 he returned to real estate as the secretary and treasurer of the new Western Realty & Investment company, apparently having dedicated himself to a life of property sales and management. He married Esther Vida Fox in the midst of this activity on June 16, 1910.[404]

It was also precisely at this time that Shirl may have purchased a hand-cranked Pathé Frères camera and begun shooting local events. The narration to *Latter-day Saint Leaders: Past and Present*, written around 1948, indicates that he filmed as early as a general conference in 1910. Video transfers of surviving Clawson footage in the Church History Library place the earliest of it at 1911, such as footage of the *Brigham Young Monument* at South Temple and Main Street. Also that year Pathé released a newsreel on the October 1911 general conference; by the 1920s the Clawsons were permanent representatives of

Pathé News, and it's possible at this point and throughout the 1910s that Shirl was already shooting footage for them. This would make more sense for Pathé than sending in a crew from the west or east coast, particularly since they were currently filming multiple anti-Mormon films and there was nothing particularly newsworthy or historic about the conference itself—beyond the fact that Shirl may have just procured a camera. In his journal entry on Sunday October 8 apostle Reed Smoot notes that there was more than one person on the film crew, implying that, if this was indeed Shirl, even in 1911 he might have enticed Chet to assist him: "Between meetings," Smoot said, "the moving picture men have taken [photographs of] the Conference crowds [and] took pictures of President Smith, the Presidency . . . and Quorum and myself."[405] In fact, the footage, the earliest-known taken of any General Authorities, was well-timed: it was advertised as including footage of the entire First Presidency, including Second Counselor John Henry Smith, who died only five days after the conference ended, and Presiding Patriarch John Smith, who died just a few weeks later on November 6.[406]

The brothers' activities become better documented by 1912, as with the Pioneer Day celebrations in Salt Lake's Liberty Park for which thirty-four different shots are catalogued, mostly of different floats and marchers in the parade. Shirl or Chet may have tried to sell more of this type of footage to Pathé, or they may have approached local theaters themselves. But a regular relationship with Pathé was still in the future, and the firm may not have been too interested in additional Mormon newsreels as it spent that year battling the Church over *An Episode of Early Mormon Days, The Mountain Meadows Massacre,* and *Marriage or Death.* Shirl's 1912 filming should therefore probably not yet be considered a full-time occupation as much as the work of an eager enthusiast attempting to break into an entirely new industry. In 1913 he finally began working full-time with film with the creation of the Education Film and Service Corporation, a Progressive Era film library mentioned earlier in connection with the Church's increased interest in movies as a didactic medium. Shirl attempted to set up a film distribution exchange for the company that could provide educational footage throughout the region. His success here is unknown, although it did associate him professionally with men like Levi Edgar Young and his half-brother Rudger, who were both on the board of advisors. Still, his obvious desire remained to work in film production rather than just distribution.[407]

One Hundred Years of Mormonism signaled an opportunity, and although the Clawsons failed to stay with *The Story of the Book of Mormon* to completion, it did firmly establish the working dynamic between Shirl and Chet. Shirl consistently displayed more dramatic and cinematic interest than his brother, and throughout their careers he tended more to the technical and artistic affairs and Chet to business, procuring new clients, handling current ones, paying bills, securing payments, and distributing copies of their work. Still, he also participated in the filmmaking—"Shirl did all the camera work while Chet assisted with the loading of film magazines, set ups and set strikings"[408]—and postproduction, and theirs was truly a joint venture.

It's hard to surmise the Clawsons' perspective on the events of 1913-15 that gave William Morton and Anton Sorensen such a low opinion of them. How was Chet pursuing fundraising for *The Story of the Book of Mormon*? What kind of production had Shirl planned? We do know their company from this period was named the Bee Hive Film Company and included Shirl's father-in-law Orson Douglas Romney as president, Shirl as vice-president, Charles Mabey as treasurer, Rudger Clawson as one of the directors, and Chet as another and the manager. They advertised their services for feature, educational, and industrial pictures, but by early 1915 it must have been clear to Shirl that the Book of Mormon project was not going to happen and the only way he could break into the industry was by leaving the parochialism of Utah and taking his family to Los Angeles. Early that year he set out, and using his screenwriter cousin Elliot as a contact he secured a position as a cameraman at Universal. Although we don't know what titles he worked on or what his specific duties were, the daily routine of filmmaking honed his abilities, teaching him skills like how to handle a camera to how to run a darkroom and properly develop a negative. When he came back to Utah in 1916, he had the knowledge to function as an autonomous filmmaking unit; all he needed was a partner to keep everything running smoothly while he focused on film production and a sponsor to provide them with steady work and income.[409]

This second item was not as difficult to procur as might have been expected. Through their family connections Shirl and Chet knew Joseph F. Smith and other General Authorities well, all of whom were probably now firm believers in the value of motion pictures as didactic and propagandistic tools. The Clawsons "proposed that they film significant Church events and people in return for a place to work and equipment necessary for the film business."[410] There were two key differences between this proposal and previous projects like *One Hundred Years of Mormonism* and *The Story of the Book of Mormon.* First, Chet and Shirl evidently wanted the Church to fund their filmmaking business as fully as possible as a long-term enterprise, not a single project to be completed within the next few months or years. While their association with the Church would technically be in the form of a contract for an independent company, they were essentially establishing a de facto filmmaking department within the Church itself and would function as permanent full-time Church employees. If this seemed like too great a commitment for cost-conscious General Authorities, it was offset by the second difference, which is that the types of films Shirl was proposing were, in a word, cheap. After seeing the difficulties the Church had with the Ellaye Motion Picture Company, the inability of *One Hundred Years of Mormonism* to earn a profit, the Clawsons' failure to raise funds for *The Story of the Book of Mormon*, and, apparently, that film's less than stellar commercial performance, Smith must have been intrigued by Shirl's proposed nonfiction filmmaking model. The brothers would have to receive salaries, rent would need to be paid on a studio space for storage and postproduction, film stock and developing chemicals would need to be replenished, and there would be an initial outlay for fixed-cost equipment like cameras, but production budgets—for costumes, sets, props, actors, shooting stages, lights, and crew members—would be nonexistent. Even publicity and distribution expenses would be minimal, as short nonfiction films could be shown for free at ward recreation halls or sold on the educational circuit as newsreels, neither of which would require the type of advertising undertaken for *One Hundred Years*. Turn-around would be a matter of days rather than months or years, and a steady stream of pro-Mormon material in bite-sized pieces just might have a larger cumulative effect on public opinion than one mammoth production that may meet bad reviews or have problems finding a ready audience outside the Mormon heartland.

In a way, the Clawsons' proposal had much more in common with the Paris Art Missionaries than with other filmmaking companies like Ellaye: like John Hafen and his associates, theirs was an audacious request for Church subsidy in return for the creation of art that might have little commercial value but would beautify Zion now and stand as a testament to future generations. We don't know specifically how the negotiations proceeded or even what the final agreement was, such as whether the camera equipment purchased was a gift or a loan. On the one hand, Church funds couldn't cover all the brothers' costs, so they also filmed projects for other clients. But on the other hand, Church funds were sufficient to allow them immense latitude in filming activities that otherwise would never have been recorded. There was no market for newsreels of a man loading a tractor or Charles Nibley's children playing, but moments like these are the heart of what the Clawsons were able to achieve as they created a longitudinal group portrait of Mormonism in the early twentieth century. There is simply no way this could have been accomplished through commercial means.

The Clawson Film Company, sometimes called the Deseret Film Company, was soon established in Brigham Young's Lion House in the present-day cafeteria. On April 9, 1916 they did their first major filming, once again at general conference. They recorded President Smith and other Church leaders, as well as the crowds outdoors on Temple Square and inside the Tabernacle and Assembly Hall. The film was called simply *The Eighty-sixth Annual Conference of the Church of Jesus Christ of Latter-day Saints*, and inasmuch as the Church hierarchy funded and oversaw it directly, it may be considered the first truly official institutional Church film. Two private screenings were held, the first the very next day at the Bishop's building, but President Smith viewed the projection quality there substandard so it was repeated a few days later at the American Theatre with organ accompaniment by J. J. McClellan. "The picture opened with several views of the conference crowds; then the overflow meetings, and finally the various dignitaries of the church were shown," the *Salt Lake Telegram* reported, adding that "as the pictures of the dignitaries were flashed upon the screen they were applauded vigorously. They expressed themselves as well pleased with the results of the film."[411] Perhaps even more intriguing are the questions over what the Church planned to do with the footage. The *Salt Lake Tribune* correspondent frankly had no idea: "Just what is to be done with the film after it has been shown privately could not be learned last night. Those who are familiar with the taking of the pictures declared that they did not know whether it was to be sent broadcast as a sort of educational topic on the Mormon church or whether it was to be placed in the archives of the church, to be kept for the private view of future generations."[412] The *Telegram* was more confident: "The film was taken for the purpose of being sent broadcast throughout the United States. At present this morning the film is 1000 feet long, and is remarkably clear and distinct . . . It is understood that the church officials plan to have similar films made from time to time, to be deposited in the archives of the church."[413] The fact that both reporters mentioned storing the film in the Church archives shows how aware everyone was of the potential of motion pictures to preserve images for the future, even starting with the Clawsons' very first Church film. Reed Smoot, a diligent diarist, noted that he again "stood for a moving picture film" after the morning priesthood session of conference the next October. It's far from certain that the Clawsons filmed each conference every six months, but at least in 1916 they started strong by recording both the spring and autumn events.[414]

The First Wave: The New Frontier

Over the next decade the duo worked intensely. They soon moved out of the Lion House across the street on South Temple, then to 133 Motor Ave. a few blocks to the west, then in the mid-1920s to their final location in the basement of the Deseret News Building on South Temple and Main Street. As mentioned, their work for the Church never made ends meet so they supplemented it creating titles for local theaters, ads for ice cream, sugar, milk, and other products—often with their children as performers—and serving as the local representatives of Pathé News, for which they shot a rescue at the Castle Gate coal mine, the burning of the Saltair resort, dinosaur excavations, and visits by Charles Lindbergh and Woodrow Wilson. In 1918 Pathé Frères released a newsreel—at least in Utah—of Joseph F. Smith and Charles Nibley playing golf, which was probably shot at the Brentwood Country Club in Santa Monica, where Smith spent much of the final years of his life engaged in this new pastime. Given their relationship with both Smith and Pathé, it seems most likely that the Clawsons accompanied him on one of these trips and brought this footage, and perhaps other scenes, back to Salt Lake City. Smith's son David A. Smith reported to him that "nearly everybody in Salt Lake city [sic], I believe, have gone to see President Smith and Bishop Nibley play golf. When I saw the announcement I was just a little bit anxious and took in the show early Monday. But I was greatly relieved in seeing a picture that you could be proud of, and in its travels over the Pathe circuit nobody will have cause to be ashamed of the President of the Mormon Church."[415] Another Pathé general conference newsreel followed in 1919, which was surely once again the Clawsons'. The full breadth of their commercial work is indicated by their initial description in a city business directory: "Motion Pictures, Animated Cartoons, Fashions, Weddings, Celebrations, Festivals, Rallies, Etc., for Advertising, Historical, and Souvenir Purposes";[416] further editions indicate that they eventually became quite involved as a film distributor for other people's productions.[417]

Still, Church films remained their passion and always took priority over any other job. They shot invaluable visual records of dozens of General Authorities on the streets, temple grounds, and in their offices and homes, gaining access to essentially all Church leaders and creating an archival treasure trove. Even a partial listing of their subjects makes an impressive roster of Mormon leadership in the early twentieth century: Melvin J. Ballard, Sylvester Q. Cannon, Rudger Clawson, Heber J. Grant, Charles H. Hart, Anthony W. Ivins, J. Golden Kimball, Anthon H. Lund, Francis M. Lyman, Richard R. Lyman, David O. McKay, Joseph McMurrin, Joseph F. Merrill, Orrin P. Miller, Charles W. Nibley, Margaret Nibley, Preston Nibley, Charles W. Penrose, Rey L. Pratt, George F. Richards,

Stephen L Richards, B. H. Roberts, David A. Smith, E. Wesley Smith, Edna L. Smith, George Albert Smith, George Henry Smith, Hyrum G. Smith, Hyrum Mack Smith, John Smith, John Henry Smith, Joseph F. Smith, Joseph Fielding Smith, Julina L. Smith, Reed Smoot, James E. Talmage, John Wells, Rulon S. Wells, Orson F. Whitney, John A. Widtsoe, Clarissa S. Williams, Levi Edgar Young, and Seymour B. Young. They recorded Joseph F. Smith's funeral in November 1918, the *Mormon Battalion Monument* cornerstone laying on April 7, 1925 and dedication in May 1927, the visit of Sweden's Crown Prince in July 1926, the dedication of the Three Witnesses Monument in April 1927, the Primary 50th Year Jubilee Parade in June 1928, and innumerable events like BYU athletic contests, MIA youth parades, Armistice Day parades at the conclusion of World War I, Old Folks' activities, and celebrations for Boys' Day, LDS University Founder's Day, and of course Pioneer Day each July 24.

While they frequently trained their camera on the Church hierarchy and official events, much of what makes their work so appealing is the egalitarian, democratic ethos behind their footage of everyday people in average situations. Many of these people were among the revelers at the parades and celebrations, but the Clawsons also occasionally caught them in even less ostentatious situations: picnics or reunions of original pioneers, for instance, or men plowing salt or working their fields, and bathers in the Great Salt Lake. We even still have eleven minutes of what amounts to home movies by Shirl of his wife, children, and mother. One exterior shot featuring Joseph F. Smith and two other adults has the scene stolen by a little girl and her dog, who are both utterly unpretentious before the camera and the ecclesiastical authority who is standing there. The Clawsons also created dozens of scenic shots of landscapes, notable buildings, and landmarks in and around Salt Lake City, plus the temple in Logan and perhaps other cities. On occasion they would travel for Pathé News stories or to document Church activities. In July 1920 they filmed a weeklong Boy Scout caravan to Bryce and Zion National Parks with 270 people, and they recorded journeys by Joseph F. Smith to Santa Monica and Heber Grant and patriarch Hyrum G. Smith to Nebraska in 1920 to lease historic sites. In this case they didn't just film the two men discussing the landscapes and signing legal documents—although they did that, perhaps with synchronized sound thanks to an early experimental technology—but they also used their camera to document the condition of sites all around Winter Quarters, which could have legal ramifications and help the men and women back in Utah who were tasked with restoring the sites. Over the years their camera recorded the aging of the Mormon hierarchy as they followed them to their offices, their public appearances, and their private lives, documenting changes in age, dress, and even facial hair. They even filmed President Grant playing golf.[418]

Their finished films were of different lengths. While the Three Witnesses Monument dedication, for instance, included eight shots, the 1925 Boys' Day parade and a 1927 BYU track meet each included forty-four, and the trips of the Church Presidents and the Boy Scout trek mentioned above were even more extended. Another example came around 1921 in the person of Clarence Neslen, mayor of Salt Lake City and bishop of the Ensign Stake Twentieth Ward. The Clawsons filmed Neslen, his family, and his ward in a degree of longitude not allowed in much of their other work, including stages of the construction of a new meetinghouse from the laying of the cornerstone until its completion. Fifteen minutes of this footage are extant, although the loss of much of it has made it unclear how often and to what extent they filmed.[419] Notwithstanding these examples, for the most part theirs were short films, much less than a full reel and sometimes only a single shot. Along with their two-man studio set up, this makes the Clawson brothers rather resemble the Lumière brothers of the 1890s, or at least their employees; these were not so much documentaries but actualities, single shot recordings of significant events or everyday life. Like with the Lumières, much of the appeal of the Clawsons' work comes from how it reveals the simple beauty of normal people and situations; even in their work with Church leaders, they created simple shots devoid of narrative purpose, just so we can see how these men looked and moved—usually the Church Historian's office describes the action in words like, "President Joseph F. Smith (close up) in front of temple, removes hat, then glasses."

As with the Lumières, however, the simplicity of the shots belie the artistry behind them. Like Robert Flaherty, often considered the father of documentary film, with his subjects in *Nanook of the North, Moana, Man of Aran* (1934), and *Louisiana Story* (1948), the Clawsons apparently felt no compunction about asking their subjects to stage certain actions. Note this description: "Stephen L. Richards in Sunday School office; George D. Pyper in and out." Obviously they did not capture Elder Pyper by chance—nor President Smith removing his glasses—but rather they were *directing* the General Authorities, treating them as actors. This is noticeable in their extant footage as the onscreen personalities obviously pause, listen to direction, then perform an action such as removing their hat or shaking hands. In one shot in front of the Salt Lake Temple several Church leaders all take off their hats in unison; in another Heber Grant shakes somebody's hand before turning and walking up the temple steps, stopping when he gets sufficiently high, as he was obviously not attempting to enter the temple at all. Records of their footage even contain references to multiple *takes*, indicating that the Clawsons desired to create the best possible footage they could of the men and women at the head of the Church and didn't mind having them repeat something to do it better. But of course the mistakes, which would have never been exhibited publicly, are today some of the most endearing and intriguing moments. In one early shot an apostle enters the frame, gets visibly confused, and winds up exiting in the same direction from which he came. In another, Joseph F. Smith climbs into an automobile and the driver, perhaps anxious for his cue, tears away before Smith can even shut the door. And in a shot of a group of apostles descending the temple steps one onlooker—perhaps it's Chet?—sees he's in the shot and runs to get out of the frame.

The Lumières were businessmen at the top of a large industrial organization, employing cameramen to shoot and exhibit the footage that earned them profit—along with many other manufacturing revenue streams. Shirl Clawson, on the other hand, was himself his own cameraman, and, as noted, his Church-related work was far from profitable, being both subsidized by the institution and supplemented by his own work for other clients. In fact, despite the clues that have already been mentioned, the least clear thing about the Clawsons is what they *did* with their Mormon films, if they were all publicly or privately exhibited or if many served a purely archival function, going straight from the camera to a storage shelf. Much of their footage would have had little immediate commercial draw, but at the same time it's hard to believe they would gather so much material on Salt Lake City and the Church without attempting to use some of it to either improve the Church's public image with viewers outside Utah, or, in contrast, to display it to local audiences who would, like their General Authority viewers in April 1916, be enthusiastic to see themselves and their people onscreen. In a 1923 *Improvement Era* article Harold Jenson talks about both he and Ed Diamond being "engaged with Clawson Brothers, in taking moving pictures of the [Willard and Farmington] flood district which moving pictures were shown in Salt Lake City."[420] From this snippet we can glean that they did both occasionally employ others and publicly exhibit their films in Utah theaters; given their Pathé work, of which this instance might have been part, it's highly likely that the Clawsons themselves came to see their films not as actualities but as newsreels, products that would have caused the thrill of recognition in their Utah viewers and helped bolster faith in the Mormons among them. By seeing the prophet up close or observing the growth of a chapel's construction over time, Mormons could themselves become galvanized to help build up the Kingdom. And when distributed further afield, their footage would have done much to fight stereotypes or at least satiate curiosity, something Church films have tried on up to the *I'm a Mormon* campaign today. In October 1922, as the British anti-Mormon campaign that yielded *Trapped by the Mormons* and *Married to a Mormon* reached its climax, Reed Smoot recorded that "the Presidency of the Church and Quorum of the Twelve had moving pictures taken of them in the office of Pres Rudger Clawson and coming from the Temple. They are to be shown in this country and England."[421] Even if this was just sent to missionaries and local Church leaders rather than to commercial cinemas in London and Manchester, clearly here was a new tool in combatting anti-Mormon animus. But they also gave future generations the opportunity to view a bygone era in a manner never before possible; imagine if there was film footage of John Taylor, Brigham Young, or Joseph Smith. In the end, their films probably served three purposes: archival, commercial, and religious.

Of course, their work did evolve from 1916 to 1929, reflecting not just growth in personal skill and maturity, but also industry-wide evolution as well. Where they began by stringing together single static shots of the April 1916 general conference, by 1929 they were creating entire documentaries that required detailed writing and editing processes—and that progression reflects what was happening in nonfiction filmmaking across the globe. In the 1910s documentaries as such didn't exist. Early nonfiction features like *Nanook of the North* (1922) and *Grass* (1925) pointed the way forward for telling longer and more complex stories, and it wasn't until 1926 that John Grierson invented the word *documentary* to describe Flaherty's *Moana* and how it documented details of life in Samoa; the Clawsons became increasingly adept at documenting life among the Utah Mormons as well. And while they had no direct influence on Grierson's work in England in the 1930s, his efforts with the Empire Marketing Board and the General Post Office film units, beginning with *Drifters* in 1929, the very year the Clawsons ceased their production work, created the same type of relationship with the British government that the Clawsons had with the Mormon hierarchy: the British government subsidized a series of roughly half-hour films that addressed pressing social needs (*Housing Problems*, 1935) and praised the government's work in managing tasks like overnight mail delivery (*Night Mail*, 1936). The effect was an egalitarian vision very similar to the Clawsons', and it's likely the brothers would have moved into this type of coherent documentary filmmaking for the Church had they been able to work beyond 1929. And while the similarities with the EMB and GPO reflect trends in the global film industry, the brothers had a much more direct effect on Mormons who would come after them. Others began imitating them even while the Clawsons were still working, with mostly amateur filmmakers recording events and prominent Mormons in their own vicinities, a trend that would explode in the Second Wave. The anonymous missionary who filmed at B. H. Roberts' Palmyra conference in 1923 was certainly following that impulse and may well have been familiar with the Clawsons' films, if not their names, before leaving to serve in the east. Later, Second Wave creators of films and other media—Gordon Hinckley, Frank Wise, and LaMar Williams—inherited the Clawsons' ethos that smaller, cheaper, and more intimate productions could be just as emotionally effective as large feature films, and they generally were much better for public relations, proselytizing, and teaching purposes. Because of the abrupt end of their careers and the loss of their footage that it entailed, we might see the Clawsons as unrelated to subsequent filmmaking efforts, but in truth they established the mindset that has dominated much Mormon filmmaking ever since. Their work set the stage for films from *Where the Saints Have Trod* (1947) to *Meet the Mormons* (2014), and if any one man deserves to be called the father of Mormon cinema it is Shirl Clawson.

Institutional Broadcasting Begins

Institutional Church radio work may appear to have no immediate connection with film, but like magic lanterns and slide shows it contributed to a culture of officially sanctioned audiovisual media that would eventually lead to a robust institutional cinema. Radio may have lacked film's visual component, but in the 1930s it paved the way for writers like Gordon Hinckley to create audio media for proselytizing and public relations work that would lead directly to the films of the Second and Third Waves. Also, in the 1940s it was the Church's business interests for radio that first expanded into television production, paving the way for the advance into electronic film distribution outlets such as VHS, closed-circuit broadcasts, satellite, and network television. Since the Third Wave Church radio, television, and film efforts have become inextricably intertwined, and online video has finally made any distinction between them completely immaterial; the connection between all these types of media is exemplified in the all-encompassing name of the Church's Audiovisual Department. As this has progressed throughout the years there have been important technological milestones, but the most important innovation introduced by radio in the First Wave was the attitude that it was proper for the Church itself to be involved with broadcasting efforts at all. This more than anything else allowed for the easy creation of permanent filmmaking institutions in the coming years.

The Church's interest in radio grew naturally out of its rich publishing history, particularly with periodicals such as the *Deseret News*, which was established June 15, 1850, three years after the pioneers arrived in the Salt Lake Valley. Radio technology is nearly as old as this, but it was in 1920 that the first major amateur and commercial broadcasts in the United States launched it as a true public communication medium. In 1921 the management of the *Deseret News*—particularly general manager Elias S. Woodruff, business manager Nathan O. Fullmer, and general circulation manager Melvin R. Ballard—saw its potential for their readers and the Church's local Boy Scout troops and decided to launch a station to serve these needs. "In an era of news competition newspaper publishers were keenly aware of the potential of the instantaneous radio signal. There were even some who feared radio would lead to the demise of the newspaper, and so in the best tradition of the marketplace, the newspaper acquired the competition."[422] President Grant wouldn't approve the $25,000 cost to purchase a transmitter, so the *News* had to construct its own, a 250-watt device that, after some major difficulties, they hauled up to a tin shack atop their roof—while the Clawsons worked out of the basement. They began experimental weekly broadcasts in March then achieved their first official broadcast at 8:00 p.m. on May 6, 1922 with the words, "Hello, hello, hello. KZN, KZN," the call letters for the new station, presumably for "Zion." This first broadcast, which went on despite flooding in the streets of the city, opened with an address by President Grant, who read from Doctrine and Covenants 76, gave his testimony of Joseph Smith's divine calling, and described the event as a momentous day in Church history. Other speakers included Mrs. Grant, Mayor Clarence Neslen, and Grant's counselor Anthony Ivins and apostle George Albert Smith, who lauded the wonders of the "wireless telephone."[423] Even though the station began with a single daily half-hour broadcast, it sparked a radio craze in Salt Lake City as people, who now had something to listen to, went out and bought receivers. The KZN program gradually expanded with news, speeches, and live dance and concert music—all reportedly provided by volunteers since the station had no budget—and could be heard as far away as Hawaii. In 1924 the newspaper sold the station to its radio engineer John Cope and his father, and they renamed it KFPT, but after a few months of private ownership they sold a majority back to the Church on June 24, 1925. The call letters were permanently changed to KSL, for "Salt Lake," and Church involvement with radio had begun.[424]

It was in these years that the Church began its two most distinctive broadcasting efforts: performances by the Mormon Tabernacle Choir and general conferences. The choir was first heard on-air in October 1922 when students from Latter-day Saint University broadcast a concert on their school station. On June 26, 1923 they had a more formal debut when they accompanied President Harding's address in the Tabernacle during his western tour just weeks before his death. The feat of installing a microphone in the Tabernacle and handling all the national attention—it was also the first time telegraph machines and automobiles were allowed on Temple Square— was accomplished by Earl J. Glade, a man who as head of KSL from 1925 to 1939 would become known as "the father of radio in the mountains" and who would be elected mayor of Salt Lake City in 1944. With this equipment in place KZN was able to broadcast portions of the October 1923 general conference, and the first presentation of the entire proceedings was by KFPT in October 1924; the signal was received by speakers around Temple Square as well as in individual homes. This is arguably one of the most important dates in the history of the semiannual conferences, as it quickly transformed them from a week-long communal gathering in the Church's central buildings to a two-day familial worship service in individual homes scattered across the world. A weekly "Church Hour" program, with sermons and worship services, began on November 16, 1924. KSL created additional religious programming, such as, in 1928, a half-hour program of sermons and music known as *Sunday Evening on Temple Square*, with themed series on a general topic running for three or even six months. Many musicians were initially opposed, as they "questioned the fidelity of radio."[425] Organist J. J. McClellan refused to ever perform on air, for instance, although ironically his funeral in 1925 was the first one broadcast from the Tabernacle. KSL became an NBC affiliate in 1929 and on July 15 the Choir performed their first coast-to-coast broadcast of the program that would become *Music and the Spoken Word,* a weekly broadcast of musical performances interpolated with inspirational but nondenominational thoughts. Thanks to the efforts of radio enthusiasts like organist Edward Kimball, this program, more than any other effort, set the stage for the Church's use of broadcasting—and even, to a great extent, filmmaking—in the Second Wave.[426]

There were plenty of growing pains with the infant medium: after KZN's initial broadcast the *Deseret News* received numerous letters asking why President Grant had said, "Turn off the heat," and a few years later Earl Glade accidentally broadcast eight minutes of the World Series across Temple Square's loudspeakers while Grant was preaching. Nevertheless, Church leaders and Utahns in general were enthralled with the new medium—"To have the voice carried for thousands of miles seems almost beyond comprehension," Grant remarked in his first broadcast general conference address.[427] The Church ran programs on the Book of Mormon and adult education as well as *Mutual Hour* for the faith's teenagers. James Talmage, now a senior apostle, embraced the new medium with weekly addresses. Latter-day Saint University's station, KFOO, was the first in the nation licensed to an educational institution, and the Radio Club of Salt Lake, primarily for boys, was the first such group in the United States. Salt Lake, with its ability to broadcast to both coasts, became something of a radio hub; even Franklin Roosevelt, who made radio such an integral component of his presidency, made a point to speak on the air from the Tabernacle during his 1932 campaign. Meanwhile some Mormons gained prominence in the broadcasting industry outside the mountain west. Arthur Burdette Church helped establish radio in the Midwest; he ran an amateur station out of Kansas City that in 1923 was purchased by the RLDS Church and moved to their headquarters in Independence, Missouri, thus launching that church's media work. Through work of men like this across the nation, radio had an auspicious introduction to Mormonism across the nation, radio had an auspicious introduction to Mormonism that ensured that, from this point on, all media would be welcome in the Church.[428]

"All Faces West"

After World War I the initial excitement from *One Hundred Years of Mormonism* had dissipated, but it seems that the slow, consistent work of the Clawsons and a desire to respond to newer anti-Mormon films like *A Mormon Maid* and *Riders of the Purple Sage* may have inspired other Church members to make new films on Mormon topics. One example that almost certainly had its origins in the Clawsons' work was a 1923 film sponsored by the Daughters of Utah Pioneers, a nonprofit historical association organized in 1901. For the 1923 Pioneer Day celebrations they planned a historical reenactment of the pioneers' entry into the valley, beginning at Echo Canyon roughly thirty miles from the city and following the trail through East Canyon, Parley's Canyon, over Little Mountain and into Emigration Canyon and then on into the valley, with a celebration held at Liberty Park. "To accomplish this accurately and true to original detail much work will be necessary," the *Deseret News* reported in June, "but once having been done, it is proposed to have a moving picture made which will perpetuate in pictorial history the events of '47."[429] The goal was almost entirely archival, to have a visual record of the event for future generations rather than to screen it immediately, and the additional expense for filming would not add much to the overall budget, which was being raised by "popular subscription." A committee of 140 prominent Church members was established, though omitting the Clawsons, and evidently the filming proceeded successfully. Brigham Young was portrayed by his grandson Ross Beatie, but other "impersonators," like participants in the the the pioneer reenactments of 1997, were uncredited, and it is more appropriate to see the film as a documentary record of a historical reenactment rather than as a fictional production in and of itself. But there are still many unanswered questions about it, including who shot it, what specific material it included, how long it was, and what happened to it in the years since.[430]

At some point that decade the Clawsons negotiated with the Church to create another feature. A few scenes were filmed but the project ground to a halt, perhaps because the Church leadership, now led by Heber J. Grant, wanted to replicate the *One Hundred Years of Mormonism* model and contract an outside company, presumably one from California that could bring in Hollywood talent. The Clawsons' test footage has been lost and even the subject matter is unknown, although it quite likely would have also been on pioneers. The Clawsons returned to making their short documentaries while Grant and the Church pursued their feature film ambitions elsewhere.[431]

This wouldn't happen until 1930, but two years before that a private enterprise created the last great Mormon film of the silent era, *All Faces West*. The driving force behind this picture was Lewis H. Moomaw, a non-Mormon filmmaker from Oregon who had been shooting in the Pacific Northwest since 1915. He wrote and directed *The Cheechakos*, the first feature film ever made in Alaska, which had been released through Pathé in 1923. A few years later he struck upon the concept of setting a film in the Mormon exodus, and when he journeyed to Salt Lake City to gauge interest he had no problem finding many others who had considered the same possibility. On March 24, 1928 the new Pioneer Film Corporation announced an epic film with the Biblical title *The Exodus of the New World*, although the final title would be the more vigorous *All Faces West*. The story would be largely the same as *One Hundred Years of Mormonism*, but with a tighter focus on the migration, which had been the most popular part of that film thirteen years earlier.

Moomaw oversaw the production but brought in many relatives and collaborators from *The Cheechakos* to complete the film. Foremost among these was George Edward Lewis. He was slated to direct and served as the public face of the company as it was getting established in Utah in spring 1928. He was replaced as the film's director, however, by Moomaw's son-in-law Raymond Johnson (sometimes Johnston), whose wife, Moomaw's daughter, Gladys Johnson was cast in a supporting role as the hero's original love interest. The major roles, however, required major stars, and Ben Lyon and Marie Prevost were secured to play the romantic leads. Though not frequently remembered today they were both extremely popular at the time—as evidenced that each received $40,000 for appearing in the picture—and securing them was quite a feat. The supporting cast included popular Danish-American actor Anders Randolf as the villain and Prevost's character's father, and character actor Russell Simpson as one of the pioneers; he would go on to play a U.S. Army Major in *Brigham Young* and Mormons twice more in *Bad Bascomb* and *Wagon Master*.[432] The crew largely consisted of Moomaw's and Lewis's associates from Oregon and Alaska, as *Picture Play* magazine noted cheekily: "Even in Salt Lake City they have the Hollywood idea of making pictures. Practically every one concerned in the film is related to the man who is producing the picture. His son-in-law is the director, the director's wife is the ingénue, and there is an assorted lot of cousins and nephews acting as property men, assistants, and general helpers."[433]

All Faces West would require buy-in from local Mormons as well, and the Pioneer Film Corporation established this connection by including many prominent Mormons in its management. David Neff, head of the Utah Radio Products Company, which produced and sold radio speakers, became the firm's president. Joseph E. Boud was the trustee, and Brigham Young's grandson Richard W. Young, the head of the state bar association, was named the firm's attorney and one of the directors of the board. The Mormon who made the largest creative contribution to the film was George Pyper, a Church leader with a thorough understanding of both pioneer history and narrative drama, who wrote the screenplay, although he apparently did not receive screen credit.[434] Levi Edgar Young was employed as a historical advisor to assure accuracy during production, and all the film's extras were locals, including many Mormons descended from the pioneers.

Moomaw must have liked what he saw in Utah, because Pioneer quickly adopted a more ambitious vision than just producing this one feature. The company capitalized at $650,000, money raised in Salt Lake and Chicago through the sales of stock. This was far more than was needed for one film, of course, and in May 1928, even before production began, Pioneer announced that it had purchased the site for a twenty-acre film studio on the eastern edge of Sugar House in the foothills of the mountains, near where Harry Revier had wanted to place his studio several years earlier. George Edward Lewis loudly promised to bolster the local economy for years to come, and, as Church leaders hoped for a public relations coup through the content of the film, local business and government leaders looked forward to establishing the film industry in northern Utah on a much more robust footing than it had ever had before. As though to show their goodwill towards the state, Pioneer's leadership first created a single-reel travelogue featuring landmarks like the temple, state Capitol Building, and, perhaps for the first time, the airport, promising to make several other short pictorial films of the city and state to encourage tourism and the growth of industry—in addition to more features. Even before *All Faces West*'s production started they signed stunt flyer Dick Grace for a series of two-reel pictures and were advertising a second feature with an Alaskan connection called *The Malemute Kid*. In December, after production was wrapped, *Picture Play* magazine wrote about the company's apparent extravagance: "Every once in a while somebody in a town remote from Hollywood gets the urge to sink a fortune in building a studio and making pictures. This Salt Lake City crowd is doing it on a really grand scale. They not only bid high for Ben [Lyon]'s services; they drafted Marie Prevost and Anders Randolf, too." Prevost, however, would presumably make the expense worth it. "I can't figure out how it can be concerned with polygamy, when Marie is playing the lead. It wouldn't be reasonable, even in a picture, to suppose that a man would have another wife if he had Marie.[435]

Filming was originally supposed to begin by May 1928, but apparently took place primarily in September. Principle photography was in Utah but included location shoots in Iowa, presumably for its rolling plains as the pioneers trekked west, and Idaho, where they shot near the Heise Hot Springs northeast of Idaho Falls to film the pioneers crossing the Snake River. One stuntman was injured when he was struck by an airplane propeller, but otherwise production seems to have gone smoothly. Filming was completed by November, with the blessing of several General Authorities who saw the footage. Even though the film had cost $55,000, the company was optimistic about its future.

In the meantime, however, the nature of cinema changed completely with the coming of sound. *The Jazz Singer*, the film most credited as ushering in the sound age, had its Salt Lake City premiere at the Victory Theater on May

19, 1928. It had cost $25,000 to convert the theater to sound projection, but audience response was so enthusiastic and the film so profitable for the theater—an event being replicated at thousands of theaters across the world—that by the time *All Faces West*'s shooting wrapped it was clear that audiences craved talking pictures and anything else was now substandard. This should not have caught anyone by surprise—trade journals had discussed the development of synchronized sound equipment for years, the Church itself had been investigating sound film, and literally the day after wrapping her part Marie Prevost was called away to add dialogue to *The Godless Girl*, a silent film she had just completed filming that was adding sound—but the Pioneer Film Corporation was completely unprepared.[436]

All Faces West would have to become a talking picture, a process that was happening not just to *The Godless Girl* (released in 1929) but to many films across the world, including Alfred Hitchcock's *Blackmail* (1929). In November 1928 the producers of *All Faces West* began advertising it as a talking picture, describing the allure "the clatter of hoofs and roaring of the wild animals" would give to the pioneer story.[437] But they were wading into unknown territory involving expensive new equipment and technical processes. In December the company started selling additional stock to raise funds for the recording of a soundtrack, but the necessary amount was not forthcoming. Eventually hopes for synchronization had to be abandoned. A score was composed by a Mormon musician in Ogden named Roland Parry, but, though it may have been recorded, it appears to have been performed live by an organist and other musicians; the music even included songs for an all-male quartet of singers. The film showed to existing stockholders around February 14, 1929, and after a few months' delay it was finally released otherwise silent on March 2, 1929.[438] It ran for a week at the Victory, perhaps still Salt Lake's only theater equipped for sound projection, for 25 cents a seat and was quite popular there. "Marie Prevost and Ben Lyon head a brilliant cast of well-known artists of the stage and screen," the *Salt Lake Tribune* raved. "Besides portraying a beautiful love tale, 'All Faces West' vividly pictures the trials and hardships, the courage and triumphs of Utah's pioneers." The film featured a buffalo stampede (from preexisting footage), an Indian attack, cattle rustling, and great comedic moments, and the sound elements proved striking as well: "Augmenting the feature picture program there has been arranged an atmospheric prologue which boasts a cast of some twenty accomplished singers and dancers. This prologue has been done under the supervision of Kenneth Scoville and there also is a specially prepared musical score interpreted by a symphonic orchestra of picked musicians."[439] The local audience obviously was impressed, and one week was a typical run, but it would cost more to launch a national release than the company had, and it was slipping out of reach.

Another plea to buy stocks was placed in the *Deseret News* on March 6, but by September the company could no longer pay stockholders interest and went into suspension. This caused one of the Chicago investors, Mox E. Miller, to file a lawsuit againt Pioneer for $150,000, with 6.5% interest, in damages. Short of this, he sought to assume ownership of the script and distribution rights for the film, noting that violation of the corporation's indenture would cause the film itself to go to one William La Plante in Los Angeles. All the company's property had to be sold as well, ending Moomaw's—and everyone else's—dream of a film factory in Sugar House. If bankruptcy proceedings held out any hope of saving the film, the stock market crash in October sealed the company's demise. *All Faces West* was presumably no less of an artistic success than *One Hundred Years of Mormonism* had been, but the industry had shifted dramatically since 1913 and it had the misfortune of being released at the time of greatest disruption in the history of world cinema; a great many films across the globe suffered a similar fate at the hands of the talkies.[440]

Research is ongoing to track the ownership of the film after 1929. After the lawsuit it was apparently sold at public auction in Los Angeles, and in September 1930 its new owners were attempting to simply sell it off as stock footage or to repurpose the footage into an entirely new film. Because of silent movies' use of intertitles rather than the spoken word, it was possible to create entire new films simply by cutting and shuffling footage and writing and shooting new titles. "The producers figure that the mob scenes are worth something," one notice read, "and that a new story can be written around them with the cast only needed to fill in on close-ups."[441] What actually happened appears to have been far less violent to the original film: the close-ups were retained—there was no sense in letting stars like Ben Lyon and Marie Prevost go to waste—and by March 1931 the distribution company Syndicate Exchange, Inc. was offering it as a part-talking film named *Call of the Rockies*.

This version, which runs for 117 minutes, is still available on video, allowing us to observe the cinematography and acting if not George Pyper's original storyline. Music runs throughout the film, and there are occasional moments of synchronized sound effects such as a barking dog, gunshots, and castanets and applause during a dance sequence in camp. But the only use of synchronized speech—and even a song—occurs in a newly shot prologue which, segueing into voice-over narration in the opening sequence, sets up the rest of the film as an extended flashback from the days of the old west. One contemporary review noted how relieving it was to watch silent footage, a reminder of how boxed-in early talkies were. It "shows how interesting the westerns can still be without a lot of talk stopping the action stuff."[442]

The film's events still occur on the "old" Mormon Trail, but the travelers are heading for California and all references to their religion has been removed; there was no reason to preserve that in this new version. Marie Prevost plays Arleta, the daughter of a horse thief and cattle rustler who ingratiates himself to the pioneers with the intent of stealing their livestock, but she falls in love with one of them, Matt (Lyon), and in the end turns against her father to save her new love. In the process she is shot, and in the film's final moments Matt's fiancé gives Arleta her engagement ring, saying she and Matt belong together, but it is unclear whether she will live or die as the film fades to black. We'll never know how much of Pyper's original screenplay survives in this version, but it's conceivable that not too much would need to be changed to remove the film's Mormonism—and we can still see its vestige in moments like when two pioneers refuse free cigars from the villain, although it's also possible that identifiable characters like Brigham Young were removed—and that major plot points conveyed through action rather than dialogue, such as the fight in which Arleta is shot, must have remained the same. If, then, we consider that *Call of the Rockies* essentially presents *All Faces West* with its religious elements removed, then we see that Pyper utilized at least two narrative tropes that would recur in many Mormon films to come: first, a romance between a Mormon and non-Mormon character who eventually joins the faith, as in *Brigham Young*, *Wagon Master,* and *Blood Arrow* (1958), and, second, outlaws stowing away with a Mormon wagon train, a trope he adapted from other westerns which would be used again in *Bad Bascomb, Wagon Master,* and even *The Duchess and the Dirtwater Fox* (1976). Ironically, the main emotional story focuses around the love triangle between Matt and the two women, and Pyper could have solved this problem by following the cue of *Hands Up!* two years earlier and having Matt marry both women. It shouldn't be surprising, however, that polygamy makes no appearance in *Call of the Rockies*, and presumably in *All Faces West* as well. In the end, in its truncated form *Call of the Rockies* proves a standard western, entertaining enough but with nothing distinct about it, and it leaves the viewer wondering whether *All Faces West,* with its Mormon elements intact, was the better film.[443]

Ironically for a silent film that was doomed to a large extent by its lack of synchronized sound, *All Faces West*'s greatest legacy was its music. The musical prologue performed at the time of the film's release was actually composed by Roland Parry to encapsulate his recorded score for the film, and in 1951 he adapted the music as a stage musical which became rather popular in Utah. The Austrian baritone Igor Gorin came to Weber College, today Weber State University, where Parry was on the music faculty, to originate the role of Brigham Young, performing songs like "Prayer for a Safe Journey," "Fly Lower, Birds" about death along the trail, "This is the Place," and "The Fluttering of a Thousand Wings," about the miracle of the gulls—as well as the pioneer anthem "Come, Come Ye Saints." An album was recorded with the Weber College Singers and Utah Symphony Orchestra, and for generations it was in this form that *All Faces West* was remembered, while the destroyed film and its financial disaster was forgotten.[444]

The End of an Era

This film's loss, however, was only a minor setback for Mormon cinema compared with other events. The Clawson brothers had continued working prodigiously for thirteen years, by this time creating a priceless visual record of the Church and region. Shirl was forty-seven and was described as a "widely known motion picture producer";[445] Chet was forty-five. Their skill and inventiveness as a two-person film studio has been largely unmatched in the history of cinema: they conceived, funded, planned, directed, lit, shot, developed, and edited all their own material, taking the mentality of 1890s film production nearly into the 1930s industry. Globally, they were in fact probably one of the last manifestations of the multitalented cameraman mode of production that, as Janet Staiger has pointed out, generally disappeared by 1907.[446] In 1929 they were embarking on yet another fictional feature and were apparently in the process of converting to synchronized sound; they had been present for and even filmed discussions on the subject between Church leaders and representatives of Electrical Research Products.[447] Their current project, however, was a documentary for the *Salt Lake Tribune* called *The World at Your Door*, about the process of creating a newspaper; it was to be exhibited at schools and civic clubs in Utah and Idaho that November.

Their basement office at No. 1 West South Temple—at the southwest corner of Main Street, across from the Temple Block—was a complete film studio, including laboratory film processing equipment. It was also essentially their library, the walls covered with canned reels of film, many of them the only copies, including their professional footage and their earlier amateur work, rare footage such as of Brigham Young's family and two hundred of Hiram Clawson's descendents inside the Salt Lake Theatre before it was razed in 1928, and even home movies of their own children. The entrance to the studio was by an iron staircase that went to street level. At the bottom was an inward-opening metal door with a glass window; near this was a small washroom with a grilled glass skylight in the sidewalk overhead.

At 11:15 on October 23, 1929 both men were working in the studio. Shirl was using a rewinding machine to dry wet film, catching it in flannel-lined baskets. A metal reel rubbing against a spindle of the machine emitted a spark which landed in one of the baskets full of nitrate-based film. Fire erupted immediately. Chet moved to escape but stopped to get Shirl, who was attempting to extinguish the flames. Chet later recounted, "The celluloid burst into flame and set fire to other rolls on the work bench. The flames shot to the ceiling and against a wall cabinet where more rolls were stored in cans. The intense heat caused these to explode." After a moment both men ran to the exit but the pressure from the heat was too great for them to pull open the swollen door. There was a second explosion as the flames reached another group of films. Desperate, Shirl began to beat the glass, but when he broke it the incoming oxygen caused a third explosion that filled the entire studio. Choking on the fumes, Shirl exclaimed, "Goodbye, Chet, our time has come." Chet, however, saw the window as a way out. Yelling for Shirl to follow him, he dove over the jagged glass and through the window, later saying that he felt lifted and shot through the small opening by a power greater than his own. The fire department was notified and Chet returned to the stairwell to try to beat down the door and save his brother. Failing this, he snatched an ax from the drugstore upstairs and chopped at the skylight in the sidewalk. The fire department arrived and took over, breaking through the sidewalk glass plates and flooding the entire basement; the city's full firefighting force was eventually called out, some evacuating the entire building while others held back the thousands of onlookers who were gathering. Chet was taken to the hospital before learning what happened to Shirl. "I thought he would follow," he told a reporter, "but the firemen found him on the floor of the washroom when they broke in." He had apparently gone there to try to escape the fumes or break through the skylight himself. Firefighters pulled him up through the skylight with a rope and spent two hours trying to revive him. He was only slightly burned but had suffocated from the nitric acid and other compounds in the toxic smoke. Fire chief Walter Knight said, "If he had been overcome by ordinary smoke, they would have succeeded, but the poison gas was too much for him." His own films had killed him. A fireman and an elevator operator were also overcome with fumes but survived. Chet was burned terribly, nearly losing his ears. He lived to age seventy-eight in 1962, but he never made another motion picture.

The fire also obviously destroyed a great deal of their work. Chet, the businessman and former fire insurance salesman, estimated a loss of $10,000 worth of developed film and $5,000 of miscellaneous film stock and equipment—worth roughly $214,000 today. What survives of their footage, centered around a core collection of three hours and fifty-two minutes of video footage at the Church History Library, generally comes from other sources. At the beginning of the chapter I mentioned that in 1945 a box of film was discovered over a radiator in the Presiding Bishopric's office, and Frank Wise was able to compile this into the film *Latter-day Saint Leaders: Past and Present*; it remains the only cohesive grouping of the Clawsons' footage publicly available on video today. In 1966 Shirl's children donated a large locker box of negatives to the BYU Motion Picture Department, and the material on Mayor Clarence Neslen mentioned earlier was discovered in 1970. With luck, more of their footage and other lost films of the silent era will yet be found. Some recent documentaries have utilized Clawson footage, such as *Faith of an Observer: Conversations with Hugh Nibley* (1985), which shows footage of Charles Nibley and his family, and Living Scriptures' *Joseph F. Smith* (1999), which uses footage of Smith and his funeral. In the 1970s David Jacobs made the first major study of their work and as a result Judge Whitaker created the reportorial *Church in Action* series to document Church news in roughly the same way the Clawsons had, although by that time the global nature of the Church meant that Whitaker's team could never cover Mormon happenings as deeply as the Clawsons had. Despite the great loss of October 1929, the detail of their surviving prints—records of the personalities and daily functioning of the Church for nearly two decades—constitutes an invaluable legacy, one that, for all the increased pervasiveness of film and media in the years since, has never quite been repeated in the Church. The Clawsons' era remains a singular moment in Mormon history.[448]

3 THE SECOND WAVE: HOME CINEMA (24 OCTOBER 1929—2 JANUARY 1953)

But Mormonism is by no means merely a closeted, holy matter. It is also a hard-headed economic system and the communicants are bustling, practical, prosperous. [Their centennial] pageant [is] calculated to impress its audience with the fact that Mormonism is a successful religion if ever there was one.

— Time *magazine, 1930* [1]

With the fire on Wednesday October 23 the Church lost the Clawsons, and with Black Thursday the very next day it soon lost what little financial ability it had to replace them: Church expenditures from tithing receipts, which before the 1950s were publicly reported in general conference, dropped from just over $4 million in 1927 to only $2.38 million in 1933, indicating the amount of activity—in construction, higher education, missionary work, and other areas—that had to be curtailed in the Depression's early years because of decreased tithes. [2] Compounding the problem, the Church had made a series of poor financial decisions, even during the boom years of the 1920s, which lost funds from its investments and business interests. "In 1927 [Heber J. Grant's] first counselor Anthony W. Ivins calculated that the church had lost $526,900 in transactions involving the church's Utah State National Bank. Five years later second counselor J. Reuben Clark noted that those losses had increased to $1,374,900. In 1930 . . . Ivins cataloged the church's loss of 'at least six million dollars' in stock and bond transactions during the previous decade." As the 1930s progressed "the combination of bad financial investments, declines in church businesses, and the Great Depression once again pushed the LDS church into deficit spending. First counselor J. Reuben Clark announced to general conferences that the church had spending deficits amounting to $100,000 in 1937 to nearly $900,000 in 1938. During the 1940s Clark allowed the church to spend only 27 percent of its annual tithing revenues." [3] There was simply no room to fund another filmmaking unit.

The Great Depression through World War II thus remains the only period since 1916 in which the Church had no official filmmaking organization. Because of this, Mormon film historian David Jacobs has called the 1930s a fruitless de-

The Second Wave: Home Cinema

cade—and he's correct in that Church filmmaking diminished in many important ways, particularly that after the Clawsons there was "an end to the type of
film coverage that had been attempted up until that time."[4] Instead of the short
quasi-ethnographic documentaries of the Clawsons, Second Wave filmmakers—full-time missionaries, mass media propagandists, and individual Church
employees—drew their inspiration from other sources, such as Mormonism's
didactic literature and magic lantern lectures of the late 1800s, and developed
innovative new approaches to making and using film and other media. Although
this yielded fewer films than the Clawsons produced, these men were trans-
planting the foundation created during the First Wave onto firmer bedrock
and making it much more integral to the Church as a whole; the Church Radio,
Publicity, and Mission Literature Committee, Deseret Film Productions, and the
temple endowment film each showed that institutional film production could
no longer take place at the periphery of the Church organization as the Clawsons' company had been; instead, it had to be brought directly into the Church's
growing bureaucracy. Through developments in filmstrips, radio, and an internal
motion picture distribution and exhibition network, the Church in this period not
only created a permanent outlet for Mormon films that has remained in place
to the present, but formed the infrastructure for an entire internal film industry,
making it a misnomer to call the entire decade fruitless.

The dearth of Mormon productions should also be seen in its broader context.
Work throughout the entire Christian film industry—films by Methodists, Congregationalists, Baptists, and others—peaked in the early 1920s, after which
it "declined precipitously. Exhibition continued unabated, but the demand for
better films outpaced supply."[5] Cinema was no longer new. It turned forty in
1935, as the Great Depression still held the United States and the world in its
grip. With film's novelty gone and the Progressive Era an increasingly distant
memory, the same societal shifts that affected Mormon film influenced other
denominations as well. "The novelty of showing religious films to attract audiences declined significantly during the early 1930s. However, church interest in
technical innovations, particularly in the advent of the 16mm sound camera and
projector, bred a generation of independent amateur filmmakers that resulted
in the emergence of fresh changes in pedagogical emphases."[6] Indeed, given
the economic and political realities as the Western world struggled against
depression and fascism, it's astounding that determined individuals like Gordon
B. Hinckley and A. Hamer Reiser devoted as much energy to the production and
distribution of religious media as they did; only a firm belief in the truthfulness
of their faith and necessity of spreading it to the world could have motivated

them to work on it as assiduously as they did.

The Second Wave differed from the First in many respects. To start with, by the 1930s the global film industry was well past its primitive pioneer era. This was no longer the era of D. W. Griffith, Sergei Eisenstein, or Buster Keaton, but of Orson Welles, Jean Renoir, and Howard Hawks, of Fred Astaire and Ginger Rogers. In the United States the studio system had perfected the classical Hollywood film, typified by titles like *Snow White and the Seven Dwarfs* (1937), *The Wizard of Oz, Gone with the Wind* (both 1939), and *Casablanca* (1942); abroad, world cinema saw movements like Italian neorealism, masterful auteurs like Yasujiro Ozu, and films like Michael Powell and Emeric Pressburger's *Black Narcissus* (1947) and *The Red Shoes* (1948). Though films and filmstrips produced by Mormons, which were often quite homely, couldn't match the sophistication of these works, they did reflect the more mature film style of the period with continuity editing, a wider range of shot sizes and angles, and more complex narratives.

The Technicolor process used in pictures like *The Wizard of Oz* and *The Red Shoes* indicates another key difference from the First Wave, which is technological advancements that allowed for greater realism and artistry. Synchronized sound is the most prominent of these, but color film, faster film stocks, and more powerful and nuanced lights all aided in the perfection of classical film style. As mentioned, for Mormons as for other religious groups one of the most important developments was the widespread adoption of 16mm gauge film in the 1930s. At half the size of 35mm stock, it could be shot and exhibited on cameras and projectors that were much smaller, lighter, and cheaper. This lowered costs for professional filmmakers like Frank S. Wise who were undertaking ambitious fiction and nonfiction projects, but it also allowed many enthusiastic amateurs to purchase their own cameras and film Church-related events; it also allowed for a much more extensive network of 16mm projectors in Mormon meetinghouses than had been achieved with 35mm equipment in the First Wave.

Third, not only had film style and technology matured, but Mormonism—and the public's perception of it—had as well. Polygamy was a relic. Danites were overtaken by new radio and comic book characters like the Lone Ranger and Superman. This was a period of rapprochement between Mormon and mainstream American societies, and Church Presidents Heber J. Grant, George Albert Smith, and especially David O. McKay were seen as practical businessmen and ecumenical leaders of an increasingly model American minority. Grant approached film and proselytizing with the savvy of a public relations expert, resulting in

The Second Wave: Home Cinema

successes like Twentieth Century-Fox's *Brigham Young* (1940). He wasn't fully responsible for this, however, as at the same time, due to Hollywood's adoption of the Hays Production Code, mainstream depictions of Mormonism changed radically toward the positive in the 1930s.

But the most important and enduring change in the Second Wave was the domestication of film by the Church and within Mormon culture. This was a time when all aspects of the medium—distribution, exhibition, and ultimately production—were integrated into Mormon social life and institutionalized by the Church itself, by the end of the period bringing film all the way into the confines of the sacred temples. Indeed, the 1930s and '40s were decades in which both the mainstream film industry and the Church reinvented the relationship between Mormonism and cinema. After these decades it would be impossible to fully understand or imagine the Church or the Mormon experience apart from its films.

The term "Home Cinema" is borrowed from Home Literature, a movement that, as mentioned in Chapter 1, lasted from around 1880 to the 1930s. Eugene England summarized it as a "highly didactic fiction and poetry designed to defend and improve the Saints but of little lasting worth."[7] In these years Mormons consciously developed their own literary tradition with two symbiotic purposes: to glorify locally made work—generally from Utah—that distanced Zion from Babylon culturally, artistically, intellectually, and morally, and to teach. Indeed, didactic writing, far from being condemned, earned the highest praise, as Nephi Anderson, one of Home Literature's best-known authors, said in his essay "Purpose in Fiction": "A good story," he declared, "is artistic preaching."[8]

Home Cinema, while not consciously based on Home Literature, emulated these characteristics. Church history and contemporary Mormon accomplishments were the most popular themes, whether that meant praising past achievements in centennial celebrations of the Church's founding in 1930 and the pioneers' arrival in Salt Lake City in 1947, or extolling the success of the Church's welfare program for the needy that was developed during the Great Depression. Essentially all of the filmstrips, radio plays, and motion pictures produced by the Church were now done for a pedagogical purpose, especially for outside audiences and not just the Mormon viewers who the Clawsons presumed might like to see Joseph F. Smith golfing. While often conflating Utah and Mormonism, virtually all films of the era glorified Latter-day Saint faith, heritage, and ethics—even in the major Hollywood pictures of the period like *Brigham Young* and *Wagon Master* (1950). Gordon Hinckley was perhaps the most concerned with proselytizing in his work at the Church Radio, Publicity, and Mission Literature Committee, but even when films were intended to only be shown to Mormons their creators were still conscious of public relations in a way completely absent from the Clawsons' work, and some films like *Corianton* (1931), which really would only appeal to Mormon audiences, were nevertheless marketed toward the general public.

But Home Cinema harked back not just to Home Literature of the 1890s but the Home Industry movement of the 1850s, an effort organized under Brigham Young that emphasized domestic production among Mormons over trafficking with outsiders. In 1847 the principal members of the valley's first settlers proclaimed their intention to not "have any trade or commerce with the gentile world, for so long as we buy of them we are in a degree dependent upon them. The Kingdom of God cannot rise independent of the gentile nations until we produce, manufacture, and make every article of use, convenience, or necessity among our own people."[9] This desire periodically received renewed emphasis, in 1852 and other years until the incursion of the transcontinental railroad in 1869. In 1868 and '69 the School of the Prophets voted to boycott all outside goods, and domestic manufacture and trade became one of the defining articles of Mormon faith. Throughout this period a desire for home industries resulted in public works, United Orders—attempts at communal industry and even living arrangements—and domestic manufacture of products like sugar, silk, paper, clothing, pottery, wool, and iron. Isolationism was difficult to maintain in the face of low-cost high-quality goods from the broader world, however, and in the late 1800s Mormons found increased prosperity the more they opened to outside trade; the School of the Prophets' boycott ended in 1882, the last United Order was established in Chihuahua, Mexico in 1893, and, as mentioned in Chapter 1, by the twentieth century the Church's economic interests transformed from communal enterprises to much more corporate guises like Zion's Savings Bank and Trust Company. Agricultural, manufacturing, and financial institutions all passed into private hands or opened up to outside trade at exactly the time the film industry was being born.[10]

Mormon cinema, then, was essentially introduced into a purely commercial world. In the First Wave, private film exhibition in the Church was seen as an extension of Progressive Era supervision of youth recreation, and the films shown were more likely to feature Douglas Fairbanks than Joseph F. Smith. With film production, Church leaders and prominent Mormons had been more than content outsourcing major projects to west coast professionals: outsiders were brought in again and again while the Clawsons, devoted Mormons, were denied the chance to create a feature film in the 1920s. But in the Second Wave—with the demise of the anti-Mormon film, the financial restrictions of the Great Depression, and the improving public image of the Church at large—Church leaders apparently felt confident enough to slow down, think smaller, and establish modest production work in-house. Like Brigham Young had said of tobacco in 1863: "Instead of buying it in a foreign market and importing it over a thousand miles, why not raise it in our own country or do without it?"[11] Now, rather than importing expensive Hollywood talent, Mormons in the Second Wave were willing to do it all themselves, even if it meant long stretches where they did indeed do without.

As had often been the case in the nineteenth century, Mormons now found their home film industry significantly behind its outside competition. Production efforts were modest and depended on a few multitasking personalities like Frank Wise and Gordon Hinckley, men who, like the Clawsons, took an artisanal approach to filmmaking's complex technical processes. The results often earned praise from other Church members whose allegiance to their tribe may have caused them to forgive any artistic shortcomings. And the home broadcasting and distribution networks they relied on to disseminate their work mimicked Home Industry's physical distribution networks in the 1800s through entities like ZCMI and the bishops' storehouses for tithing goods. Indeed, by recognizing the industrial heart at the core of film's creation and dissemination, it could be argued that Home Cinema was the last vital manifestation of the Home Industry movement begun nearly one hundred years earlier. Pure manufacturing home industries had disappeared by the 1900s, but the cultural home industry of cinema extended Brigham Young's movement into the twentieth century.

Mainstream Depictions of Mormons

The Production Code: A Kinder Hollywood

An additional reason that Mormons in the Second Wave didn't feel compelled to create positive large-scale features about their faith was that, to their delight, they found Hollywood suddenly doing it for them. American movies underwent significant changes in the 1930s with the introduction of the Motion Picture Production Code. The Code, often known as the Hays Production Code or just the Hays Code, had its roots in the early 1920s when public concern, often coming from religious groups, about the morals of the film industry threatened to saddle it with a patchwork of state and municipal censorship laws that would be practically impossible to navigate. To stave off dozens of censorship bills before state legislatures in 1922, industry representatives recruited Will H. Hays as President of a trade association called the Motion Picture Producers and Distributors of America, known since 1945 as the Motion Picture Association of America. Hays had served as the Republican National Committee Chairman from 1918-1921 and managed Warren Harding's 1920 presidential campaign; Harding rewarded him by appointing him Postmaster General, the position he was in when he joined the MPPDA in March 1922. The goal of the organization was to create an industry-wide system of self-censorship to promote self-management rather than government intervention. Because participation was voluntary and enforcement lax initial results were underwhelming, so in 1927 Hays tried to strengthen the MPPDA's hand by forming a committee of studio heads that created a list of "Don'ts" and "Be Carefuls" for films. This still didn't seem to go far enough, so in 1930 a newer, stronger set of rules, the actual Production Code, was agreed on by the MPPDA and principal Hollywood studios, and it was given additional teeth when Hays appointed the hardnosed Joseph Breen to enforce it in 1934. Crime, profanity, miscegenation, extramarital relations, and dozens of other subjects were either forbidden or allowed under strict guidelines; this was the era when married couples onscreen would have separate beds, lest a sexual relationship be even obliquely acknowledged. All the studios agreed that this voluntary self-censorship was better than compulsory federal or state censorship, and the Production Code became the governing philosophy for American films until it was replaced by the MPAA's current rating system in 1968.

Mormon leaders like Heber Grant saw Hays's appointment and the implementation of the Production Code as major victories for traditional values. Writing in August 1934, two months after the MPPDA required all new films to obtain a literal seal of approval, Elsie Talmage Brandley, associate editor of the *Improvement Era*, praised the influx of religious groups into the reform movement pushing Hays and now Breen forward. "As members of the 'Mormon' Church which has always stood for the highest type of recreation," she said, "we can take a step ahead by facing the facts concerning the movies and acting upon them."[12] This meant simply cutting off the production of offensive films. Mormon leaders, in fact, had had no qualms about proposing blatant censorship for years, dating back to pioneer leaders' complaints against novelists like Charles Dickens. We've seen the antagonistic attitudes of Joseph F. Smith and others toward early motion pictures, and of course the anti-Mormon films engendered even more energetic support of censorship in Church leaders, Mormon businessmen, and politicians like Reed Smoot. At least by the 1920s this willingness to censor films that attacked their faith spread to include any that depicted immorality and vice in any form. The greatest catalyst for this came not onscreen but off, with the Fatty Arbuckle scandal of 1921-22.

Roscoe "Fatty" Arbuckle was one of the most gifted comedians of American silent films, and throughout the 1910s he was as popular with Mormons as with everyone else. He worked closely with Mormons like James Cruze and Betty Compson, and on a 1917 coast-to-coast rail trip he made his very first stop, for two days, in the southern Utah hamlet of Milford, where an "onslaught of city officials, members of the [Mormon Church], and plain, ordinary citizens was met."[13] But then in September 1921 he attended a San Francisco party at which a young actress named Virginia Rappe mysteriously fell ill and died a few days later of a ruptured bladder. The Hearst papers immediately charged that Arbuckle had sexually assaulted her and caused her injury and death through overly vigorous coitus. Although he was eventually acquitted in court of a charge of manslaughter, the court of public opinion roundly condemned him, effectively ending his career. Three days after Rappe's death the *Deseret News* excoriated the actor, praising exhibitors who had already banned Arbuckle's films; the author admitted all suspects were technically innocent until proven guilty, "but this is not by any means to say that a nauseating degenerate is to continue to hold public favor and offend decency by either his presence or his presentations while under the foul cloud in which his alleged loathsomeness has enveloped him."[14] Calls to clean up Hollywood swept the nation, and this was the immediate impetus for Hays leaving the Harding administration and joining the MPPDA. Even though his initial efforts there on a broad scale were largely ineffectual, he did take the extreme step of specifically banning Arbuckle from appearing in films one week after a third and final jury acquitted him of any wrongdoing on April 12, 1922. Evidently elated with Hays's censure, Heber Grant telegraphed Smoot in Washington on the 21st: "The first presidency appreciate highly what Mr Hays has done in suppressing the arbuckle and other improper films," he said, adding, "We think his name should never be allowed to appear in the movies again."[15] Smoot in all likelihood conveyed this thanks to Hays personally.

After this, culturally conservative Mormons increasingly saw Hollywood as the embodiment of worldliness and sin, an attitude which has remained to the present. A few Church members continued in the vein of efforts from the 1910s to "exclude all but clean pictures from the state"[16] of Utah or "prohibiting picture shows from operating on Sunday"[17] in Logan. Eventually even the name of Hollywood caused such aversion among Mormons that in 1939 the Hollywood Stake in southern California, one of the oldest and most prosperous outside Utah, was renamed the Los Angeles Stake; many local members noted the change reflected nothing more than President Grant's distaste for the movie industry. On the other hand, in 1931 the Jewish film exhibitor Louis Marcus defeated the incumbent Mormon John Bowman to become mayor of Salt Lake City when attacks accusing Marcus of opposing film censorship actually boosted his popularity instead of hurting it. Apparently not every citizen of Salt Lake, not even every Mormon, considered censorship a virtue.[18]

When Will Hays joined the MPPDA on March 6, 1922 many Church members hoped they would finally have the ear of someone able to stop their misrepresentation on the screen. Although Heber Grant had invited Hays to Salt Lake City in 1918 to sell war bonds as part of President Wilson's Liberty Loan drive, the key to this was Reed Smoot, who knew Hays well from the 1920 campaign season when Smoot served as chairman of the Republican Senatorial Campaign Committee and Hays as the party chair. In Hays's first month at the MPPDA Smoot wrote him a series of suggestions for new guidelines, including that the industry not "produce any pictures which hold up in ridicule any religious sect or section of people, or place them in obviously false positions."[19] He found Hays, an ordained Presbyterian elder, receptive. In 1927 the MPPDA included as the final two of its eleven "Don'ts" the "ridicule of the clergy" and "willful offense to any nation, race, or creed"; after 1934 the staunchly Catholic Joe Breen saw that these stipulations were even more firmly enforced. It's easy to hear Mormons' complaints about the temple ceremonies in *A Victim of the Mormons* and *A Mormon Maid* in the 1930 Code's stipulation: "No film or episode may throw ridicule on any religious faith. Ministers of religion in their character as ministers of religion should not be sued as comic characters or as villains. Ceremonies of any definite religion should be carefully and respectfully handled."[20] Certain stereotypes suddenly evaporated from American cinema, among them the lascivious Mormon elder, the power-hungry Mormon patriarch, and those ticket-selling nubile victims of forced polygamy. Particularly from the adoption of the full Production Code in February 1930 onward, it became nearly impossible to treat Mormonism from any of the standard exploitative angles. Apparently emboldened, the next month Smoot introduced legislation prohibiting the importation of any foreign book or printed material that advocated treason or resistance to the U.S. or which "offends the moral sense of the average person." He called such books worse than opium, saying of D. H. Lawrence's *Lady Chatterley's Lover,* which he had never read, "It is most damnable to undertake to read such stuff. . . . It is written by a man with a diseased mind and a soul so black that he would obscure even the darkness of hell!"[21] After a few days of debate on the Senate floor a compromise was reached that allowed customs agents to search incoming book shipments, but with strong judicial oversight; *Lady Chatterley's Lover* specifically continued to be banned in the U.S. until a 1959 obscenity trial found it acceptable. Smoot's passionate defense of his bill indicates how thoroughly many Mormons had subscribed to using censorship to control public morality, whether concerning literature, cinema, or other forms of art and discourse.[22]

But if this was a victory in keeping negative portrayals off the screen, the Code largely eliminated positive Mormon characters as well, as approving depictions of polygamy were also nixed, thus making it impossible to approach the Church from either direction. As a 1937 handbook for screenwriters put it:

> Polygamy is considered as multiple adultery under the Code, and, therefore any story dealing with this theme must have sufficient compensating moral values to permit its dramatization on the screen. It may not be treated in a favorable or glamorous light, and no details of the intimate life of a colony devoted to polygamy may be portrayed on the screen. It must be shown as illegal, wrong, and subversive to the standards of a Christian society.[23]

Such a stipulation probably seemed a small price to pay for a universal ban against films like *A Mormon Maid*, and with the passage and strengthening of the Code in the early 1930s Mormons increasingly warmed up to the movies, as Hollywood did toward them.

Hollywood wasn't alone in this, of course. Overall opinions about the Church were changing, as President Grant noted in a 1936 address to the Institute of Human Relations at Estes Park, Colorado: Where B. H. Roberts had been refused the opportunity to speak at the Hall of Religions at the 1893 Chicago World's Columbian Exposition, in 1933 he had been invited to address an interfaith conference in Chicago, where he was greeted warmly and, despite being weak and on crutches—he passed away a few weeks later—was asked to give a second speech. Non-Mormon statesmen like Arizona Senator Henry Ashurst and Governor George W. P. Hunt were now praising Mormons, and over one thousand wards and smaller branches of the Church reached from Canada to Mexico. What Grant didn't mention was the growing popularity of the Tabernacle Choir's nationwide *Music and the Spoken Word* broadcasts, the Church's presence at other expositions and World's Fairs in Dresden (1930), Chicago (1933-34), and San Diego (1935-36), and other ways it was reaching out through public relations to modernize its image and compose a more sympathetic self-portrait. If polygamy no longer defined Mormonism, Church members, politicians, intellectuals, and even movie producers were now struggling to determine just what the public image of the Church would be.[24]

The result of all these changing attitudes and regulations was that cinematic Latter-day Saints, when present, became something of a cipher, more generally referred to by their geographic origin than their religious beliefs. The 1932 chain gang film *Hell's Highway* may be seen as the last gasp of anti-Mormon stereotyping when a prisoner jokes that hard labor is easier than his three wives back at home. Much more exemplary of the period was Monogram's western *The Man from Utah* (1934), beginning with its titular designation of the protagonist. In it a young John Wayne plays John Weston, a straight-laced rider and shooter who is continually referred to, even by himself, by his state of origin, though the film coyly never mentions that state's dominant religion. Hired by a marshal to infiltrate a gang that has been fixing rodeos by implanting needles laced with rattlesnake venom in competitors' saddles, Weston is able to best them, in part, because of his sobriety, apparently a reference to the Church's health code known as the Word of Wisdom, which increased in importance under Grant and during Prohibition. In a scene halfway through the film, after the first day's competition the gang pretends to befriend Weston and takes him to their headquarters to offer him a drugged drink. He utterly refuses, though, insisting that he never drinks. Not only this, but he spots the reflection of a thug sneaking up behind him in his glass and is able to punch out the entire gang and escape. Although he displays no qualms in courting a non-Mormon girl, he remains a paradigm of manners and decorum throughout the film, revealing an upright character that's a far cry from the vampiric missionaries of a decade before.

Most other fiction films of the '30s—generally westerns—were to greater or lesser extents variations on this theme, including two actual remakes of *The Man from Utah*: in 1937 Monogram released a version called *Trouble in Texas,* indicating how ephemeral the original's Mormon inference actually was, and in 1944 they released a third version, this time called *The Utah Kid*. The protagonist's nativity was thus switched back to the Mormon state, but there's little else to identify his religion. It gets more confusing, however, because this wasn't the first film known by that name. A previous *The Utah Kid* from 1930 inverted the formula by depicting an outlaw who reforms when he's forced into marrying a woman he's just met. The religious connotations here were minimal, as the protagonist spends most of the film brawling, dueling, and hiding out from the sheriff in a saloon before straightening out and, it seems, living up to his nickname. *Desert Mesa* (1935) had no Mormon content at all but was re-released in 1941 as *Mormon Conquest* (unrelated to the 1935 *The Mormon Conquest* discussed below), and in 1938 *Utah Trail* dealt with protecting a railroad from a gang of outlaws, apparently having nothing to do with Mormons or even the Mormon Trail implied by the title. After his death in 1938, two films depicted a fictionalized version of the real-life outlaw-turned-lawman Matt Warner from Ephraim, Utah, known in his renegade years as the Mormon Kid. The first of these was *Tenting Tonight on the Old Camp Ground* in 1943, about a group of outlaws opposing the construction of a new road, and it was followed by *Thunder Town* in 1946, where a reformed Warner serves as a foil against the protagonist, another outlaw attempting make good; this film's hero even has an outlaw sidekick ironically named Utah McGirk.

As mentioned in Chapter 2, after Reed Smoot's successful suppression of Fox's *Riders of the Purple Sage* and *The Rainbow Trail* in 1921, various other adaptations of Zane Grey novels omitted their Mormon characters. These included *The Heritage of the Desert* in 1924, 1932 (directed by Henry Hathaway), and 1939; new versions of *Riders* and *Rainbow* in 1925 with Tom Mix, 1931 and '32 with George O'Brien, and just *Riders* in 1941 with George Montgomery; and *Wild Horse Mesa* in 1925, 1932, and 1947. Nor was Grey the only author to have his Mormon characters excised in adaptation: a 1933 Hollywood version of *A Study in Scarlet* replaced the frontier American Mormons with a modern London secret society. The pattern continued through the early 1950s: the Roy Rogers musical *Utah* (1945) for Republic was about recovering a lost ranch; the outdoor adventure film *The Big Cat* (1949) was about hunting down a dangerous cougar in modern-day Utah, where the film was also shot; *Salt Lake Raiders* (1950), also for Republic, depicted a lawman sent after an escaped fugitive who claims he's innocent and how they must work together to overpower a gang of outlaws; *The Hills of Utah* (1951), a Gene Autry vehicle, was a period piece dealing with a conflict between ranchers and miners; and *Utah Wagon Train* (1951) was about a modern-day reenactment of a pioneer wagon train featuring murder and a secret cache of old California gold. None of these mentioned Mormonism, despite the obvious potential to do so. One interesting variation came from the United Kingdom in one scene in Powell and Pressburger's war film *49th Parallel* (1941), in which a German U-boat crew stranded in Canada must work their way south to the neutral United States. At one point the men come to an apparently religious community and one crew member asks a girl if the locals are Mormons; amused, she responds that they're Hutterites.[25]

In features from Hollywood and London, then, Mormons were defined as much by their absence as anything else, making it fitting that there were more rumored and unrealized films about Mormonism in the 1930s than there were actual finished films. Certainly some of these were serious projects that had to be abandoned in development, a common practice both then and now, but others probably were nothing more than evidence that Mormons' newfound respectability provided plenty of grist for the rumor mill, especially in Utah. The first of these reaches back to the First Wave in 1929, essentially on the heels of *All Faces West*'s disastrous release, when independent producer William R. Irwin created a new production company and announced a series of films based on American history, with the first, called *Souls of Mettle,* about the Mormon pioneers. A script was written by Dolores Carlyne and the film was to be executed with synchronized sound throughout and even some scenes filmed in color, another cutting-edge technology at the time. Production was to begin at the Tec-Art Studios in Los Angeles in September or October 1929, but nothing more is known of it. Given the timing of the film's demise, it's possible Irwin planned well for the talkies only to fall victim to the initial crash of the Great Depression.[26]

Starting in 1933, Paramount, MGM, and Universal all reportedly began investigating positive film subjects on Mormonism, but nothing was initiated. Paramount's project, announced in *Variety* in April 1933, was essentially a Brigham Young biopic directly inspired by James Cruze's *The Covered Wagon* (1923) and would be based "around Young's colonization accomplishments, and continuing down to the present day."[27] Multiple screenwriters were then pitching treatments, but apparently the project was never greenlit. In 1935 representatives from Universal met with Joseph Breen at the Production Code office to discuss a potential film about Brigham Young and the Mormon pioneers. They had hired a great-grandson of Young named Harvey Gage to write the screenplay, but Breen discouraged them from pursuing it, saying the polygamy angle might be too difficult to navigate, and whether for this reason or another the project was dropped.[28] On December 26, 1936 the *Deseret News* chronicled Hollywood's recent interest in the Mormon pioneer story. "Cecil B. DeMille has long been interested in this subject," it claimed. Gary Cooper, who had worked in southern Utah before, "has voiced an interest in playing such a role in a picture depicting the Pioneers and their settlement of the West," as had DeMille's frequent leading man Henry Wilcoxon. And the historian, novelist, playwright, and Oscar-nom-inated screenwriter Rupert Hughes was just finishing a story about Mormon handcart pioneers called "Sealed" that he wanted to adapt to film as well. In his story a non-Mormon "young man falls in love with a Mormon girl and goes west with them," a trope that was quickly becoming a staple in the newly positive pioneer stories. But most exciting was the announcement of a romantic drama set, uniquely, in the 1857 Utah War. It was to be produced by E. B. Derr, who apparently wasn't associated with a major studio, and feature his frequent collaborator, western star Tom Keene; the scenario was by John T. Neville, reportedly with assistance from the Church Historian's office, which was then under the direction of apostle Joseph Fielding Smith, the son of the late Joseph F. Smith and a future Church President himself. Unlike many films that climaxed with the miracle of the seagulls saving the pioneers' crops, this film, which was untitled, would begin at that point then move forward to 1857 with the approach of Johnston's Army to reign in the rebellious Mormons. Keene was to portray a U.S. soldier who, predictably, falls in love with a Mormon girl. Brigham Young would be the dominant persona yet would never appear onscreen: "His voice will be heard throughout the film, but because it is felt he can not [sic] be truly depicted he will not be shown pictorially," a strategy often used with Jesus Christ in films of the sound era. Although this is surprising, the manner in which Mormonism as a belief system was to be handled—positively but essentially as cyphers—was entirely typical of the Production Code era: "The Mormon people are to be glorified because of their great achievements," the film's announcement said. "Because of the great delicacy necessary to handle religious subjects, there will be no reference made to the gospel in the picture." Shooting of snow scenes was to begin in February 1937, but the film apparently was never completed, if it was even begun.[29]

Finally, in July 1941, ten months after Twentieth Century-Fox's *Brigham Young* came out, western producer Harry Sherman announced a film for Paramount called *Utah*. It would "trace the history of the state from its discovery to the present." Harold Lamb, who had written DeMille's *The Plainsman* in 1936, was working on the screenplay, and the budget was estimated around $1 million. One must imagine that Paramount calculated the reception of *Brigham Young* into their ultimate decision to, apparently, cancel this production; either Fox's film had performed too poorly to justify the cost or, at minimum, it had saturated the market for a historical epic on a Mormon theme. It's also possible that the attack on Pearl Harbor and the film industry's realignment to a war economy caused Paramount to jettison it, but in any case nothing more came of the project.[30]

The only apparent exception to the 1930's rule of positive if anonymous representations of Mormons came in November 1936 with a sexploitation film called *Polygamy*. The Production Code, while voluntary, provided strong incentives to major studios to comply, as they would presumably be unable to show their films and hence suffer financially without its approval. But it also created a subsidiary market for small companies that found success by pushing against the MPDDA's strictures or ignoring them entirely and playing to adults in independent theaters known as grindhouses. *Polygamy* didn't sidestep the MPDDA entirely like this, but certainly pushed the limits of what was allowed: it was an adult exploitation film emphasizing sex and set in the world of modern-day polygamy, but it surprisingly received a Production Code seal, number 2732. Historian Richard Nelson speculates that the film's strong denunciation of polygamy may have made up for its sexualized content, thus allowing it to finagle MPDDA approval; like many other films of the time, it was a case of basking in the lurid while giving just enough lip service to its condemnation.

Polygamy was produced by J. D. Kendis, who specialized in sexploitation films with names like *Gambling with Souls* (1936) and *Slaves in Bondage* (1937), through a new company called Unusual Pictures. Pat Carlyle directed and wrote the screenplay with Lillian Gaffney. Instead of looking back to Mormonism's nineteenth-century polygamous past, they found inspiration for their story in the recent revelation of a polygamous Mormon enclave in the town of Short Creek, Arizona (present day Colorado City), on the Utah border near St. George. President Grant was much harder on polygamists than President Smith had been, and in 1933 his second counselor J. Reuben Clark instigated a purge of polygamists from Church membership, including excommunicating nearly the entire population of Short Creek. Utah also made cohabitation—as well as bigamy—a felony in 1935. Polygamist leaders like Lorin Woolley and John Barlow responded by strengthening both their colony outside the state and their own ecclesiastical authority, which eventually led to the creation of the Fundamentalist Church of Jesus Christ of Latter-day Saints, the most important breakaway movement in the history of the Salt Lake City-based Church. *Polygamy* was the first of many films and television shows inspired by the Short Creek colony, with subsequent titles including *Big Love* (2006-11), *Electrick Children, Escape from Polygamy* (both 2013), and of course *Child Bride of Short Creek* (1981), as well as documentaries like *Sons of Perdition* (2010) and *Prophet's Prey* (2015).

In 1935 the Short Creek polygamists came to national attention, making a film on them topical as well as salacious. Basing their screenplay on the book *I*

The Second Wave: Home Cinema

Am a Polygamist by Peter Salia, Carlyle and Gaffney apparently found a way to tell a moralizing melodrama that would satisfy the censors but with plenty of titillation and female flesh on display. The finished film ran fifty-four minutes over nine reels, the plot dealing with a young woman (Ruth Marien) torn between duty to her polygamist family and her non-polygamist lover. It had a national release in 1936—one photograph shows a crowd waiting for a screening in Detroit—and it was released under new titles two additional times: first as *Child Marriage*, probably in 1939, and again as *Illegal Wives* in 1945.

Since we're unable to see it today, we shouldn't simply dismiss *Polygamy* as pornography, or even as the last of the early anti-Mormon films. We cannot know how prurient it was, but one can imagine that the Hays Office would not have approved anything too explicit. Inferring the protagonist's relationship with two men or the male characters' relationships with multiple wives would have been scandalous in itself, and while *Polygamy* may have included some sex it probably mirrored the pre-Code films of Mae West more closely than Hedy Lamarr's famous nudity and sex scene in *Ecstasy* (1933), and certainly much more than recent sexual films like *Basic Instinct* (1992) and *Blue Is the Warmest Color* (2013). Furthermore, *Polygamy* is a film of historical importance, simply because it's the only movie dealing with American polygamy that was made in the 1930s, a time when the movement that would become the FLDS Church was gaining strength as a serious alternative form of Mormonism to the LDS and RLDS Churches.[31]

Newsreels and Nonfiction

In the 1930s the advent of synchronized sound revolutionized newsreels and documentaries just as much as scripted features. Mormon celebrations and economic activities related to the Depression drew the attention of nonfiction filmmakers, and these types of productions were also able to deal with the contemporary Church without worrying about the thorny issue of polygamy; all nonfiction films that recounted the Mormons' pioneer past simply omitted mention of the objectionable practice. The result was a plethora of short documentary films throughout the '30s and '40s that painted a remarkably positive portrait of Utah and the Church, and if they were doctrinally vague, like contemporary fiction films, they were also quite explicit in their praise of Mormon faith and industry, making them thematically closer to later films like *Brigham Young* and *Wagon Master*, which wore their Mormonism openly, than early Production Code films like *The Man from Utah*.

In the late 1920s different studios developed their own proprietary technology in the race toward synchronized sound. At Fox, William Fox bought the Movietone system of optical sound-on-film in 1926 and used it to create music and sound effects in F. W. Murnau's *Sunrise* in 1927 and then synchronized dialogue in *Mother Knows Best* in September 1928. In between these productions Fox added sound to its newsreels, changing their name to Fox Movietone News, and one of their very first subjects announced with this new capability was the Salt Lake Tabernacle organ. Reed Smoot, who now had a cordial personal relationship with Fox, may have suggested the topic and certainly encouraged President Grant to give permission. Although *Variety* carried the announcement of the film in January 1928, initial searches in Fox Movietone archives haven't yet revealed that the project was actually completed. It probably did, however, start Grant thinking about the possibility of having a Hollywood news crew film inside the Tabernacle, and the perfect opportunity was quick in coming in the form of the centennial pageant *The Message of the Ages*, which will be discussed below.[32]

Synchronized sound also caused renewed interest in travelogues and regional portraits, and in March 1935 Warner Brothers released a ten- or eleven-minute film called *The Mormon Trail* as part of travelogue expert E. M. Newman's "See America First" series, which used Warner's Vitaphone sound system. It begins at the tombs of Abraham Lincoln and Ulysses Grant, then shifts to Utah with shots of the *Eagle Gate*, the Salt Lake Temple, the Tabernacle, and tithing house, as well as other monuments to Mormon history or possibly even recreated scenes of pioneers in Utah's founding years. The part of the production in New York City, perhaps involving Grant's Tomb, involved the Brooklyn Branch in some capacity—a branch is like a small ward. Though we don't know their involvement or if they reenacted scenes from Church history, we do know the congregation donated the $100 they earned toward the refurbishment of their chapel.[33]

Reenactments would form the heart of MGM's *The Miracle of Salt Lake* three years later. That film, also eleven minutes, follows the Mormons from their homes in Illinois, across the plains to Salt Lake City, and to their deliverance from starvation with the miracle of the gulls, which embodies the miracle of the film's title. It was written and narrated by Carey Wilson, a skillful screenwriter who already had Victor Sjöström's *He Who Gets Slapped* (1924), the Marx Brothers' *A Night at the Opera* (1935), and Frank Lloyd's *Mutiny on the Bounty* (1935) on his resume, and directed by Basil Wrangell, a Russian American best known as a film editor; he'd received an Oscar nomination for cutting *The Good Earth* just the previous year. Since *The Miracle of Salt Lake* contains so much footage of actors in period costume, one may question whether it should be considered a documentary at all or a fiction film, but it fit squarely within ideas about nonfiction filmmaking at the time, in which events were often recreated and subjects directed in their actions. Also, there was no traditional protagonist or psychological development and no speaking roles—all the action was explained through Wilson's narration. Mormon historian Ardis Parshall has described it as "more of a pageant than a movie,"[34] with one scene progressing steadily into another. In all of these ways it was apparently modeled on the federally funded films coming out of the New Deal, particularly Pare Lorentz's *The Plow That Broke the Plains* (1937), about the Dust Bowl in the Great Plains, and *The River* (1938), about the Tennessee Valley Authority. *The Plow That Broke the Plains* in particular was a landmark in documentary filmmaking, drinking deeply from the theories and work of Sergei Eisenstein in the USSR and moving the art of film music forward through Virgil Thomson's modern score, and it's likely that an accomplished film editor like Wrangell would have wanted to duplicate its style and technique as he transitioned into directing, and an accomplished writer like Wilson would have sought to match Lorentz's ornately poetic narration. How they arrived at the historical topic of the Mormon exodus is unknown, but their approach seems exactly in tune with the foremost Soviet-influenced documentary techniques of the day, including not just Lorentz's work but government-sponsored films from the United Kingdom like *Drifters* (1929) and *The Song of Ceylon* (1934) as well.

Even without knowing this cinematic pedigree, Mormons were thrilled with such a succinct and powerful portrayal of their sacred heritage onscreen, and, more surprisingly, the film was immensely popular with general audiences as well. It played across the United States and certainly showed in England—where missionary and future apostle Marvin J. Ashton estimated that one million people saw it during its eight-week run at London's Empire Theatre, helping prompt him to call 1938 "a banner year in the British Isles"[35]—and reportedly in various other countries also. The climactic miracle of the gulls appears to have been universally affecting: Parshall has written that "it wasn't only Mormon audiences who cheered at the end of the short film in tribute to a people who could not be conquered."[36] Why such a change from the sometimes violent response to *Trapped by the Mormons* sixteen years earlier? Beyond the issues already discussed about the Second Wave in general, it's likely that the Great Depression itself had much to do with it: just as it had made a surprise hit of Walt Disney's *Three Little Pigs* in 1933, the Depression made audiences newly sympathetic to the beleaguered but stoic Mormons onscreen. At a time when economies had crumbled and fields gone fallow, seeing the Mormon settlers overcome their own displacement and potential starvation through personal grit, communal effort, and, finally, the grace of God must have served as an emotional rallying cry just as much as asking, "Who's afraid of the Big Bad Wolf?" The Depression served as an equalizer: audiences now saw Mormons as stand-ins for themselves rather than the feared Other they had been for so many decades. Though a modest short film, *The Miracle of Salt Lake* therefore marks how thoroughly different this period was from the silent era. In June 1939 Salt Lake City's local MGM representative presented President Grant with a copy of the film to be stored in the Church archives, presumably the first time that had ever happened.[37]

In 1938 Utah and the Church were featured in their longest travelogue yet when Universal Pictures' Commercial Department produced *Desert Empire* for the Denver and Rio Grande Western Railroad, which began producing films to promote rail travel around 1936. A three-reel thirty-two minute film about areas surrounding the Rio Grande's Utah railroad lines, the film was produced by Robert M. Connell and directed by Carlton T. Sills, the Advertising & Publicity Manager for the Denver & Rio Grande Western railroad. The most famous crew member was Jack Foley, the artist who essentially invented the process, since named after him, of recording sounds during postproduction to match with onscreen action. In this case, however, he is credited with composing the film's score, something he also did, without receiving screen credit, on at least one other occasion, Universal's *Up for Murder* (1931), if not more.

Desert Empire's structure was familiar: "Treated in dramatic fashion, this motion picture shows the development of irrigation in Utah, completely pictures the operation of the Bingham Mine of the Utah Copper Company . . . and portrays the scenic wonders of Salt Lake City, with special emphasis on the Mormon Temple Grounds"[38] along with recreation at the Saltair Pavilion and industries like agriculture. The urban and religious content comes near the end, bearing tribute to the organizing genius of Brigham Young and praising items like the *Emigration Canyon Monument*, which would be replaced by Mahonri Young's much more massive *This Is the Place Monument* nine years later, and a large reconstruction of a beehive—the state symbol, derived from Book of Mormon imagery—out of living cacti on the Temple Square grounds. It briefly goes inside the Tabernacle for an organ recital by Frank Asper. The narrator Don Wilson again recounts the miracle of the gulls, as well as Joseph Smith's early visions, then Heber Grant speaks directly to the camera about welcoming visitors to Utah and how the desert has blossomed as the rose, an application of Isaiah 35:1 to modern Utah frequently made by Church members even today. Grant's face is double exposed over landscape shots of regions seen earlier in the film and shots of pioneer wagons and handcarts. He concludes with an interesting plug for the film's sponsor: "I was born and raised in this valley and was a passenger on the first Rio Grande train into Salt Lake City more than half a century ago." As the viewers symbolically ride away on a Rio Grande train to their next stop, the narrator emphatically declares, "Dreams do come true. Brigham Young's prophecy is fulfilled. Utah *is* the desert empire."

Though the state's economy had not returned to full force, there are tellingly no effects of the Depression seen here: prosperity is both the sign of the Mormons' industry and the region's allure for potential Rio Grande passengers. And that, ultimately, was the purpose of the film—as a half-hour advertisement. As such, all the railroad's films were "not only shown to non-theatrical audiences, but are also used for such special events as the Colorado and Utah State Fairs, travel shows in Chicago and New York, and similar events. In such events, the Rio Grande uses its own complete portable 'little theater' which is set up at the event, and a variety of films is shown throughout each day of the show."[39] Short travelogues may have been shown in traditional theaters before feature presentations, but all longer pieces like this would have had similar exhibition techniques.

In 1940 British Pathé's four-minute film *Wings of the West!* recreated an airplane journey from New York to San Francisco; while passing over Utah the narrator describes it as "the historic mecca of the Mormons," followed by shots of Temple Square—which seems to misidentify the temple as the Tabernacle—and the Bingham Canyon copper mine. While this entire sequence only takes a few seconds, it may have been the first aerial footage of the temple and its surroundings.[40]

On August 20, 1943, building off their feature film *Brigham Young*, Twentieth Century-Fox released Lowell Thomas's nine-minute *Mormon Trails,* a Technicolor film which featured some footage of the Bingham Canyon copper mine—a strong draw for visiting filmmakers—and Salt Lake City, including the temple and other Mormon sites, but focused primarily on the vistas of southern Utah like Bryce Canyon and Zion National Park.[41] The next year, 1944, MGM responded with three films, all in Technicolor, from James A. FitzPatrick's "Traveltalk" series, although one source reports that they took a combined three years to produce: *Salt Lake Diversions* in February, a nine-minute film which passes through Salt Lake City but emphasizes recreation at the Great Salt Lake; *City of Brigham Young* in June, which starts at the lake then returns to the city to discuss Young's legacy and events like the seagulls and the crickets, and show the Tabernacle Choir singing; and *Monumental Utah*, which received the highest praise, in November. This moved south to feature footage of Zion National Park, Bryce Canyon, and other sites near the Arizona border; as with *Mormon Trails*, the Technicolor footage was praised for revealing the deep reds and oranges of the rock surfaces, but in contrast to that film, this time the footage was accompanied by additional music from the Tabernacle Choir. At least the latter two films premiered at the Studio Theatre in Salt Lake to civic and Church leaders. On January 24, 1945, a young Mormon named Allen Cornwall was serving on a destroyer in the Pacific theater when he saw *City of Brigham Young* aboard the ship. His father J. Spencer Cornwall was the conductor of the choir, and it moved him deeply to watch his father leading the music back home while he was thousands of miles away fighting in the war.[42]

These films frequently dealt with the industry and success of the Mormons as a counterpoint to the realities of the Depression, but the truth is that Church members in Utah and throughout the world were hard hit, and their leaders' responses to these needs fundamentally changed how the Church has cared for its poor ever since. President Grant, a one-time Democrat, was horrified by the New Deal and its shift toward the welfare state, which he saw as breeding indolence while weakening church and family. Thus he sought to develop a relief system that could provide for the destitute while teaching the value of labor and upholding the principles of Progressivism; for decades afterwards Mormons have quoted the First Presidency's 1936 statement, read by Grant in general conference, railing against "the evils of the dole" and expressing the desire that work "be re-enthroned as a ruling principle in the lives of our Church membership."[43] Grant discovered the vigorous personification of this philosophy in the person of Harold B. Lee, stake president of the Pioneer Stake in Salt Lake City—and the youngest stake president in the entire Church. While every ward, bishop, and Relief Society was heavily taxed caring for their needy, Lee had gone one step further and established programs like cooperatively operated farms, storehouses, and canneries, in which the out-of-work were able to donate labor in return for goods. In 1935 Lee presented his "security" plan to the First Presidency, in 1936 it was adopted Church-wide, and in 1941 Lee was called to the Quorum of the Twelve, where he would become perhaps its most influential member in the entire twentieth century.[44]

The Second Wave: Home Cinema

The success of what was eventually known as the Church Welfare Program caught the attention of nonfiction film companies. In 1936 Paramount News released a short newsreel that featured the "new Mormon relief plan" along with stories about college basketball, a baby panda in the U.S., moving the Presidential inauguration to January for the first time, and a singing mouse making its radio debut.[45] While that was in theaters in December, another crew from Time Inc. spent nearly two weeks in Salt Lake City filming an episode of the acclaimed *The March of Time* series. These films grew out of a popular CBS radio program of the same name and played in theaters from 1935 through 1951, when the brand moved to television. These were not typical newsreels: installments appeared monthly rather than weekly and were longer than typical, covering just two or three topics over an entire half hour; they favored deep-dive journalism with a progressive editorial position. The series received an honorary Academy Award in 1937, the year its episode on Mormonism played in cinemas. This episode—volume three, issue six—was released on January 22, and also included stories about cancer research and Florida's winter tourism industry; the portion on the Church was simply called *Mormonism*. It included a brief history of the Church, footage of Church leaders like Grant and McKay examining and speaking about their economic relief efforts, a discussion of the one hundred employment and cooperative work initiatives then underway, a Catholic priest's perspective, and footage from around the area, particularly of sites that related to economic issues like the presiding bishop's office where members are paying their tithing, and a Church-run farm and store. Through its narration, spoken by Westbrook Van Voorhis, the film emphasized Grant's personal belief that idleness was the greatest sin and that a fundamental tenet of Mormonism was that every member should be self-sufficient. "The result," wrote *Music and the Spoken Word*'s Richard L. Evans, himself soon to become a Seventy, "was an eminently newsworthy picture, informative and entertaining—skillfully photographed, skillfully edited—dealing with Church traditions, personalities and projects,"[46] although the *Motion Picture Daily* critic found slightly less to praise, saying the entire episode was good but of "perhaps of less immediate significance than many previous issues [in the *March of Time* series], and likewise with somewhat less dramatic and emotional appeal...."[47] Still, as a *March of Time* film this episode had a tremendous national and international reach—playing in England in May 1937, for instance—and must have provided a great deal of positive publicity for the Church as the Depression dragged on through FDR's second term. In later years rights to *The March of Time* shifted from Time, Inc. to HBO to, most recently, Getty Images, which has made very brief fragments of the film available online, with the entire production available for licensing.[48]

Pathé's *Mormons Celebrate Centenary* (discussed below), the *March of Time*'s *Mormonism* episode, and *The Miracle of Salt Lake* were arguably the most important short nonfiction films from the Second Wave, but there were occasional others that were neither about the state of Utah nor the Church's welfare program. In late 1930 an unknown camera operator filmed J. Reuben Clark, in his capacity as Hoover's Ambassador to Mexico, presenting his credentials to President Pascual Ortiz Rubio; 100 feet of 16mm film footage of this is held in the Church History Library. While many of the newsreels of the 1930s recounted the 1848 episode of the seagulls and the crickets, modern farmers had to find more prosaic solutions to these pests, so in 1939 the United States Department of Agriculture produced a twenty-two minute documentary called *The Mormon Cricket*, compiling footage of the insects from many commercial films of the previous years and discussing its migratory habits and how to mitigate crop damage it could cause, a slightly comical update in how the Mormon cricket problem was addressed in the 1940s compared with the 1840s. Overall, however, there were fewer nonfiction films on the Church in the 1940s than the 1930s, although Salt Lake City's 1947 centennial celebration drew national attention. This was because, first, the end of the Depression and advent of World War II simply made Mormonism less newsworthy, and, second, by the end of the war television was poised to take over journalism from the movie theater, leading to an overall decrease in the newsreel format. One example from early in the decade was when Republican presidential candidate Wendell Willkie, who had just emerged as the dark horse nominee at the party's National Convention a few weeks earlier, spoke at Salt Lake City's Pioneer Day parade in 1940, causing the event to be filmed by Paramount and Pathé and perhaps other studios. In 1949 the Standard Oil Company released a thirty-one-minute travelogue called *Utah—The Rainbow Land*; Standard Oil was quite involved with funding location-based documentary work at this time, most famously Robert Flaherty's *Louisiana Story* from the year before. The title of this picture was probably a reference to Rainbow Bridge National Monument in southern Utah, as the film featured various landmarks, Mormon and otherwise, and landscapes from throughout the state. Likewise, in 1950 Carl Dudley Productions created an eleven-minute film for their *This Land of Ours* series title *Utah: The Center of Scenic America*. Sportswriter Henry Grantland Rice produced a few episodes of his monthly *Sportlights* newsreel in Utah, and in June 1952 the visit of new Church President David O. McKay to Stockholmwas sufficiently novel that *Paramount Svenska Journalen (Paramount Swedish Journal)* covered it, but it did not warrant much attention back home.[49]

The Second Wave: Home Cinema

Attitudes toward Mormons became so sympathetic and even admiring in this period that in December 1935 an advertiser in Lynchburg, South Carolina created a short film to compare himself with the respectable Mormons. As one LDS viewer reported:

> It was in an advertisement on the screen that I saw the great Mormon Temple; I was also thrilled at the kind remarks the advertiser made about the Mormon pioneers, of their being driven from Missouri, their trials and persecutions, and how they built a beautiful city in Utah and erected their great temple. The advertiser used the temple for only one purpose and that was to impress on the minds of the people that his business had grown and prospered under the same virtues as did the Mormons; and those virtues were faith, courage, and honesty.[50]

This was a welcome message during the Depression years, and it encapsulates how the Mormon image moved beyond the requirements of the Production Code to create an entirely new, wholesome, and admirable persona, even while perhaps conflating Mormonism with Utah too broadly. Mormons were remade into representative Americans and their history an example of American values triumphing in the West, a timely theme as Americans came together to deal with the economic downturn. Interestingly fiction films trailed behind documentaries in this respect: in the 1930s the new Code made fiction filmmakers leery of giving any depth or specificity to Mormon characters, while documentarians and journalists were able to probe the contemporary Church in an impressive degree of detail. As the Depression receded with the war and postwar era, however, three westerns and a western-themed documentary treated Mormonism with both the sympathy of Production Code features like *The Man from Utah* and the specificity of newsreels like *The Miracle of Salt Lake*. Films in the Third Wave would once again become more critical and nuanced, making these eleven years in the Second Wave the high point of Mormonism's relationship with classical Hollywood studio filmmaking. The films were *Brigham Young* (1940), *Bad Bascomb* (1946), and *Wagon Master* (1950), along with the documentary *The Mormon Battalion* (1950).

The Major Features: 1940-1950

Without question, Twentieth Century-Fox Film Corporation's *Brigham Young* was the highest profile film on Mormonism ever made to that point—and arguably ever. As mentioned in Chapter 2, William Fox had proposed making a positive film on the Church to Reed Smoot in 1921 but no action was taken. He left the studio in 1930 and, on the verge of collapse, it merged with Twentieth Century in 1935. The new company retained Twentieth Century's Joseph Schenck as Chairman and CEO and Fox's Sidney Kent as President, but creatively the studio belonged to Darryl F. Zanuck, a thirty-seven-year-old World War I veteran who'd worked his way up from a screenwriter to producer to cofounder, with Schenck, of Twentieth Century, to, now, Twentieth Century-Fox's Vice President of Production. Zanuck spent most of his career at the studio and was one of Hollywood's most powerful moguls, guiding Twentieth Century-Fox's house style, earning three Best Picture Academy Awards for himself—for *How Green Was My Valley* (1941), *Gentleman's Agreement* (1947), and *All About Eve* (1950)—and overseeing numerous other award-winning productions. "By 1940, Zanuck had brought the infant Twentieth Century-Fox studio from obscurity at its founding in 1935 to prominence as one of the top film studios boasting the commercially successful stars Alice Faye, Don Ameche, Henry Fonda, and Zanuck's own discovery, Tyrone Power."[51] His later years were somewhat less financially and artistically successful; he briefly left to work independently in the late '50s, and the studio steadily lost money in the few years before his 1971 retirement. But throughout his long career he was responsible for hits like *42nd Street* (1933), *In Old Chicago* (1938), *The Grapes of Wrath* (1940), *Twelve O'Clock High* (1949), *The Sun Also Rises* (1957), and *The Longest Day* (1962). And of the over two hundred films that he personally produced or executive produced, he once said that his favorite was 1940's *Brigham Young*.[52]

Studios like Universal and Paramount had been considering the Brigham Young story for some time, and it appears that there were several impetuses that caused Zanuck to finally undertake it at Fox in 1939. In May 1938 Eleanor Harris, a junior staff writer, submitted a twenty-eight page treatment called "Prophets of Empire" that covered the exact timeframe as the finished film, from the Mormons' expulsion from Nauvoo to the miracle of the seagulls in Salt Lake City. Zanuck rejected it twice, judging that polygamy was too difficult to navigate and the Mormon story would be hollow and artificial without it. By early 1939, however, a theater owner in Kansas submitted a nine-page treatment, and this time Zanuck decided it could be done. He briefly assigned Harris and a former Mormon named James Woolley to the project, followed by the writing team of Eleanor Griffin and William Rankin, who completed their own separate treatment as well.

Soon outside events changed the direction of the project. Lost Generation author Vardis Fisher completed his novel *Children of God*, a fictionalized version of the Mormon saga from Joseph Smith's childhood to Wilford Woodruff's Manifesto, and submitted it for consideration for the Harper Prize, which it would eventually win, in 1939. Pulitzer Prize-winning novelist Louis Bromfield, a friend of Zanuck's, was on the judging panel and immediately called Zanuck when he finished reading the unpublished manuscript, supposedly persuading him over the phone to buy the rights sight unseen. Zanuck hired Bromfield to develop it, replacing the earlier writers, and he spent eight months traveling Mormon country, corresponding with Church leaders and historians, visiting worship services, talking with pioneer descendants including three of Brigham Young's children, and researching at the Church archives in Salt Lake City. When the scope of his research proved too voluminous for him to trim down, veteran Twentieth Century-Fox executive and writer Lamar Trotti, best remembered for his collaborations with John Ford, came in to shape it into a dramatic narrative. Over the course of seven major drafts the sermons and "intricacies of Mormon history"[53] were whittled down to produce a trim and efficient narrative. There was very little left of Vardis Fisher in the final product.

The film was announced to the public in June 1939 by Fox director John Ford, implying that he might have originally been attached to direct.[54] However, fresh off the combined success of *Stagecoach* and the full-color *Drums Along the Mohawk* (both 1939), he was ultimately chosen to direct *The Grapes of Wrath*, which began principal photography in October 1939 and presumably made him unavailable for anything else. Zanuck then tried to secure Clarence Brown from MGM—Brown was known for directing Greta Garbo in *Anna Christie* (1930) and *Anna Karenina* (1935) and he had just directed Bromfield's *The Rains Came* (1939) while on loan to Fox—but ultimately forty-one-year-old Henry Hathaway, another Fox director, was selected instead.[55] Hathaway began his career in 1925 primarily as an assistant director, then in 1932 he directed his first film, an adaptation of Zane Grey's *The Heritage of the Desert.* He specialized in westerns, especially from Grey's books, and action films, reaching some of his highest critical praise with the Indian-set adventure *Lives of a Bengal Lancer* in 1935. Moving from Paramount to Fox, he directed Tyrone Power, the studio's biggest star, in the noir *Johnny Apollo* (1940), which may have prompted Zanuck to select him for this film.

Mormon Church officials had to learn about the picture from the newspaper, and Heber Grant immediately reached out to Twentieth Century-Fox President Sidney Kent to offer the Church's assistance, based on the belief that collaboration was the best way to ensure that Mormons were pleased with the result.

Zanuck quickly agreed. If there were any doubts about whether the Church should be involved with such a production—distrust of the industry may have still run high, along with memories of failed features from not many years earlier like *All Faces West* (1929) and *Corianton*—Grant must have immediately overridden them. Over 60% of Americans attended the cinema each week throughout the '30s, and "the movies were near the operative center of the nation's consciousness. They played an indispensable role in sustaining and stimulating the national imagination."[56] Eager for an opportunity to take advantage of this influence since the Church's 1930 centennial, he recognized what this film could do for the Church's public image and wasn't about to second guess an opportunity to work with a major studio to create a positive film on the Mormon story. "This film will be a friendmaker," he declared.[57] Bromfield and Trotti were both welcomed at Church headquarters to conduct their research, and Zanuck, associate producer Kenneth Macgowan, and other officials were in close contact with Church officials. Their primary host and liaison was apostle John A. Widtsoe, whom Grant assigned to be an advisor on the script; he provided Bromfield with most of his contacts and information and worked closely with Trotti as the script neared completion. When the film entered production, George Pyper, now leading the Sunday School as its general superintendent, worked on set as a historical and technical advisor. Now eighty years old, he was only one generation removed from the pioneers, and his years of dramatic experience reportedly made him an exacting presence on set as he paid strict attention to every historical detail. "Wisely juxtaposing the Church's goals with those of the studio, President Grant told Fox executives, 'Don't pay too much attention to that brother. We've got to have box office in this picture.'"[58]

But despite his public enthusiasm, Grant quietly remained worried; the potential for disaster—another *Mormon Maid,* for instance—remained high, particularly since believing Mormons viewed Vardis Fisher's *Children of God* with acrimony and saw it as an inaccurate history with too much emphasis on polygamy. The very same day he had written to Kent at Fox, Grant also wrote to Will Hays seeking his assistance in making sure that the picture would reflect well upon the Mormons, and it was primarily with the purpose of mitigating Fisher's influence that John Widtsoe was assigned to the film. Accordingly, Widtsoe repeatedly denigrated the book in his correspondence with Kenneth Macgowan, calling it an "indecent book" and "a biased and incomplete novel about polygamy," while dismissing Fisher as a neurotic author overwhelmed by the scope of his subject.[59] For months Grant confided his fears in his personal journal, and he revealed his distrust of Louis Bromfield and his enthusiasm for

The Second Wave: Home Cinema

Children of God in an October 22, 1939 letter to an associate: "I have lived in fear that perhaps there might be something in the picture that would be unfavorable to Brigham Young, because of the man who has been writing the scenario has endorsed a book that I think is about as mean as the devil."[60] In one of his many letters to Macgowan Grant explained his difficult position: "I hope we shall not appear to you to be over anxious, and we have no disposition to be oversensitive, but we are tremendously concerned that this picture shall be a true picture, and, while we are not, any of us, playwrights, or dramatists, or Movie technicians, we can appreciate the war which must constantly go on in one preparing a picture, between the highly dramatic and the sober fact."[61] In late October 1939 Grant, Widtsoe, and Grant's first counselor J. Reuben Clark "spent four days at Twentieth Century Fox consulting with executives on matters relating to the production of the film *Brigham Young*."[62] They worked their way with Trotti completely through his script, which largely placated Grant's concerns. There were still issues the Mormons wanted addressed, and Grant remained uneasy until seeing the finished picture, but through their efforts and the requirements of the Production Code, *Brigham Young* was turning out to be a much different narrative than *Children of God*.

Zanuck oversaw the film's casting. Supporting players included Mary Astor as Mary Ann Young and Jane Darwell as Eliza Kent, one of the pioneers; she received a Best Supporting Actress Oscar that same year for portraying Ma Joad in Ford's *The Grapes of Wrath*. The two romantic leads, Tyrone Power and Linda Darnell, were easy to land upon. Power was, as mentioned, Zanuck's personal discovery and the currently the studio's leading man. Darnell had only appeared in supporting roles before this—*Brigham Young* was her first lead—but she was already considered one of Fox's top stars and had appeared opposite Power in *Day-Time Wife* in 1939; their onscreen chemistry was so popular with audiences that Zanuck increased the amount of romantic material in *Brigham Young*, reportedly adding eighteen additional love scenes to develop their relationship, and then paired them again in *The Mark of Zorro* (1940), *Blood and Sand* (1941), and other films throughout the '40s.[63]

Darnell and Power played a young fictional couple and served as the audience's entry into the world of Mormonism; the roles were written for them more than they were cast to fill the roles. Casting the historical figures of Joseph Smith and especially Brigham Young proved much more difficult. There were at least twenty-five finalists for the role of Smith, and Zanuck selected a young stage actor named Vincent Price who was trying to transition into films. The fact that today he is probably the best-remembered actor who appeared in *Brigham Young*, and for horror film roles far from the idealistic founder of Mormonism, is ironic but doesn't diminish the quality of his work. His performance, in just a few scenes in the film's opening sequences, is one of the most intriguing and, hence, engaging Joseph Smiths ever committed to film. As James D'arc, the foremost authority on *Brigham Young*, has said, "Youthful Vincent Price as Joseph Smith exuded a dignity and presence"[64] in the role. And Price, in turn, became fascinated with his character, studying more about Joseph Smith, with personal assistance from President Grant, long after the picture was finished.[65]

Zanuck's search for a Brigham Young cast an even wider net. He knew that, despite the popularity of Power and Darnell in the romantic leads, a movie called *Brigham Young* would sink or succeed on the strength of its titular character. Various stars were considered for the role—Laurence Olivier, Don Ameche, and Spencer Tracy among them—but each was rejected, and Zanuck began looking among lesser-known talent. It was on the forty-sixth screen test that he found what he was looking for in stage actor Dean Jagger. Jagger had labored for years on New York's boards and occasionally tried and failed to break into Hollywood as well. It was only now, at age thirty-three, that he had a majorly successful lead role playing Jesse James in *Missouri Legend* on Broadway. This success induced him to attempt the film industry one more time, and thus Darryl Zanuck watched his half-hour screen test while vacationing in Idaho. Like Young, Jagger stood six feet two inches tall and weighed roughly two hundred pounds. On set, Jagger's appearance impressed George Pyper, who was seventeen when Brigham Young died and knew him well. "There are resemblances in facial features and in the voice," he said, adding that Jagger also effectively mimicked Young in his manner of speaking and even his gait and physical actions. "When I watched Mr. Jagger pleading in a courtroom scene, I thought I was listening again to Brigham Young," he claimed.[66] Jagger had a personal coach on Mormonism, an Ogden resident named Len Harbertson, and he dove deeply into the study of every aspect of Young's life. The work paid off: his performance anchors the film, giving Young a cool and aloof exterior that covers up intense passion and consuming self-doubt. The doubt and even the anger at injustices committed against the Mormons that fuel his portrayal make for a multi-layered characterization. He's a man who demands complete respect but who's consumed with doubt that he might not deserve it, both on a personal level and with the entire Church that he inherited from his murdered friend. Though the style may seem dated today, and many Mormons criticized this element of his characterization, it makes Jagger's by far the most interesting Brigham Young ever filmed.

The Second Wave: Home Cinema

The story begins with intense persecution against the Mormons in Nauvoo, starting with a sequence in which the fathers of the Mormon Jonathan Kent (Power) and visiting non-Mormon Zina Webb (Darnell) are killed during a mob raid on the Kent household. Joseph Smith is then arrested on trumped-up charges, leading to a trial in which Brigham gives an impassioned defense of freedom of religion, but Joseph is nevertheless convicted and imprisoned, where he's promptly murdered by a mob. Brigham assumes leadership of the Church and determines to lead it out of the city and westward across the plains, despite opposition from some Church members who rally around rebellious apostle Angus Duncan (a fictional figure played by Brian Donlevy). Brigham acts confidently in front of the others, but he's secretly unsure what God wants him to do; he never receives a clear revelation calling him as a prophet like Joseph did. As the Saints journey west much of the story focuses on a romance between Jonathan, now a scout and protégé of Porter Rockwell (John Carradine), and Zina, who has remained with the Mormons since her father's murder. Potential insurrection under Duncan festers, as some question Brigham's leadership and want to continue on to California, but he convinces them to settle in the Great Salt Lake Valley. When their first crop is threatened by the crickets, the Saints—including Brigham—lose hope, but the arrival of the seagulls shows everyone that God was caring for them after all. "You see, Brigham," his wife Mary Ann says, "he was talking to you all the time."

In part because of the Production Code, but also simply the zeitgeist of the time, Mormon doctrines were deemphasized while the people's grit and faith came to the fore—the pattern for cinematic Mormons throughout this period. As Vincent Price later recalled, "Henry Hathaway avoided any 'religious' feeling and made it a believable story of strong men and women fighting for their faith. He was particularly vehement on this score with the part of Joseph."[67] There was still the issue of polygamy, however, Early in the film's development, Zanuck told Kenneth Macgowan, "The polygamy angle should not be ducked. To do so would rip all semblance of authenticity from the story. It should be hit hard and deliberately. To make the story of Brigham Young and Mormonism and dismiss or timidly handle polygamy would be like making *Alexander Graham Bell* without the telephone, *Jesse James* without guns, or a Columbia picture without Capra."[68] Despite this initial bravado, he could not prevail against the Production Code censors to allow any inclusion of "multiple adultery" that did not also include its harsh condemnation. In the end polygamy is treated only glancingly. Brigham's dozens of wives are reduced down to two. Mary Astor's Mary Ann Young is obvious, but only the truly observant would surmise that the woman played by

Jean Rogers, largely a silent presence in the background, is a stand-in for all of Brigham's other plural wives; at one point the script supposedly called for Brigham to kiss all of them, but Hathaway shot the scene without that, for fear of it playing as comedy. At one point while complimenting Mary Ann, Brigham praises her for never being jealous of the others—though he makes no mention of *what* others he's talking about. When Brigham meets the mountain man Jim Bridger the latter starts to ask, "Say, how many—" and Brigham cuts him off, "Twelve!" Finally, two adjoining scenes in Salt Lake carefully treat it with drama then with humor. First, in a lovers' quarrel, young Eliza tearfully accuses Johnathan of wanting not her but an entire harem, and he leaves on an assignment in frustration. While he is then riding with Porter Rockwell, Porter computes how much progeny a body could get to populate the valley in just a few generations, a staggering sum. "How will we get that many women?" Jonathan asks. "Oh, that's no problem," Porter replies. "Women convert easy." But if Zanuck couldn't have a more open conversation about plural marriage in the film, he made sure to have it in the advertising. Some taglines implied a much more salacious take than the film had, and one poster showed Jagger posing with twelve women, causing *Time* magazine to lament that "only the publicity department gave him his fair share."[69]

After two years of preproduction the film went into principle photography in April 1940. Filming took place over nineteen weeks, 133 days, throughout the summer—the longest shoot since *Gone with the Wind*—with some studio work in Los Angeles but over 80% of the production occurring on six major locations in California, Nevada, and Utah; outdoor sets included Nauvoo, Fort Bridger, the Salt Lake City settlement, and a two-block long sheet of "ice" for the Mormons to cross the frozen Mississippi on foot. The principal cast numbered forty-seven actors, and total personnel totaled around 500 people who traveled almost 2,000 miles before the production concluded. All of this added up, with the finished film eventually costing $2.7 million, roughly $48 million today; numbers on the budget vary, but it seems likely that the production budget was at least $1,485,000 with the remaining amount devoted to publicity. Since the average studio picture at the time cost $200,000, this made *Brigham Young* one of the last big-budget films before the war, and the pressure to make a successful picture was intense, causing Hathaway, in the words of Mary Astor, to drive "his people unmercifully."[70]

Perhaps the most difficult scene to film was the climactic battle between the Mormons and the crickets. Luckily—for the film—an immense swarm of crickets, six miles long and between one and two miles thick, formed outside

The Second Wave: Home Cinema

Elko, Nevada that summer, and the entire crew immediately dropped their other scenes and flew there. They were to shoot among the crickets for a week but the work was so disgusting that a cast walk-out seemed possible, causing Hathaway and Bromfield to speedily rewrite the script and wrap the cricket sequence in a day and a half. Two airplanes herded the crickets out of the mountains into the valley where they could be filmed, and the intrepid actors and crew waded in in their special cricket-proof pantaloons. Astor wrote vividly about the experience:

> The first few hours of the morning were full of practical jokes, with squeals from the girls when somebody would put a cricket down the neck of a dress. But in a very short time, none of it was a joke. We had to go right into the spots where they were worst, with brooms and sacks, beating at them in the tall grain. Two days of this were all any of us could have taken. It was nauseating to walk through them piled to a foot deep in some places, and the stench was awful.[71]

Hathaway surreptitiously filmed a huge flock of seagulls when they appeared in the sky during shooting near Lone Pine, California, where most of the production took place. The crew was recording a love scene when the birds appeared, and this aerial seagull footage was later optically printed onto scenes of the crickets and the pioneers among their homes and crops. Finally, to put the two species together more convincingly, including shots of the birds actually eating the insects, the crew traveled to the Great Salt Lake with thousands of crickets packed on ice; these were let loose to attract the resident seagulls, and soon Hathaway had all the footage he needed, making for a climax as visually stunning as it was emotionally satisfying.

By August 13 the film was edited, scored by prominent composer Alfred Newman, and ready for a private screening for President Grant and a few members of the Church hierarchy at Salt Lake City's Studio Theatre. After the screening Grant told the papers, "I thank Darryl F. Zanuck for a sympathetic presentation of an immortal story. I endorse it with all my heart and have no suggestions to make for any changes. This is one of the greatest days of my life. I can't say any more than 'God bless you.'"[72] In return, Zanuck dedicated the film to Grant and the entire Church. It opened ten days later in Salt Lake City in a gala premiere, then opened nationally a month later, despite a lawsuit from Eleanor Harris, the originator of the entire project, who sought screen credit for her contribution or an injunction against the film's distribution; this was denied and the film's release went ahead as planned.[73]

Friday August 23, 1940, was a slightly rainy day in Salt Lake, but the weather couldn't dampen local enthusiasm for the biggest event in Utah—and Mormon—cinematic history. Both Governor Henry Blood and Mayor Ab Jenkins declared it a holiday, "Brigham Young Day," and shops, businesses, and even schools closed. The city's population swelled from 150,000 to 250,000, with 5,000 at the airport to meet the Twentieth Century-Fox delegation and another 100-175,000 packing the streets to glimpse a parade of Fox's stars, including all the leads of this picture and several other actors like Cesar Romero and Jane Withers—as well as four busloads of Brigham Young descendants. There were shop window competitions and special supplements in both the *Salt Lake Tribune* and *Deseret News*. The First Presidency hosted an afternoon banquet in the Lion House, Brigham Young's old home, to honor the city's guests, and that night seven theaters—the Centre, Capitol, Utah, Paramount, Victory, Studio, and Marlo, all part of the Intermountain Theatres chain—totaling more than 8,700 seats, were all sold out at a pricey $1.10 per ticket for a simultaneous showing, making this the largest world premiere a Hollywood film had yet seen. Jagger, Power, Darnell, Astor, and the other actors rushed from theater to theater to put in personal appearances, though they only made it to five, then flew back to Los Angeles at midnight, with another large crowd in the rain at the airport to send them off. With President Grant's public benediction on the film fresh in their minds, surely these ecstatic Mormons thought that they were entering a new era in how the world perceived their faith.[74]

Brigham Young's general release began on September 20 in New York City's Roxy Theatre, Los Angeles's Grauman's Chinese Theatre, and San Francisco's Paramount Theatre. Though they couldn't replicate the Salt Lake premiere, Fox's advertising team took advantage of the large number of Mormons in southern California: thirty-five Los Angeles meetinghouses had large placards advertising the film set up inside their foyers, and as many as forty-five bishops and branch presidents read President Grant's statement thanking Darryl Zanuck over the pulpit. As part of its general advertising, an ox-drawn prairie schooner was driven through the streets of L.A. and the Goodyear Blimp trolled a banner above local beaches. Reviews in general were strong. James D'arc surveyed dozens of reviews and found only a handful that could be deemed negative. *Newsweek* called it "one of the year's outstanding films," the *Los Angeles Times* "the major motion picture of the year," and movie columnist Louella Parsons said it was "the best picture ever to come out of the 20th Century-Fox Studio and one of the best pictures this reviewer has ever seen." There was dissent, of course, chiefly from the *New York Times*' Bosley Crowther, who disapproved of the film's evasion of polygamy, saying it was "too bad that *Brigham Young* had to be so monog—we mean monotonous."[75]

Tracking the film financially is slightly more difficult. War engulfed Europe and East Asia in 1940, closing up most foreign markets and obscuring the extent of international distribution, although the film did make it to Buenos Aires, as *Hijos de Dios* ("Children of God") in December 1940 and to England in the spring of 1941. *Brigham Young*'s large advertising budget therefore might have represented an attempt to make up for these lost foreign audiences with increased American attendance. The studio feared that in the eastern states the implied religiosity of the film would keep audiences away, hence the subtitle *Frontiersman* was added to emphasize the film as a western, along with taglines like, "The Great American Motion Picture." Still, the general audience was less interested than Fox executives had hoped. It had a typical opening on the U.S. west coast, for instance, but box office revenue fell steeply in the second week. Again, D'arc has synthesized large amounts of trade journal reports to determine how the film was received throughout the country: in Seattle it was "very disappointing" yet in Portland, "very strong," in San Francisco "fair," in Denver "well above average," Chicago very low, Omaha "average," Memphis low ("Mormon leader has more wives than customers in these parts"), Boston and New York average, but Providence, Pittsburgh, and Philadelphia very low. Unique in the east, in Baltimore the film received "consistent day and night trade, pointing to a most satisfying figure." Overall it appears from Twentieth Century-Fox's financial records that the film grossed over $4 million, making it highly profitable, contrary to the popular belief it was a flop, although it was no hit either. In 1941 Zanuck simply stated that the studio's experience with *Brigham Young* "convinced us that the public was not in the mood to patronize a religious picture."[76]

Critics frequently compared it with Zanuck's other large 1940 film *The Grapes of Wrath*, especially in terms of social consciousness: they were both about downtrodden people cast out of their homes through no fault of their own, and, though Zanuck was no liberal, both films seemed to call for some type of communal or even government response. *The Grapes of Wrath* was quite literally about the destitute Okies, of course, but *Brigham Young*'s social relevance played on a metaphorical level, as virtually everyone involved with *Brigham Young*, from Vardis Fisher onward, was extremely aware of the parallels between the American Mormons of the 1840s and the European Jews of the 1930s. As the film began production in spring 1940, Nazi Germany was invading Norway, Denmark, the Netherlands, Belgium, Luxembourg, and France. Some concentration camps had existed since 1938, but on May 20, 1940, while Hathaway's cameras rolled in California, the SS opened a concentration camp under the name Auschwitz outside Oswiecim in Poland—and in July more than 3,000 Alsatian Jews were impounded in Vichy France. Though Americans wouldn't grasp the full extent of the Holocaust until after the war, they were well aware of the Nazis' anti-Semitism and the persecutions European Jews faced. Eleanor Harris in one of her earliest memos connected the Mormons and the Jews in 1938: "With our eyes on today's headlines, nothing could be more topical than the story of the persecuted people who left their country because they must . . . Whose only guide was hope . . . and who, in the midst of desolation, built a triumphant Empire!" Later Fisher wrote Zanuck saying that *Children of God* could be "an antidote to the increasing spread of Fascism and anti-Semitism in this nation." Louis Bromfield was known as one of American's foremost anti-fascists, serving on the executive board of the Emergency Committee to Save the Jewish People of Europe. Zanuck, who was Jewish, compared *Brigham Young* to his earlier picture *The House of Rothschild* (1934), which was explicitly about the persecution of a Jewish banking family, in the very first story conference, comparing the Mormon's "persecution and the pogroms" with both his earlier film and "what is happening abroad today."[77]

Thus when Lamar Trotti came to the screenplay he had anti-Semitism as a firm focus in his mind. This is most evident the courtroom speech Brigham Young gives in defense of Joseph Smith (a fiction since Young was east serving a mission at the time of Smith's arrest and assassination). Instead of defending Joseph's actions or the beliefs of the Latter-day Saints, Trotti's Young gives an impassioned defense of tolerance and freedom of religion.

> Now, gentlemen, I'm not asking you to believe a single thing Joseph Smith said. But I do ask you, let him believe it—let me believe it, if we want to. Your forefathers and mine came to this country in the first place for one great reason—to escape persecution for their beliefs, and to build a free country where everybody might worship God as he pleased . . . You can't convict Joseph Smith just because he happens to believe something you don't believe. You can't go against everything your fathers fought and died for. And if you do, your names, not Joseph Smith's, will go down in history as traitors. They'll stink in the records and be a shameful thing in the tongues of your children!

Audiences did not miss the point. *The Motion Picture News* wrote, "It is difficult for us to believe that they were persecuted in Missouri and Illinois with the savage bigotry of present-day Nazism, but such was the case." And a California reviewer opined, "Religious liberty, with the U.S. Constitution as its backer, is made a serious and coherent theme in the film's motivation."[78] If the film made Brigham Young an American frontiersman, it was because the Mormons now showed the way for the entire country. "For Zanuck, a Jew very conscious of the gathering storms in Nazi Germany, the mobs terrified of Mormon subversion were the intolerant villains, and the Mormons themselves, of all people, exemplified America's promise of religious freedom and tolerance."[79] And this must be spread to all vulnerable people. Two years before *Casablanca*, *Brigham Young* was advocating resistance to anti-Semitism and, arguably, even Nazism itself.

This message would take time and ultimately require Pearl Harbor to spread to a majority of Americans. In the meantime, Mormons obviously held a different relationship with *Brigham Young*'s subject matter than general viewers. Some were thrilled: writing from Los Angeles in *Screenland* magazine, the young Mormon film journalist May Mann spoke about the response she had with her friend, actress Laraine Day:

> Faith is the motivating force and power of all religion. But to Laraine and to me and all the younger generation of Mormons, it has been strongly instilled and exemplified by our pioneer forefathers, who left their homes and properties, as shown in the picture, "Brigham Young," to seek a new refuge in the west. . . . We often discuss the picture which portrays the Mormon pioneers braving the blasts of winter—even starvation and death—because of their faith. We were both considerably enlightened by the film and Dean Jagger as Brigham Young. It was remarkably like our grandparents had told us.[80]

Others were more concerned, however, chiefly by the depiction of Young as doubtful of his calling, a concern that has only gained strength as the Church's public image has improved over the years. When the film premiered one *Deseret News* writer complained, "The Brigham Young of the picture lacks the faith and knowledge the real Brigham had, who never doubted his leadership nor its divine direction. It therefore to the Church members comes as a shock when Brigham doubts." Still, the author, like Heber Grant during the film's production, understood why that dramatic license had been taken, and thought "that Church members will readily overlook the infelicities that appear and that they only are likely to see."[81] Even when understanding the need for broad appeal and dynamic storytelling, many Mormons remained disappointed. One great-grandson of Young living in San Francisco said, "Brigham Young is characterized as altogether too vacillating in the screen portrait. He may have had some doubt of his ability as the perfect leader. But he felt called to aid his people, first in saving their lives and then in finding a peaceful haven for settlement." As a result, "it's a sympathetic and entertaining film, but not an epic."[82] Later Mormons were even less forgiving. Church President Spencer Kimball, who lived in Arizona in 1940 and may or may not have seen it in a theater there, obliquely criticized the film in "The Gospel Vision of the Arts" and decried it openly in his 1975 book *Faith Precedes the Miracle*: "The motion picture *Brigham Young* pictured President Young wondering if he was called of God. The picture showed him vacillating, unsure, and questioning his calling. In the climax of the play he is shown wavering, ready to admit he had not been inspired, that he had lied to them and misled them . . . But there was nothing vacillating or weak about Brigham Young. He knew he was God's leader."[83]

Beyond its characterization of Young, the film troubled other Mormons for its historical license, in how Brigham assumed control of the Church after Joseph's death, for instance, or even in the central fact that the real Brigham Young had returned east to gather more pioneers when the incident of the crickets and seagulls occurred in 1848. To properly assess all of these complaints we must see *Brigham Young* in its historical context. After decades of disappointing and failed projects and with the silent anti-Mormon films fresh in many minds, *Brigham Young*, even with its dramatic license, was a public relations victory of the highest order. In the October 1940 general conference President Grant said:

> I am thankful beyond expression for the very wonderful and splendid moving picture that has been made of Brigham Young. I have heard some little criticism of it, but we cannot expect the people who do not know that Brigham Young was in very deed the representative of God upon this earth, who do not know of his wonderful character, to tell the story as we would tell it. There is nothing in the picture that reflects in any way against our people. It is a very marvelous and wonderful thing, considering how people generally have treated us and what they thought of us. Of course, there are many things that are not strictly correct, and that is announced in the picture itself. It is of course a picture and we could not hope that they would make a picture at their expense, running into a couple of million dollars, to be just as we would like it."[84]

With this further endorsement from their prophet, Mormons at the time ceased to complain, while those in the future, like Spencer Kimball, were beneficiaries of *Brigham Young* and didn't even know it.

The Second Wave: Home Cinema

In 1948 Fox allowed an educational film company called Teaching Film Custodians, Inc. and the Audio-Visual Committee of the National Council for Social Studies to edit *Brigham Young* down to a thirty-one-minute version called *Driven Westward*, which was used in classroom instruction in middle and high schools for years; I myself saw this version in middle school social studies in the early 1990s. One review summarized it in a way reminiscent of the full film's original anti-fascism: "Throughout the film no reference is made to Mormon doctrine; the Mormons are shown only as a minority group. The film should be effective in developing an appreciation for the contributions of this minority group and creating an attitude of tolerance toward minorities."[85] At one point an even shorter ten-minute version was created, *Westward by Prairie Schooner*, to focus simply on pioneer travel. Incidentally, Dean Jagger, who won a Best Supporting Actor Oscar for *Twelve O'Clock High* in 1949, married Latter-day Saint Etta Norton in 1968 and was baptized himself in July 1972. Nostalgic Church members were ecstatic that "Brigham Young" was finally a Mormon. He lived in the Santa Monica Second Ward until his death in 1991, and in 1975 donated all his filmmaking papers and awards, appropriately, to Brigham Young University.[86]

A film the size of *Brigham Young* surely saturated public interest in the Mormon story, eliminating any interest other studios might have had in the subject for several years. Thus the only other fictional depiction of Mormons that decade was MGM's 1946 western *Bad Bascomb*, which placed its Mormon characters in essentially supporting roles in an entirely fictional narrative. Falling between a B-film and a monumental epic on the scale of *Brigham Young, Bad Bascomb* was what the *New York Times* called "a cheerful if somewhat lumbering and familiar Western,"[87] a highly enjoyable film with humor, intrigue, and action but no huge stars or enormous set pieces. Directed by S. Sylvan Simon, it was a vehicle for Wallace Beery and Margaret O'Brien. Beery was a heavy and character actor who had won an Academy Award for King Vidor's boxing movie *The Champ* (1931). He'd played everyone from King Richard I to Pancho Villa, and he excelled at villainous roles, hence his casting here as the aging bandit Zed Bascomb. Margaret O'Brien, in contrast, was only nine years old at the time, but she had won a Juvenile Oscar two years earlier for her show-stealing performance opposite Judy Garland in *Meet Me in St. Louis* (1944). Often seen as a successor to Shirley Temple, who was nine years her senior, O'Brien's star was on the rise: she would soon appear in adaptations of *Little Women* and *The Secret Garden* (both 1949), and although her greatest fame came as a child she continues to act up to the present. *Bad Bascomb* was tailored to their personas—Beery had already "been teamed successfully with many a moppet"[88]—and the film's trailer billed the duo as "the screen's best bad man" and "the screen's biggest little star."

The screenplay was by William Lipman and Grant Garrett, from a story by D. A. Loxley, and, though formulaic, the plot exhibits the solidification of the Church's new all-American image that *Brigham Young* so dramatically heralded. Not only were Mormons no longer the bad guys, they were now seen as so morally upright that their wagon train became the ideal hideout for a pair of outlaws on the run. Bascomb and his chief henchman Yancey (character actor J. Carrol Naish) need a place to hide from the law so they masquerade as new Mormon converts to get accepted into the group, and they're immediately interested in stealing a stash of gold intended to build a hospital in Utah. The bulk of the film and much of the comedy revolves around the attempts of these two reprobates to pass themselves off as new members of such a decent and wholesome society. The most prominent connection of course is between Bascomb and an orphan named Emmy (O'Brien) who is traveling with her grandmother; although he initially disdains her, her persistent guileless affection eventually starts to win him over to her personally and to all the Mormons as a group. And, importantly, these Mormons are relatively well-drawn characters. They are neither naïve nor pacifists, as they would be depicted in later decades, but are in turn equanimous, forgiving, intelligent, sexually attractive, and, to add some comic realism, bossy and shrewish. Again, Mormon doctrines including polygamy are completely absent, but the quality of their character and the depth of Emmy's affection induce Bascomb to begin mending his ways; he rescues Emmy from drowning during a river crossing then postpones the gold robbery in order to nurse her back to health. When, near the film's opening, Yancey shoots a Mormon in the back it is depicted as an entirely reprehensible act, used to show his complete moral blackness, and near the end it is he who decides not to wait for Bascomb anymore, so he steals the gold himself and stirs up some nearby Indians to attack the small wagon train; unlike in *Brigham Young* and *Wagon Master, Bad Bascomb*'s Native American characters are treated in stereotype, undergoing no rehabilitation similar to the film's fictional Mormons. Bascomb has by this time become converted—morally if not doctrinally—by Emmy's persistent poutiness, and he not only braves the Indian blockade to alert the cavalry, but after the battle—in which many Mormons are killed—turns himself in to be hung without ever telling Emmy who he really is. This ending is perhaps less satisfactory than if he had joined the Mormons permanently, but the Production Code stipulated that all criminals must pay for their actions, whether they reform or not. Despite this, the conclusion has the tone of a happy ending, a slightly odd moment with the optimistic Mormons waving goodbye before continuing west, more concerned with Bascomb's "temporary" departure than the dozens of their dead that lie around their feet.

The cast also included Marjorie Main, Frances Rafferty, and Marshall Thompson, as well as Russell Simpson as Elijah Walker, the second of his three turns playing Mormon pioneers. It was shot near Jackson Hole, Wyoming in 1945 and had a trade screening for industry representatives in February. It then premiered to the public in New York on May 22, 1946, traveling through the states and European territories for at least five years. Critics praised it for what it was, saying "despite its excessive length" of 112 minutes "and proneness to talkativeness, the picture kicks up quite a fuss, with all the devices dear to the heart of the lover of outdoor films," and "the sentimental is stressed in the story both in the writing and in the direction," giving "Beery a golden opportunity to play to the hilt the type of role with which he is most closely identified."[89] They described it as a highly exploitable property built, like most MGM films of the time, around its stars.[90]

Though not a prestige picture and essentially unknown today, *Bad Bascomb* reaffirmed the new positive, if doctrinally vague, depiction of Mormons under the Production Code. There is nothing about the story that requires these emigrants be religious at all; making them Mormon adds to the comedy, of course, but only if it's based on the premise that these are outstanding and scrupulous citizens, a position that now reflected American attitudes toward Mormonism at large, beyond any requirements the Hays Code may have had. And it is significant that Mormons now had sufficient cultural cachet in this way to prompt their inclusion in a film that is at heart about the relationship between an outlaw and a little girl. Though actual religion hardly plays into the picture at all, casting the incredibly popular O'Brien as the adorable Mormon girl who wins over the baddest outlaw in the country said something about the new social respectability Mormons enjoyed after World War II.

It is not surprising, then, to find Mormons featured prominently in one of the most humanistic films ever made, John Ford's *Wagon Master* (1950). Although its scale also didn't equal *Brigham Young*'s, it deserves to be remembered as one of the greatest of Mormon films. *Sight and Sound*, the magazine of the British Film Institute, listed it, with ten other Ford films, among the top 360 films ever made; it has prompted individual critics to call it Ford's most optimistic picture (Peter Bogdanovich) or even his greatest film (Andrew Sarris); it is one of his best-loved works in Europe; and Ford himself described it to his son Patrick as his favorite western[91] and to Bogdanovich as possibly his favorite film: "Along with *The Fugitive* and *The Sun Shines Bright*, I think *Wagon Master* came closest to being what I had wanted to achieve."[92] Given this and the fact that Ford remains one of cinema's best-known directors, its relative anonymity in the United States, with both Mormons and the general public, is unfortunate. It is, in fact, arguably the greatest sympathetic treatment Mormons have ever received in the cinema.[93]

Since his debut acting in his brother's *A Study in Scarlet* in 1914, John Ford, born John Martin Feeney in Maine in 1894, steadily worked to become one of the most respected directors in the world. He was incredibly prolific in the silent era and had a string of hits stretching to the 1940s with films like *The Iron Horse* (1924), *The Informer* (1935, his first of four Oscar wins), and *Stagecoach* (1939), which made John Wayne a star. *Stagecoach's* success allowed Ford and his friend Merian C. Cooper, best remembered as the creator of *King Kong*, to found the Argosy Pictures Corporation, an independent production company that would allow them greater creative control than through the studios. This had to wait for the war, however, as Ford served as the head of Navy's photographic unit, getting wounded while filming *The Battle of Midway* in 1942 and filming the D-Day invasion on Omaha Beach in 1944. After the war Cooper and Ford relaunched the company as the Argosy Pictures Corporation, although Ford also signed with Twentieth Century-Fox to ensure his personal solvency. Argosy signed a distribution deal with RKO under its new owner Howard Hughes which called for three films: *The Fugitive* from Graham Greene's book *The Power and the Glory*, *She Wore a Yellow Ribbon* about cavalry, and a project called *Wagon Master* on an unspecified subject. Ford started with *The Fugitive* (1947) then filmed the westerns *Fort Apache* (1948) and *She Wore a Yellow Ribbon* (1949), and, as mentioned in Chapter 2, these films brought him back to Utah's Monument Valley where he would discover the subject for *Wagon Master*.

Ford, usually considered a non-practicing Catholic, first encountered Mormons while filming *The Iron Horse* in Utah in 1924, and thanks to frequent location work there he often had occasion to work with them in subsequent years. While shooting *She Wore a Yellow Ribbon*, Ford's son Patrick, a screenwriter who was on the shoot because of his cavalry training, got to know some of the 200 mostly Mormon cowboys from the towns Monticello, Blanding, and Bluff who appeared on horseback in the film. One "Bishop" Perkins in particular interested him in the story of the colonization of southern Utah and the pioneers' journeys along the old Escalante Trail, near present-day Grand Staircase-Escalante National Monument, and through the treacherous Hole in the Rock formation in Glen Canyon near present-day Lake Powell (a reservoir created in 1963), where wagons had to be lowered down the near sheer face of the red rock by rope. Thus when Cooper asked him for a subject for *Wagon Master* that could be filmed for under $900,000 it seemed the best possible solution, especially when co-writer Frank Nugent became enthusiastic about it. Said the younger Ford:

> I had the idea of doing the Mormon thing because of my experiences with Bishop Perkins and those people there, and Frank grabbed onto that. And he decided if we were going to do it, we had better both read the Book of Mormon and know more about Mormons, which we did. And then we started going around with Mormon people. There's a big, huge swarm of Mormons in Los Angeles, especially in West Los Angeles. And so we got to know a lot of them, and learned a lot about their way of life. And in the meantime, all this time we were writing things, making changes, because the more you know, the more you change.[94]

They wrote the screenplay in two months. The lead Mormon character, originally actually named Bishop Perkins, became Elder Wiggs, played by longtime Ford collaborator Ward Bond. The two non-Mormon protagonists Travis and Sandy (Ben Johnson in his first lead role and Harry Carey Jr., both also regulars), were used to great advantage as a window into the Mormon world; Patrick Ford and Nugent made the characters horse traders to make them just a little shady but not unsympathetic or actual criminals. Other principle actors included Joanne Dru as Travis's love interest Denver, Charles Kemper, who died one month after the film's release, as the villainous Shiloh Clegg, and Jane Darwell and Russell Simpson in their second and third respective turns as Mormon pioneers.

Traveling to Utah in November 1949, the crew collaborated with many local Mormons during production. Ford insisted the film be shot at the authentic location—the Blanding, Mexican Hat area—but when logistics proved too difficult and expensive the company followed Bishop Perkins' advice and moved northeast to Moab where there was sufficient infrastructure like paved roads to support a film production, although it meant a compromise in the film's finale as they couldn't completely recreate the Hole in the Rock descent. As mentioned in Chapter 2, once they were in Moab, George White and Utah politicians J. A. Theobald and Ab Jenkins oversaw much of the logistics of caring for the crew throughout the shoot, and, as was his wont, Ford recruited much of the supporting cast out of locals. While Patrick and Nugent spent a great deal of time studying Mormonism, Ford père reportedly never researched the faith at all; he'd known Mormons for years, and Patrick later guessed that he simply didn't have to. "These are the people I want," he said when he saw the locals. "I want stone-age faces. I want faces of men and women who have seen people die of snakebite, whose women and babies have died in childbirth, and whose men die being bucked off horses. Just the life of primitive people."[95] This conveyed a somewhat romantic view of the cowboy as a noble savage, which some would later criticize the film for, but Ford instinctively knew such people well and how to portray them. And he wanted them to rub off on his Angeleno actors as well, so he honored their request to not work on Sundays and he set up communal tents for catering and other services that would allow the principal perform-ers to mingle with the locals; this congenial atmosphere made *Wagon Master* "literally a breath of fresh air . . . a relaxed, communal effort with some of Ford's favorite actors, crew people, stuntmen, and extras."[96] Ward Bond in particular was reported to have become "sort of an old time Mormon bishop,"[97] and Ford biographer Joseph McBride has speculated this was done on purpose to teach Bond, an egomaniac and eager collaborator with the House Un-American Ac-tivities Committee that Ford despised, a level of "tolerance by making him walk for a few weeks in the elder's shoes"[98] A ninety-year-old handcart pioneer met with the crew, and the actor-stuntman Don Summers, who played the pioneer Sam, actually converted to the Church, married a local Mormon girl, and stayed there. In addition to these human interactions, many of the props, wagons, and other equipment were sourced locally, which Patrick thought added to the film's tone and success: "That's the great thing about *Wagon Master*. That's where *Wagon Master*, in my opinion, came through, because the people were the real McCoy."[99]

Perhaps the greatest complaint about *Wagon Master*'s Mormons is their cos-tumes, which consisted of stiff black collars and flat-brimmed hats that evoked some sort of imaginary mix of stereotypical Mennonite, Amish, and Calvinist Puritans. This, however, was the invention of Howard Hughes. He famously hired only Mormons as his personal assistants so he should have known such costumes didn't reflect the faith now or in the past, but he evidently simply liked how they looked and insisted Ford use them. Ford protested, but in the end had to acquiesce on this particular battle because Hughes held the purse strings.[100] In fact, Hughes's tenure at RKO and the studio's response to the HUAC and its quest to blacklist filmmakers associated with the Communist Party strained Ford's entire relationship with RKO. *Wagon Master* shot in Moab from Novem-ber 14 to December 3, 1949, followed by twelve additional days in Los Angeles, and cost just $848,853, safely beneath the allotted $900,000. The film fulfilled Argosy's contract with RKO, and in January 1950, before *Wagon Master*'s edited negative was even complete, Ford and Cooper signed a distribution deal with Republic Pictures.

The film's story is quite simple, combining elements of Bishop Perkins's history with tropes like the outlaws who hide out in a Mormon wagon train. The unscrupulous but basically kind-hearted horse traders Travis and Sandy meet Elder Wiggs in town and refuse a position to lead his colonizing party to the San Juan River Valley. Wiggs is determined to go with or without a wagon master, and the two change their mind when they see him leading his people toward an area without water. As they travel south together they first encounter a stranded "hootchy kootchy show" which they take under their wing, then the Cleggs, an extended family of outlaws who take cover in the train. Tension mounts when one of the Clegg boys tries to rape a Navajo woman and the Mormons whip him to keep him from being scalped instead. Enraged at the indignity, Uncle Shilo Clegg takes over the wagon train at gunpoint, exploits his position, hides his boys from a posse in the Mormons' wagons, and, finally, shoots a Mormon teamster and tries to force Elder Wiggs to race the grain wagon, which the pioneers will need to survive, over a steep rocky pass. This prompts Travis and Sandy to take action with a hidden weapon; a brief gunfight ensues in which they kill all the Cleggs. The two then join the Mormons permanently and are each last seen driving a wagon with their romantic partner, heading to homestead the land.

Even with the inaccurate costumes, somewhat formal speech patterns, and, like Grace Kelly's Quaker in *High Noon* two years later, complete pacifism without a firearm among them, these Mormons are admirable in their humble determination. Wiggs cannot tell a lie even with a gun literally to his back, and the traditional cinematic allegations against the Church are thrown out in his first scene, in which he loudly and sarcastically proclaims to have horns under his hat and more wives than "Solomon hisself." To this he quietly adds, "No, we're not a big party, son. We're just a handful of people sent out to mark the trail and prepare the ground for those who will come after us." This one line humanizes the entire Mormon camp for the rest of the movie. Polygamy is henceforth dealt with tacitly, played mostly for comedy in the henpecked status of Wiggs' right-hand man Adam (Simpson), done with understated brilliance when he is forced to dance with a Navajo woman and the camera casts a series of looks between him and a formidable group of staunch-looking women. Despite Wiggs's inveterate honesty, he does require a great deal of Adam's help to refrain from profanity, another comic and humanizing touch. And Adam, for his part, shows a touch of intolerance, complaining about the group of showmen as a low class of people, but Wiggs quickly puts him in his place. This humanizing moment, where the Mormons, who are being driven out of civilization as victims of prejudice, still harbor prejudice themselves, makes them remarkably human characters—and helps drive home the theme of the entire film.

Ford's favorable disposition toward the socially marginalized found natural resonance with the Mormons. As with *Brigham Young*, the parallels between Latter-day Saints and other persecuted groups is very deliberate. Like Dallas in Ford's earlier *Stagecoach*, the Mormons are literally forced out of the community at gunpoint. If at first some of them are repulsed by the destitute performers, seeing their profession as immoral, their brotherhood as outcasts is soon demonstrated. The dancer Denver refuses alcohol in favor of water, the "Doctor" makes a magnanimous gesture to sacrifice himself to test the final dangerous road, and the group is entirely assimilated into the wagon train by film's end, not converting to Mormon doctrines but joining them as brothers, planning to settle the San Juan River Valley alongside them. The next and strongest association comes with the Navajos. In their first scene they welcome the Mormons, again explicitly identifying them as their brothers in exile. As Charles Ramirez Berg has pointed out, Ford's greatest heroes are those who treat Indians humanely, and his greatest villains, such as the Cleggs, are those who trick or violate them. "Probably the best rendering of [Ford's] cultural equivalence comes in *Wagon Master*, when the Mormons and the Native Americans each confront and tolerate the mysterious other, locking arms and circling a flickering campfire in a Navajo dance."[101] Travis and Sandy are also assimilated into the group; despite their initial avarice, charging Wiggs $50 a head for horses they previously stated are worth $30, they decide to help the Mormons purely out of human interest. They are also reluctant to fight and finally embrace the land in favor of money. Shilo Clegg, on the other hand, is Ford's worst villain because he cannot appreciate the worth of anything but money. Whereas Wiggs described their seeds as more precious than gold, Shilo's most memorable line is, "Gold *always* interests me." Since the Mormons don't have any actual gold, he attempts to destroy their seed out of pure malice. These stark contrasts all highlight Ford's empathy for the Mormons; it's quite explicit that the socially marginalized—Mormons, fallen women, Native Americans—are more moral than those who like the Cleggs undertake more socially acceptable activities, such as seeking profit.[102]

Wagon Master premiered on April 22, 1950. Ford was trying to advance Ben Johnson's career with the film, but Ward Bond was its biggest star, and without a John Wayne or Technicolor footage it received less attention in its release than the films in the Cavalry Trilogy that surrounded it; the end of Argosy's relationship with RKO may have influenced how much the studio cared to promote it as well. Reviews were mixed, with the *Hollywood Reporter* calling it a vivid and realistic drama "of the Old West that will delight everyone who enjoys outdoor adventure," but others, such as the critic at the *Hollywood Citizen-News*, missed the point entirely and criticized the film for exactly what later viewers agreed makes it great: "A good many 'peaks' of dramatic conflict were passed up, such as when the Indians accosted the wagon train. The scenarists chose to make the Indians friendly. . . . And not even the flogging of a bandit for assaulting an Indian girl compensates for the conflict that might have been." The *Los Angeles Times* complained that the final shootout was too short without enough violence, causing Joseph McBride to conclude that "it says a great deal about the cultural climate of America in 1950 that Ford's *avoidance* of racism and sadism was considered a serious commercial drawback."[103] He therefore describes *Wagon Master* as a protest film against the hysteria of McCarthyism in the early Cold War, which once again shows how Mormons as film characters were used to define exactly what America and patriotism stood for during the Second Wave. "*Wagon Master* was his way of paying tribute not only to the Mormons' pioneering courage in the face of ostracism but to the American democratic spirit as it existed in a simpler time when most people (other than Indians) were immigrants in transit from some place or another, searching for a new land to put down roots."[104]

The film earned modest returns in the States and initially only played abroad in England. In 1957 an hour-long television adaptation called *Wagon Train* premiered. This was essentially a theft of the concept behind the film: when Howard Hughes left RKO in 1955 it was in such disarray that the rights to *Wagon Master* were literally lost in the debris, leaving the concept available for anyone who wanted to take it. Ward Bond provided continuity with the film by starring in the series until he died of a heart attack in 1960—although his character was no longer Mormon—and the series ran on NBC until 1962 and then on ABC until it ended in 1965. While the show was popular the film moved toward obscurity. Though never lost, it was difficult to see and not exploited by RKO or its heirs. It wasn't released on North American DVD until 2009, but with that increased availability it has begun to be reconsidered as a major masterpiece. As Patrick Ford recalled, "*Wagon Master* was pure of heart, and simple and good, and Frank Nugent and I were pure of heart and simple and good when we wrote it, and maybe John Ford was too."[105] But in contrast to studio films like *Brigham Young, Bad Bascomb,* and *Wagon Master,* smaller-scale independent productions had a harder time getting off the ground, as Edward Finney's story shows. He entered the film industry in the 1920s, at one point working with Buster Keaton, then moved into film advertising and publicity, moving between small studios like Monogram, Grand National Films, and Republic, apparently as well as working at times as an independent contractor. In the 1930s he produced a number of standard westerns, titles like *Song of the Gringo* (1936), *Arizona Days* (1937), *Where the Buffalo Roam* (1938), and *Riders of the Frontier* (1939). Among these were Monogram's *Trouble in Texas*, which was the 1937 remake of *The Man from Utah*, and the western *Utah Trail* for the small outfit Boots and Saddles Pictures in 1938. He was also friends with the Mormon Leo J. Muir, an educator and Democratic politician from Woods Cross and Bountiful, Utah who had lived in Los Angeles since 1922. There Muir became an amateur historian and journalist, founding the *California Intermountain News* in 1935, a journal about the Church in the Golden State that ran until 1989, and writing other works on history including a two-volume history of the Church in California while serving in numerous Church leadership positions. It's possible Finney learned a fair amount about Mormon history from his friend, so when he was in San Diego to promote a film in 1950 and heard about a reenactment of the Mormon Battalion he was immediately intrigued. "It struck me that this would be a very interesting thing to film. Something that needed to be preserved."[106]

In honor of the centennial of California's statehood in 1950, the volunteer historical organization the Sons of Utah Pioneers decided to commemorate the contribution that the Battalion had made to the establishment of California. Their 1847 march through northern Mexico opened a southern route to San Diego and on to Los Angeles, where for six months they reinforced Fort Moore and strengthened the U.S. military presence, bolstering the connection between southern California and the United States and opening the way for Californian annexation and the Gadsden Purchase. In the twentieth century pioneer reenactments were an increasingly popular activity among Utah Mormons, as we saw with the Daughters of Utah Pioneers' trek into the Salt Lake Valley in 1923. It was a major component of the Salt Lake City's 1947 centennial celebrations, making it an obvious and popular way for the Sons of Utah Pioneers to commemorate the Mormon connection with California's founding. (Such reenactments were again the subject of much documentary film interest in 1997, and were depicted in the 2018 fictional film *Trek: The Movie*.)

The Battalion's entire 2,000-mile journey was obviously infeasible—and unnecessary for a Californian celebration—so the group decided to journey by bus to a few scenic and historic points in Arizona then focus on the Battalion's time in San Diego and L.A. Accordingly, around March 10, 1950 nine chartered buses with Sons of Utah Pioneers members and their wives left Salt Lake City on U.S. Route 91 and journeyed southward. They drilled by the Grand Canyon, paraded in the Mormon enclave of Mesa, and visited Yuma and other sites before meeting the San Diego branch of the Sons of Utah Pioneers outside that city on March 16. That evening they banqueted at the U.S. Grant Hotel, attended a program in the State Hall with an address from the San Diego stake president, and presented a pageant of their members dressed as Battalion soldiers. Finney had heard of them by this point, if not earlier. He quickly hired a cameraman and filmed the group from here on, with much of the footage shot silently but at least some of the speeches recorded with synchronized sound; the rest of the soundtrack would be recreated later. The next day, Friday the 17th, he was on hand as they paraded in costume through Old Town, ending at the *Mormon Battalion Monument* at Presidio Park, where San Diego Mayor Harley E. Knox and other dignitaries spoke. Then they drove north to Los Angeles and that night were joined by Church President George Albert Smith and Utah Governor J. Bracken Lee as they stayed at Knott's Berry Farm, several years before it transformed into a full-fledged amusement park. On Saturday morning they paraded up Main Street from the Hotel Alexandria to City Hall. There was another ceremony, with speeches by President Smith, Governor Lee, and California Governor Earl Warren, a few blocks further north, past the year-old Hollywood Freeway at the site of old Fort Moore, where the Battalion was mustered out of service on July 4, 1847. After another bus ride there were more speeches and pomp at the old Mormon colony of San Bernardino, all of which Finney filmed. The group rode their buses overnight and returned to Salt Lake in time for morning Sunday School.[107]

On April 17 at the spring meeting of the Los Angeles chapter of the Sons of the Utah Pioneers Finney showed the initial results of his labor, a twenty-five minute black-and-white documentary called *Sons of the Utah Pioneers Trek*. He wanted Mormon participation to make it an even longer film and exhibit it for local congregations and other interested viewers, and it seems that initially he was successful. Members of the reenactment and other Mormons sent him their own personal film footage they had recorded in Utah, Mexico, the Grand Canyon, and even Nauvoo. He did additional historical research, recorded a voice-over narration, and assembled all the footage into a six-reel, nearly hour-long documentary called *The Mormon Battalion*, which compared the original Battalion's journey with the present-day reenactment. The whole production cost him $2,000—over $20,000 in today's dollars—which he paid out of his own pocket. Years later he said he was happy to do this but didn't want to spend more personal money on an advertising and distribution campaign without participation from Church members. So he turned to his Mormon network, hoping to find willing collaborators. "But beyond the fact that Muir and several others who saw it were enthused about the film, the LDS community didn't seem to be impressed enough to carry on the commercial exhibition aspects. I was surprised because I thought this would be something the Mormons would treasure." Because there was no similar visual record of the actual Mormon Battalion, Finney saw his film as "the most authentic recreation of the whole march ever made," and it also contributed to twentieth-century Church history with, for instance, the speech of George Albert Smith, who died less than a year later. "Where else is one to hear and see this except in this film?" he asked. Anxious to exhibit it, he proposed a fifty-fifty proposition to Mormons in San Diego: "Whatever was taken in would go fifty percent to me to help defray my expenses, and the exhibitor," which could be a local ward or meetinghouse, "would keep the other fifty percent." But no willing collaborators came forward.

> Although I had a close working relationship with the Mormon leadership in California it just didn't work out financially. It became more of a bother and expense to try and follow through properly on its exhibition, and so I figured in the Church members didn't care about it enough to support it, I'd just forget about exhibiting it. The film was a personal venture to me and wasn't worth my time and financial effort if the LDS community wasn't going to be interested in it. It's a pity because I think the film is well done and of real value to the Church.[108]

He had arranged a handful of screenings in southern California and Utah in 1950, but turnout even for these was disappointing and soon he stopped trying to show it. While films like *Brigham Young* and *Wagon Master* struggled to find a sufficient national audience for a Mormon-themed picture, perhaps Finney was running up against a problem that would plague independent Mormon filmmakers up to—and even into—the Fifth Wave: an insufficient *Mormon* audience willing to pay and attend screenings of Mormon-themed pictures.

Given his interest in Church history, however, Finney did have the foresight to dispose of his film properly to ensure its preservation, or at least he hoped. He donated a copy of the negative to UCLA and a positive print to the Church archives in Salt Lake City. When Joseph Fielding Smith, who had served for years as the Church Historian, became the President of the Church in 1970 Finney thought that the Church might be interested in revisiting the film. So he wrote to President Smith, "but there seemed to be littler interest in it by the leadership and nothing came of my offer." Still, when he spoke with historian Richard Nelson in 1973 Finney said, "Actually I'm more enthusiastic today about *The Mormon Battalion* than when I first made it. Now well over twenty years have passed since then and it's got tremendous historic value."[109] As an example of a film on Mormonism from outside the faith, it evinced the same—if not more—admiration for the Mormons as every other Second Wave film, but demonstrated the limits of working outside the studio system. Finney's effort remains noteworthy as an attempt outside of the institutional Church—and even Mormon culture—to create an unpretentious artisanal film within a domestic, if ad hoc, distribution system. As such, Finney was on the same trail as A. Hamer Reiser and Frank Wise, but he was unable to pull it off given his outsider status.

There was one other opportunity for a major studio to make a movie on a Mormon topic late in the Second Wave. In 1950 the Mormon historian Juanita Brooks published a seminal work called simply *The Mountain Meadows Massacre*. This was the first comprehensive and fair look at the 1857 event; she appropriately documented the Mormons' responsibility for the affair, absolving Brigham Young of direct involvement but saying he was an accessory after the fact and documenting the actions of other more culpable Church leaders like Isaac Haight. These findings, gathered over two decades of research, caused an uproar among the Mormon faithful who had learned from folk history to scapegoat Native Americans and John D. Lee for the slaughter. There was an unsuccessful attempt to block Stanford University Press from publishing the book, Brooks was ostracized within the Mormon community, and when David O. McKay became Church President in 1951 he was pressured to excommunicate her. He resisted this, however, telling her chief accuser apostle Delbert Stapley to leave her alone.

While this response to Brooks personally represents McKay's compassionate stance toward less-than orthodox members of the faith, he was less prone to turn away from the actual messages damaging to the Church. On November 5, 1951, just months after he became Church President at the death of George Albert Smith, McKay learned that Warner Brothers had purchased the film rights to *The Mountain Meadows Massacre* and was developing it as a major production. The Mormons now had much more political, social, and legal clout than when McKay was battling *Married to a Mormon* and *Trapped by the Mormons* in England thirty years earlier—not to mention the muscle of Joseph Breen's

Production Code Administration behind them. McKay sent a delegation to Los Angeles and, though we don't know exactly what transpired, within seven days Warners agreed to drop the project. No film on the Mountain Meadows Massacre would be made until *September Dawn* at the massacre's sesquicentennial in 2007.[110] All of these positive Hollywood films about Mormonism—travelogues, newsreels, documentaries, and both tent-pole and bread-and-butter fictional studio films—suggest that Mormonism, by way of popular cinema, was gradually becoming domesticated into American life, at least within the popular mythology of the American West. As historian Matthew Bowman has written about this period, "Hollywood's embrace seemed the definitive sign of inclusion in American culture, and the Mormons accepted it gladly."[111] In fact, an increasing number of them decided to embrace Hollywood in return.

Mormons and the Mainstream Industry

At Home in the Industry

During the two decades of the Second Wave, many Mormons created a home in major filmmaking regions and in the film and now television industries themselves. As we've seen, from 1900 to 1920 the "concept of fleeing Babylon by gathering to one central location had changed to the idea of Mormons gathering as congregations throughout the world"; thus "Mormons joined the national wave of migrations from rural areas to urban centers, and Los Angeles—with its rapid growth and close proximity to the Mormon-populated areas of the rural West—became a magnet for Mormon migrants." Now in the 1930s "the Great Depression would push a second and larger wave of Mormon migrants toward urban areas" where they primarily sought white collar jobs, including creative positions in the film industry.[112] Thus at the end of the First Wave the Church was already larger in southern California than in any other area outside the Mormon heartland, and it continued to grow steadily. In April 1929 the young Hollywood Stake dedicated an impressive new tabernacle, with more chapels following soon after. In 1933 the stake, led by future apostle LeGrand Richards, had 101 convert baptisms, in addition to a continual influx of immigrating Saints. The next year President Grant began plans to build two temples in California, commissioning a search committee of local Church leaders to find a site near Los Angeles. They recommended a twenty-four-acre property on Santa Monica Boulevard in Westwood that belonged to Harold Lloyd. The Church purchased the lot from him by 1938 but found that a New York City street set that

The Second Wave: Home Cinema

Lloyd had built on the grounds was still quite popular with production companies that wanted to film there. For a while this placed the Church in the backlot business as it rented the set out, but soon work on the temple was underway. World War II delayed construction but it was dedicated in 1956, so that today the largest temple in the Church sits on a site that once was the home of one of the greatest stars of the silent era. On the opposite coast, the New York Stake, formed on December 9, 1934, was the first stake east of the Mormon Corridor since the termination of the St. Louis Stake in 1858. Many Mormons relocating to New York and especially Los Angeles worked in the entertainment industry, and some—such as Wetzel Whitaker, Nathan and Ruth Hale, and, later, Kieth Merrill and Richard Dutcher—would eventually become major participants in Mormon-related filmmaking efforts.[113]

Many of these men and women made careers within the technical and administrative side of the film and broadcasting industries. For instance, in the 1940s Karl Macdonald was both an east coast representative of Warner Brothers' foreign department, working to sell and distribute Warner films to European territories, and a bishop in a ward on Long Island, perhaps in Brooklyn or Queens. In 1939 Harold Orlob, a Mormon New Yorker originally from Logan, Utah, branched out from his usual profession as a successful Broadway composer to produce the Paramount film ...One Third of a Nation... about a repentant slumlord and featuring a young Sidney Lumet in a supporting role; he also wrote the story for the 1947 Harold Young film Citizen Saint, a film about Frances Cabrini that was sponsored by the Roman Catholic Church. That same year his song "I Wonder Who's Kissing Her Now" provided the title for a Twentieth Century-Fox musical, and it has been used onscreen at least twenty-four additional times from 1928 to a 2016 episode of the television show Gotham.[114]

Perhaps more influential than these men was Wilford J. Merrill, who was vice president and treasurer of RKO when he died, aged forty-two, in 1941. He was born to apostle Marriner W. Merrill and his plural wife Elna in 1898, the forty-fifth of Marriner's forty-six children. He grew up on a farm in Richmond in northern Utah and studied at Utah Agricultural College. After serving in World War I and working as a knit goods salesman and in the vitamin industry he studied business at Harvard, graduating with honors in 1925. In New York, he moved through executive positions at the Royal Baking Powder Company, W. & J. Sloane, and the Great Island Holding Company before joining the investment firm the Atlas Corporation. In October 1935 Atlas collaborated with Lehman Brothers to acquire a controlling interest in RKO Pictures from the Radio

Corporation of America, and while Merrill was always considered an Atlas representative he quickly moved up the RKO ranks to his final position. In the late '30s RKO was struggling to prove itself as a major studio, promoting stars like Maureen O'Hara and Ginger Rogers and forging distribution deals with production companies such as Samuel Goldwyn and Walt Disney. The company released classics like *Snow White and the Seven Dwarfs* (1937), *Bringing Up Baby* (1938), *Love Affair* (1939), *The Hunchback of Notre Dame* (1939), and *The Little Foxes* (1941); Merrill presumably oversaw the finances and revenue of all these productions. In 1938 RKO head George Schafer signed the theater and radio dynamo Orson Welles to create his first motion picture, and it must have involved Merrill extensively as *Citizen Kane*'s budget ballooned to $1 million. The weeks preceding the film's release were tumultuous for the studio due to the interference of William Randolph Hearst, and after Merrill attended a New York preview screening on April 10, 1941 he returned to the office and worked until midnight. He then went home and suffered a fatal coronary thrombosis in bed, dying alone in a scene reminiscent of the film he had just helped see to fruition. Twenty days later when it opened to the public *Citizen Kane* was hailed as a monumental advance in film art; meanwhile Merrill's funeral was held at the Riverside Memorial Chapel in Manhattan's Upper West Side and he was buried back home in Cache Valley.[115]

Hugh "Denver" Brandon also came from pioneer stock, but his life played out quite differently. A native of Castle Dale in central Utah, he moved to California and spent twenty-five years working as a Hollywood stuntman, grip, and electrician before returning to Kanab in the 1940s and pursuing various business opportunities, including a stint as a film producer. He co-founded Kanab Pictures, Inc., with local rancher and artist Loren "Dude" Larsen as president, in November 1947, when film work with Hollywood was booming in that town. They raised $50,000 and filmed the western *Stallion Canyon*, a tale of land grabbing and horse racing, around St. George in 1948. They used primarily local—and, therefore, primarily Mormon—talent, and Brandon himself was involved hands-on in much of the production. A color film, it premiered in St. George on June 15, 1949 but has since been lost. Although he apparently produced no other pictures after this, Brandon may have still pursued other film work; when he died in 1978 his tombstone was engraved with the words, "35 years in motion pictures."[116]

The Mormon who was second only to Philo Farnsworth in his influence on the television industry is today perhaps one of the least known people to have even worked in the field. Rosel H. Hyde was born in 1900 in the small Mormon farming town of Downey in southeast Idaho and studied law at George Washington University. While still a student he began his career in D.C., starting as a typist at the U.S. Civil Service Commission in 1924 and working his way up through the Office of Public Buildings and Public Parks and the Federal Radio Commission as its first disbursement officer. A Republican, in 1933 he successfully petitioned the incoming Roosevelt administration to allow him to remain in his position, and the next year when the Federal Communications Commission was created he moved there. He became a section chief over radio and television broadcasting in 1939 and assistant general counsel of the commission over broadcasting in 1942, where he was "essentially the commission's resident expert on broadcasting, which increased his contact with the commission and his visibility in the industry."[117] In 1945 he was promoted again to general counsel of the FCC, and on April 17, 1946 President Truman appointed him one of the commissioners. New television station licenses were frozen at that time while the FCC adjusted its regulations, and in 1952 Hyde engineered a plan to unfreeze the applications, allowing for the rapid spread of many new stations across the country. With this track record, it was easy for President Eisenhower to nominate him as Chairman of the FCC in April 1953, making him the first chairman nominated by a Republican President. He oversaw much of the growth of American television and satellite networks, standardizing controls over how stations functioned and supervising the introduction of color signals and the evolution of the National Television Systems Committee (NTSC) video standard, which created color standards that were compatible with existing black-and-white television sets. The NTSC standard had widespread influence beyond broadcasting, defining video production and video-based postproduction workflows and equipment, including linear and nonlinear editing systems, in the Western Hemisphere until it was overtaken by digital standards in the 2000s. He was easily appointed to a third term in 1959 but was moved to the Telephone and Telegraph Committee under Kennedy. Then in April 1966 President Johnson reappointed Hyde as Chairman, making him the first Chairman to serve two nonconsecutive terms and the first nominated by a President of the opposite political party.

In 1967 his commission created the fairness doctrine for regulating issues of bias in broadcasting. One of the first types of content to come under fire because of the doctrine was cigarette commercials, as it stipulated that for every cigarette advertisement an anti-smoking ad also had to air. Since these were public service announcements, however, and hence lost stations money, it was decided that an easier solution would be to disallow cigarette advertisements in the first place. Soon the FCC "proposed that cigarette ads should be banned, reasoning that advocating the use of a product deemed harmful by the government violated public interest, a position that proved to be both unpopular and politically volatile." Cigarettes were the largest product advertisers on television at the time, and at this point Hyde's Mormonism became a political issue as the tobacco lobby charged that he was trying to foist his religious views on the entire nation. But it was a deliberate choice, and, "once again, well established legal and policy precedents defended his stand. Eventually, the commission voted to ban tobacco advertising over the airwaves."[118] This became law in 1970, after Hyde had left the FCC, when Nixon signed the Public Health Cigarette Smoking Act. Despite this instance when Hyde's Mormonism was attacked, it generally won him respect throughout Washington. Hyde has been called the most qualified Chairman the FCC ever had; he was an expert—technical, legal, and logistical—on every issue that confronted the commission. He retired from government service at the end of his term in 1969 and practiced law for the remainder of his career, living in Washington until his death at age ninety-two. Other Mormons gained high positions in the radio and broadcasting industry in the Second Wave as well, including Eugene Hyde Merrill, a great-grandson of Orson Hyde who, as a Democrat in the Truman administration, was named an FCC commissioner in 1952. He served at the FCC until 1961, spending the rest of his career at NATO and other U.S. and Utah government posts.[119]

Undoubtedly as the film industry grew in Los Angeles many Mormons helped fill the offices of the studios, small production companies, talent agencies, and distribution firms. One of these was Mildred Gagin (perhaps spelt Gagon), who ran her own Beverly Hills-based talent agency in the late 1940s. Raised in the small town of Roosevelt, Utah, she journeyed with her husband to Bakersfield then Los Angeles in search of employment. When her husband became seriously ill she began to work outside the home, spending several years as a secretary and bookkeeper in the Church's Los Angeles Mission office. When World War II diminished the number of missionaries and the need for a full-time secretary she found work doing stenography and bookkeeping in a talent agency, eventually working her way up to become assistant manager of the Hayward-Deverish Agency, which oversaw stars like Henry Fonda, Greta Garbo, and Joseph Cotton. When that firm was acquired by the Music Corporation of America in 1945, making it the largest talent agency in the world, she briefly worked there as a personnel manager but soon decided to strike out on her own. She later took a female colleague on as a partner, making the company into the Gagin-Melton Agency. We don't know what talent she managed there, what pictures she packaged together, or how long she remained in the business, but as a women-run organization her agency was ahead of the times, particularly for a Mormon housewife who devoted all her spare time to the Young Women's Mutual Improvement Association in Beverly Hills.[120]

Even Mormon journalists moved into the film industry: Harry McPherson, a Salt Lake City reporter who became a film publicist in the 1930s, worked for Warner Brothers and Columbia Pictures throughout the decade. May Mann, born May Vasta Randall, started by writing for the *Deseret News* and *Improvement Era* but moved to Hollywood in the 1930s to freelance for trade journals like *Screenland*. A fastidious reporter and friend of many stars, including her fellow ward member Laraine Day, she eventually became known as "Hollywood's Glamour Girl Reporter," perhaps for her own style as much as the female stars she interviewed, and had her work syndicated in over 400 newspapers by the King Features, Faucett Publications, and General Features syndicates. She also worked for Twentieth Century-Fox, probably as a publicist, and the *New York Herald-Tribune*. She wrote biographies of Clark Gable and Jayne Mansfield, and her book *Elvis and the Colonel*, about Elvis Presley's relationship with his manager Tom Parker, was adapted as a film in 1993. Much of her access to the stars was due to her personal relationships with them; she was a close friend of Mansfield, for instance, as well as Marilyn Monroe, about whom she may have written an unpublished and now lost biography manuscript. Well-known for her charitable work and devotion to her faith, she died in Los Angeles on April 26, 1995.[121]

Other Mormons, also usually Utah natives, found work in the film industry's technical departments, such as Lionel Banks, head of Columbia Pictures' art department from the late 1930s to the late '40s, where he oversaw all sets, props, and other production design for the studio. His grandfather Oliver C. Bess was an 1847 pioneer, and Banks grew up in Salt Lake City, attending the Latter-day Saints High School and the University of Utah. In 1920 he began studying architecture at the University of Southern California, then he returned to Utah to begin his practice. Soon he was back in Hollywood, though, to apply his architectural skills to designing sets. His first work, probably as a sketch artist, was on *The Jazz Singer* at Warner Brothers in 1927, but he then secured a two-week position at Columbia, which lasted until 1949. In 1932 he became an associate to Columbia's chief art director Stephen Goosson, and on July 1, 1938 he succeeded Goosson to oversee Columbia's entire art department. He worked on over two hundred films, from *Moby Dick* (1930) to Frank Borzage's *Moonrise*

(1948), earning seven Oscar nominations, designing for black and white and Technicolor, and overseeing such notable titles as *You Can't Take It with You* (1938), *Mr. Smith Goes to Washington* (1939), *His Girl Friday* (1940), *The Talk of the Town* (1942), and the musical *Cover Girl* (1944). A member of the Arlington Ward in the Hollywood then Los Angeles Stake, Banks died in March 1950, less than a year after retiring from his Columbia post.[122]

At least two Mormons worked in studio costume departments. Josie L. Bird Miller grew up in the towns of Hatton, Kanosh, and Beaver in southcentral Utah. During the Depression she moved with her husband to Los Angeles in search of work, where she was able to put her skills as a seamstress to use at Paramount, where she worked in the costume department at least through the mid-1950s, when she worked on *The Ten Commandments* (1956), if not longer. It's unknown to what extent she designed costumes or if she purely executed others' designs—she worked with legendary costume designer Edith Head at one point—but she created clothes for many of Hollywood's most glamorous female stars, including Mae West, Elizabeth Taylor, Hedy Lamarr, Audrey Hepburn, Betty Grable, Shelley Winters, Nina Foch, Debbie Reynolds, and Dorothy Lamour. Among the men she clothed were Errol Flynn, Victor Mature, and the duo of Bob Hope and Bing Crosby in their *Road to...* films. Nancy Bakke, from Kanab, was a costume designer for MGM at the same time, but less is known of the specifics of her career there.[123]

It's possible that cinematographer Charles B. Lang, Jr. came from Mormon roots. His mother Mary Gertrude Lang, née Jones, was born in Salt Lake City in 1879 and married his father there in 1901. Charles Jr. was born in the small Mormon colony of Bluff in the southeast corner of Utah in 1902 but was taken by his parents to Los Angeles when he was three. He followed his father and became a negative developer at Realart Pictures Corporation in 1918 before moving on to be a still photographer, camera assistant, and finally camera operator and director of photography at Paramount in the 1930s. Working there and as a freelancer from the 1950s on he became one of Hollywood's most celebrated cinematographers, defining Paramount's lighting style and earning a record eighteen Academy Award nominations over the course of a forty-year career. His achievements would warrant more attention here were his connection to Mormonism better established beyond the possibility that his mother came from pioneer stock. But his family's journey from Salt Lake City to Bluff to Los Angeles is typical of the many Utahns who joined the film industry in the first decades of the twentieth century.[124]

The Second Wave: Home Cinema

The introduction of synchronized sound, followed a few years later by the Great Depression, was a majorly disruptive event for Mormon musicians in Utah and elsewhere. No longer able to accompany silent films in the movie theaters, some musicians found work performing and composing for the new film soundtracks that sound films required. Without doubt the most prominent Mormon film musician of this period was Leigh Harline. His parents converted to the Church in Sweden and immigrated to Salt Lake City in 1891, where he was born in 1907. After studying piano and organ performance at the University of Utah and with Mormon Tabernacle Choir conductor J. Spencer Cornwall, Harline moved to California in 1928 to work for the infant medium of radio by composing, conducting, arranging, performing, singing, and announcing for various stations in San Francisco and Los Angeles. In late 1932 he was hired by Walt Disney, one of the finest practitioners of syncopated sound in this new era, where he joined Frank Churchill and Bert Lewis to complete Disney's great trio of early composers. Harline's first score was for the Silly Symphony *Father Noah's Ark* (1933) and he quickly distinguished himself with the complexity and thematic unity of his scores. His hilarious integration of the *William Tell Overture* and "Turkey in the Straw" in *The Band Concert* (1935) illustrates this beautifully and remains one of the all-time great animation scores. His credits from the 1930s include dozens of other remarkable shorts, both Mickey Mouse films like the riotous *Mickey's Grand Opera* (1936) and Silly Symphonies, like the playful *The Grasshopper and the Ants* (1934), which showcases his songwriting ability as well as his scoring, and *The Old Mill* (1937), a somber film intended to prove the Disney studio's capability with lighting and effects animation in preparation for *Snow White*. *The Old Mill* has no dialogue, and Harline's score not only sets the tone but carries the weight of the narrative: he incorporates portions of Strauss's operetta *The Gypsy Baron* in one of the film's most beautiful moments, and his score as the scene moves from calm to storm to calm again shows his mastery of mood and orchestration, particularly in his use of ethereal female voices as the storm approaches. His music undoubtedly contributed significantly to *The Old Mill's* success; it won an Academy Award and is still considered one of the greatest short animated films. With his versatility between light fare and serious concert music, it's no wonder that Harline, along with another composer named Paul Smith, was selected by Disney to score his first feature-length film, *Snow White and the Seven Dwarfs*. Harline focused on the wicked Queen's scenes, including her conversations with the Magic Mirror and her fatal chase with the dwarfs up a stormy mountaintop.

Harline and Smith were nominated for an Academy Award and honored by Disney with the opportunity to score his next feature, *Pinocchio* (1940). For this production Harline also composed five songs with lyricist Ned Washington, including "When You Wish Upon a Star," which has been the company's theme song ever since. Harline and Smith orchestrated *Pinocchio* lavishly, for a fifty-piece orchestra and forty-voice choir, drawing on Old World sources and creating a variety of feels for the film's different locations, from Geppetto's homely puppet shop to the chaotic carnival of Pleasure Island to the treacherous encounter with Monstro the whale. Though the film was initially a financial failure, Harline won two Academy Awards, for Best Score and Best Original Song, making him the first Mormon to actually win an Oscar. Walt Disney reportedly didn't care much for *Pinocchio*'s music himself, however, and after this Harline left Disney to freelance for studios like MGM, Twentieth Century-Fox, and RKO. He worked in live action from then on, earning three more Oscar nominations and scoring films like the noir *Nocturne* (1946) and the western *Warlock* (1959)—his last scores were for NBC's *Daniel Boone* television show in 1967—but of his more than 200 credits he remains best remembered today for his work with Disney and in particular on *Pinocchio*, which has been critically reassessed and is now considered by many critics the greatest animated film of all time, thanks in no small part to Harline's score and songs. He died of throat cancer in Long Beach in 1969.[125]

The Walt Disney Studio was, in fact, something of a hub for Mormon filmmakers in the Second Wave as many artists and animators found it a stable employer in the midst of the Depression. Perhaps the first of these was Les Clark, whose mother was Mormon and who descended from pioneers, but whose father James Clark apparently was not. Les was born in Ogden in 1907 and grew up there and in Twin Falls, Idaho, so there's a chance that he may have been baptized at age eight, although he apparently didn't identify as Mormon as an adult. The family moved to Los Angeles in the 1920s and Clark, still a high school student, showed his drawings to Walt and Roy Disney and was hired immediately, working as an in-betweener, rostrum camera operator, and inker before becoming an animator in his own right. He began with the *Alice* films and was one of the few Disney employees who stayed with Walt and Roy Disney when they lost the rights to their character Oswald the Lucky Rabbit and their distribution deal with Charles Mintz, and he was involved with both the creation of Mickey Mouse and the decision to create the first sound cartoon with *Steamboat Willie* (1928). He became known as one of Disney's "Nine Old Men," Walt's team of core animators whose tongue-in-cheek nickname came from FDR's dismissive term for the Supreme Court justices, and when he retired on September 30, 1975 he had been at the company longer than any other employee. In that time he directed several short films and worked on every feature from *Snow White* to *101 Dalmatians* in 1961.[126]

Floyd Gattfredson, a young Mormon artist from Siggurd, Utah, joined the studio just two years after Clark when he moved to Los Angeles and applied for a job at Disney in 1929. Disney's new character Mickey Mouse had become an instant star with *Steamboat Willie* a few months earlier, and Disney hired Gottfredson to work with Win Smith on a new Mickey Mouse comic strip that would be released through the King Features newspaper syndicate. At the same time Gottfredson trained as an in-betweener and even began animating on the Silly Symphony *Cannibal Capers* (1930), but Smith's sudden departure in 1930 required him to take over the strip full-time, and although it was supposed to be a temporary position he wrote and drew it for the next forty-five years, eventually overseeing a large team of comic strip artists. Thus while he wasn't involved in film production directly he was attached to Mickey Mouse longer than any other artist in the history of the character. Mickey's animated films often took their tone from Gottfredson's newspaper work, with specific gags and the overall evolution in Mickey's character—from puckish to heroic—occurring in the strip first and then being picked up in the films. Sometimes entire characters, such as Donald Duck's nephews Huey, Dewey, and Louie, appeared in print before being adapted to animation.[127]

Perhaps the next Mormon to join Disney was "Judge" Wetzel Whitaker in 1932, who would prove more consequential to the history of Mormon film than Disney animation. Born on September 30, 1908, in Heber City, a town on the east side of the Wasatch Mountains near Salt Lake City and Provo, at age five he moved with his large family to Brigham City in the north of the state where his father supervised music education for Box Elder County schools. Whitaker acquired his lifelong nickname on a visit to Snowville on the Idaho border. There a stern, squat justice of the peace known as "Judge Nelson" also owned a grocery store and the only gas pump in town, and after the Whitaker family stopped at the gas station Wetzel's older brother Ferrin teased him that, with his white eyes and gap between his teeth, he would grow up to look just like the Judge. From then on Ferrin called him Judge, and soon the name caught on with the neighborhood kids and other family members, serving as his given name throughout adulthood; it's even present in the credits of Disney films like *Cinderella* (1950). "When I was a boy and young everyone knew it was a nickname," he later wrote, "but as I grew older and began to gray around the temples people who didn't know my story actually thought I was a Judge, much to my embarrassment." Once while he worked at Disney a fellow ward member wanted help getting her husband out of jail, something that this particular udge was powerless to do.[128]

When the family moved to Denver, a teenage Whitaker dabbled in acting but spent most his time playing football and participating in high school student government. His artistic career started in the mid-20s at the Morris Sign Company, where he dug post holes and painted over old signs to prepare them for reuse. Soon he developed a talent for artwork and lettering, and when his family moved to California to find work he stayed in Denver to finish high school, where he was the student body president, and keep playing right tackle and painting signs. He joined them in 1927 but didn't like it there, so he opted to go live with Ferrin in Chicago, where he was an art director at the Montgomery Ward catalog and department store retail chain. Through Ferrin, Judge landed a job doing silk screening for the company's advertisements, and simultaneously he enrolled in night classes at the Art Institute of Chicago. He briefly returned to California to propose to Doris Youkstetter, but then spent another two years on his own with Montgomery Ward before joining the *St. Louis Times* as an art director. Feeling secure in his work, he and Doris finally married, but then almost immediately the newspaper folded. In July 1932, Whitaker found himself unemployed at the height of the Depression with a baby due in September. Soon his three-person family moved back in with Ferrin in Chicago, and there Judge met Walt Pfeiffer, a childhood friend of Walt Disney who was about to join him in California as an executive for Disney's studio. Intrigued by animation, Judge mailed some samples to Disney; he was told they weren't hiring at that time but if he was ever in Los Angeles to pay them a visit. For the desperate Whitaker, that was enough: he loaded all their possessions in the family car and they moved to L.A.

Once there he went straight to Disney, where he showed his portfolio to animator Ben Sharpsteen. "Not bad, but not too good either," he recalls Sharpsteen saying.[129] Still, they were good enough to procure a position as a trainee, but in March 1933 when Roosevelt, in his first week in office, declared a bank holiday, Disney ran out of funds to pay its employees and all the trainees were laid off. Ever ambitious, Whitaker spent a few weeks cleaning up from the March 1933 Long Beach earthquake, but then found work with Disney's rival Charles Mintz, this time bringing his younger brother Scott, born in 1915 and who also wanted to be an animator, with him. Mintz's films then primarily featured the characters Krazy Kat, about a simpleton cat in love with a sadistic mouse, and Scrappy, a mischievous young boy, and they were distributed through Columbia Pictures through the label that would soon be known as Screen Gems. "Neither Scott nor I liked the cartoons that Mintz produced," Judge later said, "but it was a means of learning more about the animation business and it was a job."[130] When things picked back up at Disney the studio offered Judge and Scott $25 a week to re-join them; Mintz counteroffered at $27.50. Because Scott was single and didn't need the money he switched; while he "had gotten along well with the Mintz employees in what was a 'predominantly Jewish environment,' he wasn't 'too happy with the type of films they were doing or with their working conditions.'"[131] Judge, feeling the need to earn as much as possible, stayed on. This worked to his favor, however, because not much later he was able to move back to Disney at a salary of $35 a week.

At this point *Snow White* was in production—Scott was working as an assistant animator on it—but Judge was assigned the studio's bread and butter shorts, becoming a key member of the team overseeing the Donald Duck films. He and Doris were now able to purchase a home—allowing him to serve as the Elders' quorum president in the Huntington Park Ward—and be sealed in the Mesa Temple in time for another child to be born.[132] When Disney moved to new facilities in Burbank in January 1940 the Whitakers rented a home in North Hollywood. Judge, while not a star artist, was moving up the ranks when in May 1941 nearly all the Disney employees went on strike. This was a major event that shook the studio to the core; it would take roughly until *Cinderella* nine years later for the company to regain its footing, and Walt himself never trusted his employees the same way again. For his part, Whitaker, a conservative, claimed to be one of about five animators who voted against the strike, eventually concluding that it was entirely controlled by communist agents. Still he was forced to participate because of his union membership, but Scott had left to serve a mission in South Africa and hence avoided the episode. Judge got out of some of his picketing duties by traveling to Flint, Michigan to pick up a new car; he was delayed on the journey home by his son catching mumps and he returned the day after the strike was settled. For him the timing was suspicious:

> Peace once more settled over the studio and I always had the feeling that the strike should never have happened in the first place. It is surprising how quickly it was settled when Hitler treacherously broke his nonaggression treaty with Russia and attacked them in full force, giving me all the more reason to suspect that the strike had been fomented by communists. Russia and the United States were now allies, and the strikers must have received orders to settle quickly.[133]

With the coming of war Disney began producing instructional and other films to aid in the war effort, including several shorts Judge worked on that placed Donald Duck in the army, such as *Donald Gets Drafted, The Vanishing Private,* and *Sky Trooper* (all 1942). This public morale work exempted Judge from the draft and was his and Disney's contribution to the war effort, and at the same time he was also serving on the San Fernando Stake High Council, a group of twelve high priests who assist the stake presidency in overseeing a group of wards. After the war his career shifted to Church filmmaking, which will be discussed later, but in the 1940s and early '50s his work at Disney included multiple shorts, the low-budget features *The Three Caballeros* (1944, which featured Donald Duck as a major character), *Make Mine Music* (1946), *Fun and Fancy Free* (1947), and *Melody Time* (1948), and then contributions to the major features *Cinderella, Alice in Wonderland* (1951), and *Peter Pan* (1953), for which he worked on the Lost Boys. This would be his last film for Disney.[134]

Far more influential at that studio was animator Eric Larson. Like Les Clark he became one of Disney's Nine Old Men, guiding the studio through decades of productions, but his connection with Mormonism was much more pronounced than Clark's. One colleague jokingly described him as a "collapsed Mormon" who liked his coffee and daily sherry, but he reportedly attended Church services dutifully his whole life with the support of his Catholic wife Gertrude and, as we shall see, he invariably assisted Church filmmaking efforts whenever possible; his brother Peter described him as "devout though not 'extreme' in his faith."[135] He was born to Danish convert immigrants in 1905 in Cleveland, a town in central Utah that even today only has roughly 500 residents. Growing up on a ranch he read the comic magazines *Punch* and *Judge*, and when he studied at the University of Utah he wrote and drew cartoons for the college magazine as well as for the *Deseret News*. In 1927 a student football player got on the roof of the magazine's building and fell through the skylight of Larson's office in a fatal accident; Larson was somehow blamed for this so he dropped out of school and, like so many others, left Utah looking for work, freelancing as a magazine illustrator and working as an art director for a firm in Los Angeles that designed school yearbooks. When he tried to sell a radio play script to the station KHJ they put him in contact with Disney writer Dick Creedon, and he encouraged Larson to apply for an animator position. He was hired on June 1, 1933 and worked for five weeks as an in-betweener before being promoted to assistant animator on the Silly Symphonies, where he helped refine the process of how animators' rough drawings were cleaned up before being inked and painted on cels, vastly improving the efficiency of the workflow. He was an assistant to animator Ham

The Second Wave: Home Cinema

Luske, who brought him onto *Snow White*, and was quickly promoted to full animator, drawing the character of Bashful and much of the "Whistle While You Work" sequence. Perhaps because of his position he was able to avoid participating in the strike, which gave him even more of Walt Disney's personal confidence, and thereafter he and the other Nine Old Men were tasked with administrative duties such as hiring and firing employees; Larson distinguished himself as a calm mediating voice among so many opinionated artists. He was also heavily involved in all of Disney's features, serving, for instance, as an animation director on *Pinocchio*, overseeing much of the work on the film's animals and creating the character of Figaro the cat, an audience favorite who went on to star in six of his own short films. After this he became well-known for his animal work, including the Pegasuses in *Fantasia* (1940), the baby circus animals in *Dumbo* (1941), Sasha the bird in the "Peter and the Wolf" sequence of *Make Mine Music*, the dogs in *Lady and the Tramp* (1955) and *101 Dalmatians,* the vultures in *The Jungle Book* (1967) and *Robin Hood* (1973), and a host of animals in *Mary Poppins* (1964). He put this skill to good use as a supervising animator on *Bambi* (1942), where he oversaw a staff of ten animators and thirty assistants, and he had similar crews as he supervised animation on films like *Fantasia, 101 Dalmatians,* and *Sleeping Beauty* (1959), a difficult film on which he was eventually blamed for delays that were essentially Walt Disney's fault and removed from his directing position. Despite his reputation for animating animals his humans were some of his best work, particularly the title character of *Cinderella*; as one of two men overseeing her animation, he was credited with giving her a human grace and adult sophistication, as in the moment when she raises her eyebrows to sarcastically refer to her step-sisters' "music lesson."

As the last of the Nine Old Men at the studio in the 1970s and '80s he became something of a recruiter, teacher, and trainer, passing on the first generation's mantle to a new group of artists, setting up an entire training program that dozens of new animators went through. Having no children himself, he proved a natural teacher and father figure to them, and many of the artists responsible for Disney's animation renaissance in the late 1980s and '90s recalled fondly how Larson took them under his wing, training them technically and nurturing them emotionally as they learned their craft. This group included Ron Clements, Glen Keane, Randy Cartwright, John Musker, Brad Bird, John Lasseter, Ellen Woodbury, Mark Henn, Kathy Zielinski, and many others, and their work soon spilled outside of Disney to studios like Pixar, DreamWorks, and Aardman as well. Andreas Deja recalled how as a young artist in Germany he read about

Larson's training program so he sent him some drawings and Larson responded proposing that they meet while he was on an upcoming European cruise. The result of Larson taking time out of his vacation to talk with an aspiring young artist was that Deja moved to Los Angeles in 1980 and entered the program, eventually becoming one of Disney's top artists and animating the characters of Roger Rabbit, King Triton, Jafar, Gaston, Scar, Lilo, Mama Odie, and Hercules; many of Larson's other students have similar lists of credits. But there were also setbacks late in his career: in 1975 he had developed a half-hour film called *The Small One*, about the donkey that carried Mary to Bethlehem, that he was using to train young animators and artists. One Monday morning when they came to work they found all their offices had been cleared out and the project given to Don Bluth, another Mormon who soon left to found his own company. Larson considered this a betrayal by the studio and, hating the factionalism that he thought Bluth represented, from this point on he tried to avoid the politics that fractured the studio during its artistic and financial crisis of the 1980s. When Disney nearly suffered a hostile takeover in 1984 and the new management of Michael Eisner, Frank Wells, and Jeffrey Katzenberg moved the animation department to a bleak warehouse in Glendale, Larson saw little reason to remain with the company. He retired on February 28, 1986, after fifty-three years at Disney, and died on October 25, 1988. The new generation of animators all knew they were in his debt, and as they began the studio's comeback with *The Little Mermaid* (1989) they named the character Prince Eric in his honor.[136]

With so much activity at the Disney Studio in the 1930s and '40s, it's impossible to know exactly how many Mormons worked there in different capacities, like Leroy Beach, who was a driver for the studio and occasionally chauffeured Walt and his family. And Disney himself seemed to admire his Mormon employees. "Walt Disney had a great admiration for the Church," Larson recalled. "He respected the self-reliance of the Mormon people. He knew his Mormon employees would give an honest day's work and would get the job done."[137] Mormons, in return, have often demonstrated a love and respect for Walt Disney generally not shown for other filmmakers, bestowing awards to Disney films, emphasizing them for ward movie nights and private film distribution, and turning out in force for "Mormon Days" at Disneyland. In 1966 Connie Jean Swanson, a Mormon Disneyland tour guide, was selected as Walt Disney's personal "world ambassador," opening the It's a Small World ride and traveling to Sweden and Russia to represent the company.[138] Perhaps most importantly, when Judge and Scott Whitaker began their filmmaking program at BYU they brought along a strong belief in the types of films they had made at Disney. At least through the Fourth Wave, and

The Second Wave: Home Cinema

in many ways to the present, there has been a particular compatibility between the Mormon and Disney worldviews—and a shared aesthetic in their films.[139]

Despite their influence at studios like Disney, MGM, Paramount, and RKO, Mormon animators, composers, and technicians could never match the public recognition that Mormon actors achieved in this period. There was no slowdown from the First Wave in the number of Latter-day Saints who tried to make a career in front of the camera. Sometimes California actors came to Utah, as in the case of Don Summers, the performer who converted to the faith during the production of *Wagon Master*. But, as with other positions, typically the migration went the other way. In 1931 one J. H. Paul wrote in the *Improvement Era*, "The writer is informed that Utah is well represented in the actor population of Hollywood,"[140] and that remained true throughout the Second Wave as more and more Mormon thespians relocated to the filmmaking capital.

The best-known of these was probably Laraine Day, a great-granddaughter of pioneer apostle Charles C. Rich who was born Loraine Johnson on October 13, 1920 in Roosevelt, Utah. She later recalled that the town only showed one movie per week, but she was entranced by actress Billie Dove and wanted to follow in her footsteps. When she was twelve her family moved to Long Beach, California as a consequence of the Depression, resulting in her first public performance, a reading at the dedication of the Los Angeles Temple site; the Church further nurtured her talent as she became involved with Church and MIA dramatics, an association she would maintain throughout her life. She also trained with the Long Beach Players' Guild, eventually joining the company and appearing on stage, which led her to getting an agent and bit parts in Universal films in 1937. Soon she adopted her screen name—in memory of the Long Beach Players' director Elias Day—and signed with MGM, where she found fame playing Nurse Lamont in the *Dr. Kildare* series with Lionel Barrymore and Lew Ayres. Based on a pulp magazine character, these were medical dramas about a young doctor in New York City, and Day appeared in seven of the films between 1939 and 1941. This made her a favorite among American G.I.s, and she also later claimed to have worked many Mormon elements into the films. She filmed multiple other projects between *Kildare* pictures, including Charles Vidor's *My Son, My Son!* (1940) but most notably adopting a British accent to play the female lead in Alfred Hitchcock's *Foreign Correspondent* (1940), an impressive mark of success for a nineteen-year-old actress who still lived with her parents. She appeared in the war film *Keep Your Powder Dry* (1945) in return for the lead in the thriller *Undercurrent* (1946), but when MGM gave that role to Katharine Hepburn she broke her contract and sought to push her career forward with a psychologically complex role in the noir-ish melodrama *The Locket* (1946) for RKO. In the 1950s she began appearing on television, especially in the popular anthology programs like *The Ford Television Theatre* and *Lux Video Theatre* that portrayed individual unconnected dramas, akin to small films, in each episode. After the birth of her two children in the 1960s she diminished her amount of work overall. Her last appearances were on *Murder, She Wrote* in 1986, although she lived in retirement until 2007. She was noted throughout her career for her adherence to the Word of Wisdom and her refusal to use profanity, as well as for her patriotism and devotion to conservative political causes: she campaigned for Richard Nixon and later for her friend and one-time onscreen love interest Ronald Reagan (from *The Bad Man* in 1941). More notably, in the immediate post-war years she served on the Motion Picture Alliance for the Preservation of American Ideals, an anti-communist group that was the chief source of witnesses for the House Un-American Activities Committee's investigation into Hollywood politics. After retiring she also advocated for environmental causes, and at that point she and her third husband Michael Grilikhes, who converted to the Church while courting her in the 1950s, served two days a week as ordinance workers in the Los Angeles Temple, making her perhaps the only temple worker ever with a star on the Hollywood Walk of Fame.[141]

Unlike many others from this era, Rhonda Fleming wasn't born in Utah, although that was simply because her parents had already moved to California before she was born. Her maternal grandfather John Crosthwaite Graham was baptized as a child in Liverpool and came with his family as a pioneer to Utah. As an adult he became prominent as a newspaper editor, actor, and theater owner—he was the first to cast Maude Adams as a young child—and his daughter Effie followed this career path, leaving Utah and becoming a stage actress and model in New York. She stopped acting when she married an insurance salesman named Harold Louis, whose relationship to Mormonism is unclear, and they lived in Beverly Hills when Rhonda was born, as Marilyn Louis, in 1923. Rhonda had a troubled adolescence after her parents divorced, and at sixteen she eloped and had her only child, although the marriage only lasted a few years. This was a rocky period for her, but she later recalled, "By bringing me up in the Mormon faith, Mother had built better than I knew. The training stuck. Basically, I was a religious girl...."[142] At the same time she became interested in acting; she had reached the semifinals in Jesse Lasky's *Gateway to Hollywood* radio show at age fourteen, even though contestants had to be eighteen to enter, and after her divorce she returned to Beverly Hills High School and pursued school dramatics, landing a few film roles before she even graduated. She signed with David Selznick but had, in fact, only appeared in four films when Hitchcock cast her in a supporting role in his Freudian thriller *Spellbound* (1945) with Ingrid Bergman and Gregory Peck. This was her big break, and she appeared in over forty more films, including *Out of the Past* (1947), *A Connecticut Yankee in King Arthur's Court* (1949), *Serpent of the Nile* (1953) in which she played Cleopatra, Fritz Lang's *While the City Sleeps* (1956), and *Gunfight at the O.K. Corral* (1957), as well as several television programs and plays on Broadway and elsewhere. Regarded for her beauty even more than her acting ability, she became known as the Queen of Technicolor because of how well her lush red hair photographed. As she aged she increasingly devoted herself to philanthropy, creating a second career and legacy that rivals her film work. She sat on numerous boards and foundations and funded many initiatives, particularly focusing on child abuse and, after watching her sister battle ovarian cancer, women's cancers. Over the years she's been involved with Childhelp, the John Douglas French Alzheimer's Foundation, Stop Cancer, the Los Angeles Music Center, the Olive Crest Treatment Centers for Abused Children, the Jerusalem Film Center, the Revlon/ UCLA Women's Health Research Program, and many others, and she created the Rhonda Fleming Mann Research Fellowship at the City of Hope Hospital in Los Angeles, the Rhonda Fleming Family Center at P.A.T.H. (People Assisting the Homeless), and both the Rhonda Fleming Mann Clinic for Women's Comprehensive Care and the Rhonda Fleming Mann Resource Center for Women with Cancer at UCLA Medical Center. As of 2018 she lives in Century City, California, at age ninety-five.[143]

Like Fleming, Terry Moore was born in California, in Glendale north of central Los Angeles, in 1929. The granddaughter of Scandinavian settlers of Brigham City, Utah and Downey, Idaho—her birth name was Helen Luella Koford—she tried several stage names before settling on Terry Moore in 1948. She began as a child model and received her first part at age eleven in 1940. Signing with Columbia Pictures, she moved through various youthful roles until having her break starring opposite Glenn Ford in *The Return of October* (1948) and as the female lead in Merian Cooper and Ernest Schoedsack's *Mighty Joe Young* (1949), a follow-up film to their earlier *King Kong*—making Moore the second Mormon actress to appear opposite one of their giant apes. She was nominated for a Best Supporting Actress Oscar for the drama *Come Back, Little Sheba* in 1952 and appeared in *The Great Rupert* (1950), *Daddy Long Legs* (1955), *Between Heaven and Hell* (1956), and *Peyton Place* (1957). In the midst of that success she wrote that the Church taught her to balance her work and personal life, saying, "the mainstream of my thinking has come from my religion, and from this was shaped my character."[144] By the 1960s her career shifted toward television, particularly her role as a rancher's daughter on the NBC western *Empire* (1962-63). She semi-retired in the 1970s but made a comeback on television and film in the '80s, often in supporting roles. As of 2018, at eighty-nine, she is working as steadily as at any point in her career. In addition to her acting she has modeled—she visited the troops in the Korean War and was a popular pin-up girl among them, and she appeared naked in *Playboy* at age fifty-five in 1984—and today she is as well known for her personal life as her films. She married publicly four times, but after the death of Howard Hughes in April 1976 she claimed that she had also secretly married him aboard a yacht in international waters in 1949. She asserted they never divorced—Hughes simply tore up the ship's log—despite her three subsequent marriages during his lifetime. At one point she planned to produce a film version of one of her two books about Hughes, but instead she worked with Martin Scorsese and Leonardo DiCaprio on their Hughes biopic *The Aviator* (2004).[145]

A third native Californian was Robert Horton. Born on July 29, 1924 in Los Angeles, he suffered several childhood illnesses that resulted in a medical discharge when he enlisted in the Coast Guard in 1943. Instead of serving in the war he studied acting at the University of Miami and UCLA, receiving a bit part in *A Walk in the Sun* (1945) before appearing onstage in New York for a few years. He signed with MGM in 1952 and began acting in films. His pictures weren't notable—with titles like the Korean War film *Men of the Fighting Lady* (1954) and the science-fiction *The Green Slime* (1968)—but starting with a guest appearance on *The Lone Ranger* in 1954 he began a prolific television career, with regular appearances on magazine shows like *Alfred Hitchcock Presents* (1956-60) and *Matinee Theatre* (1955-1958), where his roles included Benedick in *Much Ado About Nothing*. He starred in *Wagon Train* and had the title role in *A Man Called Shenandoah* (1965-66), and appeared in many other series and television movies like the espionage thriller *The Spy Killer* (1969). He retired in 1989 and passed away in 2016. He has not generally been considered a Mormon actor: talking about his parents in 1962 he recalled, "They were very rigidly brought up in the Mormon religion and they brought us up this way, including no smoking and all that sort of thing—which was not for me. My family are wonderful people, but I didn't happen to want to be just like them...."[146]

There was no confusing the religion of character actor Moroni Olsen, the son of Danish convert immigrants to Utah who named him after the Book of Mormon prophet; some sources claim he was the son of the painter John Willard Clawson, but his parents were Edward Arenholt Olsen and Martha Magdaline Hoverholst Olsen, who settled in Ogden before he was born in 1889. He attended Weber State Academy and then the University of Utah while acting in Church-sponsored dramatic productions. He tried his hand at acting onstage in the eastern states, appearing in *Medea, The Trial of Joan of Arc*, and a handful of other plays, and during World War I he sold war bonds for the Navy. Returning to Ogden in 1923, he formed his own stock company, the Moroni Olsen Players, and they proved quite successful in local theaters, touring as far as Seattle. Olsen even returned to Broadway for several more productions before transitioning to film by playing Porthos in the 1935 *The Three Musketeers*, which he followed with many historical roles such as Robert E. Lee, Buffalo Bill, John Knox, Sam Houston, and, last of all, Pope Leo I in Douglas Sirk's 1954 *Sign of the Pagan*. He was in Hitchcock's *Notorious* (1946) as a Secret Service agent supporting Cary Grant, and he provided the voices for the Magic Mirror in *Snow White* and the senior angel in *It's a Wonderful Life* (1946). He also played apostle Willard Richards in *Brigham Young*, the only actual Mormon in the cast. In the 1950s he began portraying heavies on television, and he remained devoted to stage work as well: in between films he helped run the Pasadena Playhouse, frequently appearing onstage, and in the year of his death he staged an Ogden performance of Roland Parry's *All Faces West* musical, with Igor Gorin reprising his role of Brigham Young, and narrated a pageant with the Tabernacle Choir and opera singer Carl Palangi in Salt Lake City. A lifelong bachelor, he spent several years teaching the adolescents of his ward in Beverly Hills. He died of a heart attack in November 1954 and was buried in his native Ogden; fellow Ogden son David McKay spoke at his funeral, comparing him with George Washington and claiming he was too devoted to his work to ever marry.[147]

Through the Moroni Olsen Players, Olsen was partially responsible for a few other Mormon careers in Hollywood. Leora Thatcher, for instance, was born in Logan in 1894, a granddaughter of erstwhile apostle Moses Thatcher, and she studied speech and drama at Brigham Young College in Logan and the University of Utah and taught two years at Logan High School before joining Olsen as one of his first actors in 1923. She stayed with him for eight years and then joined the KSL Players, a dramatic radio troupe, for three years, while also teaching music and directing children's theater, before finally heading to Hollywood in 1935, where she played in various short comedies and a few features. She continued her association with Olsen at the Pasadena Playhouse, and she actually found more success returning to the New York stages than in Hollywood. In the city during the war, she volunteered by serving food, performing for wounded veterans, and teaching English to Jewish refugees, and afterwards she returned to radio, stage, and film but found the bulk of her work on television, including programs like *The Magnavox Theatre* (1950) and *Robert Montgomery Presents* (1954), and numerous titles of the new television soap operas, such as *The Secret Storm, Search for Tomorrow,* and *Young Dr. Malone.* She retired from the screen and returned to Logan to tend her ailing sister in 1967, though she stayed involved with regional theater there for many more years, and she died in 1984 in Salt Lake City.[148]

Another actor associated with Olsen, Frank Rasmussen, had a much briefer Hollywood career, appearing in just three films in the 1930s. Another son of Danish convert immigrants, he grew up on a farm in Fillmore, Utah, studied theater at the University of Utah, became a stage manager at the Social Hall Theater in Salt Lake, joined the Moroni Olsen Players in 1923, and spent many years with other touring groups in Utah, California—including the Pasadena Playhouse, a hub for Mormon actors—the eastern United States, Australia, and New Zealand. His films were *The Toast of New York, They Won't Forget* (both 1937), and *The Marines Come Through* (1938). After wartime missionary service he spent most of the remainder of his career teaching speech and drama in Millard High School in his hometown and working with Church and MIA dramatics.[149]

Much more prominent was Billy Barty, who was born in 1924 in Millsboro, Pennsylvania. He began his career as a child actor at the cusp of the sound era, appearing with Mickey Rooney in the *Mickey McGuire* film series that gave young Rooney his stage name. Barty's first appearance was probably with *Mickey's Pals* in 1927, and he played the baby or Mickey's little brother Billy in several dozen short films in the series over the next few years. Distinguished throughout his life by his dwarfism, even at this age Barty was noted for playing diminutive characters, as when at nine years old he played a mischievous baby in *Gold Diggers of 1933* (1933). His short stature gave him many novelty and comic roles over the years, playing imps, clowns, dwarfs, leprechauns, midgets, and a variety of creatures in costume; in this vein he is best remembered for several fantasy films from late in his career, such as *Legends* (1985), *Masters of the Universe* (1987), and especially *Willow* (1988), but over the course of nearly two hundred films he portrayed many dramatic and comic roles unrelated to his height. He also created a thriving career on television with both scripted and nonfiction shows. In addition to children's shows he appeared on adult fare like *Alfred Hitchcock Presents* (1957), *Peter Gunn* (1960), *Get Smart* (1970), *The*

The Second Wave: Home Cinema

Waltons (1972), *Charlie's Angels* (1978), *Little House on the Prairie* (1979; 1982), and *Trapper John, M.D.* (1984). In the 1950s he became a regular presence in the Spike Jones comedy band, appearing on *The Spike Jones Show* (1954) and making frequent television appearances with them, and from 1963-67 he had his own children's variety show, *Billy Barty's Big Top*. Further proof of his acting skills is his career as a voice actor for animation, including television programs like *Wildfire* (1986), *DuckTales* (1987), and *The New Batman Adventures* (1997), and the feature films *The Lord of the Rings* (1978) and *The Rescuers Down Under* (1990). He married in Malad City, Idaho in 1962, received a star on the Hollywood Walk of Fame in 1981, and died of heart failure in 2000. In 1957 he made a national appeal for all Americans with dwarfism to come to a conference in Reno, Nevada, where he founded the nonprofit organization Little People of America to support people of short stature and their families. Today the organization assists and advocates for little people through medical research, social work, employment and adoption assistance, and other areas, with over 6,000 members across the United States.[150]

Many other Mormon actors launched successful careers in this period. Edwina Booth, born in Provo in 1904, began a promising career in Hollywood in 1928, appearing in several films like *The Last of the Mohicans* and *Trapped in Tia Juana* (both 1932) before her career took a tragic turn. Cast opposite Harry Carey in an Africa-set film called *Trader Horn* (1931), she played the "White Goddess," the daughter of a missionary captured by an African tribe and now worshipped by them. On location in the African jungle, however, she contracted malaria that had her bedridden for nearly six years. Rumors of her death were rampant, and she sued MGM for over one million dollars, though the suit was settled out of court. She never acted again but remained in Los Angeles, later serving in the Los Angeles Temple. She died of heart failure in 1991. Robert Walker came from a Mormon family in Salt Lake City, and he had some acting experience at a military academy in San Diego and then the Pasadena Playhouse before studying at the American Academy of Dramatic Arts in New York. There he married actress Jennifer Jones and the two moved to Hollywood. Walker is best remembered today for his lead turn as the murderer in Hitchcock's *Strangers on a Train* (1951), and his other films include *The Clock* (1945) with Judy Garland, *Song of Love* (1947) with Katharine Hepburn, and *One Touch of Venus* (1948) with Ava Gardner. He might have become a great leading man, but when Jones divorced him he suffered a nervous breakdown and died at age thirty-two, a few months after *Stranger on a Train* was released in 1951, of an accidental combination of alcohol and the drugs he was taking to treat his condition. Gordon Westcott was a child of polygamy, born Myrthus Hickman in St. George in 1903. After his move to Hollywood he signed with Warner Brothers and appeared in supporting roles in thirty-seven films. He had the looks to make it as a leading man but he died of a head injury sustained during a polo match in 1935, cutting his career short. His daughter Helen Westcott also acted in films and television programs through the 1970s, but she was not raised in the Church and apparently had no connection with it beyond her ancestry. Marie Windsor, originally Emily Marie Bertelsen, from Marysvale, Utah, studied drama at BYU and under Moscow Art Theatre veteran Maria Ouspenskaya. Her first film role was in 1941 and by the late '40s she found success in film noir. Some of these were prestigious films, such as Stanley Kubrick's *The Killing* (1956), but she eventually starred in so many B-movies that she earned the title "Queen of the B's." Expert at playing vamps and femmes fatales, she often received Bibles in the mail from viewers who, unaware that she was a practicing Mormon, encouraged her to amend her wanton ways. She also appeared frequently on television, working steadily until 1991, and served twenty-five years on the Screen Actors Guild board of directors; she passed away at age eighty in 2000. Jean Sullivan was born in Logan, Utah in 1923. She attended UCLA and while acting in a play there was discovered by a scout for Warner Brothers; the studio signed her immediately and her first role was in Raoul Walsh's war drama *Uncertain Glory* in 1944, followed by *Roughly Speaking* and *Escape in the Desert* (both 1945). She left Hollywood, however, to pursue a dance career in New York, appearing with American Ballet Theatre and specializing in flamenco both as a dancer and musician. In this capacity she appeared on various variety shows, such as *The Steve Allen Show* and *The Jackie Gleason Show*, and she also acted in a handful of television roles in the 1960s and '70s. She died in California in 2003. Haila Stoddard worked for most of her career on the stage, but she had her first television role in the Second Wave, acting on screen through 1967. Born to Mormon parents in Great Falls, Montana, she was raised in Salt Lake City and, primarily, Los Angeles. She later recalled that it was a rebellion against her parents and their religion that led her to acting; after graduating from high school she appeared on stage first in San Francisco and then in New York, touring the South Pacific with the USO during the war and appearing in a number of plays in a career that stretched decades, in New York, London, and regional American theaters, especially in Denver. She made her first television appearance on the *Colgate Theatre* program in 1949, appearing frequently on similar televised plays for the next twenty years. She retired from the stage in the late 1980s and died, age ninety-seven, in 2011. Joi Lansing was born Joy Rae Brown in Salt Lake City in 1929. After some time in Ogden her family moved to Los Angeles in 1940 and she began modeling at age fourteen, soon signing with MGM. She gave live performances at Air Force bases and had a number of uncredited roles throughout the 1940s, while she continued to model and gained more attention as a pin-up girl than as an actress. She had bit parts in *Singin' in the Rain* (1952) and *Touch of Evil* (1958), appearing in the latter's famous opening shot as a victim of the bombing that initiates the plot—her only line was, "I keep hearing this ticking noise inside my head!"—but she also began to get higher-billed roles and launched second careers as a singer and on television. She earned her greatest fame there, with many guest appearances and continual roles on *Klondike* (1960-61) and *The Beverly Hillbillies* (1963-68). She was frustrated that her voluptuous looks often excluded her from serious dramatic roles and died of breast cancer at forty-three in 1972. Finally, one famous Mormon who had a very brief film career was Lenore Romney, née LaFount. Born in Logan in 1908, after studying at the University of Utah and George Washington University she moved to New York to study at the American Laboratory Theatre. In Hollywood she began appearing in bit parts for MGM, but she declined a contract when she married George Romney in 1931. The rest of her career was dedicated to politics—as First Lady of Michigan and a 1970 senatorial candidate—philanthropic and social work, and raising her children, including future politician Mitt Romney.[151]

The most successful Mormon screenwriter of the Second Wave was undoubtedly Casey Robinson, who was born in Logan in 1903. He studied at Cornell University, returned to Utah to teach high school English in Brigham City, then set off to New York in the mid-20s to become a journalist. There, a contact at the *New York World* got him a job writing intertitles for silent films. He moved to Hollywood in 1927, signed with Paramount in 1933, writing a series of B-pictures for them, briefly tried directing, and then moved as a writer to Warner Brothers in 1935, where he became their top screenwriter and created the tone of both their swashbuckling and romantic works throughout the next decade. His first major project for Warners was *Captain Blood* (1935), a pirate film that made a star of Errol Flynn; Robinson was nominated for an Academy Award for his script. An even greater accomplishment came two years later with *It's Love I'm After* (1937), which revitalized the career of Bette Davis after she'd had a contract dispute with the studio. Over the course of six films—including *Dark Victory* (1939) and *Now, Voyager* (1942)—Robinson solidified his reputation as a romantic writer and created a more feminine persona for Davis that would last for the rest of her career. He also developed a reputation as an excellent adapter of literature: he was Warners' choice to tackle difficult material like Henry Bellamann's novel *King's Row* (1942), an intricately plotted book that also guaranteed conflict with the Production Code office, both problems that Robinson success-fully navigated. He adapted numerous other short stories, plays, and novels—years later critic Richard Corliss called him "the master of the art—or craft—of adaptation"[152]—and this, combined with his skill with romance, is what got him assigned to the screenplay of *Casablanca* (1942). Various other screenwriters were already at work on the difficult adaptation from the stageplay *Everybody Comes to Rick's*, and Robinson oversaw changes to Ingrid Bergman's character and the flashback scenes to Rick and Ilsa's affair in Paris. Because he refused to take a writing credit with so many other contributors he missed out on winning what would have been his only Oscar.

In 1944 he also began occasionally producing. Though he only produced seven films between then and 1959—with an eighth in 1975, after he emigrated to Australia—in the first of these, a World War II film called *Days of Glory*, he cast a young stage actor named Gregory Peck in his first film role. It was also the first role for Tamara Toumanova, a Russian immigrant and dancer who Robinson married a short time later; the union lasted until 1955. He eventually moved to MGM, which he later recalled as a mistake as the studio was not known for its writing, and then to Twentieth Century-Fox. His later career included films like the Hemingway adaptation *The Snows of Kilimanjaro* (1952), Michael Curtiz's period epic *The Egyptian* (1954), and Fritz Lang's film noir *While the City Sleeps* (1956). He also wrote roughly a dozen teleplays in the 1960s, at which point he retired and moved with his third wife to her native Australia. He passed away in Sydney in 1979.[153]

Screenwriter Sloan Nibley was the grandson of Charles W. Nibley, Presiding Bishop at the time of Sloan's birth and future counselor to Heber Grant in the First Presidency. Sloan's parents Alexander and Agnes Sloan Nibley had just returned from presiding over the Church's mission in the Netherlands when he was born in 1908, and thus they lived in Portland, Oregon where Charles Nibley had a lumber business; named after his father, Sloan went by his middle name. An initial attempt to break into the industry was delayed by wartime service in the Navy in New York, but after being discharged he immediately embarked on a screenwriting career, starting with his first western for Republic Pictures, *Bells of San Angelo,* in 1947. This would be the genre and studio with which he found his greatest success, and throughout the 1940s and '50s he completed numerous other Republic westerns, often starring Roy Rogers, including *On the Old Spanish Trail* (1947), *Bells of Coronado* (1950), *Twilight in the Sierras* (1950), and *Spoilers of the Plains* (1951). He moved to Warner Brothers with *Carson City*

in 1952 and also began writing for television, penning multiple episodes for
The Adventures of Kit Carson (1952-55), *Judge Roy Bean* (1956), *Science Fiction
Theatre* (1955-56), *26 Men* (1958), *Wagon Train* (1959-63), and *Death Valley Days*
(1963-70). He switched to animation with *The Famous Adventures of Mr. Magoo*
(1964-65) for United Productions of America and situational comedies with *The
Addams Family* (1965-66). He retired in 1973 and died in Los Angeles in 1990.
His son Christopher Nibley has had a successful career as a cinematographer
and visual effects artist, working on properties like *L.A. Story* (1991), *The Santa
Clause* (1994), *Mars Attacks!* (1996), and *Herbie Fully Loaded* (2005), and the
television shows *Heroes* (2006) and Marvel's *Agents of S.H.I.E.L.D.* (2013-14).
Sloan's younger brother Hugh, born two years after him in 1910, became well
known in the Church as a prolific author and lecturer on Mormon theology and
apologetics.[154]

Given all of the Mormons who joined the industry in southern California in the
Second Wave, it's interesting that there weren't more film directors among them.
The only major Mormon director of this period in Hollywood was Joseph M.
Newman, who was born in Logan in 1909. He too must have moved to California while young, because he was working in motion pictures by age sixteen. He
began as an office bellboy, then a clerk, assistant writer, assistant director/
second unit director (job titles with much more fluidity at the time than today),
and finally director in his own right. At MGM he assisted and shot additional
material for great directors like Ernst Lubitsch and George Cukor, giving him an
ideal apprenticeship, and he was twice nominated for an Academy Award for his
second-unit work—an award category that no longer exists—for Cukor's *David
Copperfield* (1935) and W. S. Van Dyke's disaster film *San Francisco* (1936). Other
films he assisted on include *Riptide, The Merry Widow* (both 1934), *Lady of the
Tropics* (1939), and the musicals *Maytime* and *The Firefly* (both 1937), including shooting the latter's "Donkey Serenade" sequence in a moving stagecoach.
He began directing his own short films in 1938, including many newsreels and
documentaries on the war, like *Diary of a Sergeant* (1945) about the recupera-
tion of a veteran who lost his hands in combat. By 1948 Newman graduated to
directing features, working steadily for the next decade on films like *Red Skies
of Montana* (1952), *Flight to Hong Kong* (1956), and *Tarzan, the Ape Man* (1959).
He was particularly adept at film noir—as in *Abandoned* (1949), *711 Ocean
Drive* (1950), *Dangerous Crossing* (1953), and *The Human Jungle* (1954)—and is
perhaps best remembered for *This Island Earth* (1955), one of the great films of
the classical age of science fiction in the 1950s. In 1961 he made his television
debut with a crime-themed episode of *Westinghouse Desilu Playhouse*, and

from that point on he found a place within the television industry by applying his skills with film noir to programs like the television version of *The Asphalt Jungle* (1961) and especially with numerous episodes of both *The Alfred Hitchcock Hour* (1963-65) and *The Twilight Zone* (1963-64). He retired after 1965 and passed away in Simi Valley in 2006 at nearly one hundred years old.[155]

Despite the preponderance of Mormon filmmakers relocating from Utah to California in the Second Wave, surprisingly the most accomplished and important filmmaker to come out of Mormonism in this entire period was connected to neither of these places. Instead, Colin Low was born in the old polygamist colony of Cardston in Alberta, Canada on Pioneer Day, 1926, the progeny of Canadian and, going back further, Utah pioneers. Raised on a ranch outside town he didn't have many opportunities to watch movies growing up but instead read magazines and drew prolifically. During his high school summers he studied visual art at the Banff School of Fine Arts and after graduating he attended what was then known as the Calgary Institute of Technology (today the Southern Alberta Institute of Technology), intending to make his career in color printing and magazine illustration; his interest in graphic imagery informed many of his most famous films, such as *City of Gold* and *Universe*, and in addition to producing a lifetime of drawings he remained a skilled storyboard artist throughout his life. While he was preparing for an art career, however, events occurred which would eventually redirect his path. In 1938 the Canadian government invited the Scottish documentarian John Grierson to evaluate the state of government-sponsored film production in Canada; Grierson had been the chief figure in government film work in Britain in the 1930s, and due to the Depression this was a decade when many governments were attempting similar efforts at socially conscious state-funded filmmaking. Grierson's report became the foundation for the National Film Act of 1939, which established the National Film Board of Canada. With the country entering the war in 1939, almost immediately the NFB was producing propagandistic films about the Allied efforts. Back in Alberta the teenage Low saw a few of these from the *Canada Carries On* series, but he was more impressed by the NFB's advertising posters, so in 1945 he moved to Ottawa to apply for a position working on those. He was hired by the animator Norman McLaren and put to work not on posters but in the animation unit, working on titles, backgrounds, and maps under the tutelage of McLaren and other NFB luminaries like Evelyn Lambart. His first time actually animating was on George Dunning's *Cadet Rousselle* (1947), an adaptation of a French-Canadian folk song, and after a yearlong hiatus traveling and working in Europe he returned to Montreal to work on various animated films. The most notable of these was

The Second Wave: Home Cinema

The Romance of Transportation in Canada (1952), his second directorial effort and the NFB's first cel animated film. A humorous eleven-minute cartoon on the history of transportation in Canada from early canoes to the present, it was the first NFB film nominated for an Oscar and it won a BAFTA and short film Palme d'Or at the Cannes Film Festival. At the same time Low became the supervisor of the animation unit, overseeing logistics of the different films and other assignments like titles and diagrams.

Animation was part of Unit B at the National Film Board, and in the 1950s this unit became the NFB's vanguard organization, recognized globally as one of the most innovative film production units in the world; in addition to its animation, it was hugely influential in launching the global cinema verité movement which reshaped modern documentary. Low entered nonfiction filmmaking with his next major film, *Corral* (1954), at the instigation of Wolf Koenig, who was then pushing for the unit to move into live-action film. A short narrator-less documentary about a cowboy taming a half-broken horse, it was filmed on the Mormon ranches in Alberta where Low had grown up, with forty of his father's own horses and a young Mormon rider who he had known as a boy. A lyrical film that's been described as a pas de deux between a cowboy and a horse, it also helped move the NFB into regional productions and garnered international recognition, including first prize at the Venice Film Festival. Production for *Corral* and Low's next major film, *City of Gold* (1957, co-directed with Koenig) occurred within a six-week period, although postproduction on the latter took a few years longer. This film, about the Klondike Gold Rush, had a stunning narration spoken by Pierre Berton and, more importantly, used Low's experience with animation and rostrum camera movement to introduce the use of still photographs into film, a device which has since become a standard practice in historical documentary and, although it originated with this film, is today primarily associated with Ken Burns. Seven years in the making, Low's animated astronomy film *Universe* (1960, co-directed with Roman Kroitor) was a groundbreaking educational film that received immense distribution in schools and institutions throughout North America—the NFB sold 4,000 16mm prints, including 300 to NASA— and its stunning visual effects led directly to *2001: A Space Odyssey* (1968), with Stanley Kubrick initially wanting to produce that film with Low at the NFB. Instead, for Expo '67 in Montreal Low, again with Kroitor, spent five years co-directing *In the Labyrinth*, a site-specific installation that utilized 35 and 70mm film stocks and five screens. Some of the projectors were used sideways, resulting in a horizontal rather than vertical movement of the film strip, evidently Low's idea. This concept soon combined with some the mechanical tracking devices developed for *Universe* to create both the IMAX and OMNIMAX formats, with Kroitor co-founding the IMAX company in 1967. Low himself continued to occasionally work in large formats, including directing the first 3D IMAX film (*Transitions*, 1986) and the first in high-definition video (*Seville*, 1992); he was feted by the Large Format Cinema Association in 2002.

After Expo '67, Low's career took yet another sharp turn, this time into social issue documentary and political activism. That year he headed the *Challenge for Change/Societé nouvelle* series, which instructed First Nation people, minorities, and other underrepresented groups in the basics of filmmaking, provided them with equipment and technical support, and then guaranteed government-sponsored distribution of their work. Thus many groups were able to create films about their own political and social realities that otherwise would never have existed and actually engage in dialogue with the national government about what laws and programs they needed. This resulted in over 200 productions before it was ended in 1980, including some landmark verité pieces like *You Are on Indian Land* (1969). To launch this program, in 1968 Low began directing the Fogo Island Communications Experiment, eventually consisting of twenty-eight documentary films about one specific impoverished island of Newfoundland and Labrador. In 1976 he became Director of Regional Production and was instrumental in developing production centers in each of the provinces, an important step in decentralizing the NFB's work outside Ottawa and Montreal. His final film was a masterful personal essay called *Moving Pictures* (2000), in which he weaves together a fantasia about his pioneer Mormon heritage, his fascination with graphic arts and miniatures in particular, movies, horses, and the connection between print-making, propaganda, filmmaking, and war; it is one of the most understated but deft Mormon documentaries in existence, and one of the most haunting. With this film Low retired and he passed away on February 24, 2016.

Low personally contributed as a producer and director to over 200 films. He accrued nine Oscar nominations, the most by any Canadian filmmaker, and won over 100 awards, including two Palmes d'Or for *The Romance of Transportation in Canada* and *City of Gold*. He was named a member of the Order of Canada and was the first English-speaking Canadian awarded the Prix Albert-Tessier for contributions to Quebecois cinema. Over the course of his career he demonstrated an understanding of filmmaking as a stewardship, an empowerment that requires the filmmaker to strive to empower others. His work was also deeply patriotic, representing an honest and accurate portrayal of the many

The Second Wave: Home Cinema

faces of Canada's citizens, extolling the beauty of the country, its history, and its institutions while turning a critical eye on its problems such as racism and poverty. His son Stephen Low has carried on his legacy with IMAX films, directing nearly two dozen productions at the NFB and Stephen Low Company since 1980.[156]

To conclude, we should consider one final innovation in the movie theater industry in Utah in the Second Wave. Popcorn had been a popular treat at fairs, carnivals, sporting contests, and other events since its invention in the 1840s, and early movie theaters with their connection with vaudeville and fairs were no exception. This popcorn, along with peanuts and various candies, was generally sold by individual vendors, however, often men who walked up and down the movie theater aisles hawking their product. Sometimes candy vending machines were installed in theaters' lobbies, but usually they belonged to third parties and provided no revenue to the theater owners themselves; this was the type mentioned in Chapter 1 as the target of an attempted theft in Salt Lake City in 1907. As the theaters grew increasingly ostentatious in the 1910s and '20s owners eliminated all concessions and attempted to keep food out of their magnificent theaters. But the Depression saw a resurgence of popcorn, in Utah as elsewhere, simply because it was cheap and filling, providing a good profit margin for vendors, and for the first time this became part of the theater owners' business as well. Candy concessions were making a comeback by the late 1930s, but during the war sugar was rationed by the War Production Board's Sugar Policy Committee, thus eliminating most of the chocolates and candies from theater concessions entirely—and preventing patrons from having their own sweets to sneak into the theater. Thus, during the early 1940s popcorn gained its permanent status as the dominant theater concession item. A new industry was forming around the popcorn supply chain, and in 1947 Utahn William F. Gordon founded the Theater Candy Distributing Company in northern Utah, although he may have been working in that area as early as 1942. His innovation was to supply movie theaters directly with popcorn and candy to resell to patrons, and the company's rapid success throughout the Mountain West was quickly mimicked by others. This was big business: in 1951 an industry trade journal reported that nationally the "highest candy consumption per capita is in Utah, due in large part to the non-smoking Mormon population. But the population of the state is so small that the high consumption is not a major factor in the candy business,"[157] at least not nationally, but it was significant within Utah itself. While Gordon was not the only one to strike upon this concept, he was on the cusp of a major shift in movie theaters' business model: today

Utah has several wholesale concession suppliers, including the still-operating Theater Candy Distributing Company, and worldwide theaters make between forty and eighty-five percent of their profits on concessions. If Gordon himself wasn't Mormon, many of the theater owners he sold to—as well as his product's ultimate consumers, patrons throughout Utah—certainly were and still are.[158]

Independent Mormon Films

Even with so many Latter-day Saints working in the film industry, in the Second Wave, Mormons unfortunately found scant success producing films about their faith for commercial distribution. Like Edward Finney discovered with *The Mormon Battalion*, there was little market even in the postwar economic boom for a Mormon-themed picture, and the odds of success were infinitely slimmer during the Depression and war years. Part of the problem, of course, was scale: no Mormons were able to make a film with the resources Henry Hathaway had for *Brigham Young*, and therefore they were also unable to match its quality and range of distribution. A few tried to approximate it, particularly Lester Park with *Corianton* (1931), but if this had seemed possible in the 1920s such ambitious—and expensive—efforts could no longer be justified. The two features that were completed in the Second Wave—*Corianton* and *The Mormon Conquest* (1939)—exemplified many of the homemade qualities that typified the Home Cinema era, but even these gave way to a type of film that was more in tune with the period: films with no budget at all, no actors or narrative, no plans for any type of distribution, and that, in most cases, were literally meant for domestic consumption as what we today would call "home movies." This was Home Cinema in its truest sense.

"Corianton" and Commercial Productions in the 1930s

Despite the difficulties they suffered, we should not dismiss the few commercial films that were completed in this period. Both *Corianton* and *The Mormon Conquest* were major accomplishments, especially within the constraints of the Great Depression. To a large extent whatever failure the films had was due to factors far outside the filmmakers' control. Independent filmmakers in the Third Wave were not any more successful, and it would be many years before positive films on Mormonism became commercially viable with distribution on television and VHS in the Fourth Wave and in theaters and on DVD in the Fifth. But even if Mormon filmmakers like Lester Park who tried to depict their faith onscreen

The Second Wave: Home Cinema

in the 1930s were unable to create a *God's Army* they still exhibited the same optimism, tenacity, and originality as Mormon filmmakers in every other era, and their sole surviving work, *Corianton*, is just as impressive and entertaining as anything else in the corpus of Mormon cinema.

In the early days of sound film and the Production Code some Church members sought to enlist Hollywood studios to produce a Mormon-themed film. One of these was director James Cruze, an industry insider himself, who reportedly continued to pursue a pioneer saga throughout the 1930s. In November 1931 he announced a "Mormon epic" to be called *Hell and Hallelujah*, which would star his Mormon-born wife Betty Compson and be written by Hollywood screenwriter Charles Furthman. Cruze was evidently unable to package the film together, however, and the release of *Brigham Young* in 1940, combined with his declining health and fortunes, eliminated the possibility that he would ever direct such a film; as mentioned, he gradually succumbed to alcoholism and died two years after *Brigham Young*'s release, in 1942.[159]

A similar but lesser known attempt reached back into the 1920s. At the beginning of that decade, in 1923, two Mormon women, Florinda Gardner and Martha J. Ballard, published a twenty-one page "scenario" called *The Trail and Trials of the Mormon Pioneers*. Little is known of Gardner—she was a Salt Lake City resident who applied for a patent for an automobile speedometer in 1920—but Ballard was the wife of apostle Melvin Ballard and had accompanied him as a mission president in the northwestern states from 1909 to 1919. The women's scenario may have been intended for a stage production, but by the late 1920s Gardner evidently submitted it to Fox for consideration as a motion picture, and it's possible she sent it to other studios as well; it's unknown if Ballard worked with her in this. Fox declined to purchase it, but when Raoul Walsh directed his pioneer epic *The Big Trail* for that studio in 1930 Gardner recognized components of her story. In 1931 she sued the studio to block distribution of the film, and when this failed she filed plagiarism charges with the Academy of Motion Picture Arts and Sciences in 1933. Her charge was rejected, however—screenwriter Hal Evarts, who collaborated with Walsh on the screenplay, documented the film's production closely—and *The Trail and Trials of the Mormon Pioneers* evidently had no influence on Fox's *Brigham Young* in 1940 either. In a sense Gardner and Ballard were attempting to foster the kind of collaboration with professional talent that characterized *One Hundred Years of Mormonism* and *All Faces West*, but instead it became the first of many failed attempts by Mormon screenwriters to enlist Hollywood talent in telling a Mormon story.[160]

Of course, these women were probably planning their completed film exactly at the time it appeared that *All Faces West* would be a success. In 1928, near the outset of the Second Wave, events like the coming of sound and the prospect of a major studio in Salt Lake City must have seemingly heralded a bright new age for Mormon movies, and the momentum this generated was felt into the first two years of the Depression before real retrenchment occurred. At the end of the '20's, in addition to *All Faces West* two other major projects were undertaken: Lester Park's independent feature *Corianton* and Heber J. Grant's institutional film *The Message of the Ages* (discussed below).

Park, it will be remembered, had been involved in Utah's film industry since at least 1905, working as a theater owner, a distributor, and, with the formation of the Ogden Pictures Corporation in 1917, finally a producer. Though this entity only lasted a few years, he apparently nurtured his desire to create films through the 1920s, as at some point in that decade he may have partnered with one A. L. Stallings to produce racy pre-Code dramas, though we have no record of any works they completed. To re-enter higher-class filmmaking he decided to avoid any regional subjects or niche films and instead create a motion picture that would appeal to the entire Mormon population. A more astute observer of the film industry than *All Faces West*'s creators, he anticipated the lesson of that film even before its failure: if sound had been its downfall, then he would make it his greatest strength by creating not just the first Mormon talkie but a literary masterpiece. To properly bring Mormon cinema into the sound age he did the same thing as many producers of the time and turned to the stage.[161] It is fitting that *Corianton* is chronologically the first major production of the Home Cinema era as it comes from arguably the first major work of the Home Literature movement.

In July 1888 Orson Whitney published his call for Mormon Miltons and Shakespeares in the YM/YWMIA journal *The Contributor,* and immediately B. H. Roberts, then a newly ordained Seventy who had been writing for *The Contributor* since its inception in 1878, responded. He'd been analyzing the Book of Mormon at the time, publishing a series of nonfiction articles about Nephite civilization in 1888 and an "Analysis of the Book of Mormon" in the February 1889 issue, so when Whitney called for Mormon authors to look to their own heritage for inspiration Roberts naturally turned to its pages. The first result was a short story entitled "A Story of Zarahemla," about the transfer of prophetic authority and the persecution of believers at the time of Christ's birth in the opening chapters of the Book of Third Nephi, which he published under the pen name

The Second Wave: Home Cinema

Horatio in the November 1888 issue. He followed this with a more ambitious work, a longer—and better—story called "Corianton: A Nephite Story," which he published completely anonymously in five parts from March through July 1889. While Roberts had long displayed literary interests, these stories were also written out of necessity to support his family while he hid from government officials enforcing anti-polygamy laws. He was eventually arrested and spent four months in prison in 1889, but we apparently have the anti-polygamy raid to thank for *Corianton* as much as Orson Whitney.[162]

Roberts drew his story from a few chapters from the Book of Alma near the center of the Book of Mormon. In Alma 30 (about 75 BCE), an "Anti-Christ" named Korihor preaches that there is no God and there will be no Christ, but he loses a public debate with the prophet Alma and is struck deaf and dumb before being trampled to death by a breakaway group of Nephites known as Zoramites. Chapters 31-35 describe Alma's mission to these people, who have rejected the true doctrines of Christ. Although their work is not described in these chapters, Alma's sons Shiblon and Corianton accompanied him, and in chapters 39-42 Alma counsels Corianton after the mission's conclusion. Corianton is portrayed as doubting and disobedient, particularly in chapter 39 where Alma reprimands him for abandoning his ministry to go "after the harlot Isabel" (v. 3), which caused many Zoramites to not believe Alma's preaching (v. 11). Roberts weaves the Korihor story more closely into that of Corianton and the Zoramites, actually making Corianton one of Korihor's followers. As Ardis Parshall has pointed out, while contemporary Mormons generally consider Corianton's sin to be sexual, Roberts depicts his primary fault as a lack of conversion to the gospel and a mercuriality that allows him to be easily swayed; his great sin is not adultery but rejecting his calling (Alma 39:4-5). In fact, Corianton and Isabel's initial encounter is not sexual at all. Instead, masquerading as a rich socialite named Joan, she tricks him into spending the night at a riotous party in order to rouse the city's distrust of him and his companions, and when he uncovers the truth the next day instead of censuring her he quickly falls in love with her, and the pair elope to another city for a few days before Isabel just as quickly comes to despise him and sends him, a repentant prodigal, back to his father and brother.[163]

The story proved reasonably popular but would have been just one more item in Roberts' prolific output if not for Orestes Utah Bean. A schoolteacher from Richfield in south-central Utah, Bean was also an actor, first in amateur productions for the MIA and then with his own company that toured small towns near Richfield. He was memorable for his immense self-confidence bordering on egotism and his dapper personal style that has since cast him as Mormonism's greatest dandy. Around the turn of the century, when he was in his mid-twenties, Bean discovered "Corianton" as well as another melodramatic Home Literature story about the same characters, Julia A. MacDonald's "A Ship of Hagoth" from 1896-97, which invents a love triangle for Corianton and has both Shiblon and Isabel die. Bean combined these two stories into a stage play, retaining the title *Corianton*, and by 1902 had a script ready for production. The plot was significantly expanded from Roberts' work, bringing in elements from elsewhere in the Book of Mormon like the Gadianton robbers; most significant is that the Zoramites' intrigue spreads beyond religion to politics, with an eventual war between them and the Nephites and Corianton engaging in hand-to-hand combat with the Zoramite leader Seantum, a character invented by Roberts who had no military ambitions in the original story. Isabel, now rechristened Zoan Ze Isobel from her use of the false name "Joan" in Roberts' story, is wounded in the final battle and dies after revealing that Corianton is innocent of the sins the Nephites have accused him of, and in the final tableau he reconciles with his father and unites in romantic affection with an original character named Relia, who had been Shiblon's love interest before his death. Bean's dialogue veers between the contemporary and a poor pseudo-Elizabethan affectation: "Ye have chosen to join Hagoth's Emigration to that bright northern land. It is well. Hagoth is a curious man and just. He buildeth ships that ye might sail. 'Tis said this land ye seek is fruitful; may plenty be your store." Such language implies a vision of Shakespearean—or even Wagnerian—scope: Bean's very first stage direction calls for a throng of sixty Nephites to flood the stage, and he produced massive sets, commissioned original music and songs to accompany the action, and incorporated magic lantern slides into the play, which was an hour longer than a typical Salt Lake City production and ran well past midnight every night.

Salt Lake businessman George Elias Blair helped procure funds to produce all of this, and two professional actors from New York were brought in for the leads: Joseph Haworth as Corianton and Agnes Rose Lane, a Mormon and the first ward Relief Society president in Manhattan, as Zoan Ze Isobel. The other roles were filled by local thespians, including Brigham S. Young, son of apostle Brigham Young, Jr., as Alma and his half-cousin Shirl Clawson in the minor role of Melek, the leader of the revelers at the Zoramite party. The play opened at the Salt Lake Theatre on August 11, 1902 to mixed reviews and popular adulation. The first act, dealing with Korihor, was generally better received than the later portions, which strayed farther from the scriptural story and which one critic described as "too melodramatic, too senseless to be taken seriously."[164] It proved one of the greatest hits in the history of the Salt Lake Theatre, grossing $7,000 in its first week; the *Deseret News* praised it as "too ambitious an event to be ranked with local theatrical events," and when its run was extended the *Salt Lake Tribune* described it as "the most phenomenal run ever seen at this playhouse."[165] Although Bean had neglected to procure any rights to the original stories or pay their authors, B. H. Roberts, who had recently been humiliated by the First Presidency when they temporarily removed him from his office as a Seventy over his political views and by the U.S. House of Representatives' refusal to seat him due to his polygamy, was relieved to suddenly find himself the author of a hit narrative, and a lightly edited reprint of the original story in novella form brought in some much needed income, selling over 300 copies in a single weekend.

Corianton left Salt Lake to play in Ogden and Logan. Bean had arranged to tour eastward, potentially culminating in a Broadway production, but audiences outside of Utah were much less enthralled than the Mormons had been. Starting in September the production worked its way through Denver, Helena, and Omaha before failing completely in Kansas City, where Bean attempted to interest the producer Frank Perley to take the show to New York. The principal investor George Thatcher, Jr., brother of apostle Moses Thatcher, left for Utah, and individual members of the company like Shirl Clawson took advantage of the offer to have their fare home paid for, leaving for the west while Bean was still negotiating fruitlessly with Perley. To recoup costs the play reopened in Salt Lake in January 1903 with a new cast, and amateur performances proliferated throughout Utah for years. In 1909 it was professionally revived with a new tighter script at Salt Lake's Colonial Theatre. Still intent on a Broadway run, in 1912 Bean moved to New York and assembled a production. He changed the subtitle from *A Nephite Story* to *An Aztec Romance* to emphasize its ancient and oriental flavor, and he hired Mormon Broadway composer Harold Orlob to write an all-new score. The play opened on September 16 at Oscar Hammerstein's Manhattan Opera House on 34th Street across from the new Pennsylvania Station; though several blocks from the Theater District around Times Square this was a prime theater. Bean's dream of success in the Big Apple, however, was quickly smashed. Critics panned it—the *New York Times* said that "when Bean's loyal friends called for the author, a more sincere voice pleaded for ether"[166]— and the show only ran six nights before folding, and that was the last effort for a major production until the film version nearly twenty years later.[167]

Lester Park was probably familiar with the play his entire life. He may well have seen it as a fourteen-year-old boy in 1902 and again as a twenty-one-year-old film exhibitor during its 1909 Salt Lake City revival. It's unknown when he first thought of adapting it to film, but by the late 1920s he evidently remembered its popularity and saw it as the ideal vehicle to usher Mormon cinema into the approaching sound era. As early as 1927 he enlisted his brothers Byron and Allen and began negotiating for the film rights to the play with Bean, who still described himself as a playwright and probably required little persuasion. In 1929 the Parks formed the Delaware-based Corianton Corporation and began developing the project before publicly announcing it in the *Deseret News* on Saturday November 2, exactly eight months after *All Faces West's* premiere and just ten days after the Clawsons' fire and four after the Black Tuesday stock market crash. With sound films still a new phenomenon, the article emphasized the soundtrack in its opening sentence: "Music lovers and followers of the stage and screen will be interested in the announcement that an exclusive contract has been signed with the Corianton Corporation to produce the famed Taber- nacle choir and organ of the Church of Jesus Christ of Latter-day Saints, in a forthcoming talking motion picture of the well-known Book of Mormon story 'Corianton.'" Park claimed that in order to make the soundtrack as impressive as possible he had spent a year and a half negotiating with Church authori- ties, specifically David A. Smith, First Counselor in the Presiding Bishopric and the President of the Tabernacle Choir, to secure the choir for the film, which means he initiated his effort around May 1928, the same month *The Jazz Singer* brought the sound era to Salt Lake City. "It was only after the magnitude of this undertaking was shown," the *Deseret News* reported, "that permission was given and a contract signed," adding, "Though it will take over a year in the making 'Co- rianton' when produced will be made one of the outstanding masterpieces of its kind in America, principally because of its musical features."[168] Another headline on December 21 called the Tabernacle Choir "A New Movie Star!"[169] The choir's subsequent career on film and television has demonstrated that this title was more accurate than hyperbolic, and because the choir's early radio broadcasts weren't recorded *Corianton* is not only its cinematic debut but also one of its first known recordings for any purpose.

These articles also clarified that *Corianton* was not a Church production and, more importantly, assured that its finances were stable, an important point to make in the opening weeks of the Great Depression: "The entire production is al- ready financed and advance preparations are already under way."[170] At least the second half of this claim was true. A crew was in place with Park producing and the non-Mormon Wilfred North directing with the assistance of Harold Godsoe.

The Second Wave: Home Cinema

North was an Anglo-American director and actor who had been with Vitagraph since 1912. The arrival of sound proved a boon to his acting career, and *Corianton* was among the last of the over 100 films he directed. Production would take place at the Metropolitan Sound Studios in Fort Lee, New Jersey starting on November 1, 1930 and lasting through much of the winter; the huge sets were cold enough that as she played the role of Relia actress Alice Frost's shivering hands are visible in the finished film. Fort Lee, situated between Thomas Edison's laboratory in West Orange and New York City, was the United States' original filmmaking capital and still had a robust industry connected with the film industries of Manhattan and Queens. The Metropolitan Studio was built on Lewis Street in 1914 and had been known as the Fort Lee Studios before changing its name to promote its sound film production facilities. Around this time, with the George Washington Bridge under construction just a few blocks away, the studio became known for films catering to ethnic and religious minorities that were ignored by Hollywood: in addition to *Corianton* for the Mormons it was used for the Jewish film *Uncle Moses* (1932) and several Italian-language and African-American films, including *The Exile* (1931), the first talking African-American picture.[171]

The large shooting stage was necessary because, in addition to the use of the Tabernacle Choir, Park and Bean envisioned the film as a massive prestige production akin to recent Biblical epics like *The Ten Commandments* (1923) and *Ben-Hur* (1925). Initial statements indicated it would even outdo these by being shot in color, using either the two-tone Technicolor or Colorcraft process.[172] The production design was on a massive scale with the architecture devised by Broadway stage designer Joseph Physioc, reportedly an expert in archeology. His designs drew on Mesoamerican motifs, filtering them through a healthy dose of Art Deco, which was then in vogue. The costumes also adhered to Art Deco's omnivorous nature, with elements reminiscent of Arabic robes, tall Egyptian headdresses, and Roman togas; this Roman influence on depictions of Nephite dress began at least with George Reynolds' 1888 book *The Story of the Book of Mormon* and reflects how Book of Mormon people had often been depicted in visual art for years.[173] Much more notable, then, was the fact that the costumes were rather revealing on both genders. While the original proponents of the play had lauded its basis in scripture, it's likely that much of its popularity lay in the fact that Corianton's is virtually the only story in the Book of Mormon with any sex in it. The film's subtitle was changed from *An Aztec Romance* to *A Story of Unholy Love* to promote this subversive element, and the dancing girls, who had been played by chaste Mutual Improvement Association teens in 1902, were much more representative of the pre-Hays Code Jazz Age when performed onscreen by Bunny Welden's Greenwich Village Dancers in fairly translucent costumes, with one shot later in the film of partial nudity. The actors were drawn from Broadway, including Eric Elden as Corianton, Reginald Barlow as Korihor, and Theo Pennington as Zoan Ze Isobel. Perhaps the only Mormon to work in the crew was director of photography Dal Clawson. The score was by Edgar Still-man Kelley, a popular American composer who had written the music for the original *Ben-Hur* stage play in 1899 and who was associated with the Indianist movement, which incorporated Native American music into the Western classic tradition, both points of experience that surely appealed to Lester Park. Film composer Carl Edouarde worked with him, organizing the forty-piece orchestra and perhaps orchestrating some of the music as well. The score was recorded in the Tabernacle, with the choir and musicians under the baton of Anthony C. Lund. In September 1930, before the score was recorded, the *Film Daily* reported that Byron Park had actually filmed the choir and organ inside the Taberna-cle; this footage is not in the extant print of *Corianton*, however, and given the difficulty others were having filming in the Tabernacle in the early 1930s it's likely the footage was deemed unusable. In the end the choir is heard on the soundtrack, nothing more.[174]

Corianton had all the ingredients for a huge success, and in the December 21, 1929 *Deseret News* article Byron Park, acting as promoter, stated, "I predict that 'CORIANTON' will break theatre box office records in its use throughout the world ... But this statement is really not prophecy. It is an estimate based on a careful analysis of the facts ... I shall not be satisfied with less from 'CORI-ANTON' than a gross theatre box office intake of at least $5,000,000.00." His brother Lester waxed equally hyperbolic, claiming that "'CORIANTON' in my judgment is the greatest dramatic vehicle yet offered to take advantage of the tremendous possibilities now offered by the motion picture screen."[175] But if the Parks adeptly exploited the soundtrack, what they failed to foresee was the depth of the Great Depression. To raise funds they had partnered with Napoleon Hill, a self-help guru who had gained celebrity teaching people how to achieve self-confidence and financial success; he had just published an eight-volume work called *The Law of Success* in 1928, although his best-remembered book would be *Think and Grow Rich* in 1937. It could be argued that he made a habit of overpromising and associating with people who skirted the edge of the law in their business dealings. This dangerous attitude was present in 1929 when Hill and the Parks traveled throughout Idaho and Utah encouraging investment in the film and promising impossibly high returns, exemplifying the optimistic overvaluation typical of the pre-crash bubble. Once it broke, though, it hit the Corianton Corporation hard, and despite their claims in the papers the company was soon in dire financial straits. In the same article predicting a $5 million profit, the Parks were actually asking for more funds: "Owing to changed financial conditions during the past few months brought about by causes well known to the public, a limited amount of the capital stock of the Corianton Corporation, for which finances were pledged, cannot be taken up by the original subscribers."

Such appeals for additional funds proved essentially fruitless; potential investors were either now extremely cautious or simply no longer existed, and the company itself was in mortal peril of dissolving. The plans to shoot in color were dropped to save costs, but still the film wasn't ready to go into production by the April 6, 1930 centennial of the Church as the contract with Bean stipulated. This infuriated him and he pressed charges with the New York State Bureau of Securities, and the state Supreme Court suspended the company's stock on May 20, 1930, eliminating the Parks' ability to raise any more funds. However, they evidently appealed this and proved the existence of extenuating circumstances, and thus were able to press forward with development. The mercurial and irascible Bean must have been persuaded to go along as well, but he continued to cause other problems. He insisted on hiring of many of his relatives as "consultants," drawing a salary but contributing nothing to the production, perhaps out of an honest desire to use his film to care for them as their personal investments or employment disappeared. He also constantly inserted himself into the production process, causing additional delays. In fact, the crew in New Jersey took advantage of his marriage in Los Angeles in May 1931 to film as much as possible in his absence.[176]

Finally ready to be released, *Corianton* premiered on October 1, 1931 in the Playhouse Theater in Salt Lake, with a second print opening the next day in Bean's hometown of Richfield. Like all early talkies its dialogue scenes felt locked down and the acting leaden compared with the fluidity of late silent films, and the fight choreography also left much to be desired. But the film was impressive for many reasons, including its scope, production design, music, and the special effect lightning bolt that strikes down Korihor. The film, which ran an hour and forty-seven minutes, received some good reviews but was met overall with consternation by the staid Mormon public who expected the play they remembered from twenty years earlier rather than the somewhat racy film they had before them. More than the content, however, evidently the biggest problem was technical: poor sound in the Playhouse Theater. The film ran for three weeks there, at which point Park, a veteran film exhibitor, fired his distributor, a Richfield friend of Bean's named G. Stallings, ran multiple half-page ads in various newspapers apologizing for the bad sound, and tried to continue the run by installing RCA sound equipment himself in a small community theater, possibly the Cozy Theater in Duchesne near the Uintah Mountains, to launch a roadshow tour of small Utah towns. Contrary to popular belief about the film failing for purely artistic reasons, it's probable that these technical problems were the single greatest factor in *Corianton*'s demise. Even if the sound was pristine in all subsequent venues, it was a crippling blow at the outset, and with the film's poor debut in *Salt Lake Variety* reported on November 10 that the "picture is now struggling against its uphill start."[177] The distribution plan collapsed and more financial problems followed. It's possible that the association with Corianton Corporation board member Napoleon Hill, who had partaken of the stock market bubble deeply and found himself vastly overextended in late 1929, also turned problematic at this point, with money from Corianton Corporation investors moving freely into one of his separate enterprises. There were no formal charges of fraud, but this added to the film's troubles and the Parks' embarrassment and, unable to recoup its costs, the Corianton Corporation was suspended on April 4, 1932 for failure to pay taxes.

It's unknown what, if anything, B. H. Roberts thought of the film; he suffered acutely from diabetes in his final years and passed away in September 1933. Orestes Bean, however, was furious with many of the changes to his play—perhaps particularly those made in his absence—and he initiated a flurry of what eventually became ten lawsuits and countersuits to wreak his vengeance on Lester, Byron, and Allen Park. In a way he was successful, as these suits may have tied up enough of the Parks' resources to hobble the film's distribution, and the chief result was to increase the ignominy surrounding the film, helping lead to its eventual disappearance. They also shed light on the film's public reception, or at least Bean's perception of it. In one of his affidavits, he reported the audience's shocked and disappointed response to the film:

> ...When the general public, who saw such advertising, went to said playhouse to see "Corianton," they indeed saw "A Story of Unholy Love" not written in and a part of said play as written by this defendant, its author, but on the contrary they saw, and the plaintiffs then and there showed, a lewd, low, vulgar and licentious picture of "Bunny Welden's Greenwich Dancers" in hoo-chee-coochi riotous scenes in scant

clothing, and which then and there offended all who came to see said
"Corianton" play which was, and is, known to them as a high class dramatic work of affiant, O. U. Bean ... and all of said play-goers thereby
became disgusted with such filth and advised their friends to avoid
attending such "play" and to keep their children away from same, and
by reason thereof, the said motion picture "Corianton" was ruined, lost
and destroyed....[178]

These lawsuits filled the last six years of Bean's life; at one point he spent five
days in jail for talking back to a judge during one of the hearings. He moved to
Los Angeles, where he was involved with an attempted stage revival of the play
in 1933 which was fully prepared and rehearsed but, like the film, failed from
poor financial management and insufficient ticket sales to make up the difference in funding and allow the show to open, allegedly despite great interest
from the Mormon population around L.A. While living there Bean also lectured
on the Book of Mormon—even passing off his own dialogue as scriptural
text—and he died in 1937; Eric Samuelsen has said that while Bean is primarily
remembered as a colorful eccentric, we should also remember that "his work
was uniquely popular in the Mormon culture of his day."[179] In 1963 his widow
Zoan E. Houtz Bean—she had legally changed her name to that of *Corianton*'s
female lead—revised the play again under the title *Out of the Dust*, a popular
Mormon phrase from Isaiah 29:4 regarding the Book of Mormon. This version
featured Zoan Ze Isobel as the protagonist and might have been intended for
performance on television as well as, or instead of, onstage, but no studio ever
purchased it. Lester Park never attempted a similar venture again, perhaps
because of the Depression and the war or perhaps out of loss of interest or
sheer despair at the film's failure; he died in San Mateo in 1952. Over the years
the film, for those who remembered it, saw its reputation as a financial and
artistic fiasco grow. For instance, one Utah family that had invested heavily in
the film converted the term "Corianton" to mean "an ill-considered investment."
For everyone else, Lester Park ensured that *Corianton*'s demise was absolute: all
negatives, prints, and other materials disappeared so completely that for years
historians claimed it was never even completed, let alone screened, and the
vast majority of American Church members today have never heard of the film
or the play.[180]

That was the state of affairs until 2004, when BYU Motion Picture archivist
James D'arc discovered that Lester Park's surviving daughters still possessed
a 16mm print of the film. It had been stored in a barn for years and was badly

degraded, but he was able to convince them of its historical importance and they donated it to BYU, where he set about digitally restoring it. The results aren't perfect, but given the project's constraints—working with a 16mm print of a 35mm film and simply not having the budget to deal with every scratch and instance of image degradation—the high-definition video looks wonderful. D'arc has held several screenings in the BYU Special Collections theater and a few other locations, but the film is not publicly available as per the Park family's conditions. Regardless, this is easily the most exciting development in recent Mormon film history. The donors should be commended for making the film as available as they have, and those who have seen it, while noting its many flaws, have also seen that the film is entertaining for its own sake and an impressive memorial to the Park brothers specifically and Mormon filmmaking in general in this very difficult period at the start of the Great Depression. As for its status as the first major sound Mormon film, *Corianton* leaves nothing to be desired and stands on par with any other independent film from the early '30s. Although *Corianton* wasn't the first Mormon feature film made completely independently of the Church—that title goes to *The Story of the Book of Mormon* in 1915—it was nevertheless a milestone in the history of Mormon film. Hopefully the restored version will become even more widely available and viewers and critics will reassess its aesthetic merits and its place within what is now a long and varied tradition of adapting the Book of Mormon to the screen.[181]

The only other major Mormon-made feature of the Second Wave was *The Mormon Conquest* (1935), and its genesis apparently came not from pictures like *All Faces West* and *Corianton* but from the increased presence of Hollywood film crews in southern Utah. As mentioned in Chapter 1, the town of Kanab had been a filming location since at least 1924, and major investments in the late 1930s poised to make it into a filmmaking hub. Thus in 1938 Denver Dixon, a local Mormon who had worked in minor producing and directing roles for Monogram in Hollywood, founded Security National Pictures and built the "Utah's Hollywood" studio facilities, the area's first local film production company. To inaugurate homegrown filmmaking in this ambitious little town, Dixon chose a local story, writing the screenplay for a film called *The Mormon Conquest* about the pioneers of the San Juan Expedition and the settlement of Utah's southernmost frontier; the fact that later films like *Wagon Master* treated roughly the same topic shows how appealing the desert pioneer saga was. We don't know the film's plot or, therefore, how focused it was on Mormonism, although its title indicates quite a bit. We do know that Dixon met with Church leaders in Salt Lake City "to make his film as authentic as possible," and, as with many travelogues and other pictures from this decade, he filmed views of contemporary Salt Lake City, including the temple, to juxtapose against the movie's nineteenth-century story.

Dixon also tried to enlist Hollywood talent in the form of George O'Brien—star of F. W. Murnau's *Sunrise* (1927) and many silent and now sound westerns, including playing Jim Lassiter in Fox's 1931 *Riders of the Purple Sage* and John Shefford in the 1932 *The Rainbow Trail*—and Monte Blue, a prolific leading man of silent films who was forced to move back into B-pictures after the stock market crash. Neither man agreed to participate, however, so Dixon pressed forward with an entirely local cast and crew, including a child actress named Bonnie Chamberlain, the daughter of his business partner, as an orphan girl akin to Margaret O'Brien's role in *Bad Bascomb* a few years later. Production took place on Dixon's outdoor set of a western town and outside Kanab in the Three Lakes area north of town, Bryce Canyon, Zion Canyon, the Grand Canyon, and possibly Peek-a-Boo Canyon and the scenic Vermillion Cliffs area in Arizona. Civic and religious pride in the production ran high, with the local newspaper covering the work regularly, proclaiming, "The trek of the pioneers to southern Utah, incidents in the settlement of Kanab, the discovery of Zion canyon by Nephi Johnson and the incident of Jacob Hamblin at the Navajo Indian lodge will be portrayed in the movie production."[182] Dixon had to postpone the work at least once, in February 1939, to return to Hollywood to earn more money for his own film. He also wrote another screenplay, *Roll Wagons Roll* (1940), and not only sold it to Monogram but negotiated for them to use his studio for that film and *Westbound Stage* (1939). With that money in place he could move forward with *The Mormon Conquest* in the spring of 1939. He had shot the picture silently, so once editing was finished he took the film to Hollywood to dub the dialogue and lay the sound, and the finished picture played in Kanab on July 11 and 12, 1939. Nothing seems to have happened with it after that, however. There are no records of additional screenings or even any attempts to distribute it, even in the Mormon heartland around the Salt Lake Valley. The film was lost and even more surprisingly Dixon's entire studio closed soon after that. In researching the history of Kanab filmmaking James D'arc was unable to find anyone except Bonnie Chamberlain Cutler who remembered Denver Dixon, let alone *The Mormon Conquest*. It remains one of the most important lost films of the Second Wave.[183]

There would be no attempts at another Mormon feature for many years, but in this period at least one Church member produced short films for commercial or educational audiences. This was documentarian Sullivan C. Richardson, who would also contribute to many Church media projects over the years. Born to a plural wife in the Mormon colony of Colonia Diaz in Chihuahua, Mexico, in 1902, young Richardson fled Pancho Villa with his family in 1912 and spent his adolescence in Arizona.[184] As an adult he lived in Detroit and Chicago, working as a journalist and in advertising before moving into educational filmmaking. He was also an enthusiastic amateur adventurer, an avocation which opened the door to creating first-person travelogue films. The first of these that we know of began in 1939, when he determined to travel the Hole in the Rock pioneer trail and record it on color film to commemorate the sixtieth anniversary of the Mormon San Juan Expedition; although the trip was catalyzed by a recent article about the pioneers, Richardson had surely learned about them growing up in the Mormon communities of Arizona. Enlisting a friend named Arnold Whitaker, a mechanic from one of Detroit's large automobile plants who was also originally from the west and may have been Mormon as well, Richardson traveled to southern Utah and, on June 22, 1939, set out on the trail. The group, which included Ezekiel Johnson, a Mormon and the National Park Service's first custodian-ranger of the Natural Bridges Monument, and Jim Mike, a Ute Indian who had participated in the 1909 discovery of Rainbow Bridge, traveled with five pack horses, four saddle horses, two 16mm movie cameras, three 35mm still cameras, and "two pack-bags full of film, tripods, and other picture-taking impedimenta."[185] They didn't list any sound recording equipment among their gear, implying they intended to record a narration afterward.

It was a hot and dusty eight-day trip along a difficult and sometimes nonexistent trail. They periodically stopped to film along the way, including guiding the horses back up and down rock faces they had just crossed so that Richardson could film them descending. On the fourth day in the shadow of the Hole in the Rock crevice itself he floated out into the Colorado River on a tin raft they found in order to film a horse swimming in close-up; they would use this footage while discussing the eighty-two wagons that floated across in January 1880. Finally they filmed in Hole in the Rock itself before returning to the town of Blanding. There they filmed and photographed ten survivors of the original 1879 pioneer company, including Kumen Jones, then eighty-three, who had scouted out the route and driven the first wagon down the perilous stone descent in Hole in the Rock.

When the film was completed back in Detroit, Richardson eschewed commercial theaters, instead distributing gratis copies of his motion picture and his black and white photographs to his own employer the *Detroit News* and to *National Geographic,* the *Saturday Evening Post*, Twentieth Century-Fox, and private firms like the Motion Picture Publicity department of the Ford Motor Company; he also wrote about his journey and published several photographs in the Church's *Improvement Era.* His motivation must have been to sell the film to a company which would distribute it to classrooms, educational film libraries, or similar outlets, but it's unknown if he succeeded. In fact we don't even know the name of the finished film. But regardless of how extensively it was distributed it was the first of many such projects for Richardson and Whitaker. Two years later the duo took another frequent traveling companion and drove the length of what would soon become the Pan-American Highway, journeying from their base in Detroit to Tierra del Fuego in Chile's southern tip, traversing areas with paved roads, dirt roads, and, often, no roads at all. This adventure, frequently considered one of the greatest automobile journeys of all time, resulted in the book *Adventure South* and two roughly half-hour films, *Road to Panama* (1946) and *Rugged Road to Cape Horn* (1947), released through the educational film company 20th Century Vikings. *Road to Panama* includes brief footage from the Hole in the Rock film, of beautiful red rock formations and horses descending a steep stone slope.

Richardson created other educational films, such as *South of Monterrey* and *Rubber River* (both 1946), which were shorter pieces drawn from his Pan-American expedition, and in 1947 he focused intently on the Mormon pioneer story in a series of films that will be discussed below. But his initial film from southern Utah contains the only known footage of horses traversing Hole in the Rock and other portions of the San Juan Expedition trail before the Lake Powell reservoir flooded much of the area in 1963. Its location is currently unknown, making it an important lost film of the Second Wave.[186]

The Parks' *Corianton*, Dixon's *The Mormon Conquest*, Richardson's Hole in the Rock film, and Finney's *The Mormon Battalion* all demonstrate that in the Second Wave there was not enough interest to support a commercial Mormon film industry. But each of these projects in its own way also shows that there was room for a viable noncommercial independent cinema. By removing the need to make money, filmmakers achieved success with a broad variety of mostly documentary material. In this way the work of the Clawsons in documenting the Mormon story was continued and spread among a large cadre of untrained amateur filmmakers. And this, of course, was emblematic of the ethos of Home Cinema: domestic films for domestic consumption.

Home Movies as Home Cinema

One way to understand the dynamics of the Second Wave is to see a general movement away from large film productions intended for mass commercial exhibition toward small inexpensive films intended for local congregational or home viewing. This in fact tied into a strong tradition in Mormon culture celebrating family life, domesticity, and quiet unsung demonstrations of faith and service that has existed since the faith's founding. William A. Wilson has spoken about this, and researchers' tendency to overlook it, in relation to Mormon folklore: "…In my work with Mormon traditions in general I let myself be too easily influenced by what folklorists generally have considered to be memorable in religious folklore—that is, with dramatic tales of the supernatural—rather than with the quiet lives of committed service that I knew really lay at the heart of the Mormon experience."[187] The same is true with cinema: it's easy to focus on large-scale features like *Brigham Young* and turning points like *God's Army*, but in doing so we cannot ignore the growing body of Mormons who from the Second Wave on have used film and video to record their daily lives and expressions of their faith, which are indeed "the heart of the Mormon experience." These amateur filmmakers couldn't make a living this way, but they have contributed to a movement that, in the 1930s, '40s, and '50s, spread beyond the reach of the Clawson brothers, who originated this type of filmmaking, to approach a global mosaic group portrait of Mormonism. These men and women's use of private film equipment to record important Church sites, current events in Church activity, and even just their own lives perpetuated an autobiographical approach to film that's resonated throughout Mormonism in the ensuing years, evolving into the multitude of personal essay-style Instagram and YouTube videos that we see today.

Key to the birth of this new type of cinema was the ability of non-specialists to access inexpensive and easy-to-use motion picture cameras. A popular 35mm camera such as the Mitchell BNC cost thousands of dollars and weighed thirty pounds. Eastman Kodak's introduction of smaller and cheaper 16mm stock in 1923 led by the 1930s to relatively affordable cameras that put filmmaking within the public's grasp. The Bolex H-16 camera, for instance, introduced in 1933, was light enough—around five pounds—for easy handheld operation. It used a wound spring mechanism to drive the film forward and thus didn't require any battery or electric charge, and its eyepiece and lens system, featuring a turret that allowed for switching between multiple focal lengths without stopping to change lenses, were easy to use; some models included features like

The Second Wave: Home Cinema

automatic in-camera fades and, by the 1950s, a reflex viewfinder that allowed for viewing through the camera's actual lens rather than an eyepiece that ran parallel to it. Intended for newsreel work, the H-16 quickly became popular with avant-garde filmmakers, animators, and the general public, remaining a favorite device for home movies through the 1940s and '50s. Bolex introduced 9.5mm and 8mm cameras in 1936 and '38, and after the war continued refining its 8mm cameras; with Super-8, developed by Kodak in 1965, the film is housed inside a cartridge rather than being loaded into a magazine, which made it the simplest format for amateur use until the arrival of consumer video in the 1980s. In the Second Wave 16mm cameras were developed by Auricon in 1931, Éclair in 1932, Caméflex in 1947, and others, with both 16 and 8mm formats providing many options for home moviemakers; compact and affordable film projectors were developed to match.[188]

American Mormons, of course, were just as interested in these devices as their non-Mormon counterparts. At the same time, the Church was taking an increasingly proactive stance toward Mormon-themed media, such as the film-strips and radio plays of the ebullient Gordon Hinckley, and this inspired some aspiring filmmakers, historians, and evangelists, like LaMar Williams, to acquire a motion picture camera and record Church events. Women were often active in filming familial events, but for the most part the amateur filmmakers who moved into the public sphere to record functions like missionary meetings or temple dedications were men. In either case their work was modest: short films that were often no more than visual artifacts without soundtracks—the Auricon camera had a sound-on-film capability, but for the most part 16mm cameras shot picture only—focusing around Church history or the filmmakers' personal activities or geographical location; many of the most notable films, interestingly, were made far from Salt Lake City and even Los Angeles as the first major component of Mormon cinema to reflect the burgeoning global Mormon diaspora. Some productions were genuine home movies, while others were quite polished. Many believed they were filming simply for their own memories, while others had a sense of mission that made them willing to create films to build up the Church at their own cost and entirely without institutional oversight or support

Perhaps the best known of the latter group was Wilford C. Wood, although he is not primarily remembered for his filmmaking. The grandson of Daniel Wood, the founder of Woods Cross just north of Salt Lake City, Wilford was born there in 1893. He made his profession in the fur trade but his passion was Church history, particularly the life of Joseph Smith. Beginning in 1915 he served in the Northern States Mission, where he learned about his mission president German E. Ellsworth's 1907 attempt, with George Albert Smith, to purchase the Hill Cumorah in New York state. On his way home to Utah in 1918 Wood stopped in Nauvoo and made the decision to dedicate his life to preserving the sites and physical artifacts connected with Joseph Smith's life, and this remained his driving vision for the next fifty years. He's best remembered for the historical sites that he procured, buying them with his own money then selling them at cost or even at a loss to the Church; his business as a furrier required frequent sales trips to the East Coast, and he used these to investigate the ownership of important Church history sites. In this way he eventually acquired and passed on to the Church most of the Martin Harris farm outside Palmyra; a site on the Susquehanna River in western Pennsylvania associated with the Aaronic priesthood restoration; the Newel K. Whitney store in Kirtland and John Johnson home in Hiram, Ohio; Adam-ondi-Ahman and Liberty Jail in Missouri; and the Masonic Lodge, John Taylor home/*Times and Seasons* office, and eight of the ten plots of the temple block in Nauvoo. A combined four of these plots contained the Nauvoo Opera House, which was actually the city's movie theater. Purchased by Wood in 1937, it continued to operate under his and then the Church's ownership until a projection booth fire during a screening of *Kentucky Moonshine* in 1938 burned it to the ground, after which the lot laid vacant awaiting restoration as a historic site and, in 2002, the completion of the restored temple.[189] Wood formed relationships with other property owners in Palmyra and served on the Church's historical committee of the time, providing motivation and paving the way for organizations like Nauvoo Restoration, Inc. and the Mormon Historic Sites Foundation to acquire and restore other sites from the Sacred Grove to Winter Quarters.

He used a similar strategy with the physical artifacts he collected, donating many to the Church but retaining others for himself, which he eventually used to create the small Wilford C. Wood Museum in Woodland by North Salt Lake, which is still extant today. The physical artifacts he acquired include the original organ pipes from both the Salt Lake Theatre and the Tabernacle, the Tabernacle's original pulpit and several benches, Philo Dibble's seer stone and death masks of Joseph and Hyrum Smith, a crystal sacrament goblet from Nauvoo, Emma Smith's leather wallet, Brigham Young's fountain pen case, and Joseph Smith's alleged Jupiter talisman and his ivory whip handle from the Nauvoo Legion, as well as rare printed works like part of the handwritten Book of Abraham manuscript, an original edition of the Book of Commandments (a brief predecessor to the Doctrine and Covenants), the uncut printer's copy sheets of

The Second Wave: Home Cinema

the original Book of Mormon, Kirtland Safety Society script, handwritten notes on the trial of Joseph and Hyrum's murderers, a hymnal owned by Emma Smith, some of Joseph Smith's childhood books, and various deeds, letters, photographs, maps, and broadsheets.

This immense amount of preservation work was the context for Wood's filming, helping us surmise what types of locations and events he would have deemed important to record. In the early 1930s he volunteered as a photographer for the Utah Trails and Landmarks Association, and in 1934 this led him to purchase a 16mm motion picture camera and take moving pictures as well, an activity he continued until at least 1947. Essentially, he would take the camera with him as he traveled and record the vistas he saw, much as George Edward Anderson and others had done earlier with still photography. Not everything he filmed was related to Church history: among his footage are scenic vistas like New York City, Niagara Falls, Salt Lake's Little Cottonwood Canyon, and southern Utah's stone arches, complete with some wild foxes, as well as individuals he knew personally—one features "Mary, Leilah, and pony"—and local scenes like a prominent florist shop in Farmington, Utah. But he also recorded extensive footage of historical sites all along the route of the Mormons from Palmyra to Utah. This included sites like the Hill Cumorah, Kirtland Temple, and Temple Square, and some that he eventually helped purchase like Liberty Jail, but he also filmed less likely locations such as the trail that Zion's Camp took from Ohio to Missouri in 1834 and buildings belonging to the RLDS Church in Independence, Missouri. On occasions he accompanied General Authorities to these sites, such as Heber Grant visiting Joseph Smith's place of death in Carthage, Illinois—Wood was probably the first person to film inside the Carthage Jail—and George Albert Smith and John D. Giles at Winter Quarters and on the Mormon Trail. With a burgeoning relationship with Church leaders, he was also able to film them at home, recording footage of David McKay and President Grant's eightieth birthday celebration. At home he filmed activities of the South Davis Stake, and outside Utah he recorded the dedications of the monuments at the Hill Cumorah in 1935 and Winter Quarters in 1936 and the laying of the Idaho Falls Temple cornerstone in 1940; he also filmed during his visit to the 1939 Chicago World's Fair, which may have included the Tabernacle Choir and Mormon delegation. One item in his catalog is given a tantalizing title, "From Palmyra, New York, to Nauvoo, Illinois, with President David O. McKay and George D. Pyper." It's possible this represents a completed film by another filmmaker, but at the same time, elsewhere in his collection he has original footage of McKay, who was then Second Counselor in the First Presidency, and Pyper in Independence from 1941, so it could be that Wood accompanied them along that entire route and this is a collection of footage from that trip. It's unknown just how much footage he shot before abandoning filmmaking around 1947, the year when Frank Wise and others began filming in earnest for the Pioneer Centennial, but in 1978 his widow and daughters donated five hours of footage to the Church Historical Department; Wood himself had passed away in January 1968. His filmmaking output over two decades is sufficient that he should be remembered for this alone, beside his work with historic sites and artifacts.[190]

Wood wasn't alone in wanting to preserve nineteenth-century Church history through film. While serving in the Eastern States Mission in the early 1930s, a young missionary named Joseph Smith Peery was impressed by his mission president James H. Moyle's use of the radio and motion pictures to teach the gospel. As discussed below, Moyle had shot a film of ruins in Central America, which many Mormons at the time saw as evidence of Book of Mormon historicity, and had his missionaries use it in public meetings. Peery later recalled:

> I had seen pictures that President Moyle had taken the year before down in Central America, because he had one of the first movie cameras that was ever available to the public. I had seen those pictures, and it seemed to me that this was a wonderful way of showing Church history. So I tried to get the Church interested in buying the film for me, because I bought a used car, and I said, "When I'm released from a mission I would like to go all over Church history sites, and take pictures of Church interest, just for the Church."[191]

Specifically, he wrote to his uncle David Smith of the Presiding Bishopric; Smith had recently given permission for the Tabernacle Choir's participation in *Corianton*, and around this time he was also involved with the growth of filmstrips in missionary work, so he was an excellent person for Peery to proposition regardless of their relationship. Peery first asked whether the Presiding Bishopric would sponsor a film for Church-wide distribution, but Smith responded that the Depression had hit the Church too hard for any project near that scale. Peery then requested just $500 to cover his production costs, but even this was too much. In the end, when he was released in 1933 Peery simply bought a 16mm camera with a 100-foot magazine and a few rolls of film. His sister came to New York to travel with him, and they set off in his used car on a self-guided tour of Church history sites, driving and filming all the way back to Utah. Today the Church History Library has a nine-minute film of Peery's footage from Sharon,

The Second Wave: Home Cinema

Palmyra, Kirtland, and Nauvoo, but he probably shot much more than that, even if the Depression prevented him from distributing it.[192]

David A. Smith surely would have funded his nephew if he could. He had in fact begun shooting his own footage just two years earlier; today the Church has three reels of 35mm and four reels of 16mm film in his collection. The son of Joseph F. Smith, he was called as the Second Counselor in the Presiding Bishopric in 1907, then the First Counselor in 1918, and he served on the general Sunday School board and as the President of the Tabernacle Choir since 1908. He seems to have been eager to find new ways to spread the gospel, which caused his film footage to be interestingly split between domestic life—babies, parties, group poses, even a performing acrobat—and material that could be used in educational situations—temples, Church history sites, and Central American ruins. Some of this was motion picture film, some still filmstrips, and it's quite likely that Smith gathered much of it from other people rather than shooting it all himself. But even in that case it demonstrates a Church leader eager to use new audiovisual media to preach the gospel and instruct Church members, who, as a member of the organizational unit charged with overseeing much of the Church's finances, was perhaps frustrated by the constraints of the Great Depression.

The Church History Library also holds footage of historic sites by at least two other men. Lisle Chandler Updike was born in Erie, Pennsylvania in 1890 and at eleven found his life's work from a photographer who lodged next to his family in Abilene, Texas. Within two years he began a profession in photography, traveling the country to shoot at fairs, circuses, and carnivals. In 1912 he converted to the Church, married, and settled in St. Johns, Arizona near the New Mexico border, where he stayed until relocating to Phoenix in 1932. He took many photographs of the local countryside and Zuni Native Americans, and although photography always remained his profession during the Depression he began to work with motion pictures when he and a young Barry Goldwater began shooting color 16mm film of scenes throughout Arizona. The Church History Library holds color footage he shot of Mormon subjects from the 1930s and '40s. In particular on a trip through the northeast United States in 1945 he shot extensive footage, including the Smith family farm and its surroundings in Sharon, Vermont; the Sacred Grove, Hill Cumorah, the grave of Joseph's brother Alvin Smith, and the Martin Harris farm around Palmyra; the temple and cemetery in Kirtland; the Clay County courthouse and David Whitmer grave in Missouri; and numerous houses and sites around Nauvoo, including inside the Carthage Jail. He also documented Temple Square in Salt Lake and every temple throughout Utah, Arizona, and Idaho, and he filmed a range of General Authorities spanning the Church's twentieth-century leadership, including Richard Evans, Harold Lee, Ezra Taft Benson, Alma Sonne, Charles Callis, George Albert Smith, Delbert Stapley, Matthew Cowley, David McKay, J. Reuben Clark, and Albert Bowen. Updike also helped invent the automatic photo booth and Polaroid film; today his photography studios remain open in Salt Lake City and Phoenix.[193]

The Church History Library's third set of footage of historic sites comes from Antoine R. Ivins. The grandson of apostle Erastus Snow, Ivins was born in St. George in 1881 but spent several years in Mexico as his father Anthony W. Ivins avoided prosecution for polygamy; the older Ivins was called as an apostle in 1907 and served in the First Presidency from 1921 to his death in 1934. In the June 1918 *Improvement Era* he published photographs of the devastation caused in the Mormon colony Colonia Díaz by the Mexican Revolution, demonstrating a family interest in still photography. Antoine Ivins, after studying law in Mexico City, Ann Arbor, and Salt Lake, was placed in charge of the Church's sugar plantation in Laie, Hawaii, a position he held from 1921 to 1931. He was then called to the Quorum of the Seventy and made president of the Mexican Mission. He may have taken a motion picture camera with him to Mexico City at that point, as his catalogued footage includes views of the Federal District, but he certainly had one by October 1940 when he filmed color footage of David McKay and J. Reuben Clark placing a time capsule in the Idaho Falls Temple cornerstone, and the next year he took his camera east where he filmed black and white footage of the Kirtland Temple, Peter Whitmer home in Fayette, New York where the Church was founded, and missionaries gathering at the Hill Cumorah.[194]

Joseph Smith Peery may have been the only one of these men to exclusively film historical sites: Wood, Smith, Updike, and Ivins all recorded contemporary personalities or events as well. And there were a great many others whose work fell along these same lines, either purposely filming Church events as a historical record, like the Clawsons before them, or simply filming their own personal lives and catching glimpses of unfolding Church history incidentally. Among the first group, perhaps the only person to transition from amateur filmmaking to a full-time position making films for the Church was LaMar S. Williams. Today Mormons remember him primarily for his work in the 1960s establishing the Church in western Africa, but in his thirties he was instrumental in relaunching institutional Church filmmaking through his work with Frank Wise at Deseret Film Productions. Born in 1911 in Groveland, Idaho, not far south of Idaho Falls, by the late 1930s he thought that the Church should be doing more with audiovisual instruction, so he purchased his own 16mm camera—but no sound equipment or even a light meter—and took it upon himself to film scenes he thought could be useful in teaching situations. After some small projects his first major undertaking was recording some of the construction of the Idaho Falls Temple and then the laying of the cornerstone on October 19, 1940. Like the dedication of the Hill Cumorah monument five years earlier this was, in fact, one of the most documented events by early amateur filmmakers: LaMar Williams, Wilford Wood, and Antoine Ivins were all present with their cameras—Williams and Ivins might have even worked together—and at the time the temple was rededicated in 2017 one local resident discovered a box of color 8mm film in her basement that included additional footage of the event. Not content to simply film events like this on his own, however, the next year Williams moved to Utah to study education and the use of audiovisual aids at Brigham Young University, and, while he completed his bachelor's and master's degrees at BYU by 1949, well before that he was in Salt Lake City trying to get a job with Frank Wise at the new Deseret Film Productions, a story discussed below.[195]

Perhaps the most notable class of people to film Church events at this time were full-time missionaries called, increasingly, to live and teach throughout the world. This started at least in the 1920s when some anonymous missionaries created an eighteen-minute 35mm film of the Catawba Native American tribe on a reservation just south of Charlotte in northern South Carolina. Mormons had had a strong presence among the Catawba since 1885, and by the 1900s as many as 95% were LDS. The film features Chief Samuel Taylor Blue, who would speak in general conference in April 1950, performing a traditional Bear Dance and standing with his sister Sally Brown, who with him was one of their language's last native speakers. It's a polished film, complete with intertitles, and most of the footage was shot in the winter and features scenes like Mormon schoolchildren filing into class and then enjoying a snowball fight at recess. There's no mention of the Church beyond a shot featuring an Elder Davis, who we're told was serving among the Catawba with his family, and the rest of the film has a more ethnographic—if ethnocentric—air like the films of Robert Flaherty or Merian Cooper from that decade: the Catawba demonstrate traditional methods of fishing, hunting, and creating pottery, with an intertitle identifying the female potters as the "last Indian potters east of the Mississippi."[196] Also around 1925 Ezra Christian Lundahl, a missionary in the Eastern States Mission, filmed footage of missionaries holding street meetings in New York City, the new meetinghouse on the corner of Gates and Franklin Avenues in

Bedford-Stuyvesant in Brooklyn, and Mission President B. H. Roberts; additional footage included Niagara Falls, Washington D.C., and historic sites around Palmyra.

Missionaries have continued to film their experiences ever since, most of which we'll never know about because they kept their footage in their personal possession, but the work of a few from this period is now housed in the Church History Library. For instance, Henry Castle Hadlock Murphy, an early missionary to Hawaii, returned there as a mission and temple president in the 1930s and '40s. Between 1930 and 1947 he made extensive audio recordings of sermons and filmed silent footage of various meetinghouses and the temple in Laie, visits by Church leaders like Heber Grant, David McKay, and J. Reuben Clark, and scenes of local Church members, including Chinese, Japanese, and Japanese-American Mormons. While serving in the British Mission from 1936-37 Robert Stringham Stevens filmed footage of a missionary choir called the Millennium Chorus and the 1937 British Mission Centennial celebrations; he also filmed in London at the coronation of King George VI on May 12, 1937. Also in 1936 Blythe M. Gardner filmed 16mm footage while serving in the German-Austrian Mission; when he returned as a mission president in the early 1960s he brought an 8mm camera. David Evans also filmed on his mission in New Zealand in 1936, as did Erin Boley Bigler, on 8mm, from 1936-39, including American missionaries, Maori Church members, Princess Te Puea Herangi, and an annual mission conference and Maori cultural celebration known as the Hui Tau; the Hui Tau was filmed again in 1940 by R. G. Harwood Manley.[197] From 1938-46 Wallace Felt Toronto served as president of the Czechoslovak Mission, filming black and white and color footage of the mission home where he lived in Prague, the countrysides of Czechoslovakia, Germany, and Switzerland, visiting Church leaders like Joseph Fielding Smith and Hugh B. Brown, Nazi soldiers marching through an unidentified German city, Czech Mormons' celebration at a Church monument near Karlstejn Castle southwest of Prague of the ten-year anniversary of John Widtsoe's 1929 dedication of the country for proselytizing, and a post-war Communist rally in Prague. From 1944-48 June Bennion Sharp documented his service as president of the South African Mission with silent color footage of his family and young missionaries, animals, the South African landscape and "native villages," as well as at least one sightseeing trip to the grave of Cecil Rhodes in Zimbabwe. Around 1947 George E. Magnusson was called as one of the first four missionaries to reopen Tahiti to missionary work after the war, and he filmed silent footage of the sites—the ocean, beaches, docks, and local people—as well as a makeshift meetinghouse for worship services. Harrison Theodore "Ted" Price filmed Church activities in Japan and the Pacific from 1948-49; this appears to be the only time he filmed regularly, although he spent most of his life in Hawaii and various Pacific nations. His footage includes the Hawaii Temple, Central Pacific Mission office, historic sites and Mormon servicemen in Japan, and Church members and missionaries in both Japan and Hawaii. Also serving from 1948-49, Le Roy Ronald Folkersen filmed moments from his mission service, which probably took place in Sweden, where he served as a mission president from 1969-75. Also serving in the Swedish Mission in 1950, George Damstedt recorded footage of missionaries, local members, Church buildings, and celebrations of the centennial of the Church in Sweden. He also filmed the local people, the Swedish countryside, and scenes in and around Stockholm. From 1949-51 Gordon R. Woolley filmed 8mm footage of his mission in the Swedish-speaking areas of Finland, including missionary activity in Vaasa and Larsmo. He also recorded the aftermath of World War II, such as tanks and other equipment, the destruction he saw on a trip to Germany, and ships being sent to the Soviet Union as war reparations. In 1953 Ernest D. Rose created an entire documentary about the Church in Tonga and its school there called Liahona College. Years later he and two associates added a voice-over narration to the silent film. Finally, one of the most interesting pieces of missionary footage was the wedding of Thayle Nielsen and Renee Johnson in the mission home in São Paulo, Brazil. A twenty-seven-year-old combat veteran of the Battle of the Bulge, Nielsen was older than the typical missionary and thus received permission from President McKay to have Johnson, who he had been courting back in Utah, called as a missionary and assigned as his companion; the two were married in June 1947, soon after her arrival, in a ceremony filmed by fellow missionary Wayne M. Beck—who was also married—and served the rest of their mission together.[198]

Perhaps most interesting are not the films made by American missionaries abroad but by the Church members themselves who lived far from Salt Lake City, such as a five-reel silent 8mm film entitled *Life Among the Saints in Hawkes Bay, New Zealand,* which was filmed by Ra Puriri between 1938 and '48. Depicting a community of Maori Mormons on the eastern shore of the North Island, this footage shows family reunions and events, Church activities, and other scenes. There are shots of visiting Americans, such as mission presidents Matthew Cowley and A. Reed Halverson, but this is primarily footage of the Maori community. More importantly, since all the previous footage filmed in Native American reservations, Japan, Hawaii, and even Eastern Europe was shot by white Americans, this was the first time a group of non-Caucasian non-American Mormons picked up a camera to depict their faith and their own culture.

Maori Mormons have continued to maintain a tradition of cultural differentiation and pride up to the present in the film work of Rangi Parker and other
writers, artists, and activists. Around the same time in 1938 some 8mm footage
was shot of Church members in Argentina, which may have come from American
missionaries or Argentine Saints. And from 1945-55 Jack Sing Kong, a native
of Guangdong, China who had moved to Hawaii as a child before contracting
leprosy and converting to the Church, served as branch president of the Kalaupapa Branch on the Hawaiian island of Molokai, where he filmed people in the
leper settlement there—even after overcoming the disease himself—as well as
missionaries and visiting General Authorities, the Hawaii Temple, parades and
pageants, and nature scenes, including the eruption of the Mauna Loa volcano
in June 1950.[199]

While cameras were capturing the Mormon people in Europe and the Pacific, there was a great amount of activity in the Mormon heartland as well. The
Church History Library contains home movies by Clifford G. Snow from 1938-62,
including the April 1938 general conference and construction of the Los Angeles
Temple, and by Ivan R. Walton from 1939-69, including scenes of President
McKay and a trip to the Hill Cumorah. Similarly, Juel LeRoy Andreasen filmed
from 1935 into the 1950s. This silent 8mm footage, in both color and black and
white, follows Andreasen's son McKay from age two until he leaves for college.
This alone constitutes a wonderful longitudinal record, but in the periphery
Andreasen captured much of the history of Vineyard, Utah on the northeast
coast of Utah Lake: there are views of the town, the new Geneva Steel plant that
opened in 1944 as an industrial base that would be safe from Japanese bombing, the Provo airport, a Pioneer Day parade in nearby American Fork, President Truman's visit to BYU in October 1952, and, during World War II, footage of
servicemen from Fort Ord near Monterey, California where Andreasen served in
the U.S. Army Dental Corps. North of Vineyard in Logan, Samuel LeRoy Mitton
created a similar record of his family's life from 1937-44. His silent footage, also
alternating between black and white and color, included Temple Square during
general conference, a family wedding at the Logan Temple, the Logan Tabernacle, scenic shots around the Bear River Mountains in northeast Utah and
Flaming Gorge in southwest Wyoming, and other shots of Church leaders, military personnel, and family vacations. In Berkeley, California, stake president W.
Glenn Harmon was an avid photographer and filmmaker, filming silent footage
from 1939-67, including the entire development of the Oakland Temple—on a
site that he selected and purchased—as well as events like the Berkeley Ward's
fiftieth anniversary celebration, visits by Herbert Hoover and various Church of-

The Second Wave: Home Cinema

ficials, the 1939 Golden Gate International Exposition (quite likely including the Church's exhibit there), and several ward plays and a minstrel show; some of this footage was later edited together and given voice-over narration. Farrest Rudd in 1943 was assigned to a U.S. Army base in Fort Lauderdale, where he made a short documentary with synchronized sound and narration by himself and his son Clive about the new Fort Lauderdale Branch, its members, and how the war effort was affecting the city. From 1948-59 former South African Mission President June Sharp and his wife Ida continued their filmmaking career by recording their family at home in Salt Lake City and on trips to Wendover, Bryce Canyon, Tennessee, London, and Los Angeles, where they filmed the excavation taking place for the temple. Beginning in 1949 Santa Barbara resident Karl N. Haws filmed, like many others, the progress of that temple over several years as well as visits by Church authorities, trips to Yellowstone and Yosemite, and civic and Church events in Santa Barbara. Such activities continued into the Third Wave: on October 1, 1953, for instance, amateur filmmaker Richard Vernon Thiriot filmed the groundbreaking of the Relief Society Building at Temple Square, despite the presence of Frank Wise as an official cinematographer for the Church.

One film of particular note was *General Authorities at Christmastime*, shot by Mark Brimhall Garff in 1945. Garff worked in construction—his firm the Garff, Ryberg, and Garff Construction Company built many prominent buildings on BYU's campus, in Salt Lake City, and throughout the western states, and starting in 1965 he chaired the new Church Building Committee—but as a missionary in Denmark in 1932 he had written in the *Improvement Era* about Mission President Holger Larsen's filmstrip lectures, and experiences like this may have kindled an interest in visual media like film. *General Authorities at Christmastime* was evidently intended for public exhibition, but it was somewhat antiquated, especially for 1945, by its black and white film stock and complete lack of a soundtrack. Still, it's a valuable visual record in the tradition of the Clawsons: running eighteen minutes, it includes footage of George Albert Smith, J. Reuben Clark, David McKay, and other Church leaders, as well as shots of the Salt Lake Temple—including close-ups of the Angel Moroni sculpture on the spire—the Church Administration Building, the Hotel Utah, Deseret Gym, Welfare Square, the Brigham Young Monument, the Deseret News Building, the Church department store ZCMI, and the state Capitol Building.

While many of these people served in prominent Church positions, some of the most interesting home movies come from actual General Authorities and their families. J. Reuben Clark's daughter Marianne Clark Sharp filmed her family life in the Jackson Heights neighborhood of Queens in the mid-1930s, including footage of when her parents came to visit. There is, in fact, a great deal of amateur footage of Clark and his wife Lute from 1930-52. This includes the family not just in New York but in Hawaii on a trip with Grant and his wife to organize the Oahu Stake; Salt Lake City, such as hosting a dinner for General Authorities in their home; southern Utah's National Parks; Clark's hometown of Grantsville, Utah, where they visited his brother and mother; and Mexico City, where they are seen outside the embassy and chancery, touring the Floating Gardens of Xochimilco, and visiting outgoing U.S. ambassador Dwight Morrow's residence in Cuernavaca. Others might not have been as prolifically filmed, but Edward Riggs McKay with his wife Lottie shot silent color footage of his parents David and Emma McKay at the Swiss Temple dedication on September 11, 1955, a privileged up-close look at President McKay completing one of his signature achievements. The McKays also included many shots of Church leaders like Spencer Kimball and Henry Moyle, missionaries, and other faces in the crowd, as well as the temple itself and the nearby temple president's home. It's likely other apostles' families created similar material—for instance, having sponsored the legislation that created the National Park Service, on a July 1927 trip to Yellowstone Reed Smoot recorded that his son Harlow and daughter Zella each had "a moving picture camera and will have reels by the hundred yards of Animals of the Park and the natures greatest sights." They apparently even filmed their father feeding candy to a bear.[200]

Interestingly, filmmaking work often went beyond private individuals and became group projects for Mormon congregations, becoming part of the recreational and historical work that was common in this period. For instance, members of the branch in Washington, D.C. documented the entire construction process of their new chapel from the groundbreaking in 1930 to the cornerstone-laying ceremony on April 21, 1932, to the building's dedication on November 5, 1933. Located two miles straight north of the White House at 2810 16th Street NW, this was a prominent building designed by Don Carlos Young and Ramm Hansen with exterior artwork by Mahonri Young and an Angel Moroni statue, the only one ever placed on a meetinghouse, by Torlief Knaphus. The footage, while black and white, includes sound and features Reed Smoot, Washington Branch president Edgar Brossard of the U.S. Tariff Commission, the entire First Presidency of Heber Grant, Anthony Ivins, and J. Reuben Clark, and organ music by Edward Kimball, who moved from Utah to give daily recitals there; Joseph Smith Peery also filmed the nearly completed building during his tour of 1933. Members of the Twenty-ninth Ward in the Riverside Stake in northwest

The Second Wave: Home Cinema

Salt Lake City also recorded their activities for over thirteen years, from 1936-49. This included all the ward members, the leadership and various priesthood and auxiliary groups like the Relief Society, and informal events like the children parading on Pioneer Day. Other Church units dabbled in similar attempts, such as in 1939 when a ward from Holladay in south Salt Lake filmed its Boy Scout troop, under scoutmaster Doral Cutler, in the Uintah Mountains camping, backpacking, playing water sports, raising the flag, and even eating their meals; in 1948 when the Orchard Ward in Bountiful, Utah filmed silent footage of a ward barbecue, complete with ward members cooking, serving, cleaning up, and enjoying a post-meal dance; in 1948 when a ward in California filmed its Blazer Scouts meeting Presiding Bishop LeGrand Richards and in a variety of other activities; in July 1949 when a demonstration of the hukilau fishing technique, probably held as a fundraiser, was filmed on a beach in Laie, Hawaii; on June 25, 1950 when the Manchester Ward in Los Angeles filmed David McKay dedicating their new chapel; and on August 12, 1955 when the Second Ward in Salt Lake's Liberty Stake filmed its tenth birthday celebration. Finally, while all of these were essentially observational documentaries, in 1936 the Brooklyn Ward in New York attempted to create more polished productions in two documentaries explaining the history of the Mormon pioneers and the purpose of modern temples, aiming at education as much as historical preservation. These were silent films but were accompanied by live oration and Foley-type sound effects by Dr. Howard R. Driggs, a son of pioneers who at that time taught English at New York University. The films premiered on March 30 and 31 as part of a Church-wide centennial celebration of Elijah restoring the sealing keys to Joseph Smith in the Kirtland Temple in 1836, and they were accompanied by an exhibit on genealogy and a live pageant that ran for two weeks in the Brooklyn chapel.[201]

Enough Americans were pursuing filmmaking as a hobby that in 1926 the Amateur Cinema League (ACL) formed in New York, lasting until 1954, with at least two active branches in Utah. The Utah Amateur Movie Club in Salt Lake ran throughout this period and in 1942 Alton Morton co-founded the Utah Cine Arts Club. Morton's mother came from a polygamous family and his father, a Scottish immigrant, converted to the Church as a twelve year old in Idaho in 1863. Al, who was born in 1905, found work as a mail carrier late in the Depression and used his earnings to buy an 8mm camera, launching a prolific filmmaking hobby for both himself and his wife Thelma. They soon obtained other equipment, shooting on 16mm Kodachrome color stock, which Kodak had introduced in 1935, and frequently building their own equipment such as tripods, butt splicers for editing, and even an entire boat with a built-in camera mount. Al was an avid outdoorsman, so the majority of their films consist of nature scenes, particular-ly rafting trips down Utah's rivers: titles include *The Utah Trail* (1942), *Adventures on the Colorado* (1947), *Green River Expedition* (1950), *Waters of Lodore* (1951), *Grand Canyon Voyage* (1951), *Wild Water and Bouncing Boats* (1957), and *Trailer in the Pines* (1959). Their films were generally around half an hour long, and often used innovative double exposures and lyrical editing techniques to expand their stylistic range, on top of the skill it took to film while navigating white wa-ter. His fiction film *Worth Scouting For* (1945) is notable: Morton frequently gave free public screenings to local groups like Scout troops, which gave him the idea to make a scripted fiction film—with extensive documentary elements—about scouting. Several years in the making, the film required him to work closely with a local Mormon troop, involving the ward bishopric, parents, and boys in its planning and execution. Accordingly, although the story makes no mention of the Church it does include a Word of Wisdom element when some of the boys ill-advisedly smoke some stolen cigarettes. Starting with the film *Call of the Canyons* in 1947 Morton began to receive commissions from the Utah State Tourist and Publicity Council and other agencies, making him a professional filmmaker. He continued to shoot films and photographs until 1968 when his health prevented him from working, by which time he was arguably the most prolific twentieth-century documentarian of Utah's nature and landscapes.[202]

Another prominent member of the Utah Amateur Movie Club was Glen H. Turner. A resident of Springville south of Provo in Utah Valley, Turner was a photogra-pher and painted landscapes in watercolor and oil. He worked as director of a popular art gallery in Springville, which in 1937 became the Springville Museum of Art, and in 1948 he joined the art faculty at Brigham Young University. A pro-lific filmmaker, Turner worked primarily in nonfiction; the Church History Library contains twenty-one reels of 16mm footage and eighteen reels of 8mm footage of documentary work that he either shot or compiled from other filmmakers between 1947-77. This includes home movies, footage of Brigham Young's home in St. George, material on Native Americans, and finished documentaries about his grandmother and other people and places in Utah. A great deal of footage deals with art, including instruction at BYU and the creation of the doors for the Washington, D.C. Temple in the early 1970s. For competitions sponsored by the ACL he created lyrical documentaries reminiscent of the quiet perceptiveness of Joris Ivens' *Rain* (1929) and the mystical special effects of Jean Cocteau's *The Blood of a Poet* (1930), such as *Water Wheel* (1958), about the role of water in the Utah desert, with melting snow, bubbling streams, and a spinning water wheel, and *Caineville* (1953), a city symphony of a Utah ghost town that uses in-camera dissolves to portray a young actor as a ghost. His fiction film *One Summer Day* (1949) uses stop-motion animation to recreate a child's fantasy about his toy boat, and *Little Girl* (1955) is a short film about a young girl exploring her family farm with a guileless perspective that anticipated Albert Lamorisse's *The Red Balloon* the next year.[203]

Other principal members of the Utah Cine Arts Club and Utah Amateur Movie Club, not all of whom were necessarily Mormon, were L. Clyde Anderson, Mildred Greene, Richard Thiriot, Albert "Al" Londema, Orland Lavell "O. L." and Irene Tapp, James Sanders, Richard Carman, Edward A. Burgess, and W. R. Anderson. L. Clyde Anderson, born in 1895, began creating film trailers and other marketing material for Utah's film exhibitors in 1919, and in 1934 he opened the L. Clyde Anderson Film Laboratory to evidently not only develop still and motion film negatives but produce his own films and photographs as well. In addition to the hundreds of short advertisements and other films he produced in this way he and his wife shot their own travelogues and scenic pictures: his early film *A Day in the Country* (1930) is essentially a home movie of him and his wife around the foothills of Mount Timpanogos, but by *October Byways* in 1935 they used Kodachrome to show the autumn leaves in the same area with a technique that won them an award from the ACL for color cinematography; he also loved sailing on the Great Salt Lake and filmed it in productions like *Weekend Cruise* (1950) and *Cruise on the Minnie-Lee* (1960), although in the latter title he also included footage taken on vacation on the beaches of Central America. The majority of films by ACL members were essentially scenic documentaries or travelogues—such as John Walter's *Midsummer Night's Dream* (1937) of Cedar Breaks, and Bryce, Zion, and the Grand Canyon, O. L. Tapp's *I Walked a Crooked Trail* (1950) of Arches National Park, and Stanley Midgley's series of comic travelogues, which he called "chucklelogues," about his travel on bicycle and Jeep through southern Utah. But some filmmakers branched into other genres, such as Al Londema's short western *The Black Satchel* (1951). Mildred Greene's *A Greene Christmas* (1939) was a twelve-minute fiction film shot over five months, using her own family playing themselves to depict a warm domestic holiday in their Salt Lake City home. In contrast, Tapp's *Rainbow Trail* (1948) is a twenty-minute comic film in the vein of Laurel and Hardy about two friends fishing in a stream. In 1932 ACL member Riley Hess of Ogden shot a film about seagulls, which may have actually been a scripted fictional film and which included the miracle of the gulls as its climax, with much of the footage of the birds shot on Bird Island in Utah Lake. In all, today the website *Amateur Cinema* lists exactly fifty films from this period related to Utah or Utah-based filmmakers, a rich trove of footage which is by and large still extant at the University of Utah film archives.[204]

In sum, Mormons took to the new ability to record their own films with an eagerness that has never abated. During the Second Wave additional anonymous filmmakers recorded events like Heber Grant's funeral in May 1945, artists like Mahonri Young and Avard Fairbanks at work, and Church leaders in a variety of situations. And in the following years missionaries and other Church members continued this new cinematic tradition: the Church History Library contains items such as film footage of the Danish Mission from 1952-60, President McKay's visit to Uruguay in 1954, Melvin R. Richards' service as the East Central States Mission President from 1955-60 and the Gulf States Mission President from 1961-65, Stuart L. Poelman's footage and sound recordings of his mission in the Netherlands from 1957-59, the construction of meetinghouses in Whitney and El Camino in northern California from 1959-62, films of the Hill Cumorah pageant and its participants in 1962 and '63, Milton W. Moody's record of his mission to Rarotonga in the Cook Islands in 1962-66, and Rendell N. Mabey's footage of mission work in Nigeria and Ghana in 1978 and '79—immediately after the revelation granting the priesthood and temple attendance to black Mormons—including the first baptisms in Nigeria, with James Faust, a seventy who would become an apostle the next year, baptizing some converts in a small creek. Even in 2008, when an Angel Moroni statue was placed atop the London Temple, Church members like thirteen-year-old Aaron Glover and a grandfather named Bob Horton journeyed 150 miles to Surrey to record the event for posterity on video.[205] Such a propensity is now so common as to not warrant mention, and while it is a movement which originated with Chet and Shirl Clawson it found its first expression with the general Mormon populace in the Home Cinema moment of the Second Wave.

Institutional Films

The Church Centennial and "The Message of the Ages"

Even before the Clawsons' fire some General Authorities desired to expand the Church's filmmaking capability beyond what two individuals could accomplish; Shirl and Chet themselves may have even felt this way. As the Church's centennial on April 6, 1930 approached, an aging B. H. Roberts, hard at work on a multivolume history of the Church, "dreamed of a major motion picture with a script built upon one or more of the epic civilizations portrayed in the [Book of Mormon]."[206] The Church would have been an ideal agent to produce such a film— as *Corianton*'s subsequent failure as a private enterprise arguably showed—but it was not to be. Church President Heber J. Grant harbored similar desires. He had been impressed by the potential of talking pictures for years, and in his opening remarks at the April 1930 general conference he ended a recitation of mankind's achievements over the past hundred years with a tribute to the phonograph and radio:

> Undoubtedly the greatest miracle of the century is the accomplish-
> ment by which the human voice, with the personality of the speaker,
> may be indefinitely preserved and reproduced with every detail of orig-
> inality. Whether uttered in the frozen arctics, or from the jungles of the
> tropics, without visible means of conduct, the human voice instantly
> circles the earth, thus overcoming the hitherto insurmountable barrier
> of both time and space.[207]

Though he didn't mention moving pictures in that statement, they were very much on his mind; indeed, he delivered this sermon standing on a stage that he would try to use for a film production in the coming days. Despite the Church's financial pressures, he had been determined to make its centennial celebrations as awe inspiring as possible, and to use motion picture technology to reach Church members—and others—everywhere.

At the center of the centennial celebration was a two-hour pageant called *The Message of the Ages* that was staged inside the Tabernacle itself. This type of dramatic pageantry, with huge casts depicting sweeping historical narratives, had been popular in the United States for decades, and had caught on in the Church after B. H. Roberts' 1920 missionary conference at the Hill Cumorah. Quickly becoming an annual event, these celebrations featured missionaries acting out scenes from the Book of Mormon on the hillside, a natural stage that allowed for great visibility from the fields off its western slope. These perfor-mances grew in scope until July 24, 1930, three months after *The Message of the Ages* premiered in Salt Lake, when the Cumorah pageant would receive its first title, "Footprints on the Sands of Time"; in 1937 it was rewritten as "Ameri-ca's Witness for Christ," a major production that has played, with some addition-al rewrites, every summer since, with the exception of a few years during World War II. While this grassroots production was gradually growing throughout the 1920s, *The Message of the Ages* was the Church's first officially sponsored and preplanned large-scale pageant, and lacking any outdoor amphitheaters similar to the Hill Cumorah in Salt Lake City the only space that would accommodate it was inside the Tabernacle. That made this an indoor pageant, but it set the precedent for future outdoor productions—at Calgary, Manti, Auckland, Nauvoo, and other cities—in every other way.

In 1929, soon after he had finished his work on *All Faces West*, George Pyper was named chairman of the pageant committee, with Elder George Albert Smith serving as chairman of the entire centennial celebration. The pageant committee members, while aware of the Hill Cumorah event, evidently found their true inspiration in the Passion Play at Oberammergau in Germany, a large-scale decennial production about Christ's death and resurrection that dates back to 1634. Aiming for a similar effect, Pyper's committee spent over six months identifying scriptural and historical stories to fit into a compelling narrative. Their work was synthesized into a finished poetic script by Bertha A. Kleinman of Mesa, Arizona, who also borrowed from Orson Whitney's poem "Elias: An Epic of the Ages"; Whitney, the founder of Home Literature, must have been gratified by this production, and he passed away thirteen months later. An enormous stage was designed by architects Joseph Don Carlos Young and his son George Cannon Young, complete with a large drapery backdrop and an array of elevated platforms, like stairs, running across its width. Like performing on a hillside, this allowed for greater visibility from the rear of the house, but the play's blocking also took full advantage of it artistically. Additional electric lighting—"batteries of foot, flood and spot lights"[208]—was installed using the old switchboard from the Salt Lake Theatre, which had been razed a little over a year earlier, and new music was composed for the Tabernacle Choir. Over 1,500 people in all worked on the pageant, including 312 members of the choir as the performers, 187 ushers, fifty orchestra musicians, and fifty staff and stage directors.

The finished production was two hours long. A printed program described it as "divided into a prologue and three periods, viz.: the Ancient Dispensations; the Messianic Dispensation; the Dispensation of the Fulness of Times [sic]. The story is told in narrative, tableau, and processional with organ, orchestral, and choral music."[209] Scenes included the creation of the world, Adam and Eve in the garden, Noah and the deluge, the Israelites fleeing Egypt, Moses receiving the Ten Commandments, Jesus' nativity, the Sermon on the Mount, the resurrection, Joseph Smith's First Vision, pioneers and handcarts, and a final tableau suggesting the glory of the contemporary Church. Its initial run was planned around April conference—as mentioned, sermons were given from the stage—but demand proved higher than expected so the run was extended from one week

The Second Wave: Home Cinema

to a full thirty nights, from April 6 to May 5, with each performance dedicated to President Grant. The Church gave away tickets for free but many were scalped for $1. Audience capacity was increased by letting in about 1,000 additional patrons each night to stand around the perimeter and aisles of the Tabernacle. In the end an estimated 200,000 people saw it; 30,000 more had applied for tickets but couldn't be accommodated, meaning that it easily could have run to the end of June. Thinking of these would-be viewers, President Grant surely wasn't the only one who thought that transforming the entire production into a motion picture would make it available to the entire Church membership.[210]

First, however, one group of people whose interest was already raised was Pathé Sound News, the renamed journalistic department of the studio that had invented the newsreel format. A Seattle-based crew arrived in Salt Lake City on April 16, planning to stay for a week or more. While in the area they filmed at the Bingham copper mine in the mountains west of the city, which as the largest open-face mine in the world was of national interest. They may have investigated other stories as well, but their main task was to produce a piece about the centennial and the pageant that celebrated it. President Grant was probably quick to give permission to record the performance, and the crew set about determining how to film inside the capacious space of the Tabernacle.

The first problem that had to be overcome was recording the soundtrack, and to do this the film utilized groundbreaking technology in the recording device known as the RCA Photophone. Most sound recording equipment at this point filled an entire production truck and wouldn't fit into the building, but the Photophone was compact and portable. A sound-on-film recorder, it looked rather like a camera on a baby tripod, its compactness allowed by its use of a relatively small single-ribbon microphone. It lacked important features like ground-noise elimination, but still yielded impressive results and allowed location work for the first time in the sound era. In this case, the Pathé crew was able to record the choir inside the Tabernacle, and, later, the actors on the steps of the Capitol Building. Pathé considered the audio recording, which predated *Corianton*'s recording by a few months, so impressive that they played it a full year later at the spring 1931 convention of the Society of Motion Picture Engineers in Los Angeles—it's unclear whether the recording was accompanied by any film footage of the choir—and then again on July 16, 1931 for an industry screening in the RCA Photophone projection room. In this recording the choir sings several "choruses" and the organ plays several others. During some of the numbers a film showed a graphic representation of the soundtrack, like a waveform, so the audio professionals in the audience could visualize the modulations of the sound.[211]

Obtaining a proper image, however, proved more difficult. Despite the additional lights that had been installed for the production, the Tabernacle remained a dimly lit space, suitable for the human eye but too dark to properly expose the 35mm film. This was particularly true because filming the pageant required taking wide shots that encompassed much or all of the stage, and such a broad area, as opposed to a close up, simply couldn't be sufficiently lit to allow for a suitable exposure. This could have put an end to the entire production, but someone—most likely a local who knew the surrounding area—suggested that the pageant be staged outside after all, using the exterior steps of the Utah State Capitol to substitute for the tiered stage. These three levels of grey granite steps, which would later be seen in films like *Legally Blonde 2* (2003), were more than sufficient to contain the action as originally blocked, and the naked sunlight obviously worked for the camera crew.

Just a few minutes of the production were selected to be filmed. Given the centennial theme of the newsreel, these scenes and tableaus focused primarily on the modern Church. There were six segments, each including multiple shots: first was an introductory narration and views of Salt Lake Valley; second, Joseph Smith, played by Hyrum J. Smith, kneels in the Sacred Grove—the smaller rear Capitol steps, with a backdrop—and rises when he sees a vision; third, six men gather around a table on a landing in the center of the steps and organize the Church; fourth, the pioneers struggle along at different levels on the staircase, with Brigham Young watching from the top—at one point they carefully lower a handcart onto a landing—fifth, in a section called "The Past Sets forth Commandments for the Present," Moses stands at the top of the staircase, representing Sinai, and descends to a crowd of his clamoring followers; and sixth, to represent Mormonism's contemporary stature, a line of men and a line of women come from the edges of the frame to meet in the middle, turn to ascend, and then use flags and other props to perform a final pantomime.

The finished newsreel, *Mormons Celebrate Centenary*, part of Pathé Sound News No. 38 of 1930, was copyrighted on April 30. The centennial celebration was the lead item in the episode, followed by the unveiling of a monument to pioneer women in Oklahoma, French women riding motorcycles, military officers drilling in Rhode Island, Catholics sailing to Tunisia for the Thirtieth International Eucharist Congress, and a police parade in New York City. It was released in early May, and the Church's Centennial News Bureau, under chairman James M. Kirkham, declared that the newsreel was well reviewed and "exhibited all over the nation to millions of people."[212] A sprawling two-page Pathé advertisement in *Film Daily* reported that "Heber J. Grant, President of the Mormon Church, praises Pathé Sound News for giving the whole world a chance to see this great and costly spectacle through the medium of the Pathé newsreel."[213]

We don't know when Grant decided that the pageant would make an excellent feature film. It may have been before the play even premiered in April or during its initial run in the Tabernacle, but it was at least by this point when the Pathé crew was already filming portions of it. On April 30, after that crew had left and as the stage production was nearing its end on May 5, *Variety* reported that the "industrial department of Metropolitan studios will film the Mormon Church pageant to be held at Salt Lake City next month."[214] The fact that Grant or other Church leaders selected an educational film company indicates their desire, even though it would be a feature-length production, to not release it commercially, as *All Faces West* had just attempted, but to use the Church's well-established domestic film distribution apparatus that had grown over the previous decade.

Another problem arose, however. Even though the newsreel crew had already solved the lighting problem, Grant wanted to shoot this version in color and, evidently, do so indoors, back inside the Tabernacle. As could have been expected, lighting again became the limiting factor, as A. Hamer Reiser, secretary of the pageant committee, later recalled:

> President Grant wanted to have it photographed in motion pictures in color so that it might be available in that fashion to be presented in many places all over the Church. An effort was made to get it in color and finally the people who were working with technicolor photography motion pictures persuaded President Grant that it couldn't be done that there was not enough light on the sets and the scenes to expose the film. And closeups [sic] would be very disillusioning because they would reveal young men with whiskers and all the rest of the paraphernalia of an ancient prophet just stuck on his face & In other words they talked President Grant out of the project.[215]

We learn a few things from this. First, Grant was envisioning a classically edited film, probably with medium shots, close ups, reverse angles, and so forth, and not just a wide-angle view of the entire stage; this was to be a movie in its own right, not a record of a theatrical production. Second, of course, is that he wanted to film in color. Technically this was very ambitious: the additive Technicolor process that used three strips of film—with one strip each soaked in cyan, magenta, and yellow dye—and that was used throughout Hollywood's golden years in films like *The Wizard of Oz* wasn't developed until 1932. Instead what was available was different versions of a subtractive two-color system, that exposed two strips of black and white negative with a red and a green filter. Results could be good, and increasingly color sequences were inserted into otherwise black and white films in the late 1920s, with a few shot entirely that way, but the colors were still dull, especially in the reds. Incidentally, more light was needed to expose two strips of film simultaneously than was needed for one, so if Pathé experienced difficulty with their black and white newsreel then the Technicolor personnel would surely have found the Tabernacle impossible to film in. But Grant had good reason to attempt a color shoot, as color was an integral component of *The Message of the Ages*' design, particularly in the climactic tableau. At that point, the costumes of the groups of people on the different tiers of the stage identify them with different organizations within the Church, as the *Improvement Era* explained: "At the topmost point of the stage the Priesthood quorums are represented, robed in tones of cream and pale yellow. Light, radiating from above, makes of them almost unearthly beings, through whom the organizations and activities of today are directed." The other groups were the temple and genealogical workers, the Sunday School, the Relief Society, the MIA, and, at the bottom, the children's Primary. Through costuming "the color scheme of the final picture merges from ivory white through deepening shades of cream, corn-color, yellow, peach, pink, violet and purple. Arranged in transverse lines, the costumes complete an effective color harmony, into which the audience is drawn, when at a signal word with arms raised high all join in a song of praise to him who is the Creator of heaven and earth, and all the inhabitants thereof."[216] For those who had labored to create this effect, the prospect of filming it in black and white must have been discouraging.

The third and fourth things we learn from Reiser are that, for whatever reason, this production was still occurring indoors and in the end, therefore, it never occurred at all. Nothing in the historical record addresses why this version didn't shoot at the Capitol Building as well—perhaps the pageant's creators were dissatisfied with the makeshift staging, but holding to that artistic standard at the expense of the entire production is surprising. Thus, while for decades historians have considered the lack of lighting as the prime reason *The Message of the Ages* was never filmed in its entirety, it's possible it was due to other causes. Reiser's mention of the make-up is one: perhaps Grant decided that the production that was inspiring in the vastness of the Tabernacle would simply look fake with the proximity of the movie screen; Richard Nelson has posited this as the primary cause, and the next year *Corianton* suffered somewhat from the same problem.[217] Fatigue is another possibility: perhaps after all the months of preparation and rehearsal, a theatrical run of six shows a week lasting four times as long as expected, and the simultaneous shooting of the newsreel footage in the daytime before a performance in the evening, now the volunteer cast and crew—including Tabernacle Choir members with duties including weekly broadcasts of *Music and the Spoken Word*—were eager to move on and return to their lives rather than undertake another two- to three-week film shoot. Logistically keeping the hundreds of people there that much longer may have proven difficult as well. This, in a way, combines with the most likely cause, that the Church was out of funds to not only pay Metropolitan studios but then to develop and edit the footage and strike hundreds of prints and ship them to the various wards and branches. Within three years Bishop David A. Smith would be telling his nephew that the Church couldn't even front a 16mm home movie camera, so it's very likely that this much more ambitious scheme was simply beyond the reach of the Church six months into the Great Depression. Hamer Reiser recorded his memory of the pageant with David Jacobs in 1966, thirty-six years after the events, so it's possible that he was unaware or simply forgot some of these other possible factors. At any rate, what we do know is that President Grant's dream of a feature length *Message of the Ages* film was not to be, making the Pathé Sound News footage—which constitutes the first known Mormon film with synchronized sound—all the more precious today. *The Message of the Ages* had a bit more life in it, as the pageant was restaged in 1947 for the Pioneer Centennial of Salt Lake City, when it was photographed and turned into a still filmstrip for slideshow presentations. Still, after 1930 official Church efforts at motion picture production halted for fifteen years, though President Grant remained proactive throughout the period, culminating in his involvement with *Brigham Young* in 1939-40.

Later in the 1930s individual Church departments may have desired to produce films but they were simply unable to pay for them, as David Smith's correspondence with Joseph Smith Peery shows. As mentioned in Chapter 2, Church leaders like Grant had investigated sound film before the stock market crash, and this KSL film must have further proved its value in classroom instruction. Thus at a Sunday School training conference in October 1932 attendees were greeted by a film featuring Grant and Ivins, again speaking to the camera. "This display was part of a demonstration by the Deseret Sunday School Union [the Sunday School's full name] of the possibilities of teaching religion through talking pictures and the available facilities for such instructions."[218] But even with the reduced cost of 16mm film not too many resources could be devoted to fully moving pictures. The Sunday School and the entire Church were already finding that they could stretch their dollars much further with still filmstrips, making the 1930s the golden decade of the Mormon slideshow.

Home Media: Filmstrips and Missionary Media

Besides 16mm film, the signature innovation for Mormon media in the Second Wave was the filmstrip. While perhaps seen as somewhat quaint today, this medium was revolutionary in its time, quickly proving its effectiveness and becoming a dominant instructional medium for presenting lectures to both Church members and the general public. Filmstrips were much cheaper and easier to produce than motion pictures—perfect for a cash-strapped organization—and could be shown with small and inexpensive projectors easily transported by Sunday School teachers or missionaries to churches, homes, or other settings. This medium became so central to the missionary program, Sunday School, seminaries, and other Church organizations during the Second Wave that it lasted well into the 1980s. And in the 1940s its ubiquity made it completely natural for Mormons to want to graduate to institutionally produced motion pictures once it became fiscally practical.

Filmstrips and slideshows were of course the twentieth-century descendent of the magic lantern. While magic lanterns were still used throughout the Church's missions in the 1920s, as the work of Andrew Jenson, Gustive Larson, and others like James Gunn McKay shows, technology was advancing that would soon make illustrated lectures much easier to deliver. In 1925 the first 35mm still film projector was invented, which, like the magic lantern, displayed one image until it was manually advanced, but which substituted a single roll of 35mm film for the lantern's glass slides. This proved a tremendous boon for educators everywhere, as a filmstrip was virtually weightless and could be rolled up and stored in a small tube or box, whereas lantern slides were large, heavy, and fragile. The presentation format remained the same, with a lecture, group discussion, or even a phonograph playing an accompanying recording while each image was shown. In 1935 the slide projector was invented, which allowed for individual frames of 35mm film to be inserted like the old glass slides; while this allowed for greater versatility for presenters who wanted to add, subtract, or rearrange images, Mormons tended to favor the continuous strip, which allowed for greater uniformity and mass production of standardized narratives, with reduced probability of error across a global missionary force. Also, it remained simpler to transport strips of film and faster to thread them into a projector than load slides into a slide projector carousel. In either case, both machines were an improvement over magic lanterns and caught on quickly with schools, church-es, libraries, governments, and other institutions, none more enthusiastic than the Mormons, who found it useful in classroom instruction but especially for itinerant missionaries who would give lectures in different venues like churches and rented halls—and eventually right in people's living rooms. In 1936 Gordon Hinckley summarized the format's strengths:

> The celluloid strip is a film slide the size of a spool of thread. The beam of light is a tiny projector that weighs less than a big book and is as easy to carry as a camera.... The machines are portable. Moreover, they are not costly. One excellent for cottage meeting work may be obtained for the price of the most ordinary kind of camera. Nor are the films expensive when their cost is compared with other things. A film of fifty selected colored views may be had for the price of three or four colored glass slides. And they are more easily carried and are not in great danger of breakage.[219]

As with other formats, we don't know precisely when a filmstrip was first used in the Church, but the new format was promising enough that a filmstrip projec-tor was demonstrated at a 1930 conference of European mission presidents "and was found to possess high possibilities."[220] This may have been the work of the forward-thinking Bishop David Smith, because on October 18, 1930 he announced the creation of a filmstrip about Latin American ruins, which many Mormons viewed as evidence of Book of Mormon historicity, for use by mission-aries throughout the Church. The *Deseret News* reported:

> A new method of preaching the Gospel was announced by Bishop David A. Smith, of the presiding bishopric, upon his arrival in Salt Lake Friday. Lectures on film, will be supplied the missionaries of the Church. The old method of lantern lectures will be done away with, and a modern outfit, weighing approximately 6 pounds, will replace the old style lec-ture equipment weighing 45 pounds.
>
> One feature of the new machine is that any missionary can manipulate it alone. Instead of bothering with 30 pounds of assorted slides, a few cans containing rolls of motion picture film will be carried. Each picture or frame, may be held indefinitely in position on the screen, while ques-tions pertaining to it may be asked and answered.

Accompanying the pictures will be passages from the Bible, from the Book of Mormon, and other Church works, as well as statements by famous historians, both ancient and modern.

The lectures will prove that the inhabitants of America, up to the advent of the Spaniards, had a knowledge of the earth's creation, of the flood, of the Tower of Babel, of a hell, whose only punishment is absolute darkness, of the dispersion of the Tribes of Israel, of God, of degrees of glory in heaven, of Jesus Christ, or Quetzalcoatl as they know him. Also, that they looked for the second coming of the white God, and for a reign of peace and prosperity, according to Bishop Smith.[221]

Besides Smith, whose enthusiasm for visual media has already been discussed, the driving force behind this project seems to have been Joseph F. Merrill, who arguably had a greater influence on Church education than any other person in its history. The son of apostle Marriner Merrill—and, through a different plural wife, much older half-brother of RKO vice president Wilford Merrill—in 1912 he had created the Church's seminaries for weekday religious instruction of adolescents, first in the Granite Stake and then Church-wide. After a long career on the faculty at the University of Utah, in 1928 he was appointed Commissioner of Church Schools. His major responsibility at this time was transferring the Church's remaining academies to state control, with the exceptions of Brigham Young University, which he retained as a center for the training of future seminary instructors, and Ricks College, which the state of Idaho refused to take over. He also developed an institute program for university students at these now secular colleges that mirrored the program he'd developed for high school students nearly two decades earlier. The increased need for more effective weekday instructors of Mormon youth coincided with a drop in the number of full-time proselytizing missionaries occasioned by the economic realities of the 1930s: where 800-1,300 young men were called each year in the 1920s, by 1932 only 399 were called, and 5% of missionaries already in their assigned areas returned home early to seek employment. This required those remaining to increase their effectiveness, and the filmstrip on ancient America played a key role as missionaries "employed more favorable techniques to find interested persons to teach." This included such innovations as a missionary chorus in England and Ireland, a missionary basketball team in Czechoslovakia, and four missionaries in Berlin who were recruited to judge basketball for the 1936 Olympics. "Lectures featuring colored slides of ancient America were particularly productive in making contacts."[222]

The Second Wave: Home Cinema

Given his position over Church education Merrill probably coordinated with Smith and the Presiding Bishopric for this first project, but even before its release he was probably working on a much more ambitious filmstrip of his own, *The History of the Church of Jesus Christ of Latter-day Saints in Film*, completing it by March 21, 1931. For this, Merrill appointed a special committee, headed by Samuel D. Moore, Jr., and, working with the Church Historian's office, the Presiding Bishopric, and private collectors, they compiled 405 photographs which they divided into ten reels, each on different periods of Church history: one on the Vermont period, one on the New York and Pennsylvania period, one on Ohio and Missouri, one on Nauvoo, two on the pioneer journey, two on nineteenth-century Utah, one on temples, and one on current General Authorities. As with many magic lantern lectures, a written script accompanied the films so that lecturers would know precisely what to say. The General Authorities featured in the final reel included some of the most cinematically forward-thinking leaders of the Church: Heber Grant, Anthony Ivins, and David McKay, along with David Smith and his superior Presiding Bishop Sylvester Q. Cannon. Soon these filmstrips were in use throughout the Church's missions, and when Orson Whitney passed away that May, Merrill was called to take his place in the Quorum of the Twelve.[223]

Even while missionaries enthusiastically embraced this new material provided from Church headquarters, others set out to create their own media presentations, including even 16mm motion pictures. The most prominent of these was James Henry Moyle, president of the Eastern States Mission from 1929 to 1933. Moyle was born in Salt Lake City in 1858, the son of Cornish pioneers on his father's side and the grandson of Daniel Wood on his mother's, making him a cousin or half-cousin of Wilford Wood. After serving a mission in North Carolina and earning a law degree at the University of Michigan he returned to the territory and was elected county attorney in 1886. A long career in politics followed: he founded the Utah Democratic Party and served in the territorial legislature in the years before statehood, followed by unsuccessful campaigns for governor in 1900 and 1904 and the Senate, against the incumbent Reed Smoot, in 1914. Though he failed to gain elected office he served many years on the Democratic National Committee and was Assistant Secretary of the Treasury in Woodrow Wilson's administration; there he became friends with Franklin Roosevelt, who appointed him Commissioner of the U.S. Customs Service in 1933, where he served until being named a special assistant to the Secretary of the Treasury at the outset of the European war in 1939.

It was between his service in the Wilson and Roosevelt administrations that Moyle, from the mission's headquarters in Brooklyn, oversaw the growth of the Church from Washington, D.C. to Maine. Although seventy years old, he brought an energetic innovation to the work, embracing new technologies and quickly beginning a groundbreaking public relations campaign that would influence similar projects throughout the entire Church. When he arrived he was surprised that missionary work was essentially identical to when he had served half a century earlier. "I was immediately impressed with the importance of modernizing the missionary activities," he recalled, "and wrote the First Presidency urging that if they could give us some time of Dr. James E. Talmage or B. H. Roberts, we could do a great work over the radio in New York."[224] Instead, the young missionaries themselves began appearing on the air, often through the assistance of local Church member Stanley McAllister, a mechanical engineer at the Columbia Broadcasting Company who had helped to first get the Tabernacle Choir on the radio a few years earlier. Many individual speeches were delivered, and in August 1930 missionaries in Wiles-Barre, Pennsylvania procured a weekly half-hour spot on Sunday afternoons. In 1932 Moyle and McAllister arranged for a thirteen-part series on the Church to air on CBC, which served ninety-two stations nationwide. There was so much radio work underway that Moyle called an Elder Brown as Mission Radio Director, and he oversaw more than one thousand radio speeches over at least twenty-one stations during Moyle's tenure. In his 1951 biography of Moyle, Gordon B. Hinckley, who did as much as any other person to advance the Church's radio work, wrote, "This pioneer effort was taken up by the Church in other sections, until at the date of this writing, hundreds of Mormon radio programs are presented each week in various parts of the nation."[225]

This was the first attempt by an individual mission to use radio in an organized campaign, and Moyle wrote that "the success with radio convinced me that other forms of publicity were necessary."[226] Thus he called twelve missionaries as publicity directors for their individual districts and had others start presenting at public fairs and exhibitions, beginning with the Eastern States Exposition in Springfield, Massachusetts in the fall of 1930; when Salt Lake City couldn't provide any material for a booth, the missionaries created it themselves, including a miniature replica of the Salt Lake Temple. But perhaps most importantly, Moyle had purchased one of the earliest consumer model 16mm cameras in 1928 and in February 1931 he left his mission with his wife, son, and daughter-in-law and journeyed to the Yucatán Peninsula, where his son James, Jr. filmed the Mayan ruins at Chichen Itza and Uxmal. They also visited J. Reuben Clark in

The Second Wave: Home Cinema

Mexico City and filmed the Temple of the Feathered Serpent and other monuments at Xochicalco in the central state of Morelos. Upon returning to New York some footage of the Sacred Well at Chichen Itza was found to be underexposed but the rest was spliced together, duplicated, and distributed to missionaries to exhibit; whether missionaries also obtained their own film projectors or relied on finding venues that already had them is unknown, but their use of the film multiplied its influence far beyond what Moyle could have achieved on his own.[227]

All of this had a galvanizing effect on his missionaries like Joseph Peery who saw the potential of being able to show their own films and proselytize on the airwaves, and Moyle did similar work with newspapers, libraries, printed tracts, and standardization of missionary rules and accountability metrics. Given his prominent position in the Church in the eastern United States, his innovations in proselytizing, and his work formalizing the annual meeting and pageant at Palmyra, it was appropriate that when sculptor Torlief Knaphus was commissioned to create a monument at the Hill Cumorah he chose Moyle as his model for the Angel Moroni; he had used Moyle's grandfather John Rowe Moyle, a stonemason on the Salt Lake Temple, as the model for his *Handcart Pioneer Monument* at Temple Square just a few years earlier in 1927, making this a conscious tribute to the Moyle family as well—and the only Angel Moroni statue with a beard. The First Presidency and Quorum of the Twelve also recognized the importance of Moyle's work, and in 1930 nearly ordained him an apostle, ultimately declining only because of his advanced age. Instead, in 1947 they called his son Henry D. Moyle, in large part out of respect for his father who had passed away the previous year.[228]

A decade later missionary John M. Goddard used a similar 16mm film in the North Central States Mission. After serving as an Air Force pilot in World War II, Goddard traveled with his father to Central America where they filmed, in color, the ruins of Yucatán. Inveterate explorers, they also added footage of the people, animals, and natural wonders of the area, including two Mexican volcanos, the open-air market in Chichicastenango in the Guatemalan highlands, and a two-hundred-mile trek through what they claimed was an unexplored jungle in Nicaragua. Back home in Los Angeles Goddard assembled this footage into a film he called *Off the Beaten Path*, and while he used it to help gain membership into the Adventurers' Club he evidently had no further designs for it until he was called to preach the gospel and found it could be useful: in November 1948 he began showing it to audiences, along with a half-hour lecture on Book of Mormon peoples. Over the next seven months he presented it to an estimated

8,000 people in cities and towns throughout Minnesota, Wisconsin, the Dakotas, Montana, and southern Saskatchewan and Manitoba, with possibly more screenings later in 1949. This was a unique case of a home movie coming to be used for proselytizing purposes, and although Goddard did not continue to film he did spend the rest of his life as a world-renowned explorer, adventurer, speaker, and author.[229]

But 16mm motion pictures were the exception rather than the rule. Soon after David Smith and Joseph Merrill introduced filmstrips to the Church the volume of filmstrip use far outstripped all previous use of magic lanterns or motion pictures by the Clawsons or any other filmmakers. Many Church organizations became involved with the medium, such as A. Hamer Reiser's work at the Sunday School and Deseret Book (discussed below), and the Genealogical Society of Utah's use of colored filmstrips to create interest in family history work, although they also exhibited locally made motion pictures about the wanderings of the ancient Israelites. But the most enthusiastic adopters of filmstrips were the Church's full-time missionaries. Mission President Holger M. Larsen had great success touring Denmark in 1932 with an illustrated lecture "on Utah and its people, showing—with pictures—the homes of the Mormons."[230] The next year Joseph Merrill, as a junior apostle, was called to preside over all the Church's missions in Europe, and he took his opinions about visual education with him to London. Missionaries serving under him in Merthyr Tydfil, Wales premiered the filmstrip *Joseph Smith—An American Prophet* in January 1935 and it quickly spread throughout Great Britain, proving the power of the new format more than any other filmstrip to date. In a district conference in February 1935 "one thousand people packed the New Royal Cinema at Pontypool, Monmouthshire"[231] in southern Wales to see the lecture presented by missionary and future Seventy G. Homer Durham and hear Merrill and other missionaries speak, with one thousand more turned away for lack of space. While this audience was largely made up of Mormons, it showed the attraction of filmstrips for the general public as well. Merrill already believed strongly in the medium, of course, but this filmstrip helped cement their value in the mind of his closest and most important protégé, a young missionary named Gordon Bitner Hinckley, who would become the fifteenth President of the Church in 1995.

Hinckley was born in Salt Lake City in 1910, the nephew of apostle of Alonzo A. Hinckley and son of Bryant S. Hinckley, a prominent stake president and author as well as principal of the Latter-day Saint High School where Gordon attended. He absorbed his father's bibliophilism and after studying English and ancient languages at the University of Utah considered graduate school at Columbia and a career in journalism, but first accepted a mission call to England in 1933. While studying at the Mission Home in Salt Lake City, the forerunner of today's Missionary Training Center, he wrote an essay on what it means to be a missionary that so impressed David McKay that he called him into his office to congratulate him; Hinckley "had indelibly impressed this prominent apostle,"[232] who was called into the First Presidency in October 1934, and this connection would deeply influence his career upon his return home. On his way to England Hinckley passed through Chicago to take in the World's Fair, his first exposure to a large exposition, then arrived in Plymouth on July 1. While staying at the European Mission headquarters in London awaiting his assigned area he became reacquainted with mission president John Widtsoe, a friend of his father's, in a second fateful meeting with a member of the Quorum of the Twelve.[233] His first area was in Preston near the west coast of Lancashire, and while there he began using his writing abilities to publish in the British Church journal the *Millennial Star*, but after nine months there and in nearby Nelson he was called back to the south to be an assistant to the new mission president Joseph Merrill, who as a fellow educator probably also knew Bryant Hinckley. Soon after this, Merrill followed James Moyle's lead and appointed Gordon the Director of Publicity in the British Mission in addition to his other responsibilities, and from his office near the British Museum the young missionary set about working with newspapers to gain good coverage and advertise Church conferences, using baseball to gain recognition for the missionaries, interfacing with publishers and opinion makers about the Church, and assisting elders in the Newcastle District when they developed a small exhibition about the Word of Wisdom that they displayed in a series of rented halls.[234]

When Hinckley arrived in the UK there were only 85 missionaries in Britain and 525 in all the world, and he was quickly convinced of the critical necessity of mass media beyond just the *Millennial Star* to amplify their voices as much as possible. Though he was apparently not involved in the creation of the filmstrip *Joseph Smith—An American Prophet* in Wales he was on hand to oversee its implementation among missionaries in England and Scotland. He was also invaluable to President Merrill in other ways, and when the end of Hinckley's service approached in the spring of 1935 Merrill initially asked him to remain six months longer than planned. A few days later, however, he not only rescinded the extension but asked Hincklely to return to Utah as quickly as possible with a new assignment. He had received a letter from the First Presidency declining a request for additional filmstrips and teaching aids, so he told the young missionary, "I want you to go home, meet with the First Presidency in person, and explain our needs to them. Perhaps you can describe our situation in a way I can't seem to put across in a letter."[219] Though hesitant to lecture the First Presidency about anything, Hinckley accepted and, after concluding his service and briefly visiting continental Europe and New York City on his way home, arrived in Salt Lake and made an appointment for Tuesday, August 20, 1935. Once again Hinckley already had connections with the First Presidency: President Grant was a close friend of his father, First Counselor J. Reuben Clark was well acquainted with his mother Ada Hinckley from when they both taught at the same college, and Second Counselor David McKay remembered him from their encounter in 1933.

The meeting was scheduled to run fifteen minutes but lasted a full hour longer; given his own specialty in journalism the bulk of their conversation evidently centered around his work with the British press, but they discussed all of Elder Merrill's desires for the European Mission as well. After the conversation Hinckley left, satisfied that he had fulfilled his mentor's assignment, but he was ignorant that this meeting was connected to a larger movement in the upper echelons of the Church. For some time Elder Stephen Richards had been nominally overseeing Church-wide efforts in radio and media, with much of the actual work falling to David Smith and the leaders of the Church's various auxiliaries. The Church was not reaching its potential with this system, and Merrill's predecessor in Europe Elder John Widtsoe had noticed the same lack of modernization and effectiveness that his fellow mission president James Moyle saw in the Eastern States; this was particularly unfortunate because it meant that the Church's missionary force was squandering the mellowing public opinion that dismissed polygamy and produced films like *The Man from Utah*. He wrote from London, "We have not been [in] a position . . . to make full use of this tolerant feeling which is developing concerning us—that will be one of the big steps forward in the near future . . . The entrance of our cause into newspaper fields, into radio activities, into the usual advertising methods, is right ahead of us and must be brought into use if we are to make use of the means the Lord has given us, for the promulgation of His cause in these days."[220] And he had a degree of success: in the October 1930 general conference Grant noted that Widtsoe was obtaining favorable publicity with the European press—saying "the newspapers are open to" him—that was completely out of Grant's own reach when he presided over that mission in the early 1900s.[221] Thus, when Widtsoe returned from his three-year assignment, Grant decided to place him over the Church's growing media efforts. "On 26 February 1934, Rudger Clawson, president of the Quorum of the Twelve, wrote to him, 'Please be advised that you have been appointed to act as chairman of a committee of three to 'Organize the Available Material for Publicity Purposes Among the Missions of the Church.' The other members of the committee are Bishop David A. Smith and President Samuel O. Bennion, who have been notified of this appointment.'"[222]

This trio solicited advice from visiting mission presidents during the April general conference and received a prescient written response from Northern States Mission President George S. Romney, uncle of future Michigan governor George W. Romney and father of future Church leader Marion G. Romney, that "outlined six specific areas of focus: newspapers, radio talks, window displays, Church-oriented dramas, big-screen advertisements for local movie theaters, and slide shows with prepared lectures."[223] Joseph Daynes of the Western States Mission and LeGrand Richards of the Southern States Mission gave similar suggestions, which was sufficient for Widtsoe, Smith, and Bennion to call themselves the Publicity Committee and start working in these areas, although the name would eventually be changed to the LDS Publicity Bureau and then the Mission Publicity Committee. They submitted a report to the First Presidency recommending that the *Church News*, a weekly tabloid-size supplement to the *Deseret News* launched on April 6, 1931, have international distribution; that KSL be affiliated with BYU for broader penetration of the radio market and the creation of more radio dramas; and that their team be expanded to handle all radio, magazine, news, and motion picture publicity. Though the Church was unable to respond to any of these requests, the LDS Publicity Bureau such as it was still got to work. They created some 16mm "film sermons" with General Authorities addressing the camera directly as well as lectures and filmstrips; they even planned a motion picture about the Book of Mormon which evidently was never produced.[224] When Northwestern States Mission President Joseph Quinney, Jr. requested a series of talks suitable for the radio, the committee promptly provided scripts for thirteen. But they were still overwhelmed, particularly with their other duties, and were far less effective than they would have liked. Just a month after receiving this assignment Widtsoe was also named Church Commissioner of Education, giving him responsibility over all the Church's educational institutions, and the following year he added state government work and the editorship of the *Improvement Era* to his workload. Not only were the three men overworked, they found that coordinating work across the Church's vast missions and other organizations was nearly impossible. In August of 1934 Widtsoe confided in LeGrand Richards that their work was at a virtual standstill, and in a September 24, 1934 report to Rudger Clawson the three wrote about how much bigger a task this was than originally thought, adding, "The attempt to place upon young missionaries the burden of publicity direction, often involving the preparation of the materials themselves, without adequate supervision from the head-quarters of the Church, has seldom been successful. Some good has of course resulted, but too much cannot be expected from the young people sent into the field. Moreover, the efforts made in this field need review and coordination. There is an unnecessary and wasteful duplication, owing to the lack of organization for mission publicity."[225] This was the situation that caused Joseph Merrill to find the First Presidency unresponsive to his requests for more filmstrips, and the background for Gordon Hinckley's meeting with them on August 20, 1935.

All three members of the First Presidency were impressed by Hinckley, Grant enough so to write in his journal that night about the young man's success with the British press. And while Hinckley thought this marked the end of his full-time Church work, the First Presidency began to see an opportunity. In that same September 1934 report Widtsoe had asked for two things: first, that "suitable returned missionaries, many of whom have already volunteered, be called to the aid of the Committee, on an unpaid basis, or at the most to be paid for actually accepted productions." Second, "That for general supervisory and coordinating purposes the part or full time of a paid man be placed at the disposal of the work."[226] No one had appeared in the intervening months who could possibly fit the bill, but the highly literate son of Bryant Hinckley, who had served under Widtsoe in England and then been personally trained for a year and a half by Joseph Merrill, could conceivably do it. Two days after his meeting with the First Presidency Hinckley received an unexpected phone call from President McKay, who asked him to come back in for a more in-depth personal interview, although he was initially kept in the dark about its purpose. McKay was again so impressed he offered him a job even before working out the logistics of reorganizing the Mission Publicity Committee with Widtsoe. The funding to pay Hinckley's salary was probably the greatest obstacle—this was only six years after the Clawsons' fire and start of the Great Depression, and no one had been working in a similar capacity for the Church in all that time—but Widtsoe was optimistic, writing McKay on September 19 about a conversation with David Smith and Samuel Bennion: "The Committee felt that if a small sum, say not to exceed one hundred dollars a month, could be allowed by the Presidency, helps such as that offered by Brother Hinckley could be secured from time to time, to get the work under way. Really, I have a feeling that in these changing times mission publicity is one of the outstanding needs connected with our proselyting."[227] Eventually the offer was made to pay him much less than this—just $65 dollars a month—but Widtsoe, who headed the Church's education system, also offered him a part-time position teaching seminary at South High School for another $35 a month, and this combined $100, roughly the equivalent of $1,800 today, was sufficient for him to drop his journalistic aspirations and begin work in October.[228]

The reorganized department, now known as the Radio, Publicity and Mission Literature Committee, was chaired by Stephen Richards and included Widtsoe along with the apostles Melvin Ballard, Charles Callis, Albert Bowen, and Hinckley's uncle Alonzo. Hinckley's job title was executive secretary of the committee, but he was its entire workforce; much of the point of his hiring, after all, had been that the apostles were unable to devote much attention to this work. Richards assigned him the vacant office next to his own, but when he stepped inside Hinckley found it was absolutely bare, making his first task procuring a free chair and table; the latter had been discarded by a friend's father's office supply store because it was warped and wobbled, but Hinckley propped up the short leg and went to work. He brought his own typewriter from home and, in a story he told frequently in later years, found the man who dispensed office supplies to ask for a ream of paper. "...The employee responded with astonishment, 'Do you realize how much paper is in one ream?' 'Yes, five hundred sheets,' Gordon replied. 'What in the world are you going to do with five hundred sheets of paper?' the secretary asked, apparently having never entertained such a request. 'I am going to write on it one sheet at a time,' Gordon answered."[229] And that's exactly what he did. At a time the Church could only afford ten full-time employees he became the eleventh, an indication of President Grant's interest in audiovisual media. The decision paid great dividends, however, both for the Church and for Hinckley. John Widtsoe, one of Mormonism's most prolific authors of proselytizing literature, and Stephen Richards, an exacting and deliberate supervisor who others often found difficult, became his closest mentors, and his position put him in close contact with all the General Authorities, an important phase in what was perhaps the most exquisite training that any apostle or Church President has ever had. In return, Hinckley proved an indefatigable and innovative employee, enhancing the Radio, Publicity and Mission Literature Committee's output far beyond what anyone expected. Widtsoe nicknamed him "the Slave."[230]

In his first month, Hinckley and Widtsoe co-wrote a handbook for missionaries, began a booklet about temples, and continued work on a filmstrip that Hinckley had begun in England. Despite work writing pamphlets and radio programs, filmstrips constituted the majority of his early work. He wrote scripts, interfaced with scholars, oversaw the photography and artwork—or took photographs himself—supervised the physical production of material, and continually revised his scripts and plans to match the exacting feedback Richards and other General Authorities gave him. Despite the workload he remained enthused, at one point writing to Joseph Merrill in England, "There is a terrific lot of work ahead, but I am not afraid of it."[231] The most ambitious of the early filmstrips were *Down Pioneer Trails* (1935, with fifty-one frames) on pioneers and *Forgotten Empires* and *Before Columbus* (both 1936 and both with fifty frames each) on ancient American civilizations. Strongly preferring color to black and white, he hired six young women, including his sister Ramona, to hand paint the films for five cents a frame, an expensive process that bottlenecked the entire operation. In a memo to Richards he wrote, "This is the most expensive item in the process, but I do not think these people are over-paid, one girl having recently discontinued because of eye strain."[232] Even when he convinced Cecil B. DeMille to authorize the use of ninety-one frames from *The King of Kings* (1927), Hinckley still preferred a colorized version and submitted it to the same process. In addition to these four strips, other titles made after 1935 include *Fascinating Salt Lake City, Ancient American Landscapes, Landmarks of Church History, In the Top of the Mountains, Latter-day Saint Temples, Historic Highlights of Mormonism, The Church Welfare Plan, Beautiful Britain, Latter-day Saint Leadership, Accomplishments of the Mormon People, The Apostasy, The Abundant Life, Early Empires of America, The Stick of Joseph* about the Book of Mormon, and *Everlasting Hills*, as well as more prosaic projects like *A Systematic Program for Teaching the Gospel*; in 1937 the book *The House of the Lord* was adapted as a filmstrip with new photographs of the Salt Lake Temple interior, the first time pictures had been taken there since 1911. Hinckley later said, "We worked at this very energetically and very industriously. We produced strips by the thousands."[233] Within a year every pair of missionaries in the world was provided with a projector, and because of these efforts and the microfilming of genealogical records, by 1936 Hinckley learned that the Church was the largest user of film stock outside the federal government, including all major film studios.[234]

Missionaries everywhere were soon converted to what Hinckley in a May 1936 *Church News* article called "The Romance of a Celluloid Strip." Despite the committee's prolific output, requests continued to pour into Salt Lake City from around the world. From London President Merrill pled, "We need more films at once. Our mission presidents in Europe are finding them very effective in making contacts." In Berlin Roy A. Welker reported that missionary activity was up an astonishing 1,400%, however he calculated this, adding that filmstrips "have a tendency in breaking down prejudice better than any word we have of our own." And in Amsterdam T. Edgar Lyon claimed that "the missionaries are reporting new investigators found through the use of this material, and avenues of contact are being opened which have heretofore been unheard of. As a rule when given in halls, [illustrated lectures] are well attended by non-members and favorable newspaper reviews of the same have appeared in local newspapers. Their use at cottage meetings, however, has up to the present time been of greater value than the public presentations." Hinckley explained what these cottage or fireside meetings were like:

> Here the group is small and congenial. The informality of the occasion allows for a closer personal association between the lecturer and those listening. Exchange of thought and opinion is easy; differences can be quickly cleared up and questions may be asked. In fact, the lectures are designed with the principal thought of piquing the interest of the listener so that he will want to hear more and ask questions. Every precaution is taken to avoid being dogmatic or argumentative, or of appearing in any way to foist doctrines on those who have been so gracious as to welcome the elders. More than that, the cottage meeting allows the bearing of personal testimony.

For the most part such meetings, large and small, were successful in reshaping public opinion, especially compared with the anti-Mormon sentiment of the 1910s and '20s. "In most cases the old prejudice vanishes and the way is opened for questions," Hinckley wrote. "Likely an invitation is extended to come again. Those listening have been entertained and at the same time instructed. Moreover, it is a dignified manner of preaching the gospel. Without the odium of propaganda, it catches the interest of the listener. There is none of the thought that he is being fooled into something, for it was never designed that such a thing should be."[235]

Feedback from missionaries on the ground echoed Hinckley's optimism. Four elders in California spent much of 1937 traveling the state and showing either *Forgotten Empires* or *Before Columbus* to an estimated 50,000 viewers in various "service clubs, colleges, high schools, hospitals, department stores, and hotels,"[236] and distributing 13,387 Books of Mormon in the process. In England in 1935 Joseph Merrill was so encouraged by the success his missionaries were having with *Joseph Smith—An American Prophet* that he wrote an article called "The Missionary and His Tools" in the *Improvement Era*. He recounted the success of the British missionaries with that filmstrip and of the Czechoslovakian missionaries with a radio broadcast called "Mormons and their Beliefs," then described the potential that radio and cinema had for proselytizing. "By their use it would be possible to preach the gospel to all the world in a day." Based on the success the Roman Catholics were having with original film production, he proposed the Church make a motion picture about how Joseph Smith translated and published the Book of Mormon: "Could not the story of how the modern world got this book be made to grip a movie audience?" Indeed, many short and feature length films have since been made on precisely this topic, but at the time this was little more than enthusiastic rhetoric spurred by the success that even filmstrips promised.[237]

Because of their portability filmstrips also proved an ideal medium for use during the war. On November 25, 1941, thirteen days before the attack on Pearl Harbor, Northwestern States missionary B. Grant Pugh gave an illustrated lecture on Utah to one thousand Italian POWs in Fort Missoula, then the largest Alien Detention Camp in the country. A Mormon guard helped arrange the event and one of the prisoners translated into Italian. The literally captive audience seemed relieved by the diversion but no baptisms came from it. Some returned missionaries serving in the American Armed Forces, particularly chaplains, probably carried their old Church filmstrips with them, and we know that a group of Mormon sailors on the USS Saginaw Bay gave multiple presentations aboard ship in 1945 and '46. This was a troop transport vessel in the Pacific, and after the war's end as it brought soldiers, Mormon and not, toward the United States images of Utah caused spontaneous cheers. The LDS crewmen reported, "After viewing these films the returning veterans usually express a siege of homesickness and concern over the ship's low rate of speed."[238]

Radio was the mass medium of home entertainment in the 1930s and on-air dramas were big business, from children's series to adult fare like Orson Welles' "The Mercury Theatre on the Air," which ran from July to December 1938 with its famous *War of the Worlds* episode airing on October 30. As we've seen, Mormons were anxious to utilize the new medium as well, and, while filmstrips took up much of his time, Hinckley quickly began writing for the radio, initially focusing on short Sunday evening broadcasts, missionary material, and KSL's popular programs *"Church Hour"* and, later, "Church of the Air." A Missionary Broadcast Division was formed to differentiate between programs aimed at Church members and those for outsiders and potential converts, but Hinckley oversaw both departments and was soon working on something that spanned across these audiences. This was his first major radio program, "The Fulness of Times," a thirty-nine-episode series on the history of the Church that he began in 1937. This actually didn't originate as an internal Church project: instead, the Mertens and Price Radio Feature Service, a Los Angeles radio production company, approached the Church with a proposal. Hinckley did all the historical research and outlined the entire series, frequently travelling to L.A. to consult on its production, and when the original writer had to drop out he took over the entire scripting process. This was a major undertaking on top of all his other assignments. Partway through he wrote to the producer, "I'm losing weight, hair and my good disposition trying to meet half a dozen deadlines, among which I rank the 'Fulness of Times' as the most important. Writing does not come easy to me. It's slow, hard labor and because I have so many other things demanding attention, I do not get things out as rapidly as I should."[239] Nevertheless, he was able to complete it on time and arrange for it to air on over 125 U.S. stations over two seasons, the first in 1938-39 and the second 1940-41, although with additional broadcasts over the next five years it reached a total of 400 stations, from small towns in the rural U.S. to broadcasters in South Africa, New Zealand, Canada, and even at least in Sweden in the non-English-speaking world. This lengthy release was possible because Hinckley and the producers recorded each program beforehand rather than broadcast live, which also allowed him to produce hundreds of 78 rpm records to send to each mission, stake, and ward in the Church, as well as making them available to purchase. He also implemented the sale of souvenir records of the Tabernacle Choir at Temple Square and continued to produce and usually write regular radio programs as well as additional series like "A New Witness for Christ" about the Book of Mormon and "The Church's Attitude" about the Mormons' response to contemporary social problems. While working on this latter series he wrote to the producer, now his friend, at Mertens and Price, "I had hoped that once we got the Fulness of Times out of the way and the film on which we are now completing production, together with one or two other worrisome jobs that are now winding up, that there would be something of a respite and I could sorta loaf along. But whenever I get to a spot like that, something else bobs up to smash the picture. But, life's like that—and it wouldn't be very interesting if it were not."[240]

One of the things that bobbed up was the committee's expansion into live events at fairs and expositions. He obviously wasn't the first to do this, as the Church's involvement with such events dates back to the Tabernacle Choir's performance at the 1893 World's Columbian Exposition. More recently, the Church created an exhibit about the Word of Wisdom for the Second International Hygiene Exposition in Dresden in 1930, its first participation in a major international exposition, followed by the 1933-34 Chicago World's Fair, featuring sculptures by Avard Fairbanks in the Hall of Religion, and the 1935-36 California-Pacific International Exposition in San Diego. Individual missionaries also continued to make booths at fairs and even just to display on their own, such as a group of elders in Milwaukee who in 1936 rented a store and created a "Mormon Reading Room" in a busy shopping district, with street-level window displays and a plethora of reading material; this was copied throughout the Northern States Mission, and in 1937 similar reading rooms were created in Texas, California, New Zealand, and Prague.[241] For major expositions, though, the General Authorities now assigned responsibility to the Radio, Publicity and Mission Literature Committee, beginning with the Golden Gate International Exposition in San Francisco in February 1939. Inspired by his visit to the Church's booth at the 1933 Chicago World's Fair and the exhibits he'd helped with in England, Hinckley decided to go big and capitalize on the popularity of the Tabernacle Choir by building a smaller-scale replica of the Salt Lake Tabernacle with an electric organ and seating for fifty visitors. Several times a day a missionary played an organ recital, followed by a filmstrip lecture displaying images of Temple Square and Mormon history and doctrine; Hinckley prepared new printed literature centering around Temple Square and revised a booklet called *Joseph Smith's Own Story* as well. The exhibit proved extremely popular: one conservative estimate calculated that roughly 1,400 visitors passed through on opening day, with 700 on an average day but over 320,000 total by the time it closed in March 1940. Hinckley himself, however, calculated the number at over 1.25 million total visitors, with 8,211 presentations given and 200,000 Joseph Smith booklets distributed, along with 264 copies of the Book of Mormon, eighty-seven of his *Short History of the Church*, and numerous other publications. Although the Church itself didn't have an exhibit at the massive New York World's Fair in Queens that year, the state of Utah maintained the same theme with a twenty-three by twelve-foot diorama of Temple Square. Ten years later when California celebrated the centennial of the Mormon Battalion's arrival—at which Edward Finney filmed the Sons of Utah Pioneers' reenactment—Hinckley replicated a cabin in which the soldiers would have barracked; this and his work photographing Mormon historic sites began a lifelong interest in restoring such sites that ultimately culminated with his reconstruction of the Nauvoo Temple in 2002.[242]

With the Radio, Publicity and Mission Literature Committee proving the effectiveness of filmstrips and radio plays as pedagogical and propagandistic media, other Church entities occasionally created original work—despite the volume of material that Hinckley produced. The Sunday School, for instance, made numerous filmstrips, such as a fifty-frame filmstrip on the Word of Wisdom in 1935 and another about the life of Jesus called *Peace on Earth* that featured thirty-seven hand-colored pictures of artwork with printed captions from the New Testament. At Brigham Young University the physics professors Wayne Hales, Carl Eyring, and Milton Marshall produced a filmstrip specifically designed for the European Mission showing how Mormons had prospered in the desert climate of the American west. As others, including Eyring, began working with radio broadcasting and 16mm film production (discussed below), faculty and students produced programs like "The Purposes and Values of a Mission" (1938) in the Radio, Publicity and Mission Literature Committee mold.[243]

Hinckley and others at Church headquarters experimented with other types of visual media as well, such as *A Picture Story of Mormonism*, a "loose leaf" book that, in the tradition of George Reynolds's *Story of the Book of Mormon*, included over one hundred full-page pictures of Church history compiled by John Davis Giles. While not intended for group presentations, it was better equipped to grab the attention of someone in their home or even on the street without the need to set up even a filmstrip projector, and its format has been replicated in missionary materials for years.[244] Motion pictures, however, remained an elusive goal that remained outside Hinckley's reach. Though convinced of films' potential, he simply didn't have time to learn the craft. This would have to wait for the arrival of Frank S. Wise from England.

Born in south London in 1906, Wise spent his childhood in Bournemouth on Great Britain's southern coast and his adolescence in Walton-on-Thames southwest of the capital. This was the location of the Hepworth Studios, one of England's premiere film studios and creator of the *Tilly* comedies, and when Wise became friends with the brother of star Alma Taylor he was allowed to wander the lot, learning film production by observation. He installed a 35mm projector in the loft of his family's home, and after purchasing one of Pathé's first consumer cameras he also created a dark room in a closet. In 1929 he moved to London to work at the Ensign Camera Company's factory in Walthamstow, the largest camera factory in the UK, where he designed accessories like rewinders, splicers, and cans; he also shot newsreel footage and helped start the company's 16mm film library. He then met the missionaries, and one named Ralph Hardy invited him to visit Utah, which he did in 1937. Of course he brought a camera and spent three weeks photographing the scenic vistas of Yellowstone in Wyoming and Zion National Park and Bryce Canyon in southern Utah, arranging the pictures into a filmstrip called *Western Wonderlands* when he returned home. When he presented this to a missionary conference at Bradford in northern England it was so beautiful it reportedly made the American missionaries homesick. This was in 1939, and that May he returned to Utah; if he had intended another short trip, his plans were changed by Hitler's invasion of Poland on September 1 and the United Kingdom's subsequent declaration of war—he decided to stay in the U.S. permanently.

Ralph Hardy, who worked at KSL radio, was good friends with Gordon Hinckley, and he introduced the two men through the "Windsor Club," an informal group of returned missionaries who had served in Britain, with Wise the only British non-Mormon among them. Although he wasn't a member of the Church Hinckley recognized his talent and wanted to hire him, but before he could Wise, deeply moved by the October 1939 general conference as well as the returned missionaries he had met, was baptized in the Tabernacle's basement font. Meanwhile Hinckley procured a $100 a month salary for him—Church staff was still miniscule, but funding was evidently not as large an impediment as it had been—and brought him onboard as the committee's second full-time employee in early 1940, making space for him in his own office. Wise began his work with the same energy that Hinckley had shown five years earlier. He frequently focused on technical issues that were beyond Hinckley's skillset and his first major accomplishment, with the Church's Technicolor liaison George Cave, was devising a method to mass produce colored 35mm filmstrips from a Kodachrome original, eliminating the unwieldy and expensive hand painting of frames. The committee also helped create a combination record player/film projector to play recorded narrations along with slideshows.

Wise also became the committee's primary photographer, and between 1939 and 1942 he helped shoot three major filmstrips, *In the Tops of the Mountains, Historic Highlights of Mormonism,* and *Latter-day Saint Temples. In the Tops of the Mountains*, finished May 1941, was the first done in Technicolor and the first with recorded rather than live narration; it grew out of Wise's success with *Western Wonderlands* and his interest in landscape photography. *Historic Highlights* was finished the following January with sixty pictures and eight maps, one of the most comprehensive filmstrips yet made on Church history. With Wise's technical expertise, it was a short step for the two men to create their first motion picture, an untitled 200-foot film on the Aaronic priesthood that they shot on their own, without any Church funding, in the early 1940s. Perhaps because of lack of funds the film was never even printed, and further work was interrupted by the war when Wise enlisted with the Signal Corps to create filmstrips and movies for the military in Long Island; he was discharged in September 1945, around the same time he received U.S. citizenship. Hinckley, meanwhile, contributed to the war effort as a civilian, moving to Colorado to work for the Rio Grande Western Railroad.[245]

After the war he returned to Salt Lake City and resumed his position with the Radio, Publicity and Mission Literature Committee. Times had changed, however, from when it was just him in an empty office, as the Church's bureaucracy—and its payroll—were both quickly expanding. He still wrote a great deal of original material, such as a steady stream of literature for individual missions, the centennial radio play "What of the Mormons?" broadcast on July 24, 1947, and the radio series "A New Witness for Christ" (1950-57) and "Faith in Action" (1951-57). But he also oversaw more of the Church's growing broadcasting capabilities, an interest he maintained through the Fourth Wave and into his own presidency over the Church. He set up an expanded radio broadcast network for general conference and assisted with its initial television broadcasts; in April 1952 he oversaw the first closed circuit wire transmission of the general conference priesthood session from the Tabernacle to meetinghouses, and during the Church's April 1980 sesquicentennial it was his idea to broadcast part of the conference from the Peter Whitmer farmhouse in Fayette, where the Church had been founded, back to the Tabernacle in Salt Lake City and television sets everywhere, and he continued to oversee the expansion of the Church's satellite network. Foreign language translation also now fell under his purview, as proselytizing literature, scriptures, hymns, and filmstrip scripts all had to be rendered in dozens of European and Asian languages. While far from his original duties in 1935, this work did create a network of translators and prepare him for the creation of the filmed temple endowment ceremony a few years later. In 1951 when David O. McKay became Church President and Stephen L Richards his First Counselor, Church departments were reorganized and the Radio, Publicity and Mission Literature Committee was brought under Richards' larger Missionary Committee. Richards appointed Hinckley this committee's executive secretary, and he now oversaw all missionary work rather than just their audiovisual aids. In 1957 the new Church Information Service took over all material meant for explicit proselytizing, while general public relations work remained with the Radio, Publicity and Mission Literature Committee. Finally, in 1972, long after Hinckley had been assigned to other duties in the Quorum of the Twelve, the Church replaced the old committee with the Public Communications Department—which oversaw all press relations, new radio and television programs, visitors' centers, and pageants—with Hinckley's childhood friend and mission associate Wendell J. Ashton as its first director.[246]

Before this, though, and after focusing on so many different types of media for so many years, Hinckley finally became a screenwriter and film producer in 1951 when the Radio, Publicity and Mission Literature Committee produced a series of short 16mm films about the dangers of cigarettes. Intended for television broadcast or distribution through Deseret Book, these were produced in southern California by Signal Productions, Inc., a professional production company, but relied heavily on the Mormon community in Glendale and Hollywood. Mormon film agent Mildred Gagin acted as liaison between the film crew and Hinckley. Filming took place in Mormon homes as well as the Hal Roach Studios and other locations. Some of the leads were filled by professional television actors but many Church members appeared in the cast as well, most importantly Nathan and Ruth Hale, playwrights and thespians who ran the Glendale Center Theater, a hub for Mormon actors, and who would later have an enormous impact on theater in Utah as well as Church films throughout the Third and Fourth Waves. The films were well received in the educational market, and producing them was one of the most ambitious projects Hinckley had yet undertaken, although it prepared him specifically for his next and most difficult project ever, the filming of the temple endowment ceremony.[247]

Though not really a filmmaker beyond a few projects like these, Hinckley's influence on the Church's institutional media production, including filmmaking, is immense. Before Hinckley's arrival at Church headquarters, there were individuals working in Church media, but no concentrated effort. The Clawsons, KSL, early pageants, panoramas, and magic lantern lectures, publications like *The House of the Lord*, and individual films like *One Hundred Years of Mormonism* were all impressive but not coordinated. In the Second Wave, the motives and methods for Church media realigned to serve the Church's educational programs and missionary work, presaging the Church-wide coordination that would occur under Correlation and effectively creating a demand that would help bring about a renewal and expansion of Church film production. Gordon Hinckley's mentality of bringing all media under a single umbrella may have yielded little by way of finished motion pictures but did create the atmosphere in which institutional films could flourish under Judge Whitaker, which is why the 1930s should be far from considered a fruitless decade.

In fact, with the success of Hinckley's committee and the relative affordability of 16mm film, many Mormons thought the Church should have a greater role in the production and distribution of films. Even in 1936, when the Radio, Publicity and Mission Literature Committee was brand new, Elder Widtsoe was already anxious to move beyond filmstrips and to motion picture production, but he knew realistically that this couldn't fall to the already overworked Hinckley. Instead, he wrote a letter on May 25 to A. Hamer Reiser, a member of the Sunday School general board and head of the Church-owned Deseret Book Company, with the suggestion. Reiser was already of the same mind and was in the process of building up a massive film rental library, and it was from this work in home exhibition of motion pictures that full-fledged institutional film production would be reborn.[248]

Home Distribution and Exhibition

While filmstrips evolved from an experimental medium to a staple of Mormon instruction and proselytizing, the Church was also evolving its use of motion pictures and the infrastructure that would support them. For the average Mormon, the only connection with cinema remained that of consumption. In the final years before television Americans continued to attend the cinema frequently, although for Mormons the option to attend ward-sponsored screenings, which may have been discounted or even free, proved an enticing alternative to commercial theaters during the Great Depression. Thus if anything the economic crisis made communal film watching an even more integral component of American Mormon culture, not just socially but also financially as regular film screenings presented an opportunity for wards to fill their coffers. During good economic times Church leaders had counselled against using films to raise funds, but the Depression changed that as decreased tithing revenue meant wards needed new ways to cover their costs, particularly when they had to pay for large construction projects. Ward movies were an established activity that presented an easy way to generate revenue, and this precipitated a change in practice that led to film screenings serving as some of the biggest fundraisers of the Third and Fourth Waves. This wasn't limited to films, of course; in St. George when the Church's popular Dixie Junior College transferred ownership to the state in 1935, Church members from three wards there held dances to raise funds for another hall, and in 1940 the Adams Ward in the Hollywood Stake raised $3,000 for a recreation center with a playground and indoor and outdoor athletic facilities.[249] While the vast majority of "ward shows" or "movie evenings" continued in their original venues of ward meetinghouses or old amusement halls—with some wards that didn't have a projector convincing local exhibitors to set aside one night a week for MIA youth[250]—occasionally this impulse branched into Church units owning and operating their own commercial cinemas. Recall that the Fountain Green Ward in northern Utah ran its dance hall and movie theater from 1918 all the way through the Depression, not closing it until 1944. And as mentioned earlier, in 1937 Wilford Wood purchased the Nauvoo Opera House, the only movie theater in Nauvoo, and donated it to the Church six months later; whether the Church would have continued to run it if it hadn't burned down the following year remains a mystery.

But the most famous example came in the Sharon area of Orem, Utah, a community named after Joseph Smith's birthplace in Vermont that had been subsumed within the city of Orem when it incorporated in 1919. With the onset of the Depression and President Grant's aversion to the new policies of Franklin Roosevelt, the First Presidency in 1933 requested that all local Church leaders oversee recreation for their communities, a call not very different from what the MIA and Social Advisory Committee had counseled in the past but given new impetus by the trying economic conditions. Sharon Stake President Arthur V. Watkins, who would serve from 1947-59 in the U.S. Senate, responded by forming the Sharon Community Educational and Recreational Association, or SCERA, essentially as a stake amusement committee. Although initially run under stake auspices, to procure proper legal standing SCERA registered as a nonprofit cooperative in the state of Utah. The stake already held occasional film screenings in the local high school; these were free but required a pass from a bishop stating that the ticket holder had paid their share of the ward budget. Now, a committee decided that the most pressing recreational need on the hot Provo Bench was a community swimming pool, and they transformed these high school film screenings into fundraisers for the pool's construction. SCERA administrators, though probably all LDS, frequently emphasized that the program was open to all residents, not just Mormons. Tickets were sold by subscription rather than at the door: "Annual dues were set at $1 for heads of families and single adults over eighteen, with additional assessments based on the degree of individual participation. Thus, for a program of five dances, a play, a road show, subscription to the stake newspaper, and fifty-two movies, the annual cost ranged from $7 for a single person to $13 for a family. The advantages, contrasted to an estimated $40 charged for the same activities by comparable commercial enterprises, were obvious."[251] SCERA had purchased a new sound projector for these screenings in 1934, and by the time the pool was completed in June 1936 the film screenings had become so popular that the need for a proper movie theater was apparent. The Church agreed to donate the land next to the pool on condition the theater be closed on Sundays. Bonds were sold to

the amount of $6,000 and the design and construction labor was donated by lo-
cal residents in the spirit of public works like the Works Progress Administration
and the Public Works Administration, except that they opted for de facto Church
guidance to run their government program. "By 1937, SCERA had the active
support of 3,000 members and enjoyed the interest of publications ranging from
the Church-distributed *Improvement Era* to the worldlier *Reader's Digest*."[252] The
SCERA Theatre opened on Labor Day, September 1, 1941 with Henry Hathaway's
John Wayne film *The Shepherd of the Hills*, Hathaway's next movie after *Brigham
Young*, with Utah's Mormon governor Herbert Maw and Marvin J. Ashton, First
Counselor in the Presiding Bishopric, in attendance. Its completion was hardly
a small feat for a fruit farming town of 3,000 emerging from the Depression.
In the tradition of Progressive Era activists, Watkins and his associates saw
SCERA primarily as an agent of social reform, and despite the predominance
of Mormons in the community they sought to keep it nondenominational, even
though, as Frank Wise, a longtime Orem resident, said, "Of course the idea . . .
was to use films that were suitable for LDS consumption."[253] The organization
and its new indoor space worked with the Boy Scouts and other groups, and
during World War II SCERA handled the community's war bonds because Orem
had no bank. A second screen, a legitimate theater, an outdoor amphitheater,
and a museum of city history have since been added, with the pool replaced by
an entire waterpark, and today the SCERA, as it is often called, is perhaps the
oldest public building and one of the best-known landmarks in the city, continuing to use volunteer labor, close Sundays, and show only family-friendly fare,
despite the financial difficulties that this has presented in today's market. Since
2005 it has appropriately been the home of the LDS Film Festival. Although this
is an extreme case, the use of films as fundraisers in the Church continued for
over fifty years.[254]

The actions of autonomous Church units like the Sharon Stake also demonstrate that, despite the prevalence of films being shown in Mormon buildings,
exhibition at the beginning of the Second Wave was largely governed at the local
level. Over the course of the next twenty years it too would undergo a consol-
idating process akin to Hinckley's work with filmstrips and other media, and
more than anyone else this was due to A. Hamer Reiser. The grandson of Swiss
pioneers, Reiser was born in Salt Lake City in 1897 and spent his life involved
in numerous civic and Church affairs, serving in the Boy Scouts, the University
of Utah Board of Regents, the Utah State Parks and Recreation Commission,
and the state committee for the 1947 centennial of the state's founding. He also
served in a number of Church posts, such as secretary to the 1930 *Message of*

the Ages pageant committee. His longest-lasting position, however, was with the Deseret Sunday School Union. David McKay called him as secretary to the Sunday School's general board in 1921 when he was just twenty-four years old, and over the next twenty years he rose through the ranks, overseeing projects and writing a great deal of curricula, eventually becoming the first assistant to general superintendent Milton Bennion in 1949; he only left the Sunday School when he was called to preside over the British Mission in 1952. It was his early collaboration with McKay, however, that set the tone for his work with films and filmstrips. Since the anti-Mormon film era, McKay believed fervently in the power of film, and for the rest of his life he remained the most ardent advocate for Church filmmaking and film distribution out of all the General Authorities. Reiser once said that all of his work with film and media sprang from McKay's interest and help, and speaking of his time at the Radio, Publicity and Mission Literature Committee, Frank Wise said that while Stephen Richards was supportive nobody was truly excited about audiovisual media except McKay.[255] Having worked in the Sunday School since 1906, becoming its superintendent in 1918, when he called Reiser three years later they set about to fully domesticate film and filmstrip distribution within the institution of the Church.

It's possible that Reiser assisted in obtaining 35mm film projectors for wards in the 1920s, but in 1927 private Church film distribution faced its greatest crisis yet with the coming of synchronized sound. Of course, sound films had a lasting effect on the social nature of the experience by replacing homemade music or friendly chatter with the canned soundtrack. The greater initial challenge, however, was procuring new projection equipment that could play a soundtrack. David Smith discussed the problem in the April 1933 *Improvement Era*: "With the development of the sound motion picture, the bishops of these wards [that had purchased silent projectors] discovered that it was difficult to secure suitable pictures to meet their purposes. They found expensive equipment on hand, in some cases not fully paid for, and yet useless." Some congregations simply continued to watch old silent movies several years into the sound era, finding prints as best they could, but a few enterprising wards "entered into contracts for sound equipment," a generally unwise decision during what was a rather volatile period to make large capital expenditures. First, as an individual customer rather than a large film theater circuit, a ward often had to pay more or received lower-quality equipment. Second, sound film technology was rapidly evolving, and "in a few cases after only a few months some of this equipment . . . became obsolete" and had to be discarded. The First Presidency was made aware of the problem and formed a committee with McKay, Bishop Smith, and others, with Reiser again as secretary, to conduct a nearly year-long investigation into the uses of sound cinema and how to protect wards from huckster salesmen seeking to dump bad projectors. The solution they proposed was collective bargaining, and the First Presidency then assigned the committee to attempt to enter a contract with a reliable supplier to outfit all the wards, with a reasonable payment plan, rather than allow the wards to deal with suppliers one at a time. But, despite a rumored deal with RCA in February 1932 that sparked protests among Utah's commercial film exhibitors, finding that supplier proved elusive.[256]

Fortunately, McKay was also a member of the Rotary Club and attended their meetings every Tuesday afternoon. On one particular day in August 1932 he came back to the office and told Hamer Reiser that he had to show him something at the nearby Hotel Utah. The firm Electrical Research Products Incorporated, a subsidiary of Western Electric, had demonstrated their sound film projectors with a twelve-minute documentary on the life cycle of a pea plant. When the two returned the ERPI personnel were already dismantling the equipment, but McKay's enthusiasm initiated a good relationship with them—instead of returning home they remained in Salt Lake City for several weeks—and he assigned Reiser to strike a deal to outfit all 500 wards in the Church with 35mm projectors. Various proposals went back and forth, with ERPI's final offer being to outfit fifty wards with a projector, screen, and a supply of films, including two entertainment films and other educational films per month, for $49.50 per month per ward. The firm would also produce five educational films on Mormon topics each year. In the end the committee decided the cost was prohibitive and dealt with too small a percentage of the wards to move forward and that the funds could be better used in the growing welfare program. But the offer, minus the production of original films, was made available to individual wards that could raise the funds. The Hawthorne Ward in central Salt Lake City in this way ran a successful film program for many years, and in the tiny town of Ferron in central Utah theirs was the only film projector for miles; once or twice a month people would gather from all around to see a film, making Ferron the entertainment capital of that small portion of rural Utah. Ticket sales paid for the projection equipment and a new chapel as well. Nevertheless, the arrangement was still difficult, especially for those wards projecting films in multipurpose spaces, as "the projection equipment for 35mm was unwieldy and could not be easily moved from room to room [and] the films were too costly to be used extensively."[257]

Despite this limited success, throughout 1932 Reiser experimented with showing secular educational films in Church settings—such as *The Brass Choir, Plant*

Growth, The Study of Infant Behavior, and *Jack and Jill in Songland*—and grew as passionate as his mentor McKay about their pedagogical potential. He was so encouraged that he oversaw the filming of President Grant and his First Counselor Anthony Ivins speaking on the potential of talking pictures in religious instruction, along with speeches by David O. McKay, Presiding Bishop Sylvester Q. Cannon, a performance by Edward Kimball at the Tabernacle organ, and the Tabernacle Choir singing "Let the Mountains Shout for Joy." As mentioned earlier, the footage of Grant and Ivins premiered at the October 1932 Sunday School convention with great success—the first use of film in a general Church meeting—and continued to be shown in various wards. In one case the congregation had been told that President Grant would be visiting, so the chapel was packed with people wondering where the prophet was when the services began without him. Without explanation the lights were lowered and the film projected onto a screen by the pulpit. These people were quite familiar with silent films, but hearing Grant while seeing his moving image was reportedly electrifying. "I doubt if you realize the true value these church films are going to bring to the outlying wards," one worshipper wrote. "Religious or educational pictures are going to do much to help bring out the attendance." For precisely that reason one ward even began showing a film each week during sacrament meeting.[258]

Still, despite these early encouraging results further work with sound pictures was postponed. It's likely that insufficient financing was once again the culprit, as in July 1932 the Sunday School instead began an extensive rental program of still filmstrips, some original and some purchased from outside suppliers. This was a natural extension of the circulating library of books that the Sunday School made available to its members; by the end of the year the general board offered Merrill's *The History of the Church of Jesus Christ of Latter-day Saints in Film* and forty-seven filmstrips on the Old Testament and forty-four more on the New Testament. A unique item made by the Sunday School itself—perhaps with Reiser's involvement—was two filmstrips of their previous two conferences along with a transcript of the speeches so that students could read the sermons while looking at the original speakers and thus recreate the experience of being at the meeting.

In 1935 they added a fifty-frame filmstrip on the Word of Wisdom and another, as already mentioned, about the life of Jesus called *Peace on Earth.* These and many more items were available free of charge except for postage—about ten cents for a filmstrip—and by November 1932 the Sunday School began offering filmstrip projectors for rental as well; previously individual wards had to purchase their own. In September 1933 Reiser oversaw the creation of a permanent display about visual instruction at the Sunday School's headquarters at 50 North Main Street next to Temple Square. This presumably is also where the Sunday School held its filmstrip collections, the center of a sprawling distribution network that utilized stake-level board members, volunteers serving in local Sunday School callings, as intermediary distributors to get filmstrips and projectors in the hands of the correct customers. This served as the prototype for Reiser's immense motion picture distribution apparatus at Deseret Book.[259]

The Sunday School continued to produce and distribute filmstrips throughout the Second Wave. The general board also pushed for individual wards to equip their meetinghouses with a small library or resource center, a process begun a generation earlier in the Progressive Era, and this eventually allowed for local buildings to maintain a permanent catalog of titles themselves rather than having to request filmstrips in advance from Salt Lake. By 1939 a filmstrip like *Dazzy Shows His Album*, a dramatic narrative about the Word of Wisdom with a soundtrack on an accompanying record, was shipped for free to each ward for placement in this resource center. A robust teacher training program continued for years to ensure maximum returns from the filmstrips; *You Can Teach It Better With Pictures* (1951) was even a filmstrip about how to use filmstrips and other visual aids, explained in enough detail to require sixty-seven images; later that year it was followed by *Special Aids to Teaching and Making Lessons Live*. The accumulation of these resources in local meetinghouses, though taken for granted today, marked a major shift in Mormon culture from the days when wards had no supplies beyond each member's personal possessions. Meetinghouse libraries are now an integral feature of every sizeable meetinghouse throughout the world, over the years housing reels of film, projectors, televisions, videocassettes, and DVDs in addition to printed material and items like blackboard chalk.[260]

In 1942 Reiser was named general manager of the Deseret Book Company, a position which would allow him much greater control over the Church's motion picture distribution apparatus. This Church-owned publisher actually had its roots in the Sunday School, making it easy for Reiser to coordinate between them. The first Mormon Sunday schools were created by Richard Ballantyne in 1849 soon after arriving in the Salt Lake Valley, but in 1866 apostle George Q. Cannon formed the Deseret Sunday School Union as an organization to unite and coordinate these isolated, disparate classes. To facilitate teaching he also began publishing the *Juvenile Instructor* magazine and other literature geared toward Mormon readers. To sell this material he founded various bookstores under different names, including the Deseret Sunday School Union Bookstore, and by 1920 these were all merged under Church ownership and renamed the Deseret Book Company, one of the Church's largest commercial interests in the years after the Great Accommodation. The company still published much of the material used in Sunday instruction, as well as for Mormons' personal study, and thus the appointment of Reiser, a lifelong Sunday School operative and author of many such doctrinal and historical works, to oversee Deseret Book was a natural choice. And while there was much to supervise on the publishing and retail end of his new position, he attacked film distribution with a degree of enthusiasm that simply reflects his own personal interest in it.

Of course his appointment at Deseret Book occurred as the United States was shifting into a war mentality, and beyond just anti-German or Japanese propaganda Hollywood began producing numerous instructional films about details of the war effort. This massive display of the effectiveness of educational films had a profound impact on both General Authorities and filmmakers in the Church, even those like Reiser who were already interested in the medium. As Wise, who spent the war producing training films for the Army, put it, "It was the war that taught us that you can teach people quicker and better by using visual images with audible commentary . . . We sensed it before that time, in the little efforts that we made in the filmstrip program, but we did not really know. The war was the proving ground for using motion pictures in training."[261] This was not a unique experience for Wise alone but a major shift across the entire nation: "World War II caused an explosion in the use of films as means of informing and educating. Following the war the non-theatrical field, with industrially sponsored and class-room films predominating, expanded enormously compared to pre-war."[262]

In line with these national trends, Reiser's ultimate goal was to acquire motion picture prints and make them available to the wards. He would have to do this on a commercial basis, even if the prices were steeply discounted, as Deseret Book couldn't rely on Church funding and had to remain in the black. Thus, al-though wards had been successfully showing movies throughout the 1930s, the rise of inexpensive 16mm film in that decade may in fact have caused him some buyer's remorse for the 35mm projectors from Electrical Research Products Incorporated—purchasing and renting out 16mm film prints would have been much less expensive and much easier to ship, and he would be able to buy many more of them. In February 1945 he traveled to Chicago with LeGrand Richards, who was now Presiding Bishop and oversaw much of the Church's finances, to strike a deal with the Bell & Howell Company, a well-known manufacturer of cameras and projectors that wanted to expand into the educational film distribution market with 16mm films and equipment. Projectors, sound equipment, and screens were sold to wards outright at the wholesale cost of $1,000, with the ward paying half the cost and the institutional Church through the Presiding Bishopric paying half. Thereafter Bell & Howell, in conjunction with the Encyclopedia Britannica, supplied film prints to Deseret Book, which it could then rent to the wards from what was called the Deseret Book Store Film Library, making it a vast film rental house for the wards and stakes with hundreds of educational and entertainment titles available—not one of which was produced by the Church. Bell & Howell even provided equipment to wards in Britain and the Continent at roughly the same rates, even though they were far beyond Deseret Book's distribution reach. In the U.S. Reiser caught onto the idea of using evening film screenings as fundraisers for building projects, thus giving some official approval to a concept already well established among the various wards. As rental rates increased the library was so well managed by Beth Soffe that the entire program's weakest link threatened to be the viewers at the ward level who might damage the films or their projectors. Thus in 1946 the Church, probably through the MIA, initiated a film projectionist training program, especially for young men visiting general conference from outlying areas. Hundreds of teenage boys learned how to thread film through a projector, how to rewind and care for the film, and how to clean projectors and make basic repairs. Film was now so popular that it even threatened to influence Mormon architecture: in 1949 Frank Wise devised a plan that would place projectors in a soundproof booth between two adjacent classrooms so that it could serve either one. Drawing on his vast knowledge of the mechanics of film equipment, he even devised a way to allow projection of a large image in half the space by bouncing the beam off a mirror and onto the screen, thus increasing its cast without increasing the size of the classroom. Though apparently never implemented, this does show how integrated film was in Mormon worship and study, besides the evening screenings of Hollywood films that so shaped Mormon social life. In 1950 the relationship with Bell & Howell had placed projectors in more than 700 wards, and within a year that number had grown to include nearly 1,200 wards, stakes, and missions: an efficient—and unprecedented—distribution and exhibition network was firmly in place, which Hamer Reiser estimated may have been the largest private film distribution network in the world.[263]

Such a vast undertaking raised questions. The first was a variation on something that Mormon leaders had been asking since the early 1900s: With ward shows now so easy to hold, how can we be sure that the films themselves are of high moral quality? Church leaders, as they had done in previous decades, decided to pay closer attention and exercise greater control over what was being shown. When the Social Advisory Committee disbanded in 1922 the youth MIA program, particularly its Community Activity Department under Ephraim Edward Ericksen and Emily C. Adams, began to publish periodic film reviews in the *Improvement Era*, sometimes original but more often reprints or summaries of national stories. In late 1929, as churches and civic voices across the country called for greater moral regulation of the film industry, the MIA launched an entire curriculum about how to best use motion pictures for education and recreation, followed periodically for several years by lists of approved titles and brief reviews taken from "The Motion Picture"—a small film magazine published by a consortium of companies wishing to reform Hollywood—the General Federation of Women's Clubs, and similar sources; they also addressed the physical conditions of ward screenings, such as fire safety and ventilation. In April 1932 this article adopted the name "Lights and Shadows on the Screen" and served as the primary outlet for Mormon voices like Elsie Talmage Brandley who spoke in harmony with the Catholic League of Decency and others who supported the nascent work of Will Hays and Hollywood's reformers. This column also provided the continual procession of approved film titles, from RKO's children's film *Little Orphan Annie* (1932) to the swashbuckling blockbuster *Mutiny on the Bounty* (1935), with plenty of documentaries, short films, and foreign films included. There were even the profiles and anecdotes a typical fan magazine would carry but with a distinctly Mormon flavor, as when Hollywood makeup magnate Max Factor Jr. endorsed keeping the Word of Wisdom to increase personal beauty.[264]

Such articles were a valuable resource but still relied on outsiders for evaluation of what was appropriate for Mormon youth, which may have made some leaders slightly uncomfortable. Also, they peaked in 1935 and greatly diminished in subsequent years. And perhaps most importantly, with the advent of the film library at Deseret Book some—most likely those who were most involved, such as Reiser, McKay, and Richards—felt the need to bring the Church's film criticism into closer symbiosis with the films they had available. Hence, on January 3, 1948 Reiser announced that the First Presidency was creating an LDS Film Council, later called the Church Film Screening Council, to "appraise motion pictures and decide upon their suitability for entertainment and teaching purposes for the various organizations of the Church" and advise Deseret Book of their findings.[265] Reiser was named chairman over at least eighteen other committee members of both genders, including Bryant Hinckley. As a Church, not Deseret Book, entity, the whole group fell under the supervision of Bishop Richards. Al-

The Second Wave: Home Cinema

though Reiser's description may seem to indicate an organization prone to censorship, the Council actually proved quite generous in their recommendations, giving nuanced if short critiques that recognized the different maturity levels within the Church membership. For several afternoons and evenings each week, they came with their families to Deseret Book's projection-equipped auditorium at 1400 Indiana Avenue and screened the incredible backlog of titles already in stock there, starting with feature films from Hollywood and foreign countries before moving on to nonfiction and educational films, presumably because entertainment films were more likely to contain objectionable material. Until approved, individual films were evidently frozen from rental, but by May much of the catalog was circulating again and Council members began publishing brief reviews in the *Improvement Era* and *Church News*. The films recommended in their first article were the Nathaniel Hawthorne adaptation *The House of Seven Gables* (1940), the backstage story *Cowboy in Manhattan* (1943), the Hal Roach social picture *Captain Fury* (1939), the Bing Crosby musical *East Side of Heaven* (1939), and the thriller *Lady on a Train* (1945), representing an attempt to reach into a broad generic range for multiple age groups. Each title included a pithy statement such as, "Excellent entertainment. Good standards. Acceptable and wholesome," for *Cowboy in Manhattan* or, "Good entertainment, thriller. Good mystery, interesting to everyone, though a little severe for children," for *Lady on a Train*. Future articles greatly expanded the number of films covered, with more editorials on film-related issues.[266]

Before the LDS Film Council could start publishing their findings, however, the stage was set by a short-lived column called "...And So the Movies!" by *Improvement Era* associate editor Marba C. Josephson. She constantly maintained the Mormon fascination with the moral quality and effect of films, but her goal was to enhance readers' cinematic literacy. She stated her thesis in her very first article by saying that "the more accurately we can judge a movie, the better will be our enjoyment of the good movies which we elect to attend."[267] Thus she tried to increase viewers' awareness of what they were watching by handling topics like humor, plot and how it differs from story, and verisimilitude, and she tried to increase appreciation for elements like tragic endings which viewers might easily dismiss. For instance, despite its fantasy element she praised the realism of Frank Capra's *It's a Wonderful Life* (1946), saying it "is a movie in which the fanciful and the real are well treated to indicate how a well-written and produced movie can handle the unusual." She then added a touch of Mormon perspective: "One thing that we should take issue with in this play is the drinking scene, which was not essential to the plot. But the play as a whole was good, and Latter-day Saints should learn to discriminate by discarding the bad and holding the greater amount of good."[268] Since her goal was greater understanding of movies she rarely dismissed any, although Hitchcock's *Notorious* (1946) is an example of a film that earned her scorn for its implausibility. She had an effect on her readers, because in her last column, which was co-written with Reiser, she reported that so much mail had come into Church headquarters agreeing and disagreeing with her points and discussing how to implement them in ward movie screenings that she turned it all over to LeGrand Richards. He in turn contacted Reiser, who hoped that the work of the LDS Film Council could help continue exactly this type of conversation. Internationally this was the first great era of film criticism, and though Josephson, an untrained volunteer amateur, wasn't equal to the great theorists and critics of the mid-century—men like André Bazin, Rudolf Arnheim, Bosley Crowther, Otis Ferguson, James Agee, Manny Farber, and Parker Tyler—her writing was thoughtful and her approach remarkable for a religious organization, and it helped influence how Mormons have seen film ever since. Between the MIA in the 1930s and LDS Film Council in the '40s these were the golden years of institutional film criticism; nothing like it has ever been attempted since.[269]

Having an entire committee to address film issues allowed them to try other ways to improve the cinematic experiences of the various wards. They took over the projectionist training program and, to foster even better care of the equipment, initiated Deseret Book's Mobile Service Laboratory, a well-marked van which employees drove around the Mormon Corridor to visit each unit as often as possible to deliver and pick up films and inspect, clean, and repair projection equipment. And this brought them to the second question raised by such a vast distribution and exhibition apparatus. As Frank Wise put it years later, "'Well, we've got these machines and we're going to put them in. What are we going to put in them? What are we going to feed them?'"[270] It was decided the time was right for the Church through Deseret Book to re-enter the film production business. Reiser, in his "...And So the Movies!" article, enthusiastically proclaimed, "As the Church has been a leader in the use of radio and more recently of television in communicating its message to the world, so now it is in the forefront of the use of motion pictures for ward recreational and educational programs."[271] This effort came in the form of Deseret Film Productions, but the LDS Film Council itself undertook some unsuccessful production work of its own in the form of a series of short educational films on music, basketball, homemaking, and art education that unfortunately never materialized. Instead, in the summer of 1948 they gained a fair amount of publicity for the acquisition of two major

The Second Wave: Home Cinema

projects from outside Deseret Book's regular Bell & Howell supplier. The first was a series of films on Scouting produced by the Boy Scouts of America's executive office; individual titles covered topics from Cub Scouts to Senior Scouts, with titles like *The Patrol Method, Camping with the Troop, Winter Camping, The Scout in the Forest, The Scout Trail to Citizenship*, and a film for older boys aerodynamics. The second title was *God Is My Landlord,* a nearly hour-long film from the Dynamic Kernels Institute about a Quaker farmer who from 1940-46 conducted an experiment in planting wheat, paying a tithe on the harvest, and replanting the remaining kernels to measure how great the yield would grow. The experiment had gained national recognition among tithe-paying religions, and the Technicolor film, coming fifteen years before *Windows of Heaven* (1963), was the first film shown in the Church about the principle of tithing. Given the size of the Church's film exhibition network the LDS Film Council negotiated a reduced rate to screen the film, charging $12 for a screening of at least 120 spectators, or ten cents per person; appropriately, the Dynamic Kernels Institute allowed customers to deduct ten percent of their earnings to pay as tithing. In these years the LDS Film Council was quite successful, but, as with the Social Advisory Committee, once it had done the hard work of organizing the Church's film viewing, it became less necessary. Thus the work of the Council continued for several years before gradually fading away, but the infrastructure for film exhibition that it along with Deseret Book created has remained in place up to the present, even with the disappearance of the regular ward movie night and the substitution of satellite dishes and video equipment for film projectors.[272]

Besides the Radio, Publicity and Mission Literature Committee and the Sunday School/Deseret Book, the Church-owned entity that saw the most activity with motion pictures and visual media in the 1930s was Brigham Young University. Though a small collection of charts and magic lantern slides were made available to faculty in 1924, the big leap came in 1933. In keeping with the Church's new excitement over filmstrips in that year, the university offered a summer course in visual instruction. Following this, Dr. Lowry Nelson, director of the school's Extension Division over public outreach and education, asked university President Franklin S. Harris for funds to create a permanent Bureau of Visual Instruction. Once funded, Nelson organized the Bureau with the assistance of F. Wilken Fox, a recent graduate who would become the Bureau's director, but especially Dr. Ellsworth Dent, the director of the Audiovisual Bureau at the University of Kansas and an editor of *Educational Screen* magazine who was at BYU as a visiting faculty member.

The Bureau of Visual Instruction opened in the Education Building on the lower campus with 150 reels of motion pictures and 500 filmstrips "for use in teaching agriculture, athletics, biology, general science, geography, history, industrial arts, L.D.S. Church history, literature, New Testament, Old Testament, physical science, physiology, and other subjects." Other items included a 35mm camera that had once belonged to Rudolph Valentino and a 16mm camera that had no such history but evidently saw much more use from students and faculty. Perhaps most notable of all was the film stock that was used in this camera, which BYU claims was the very first reel of 16mm color film that Eastman Kodak had ever released commercially. The first thing filmed was a football game in the fall of 1933, footage that the university still has today, and "other attempts in the 1930s included a slow-motion film of the state high school typing championship contest, the twenty-fifth annual invitational track meet, a film for the Boy Scouts of America, and a film on creative dancing."[273]

Ellsworth Dent proved to be a worthwhile addition to the university, as he knew pedagogy well and had a skilled eye for successful magic lantern slides, stereopticons, charts, maps, and other formats besides filmstrips. Perhaps it was thanks to his influence that, as mentioned earlier, the physics professors Wayne Hales, Carl Eyring, and Milton Marshall produced a filmstrip specifically designed for the European Mission showing how Mormons had prospered in the desert climate of the American west. A. Hamer Reiser audited Dent's summer classes on visual instruction in 1934 and was so impressed he continued during the school year and into the next summer. In return, he convinced Dent and the university to open an extension course in Salt Lake City, with the Sunday School general superintendency underwriting half the cost of all registrations and tuitions for any stake board members who finished the course. Over one hundred students attended each week for the duration of this course, which was held in the old LDS University campus where the Church Office Building stands today, and thus Dent influenced the creation and implementation of filmstrips in the Sunday School as well.

As part of the Extension Division the Bureau's purpose was to reach every college and department on campus as well as the surrounding community in Utah Valley. "The chief function of the Bureau is to provide suitable motion pictures, filmstrips, and other materials for the use of the schools and seminaries, stakes and wards."[274] Public schools were courted as well: Fox was soon telling local parents about the use of films and filmstrips in the classroom and perhaps even the home. In January 1936, for instance, he spoke about the merits of visual

The Second Wave: Home Cinema

instruction at an evening PTA meeting in Springville south of Provo, of course using a filmstrip to illustrate his points. "During the early part of the Wilkinson Administration, the rapid growth of the audiovisual center continued, especially in the areas of circulation, equipment, and personnel. By 1958 the services of the center were extended to seven western states and three foreign countries, with a catalog circulation of 3,511."[275]

Within the university, this Bureau became the forerunner of all the subsequent film and video holdings in the library, the BYU Motion Picture Department, and all student instruction in filmmaking in the College of Fine Arts. In the following decades visual instruction continued to expand in every department, eventually growing to include dozens of classrooms with video projection capabilities; a trove of audio and video resources in the Learning Resource Centers Department that evolved into the Harold B. Lee Library's current Media Center; extensive film and video holdings in the library's L. Tom Perry Special Collections, with its own basement theater completed with the building's renovation in 1999; a small theater in the lower level of the university's Museum of Art; and two large theaters for entertainment.[276]

The first of these, the Varsity Theatre, opened as a commercial cinema in the Wilkinson Student Center in 1964, charging admission for students to see films like *Don't Go Near the Water* (1957) and *The Wackiest Ship in the Army* (1960). For years the theater was famous for editing objectionable content out of mainstream films with R and PG-13 ratings in order to meet university standards, but in the summer of 1998 copyright concerns ended this practice and today the theater shows PG- and G-rated films as well as classics like *The African Queen* (1951) and *Rebel without a Cause* (1955). Like with the SCERA a few miles away, this unfortunately has caused it to lose its once prestigious reputation among students and struggle to remain profitable, as it now has no comparative advantage to leverage over nearby off-campus theaters that offer all Hollywood's latest products regardless of rating. The university's second public theater is less known but more remarkable: the College of Humanities' International Cinema program, housed since 1981 in a spacious theater on the ground level of the Spencer W. Kimball Tower. This began in the 1950s when the college's French, German, and Spanish programs screened occasional films for students. In 1968 German instructor Joseph Baker expanded this into a larger International Film Festival and a weekly film series. In 1975 Donald Marshall took over the program and christened it the BYU International Cinema, and under his guidance it moved to its current home and greatly expanded the number of screenings. Today it offers an average of eighty-two films per year, with roughly 164 screenings each semester, primarily of 35mm prints. Titles range from new films like Anne Fontaine's *The Innocents* (2016, France) to classics like Ingmar Bergman's *The Seventh Seal* (1957, Sweden), including English-language and silent films like Stanley Kubrick's *Dr. Strangelove* (1964) and Abel Gance's *Napoléon* (1927). Free and open to the public, the International Cinema is today one of the most robust and oldest university cinema programs anywhere in the country. While students are still assigned to attend screenings for foreign language or other course-work, the International Cinema primarily serves as an entertainment resource, providing a broad selection of high-quality curated films for the population of an entire county that otherwise lacks any arthouse cinema.[277]

By the 1950s the men who created the Church's nascent film production and distribution apparatus were moving on to other things. David A. Smith was released from the Presiding Bishopric—and the Tabernacle Choir—in 1938 and passed away in 1952; LeGrand Richards was called into the Quorum of the Twelve in 1952; A. Hamer Reiser presided over the British Mission from 1952-55 then spent the last ten years of his career still with David O. McKay as an assistant secretary in the First Presidency's office; and Gordon B. Hinckley was called as an Assistant to the Quorum of the Twelve in 1958.[278] Frank Wise was the only one who remained involved with Church film as he transitioned to working with Judge Whitaker at the BYU Motion Picture Department in 1953, although he no longer had any input on film distribution. But the infrastructure of what they created was robust and outlasted them, only growing stronger through the subsequent work of BYU and the Presiding Bishopric. Reiser and Hinckley in particular can be credited with creating a cinematic culture that helped create Mormons' entire self-image and influenced a great many aspects of their devotional and recreational life.

This legacy wasn't all these men's doing, of course. As we've seen, natural forces were driving Mormons and the movies into closer contact in these years, with large groups of Mormons working in the industry, surprisingly positive films like *Bad Bascomb* and *Wagon Master* coming from Hollywood, and a willingness on the part of Church leaders at both the general and local level to champion motion pictures as not just a great form of propagandizing but a great form of art. If today Church leaders often seem to exude cautious disapproval of popular films and television, in the more open atmosphere of the Second Wave, exemplified by the Production Code's restraints on the industry—with a lack of concern about ratings, which didn't even exist yet—and the generous attitude of the LDS Film

The Second Wave: Home Cinema

Council, it was much more common for Church authorities to attend the cinema or commend its virtues in public and private. Church President Heber J. Grant and the apostle-senator Reed Smoot were foremost examples in this regard, with Smoot in particular forming close working relationships not just with Will Hays and William Fox but with many Californians representing the film industry. In September 1927, at the outset of this period, he was invited to see Cecil B. DeMille's *The King of Kings* and recorded in his diary that "it was a marvelous presentation and preached Mormonism in every particular. It is the greatest picture ever produced in my opinion. I would like to get a reel and show it to the Authorities of the church before I leave for Washington."[279] His enthusiasm may have led to Hinckley adapting it as a filmstrip a few years later. Similarly, on December 1, 1941 President McKay, then Grant's Second Counselor, recorded in his journal that he and his wife Emma saw *Citizen Kane* at the Paramount Theatre at 53 South Main Street, half a block from Temple Square. As Church President during the Third Wave his personal friendship with Cecil DeMille was well-known among Church members, and he and other General Authorities often recommended films, as in the April 1955 general conference when McKay publicly endorsed *A Man Called Peter* (1955), saying it "is well worth seeing, and has a message of spirituality most timely for the nation at this time" and reading an invitation for all bishops and stake presidents to attend a free preview screening at the Utah and Capitol Theatres. While he prefaced this invitation by joking that he didn't want to set any precedent, in the Second and early Third Waves such endorsements would not have seemed unusual, and nor would the marketing technique of inviting Church leaders in for a free screening. Even local leaders were occasionally treated as VIPs by film marketing campaigns hoping to foster strong word of mouth for their product: for instance, local Church authorities in Ogden were invited to a free preview of Errol Flynn's *The Adventures of Robin Hood* in July 1938 in hopes that they would spur their numerous ward and quorum members to see it as well—with a full-priced ticket.[280]

We've seen how assiduously President Grant courted Hollywood's favor, climaxing with the premiere of *Brigham Young* in 1940, but the year before he hosted another public event for the seventieth anniversary of the transcontinental railroad and premiere of DeMille's film *Union Pacific*. In late 1938 Paramount arranged with Grant personally to hold a preview screening of the film in the Tabernacle, the first and perhaps only time a Hollywood feature film has ever shown there. This probably occurred on April 1, 1939, and later that month DeMille traveled via rail with the Union Pacific railroad's president William M. Jeffers and various Paramount stars and Los Angeles dignitaries to the film's premiere in Omaha, making stops along the way. The party passed through Salt Lake City on April 25 and was greeted by Grant—a director of the railroad—J. Reuben Clark, Governor Harry Blood, and other local officials for a parade and luncheon, with speeches by DeMille and the eighty-two-year-old Grant, who was perhaps the only person present who remembered the actual 1869 ceremony, before continuing on their way to Ogden and Promontory Point. The visiting party then left for Nebraska, with President Grant going along for the premiere and celebrations in Omaha, while the rest of the locals, an estimated 10,000 of them, stayed for a dance at Ogden's Union Station. *Union Pacific* premiered in Omaha on Friday April 28, opening at Salt Lake City's Centre Theater the next day, but this type of celebration of a film by a Church president seems unlikely today.[281]

In his 1942 book *Mormon Country*, a lyrical but precise portrait of small town Latter-day Saint culture, the western novelist and historian Wallace Stegner aptly described the Mormons' relationship with recreation through its youth Mutual Improvement Association:

> The social life of Mormonism is centered in the Ward House as surely as the religious life is . . . Especially in the smaller and more isolated towns, but to some extent in the cities as well, the M.I.A. focuses the social life of the Wards . . . Young people will dance and play no matter what the Church does. The Church therefore gives them the opportunity—in fact by social pressures almost forces them—to dance and play in the place where the priesthood can keep an eye on them . . . All the way from hikes, outings, picnics, swimming parties, and hayrides to movies, dances, community singing, amateur theatricals, and athletic contests, the M.I.A. is the orbit within which the young Saint's life moves. The M.I.A. is by no means all of Mormonism, and by no means all the strength of the Mormon system. But put it partly down to the M.I.A. that the Mormons are an extremely law-abiding people. Put it partly down to the M.I.A. that there is as little apostasy, as little inclination to break with the parental system, as there is. Missionaries sometimes come home agnostics or jack-Mormons. Boys and girls in the larger towns, where the Gentile population is strong and the opportunities for wandering are greater, sometimes stray. But the boys and girls who stay at home in the small towns don't often get far from the Ward House. Radio and movie houses may have cut down Mutual attendance somewhat, and the hold of the church over its youth may be weaker than it was a generation ago. But it is still strong. You can't

> play basketball over the radio; you can't dance as well to the radio, in
> a crowded living room, as you can on a large amusement hall floor to a
> stomp band of Koosharem Koyotes. You can't *participate* in movies or
> the radio, and it is participation, shrewdly calculated and carefully nur-
> tured, that maintains the group spirit and Mormon belief in the small
> towns of Zion long after one would have expected the American system
> to dilute and destroy it.[282]

This is an excellent analysis that only misses one point: the Mormons had devised a method by which you *could* participate in movies. From selecting titles to
organizing ward shows, to running and cleaning the projectors, to receiving and
returning film prints, to handling the revenue and keeping the books, to simply
transforming the makeshift movie theater into a social space where a ward
unites to see a specific film together, Mormons had made movies social. And the
strength of that cinematic culture, though altered by film viewing technology
and practices, remains embedded deep within Mormonism today.

Postwar: Deseret Film Productions and the 1947 Utah Centennial

By the end of the war, with the Bell & Howell contract providing projection
equipment to every ward in the Church and creating a content vacuum, and
World War II demonstrating the power that educational film could exert and
how that vacuum could be filled, the need was clear for the Church to once
again produce its own films, and Reiser was convinced that Deseret Book
was the place to do it. Another factor that made this possible was the booming wartime and postwar economy. During the Depression Deseret Book had
required constant subsidies from the Church to remain afloat, and when Reiser
arrived in 1942 it was still struggling. Most of his effort, therefore, went into
strengthening the publishing and bookselling arms of the business, its bread
and butter, but then as sales increased he also realized that he could increase
profitability by channeling revenue into motion pictures and visual aids rather
than counting it as profit, thus reducing the company's overall tax burden. "We
finally took some dormant franchises we had and put the money into them, and
in film production," he recalled. "In a certain sense the profits that the Deseret Book Company made, subsidized the development of motion pictures and
visual aids."[283]

With the funds to pay for it he still needed somebody to do the work, and the
choice was obvious. Reiser offered Frank Wise a position as soon as he returned
from his military service in 1946. Wise accepted and thus became the head—

and in fact the staff—of a new division dubbed Deseret Film Productions. He started out much like Hinckley had, in a bare office:

> We were first located in an office in the Union Pacific Annex, one room. And at that time we had to build everything we wanted. We built our own animation camera and stand; we built our own benches. We just had simple little rewinds and the simplest kind of splices. Later we went into Richards Street down to a part of the Deseret News Building and had a room there. We never were located actually in the building of the Deseret Book Company because there wasn't space for us.[284]

Despite all the polished documentaries that Wise would complete at Deseret Film Productions, perhaps his most important work there appeared on the surface to be the most banal: the filming of General Authorities. Although this sounds akin to the Clawsons' films, with action shots and close-ups of Church leaders in various locations, it actually launched a different tradition that includes the filming and now broadcast of general conference and other addresses. This of course was made possible because of the advent of sound film and had been attempted by Reiser in 1932, but it was Frank Wise who solved all the technical and artistic problems and made the filming of sermons a standard component of general conference. It became a continual, or at least semiannual, project that he worked on from his hiring in 1946 until KSL television took over the recording of all general conferences in 1953, and thus it occupied his time in preparing, shooting, and editing, even while he worked on Deseret Film Production's other individual projects.

It was also Wise who pushed these humble films into existence. Some General Authorities expressed skepticism about the need for filming speeches, but, as he later said, "Now that we had the means to record the image and voice of our leaders, I was determined to do something about it."[285] To make his case he appealed to history. "The only argument that I used," he said, "was what would Brigham Young have done if he'd had this facility. And what would we give today to have pictures of Brigham Young and the Prophet Joseph speaking, so that we could see what they looked like and hear them."[286] As a test, he at first actually tried to do something more in the vein of the Clawsons, separately filming junior apostles Mark E. Petersen and Ezra Taft Benson in a makeshift studio dressed like an office on the top floor of the Church Administration Building. Both men's delivery was so stilted and halting, however, that Wise decided to shift his efforts to filming them in their natural element, behind the Tabernacle podium at general conference.

The Second Wave: Home Cinema

This presented its own set of challenges, beyond another round of conversations with General Authorities. Again many were resistant, but J. Reuben Clark took up Wise's cause and pulled all the strings necessary to get him permission. Also, although Wise was shooting a smaller subject, the lighting problem from *The Message of the Ages* remained and he found it almost impossible to get an adequate exposure. It appears that he initially installed some spotlights in the house, but they shone in the speakers' eyes and one person even asked from the podium that they be turned off. Finally, with the help of Bishop Marvin Ashton he received permission to install six fluorescent tubes directly over the Tabernacle pulpit. These cast enough light but came from the wrong direction and looked horrible, darkening the eyes and face while the top of the head glowed like an angel. To solve this problem, Wise replaced the red velvet cover of the pulpit with a white oil cloth; this served as a reflector, bouncing enough light back into the speaker's face to properly illuminate it. Combined with a very wide aperture lens and very fast, or light-sensitive, film stock, Wise was finally able to achieve an acceptable result.

The next problem was where to place his camera. Much of the resistance he encountered stemmed from concerns that a motion picture camera running in the middle of the Tabernacle pews would disrupt what should be a spiritual event. Ever the engineer, Wise used his mechanical knowledge to devise a solution: he cut a hole in the floor forty feet in front of the pulpit, about in the third row, and essentially installed a periscope with a twelve-inch square opening, allowing him to film the image of the speaker on a mirror in a small space below ground level. This was much less obtrusive than a camera on a tripod, but the congregation didn't know what this strange new "protrusion was from the floor of the Tabernacle, and many times orange peels and other cast off materials came charging down,"[287] dropped in by hungry but litter-conscious worshippers. He later joked that incoming rubbish proved quite perilous, so he quickly devised a remote-control system and operated the camera from the balcony in the main hall. More disruptive to the finished product was when somebody would lean on the tube, which would wobble the mirrors and distort the filmed image.

He shot with a 16mm Auricon sound-on-film camera that they used on all their productions, perhaps the Berndt-Maurer Sound-Pro model, which as the name implies used a light pulse to record sound directly onto the film stock. He was unable to use this feature, however, probably from an inability to properly place a microphone to pick up a good sound and be inconspicuously connected to the camera underneath the floor. Instead, the film was shot silently and sound was taken from the vinyl records that KSL recorded for later radio broadcast, which had a direct feed to the speaker's microphone and better sound quality anyway. Synchronizing the picture and the soundtrack would require some effort in postproduction, but Wise had even more ambitious plans. To add some visual variety and make the films as pleasant to watch as possible, he installed a second camera. While his main Auricon shot a frontal medium close-up with a six-inch telephoto lens, he used an old silent Bell & Howell camera with a wide lens in the balcony to get a different angle and show the surrounding space, despite the exposure problems in the choir seats; this set-up, expanded to three cameras, is essentially how conference is still shot today. Because the crowded building was prone to vibrate and any movement in the camera could ruin the image, especially with a very long lens, he also built a shock absorption system for both cameras. In addition, the cameras' film magazines were too small to film most sermons—the Bell & Howell came with a 400-foot magazine, which would film for roughly ten minutes—so he built customized 1200-foot magazines for each camera, allowing him to shoot up to thirty minutes without changing. To save footage he even cut in camera, remotely stopping the Auricon while filming with the Bell & Howell and then starting the Auricon back up again before stopping the Bell & Howell; this allowed him to change one camera's magazine while the other was running, and he could get through an entire two-hour session of conference with four magazines. This system, however, created a mammoth synchronization problem. In traditional film shoots a clapperboard is used before the scene starts to give both a visual and an aural signal at the same moment when the board claps shut, thus allowing editors to line up that instant in both the sound and the picture and relieving them from trying to match voices with lip movement by eye. Wise, of course, was unable to do this before every speaker, so he created an electronic solution, installing one tiny lightbulb on the organ behind the speaker for the frontal camera and another on the podium itself for the wide angle camera. He would pulse these lights when both cameras were running, and a small electronic buzz would be recorded on the soundtrack as well. Thus he could silently slate the shots while the speaker was still going, and afterwards at his editing table it was a relatively simple affair to line up all the pictures with the soundtrack. "I was never more than two frames out of sync," he recalled, "which is really fantastic," particularly given the soundtrack's origin on the 33 1/3-inch record and then transfer onto film stock, where it was synchronized and edited, and then transferred again onto a print where the sound was married to the picture.[288]

The Second Wave: Home Cinema

The results were worth the effort. Not every talk was filmed; emphasis was placed on the First Presidency and the oldest men who were, frankly, the most likely to die, but Wise also thought that he recorded at least one film of every General Authority who spoke in those years. Over six years he shot at least 120 speeches, or about ten from each conference, though as many as forty-five more were apparently recorded on film as late as 1967, when the process was completely taken over by video. The General Authorities had to approve each film before Deseret Book offered it for rental, and not everything got approved. After David O. McKay was sustained as the President of the Church in the April 1951 conference he was describing George Albert Smith's death when he broke down and cried at the podium. Wise found this profoundly moving, but some of the General Authorities thought that some people might laugh at it. It was therefore rejected and apparently never offered for rental; Wise took a print home for his personal collection and another copy was stored with Deseret Book. At first many General Authorities were uncomfortable watching themselves speak, but they soon warmed up to the idea and eventually all came to see the wisdom in Wise's vision. In evaluating his entire career after his retirement, Wise said he considered these general conference speeches the most notable films Deseret Film Productions ever made, on another occasion saying, "May I say that I think that that project is possibly the greatest contribution that I've ever been privileged to make, because we have a record now of people before the time of TV."[289] This is a powerful statement about a career that included hundreds of films, including the filmed temple endowment.

The initial process of obtaining permission and arranging the lights and cameras took a few years, so that Deseret Book's conference films weren't mentioned in the *Church News* until 1950. In the meantime, Wise directed and produced several other notable films. But nothing of value could be achieved by one man working alone, even one as multitalented as him. Reiser wanted to assist, but had no practical knowledge of filmmaking, besides the demands of his other responsibilities. The answer came in the person of LaMar Williams, who since beginning to work with his camera in Idaho had attended one of Ellsworth Dent's audiovisual instruction courses at BYU. He still lacked the skills Wise was looking for in an assistant, but he returned to call on Wise every week or two until the older man relented and gave him a job. "He finally hired me I think out of desperation more than anything else," Williams recalled.[290] With the 1947 centennial of the Mormon's arrival in Utah, which would occasion several major projects, fast approaching, Wise must have decided to take whatever help he could get. It was a good decision, though, as Williams proved up to the challenge.

With his hiring, Deseret Film Productions became an actual filmmaking unit, the Church's first since the Clawsons, and one which Reiser, Wise, and others considered a necessary step to the creation of the larger BYU Motion Picture Department in 1953.

The state legislature in 1939 had created the Utah Centennial Commission, with David McKay as chair and, at his request, Hamer Reiser as secretary. Celebrating 1947 as the "Utah Centennial" was a bit of marketing bravado by the state, as 1947 marked the centennial of Salt Lake City alone—the state of Utah was technically only fifty-one years old. But honoring the arrival of the Mormons in the Salt Lake Valley as the beginning of the entire region's settlement allowed the celebrations to spread beyond the capital, generating civic pride and, hopefully, economic growth from Logan to Kanab. McKay's commission reportedly had an even broader initial vision, hoping to host a major world's fair throughout the year and, since this was a decade before the Interstate Highway System, build parks and highways throughout Utah to connect it with neighboring states. This prospect was doomed by the war, though, which ate up not just the necessary capital but raw material like steel and aluminum as well; the famed Trylon and Perisphere structures from New York's 1939 World's Fair had just been dismantled and donated to the military to be turned into weapons. Not only this, but *all* plans for the celebration were suspended after Pearl Harbor. But on November 10, 1944, as an Allied victory looked increasingly likely, Governor Herbert Maw recommended the resumption of planning. The affair would have to be reduced, but it would still be a major event, with the dedication of Mahonri Young's *This Is the Place Monument* on Pioneer Day and celebrations occurring across the state from May 15 until October 15. The entire festivities were a state governmental effort, but years later when historian William G. Hartley asked Reiser to confirm that point, he laughed and responded, "Right. But of course we used the Church, always, with a vengeance."[291]

The celebration, with such ecclesiastical support, came off wonderfully. In addition to the many events sponsored by the Utah Centennial Commission, this also meant a surge in filmmaking activity. Hamer Reiser thought that the Church should have some type of official film, so he conceived of the project that would become *Where the Saints Have Trod*, a documentary about the pioneers as seen through the eyes of George Albert Smith, who had assumed the Church Presidency upon Heber J. Grant's death in 1945. The central idea of the project lay in Smith's deep affinity for the outdoors, history, and, specifically, historical geography. Born in 1870 as the son of apostle John Henry Smith and namesake of his grandfather, another apostle and first cousin of Joseph Smith, George Albert had been interested in Church history in particular from a young age, and as he rose through the Church hierarchy he, rather like Wilford Wood, focused on the acquisition of key historical sites and emphasized the importance of monuments and historical markers, writing to a friend in 1937, "In this part of the world there are many points of interest that are being forgotten and the people have felt that it was desirable to mark them in a substantial way so that those who follow will have their attention called to important events." His biographer clarified, "The 'people' referred to here consisted of a group of dedicated history buffs among whom George Albert Smith was a conspicuous member."[292] He hadn't always had such a peer group; a frequently solitary man who suffered from lifelong depression and anxiety disorder, he had spent many years pursuing his historical interests in solitary. But to foster a community and have a physical impact on the landscape, in September 1930 he formed and served as the first president of the Utah Pioneer Trails and Landmarks Association. In the subsequent years this group placed 120 markers from Nauvoo to San Diego and sponsored hugely popular memorial motorcades to Independence Rock—a Wyoming landmark on the Mormon, Oregon, and California Trails—in 1931 and from Florence, Nebraska, to Utah in 1936. In 1934 Smith conceived of placing a large monument at the mouth of Emigration Canyon where the pioneers had entered the valley, replacing the old plaque there, and as the Utah Centennial approached he launched a fundraising and letter-writing campaign, convincing the state legislature to create a Monument Commission as part of the festivities; Heber Grant was its first president, and Smith assumed the position upon his death. With this funding in place, the Utah Pioneer Trails and Landmarks Association commissioned sculptor Mahonri Young to create a massive monument, to be called the *This Is the Place Monument*, in the largest project the Association had ever undertaken. Groundbreaking was to take place on Pioneer Day, July 24, 1945, with the cornerstone of the base laid on Pioneer Day 1946, and the finished monument unveiled and dedicated exactly one year later in 1947.

Smith's original conception for the monument was very ecumenical, with a pyramid structure that included Catholics and Native Americans in its tributes. Though the finished design was quite different, this idea carried through to the large plaques on each side of the monument. He worked to get news of the monument's progress to the media, and he allegedly even journeyed to the site every day to feed the seagulls to train them to be there for the monument's unveiling. It might have been Smith, Reiser, or a different member of the Association who first thought of hosting another memorial motorcade, but it was Reiser's idea that this would make a good film. The motorcade would have to be held—and filmed—in 1946 in order for the picture to be ready for release by the summer of 1947, but this was presumably accommodated by the fact that the original pioneers had made half their journey, from Nauvoo to Winter Quarters, in 1846, so centennial celebrations of this portion of the journey could be held along the way, providing good subject matter for the motion picture.

George Albert Smith had recently returned from a trip to Mexico City on Church business and was struggling to return to full form, though due to the stigma surrounding mental illness at the time it's unclear what exactly he was suffering from. Nevertheless, when the time came for the two-week journey he was ready. "Accompanied by friends from the Trails Association, the Prophet left Salt Lake City on July 11, 1946, on the Denver & Rio Grande."[293] The group consisted of just thirteen men besides President Smith, including Frank Wise and LaMar Williams, who brought along a new sound-on-film Auricon camera—the one that would come to be used for general conferences—and other brand new equipment that Reiser had purchased just for this production. Wise recalled that "the Church was still dragging its feet on providing either personnel or money to run anything like this,"[294] so Reiser had been forced to dip into Deseret Book's general funds to provide them with the bare minimum equipment and film stock. One item that was either purchased or donated was a used truck that they—probably Wise—outfitted with a shooting platform to get high-angle exterior shots, so it's possible that Wise and Williams drove this to meet President Smith's group rather than riding on the train with them.

Stopping in Pueblo, Colorado, Smith dedicated a monument to the first white settlers of the state, while Wise and Williams commenced their filming. The final stop via rail was in Kansas City, Missouri, where the group switched to automobiles, launching the memorial caravan. They visited various sites around Independence and Far West then went due east to Quincy, Illinois, then upriver to Nauvoo, where they held a memorial service for Joseph and Hyrum Smith. They now switched directions and headed westward in the footsteps of the pioneers, holding centennial observances of 1846 sites as they went. "The history buffs in the party told stories along the way to give the trekkers a vicarious sense of what the Mormon Pioneers had experienced."[295] They passed through Winter Quarters then headed west toward Fort Laramie, traveling along the Platte River and visiting the well-known grave of pioneer Rebecca Winters near Scottsbluff, Nebraska. By July 20 they were in Casper, Wyoming, where they attended church then visited Independence Rock; over the next two days they visited Sacagawea's purported gravesite in Wyoming and held a memorial service for the ill-fated Willie handcart company. They had a bonfire at Fort Bridger on July 23, then the next day President Smith led the caravan to Henefer, northeast of Salt Lake City, where they were met by Governor Maw, and the entire entourage drove to Salt Lake City where, in the afternoon, Smith laid the cornerstone for the monument, exactly one year after its groundbreaking ceremony.

Wise and Williams recorded all of this. Their film is exemplary of Home Cinema, with two Church-employed filmmakers using color 16mm film to record a journey of the Mormon prophet traveling in the footsteps of the pioneers, with music provided by the Mormon Tabernacle Choir. The result is an intimate portrait of this often-overlooked Church President, and it includes interesting moments such as the circling of cars like nineteenth-century wagons. They shot parts without sound to allow for narration, recorded in Utah by Paul Royall, while other scenes had sound recorded straight into the Auricon camera. In one engaging moment the men are gathered in the upper room of the Carthage Jail where Joseph and Hyrum Smith were killed. John D. Giles holds the microphone for Preston Nibley while he delivers an impromptu narration about the martyrdom. The scene was so remarkable that it's "become a historic document in many ways," as Wise later said.[296] The finished product was four reels and seventy minutes long, making it by far the longest movie any Church-employed filmmaker had yet made, an auspicious way to relaunch institutional filmmaking. Even the unused footage, thirty-one minutes of which are stored at the Church History Library, is an invaluable historical record in the vein of the amateur filmmakers discussed earlier, with shots of President Smith visiting Council Bluffs, Iowa, where his father was born in 1848, and speaking at Adam-ondi-Ahman in Missouri, where some Mormons believe the Garden of Eden was located.

Wise and Williams previewed *Where the Saints Have Trod* for a group of General Authorities and auxiliary organization leaders in December 1946. No objections were raised, so it was released through Deseret Book on January 4 as the kickoff of the yearlong celebration. "It is expected that the film will have a special appeal to members of the Church who are interested in Church History and who desire to hear the voice of President Smith as he speaks to them from the screen," the *Church News* reported. It's also probably the most important picture Deseret Film Productions made, as it represents the re-beginning of institutionally sponsored filmmaking eighteen years after the Clawsons' fire and is a wonderful historical record in its own right, commemorating the Church and its members in both 1847 and 1947. While it and other Deseret Film Productions titles have been preserved at the Church History Library—Frank Wise saved two copies of every film to ensure against their loss, although proper storage vaults weren't built for several more years—they have unfortunately never been made available on video for later generations of Mormons to see, one of the most glaring holes in the current state of Mormon film preservation and scholarship, particularly given how little footage there is of George Albert Smith and how monumental an achievement this film was on Wise and Williams' part.[297]

Where the Saints Have Trod ends with the laying of the *This Is the Place Monument* cornerstone, which is how their next film, *Tribute to Faith*, opens. This seventeen-minute color documentary chronicles the construction of the monument, as Reiser put it, "from the first breaking of the ground through every stage of construction, including clearing the ground, quarrying and preparing the granite, placing the bronze plaques and figures and concluding with the dedicatory services on July 24, 1947," in particular the address given by J. Reuben Clark.[298] July was of course the busiest month for Wise and Williams, as in addition to the dedication the two men also filmed a Boy Scout camp that ran from July 21-26 at Fort Douglas, east of the city on part of the old Pioneer Trail. Future apostle George Q. Morris chaired the Centennial Scout Committee, organizing various events leading up to this massive camp that attracted roughly 5,000 youth and their leaders, drawing in troops from many states and even England and the Netherlands. Switching to black and white film stock, Wise and Williams probably filmed in the camp's first few days and then went to the nearby monument on July 24 to film *Tribute to Faith*. The result with the scouts was a twenty-two-minute film on a single reel, which they called *Centennial Scout Camp* and which Deseret Book probably marketed toward ward troops and youth leaders. This was a popular topic among youth work at the time; it was the next year as Reiser was advertising *Centennial Scout Camp* in the *Church News* that the LDS Film Council procured the set of Boy Scout films mentioned earlier.[299]

Deseret Film Productions may have shot or attempted to shoot other events as well, as might other Church departments have done. One that was completed came from Gordon Hinckley working for Stephen Richards in the Missionary Department. Called *Pioneer Trails*, this was a documentary that covered much the same material as *Where the Saints Have Trod*, but in a more traditional travelogue format with a narrator explaining shots of historic sites and other vistas. The film is essentially a motion-picture remake of Hinckley's 1935 filmstrip *Down Pioneer Trails*, and, coming between his incomplete Aaronic priesthood film with Frank Wise and his anti-tobacco films of 1951, it marks the first time he worked on a finished film. He recruited LaMar Williams to help him with the production, and the two shot footage all the way from the Smith home in Vermont to contemporary Utah, where they emphasized how the Mormon settlers had "developed the wasteland into the beautiful valley of today."[300] This was the first time these two men worked together, and a few years later when Williams went to work for Hinckley in the Missionary Department their collaboration became permanent, and they served together for nearly three decades—in contrast, for instance, to the relatively brief time they each spent working with Frank Wise—vastly shaping the course of the Church's proselytizing work.

One other Church production deserves to be mentioned. Remembering its success in 1930, Church leaders decided to revive *The Message of the Ages* in the Tabernacle as the Church's major contribution to the festivities, with Hamer Reiser, who had been the secretary of that committee in 1930, assuming the chair from George D. Pyper, who had passed away in 1943. The script and dramaturgy essentially remained the same, but this time Frank Wise was on hand to enhance the productions with two major innovations. First he helped erect a huge lighting grid that held around one hundred colored spotlights that he integrated into the action of the play; Reiser claimed there were more lights on this stage than in all of Salt Lake's other theaters combined. While the lighting was surely a deep collaboration with experienced stage artists—roughly 1,400 people worked on the production—Wise was more personally responsible for the special effect of the stage's huge backdrop, which used rear projection to transport viewers along the sweeping scope of the narrative's various locations. To do this he procured an enormous translucent screen which he installed in front of the organ. Since the image would be projected from behind, he wasn't left with much space in which to cast the image and allow it to grow to fill the size of the screen. The first part of the solution, then, was to use a stereopticon, which originated its image with a four-by-five-inch glass slide rather than a mere thirty-five millimeter frame of film. Thus the 1947 *Message of the Ages*, a celebration of the Church's hundred years centered in the American west, appropriately became the apotheosis and conclusion of its use of magic lanterns, a medium which had been incredibly integral to Mormon culture for much of that time. Wise didn't have one, though, so he purchased two new machines, allowing him to create the double exposures and dissolves that lanterns were famous for. We don't know the details on the productions of the slides—how much they represented Wise and Williams' own work or to what extent other visual artists were brought into the process—but there were about forty images used over the course of the show. The second part of the solution was to devise a way to position the lanterns, as Reiser put it, "down in the bowels of the organ underneath,"[301] pointing from below the organ's pipes at the screen. This still wouldn't allow the image to fill the whole screen, so Wise designed a new extra-wide angle lens to cast a particularly wide beam of light and thus accommodate for the short focal distance.

Technology was used in other ways as well: in order to reduce the complexity and cost of performances, live musicians were replaced by a recorded soundtrack which the actors sang along to. Aware of the failure to film the pageant in 1930, Reiser looked into having Deseret Film Productions attempt it again, but once more lighting and exposure prevented it: raising the lights' intensity enough for the film stock to expose would wash out the rear projection. Wise and Williams did, however, take enough still photographs of the show to result in multiple different filmstrip versions, all accompanied by an audio recording of the performance. The actual stage production itself was once again a great success, showing to over 130,000 spectators between May 5 and June 6. The railroads asked Reiser to extend the run because enough viewers were coming from out of town that it was helping their business, and at least one family flew in from Denver. Just as in 1930, many more wanted to attend than could, and, according to Temple Square Bureau of Information chief Richard L. Evans, for the first time in its history over one million visitors—1,003,218, to be exact—came to Temple Square in the course of a single year, up from 719,765 in 1946.[302]

In addition to these institutionally sponsored productions, the centennial was a magnet for independent filmmakers, including some of the amateurs and professionals discussed earlier. Undoubtedly the busiest independent Mormon filmmaker that year was Sullivan Richardson, now of Chicago, who since his Pan-American expedition of 1941 had become known as an educational filmmaker through his production company the Viking Corporation. That summer the Sons of Utah Pioneers organized a reenactment trek from Nauvoo to Salt Lake, much like they would do to commemorate the Mormon Battalion journey in 1950, and Richardson, now one of the world's most experienced long-distance automobile drivers, came along and filmed the caravan, resulting in the twenty-minute color picture *This Is the Place*. The group took the same number of people as the vanguard 1847 pioneer company—143 men, three women, and two children—and the same number of vehicles—seventy-three—although these were cars rather than wagons. Because of this they made slightly better time than the pioneers, covering the distance in eight days rather than a year and a half and arriving in the Salt Lake Valley on July 22. Participants dressed in period costume, with some taking on specific roles like Brigham Young, and many even disguised their cars with canopies akin to covered wagon tops or placed wagon boxes around the frames. They noticed that Nauvoo's lone cinema, the Mormon Theatre, was showing the seven-year-old *Brigham Young* in commemoration of the pioneers' centennial. Spencer and Camilla Kimball were the most prominent members of the caravan; he used it as a missionary opportunity and delivered thirty addresses in person or over the airwaves in the course of their journey, beginning with a small radio station in Carthage, Illinois. The night before the company left Nauvoo they held a large outdoor fete with 2,000 spectators. The main presentation was a miniature pageant about the rise and fall of the Mormons in Nauvoo, directed by Francis L. Urry, a radio actor for KSL who today is best remembered for his roles in Church films like *Johnny Lingo* and *Windows of Heaven*. The vehicles were numbered and, as they set out, each day's progress carefully monitored. Unlike President Smith's 1946 group, which stayed in hotels, members of this caravan camped, rising at 5 a.m. each day just like the pioneers. They were met at Fort Bridger by President McKay and Elder Harold Lee, then at Henefer by President Smith in his Boy Scout uniform, who accompanied them all the way to Sugarhouse Park in Salt Lake City where he and Governor Maw spoke. While Richardson was the only professional cinematographer in the group, Wendell Ashton reported that "scores of cameras, from small 'Brownies' to modern movie machines, continued to click along the highway as the caravan rolled westward."[303]

Richardson followed this with a documentary on Salt Lake City entitled *Valley of Triumph*. A forty-five-minute film, it's a mixture of travelogue and history, based on the popular Mormon theme that "the desert shall blossom like the rose." In practical terms this meant that in his first film he focused on pioneers in 1847, and now he wanted to look at the history of Utah from 1847 to the present. Scenes include the Great Salt Lake and salt flats, Bear River Migratory Bird Refuge on the northeast bank of the lake, and Temple Square, the Tabernacle, and the organ. The Tabernacle Choir appears onscreen, singing "Let the Mountains Shout for Joy" while their image is replaced by footage of the valley's mountains. For six minutes the audience is encouraged to sing along with choir, as the lyrics appear at the bottom of the screen with an animated bouncy ball, in the style of Max and Dave Fleischer's *Song Car-Tunes* films from the 1920s.

Usually Richardson marketed his productions to educational film libraries, but in this case he seems to have wisely approached the Church, or Deseret Book,

directly; at least one preview screening of *Valley of Triumph* had several Tabernacle Choir members in attendance, and it's possible he was pitching the finished
product to potential buyers in the Church. But even before selling the films'
rights he procured corporate sponsors to defray his expenses. A Detroit man, he
secured sponsorship from Dodge for *This Is the Place*, essentially a film about
cars, and *Valley of Triumph* was made in collaboration with the Utah Department
of Publicity & Industrial Development. Today both films are held by the Church
History Library, and LaMar Williams reported that a condensed version of the
latter film became the first motion picture ever shown at the Bureau of Information at Temple Square, making it the first film shown at a Mormon visitors'
center anywhere and an important precedent given how oriented contemporary
visitors' centers are toward video and interactive displays. Not only did *Valley
of Triumph* play in the heart of the Mormon capital, it was used in missionary
work as far away as Brazil. In June 1951 Elder J. H. Whitaker reported that he
and his fellow missionaries in São Paulo had translated the film's soundtrack
into Portuguese and were using it to give lectures and screenings in spaces like
public squares and sports clubs. These screenings each were attended by over
one hundred spectators, providing the missionaries "a good chance to tell of
the teachings of the Church."[304] With filmstrip projectors so successful, it would
be hard for missionaries to adopt full-motion movies, but screenings like these
indicate that this was always the direction Church audiovisual instruction was
heading.

Although this was a Utah celebration, the centennial extended slightly to the
outside world. Church members in far-flung places participated in honoring the event; one group of Mormons in Maui made an audio recording of the
hymn "High on the Mountain Top" while gathered around the volcanic crater
of Haleakala which they later broadcast on the radio, and another in Sweden made a small film about pioneers to advertise the anniversary. Likewise,
non-Mormon newsreel companies came to Utah especially to record the parade
that advanced down Salt Lake's downtown streets. And now the Mormons who
lined the parade route often had still and moving picture cameras of their own.
Amateur footage of the parade moving past, with hundreds of marchers and
Torleif Knaphus's *Handcart Pioneer Monument* sculpture perched atop a float, is
the perfect embodiment of Home Cinema: homemade movies recording a local
holiday celebrating the creation of Mormons' mountain home.[305]

Other events occurred as part of the centennial that related to film. Some
members of the Utah Centennial Commission wanted to name an official cen-

tennial picture out of those Hollywood productions shot in the state. At the time there was conflict between Truman's Department of the Interior and Hollywood studios and Utah businessmen over permission to film in the state's National Parks. Under Interior Secretary Harold Ickes parks had been declared off-limits for large film crews, and a great deal of lobbying occurred before Utah's Department of Publicity & Industrial Development secured permission once again for limited shooting within the parks. The first film to take advantage of this was Enterprise Production's *Ramrod*, a western starring Joel McCrea and Veronica Lake which shot in Zion National Park in 1946. Due to this, the Commission selected it as the official film of the centennial, and it premiered in February 1947 in a spectacle that possibly exceeded that surrounding *Brigham Young* seven years earlier. More than fifty stars and studio executives came to the city, and there was plenty of pomp and celebration, from a Tabernacle organ concert to the obligatory parade; Mayor Earl J. Glade, who as head of KSL had transformed it into a thriving radio station, even issued a declaration renaming Salt Lake City as Veronica Lake City. After the film premiered at the Utah Theater the papers and public seemed to like it, but some members of the Centennial Commission were scandalized: sometimes known as the first "adult western," *Ramrod* contained a level of violence and sexual frankness they may not have expected. Still, their response might have had less to do with *Ramrod*'s faults and more with the expectations the Mormons had for it: things had come so far since the First Wave that by 1947 they actually expected Hollywood to lionize their pioneer progenitors, and the fact that the film dealt with a ranching feud between cattlemen and sheep farmers rather than their great state was disappointing. State Senator Rue L. Clegg called it a "fourth class, trashy picture . . . It typifies and exemplifies nothing of the pioneer spirit which we observe this year."[306] Soon politicians, film critics, and the public were arguing about the film's merits, with several officials reprimanding those who bit the hand that fed them after *Ramrod* had brought so much economic activity—$750,000 worth—and national publicity to the state—regardless of its cinematic merits. It was too late, however, as the caustic response apparently may have, in fact, deterred California studios from filming in Utah for a few years.[307]

Despite all the attention paid to *Ramrod* at the time, an arguably more notable event for the history of cinema was Orson Welles' theatrical production of *Macbeth* in May 1947 as part of the centennial's cultural events. Welles wanted to film the play, but Republic Pictures was hesitant; there had been very little cinematic Shakespeare made since the coming of sound, and Welles' films after *Citizen Kane* had been less than stellar successes. This stage production was part of a campaign by Welles to convince Republic *Macbeth* would make a viable motion picture, and the support of the Festival allowed him to get it on the boards and test his ideas before committing them to film. The production, which reportedly did well at the box office, retained some elements of his famous black "Voodoo" *Macbeth* from New York City in 1936, but Welles transferred the action from the Caribbean back to Scotland—he himself played the title role—and he famously had his cast speak with a thick Scottish brogue. Republic gave him a greenlight for the film and he shot it, his first Shakespearean film, that fall, with a release the next year. Not only did he use the same script and cast, the actors even recorded their dialogue in Utah and lip-synched to playback while filming in Los Angeles. Many viewers, including Republic's top management, couldn't understand the accents, so studio executives had the entire soundtrack re-dubbed, much to the film's detriment, but the original Utah recording was reinstated as far as possible when UCLA restored the film in 1979.[308]

With cinema still such an integral part of people's lives in 1947, in the actual days surrounding the July 24 anniversary as many people were going to the movies as ever, with all local cinemas reportedly doing good business. On July 23 Burt Lancaster and Lizabeth Scott, stars of Paramount's *Desert Fury*, came to town and participated in "Covered Wagon Days." Before the premiere of the film, Scott, a famed femme fatale, presented George Albert Smith with a California rose tree, which the trade press, unaware of President Smith's busy schedule with Hollywood royalty that year, mistakenly reported as the first time he had ever met a movie star. Even films that weren't officially part of the celebration did well, with commercial cinemas showing films like *Carnival in Costa Rica* (1947) and *The Yearling* (1946), and a new Capitol Theater timed its opening to happen directly during the celebrations.[309]

It's safe to say that nobody, not even Hamer Reiser or Frank Wise, saw the Utah Centennial as a cinematic event. Nevertheless, motion pictures were completely integral to the festivities, which would not have been the same without them. This could be felt from the Deseret Book Store Film Library to the streets of São Paolo. As Utah's population passed the one million mark in 1947, Home Cinema may have reached its natural zenith; although many of the characteristics that defined the era remained for decades, from this point on Mormon cinema was infused with inevitable growth. The gears were in motion that would lead to the BYU Motion Picture Department in the Third Wave, the massive video infrastructure and broadcasts of the Fourth, and the theatrical feature films of the

The Second Wave: Home Cinema

Fifth. Home Cinema, like Home Literature, had no ambitions to reach beyond the borders of its province. After the Utah Centennial, it was clear that that province could no longer contain Mormon film.

Of course, all that Reiser, Wise, and Williams could see at the time was that Deseret Film Productions was a secure and efficient, if small, enterprise. Pleased with their films from 1947, they launched straight into their third major production, which was in a way an even more ambitious project: *Temple Square*. They also moved from the small space on Richards Street into the building on Indiana Avenue that housed the circulating film library. "We really thought we had arrived," Wise said. "Here was quite a big building [that] had a number of rooms that we could spread out into. We built a theatre with projection booths and everything we should have and there was space out the back where we had plans to build a studio."[310] Despite the excellent work from Wise and Williams, however, Deseret Film Productions remained a passion project for Hamer Reiser rather than a money-maker; Wise believed that it never paid for itself, but always received a subsidy from Deseret Book's publishing operations, and there would be no backlot on Indiana Avenue. In fact, by mid-1948 finances proved sufficiently tight that Reiser transferred LaMar Williams to be the head of Deseret Book's visual aids department in order to justify his payroll. This actually might have been a better fit as well: Williams was about to complete a master's degree in education, with an emphasis on visual aids. He continued to help Wise whenever he could until he was called on a mission to Uruguay. Upon returning he stayed in the field of visual education, working for Gordon Hinckley as the photo technician for the Missionary Department, where he remained for twenty-seven years. In that capacity he was assigned in 1961 to investigate the situation in Nigeria and Ghana where hundreds of people were requesting baptism but the Church couldn't operate due to its policy of barring the priesthood, necessary for units like wards to function, from blacks. Williams received a calling to oversee the Church's presence in West Africa for several years , and his work with the people there helped prompt Church leaders to reconsider the prohibition, which Spencer Kimball rescinded in 1978. After returning home, in 1968 Williams was producing the Missionary Department's radio program "Sunday Evening on Temple Square" and had the idea to create an orchestral musical group for Mormon youth for broadcasting and live performances. The Mormon Youth Symphony and Chorus was one of the Church's premiere musical ensembles until it was absorbed into the Orchestra at Temple Square in 1999. Williams himself passed away, while attending a Church service, in 1996.[311]

As it happened, Williams left partway through the work on *Temple Square*. The film was structured around a documentary framework now familiar from a dozen travelogues, most recently Richardson's *Valley of Triumph*. But embedded within the nonfiction narrative of a tour of Temple Square were scripted reenactments. "What we tried to do in the film was what the guides were doing at that time on Temple Square. In other words we would go to the monument of the Prophet Joseph and have a few people standing around them and instead of hearing the guide talk about it we went back and saw Joseph as a boy."[312] Dwayne Hill played young Joseph, and the other actors were local volunteers, some with theatrical experience. As with *Where the Saints Have Trod*, Paul F. Royall narrated. Fictional reenactments included early moments in Joseph Smith's life, the formation of the Church, the handcart journey, the miracle of the gulls, and other events, although they purposely avoided the First Vision, choosing to tell about it instead. The thirty-five-minute run time wasn't too daunting, but this was the first time Deseret Film Productions had featured actors in scripted scenes like these, and, as Wise himself admitted, for all his other skills he was not a good director of actors. "We were happy to get the images on the screen in sequence."[313] Of course it probably didn't help that the performers were all local volunteers, but cast and crew worked through this, however, and had some major technical successes as well. Most importantly, Wise was determined to overcome the nineteen-year-old problem of lighting the Tabernacle's choir seats, and with his experience on *The Message of the Ages* it seemed like he should be able to do it. Perhaps getting permission was the most difficult part of the process, but once he had that he constructed and installed a network of makeshift sixty-one-foot battens, or metal pipes, with an array of spotlights using 500,000 watts of power, attached to them. This entire rig was wired and hung from the ceiling "with some difficulty."[314] The choir, appropriately, sang the "Hallelujah" segment from Beethoven's *Christ on the Mount of Olives*.

To capture this performance, Wise used his experience from general conference and set up three cameras in the left, center, and right of the house, further cementing the house style that has been used for film or video recordings of the choir ever since. These were manned by himself, Williams, and Joe Osmond, and, like with general conference addresses, Wise had predetermined when to cut from one camera to another, to reduce their shooting ratio and save as much film stock as possible. Once incorrectly considered the first film footage of the Tabernacle Choir, we can now say that it is the first color sound footage of them—and more importantly the permanent lighting rig allowed for their continual appearances in more film and television productions down the road.

The Second Wave: Home Cinema

Temple Square also included Deseret Film Production's first dolly shot, taken out of the trunk of a moving car, and Wise achieved a good special effect in recreating the miracle of the gulls, something which had taken Henry Hathaway a huge crew, multiple locations, and matting. Wise simply traveled to Idaho and collected live crickets by hand. He then deposited them in a six-foot-square pen where he could film a variety of close ups. Seagulls were simply shot at the dump. Production progressed throughout 1948, and it was released on May 15, 1949.[315]

In the meantime Wise came into possession of several reels of footage from Shirl and Chet Clawson, as mentioned in Chapter 2. One day he got a phone call from the Presiding Bishopric's office asking him to come investigate several old film cans that they'd discovered in the basement. The first can had nothing but dust, the film having completely disintegrated. Since this cellulose nitrate film was stored near a radiator there was a slight danger of combustion, but decomposition was much more likely, and that's indeed what Wise found. As he weeded out the segments of film that were still usable, the value of what he had became clear, and the prospect of assembling it and releasing it to the wards became very exciting, perhaps particularly because, first, it would cost very little and, second, LaMar Williams had just been transferred and this was a project that Wise could complete on his own at his editing table; he was even able to finish it before *Temple Square*. The first step was to transfer the film to more usable stock, first because Wise needed to work with 16 rather than 35mm stock (which run at different feet per second), second to avoid working with the dangerous cellulose nitrate footage, and third because silent film and sound film run at different frame rates. This third point meant that the film couldn't be simply copied frame by frame but certain frames had to be repeated in order to stretch out the running time and make the action look natural when running at 24 frames per second on a 16mm projector. This step frame process was all done in 35mm, and then the footage was shrunk down to 16mm.

All of that was done to the salvageable raw footage and constituted the most technical and crucial part of the process, after which putting a film together was simple. Not knowing the Church leaders from this period well himself, Wise needed help in identifying them; he wrote the voice-over narration and it was read by Wayne Richards. While this text is quite informative, if anything there might be slightly too much of it, with no time for the images to breathe on their own, although wisely there is no music beyond an organ during the opening title. *Latter-day Saint Leaders: Past and Present* remains gripping today as a wonderful record of a bygone era. Viewers in 1948 thought so too, and it quickly became one of Deseret Book's most popular titles. It also apparently inspired Wise to attempt something similar himself, as Hamer Reiser announced in June 1948 that "production has started on a series of intimate pictures and messages of each of the present General Authorities of the Church."[316] This, however, never happened, and as mentioned the film project that owes its closest lineage to the Clawsons is Judge Whitaker's *Church in Action* series begun in 1970.[317]

Other unfinished or aborted profiles that we know of include several twelve-minute films for Sunday School classes and a film to prepare Mormon servicemen to deploy overseas. Such dropped projects were not uncommon, however, and even on his own Frank Wise had proven the value of Deseret Film Productions and institutional filmmaking, enough so that various Church departments began reaching beyond what he alone could provide to satisfy their needs. A few apostles recruited Judge Whitaker at Disney to produce films about the Church's welfare program, Gordon B. Hinckley was tasked with creating a filmed version of the temple endowment ceremony, and KSL was moving beyond radio into television production. In fact, after the war this new medium, invented by a Mormon scientist in 1929, was poised to revolutionize not just Church filmmaking but the entire world. Just as Gordon Hinckley found himself producing anti-tobacco films for television distribution in 1951, many Church departments beyond KSL—from the Primary to the Tabernacle Choir—would now become involved in broadcasting. In that year even Deseret Film Productions was entering the brave new world of television. When President Smith passed away on April 4, 1951 Wise made another film primarily through the assemblage of preexisting footage. Called *George Albert Smith—In Memorium,* it ran nineteen minutes, in color, and included original footage of Smith's funeral as well as scenes shot earlier about his life and ministry. Most remarkable is that it was broadcast on television, and the Church History Library lists it as being produced by Deseret Film Broadcasting. The connection between film and television was already drawn.

Home Broadcasting: From Radio to Television

Mormon broadcasting developed on several fronts in the Second Wave. One that's been discussed in some detail is missionaries' use of radio to present their message in their assigned areas, which became centralized in Gordon Hinckley's work at the Radio, Publicity and Mission Literature Committee. This committee oversaw all of the Church's radio work in departments dedicated to the Tabernacle Choir, "Church of the Air," Sunday evening broadcasts from

The Second Wave: Home Cinema

Temple Square, and "mission broadcasts," which essentially included everything else.[318] Multi-episode series like "The Fulness of Times" were primarily broadcast over KSL but reached numerous other stations through hard promotional work. The very scope and variety of programs like these gives some idea of the nature of radio in its golden age. Like similar stations all over the world, since its birth as KZN in 1922 KSL had quickly grown past its initial experimental phase to become a well-established profitable business and part of the most important mass medium to enter people's homes since the printing press, surpassing even the daily newspapers in their heyday of the late 1800s. No longer just for budding engineers or ham radio operators sitting in their garages and attics trying to pick up or send out a signal, radio was now in the parlors and the living rooms of America, a mass-produced object fully domesticated into middle-class life. Radio listeners had become consumers: they turned it on not to talk but to listen. And those who created the content—storytellers, advertisers, politicians, and religionists—did everything they could to make sure people heard what they had to say.

KSL in these years was much like any other station, carrying national programs through its affiliations with NBC then CBS and airing a mix of fiction, news, music, and nonfiction opinion or propaganda-type pieces. It was in these latter two areas that Mormon broadcasters, at KSL and elsewhere, excelled. Even though he preferred to have others read his words than speak on-air himself, Hinckley is a prime example of someone who developed a marvelous voice for the medium, propagandizing in a way that made it seem less odious, as he wrote in "The Romance of a Celluloid Strip," and instead building bridges and inviting listeners to share in his worldview—and his testimony. And despite the breadth of what he accomplished this nonconfrontational voice is not unique to him; we see the same impulse in many filmstrips and tracts, and the short speeches that another future apostle, Richard L. Evans, delivered every week between musical numbers sung by the Tabernacle Choir.

As mentioned in Chapter 2, when *Music and the Spoken Word* began at 3 p.m. on Monday, July 15, 1929, it was just an experiment with new technology undertaken at the behest of KSL head Earl Glade, despite the misgivings of many of the musicians and Church leaders who thought the power and beauty of the choir couldn't be conveyed through a little tin box in somebody's kitchen. The program started as a pure recital: emphasis was on the music, while the spoken thoughts were initially just announcements delivered by various hosts. The first of these was organist Edward Kimball's nineteen-year-old son Ted, who essentially was asked to do it because he was there. He stayed on just three more episodes before leaving on a mission, then this position passed through a few hands until June 1930 when it was taken over permanently by Evans. With his pen and voice he reshaped the program into something completely different, holding to broadly ecumenical language—delivered from the wholesome "crossroads of the west"—and establishing the program as a spiritual refuge for thousands of listeners who had no idea of its connection with Mormonism. The broadcast, at CBS since September 1932, finally took the form of *Music and the Spoken Word* in 1936. Technical improvements were made throughout that decade, both in the microphones and equipment used in recording and in the network's broadcasting capability. This weekly program has continued uninterrupted on both radio and television and today is the longest-running program in the history of both media. J. Spencer Cornwall, conductor of the choir from 1935-57, noted, "The development of American radio can be traced by following the development of the broadcasting of the Tabernacle Choir and Organ from the Mormon Tabernacle in Salt Lake City, for the simple reason that many of the important steps in the history of the transmission of sound by radio has been a successive part of the broadcasting of the choir."[319] While each episode by itself may not seem overly remarkable, its relentless consistency has accumulated into an exceptional body of work. Because of its longevity and its immense broadcast range, it is undoubtedly the most important broadcast program in the history of the Church, and for millions of people across the globe the Mormon Tabernacle Choir is the most recognizable ambassador for the faith. When the choir was inducted into the Broadcasting Hall of Fame in 2004, Church President Gordon Hinckley summarized this legacy: "No medium has touched the lives of so many for so long as has the weekly broadcast of *Music and the Spoken Word*."[320]

But *Music and the Spoken Word* was far from the only media appearance the choir made. Its film work was impressive; even in these early years of the Second Wave it participated, either onscreen or on the soundtrack, in the films *Mormons Celebrate Centenary* (1930), *Corianton* (1931), A. Hamer Reiser's experimental short films (1932), *City of Brigham Young* (1944), *Monumental Utah* (1944), *Where the Saints Have Trod* (1947), *Valley of Triumph* (1947), and *Temple Square* (1949), as well as live productions of *The Message of the Ages* in both 1930 and 1947 and other performances, like at the 1939 Chicago World's Fair. World War II constricted the choir's ability to travel, but they innovated on the airwaves and in their use of technology, such as making the first stereophonic recording with Harvey Fletcher and Leopold Stokowski in April 1940, broadcasting a reenactment of the Salt Lake Temple dedication on April 6, 1943, making their first international broadcast, to the British Isles through the U.S. Army Special Services radio network, on January 6, 1944, and making their first coast-to-coast broadcast in the U.S. on April 12, 1945 as part of an impromptu memorial service on the day Franklin D. Roosevelt died. They did additional film work as well: On July 11, 1944 they recorded music from Fauré's Requiem, arranged by Hollywood composer Dmitri Tiomkin, for use in John Huston's controversial half-hour documentary The Battle of San Pietro (1945); this music was used over footage of American soldiers entering a decimated Italian village, finding particular value in an optimistic sequence as Italian children laugh and play among the rubble. In 1952 they sang three numbers in This Is Cinerama, an experimental feature film designed to demonstrate the power of a new widescreen technology that required three projectors to cover the curved screen. "Lowell Thomas, the news commentator, was producing the film, and to produce an equally spacious sonic effect, he utilized the stereophonic sound system developed by Dr. Fletcher. For the first time, a movie used multichannel sound. The Choir was recorded in six-track stereo in the Tabernacle, and the effect on audiences was staggering, greatly widening the Choir's following."[321] There were further film and television appearances going into the Third Wave, such as on a CBS television program called Choir's Rehearsing for Easter and on Edward R. Murrow and Fred Friendly's See It Now, both in April 1954 and with at least the latter program offered in color. When the choir appeared on Wide, Wide World in October 1955 one viewer wrote in to commend all the show's content before saying, "But I felt most rewarded by the great Mormon Tabernacle Choir, often heard by radio but now seen as well in homes over the nation."[322]

Earl Glade saw broadcasting as "a tremendous factor in establishing the fact of Utah culture to the world." As early as 1931 he estimated that "now 10,000,000 people once a week hear the Tabernacle organ and choir. Hundreds of thousands also listen in on other local broadcasts."[323] For a musical group that just a few years earlier had its audience limited to the size of its namesake building, this was an amazing leap. The next year the switch from NBC to CBS expanded the potential audience even more: where KSL was broadcasting at 5,000 watts, in 1932 they moved to a new transmitter with 50,000 watts, the maximum strength allowable under federal regulations, thus vastly increasing their broadcast range. The May 12, 1935 episode of "Church of the Air," which began with an address by President Grant, aired to sixty-eight stations in the United States and Canada, the largest audience he had ever spoken to. One general conference session held on April 5, 1936 saw two new landmarks when a half hour of the proceedings were broadcast coast to coast on the entire North American

CBS network and via shortwave radio to locations in Europe. In April 1941 the full conference was broadcast outside of Utah for the first time, and on December 26, 1946 KSL-FM went on the air, improving sound quality for those within its range; Church leaders chose to keep this FM station going for decades out of pure faith in the persuasive power of radio, despite consistently disappointing revenue. At the same time, the amount of original content was keeping pace: in 1932 there were nineteen Mormon broadcasts in a typical week in the United States, and while this was an 800% increase from just a few years earlier any future growth would require more original productions. Perhaps the most popular program was "Church of the Air," which covered a variety of topics germane to Mormonism and which constantly required new material. By the 1940s specially produced programs like "The Fulness of Times" were commonplace, partly through the influence of the Radio, Publicity and Mission Literature Committee and partly from the broader trend of churches using the radio for preaching and ministering. In March 1949 one small station in northern Utah even broadcast the local stake conference, showing just how integrated worship and radio had become in Mormon communities.[324]

President Grant was obviously enthusiastic about radio, and this commitment was continued after his death by George Albert Smith. In the October 1946 conference he spoke about a recent address he'd given to U.S. troops via radio:

> Short-wave broadcasting will continue to improve, and it will not be long until, from this pulpit and other places that will be provided, the servants of the Lord will be able to deliver messages to isolated groups who are so far away they cannot be reached. In that way and other ways, the gospel of Jesus Christ our Lord . . . will be heard in all parts of the world, and many of you who are here will live to see that day.[325]

At the same time, there were already intimations of an even more powerful technology on the horizon. "As early as 1934, KSL's Vice President, John Fitzpatrick had discussed television's potential with Columbia Broadcasting System executives."[326] The next year Presiding Bishop Sylvester Cannon, who also served as president of the Radio Service Corporation, urged KSL executives to stay on top of developments with television, advice which was echoed in a letter to them from Philo Farnsworth. Television had its first public demonstration in Utah at an exhibition on September 16, 1939. President Grant, who knew of the work of both Farnsworth and Harvey Fletcher, spoke at the event, and at that point it may have seemed that the public would have access to the device very shortly. The war, however, caused the government to put a freeze on private television

The Second Wave: Home Cinema

development as resources were diverted elsewhere, and during this period KSL's board of directors lost any enthusiasm they might have had. Minutes from a March 26, 1945 meeting read, "In respect to television . . . operations require such a tremendous amount of operating equipment and personnel, there appears to be a long way to go before television broadcasting will emerge from the present experimental basis to one based on practical business procedures."[327] When the nationwide freeze was lifted in 1946, KSL found itself behind Utah's other main radio station KDYL in preparing for a television launch. Recording equipment had to be procured, broadcasting facilities constructed, and licenses obtained from the FCC. This work began in 1947, making 1948 the year in which television exploded across the United States.[328]

KSL-TV's launch wasn't the first contact an individual Mormon had with television, of course, particularly with much of the original technology coming from the hands of Philo Farnsworth. While Pem Farnsworth was the first Mormon—and first person—to have her likeness sent via video technology, it would be several more years until the television broadcasting industry was sufficiently established to allow Mormons to appear on a broadcast program. Given how events unfolded in the United States, we shouldn't be surprised that this apparently first occurred in Sweden. In September of 1938 four male missionaries named Don A. Carlson, Claudell Johnson, E. LeRoy Olson, and Joseph L. Mattson formed a singing quartet, the American Harmony Singers, under the tutelage of Virginia B. Larson. Simultaneously the Phillips Company and the *Stockholms-Tidningen*, Sweden's largest newspaper, were organizing what today we would call a variety show to air in Stockholm throughout the first week in November. The missionaries managed to get a spot on the show and thus performed three different songs, perhaps over the course of multiple evenings. "The appearance of the four young inexperienced singers on the same program with many of Sweden's leading entertainers was more surprising to themselves than to the public." In responding to the call to use innovative public relations methods, these four also earned the distinction of being the first Mormons to ever appear on a television show. Their success was repeated by other missionaries in what may have been the second time Mormons were televised, when a ten-man missionary chorus appeared on a program in Buffalo, New York, in late 1947.[329]

Also in 1947, KSL managed to stay in step with other budding television broadcasters, and the launch of institutional Mormon television—as well as television in Utah—occurred at the April 1948 general conference, before KSL even had its broadcasting license. Instead, two cameras in the Tabernacle sent a signal to television sets in the neighboring buildings. The *Improvement Era* explained how this was done: "The electrical impulses activated by the television camera, were taken by wire to the seven television receiving units located at various places in the Assembly Hall, and one set in the Bureau of Information. Television cameras were set up in the Tabernacle to catch the speaker as well as a three-quarter view of the Tabernacle choir and organ." [330] The *Church News* captured more of the feel of the event, reporting that, amazingly, conference visitors could see the proceedings "even if they were unable to get inside the packed Tabernacle. One of the most interesting innovations on Temple Square, the telecasts drew lavish praise from those seeing the presentations. Thousands saw television for the first time." [331] The black and white image was dull, and the screens miniscule compared with Frank Wise's magic lantern displays from the previous year, but crowds were impressed nevertheless. In opening the conference President Smith noted the innovation and added, "The television pictures will not be all that we hope they will become some day, but they will be sufficiently good to be a great help to those who are seated in the Assembly Hall." Then he began his opening remarks by continuing, "I am sure that all present, this morning, have every reason to be grateful to the Lord for our blessings. Seated, as we are, in this comfortable Tabernacle, although the weather is inclement, we here, and in the adjoining building, are comfortable and because of the intelligence of men, devices have been provided so that we can both see and hear even in separate buildings and some distance apart." [332] But this was just the beginning for this striking new technology: "Future conferences are expected to be seen via television, by many thousands more when, it is anticipated, they will go into homes and perhaps in ward chapels in the Salt Lake Valley as the sound broadcasts do today." [333] KSL manager Ivor Sharp said that the two cameras would be kept in use throughout the year, though the company hadn't yet determined how.

With this successful test complete, the next task for KSL was to launch their broadcasting capability. They applied for a television license on May 26, 1948, just months before the FCC put a freeze on new licenses, mentioned earlier in connection with Rosel Hyde. Despite a complaint from a competing radio station, construction of a broadcasting tower began with an FCC deadline to be on the air on March 22, 1949. General manager C. Richard Evans went east to secure a network contract, returning with offers from ABC, CBS, and the Du Mont Television Network; following the lead with the radio station, CBS was chosen. Meanwhile advertisers were secured through a representative named Radio Sales. Though missing the March deadline in order to increase their broadcast signal, KSL-TV was launched on June 1, 1949, just slightly after KDYL launched their channel, with a survey area that included seven states. One other influential player in KSL-TV's development who should be mentioned was Scott Clawson, Shirl Clawson's son who had been with the company since returning from wartime service. He remained with KSL his entire career, forty-five years, becoming a production manager, Program Director, and finally Vice President of Programming.[334]

Just as President Smith predicted, over the next years the quality of general conference broadcasts improved. With KSL-TV now fully functioning, conference was broadcast on television for the first time in October 1949, and with the cameras and equipment in place *Music and the Spoken Word* began television broadcast that year as well. Television was adopted quickly throughout the country and KSL strove to spread conference broadcasts as far as possible, just as had been done with radio over the previous years. In April 1952, for instance, the session for priesthood holders, which Church leaders chose not to publicly broadcast, were sent via telephone wire to nearby meetinghouses. At the closing of the October 1953 conference President McKay spoke about the warm reception telecasts of the sessions were receiving along the west coast, reading brief statements from a viewer in Seattle and California Mission President Bryan L. Bunker, who praised the image and predicted it would prove a boon to missionary work. By 1961, television had become general conference's dominant medium: twenty-seven television stations broadcast conference, opposed to just eighteen on the radio.[335]

A final unseen but critical change had to take place to make the transition to video complete. Like radio broadcasts, television broadcasts are simply transmissions of signals, with no way to store the information sent. We tend to overlook this today based on the amount of television that is prerecorded and the consistent use of technology to record and save any live broadcasts, but early television had no such ability: programming was performed live, and once sent across the airwaves the images were lost. This is why Frank Wise continued to film conference addresses after KSL was broadcasting, because it was only through his films that speeches would be saved for posterity, or even ward viewing a few months later. Technicians the world over were working on the problem, of course, and the best early solution was a machine known as a kinescope. Essentially a film camera trained on a video monitor, kinescopes could transfer live video to film and thus preserve performances indefinitely. April 1957 was the first time it was used in general conference, for the First

Presidency's messages only. "These 'sight and sound' recordings will be sent to the distant missions of the Church so the members may see and hear as well as read the Presidency's messages."[336] This is actually a rather late date to adopt a kinescope, and it's possible that KSL would have done so earlier had Wise not already been filming and preserving the talks. Different formats of videotape were also being explored in the 1950s, and soon the entire procedure could be shot, broadcast, and recorded electronically. There have been regular milestones broadcasting conference throughout the Third, Fourth, and Fifth Waves, as in April 1962 when for the first time it was broadcast in its entirety throughout the United States and Canada, and in April 1967 when it was first shown on Mexican television. Of course, all of this is thanks to the pioneering work of Frank Wise, who must have been bemused by the opposition he initially received contrasted with the Church's vast broadcasting capability today; in 1980 he said it was "an interesting thing" that the hole he carved for his periscope was now the base for KSL's hydraulic camera platform.[337]

With the arrival of broadcast television, Mormons began creating content. The first Church organization to use the new medium was the children's Primary. This grew out of a long tradition in radio—such as KSL's programs "Story Telling Time," "The Family Hour," and "The Story Princess"—and publishing that dated back to the Home Literature movement, which had a strong element of didactic concern over the reading material available to youth. In the 1880s and '90s authors like Nephi Anderson and Susa Young Gates published much of their material in the *Juvenile Instructor*, which had begun publication in 1866. In time this journal changed its name to the *Instructor*, an adult magazine that featured information for teachers, and starting in 1902 it was supplemented by the *Children's Friend*, written for the children themselves. Both magazines were supplanted in 1970 by the *Friend*, but, before that, other areas of Mormon children's media grew primarily from these early publications. Just as the MIA and LDS Film Council were concerned about teenagers' consumption of motion pictures, with the advent of children's radio programming in the 1930s the Primary hoped to insure that children would only consume the best material. During World War II Miriam Taylor began a column in the *Children's Friend* titled "We Listen to the Radio," which discussed a broad range of children's radio programming available along the Mormon Corridor, as well as frequent film recommendations and, starting in March 1946, information about television. In July 1946 Taylor discussed a Primary-sponsored radio program named the "Children's Friend of the Air," which had begun weekly broadcasts on KDYL on June 15; it was written by Olive Milner and directed and produced by Beckie Thompson, with assistance from Forrest Hobbs. The program took more than its name from the magazine: like the *Children's Friend*, it created a virtual "sharing time" by allowing local children to introduce themselves, read poems, or present their pets. In addition, a cast of three girls and three boys—the Primary Players—appeared every week under Thompson's direction. Initially programmed for just twelve weeks, the program was popular enough to run for years, and the June 1948 *Children's Friend* announced plans for a television version.

Like the radio version, this would air on KDYL television. The Primary series, to be renamed *Junior Council*, was among the first of its offerings, premiering one month after KDYL went on the air; this also made it the first children's television program in the state. General Primary President Adele Cannon Howells was credited with pushing this adaptation of the "Children's Friend of the Air" into the new medium. Olive Milner directed and Jim Baldwin produced, and the show featured a cast of four children and one adult. As with the radio program, this official sponsorship was a central characteristic; it was not uncommon, for instance, to refer to *Junior Council* as "the Primary Television Show" or "the *Children's Friend* television show." Again, local children came in, pets in tow, to enliven the production, making it a virtual interactive community for the large percentage of Primary children who lived within its broadcast range. Initially airing on Friday evenings, the show eventually switched to KTVT Channel 4 and ran until at least 1960, with several sets of cast members; a tenth anniversary episode in 1958 brought back previous performers for a celebration. Like all television programming from this era, it was broadcast live with no kinescope, so it is apparently lost today.[338]

KSL also increased its offerings. On the morning of April 9, 1950, before the final sessions of that fall's general conference, the "Church of the Air" program was televised for the first time, with an address by J. Reuben Clark and music by the Tabernacle Choir. Although the radio broadcast went out over CBS's network, the telecast was limited to KSL-TV.[339] When he became Church President in 1951, David McKay "inherited a nascent broadcasting apparatus with largely unrealized potential" that he began to develop.

> In October 1953, general conference was televised outside of Utah for the first time; and six months later, out-of-state coverage expanded to ten stations in six Western states, an estimated potential audience of twelve million viewers. Speaking at a special conference session at which a new proselytizing plan was unveiled, McKay spoke of electronic media's potential in carrying the message of Mormonism to the world:

"Today it is a simple matter for us to teach all nations. The Lord has giv-
en us the means of whispering through space, of annihilating distance.
We have the means in our hands of reaching the millions in the world."[340]

But while McKay was an enthusiastic supporter of Church broadcasting in
radio and television, not all Mormons trusted the new medium, raising the
same concerns that others had had for generations about new media like the
novel, vaudeville, and motion pictures. In general conference in October 1949, J.
Reuben Clark complained about the sexualization of culture, adding, "Our art,
literature, drama, movies, television, music, the ads in magazines—in great part
run to sex," making this the first negative comment about television in a general
conference.[341] Other General Authorities would pick up the gauntlet against
television again and again as it became increasingly intertwined with American
life. This was one way television challenged Mormon culture; a different type
of complication hounded KSL specifically in that it was difficult for them, even
in the days of radio, to avoid programming sponsored by alcoholic beverage
companies, or commercials advertising alcohol directly. J. Reuben Clark had
at one point suggested that all broadcasting simply be shut down rather than
tangle with the issue, but he eventually became more sympathetic. In 1951
KSL "reluctantly" decided "to sacrifice the strict application and interpretation
of religious philosophy in order to make the stations profitable and have them
provide leadership within local and national media communities." This caused a
great deal of consternation among Church members, but merely illustrated that
"KSL's operational policy clearly had progressed from one of primarily religious
proselytizing to one of business and economics."[342] Today KSL's commercials are
indistinguishable from its competitors'.

Advertising, in fact, is perhaps the most surprising way in which Mormons took
to broadcasting in the Second Wave. We may not think of this as remarkable
today, in part because our current culture is so saturated with commercials,
but it was quite innovative in 1948 when the Church-owned department store
ZCMI began preparing fifteen-minute programs in a newsreel format, changing every week, for broadcast on local stations, detailing the items that were
for sale in their stores that week. An alternative to the traditional model from
radio of having brands sponsor content, this form of direct selling was on the
cusp of such television advertising efforts, predating the concept of sixty- or
thirty-second commercials, and making ZCMI contemporary with other stores
like Macy's in New York. Still, while Macy's spent 8% of its advertising budget
on television, ZCMI spent 17%; though not the highest rate out of American de-

partment stores—Robert Hall Clothes spent as much as 40%—it does indicate a strong faith in the ability of television to sell products. In monitoring the value of this new type of advertising, ZCMI kept careful records of the "more than 20 different items receiving TV plugs, and reports that in addition to these sales, TV has frequently brought in customers for purchases of other than the television featured items."[343]

As with filmstrips, Brigham Young University was once again the Church's most important institution, outside KSL, that entered the field of radio and television broadcasting in these years. BYU's broadcasting efforts, while distinct from its filmmaking departments, have often overlapped with cinema. What began as an extracurricular program in the Physics Department to teach the laws of radio waves and have some fun with amateur ham radio culture has grown into an immense broadcasting and filmmaking apparatus, including KBYU radio and television, BYUtv, and even the LDS Motion Picture Studio. Today BYU Theatre & Media Arts students frequently train at BYU Broadcasting facilities, and BYU Broadcasting brings all professional productions under one roof to pursue increasingly cinematic aspirations, as series like *Granite Flats* (2013-15) and *Extinct* (2017) demonstrate.

Professor Carl F. Eyring began fostering physics students' interest in radio in the early 1920s. By 1922, the same year KZN debuted in Salt Lake City, BYU's Physics Department was running the radio station 6APL, reaching and receiving broadcasts from as far away as Denver and California. Elsewhere on campus, a few years earlier in 1919, T. Earl Pardoe, an actor and instructor at Weber Academy in his native Ogden, was hired to coach tennis and teach speech and drama. Six years later on April 21, 1925 his work helped create the College of Fine Arts, under Dean Gerrit de Jong, Jr., including departments in speech, music, art, and dramatic arts. This was part of the reforms that took place under university President Franklin S. Harris to gain the school national accreditation. Through the work of Pardoe and others a robust speech and drama program was developed, while simultaneously the influence of Ellsworth Dent's visual aids department and the vision for Church radio work led to some advanced amateur filmstrip and radio productions, such as the aforementioned faculty- and student-produced program "The Purposes and Values of a Mission" that was broadcast in 1938 on KSL. While this relied on a professional station for distribution, BYU's own broadcasts expanded: students hoping to practice their French and German achieved the first campus-wide broadcast, with a range of about two blocks, on May 20, 1931. They continued achieving wider ranges until

1939, when the obvious confluence between those studying speech and journalism and those creating radio programs led Pardoe to create KBYU, the first
collegiate radio station west of Chicago.

There were various growing pains for the young station, and for Pardoe, the
Director of Radio who became known as the Father of Broadcasting at BYU. The
actual studio space was developed by speech student Norman Geertsen, who
had been trying to create a space to amplify sounds for the hearing impaired,
and with this permanent facility the infant station was quickly linked via wire
with commercial station KOVO in Provo, run by Arch Madsen, who would play
a major role in Church broadcasting in the following decades. In October 1940
the broadcasting studio was dedicated, but again all planned expansions were
cancelled by the war and the station contracted. In 1946 a planned new student
station, WBYU, failed to even go on the air, so Pardoe and others worked to
expand the university's existing broadcast capability. This slow and steady work,
intent on focusing on building a firm foundation at home rather than trying too
quickly to broadcast thousands of miles away, was typical of the Second Wave
and the home broadcasting mentality—and it created a base that BYU Broadcasting has stood on ever since. Finally, KBYU relaunched in October 1946, with
its strongest signal going to a few on-campus dormitories. It was able to join the
Intercollegiate Broadcasting System, and by 1948 had expanded to cover much
of Provo with a ten-watt station, the first such student-operated station west of
the Mississippi.

Meanwhile the Department of Speech had offered its first class in broadcasting in 1939, with an increasing number of courses in subjects like speaking for
the microphone and writing for the radio in the following years. With the surge
of new students after the war KBYU was brought into the curriculum directly
rather than remaining an extracurricular entity. With students now learning
radio work in class, for extracurricular development they formed the BYU Radio
Club in early 1946, with student Lester Card as president. By 1951 the university was teaching courses in Radio and Television Production, and with a new
sufficiently robust radio program university administrators began to wonder if
television facilities, or even a functioning television station, should be added as
well. An official investigation began, but part of what would be needed to make
this viable was experienced faculty members who could teach video or film
production, and while this problem was under consideration events occurred
that brought just such a person all the way from the Walt Disney Studio to
BYU's doorstep.[344]

The Welfare Films

As mentioned, Church authorities had been greatly impressed with the government's use of film during World War II to train the military and motivate and mobilize the entire citizenry for the war effort. Particularly useful in the latter regard was the *Why We Fight* series, seven feature-length films directed by Frank Capra that showed Americans the threat the Axis powers posed, the nature of the conflict in different theaters, and how U.S. efforts could overcome the enemy. At the war's end Hamer Reiser wasn't the only Mormon interested in pursuing similar efforts within the Church. Others did experiments to prove that films could be used in Church settings even during the war; for instance, in March and April 1942 the film *Fighting the Fire Bomb* from the Office of Civilian Defense was shown in Salt Lake City wards, and in March 1945, the local Sunday School in the Bonneville (Utah) Stake used Navy training filmstrips with a synchronized vinyl record soundtrack to instruct their teachers in methods of pedagogy, with favorable results. And a few years later at Deseret Film Productions Frank Wise wrote, "The Church generally is aware of these valuable teaching tools which science has put into our hands. It is also not insensitive to the findings growing out of one the greatest teaching jobs ever attempted, the training of fighting forces in World War II . . . This is probably the first time that visual aids were given a chance to prove their worth . . . The worth of visual aids is no longer a problematical quantity, but a known fact, and few will challenge the ability of these tools to aid in promoting the ways of peace just as efficiently as they served in teaching the arts of warfare."[345]

This opinion was shared by Elder Harold B. Lee of the Twelve, who one day in 1946 discussed it on the phone with Judge Whitaker in California. The two men knew each other from when they each lived in Denver, when Whitaker was a high school football player and Lee the president of the district, or a small stake. Now Whitaker was on his own stake's high council, so he was discussing some Church business with Lee when the *Why We Fight* films came up. Disney had provided the animation for these pictures, such as maps with moving armies, and Whitaker told Lee, "Come on over and I will take you through" the studio.[346] Lee came, bringing along his fellow apostles Mark E. Petersen and Matthew Cowley, and Whitaker gave them a tour of the studio. Specifically, Lee was interested in promoting and explaining the Church's welfare program, of which he was the primary architect. Sitting in a screening room after watching part of one of the *Why We Fight* films, the four men were discussing how they might make a similarly compelling narrative about how the Church cared for its poor when Whitaker made what he later called "kind of a rash offer": he and some of his Mormon colleagues at Disney would produce the film for them. If the Church could pay for the materials, he was sure that his friends would lend their time for free. This seemed like exactly the solution the apostles were looking for, but as they excitedly discussed the potential it became clear that "they wanted everything but the kitchen sink in it"[347] and Whitaker started feeling uneasy that he had promised the impossible. Still, he left the offer on the table and the apostles went back to Salt Lake to discuss it with the General Welfare Committee. When they accepted, the project was a go.

For the first time in his life Judge Whitaker was now a film producer. First was the matter of gaining permission and putting together a crew. He approached Walt Disney personally, who admired Whitaker's loyalty and immediately okayed the outside project with a promise to help however needed; Disney cameras, studio space, and editing tables would be available. For the crew, Whitaker started with a core group just as enthusiastic as himself: his brother Scott, who had moved from animation to the story department at Disney, and would spend the rest of his career as a screenwriter; Eric Larson; and W. Cleon Skousen, then a newly minted FBI agent who Whitaker described as having "a keen story mind."[348] As the work progressed others came onboard: John Lewis, a local newspaper journalist; cameraman Kenneth Peach, who shot the live-action footage in California; Bob Adams, who edited and shot some of the footage; animators Grant Simmons, Charles Otterstrom, and Al Coe, who assisted Judge and Scott with the animation; radio presenter Wendell Noble, who narrated both films; Norma Jean Wright, who found archival footage and secured permission for its use; and Nathan and Ruth Hale, who oversaw the acting, especially in *The Lord's Way*. Those, like Coe, who were not Mormon accepted a small fee, while the Church members donated their time entirely. There was support from Salt Lake as well: Donald Davis of the General Welfare Committee was the Church's main liaison with the crew. To discuss Church welfare required shooting many events and locations in Salt Lake City, so Frank Wise and LaMar Williams at Deseret Film Productions provided contemporary footage of "Church welfare in action" for both films.[349]

Work commenced in October 1946 and continued, perhaps unexpectedly, for two full years. These collaborators were spread out around Los Angeles in neighborhoods like La Cañada Flintridge, North Hollywood, and Westchester, but they still managed to meet regularly in their homes at night to discuss their research and possible storylines. They determined they would need to make two productions to cover everything the General Authorities wanted, which their sponsors in Salt Lake happily agreed to. Eric Larson took charge of the film *Church Welfare in Action* and Whitaker *The Lord's Way*. "We soon learned what a herculean task it was to hold down full-time jobs, fulfill our heavy Church responsibilities, and try to make the films in our spare time . . . Our progress was so slow that a year later we didn't have even one script ready for production, and I was very discouraged."[350] Starting to fear for his health, let alone the films, Whitaker decided to violate a norm of Mormon culture and seek out a special blessing from his stake patriarch Albin Hoglund, a man whose usual function was to give one-time-only blessings to Church members detailing what types of blessings the Lord had in store for them in their lives, akin to the blessings given by the Old Testament patriarchs in Genesis. There is generally one patriarch per stake, and because of the heavy demands of their calling Church members are advised not to solicit "extra" blessings from these men, but in this case Whitaker felt prompted by the Spirit to do so; he set out one evening, at one point turning the car around and almost returning home, but in the end he arrived at Hoglund's door. He was alone, his family out for the evening, and agreed to give Whitaker a blessing. Immediately when Hoglund placed his hands on his head Whitaker felt a surge of the Holy Ghost. "Strangely enough," he recalled, "he spent little time in reassuring me about the welfare films except to say that I shouldn't be unduly concerned, things would work out all right...." Instead, the thing that most impressed Whitaker was this: "The time will come when you will be called to an assignment which will literally revolutionize the teaching methods of the Church. Thousands of people throughout the Church will know of the work you will do and will bless you and those associated with you."[351] Though perplexed by this, Whitaker felt his anxiety dissipate. As he later recalled,

> We walked back to the living room and sat quietly for a few minutes and he said, "Brother Whitaker, I know what you are thinking. You are wondering how this could ever come about, aren't you?" I said, "Brother Hoglund, indeed I am." He said, "As sure as we are here tonight, it will come about, and you will bear testimony to it. I won't live to see it, but you will."... I was so impressed when I got home to my family from that blessing that I called my family and said, "Listen, and listen carefully ... If I live for it, the things that this good man has told me tonight will come true. I want you to remember it." Long after my wife and children were in bed I sat down and wrote out in detail the blessing as I remembered it. It was all very vivid in my mind and in spite of nearly twenty years of intervening time I still remember almost word for word the blessing I received that night.[352]

Hoglund was only fifty-four and in good health, so Whitaker thought it would be a very long time before any of this happened. But that very night after Whitaker left he fell ill. He was soon in the hospital—where Whitaker visited him and gave him a blessing of his own—and passed away three weeks later; Whitaker's was the last blessing he ever gave.

As far as the films were concerned, Whitaker was reassured and jumped back into the work. Things didn't necessarily go any quicker, but the crews did push forward with good spirits until the films were finished, with *Church Welfare in Action* complete on October 3, 1948 and *The Lord's Way* a month later. The former title was closer to what was originally envisioned by Elder Lee: a half-hour black and white documentary on what the welfare system is and how it functions. The story was by Skousen, who worked with Scott Whitaker, and vocal music was provided by members of the Wilshire Ward in Hollywood; it's unclear who composed or performed the orchestral score. Norma Jean Wright secured archival footage from Twentieth Century-Fox, Warner Brothers, RKO, and Time, Inc., which allowed use of their 1937 *March of Time* newsreel on Church welfare. The finished film gives a history of the program and discusses various components of it, like volunteer-run orchards, farms, and canning operations—as well as the entire operation's management by priesthood leaders—along with the spiritual characteristics this work helps foster; at one point the narrator points out that the volunteer work "meant fully as much to the brother with plenty as to the brother in need," a perfect encapsulation of Heber J. Grant's original intent in fostering the welfare program and teaching the value of hard work as a spiritual necessity even if it's not a temporal one.

If *Church Welfare in Action* teaches the nuts and bolts of the program—like the segments of *Why We Fight* that explain in minute detail the strategic necessity of forming an alliance with the Soviet Union, or the movement of troops in the Pacific theater—then *The Lord's Way* puts a human face on it and tells why all this organization and effort remains necessary even in the booming postwar economy when its need is less apparent. This film is a few minutes shorter, with approximately two-thirds of it dedicated to two fictional case studies of Church welfare assisting families who encounter an unexpected need; this is where the Hales and their company of Glendale Theater Players came in, with Nathan Hale and Scott Whitaker working together to direct the actors. The other third contains animated sequences, original and archival. Whitaker knew that Disney had already made the perfect film to teach the value of hard work and avoiding laziness—what Grant had called "the evils of the dole"—in the 1934 Silly Symphony

The Grasshopper and the Ants, from Aesop's fable. In this film a carefree grasshopper, voiced by Goofy voice actor Pinto Colvig, mocks the industrious ants who are busy preparing for winter, but when the cold weather arrives he learns to appreciate work and self-preparedness as he nearly starves and freezes in the snow, although the ants eventually take him in for a musical climax in which he sings, "I owe the world a living." Once again Walt Disney himself authorized the use of part of this film, giving *The Lord's Way* some lightness that it would otherwise have lacked. The film footage for both pictures was developed in laboratories at commercial rates, but everything else was done for free or on a steep discount, and Judge Whitaker and Eric Larson estimated that "without the donated labor of the producers, writers, actors, animators, musicians, editors, and others, the films would have cost in excess of $50,000."[353]

George Albert Smith personally paid for train tickets for the filmmakers and their wives to come to a preview of the films in Salt Lake. Though the experience was nerve-wracking for Whitaker, both films were well received: David McKay even went so far as to tell Scott Whitaker that these were the best films to ever come out of Hollywood. They were shown in the Tabernacle—a huge space which Judge thought made the films look like a postage stamp—and were put into distribution by Deseret Book the following April, remaining popular for many years; prints of the films were also shown at stake welfare meetings throughout a six-month period in 1949 and '50. More importantly, they indicated to several Church leaders, perhaps McKay foremost among them, that there was a need for a greater Church-sponsored filmmaking effort than was available through Deseret Book; Scott later commented on McKay's compliment, "It was a great thrill in my life and, in fact, I believe gave us a vision of things to come. It kind of set the stage for future production."[354] At the time, though, Judge, Scott, and all their associates thought their work was done. "After those films were completed," Judge said, "it seemed as if the weight of the world had been lifted from my shoulders. Our little committee was disbanded, and we all went back to living normal lives."[355] For Judge this meant he forgot Albin Hoglund's blessing and returned to Disney, where he contributed to *Cinderella* (1950), *Alice in Wonderland* (1951), and *Peter Pan* (1953).

A Sacred Film: The Temple Endowment

In hindsight, we can see that forces were now moving inexorably toward the establishment of the BYU film studio; the welfare films were just further testament of this. At the time, however, this was by no means clear. By March 7, 1951 Frank Wise's contribution to the Sunday School was so apparent that he was placed on the general board; at this time they considered but rejected making Church films on a larger scale, and his work therefore remained primarily connected to filming general conference. Television had popularized the concept of watching conference in ways other than in person, and an extremely high demand existed for talks to be distributed on film—in 1949 the prints were booked solidly among the 700-plus wards then equipped with 16mm equipment.[356] And Hinckley, as busy as ever, turned to other tasks after making the anti-tobacco films, with no thought about returning to film production work. A call from President McKay would change the situation for both men.

Although the filmed endowment was not completed until 1955, its creation began in 1952 and it should rightly be seen as the apex of Home Cinema: it's a film that is integrally featured in one of the holiest of Mormon rites; it's shown in a Church building where not even all Mormons are allowed, let alone outsiders; and its content, which deals with family and covenants, is believed to be given through revelation and is the most didactic film the Church has ever produced. Its production methods also reflected Home Cinema perhaps more than any other film, with a small group of faithful Church members working and multitasking as part of a Church assignment, with no remuneration or industry assistance at any stage, even filming within the walls of the Salt Lake Temple. While all of this speaks to its nature as a work of Home Cinema, the breadth of its distribution points toward things to come: in its various versions throughout the years it has screened multiple times daily in nearly every temple in the world, making it quite certainly the most-screened picture in the history of Mormon cinema.

While Mormons don't discuss the content of temple work outside the temple, a great deal of information about the endowment has been made available by General Authorities, in archives, and in the Church's own publications. As discussed in Chapter 1, the temple endowment ceremony was developed in Nauvoo in the form of a medieval morality play, with actors taking on various roles like God and Lucifer to depict the creation of the world and all mankind's journey through it; this is done by making Adam and Eve into a type of Everyman character, standing in for the worshippers who are watching the performance; at certain moments in the story all the congregation makes individual covenants which they promise not to disclose outside the temple walls. This is one of the endowment's greatest innovations—making the narrative participatory and relevant, through specific promises, to the initiate's everyday life.

It also could be very long. There was no written script until 1877 when an ailing Brigham Young first wrote it down, meaning that all previous endowment sessions were improvised as part of an oral tradition, which could result in lengthy performances and irregular runtimes, making it very difficult to schedule multiple sessions in a row with predetermined start times as happens in temples today.[357] An endowment ceremony under Young could take hours, making time for all the material, the embellished performances of actors like William W. Phelps, hymn singing, impromptu lectures and sermons, and the procession between rooms that represent different stages of the narrative. It required a full cast of temple workers to deliver the presentation, which helped make staffing a temple a difficult logistical affair; this in turn helped restrict temples to areas where a sufficiently large Mormon population could both run and attend them. Mormons had not been counseled to gather together geographically for half a century, placing temples at the center of a new paradox for the faith that hadn't existed in the 1800s: how to make the endowment ceremony and eternal marriages—which were seen as essential for salvation but could only be performed in temples—available to the increasingly diasporic Mormon population that lived far from the old places of gathering in the American west? A second question had been partially addressed when the endowment was presented in Spanish for the first time in the Arizona Temple in 1945,[358] but now in examining areas with lower Mormon populations there was the question of how to present the endowment to people in their native languages without a full complement of temple workers who also speak that language? A third problem was cost: temples were the largest and most expensive buildings the Church erected, and the price tag not just for construction but for land and maintenance made it a prohibitively expensive endeavor, one you wouldn't want to get wrong by building a temple in a far-off locale that then primarily sits unused.

This was the situation that faced David O. McKay when he assumed the Church presidency in 1951. At the time there were eight operating temples: four in Utah, one in Hawaii, one in Arizona, one in Alberta, and the newest one in Idaho, with another underway in Los Angeles, an extremely expensive structure which even today remains the largest temple the Church has ever built. McKay felt impressed to build smaller temples in areas of lower Church membership, specifically in Europe and New Zealand, but it was unclear how or whether such an audacious plan would work.

> The move was unprecedented on two levels: It was the first time temples were constructed outside North America (including Hawaii) and the first time they were constructed where stakes did not already exist. It was a calculated risk on McKay's part, but he was confident that

such temples would anchor church members in their native countries, thus curtailing emigration to the United States and allowing the creation of overseas stakes.[359]

Eight months after becoming president, McKay authorized the purchase of property that mission president Hamer Reiser had found in Surrey, south of London, for a British temple, and a month later, in January 1952, he proposed building a second temple on the continent. West Germany was initially considered because it had the largest Mormon population, but fear of Soviet and East German expansion made Church leaders opt for neutral Switzerland; despite its small Mormon population of just 3,000 people—out of 40,000 Mormons throughout all Europe—McKay considered it "probably the safest country in Europe, and more accessible than England to most of the other European countries." Ironically, then, "at the same time that the church's largest temple was under construction in Los Angeles, plans for the European temples moved in the opposite direction."[360] The capital of Bern, nestled between the Jura Mountains to the north and Western Alps to the south, was selected, and when McKay visited later that year he assigned Swiss-Austrian Mission President Samuel E. Bringhurst—who McKay would call as the temple's first president—to purchase the property.

Back in Utah, McKay presented his concept of smaller temples to the Quorum of the Twelve. He had enough experience with audiovisual devices that with Church Architect Edward O. Anderson he could devise something of what he wanted: "It is not contemplated that an expensive edifice would be erected but that temples be built that would accommodate the people under a new plan whereby temple ceremonies can be presented in one room without moving from one room to another, utilizing modern inventions therefore. It is thought that one room might be used and the scenery changed as needed and seats adjusted to accommodate the situation. It is felt that such a building could be erected and adequately equipped for about the cost of one of our present meeting houses, namely, two hundred to two hundred fifty thousand dollars."[361]

This wasn't the first time that the use of new technology in the temple had been discussed. In 1927 a Church member named Pearl W. Peterson had written from Gunnison, Utah to the First Presidency to ask about the Church's interest in staging a play or even a film about the life of Jesus. While we don't know specifically what type of content she was proposing, in their response of August 27 Heber Grant, Anthony Ivins, and Charles Nibley responded that "the only proper place for such a presentation would be a holy temple, if the time could ever come when it might be deemed wise and proper to use the motion picture in these sacred places. We have no such intention at the present time...."[362] Church leaders may not have deemed film appropriate to use in temples, but Mormon architects, on the other hands, were discussing the possibility as early as the 1930s, essentially as soon as sound film became available.[363] Even after the first of the smaller temples were in place in Europe and New Zealand, McKay remained troubled by temples' inaccessibility to as many as one third of all Church members. In 1967 he assigned the Building Committee Chairman Mark Garff, mentioned earlier for his 1945 film *General Authorities at Christmastime*, to study the problem; after traveling to congregations around the Pacific he recommended the Church outfit and dedicate an ocean liner as a traveling temple that could visit LDS communities in different ports. Though McKay ultimately rejected the idea, its consideration for a few months shows how willing he remained to innovate with changes that others might consider improper for the holy precincts of the temple.

The main idea of the smaller temples was to save costs by eliminating the numerous rooms that worshippers moved through in the large temples in the western U.S. While McKay's concept with moving backdrops and chairs would save money, staffing and language issues remained unresolved. What he needed was a method to economically present the endowment in various languages with *fewer* workers than traditionally required. It's unclear what progress was made in 1953 while the building's superstructure progressed in Bern—the groundbreaking was on August 5, 1953—but evidently no solution was in sight so in early 1954 a committee was formed that included Edward O. Anderson and apostles Joseph Fielding Smith, Harold Lee, and Richard Evans, who joined the Twelve in October 1953—but once again the entire burden essentially fell upon the shoulders of Gordon Hinckley, who was given a room on the fifth floor of the Salt Lake Temple where he worked on the problem on his own for some time, consulting frequently with President McKay. He eventually brought in Paul Evans and Joseph Shaw of KSL and Frank Wise to provide technical expertise. First they considered slides or filmstrips, but Wise suggested making a 16mm film. They would produce a different film for every language with large Mormon populations in the countries surrounding Switzerland, including all the narrative portions of the endowment; only a few temple workers would need to be present to administer the actual ordinances. The films would visually replace wall murals, allowing for single movie theater-type spaces to take the place of a series of themed rooms, thus reducing the size of the temples exactly how McKay desired. Though audacious, this was the most workable solution. "A large scale model of the temple was built, including a motion picture projector, that enabled them to visualize the procedure of the endowment in the new type of temple."[364] It was soon approved and, with a September 11, 1955 dedication date looming, the committee began the hard work of producing the films.

A major component of the project took place in preproduction with the translation of the script into the different languages, followed by the casting of actors who could deliver that dialogue; these came from native speakers and some returned missionaries. The committee chose not to dub foreign languages over a single film but to film the entire endowment multiple times with different casts speaking in English, German, Dutch, French, Danish, Swedish, Norwegian, and Finnish; later, in preparation for the new temple in Hamilton, New Zealand, they created Samoan, Tahitian, Tongan, and Maori versions as well. Luckily, one of Hinckley's current assignments was the translation of the scriptures into different languages, so he already had a network in place to assist with this work, and the translations were quickly underway while he proceeded with the English version of the film. This was shot first and shown to the General Authorities on the committee, and probably to at least the First Presidency as well, and once this was approved they proceeded with the other versions.

The crew worked entirely as volunteers on Saturdays and holidays, which made the production take over a year to complete. Hinckley produced and oversaw the entire process, with Harold I. Hansen, a BYU theater professor and longtime director of the Hill Cumorah pageant, directing and Frank Wise shooting and editing. Other crew members included Paul Evans on sound, Joe Shaw, the Church's electrician Joe Osmond as a gaffer, Winnifred Bowers on costumes, and Bill Demos as production designer. All of these were believing, practicing Church members to allow them to work with this material. Mormons consider the endowment and other temple work so sacred that they never enact it or even repeat its content outside the temple. In order to actually stage and film the endowment ceremony, therefore, it was necessary to do so inside the Salt Lake Temple itself. The obvious choice of space was the assembly room, a three-story space on the uppermost floor used for large meetings, such as the actual dedication of the temple in 1893. A set of the Garden of Eden was constructed without damaging the ornate room by hanging a backdrop from lighting gantries extending out from the room's balcony seats. Although realism was not the goal of this production, Demos's designs did require lifting some large items through the windows with heavy tackle, surely an interesting sight from the grounds of Temple Square. Because the endowment retells the creation story from Genesis, the film also involved some outdoor documentary filmmaking to capture footage of plants, animals, and natural phenomena to represent the earth as it was created. This was shot in the American South to find warm enough weather during winter in early 1955, and of course these portions could be shot without any worries about revealing content from the endowment itself. They even called upon their Disney contacts and received permission, again directly from Walt himself, to use a portion of the "Rite of Spring" segment from *Fantasia* (1940) to show lava and volcanic activity as the earth was formed. Wise also edited the films inside the temple, but the raw footage had to be developed elsewhere. For this Hinckley worked through a friend named James B. Keysor, a Mormon and future state assemblyman who at the time worked at Capitol Records in Burbank, to insure that only LDS lab technicians worked on the footage. The sound had not been synchronized, of course, but everyone concerned wanted to err on the side of caution, even giving the project a fake name of *In the Beginning* for the laboratory reports and bookkeeping.

Producing eight entire films—seven of them in languages the crew didn't speak—proved a race against the clock. Nevertheless, they were all edited and ready well in advance of the September 11 dedication, time that Hinckley would need onsite in Switzerland: "Projection and sound equipment had to be installed in the temple, the audio [on 16mm magnetic film stock] and filmed segments synchronized, and any potential problems detected and corrected so that ordinance work could commence upon conclusion of the last dedicatory session."[365] Traveling with his wife, Hinckley was preoccupied with keeping the finished endowment ceremony from being seen by non-Mormons while he was en route to the temple. He packed the sound and image reels in different suitcases, but when he arrived in Basel on a Saturday the Swiss Customs agent said that all the footage would need to be approved by the national film board; he was forced to leave the reels with the agent over the weekend. One full-time missionary remembered that Hinckley "and Swiss-Austrian Mission President William F. Perschon requested that the missionaries join them in fasting and prayer over the weekend that the material would be kept sacred and permitted into the country."[366] Early Monday morning the two men were back answering the same set of questions with a national film board agent, declaring the content of the reels as "Church film and lectures." "What is its purpose?" the agent asked. "'It will be used in the new temple we are building in Zollikofen.' 'What is its title?'. . .'This is just a lecture, and we don't title every lecture given in our church.' . . . Finally the agent stamped the papers with the necessary seal and indicated the number of Swiss francs due. 'I've never seen anyone reach for money faster than did President Perschon,' Gordon remembered."[367] In the end the films arrived at the temple without any non-Mormon viewing them, an accomplishment that Hinckley felt as a divine gift.

He finally arrived at the temple itself and could now see how their little model looked in real life. The architectural design of the temples in Bern, London, and Hamilton, New Zealand turned out to be nearly identical: on the exterior, a blocky design reminiscent of the basic shapes of the Salt Lake Temple but at a much smaller scale—the Swiss Temple was just 35,000 square feet—with the interior designed completely around the film projection facilities. One last flurry of activity ensued as Hinckley, "Paul Evans, Joe Shaw, and Hans Lütscher, the newly appointed temple engineer, began installing the projectors and audio equipment, synchronizing the film and audio segments, and reviewing each language version of the film."[368] The work was nonstop day and night, but by dedication Sunday everything was ready. The dedication was held and then Hinckley suddenly found himself serving as the projectionist as Lütscher had not yet been endowed himself. Several large groups of German, French, Swedish, and Dutch Saints who had come for the dedication were accommodated before the local members could finally take over and Hinckley and the others could rest. The next month in conference President McKay praised Hinckley's indefatigable efforts, and two and a half years later in April 1958 he called him to be an Assistant to the Twelve; he was called as an apostle in October 1961.[369]

The Swiss temple set the pattern for all temples constructed since; in addition to bridging language boundaries, it has also allowed multiple endowments to be presented simultaneously in multiple projection rooms. In fact one of the most important side effects of the filmed endowment, especially in areas with large Mormon populations, is that the ceremony is now quicker and of a uniform duration, allowing for predictable scheduling. Over the years the endowment has been further modified, primarily by removing material and making it even shorter, and as new films have been produced efficiency has become as important as any other result of a filmed endowment. A desire to increase speed while reducing staff has caused nearly all the temples built before Switzerland's to have been retrofitted to adopt a video presentation. President McKay anticipated this in 1959 as the wave of temples in Switzerland, New Zealand, England, and California bothered some Mormons in Utah. As they complained that the temples in Salt Lake and Logan were overcrowded and petitioned for a new temple in Ogden to help relieve this, McKay "expressed the opinion that the crowded condition in the Salt Lake and Logan Temples . . . can be overcome in part by introducing the more efficient way of conducting the sessions."[370] Though he didn't say it, in 1959 a more efficient endowment session meant one presented on film. The Alberta Temple in 1962 was the first to receive such a renovation, followed by Arizona (1975), St. George (1975), Hawaii (1978), Logan (1979), and Manti (1985).[371] New buildings designed in this same period—and since—have been designed from their inception to take advantage of film to perform at peak efficiency, executing dozens of endowment sessions each day. The Provo Temple (1972), one of the Church's busiest, has six endowment rooms with video projection radiating out around the central Celestial Room, a floorplan that allows a new session to begin every twenty minutes; the Ogden and Washington, D.C. Temples were designed with six endowment rooms as well. Without a filmed endowment presentation such high volumes of ordinance work would require hundreds of workers simultaneously, a logistical impossibility. In one instance a temple architect went the other way: in designing the Oakland Temple (1964) in the early 1960s architect Harold Burton wanted to take advantage of the new widescreen aspect ratios that had become popular in the 1950s. He thus designed the two endowment rooms in that temple with larger screens, designed for 35mm projection, than any other temple in the Church, and originally slide projectors shown images on the walls to recreate the murals of the early temples. The combined effect was an audiovisual immersion that only film could produce.[372]

In addition to allowing more endowment sessions and vicarious ordinance work to be done, the filmed endowment has also allowed for more temples to be built. Most Church members believe that Hinckley's role with the Swiss Temple was not coincidental. Soon after becoming Church President in 1995 he too felt impressed to once again cut temple sizes in half and reduce or even eliminate full-time staff, allowing for the Church's greatest surge yet in temple building. He made a particular push in 1999 and 2000, resulting in 102 finished temples by the end of 2000—and 169 by 2018. The endowment film itself has been remade, always under Hinckley's supervision during his lifetime, first with Judge Whitaker in 1967 then again with two different versions in 1988 and 1990, and three more in 2013-14. As mentioned, these have included changes in content, but they also reflect the addition of music and improvements in technical proficiency and production design.[373]

Creating the BYU Motion Picture Department

By the early 1950s, multiple factors had come together to encourage the creation of a large-scale filmmaking entity, eventually to be placed at Brigham

Young University. These included the widespread use of 16mm stock; the Church's domestic film distribution network and the subsequent need for product; the success of filmstrips, Deseret Film Productions, and the welfare films; and, crucially, the ordination of David O. McKay as President of the Church. The diverse ways the Church had already used film, even in the past few years, suggested only a greater need for home production in the future. Locating production facilities at Church-owned Brigham Young University made sense for many reasons: the instructional nature of Church films and the ability this would give filmmakers to make non-religious pictures for the educational market; the educational opportunities it would afford rising generations of Mormon filmmakers; the growing use of media like filmstrips and 16mm film at the university; increasing efforts in collegiate broadcasting; and a growing pool of talent in the university community from which to draw for all aspects of film production. It also had more prosaic features such as buildings with vacant spaces, security, vehicles, and support staff that would allow a young film studio to grow. Creating a BYU motion picture studio seemed as much part of the destiny of the university as of its parent institution.

One other new player who would help insure the success of film at BYU was the new University President Ernest L. Wilkinson, who began his administration in February 1951. He was already aware of the challenges film and broadcasting presented the university when, on May 8, 1952, Weston N. Nordgren, Provo bureau chief for the *Salt Lake Tribune* and the husband of one of Wilkinson's secretaries, submitted a highly researched twelve-page single-spaced memo to Wilkinson. Written at the urging of Nordgren's former mission president John A. Widtsoe—who would pass away that November without seeing the new film studio take form—this short document seems prophetic today. In it Nordgren proposes three projects that would better equip the university to carry out the work of the Church. In order of importance, they were: 1) to transfer all film, radio, and television work of the Church from Salt Lake to Provo, establishing a motion picture studio on BYU campus; 2) to establish a three-month missionary training course along with a mission home or dormitory for newly called missionaries; and 3) to construct a temple on what had always been called Temple Hill, north of campus near the mouth of Rock Canyon and where the current campus was then taking shape. He also outlined what would be necessary to form a motion picture studio and a Department of Motion Picture, Radio, and Television Arts for training students, with sample scripts to begin building a cinematic library. In connection with this, he also recommended the university create a "commercial channel television station" for training students and broadcasting Church-related programs. It's unclear if Wilkinson decided to pursue any of these because of Nordgren's recommendation, but at any rate every single item he suggested was accomplished within twenty years.

As a result of all the activity regarding radio and television broadcasting at the university, even before receiving Nordgren's memo Wilkinson authorized the creation of a Radio and Television Committee to investigate the feasibility of launching television production at the school. W. Cleon Skousen, who had worked on the welfare films, had moved to Provo to teach at the university, and he now was a chief assistant to the new president, and Wilkinson appointed him chairman of the Radio and Television Committee; though best remembered for his books and conservative political ideology, in these months Skousen played a crucial role in forming the course that Mormon film would take in the subsequent decades. Perhaps the most important thing he did—more than any official recommendations—was contact Judge Whitaker.

In 1951 Whitaker's family vacationed with his brother Ferrin and his family around the Schneitter Hot Pots near Midway in Heber Valley, northeast of Provo and Orem via Provo Canyon. They had fond memories of visiting these hot pots as children, and now they thought that if the facilities were spruced up it could be a nice spot for tourists and locals, a sort of country inn featuring bathing in the warm water. They discovered that the property was indeed for sale, so with two other brothers they purchased it. It would require a great deal of work to fix up, however, which would be applied primarily through their own elbow grease, and therefore Whitaker returned to California to ask Walt Disney for a year-long leave of absence. "He listened with great interest, and his eyes sparkled as he said, 'All my life I have wanted to do something like that, and here I am stuck with this,' as he gestured with mock disdain toward his multi-million dollar studio. 'Take your year, then come back, and your job would be waiting.'"[374] How facetious Disney was being is unclear, because at that point he was beginning to toy with the idea of opening a resort of his own, and Disneyland opened on July 17, 1955. The Whitakers' ambitions were humbler, but they worked just as hard to get what they renamed the Homestead ready as soon as possible; today the Homestead Resort is a quaint hotel and recreational resort with golfing and various aquatic attractions.

Whitaker, then, was living fairly close to Provo in 1952, so Skousen asked him to participate as an ex officio member of his committee. He gladly accepted, but through his relationship with Harold B. Lee he was already discussing prospects for increased Church filmmaking in Salt Lake City with Lee, Elder Henry Moyle, and the new Presiding Bishop Joseph L. Wirthlin. *Church Welfare in Action* and *The Lord's Way* had made an impression, and now, as Whitaker recalled, "Church officials, educators, mission presidents, and lay members had all voiced the need for films for the priesthood, for the Anti-Liquor-Tobacco Committee, for missionary work, the Welfare Program, to train bishops, and for various other purposes. It was clear that there was a definite need for increasingly effective means of communicating with the Church membership and the world at large. Motion pictures could help fulfill that need." It seemed at many points as though Lee were trying to recruit Whitaker to run such a department, and as he got to know Ernest Wilkinson that winter he did as well. "He asked me if I would be interested, should the opportunity arise, in accepting an assignment to head a motion picture department at the University."[375] It seemed that a consensus was being reached that BYU was the right place to house the facility, with Elder Lee agreeing.[376] Whitaker may have agreed on the need for films and that BYU was the best location, but he was still hesitant to head the effort himself. For one thing, it was completely outside his experience as an animator, but for another it would mean giving up a comfortable position at Disney that he loved for a job with less pay, more work and responsibilities, and less certainty. Then he remembered the blessing he'd received in 1947 from Albin Hoglund saying that one day the work he would do would revolutionize the entire Church. "Suddenly, the promises made in my blessing rang in my ears, and I thought, "Well, maybe this is it."[377]

Whitaker developed a hypothetical filmmaking scheme while Bishop Wirthlin developed a financial plan and promised to commission many films. In October 1952 a meeting was held with Whitaker, Wirthlin, Wilkinson, and the BYU finance committee, at which they concluded to establish the Department of Motion Picture Production the following January. Whitaker was asked to head the project and create the studio, which he accepted. Because he was not qualified to teach he requested it be a staff and not a faculty position, meaning that it would be a few more years before film instruction would begin at the university. Whitaker wrote a sad resignation letter to Walt Disney, who replied wishing him well with the new studio; indeed, Disney proved of great assistance with the fledgling Motion Picture Department, and it was probably through this relationship with Whitaker that he allowed the footage from *Fantasia* to be used in the endowment. And with that he moved with his family to Provo and began work on January 3, 1953.[378]

With so many variables coming together all at the same time, we could ask who is primarily responsible for the creation of the BYU Motion Picture Department? As Frank Wise said, it never would have happened without David O. McKay at the head of the Church. No one else was interested enough in it to back such a risky venture. At the same time, much of McKay's faith in motion pictures may have come from Hamer Reiser—it seems they equally inspired each other. And so although Reiser was never involved with the BYU film department, Wise gave him the lion's share of credit for its creation simply because it grew out of his initial vision—and he may have even influenced David McKay to increase his belief in and support of institutional films. Speaking years later, Wise said that Reiser in the 1940s had the vision for training and bettering the Saints through film, but the resources simply weren't available until the BYU studio formed. "Hamer Reiser's concept was that one of these days there would be a film-producing unit for the Church and by the Church. He was just trying to get the thing going, and he did get it going. The credit lies really in his hands, in Hamer Reiser's hands. We were just pawns that were used in order to further the game . . . He had the vision. He had the contact, especially after President George Albert Smith passed away and President McKay came into the picture."[379] This assessment appears accurate, but Reiser himself would have been quick to deflect the credit. In his own interview near the end of his life, he gave credit to Wise, calling him "a genius, a true genius," and adding, "Frank I think has been a cornerstone of the BYU development in motion picture" production.[380]

The creation of the Motion Picture Production Department at BYU represents the culminating act in the establishment of a Mormon film industry, done after the Church had put firmly into place a ubiquitous exhibition system in every ward, branch, and mission in the world, sanctioned by critical discussion about film through official channels. The films that were produced at this time should be measured less by their quality or success than by their range of application and by how they were received in the Church, meaning, yes, with General Authorities, but primarily with the rank and file members attending the ward movie shows every month. During the Home Cinema era, cinema became at home in the Church; by the end of this period it was firmly accepted within Mormon culture that film was fit for all aspects of Church activity.

In addition to the establishment of the technical and cultural infrastructure necessary for a nascent LDS film industry, the Second Wave also helped crystallize the forms of native LDS film genres that are now recognized staples of institutional film. These "home genres" (which overlap somewhat) include the Church leader film (*Latter-day Saint Leaders: Past and Present*), the commemorative documentary film (*Message of the Ages, Where the Saints Have Trod*), the public service film (Hinckley's anti-tobacco films); the training film (*Church Welfare in Action*), the visitors' center/public relations film (*Valley of Triumph, Pioneer Trails*), and the temple endowment film. These reflect the diverse purposes to which Latter-day Saints believed film could be applied, and together they constitute a major effort, institutionally and independently, to establish a Home Cinema—and they would reach a degree of perfection and have their message amplified many times over through Judge Whitaker's work in the Classical Era of Mormon film.

Despite the challenges facing would-be filmmakers in this period, the Second Wave was anything but a hiatus. Indeed, looked at holistically—recognizing the connections between Hollywood films, independent Mormon films, and institutionally produced films—it is easy to see how cinematic work grew consistently during the 1930s and '40s. At the beginning of the period the tempered enthusiasm for *All Faces West* moved directly into the simultaneous production of *Corianton* and *Message of the Ages,* the increased use of amateur Mormon-themed home movies, the growth of Deseret Book's distribution network, improved representations by Hollywood, and the use of southern Utah as a filming location. This was followed by films like *The Mormon Conquest, Brigham Young,* the multiple productions surrounding the 1947 celebrations, and then *The Mormon Battalion* and *Wagon Master.* Current and future Church Presidents—Heber J. Grant, George Albert Smith, David O. McKay, Harold B. Lee, and Gordon B. Hinckley—all played primary roles in the promotion and development of filmmaking for use across Church programs, in proselytizing, and even in temple worship. Despite the break in regular institutional productions after the loss of the Clawsons, all of this came together to create a cinematically engaged culture unique among religious grops—and a Church completely committed to film's numerous applications. In other words, it was time for Mormon cinema to look to the future and enter its classical phase in the Third Wave.

NOTES

Preface

01 M. Russell Ballard, "The Importance of a Name," *Ensign*, November 2011, 81. The second-highest governing body of the Church is the Quorum of Twelve Apostles, modelled after Jesus' closest disciples in the New Testament Gospels.

02 In 2001 Ballard preached against sanctimoniousness in predominantly Latter-day Saint communities by saying, "I believe it would be good if we eliminated a couple of phrases from our vocabulary: 'nonmember' and 'non-Mormon.' Such phrases can be demeaning and even belittling. Personally, I don't consider myself to be a 'non-Catholic' or a 'non-Jew.' I am a Christian. I am a member of The Church of Jesus Christ of Latter-day Saints. That is how I prefer to be identified—for who and what I am, as opposed to being identified for what I am not. Let us extend that same courtesy to those who live among us. If a collective description is needed, then 'neighbors' seems to work well in most cases." M. Russell Ballard, "Doctrine of Inclusion," October 2001, http://www.lds.org/general-conference/2001/10/doctrine-of-inclusion?lang=eng (accessed January 26, 2013). In Mormon terminology, an *elder* denotes an adult male who has been ordained to the Melchizedek priesthood and to the office of an elder within that priesthood; the capitalized title *Elder*, as in "Elder Ballard," is often used to refer to both full-time male missionaries, young men between eighteen and twenty-five years old, and members of the Church's governing quorums of the Seventy and Twelve Apostles. The president of the Church and his two counselors, who comprise the First Presidency, as well as presidents of all other priesthood quorums, are referred to as *President*.

03 Richard L. Bushman, *Joseph Smith: Rough Stone Rolling* (New York: Vintage Books, 2005), xxi-xxii.

Introduction

01 William Blake, *The Complete Poetry and Prose of William Blake* (Berkeley: University of California Press, 1982), 207.

02 Similarly, Kimball's landmark 1969 book *The Miracle of Forgiveness* contains a brief section called "Trying Is Not Sufficient" in which he counsels: "Adults ... must determine what they will do, then proceed to do it. To 'try' is weak. To 'do the best I can' is not strong. We must always do better than we can.... With the inspiration from the Lord we can rise higher than our individual powers, extend far beyond our

own personal potential." Such instruction would be appropriate for Luke's training in Empire, as when, later in the same scene, Yoda chides his unbelief after raising his X-wing starfighter from the swamp. Spencer W. Kimball, *The Miracle of Forgiveness* (Salt Lake City: Bookcraft, Inc., 1969), 164-165.

03 Outside of Mormonism the most commonly cited human model for Yoda is Albert Einstein, generally in combination with the *Star Wars* films' head puppet builder Stuart Freeborn, executing a bit of a self-portraiture. Nick Maley, who worked as a puppet maker under Freeborn (who himself was working from Ralph McQuarrie's drawings), acknowledged the Einstein connection but indicated it was incidental: "The defining element that controlled Yoda's proportions, which ultimately altered his character, were the length and breadth of Frank Oz's arm . . . A picture of Einstein ended up on the wall behind the Yoda sculptures and the wrinkles around Einstein's eyes somehow got worked into the Yoda design. Over the course of this evolutionary process Yoda slowly changed from a comparatively spritely [sic], tall, skinny, grasshopper kind of character into the wise old spirited gnome that we all know today. The final step in that transformation was Frank's insistence that the puppet should have no jaw fitted. That allowed him more freedom for expression as a puppeteer but it also meant that the skin hung loosely below the cheeks and that gave Yoda an older, rather chinless look that is quite different to the drawings Ralph did." It is precisely these jowls, combined with the ears, that give the puppet such a striking resemblance to President Kimball. "The Making of Yoda, Part 1," http://netdwellers.com/1001/hosting/users/cinesecrets/pmMakingYoda1.html (accessed November 24, 2009). Today there are a number of Mormon websites that debunk the Kimball connection, such as "Yoda was based on President Spencer W. Kimball," *Holy Fetch*, http://www.holyfetch.com/entertainment/yoda_kimball.html (accessed January 25, 2013). A 2008 documentary called *Mormon Myth-ellaneous* (based on a book by the same name) also includes and disproves this belief along with other instances of Mormon folklore. Cody Clark, "Reel LDS rumors," *Daily Herald*, January 21, 2009, http://www.heraldextra.com/entertainment/reel-lds-rumors/article_b40d0a35-5957-5bb8-841a-d61ae881a9a6.html (accessed January 3, 2013).

04 Some populist websites assert that Kurtz inserted his religious beliefs into the *Star Wars* mythology, guiding Lucas in the development of the Jedi and the Force and thus putting covertly Mormon characters into the film. Amuleki, "How Gary Kurtz, The Mormon, Affected The World That You Live In," *Amuleki's blog*, December 6, 2013, http://amuleki.skyrock.com/3198573611-How-Gary-Kurtz-The-Mormon-Affected-The-World-That-You-Live-In.html (accessed August 9, 2014). Other sources, however, refute such claims. J. W. Rinzler, in his exhaustive chronicle of *Star Wars*' production, makes no mention of Kurtz's influence on the spiritual or mythical components of the script. J. W. Rinzler, *The Making of Star Wars: The Definitive Story Behind the Original Film* (New York: Ballantine Books, 2007). In his biography of Lucas, John Baxter indicates that Kurtz was initially opposed to the inclusion of a religious dimension to the film, out of fear that it would require too much exposition or explanation. Once he agreed with Lucas about the inclusion of a Joseph Campbell-influenced mythology, Kurtz introduced him to Eastern religions and advocated for a generic spirituality that would resonate with viewers of many religious traditions. "'Comparative Religion is one of the things I studied in university,' says Kurtz. 'I also studied the Buddhist and Hindu sects, and studied Zen and Tibetan Buddhism, and also Native American spirituality;

shamanistic methods and so on. I got out a lot of my old books and we talked about it. If you trace back most religious thought to the teachings of the great prophets, whether Judeo-Christian, or Muslim, or even Hindu or Buddhist, you start to see a lot of similarities. The core philosophies are very, very similar. The most obvious one is the Buddhist tradition about karma—the karmic action that comes out of cause and effect. So the Force is an amalgamation of lots of different things." John Baxter, *Mythmaker: The Life and Work of George Lucas* (New York: Avon Books, 1999), 163-166. No source I've found details Kurtz's religious beliefs at the time of his collaborations with Lucas, which stretched from American Graffiti (1973) to The Empire Strikes Back (1980), although his vegetarianism (Baxter, p. 129) could have been influenced by Eastern religions.

05 Benjamin Urrutia, "The Force That Can Be Explained Is Not the True Force," *Dialogue: A Journal of Mormon Thought* 11:3 (Autumn 1978), 101.

06 Richard L. Bushman, "Joseph Smith in the Current Age," *Joseph Smith: The Prophet, the Man*, ed. Susan Easton Black and Charles D. Tate, 1992, http://gospelink.com/library/doc?doc_id=271121&highlight_p=1 (accessed July 10, 2007).

07 Christopher Ingraham, "This is the state where people are most nuts about Star Wars," *Washington Post*, December 17, 2015, https://www.washingtonpost.com/news/wonk/wp/2015/12/17/this-is-the-state-where-people-are-most-nuts-about-star-wars (accessed December 17, 2015), which indicates that Utah had the most Google searches for *Star Wars*-related terms leading up to the 2015 release of *The Force Awakens*; Matthew Bowman, "Everybody loves Star Wars. But here's why Mormons especially love Star Wars," *Washington Post*, December 21, 2015, https://www.washingtonpost.com/news/acts-of-faith/wp/2015/12/21/everybody-loves-star-wars-but-heres-why-mormons-especially-love-star-wars (accessed December 22, 2015); an introspective personal look by blogger Blake L., "A Gay Mormon's Take on 'The Force Awakens,'" *[Awkward Pause] My Musings*, December 22, 2015, https://whatdoesthatsayaboutus.wordpress.com/2015/12/22/a-gay-mormons-take-on-the-force-awakens (accessed December 22, 2015); and a video of the Mormon Tabernacle Choir singing to *The Last Jedi* director Rian Johnson the week that film came out, in Herb Scribner, "Watch the Mormon Tabernacle Choir sing 'Happy Birthday' to Star Wars director," *Deseret News*, December 17, 2017, https://www.deseretnews.com/article/900005912/watch-the-mormon-tabernacle-choir-sing-happy-birthday-to-star-wars-director.html (accessed December 18, 2017).

08 Brad Goldfarb, "Amy Adams," *Interview*, February 2008, 105.

09 J. Michael Hunter, "Maude Adams and the Mormons," *Mormons and Popular Culture: The Global Influence of an American Phenomenon*, Vol. 1, ed. J. Michael Hunter (Santa Barbara: Praeger Publishers, 2013), 137. Hunter notes that although "there is no known record of her baptism as a member" of the Church, Adams "considered herself a cultural Mormon" and "spoke fondly of her Utah beginnings and her Mormon relatives," p. 139. For an example of Adams' enthusiastic hometown reception among Utah audiences see "Events of the Month," *Improvement Era* 7:9 (July 1904), 730; see

also Annie Adams Kiskadden and Verne Hardin Porter, "The Life Story of Maude Adams and Her Mother," *Green Book Magazine* 11-13 (June 1914-January 1915). Mormon children are not baptized until age eight, making it akin to a cross between other Christian denominations' infant baptisms and a coming-of-age ceremony like a Jewish bar or bat mitzvah, and it is this rite and the accompanying ordinance of confirmation that officially make any person a member of the Church. The age of eight was given to Joseph Smith in a revelation now found in Doctrine and Covenants [hereafter D&C] 68:27, with the understanding that children below that age have not reached the "age of accountability" and thus cannot comprehend the significance of the baptismal covenant. The eighth chapter of Moroni, near the end of the Book of Mormon, gives a particularly strong malediction against infant baptism that holds sway within Mormon thought today. Thus there is a long period between a child's birth and their baptism and confirmation, and children like Adams may be born into Mormon families but not receive these ordinances eight years later. Therefore they would not technically qualify as members of the Church as adults, although they may consider themselves culturally Mormon. This can make a person's relationship to the Church slightly more problematic than in faiths like Roman Catholicism that baptize infants or others that don't have such a specific moment of entry into the church's official membership records. Throughout this book I tend to err by including people who were born into Mormon families regardless of whether or not we have a clear record of their baptism at age eight or later.

10 As with Maude Adams, while there is no evidence of Wray's baptism into the Church her ethnic Mormonism—her childhood roots within the faith and culture—is intriguing in itself. I discuss Wray in greater detail in Chapter 2.

11 Philip Boroff, "'Mormon Tickets Soar to $487 as Satire Breaks Broadway Records,'" *Bloomberg*, June 16, 2011, http://www.bloomberg.com/news/2011-06-16/-book-of-mormon-tickets-soar-to-487-as-musical-breaks-broadway-records.html (accessed January 26, 2013); "The Book Of Mormon breaks West End records in first week," *Metro.co.uk*, March 24, 2013, http://metro.co.uk/2013/03/24/the-book-of-mormon-breaks-west-end-records-in-first-week-3557179 (accessed February 20, 2014). *Broadway World* commemorated the show's 1,000th performance on West 49th Street by noting its original rave reviews, its two touring companies' record-setting success in Chicago and throughout the U.S., and the fact that "the London production set a record for highest single day gross in theatre history for both sides of the Atlantic." "THE BOOK OF MORMON Celebrates 1,000th Performance on Broadway Today," *Broadway World*, August 17, 2013, http://www.broadwayworld.com/article/THE-BOOK-OF-MOR-MON-Celebrates-1000th-Performance-on-Broadway-Today-20130817# (accessed February 20, 2014).

12 Gideon Burton, "Making Mormon Cinema: Hype and Hope," *LDS Film Forum*, ed. Randy Astle (Provo: Brigham Young University Department of Theatre and Media Arts, 2002), 8. A ward is a Mormon congregation, based on the similar use of the term for parish or municipal divisions, particularly on the American frontier and in northern England where many Mormon converts hailed from in the 1840s. Since their creation in Nauvoo in 1844 and Nebraska in 1846 Mormon wards have been geographically administered, with all Church members within a designated area belonging to the same ward and attending all meetings together; there is strong institutional and cultural discouragement against attending a ward where you do not live, and hence

Mormons have no equivalent to the Protestant practice of selecting a church or a pastor that fits their taste. A ward is under the supervision of a bishop assisted by two counselors who together comprise a bishopric. A group of wards—usually five to twelve—composes a stake, a larger administrative area akin to a Catholic diocese that is supervised by a stake president and his counselors. The term *stake* derives from Isaiah 54:2 and its invocation of the Israelites' portable Tabernacle as a spiritual metaphor: "Enlarge the place of thy tent, and let them stretch forth the curtains of thine habitations: spare not, lengthen thy cords, and strengthen thy stakes." Joseph Smith's revelations designated the Mormons' aborted settlement in Jackson County, Missouri as Zion, the location for the future city of New Jerusalem (see D&C 58:49-50; 62:4; 63:48; 72:13; 84:76; 104:47; and Article of Faith 10), and when the Church moved elsewhere each of its major communities was seen as a metaphorical stake surrounding and upholding that central gathering place in Missouri or, later, the metaphorical vision of a global Zion. As of 2017 there are 23,054 wards within 3,282 stakes in the Church. Regarding Burton's reference to his teachers quorum, Mormon men within these wards and stakes typically belong to a priesthood quorum, which may consist of deacons (typically ages twelve and thirteen), teachers (fourteen and fifteen), priests (sixteen to eighteen), and elders or high priests (eighteen and above). Although they do not presently hold the priesthood, similar age-distinguished groups and classes exist for adolescent girls (Beehives, Mia Maids, and Laurels) and adult women (the Relief Society). For an overview of wards see Douglas D. Alder, "Ward," *Encyclopedia of Mormonism*, Vol. 4, ed. Daniel H. Ludlow (New York: Macmillon Publishing Company, 1992), 1541-1543; for an analysis of how wards affect Mormon culture and social life, see Terryl L. Givens, *People of Paradox: A History of Mormon Culture* (Oxford: Oxford University Press, 2007), 103-104.

13 Travis Anderson, "Faith on Film/Film on Faith," *LDS Film Forum*, 22.

14 Frank S. Wise, "The 'EYES' have it," *Improvement Era* 52:1 (January 1949), 20—see also pages 21 and 58—also at https://archive.org/stream/improvementera5201un-se#page/n21/mode/2up.

15 Frank S. Wise, "Pertinent Suggestions Given for Showing Films in Wards," *Church News*, November 17, 1962, 6.

16 Joanna Brooks, *The Book of Mormon Girl: A Memoir of an American Faith* (New York: Free Press, 2012), 19.

17 Ibid., 23-24.

18 In early 2018 a YouTube search for the term "Mormon" yielded "about 1,770,000" videos. *YouTube.com*, https://www.youtube.com/results?search_query=mormon (accessed February 4, 2018).

19 The Los Angeles LDS Singles Film Festival began around 1997 and is held in the Santa Monica Stake center, or central meetinghouse, in July or August of each year. "16th or 17th Annual YSA/MSA Film Festival," *YouTube.com*, June 5, 2013, http://www.youtube.com/watch?v=ZZEPzECC6HI&list=PLjxPVXyu9pMv76R2SBUPT3bU-RU_ImqCbD (accessed August 22, 2013); Matthew Stumphy, "How an Epic Movie is Made," *The Guru Blog: The Minor Rantings of a Single LDS Male, Flailing through Eter-

nity, August 18, 2011, http://www.gurustump.com/blog/how-an-epic-movie-is-made (accessed August 22, 2013). The Lingos Film Festival (occasionally called the Lingos! Short Film Festival) in Manhattan began at least by the early 2000's and is currently held each winter at Manhattan's Lincoln Square or East 87th Street church buildings. "Lingos! Short Film Festival," http://backporchmedia.ca/lingos/Lingos_Short_Film_Festival/Home.html (accessed August 22, 2013). Its name derives from *Johnny Lingo*, a popular Church-produced film from 1969.

20 Perry has frequently admitted that her religion shapes her writing. See Richard R. Robertson, "Anne Perry: LDS British Novelist with 'a Commitment to Morality,'" *Ensign*, January 1984, https://www.lds.org/ensign/1984/01/anne-perry-lds-british-novelist-with-a-commitment-to-morality?lang=eng, and Katherine Morris, "Anne Perry," *Mormon Artist*, October 29, 2010, http://mormonartist.net/interviews/anne-perry. One moment of overt Mormon content occurs in her 1990 novel *Bethlehem Road*, in which a Mormon convert is starved to death by her abusive husband who disapproves of her religious decisions.

21 Thomas Elsaesser, *New German Cinema: A History* (New Brunswick: Rutgers University Press, 1989), 9.

1 - Origins

01 Andrew D. White, "Walks and Talks with Tolstoy," *McClure's Magazine* 16, April 1901, 511, also in Andrew D. White, *Autobiography*, Vol. II (New York, 1906), 86-87; quoted in Leland A. Fetzer, "Tolstoy and Mormonism," *Dialogue: A Journal of Mormon Thought* 6:1 (Spring 1971), 23.

02 A comprehensive history of the Church obviously cannot be presented here, and for brevity I am omitting many details and any discussion of controversies over historical claims, but there are innumerable books and publications to which the reader can refer. For a brief officially sanctioned version see Gordon B. Hinckley, *Truth Restored: A Short History of the Church of Jesus Christ of Latter-day Saints* (Salt Lake City: Deseret Book Company, 1990), an extract from his earlier work *What of the Mormons?*. For unofficial but favorable versions see Claudia Lauper Bushman and Richard Lyman Bushman, *Building the Kingdom: A History of Mormons in America* (New York: Oxford University Press, 2001), which includes an excellent discussion on Mormon women, and Matthew Bowman, *The Mormon People: The Making of an American Faith* (New York: Random House, Inc., 2012). For a critical outside perspective see Richard Abanes, *One Nation Under Gods: A History of the Mormon Church* (New York: Basic Books, 2003).

03 The Pearl of Great Price is one of the four canonized works of scripture of the Church, the others being the Bible, Book of Mormon, and Doctrine and Covenants. The shortest book of Mormon scripture, it contains four sections: Joseph Smith's inspired revision of the opening chapters of Genesis, an ancient autobiographical record of Abraham, the beginning of Joseph Smith's personal history (cited here) taken from the seven-volume *History of the Church*, and an excerpt from an 1842 letter by Smith outlining thirteen core tenets of Church doctrine known as the Articles of Faith.

04 The Doctrine and Covenants, or D&C, is the Church's only contemporary book of scripture—the other three all purport an ancient origin (with the exception of a portion of the Pearl of Great Price)—and contains inspired writings by and revelations to Joseph Smith and his associates and successors. The vast majority of material comes from the 1830s, while the most recent addition is from 1978.

05 At present the best study of the demographics of plural marriage is Kathryn M. Daynes's *More Wives Than One: Transformation of the Mormon Marriage System 1840-1910* (Urbana and Chicago: University of Illinois Press, 2001).

06 D. Michael Quinn, *The Mormon Hierarchy: Extensions of Power* (Salt Lake City: Signature Books in association with Smith Research Associates, 1997), 749 (which tells how Brigham Young instructed the Utah Legislature in 1852 to legalize slavery because "we must believe in slavery"), 758 (in which Young told newspaperman Horace Greeley he considered slavery "a divine institution, and not to be abolished until the curse pronounced on Ham shall have been removed from his descendants"), and 273-277 (which discusses Mormon polygamists' affinity with Southern slaveholders once the war started and how close Young and his associates came to secession from the Union in 1861 and '62). The South's eventual defeat—and the implicit supremacy of the federal government that the Mormons saw as hostile to their way of life—was a bitter pill to swallow. See also Doctrine and Covenants 87, an 1832 revelation in which Joseph Smith prophesied of the Civil War beginning in South Carolina over the slavery question, and 134:12, an official statement from 1835, four years after Nat Turner's Rebellion, professing Mormons' belief that they should not preach to "bond servants" without their masters' consent nor incite them to rebel. Young took a much more forceful stance on slavery and blacks' racial inferiority to whites than did Smith, who ordained some African Americans to the priesthood and advocated for gradual emancipation and the return of black freemen to Africa, a not uncommon position of the time, as part of his 1844 presidential platform.

07 Wyoming granted women suffrage in 1869 but held no election until September 1870, while Utah women received the vote on February 12, 1870 and voted just two days later, thus making them—and one Seraph Young in particular—the first American women to exercise the franchise. This right was granted by Utah's non-Mormon governor partly on the mistaken assumption that Mormon women would vote against polygamy; they did not. Utah women could not yet hold office or exercise certain other civil rights. Quinn, *The Mormon Hierarchy: Extensions of Power*, 766.

08 Peggy Fletcher Stack, "Africa's 'Mormon superstar' is first black African LDS general authority," *Salt Lake Tribune*, April 20, 2009, http://www.sltrib.com/ci_12148790 (accessed February 23, 2014); Stack, "Mormonism is growing in Africa, but is its rise 'exponential'?," Salt Lake Tribune, February 25, 2016, http://www.sltrib.com/life-style/faith/3582770-155/mormonism-is-growing-in-africa-but (accessed February 28, 2016). In this article, the Church claims over 500,000 African members in 1,600 congregations—a twenty-fold increase from 1985—but demographer Matt Martinich challenges claims of "exponential" growth, claiming more modest membership increases in Ghana, Nigeria, the Democratic Republic of the Congo, and Cote d'Ivoire—the countries "where more than half of African Mormons reside"—with an incredibly minor presence in the rest of Sub-Saharan Africa.

Notes - Origins

09 "Statistics: World," *Temples of The Church of Jesus Christ of Latter-day Saints*, http://www.ldschurchtemples.com/statistics/units/world (accessed February 25, 2013).

10 "List of Book of Mormon translations," *Wikipedia*, http://en.wikipedia.org/wiki/List_of_Book_of_Mormon_translations (accessed February 25, 2013).

11 "Book of Mormon Reaches Another Milestone: 150 Million and Counting," *Mormon Newsroom*, April 18, 2011, http://www.mormonnewsroom.org/article/book-mormon-150-million (accessed February 25, 2013).

12 Stephanie Grimes, "LDS Church announces 58 new missions," *KSL.com*, February 22, 2013, http://www.ksl.com/index.php?sid=24168317&nid=1016&title=lds-church-announces-58-new-missions&fm=home_page&s_cid=featured-1 (accessed February 25, 2013); Peggy Fletcher Stack, "From surge to slump? No, but Mormon missionary tally has dropped by 12%," *Salt Lake Tribune*, January 22, 2016, http://www.sltrib.com/lifestyle/faith/3450134-155/from-surge-to-slump-no-but (accessed January 22, 2016). Stack traces missionary numbers as beginning at 58,000 in 2012, 85,000+ at the end of 2014, and 75,000 in January 2016, a 12% drop from the 2014 high but 30% increase from 2012, before the age change. Earlier, in 2013, Elder L. Tom Perry of the Quorum of the Twelve Apostles indicated that Church leaders estimate there would be as many as 80,000 full-time missionaries serving by July 2014, though this number was reached months earlier. L. Tom Perry, untitled speech in multi-stake conference for the New England area, May 19, 2013; "Facts and Statistics: Worldwide Statistics," *Mormon Newsroom*, http://www.mormonnewsroom.org/facts-and-stats (accessed March 29, 2014). For more information on the international growth of the Church see *Cumorah.com* at http://www.cumorah.com and BYU's *Global Mormonism Project* at http://globalmormonism.byu.edu, which includes excellent introductory bibliographies for eight major geographical regions. See also footnotes 27 and 32.

13 The Church is presided over by a President with two counselors who together comprise a quorum of the First Presidency (see D&C 107:22 and 124:124-126); the President alone is considered the Church's Presiding High Priest and the sole person responsible for and capable of receiving revelation for the entire Church (D&C 81:2; 107:64-66, 91-92), but his counselors are also considered prophets; Peter, James, and John are often seen as the New Testament prototype for this modern-day presidency. Underneath the First Presidency is a Quorum of Twelve Apostles patterned on the group of Jesus' closest disciples in the New Testament, who are also sustained as prophets (Matt. 10:1-4; Mark 3:14-19; Mark 6:7; Luke 6:13-16; D&C 18:26-38; 102:30-31; 107:23, 33, 35, 58). Next in authority comes the quorum(s) of seventy (Luke 10:1, 17) who are not sustained as prophets but are still considered general—that is, global—authorities of the Church (D&C 107:25-26, 34). As of 2012 there were eight quorums of seventy with a total of 305 members, some considered global and some area-specific authorities, although scripture allows for up to seven global quorums of seventy members each (D&C 107:93-98). "Quorums of the Seventy," *LDS.org*, http://www.lds.org/church/leaders/quorums-of-the-seventy?lang=eng (accessed February 15, 2013); "List of area seventies of The Church of Jesus Christ of Latter-day Saints," *Wikipedia*, http://en.wikipedia.org/wiki/List_of_area_seventies_of_The_Church_of_Jesus_Christ_of_Latter-day_Saints (accessed February 15, 2013). Both apostles and seventies—as well as the Church's larger cadre of young male full-time missionaries—are

generally referred to by the title "Elder," referring to an office in the priesthood.

14 "Mormon Women Leaders Announce International Board Members," *Mormon Newsroom*, February 7, 2014, http://www.mormonnewsroom.org/article/mormon-auxiliary-leaders-announce-international-board-members (accessed February 7, 2014). For a discussion of internal and external tensions as Mormonism expands internationally, see Lawrence A. Young, "Confronting Turbulent Environments: Issues in the Organizational Growth and Globalization of Mormonism," *Contemporary Mormonism: Social Science Perspectives*, ed. Marie Cornwall, Tim B. Heaton, and Lawrence A. Young (Urbana: University of Illinois Press, 2001), 43-63.

15 Matt Martinich, "Overall LDS Growth Trend Case Studies," *Cumorah.com*, http://cumorah.com/index.php?target=view_case_studies&story_id=474&cat_id=8 (accessed January 3, 2017).

16 "List of Latter Day Saints: Politicians outside the United States," *Wikipedia*, http://en.wikipedia.org/wiki/List_of_Latter_Day_Saints#Politicians_outside_the_United_States (accessed May 28, 2013).

17 For Samaké, see Katrina Hoije, "Mormon makes bid to lead Muslim-majority Mali out of post-war chaos," *Christian Science Monitor*, May 24, 2013, http://www.csmonitor.com/World/Africa/2013/0524/Mormon-makes-bid-to-lead-Muslim-majority-Mali-out-of-post-war-chaos?nav=87-frontpage-entryNineItem (accessed May 28, 2013). The former Prime Minister Ibrahim Boubacar Keita won in a two-round runoff election. "Keita wins Mali election after Cisse concedes," *Al Jazeera*, August 12, 2013, http://www.aljazeera.com/news/africa/2013/08/201381222306327330.html (accessed August 12, 2013); Abby Stevens, "Mali Mormon presidential hopeful loses election," *Deseret News*, August 2, 2013, http://www.deseretnews.com/article/865584005/Mali-Mormon-presidential-hopeful-loses-election.html?pg=all (accessed August 12, 2013). For Ardern, see Lydia Smith, "New Zealand prime minister Jacinda Ardern left Mormon church to support LGBT rights," *Independent*, October 21, 2017, http://www.independent.co.uk/news/world/australasia/new-zealand-prime-minister-jacinda-ardern-quit-mormon-church-lgbt-rights-a8012676.html (accessed November 18, 2017); Ally Foster, "Why the New Zealand Prime Minister left the Mormon church," *News.com.au*, October 23, 2017, http://www.news.com.au/finance/work/leaders/why-the-new-zealand-prime-minister-left-the-mormon-church/news-story/45fe1c1039e-7a62ef73dfc1871a2848d (accessed November 18, 2017). Prince Ata of Tonga, the third son of King Tupou VI, was baptized in 2015, but he is several steps removed from inheriting the throne.

18 "Facts and Statistics: Worldwide Statistics," *Mormon Newsroom*, http://www.mormonnewsroom.org/facts-and-statistics (accessed December 15, 2017). These members meet in 30,304 congregations. This number is produced by the Church and is occasionally contested by outside observers, as noted below.

19 "International LDS Database: United States," *Cumorah.com*, http://www.cumorah.com/index.php?target=main&wid=231 (accessed February 26, 2013); "Jewish Population Statistics," *Mandell L. Berman Institute North American Jewish Data Bank*, http://www.jewishdatabank.org/study.asp?sid=90194&tp=6 (accessed February 26, 2013); Ner LeElef, "World Jewish Population," *SimpleToRemember.com*, http://www.simpleto-

remember.com/vitals/world-jewish-population.htm (accessed February 26, 2013).

20 "17 Mormons will serve in next Congress," *The Salt Lake Tribune*, November 16, 2012, http://www.sltrib.com/sltrib/politics/55286186-90/congress-elect-faith-idaho. html.csp (accessed February 23, 2013).

21 Peter Applebome, "A Mormon Spectacle, Way Off Broadway," *New York Times*, July 13, 2011, http://www.nytimes.com/2011/07/14/nyregion/hill-cumorah-pageant-of-fers-mormon-spectacle-way-off-broadway.html?pagewanted=1&_r=1&ref=todays-paper (accessed July 31, 2011); Walter Kirn, "The Mormon Moment," *Newsweek*, June 5, 2011, http://www.newsweek.com/mormon-moment-67951 (accessed July 31, 2011); Walter Kirn, "Mormons Rock!," *Newsweek*, June 13 & 20, 2011, 38-45, also available at http://www.thedailybeast.com/newsweek/2011/06/05/mormons-rock.html (accessed July 31, 2011). The title "Mormon Moment" generated much discussion among Mormons themselves; a video of one thoughtful panel discussion is at "Perspectives on the 'Mormon Moment,'" *Dialogue: A Journal of Mormon Thought*, February 27, 2013, https://www.dialoguejournal.com/2013/perspectives-on-the-mormon-moment (accessed February 27, 2013).

22 Neil J. Young, "Is the Mormon Moment Over?," *Huffington Post*, November 11, 2012, http://www.huffingtonpost.com/neil-j-young/is-the-mormon-moment-over_b_2160270.html (accessed February 11, 2014); Cristine Hutchison-Jones, "Romney Lost. Is the Mormon Moment Over? And What Would That Mean, Anyway?," *Juvenile Instructor,* November 7, 2012, http://www.juvenileinstructor.org/romney-lost-is-the-mormon-moment-over-and-what-would-that-mean-anyway (accessed March 29, 2014); Electa Draper, "LDS scholars: 'Mormon moment' could expand into cultural shift," *Denver Post*, December 23, 2012, http://www.denverpost.com/ci_22247809/lds-scholars-mormon-moment-could-expand-into-cultural (accessed March 29, 2014); Joseph Walker, "Are LDS learning to swim in the mainstream in this post-Mormon moment?," *Deseret News*, August 7, 2013, http://www.deseretnews.com/article/865584281/Are-LDS-learning-to-swim-in-the-mainstream-in-this-post-Mormon-moment.html (accessed March 29, 2014); Linda Davidson, "What lies ahead for the Mormons?," *Washington Post*, November 8, 2012, http://www.faithstreet.com/onfaith/2012/11/08/what-lies-ahead-for-the-mormons/12096 (accessed March 29, 2014); Michael Otterson, "More than a 'Mormon moment,'" *Washington Post*, March 15, 2012, http://www.faithstreet.com/onfaith/2012/03/15/more-than-a-mormon-moment/11006 (accessed March 29, 2014); and Brittany Karford Rogers, "Mitt Romney and the Mormon Moment," *BYU Magazine*, Winter 2013, http://magazine.byu.edu/?act=view&a=3112 (accessed March 29, 2014), which includes a four-minute video of scholars discussing the Mormon moment's ramifications. A wave of disciplinary proceedings within the Church against several heterodox members, primarily Kate Kelly and John Dehlin, resulted in many commentators pronouncing that "the era of Mormon PR victories" was definitively ended. Jim Dalrymple II, "The Mormon Moment Is Finally (Really) Over," *BuzzFeed*, June 12, 2014, http://www.buzzfeed.com/jimdalrympleii/the-mormon-moment-is-finally-really-over (accessed July 26, 2014); Cadence Woodland, "The End of the 'Mormon Moment,'" *New York Times*, July 14, 2014, http://www.nytimes.com/2014/07/15/opinion/the-end-of-the-mormon-moment.html (accessed July 26, 2014). For a brief overview of some of the Church members threatened with discipline see Laurie Goodstein, "Mormons Say Critical Online Comments Draw Threats From Church," *New York Times*, June 18, 2014, http://www.nytimes.

com/2014/06/19/us/critical-online-comments-put-church-status-at-risk-mormons-say.html?smid=fb-share&_r=2 (accessed June 20, 2014).

23 There is evidence, however, that increased exposure has not resulted in increased acceptance. A Pew Research survey in spring 2014 found that only 48% of Americans viewed Mormons "warmly," below Jews (63%), Catholics (62%), Evangelicals (61%), Buddhists (53%), and Hindus (50%), but above atheists (41%), and Muslims (40%). One scholar of religion expressed surprise that Pew found "there hasn't been any real change in views on Mormons in spite of the [hit Broadway play] 'The Book of Mormon' and Mitt Romney's presidential campaign and all the attention to the so-called 'Mormon Moment.'" "Religion survey: Jews score highest, Muslims lowest," *Salt Lake Tribune*, July 16, 2014, http://www.sltrib.com/sltrib/news/58190745-78/groups-evangelicals-jews-pew.html.csp?page=1 (accessed July 16, 2014). This verified results from an earlier Pew survey that indicated very little shift in the public perception of Mormonism during Romney's campaign. Joanna Brooks, "The 'Mormon Moment' Yields . . . Not So Much," *Religion Dispatches*, December 19, 2012, http://religiondispatches.org/the-mormon-moment-yields-not-so-much (accessed December 23, 2012).

24 Terry Lindvall, *Sanctuary Cinema: Origins of the Christian Film Industry* (New York: New York University Press, 2007), 19.

25 Michael Hicks, *Mormonism and Music: A History* (Urbana and Chicago: University of Illinois Press, 1989), 10-11.

26 The full text of the thirteenth Article of Faith reads: "We believe in being honest, true, chaste, benevolent, virtuous, and in doing good to all men; indeed, we may say that we follow the admonition of Paul—We believe all things, we hope all things, we have endured many things, and hope to be able to endure all things. If there is anything virtuous, lovely, or of good report or praiseworthy, we seek after these things." The "admonition of Paul" is found in Philippians 4:8, where he makes a similar appeal to the virtuous and lovely.

27 John S. Tanner, "Shakespeare Among the Saints," *Journal of Mormon History* 32:1 (Spring 2006), 82-115; Leland H. Monson, "Shakespeare in Early Utah," *Improvement Era* 63:10 (October 1960), 718-721, 763-764.

28 Terryl L. Givens, *People of Paradox: A History of Mormon Culture* (Oxford: Oxford University Press, 2007), xiv.

29 Roger K. Petersen and Carole Reid Burr, "A Genius for Beauty: Swimsuit Designer Rose Marie Reid," *Mormons and Popular Culture: The Global Influence of an American Phenomenon*, Vol. 1, ed. J. Michael Hunter (Santa Barbara: Praeger Publishers, 2013), 225. Reid, who in the 1950s redesigned the Mormon undergarment for those who had received ordinances in the temple, exhibited her progressive tendencies by advocating for a two-piece women's garment, a radical idea that was not accepted by conservative Church authorities until two years after her death in 1978 (p. 224). Throughout the history of the Church the temple garment has proven an interesting locus for conservative-progressive tension, with impassioned—though often whispered—arguments for or against innovations like two-piece sets rather than full-body suits and short sleeves and legs replacing the original long versions. The debate continues today, as

seen in a recent thoughtful article and discussion highlighting numerous issues with women's garments that advocates for accurate sizing, more variety, better nursing and pregnancy garments, and even camisole straps. Angela C, "Female Garments: The Underwear Business," *By Common Consent*, May 13, 2013, http://bycommonconsent. com/2013/05/13/female-garments-the-underwear-business (accessed May 14, 2013). After soliciting extensive public feedback the Church announced new sizing and styles in women's garments in the fall of 2015, though not with as extreme changes as proposed by Angela C. "New Sizing for Women's Garments," *Ensign*, September 2015, https://www.lds.org/ensign/2015/09/news-of-the-church/new-sizing-for-womens-garments?lang=eng (accessed April 11, 2016).

30 "BYU Bans Rodin Nudes," *Sunstone* 20:4 (November-December 1997), 76.

31 University President and Church Seventy Merrill J. Bateman, who had earlier described *Monument to Balzac* as a "nude male in the act of self-gratification," took ultimate responsibility for the decision. Administrators' public statements emphasized the sculptures weren't censored because they were nude but because they were undignified; *USA Today* quoted museum director Campbell Gray as saying, "We have felt that the nature of those works are such that the viewer will be concentrating on them in a way that is not good for us." The student demonstration, extremely rare at an institution that barely protested against Vietnam or for civil rights, was criticized by Bateman and Church President Gordon B. Hinckley. "BYU Bans Rodin Nudes," 76-77. For the *Bacchae*, or *Bakkhai*, event, see *Steve Heimoff*, "Wine, sex and Mormons: an inquiry," Steve Heimoff, September 25, 2009, http://www.steveheimoff.com/index. php/2009/09/25/wine-sex-and-the-mormons-a-rant (accessed April 9, 2016). As this more recent example shows, these issues remain salient in Mormon culture: in spring 2013 residents of the small town of Coalville, Utah started putting clothes on a public statue of a female figure that they deemed immodest. The sculptor Mitt Neely reportedly saw this as a form of public engagement with his work and soon the city government institutionalized the practice by having residents apply for a weeklong timeslot to dress the statue. Carole Mikita, "Coalville residents dress up 'immodest' statue," *KSL.com*, June 3, 2013, http://www.ksl.com/?sid=25451096&nid=148&title=-coalville-residents-dress-up-immodest-statue&fm=home_page&s_cid=featured-2 (accessed June 4, 2013). Neil LaBute, who graduated from BYU in 1985, opened his play-turned-film *The Shape of Things* (2001; 2003) with a discussion of covering sculptural anatomy, and both the opening scene and entire play/film are an exploration of what is appropriate in art, particularly at a religious university modeled on BYU.

32 Hicks, *Mormonism and Music*, 18-20; see also p. 21-34. For additional sources on Mormon hymnody, see George D. Pyper, *Stories of Latter-day Saint Hymns, Their Authors and Composers* (Salt Lake City: Deseret Book Company, 1939); J. Spencer Cornwall, *Stories of Our Mormon Hymns*, 2nd ed. (Salt Lake City: Deseret Book Company, 1963); and Karen Lynn Davidson, *Our Latter-day Hymns: The Stories and the Messages* (Salt Lake City: Deseret Book Company, 1988). These and other resources on Mormon music are included in Michael Hicks, "The Performing Arts and Mormonism: An Introductory Guide," *Mormon Americana: A Guide to Sources and Collections in the United States*, ed. David J. Whittaker (Provo: BYU Studies Monographs, 1995), 540-546.

33 Because several original hymns had no attribution, Smith's biographers Linda King Newell and Valeen Tippetts Avery believe she may have been the author. Linda

King Newell and Valeen Tippetts Avery, *Mormon Enigma: Emma Hale Smith*, 2nd ed. (Urbana and Chicago: University of Illinois Press, 1994), 57.

34 Hicks, *Mormonism and Music*, 10; see Newell and Avery, *Mormon Enigma*, 57-58, for the fact Smith included forty-two extant hymns.

35 Hicks, *Mormonism and Music*, 116, 140. In one instance from the twentieth century the tension between conservatism and progressivism played out behind closed doors via a controversy over installing electric rather than bellows-based pipe organs in Mormon chapels. In this case, engaging with the modern invention of electric organs would prove cost-effective and practical but was opposed by musicians, particularly those on the Church's own Music Committee, who thought the timbre and solemnity of a traditional pipe organ could not be matched by an electronic instrument or pianos. By the 1960s cost won the day, however, and today any Mormon meetinghouse large enough to have an organ is outfitted with the electronic variety. Hicks, *Mormonism and Music*, 133, 141.

36 See, for instance, Hicks's chapter on "The Immigrant Professors," *Mormonism and Music*, 91-108; also Hicks, "The Performing Arts and Mormonism," 543-544, which lists other sources, current through 1995, on most of these musicians and the Tabernacle Choir and organ. A more recent source on the choir is Heidi S. Swinton, *America's Choir: A Commemorative Portrait of the Mormon Tabernacle Choir* (Menomonee Falls, Wisconsin: Shadow Mountain and Mormon Tabernacle Choir, 2004).

37 David Kent Jacobs, "The History of Motion Pictures Produced by The Church of Jesus Christ of Latter-day Saints" (master's thesis, Brigham Young University Dept. of Dramatic Arts, 1967), 17; Richard Alan Nelson, "The History of Utah Film: An Introductory Essay," unpublished paper for BYU course Communications 691R (1973), f 3-4. The American Theater, which is discussed in Chapter 2, was located at 241 South Main Street in Salt Lake City. "American Theater (Granada Theatre)," *Utah Theaters*, http://utahtheaters.info/TheaterMain.asp?ID=63 (accessed May 18, 2013). McClellan's role at the American is discussed in greater detail in Chapter 2.

38 Hicks, "The Performing Arts and Mormonism," 545.

39 This is a major theme running throughout Hicks's *Mormonism and Music*. His chapter on evolving Mormon rhetoric toward jazz and rock, for instance, is particularly pertinent, showing how hardline stances against certain styles softened in subsequent decades as new (threatening) styles emerged; p. 189-208.

40 Hicks, *Mormonism and Music*, 79. See p. 78-80 for the use of fiddle music with dances, and, for a pioneer fiddler's full autobiography, Kenner C. Kartchner, *Frontier Fiddler: The Life of a Northern Arizona Pioneer*, ed. Larry V. Shumway (Tucson: University of Arizona Press, 1990).

41 Hicks, *Mormonism and Music*, 63, for instance, states that by 1853 fiddles had joined the Deseret Dramatic Association's orchestra, the "more or less official band" of the Church and Utah Territory. See also Hicks, "The Performing Arts and Mormonism," 541.

42 Michael Hicks, "Mormons and the Music Industry," *Mormons and Popular Culture*,

vol. 2, 199, footnote 34. Kimball played in northern Arizona while Hunter, who organized his own five-piece orchestra Hunter's Croonaders in 1924, played in and around Boise, Idaho, including 53 gigs in 1925 and a two-month Oriental cruise in 1927. Eleanor Knowles, *Howard W. Hunter* (Salt Lake City: Deseret Book Company, 1994), 45-46. For Paul Whiteman's performance, see "Paul's Welcome," *Variety*, March 4, 1925, 41, http://www.archive.org/stream/variety78-1925-03#page/n39/mode/2up (accessed May 8, 2014). Quinn, *The Mormon Hierarchy: Extensions of Power*, 782 lists other popular musicians who played in the Tabernacle starting on April 1, 1884: opera singer Adelina Patti, "Ernestine Schumann-Heink, Lili Pons, Ignace Padewerski, John Philip Sousa, Fritz Kreisler, Vladimir Horowitz, Artur Rubinstein, Marian Anderson Yehudi Menuhin, Van Cliburn, and others."

43 *Daily Universe*, October 5, 1971, quoted in Hicks, "Mormons and the Music Industry," 192. Since *Saturday's Warrior* premiered in 1974 and *My Turn on Earth* in 1977 it should be noted that Elder Benson was not speaking about these works specifically.

44 Thomas L. Kane, quoted in Daniel Tyler, *A Concise History of the Mormon Battalion in the Mexican War, 1846-47* (Salt Lake City: n.p. 1881), 82, and in Givens, *People of Paradox*, 136.

45 Pioneer Helen Mar Kimball told "how her company dealt with the chill of nights on the plains: 'Everyone danced to amuse ourselves as well as to keep our blood in proper circulation.'" Bowman, *The Mormon People*, 102.

46 Quinn, *The Mormon Hierarchy: Extensions of Power*, 748.

47 This phenomenon is not new. In the early twentieth century, "despite the chaperoning of Mormon elders, 'belly-rubbing' dances such as the tango, the turkey trot, the bunny hug, and the grizzly bear entered Latter-day Saint social gatherings." Hicks, *Mormonism and Music*, 189.

48 Georganna Ballif Arrington, "Dance in Mormonism: The Dancingest Denomination," *Focus on Dance X: Religion and Dance*, ed. Dennis J. Fallon and Mary Jane Wolbers (Reston, Virginia: National Dance Association, 1982), 31-35; Georganne Ballif Arrington, "Mormonism: The Dancingest Denomination," *Century 2*, vol. 5 (Fall 1980), 42-56; Phyllis C. Jacobson, "Dance," *Encyclopedia of Mormonism*, Vol. 1, 354-355; Larry V. Shumway, "Dancing the Buckles Off Their Shoes in Pioneer Utah," *BYU Studies* 37:3 (1997-98), 6-50; Leona Holbrook, "Dancing as an Aspect of Early Mormon and Utah Culture," *BYU Studies* 16:1 (1975), 1-20; Givens, *People of Paradox*, 131-137, 261-263; Hicks, *Mormonism and Music*, 74-90. Hicks gives numerous other sources in "The Performing Arts and Mormonism," 546-547. In contrast to this image of dance's long-lasting stature in Mormonism, BYU dance professor Pat Debenham has said that, like ballet, "modern dance is just beginning to find its voice. I think that as a Mormon art form, it's just starting to get its feet underneath itself, which seems to be an appropriate metaphor to use here." J. Scott Bronson, "The Sacredness of Moving in Our Bodies: An Interview with Pat Debenham," *Irreantum: A Review of Mormon Literature and Film* 8:2 (2006), 159.

49 Carol A. Edison, "Material Culture: An Introduction and Guide to Mormon Ver-

nacular," *Mormon Americana*, 309; Craig D. Galli, "Building Zion: The Latter-day Saint Legacy of Urban Planning," *BYU Studies* 44:1 (2005), 111-136; Richard H. Jackson, "The Mormon Village: Genesis and Antecedents of the City of Zion Plan," *BYU Studies* 17:2 (1977), 1-14.

50 Edison, "Material Culture," 310-313. For a revisionist history on this point, including a discussion of sacred architecture beyond the Kirtland and Nauvoo temples, see W. Ray Luce, "Building the Kingdom of God: Mormon Architecture before 1847," *BYU Studies* 30:2 (Spring 1990), 33-45.

51 Marjorie Hopkins Bennion, "The Rediscovery of William Weeks' Nauvoo Temple Drawings," *Mormon Historical Studies* 3:1 (2002), 73-90; J. Earl Arrington, "William Weeks, Architect of the Nauvoo Temple," *BYU Studies* 19:3 (Spring 1979), 337-359; see also Don F. Colvin, *Nauvoo Temple: A Story of Faith* (American Fork, UT: Covenant Communications, 2002) and Heidi S. Swinton, *Sacred Stone: The Temple at Nauvoo* (American Fork, UT: Covenant Communications, 2002).

52 Angell, "Truman O. Angell, 1810-1887"; Allen D. Roberts, "More on Utah's Unknown Pioneer Architects: Their Lives and Works," *Sunstone* 1:3 (1976), 42-56.

53 Nathan D. Grow, "One Masterpiece, Four Masters: Reconsidering the Authorship of the Salt Lake Tabernacle," *Journal of Mormon History* 32:3 (Fall 2005), 171. The whole article, p. 170-197, discusses the building's design process in detail. For a complete history of the Salt Lake Tabernacle see Elwin C. Robison, *Gathering as One: The History of the Mormon Tabernacle in Salt Lake City* (Provo: BYU Press, 2013); Stewart L. Grow, *A Tabernacle in the Desert* (Salt Lake City: Deseret Book Company, 1958); and Paul L. Anderson, "Tabernacle, Salt Lake City," *Encyclopedia of Mormonism*, Vol. 4, 1433-1434.

54 Quinn, *The Mormon Hierarchy: Extensions of Power*, 855; Paul L. Anderson, "Mormon Moderne: Latter-day Saint Architecture, 1925-1945," *Journal of Mormon History* 9 (1982), 71-84; Brad Westwood, "Architectural Records," *Mormon Americana*, 362. For a compendium of Mormon chapel architecture, often featuring works from this period, see Jonathan Kland's blog *LDS Architecture*, http://ldsarchitecture.wordpress.com (accessed February 3, 2013). For an in-depth study of a single representative building, see Paul L. Anderson, "A Jewel in the Gardens of Paradise: The Art and Architecture of the Hawai'i Temple," *BYU Studies* 39:4 (2000), 164-182.

55 Westwood, "Architectural Records," 382.

56 See Martha Sonntag Bradley, "'The Church and Colonel Saunders': Mormon Standard Plan Architecture," (master's thesis, Brigham Young University Dept. of History, 1981). On p. 131-132 she writes: "Many saw in the use of worldwide standardization an alarming insensitivity to local cultures and styles. The cry of regionalism was common among those who recognized the incongruity of an American Chapel in Western Samoa or some other foreign setting . . . With the emphasis on function it was natural for the [building] department to consider regionalism a less important priority and, as in the case of a chapel in Japan, to completely miss the significance of local design elements." Bradley's title comes from the blithely ethnocentric statement of one anonymous Church member (p. 134) who described Mormon chapels like American comfort food: "Coming upon a Mormon meetinghouse in a strange town is like finding your

favorite food franchise when you are traveling. Once you've located the church and Colonel Saunders it's as if you never left home." One of Bradley's earlier studies is currently available online: Martha Sonntag Bradley, "The Cloning of Mormon Architecture," *Dialogue: A Journal of Mormon Thought* 14:1 (Spring 1981), 20-31, available at http://www.dialoguejournal.com/wp-content/uploads/sbi/articles/Dialogue_V14N01_22.pdf. The Church has made examples of meetinghouse standard plans available at http://aec.ldschurch.org/aec/standard_plans. It should be noted that temples are sometimes more prone to incorporate local motifs, as seen in the details of the Laie, Hawaii (1919) and Mexico City (1983) temples. Anderson, "A Jewel in the Gardens of Paradise."

57 See also Givens, *People of Paradox*, 101-116, 241-252; Jonathan Kland, "Mormon Architecture," *By Common Consent*, January 30, 2012, http://bycommonconsent.com/2012/01/30/mormon-architecture (accessed May 21, 2013); Richard W. Jackson, *Places of Worship: 150 Years of Latter-day Saint Architecture* (Provo: Religious Studies Center, Brigham Young University, 2003); Franklin T. Ferguson, "Architecture," *Encyclopedia of Mormonism*, Vol. 1, 63-65; and, for a comprehensive list of sources through 1995, Westwood, "Architectural Records," 336-405.

58 This temple is part of a complex at 16th and Vine Streets, primarily designed by the New York firm of Robert A. M. Stern, that was announced in February 2014. The temple itself incorporates elements of historic Philadelphia such as the Independence Hall clock tower, but the overall complex, which includes a standard-plan meetinghouse and 250-unit 32-story apartment tower has been highly criticized as an inappropriate use of Church funds and for its bland and imposing design. Inga Saffron, "Changing Skyline: Mormon development combines civic-mindedness, awful architecture," *Philly.com*, February 22, 2014, http://articles.philly.com/2014-02-22/entertainment/47563073_1_mormons-tower-architecture (accessed April 2, 2014).

59 Though the only (somewhat oblique) Biblical reference to baptism for the dead comes from Paul in 1 Corinthians 15:29, for their oxen-based font Smith and Weeks followed the Old Testament pattern of Solomon's "molten sea" found in 1 Kings 7:23-26—a Christianization of the Old Testament typical of Smith's theology.

60 Richard G. Oman and Robert O. Davis, *Images of Faith: Art of the Latter-day Saints* (Salt Lake City: Deseret Book Company, 1995), 5. Suppositions that the Moroni statue may have been preserved as a weathervane in Cincinnati have been largely disproved.

61 Martha Sonntag Bradley, "Folk Art," *Encyclopedia of Mormonism*, Vol. 2, 517; Edison, "Material Culture," 322-324.

62 Thomas Carter, "Building Zion: Folk Architecture in the Mormon Settlements of Utah's Sanpete Valley, 1849-1890," (Ph.D. dissertation, Indiana University, 1984), which examines the Scandinavian tradition in much Mormon furniture; Richard G. Oman, "Sources for Mormon Visual Arts," *Mormon Americana*, 647-649; Oman and Davis, *Images of Faith*, 16-19; Edison, "Material Culture," 317-319, and, for a brief discussion of homemade pioneer toys, 322.

63 Oman and Davis, *Images of Faith*, 18.

64 Oman, "Sources for Mormon Visual Arts," 609-610. Ramsay, whose name is occasionally spelled Ramsey, is also remembered for sculptures at the Beehive House, the post and banister at the Devereaux House in downtown Salt Lake, and a bas-relief horse head on a home in Snowflake, Arizona.

65 See footnote 9 of the Introduction.

66 Orvill Paller, "I Have a Question," *Ensign*, October 1990, https://www.lds.org/ensign/1990/10/i-have-a-question?lang=eng (accessed April, 4, 2016).

67 Oman and Davis, *Images of Faith*, 52.

68 Ibid., 46-47, 50-53, 83-89; Oman, "Sources for Mormon Visual Arts," 608-614.

69 Oman, "Sources for Mormon Visual Arts," 614-620. In 2002 Rocky Hansen and I co-directed a short documentary about Smith and the sesquicentennial of the Church in Denmark entitled *Till We Meet Again: The Story of Kristina*.

70 Eugene England, "Mormon Literature: Progress and Prospects," *Mormon Americana: A Guide to Sources and Collections in the United States*, ed. David J. Whittaker (Provo: BYU Studies Monographs, 1995), 462. This entire essay (p. 455-505), except the appendix (p. 483-493), is online at http://mldb.byu.edu/progress.htm. For an earlier version, see his "The Dawning of a Brighter Day: Mormon Literature after 150 Years," *BYU Studies* 22:2 (Spring 1982), 131-160. It was originally given as a Charles C. Redd Address at BYU in February 1980 and was published as part of the Charles C. Redd Lecture Series, No. 13, *Mormonism after 150 Years*.

71 England, "Mormon Literature," 462-465.

72 Young's full comments read: "Novel reading—is it profitable? I would rather that persons read novels than read nothing. There are women in our community, twenty, thirty, forty, fifty, and sixty years of age, who would rather read a trifling, lying novel than read history, the Book of Mormon, or any other useful print. Such women are not worth their room. It would do no good for me to say, Don't read them; read on, and get the spirit of lying in which they are written, and then lie on until you find yourselves in hell. If it would do any good, I would advise you to read books that are worth reading; read reliable history, and search wisdom out of the best books you can procure. How I would be delighted if our young men would do this, instead of continually studying nonsense." Brigham Young, "Necessity of Paying Due Attention to Temporal Duties, &c," *Journal of Discourses* 9:173 (January 26, 1862). Richard Cracroft, one the founding scholars of Mormon literature, opens an article on Young's attitude toward fiction by noting he "dismissed novels as 'nonsense,' called reading them a waste of life, and reminded the Saints that they have more important ways to spend their time—that, like the daughters of Zion, they 'have got cows to milk instead of novels to read.'" The rest of the article delves deeper into the nuances and causes of Young's beliefs. Richard H. Cracroft, "'Cows to Milk Instead of Novels to Read': Brigham Young, Novel Reading, and Kingdom Building," *BYU Studies* 40:2 (2001), 103.

73 Matthew Durrant and Neal E. Lambert, "From Foe to Friend: The Mormon Embrace of Fiction," *Utah Historical Quarterly* 50:4 (Fall 1982), 329; England, "Mormon Literature," 465. After the completion of the transcontinental railroad in 1869 cheap dime

novels inundated the Mormons and may have prompted an increase in anti-literary comments like these.

74 Orson F. Whitney, "Home Literature," *A Believing People: Literature of the Latter-day Saints*, ed. Richard H. Cracroft and Neal E. Lambert (Salt Lake City: Bookcraft, 1979), 129-133. The rise of Home Literature is discussed, among other sources, in Durrant and Lambert, "From Foe to Friend," 325-339, and England, "Mormon Literature," 465-469. One in-depth biographical study is Richard H. Cracroft, "Nephi, Seer of Modern Times: The Home Literature Novels of Nephi Anderson," *BYU Studies* 25:2 (1985), 1-13.

75 Edward A. Geary, "Mormondom's Lost Generation: The Novelists of the 1940s," *BYU Studies* 18:1 (Fall 1977), 89-98; England, "Mormon Literature," 469-471, 487-488.

76 England, "Mormon Literature," 471-482, 488-489. Articles on Mormon literature are far too numerous to list, but for a general overview of various issues and genres in fiction see Gideon Burton and Neal Kramer, "The State of Mormon Literature and Criticism," *Dialogue* 32:3 (Fall 1999), 1-12; Eugene England, "Beyond 'Jack Fiction': Recent Achievement in the Mormon Novel," *BYU Studies* 28:2 (Spring 1988), 97-109; Toni Elise Pilcher, "Mormon Contributions to Young Adult Literature," *Mormons and Popular Culture*, Vol. 2, 23-37; Christopher Kimball Bigelow, "Orthodox vs. Literary: An Overview of Mormon Fiction," *Mormons and Popular Culture*, Vol. 2, 51-63; John Bennion, "Popular and Literary Mormon Novels: Can Weyland and Whipple Dance Together in the House of Fiction?," *BYU Studies* 37:1 (1997-98), 159-182; and Rick Walton, "Mormon Picture Book Authors," *Mormons and Popular Culture*, Vol. 2, 65-79. The Association for Mormon Letters, founded in 1976, hosts an annual conference and promotes Mormon literature in other ways; its website is at http://www.aml-online.org and blog *Dawning of a Brighter Day* is at http://blog.mormonletters.org. I discussed the relationship between Mormon film and literature in "LDS Cinema and LDS Literature: Kid Brother or Two-Ton Gorilla?," a presentation at the 2006 Annual Conference for the Association for Mormon Letters, Utah Valley University, February 25, 2006.

77 England, "Mormon Literature," 460.

78 Ibid., 477.

79 *The Mormon Archipelago* at http://www.ldsblogs.org is one of the most comprehensive gateways into the Bloggernacle. The specific sites mentioned in the text are at http://bycommonconsent.com, http://timesandseasons.org, http://www.motleyvision.org, http://www.feministmormonhousewives.org, http://www.modernmormonmen.com, and http://www.juvenileinstructor.org.

80 One gateway to these blogs is at http://www.mormonmommyblogs.com. For two perspectives on Mormon mommy blogs from non-Mormon readers see Emily Matchar, "Why I can't stop reading Mormon housewife blogs," *Salon*, January 15, 2011, http://www.salon.com/2011/01/15/feminist_obsessed_with_mormon_blogs (accessed June 2, 2013) and Elizabeth Orpina, "Column: Mormon mommy blogs," *The California Aggie*, October 11, 2012, http://www.theaggie.org/2012/10/11/column-mormon-mommy-blogs (accessed June 2, 2013).

81 England, "Mormon Literature," 477.

82 Joseph J. Ellis, *After the Revolution: Profiles of Early American Culture* (New York: Norton, 1979), 129, quoted in Givens, *People of Paradox*, 144.

83 Givens, *People of Paradox*, 145-146.

84 Ibid., 146; John S. Lindsay, *The Mormons and the Theatre* (Salt Lake City: n.p., 1905), 6-7; Ila Fisher Maughan, *Pioneer Theatre in the Desert* (Salt Lake City: Deseret Book Company, 1961), 8; Tanner, "Shakespeare Among the Saints," 84-86. Others histories that cover pre-Utah theater include Noel A. Carmack, "A Note on Nauvoo Theater," *BYU Studies* 34:1 (Winter 1994), 94-100; Harold I. Hansen, *A History and Influence of the Mormon Theatre from 1839-1869* (Provo: Brigham Young University Press, 1967); Preston Ray Gledhill, "Mormon Dramatic Activities" (Ph.D. dissertation, University of Wisconsin, 1950); Edmund Emil Evans, "A Historical Study of the Drama of the Latter Day Saints," (Ph.D. dissertation, University of Southern California, 1941); and William Henry Thorpe, "The Mormons and Drama," (master's thesis, Columbia University, 1921).

85 Richard L. Bushman, *Joseph Smith: Rough Stone Rolling* (New York: Vintage Books, 2005), 527.

86 Megan Sanborn Jones, "Mormons and Melodrama," *Mormons and Popular Culture*, Vol. 1, 121. See also Quinn, *The Mormon Hierarchy: Extensions of Power*, 750.

87 Quinn, *The Mormon Hierarchy: Extensions of Power*, 761.

88 Carmack, "A Note on Nauvoo Theater," 95-96; Ronald W. Walker and Alexander M. Starr, "Shattering the Vase: The Razing of the Old Salt Lake Theatre," *Utah Historical Quarterly* 57:1 (Winter 1989), 64-88; Levi Edgar Young, "A Tabernacle and a Theater in the Wilderness," *Church News*, July 30, 1938, 4; "The Spirit of the Old Theatre," *Church News*, Mar. 29, 1947, 10; "Pioneer Drama Born Century Ago in Old Social Hall," *Church News*, Dec. 27, 1952, 1; "Salt Lake Theatre Culture of the Old West," *Church News*, Mar. 7, 1959, 12; Alfred Lambourne, "Reminiscences of the Salt Lake Theatre," *Improvement Era* 15:6 (April 1912), 529-541 and 15:8 (June 1912), 696-702; Horace G. Whitney, "The Story of the Salt Lake Theatre," *Improvement Era* 18:6-9 (April-July 1915), 509-516, 580-592, 686-695, 790-804; Leland H. Monson, "Pioneer Interest in the Drama," *Improvement Era* 67:4 (April 1964), 264-265, 290, 292. For a good general history of the Utah period see Maughan, *Pioneer Theatre in the Desert*, in its entirety. For some oft-overlooked economic information on the Salt Lake Theatre, including the public-works nature of its construction and the fact patrons paid for tickets in kind such as produce, poultry, and livestock, see Leonard J. Arrington, *Great Basin Kingdom: An Economic History of the Latter-day Saints, 1830-1900*, New Edition (Urbana and Chicago: University of Illinois Press, 1958), 211-213.

89 Jones, "Mormons and Melodrama," 131-132, 141-144. Acting on stage, which was particularly encouraged for young single adults, allowed performers to feel the consequences of good and evil without literally indulging in the latter (p. 132) and was often seen as a missionary opportunity akin to going abroad to preach the gospel (also p. 132). This perspective of acting as religious service—along with literal calls from Church leaders—continues today for many who participate in the Church's pageants in Palmyra, Nauvoo, and other sites.

90 Jones, "Mormons and Melodrama," 126; Quinn, *The Mormon Hierarchy: Extensions of Power,* 750.

91 See Jones's entire article, "Mormons and Melodrama," 121-132, 141-147; pages 130-131 discuss the seating arrangement of the Salt Lake Theatre audience and how it reflected the social structure of the city, so that an actor looking at the house would see a representation, essentially, of the structure of Zion, "with the prophet at the center, family units prominently placed closest to him, with wives and single women in places of honor and single men, not yet joined in family bonds, on the peripheries." For another discussion of Mormon melodrama see Shelley T. Graham, "Dramaturgical Perspectives of the Mormon Stage," *Irreantum: A Review of Mormon Literature and Film* 8:2 (2006), 17-21.

92 Clarissa Young Spencer and Mabel Harmer, *Brigham Young at Home* (Salt Lake City: Deseret News Press, 1947), 140.

93 "The New Theatre," *Deseret News* 11:37, March 12, 1862, quoted in Jones, "Mormons and Melodrama," 129.

94 Brigham Young, "Propriety of Theatrical Amusements—Instructions Relative to Conducting Them," *Journal of Discourses* 9:245 (March 6, 1862).

95 Brigham Young, "Theatricals," *The Semi-Weekly Telegraph*, January 12, 1865, quoted in Graham, "Dramaturgical Perspectives of the Mormon Stage," 19.

96 Eric Samuelsen, "Mormon Drama," *Mormons and Popular Culture*, Vol. 1, 149-158; for a complete view of Mormon theater see Givens, *People of Paradox*, 143-156, 165-271, and Hicks, "Performing Arts and Mormonism," 547-551, which lists many additional sources; see also Eric Samuelsen, "Whither Mormon Drama? Look First to a Theatre," *BYU Studies* 35:1 (1995), 81-103 and Lael J. Woodbury, "A New Mormon Theatre," *BYU Studies* 16:1 (Autumn 1975), 85-94.

97 Richard Neitzel Holzapfel and T. Jeffery Cottle, "The City of Joseph in Focus: The Use and Abuse of Historic Photographs," *BYU Studies* 32:1, 2 (1992), 249-268. They record that later photographers to document Nauvoo included Thomas Easterly, B. H. Roberts, F. Goulty, James Ricalton, George Edward Anderson, and Harold Allen.

98 "Is this Joseph Smith?," *Runtu's Rincón*, http://runtu.wordpress.com/2008/03/20/is-this-joseph-smith (accessed June 9, 2013); Kim Marshall, *Joseph Smith Jr.: A True Photograph of the Mormon Prophet*, March 21, 2009-June 28, 2011, http://josephsmithjrphoto.blogspot.com (accessed June 9, 2013); Reed Simonsen, *Photograph Found a 20 year perspective*, 2009, http://www.photographfound.com/Photograph_Found/Welcome.html (accessed June 9, 2013); Ardis E. Parshall, "Rumor-Mongering: Joseph Smith Daguerreotype," *Times and Seasons*, March 17, 2008, http://timesandseasons.org/index.php/2008/03/rumor-mongering-joseph-smith-daguerreotype (accessed June 9, 2013); and LDS Anarchist, "Joseph Smith's Daguerreotype – An Appeal for Help," *LDS Anarchy*, March 2008, http://ldsanarchy.wordpress.com/2007/10/15/joseph-smiths-daguerrotype-an-appeal-for-help (accessed June 9, 2013). Alexander L. Baugh, "Parting the Veil: The Visions of Joseph Smith," *BYU Studies* 38:1 (1999), 22 indicates that the Church History Library in Salt Lake City considers one of these an

authentic photograph of Smith and holds it in the Charles W. Carter collection. The 48-minute documentary *Picturing Joseph* (2008), directed by Nick Galieti, explores these issues in depth.

99 Woodruff noted having his picture taken by a traveling (that is, non-Mormon) daguerreotypist named Miller on August 28, 1843, before Foster arrived in Nauvoo. Kim Marshall, "The Daguerreotype and Joseph Smith Jr.," *Joseph Smith Jr.: A True Photograph of the Mormon Prophet*, May 24, 2011, http://josephsmithjrphoto.blogspot.com/2011/05/daguerreotype-and-joseph-smith-jr.html (accessed June 9, 2013). Willard Richards and his wife and son were photographed by Foster. Reed Simonsen, "Daguerreotypy & Lucien Foster in Nauvoo," *Photograph Found a 20 year perspective*, http://www.photographfound.com/Photograph_Found/Lucien_Foster.html (accessed June 9, 2013). For the Nauvoo temple photograph and a description of the Church History Library' photography holdings, see Glenn N. Rowe, "The Historical Department and Library of the LDS Church," *Mormon Americana*, 165-167.

100 William W. Slaughter and W. Randall Dixon, "Utah Under Glass: An Introduction to Four Prominent Pioneer Photographers of 19th-century Utah," *Sunstone* 2:2 (Summer 1977), 28-39; Nelson Wadsworth, "Zion's Cameramen: Early Photographers of Utah and the Mormons," *Utah Historical Quarterly* 40:1 (Winter 1972), 24-54; Richard Neitzel Holzapfel and Thomas R. Wells, "A Superlative Image: An Original Daguerreotype of Brigham Young," *BYU Studies* 44:2 (2005), 96-102; Madeleine B. Stern, "A Rocky Mountain Book Store Savage and Ottinger of Utah," *BYU Studies* 9:2 (Winter 1969), 144-154; Oman and Davis, Images of Faith, 39.

101 Oman and Davis, *Images of Faith*, 65-68, 104-105, 108-111, 128-129; Richard Neitzel Holzapfel and T. Jeffrey Cottle, "Mormon-Related Material in Photoarchives," *Mormon Americana*, 507-508; Oman, "Sources for Mormon Visual Arts," 623. See also Mary Campbell's book, still forthcoming as of this writing, *Charles Ellis Johnson and the Erotic Mormon Image* from the University of Chicago Press, in which Campbell analyzes Johnson's 1890s photography of important Church sites as well as stereoviews of erotica.

102 See for instance James R. Swenson, "Dorothea Lange's Portrait of Utah's Great Depression," *Utah Historical Quarterly* 70:1 (Winter 2002), 39-62.

103 Colleen Whitley, "Thomas Farrar Whitley's Mission Photos of Tonga, 1935-1938," *BYU Studies* 48:1 (2009), 89-121; Rowe, "The Historical Department and Library of the LDS Church," 167.

104 Oman, "Sources for Mormon Visual Arts," 624.

105 Ibid., 623.

106 Oman and Davis, *Images of Faith*, 5-15, 20-33; Givens, *People of Paradox*, 179-186; Oman, "Sources for Mormon Visual Arts," 620-628.

107 Givens, *People of Paradox*, 325-338; Noel A. Carmack, "Mormons and American Popular Art," *Mormons and Popular Culture*, Vol. 2, 95-120; Robert T. Barrett and Susan Easton Black, "Setting a Standard in LDS Art: Four Illustrators of the Mid-Twentieth Century," *BYU Studies* 44:2 (2005), 24-80.

Notes - Origins

108 Wetzel O. Whitaker, "Pioneering with Film: A History of Church and Brigham Young University Films," unpublished manuscript, n.d. (est. 1983), L. Tom Perry Special Collections, Harold B. Lee Library, Brigham Young University, 1.

109 C. C. A. Christensen, "C. C. A. Christensen on Art from the Salt Lake City *Bikuben* February—March 1892," introduced and translated by Richard L. Jensen, *BYU Studies* 23:4 (Fall 1983), 404.

110 Oman and Davis, *Images of Faith*, 25.

111 Noel A. Carmack, "'One of the Most Interesting Seeneries That Can Be Found in Zion': Philo Dibble's Museum and Panorama," *Nauvoo Journal* Vol. 9 (Fall 1997), 25-26, also available at http://mormonhistoricsites.org/wp-content/uploads/2013/05/NJ9.2_Carmack.pdf (accessed June 19, 2013).

112 Ibid., 25; Givens, *People of Paradox*, 184-185.

113 Joseph Earl Arrington, "Panorama Paintings in the 1840s of the Mormon Temple in Nauvoo," *BYU Studies* 22:2 (Spring 1982), 1-13. The subject matter of the Mississippi was not surprising: genre painting of life along American rivers was popularized in this decade by artists like George Caleb Bingham, who exhibited his recent paintings of fur traders, gamblers, and fishermen on the Missouri River at the American Art-Union Gallery in New York City in 1845, helping launch national enthusiasm for this style of painting.

114 Ryan Tobler, "John Wesley Jones's Pantoscope of California, Nebraska, Utah, and the Mormons (1852)," *Juvenile Instructor*, May 30, 2013, http://www.juvenileinstructor.org/john-wesley-joness-pantoscope-of-california-nebraska-utah-and-the-mormons-1852 (accessed April 10, 2014).

115 Philo Dibble, "Journal of Philo Dibble, Sr.," typescript in the possession of Edwin S. Dibble, Provo, Utah, quoted in Carmack, "One of the Most Interesting Seeneries," 26.

116 Jill C. Major, "Artworks in the Celestial Room of the First Nauvoo Temple," *BYU Studies* 41:2 (2002), 58.

117 Mary J. Finley, *A History of Springville* (Springville, Utah: Art City Publishing, 1988), 58, quoted in Carmack, "One of the Most Interesting Seeneries," 32-33.

118 Carmack, "One of the Most Interesting Seeneries," 25-38, especially footnote 33 on page 36; Alfred Bush, "Mormon Americana at Princeton University," *Mormon Americana*, 285.

119 Untitled advertisement, *Salt Lake Herald*, November 10, 1881, 1, http://chroniclingamerica.loc.gov/lccn/sn85058130/1881-11-10/ed-1/seq-1 (accessed April 10, 2014).

120 Quoted in Givens, *People of Paradox*, 185.

121 Ibid., 185; see also Donna L. Poulton, *Reuben Kirkham: Pioneer Artist* (Springville, Utah: Cedar Fort, Inc., 2012).

122 Noel A. Carmack, "'A Picturesque and Dramatic History': *George Reynolds's Story of the Book of Mormon*," *BYU Studies* 47:2 (2008), 115.

123 Givens, *People of Paradox*, 188; see also Oman and Davis, *Images of Faith*, 27-29.

124 Oman, "Sources for Mormon Visual Arts," 654.

125 "The Signs of the Times," *Salt Lake Herald*, September 20, 1887, 8, http://chroniclin-gamerica.loc.gov/lccn/sn85058130/1887-09-20/ed-1/seq-8 (accessed April 10, 2014).

126 "Miscellaneous," *Salt Lake Herald*, June 14, 1892, 3, http://chroniclingamerica.loc.gov/lccn/sn85058130/1892-06-14/ed-1/seq-3 (accessed April 10, 2014).

127 The Nephites were one of the major civilizations discussed in the Book of Mormon, and the one that kept the record from which the golden plates were abridged. The civilization was named after their prophet-founder Nephi, whose autobiographical record is contained in the books of 1 and 2 Nephi. The noncontiguous books of 3 and 4 Nephi take place roughly six centuries later and are named after the first Nephi's descendent and namesake; it is in 3 Nephi that the visit of the resurrected Christ to the people of ancient America is recorded, the scene that Armitage depicted here. Other Book of Mormon peoples are the Lamanites, chief rivals of the Nephites who eventually destroy them, the Mulekites (called the people of Zarahemla in the text), who are subsumed into Nephite culture, and the Jaredites, who predate all the other groups and whose thousand-year history is recorded in the Book of Ether.

128 Oman and Davis, *Images of Faith*, 26; Oman, "Sources for Mormon Visual Arts," 622. In 1905 the *Salt Lake Tribune* reprinted a nostalgic article from the *New York Sun*, reminiscing about the days of the panorama and the loss of a golden era: "...By degrees panoramas have ceased to be a recognized form of popular entertainment. The prejudice against theaters has been effaced, scene painting has greatly improved, and the larger towns are equipped with theaters. The improvement of railroad connections has made it possible for the residents of smaller towns to obtain a fair share of theatrical novelties, and they are no longer dependent upon companies traveling, as panorama companies often did, by van from town to town. There survive a few old panorama managers who are reminiscent of the old days, and some of the old storage houses have unclaimed in some dusty corner the hundreds of yards of canvas which have delighted hundreds nightly, as laboriously they were unrolled to the accompaniment of the monotone lecturer." "Where's the Panorama?," *Salt Lake Tribune* reprinted from the *New York Sun*, February 12, 1905, magazine section, 14, http://chroniclingamerica.loc.gov/lccn/sn83045396/1905-02-12/ed-1/seq-30 (accessed April 19, 2014).

129 Carmack, "'A Picturesque and Dramatic History,'" 115-141.

130 Ardis E. Parshall, "George Reynolds and C.C.A. Christensen: Illustrated Book of Mormon Stories," *Keepapitchinin*, March 10, 2009, http://www.keepapitchinin.org/2009/03/10/george-reynolds-and-cca-christensen-illustrated-book-of-mormon-stories (accessed April 15, 2014).

131 William Clayton, *An Intimate Chronicle: The Journals of William Clayton*, ed. George D. Smith (Salt Lake City: Signature Books, 1991), 206, also cited in Major, "Artworks in the Celestial Room of the First Nauvoo Temple," 47.

132 Major, "Artworks in the Celestial Room of the First Nauvoo Temple," 47-56.

133 Ibid., 58-59.

134 Scott, "LDS Temple Murals – Pt 1 – The Beginnings of Temple Murals," March 20, 2011, *The Trumpet Stone*, http://thetrumpetstone.blogspot.com/2011/03/lds-temple-murals-pt-1-begginings-of.html (accessed June 19, 2013). The Manti temple murals were originally painted by Danquart Weggeland and C. C. A. Christensen; when these could not be restored in the 1940s new murals were painted by Minerva Teichert and Robert L. Shepherd. Doris R. Dant, "Minerva Teichert's Manti Temple Murals," *BYU Studies* 38:3 (1999), 8.

135 Paul C. Richards, "The Salt Lake Temple Infrastructure: Studying It Out in Their Minds," *BYU Studies* 36:1 (1996-97), 208-209.

136 Christopher Smith, "Costume Drama in the Early Endowment Ceremony," *Worlds Without End: A Mormon Studies Roundtable*, October 31, 2015, http://www.withoutend.org/costume-drama-early-endowment-ceremony (accessed April 5, 2016).

137 Letter from John Hafen to George Q. Cannon, March 25, 1890, quoted in Martha Elizabeth Bradley and Lowell M. Durham Jr., "John Hafen and the Art Missionaries," *Journal of Mormon History* 12 (1985), 93.

138 Oman, "Sources for Mormon Visual Arts," 629; W. V. Smith, "Your Sunday Brunch (Before-After Church) Special (#4). Utah Artist James T. Harwood, 3: Painting, Marriage and Marriage," *By Common Consent*, May 15, 2011, https://bycommonconsent.com/2011/05/15/your-sunday-brunch-before-after-church-special-5-utah-artist-james-t-harwood-3-painting-marriage-and-marriage (accessed April 9, 2016); Quinn, *The Mormon Hierarchy: Extensions of Power*, 791.

139 Givens, *People of Paradox*, 326-327.

140 John B. Fairbanks, *Diary of John B. Fairbanks*, L. Tom Perry Special Collections, Harold B. Lee Library Brigham Young University, 1, quoted in Bradley and Durham, "John Hafen and the Art Missionaries," 94.

141 Givens, *People of Paradox*, 327.

142 Bradley and Durham, "John Hafen and the Art Missionaries," 91-105; Oman and Davis, *Images of Faith*, 41-46; Givens, *People of Paradox*, 326-328; Rachel Cope, "'With God's Assistance I Will Someday Be an Artist': John B. Fairbanks's Account of the Paris Art Mission," *BYU Studies* 50:3 (2011), 133-159. The Paris-trained artists were joined on the temple murals by Danquart Weggeland, the master of landscape painting in nineteenth-century Utah, the fusing of styles making the resulting work even more intriguing; Oman and Davis, *Images of Faith*, 44.

143 Oman and Davis, *Images of Faith*, 42; Joyce Athay Janetski, "Stained Glass Windows: A Latter-day Saint Legacy," *Ensign*, January 1981, http://www.josephsmith.net/ldsorg/v/index.jsp?hideNav=1&locale=0&sourceId=d001f-c3157a6b010VgnVCM1000004d82620a____&vgnextoid=2354fccf2b7db010Vgn-

VCM1000004d82620aRCRD (accessed June 23, 2013); Joyce Athay Janetski, "Louis Comfort Tiffany: Stained Glass in Utah," UP/R 3 (1981), 20-25; and Allen D. Roberts, "Art Glass Windows in Mormon Architecture," *Sunstone* 1 (Winter 1975), 8-13.

144 Richards, "The Salt Lake Temple Infrastructure," 217-218.

145 Ibid., 213-216.

146 Levi Edgar Young, "The Angel Moroni and Cyrus Dallin," *Improvement Era* 56:4 (April 1953), 234-235, 268; Oman, "Sources for Mormon Visual Arts," 610.

147 William Cupp Darrah, *Stereo Views: A History of Stereographs in America and Their Collections* (Gettysburg: Times and News Publishing Company, 1964), 167, quoted in Richard Neitzel Holzapfel, "Stereographs and Stereotypes: A 1904 View of Mormonism," *Journal of Mormon History* 18:2 (1992), 158.

148 Holzapfel, "Stereographs and Stereotypes," 166-173; see the entire article, p. 155-176. Holzapfel gives the number of photographs included in the series as twenty-nine. The contemporary Annual American Catalog, however, lists the number as thirty-eight. *The Annual American Catalog*, 1905 (New York: Office of the Publishers Weekly, 1906), 241. In late 2017 Signature Books released a new edition of the photographs and Roberts' booklet.

149 Mike Gorrell, "Majority Owner Robert Fuller Completes 11 Year Dream with the Grand Opening of the $90 million Dolce Operated Zermatt Resort & Spa in Midway, Utah," *Hotel Online*, http://www.hotel-online.com/News/PR2006_3rd/Sep06_Zermatt.html (accessed November 11, 2017); untitled notice, *Salt Lake Herald*, July 3, 1880, 3, http://chroniclingamerica.loc.gov/lccn/sn85058130/1880-07-03/ed-1/seq-3 (accessed April 15, 2014); "Fuller's Hill," *Salt Lake Herald*, May 1, 1881, 3, http://chroniclingamerica.loc.gov/lccn/sn85058130/1881-05-01/ed-1/seq-3 (accessed April 15, 2014); "Fuller's Hill," *Salt Lake Herald*, April 29, 1882, 1, http://chroniclingamerica.loc.gov/lccn/sn85058130/1882-04-29/ed-1/seq-1 (accessed April 15, 2014). The park stretched over four or five square blocks near downtown Salt Lake City, from South Temple to 400 South and from 1000 East to 1300 East (other sources place it between South Temple and 500 South and 900 and 1400 East), and its artificial lake became the namesake of Reservoir Park. Lotta Ankle, "My Quest to Learn the Truth about Fuller's Hill Pleasure Garden," *The Villainous Arts of Practiced Voluptuaries*, https://practicedvoluptuary.wordpress.com/my-quest-to-learn-the-truth-about-fullers-hill-pleasure-garden (accessed November 11, 2017).

150 Lindvall, *Sanctuary Cinema*, 46-47.

151 For Presbyterians, see "The News in Ogden," *Salt Lake Herald*, June 5, 1889, 3, http://chroniclingamerica.loc.gov/lccn/sn85058130/1889-06-05/ed-1/seq-3 (accessed April 19, 2014); for Unitarians, "Unitarian Coffee," *Salt Lake Herald*, April 1, 1892, 5, http://chroniclingamerica.loc.gov/lccn/sn85058130/1892-04-01/ed-1/seq-5 (accessed April 19, 2014) and "At the University: Dr. Utter Entertains a Large and Interested Audience," *Salt Lake Herald*, November 12, 1892, 8, http://chroniclingamerica.loc.gov/lccn/sn85058130/1892-11-12/ed-1/seq-8 (accessed April 19, 2014). One notable lecture was the farewell address of the Unitarian Reverend Stanley Hunter on Sep-

tember 25, 1895, given under the title "Utah: Her People and Her Prospects; or Saints and Sinners of the Promised Land." This treated the Mormon story with deference and spoke about a broader movement of Christians grouped together in the mountain west. "Farewell Address: Rev. Stanley Hunter's Lecture at Unity Hall," *Salt Lake Herald*, September 26, 1895, 8, http://chroniclingamerica.loc.gov/lccn/sn85058130/1895-09-26/ed-1/seq-8 (accessed April 19, 2014).

152 Untitled notice, *Evening Dispatch*, January 16, 1894, 4, http://chroniclingamerica. loc.gov/lccn/sn86091038/1894-01-16/ed-1/seq-4 (accessed April 19, 2014).

153 Among many articles, see "Hammond Hall Lecture," *Salt Lake Herald*, December 19, 1884, 1, http://chroniclingamerica.loc.gov/lccn/sn85058130/1884-12-19/ed-1/seq-1 (accessed April 19, 2014) and "Lecture on Astronomy," *Salt Lake Herald*, May 8, 1890, 8, http://chroniclingamerica.loc.gov/lccn/sn85058130/1890-05-08/ed-1/seq-8 (accessed April 19, 2014).

154 "General Notes," *Salt Lake Evening Democrat*, March 7, 1887, 3, http://chroniclingamerica.loc.gov/lccn/sn85058117/1887-03-07/ed-1/seq-3 (accessed April 5, 2016). The entire notice reads: "A number of deputy marshals and Ogdenites went to Brigham City to-day to see the Saints 'swallowing the rats,' as the taking of the oath by them is now termed. A recent magic lantern scene furnished the idea." This phrasing slightly obscures whether it was the Mormons or non-Mormons who coined and used the term, though it's quite possible it was common among both groups. *The Ratcatcher* was an extremely popular drawn presentation that consisted of two slides: a snoring man with a rat perched on his bed, and then an image of the man with the rat halfway inside his open mouth; the affect was of a primitive animation of the rat running into his mouth, and audiences would produce the sound effects of snoring and choking along with the images. Terry Borton, "Film History Began with the Magic-Lantern," *Magic-Lantern Shows*, http://www.magiclanternshows.com/history.htm (accessed November 11, 2017).

155 "Calder's Park – Salt Lake City, UT, USA," *Waymarking.com*, http://www.waymarking.com/waymarks/WMG7MR_Calders_Park_Salt_Lake_City_UT_USA (accessed November 11, 2017). See also "Fuller's Hill," *Salt Lake Herald*, May 1, 1881, 3.

156 "Street Stereopticon," *Salt Lake Herald*, February 5, 1884, 8, http://chroniclingamerica.loc.gov/lccn/sn85058130/1884-02-05/ed-1/seq-8 (accessed April 16, 2014).

157 "The School Exhibition: The Lecture on Bonaparte at the Theatre To-day," *Salt Lake Herald*, November 8, 1884, 8, http://chroniclingamerica.loc.gov/lccn/sn85058130/1884-11-08/ed-1/seq-8 (accessed April 16, 2014); "Local and Other Briefs," *Salt Lake Herald*, January 30, 1891, 8, http://chroniclingamerica.loc.gov/lccn/sn85058130/1891-01-30/ed-1/seq-8 (accessed April 16, 2014); for the clock show see "Local Briefs," *Salt Lake Herald*, November 10, 1888, 8, http://chroniclingamerica.loc.gov/lccn/sn85058130/1888-11-10/ed-1/seq-8 (accessed April 16, 2014), and "Local Briefs," *Salt Lake Herald*, November 16, 1888, 8, http://chroniclingamerica.loc.gov/lccn/sn85058130/1888-11-16/ed-1/seq-8 (accessed April 16, 2014).

158 Untitled advertisement for the Salt Lake Theatre, *Salt Lake Herald*, February 1, 1881, 2, http://chroniclingamerica.loc.gov/lccn/sn85058130/1881-02-01/ed-1/seq-2

(accessed April 16, 2014); "Worlds: Their Lives and Death—and How They are Distinguished," *Salt Lake Herald*, February 9, 1881, 3, http://chroniclingamerica.loc.gov/lccn/sn85058130/1881-02-09/ed-1/seq-3 (accessed April 16, 2014).

159 "The Lecture," *Salt Lake Herald*, March 25, 1884, 4, http://chroniclingamerica.loc.gov/lccn/sn85058130/1884-03-25/ed-1/seq-4 (accessed April 16, 2014); see also "Lecture on St. Helena," *Salt Lake Herald*, March 22, 1884, 8, http://chroniclingamerica.loc.gov/lccn/sn85058130/1884-03-22/ed-1/seq-8 (accessed April 16, 2014).

160 The event in question was two medical lectures by Dr. J. C. Harrison on various diseases; because of the subject matter women and boys under fifteen were not admitted. "Salt Lake Theatre, For Men Only," *Salt Lake Herald*, May 1, 1890, 1, http://chroniclingamerica.loc.gov/lccn/sn85058130/1890-05-01/ed-1/seq-1 (accessed April 16, 2014); "Pictorial Physiology: Dr. J. C. Harrison Will Deliver Two Lectures to Men Only," *Salt Lake Herald*, May 2, 1890, 8, http://chroniclingamerica.loc.gov/lccn/sn85058130/1890-05-02/ed-1/seq-8 (accessed April 16, 2014).

161 Untitled notice, *Salt Lake Herald*, September 20, 1888, 8, http://chroniclingamerica.loc.gov/lccn/sn85058130/1888-09-20/ed-1/seq-8 (accessed April 16, 2014).

162 "The B. Y. Summer School," *Salt Lake Herald*, June 27, 1893, 3, http://chroniclingamerica.loc.gov/lccn/sn85058130/1893-06-27/ed-1/seq-3 (accessed April 16, 2014); "Territorial Topics: Teachers' Work at the Provo Summer School," *Salt Lake Herald*, August 12, 1893, 6, http://chroniclingamerica.loc.gov/lccn/sn85058130/1893-08-12/ed-1/seq-6 (accessed April 16, 2014). This lecture evidently dealt with history, travel, or geography, and the Herald reporter recorded how "all felt how much more vivid impressions may be made when pictures supplement words in teaching," an oft-repeated mantra in Mormon pedagogy.

163 "Dallin's Lecture," *Salt Lake Herald*, April 9, 1884, 8, http://chroniclingamerica.loc.gov/lccn/sn85058130/1884-04-09/ed-1/seq-8 (accessed April 16, 2014); "University Library Lecture," *Salt Lake Herald*, January 22, 1893, 3, http://chroniclingamerica.loc.gov/lccn/sn85058130/1893-01-22/ed-1/seq-3 (accessed April 16, 2014).

164 John R. Talmage, *The Talmage Story: Life of James E. Talmage—Educator, Scientist, Apostle* (Salt Lake City: Bookcraft, 1972), 81; see also p. 65.

165 "Provo Points: A Batch of Items From Utah County's Capital," *Salt Lake Herald*, February 26, 1885, 7, http://chroniclingamerica.loc.gov/lccn/sn85058130/1885-02-26/ed-1/seq-7 (accessed April 16, 2014); "Local Briefs," *Salt Lake Herald*, April 3, 1887, 8, http://chroniclingamerica.loc.gov/lccn/sn85058130/1887-04-03/ed-1/seq-8 (accessed April 16, 2014); "Dr. Talmage's Lecture," *Deseret News*, November 15, 1890, 3, http://chroniclingamerica.loc.gov/lccn/sn83045555/1890-11-15/ed-1/seq-3 (accessed April 16, 2014); "Fragments," *Deseret News*, February 16, 1894, 8, http://chroniclingamerica.loc.gov/lccn/sn83045555/1894-02-16/ed-1/seq-9 (accessed April 16, 2014); W. E. Rydalch, "Dr. Talmage Will Lecture," *Evening Dispatch*, November 20, 1894, 1, http://chroniclingamerica.loc.gov/lccn/sn86091038/1894-11-20/ed-1/seq-1 (accessed April 16, 2014); "Notes," *Salt Lake Herald*, November 21, 1894, 7, http://chroniclingamerica.loc.gov/lccn/sn85058130/1894-11-21/ed-1/seq-7 (accessed April 16, 2014); "University of Utah: President Talmage's Lecture This Evening—Delta Phi

Society," *Salt Lake Herald*, March 14, 1895, 5, http://chroniclingamerica.loc.gov/lccn/
sn85058130/1895-03-14/ed-1/seq-5 (accessed April 16, 2014); "University Lectures: Full Course Arranged for the Coming Season," *Salt Lake Herald*, November 17,
1895, 7, http://chroniclingamerica.loc.gov/lccn/sn85058130/1895-11-17/ed-1/seq-7
(accessed April 16, 2014); "Town Talk," *Salt Lake Herald*, January 23, 1896, 8, http://
chroniclingamerica.loc.gov/lccn/sn85058130/1896-01-23/ed-1/seq-8 (accessed April
16, 2014). The first of these reports, from 1885, records that "the hall was crowded and
many were turned away, not being able to gain admittance. The lecture was instructive
and was highly appreciated." And his 1890 lecture on insects was described in more
colorful terms, the reporter saying the event "was handled in a very instructive and
interesting manner, the stereopticon views adding a most pleasing effect. The hall was
crowded to its fullest capacity. A synopsis would not do the lecture justice; it should be
heard to be appreciated."

166 "'The Eternal City.' Professor Talmage's Lecture For Benefit of the Kindergar-
ten," *Salt Lake Herald*, December 4, 1897, 8, http://chroniclingamerica.loc.gov/lccn/
sn85058130/1897-12-04/ed-1/seq-8 (accessed April 16, 2014).

167 "The Land of the Czar: Dr Talmage Interests a Large Audience at the Tabernacle," *Salt Lake Herald*, January 24, 1898, 2, http://chroniclingamerica.loc.gov/lccn/
sn85058130/1898-01-24/ed-1/seq-2 (accessed April 16, 2014). See also "Amusements," *Deseret Evening News*, January 19, 1898, 2, http://chroniclingamerica.loc.gov/
lccn/sn83045555/1898-01-19/ed-1/seq-2 (accessed April 16, 2014) and "Sights and
Scenes in Russia," *Deseret Evening News*, January 24, 1898, 2, http://chroniclingamer-
ica.loc.gov/lccn/sn83045555/1898-01-24/ed-1/seq-2 (accessed April 18, 2014); "Town
Talk," *Salt Lake Herald*, March 31, 1897, 8, http://chroniclingamerica.loc.gov/lccn/
sn85058130/1897-03-31/ed-1/seq-8 (accessed April 16, 2014); Talmage, *The Talmage
Story*, 91, 105-107 (for a trip through western Europe including Rome and Pompeii),
110, 116 (for his presentation of photographs of rock deposits in Utah to an audience
in Edinburgh), 143-144 (for his 1897 trip through Russia and Scandinavia).

168 "Local Briefs," *Salt Lake Herald*, April 3, 1887.

169 "Twentieth Ward Sunday School Party," *Salt Lake Herald*, January 5, 1882, 8,
http://chroniclingamerica.loc.gov/lccn/sn85058130/1882-01-05/ed-1/seq-8 (accessed April 18, 2014); "Local Briefs," *Salt Lake Herald*, January 17, 1886, 12, http://
chroniclingamerica.loc.gov/lccn/sn85058130/1886-01-17/ed-1/seq-12 (accessed
April 18, 2014); "Local Briefs," *Salt Lake Herald*, February 9, 1887, 8, http://chroniclin-
gamerica.loc.gov/lccn/sn85058130/1887-02-09/ed-1/seq-8 (accessed April 18, 2014);
G. G. Bywater, "Mr. Ward's Lecture," *Deseret Evening News*, July 11, 1890, 3, http://
chroniclingamerica.loc.gov/lccn/sn83045555/1890-07-11/ed-1/seq-3 (accessed April
18, 2014); "Egypt, The Wonderful Land," *Salt Lake Herald*, June 1, 1894, 5, http://chron-
iclingamerica.loc.gov/lccn/sn85058130/1894-06-01/ed-1/seq-5 (accessed April 19,
2014); "Stereopticon Entertainment," *Deseret Evening News*, January 27, 1897, 2, http://
chroniclingamerica.loc.gov/lccn/sn83045555/1897-01-27/ed-1/seq-2 (accessed
April 19, 2014); "Stereopticon Entertainment," *Deseret Evening News*, January 28,
1897, 8, http://chroniclingamerica.loc.gov/lccn/sn83045555/1897-01-28/ed-1/seq-8
(accessed April 19, 2014); "Ward Entertainment," *Deseret Evening News*, February 1,
1898, 2, http://chroniclingamerica.loc.gov/lccn/sn83045555/1898-02-01/ed-1/seq-3
(accessed April 18, 2014).

170 "News From Near-by Towns," *Salt Lake Herald*, March 19, 1896, 7, http://chroniclingamerica.loc.gov/lccn/sn85058130/1896-03-19/ed-1/seq-7 (accessed April 19, 2014).

171 "Amusements," *Salt Lake Herald*, April 5, 1898, 5, http://chroniclingamerica.loc.gov/lccn/sn85058130/1898-04-05/ed-1/seq-5 (accessed April 19, 2014).

172 "Town Talk," March 31, 1897, 8; "Dr. James E. Talmage Will deliver a lecture entitled A Visit to Pompeii," March 31, 1897, 5, http://chroniclingamerica.loc.gov/lccn/sn83045555/1897-03-31/ed-1/seq-5 (accessed April 16, 2014).

173 "Amusements," *Deseret Evening News*, April 6, 1899, 8, http://chroniclingamerica.loc.gov/lccn/sn83045555/1899-04-06/ed-1/seq-12 (accessed April 19, 2014).

174 "Sights and Scenes in Russia," 2; "Amusements," *Salt Lake Herald*, May 4, 1898, 2, http://chroniclingamerica.loc.gov/lccn/sn85058130/1898-05-04/ed-1/seq-2 (accessed April 19, 2014); "Lecture on California: It Will be Illustrated and Will be Delivered at the Tabernacle," *Deseret Evening News*, April 30, 1898, 2, http://chroniclingamerica.loc.gov/lccn/sn83045555/1898-04-30/ed-1/seq-2 (accessed April 19, 2014).

175 Quinn, *The Mormon Hierarchy: Extensions of Power*, 782; see footnote 58.

176 "Lecture on California," 2; "Amusements," *Salt Lake Herald*, May 4, 1898, 2. Kelleher's name is elsewhere given as Keliher.

177 "Local Briefs," *Deseret Evening News*, April 17, 1899, 8, http://chroniclingamerica.loc.gov/lccn/sn83045555/1899-04-17/ed-1/seq-8 (accessed April 19, 2014).

178 "Will Lecture on India: Father Younan In Theatre Friday Night—Tabernacle Tonight," *Salt Lake Herald*, June 4, 1899, 9, http://chroniclingamerica.loc.gov/lccn/sn85058130/1899-06-04/ed-1/seq-9 (accessed April 19, 2014).

179 L. L. Marcy, *The Sciopticon Manual: Explaining Lantern Projections in General, and the Sciopticon Apparatus in Particular* (Philadelphia: James A. Moore, Printer, 1877), 59, http://www.archive.org/stream/sciopticonmanual00marcrich#page/286/mode/2up (accessed May 9, 2014); "To Lecture on Salt Lake," *Salt Lake Herald*, August 30, 1890, 8, http://chroniclingamerica.loc.gov/lccn/sn85058130/1890-08-30/ed-1/seq-8 (accessed April 19, 2014).

180 "Town Talk," *Salt Lake Herald*, February 22, 1897, 8, http://chroniclingamerica.loc.gov/lccn/sn85058130/1897-02-22/ed-1/seq-8 (accessed April 19, 2014).

181 "The Pioneer Jubilee," *Salt Lake Herald*, July 3, 1897, 8, http://chroniclingamerica.loc.gov/lccn/sn85058130/1897-07-03/ed-1/seq-8 (accessed April 19, 2014).

182 "In the Social Realm," *Salt Lake Herald*, June 1, 1898, 8, http://chroniclingamerica.loc.gov/lccn/sn85058130/1898-06-01/ed-1/seq-9 (accessed April 19, 2014).

183 "Local Briefs," *Deseret Evening News*, November 2, 1899, 8, http://chroniclingamerica.loc.gov/lccn/sn83045555/1899-11-02/ed-1/seq-8 (accessed April 19, 2014).

184 "Dr. Talmage's Lectures Abroad," *Deseret Evening News*, August 26, 1898, 4, http://chroniclingamerica.loc.gov/lccn/sn83045555/1898-08-26/ed-1/seq-4 (accessed April 19, 2014).

185 Talmage, *The Talmage Story*, 145-152.

186 Modern historian Konden R. Smith summarizes: "The power of the choir in fashioning public opinion was not lost upon Mormon leaders, bringing forth direction and focus regarding LDS policy at the beginning of the twentieth century." And in that century film would often fill this role, becoming one of the primary media for Church proselytizing and public relations. Konden R. Smith, "The Dawning of a New Era: Mormonism and the World's Columbian Exposition of 1893," *Mormons and Popular Culture*, Vol. 2, 199; a passage from p. 203 might as well be summarizing the Church's broadcast public service announcements from the 1970s: "Leaving explicit evangelizing efforts behind, the new Mormon policy avoided even the appearance of proselytizing and stirring up controversies, seeking instead to bridge differences and assuage enmities." See also Givens, *People of Paradox*, 253-254; Hicks, *Mormonism and Music*, 152-153.

187 Richard Neitzel Holzapfel and Steven C. Harper, "'This Is My Testimony, Spoken by Myself into a Talking Machine': Wilford Woodruff's 1897 Statement in Stereo," *BYU Studies* 45:2 (2006), 112-116.

188 Richards, "The Salt Lake Temple Infrastructure," 218-219.

189 Givens, *People of Paradox*, 326.

190 Leonard Arringtom, B. C. Hardy, and others have argued that the 1880s are an "axial age" that must be included in any discussions of "the drama of Mormon transformation." Daymon Mickel Smith, "The Last Shall Be First and the First Shall Be Last: Discourse and Mormon History," (Ph.D. dissertation, University of Pennsylvania Dept. of Anthropology, 2010), 286. The specific passages that Smith cites are Arrington's *Great Basin Kingdom*, 354-356, and Hardy's *Solemn Covenant: The Mormon Polygamous Passage* (Urbana: University of Illinois Press, 1992), 55.

191 "When the church president capitulated to the supremacy of federal authority in 1890 by publicly abandoning polygamy, the surrender of more central features of the Mormon commonwealth would paradoxically become easier." Quinn, *The Mormon Hierarchy: Extensions of Power*, 330.

192 The text of the Manifesto and some commentary from 1890-1893 can be read in Official Declaration—1 of the Doctrine & Covenants, pages 291-293 of modern editions. How the language of covert resistance from the 1870s and '80s influenced Mormons' interpretation of the Manifesto is discussed throughout Smith, "The Last Shall Be First and the First Shall Be Last," particularly in the first section, Discourse and the Mormon Underground, p. 11-112, and Chapter 6 in the second section, p. 113-137, on internal mental discourse and spoken verbal discourse. The language of coded resistance was so ingrained into Mormonism that it became practically impossible for Church members to know how to interpret the "official announcements" of the end of polygamy.

193 Rutherford B. Hayes diary, January 9, 1880, in T. Harry Williams, ed., *Hayes: The*

Diary of a President, 1875-1881 (New York: David McKay Co., Inc., 1964), 258-259, and quoted again in Quinn, *The Mormon Hierarchy: Extensions of Power*, 329. President Hayes added, "The Union of Church and State is complete. The result is the usual one [—] usurpation or absorption of all temporal authority and power by the Church. Polygamy and every other evil sanctioned by the Mormon Church is the end in view. This requires agitation. The people of the United States must be made to appreciate[,] to understand the situation. Laws must be enacted which will take from the Mormon Church its temporal power. Mormonism as a sectarian idea is nothing, but as a system of government it is our duty to deal with it as an enemy to our institutions, and its supporters and leaders as criminals." Quinn, *The Mormon Hierarchy: Extensions of Power*, 43, 264.

194 This was *The Springfield Union* of February 1885, reprinted in the *Salt Lake Daily Tribune*, February 15, 1885 and quoted in Gustive O. Larson, "Federal Government Efforts to 'Americanize' Utah before Admission to Statehood," *BYU Studies* 10:2 (Winter 1970), 1. Another 1885 commentator echoed essentially the same view: "It is the general sentiment that religion has nothing to do with the Utah question—that it is simply a matter of law and government. There is no hostility against the common people who call themselves Mormons. The hostility is against their illegal system of government." Quoted in John Sorenson, "Mormon World View and American Culture," *Dialogue: A Journal of Mormon Thought* 8 (Summer 1973), 20. Finally, as Quinn summarizes, "Polygamy had become symbolic of the chasm that separated Mormon culture from 'American' society. In one sense polygamy was an inappropriate symbol because Mormons had been accused of being 'un-American' long before polygamy became significant. One historian concluded that Mormon 'anti-pluralism was the main cause of persecution.'" Quinn, *The Mormon Hierarchy: Extensions of Power*, 329.

195 Quinn, *The Mormon Hierarchy: Extensions of Power*, 340.

196 Ibid., 347.

197 Michael Lipka, "U.S. religious groups and their political leanings," *Pew Research Center*, February 23, 2016, http://www.pewresearch.org/fact-tank/2016/02/23/u-s-religious-groups-and-their-political-leanings (accessed April 9, 2016). A complete history of the Church's involvement in partisan politics in the nineteenth and early twentieth centuries can be found in Quinn, *The Mormon Hierarchy: Extensions of Power*, 314-363; see especially p. 336, 340, 346-347, and 791-792 for details on the Church's involvement with Republicanism around the period in question, including the party's influence on Woodruff releasing the Manifesto. Smith, "The Last Shall Be First and the First Shall Be Last," 108-109, notes that several members of the California lobby owned stock in Church mining interests and could cause significant financial problems were their suggestion to end polygamy via manifesto ignored. See also E. Leo Lyman, "The Political Background of the Woodruff Manifesto," *Dialogue: A Journal of Mormon Thought*, 24:3 (Fall 1991), 21-39.

198 Harold R. Laycock, "Academies," *Encyclopedia of Mormonism*, Vol. 1, 11-13; "Education in Utah," *Utah History Encyclopedia*, http://www.uen.org/utah_history_encyclopedia/e/EDUCATION.html (accessed June 25, 2013); Quinn, *The Mormon Hierarchy: Extensions of Power*, 771, 792. Weber State University, formerly Weber State Academy, was one of the last major institutions to shift control away from the Church, in 1933.

Notes - Origins

199 Leonard J. Arrington quoted in Caroline Winter, "How the Mormons Make Money," *Bloomberg Businessweek*, July 18, 2012, http://www.businessweek.com/articles/2012-07-10/how-the-mormons-make-money#p1 (accessed November 10, 2014).

200 Arrington, *Great Basin Kingdom*, 403.

201 Ibid., 409.

202 Quinn, *The Mormon Hierarchy: Extensions of Power*, 329-330 (Council of Fifty), 798 (fast day), 806 (interpreting dreams), 808 (speaking in tongues).

203 Edward Leo Lyman, "Utah Statehood," *Encyclopedia of Mormonism*, Vol. 4, 1502-1503; for a detailed record of the progress toward statehood written shortly after the event, see William H. King's serialized article "Statehood and How It Was Achieved," *Improvement Era* 1:1-4, November 1897-February 1898, 26-33, 104-110, 201-203, 231-236. Relatively late in the campaign a robust Republican presence in the potential state seemed more certain—evidenced by events like a Republican victory in a March 9, 1892 election in the Democratic stronghold of Logan—and Democratic support in Washington began to wane. Ultimately those negotiating for statehood had to pull together a bipartisan coalition of support. The Tabernacle Choir's appearance at the 1893 World's Fair also helped present the Mormons in a more American light to eastern legislators. Smith, "The Dawning of a New Era," 187-188. There are several additional sources that discuss the Mormons' accommodations and Utah's movement toward statehood. They include Arrington's *Great Basin Kingdom*; Larson's expanded work *The "Americanization" of Utah for Statehood* (San Marino: Huntington Library, 1971); Edward Leo Lyman, *Political Deliverance: The Mormon Quest for Utah Statehood* (Urbana: University of Illinois Press, 1986); and Jan Shipps, "The Mormons in Politics: The First Hundred Years," (Ph.D. dissertation, University of Colorado, 1965).

204 Judson Callaway and Su Richards, "'Electricity for Everything': The Progress Company and the Electrification of Rural Salt Lake County, 1897-1924," *Utah Historical Quarterly* 70:3 (Summer 2002), 239.

205 Callaway and Richards, "'Electricity for Everything,'" 239-240; John S. McCormick, "The Beginning of Modern Electric Power Service in Utah, 1912-22," *Utah Historical Quarterly* 56:1 (Winter 1988), 6.

206 Richard R. Lyman, "The Pioneer Use of Electricity in Utah," *Improvement Era* 29:5, March 1926, 410-412.

207 Paolo Cherchi Usai, "Origins and Survival," *The Oxford History of World Cinema*, ed. Geoffrey Nowell-Smith (Oxford: Oxford University Press, 1996), 6-13; Roberta Pearson, "Early Cinema," *The Oxford History of World Cinema*, 13-23, esp. 14.

208 Daniel H. Olsen, "Touring Sacred History: The Latter-day Saints and Their Historical Sites," *Mormons and Popular Culture*, Vol. 2, 231; one of the foundational essays on Mormonism's faithful history, including its causes and problems and the challenges in writing it, is Richard L. Bushman's essay "Faithful History," *Dialogue: A Journal of Mormon Thought* 4:4 (Winter 1969), 11-25.

209 Nathan O. Hatch, *The Democratization of American Christianity* (New Haven: Yale University Press, 1989), 226.

210 After hiring out the printing of the Book of Mormon to Egbert Grandin's press in Palmyra, Mormons undertook their own printing, primarily of pamphlets and scriptures, with important presses in Kirtland, Independence, Nauvoo, Salt Lake City, Liverpool, New York, and San Francisco. As mentioned, it was this last press, owned and operated by Samuel Brannan, that announced the discovery of gold at Sutter's Mill and sparked the 1849 Gold Rush.

211 *Deseret News Extra*, December 1, 1866, quoted in Arrington, *Great Basin Kingdom*, 229; Sherry Pack Baker, "Mormon Media History Timeline, 1827-2007," *BYU Studies* 47:4 (2008), 120-121.

212 Brigham Young, "Instructions to the Latter-day Saints, in the Settlements South of Great Salt Lake City," *Journal of Discourses* 10:225 (April 1, 1863).

213 Levi Edgar Young, "'Mormonism' in Picture," *Young Woman's Journal* 24:2 (February 1913), 75, 80.

214 John A. Widtsoe, *In a Sunlit Land: The Autobiography of John A. Widtsoe* (Salt Lake City: Deseret News Press, 1952), 202-203.

215 Brent L. Top, "A Lengthening of Stride, 1951 through 1999," *Out of Obscurity: The LDS Church in the Twentieth Century* (Salt Lake City: Deseret Book Company, 2000), 38.

216 Sarah Jane Weaver, "Share More Gospel Messages on Social Media, Elder Bednar Says," *Church News*, August 19, 2014, https://www.lds.org/church/news/share-more-gospel-messages-on-social-media-elder-bednar-says?lang=eng (accessed August 27, 2014). For an overview of the literature treating science/technology and Mormonism, as of 1995, see Richard F. Haglund Jr. and Erich Robert Paul, "Resources for the Study of Science, Technology, and Mormon Culture," *Mormon Americana*, 559-606. On page 560 they note: "By comparison with other religious denominations, the Latter-day Saint community has not only produced an unusually large number of scientists for its size, but also managed to retain the commitment and activity of a large proportion of those scientists. Sterling McMurrin noted in 1959 and Robert Miller affirmed in 1992 that this well-documented hospitality of Mormon culture toward science and technology was firmly rooted in Mormonism's revealed theology . . . On numerous occasions since the Church was organized in 1830, its leaders have publicly corroborated [a] positive attitude toward science and technology." However, page 579 notes that "the Church has rarely been at the forefront of technological change, and thus far the Church has made no systematic effort to incorporate technology planning into its programs," although this has changed somewhat in the twenty years following this work's publication.

217 "The Latest Miracle," *Deseret Evening News*, July 2, 1891, 3, http://chroniclingamerica.loc.gov/lccn/sn83045555/1891-07-02/ed-1/seq-3 (accessed August 12, 2013). The article observes that the kinetograph records forty-six frames per second (opposed the later cinematic standard of twenty-four), uses gelatin film, and records images in synchronicity with the sound recorded by the phonograph. "One part of the

miracle is thus accomplished, the photographing of the continuous picture and the recording of the sounds that goes with the series of pictures. Another part remains no less difficult to be accomplished, and that is reproducing both to the eye and ear." This wouldn't be done to the extent predicted here until the late 1920s.

218 Besides the already cited ways in which Protestants and Mormons saw proto-cinematic technologies like the magic lantern as means to propagate the faith, Terry Lindvall in *Sanctuary Cinema* notes some other synchronicities between early film and religiosity. The Episcopalian Reverend Hannibal Goodwin created and patented a flexible film base in Newark around the same time as George Eastman's company, for instance. Though he lost a suit to Eastman he was still known enough to receive praise throughout the 1910s for creating motion film stock for religious purposes (p. 56). And Hollywood itself, which would soon be seen by many as a den of sin par excellence, actually began as a religious community, growing out of the campaign of Horace Wilcot, "a God-fearing real estate speculator" who envisioned the town and its orange groves as a model Christian community with "no saloons, no liquor stores, with free land offered to Protestant Churches locating within the city limits" (p. 59).

2 - The First Wave: The New Frontier

01 Terry Lindvall, *Sanctuary Cinema: Origins of the Christian Film Industry* (New York: New York University Press, 2007), 55.

02 David Bordwell, Janet Staiger, and Kristin Thompson, *The Classical Hollywood Cinema: Film Style & Mode of Production to 1960* (London: Routledge, 1985), 262.

03 "The Church Moves On: One of Last of 1847 Pioneers Passes," *Improvement Era* 43:7 (July 1940), 414. Another article on the same page notes a survivor of the 1846 ship Brooklyn expedition carrying Mormon emigrants from New York to San Francisco, and a November 1940 article notes the hundredth birthday of a member of the famous 1856 Martin handcart company. "The Church Moves On: Survivor of Martin Handcart Company Reaches Century Mark," *Improvement Era* 43:11 (November 1940), 670. For Erickson, see D. Michael Quinn, *The Mormon Hierarchy: Extensions of Power* (Salt Lake City: Signature Books in association with Smith Research Associates, 1997), 857.

04 For instance, in the very title of the most prominent and groundbreaking study of Mormon film in this period: Richard Alan Nelson, "A History of Latter-day Saint Screen Portrayals in the Anti-Mormon Film Era, 1905-1936" (master's thesis, Brigham Young University Dept. of Communications, 1975).

05 "The Kinetograph: Edison's Latest Invention Whereby Motion is Recorded the Same as Sound," *Salt Lake Herald*, May 29, 1891, 1, http://chroniclingamerica.loc.gov/lccn/sn85058130/1891-05-29/ed-1/seq-1 (accessed August 12, 2013).

06 "People," *Salt Lake Herald*, May 10, 1897, 3, http://chroniclingamerica.loc.gov/lccn/sn85058130/1894-05-10/ed-1/seq-3 (accessed May 12, 2014); "A Look into the Kinetoscope," *Salt Lake Herald*, September 3, 1894, 1, http://chroniclingamerica.loc.gov/lccn/sn85058130/1894-09-03/ed-1/seq-1 (accessed August

12, 2013).

07 For Mrs. De Moisy, see "In the Social Realm," *Salt Lake Herald*, Sunday January 30, 1898, 16, http://chroniclingamerica.loc.gov/lccn/sn85058130/1898-01-30/ed-1/seq-16 (accessed August 12, 2013); see also the practical explanation of moving picture technology in William J. Hopkins, "VI—Moving Pictures," *Salt Lake Herald*, May 8, 1900, 4, http://chroniclingamerica.loc.gov/lccn/sn85058130/1900-05-08/ed-1/seq-4 (accessed August 12, 2013). For the *Popular Science* article, see "Notes," *Improvement Era* 3:10 (August 1900), 786. Likewise, a *Salt Lake Herald* article from late 1899 described advances in the kinetscope, bioscope, and similar devices, discussing the moving picture's use for medicine, microscopy, law enforcement, astronomy, and other fields. The author, taking a cue from Edison's frequent pronouncements, predicts a day in which mutoscopes would be in people's homes and allow them to watch performances or athletic events from far away: "Sets of pictures showing the exciting scenes—the yacht race, athletic game, court scene or other event—will be made in such quantities and so reasonably as to be distributed daily like newspapers for home use in the cabinets; thus we may see the day's notable occurrences as well as read the reports." "Advance of the Kinetoscope," *Salt Lake Herald*, November 20, 1899, 6, http://chroniclingamerica.loc.gov/lccn/sn85058130/1899-11-20/ed-1/seq-6 (accessed May 13, 2014). Equally visionary was a *Herald* article from the next May (1900), which describes persistence of vision and motion picture apparatuses from the zoetrope to multiple-camera processes like Eadweard Muybridge's to the newest invention, the Projectoscope. "The chief use to which moving pictures have been applied thus far is that of entertainment, and unfortunately the subjects which have aroused the most interest have been prize fights," but other uses are possible, such as footage of Boer War combat and time-lapse of sprouting plants. William J. Hopkins, "Recent Scientific Discoveries: VI – Moving Pictures," *Salt Lake Herald*, May 8, 1900, 4, http://chroniclingamerica.loc.gov/lccn/sn85058130/1900-05-08/ed-1/seq-4 (accessed May 15, 2014). A comprehensive explanation of the kinetoscope is in Roberta Pearson, "Early Cinema," *The Oxford History of World Cinema*, ed. Geoffrey Nowell-Smith (Oxford: Oxford University Press, 1996), 14-15.

08 "Local Briefs," *Salt Lake Herald*, February 27, 1895, 7, http://chroniclingamerica.loc.gov/lccn/sn85058130/1895-02-27/ed-1/seq-7 (accessed May 12, 2014).

09 "Personal," three untitled items, *Salt Lake Herald*, May 11, 1896, 8, http://chroniclingamerica.loc.gov/lccn/sn85058130/1896-05-11/ed-1/seq-8 (accessed May 12, 2014); "Edison Phonograph and Kinetoscope Parlors," *Deseret Evening News*, May 7, 1896, 4, http://chroniclingamerica.loc.gov/lccn/sn83045555/1896-05-07/ed-1/seq-4 (accessed May 12, 2014). My thanks to John Hatch for pointing out that Tuttle did not stay in the business, but later married a man named Thomas Ellerbeck and moved to Long Beach, California, where she died, quite young, in 1911.

10 "Advertising Novelty: The Mutoscope at the Union Pacific Office Draws Crowds," *Salt Lake Herald*, April 13, 1900, 5, http://chroniclingamerica.loc.gov/lccn/sn85058130/1900-04-13/ed-1/seq-5 (accessed May 13, 2014); the "conference visitor" was attending the Mormon Church's semiannual general conference, a point I will return to shortly. See also the short notice "Mutoscope,"

Deseret Evening News, April 16, 1900, 8, http://chroniclingamerica.loc.gov/lccn/sn83045555/1900-04-16/ed-1/seq-8 (accessed May 13, 2014).

11 "Amazing Growth of Penny in the Slot Business," *Salt Lake Herald*, May 19, 1902, 6, http://chroniclingamerica.loc.gov/lccn/sn85058130/1902-05-19/ed-1/seq-6 (accessed May 13, 2014).

12 "Amusements," *Deseret Evening News*, Wednesday March 17, 1897, 5, http://chroniclingamerica.loc.gov/lccn/sn83045555/1897-03-17/ed-1/seq-5 (accessed August 12, 2013). Information on the Lyceum Theatre is at "Lyceum Theatre," *Utah Theaters*, http://utahtheaters.info/TheaterMain.asp?ID=837 (accessed August 12, 2013); see also Mary Bellis, "The Life of Thomas Edison: Phonograph and Motion Pictures," *About.com*, http://inventors.about.com/od/estartinventors/a/Thomas_Edison_4.htm (accessed August 12, 2013). On Thursday March 18 the *Herald* called the machine the "Vivescope": "Lyceum: Friday and Saturday Nights," *Salt Lake Herald*, Thursday March 18, 1897, 4, http://chroniclingamerica.loc.gov/lccn/sn85058130/1897-03-18/ed-1/seq-4 (accessed August 12, 2013); the day of the performance in the *News* this was changed to the "Vivrescope," indicating the vaudeville company may not have cared what they called it as long as it was "the latest and best motion picture machine." "Lyceum: Friday and Saturday Nights...," *Deseret Evening News*, Friday March 19, 1897, 4, http://chroniclingamerica.loc.gov/lccn/sn83045555/1897-03-19/ed-1/seq-4 (accessed August 12, 2013).

13 "The Kickapoos," *Coalville Times* 9:47, November 28, 1902, 8, http://chroniclingamerica.loc.gov/lccn/sn85058217/1902-11-28/ed-1/seq-8 (accessed September 5, 2013); Morgan J. Kavanagh, "Letters and Answers," *Intermountain Catholic*, January 24, 1903, 5, http://chroniclingamerica.loc.gov/lccn/sn93062856/1903-01-24/ed-1/seq-5 (accessed May 18, 2014).

14 "City and County," *Logan Republican*, May 26, 1906, 5, http://chroniclingamerica.loc.gov/lccn/sn85058246/1906-05-26/ed-1/seq-5 (accessed August 12, 2014); H. W. Pickering, "Salt Lake City, Utah, Registers a Few Exhibitors," *Moving Picture World*, July 15, 1916, 387-388, http://www.archive.org/stream/moviwor-29chal#page/n449/mode/2up (accessed August 19, 2014).

15 "Ogden Briefs," *Salt Lake Herald*, June 20, 1902, 7, http://chroniclingamerica.loc.gov/lccn/sn85058130/1902-06-20/ed-1/seq-7 (accessed May 13, 2014); "Amusements," *Salt Lake Tribune*, June 21, 1905, 12, http://chroniclingamerica.loc.gov/lccn/sn83045396/1905-06-21/ed-1/seq-12 (accessed May 18, 2014). For a brief discussion of the construction of Saltair, including that the Church covered at least $185,000 of the $350,000 cost, see Leonard J. Arrington, *Great Basin Kingdom: An Economic History of the Latter-day Saints, 1830-1900*, New Edition (Urbana and Chicago: University of Illinois Press, 1958), 392.

16 "Orpheum," *Goodwin's Weekly*, January 13, 1906, 8, http://chroniclingamerica.loc.gov/lccn/2010218519/1906-01-13/ed-1/seq-8 (accessed November 26, 2013). Similarly, a 1909 *Deseret News* article reportedly warned against cinema's deleterious effects. Richard Alan Nelson, "The History of Utah Film: An Introductory Essay," unpublished paper for BYU course Communications 691R (1973), Richard Alan Nelson Collection, L. Tom Perry Special Collections, Harold B. Lee Library,

Brigham Young University, 19.

17 Joseph F. Smith, "Editor's Table: Clean Dramatic Amusements," *Improvement Era* 13:5 (March 1910), 459. Smith, the nephew and namesake of Church founder Joseph Smith, served as Church President from 1901 to 1918, the period when film was first popularized in Utah and among the Mormons.

18 Richard Alan Nelson, "Utah Filmmakers of the Silent Screen," *Utah Historical Quarterly* 43:1 (Winter 1975), 5. I myself have not found many of these editorials in primary sources, but one excellent example is "Moving Picture Shows," *Deseret Evening News*, June 30, 1909, Journal History of the Church, Church History Library, The Church of Jesus Christ of Latter-day Saints, Salt Lake City, Utah, June 30, 1909, 1-2, https://dcms.lds.org/delivery/DeliveryManagerServlet?dps_pid=IE403421 (accessed January 14, 2018).

19 Joseph F. Smith, "Sermon on Home Government," *Millennial Star* 74:4 (January 25, 1912), 53.

20 J. M. S., "Dangers of Large Cities," *Millennial Star* 77:38 (September 23, 1915), 601.

21 "John Cort Ties Up Salt Lake; But One House Next Season," *Variety*, May 25, 1912, 12, http://www.archive.org/stream/variety26-1912-05#page/n129/mode/2up (accessed November 19, 2014); "Artists' Forum," *Variety*, January 1, 1910, 9, http://www.archive.org/stream/variety17-1910-01#page/n7/mode/2up (accessed November 19, 2014); "Lauder Skips Salt Lake," *Variety*, January 8, 1910, 1, http://www.archive.org/stream/variety17-1910-01#page/n37/mode/2up (accessed November 19, 2014).

22 One 1908 want ad in the *Salt Lake Tribune* advertised for a "bright, clever young lady to sell tickets for traveling moving picture show" to tour through Oregon, Washington, and British Columbia. Untitled want ad, *Salt Lake Tribune*, December 13, 1908, 25, http://chroniclingamerica.loc.gov/lccn/sn83045396/1908-12-13/ed-1/seq-25 (accessed May 18, 2014). The year before, one Professor Randolph was showing films at the Auditorium skating rink on Richards Street in Salt Lake City, traveling through town with 1,500 feet of motion pictures. "At the Skating Rinks," *Deseret Evening News,* February 6, 1907, 2, http://chroniclingamerica.loc.gov/lccn/sn83045555/1907-02-06/ed-1/seq-2 (accessed May 28, 2014); untitled Auditorium advertisement, *Salt Lake Herald*, February 10, 1907, 11, http://chroniclingamerica.loc.gov/lccn/sn85058130/1907-02-10/ed-1/seq-11 (accessed May 28, 2014). And that same month a traveling lecturer visited the city with what we would today call various documentary films on urban social problems. "Bert Levy to Speak," *Deseret Evening News*, February 22, 1907, 2, http://chroniclingamerica.loc.gov/lccn/sn83045555/1907-02-22/ed-1/seq-2 (accessed May 28, 2014).

23 Nelson, "The History of Utah Film," 2; "A Grand Treat," *Salt Lake Herald*, October 21, 1902, 5, http://chroniclingamerica.loc.gov/lccn/sn85058130/1902-10-21/ed-1/seq-5 (accessed May 19, 2014); Ronald W. Walker and Alexander M. Starr, "Shattering the Vase: The Razing of the Old Salt Lake Theatre," *Utah Historical*

Quarterly 57:1 (Winter 1989), 75.

24 "Around Town," *Lehi Banner*, October 13, 1904, 4, http://chroniclingamerica.loc.gov/lccn/sn85058090/1904-10-13/ed-1/seq-4 (accessed November 24, 2013); this was repeated verbatim in "Around Town," *Lehi Banner*, October 20, 1904, 4, http://chroniclingamerica.loc.gov/lccn/sn85058090/1904-10-20/ed-1/seq-4 (accessed November 24, 2013); "Briefs and Personals," *Deseret Evening News*, November 5, 1904, 11, http://chroniclingamerica.loc.gov/lccn/sn83045555/1904-11-05/ed-1/seq-11 (accessed November 24, 2013); "The Bioscope Co.," *Lehi Banner*, October 5, 1905, 5, http://chroniclingamerica.loc.gov/lccn/sn85058090/1905-10-05/ed-1/seq-5 (accessed November 24, 2013); "Grand Opera House," *Utah Theaters*, http://utahtheaters.info/TheaterMain.asp?ID=90 (accessed May 20, 2014).

25 The manager of the traditional theatrical and cinematic offerings at the Salt Palace was L. R. Carr; his system for film projection was dubbed "the palace-scope." The more recent Salt Palace at 100 W. South Temple is a completely different structure. "Salt Palace Opening: Resort Will Furnish Patrons With Superb Attractions," *Salt Lake Tribune*, May 30, 1906, 9, http://chroniclingamerica.loc.gov/lccn/sn83045396/1906-05-30/ed-1/seq-9 (accessed May 28, 2014). For the Capitol Theatre, see "Capitol Theatre," *Utah Theaters*, http://utahtheaters.info/TheaterMain.asp?ID=69 (accessed November 13, 2013); Joseph Bauman, "Movie theaters have a long, rich history in the Salt Lake area," *Deseret News*, March 9, 2009, http://www.deseretnews.com/article/705289656/Movie-theaters-have-a-long-rich-history-in-the-Salt-Lake-area.html (accessed November 13, 2013). The Capitol Theatre today is home to Utah Opera, the Ririe-Woodbury Dance Company, and Ballet West, for which it was the setting of the 2013 CW reality television series *Breaking Pointe*. A 1912 renovation of another theater, the Mission Theater, is detailed by Epes Winthrop Sargent, "Advertising for Exhibitors," *Moving Picture World*, July 6, 1912, 1272.

26 Nelson, "The History of Utah Film," 2; Nelson, "Utah Filmmakers of the Silent Screen," 5-6.

27 "Young Woman Swallows Laudanum at Babies' Matinee of Picture Show," *Salt Lake Herald*, October 24, 1907, 12, http://chroniclingamerica.loc.gov/lccn/sn85058130/1907-10-24/ed-1/seq-12 (accessed May 21, 2014); "Drinks Poison in a Theater," *Salt Lake Tribune*, October 24, 1907, 12, http://chroniclingamerica.loc.gov/lccn/sn83045396/1907-10-24/ed-1/seq-12 (accessed May 21, 2014). The woman's name is not given; she is identified via her husband Mr. Benjamin Booth of 855 Kimball Avenue. After her stomach was pumped she was questioned by police—and journalists—and, putting on a game face, she "alternately laughed and scoffed at the idea of her committing suicide. Why she had attempted self-destruction was as much a mystery to her as to anyone else, she declared." For the candy machine incident, see "In Police Circles," *Salt Lake Herald*, November 8, 1907, 8, http://chroniclingamerica.loc.gov/lccn/sn85058130/1907-11-08/ed-1/seq-8 (accessed May 21, 2014). Two other early Utah notices of nickelodeons on the national scene are Frederic J. Haskin, "Straws in the Trade Winds," *Salt Lake Tribune*, July 29, 1907, 6, http://chroniclingamerica.loc.gov/lccn/sn83045396/1907-07-29/ed-1/seq-6 (accessed May 21, 2014), which discuss-

es the run on cheap chairs that the nickelodeon boom occasioned, and "Timely Gossip from Chicago," *Deseret Evening News*, Febrary 26, 1908, 5, http://chroniclingamerica.loc.gov/lccn/sn83045555/1908-02-26/ed-1/seq-5 (accessed May 21, 2014), which notes how film prices are rising and cheap nickelodeons are closing throughout that city.

28 "Week Beginning Monday December 25th," *Salt Lake Tribune*, December 21, 1905, 8, http://chroniclingamerica.loc.gov/lccn/sn83045396/1905-12-21/ed-1/seq-8 (accessed November 26, 2013). It's unknown what pictures showed in the initial Christmas evening program—one review describes them as "a number of new and entertaining motion pictures"—but the vaudeville acts that preceded the film included the one-act play *The Night Before*, the singing and dancing Hengler Sisters, a Grand Opera Trio, the comedienne Nelle Florede, and the "physical culture artists" the Three Jacksons. Performances were every evening except Sundays. The advertisement announcing this program was duplicated in both the *Salt Lake Herald* and *Deseret News*, though in the latter "kinodrome" was misspelled "Rinodrome." The *Herald* indicates this bill had a weeklong run. "Dramatic," *Deseret Evening News*, December 23, 1905, 12, http://chroniclingamerica.loc.gov/lccn/sn83045555/1905-12-23/ed-1/seq-12 (accessed November 26, 2013); "Orpheum," *Deseret Evening News*, December 21, 1905, 4, http://chroniclingamerica.loc.gov/lccn/sn83045555/1905-12-21/ed-1/seq-4 (accessed November 26, 2013); "The Theatres," *Salt Lake Herald,* December 24, 1905, section two page 5, http://chroniclingamerica.loc.gov/lccn/sn85058130/1905-12-24/ed-1/seq-13 (accessed November 26, 2013); "Orpheum," *Goodwin's Weekly*, January 13, 1906; "Dramatic," *Deseret Evening News*, January 20, 1906, 14, https://chroniclingamerica.loc.gov/lccn/sn83045555/1906-01-20/ed-1/seq-14 (accessed November 25, 2017), which lists "motion pictures dealing with a coal mine disaster in Germany and showing the explosion and subsequent breaking in of water and rescue of the survivors"; "How the Wonderful Kinodrome Pictures Are Secured," *Deseret Evening News*, February 3, 1906, part two page 17, http://chroniclingamerica.loc.gov/lccn/sn83045555/1906-02-03/ed-1/seq-17 (accessed May 23, 2014); "Amusements," *Truth*, February 10, 1906, 6, http://chroniclingamerica.loc.gov/lccn/sn85058310/1906-02-10/ed-1/seq-6 (accessed May 23, 2014); "Dramatic," *Deseret Evening News*, February 10, 1906, part two page 14, http://chroniclingamerica.loc.gov/lccn/sn83045555/1906-02-10/ed-1/seq-14 (accessed May 23, 2014); "Vaudeville," *Salt Lake Herald*, February 18, 1906, 5, http://chroniclingamerica.loc.gov/lccn/sn85058130/1906-02-18/ed-1/seq-21 (accessed May 23, 2014); "At the Orpheum," *Salt Lake Herald*, February 25, 1906, 5, http://chroniclingamerica.loc.gov/lccn/sn85058130/1906-02-25/ed-1/seq-21 (accessed May 23, 2014); "Orpheum," *Salt Lake Herald*, March 4, 1906, 5, http://chroniclingamerica.loc.gov/lccn/sn85058130/1906-03-04/ed-1/seq-21 (accessed May 23, 2014); "Amusements," *Truth*, March 17, 1906, 6, http://chroniclingamerica.loc.gov/lccn/sn85058310/1906-03-17/ed-1/seq-6, two items (accessed May 23, 2014); "Vaudeville," *Salt Lake Herald*, March 18, 1906, 7, http://chroniclingamerica.loc.gov/lccn/sn85058130/1906-03-18/ed-1/seq-19 (accessed May 23, 2014); "Vaudeville," *Salt Lake Herald*, April 1, 1906, 5, http://chroniclingamerica.loc.gov/lccn/sn85058130/1906-04-01/ed-1/seq-21 (accessed May 23, 2014); "Dramatic," *Deseret Evening News*, April 14, 1906, part two page 20, http://chroniclingamerica.loc.gov/lccn/sn83045555/1906-04-14/ed-1/seq-16 (accessed May 23, 2014);

Notes - The First Wave: The New Frontier

"Orpheum," *Deseret Evening News*, April 17, 1906, 10, http://chroniclingamerica. loc.gov/lccn/sn83045555/1906-04-17/ed-1/seq-10 (accessed May 23, 2014), which reports *Rarebit Fiend* was "the most laughable set of motion pictures yet seen in the house"; "Amusements," *Salt Lake Tribune*, April 18, 1906, 6, http:// chroniclingamerica.loc.gov/lccn/sn83045396/1906-04-18/ed-1/seq-6 (accessed May 23, 2014); "The Theatres," *Salt Lake Herald*, August 26, 1906, 5, http://chroniclingamerica.loc.gov/lccn/sn85058130/1906-08-26/ed-1/seq-15 (accessed May 27, 2014); "Vaudeville at Orpheum," *Salt Lake Herald*, September 16, 1906, part two page 5, http://chroniclingamerica.loc.gov/lccn/sn85058130/1906-0916/ed-1/seq-21 (accessed May 27, 2014); "Dramatic," *Deseret Evening News*, October 13, 1906, part two page 20, http://chroniclingamerica.loc.gov/lccn/ sn83045555/1906-10-13/ed-1/seq-20 (accessed May 27, 2014); "Vaudeville at Orpheum," *Salt Lake Herald*, November 11, 1906, 5, http://chroniclingamerica. loc.gov/lccn/sn85058130/1906-11-11/ed-1/seq-21 (accessed May 27, 2014); "Amusements," *Salt Lake Herald*, November 14, 1906, 3, http://chroniclingamerica.loc.gov/lccn/sn85058130/1906-11-14/ed-1/seq-3 (accessed May 27, 2014); "Promise of the Theatres," *Salt Lake Herald*, November 25, 1906, 5, http://chroniclingamerica.loc.gov/lccn/sn85058130/1906-11-25/ed-1/seq-21 (accessed May 27, 2014); "Dramatic," *Deseret Evening News*, December 29, 1906, part two page 16, http://chroniclingamerica.loc.gov/lccn/sn83045555/1906-12-29/ed-1/seq-16 (accessed May 27, 2014); "Cheer Up," *Truth*, February 2, 1907, 11, http://chroniclingamerica.loc.gov/lccn/sn85058310/1907-02-02/ed-1/seq-11 (accessed May 28, 2014); untitled Orpheum advertisement, *Salt Lake Herald,* February 10, 1907, 11, http://chroniclingamerica.loc.gov/lccn/sn85058130/1907-02-10/ ed-1/seq-11 (accessed May 28, 2014); "Orpheum," *Goodwin's Weekly*, March 2, 1907, 8, http://chroniclingamerica.loc.gov/lccn/2010218519/1907-03-02/ed-1/ seq-8 (accessed May 23, 2014); "Salt Lake City, Utah," *Variety*, October 1907, 25, http://www.archive.org/stream/variety08-1907-10#page/n67/mode/2up (accessed May 28, 2014); "Orpheum Theatre," *Truth*, November 9, 1907, 7, http:// chroniclingamerica.loc.gov/lccn/sn85058310/1907-11-09/ed-1/seq-7 (accessed September 5, 2013); "Orpheum Theatre," *Goodwin's Weekly*, November 27, 1909, 9, http://chroniclingamerica.loc.gov/lccn/2010218519/1909-11-27/ed-1/seq-9 (accessed September 5, 2013); "With the Plays, Players and Playhouses All of Next Week," *Goodwin's Weekly*, August 2, 1913, 8-9, http://chroniclingamerica.loc. gov/lccn/2010218519/1913-08-02/ed-1/seq-8 (accessed September 5, 2013), which indicates that the films shown were generally news items; "Promised Valley Playhouse," *Utah Theaters*, http://utahtheaters.info/TheaterMain.asp?ID=97 (accessed November 13, 2013); Grant Smith, "Promised Valley Playhouse," *Cinema Treasures*, http://cinematreasures.org/theaters/916 (accessed September 5, 2013). I personally remember being taken to this theater with Church youth groups in the 1990s to watch both religious productions and revues with songs from shows like *Les Misérables*.

29 New Grande Theatre advertisement, *Salt Lake Herald*, April 2 1906, 4, http:// chroniclingamerica.loc.gov/lccn/sn85058130/1906-04-02/ed-1/seq-4 (accessed May 23, 2014); "'A Parisian Princess'" and New Grand Theatre advertisement, *Salt Lake Herald*, May 6, 1906, section two page 5, http://chroniclingamerica.loc.gov/ lccn/sn85058130/1906-05-06/ed-1/seq-21 (accessed May 23, 2014).

30 "Lyric Theatre," *Utah Theaters*, http://utahtheaters.info/TheaterMain.asp?ID=522 (accessed May 29, 2014); "Amusements: Lyric," *Deseret Evening News*, April 2, 1906, 2, http://chroniclingamerica.loc.gov/lccn/sn83045555/1906-04-02/ed-1/seq-3 (accessed May 29, 2014); "Amusements: Lyric," *Deseret Evening News*, March 26, 1907, 2, http://chroniclingamerica.loc.gov/lccn/sn83045555/1907-03-26/ed-1/seq-2 (accessed May 29, 2014); untitled notice ("The Byrne Kenyon Four..."), *Salt Lake Tribune*, March 27, 1907, 2, http://chroniclingamerica.loc.gov/lccn/sn83045396/1907-03-27/ed-1/seq-2 (accessed May 29, 2014); Lyric Theatre advertisement, *Goodwin's Weekly*, March 30, 1907, 9, http://chroniclingamerica.loc.gov/lccn/2010218519/1907-03-30/ed-1/seq-9 (accessed May 29, 2014); Lyric Theatre advertisement, *Salt Lake Herald*, May 17, 1907, 10, http://chroniclingamerica.loc.gov/lccn/sn85058130/1907-05-17/ed-1/seq-10 (accessed May 29, 2014).

31 "How the Wonderful Kinodrome Pictures Are Secured," *Deseret Evening News*, part two page 17; Jay E. Johnson, "Salt Lake City, Utah," *Variety*, October 5, 1907, 25, http://www.archive.org/stream/variety08-1907-10#page/n67/mode/2up (accessed August 12, 2014).

32 Pickering, "Salt Lake City, Utah, Registers a Few Exhibitors," 387. For the Isis, see "Isis Theater," *Utah Theaters*, http://utahtheaters.info/TheaterMain.asp?ID=94 (accessed November 13, 2013).

33 H. W. Pickering, "Salt Lake Screen Club," *Moving Picture World*, April 1, 1916, 128, http://www.archive.org/stream/movwor28chal#page/128/mode/2up (accessed September 2, 2014). Though oriented towards their communal bottom line, some of the organization's first activities were meant to build a communal spirit, hence numerous suppers and both a bowling and baseball team. For the strike, see "Salt Lake Moving Picture Men Hit by Walkout," *Ogden Standard*, January 27, 1920, 7, http://chroniclingamerica.loc.gov/lccn/sn85058396/1920-01-27/ed-1/seq-7 (accessed September 2, 2014). Employees wanted a wage increase of $2.50 a week plus a six-hour day; managers assented to the former but not the latter, resulting in the strike and Salt Lake exhibitors advertising in Ogden for new employees.

34 "Empire Theatre Opens," *Salt Lake Herald-Republican*, October 24, 1909, 10, http://chroniclingamerica.loc.gov/lccn/sn85058140/1909-10-24/ed-1/seq-10 (accessed August 11, 2014); "The New Empire Theatre," *Salt Lake Herald-Republican*, October 24, 1909, Real Estate-Classified Section, 10, http://chroniclingamerica.loc.gov/lccn/sn85058140/1909-10-24/ed-1/seq-33 (accessed August 10, 2014); "The New Empire Theatre," *Salt Lake Herald-Republican*, October 25, 1909, 5, http://chroniclingamerica.loc.gov/lccn/sn85058140/1909-10-25/ed-1/seq-5 (accessed August 11, 2014); "The New Empire Theatre (Reopened.)," *Goodwin's Weekly*, October 30, 1909, 11, http://chroniclingamerica.loc.gov/lccn/2010218519/1909-10-30/ed-1/seq-11 (accessed August 11, 2014); "The New Empire Theatre (Reopened.)," *Goodwin's Weekly*, November 6, 1909, 9, http://chroniclingamerica.loc.gov/lccn/2010218519/1909-11-06/ed-1/seq-9 (accessed August 11, 2014); "The New Empire Theater," *Goodwin's Weekly*, November 27, 1909, 9, http://chroniclingamerica.loc.gov/lccn/2010218519/1909-11-27/ed-1/seq-9 (accessed September 5, 2013). One specific picture Rand showed at the

Empire, perhaps through his distribution deal with Biograph, was a boxing match between Messrs. Johnson and Ketchel. "Fight Pictures of Ketchel-Johnson," *Salt Lake Tribune*, November 29, 1909, 9, http://chroniclingamerica.loc.gov/lccn/ sn83045396/1909-11-29/ed-1/seq-9 (accessed August 11, 2014). See also Grant Smith, "Empire Theatre," *Cinema Treasures*, http://cinematreasures.org/the-aters/1470 (accessed May 9, 2006); and "Empire Theatre," *Utah Theaters*, http:// utahtheaters.info/TheaterMain.asp?ID=82 (accessed November 13, 2013). The primary source advertisements contradict some of the information on the *Cinema Treasures* and *Utah Theaters* websites: that is, that the building's location was at 156 rather than 158 or 160 South State Street, although it was rather surrounded by a complex of theaters and the street number could have been adjusted over the years; and Rand's middle initial was R rather than S, though other contemporary articles give it as H. My thanks to Travis Anderson for initially pointing out the existence of this theater to me.

35 "Salt Lake City to Have the Largest Life Motion Picture Theater in America," *Salt Lake Tribune*, December 18, 1910, 32, http://chroniclingamerica.loc.gov/ lccn/sn83045396/1910-12-18/ed-1/seq-32 (accessed August 11, 2014). See also "Another Vaudeville and Motion Picture House," *Salt Lake Tribune*, December 4, 1910, 23, http://chroniclingamerica.loc.gov/lccn/sn83045396/1910-12-04/ed-1/ seq-23 (accessed August 11, 2014). The December 23, 1910 opening gala was a Christmastime benefit for Salt Lake City's poor. "Will Give Shows for Poor People: Harry H. Rand of Daniels Theater to Donate Gross Receipts for Christmas Charity," *Salt Lake Tribune*, December 21, 1910, 12, http://chroniclingamerica.loc.gov/lccn/ sn83045396/1910-12-21/ed-1/seq-12 (accessed August 11, 2014); "Receipts Are Given to Elks' Charity Fund," *Salt Lake Herald-Republican*, December 25, 1910, 3, http://chroniclingamerica.loc.gov/lccn/sn85058140/1910-12-25/ed-1/seq-3 (accessed August 11, 2014).

36 "Big Picture House Is Being Planned," *Evening Standard*, April 30, 1912, 5, http://chroniclingamerica.loc.gov/lccn/sn85058397/1912-04-30/ed-1/seq-5 (accessed August 11, 2014).

37 Pickering, "Salt Lake City, Utah, Registers a Few Exhibitors," 387. Rand's son Walter oversaw the family firm's Denver theaters, which caused him and his bride, a Salt Lake City native, to create what may have been one of the first wedding films when they recorded their nuptials for their absent parents in 1913. "Take Moving Picture of Wedding That Absent Parents Can Later View Scene," *Salt Lake Tribune*, April 17, 1913, 1, http://chroniclingamerica.loc.gov/lccn/ sn83045396/1913-04-17/ed-1/seq-1 (accessed August 11, 2014). It could also be noted that Mormon-born director James Cruze also filmed his wedding, this time in Hollywood, to actress Marguerite Snow that same year.

38 "Personal Mention," *Park Record*, November 14, 1908, 3, http://utahtheaters. info/Article.asp?ArticleID=1575 (accessed November 13, 2013); Isis Theater, *Utah Theaters*, http://utahtheaters.info/TheaterMain.asp?ID=94; "Max Florence," *Wikipedia*, https://en.wikipedia.org/wiki/Max_Florence (accessed March 3, 2016).

39 Pickering, "Salt Lake City, Utah, Registers a Few Exhibitors," 387-388; F. H. Richardson, "Richardson Among the Ranchers," *Moving Picture World* June

30, 1917, 2077-2078, http://www.archive.org/stream/movingpicturewor32n-ewy#page/2076/mode/2up (accessed August 27, 2014); H. W. Pickering, "Swanson's Theater Party for Old Folks," *Moving Picture World*, November 18, 1916, 1050, http://www.archive.org/stream/movingpicturewor30newy#page/1050/mode/2up (accessed August 27, 2014); H. W. Pickering, "Big Organ's Premier: Salt Lake City's American Has Immense Instrument," *Moving Picture World*, June 3, 1916, 1736, http://www.archive.org/stream/moviewor28chal#page/n145/mode/2up (accessed August 23, 2014); H. W. Pickering, "C. W. Meighan With Swanson Circuit," *Moving Picture World,* June 3, 1916, 1736, http://www.archive.org/stream/moviewor28chal#page/n145/mode/2up (accessed August 23, 2014). Old Folks were generally over seventy. The organization for them, which was much more like a club than a formal organization such as a ward priesthood quorum, was founded by photographer Charles Savage in 1875 and lasted until the 1960s. See Joseph Heinerman, "The Old Folks Day: A Unique Tradition," *Utah Historical Quarterly* 53:2 (Spring 1985), 157-169.

40 "America's Biggest Picture Theatre," *Motion Picture News*, January 10, 1914, 19, http://www.archive.org/stream/picturen09moti#page/n5/mode/2up (accessed August 15, 2014).

41 "Harry A. Sims Has Resigned His Position," *Ogden Standard*, May 1, 1916, 4, http://chroniclingamerica.loc.gov/lccn/sn85058396/1916-05-01/ed-1/seq-4 (accessed May 2, 2016); H. W. Pickering, "Will Build Theatre at Salt Lake," *Moving Picture World*, September 2, 1916, 1579, https://books.google.com/books?id=1qEb-AQAAMAAJ&pg=PA1579&lpg=PA1579&dq (accessed May 2, 2016).

42 Nelson, "Utah Filmmakers of the Silent Screen," 15.

43 "Small Theater Fire: Moving Picture Machines and Some of Films are Destroyed At Electric," *Ogden Standard Examiner*, February 8, 1908, 5, http://utahtheaters.info/Article.asp?ArticleID=1217 (accessed November 14, 2013). For the Grand Theater venture, see "With the Theaters," *Salt Lake Tribune*, July 5, 1908, 26, http://chroniclingamerica.loc.gov/lccn/sn83045396/1908-07-05/ed-1/seq-26 (accessed August 12, 2014); "Grand Theater," *Salt Lake Tribune*, July 5, 1908, 26, http://chroniclingamerica.loc.gov/lccn/sn83045396/1908-07-05/ed-1/seq-26 (accessed August 12, 2014).

44 "America's Biggest Picture Theatre," *Motion Picture News*, 19-20, 38; Pickering, "Salt Lake City, Utah, Registers a Few Exhibitors," 388; "American in Salt Lake Contracts for Fox Films," *Motion Picture News*, May 29, 1915, 53, http://www.archive.org/stream/motionpicturenew112unse#page/n871/mode/2up (accessed November 19, 2014); "Among the Picture Theaters: News and Views of Photoplay Houses Everywhere," *Moving Picture World*, July 10, 1915, 275, http://www.archive.org/stream/movingpicturewor25newy#page/274/mode/2up (accessed November 17, 2014). This last article gives the price of the organ at a more affordable $8,000.

45 "Salt Lake City," *Variety*, May 4, 1912, 30, http://www.archive.org/stream/variety26-1912-05#page/n109/mode/2up (accessed August 15, 2014).

46 "Amusements," *Ogden Standard*, April 26, 1916, 3, http://chroniclingamerica.loc.gov/lccn/sn85058396/1916-04-26/ed-1/seq-3 (accessed November 13, 2013); "Alhambra Theatre," *Utah Theaters*, http://utahtheaters.info/TheaterMain.asp?ID=258 (accessed November 13, 2013); Grant Smith, "Peery's Egyptian Theater," *Utah Theaters*, September 18, 2004, http://utahtheaters.info/TheaterMain.asp?ID=167 (accessed September 6, 2013).

47 Nelson, "The History of Utah Film," 3-5, 23; Roger Roper, "Going to the Movies: A Photo Essay of Theaters," *Utah Historical Quarterly* 67:2 (Spring 1999), 113-115; Grant Smith, "Tower Theater," *Cinema Treasures*, http://cinematreasures.org/theater/1112 (accessed May 9, 2006). For another prominent Salt Lake theater opening from 1938, see "Center Theatre Opening Campaign," *Motion Picture Herald*, February 12, 1938, 74, http://www.archive.org/stream/motionpictureher130unse#page/n739/mode/2up (accessed November 19, 2014).

48 Roper, "Going to the Movies: A Photo Essay of Theaters," 112.

49 Although, light musical theater continued in Salt Lake City for decades and, in some forms, up to the present. In 1930 two vaudeville performers, Roy Zastro and Sunny Schuck, gained national renown by wedding on stage at the R-K-O theater in Salt Lake. Their honeymoon consisted of continuing their contractual tour. "Wedding Stunt for R-K-O Stage, Salt Lake," *Variety*, July 2, 1930, 49, http://www.archive.org/stream/variety99-1930-07#page/n47/mode/2up (accessed November 19, 2014).

50 "Stageland," *Logan Republican*, March 16, 1912, 6, http://chroniclingamerica.loc.gov/lccn/sn85058246/1912-03-16/ed-1/seq-6 (accessed August 12, 2014).

51 Pickering, "Salt Lake City, Utah, Registers a Few Exhibitors," 387; for Brigham City see "Among the Picture Theaters," *Moving Picture World*, December 12, 1914, 1509, http://www.archive.org/stream/movingpicturewor22newy#page/1508/mode/2up (accessed November 19, 2014); for Nephi, see Philip Rand, "'California or Bust!,'" *Exhibitor's Herald*, November 24, 1923, 40, http://www.archive.org/stream/exhibitorsherald17exhi#page/n951/mode/2up (accessed November 19, 2014). Brigham City's other movie theater at the time was the Alta; both houses were owned by Messrs. Koford & Ryan.

52 "Regional News from Correspondents: Salt Lake City," *Motion Picture News*, August 26, 1927, 605, http://www.archive.org/stream/motion36moti#page/612/mode/2up (accessed November 19, 2014); "Utah Squatters Watch Bishop's Old Silents for Petty Cash—Cabbages," *Variety*, February 4, 1931, 1, 87, http://www.archive.org/stream/variety101-1931-02#page/n0/mode/2up (accessed November 19, 2014). For the definitive resource Utah's early rural theaters, see Carrie Richter, "Glitz and Glamour on Main Street: A History of the Small Town Movie Theater in Utah, 1915-1945" (master's thesis, University of Utah Graduate School of Architecture, 1997).

53 "The Theatres," *Salt Lake Herald*, April 1, 1906, Section 2, page 5, http://chroniclingamerica.loc.gov/lccn/sn85058130/1906-04-01/ed-1/seq-21 (accessed August 31, 2014).

54 Jay E. Johnson, "Salt Lake City, Utah," *Variety*, April 14, 1906, 13, http://www.archive.org/stream/variety02-1906-04#page/n39/mode/2up (accessed November 19, 2014); Johnson, "Salt Lake City, Utah," October 5, 1907, 25.

55 Jay E. Johnson, "Salt Lake City, Utah," *Variety*, April 13, 1907, 20, http://www.archive.org/stream/variety06-1907-04#page/n51/mode/2up (accessed November 19, 2014); Epes Winthrop Sargent, "Advertising for Exhibitors," *Moving Picture World*, December 8, 1917, 1497, http://www.archive.org/stream/moving34chal#page/n285/mode/2up (accessed November 19, 2014); "Industrial Activity in Salt Lake City Continues to Be Reflected in Business," *Talking Machine World*, April 15, 1925, 141, http://www.archive.org/stream/talkingmachinewo-21bill#page/n825/mode/2up (accessed November 19, 2014); Glenn Perrins, "Salt Lake City," *Variety*, April 14, 1926, 48, http://www.archive.org/stream/variety82-1926-04#page/n113/mode/2up (accessed November 19, 2014); "Key City Reports," *Motion Picture News*, April 22, 1927, 1455, http://www.archive.org/stream/motion35moti#page/n371/mode/2up (accessed November 19, 2014), which indicates what pictures each of the major theaters were showing; Philip G. Lasky, "Chatter: Salt Lake City," *Variety*, April 15, 1931, 60, http://www.archive.org/stream/variety102-1931-04#page/n195/mode/2up (accessed November 19, 2014); "Chatter: Salt Lake City," *Variety*, April 26, 1932, 39, http://www.archive.org/stream/variety106-1932-04#page/n229/mode/2up (accessed November 19, 2014); "Special Showing," *Motion Picture Daily*, April 9, 1938, 1, http://www.archive.org/stream/motionpicturedai43unse_0#page/n55/mode/2up (accessed November 19, 2014). For *The Birth of a Nation*, see H. W. Pickering, "Business Notes," *Moving Picture World*, April 1, 1916, 128, http://www.archive.org/stream/movwor28chal#page/128/mode/2up (accessed August 12, 2014).

56 "Mysterious Entertainers Stunt Gets Much Attention," *Motion Picture News*, March-June 1920, 3082-3083, http://www.archive.org/stream/motionpicturenew212unse#page/n309/mode/2up (accessed August 16, 2014); for the phonograph company, see "Salt Lake Dealers Enjoy Good Business," *Talking Machine World*, May 15, 1925, 66, http://www.archive.org/stream/talkingmachinewo-21bill#page/n941/mode/2up (accessed November 19, 2014); and for the *Sahara* leaflets, "'Bomb' Mormon City in Exploiting 'Sahara,'" *Motion Picture News*, July 5, 1919, 368, http://www.archive.org/stream/motionpicturenew201unse#page/368/mode/2up (accessed November 20, 2014).

57 "'Turkish' Girl Gets Attention of Salt Lake City," *Motion Picture News*, March-June 1920, 3833, http://www.archive.org/stream/motionpicturenew212unse#page/n1209/mode/2up (accessed August 12, 2014).

58 "Pretty Girl Has Her Legs Painted," *Exhibitors Trade Review* 12:21 (October 21, 1922), 1356, http://www.archive.org/stream/exhibitorstr00newy#page/1356/mode/2up (accessed August 16, 2014).

59 Richard Koszarski, *An Evening's Entertainment: The Age of the Silent Feature Pictures, 1915-1928* (Oakland: University of California Press, 1994), 193.

60 Nelson, "Utah Filmmakers of the Silent Screen," 6-7.

61 "Ushers and Ushering," *Motography*, July 17, 1915, 119, https://archive.org/stream/motography00test#page/118/mode/2up (accessed August 30, 2014). Also see a letter from Anthony Slide of the American Film Institute to Richard Alan Nelson, January 4, 1974, in the Richard Alan Nelson Collection, box 2 folder 16. For a detailed summary of Carpenter's career up to 1920, see "Real Showmen – and Why," *Film Daily*, January 4, 1920, 6, 9, http://www.archive.org/stream/filmdailyvolume11112newy#page/18/mode/2up (accessed November 20, 2014).

62 "The Orpheum," *Goodwin's Weekly*, December 30, 1905, 8, http://chroniclingamerica.loc.gov/lccn/2010218519/1905-12-30/ed-1/seq-8 (accessed November 26, 2013); "With the Plays, Players and Playhouses All of Next Week," *Goodwin's Weekly*, 8-9; "Death Certificate of Willard Erastus Weihe, June 5, 1926," *Jared Pratt Family Association*, http://jared.pratt-family.org/orson_family_histories/willard-weihe-death.html (accessed August 31, 2014). Weihe's death certificate indicates he was employed at the LDS School of Music at the time of his death.

63 "The Theatres," *Salt Lake Herald*, section two, page 5.

64 "With the Theaters," *Salt Lake Tribune*, 26.

65 D. J. G., "About This That and T' Other," *Ogden Standard Examiner*, July 15, 1923, 10, http://utahtheaters.info/Article.asp?ArticleID=2860 (accessed November 24, 2013).

66 Pickering, "Salt Lake City, Utah, Registers a Few Exhibitors," 387.

67 "Salt Lake City," *Variety*, 30. The article names the organist as Edwin Kimball; this is apparently a mistake, as Edward Partridge Kimball was a prominent Tabernacle organist and composer active from 1905 until his death in 1937. "Edward P. Kimball," *Wikipedia*, http://en.wikipedia.org/wiki/Edward_P._Kimball (accessed August 18, 2014). The Tabernacle organ was widely seen as one of the highest quality in the country, resulting in many church and theater organs designed to approximate its scope and timbre. One of these was in the Rialto Theater, which opened in Times Square in April 1916, where some of the organ's stops imitated the Tabernacle instrument's alleged ability to give "the effect of scores of violins, gambas, cellos and double basses." But years earlier in 1910 a San Francisco theater took this imitation much further: "One special feature will be a dome shaped interior, patterned after the Mormon tabernacle in Salt Lake City, which is known the world over for its excellent acoustic properties." "Rialto Theater Formally Opened," *Moving Picture World*, May 6, 1916, 945, http://www.archive.org/stream/movpic28chal#page/n65/mode/2up (accessed November 17, 2014); "Among the Picture Theaters," *The Nickelodeon*, September 1, 1910, 138-143, http://www.archive.org/stream/nickelodeon04elec#page/140/mode/2up (accessed November 18, 2014).

68 W. H. Bennett, Jr., "Salt Lake City Business Near Normal: Audiences Composed Mostly of Men and Boys—Managers Agree to Bar Children Under Fourteen," *Moving Picture World*, January 11, 1919, 225, http://www.archive.org/stream/movingwor39chal#page/224/mode/2up (accessed August 31, 2014); H. W. Pickering, "A Fine Salt Lake Theater: Paramount-Empress, Under Management

of H. E. Ellison, Succeeds," *Moving Picture World*, June 24, 1916, 487, http://www.archive.org/stream/movwor28chal#page/486/mode/2up (accessed August 18, 2014).

69 "Col. Cody and Sells-Floto Circus Given Honorary Organ Recital in Salt Lake City," *New York Clipper*, June 27, 1914, 22, http://www.archive.org/stream/clipper62-1914-06#page/n95/mode/2up (accessed November 17, 2014). Cody also frequently met with Joseph F. Smith and other Church leaders. Among the numbers on McClellan's program in 1914 were selections from Wagner's opera *Tannhäuser*, Edwin Lemare's "Andantino" in D flat, and numbers by Théodore Dubois, Niccoló van Westerhout, and some others.

70 "Merger Negotiations Off until Monday Conference," *Variety*, February 5, 1910, 4, http://www.archive.org/stream/variety17-1910-02#page/n3/mode/2up (accessed November 17, 2014); "Seeley Has Some News," *Variety*, February 26, 1910, 1, http://www.archive.org/stream/variety17-1910-02#page/n125/mode/2up (accessed November 17, 2014); "Mormon Organist in Theatre," *Variety*, March 5, 1910, 4, http://www.archive.org/stream/variety18-1910-03#page/n3/mode/2up (accessed August 18, 2014); "Incorporates for Salt Lake," *Variety*, February 12, 1910, 4, http://www.archive.org/stream/variety17-1910-02#page/n43/mode/2up (accessed November 17, 2014). This latter article primarily concerns the creation of the American Music Hall Company, whose officers and chief shareholders included William Morris president, Walter Hoff Seeley vice president, and Joel Nibley treasurer; Nibley was the son of Charles W. Nibley, who was then the Church's Presiding Bishop and who would serve in the First Presidency from 1925 until 1931, showing that belonging to a prominent Mormon family was no deterrent to getting involved in the (potentially lucrative) business of show business. Given the prominence of the William Morris Endeavor talent agency today, the personal interest Morris took in his Utah properties is intriguing.

71 George E. Carpenter, "American Theater Orchestra: Prof. J. J. McClellan, Organist and Leader in Big Salt Lake Picture House," *Moving Picture World*, January 2, 1915, 989, http://www.archive.org/stream/movingpicturewor23newy#page/988/mode/2up (accessed August 18, 2014).

72 H. W. Pickering, "Big Organ's Premier: Salt Lake City's American Has Immense Instrument," *Moving Picture World*, June 3, 1916, 1736, http://www.archive.org/stream/moviewor28chal#page/n145/mode/2up (accessed August 23, 2014); Pickering, "Business Notes," 128.

73 "John J. McClellan," *Wikipedia*, http://en.wikipedia.org/wiki/John_J._McClellan (accessed August 18, 2014); "America's Biggest Picture Theatre," *Motion Picture News*, 19-20, which reveals that instruments at the American included "three violins, viola, 'cello, bass, flute, oboe, first clarinet, second clarinet, bassoon, trumpet, trombone, piano, organ, [and] tympani" and that McClellan's assistant conductor was Levi N. Harmon, Jr.; H. W. Pickering, "Salt Lake a Film Center," *Moving Picture World*, September 25, 1915, 2222, http://www.archive.org/stream/movingpicturewor25newy#page/2222/mode/2up (accessed November 17, 2014); S. Clark Patchin, "Clemmer Theater Celebrates Its Birthday," *Moving Picture World*, March 17, 1917, 1810, http://www.archive.org/stream/movpict31chal#page/n599/

mode/2up (accessed August 23, 2014); untitled Bendix advertisement, *Variety*, May 26, 1916, 43, http://www.archive.org/stream/variety42-1916-05#page/n177/mode/2up (accessed August 23, 2014); Norman Stuckey, "Music for the Photoplay," *Exhibitor's Trade Review*, April 15, 1922, 1432, http://www.archive.org/stream/exhibitorstrad00newy#page/1432/mode/2up (accessed August 31, 2014).

74 Daniel Frederick Berghout, *Alexander Schreiner: Mormon Tabernacle Organist* (Provo: Joseph Fiedling Smith Institute for Latter-day Saint History, Brigham Young University, 2001), 9-10, 15-16, 41-47; "Mormon Organist Signed," *Variety*, October 5, 1927, 55, https://archive.org/stream/variety88-1927-10/Variety88-1927-10#page/n53/mode/2up (accessed November 18, 2014); "Regional News from Correspondents: Salt Lake City," 605; "Alexander Schreiner," *Wikipedia*, http://en.wikipedia.org/wiki/Alexander_Schreiner (accessed November 18, 2014). The Capitol Theatre's selling price is at "Building & Backstage Tours," *USUO Education*, http://www.usuoeducation.org/index.php/for-schools/building-and-backstage-tours (accessed November 19, 2014).

75 Untitled advertisement, *Salt Lake Herald*, November 2, 1902, 8, http://chroniclingamerica.loc.gov/lccn/sn85058130/1902-11-02/ed-1/seq-8 (accessed September 5, 2013).

76 *Utah State Gazetteer and Business Directory, 1903-1904*, Vol. 2 (Salt Lake City: R. L. Polk & Co., 1904), 379; "Charles P. Madsen," *Google Patents*, http://www.google.com/search?tbo=p&tbm=pts&hl=en&q=ininventor:%22Charles+P.+Madsen%22 (accessed September 5, 2013); *Distribution List of the Chemical Engineering Catalog* (New York City: The Chemical Catalog Company, Inc., 1917), 78; untitled advertisement, *Salt Lake Herald*, September 27, 1903, 8, http://chroniclingamerica.loc.gov/lccn/sn85058130/1903-09-27/ed-1/seq-8 (accessed August 26, 2014). This last item indicates that Madsen sold both the 1903 model Universal kinetoscope (a projecting device) and the earlier exhibition kinetoscope.

77 "Personal Mention," *Park Record*, 3.

78 "Motion Picture Men in the City," *Ogden Standard*, March 3, 1917, 14, http://chroniclingamerica.loc.gov/lccn/sn85058396/1917-03-03/ed-1/seq-14 (accessed August 26, 2014); Pickering, "Salt Lake a Film Center," 2222; "Ben Simpson Leaves San Francisco," *Moving Picture World*, June 14, 1919, 1664, http://www.archive.org/stream/mopicwor40chal#page/n295/mode/2up (accessed November 19, 2014); "Regional News from Correspondents: Salt Lake City," 605; see also Pickering, "Salt Lake City, Utah, Registers a Few Exhibitors," 387-388.

79 Manuscript material in the Richard Alan Nelson Collection, L. Tom Perry Special Collections, Harold B. Lee Library, Brigham Young University, box 2 folder 5.

80 "Leading Managers Combine Forces," *Ogden Standard*, July 13, 1914, 12, http://chroniclingamerica.loc.gov/lccn/sn85058396/1914-07-13/ed-1/seq-12 (accessed September 2, 2014); "Regional News from Correspondents: Salt Lake City," 605. Herman Wobber succeeded Marcus in his Paramount position.

81 "William Wadsworth Hodkinson," *Wikipedia*, http://en.wikipedia.org/wiki/

William_Wadsworth_Hodkinson (accessed August 26, 2006); D. J. G., "About This That and T' Other," *Ogden Standard Examiner*, 5; "Uptown Theatre," *Utah Theaters*, http://utahtheaters.info/TheaterMain.asp?ID=128 (accessed August 31, 2014); Pickering, "Salt Lake City, Utah, Registers a Few Exhibitors," 388; Pickering, "A Fine Salt Lake Theater," 487. The Empress was originally known as the Sullivan & Considine theater when a vaudeville hall; it had only briefly operated under its new name "as a combination musical comedy-motion picture house" and then stock theater when purchased by Paramount, and it was under Paramount that it dropped vaudeville entirely from its offerings. Pickering, "Salt Lake a Film Center," 2222 states that the theater reopened after renovations in 1915, which is when Weihe was hired to lead the music, although some renovations apparently continued until 1916.

82 Koszarski, *An Evening's Entertainment*, 69.

83 J. A. Aberdeen, "W. W. Hodkinson: The Man Who Invented the Movie Business," *Hollywood Renegades Archive*, http://www.cobbles.com/simpp_archive/hodkinson_system.htm (accessed August 26, 2006).

84 The MPPC, also commonly known as the Edison Trust, was an attempt among a few American film stock, camera, and motion picture production companies to control the basic technology underpinning filmmaking and, hence, the lucrative filmmaking business itself. Primary partners included Edison, Biograph, Vitagraph, Essaney, Selig, Lubin, Kalem, Star Film Company, the American branch of Pathé, Eastman Kodak, and distributor George Kleine. Founded at the end of 1908 it held considerable influence for several years, though never as monopolistically as its founders hoped, and many independent studios continued to operate throughout its existence without the payment of patent royalties. The trust's original patents expired in September 1913, around the same time it came under the trust-busting scrutiny of the federal government; in October 1915 the federal court decision United States v. Motion Picture Patents Co. broke up the company under the provisions of the Sherman Antitrust Act. There are many sources on the MPPC, including Koszarski's *An Evening's Entertainment*, but for a quick overview see "Motion Picture Patents Company," *Wikipedia*, http://en.wikipedia.org/wiki/Motion_Picture_Patents_Company (accessed September 2, 2014).

85 Koszarski, *An Evening's Entertainment*, 69.

86 After his ouster from Paramount Hodkinson attempted several other endeavors, helping form the production company Superpictures Incorporated in 1916 before being named president of the distribution arm of the Triangle Film Corporation, where he maintained an active interest in the Utah market. His final film-related venture was the W. W. Hodkinson Company, which lasted until 1929; he later went into aircraft manufacture in the U.S. and Guatemala and lived until 1971. "Come In—It's Paramount Week," *Ogden Standard-Examiner*, September 5, 1920, 11, http://chroniclingamerica.loc.gov/lccn/sn85058393/1920-09-05/ed-1/seq-11 (accessed September 2, 2014); Nelson, "The History of Utah Film," 13-15; John Douglas Eames, *The Paramount Story* (New York: Crown Publishers, Inc., 1985), 9, 11; "W. W. Hodkinson and Wife Guests," *Ogden Standard*, March 19, 1917, 3, http://chroniclingamerica.loc.gov/lccn/sn85058396/1917-03-19/ed-1/

seq-3 (accessed September 2, 2014). For a good online introduction and portal to primary sources on Paramount, see Nicholas Rombes, "The Invention of Paramount Pictures," *Filmmaker*, September 5, 2013, http://filmmakermagazine. com/75946-the-invention-of-paramount-pictures/#.VAX96hxLhLl (accessed September 5, 2013), which includes several links and information such as Paramount's first film, *The Lost Paradise*, directed by Henry Churchill de Mille. Like Paramount, most major film studios began in distribution; see Bordwell *et al, The Classical Hollywood Cinema*, 398.

87 Marcus was also a Republican, a party he shared with the unpopular President Hoover and which held far less sway in Utah politics than it does today; Utah went overwhelmingly for Roosevelt in 1932, and even today Salt Lake City is more liberal than the rest of the state, as of this writing having not elected a Republican mayor since 1976. "Par-F.&M. Pool Being Discussed for Salt Lake," *Variety*, January 9, 1934, 4, http://www.archive.org/stream/variety113-1934-01#page/ n131/mode/2up (accessed November 19, 2014); "Paramount Theatre," *Cinema Treasures*, http://cinematreasures.org/theaters/26282 (accessed November 19, 2014); Pickering, "Business Notes," 128. There is a variety of sources for Marcus's political career, and his personal papers, reflecting 1902-1939 and including his personal diary, are held at the J. Willard Marriott Library Manuscripts Division at the University of Utah and, concerning his work from 1911-1936, at the Harold B. Lee Library at BYU. For more on the early history of Jewish politicians in Utah, including governor Simon Bamberger (elected in 1916), see Quinn, *The Mormon Hierarchy: Extensions of Power*, 815, 819.

88 "David P. Howells Dies in Hollywood," *Motion Picture Daily*, March 31, 1939, 2, http://www.archive.org/stream/motionpicturedai45unse#page/2/mode/2up (accessed August 22, 2014); J. C. Jenkins, "J. C. Jenkins—His Colyum," *Motion Picture Herald*, June 29, 1935, 82, http://www.archive.org/stream/motionpicture-her119unse#page/82/mode/2up (accessed November 20, 2014).

89 David Kent Jacobs, "The History of Motion Pictures Produced by The Church of Jesus Christ of Latter-day Saints" (master's thesis, Brigham Young University Dept. of Dramatic Arts, 1967), 11.

90 Richardson, "Richardson Among the Ranchers," 2077.

91 "Visual Instruction President Will Visit Eastern Centers With View of Introducing Movies Into Schools," *Deseret Evening News*, August 3, 1921, Journal History of the Church, August 3, 1921, 3, https://dcms.lds.org/delivery/Delivery-ManagerServlet?dps_pid=IE375112, Image 12.

92 "Salt Lake Styled 'Dead Head City of America,'" *Deseret Evening News*, November 24, 1914, Journal History of the Church, November 24, 1914, 4, https:// dcms.lds.org/delivery/DeliveryManagerServlet?dps_pid=IE307563, Image 144. The *Variety* article goes into detail about how two newspapers were distributing tickets for free and how it was having tangible consequences on legitimate theaters' profits, such as causing the Loew's Empress to only open three days a week. Due to such hampered income this theater would be sold to Hodkinson the next year and converted into the Paramount-Empress, a film-only house. "Long

Distance Split-Week on Loew's Western Time," *Variety*, January 16, 1915, 5, http://www.archive.org/stream/variety37-1915-01#page/n87/mode/2up (accessed November 20, 2014).

93 Ogden Trades and Labor Assembly Committee members, "Labor Unions Explain Attitude On Free Coupons and Free Ticket System," *Ogden Standard*, June 9, 1915, 6-7, http://chroniclingamerica.loc.gov/lccn/sn85058396/1915-06-09/ed-1/seq-6 (accessed September 2, 2014). A 1911 article describes the extent of the discount pricing that engendered this animus: "...A ticket issued by Keith O'Brien, the largest store in the Mormon capital . . . is given every purchaser in the 'Bargain Basement,' whatever that is. The tickets are sold to the merchant at six cents each, cash in advance. A second slip admits two to any matinee and is issued by the Herald-Republican in a scheme to boom the want ads. [Readers had to search through them to piece together the coupon.] One thousand of the tickets pay for such advertising as the house obtains that is not given free in connection with this offer . . . There are no blanks in this scheme. Any person who will present the coupon properly fixed up gets the tickets." Epes Winthrop Sargent, "Advertising for Exhibitors," *Moving Picture World*, December 23, 1911, 979, http://www.archive.org/stream/moviwor10chal#page/n981/mode/2up (accessed November 20, 2014).

94 "Passing Events," *Improvement Era* 26:6 (April 1923), 584.

95 Untitled photograph, *Improvement Era* 21:7 (May 1918), 622.

96 Charles Chaplin, *My Autobiography* (London: The Bodley Head, 1964), 237-239; Howard Pearson, "'The Kid' Was Edited In Salt Lake Hotel," *Deseret News*, September 30, 1964, B3, http://news.google.com/newspapers?nid=336&dat=19640930&id=hGMvAAAAIBAJ&sjid=N0gDAAAAIBAJ&pg=7234%2C6441442 (accessed September 18, 2011). The edit continued to be refined on the East Coast, and the custody battle continued as well. Mildred Harris Chaplin's lawyers placed a value of $750,000 on the film, but before its premiere Charlie was getting sales offers of over $1,000,000. Herbert Howe, "What's the Matter with Chaplin?," *Picture Play* 13:4 (December 1920), 28, http://www.archive.org/stream/pictureplaymagaz13unse#page/n357/mode/2up (accessed November 20, 2014). Still, the film premiered in New York on January 21, 1921.

97 F. L. W. Bennett, "Salt Lake City," *Variety*, August 30, 1923, 54, http://www.archive.org/stream/variety71-1923-08#page/n245/mode/2up (accessed September 2, 2014).

98 Quinn, *The Mormon Hierarchy: Extensions of Power*, 292. Quinn describes how Church leaders were involved in various types of familial, community, and political decisions as well as issues such as crop irrigation.

99 Rex Skidmore, "Mormon Recreation in Theory and Practice: A Study in Social Change," (Ph.D. dissertation, University of Pennsylvania, 1941), 5, quoted in Terryl Givens, *People of Paradox: A History of Mormon Culture* (Oxford: Oxford University Press, 2007), 45.

100 Thomas G. Alexander, "Between Revivalism and the Social Gospel: The Latter-day Saint Social Advisory Committee, 1916-1922," *BYU Studies* 23:1 (Winter 1983), 19.

101 Carol Cornwall Madsen, "Retrenchment Association," *Encyclopedia of Mormonism*, Vol. 3, ed. Daniel H. Ludlow (New York: Macmillon Publishing Company, 1992), 1223-1225.

102 As with other Church organizations like the Sunday School and children's Primary, the young men's organization began as an innovation in a single unit, the Salt Lake Thirteenth Ward, in June 1875 and was then adopted Church-wide in December 1876. Quinn, *The Mormon Hierarchy: Extensions of Power*, 771.

103 Matthew Bowman, *The Mormon People: The Making of an American Faith* (New York: Random House, 2012), 138-139. Similar changes characterized American Protestantism at this time.

104 Ibid., 140.

105 Matthew Bowman, "Mormonism's Surprisingly Deep Affinity For Progressive Politics," *New Republic*, November 21, 2011, https://newrepublic.com/article/97613/romney-mormonism (accessed June 13, 2015).

106 Alexander, "Between Revivalism and the Social Gospel," 20-21; see the entire article.

107 Bowman, *The Mormon People*, 164. The education that Bowman is referring to demonstrates how Mormons valued institutions like educational societies even before the Progressive Era emerged as a national phenomenon. For instance, in the 1870s B. H. Roberts "had belonged to the Young Men's Club of Centerville, Utah. This remarkable, independent group of boys paid the then hefty initiation fee of $2.50 (and $.50 monthly) 'all of which was turned into books.' The group existed expressly 'to encourage reading and meet . . . at stated periods—usually once a week—and to retell the stories of their reading.' They amassed 'a rather considerable library' and even raised enough funds to build their own public hall." Givens, *People of Paradox*, 93-94; the quotations are from Gary James Bergera, ed., *Autobiography of B. H. Roberts* (Salt Lake City: Signature Books, 1990), 54.

108 Indeed, leaders worked throughout the early twentieth century to once again reform all priesthood quorums, this time in accordance with Progressive principles. This Priesthood Reform Movement lasted from 1908 to 1922 and stemmed from a lack of uniformity among different wards, emphasizing activities like standardizing curricula and creating ward-level groups for Seventies and High Priests. William Hartley, "The Priesthood Reform Movement, 1908-1922," *BYU Studies* 13:2 (1973), 1-16.

109 James B. Allen, "The LDS Family History Library, Salt Lake City," *Mormon Americana: A Guide to Sources and Collections in the United States*, ed. David J. Whittaker (Provo: BYU Studies Monographs, 1995), 138. The Genealogical Society of Utah was founded in 1894, in part in response to the loss of polygamy—Mor-

mons would hereafter emphasize their vertical family structures through time rather than their horizontal family structures here and now—but it also represents a progressive approach, through an institutional body, to the issue of family history. The society became the Genealogical Department of the Church in 1975, when Correlation emphasized the consolidation of many such programs.

110 Quinn, *The Mormon Hierarchy: Extensions of Power*, 812.

111 Wallace Stegner, *Mormon Country* (Lincoln and London: University of Nebraska Press, 1970), 16-17, which includes information on the nineteenth-century organization, known as the "Hope of Israel"; Lowell M. Snow, "Scouting," *Encyclopedia of Mormonism*, Vol. 3, 1275-1277; Quinn, *The Mormon Hierarchy: Extensions of Power*, 811 (which points out that "one of Lord Baden-Powell's original English Scout troop [was] LDS Arthur William Sadler"), 864 (which states that in 1973 one in every twenty American Boy Scouts was Mormon); L. R. Martineau, "M.I.A. Scouts," *Improvement Era* 15:5 (March 1912), 354-361; Joseph F. Smith, "Editors' Table: Boy Scouts," *Improvement Era* 17:4 (February 1914), 385-386; Oscar A. Kirkham, "Mutual Work: What Can Be Done With the Boys, Brethren?," *Improvement Era* 17:5 (March 1914), 488-491, which indicates, on p. 488, that MIA Scouting "is no longer in the experimental stage"; "Good Progress in Utah," *Improvement Era* 17:12 (October 1914), 1181, which quotes a report on Mormons' high enrollment in that August's *Scouting* magazine, including the following: "Boy Scout work has been taken up with a great of thoroughness by the 'Mormon' Church, and under Scout Commissioner John H. Taylor the enrollment has been very high. The Y.M.M.I.A., the 'Mormon' organization, which corresponds to the Y.M.C.A., published in their hand-book an exhaustive account of the Scout work"; "In 22 Years L.D.S. Scouting Encircles Globe," *Improvement Era* 38:2 (February 1935), 78, which states that it was the YMMIA's Athletic Committee that actually investigated and approved adopting the BSA program; D. L. Roberts, "Scouting for 40 Years," *Improvement Era* 56:6 (June 1953), 394-395, 470. The April 1921 *Improvement Era* was a special issue devoted to Scouting. In 2017, an estimated 330,000 Mormon youth participated in the BSA, comprising roughly 20% of the BSA's total membership. But in October 2017, after the BSA announced it would admit girls the Church responded that it would no longer sponsor units for boys fourteen and over; as of this writing the future of the relationship regarding boys under that age is uncertain. Joe Sutton, "Mormon church is pulling older teens from Boy Scouts' programs," *CNN*, October 11, 2017, http://www.cnn.com/2017/05/11/health/lds-teens-boy-scouts-trnd/index.html (accessed October 19, 2017); Benjamin Park, "Mormons and the Boy Scouts: Heading down different trails," *Religion News Service*, October 17, 2017, http://religionnews.com/2017/10/17/mormons-and-the-boy-scouts-heading-down-different-trails (accessed October 19, 2017).

112 Nationally, Libraries and gymnasiums were often combined, as they eventually were in Mormon meetinghouses, into single structures that could nourish both mind and body and that could counteract the dangers of saloons and other deleterious locales. By the late 1920s not only did all new Mormon meetinghouses have cultural halls attached, but many old recreational halls were remodeled for use as meetinghouses themselves. It is largely thanks to the work of the architect Hyrum Pope—best known for the Laie, Hawaii and Cardston, Alber-

ta temples—in the 1930s-50s that the recreational or social hall was placed, with a retractable wall, as an overflow seating area for the chapel itself. Martha Sonntag Bradley, "'The Church and Colonel Saunders': Mormon Standard Plan Architecture," (master's thesis, Brigham Young University Dept. of History, 1981), 25, 33, 48, 53, 137. This practical design has been one of the most criticized aspects of Mormon meetinghouse architecture from an aesthetic standpoint. See the roundtable discussion "Mormon Architecture Today," *Dialogue: A Journal of Mormon Thought* 3:1 (Spring 1968), 18, 20. Scouting and gyms were often linked in Mormon thought, such as a joint headline in the *Improvement Era* reading "Athletic and Scout Work," all major Scouting conferences took place inside the Deseret Gym, and MIA Scout Commissioner John H. Taylor actually had his office there. "Mutual Work: Of Interest to Scouts," *Improvement Era* 17:10 (August 1914), 994. The Deseret Gym remained in use until May 1997 when it was demolished to make way for the Conference Center just north of Temple Square.

113 Clayne R. Jensen, "Sports," *Encyclopedia of Mormonism,* Vol. 3, 1409-1411.

114 "Mutual Work: Dramas for M.I.A.," *Improvement Era* 13:5 (March 1910), 470-471; Horace G. Whitney, "A Word to Dramatic Clubs," *Improvement Era* 13:6 (April 1910), 559-563; Edward H. Anderson, "Social Affairs," *Improvement Era* 14:11 (September 1911), 1056, which discusses the first road show and predicts "the scheme [will] eventually prove a very great success, and that a great deal of good can be accomplished in this particular field"; Horace G. Whitney, "Special Exercises in the M.I.A.," *Improvement Era* 15:4 (February 1912), 323-329; "Nineteenth General Annual Conference of the Y.M. and Y.L.M.I.A. June 12, 13, and 14, 1914," *Improvement Era* 17:10 (August 1914), 950; "Mutual Work: The Short Drama," *Improvement Era* 17:11 (September 1914), 1087; "Mutual Work: M.I.A. Day Play Production," *Improvement Era* 19:7 (May 1916), 664; "Mutual Work: Lists of Dramas, Debates, and Declamations," *Improvement Era* 19:12 (October 1916), 1119; "Mutual Work: Special Activities: About Plays," *Improvement Era* 20:3 (December 1916), 278; Maud May Babcock, "The Social Hall," *Improvement Era* 21:11 (September 1918), 1012. For some examples from when Merry-Go-Rounds or road shows were well established, see "Mutual Work: Utah Stake Recreation Road Show," *Improvement Era* 27:7 (May 1924), 698-699; "Granite Stake Merry-Go-Round," *Improvement Era* 29:7 (May 1926), 690; "M.I.A. Merry-Go-Round," *Improvement Era* 30:4 (February 1927), 383, about an event in the Shelley, Idaho stake; and "M.I.A. Road Shows Delight: Originality Rules in Drama Contest: Project Now Churchwide," *Church News*, October 8, 1932, 2. Some wards had been staging comic operas and minstrel shows, often as fundraisers, well before the road show movement of the early twentieth century: "Amusements," *Salt Lake Herald*, May 4, 1898, 2, http://chroniclingamerica.loc.gov/lccn/sn85058130/1898-05-04/ed-1/seq-2 (accessed April 19, 2014), which announces a comedy and opera presented at the Salt Lake Eighteenth Ward; "State Society: Manti," *Salt Lake Herald-Republican*, October 31, 1909, https://chroniclingamerica.loc.gov/lccn/sn85058140/1909-10-31/ed-1/seq-34 (accessed November 17, 2017), which gives one example of a Church-sponsored minstrel show to raise money for a new chapel.

115 "Editors' Table: 'The Time Has Come for the Latter-day Saints to Look After Their Children,'" *Improvement Era* 13:1 (November 1909), 81-82; "Editors' Table: The Love of Mother," *Improvement Era* 13:3 (January 1910), 276; Zina B. Can-

non, "Social Affairs," *Improvement Era* 14:11 (September 1911), 1060; "Editors' Table: Duty of Parents to Children, and Officers to Members," *Improvement Era* 18:6 (May 1915), 636; "Editors' Table: Home Evening," *Improvement Era* 18:8 (June 1915), 733-734; "Editors' Table: About Our Conference," *Improvement Era* 18:10 (August 1915), 923; Quinn, *The Mormon Hierarchy: Extensions of Power*, 814 (about its creation), 825 (about the program's reemphasis in 1937), 832 (and again in 1946), 852 (and again, under the new Correlation program, in 1964).

116 R. Wayne Boss, "Home Teaching," *Encyclopedia of Mormonism*, Vol. 2, 655; Quinn, *The Mormon Hierarchy: Extensions of Power*, 768.

117 "Our Work: Amusements and Entertainments," *Improvement Era* 7:2 (December 1903), 146; "Priesthood Quorum's Table: Summer Amusements, Davis Stake," *Improvement Era* 21:8 (June 1918), 742-743, which after excoriating the cities and their pleasure resorts and praising Scout work, bicycle races, and other athletic contests mentions "the evils of automobiling, treating and cigarette smoking"; Bryant S. Hinckley, et al, "Preliminary Programs and Social Affairs," *Improvement Era* 14:11 (September 1911), 1047-1061. Edith R. Lovesy presented the thought: "If you would save these young people, you must plan, and provide better places for their amusements—especially in the outlying districts—and plan more forms of recreation for them . . . We must furnish more forms of recreation for the young people, for without them religion will not have the same power to reach their hearts" (p. 1052). Such sentiments have lasted, essentially, up to the present. In 1923, after Church-sponsored film screenings were well established, apostle Melvin Ballard recapitulated that "the ultimate purpose of our being interested in this recreational work is to keep our young people safe, pure, and under the influence of the Church...." Melvin J. Ballard, "Timely Thoughts from the June Conference: Church Organization for Recreation," *Improvement Era* 26:10 (August 1923), 924.

118 "Ward Entertainments," *Salt Lake Herald*, November 22, 1901, 3, https://chroniclingamerica.loc.gov/lccn/sn85058130/1901-11-22/ed-1/seq-3 (accessed July 2, 2012). Patriotism from the Spanish-American War still ran strong, and the other lantern views included "soldiers marching to war, battle of San Juan hill, battleship Maine starting on her last voyage, burial of the Maine victims."

119 In 1909 a missionary in Britain mused that if he lived today Joseph Smith would be making motion pictures about ancient America. "Deadly Blunders in Joseph Smith's Work, if He Was an Imposter," *Millennial Star* 71:34 (August 26, 1909), 529.

120 "Motion Pictures Illustrate Talk: Innovation at First Methodist Church Proves to be Flattering Success," *Salt Lake Herald-Republican*, June 26, 1911, Journal History of the Church, June 26, 1911, 3, https://dcms.lds.org/delivery/DeliveryManagerServlet?dps_pid=IE497552 (accessed November 16, 2017). Short's topic was "Your Life—What Is It? What Will You Do With It?" and the three films were *The Walled City of Pekin (or Pekin, the Walled City)*, *The Construction of Flying Machines*, and *Judas Betraying Christ*.

121 "Mormon Church Will Use Motion Pictures," *Salt Lake Tribune*, August 30,

1913, 16, https://chroniclingamerica.loc.gov/lccn/sn83045396/1913-08-30/ed-1/seq-16 (accessed November 17, 2017).

122 Untitled editorial, *Deseret News*, September 6, 1913, Journal History of the Church, September 6, 1913, 2, https://dcms.lds.org/delivery/DeliveryManagerServlet?dps_pid=IE304777 (accessed November 16, 2017). The author claims that local Catholics had been much more enthusiastic in showing films than the more iconoclastically inclined Protestants. See also "Mormon Church Will Use Motion Pictures," *Ogden Standard*, August 30, 1913, 16, https://chroniclingamerica.loc.gov/lccn/sn85058396/1913-08-30/ed-1/seq-16 (accessed November 24, 2017); "At the Theater," *Salt Lake Tribune,* September 7, 1913, magazine section page 4, https://chroniclingamerica.loc.gov/lccn/sn83045396/1913-09-07/ed-1/seq-44 (accessed November 24, 2017).

123 "Roll of States: Utah," *Motography*, August 23, 1913, 152, http://www.archive.org/stream/motography10elec#page/152/mode/2up (accessed March 2, 2018); "Mormon Church Adopt Simplex," *Motion Picture News*, May 31, 1919, 3596, http://www.archive.org/stream/motionpicturenew192unse_0#page/3596/mode/2up (accessed December 1, 2017), which announces the purchase of Simplex brand projectors for two wards in Salt Lake City and one each in Roosevelt and Bountiful, Utah; S. Clark Patchin, "Mormon Church Spent $60,000 for Films Last Year," *Moving Picture World*, December 30, 1916, 2002, http://www.archive.org/stream/movingpicturewor30newy#page/2002/mode/2up (accessed December 1, 2017).

124 Alexander, "Between Revivalism and the Social Gospel," 25.

125 "Mutual Work: Preaching the Gospel of Better Recreation," *Improvement Era* 27:7 (May 1924), 696; Alexander, "Between Revivalism and the Social Gospel," 26-37. See also "Preliminary Announcement by the N.E.A. Press Service," *Visual Education* 1:2 (April 1920), 34, http://www.archive.org/stream/visualeducation-01soci#page/n83/mode/2up (accessed December 1, 2017), which announces a national social work conference to be held in Salt Lake City.

126 Alexander, "Between Revivalism and the Social Gospel," 25.

127 "Extension Courses To Be Given Here," *Ogden Standard-Examiner*, September 22, 1920, 14, https://chroniclingamerica.loc.gov/lccn/sn85058393/1920-09-22/ed-1/seq-14 (accessed November 26, 2017). For other examples of educational films in the Mormon press, see "The 'Movies' for Publicity," *Deseret Evening News*, December 4, 1917, Journal History of the Church, December 4, 1917, 1, https://dcms.lds.org/delivery/DeliveryManagerServlet?dps_pid=IE375650 (accessed November 25, 2017), on educational films about the Philippines; "Motion Pictures vs. Books," *Deseret Evening News*, May 17, 1921, Journal History of the Church, May 17, 1921, 2, https://dcms.lds.org/delivery/DeliveryManagerServlet?dps_pid=IE305272 (accessed November 24, 2017); "Visual Instruction President Will Visit Eastern Centers With View of Introducing Movies Into Schools," *Deseret Evening News*, August 3, 1921, Journal History of the Church, August 3, 1921, 3, https://dcms.lds.org/delivery/DeliveryManagerServlet?dps_pid=IE375112 (accessed November 26, 2017); "Movies Reach Wider Field," *Deser-*

et *Evening News*, August 5, 1923, Journal History of the Church, August 5, 1921, 3; "Messages from the Missions: The Sixth Annual Farmers' Encampment," *Improvement Era* 29:8 (June 1926), 801, about a conference at the Agricultural College in Logan (now Utah State University) that featured instructional films among other activities.

128 Lindvall, *Sanctuary Cinema*,110-111.

129 Ibid., 163. Methodist film production also swelled in the 1920s.

130 "Passing Events: Moving Pictures," *Improvement Era* 23:1 (November 1919), 89.

131 Alexander, "Between Revivalism and the Social Gospel," 32.

132 Stephen L Richards, "Some Social Sentiments," *Improvement Era* 24:3 (January 1921), 199-204. He admonishes social purity from the world's contaminated influences and the regulation of motion picture exhibition among Church members.

133 Edward H. Anderson, "Social Affairs," *Improvement Era* 14:11 (September 1911), 1055.

134 James E. Talmage, "'Mormon' Temporalities," *Improvement Era* 24:10 (August 1921), 923.

135 "Mutual Work: Instructions to Stake and Ward Committees on Recreation," *Improvement Era* 27:3 (January 1924), 265. See also F. C. Steele, "The Program on Recreation," *Improvement Era* 29:12 (October 1926), 1204-1205, which suggests a method of splitting fundraising revenue between the sponsoring organization and a general ward recreation fund. For Elder Ballard's comment, see Melvin J. Ballard, "The Mission of the M.I.A.," *Improvement Era* 27:10 (August 1924), 935.

136 "Movies Suitable for Ward Presentation," *Improvement Era* 27:3 (January 1924), 251; "Mutual Work: Movies Suitable for Ward Presentation," *Improvement Era* 27:4 (February 1924), 394; "Editor's Table: Acceptable Movies," *Improvement Era* 27:5 (March 1924), 485; "Mutual Work: Acceptable Movies," *Improvement Era* 27:6 (April 1924), 571-572; "Mutual Work: Acceptable Movies," *Improvement Era* 27:7 (May 1924), 699; "Editors' Table: Acceptable Movies," *Improvement Era* 27:11 (September 1924), 1100; "Priesthood Quorums: Motion Pictures," *Improvement Era* 28:2 (December 1924), 174; W.H. Boyle, "Picture Shows: An Asset or a Liability—for Me and Mine?," *Improvement Era* 28:6 (April 1925), 527-528; "Mutual Work: Motion Pictures," *Improvement Era* 29:2 (December 1925), 205; "Mutual Work: Pictures Previewed and Recommended by the M.I.A. Committee," *Improvement Era* 29:6 (April 1926), 601-602; Steele, "The Program on Recreation," 1204-1205; Oscar A. Kirkham, "Third International Boys' Work Conference: Held at Edgewater Beach Hotel, Chicago, Ill., Nov. 30, Dec. 1 and 2, 1926," *Improvement Era* 30:5 (March 1927), 440; "Course of Study: Motion Pictures," *Improvement Era* 33-41:1 (November 1929), 76-80, a series of topics related to cinema for class study and discussion; "Motion Pictures," *Improvement Era* 33:8 (June 1930), 576-577, 582; "Community Activity Dept. Committee: Motion Pictures," Improve-

ment Era 34:5 (March 1931), 293, which proposing centralizing control over ward screenings; "Community Activity Dept. Committee: Motion Pictures," *Improvement Era* 34:6 (April 1931), 348; "Community Activity Dept. Committee: Motion Pictures," *Improvement Era* 34:7 (May 1931), 419; and slightly on into the 1930s. See also "Mormon Church Takes Up Movies," *Educational Film Magazine* 3:1 (January 1920), 14, and "Flashes on the World's Screen," *Educational Film Magazine* 3:1 (January 1920), 30, which are about the implementation of films into the Latter-day Saint University.

137 "Movie Pictures Are Denounced: Stake President Declared Film Productions Are Cause of Juvenile Deliquency," *Salt Lake Tribune*, February 13, 1922, Journal History of the Church, February 13, 1922, 3; "The Week in Review: Friday, December 18," *Exhibitors Trade Review*, December 19, 1925, 6, http://www.archive.org/ stream/exhibitorstrade00new#page/n197/mode/2up (accessed December 1, 2018); "Passing Events," *Improvement Era* 31:2 (December 1927), 178.

138 "Fountain Green Theatre," *Utah Theaters*, http://utahtheaters.info/Theater/ History/273/Fountain-Green-Theatre (accessed December 2, 2017); Fountain Green Theatre financial records, 1929-1935, one box, Church History Library, The Church of Jesus Christ of Latter-day Saints, Salt Lake City, which includes an account book listing movies shown as well as all other financial records; Suzanne Dean, "Old dance hall kicks up heels," *Deseret News*, July 13, 2004, https://www. deseretnews.com/article/595076908/Old-dance-hall-kicks-up-heels.html (accessed December 2, 2017); Susan Whitney, "New life for an old building," *Deseret News*, November 15, 2004, https://www.deseretnews.com/article/595105030/ New-life-for-an-old-building.html (accessed December 2, 2017); "Exhibitors' Personals: Wyoming," *Motion Picture News*, May 4, 1918, 2728, http://www.archive. org/stream/motionpicturenew172unse#page/2728/mode/2up; "Wyoming movie theatres: Includes Casper and Cheyenne," *Movie Theatre*, January 4, 2012, http:// www.movie-theatre.org/usa/wy/WY%20Wyoming.pdf, 10 (accessed December 2, 2017). For a detailed explanation of the finances and logistics involved for a ward to build a traditional amusement hall—which may have included a film exhibition space—see Melvin Lemon, "How Hyrum Second Ward Built Its Recreation Hall," *Improvement Era* 28:10 (August 1925), 976-977.

139 Konden R. Smith, "The Dawning of a New Era: Mormonism and the World's Columbian Exposition of 1893," *Mormons and Popular Culture: The Global Influence of an American Phenomenon*, Vol. 2, ed. J. Michael Hunter (Santa Barbara: Praeger Publishers, 2013), 187-208; for the Seattle event see "Events and Comments: The 'Mormons' and the West," *Improvement Era* 12:7 (May 1909), 580 and "Events and Comments: The Alaska-Yukon-Pacific Exposition," *Improvement Era* 12:10 (August 1909), 844; for the Bureau of Information see the following: "Editor's Table: Bureau of Information and Church Literature," *Improvement Era* 5:11 (September 1902), 899-901; "Events of the Month," *Improvement Era* 7:8 (June 1904), 632; "Passing Events: The Bureau of Information," *Improvement Era* 14:1 (November 1910), 92; Joseph S. Peery, "The Bureau of Information," *Improvement Era* 14:8 (June 1911), 687-694; Edward H. Anderson, "The Bureau of Information," *Improvement Era* 25:2 (December 1921), 130-139; Sherry Baker, "Mormon Media History Timeline, 1827-2007," http://contentdm.lib.byu.edu/cdm/ref/collection/ IR/id/157, 36, 41 (accessed August 2, 2014). See also Gareth W. Seastrand, "Visi-

tors Centers," *Encyclopedia of Mormonism*, Vol. 4, 1517-1518.

140 Woods, Fred E., "Andrew Jenson's Illustrated Journey to Iceland, the Land of Fire and Ice, August 1911," *BYU Studies* 47:4 (2008), 101-103, 106, 111; "Messages from the Missions," *Improvement Era* 15:1 (November 1911), 90-91.

141 "Messages from the Missions: Nevada Conference Organized," *Improvement Era* 26:4 (February 1923), 387; "Messages from the Missions: Conference in Nevada," *Improvement Era* 26:12 (October 1923), 1152; "Mutual Work: The Gospel Presented in Picture and Song," *Improvement Era* 27:1 (November 1923), 85; "Messages from the Missions: The Arizona Conference," *Improvement Era* 27:5 (March 1924), 458; "Messages from the Missions: Los Angeles Missionary Conference," *Improvement Era* 27:6 (April 1924), 545; Gustive O. Larson, "Messages from the Missions: Illustrated Lectures in California Mission," *Improvement Era* 27:9 (July 1924), 841-842; "Messages from the Missions: Enjoyable Conference in San Francisco," *Improvement Era* 27:11 (September 1924), 1077; "Messages from the Missions: Fresno, California Has 380 at Conference," *Improvement Era* 28:4 (February 1925), 371-372; "Messages from the Missions: Mission Work in California," *Improvement Era* 28:6 (April 1925), 592.

142 "Messages from the Missions," *Improvement Era* 16:11 (September 1913), 1154 (the Eastern States Mission); James Gunn McKay, "Messages from the Missions: In Great Britain: Lantern Slide Lectures," *Improvement Era* 24:5 (March 1921), 453; James Gunn McKay, "Messages from the Missions: Successful Lantern Slide Lectures in England," *Improvement Era* 24:7 (May 1921), 658 (in print this issue was incorrectly labeled as 24:6, April 1921); "Messages from the Missions: The Work in Oregon," *Improvement Era* 28:8 (June 1925), 771-772; J. Henricksen, "Messages from the Missions: The Gospel for All," *Improvement Era* 29:1 (November 1925), 72 (Texas); "Diamond Anniversary of Hawaiian Mission," *Improvement Era* 29:6 (April 1926), 600; William H. Allen, "Messages from the Missions: Bright Prospects for South Texas Conference," *Improvement Era* 29:8 (June 1926), 797-798; "Messages from the Missions: First Baptisms in Montpelier, France," *Improvement Era* 31:2 (December 1927), 158; Klenner F. Sharp, "Messages from the Missions: Paris, France, Open for Missionary Work," *Improvement Era* 31:4 (February 1928), 327-328; Melvin B. Watkins, "Messages from the Missions: Utah Scenes Shown in Germany," *Improvement Era* 32:7 (May 1929), 596-597; Alvin G. Pack, "Illustrated Lecture Experiences in the British Mission," *Improvement Era* 32:10 (August 1929), 861-865; Thomas G. Alexander, *Mormonism in Transition: A History of the Latter-day Saints, 1890-1930* (Urbana: University of Illinois Press, 1986), 219. For notices of missionaries using phonograph records of the Tabernacle Choir, see "Messages from the Missions," *Improvement Era* 14:7 (May 1911), 649 (Kansas), and "Messages from the Missions," *Improvement Era* 16:6 (April 1913), 640 (Alaska).

143 "Mormon Exhibitors," *Film Daily*, December 16, 1925, 1, http://www.archive.org/stream/filmdaily3134newy#page/n1429/mode/2up/search/mormon (accessed December 2, 2017).

144 "Mormon Circuit," *Film Daily*, December 17, 1925, 1, 6, http://www.archive.org/stream/filmdaily3134newy#page/n1437/mode/2up (accessed December 2,

2017);

145 "Salt Lake Rulings Delay Church Shows," *Motion Picture Daily*, August 7, 1934, http://www.archive.org/stream/motionpicturedai36unse#page/n289/ mode/2up (accessed November 26, 2017).

146 "Passing Events," *Improvement Era* 28:3 (January 1925), 305; "Passing Events," *Improvement Era* 28:3 (January 1925), 307; "Passing Events," *Improvement Era* 28:5 (March 1925), 493; "Passing Events," *Improvement Era* 28:8 (June 1925), 799; "Passing Events: 'Movies' at home," *Improvement Era* 31:11 (September 1928), 983; untitled advertisement, *Improvement Era* 32:3 (January 1929), front matter across from table of contents. This last item advertises a $107 "complete home motion picture outfit," with the tagline "Why not use this in genealogical work—Get a LIVING record of the Family?" It was manufactured by the Q.R.S. Company and sold at Daynes-Beebe Music Co. on Salt Lake City's Main Street.

147 Claudia Lauper Bushman and Richard Lyman Bushman, *Building the Kingdom: A History of Mormons in America* (New York: Oxford University Press, 2001), 81 (which notes that Los Angeles' first stake president George W. McCune was called by Church leaders to move from his home in Ogden, Utah to oversee this group of southern California Saints); Richard O. Cowan, "The Latter-day Saint Century," *Out of Obscurity: The LDS Church in the Twentieth Century* (Salt Lake City: Deseret Book Company, 2000), 18; J. B. Haws, *The Mormon Image in the American Mind: Fifty Years of Public Perception* (Oxford: Oxford University Press, 2013), 21; and Chad M. Orton, *More Faith Than Fear: The Los Angeles Stake Story* (Salt Lake City: Bookcraft, 1987), ix, 55-74. For an overview of the history of the Church in the state, see Richard O. Cowan and William E. Homer, *California Saints: A 150-Year Leagacy in the Golden State* (Provo: Religious Studies Center, Brigham Young University, 1996). For a contemporary account of the new Los Angeles Stake, see Gustive O. Larson, "The Los Angeles Stake of Zion," *Improvement Era* 26:5 (March 1923), 467-470; and for a longitudinal primary source on the history of the Church in California from 1935 until the 1980s, see the weekly periodical *California Intermountain News*, which is presently not yet digitized and is hence available only at the University of Utah and certain physical repositories in California.

148 Grace Lamb, "James Cruze, of the Thanhouser Company," *The Motion Picture Story Magazine*, January 1914, 102, http://www.archive.org/stream/motionpicturesto06moti#page/n995/mode/2up (accessed December 8, 2014).

149 George N. Fenin and William K. Everson, *The Western: From Silents to the Seventies* (New York, New York: Penguin Books, 1973), 130-135; "James Cruze Joins Metro for 'The Snowbird,'" *Motion Picture News*, April 15, 1916, 2198, http://www.archive.org/stream/motionpicturenew132unse#page/2198/mode/2up (accessed December 8, 2014); "Motion Picture Men in the City," *Ogden Standard*, 14; Nelson, "The History of Utah Film," 37; Nelson, "A History of Latter-day Saint Screen Portrayals," 175; "James Cruze," *Wikipedia*, http://en.wikipedia.org/wiki/James_Cruze (accessed December 8, 2014); Q. David Bowers, "CRUZE, James," *Thanhouser Company*, http://thanhouser.org/people/cruzej.htm (accessed De-

cember 7, 2014); Koszarski, *An Evening's Entertainment*, 246-248. Kozarski, also my source on Cruze's association with Arbuckle and Reid, gives the best critical evaluation of Cruze's films: of *The Covered Wagon*, he says (on p. 248) it was "a film whose value, even at the time of its initial release, was the subject of some debate" due to its shift of emphasis, at Jesse Lasky's behest, from characters to scenery. But it still "set a visual standard for Western epics to come and was the dominant critical and commercial success of the season." The film's success cut into its reputation and helped lead Paramount to drop Cruze's contract in 1928, precipitating his troubles in the 1930s. For a complete biography of Cruze by his sister, recently released as an e-book, see Helen May Cruze, *My Big Brother, James Cruze* (Sea Angel Enterprises, 2007).

150 "Utah Stars Add Brilliance to Photoplay Firmament," *Deseret Evening News*, December 16, 1916, 77. My thanks to Kjerste Christensen, Contemporary Mormonism and Utah History Cataloger at BYU's Harold B. Lee Library, for scanning this article from microfilm for me when I was unable to locate it in online databases. "Ward Entertainments," *Deseret Evening News*, February 3, 1906, 2, http://chroniclingamerica.loc.gov/lccn/sn83045555/1906-02-03/ed-1/seq-2 (accessed January 7, 2015); "Amateurs to Give Play," *Salt Lake Herald*, April 14, 1906, 8, http://chroniclingamerica.loc.gov/lccn/sn85058130/1906-04-14/ed-1/seq-8 (accessed January 7, 2015); "Wanted: Girls between ages of 16 and 20," *Salt Lake Herald*, March 27, 1908, 9, http://chroniclingamerica.loc.gov/lccn/sn85058130/1908-03-27/ed-1/seq-9 (accessed January 7, 2015); "With the Plays, Players and Playhouses All of Next Week," *Goodwin's Weekly*, 8; "Behind the Screen," *Ogden Standard-Examiner*, December 17, 1922, 7, http://chroniclingamerica.loc.gov/lccn/sn85058393/1922-12-17/ed-1/seq-14 (accessed January 7, 2015); "F. Harmon Weight," *Internet Movie Database*, http://www.imdb.com/name/nm0917857/?ref_=fn_al_nm_1 (accessed January 7, 2015); Nick Bruno, "Treasures from the UCLA Archive: MANTRAP – Newly Restored 35mm Print!," *NW Film Center Newsroom*, January 12, 2014, http://newsroom.nwfilm.org/tag/f-harmon-weight (accessed January 7, 2015).

151 "Jack Jevne," *Internet Movie Database*, http://www.imdb.com/name/nm0422382/?ref_=fn_al_nm_1 (accessed December 8, 2014); "Jack Jevne," *Wikipedia*, http://en.wikipedia.org/wiki/Jack_Jevne (accessed December 8, 2014).

152 "Elliot J. Clawson," *Internet Movie Database*, http://www.imdb.com/name/nm0165470/?ref_=fn_al_nm_1 (accessed December 8, 2014); "Elliot J. Clawson," *Wikipedia*, http://en.wikipedia.org/wiki/Elliott_J._Clawson (accessed December 8, 2014).

153 I. S. Mowis, "Waldemar Young: Biography," *Internet Movie Database*, http://www.imdb.com/name/nm0950150/bio?ref_=nm_ov_bio_sm (accessed December 8, 2014); "Waldemar Young," *Wikipedia*, http://en.wikipedia.org/wiki/Waldemar_Young (accessed December 8, 2014).

154 "Utah Stars Add Brilliance to Photoplay Firmament," 77; "Farewell Concert Tonight: Entertainment in Honor of Elder Harvey Gates, Who Leaves on a Mission," *Salt Lake Herald*, June 18, 1907, 2, http://chroniclingamerica.loc.gov/lccn/sn85058130/1907-06-18/ed-1/seq-2 (accessed January 5, 2015); "Salt

Lake," Variety, September 26, 1919, 53, http://www.archive.org/stream/variety56-1919-09#page/n227/mode/2up (accessed February 2, 2015); "Harvey Gates," Internet Movie Database, http://www.imdb.com/name/nm0309567 (accessed January 1, 2015); "Harvey Gates," Wikipedia, http://en.wikipedia.org/wiki/Harvey_Gates (accessed January 1, 2015).

155 L. P. Roberts, "Is Utah Civilized?," Improvement Era 30:6 (April 1927), 511. Many sources discuss Mathis's Spiritualism, which evidently began after her mother's death. Koszarski, An Evening's Entertainment, 100 describes how mystical "philosophizing was quite popular in Hollywood in the boom years of the immediate postwar era, especially among the circle around [Alla] Nazimova, [Rudolph] Valentino, and June Mathis." Mathis's beliefs were said to be on display in many of her films, Young Rajah (1922) being a prime example.

156 Emily W. Leider, Dark Lover: The Life and Death of Rudolph Valentino (New York: Farrar, Straus and Giroux, 2003), 114-116, 151, 323-324; Natacha Rambova & Hala Pickford, Rudolph Valentino: A Wife's Memories of an Icon (Hollywood: Theodosia Tramp Publishing, 2015), 275-296, especially 276-277 (the original version is Rudy: An Intimate Portrait of Rudolph Valentino by His Wife (London: Hutchinson & Co., 1926)); Leonard Gmür, Rex Ingram: Hollywood's Rebel of the Silver Screen (Berlin: Druck und Verlag, 2013), 352; "June Mathis," Wikipedia, http://en.wikipedia.org/wiki/June_Mathis (accessed December 10, 2014); "June Mathis," Internet Movie Database, http://www.imdb.com/name/nm0558923/?ref_=nmbio_bio_nm (accessed December 10, 2014); "June Mathis," Women Film Pioneers Project, https://wfpp.cdrs.columbia.edu/pioneer/ccp-june-mathis (accessed December 10, 2014); "June Mathis," Rudolph Valentino Society, July 10, 2012, http://rudolphvalentino.org/june-mathis (accessed December 10, 2014).

157 Leider, Dark Lover, 127-137 (these pages focus on her youth and Mormon background, though her career and stormy relationship with Valentino are discussed throughout the book); "Natacha Rambova," Wikipedia, http://en.wikipedia.org/wiki/Natacha_Rambova (accessed December 10, 2014). See also her book, Rambova, Rudy: An Intimate Portrait of Rudolph Valentino by His Wife. For the record of the Tabernacle séance, see Michael Morris, Madame Valentino: The Many Lives of Natacha Rambova (New York: Abbeville Press, 1991), 195-196.

158 "Oliver Morosco," Wikipedia, http://en.wikipedia.org/wiki/Oliver_Morosco (accessed September 7, 2014); "Oliver Morosco," Internet Movie Database, http://www.imdb.com/name/nm0606092 (accessed September 7, 2014); "Morosco Announces New Captures," Moving Picture World, August 14, 1915, 1140, https://books.google.com/books?id=eUs_AAAAYAAJ&pg=PA1140&lpg#v=onepage&q&f=false (accessed September 9, 2014); "Edna Goodrich in Next Morosco Offering," Moving Picture World, September 9, 1916, 1718, https://books.google.com/books?id=1qEbAQAAMAAJ&pg=PA1718&lpg=PA1718&dq#v=onepage&q&f=false (accessed September 9, 2014); John C. Tibbetts, The American Theatrical Film: Stages in Development (Madison: University of Wisconsin Press, 1985), 93; Oliver Morosco, Helen McRuer Morosco, and Leonard Paul Duggar, Life of Oliver Morosco: The Oracle of Broadway, Written from His Own Notes and Comments (Caldwell, Idaho: Caxton Printers., Ltd., 1944), 107; Samuel Dickson, The Streets of San Francisco (Stanford: Stanford University Press, 1955), 122-

129; "Walter Morosco," *Wikipedia*, http://en.wikipedia.org/wiki/Walter_Morosco (accessed September 7, 2014); "Walter Morosco," *Internet Movie Database*, http://www.imdb.com/name/nm0606094 (accessed September 7, 2014).

159 "Ralph J. Pugh," *Internet Movie Database*, http://www.imdb.com/name/nm1818438/?ref_=fn_al_nm_1 (accessed December 10, 2014); Harvard S. Heath, ed., *In the World: The Diaries of Reed Smoot* (Salt Lake City: Signature Books in association with Smith Research Associates, 1997), 544; Rachael Low, *The History of the British Film 1918-1929* (London: George Allen & Unwin Ltd., 1971), 227. As the film studio in Wembley didn't materialize, the most lasting edifice to remain from the Exhibition was the original Wembley Stadium, known at first as the Empire Stadium and used until its demolition in 2002. "British Empire Exhibition," *Wikipedia*, http://en.wikipedia.org/wiki/British_Empire_Exhibition (accessed December 10, 2014).

160 "Utah Stars Add Brilliance to Photoplay Firmament," 76. The author goes on to say, "The foremost actors of the stage gradually receded from their first position of bitter opposition to the new art until, today, practically every actor of note has 'registered' for the camera. It was to be expected, therefore, that some of the Utah talent would join the motion picture 'recruits.'"

161 Leatrice Gilbert Fountain, *Dark Star* (New York: St. Martin's Press, 1985), 6-18 (these pages relate primarily to his youth and relationship with his Mormon relatives; the remainder of the book covers the rest of his life); Elizabeth Peltret, "The Best Thing in Life," *Motion Picture Classic*, April-May 1921, 83, http://www.archive.org/stream/motionpicturecla1920broo#page/n411/mode/2up (accessed December 22, 2014); Koszarski, *An Evening's Entertainment*, 309-312; "John Gilbert (actor)," *Wikipedia*, http://en.wikipedia.org/wiki/John_Gilbert_(actor) (accessed December 22, 2014); "John Gilbert," *Internet Movie Database*, http://www.imdb.com/name/nm0318105 (accessed December 22, 2014); "Utah Stars Add Brilliance to Photoplay Firmament," 77.

162 "Utah Stars Add Brilliance to Photoplay Firmament," 76; "Betty Compson," *Wikipedia*, http://en.wikipedia.org/wiki/Betty_Compson (accessed December 29, 2014); "Betty Compson," *Internet Movie Database*, http://www.imdb.com/name/nm0173993 (accessed December 29, 2014); Tim Lussier, "The Incomparable Compson: A Tribute to Betty Compson," *Silents Are Golden*, http://www.silentsaregolden.com/compsonarticle.html (accessed December 29, 2014).

163 Fay Wray, *On the Other Hand: A Life Story* (New York: St. Martin's Press, 1989), 6-29 (as with Gilbert's biography, these early pages cover Wray's childhood and experiences in Mormon Utah); "Fay Wray," *Wikipedia*, http://en.wikipedia.org/wiki/Fay_Wray (accessed December 22, 2014); "Fay Wray," *Internet Movie Database*, http://www.imdb.com/name/nm0942039 (accessed December 22, 2014); "Fay Wray, Beauty to Kong's Beast, Dies at 96," *New York Times*, August 9, 2004, http://www.nytimes.com/2004/08/09/movies/09CND-WRAY.html (accessed December 22, 2014). For an example of Wray's stardom at its zenith, see Laura Benham, "The Busiest Bee," *Picture Play Magazine*, June 1934, 42-43, 52, http://www.archive.org/stream/pictureplay3941stre#page/n371/mode/2up (accessed December 22, 2014).

164 Chris Hicks, "Restored 'King Kong' maintains emotion and draws sympathy even after 70 years," *Deseret News*, November 25, 2005, http://www.deseretnews.com/article/635163657/Restored-King-Kong-maintains-emotion-and-draws-sympathy-even-after-70-years.html?pg=all (accessed December 22, 2014); Lindsay Bird, "King Kong in HBLL," *Digital Universe*, September 15, 2005, http://universe.byu.edu/2005/09/15/king-kong-in-hbll (accessed December 22, 2014).

165 Aileen St. John-Brenon, "Manhattan Medley," *Picture Play*, December 1927, 56, 114; "Margaret Livingston," *Internet Movie Database*, http://www.imdb.com/name/nm0515272 (accessed December 15, 2014); "Margaret Livingston," *Wikipedia*, http://en.wikipedia.org/wiki/Margaret_Livingston (accessed December 15, 2014); "Ivy Livingston," *Internet Movie Database*, http://www.imdb.com/name/nm0515249/?ref_=fn_al_nm_1 (accessed December 15, 2014).

166 Untitled Mary Thurman obituary, *Photoplay*, February 1926, 115, http://www.archive.org/stream/photo29chic#page/n249/mode/2up (accessed December 14, 2014).

167 "Utah Stars Add Brilliance to Photoplay Firmament," 76; "Mary Thurman," *Wikipedia*, http://en.wikipedia.org/wiki/Mary_Thurman (accessed December 14, 2014); "Mary Thurman," *Internet Movie Database*, http://www.imdb.com/name/nm0862197/?ref_=fn_al_nm_1 (accessed December 14, 2014); Jessica Keaton, "Miss Mary Thurman," *Silence is Platinum*, June 7, 2013, http://silenceisplatinum.blogspot.com/2013/06/miss-mary-thurman.html (accessed December 14, 2014); Ruth Waterbury, "The Final Fade-outs," *Photoplay*, March 1926, 34, http://www.archive.org/stream/photo29chic#page/n313/mode/2up (accessed December 14, 2014).

168 Ruth Kingston, "How Ora Puts Over Her Aura," *Motion Picture Magazine*, February 1919, 82, http://www.archive.org/stream/motionpicturemag-17moti#page/n83/mode/2up (accessed January 1, 2015).

169 Ibid.; "Utah Stars Add Brilliance to Photoplay Firmament," 76; "Ora Carew," *Internet Movie Database*, http://www.imdb.com/name/nm0136876/?ref_=fn_al_nm_1 (accessed January 1, 2015); "Ora Carew," *Wikipedia*, http://en.wikipedia.org/wiki/Ora_Carew (accessed January 1, 2015).

170 "Utah Stars Add Brilliance to Photoplay Firmament," 76; "Mack Swain," *Internet Movie Database*, http://www.imdb.com/name/nm0841501 (accessed January 1, 2015); "Mack Swain," *Wikipedia*, http://en.wikipedia.org/wiki/Mack_Swain (accessed January 1, 2015); "Mack Swain (1876-1935)," *Golden Silents*, http://www.goldensilents.com/comedy/mackswain.html (accessed January 1, 2015); "Stars of Slapstick #71: Mack Swain," *Travalanche*, February 16, 2013, https://travsd.wordpress.com/2013/02/16/stars-of-slapstick-71-mack-swain (accessed January 1, 2015).

171 "Utah Stars Add Brilliance to Photoplay Firmament," 76-77; "Art Acord," *Internet Movie Database*, http://www.imdb.com/name/nm0010134/?ref_=fn_al_nm_1 (accessed December 16, 2014); "Art Acord," *Wikipedia*, http://en.wikipedia.org/wiki/Art_Acord (accessed December 16, 2014); "Charles Meakin," *Internet*

Movie Database, http://www.imdb.com/name/nm0575124/?ref_=fn_al_nm_1 (accessed December 17, 2014); "Lee Shumway," *Internet Movie Database*, http://www.imdb.com/name/nm0795884/?ref_=fn_al_nm_1 (accessed December 16, 2014); "Lee Shumway," *Wikipedia*, http://en.wikipedia.org/wiki/Lee_Shumway (accessed December 16, 2014); "Hazel Dawn," *Internet Movie Database*, http://www.imdb.com/name/nm0206008/?ref_=fn_al_nm_1 (accessed December 17, 2014); "Hazel Dawn," *Wikipedia*, http://en.wikipedia.org/wiki/Hazel_Dawn (accessed December 17, 2014); Mavis Gay Gashler, "Three Mormon Actresses: Viola Gillette, Hazel Dawn, Leora Thatcher," (master's thesis, Brigham Young University, 1970), 65-122; Quinn, *The Mormon Hierarchy: Extensions of Power*, 810; "Frank Jonasson," *Internet Movie Database*, http://www.imdb.com/name/nm0427342/?ref_=fn_al_nm_1 (accessed December 18, 2014); "Frank Jonasson," *Wikipedia*, http://en.wikipedia.org/wiki/Frank_Jonasson (accessed December 18, 2014); "May Cruze," *Internet Movie Database*, http://www.imdb.com/name/nm0190519/?ref_=fn_al_nm_1 (accessed December 7, 2014); Bowers, "CRUZE, James," http://thanhouser.org/people/cruzej.htm; "Mae Bosen Cruze," *Billion Graves*, http://billiongraves.com/pages/record/Mae-Bosen-Cruze/1319272 (accessed December 7, 2014); J. Michael Hunter, "Profiles of Selected Mormon Actors," *Mormons and Popular Culture*, Vol. 1, 229 (Art Acord), 233 (May Cruze), 234 (Hazel Dawn), 243 (Charles Meakin), 250-251 (Lee Shumway and Mack Swain), 252 (Mary Thurman).

172 "Utah Stars Add Brilliance to Photoplay Firmament," 77; "The Eastern Studios," *Motion Picture News*, June 3, 1916, 3397, http://www.archive.org/stream/motionpicturenew133unse#page/3396/mode/2up (accessed November 2, 2014); "Eighteen and Eighty Will Make Premier in a Fox," *Motion Picture News*, July 22, 1916, 440, http://www.archive.org/stream/motionpicturenew141unse#page/440/mode/2up (accessed November 2, 2014); "Sara Alexander," *Internet Movie Database*, http://www.imdb.com/name/nm0018727 (accessed November 3, 2014); "Lisle Leigh," *Internet Movie Database*, http://www.imdb.com/name/nm0500256 (accessed November 3, 2014).

173 "Utah Stars Add Brilliance to Photoplay Firmament," 76-77; "Arthur Moon," *Internet Movie Database*, http://www.imdb.com/name/nm0600592 (accessed December 27, 2014); "Arthur Morse Moon," *FamilySearch*, https://familysearch.org/ark:/61903/1:1:F8GM-24W (accessed December 27, 2014); "Salt Lakers in Gotham," *Deseret Evening News*, December 5, 1908, part 2, page 23, http://chroniclingamerica.loc.gov/lccn/sn83045555/1908-12-05/ed-1/seq-23 (accessed December 27, 2014); "Salt Lakers in Gotham," *Deseret Evening News*, April 10, 1909, part 2, page 16, http://chroniclingamerica.loc.gov/lccn/sn83045555/1909-04-10/ed-1/seq-16 (accessed December 27, 2014); "Donna Drew," *Internet Movie Database*, http://www.imdb.com/name/nm0237651/?ref_=fn_al_nm_1 (accessed December 27, 2014); "Vera Sisson," *Wikipedia*, http://en.wikipedia.org/wiki/Vera_Sisson (accessed December 27, 2014); "Vera Sisson," *Internet Movie Database*, http://www.imdb.com/name/nm0803103 (accessed December 27, 2014); "Vera Sisson," *Find a Grave*, http://www.findagrave.com/cgi-bin/fg.cgi?page=gr&GRid=8990 (accessed December 27, 2014); "Marguerite Clayton," *Wikipedia*, http://en.wikipedia.org/wiki/Marguerite_Clayton (accessed December 27, 2014); "Marguerite Clayton," *Internet Movie Database*, http://www.imdb.com/name/nm0165744/?ref_=fn_al_nm_1 (accessed December 27, 2014); Hans J.

Notes - The First Wave: The New Frontier

Wollstein, "Marguerite Clayton," *All Movie*, http://www.allmovie.com/artist/marguerite-clayton-p185800 (accessed December 27, 2014); "Julia Dean (actress)," *Wikipedia*, http://en.wikipedia.org/wiki/Julia_Dean_(actress) (accessed December 27, 2014); "Julia Dean," *Internet Movie Database*, http://www.imdb.com/name/nm0212828/?ref_=fn_al_nm_1 (accessed December 27, 2014); "Alfred Wertz," *Internet Movie Database*, http://www.imdb.com/name/nm0921640 (accessed December 1, 2014); "Willard Wayne," *Internet Movie Database*, http://www.imdb.com/name/nm0915654/?ref_=fn_al_nm_1 (accessed December 1, 2014); Hal Erickson, "Movies & TV: DeWitt Jennings," *New York Times*, http://www.nytimes.com/movies/person/35485/DeWitt-Jennings (accessed December 31, 2014); "DeWitt Jennings," *Internet Movie Database*, http://www.imdb.com/name/nm0421138 (accessed December 31, 2014); "DeWitt Jennings," *Wikipedia*, http://en.wikipedia.org/wiki/DeWitt_Jennings (accessed December 31, 2014); "Charles A. Post," *Internet Movie Database*, http://www.imdb.com/name/nm0692809 (accessed January 17, 2015); "Salt Lake," *Variety*, September 26, 1919, 54. This last article also mentions a Salt Lake-native actress named Hazel Craig, known as Hazel Richmond, working in films at the time (p. 53-54).

174 "Utah Stars Add Brilliance to Photoplay Firmament," 76.

175 "Dal Clawson," *Internet Movie Database*, http://www.imdb.com/name/nm0165469 (accessed November 3, 2014); "L. D. Clawson," *Wikipedia*, http://en.wikipedia.org/wiki/L.D._Clawson (accessed November 3, 2014); "Personals," *Salt Lake Tribune*, June 30, 1912, second news section page 25, http://chroniclingamerica.loc.gov/lccn/sn83045396/1912-06-30/ed-1/seq-25 (accessed November 3, 2014), which states that Clawson was in L.A. at this time; "Utah Stars Add Brilliance to Photoplay Firmament," 77.

176 "Grant Whytock," *Internet Movie Database*, http://www.imdb.com/name/nm0926705/?ref_=nmbio_trv_2 (accessed December 15, 2014); "Grant Whytock," *Wikipédia* (French), http://fr.wikipedia.org/wiki/Grant_Whytock (accessed December 15, 2014).

177 "Harvey Fletcher," *Utah History to Go*, http://historytogo.utah.gov/people/utahns_of_achievement/harveyfletcher.html (accessed August 2, 2014).

178 Harrison R. Merrill, "Harvey Fletcher—Friend of the Listener," *Improvement Era* 35-41:3 (January 1930), 198.

179 "Harvey Fletcher," *Wikipedia*, http://en.wikipedia.org/wiki/Harvey_Fletcher (accessed August 2, 2014); "Harvey Fletcher," *Reference.com*, http://www.reference.com/browse/wiki/Harvey_Fletcher (accessed July 4, 2005); "Stereophonic Sound," http://history.acusd.edu/gen/recording/stereo.html (accessed July 4, 2005); "The history of Stereo," *Rocking & Stomping*, http://www.stomping.nl/vinyl/stereo.html (accessed August 2, 2014); Tom Fletcher, "In Memory of Harvey Fletcher," http://www.et.byu.edu/~tom/family/Harvey_Fletcher/harvey_fletcher.html (accessed July 4, 2005); *A Tribute to Harvey Fletcher*, http://www.et.byu.edu/~tom/family/Harvey_Fletcher/Harvey_Tribute.html (accessed July 4, 2005); Stephen H. Fletcher, "Harvey Fletcher: 1884—1981," *Biographical Memoirs*, Vol. 61 (Washington D.C.: National Academy of Sciences, 1992), 163-193, http://www.

Notes - The First Wave: The New Frontier

nasonline.org/publications/biographical-memoirs/memoir-pdfs/fletcher-harvey.
pdf (accessed August 3, 2014), especially see pages 182-185 for the development of sound film and stereo; Baker, "Mormon Media History Timeline, 1827-
2007," http://contentdm.lib.byu.edu/cdm/ref/collection/IR/id/157, 46; Matthew
Piper, "Utahn who pioneered synthesized stereo sound will receive posthumous
Grammy," *Salt Lake Tribune*, January 13, 2016, http://www.sltrib.com/entertain-
ment/3414263-155/utahn-who-pioneered-synthesized-stereo-sound (accessed
January 14, 2016); J. Michael Hunter, "Stereophonic Sound," *Mormons and Popular Culture*, Vol. 1, 185-186. See also Edward L. Kimball, "Harvey Fletcher and
Henry Eyring: Men of Faith and Science," *Dialogue: A Journal of Mormon Thought*
15:3 (Autumn 1982), 74-86 and especially Harvey Fletcher, *Autobiography of Harvey Fletcher* (Provo: self-published, 1968), which is also quoted in some of these
sources.

180 Albert Abramson, quoted in Donald G. Godfrey, "'Flights of Imagination': Philo T. Farnsworth and the Invention of Television," *Mormons and Popular Culture*,
Vol. 1, 81.

181 Both McKay and Farnsworth are quoted in Donald G. Godfrey, *Philo T.
Farnsworth: The Father of Tevlevision* (Salt Lake City: University of Utah Press,
2001), 181. This work is the most complete scholarly source on Farnsworth's life:
see, for instance, p. 11-12 on his inspiration on the farm, p. 28-31 on his initial work in San Francisco, p. 165-169 on his initial fusion work, p. 180-184 for
evaluations of his faith, p. 195-198 (Appendix B: The Chronology of "Firsts") for a
balanced account of the competing claims of Farnsworth and Zworykin. Godfrey
summarizes his biography in "'Flights of Imagination': Philo T. Farnsworth and
the Invention of Television," *Mormons and Popular Culture*, Vol. 1, 71-90. There
are other biographies as well, including one by his wife: Elma G. Farnsworth,
Distant Vision: Romance and Discovery on an Invisible Frontier (Salt Lake City:
Pemberly Kent, 1989). Pem, who outlived her husband, was in fact his tireless
advocate, helping secure a memorial postage stamp (see "Postage Stamp Honors
TV Camera Inventor", Church News, September 25, 1983, 6, and Godfrey, *Philo T.
Farnsworth*, 184-185), and being involved with the Philo T. Farnsworth Society,
whose website was previously at "Philo T. Farnsworth Society," *BYU Broadcasting*,
www.byubroadcasting.org/philo/story.asp (accessed July 4, 2005) and that is
now described at "Major Donors: Philo T. Farnsworth Society," *KBYU*, http://www.
kbyutv.org/support/membership/majordonors (accessed August 5, 2014). "Philo
Farnsworth," *Wikipedia*, http://en.wikipedia.org/wiki/Philo_Farnsworth (accessed
February 3, 2015); "The Time 100: Philo Farnsworth", *Time*, http://www.time.
com/time/time100/scientist/profile/farnsworth.html (accessed July 4, 2005);
"Passing Events," *Improvement Era* 30:7 (May 1927), 663 (the earliest mention of
television in the Church periodical); Fay Ollerton, "The Story Behind Farnsworth
Television," *Improvement Era* 39:6 (June 1936), 347-351 (with an introduction by
Mormon physicist Carl Eyring); "Philo T. Farnsworth's 100th Birthday marked in
Rigby, Idaho," *East Idaho Online*, http://www.eastidahoonline.com/philo-t-farn-
sworth-rigby-idaho (accessed February 3, 2015). Godfrey's works of course cite
many more sources on Farnsworth, and his papers have recently been donated to
the University of Utah: Donald G. Godfrey papers, 1924-2013, Special Collections,
J. Willard Marriott Library, University of Utah.

182 James V. D'arc, *When Hollywood Came to Town: The History of Moviemaking in Utah* (Layton: Gibbs Smith, 2010), 14, 17.

183 Ibid., 16.

184 Ibid., 17.

185 Ibid., 14. Films and their locations are listed throughout the book, of course, as well as the appendix on p. 286-304. Other summaries of films made in the state include Nelson, "The History of Utah Film," (with information on films shot in southern Utah on 38, 41, 48-49; this essay is current through 1973); "Filmed in Utah!," an anonymous brochure for the Utah Film Commission, 2004;.John A. Murray, *Cinema Southwest: An Illustrated Guide to the Movies and Their Locations* (Flagstaff: Northland Publishing, 2000), 77-92; Katie Harmer, "50 movies filmed in Utah: 'The Sandlot,' 'Hulk' and more," *Deseret News*, July 10, 2013, http://www. deseretnews.com/top/1633/00/50-movies-filmed-in-Utah-The-Sandlot-Hulk-and-more.html (accessed July 15, 2013); and Betty L. Stanton, *Where Got Put the West: Movie Making in the Desert* (Moab, Utah: Canyonlands Natural History Association, 1994

186 D'arc, *When Hollywood Came to Town*, 20.

187 *Iron County Record*, September 5, 1924, quoted in D'arc, *When Hollywood Came to Town*, 38. See p. 32-39 for the complete account of *The Deadwood Coach*'s production.

188 D'arc, *When Hollywood Came to Town*, 40-42, 63-64.

189 John W. Thomas, "Chauncey Gardner Parry — Modern Pioneer," typescript biography, Special Collections, Gerald R. Sherratt Library, Southern Utah University, quoted in Janet B. Seegmiller, "Selling the Scenery: Chauncey and Gronway Parry and the Birth of Southern Utah's Tourism and Movie Industries," *Utah Historical Quarterly* 80:3 (Summer 2012), 254.

190 Seegmiller, "Selling the Scenery," 255.

191 D'arc, *When Hollywood Came to Town*, 43-59.

192 D'arc, *When Hollywood Came to Town*, 116 indicates that the investors were Chauncey and Gronway, but the picture caption on page 117 indicates it was Chauncey and Whit. Since Whit was joining his older brothers around this time the former scenario seems to be more likely, though it is possible all three brothers invested in different ways in that film and *El Diablo Rides*.

193 D'arc, *When Hollywood Came to Town*, 115-120.

194 Ibid., 59.

195 Ibid., 120-203.

196 Seegmiller, "Selling the Scenery," 255.

197 D'arc, *When Hollywood Came to Town*, 115-116, 198-199, 202; "R. Fay Hamblin," *BillionGraves*, http://billiongraves.com/pages/record/R-Fay-Hamblin/6012769#given_names=R.&family_names=Hamblin (accessed July 16, 2013).

198 D'arc, *When Hollywood Came to Town*, 140, 145.

199 Ibid., 139; Seegmiller, "Selling the Scenery," 256-257. Similar encounters between locals and stars were common in other Utah towns as well, such as during production of The Proud Rebel when Bryce Canyon naturalist J. L. Crawford spent thirty minutes discussing the canyon's trails and flora with Olivia de Havilland without recognizing her (D'arc, *When Hollywood Came to Town*, 58) and when the entire cast of John Ford's *Rio Grande*—including Maureen O'Hara, John Wayne, Victor McLaglen, Ben Johnson, and Harry Carey, Jr.—put on a lively variety show in the Moab High School auditorium (p. 233).

200 D'arc, *When Hollywood Came to Town*, 28, 31.

201 Seegmiller, "Selling the Scenery," 257; this indicates Whit ran the lodge until his death, something disproven by D'arc, *When Hollywood Came to Town*, 198; see also p. 132. Much of the preceding information on the Parry brothers comes from Seegmiller's entire article, p. 242-257.

202 D'arc, *When Hollywood Came to Town,* 49; see p. 46-49.

203 Keith Phipps, "The Easy Rider Road Trip," *Slate*, November 17, 2009, http://www.slate.com/articles/arts/dvdextras/features/2009/the_easy_rider_road_trip/monument_valley_where_peter_and_henry_fondas_careers_intersected.html (accessed March 1, 2015).

204 D'arc, *When Hollywood Came to Town*, 209.

205 Andrew Sinclair, *John Ford* (New York: Dial Press/J. Wade, 1979), 82, also quoted in D'arc, *When Hollywood Came to Town*, 208-209.

206 Thomas J. Harvey, *Rainbow Bridge to Monument Valley: Making the Modern Old West* (Norman, Oklahoma: University of Oklahoma Press, 2011), 81; see p. 79-108 for his entire treatment of Ford, Goulding and his wife and partner Leone ("Mike"), and the area. For more on the Gouldings also see Samuel Moon, *Tall Sheep: Harry Goulding, Monument Valley Trader* (Norman, Oklahoma: University of Oklahoma Press, 1992); D'arc, *When Hollywood Came to Town*, 206-207; Lee Benson, "About Utah: Harry and Leone 'Mike' Goulding put Utah on movie map," *Deseret News*, January 6, 2013, http://www.deseretnews.com/article/765619619/Harry-and-Leone-Mike-Goulding-put-Utah-on-movie-map.html?pg=all (accessed March 2, 2015); Buzz Bissinger, "Inventing Ford Country," *Vanity Fair*, March 2009, http://www.vanityfair.com/culture/2009/03/monument-valley200903 (accessed March 1, 2015); K. C. DenDooven, Bruce Hucko, and Mary Ellen Conner, *Monument Valley: The Story Behind the Scenery* (Whittier, California: KC Publications, 2002); and the website for Goulding's Lodge, the base from which Ford and others shot their films which is now a hotel, gift shop, and museum of the area's cinematic history: *Goulding's Lodge*, http://www.gouldings.com (accessed March 1, 2015).

Notes - The First Wave: The New Frontier

For more revisionist/critical views on Goulding's activities and relationship with the local Navajo, see Peter Limbrick, *Making Settler Cinemas: Film and Colonial Encounters in the United States, Australia, and New Zealand* (New York: Palgrave Macmillan, 2010), 84-88, and Nancy C. Maryboy and David Begay, "The Navajos of Utah," *Utah History to Go*, http://historytogo.utah.gov/people/ethnic_cultures/the_history_of_utahs_american_indians/chapter7.html (accessed March 17, 2015), which discusses his involvement with uranium mining on the Navajo reservation.

207 D'arc, *When Hollywood Came to Town*, 209, 220-221; "List of appearances of Monument Valley in the media," *Wikipedia*, http://en.wikipedia.org/wiki/List_of_appearances_of_Monument_Valley_in_the_media (accessed March 2, 2015).

208 D'arc, *When Hollywood Came to Town*, 224-261; Kristin Millis, "Conversation with Essie—Performance by Gerald Elias and ensemble," *Back of Beyond Books*, http://www.backofbeyondbooks.com/events.cfm?mode=detail&id=1345839021724 (accessed April 2, 2015); "Moab Movies," *Canyonlands by Night*, http://www.canyonlandsbynight.com/mallory_graphics/Movie%20Guide.pdf (accessed April 2, 2015); "Movies Filmed in the Moab Area," *Discover Moab*, http://www.discovermoab.com/movie.htm (accessed April 2, 2015); "Museum of Moab," *Moab Happenings*, http://www.moabhappenings.com/museum.htm (accessed April 2, 2015).

209 D'arc, *When Hollywood Came to Town*, 198, 200, 225, 233, 238-239, 253-255, 267-269. Stanton served as the Moab Film Commission's head from 1984 to 1993; after helping create the Moab Film and Heritage Museum she retired in 1996. Ray Boren, "Utah's Desert Hollywood," *Deseret News*, November 6, 1998, http://www.deseretnews.com/article/661462/Utahs-desert-Hollywood.html?pg=all (accessed April 2, 2015); Laura Haley, "Generations: Bette Stanton," *Times-Independent* (Moab), http://www.moabtimes.com/view/full_story/23695513/article-Generations-Bette-Stanton (accessed April 2, 2015); Vicki Barker, "From Cowpoke to Paintstroke," *Moab Happenings*, http://www.moabhappenings.com/Archives/historic1108FromCowpokeToPainstroke.htm (accessed April 2, 2015). For a very brief summary of Von der Esch's career, see Robert Gehrke, "Long-time Utah film and tourism director retires," *Salt Lake Tribune*, December 27, 2012, http://www.sltrib.com/sltrib/politics/55533825-90/director-tourism-utah-office.html.csp (accessed April 2, 2015).

210 "Film commission," *Wikipedia*, http://en.wikipedia.org/wiki/Film_commission (accessed April 2, 2015); "History," AFCI.org, http://www.afci.org/about-afci/history (accessed April 2, 2015). Moab's Mormon population diminished after the uranium mining boom and with the rise of the outdoor recreational industry, so that its percentage of Mormons (31%) is lower than that of Cedar City (69%), Kanab (58%), or St. George (68%). Still, the influence of Mormons during the town's founding period as well as their initial involvement with the film industry and film commission warrants, I think, the praise given here.

211 Bowman, *The Mormon People*, 153.

212 Quinn, *The Mormon Hierarchy: Extensions of Power*, 800.

213 Thomas Hull, "Events of the Month," *Improvement Era* 1:8 (June 1898), 623, indicates that on May 15, 1898, ten days after Utah's infantry volunteers were mustered into service and six days after Utah's two artillery batteries were mustered, "the Utah company of rough riders left Salt Lake City . . . for Cheyenne." However, A. Prentiss, *The History of the Utah Volunteers in the Spanish-American War and in the Philippine Islands* (Salt Lake City: W.F. Ford, 1900), 51, indicates that they reached Fort Russell on May 15 and were already mustered when Col. Torrey arrived on May 16. It's probable the entire company did not depart Utah and was not mustered into service simultaneously: in her personal history Emily Partridge Young notes that on Friday May 20 she "went up to town to see some of the Utah troops off for the war." Emily Dow Partridge Young, *Diary and Reminiscences*, unpublished m.s., February 1874—November 1899, 13, https://archive.org/stream/MS2845F0001/MS%202845_f0001#page/n299/mode/2up (accessed March 7, 2018). It is interesting to note that future filmmaker Chet Clawson was there with her to wish the troops farewell.

214 Richard I. Reeves II, "Utah and the Spanish-American War" (master's thesis, Brigham Young University Dept. of History, 1998), 105. Such praise is even more remarkable considering that Cannon had been excommunicated from the Church in 1886 after assaulting a *Tribune* reporter who had written an article about Cannon that he deemed offensive; he was re-baptized into the Church in 1888 and took his position at the *Deseret News* in 1892. See also Quinn, *The Mormon Hierarchy: Extensions of Power*, 776, 783. The official name of the Rough Riders company was the Second United States Volunteer Cavalry.

215 Elias Savada, comp., *The American Film Institute Catalog of Motion Pictures Produced in the United States: Film Beginnings, 1893-1910* (Metuchen, N.J.: The Scarecrow Press, Inc., 1995), 938. *Salt Lake City Company of Rocky Mountain Riders* has the alternate title—it may not have been titled at all at the time—of Rocky Mtn. Riders Salt Lake City. The additional films—and others on Theodore Roosevelt and units under other commanders—are listed on pages 913, 920, 205, and 206.

216 Untitled notice, *Bourbon News*, September 6, 1898, 5, https://chroniclingamerica.loc.gov/lccn/sn86069873/1898-09-06/ed-1/seq-5 (accessed December 2, 2017).

217 Untitled Orpheum advertisement, *Los Angeles Herald*, August 3, 1898, 2, https://chroniclingamerica.loc.gov/lccn/sn85042461/1898-08-03/ed-1/seq-2 (accessed December 2, 2017); untitled Orpheum advertisement, *Los Angeles Herald*, August 4, 1898, 2, https://chroniclingamerica.loc.gov/lccn/sn85042461/1898-08-04/ed-1/seq-2 (accessed December 2, 2017); "New Theaters, New Plays and the New Season," *San Francisco Call*, August 21, 1898, 29, https://chroniclingamerica.loc.gov/lccn/sn85066387/1898-08-21/ed-1/seq-29 (accessed December 2, 2017); untitled notice, *Bourbon News*, September 6, 1898, 5; untitled New Grand theater announcement, *Times*, November 19, 1899, 5, https://chroniclingamerica.loc.gov/lccn/sn85054468/1899-11-19/ed-1/seq-17 (accessed December 2, 2017).

218 For further information on the Utah Company see Reeves, *Utah and the*

Spanish-American War, 98-105; Prentiss, *The History of the Utah Volunteers*, 50-57 (p. 53-55 give a complete roll for the company, therefore giving us the names of the men who were filmed, though we can't know which ones appeared on screen and which didn't; p. 56-57 give a profile of Cannon); and D. Michael Quinn, "The Mormon Church and the Spanish-American War: An End to Selective Pacifism," *Pacific Historical Review* 43 (1974), 342-366. After helping establish American control in Havana, the Rocky Mountain Rough Riders returned to Jacksonville where they were mustered out of service in mid-October. "Torrey's Troopers to Be Mustered Out," *Evening Star*, October 12, 1898, 11, https://chroniclingamerica.loc.gov/lccn/sn83045462/1898-10-12/ed-1/seq-11 (accessed December 2, 2017). Thomas Hull, "Events of the Month," *Improvement Era* 4:1, November 1900, 77, indicates that the local Rough Riders gave Roosevelt a warm reception as he campaigned for the vice presidency in Salt Lake City, indicating the cohesiveness of the group in later years. Mormons served in the Philippine theater as well, and the first LDS combat casualty of any United States war was George Hudson, who was killed in the Philippine Insurrection on August 24. Quinn, *The Mormon Hierarchy: Extensions of Power*, 800.

219 "Ward Entertainments," *Salt Lake Herald*, November 22, 1901, 3; "Around Town," *Lehi Banner*, October 13, 1904, 4; "Briefs and Personals," *Deseret Evening News*, November 5, 1904, 11.

220 Bowman, *The Mormon People*, 157. In particular, Progresives who were otherwise generally allied with the Mormons "harbored deep suspicion of monopolies, organizations that appeared to deny American citizens freedom of choice, be it political, moral, or economic. Their most famous crusades were waged against the great business trusts, but they saw in Mormonism (as they did in Catholicism) a religious monopoly. To Progressives, that the Mormon prophet Joseph F. Smith and the other apostles quietly discouraged Mormon Democrats from opposing Smoot seemed to confirm that Mormons still sought to govern through their autocratic hierarchy. That they had sent Smoot, an apostle himself, as Smith's viceroy seemed to add insult to injury," p. 157-158.

221 Kathryn M. Daynes, *More Wives Than One: Transformation of the Mormon Marriage System 1840-1910* (Urbana and Chicago: University of Illinois Press, 2001), 208.

222 Ibid., 186.

223 My polygamous great-grandparents were married in 1884, but clearly cohabitated as a married couple well after the 1890 Manifesto. Indeed, entire books could be and have been written about post-Manifesto polygamy. Many resources are listed in David J. Whittaker, "The Study of Mormon History: A Guide to the Published Sources," *Mormon Americana,* 80, and a fantastic audio resource covering the history and sociology of polygamy across the entire Mormon movement from the 1830s to today is Lindsay Hansen Park's *Year of Polygamy* podcast at http://www.yearofpolygamy.com. See also Daynes, *More Wives Than One*, 182-183, 186-187, 196, 208. Page 182, for example, points out that "the last monogamist of the nineteenth-century hierarchy who married polygamously was Abraham Owen Woodruff. He became an apostle in 1897 and took an additional wife in 1901.

This was more than ten years after his father, LDS president Wilford Woodruff, formally announced that there would be no more polygamous marriages." Rudger Clawson and other leaders did the same.

224 "The Smoot Hearings," *The Mormons*, http://www.pbs.org/mormons/themes/smoot.html (accessed August 22, 2013). This contains a transcript from the 2007 PBS documentary *The Mormons* by director-producer Helen Whitney.

225 Quinn, *The Mormon Hierarchy: Extensions of Power*, 144. See D. Michael Quinn, "LDS Church Authority and New Plural Marriages, 1890-1904," *Dialogue: A Journal of Mormon Thought* 18 (Spring 1985): 86-88.

226 These lyrics are available from multiple sources, including Ian Shin, "'Scoot—Smoot—Scoot': The Seating Trial of Senator Reed Smoot," *Gaines Junction* 3:1 (2008), 164, http://web.archive.org/web/20080309131303/http://gaines-junction.tamu.edu/issues/vol3num1/ishin/ishin.pdf (accessed August 31, 2013). "The Mormon Coon" was also known as "The Mormon Coon Song." See "Music and Song," *New York Clipper*, February 11, 1905, 1200, http://www.archive.org/stream/clipper52-1905-02#page/n1931/mode/2up (accessed December 3, 2017), "Music and Song," *New York Clipper*, April 15, 1905, 191, http://www.archive.org/stream/clipper53-1905-04#page/n33/mode/2up (accessed December 3, 2017), and "Music and Song," *New York Clipper*, April 22, 1905, 230, http://www.archive.org/stream/clipper53-1905-04#page/n71/mode/2up (accessed December 3, 2017), which all mention "The Mormon Coon Song" as a popular number; Smith & Browne, Inc., Music Publishers advertisement, *New York Clipper*, October 5, 1912, 9, http://www.archive.org/stream/clipper60-1912-10#page/n7/mode/2up (accessed December 3, 2017) advertises sheet music of "The Mormon Coon," showing the song's longevity.

227 Michael Harold Paulos, "'Horribly Caricatured and Made Hideous in Cartoons': Political Cartooning and the Reed Smoot Hearings," *Mormons and Popular Culture*, Vol. 2, 125. See also his article "Political Cartooning and the Reed Smoot Hearings," *Sunstone* 144 (December 2006), 36-40. For a broader perspective of Mormonism in printed cartoons, see Gary L. Bunker & Davis Bitton, *The Mormon Graphic Image, 1834-1914: Cartoons, Caricatures, and Illustrations* (Salt Lake City: University of Utah Press, 1983).

228 Joseph F. Smith to Reed Smoot, April 9, 1904, Reed Smoot Papers, L. Tom Perry Special Collections, Harold B. Lee Library Brigham Young University, also quoted in Paulos, "'Horribly Caricatured and Made Hideous in Cartoons,'" 121.

229 W. K. L. Dickson, Edison's early collaborator on cinematographic technology, founded the American Mutoscope Company in 1895 and oversaw its recording and projection technology. Roberta Pearson, "Early Cinema," *The Oxford History of World Cinema*, 16. Vitagraph from the United States and Pathé Frères from France were the other major players in the American market, with the latter soon coming to dominate all domestic film production companies. *A Trip to Salt Lake City*'s June 5, 1905 copywrite date was printed on a surviving (not original) 16mm print distributed by Blackhawk Films.

230 Barry Salt, *Film Style & Technology: History & Analysis*, 2nd ed. (Southampton, England: Starword, 1992), 42. Cooper-Hewitt was the principle manufacturer of mercury vapor lamps, "large glass tubes about three feet long and three inches in diameter which produced monochromatic blue light from mercury vapour ionised by an electric current passing through it," p. 41. See also p. 67-68 on Biograph's lighting methods from 1907-1913. Other sources say that while in the Roosevelt Building American Mutoscope filmed exclusively on the rooftop and it wasn't until a 1906 move to a brownstone on nearby East 14th St. that they first began shooting indoors. A 1903 fire damaged the Roosevelt Building's upper stories, but the basic machinery for the studio's rotating floor is reportedly still intact today. "Biograph Company," *Wikipedia.org*, http://en.wikipedia.org/wiki/American_Mutoscope_and_Biograph_Company (accessed August 12, 2013); Christopher Gray, "A Family's Legacy, Burnished Anew," *The New York Times*, April 13, 2008, http://www.nytimes.com/2008/04/13/realestate/13scap.html (accessed August 12, 2013). The sun of course casts hard light on a clear day, implying that if *A Trip to Salt Lake City* was shot with sunlight, diffusion was used, because the light appears reasonably soft.

231 As of Decembrer 2017, the film is available on YouTube at http://www.youtube.com/watch?v=9bZvA1qeHwQ. This was posted on March 6, 2013 and seems to be ripped from the 2005 DVD of *Trapped by the Mormons* (1922), where it was included as a bonus feature.

232 Paulos, "'Horribly Caricatured and Made Hideous in Cartoons," 132.

233 Ibid., 133-134. He is quoting Stephen Hess and Sandy Northrup, *Drawn and Quartered: The History of American Political Cartoons* (Montgomery, AL: Elliott & Clark Publishing, 1996), 20.

234 He also declined the opportunity to serve as President Harding's Secretary of the Treasury. Quinn, *The Mormon Hierarchy: Extensions of Power,* 817.

235 For more on *A Trip to Salt Lake City*, see Nelson, "Utah Filmmakers of the Silent Screen," 7; Nelson, "The History of Utah Film," 6; Nelson, "A History of Latter-day Saint Screen Portrayals," 23; Richard Alan Nelson, "From Antagonism to Acceptance: Mormons and the Silver Screen," *Dialogue: A Journal of Mormon Thought* 10:3 (Spring 1977), 61. For more on the Smoot hearings, see Shin, "'Scoot—Smoot—Scoot,' 143-164; Michael Harold Paulos, *The Mormon Church on Trial: Transcript of the Reed Smoot Hearings* (Salt Lake City: Signature Books, 2008); Heath, *In the World: The Diaries of Reed Smoot; Church History in the Fulness of Times Student Manual,* (Salt Lake City: The Church of Jesus Christ of Latter-day Saints, 2003), 465-479; Harvard S. Heath, "Smoot Hearings," *Encyclopedia of Mormonism*, Vol. 3, 1363-1364; Milton R. Merrill, *Reed Smoot: Apostle in Politics* (Logan: Utah State University Press and Department of Political Science, 1990); Harvard S. Heath, "Reed Smoot: The First Modern Mormon," (Ph.D. dissertation, Brigham Young University, 1990); and Quinn, *The Mormon Hierarchy: Extensions of Power*, 301-302.

236 Sally Shuttleworth, "Introduction," Charlotte Brontë, *Jane Eyre* (Oxford: Oxford University Press, 2000), xxix. The quote from the text is from page 297 of

this edition.

237 Lester E. Bush, Jr., "'Mormon Elders' Wafers: Images of Mormon Virility in Patent Medicine Ads," *Dialogue: A Journal of Mormon Thought* 10:2 (Autumn 1976), 89-93.

238 Carol Cornwall Madsen, *Journey to Zion: Voices from the Mormon Trail* (Salt Lake City: Deseret Book Company, 1997), 82.

239 Michael Austin, "The 'Anti-Mormon' Card," *By Common Consent*, March 30, 2015, https://bycommonconsent.com/2015/03/30/the-anti-mormon-card (accessed December 18, 2017).

240 Richard H. Cracroft, "Distorting Polygamy for Fun and Profit: Artemus Ward and Mark Twain among the Mormons," *BYU Studies* 14:2 (1974), 1-14.

241 Haws, *The Mormon Image in the American Mind*, 8. The general overview of nineteenth-century anti-Mormonism in J. Spencer Fluhman, *"A Peculiar People": Anti-Mormonism and the Making of Religion in Nineteenth-Century America* (Chapel Hill: University of North Carolina Press, 2012) shows the shades of nuance and the social conditions that helped determine the positions of actors on all sides of the Mormon question.

242 Ibid., 7; see also Dean C. Jessee, "Sources for the Study of Joseph Smith," *Mormon Americana*, 15.

243 For an overview of the Danites' founding, see Leland H. Gentry, "The Danite Band of 1838," *BYU Studies* 14:4 (Summer 1974), 1-26; Richard L. Bushman, *Joseph Smith: Rough Stone Rolling* (New York: Vintage Books, 2005), 349-355; Bowman, *The Mormon People*, 61; Fluhman, *"A Peculiar People,"* 90-93; and Rebecca Foster Cornwall and Leonard J. Arrington, "Perpetuation of a Myth: Mormon Danites in Five Western Novels, 1840-90," *BYU Studies* 23:2 (1983), 147-148; for their discussion of *Monsieur Violet*, see p. 149, 152-153.

244 Cornwall and Arrington, "Perpetuation of a Myth," 148.

245 Quinn, *The Mormon Hierarchy: Extensions of Power*, 757.

246 Ibid., 750 (Hickman claims Brigham Young instructs him to "kill Gentiles and take their property for the good of the Church," a claim Young denies; Hickman also murders Ike Hatch); 751 (Hickman murders Jesse T. Hartley); 752 (Young threatens to murder a non-Mormon U.S. Army lieutenant who is courting his daughter); 754 (Young supports Bishop Warren Snow, who castrated a twenty-four-year-old man for an unknown sexual offense; several people leaving the Church and territory claim that a number of assassinations occurred in the winter of 1856-57); 756 (Hickman's brother openly wears the sword of a supposedly murdered Army soldier; Hickman murders non-Mormon Richard Yates for attempting to transport munitions to the Army and implicates Young, Second Counselor Daniel Wells, and Joseph A. Young in the decision to kill him; Rockwell, Hickman, and other be'hoys murder five California-bound emigrants who were "supposed spies"); 757 (a group of Mormons disguised as Native Americans

castrate a man in his bed at night; the bishop of Payson, Utah leads a group of men in murdering a woman, castrating and murdering her son, and murdering her infant when the mother and son are suspected of incest); 757-758 (in separate events two women's severed heads—one had been frequenting the U.S. military camp—are discovered near Salt Lake City); 758 (the Parrish family is shot to death and has their throats slit under the order of the bishop of Springville, Utah because they were attempting to leave Utah without paying tithing; U.S. Army sergeant Ralph Pike is shot and killed in broad daylight in Salt Lake City, with the *Deseret News* later editorializing that he richly deserved his fate); 759 (Rockwell murders Martin Oats after Oats accuses him of stealing cattle; Salt Lake City's mayor warns Young that Hickman, though useful, is now killing too many Mormons; alleged horse thief A. B. Baker is lynched, with the approval of the *Deseret News* editors); 760 (apostle Orson Hyde intervenes to keep Hickman from being excommunicated); 761 (after allegedly insulting a Mormon woman Utah Governor John Dawson is assaulted and nearly beaten to death at Ephraim Hanks's coach station, and is forced to flee the territory to avoid castration or murder; Rockwell murders Lot Huntington for the Dawson beating, and Salt Lake City policemen murder Moroni Clawson and John P. Smith while escorting them to jail for the beating; a government-sanctioned Mormon "posse" attacks the schismatic community of Joseph Morris and kills its leaders in what is known as the Morrisite War); 763 (S. Newton Brassfield is murdered for polygamously marrying the wife of an absent missionary, with Young publicly approving of the killing); 764 (Dr. J. King Robinson is murdered, apparently by Salt Lake City policemen; an African American corpse is found in Salt Lake City with a note pinned to it warning other "niggers" of meddling with white women); 768 (from prison Hickman publishes *Brigham's Destroying Angel* and is excommunicated, although his membership is posthumously restored by the First Presidency in 1934); 769 (a mob lynches apostate and suspected murderer Charles A. Benson); 776 (three men attack John C. Young, the editor of the *Salt Lake Tribune*); 777 (an agent of the Presiding Bishopric and others assault the son of the U.S. Solicitor, to the praise of the *Deseret News*); 782 (an African American is lynched in Salt Lake City for the murder of bishop Andrew Burt).

247 Ibid., 751-752.

248 Ibid., 754. See also p. 747 (Young gives a general call for the decapitation of sinners and one man is almost killed as a result; Young recommends the beheading of a prison inmate); 755 (Samuel Sprague, the leader of a weekly prayer circle, teaches that those who are anointed in the temple are empowered to avenge the blood of Joseph and Hyrum Smith; apostle George A. Smith tours southern Utah with a series of fiery sermons on blood atonement that contribute to causing the Mountain Meadows Massacre); 756 (a member of Sprague's prayer circle advocates murdering those responsible for killing Joseph and Hyrum Smith); 760 (Young preaches to congregations in southern Utah that the victims of Mountain Meadows deserved their fate); 762 (Kimball teaches that men can kill for blood atonement without seeking Church approval but they should be careful to obtain all the relevant facts first); 764 (a *Deseret News* editorial advocates death as the fitting punishment for "adultery, seduction, and whoredom"; the *News* praises a father for shooting "his daughter's seducer"); 765 (the *Deseret News* praises

unnamed assailants who attacked a young non-Mormon man who tried to visit a Mormon woman; George Cannon preaches "we will kill you" to those who practice "whoredoms, seductions and adulteries"); 805 (in a 1902 editorial the *Deseret News* affirms that "the only atonement a murderer can make for his guilt is the shedding of his blood according to divine mandate"); see also p. 241 on the culture of violence that formed around the be'hoys in pioneer Utah.

249 Givens, *People of Paradox*, 196.

250 Although by far the largest, Mountain Meadows was not the only massacre perpetrated by Mormons during these years. One incident was the Circleville Massacre during the 1866 Black Hawk War, in which Mormon militiamen tied and shot several captured Piede Indian men then slit the throats of the women and children. Albert Winkler, "The Circleville Massacre: A Brutal Incident in Utah's Blackhawk War," *Utah Historical Quarterly* 55:1 (1987), 17-18, see the entire article p. 4-21; Quinn, *The Mormon Hierarchy: Extensions of Power*, 256, 763. In the earlier 1850 Battle at Fort Utah, the first Indian war in Utah Valley, members of the Nauvoo Legion shot around one hundred Timpanogos Indians not only in battle but after their capture. Over fifty Native American heads were removed and displayed at Fort Utah as a warning. "Battle at Fort Utah," *Wikipedia*, https://en.wikipedia.org/wiki/Battle_at_Fort_Utah (accessed December 19, 2017).

251 For the use of exit or travel passes, see Quinn, *The Mormon Hierarchy: Extensions of Power*, 751 (in 1854 excommunicant Jesse Hartley receives a travel pass from Brigham Young but is nevertheless killed by William Hickman en route to the eastern states); 756 (Young gives someone a travel pass to journey "freely and safely through this Territory on his way to California" in 1857; it's reported that "it is dangerous for Mormons to attempt to leave Salt Lake City for the East without a pass from Brigham Young"); 758 (in 1859 the Parrish family is murdered for attempting to leave Utah without a pass); 764 (in 1867 Young gives William Hickman an exit pass to journey east; the pass states, "I know of no reason why he should not be permitted to attend to his business and leave, when he gets ready, in peace and quietness").

252 Michael Austin, "Troped by the Mormons: The Persistence of 19th Century Mormon Stereotypes in Contemporary Detective Fiction," *Sunstone* 21:3 (August 1998), 62-63.

253 Nelson, "A History of Latter-day Saint Screen Portrayals," 66.

254 Cornwall and Arrington, "Perpetuation of a Myth," 158.

255 Ibid., 153-160; Michael Austin, "'As Much as Any Novelist Could Ask': Mormons in American Popular Fiction," *Mormons and Popular Culture*, Vol. 2, 3-8. The most complete source on the entire period is Terryl Givens, *The Viper on the Hearth: Mormons, Myths, and the Construction of Heresy* (New York: Oxford UP, 1997). See also Neal Lambert, "Saints, Sinners and Scribes: A Look at the Mormons in Fiction," *Utah Historical Quarterly* 36:1 (Winter 1968), 63-76; Leonard Arrington and John Haupt, "Intolerable Zion: The Image of Mormonism in Nineteenth-Century American Literature," *Western Humanities Review* 22:3 (Summer

1968), 243-260; Leonard Arrington and John Haupt, "Community and Isolation: Some Aspects of 'Mormon Westerns'," *Western American Literature* 8:1&2 (Spring/Summer 1973), 15-31; R. Philip Loy, "Saints or Scoundrels: Images of Mormons in Literature and Film About the American West," *Journal of the American Studies Association of Texas* 21 (1990), 57-74; R. Douglas Brackenridge, "'Are You That Damned Presbyterian Devil?' The Evolution of an Anti-Mormon Story," *Journal of Mormon History* 21:1 (Spring 1995), 80-105; Gregory Pingree, "'The Biggest Whorehouse in the World': Representations of Plural Marriage in Nineteenth-Century America," *Western Humanities Review* 50:3 (Fall 1996), 213-232; Neal E. Lambert and Richard H. Cracroft, "Through Gentile Eyes: A Hundred Years of the Mormon in Fiction," *New Era,* March 1972, 14-19; and Craig L. Foster, "Victorian Pornographic Imagery in Anti-Mormon Literature," *Journal of Mormon History* 19:1 (Spring 1993), 115-132. For the National Democrats, see David Herbert Donald, *Lincoln* (New York: Simon & Schuster Paperbacks, 1995), 212-213. Lincoln preferred to coordinate his work with these Danites through an intermediary rather than directly engaging with them himself.

256 Davis Bitton and Gary L. Bunker, "Mischievous Puck and the Mormons, 1904-1907," *BYU Studies* 18:4 (1978), 2.

257 Haws, *The Mormon Image in the American Mind*, 14. This is from Martin E. Marty, *The Irony of It All: 1893-1919, vol. 1, Modern American Religion* (Chicago and London: The University of Chicago Press, 1986), 301.

258 Loy, "Saints or Scoundrels," 64. One example was James Oliver Curwood's story *The Courage of Captain Plum*, which featured an island stronghold of lecherous Mormons. Austin, "'As Much as Any Novelist Could Ask,'" 8.

259 Melvin L. Bashore, "'The Bloodiest Drama Ever Perpetrated on American Soil': Staging the Mountain Meadows Massacre for Entertainment," *Utah Historical Quarterly* 80:3 (2012), 258-271; DeWolf Hopper and Wesley Winans Stout, *Once a Clown, Always a Clown: Reminiscenes of DeWolf Hoppper* (Boston: Little, Brown, and Company, 1927), 15.

260 "The Mormon Wife," *Internet Broadway Database*, https://www.ibdb.com/broadway-production/the-mormon-wife-5478 (accessed December 18, 2017); "New York State: Buffalo," *New York Clipper*, June 20, 1903, 394, http://www.archive.org/stream/clipper51-1903-06#page/n45/mode/2up (accessed December 18, 2017); Selwyn & Co. Play Brokers advertisement, *New York Clipper*, February 20, 1904, http://www.archive.org/stream/clipper51-1904-02#page/n73/mode/2up (accessed December 18, 2017); Selwyn & Co. Play Brokers advertisement, *New York Clipper*, August 13, 1904, 576, http://www.archive.org/stream/clipper52-1904-08#page/n45/mode/2up (accessed December 18, 2017); "Louisiana: New Orleans," *New York Clipper*, November 12, 1904, 885, http://www.archive.org/stream/clipper52-1904-11#page/n35/mode/2up (accessed December 18, 2017); "Charles E. Blaney's Plays for Repertoire," *New York Clipper*, April 22, 1905, 226, http://www.archive.org/stream/clipper53-1905-04#page/n67/mode/2up (accessed December 18, 2017). After 1904 the play was apparently known as *A Mormon Wife.*

261 For *The Mormon Wife* see Charles Gatchell, "The Movie Almanac," *Picture Play*, September 1921, 34, http://www.archive.org/stream/pictureplaymaga-z15unse#page/n39/mode/2up (accessed December 20, 2017). For *The Mormon* see "Maryland: Baltimore," *New York Clipper,* December 5, 1903, 976, http://www.archive.org/stream/clipper51-1903-12#page/n7/mode/2up (accessed December 18, 2017). For *The Mormon Queen* see "Vaudeville and Minstrel," *New York Clipper*, July 9, 1904, 454, http://www.archive.org/stream/clipper52-1904-07#page/n31/mode/2up (accessed December 18, 2017); "Vaudeville and Minstrel," *New York Clipper,* July 30, 1904, 520, http://www.archive.org/stream/clipper52-1904-07#page/n97/mode/2up (accessed December 18, 2017); "Wanted, Chorus Girls and Acts," *New York Clipper*, July 30, 1904, 528, http://www.archive.org/stream/clipper52-1904-07#page/n105/mode/2up (accessed December 18, 2017). For *Richard Loraine* see "Wanted, Manager for 'Richard Loraine,'" *New York Clipper,* July 9, 1904, 458, http://www.archive.org/stream/clipper52-1904-07#page/n35/mode/2up (accessed December 18, 2017); "To Let. 'Richard Loraine,'" *New York Clipper*, October 1, 1904, 747, http://www.archive.org/stream/clipper52-1904-10#page/n25/mode/2up (accessed December 18, 2017). For *The Mormon's Troubles* see "Our Chicago Letter," *New York Clipper*, October 15, 1904, 778, http://www.archive.org/stream/clipper52-1904-10#page/n57/mode/2up (accessed December 18, 2017). For *The Mormons* see "New York City: Brooklyn," *New York Clipper*, January 21, 1905, 1135, http://www.archive.org/stream/Clipper52-1905-01#page/n61/mode/2up (accessed December 18, 2017); Frank Wiesberg, "Correspondence: Chicago," *Variety*, January 12, 1907, 11, http://www.archive.org/stream/variety05-1907-01#page/n31/mode/2up (accessed December 20, 2017). For *The Wanderer* see "The Wanderer," *New York Clipper*, July 15, 1905, 531, http://www.archive.org/stream/clipper53-1905-07#page/n65/mode/2up (accessed December 18, 2017). For *Utah* see "World of Players," *New York Clipper*, May 5, 1906, 302, http://www.archive.org/stream/clipper54-1906-05#page/n7/mode/2up (accessed December 19, 2017). For *The Mormon Senator* see "Illinois: Peoria," *New York Clipper*, July 13, 1907, 564, http://www.archive.org/stream/clipper55-1907-07#page/n43/mode/2up (accessed December 19, 2017). For *The Mormon* see Walter K. Hill, "Chicago," *Variety*, May 7, 1910, 24, http://www.archive.org/stream/variety18-1910-05#page/n23/mode/2up (accessed December 20, 2017). For an example of a Mormon song, see "Burlesque Review," *New York Clipper*, September 16, 1916, 12, http://www.archive.org/stream/Clipper64-1916-09#page/n85/mode/2up (accessed December 20, 2017).

262 "New York City: American Theatre," *New York Clipper,* October 12, 1907, 938, http://www.archive.org/stream/clipper55-1907-10#page/n49/mode/2up (accessed December 20, 2017); "New York City: Fourteenth Street Theatre," *New York Clipper*, November 9, 1907, 1056, http://www.archive.org/stream/clipper55-1907-11#page/n47/mode/2up (accessed December 20, 2017); Mormon Artists Group, *The Glen & Marcia Nelson Collection of Mormon Art*, 2nd ed. (New York: Mormon Artists Group, 2015), 278.

263 Austin, "Troped by the Mormons," 53; *"The Girl from Utah," Wikipedia*, https://en.wikipedia.org/wiki/The_Girl_from_Utah (accessed December 20, 2017); "The Girl from Utah," *Internet Broadway Database*, https://www.ibdb.com/broadway-show/the-girl-from-utah-3897 (accessed December 20, 2017); "This

Notes - The First Wave: The New Frontier

'Girl from Utah' is a Dancer, Not a Mormon Maid," *Day Book*, March 30, 1915, 15, https://chroniclingamerica.loc.gov/lccn/sn83045487/1915-03-30/ed-2/seq-15 (accessed December 20, 2017); "'The Girl from Utah,'" *New York Clipper*, August 29, 1914, 6, http://www.archive.org/stream/clipper62-1914-08#page/n101/mode/2up (accessed December 20, 2017). For some reports from Mormon missionaries in Britain about *The Girl from Utah* and other anti-Mormon plays, see "Messages from the Missions," *Improvement Era* 17:4 (February 1914), 39 (Belfast); "Messages from the Missions," *Improvement Era* 17:7 (May 1914), 689 (Manchester); "Messages from the Missions," *Improvement Era* 17:10 (August 1914), 989 (Nottingham); "Messages from the Missions," *Improvement Era* 17:11 (September 1914), 1082 (York, featuring a play called *A 'Mormon' and His Wives*).

264 For the play *Polygamy, or Celestial Marriage* (1914), see "'Polygamy,'" *New York Clipper*, December 12, 1914, 4, http://www.archive.org/stream/clipper62-1914-12#page/n27/mode/2up (accessed December 20, 2017); "Real Tales About Reel Folk," *Reel Life*, February 27, 1915, 20, http://www.archive.org/stream/reellife05unse#page/n825/mode/2up (accessed December 20, 2017). For *His Little Widows* (1917), see "'His Little Widows' Boasts a Sure Enough Comic Opera Plot," *New York Tribune*, May 1, 1917, 9, https://chroniclingamerica.loc.gov/lccn/sn83030214/1917-05-01/ed-1/seq-9 (accessed December 29, 2017); "'His Little Widows' a Laughing Success at the Astor," *New York Clipper*, May 2, 1917, 10, http://www.archive.org/stream/Clipper65-1917-05#page/n9/mode/2up (accessed December 20, 2017); "His Little Widows," *Variety*, May 4, 1917, 15, http://www.archive.org/stream/variety46-1917-05#page/n13/mode/2up (accessed December 20, 2017). For *Some Little Girl* (1918), an adapatation of *His Little Widows*, see "Some Little Girl," *Variety*, March 29, 1918, 15, http://www.archive.org/stream/variety50-1918-03#page/n231/mode/2up (accessed December 20, 2017). For the vaudeville play *The Mormons* (1919), see "The Mormons," *New York Clipper*, March 12, 1919, 13, http://www.archive.org/stream/Clipper67-1919-03#page/n47/mode/2up (accessed December 20, 2017). For *The Mormon and His Wives* (1922), see "In London," *Variety*, October 13, 1922, 2, http://www.archive.org/stream/variety68-1922-10#page/n49/mode/2up (accessed December 20, 2017). And for the most comprehensive overview of anti-Momon theater, see Megan Sanborn Jones, *Performing American Identity in Anti-Mormon Melodrama* (Routledge: New York, 2009); see also Stuart W. Hyde, "The Anti-Mormon Drama in the United States," *Western Humanities Review* 9 (Spring 1955), 177-181.

265 Sherry Baker, "Mormon Media History Timeline, 1827-2007," 37, http://scholarsarchive.byu.edu/cgi/viewcontent.cgi?article=1958&context=facpub; Brian Q. Cannon and Jacob W. Olmstead, "'Scandalous Film': The Campaign to Suppress Anti-Mormon Motion Pictures, 1911-12," *Journal of Mormon History* 29 (Fall 2003), 44.

266 Alexander, *Mormonism in Transition*, 242; Malcolm R. Thorp, "The British Government and the Mormon Question, 1910-22," *Journal of Church and State* 21 (Spring 1979), 305-322; Malcolm R. Thorp, "'The Mormon Peril': The Crusade against the Saints in Britain, 1910-1914," *Journal of Mormon History* 2 (1975), 69-88; Malcolm R. Thorp, "Winifred Graham and the Mormon Image in England," *Journal of Mormon History* 6 (1979), 107-121; Peter J. Vousden, "The English Editor and the 'Mormon Scare' of 1911," *BYU Studies* 41:1 (2002), 65-75; Cannon

and Olmstead, "'Scandalous Film,'" 48-50; "Messages from the Missions," *Improvement Era* 14:5 (March 1911), 459; "Passing Events: Investigation of 'Mormon' activity in England," *Improvement Era* 14:6 (April 1911), 565; Joseph F. Smith, Anthon H. Lund, and John Henry Smith, "Magazine Slanders Confuted," *Improvement Era* 14:8 (June 1911), 719-724; "Messages from the Missions," *Improvement Era* 14:11 (September 1911), 1062; "Messages from the Missions," *Improvement Era* 15:4 (February 1912), 330; "The Government Investigation of 1911," *Millennial Star* 76:24 (June 11, 1914), 376-380; Arthur L. Beeley, "Government Investigation of the 'Mormon' Question: A Summary Statement of the Investigation Made by the British Government of the 'Mormon' Question in England," *Improvement Era* 18:1 (October 1914), 56-62.

267 Givens, *The Viper on the Hearth*, 4.

268 Ibid., 151.

269 Austin, "Troped by the Mormons," 68.

270 Cornwall & Arrington, "Perpetuation of a Myth," 164-165.

271 Nelson, "From Antagonism to Acceptance," 63. For information on Hale's Tours see Gunnar Iverson, "Norway in Moving Images—Hale's Tours in Norway in 1907," http://www.hf.ntnu.no/estetisk_teknologi/personer/Gunnarmappe/Hale's_Tours_in_Norway.pdf (accessed May 13, 2006); "Hale's Tours of the World," *Wikipedia*, https://en.wikipedia.org/wiki/Hale%27s_Tours_of_the_World (accessed February 25, 2018); Raymond Fielding, "Hale's Tours: Ultrarealism in the Pre-1910 Motion Picture," *Film Before Griffith*, ed. John L. Fell (Berkley: University of California Press, 1983), 116-130; Charles Musser, *The Emergence of Cinema – The American Screen to 1907* (New York: Charles Schribner's Sons, 1990), 429-431; Lynn Kirby, *Parallel Tracks – The Railroad and Silent Cinema* (Exeter: University of Exeter Press, 1997), 46, 57.

272 Nelson, "Utah Filmmakers of the Silent Screen," 9, also see p. 8; "Edison: Salt Lake City, Utah, and its Surroundings," *Moving Picture World*, November 9, 1912, 586, http://www.archive.org/stream/movinwor14chal#page/n591/mode/2up (accessed February 26, 2018).

273 Nelson, "A History of Latter-day Saint Screen Portrayals," 70-71; Nelson, "The History of Utah Film," 8, 11.

274 At the present time two short films are still available: *A Trip to Salt Lake City* (1905) and *My Sister-in-Law from America* (1917). For a concise history of the entire period, see Richard Alan Nelson, "Mormons as Silent Cinema Villains: Propaganda and Entertainment," *Historical Journal of Film, Radio, and Television* 4:1 (1984), 3-14.

275 In some older sources about this film the title is given as *Tilly and the Morman Missionary*, spelling Mormon with an "a." This is probably how it was spelled on the actual release print, but since the film is lost we cannot be sure. Denis Gifford, *The British Film Catalogue, 1895—1970: A Guide to Entertainment Films* (Newton Abbot, UK: David and Charles, 1973), entry number 03117 (no

pagination); Alan Goble, ed., *The International Film Index, 1895—1990, Vol. 1: Film Titles* (London: Bowker-Saur, 1991), 841; Brian McFarlane, ed., The Encyclopedia of British Film (London: Methuen, 2003), 655; "Tilly and the Mormon Missionary," *Complete Index to World Film*, http://www.citwf.com/film351887.htm (accessed December 21, 2017); "Tilly and the Fire Engines," *British Film Institute,* https://player.bfi.org.uk/free/film/watch-tilly-and-the-fire-engines-1911-online (accessed December 21, 2017); "Tilly's Party," *British Film Institute*, https://player.bfi.org.uk/free/film/watch-tillys-party-1911-online (accessed December 21, 2017). For an analysis of how Mormons were conflated with gypsies, particularly in *Trapped by the Mormons*, see James V. D'arc, "The Mormon as Vampire: A Comparative Study of Winifred Graham's The Love Story of a Mormon, the Film *Trapped by the Mormons*, and Bram Stoker's *Dracula*," *BYU Studies* 46:2 (Summer 2007), 172-173, 177.

276 "Messages from the Missions," *Improvement Era* 14:11 (September 1911), 1062.

277 Michael Mitchell, "The Mormons in Wilhelmine Germany, 1870-1914: Making a Place for an Unwanted American Religion in a Changing German Society" (master's thesis, Brigham Young University Dept. of History, 1994), 163-164; Cannon and Olmstead, "'Scandalous Film,'" 44; Nelson, "A History of Latter-day Saint Screen Portrayals," 25; Edward H. Tripp and J. A. Lockwood, "Protests Against False Reports," *Millennial Star* 70:36 (September 3, 1908), 572-575; "Passing Events: The Press of Norway," *Improvement Era* 13:10 (August 1910), 957-958 (about women being abducted); George F. Richards, "Why Are 'Mormon' Missionaries Expelled From Germany?," *Improvement Era* 13:11 (September 1910), 1004-1007; "Messages from the Missions," *Improvement Era* 13:11 (September 1910), 1039 (on Clawson's arrest); "Messages from the Missions," *Improvement Era* 13:12 (October 1910), 1136-1137 (on the German banishment issue); "Messages from the Missions," *Improvement Era* 14:4 (February 1911), 356-358, 360 (on anti-Mormonism in Ireland and Freece's tour there); "Messages from the Missions," *Improvement Era* 14:8 (June 1911), 744-746 (a report about driving missionaries from Heywood, England, and the work in Middlesbrough); "Passing Events: An Anti-'Mormon' mass meeting," Improvement Era 14:8 (June 1911), p. 757-758 (in London); "Messages from the Missions," *Improvement Era* 14:9 (July 1911), 839 (a report about opposition in Denmark and Barnsley, England); "Messages from the Missions," *Improvement Era* 14:10 (August 1911), 940 (opposition in Norway); "Passing Events: Freece, the Anti-Mormon Agitator," *Improvement Era* 14:10 (August 1911), 949; "Messages from the Missions," *Improvement Era* 14:11 (September 1911), 1042 (a mobbing of missionaries in Bury, Lancashire); "Editor's Table: The Work of the Lord in Europe," *Improvement Era* 14:12 (October 1911), 1113-1114 (mostly a report by Rudger Clawson); Joseph F. Smith, "Reasons for Opposition to the Latter-day Saints," *Improvement Era* 15:1 (November 1911), 70-76, and 15:2 (December 1911), 137-143; "Messages from the Missions," Improvement Era 15:1 (November 1911), 85 (opposition in Sheffield); "Messages from the Missions," *Improvement Era* 15:1 (November 1911), 87 (opposition in Mosjoen, Norway); "Messages from the Missions," *Improvement Era* 15:1 (November 1911), 90 (opposition in Ireland); John Halversen, "An Interview with King Haakon VII of Norway," *Improvement Era* 15:2 (December 1911), 146-148; "Passing Events:

The exile of some elders from Sweden," *Improvement Era* 15:2 (December 1911), 190-191; "Messages from the Missions," *Improvement Era* 15:2 (December 1911), 178-179 (opposition in Nottingham); "'Mormon' Missionaries Mobbed at Nuneaton," *Millennial Star* 74:12 (March 21, 1912), 177-178 (a mobbing of missionaries in Warwickshire).

278 Julie K. Allen, "The White Slave Trade Gets Religion in 'A Victim of the Mormons,'" May 31, 2013, http://www.kosmorama.org/ServiceMenu/05-English/Articles/A-Victim-of-the-Mormons.aspx (accessed July 1, 2013).

279 Jacob W. Olmstead, "*A Victim of the Mormons* and *The Danites*: Images and Relics from Early Twentieth-Century Anti-Mormon Silent Films," *Mormon Historical Studies* 5 (Spring 2004), 205; Allen, "The White Slave Trade Gets Religion," http://www.kosmorama.org/ServiceMenu/05-English/Articles/A-Victim-of-the-Mormons.aspx. This was the era of women's suffrage, when concern about women's morality and personhood was spreading internationally, thus paving the way for the genre to expand beyond Denmark, as with the American film *Traffic in Souls* (1913).

280 Edwin D. Hatch, "Moving Picture Misrepresentations," *Millennial Star* 73:45 (November 9, 1911), 710.

281 Cannon and Olmstead, "'Scandalous Film,'" 51; Mark B. Sandberg, "Location, 'Location': On the Plausibility of Place Substitution," *Silent Cinema and the Politics of Space*, ed. Jennifer M. Bean, Anupama P. Kapse, and Laura Evelyn Horak (Bloomington: Indiana University Press, 2014), 35-36; Allen, "The White Slave Trade Gets Religion," http://www.kosmorama.org/ServiceMenu/05-English/Articles/A-Victim-of-the-Mormons.aspx; Hatch, "Moving Picture Misrepresentations," 710—he compared the building at the Copenhagen Zoo that stood in for the temple to "the entrance to a modern Wesleyan chapel or the front of the church of the Madeline in Paris," inadvertently showing that the filmmakers did a good job finding a location that suggested a large church without filming at any recognizable Danish landmark or flying all the way to Salt Lake City, where they would not have been allowed to film anyway. For a discussion of the film's directorial style (and for the characters' names in the Danish version) see David Bordwell, "Sometimes two shots...," *Observations on film art*, http://www.davidbordwell.net/blog/2013/01/22/sometimes-two-shots (accessed January 1, 2018). See also "Mormonens Offer," *Danish Film Institute*, http://www.dfi.dk/faktaomfilm/film/da/20932.aspx?id=20932 (accessed February 24, 2018).

282 Cannon and Olmstead, "'Scandalous Film,'" 45; p. 46 notes other advertisements that claimed this film "should do more to counteract the growth of Mormonism in this country than all the preaching against it, even by the most noted clerics," particularly for weak-minded women who were Mormons' chief targets.

283 Ibid., 48.

284 Thorp, "Winifred Graham and the Mormon Image in England," 108-110; "Messages from the Missions," *Improvement Era* 15:6 (April 1912), 560-561; Cannon and Olmstead, "'Scandalous Film,'" 47-50; Rudger Clawson, "The An-

ti-'Mormon' Moving Pictures and Play," *Millennial Star* 73:51 (December 21, 1911), 808-811; Hatch, "Moving Picture Misrepresentations," 710-711; J. E. Salisbury and J. Thurman Smith, "Combatting Anti-'Mormon' Pictures in Bristol," *Millennial Star* 74:20 (May 16, 1912), 315-316; F. D. Ashdown and A. R. Cook, "The Anti-'Mormon' Drama," *Millennial Star* 74:8 (February 22, 1912), 124-125, about *Through Death Valley* in Ipswich; "Messages from the Missions," *Improvement Era* 15:4 (February 1912), 330-331, for a discouraging report from Stavanger, Norway in October 1911, early in the film's release; "Convention of Conference Presidents," *Millennial Star* 74:9 (February 29, 1912), for a report from Nottingham, 74:10 (March 7, 1912), 158, for Newcastle, and 74:11 (March 14, 1912), 172, for a general report on England and the 173,000 tracts figure; "Messages from the Missions," *Improvement Era* 15:5 (March 1912), 427-428, for an encouraging report from Newport; "President Andrew Jenson's Release," *Millennial Star* 74:22 (May 30, 1912), 348-349, in which Preisdent Jenson describes *Victim* and *Flower* by saying, "Living picture shows have been concocted, manufactured and exhibited, misrepresenting and vilifying us in the most scandalous manner"; Stephen H. Chipman, "Scenes in Denmark," *Improvement Era* 15:8 (June 1912), 707-709; "Messages from the Missions," *Improvement Era* 15:8 (June 1912), 745, for an encouraging report from Haugesund, Norway in February 1912; "Messages from the Missions," *Improvement Era* 15:8 (June 1912), 748, for the use of the "£200 Reward" pamphlet in Carlisle, England; "Messages from the Missions," *Improvement Era* 15:12 (October 1912), 1123-1124, about waning anti-Mormon activity in Norway. For *Victim*'s French release, see an untitled advertisement, *Ciné-Journal*, December 16, 1911, 70, http://www.archive.org/stream/cineaugde04gdur#page/n781/mode/2up (accessed December 28, 2017); "Messages from the Missions," *Improvement Era* 16:1 (November 1912), 75, for an encouraging report from Sheffield in August; "Messages from the Missions," *Improvement Era* 16:2 (December 1912), 171-172, for an encouraging report from Norway; "Messages from the Missions," *Improvement Era* 17:11 (September 1914), 1084, about calming agitation in Norwich. For the Sutherland riot, the same report was printed as both "Moving Picture Film Angers Mormon Band," *Salt Lake Tribune*, December 17, 1911, 27, https://chroniclingamerica.loc.gov/lccn/sn83045396/1911-12-17/ed-1/seq-27 (accessed December 28, 2017) and "Mormons Enraged at Moving Picture Show," *Logan Republican*, December 21, 1911, 5, https://chroniclingamerica.loc.gov/lccn/sn85058246/1911-12-21/ed-1/seq-5 (accessed December 28, 2017).

285 "Messages from the Missions," *Improvement Era* 16:4 (February 1913), 386.

286 "Mormonbyens Blomst," *Danish Film Institute,* http://www.dfi.dk/faktaomfilm/film/en/36200.aspx?id=36200 (accessed February 24, 2018); Cannon and Olmstead, "'Scandalous Film,'" 46-50; Thorp, "'The Mormon Peril,'" 72-86; "From the Mission Field: Anti-'Mormon' Pictures in Edinburgh," *Millennial Star* 74:29 (July 18, 1912), 462; Albert T. Smith, "Anti-'Mormon' Rowdyism at Birmingham," Millennial Star 74:35 (August 29, 1912), 555-556; "The Anti-'Mormon' Mass Meeting at Sunderland," *Millennial Star* 74:22 (May 30, 1912), 344-347; "Messages from the Missions," *Improvement Era* 15:12 (October 1912), 1124-1125, a further report about the violence in Sunderland; "Minutes of Norwich Conference," *Millennial Star* 74:43 (October 24, 1912), 683; Amos R. Cook and Rudger Clawson, "Further Mob Violence at Ipswich," *Millennial Star* 75:6 (February 6, 1913), 81-86;

"Messages from the Missions," *Improvement Era* 16:7 (May 1913), 722, for more on violence in Ipswich; "Messages from the Missions," *Improvement Era* 16:4 (February 1913), 386 (distribution in Amsterdam); "Mormonsbyens Blomst," *Danish Film Institute,* http://www.dfi.dk/faktaomfilm/film/en/36200.aspx?id=36200 (accessed December 29, 2017). Many of the articles cited in footnote 283 refer to both *Victim* and *Flower* together.

287 An untitled advertisement quoted in Nelson, "A History of Latter-day Saint Screen Portrayals," 50. The amount of footage is from "Vacant Dates on Feature Films After July 1st," *Moving Picture World,* July 8, 1912, 97, http://www.archive.org/stream/moviwor13chal#page/n101/mode/2up (accessed January 1, 2018) and "Films for Sale or Rent," *Moving Picture World,* September 14, 1912, 1128, http://www.archive.org/stream/moviwor13chal#page/n1131/mode/2up (accessed January 1, 2018).

288 *O Estado de São Paulo,* February 2, 1912, page unknown. My thanks to Kent Larsen for alerting me about this notice. "Will Present Big Productions," *Moving Picture World,* January 13, 1912, 109, http://www.archive.org/stream/movingpicturewor11newy#page/108/mode/2up (accessed December 28, 2017); Cannon and Olmstead, "'Scandalous Film,'" 51-52.

289 "Will and Effort to Suppress Films," *Salt Lake Tribune,* February 11, 1912, 16, https://chroniclingamerica.loc.gov/lccn/sn83045396/1912-02-11/ed-1/seq-16 (accessed December 31, 2017), in which William Swanson refers to *The Mountain Meadows Massacre* as "a foreign film," (his distribution organization only deals with American films, so he had no influence over it), and "Lecture Against Mormons Suppressed," *Salt Lake Tribune,* February 24, 1912, 7, https://chroniclingamerica.loc.gov/lccn/sn83045396/1912-02-24/ed-1/seq-7, in which Ben E. Rich says he is waiting for prints of *Marriage or Death* to arrive in America.

290 Nelson, "A History of Latter-day Saint Screen Portrayals," 56-57, 62-63; Cannon and Olmstead, "'Scandalous Film,'" 62; "Complete Record of Current Films," *Motography,* December 1911, 295, http://www.archive.org/stream/motography56elec#page/294/mode/2up (accessed December 31, 2017); "Data from Manufacturer's List of Releases," *Moving Picture News,* December 2, 1911, 49, http://www.archive.org/stream/movingpicturenew04unse#page/n1517/mode/2up (accessed December 31, 2017); "Calendar of Licensed Releases," *Moving Picture World,* December 9, 1911, 826, http://www.archive.org/stream/moviwor10chal#page/n829/mode (accessed January 1, 2018); "Licensed Release Dates: Pathé," *Moving Picture World,* December 9, 1911, 846, http://www.archive.org/stream/moviwor10chal#page/n849/mode/2up (accessed January 1, 2018).

291 Interestingly, white slave trade films were a particularly thorny issue for the Board. Hence in 1913 the film *Traffic in Souls* was approved because it portrayed a woman's campaign to save others before they fell into prostitution, while the *The Inside of the White Slave Traffic,* which took a more complex look at the causes and social stigma of prostitution, was deemed too vague and hence was rejected. Robert W. Morrow, *Sesame Street and the Reform of Children's Television* (Baltimore: Johns Hopkins University Press, 2006), 13; Cannon and Olmstead, "'Scandalous Film,'" 56.

292 Cannon and Olmstead, "'Scandalous Film,'" 54.

293 Elizabeth Atwood, "Moving Pictures and the Child," *Implet*, June 1, 1912, 2, http://www.archive.org/stream/implet01bedd#page/n177/mode/2up (accessed December 31, 2017); Cannon and Olmstead, "'Scandalous Film'" 52-55; Nelson, "A History of Latter-day Saint Screen Portrayals," 58-62; Nelson, "From Antagonism to Acceptance," 61.

294 Cannon and Olmstead, "'Scandalous Film,'" 63.

295 "Mormon Pictures in Demand," *Moving Picture World*, February 10, 1912, 470, http://www.archive.org/stream/movingpicturewor11newy#page/470/mode/2up (accessed December 31, 2017);

296 Joseph Lippman, "Enjoy Delightful Sightseeing Trip," *Salt Lake Tribune*, April 19, 1912, 16, https://chroniclingamerica.loc.gov/lccn/sn83045396/1912-04-19/ed-1/seq-16 (accessed December 31, 2017).

297 Cannon and Olmstead, "'Scandalous Film,'" 71.

298 Ibid., 56-67; Olmstead, "*A Victim of the Mormons and The Danites*," 203-207; Nelson, "A History of Latter-day Saint Screen Portrayals," 24-46; Nelson, "The History of Utah Film," 7; Nelson, "From Antagonism to Acceptance," 61; James V. D'arc, "The Saints on Celluloid: The Making of the Movie 'Brigham Young'," *Sunstone* 1:4 (Fall 1976), 12; Quinn, *The Mormon Hierarchy: Extensions of Power*, 811; "The Sectarian Film Once More," *Moving Picture World*, January 2, 1912, 282, http://www.archive.org/stream/movingpicturewor11newy#page/282/mode/2up (accessed December 31, 2017), which also discusses *The Mormon*; "'A Victim of the Mormons' advertisement," *Moving Picture News*, February 3, 1912, 33, http://www.archive.org/stream/movingpicturenew05unse#page/n229/mode/2up (accessed December 31, 2017); "Heeds Request for Suppression of Film," *Salt Lake Tribune*, February 4, 1912, 28, https://chroniclingamerica.loc.gov/lccn/sn83045396/1912-02-04/ed-1/seq-28 (accessed December 31, 2017); "Serves But to Advertise," *Salt Lake Tribune*, February 5, 1912, 4, https://chroniclingamerica.loc.gov/lccn/sn83045396/1912-02-05/ed-1/seq-4 (accessed December 31, 2017); "Great Northern Feature Film Company," *Moving Picture News*, February 10, 1912, 24, http://www.archive.org/stream/movingpicturenew05unse#page/n273/mode/2up (accessed December 31, 2017); "Greatest Box-Office Feature Of the Day: 'A Victim of the Mormons,'" *Moving Picture World*, February 10, 1912, 507, http://www.archive.org/stream/movingpicturewor11newy#page/506/mode/2up (accessed December 31, 2017); "Will and Effort to Suppress Films," *Salt Lake Tribune*, 16; "The Talk of the Trade: Victim of the Mormons," *Moving Picture News*, February 24, 1912, 28, http://www.archive.org/stream/movingpicturenew05unse#page/n385/mode/2up (accessed December 28, 2017); "The Talk of the Trade: Victim of the Mormons," *Moving Picture News*, February 24, 1912, 28, http://www.archive.org/stream/movingpicturenew05unse#page/n385/mode/2up (accessed December 31, 2017); Epes Winthrop Sargent, "Advertising for Exhibitors," *Moving Picture World*, February 24, 1912, 666, http://www.archive.org/stream/movingpicturewor11newy#page/666/mode/2up (accessed December 31, 2017), about how to market the film; "Across the Pond: Our Letter from America," *Cinema News*

and Property Gazette, March 1912, 13, http://www.archive.org/stream/cinenew-
gaz01cine#page/n49/mode/2up (accessed December 28, 2017); "Passing Events:
'A Victim of the Mormons,'" *Improvement Era* 15:6 (April 1912), 576. For missionaries working outside the theaters, see "Messages from the Missions," *Improvement Era* 15:9 (July 1912), 850, from Billings, Montana, and "Messages from
the Missions," *Improvement Era* 15:12 (October 1912), 1123-1124, from Battle
Creek, Michigan. For the extent of *Victim*'s distribution in the United States, see
"'A Victim of the Mormons,'" *Amarillo Daily News*, February 14, 1912, 4, https://
chroniclingamerica.loc.gov/lccn/sn85042551/1912-02-14/ed-1/seq-4 (accessed
December 28, 2017) in Amarillo, Texas; "The Moving Pictures Begin for 1912,"
Abbeville Press and Banner, March 13, 1912, 5, https://chroniclingamerica.loc.
gov/lccn/sn84026853/1912-03-13/ed-1/seq-5 (accessed December 31, 2017) in
Abbeville, South Carolina; "Amusements," *Bryan Daily Eagle and Pilot*, March 16,
1912, 6, https://chroniclingamerica.loc.gov/lccn/sn86088651/1912-03-16/ed-1/
seq-6 (accessed December 31, 2017) in Bryan, Texas; "A Victim of the Mormons,"
Daily Ardmoreite, March 31, 1912, 9, https://chroniclingamerica.loc.gov/lccn/
sn85042303/1912-03-31/ed-1/seq-9 (accessed December 31, 2017) in Ardmore,
Oklahoma; "At the Theatres This Week," *Times Dispatch*, May 26, 1912, 7, https://
chroniclingamerica.loc.gov/lccn/sn85038615/1912-05-26/ed-1/seq-39 (accessed December 31, 2017), in Richmond, Virginia; "At the Arcade Today, Monday,"
Herald and News, June 18, 1912, 8, https://chroniclingamerica.loc.gov/lccn/
sn86063758/1912-06-18/ed-1/seq-8 (accessed December 31, 2017), in Newberry,
South Carolina; "Short Local News," *Interior Journal*, August 2, 1912, 3, with an
advertisement, https://chroniclingamerica.loc.gov/lccn/sn85052023/1912-08-
02/ed-1/seq-3 (accessed December 31, 2017), in Stanford, Kentucky.

299 "Comments on the Films," *Moving Picture World,* February 3, 1912, 393,
http://www.archive.org/stream/movingpicturewor11newy#page/392/mode/2up
(accessed January 1, 2018); Nelson, "A History of Latter-day Saint Screen Portrayals," 50-53; Cannon and Olmstead, "'Scandalous Film,'" 57-58; "Answers to
Inquiries," *Motion Picture Story Magazine,* 150, http://www.archive.org/stream/
motionpicturesto03moti#page/150/mode/2up (accessed December 31, 2017);
"A Breezy Westerner Fresh from Range and Cattle-Corral," *Moving Picture World*,
January 20, 1912, 229, http://www.archive.org/stream/movingpicturewor11n-
ewy#page/228/mode/2up (accessed January 1, 2018); "Independent Film Stories:
American," *Moving Picture World*, January 20, 1912, 242, http://www.archive.org/
stream/movingpicturewor11newy#page/242/mode/2up (accessed January 1,
2018); "A Breezy Westerner Fresh from Range and Cattle-Corral," *Moving Picture
News*, January 13, 1912, 35, http://www.archive.org/stream/movingpicture-
new05unse#page/n83/mode/2up (accessed January 1, 2018); "The Mormon,"
Moving Picture News, December 30, 1911, 20, http://www.archive.org/stream/
movingpicturenew04unse#page/20/mode/2up (accessed January 1, 2018).

300 Nelson, "A History of Latter-day Saint Screen Portrayals," 64-69; Cannon
and Olmstead, "'Scandalous Film,'" 68-69; Olmstead, "*A Victim of the Mormons*
and *The Danites*," 207-209, 217-219; Cornwall and Arrington, "Perpetuation of a
Myth," 156-158; "The Danites: Plot," *Internet Movie Database*, http://www.imdb.
com/title/tt0429977/plotsummary?ref_=tt_ov_pl (accessed January 1, 2018);
untitled advertisement, *O Estado de São Paulo*, January 23, 1912, 10; "Palace

Bioscope," *Beira Post*, June 13, 1913—my thanks to Kent Larsen for alerting me to these two screenings; "Events of the Month," *Improvement Era* 15:12 (October 1912), 1144-1145 for the South African report. For additional information on the American release of *The Flower of the Mormon City*, see Nelson, "From Antagonism to Acceptance," 61, which notes that *Flower* was among the "other foreign melodramas [besides *Victim* that] brought vigorous protests from both LDS Church and Utah civic officials"; Nelson, "A History of Latter-day Saint Screen Portrayals," 46-50; untitled Davis Film Exchange Company advertisement, *Moving Picture World*, April 27, 1912, 42, http://www.archive.org/stream/movingpicture-new05unse#page/n881/mode/2up (accessed December 29, 2017), and again in *Clipper*, April 27, 1912, 7, http://www.archive.org/stream/clipper60-1912-04#page/n77/mode/2up (accessed January 1, 2018), both about state's rights distribution in Wisconsin; Vacant Dates on Feature Films After July 1st," *Moving Picture World*, July 8, 1912; "Films for Sale or Rent," *Moving Picture World*, September 14, 1912, both ads for national rights from a distributor in Philadelphia; "Live Exhibitors, Look," *Moving Picture World*, December 7, 1912, 1011, http://www.archive.org/stream/movinwor14chal#page/n1015/mode/2up (accessed January 1, 2018), an ad from a distributor in Cleveland.

301 Nelson, "A History of Latter-day Saint Screen Portrayals," 63-64; Cannon and Olmstead, "'Scandalous Film,'" 67-68; "Lecture Against Mormons Suppressed," *Salt Lake Tribune*, February 24, 1912; "Objectionable Film Passes the Censors," *Salt Lake Tribune*, February 25, 1912, 10, https://chroniclingamerica.loc.gov/lccn/sn83045396/1912-02-25/ed-1/seq-10 (accessed January 1, 2018).

302 "Salt Lake City Woman Brands Lecturer on Mormons as 'Liar,'" *Salt Lake Telegram*, January 16, 1914, Journal History of the Church, January 16, 1914, 3, https://dcms.lds.org/delivery/DeliveryManagerServlet?dps_pid=IE306618 (accessed March 4, 2018).

303 "The Church of Jesus Christ of Latter-day Saints membership history," *Wikipedia*, https://en.wikipedia.org/wiki/The_Church_of_Jesus_Christ_of_Latter-day_Saints_membership_history (accessed December 30, 2017).

304 Joseph O. Stone, "Free from Persecution," *Improvement Era* 18:8 (June 1915), 738-739.

305 Nelson, "A History of Latter-day Saint Screen Portrayals," 81-82.

306 *Kinematograph Monthly Film Record*, November 1914, quoted in "Who can solve the mystery of the missing Sherlock Holmes film?," *British Film Institute*, August 15, 2014, http://www.bfi.org.uk/news-opinion/news-bfi/announcements/who-can-solve-mystery-missing-sherlock-holmes-film (accessed January 4, 2018).

307 Nelson, "A History of Latter-day Saint Screen Portrayals," 83-87; George Pearson, *Flashback: The Auto-Biography of a British Filmmaker* (London: Ruskin House, 1957), 36-38; Michael W. Homer, "The Mormon Subplot in *A Study in Scarlet* and *Angels of Darkness*," in Arthur Conan Doyle, *Angels of Darkness: A Drama in Three Acts* ed. Peter E. Blau (New York: Baker Street Irregulars, 2001), 166-183;

"Who can solve the mystery of the missing Sherlock Holmes film?," *British Film Institute*; "Isleworth Studios," *Wikipedia*, https://en.wikipedia.org/wiki/Isleworth_Studios (accessed January 4, 2018).

308 "Independent Specials," *Moving Picture World*, January 2, 1915, 77, http://www.archive.org/stream/movingpicturewor23newy#page/76/mode/2up (accessed January 4, 2018); "A Study in Scarlet (Movie 1914 with Ford)," *The Arthur Conan Doyle Encyclopedia*, https://www.arthur-conan-doyle.com/index.php/A_Study_in_Scarlet_(movie_1914_with_Ford) (accessed January 4, 2018).

309 For *The Latter-day Saints*, see "Film Flashes," *Variety*, February 20, 1915, 24, http://www.archive.org/stream/variety37-1915-02#page/n111/mode/2up (accessed February 24, 2018); James B. Allen, *The Latter-day Saints: A Study of the Mormons in the Light of Economic Conditions*, by Ruth Kauffman and Reginald Wright Kauffman (Williams and Northgate, 1912)," BYU Studies 35:3 (1995-96), 190-191. For *Polygamy*, see "Polygamy," *Internet Broadway Database*, https://www.ibdb.com/broadway-production/polygamy-8099 (accessed February 24, 2018); "Equitable's Producing Plans," *Moving Picture World*, September 25, 1915, 2188, http://www.archive.org/stream/movingpicturewor25newy#page/2188/mode/2up (accessed February 24, 2018); William Thompson Price, ed., *The American Playwright*, (New York: William Thompson Price, 1915), 8-9.

310 "'A Mormon Maid,'" *Variety*, February 16, 1917, 23, http://www.archive.org/stream/variety45-1917-02#page/n125/mode/2up (accessed September 1, 2017), and quoted in Richard Alan Nelson, "Commercial Propaganda in the Silent Film: A Case Study of *A Mormon Maid* (1917)," *Film History* 1:2 (1987), 154.

311 Edje Jeter, "Graphical Representations of Hooded Mormon Vigilantes," *Juvenile Instructor*, October 20, 2013, http://juvenileinstructor.org/graphical-representations-of-hooded-mormon-vigilantes (accessed January 2, 2018); Nelson, "A History of Latter-day Saint Screen Portrayals," 103-105; Nelson, "Commercial Propaganda in the Silent Film," 154. See also Edje Jeter, "Mormon Horns 3/7: What Makes Horns Stick?," *Juvenile Instructor*, February 2, 2010, http://juvenile-instructor.org/mormon-horns-3o7-what-makes-horns-stick (accessed January 2, 2018). Many books, essays, and documentaries have been made about *The Birth of a Nation*'s controversy, but for one short summary see Dorian Lynskey, "'A Public Menace,'" *Slate*, March 31, 2015, http://www.slate.com/articles/arts/history/2015/03/the_birth_of_a_nation_how_the_fight_to_censor_d_w_griffith_s_film_shaped.html (accessed January 2, 2018).

312 Gene Ringgold and DeWitt Bodeen, *The Films of Cecil B. DeMille* (New York: The Citadel Press, 1969), 9-10. In one source Leonard claimed to have written the script from West's story which, in the early silent days of studio filmmaking, was actually quite likely. Jane Ardmore, *The Self-Enchanted: Mae Murray: Image of an Era* (New York: McGraw-Hill Book Company, Inc., 1959), 79, http://www.archive.org/stream/selfenchanted00jane#page/n97/mode/2up (accessed February 21, 2018).

313 Nelson, "Commercial Propaganda in the Silent Film," 154.

314 Ardmore, *The Self-Enchanted*, 79.

315 George W. Graves, "'A Mormon Maid,'" *Motography*, March 3, 1917, 483, http://www.archive.org/stream/motography17elec#page/482/mode/2up (accessed September 2, 2017).

316 Peter Milne, "'A Mormon Maid,'" *Motion Picture News,* March 3, 1917, 1419, http://www.archive.org/stream/motionpicturenew152unse#page/1418/mode/2up (accessed September 2, 2017).

317 Julian Johnson, "The Shadow Stage," *Photoplay*, April 1917, 81-82, http://www.archive.org/stream/photoplayvolume11112chic#page/434/mode/2up (accessed September 3, 2017). For a sampling of contemporary notices and reviews, see "Five Lasky Pictures for January," *Motography*, December 30, 1916, 1438, http://www.archive.org/stream/motography162elec#page/1438/mode/2up (accessed September 2, 2017); "Paramount Has Dickens Week," *Moving Picture World,* January 6, 1917, 103, http://www.archive.org/stream/movwor31chal#page/102/mode/2up (accessed September 1, 2017); *A Mormon Maid* trade showing ticket, *Variety*, February 9, 1917, 21, http://www.archive.org/stream/variety45-1917-02#page/n71/mode/2up (accessed September 6, 2017); "'Mormon Maid' Propaganda," *New York Clipper*, February 14, 1917, 33, http://www.archive.org/stream/Clipper65-1917-02#page/n69/mode/2up (accessed September 1, 2017); "New Open Market Concern," *Motography*, February 24, 1917, 412, http://www.archive.org/stream/motography17elec#page/412/mode/2up (accessed September 2, 2017); "'A Mormon Maid,'" *Motography*, March 3, 1917, 452, http://www.archive.org/stream/motography17elec#page/452/mode/2up (accessed September 3, 2017); "'Mormon Maid' Attracts Buyers," *Moving Picture World*, March 3, 1917, 1382, http://www.archive.org/stream/movpict31chal#page/n135/mode/2up (accessed September 2, 2017); George Blaisdell, "'A Mormon Maid,'" *Moving Picture World,* March 3, 1917, 1372, http://www.archive.org/stream/movpict31chal#page/n125/mode/2up (accessed September 2, 2017); untitled two-page *A Mormon Maid* advertisement, *Motion Picture News*, March 10, 1917, 1504-1505, http://www.archive.org/stream/motionpicturenew152unse#page/1504/mode/2up (accessed September 1, 2017); untitled *A Mormon Maid* Park Theatre advertisement, *Sun*, April 19, 1917, 7, https://chroniclingamerica.loc.gov/lccn/sn83030431/1917-04-19/ed-1/seq-7 (accessed August 3, 2017); "'A Mormon Maid' Park Theatre Film," *Evening World*, April 21, 1917, 9, https://chroniclingamerica.loc.gov/lccn/sn83030193/1917-04-21/ed-1/seq-9 (accessed August 3, 2017); "Mae Murray Becomes Bluebird," *Motography*, August 4, 1917, 244, http://www.archive.org/stream/motography18elec#page/244/mode/2up (accessed September 1, 2017), a profile of Murray after her success with that film. See also "Bosworth Injured," *Seattle Star*, October 29, 1917, 4, https://chroniclingamerica.loc.gov/lccn/sn87093407/1917-10-29/ed-1/seq-4 (accessed January 30, 2018) about how Bosworth crushed his foot during production and "was confined to his home for three weeks."

318 "'Mormons' in the Movies," *Deseret Evening News*, December 27, 1916, quoted in Nelson, "Commercial Propaganda in the Silent Film," 150; the full text of Monson's letter is in "'Mormons' in the 'Movies,'" *Deseret Evening News*, December 27, 1916, Journal History of the Church, December 27, 1916, 2, https://dcms.lds.

org/delivery/DeliveryManagerServlet?dps_pid=IE387974 (accessed February 21, 2018).

319 "Anti-Mormon Film Halted by Protests," *New York Tribune*, April 23, 1917, 5, https://chroniclingamerica.loc.gov/lccn/sn83030214/1917-04-23/ed-1/seq-5 (accessed August 7, 2017); "Mormon Intrigue Shown in Filmed 'Mormon Maid' at the Park Theatre," *Evening World,* April 24, 1917, 13, https://chroniclingamerica. loc.gov/lccn/sn83030193/1917-04-24/ed-1/seq-13 (accessed August 7, 2017); "Park's Added Feature," *Variety*, April 27, 1917, 24, http://www.archive.org/stream/ variety46-1917-04#page/n171/mode/2up (accessed August 8, 2017).

320 Cannon and Olmstead, "'Scandalous Film,'" 75-76; "Mormons Oppose Film," *Variety*, February 9, 1917, 18, http://www.archive.org/stream/vari- ety45-1917-02#page/n69/mode/2up (accessesd January 31, 2018); "Film Flashes," *Tulsa Daily World*, February 11, 1917, 11, https://chroniclingamerica. loc.gov/lccn/sn85042344/1917-02-11/ed-1/seq-11 (accessed January 30, 2018); "'Mormon Maid' New York and Jersey Rights Sold," *Moving Picture World*, April 21, 1917, 461, http://www.archive.org/stream/movingpicturewor32newy#page/460/ mode/2up (accessed September 1, 2017); "Mormons Object to 'Mormon Maid' in Utah and Idaho," *Motion Picture News*, April 21, 1917, 2482, http://www.archive. org/stream/motionpicturenew153unse#page/2445/mode/2up (accessed January 30, 2018); "'The Mormon Maid' May Come to Utah," *Salt Lake Tribune*, April 22, 1917, Journal History of the Church, April 22, 1917, 10, https://dcms.lds.org/deliv- ery/DeliveryManagerServlet?dps_pid=IE399238 (accessed February 22, 2018); *A Mormon Maid* full-page advertisement, *Moving Picture World*, May 12, 1917, 907, http://www.archive.org/stream/movingpicturewor32newy#page/n997/mode/2up (accessed February 21, 2018); "'Mormon Maid' Sub-Titled After Investigation," *Motion Picture News*, May 26, 1917, 3285, http://www.archive.org/stream/motion- picturenew153unse#page/3247/mode/2up (accessed January 31, 2018).

321 Nelson, "Commercial Propaganda in the Silent Film," 157.

322 "Opens Chicago Branch," *Motography*, March 17, 1917, 574, http://www. archive.org/stream/motography17elec#page/574/mode/2up (accessed Septem- ber 2, 2017). For the 896 interested buyers see *A Mormon Maid* full-page adver- tisement, *Moving Picture World*, March 24, 1917, 1887, http://www.archive.org/ stream/movpict31chal#page/n691/mode/2up (accessed September 1, 2017).

323 "Official Cut-Outs Made by the Chicago Board of Censors," *Exhibitors Herald*, September 8, 1917, 33, http://www.archive.org/stream/exhibitorsheral- d05exhi#page/n531/mode/2up (accessed January 30, 2018); "The Mormon Maid," *Motography*, November 10, 1917, 966, http://www.archive.org/stream/motogra- phy18elec#page/966/mode/2up (accessed September 5, 2017) for the quote; "State Rights and Specials: The Mormon Maid," *Motography*, January 26, 1918, 154, http://www.archive.org/stream/motography19elec#page/154/mode/2up (accessed September 2, 2017). For more information on sales and exhibition in Chicago see James S. McQuade, "Chicago News Letter," *Moving Picture World*, April 28, 1917, 621-622, http://www.archive.org/stream/movingpicturewor32n- ewy#page/620/mode/2up (accessed September 2, 2017); "Mormon Maid in Chicago," *Variety*, August 17, 1917, 25, http://www.archive.org/stream/vari-

ety47-1917-08#page/n111/mode/2up (accessed September 2, 2017); "'Split Reel' Notes for Theater Men: How Others Are Steering the Ship," *Motography*, September 29, 1917, 676, http://www.archive.org/stream/motography18elec#page/676/mode/2up (accessed September 1, 2017); "States Rights and Specials," *Exhibitors Herald and Motography*, September 7, 1918, 56, http://www.archive.org/stream/exhibitorsherald07exhi#page/n601/mode/2up (accessed September 2, 2017).

324 Nelson, "Commercial Propaganda in the Silent Film," 157-158; "Friedman Reports Mid-West Taking War Calmly," *Motion Picture News,* June 2, 1917, 3439, http://www.archive.org/stream/motionpicturenew153unse#page/n1377/mode/2up (accessed September 4, 2017). For general sales see *A Mormon Maid* full-page advertisement, *Moving Picture World*, March 17, 1917, 1714, http://www.archive.org/stream/movpict31chal#page/n491/mode/2up (accessed September 3, 2017); "State Rights Field Expanded Remarkably, Says Friedman," *Motion Picture News* March 17, 1917, 1700, http://www.archive.org/stream/motionpicturenew152unse#page/1700/mode/2up (accessed September 3, 2017); "Keen Competition for 'A Mormon Maid,'" *Moving Picture World*, March 24, 1917, 1960, http://www.archive.org/stream/movpict31chal#page/n765/mode/2up (accessed September 2, 2017); "Territory for 'A Mormon Maid' Is Selling Rapidly," *Motion Picture News* March 24, 1917, 1851, http://www.archive.org/stream/motionpicturenew152unse#page/1850/mode/2up (accessed September 2, 2017); "Trade-Showing Tour for 'A Mormon Maid,'" *Moving Picture World*, March 24, 1917, 1958, http://www.archive.org/stream/movpict31chal#page/n763/mode/2up (accessed September 1, 2017), and "'A Mormon Maid' to Be Given Trade Showing Tour," *Motion Picture News*, March 31, 1917, 2014, http://www.archive.org/stream/motionpicturenew152unse#page/2014/mode/2up (accessed September 2, 2017) both discuss a sale trips Friedman took to Chicago, Minneapolis, Denver, and San Francisco; "Hiller & Wilk Take New Offices," *Motography*, May 5, 1917, 958, http://www.archive.org/stream/motography17elec#page/958/mode/2up (accessed December 1, 2017); "Hiller & Wilk Expand," *Moving Picture World*, May 5, 1917, 822, http://www.archive.org/stream/movingpicturewor32newy#page/822/mode/2up (accessed September 1, 2017); "Wilk on Intrinsic Value of Picture Publicity," *Motion Picture News,* May 26, 1917, 3269, http://www.archive.org/stream/motionpicturenew153unse#page/3231/mode/2up (accessed September 4, 2017). For Detroit and Michigan see "Butterfield in State Right Field," *Moving Picture World*, February 17, 1917, 1041, http://www.archive.org/stream/moviwor-31chal#page/n483/mode/2up (accessed September 3, 2017); "Many Big State Right Films," *Moving Picture World*, March 10, 1917, 1647, http://www.archive.org/stream/movpict31chal#page/n421/mode/2up (accessed September 3, 2017); "State Film Co. Picture Opens," *Moving Picture World*, March 17, 1917, 1805, http://www.archive.org/stream/movpict31chal#page/n593/mode/2up (accessed September 3, 2017); "In Market for Territorial Subjects," *Motion Picture News*, March 17, 1917, 1672, http://www.archive.org/stream/motionpicturenew152unse#page/1672/mode/2up (accessed September 1, 2017); "To Spread on 'Mormon Maid' Advertising,' *Moving Picture World*, May 12, 1917, 1003, http://www.archive.org/stream/movingpicturewor32newy#page/1002/mode/2up (accessed September 3, 2017); "Big Michigan Exploitation on 'Mormon Maid,'" *Motion Picture News,* May 12, 1917, 2983, http://www.archive.org/stream/motionpicturenew153unse#page/2945/mode/2up (accessed September 4, 2017); "State Right Film for

Week at Drury Lane," *Moving Picture World*, August 25, 1917, 1255, http://www. archive.org/stream/mowor33chal#page/1254/mode/2up (accessed September 1, 2017); "Theaters and Programs—Business Notes," *Moving Picture World*, October 13, 1917, 277, http://www.archive.org/stream/movewor34chal#page/n353/ mode/2up (accessed September 1, 2017); "Newsy Notes from Michigan," *Moving Picture World*, October 27, 1917, 565, http://www.archive.org/stream/movewor-34chal#page/n717/mode/2up (accessed September 1, 2017); Jacob Smith, "Higher Admissions in Detroit Probable: State Film Again Changes Hands," *Moving Picture World*, August 24, 1918, 1147, http://www.archive.org/stream/movwor-37chal#page/1146/mode/2up (accessed February 21, 2018). For New York and New Jersey see "News of the Film World," *Variety*, March 10, 1917, 28, http://www. archive.org/stream/variety46-1917-03#page/n131/mode/2up (accessed September 3, 2017); "News of the Film World", *Variety*, March 16, 1917, 28, http:// www.archive.org/stream/variety46-1917-03#page/n131/mode/2up (accessed February 21, 2018); "Backer Buys Two for Jersey," *Moving Picture World*, April 7, 1917, 130, http://www.archive.org/stream/movingpicturewor32newy#page/130/ mode/2up (accessed September 1, 2017), for New Jersey; "'Mormon Maid' New York and Jersey Rights Sold," *Moving Picture World*, April 21, 1917, 461; "Films—Advertising Stunts—Business Notes," Moving Picture World, June 16, 1917, 1818, http://www.archive.org/stream/movingpicturewor32newy#page/1818/mode/2up (accessed September 1, 2017), for the Buffalo advertising stunt; "List of Current Film Release Dates: Feature Releases," *Moving Picture World*, June 1, 1918, 1348, http://www.archive.org/stream/morewor36chal#page/n757/mode/2up (accessed February 21, 2018). For Minneapolis and the Midwest see "Minneapolis News Notes of Convention Week," *Moving Picture World*, May 26, 1917, 1325, http://www. archive.org/stream/movingpicturewor32newy#page/1324/mode/2up (accessed September 1, 2017); "Business Notes From Film Row," *Moving Picture World*, October 6, 1917, 117, http://www.archive.org/stream/movewor34chal#page/n149/ mode/2up (accessed September 1, 2017); "Friedman Leaves for Minneapolis," *Moving Picture World*, June 9, 1917, 1633, http://www.archive.org/stream/ movingpicturewor32newy#page/1632/mode/2up (accessed September 1, 2017), which also mentions the runs in Cleveland and Buffalo; "Shoppers Guide," *Motography*, July 28, 1917, 215, http://www.archive.org/stream/motography18e-lec#page/214/mode/2up (accessed September 4, 2017), for sales in the Midwest out of Friedman's Minneapolis office; "'A Mormon Maid' Is Sold in Two Mid-West States," *Exhibitors Herald*, September 8, 1917, 46, http://www.archive.org/stream/ exhibitorsherald05exhi#page/n545/mode/2up (accessed September 4, 2017); "'A Mormon Maid' Sold for Two States," *Moving Picture World*, September 8, 1917, 1548, http://www.archive.org/stream/movpict33chal#page/n319/mode/2up (accessed September 2, 2017); John L. Johnston, "Minneapolis Film News Items Last Week," *Moving Picture World*, October 20, 1917, 427, http://www.archive.org/ stream/movewor34chal#page/n545/mode/2up (accessed September 2, 2017). For New England see "About State Rights Plays," *Motography*, September 22, 1917, 617, http://www.archive.org/stream/motography18elec#page/616/ mode/2up (accessed September 1, 2017); Ben H. Grimm, "State Rights Depart-ment: 'A Mormon Maid' Sold for New England," *Moving Picture World*, September 22, 1917, 1863, http://www.archive.org/stream/movpict33chal#page/n699/ mode/2up (accessed September 4, 2017); "Boston Photoplay Secures 'Mormon Maid,'" *Motion Picture News*, September 22, 1917, 2023, http://www.archive.org/

stream/motionpicturenew162unse#page/2022/mode/2up (accessed September 4, 2017). For Washington, Oregon, Idaho, and Montana see "News of the Film World," *Variety*, September 21, 1917, 37, http://www.archive.org/stream/variety48-1917-09#page/n149/mode/2up (accessed September 4, 2017); "Buys 'Mormon Maid' for Pacific Coast," *Moving Picture World*, October 6, 1917, 96, http://www.archive.org/stream/movewor34chal#page/n129/mode/2up (accessed September 1, 2017); "About State Rights Plays: Secures 'A Mormon Maid,'" *Motography*, October 6, 1917, 727, http://www.archive.org/stream/motography-18elec#page/726/mode/2up (accessed September 1, 2017); "Greater Features Company Moves," *Moving Picture World*, October 27, 1917, 570, http://www.archive.org/stream/movewor34chal#page/n723/mode/2up (accessed September 3, 2017). For California, Nevada, and Arizona see "Turner and Dahnken Buy 'A Mormon Maid,'" *Motion Picture News*, October 20, 1917, 2753, http://www.archive.org/stream/motionpicturenew162unse#page/2752/mode/2up (accessed September 3, 2017); "'A Mormon Maid' Sold for Pacific Coast," *Motography*, October 27, 1917, 875, http://www.archive.org/stream/motography18elec#page/874/mode/2up (accessed September 2, 2017); "Hiller & Wilk Astir," *Moving Picture World*, October 20, 1917, 403, http://www.archive.org/stream/movewor34chal#page/n521/mode/2up (accessed September 1, 2017). American newspapers from this summer are full of advertisements for the film, in Tulsa in May, New Orleans in July, El Paso in August, Seattle in October, Everett, Washington in November, Williston, North Dakota and Ashland, Oregon in December, Grants Pass, Oregon in January 1918, Tacoma in February, and Bisbee, Arizona all the way in June.

325 Nelson, "A History of Latter-day Saint Screen Portrayals," 115-120; Nelson, "Commercial Propaganda in the Silent Film," 158-159; Chester B. Bahn, "Syracuse, N.Y.," *Variety*, July 5, 1918, 25, http://www.archive.org/stream/variety51-1918-07#page/n23/mode/2up (accessed February 21, 2018), in which lecturer Myrtle Edwards is accompanying the film around Utica, New York, after just recovering "from injuries received during an attack by Mormon elders"; "Rochester, N.Y.," *Variety*, September 20, 1918, 39, http://www.archive.org/stream/Var52-1918-09#page/n37/mode/2up (accessed February 21, 2018); "Syracuse, N.Y.," *Variety*, September 27, 1918, 38, http://www.archive.org/stream/Var52-1918-09#page/n87/mode/2up (accessed February 21, 2018); L. B. Skeffington, "Rochester News Letter," *Moving Picture World*, October 5, 1918, 113, http://www.archive.org/stream/moviwor3738chal#page/n749/mode/2up (accessed February 21, 2018).

326 For South America and Scandinavia see "News of the Film World," *Variety*, May 25, 1917, 19, http://www.archive.org/stream/variety46-1917-05#page/n257/mode/2up (accessed September 4, 2017); "South America Gets 'Mormon Maid,'" *Moving Picture World*, June 9, 1917, 1632, http://www.archive.org/stream/movingpicturewor32newy#page/1632/mode/2up (accessed September 1, 2017); F. G. Ortega, "Film Export Notes," *Moving Picture World*, June 16, 1917, 1768, http://www.archive.org/stream/movingpicturewor32newy#page/1768/mode/2up (accessed September 1, 2017); "'Joan' for Crest in South America," *Motion Picture News*, July 7, 1917, 83, http://www.archive.org/stream/motionpicturenew161unse#page/82/mode/2up (accessed September 4, 1917). For Australia see "Mormon

Maid for Australia and New Zealand," M*oving Picture World*, May 5, 1917, 825, http://www.archive.org/stream/movingpicturewor32newy#page/824/mode/2up (accessed September 3, 2017); "News of the Film World," *Variety*, June 15, 1917, 24, http://www.archive.org/stream/variety47-1917-06#page/n111/mode/2up (accessed September 3, 2017); "Australasian Films, Ltd., Gets Rights to Chaplin Comedies," *Motion Picture News,* July 28, 1917, 684, http://www.archive.org/stream/motionpicturenew161unse#page/684/mode/2up (accessed September 4, 2017); "Australian Notes," *Moving Picture World*, July 28, 1917, 635, http://www.archive.org/stream/movwor33chal#page/n743/mode/2up (accessed February 13, 2018); "Success of 'A Mormon Maid' in Australia," *Moving Picture World*, August 11, 1917, 961, http://www.archive.org/stream/mowor33chal#page/960/mode/2up (accessed September 2, 2017); "Australian Notes," *Moving Picture World*, August 18, 1917, 1063, http://www.archive.org/stream/mowor33chal#page/1062/mode/2up (accessed September 2, 2017); "Messages from the Missions," *Improvement Era* 21:5 (March 1918), 453, a report from a missionary in Tasmania. For the United Kingdom see F. G. Ortega, "Foreign Trade News: Robertson-Cole in Foreign Markets," *Moving Picture World,* July 27, 1918, 555, http://www.archive. org/stream/movwor37chal#page/554/mode/2up (accessed February 21, 2018). For Canada see W. M. Gladish, "Toronto Has Fine New Uptown Theater: St. Denis Begins Two Changes a Week," *Moving Picture World*, November 24, 1917, 1211, http://www.archive.org/stream/mopict34chal#page/1210/mode/2up (accessed September 4, 2017). For South Africa see H. Hanson, "South Africa," *Variety*, April 18, 1919, 47-48, http://www.archive.org/stream/Var54-1919-04#page/n183/mode/2up (accessed September 4, 2017); and for Ohio see K. E. Wall, "The Sunday Night Problem," *Moving Picture Age*, February 1922, 32, http://www.archive.org/stream/movingpictureage05unse#page/n73/mode/2up (accessed September 4, 2017). For its availability in Boston in 1923 see "Independent Exchanges: Massachusetts: Boston," *Film Yearbook: 1922-23* (New York: Wid's Films and Film Folks, Inc., 1923), 220, http://www.archive.org/stream/filmyearb1922192223n-ewy#page/220/mode/2up (accessed February 21, 2018). *National Cinema Service presents the 1942-1943 Film Rental Library Catalog* (New York: National Cinema Service, 1943), 2. For more on *A Mormon Maid*, see also Nelson, "A History of Latter-day Saint Screen Portrayals," 95-120; Nelson, "The History of Utah Film," 20-21, 23; Nelson, "From Antagonism to Acceptance," 59; D'arc, "The Saints on Celluloid," 13; Richard Alan Nelson, "Mormons as Silent Cinema Villains: Propaganda and Entertainment," *Historical Journal of Film, Radio, and Television* 4:1 (March 1984), 3-14.

327 "Not Distinctive But Action Holds Interest and Will Carry This," *Film Daily,* September 22, 1918, 18, http://www.archive.org/stream/filmdailyvolume556n-ewy#page/404/mode/2up (accessed February 22, 2018).

328 "Feature Star and Mormon Angle and Soft Pedal Trick Finish: William Farnum in 'Riders of the Purple Sage,'" *Film Daily*, September 15, 1918, 8, http://www.archive.org/stream/filmdailyvolume556newy#page/334/mode/2up (accessed February 22, 2018). For information on the films' production, see "Adventure Tales for Farnum," *Motography*, May 4, 1918, 853, http://www.archive.org/stream/motography19elec#page/852/mode/2up (accessed February 22, 2018); "Old Friends Are Star and Author of Fox Screen Story," *Moving Picture World*, July 13,

1918, 220, http://www.archive.org/stream/movwor37chal#page/220/mode/2up
(accessed February 22, 2018); "Adventure Tale for Farnum," *Motography*, May
4, 1918, 853, http://www.archive.org/stream/motography19elec#page/852/
mode/2up (accessed February 22, 2018); "Lloyd to Direct Zane Grey Stories,"
Motography, May 4, 1918, 877, http://www.archive.org/stream/motography19e-
lec#page/876/mode/2up (accessed February 22, 2018); "Farnum Again at Work,"
Motography, May 18, 1918, 950, http://www.archive.org/stream/motography-
19elec#page/950/mode/2up (accessed February 22, 2018); "His Many-Horned
Dilemma," *Moving Picture World*, June 1, 1918, 1302, http://www.archive.org/
stream/morewor36chal#page/n711/mode/2up (accessed February 22, 2018);
"Civil War Veterans Come to Farnum's Rescue," *Motion Picture News*, June 8, 1918,
3426, http://www.archive.org/stream/motionpicturenew172unse#page/3426/
mode/2up (accessed February 22, 2018); "Farnum Completing Grey's 'Riders of
the Purple Sage,'" *Moving Picture World*, June 8, 1918, 1448, http://www.archive.
org/stream/morewor36chal#page/n857/mode/2up (accessed February 22, 2018);
"Farnum Scenes Filmed in Wild Canyon," *Motography*, June 15, 1918, http://
www.archive.org/stream/motography19elec#page/1128/mode/2up (accessed
February 22, 2018); "Farnum Starts Work on Second Zane Grey Story," *Moving
Picture World*, June 22, 1918, 1734, http://www.archive.org/stream/morewor-
36chal#page/n1149/mode/2up (accessed February 22, 2018); "Farnum Begins
Sequel," *Motography*, June 22, 1918, 1176, http://www.archive.org/stream/mo-
tography19elec#page/1176/mode/2up (accessed February 22, 2018); "Farnum
Begins Zane Grey Picturization," *Motion Picture News*, June 22, 1918, 3712, http://
www.archive.org/stream/motionpicturenew172unse#page/3712/mode/2up (accessed February 22, 2018); and "Farnum Starts 'Rainbow Trail,'" *Motography*, June
29, 1918, 1207, http://www.archive.org/stream/motography19elec#page/1206/
mode/2up (accessed February 22, 2018). For reviews, see "Not Distinctive But Action Holds Interest and Will Carry This," *Film Daily*, September 22, 1918; "Should
Pull As Sequel And Will Get By Despite Its Weaknesses," *Film Daily*, September 22,
1918, 18, http://www.archive.org/stream/filmdailyvolume556newy#page/404/
mode/2up (accessed February 22, 2018); Edward Weitzel, "'The Rainbow Trail':
William Farnum Scores Success in Fox Screen Version of of Zane Grey Novel,"
Moving Picture World, October 12, 1918, 272, http://www.archive.org/stream/mov-
iwor3738chal#page/n915/mode/2up (accessed February 22, 2018); "The Rainbow
Trail," *Variety*, October 18, 1918, 39, http://www.archive.org/stream/Var52-1918-
10#page/n69/mode/2up (accessed February 22, 2018); and "William Farnum
in 'Riders of the Purple Sage,'" *Exhibitors Herald and Motography*, September
21, 1918, 34, http://www.archive.org/stream/exhibitorsherald07exhi#page/34/
mode/2up (accessed February 22, 2018).

329 Nelson, "A History of Latter-day Saint Screen Portrayals," 128.

330 "Messages from the Missions: Missionary Work Resumed in South Africa,"
Improvement Era 25:3 (January 1922), 265-266.

331 Heber J. Grant, letter to Reed Smoot, October 14, 1921, Richard Alan Nelson
Collection, L. Tom Perry Special Collections, Harold B. Lee Library, Brigham Young
University, Box 2. Folder 13; "Fox to Film True Story of Utah," *Millennial Star* 84:28
(July 13, 1922), 445-446. Unfortunately we have little to no record of what other
cinematic proposals President Grant is referencing.

332 Milton R. Merrill, *Reed Smoot: Apostle in Politics* (Logan: Utah State University Press and Department of Political Science, 1990), 153; Heath, *In the World: The Diaries of Reed Smoot*, 477, 587; Nelson, "A History of Latter-day Saint Screen Portrayals," 121-141; Quinn, *The Mormon Hierarchy: Extensions of Power*, 817-818; D'arc, *When Hollywood Came to Town*, 35.

333 "Some Stories Now Available Through Film Fiction Mart," *Motion Picture News*, April 3, 1920, 3174, http://www.archive.org/stream/motionpicture-new212unse#page/n401/mode/2up (accessed February 22, 2018).

334 For just one example of many articles about *The Fighting Shepherdess*, see "Coast Brevities," *Film Daily*, December 18, 1919, 2, http://www.archive.org/stream/filmdailyvolume9910newy#page/1024/mode/2up (accessed February 22, 2018); for *The Mormon* see "Chicago Notes," *Variety*, September 19, 1919, 8, http://www.archive.org/stream/variety56-1919-09#page/n141/mode/2up (accessed February 22, 2018); Orvis F. Jordan, "The Larger Christian World: Fight Mormonism with Movies," *Christian Century: A Journal of Religion*, April 4, 1918, 20; "Fidelity Picture Plays Syndicate Stock Certificate," *icollector.com*, http://www.icollector.com/Fidelity-Picture-Plays-Syndicate-Stock-Certificate_i11280956 (accessed February 22, 2018); "Mormon Evil to be Attacked by Photoplay," *Continent*, March 7, 1918, 255, https://books.google.com/books?id=2St-KAQAAMAAJ&pg=PA255&lpg=PA255&dq#v=onepage&q&f=false (accessed February 22, 2018); for *The Mormon Trail*, see "'Mormon Trail' First Of Star Ranch Series," *Exhibitors Herald*, November 13, 1920, 76, http://www.archive.org/stream/exhibitorsherald11exhi_1#page/n857/mode/2up (accessed February 22, 2018); "C. B. C. Film Sales Corp.," *Film Daily*, December 19, 1920, 18, http://www.archive.org/stream/filmdailyvolume11314newy#page/1378/mode/2up (accessed February 22, 2018); "Guide to Short Subjects—Cont'd: Rialto Productions, Inc.," *Exhibitors' Trade Review*, December 3, 1921, 66, http://www.archive.org/stream/exhibitorstrade00test#page/66/mode/2up (accessed February 22, 2018); "'The Mormon Trail'—C. B. C. Film Sales," *Film Daily*, February 6, 1921, 24, http://www.archive.org/stream/filmdailyvolume11516newy#page/316/mode/2up (accessed February 22, 2018).

335 "Pelted Mormons," *Variety*, June 17, 1925, 2, http://www.archive.org/stream/variety79-1925-06#page/n111/mode/2up (accessed February 24, 2018).

336 Nelson, "A History of Latter-day Saint Screen Portrayals," 152, 154.

337 Jolo, "New Films in London," *Variety*, March 31, 1922, 43, http://www.archive.org/stream/variety66-1922-03#page/n233/mode/2up (accessed February 24, 2018).

338 "London Film News," *Variety*, April 7, 1922, 42, http://www.archive.org/stream/variety66-1922-04#page/n41/mode/2up (accessed February 24, 2018). For additional reviews see "British Film News," *Variety*, April 14, 1922, 41, http://www.archive.org/stream/variety66-1922-04#page/n87/mode/2up (accessed February 24, 2018).

339 G. Osmond Hyde, "Movie Campaign Against 'Mormons' Leads Many to In-

vestigate Message," *Deseret Evening News* April 30, 1922, Journal History of the Church, April 30, 1922, 5, also in "Messages from the Missions: Persecution has Helped to Fill the Meeting Halls," *Improvement Era* 25:10 (August 1922), 937-938; "Trapped by the 'Mormons,'" *Millennial Star* 84:14 (April 6, 1922), 223. See also "From the Mission Field: Priesthood Meetings," *Millennial Star* 84:16 (April 20, 1922), 254-255.

340 Sheri L. Dew, *Ezra Taft Benson: A Biography* (Deseret Book Company: Salt Lake City, 1987), 57.

341 Ibid., 61-63.

342 A. Lewis Elggren, "Messages from the Missions: Better Conditions in Norwich," *Improvement Era* 26:9 (July 1923), 845; see also "Messages from the Missions: Interesting Celebrations at Hull," *Improvement Era* 28:1 (November 1924), 16-17.

343 Nelson, "A History of Latter-day Saint Screen Portrayals," 145-164; Nelson, "From Antagonism to Acceptance," 63; Thorp, "Winifred Graham and the Mormon Image in England," 112-114; Hyde, "Movie Campaign Against 'Mormons' Leads Many to Investigate Message," 5. For some additional primary sources on the films and events in England see "Editor's Table: Defending the Latter-day Saints," *Improvement Era* 23:2 (December 1919), 174-175; James E. Talmage, "Christianity Falsely So-Called," *Improvement Era* 23:3 (January 1920), 196-205, the speech he was unable to deliver at a conference in Pittsburgh after Winifred Graham's performance; Dan C. Smedley, "Messages from the Missions: Progress of the Church in Sheffield, England," *Improvement Era* 25:2 (December 1921), 168-169, which gives an optimistic appraisal of the Church before the anti-Mormon campaign picked up steam; Orson F. Whitney, "Editorial: An Unaccepted Challenge," *Millennial Star* 84:13 (March 30, 1922), 200-203; "Passing Events," *Improvement Era* 25:5 (March 1922), 472; untitled comment on *Trapped by the Mormons, Millennial Star* 84:15 (April 13, 1922), 231; "That Unclaimed Reward," *Millennial Star* 84:15 (April 13, 1922), 237-238; "Passing Events," *Improvement Era* 25:6 (April 1922), p. 570, which reports a mob attack on the London mission home uncannily similar to that at the climax of *Trapped*; "Editor's Table: A Tempest in England," *Improvement Era* 25:7 (May 1922), 643-645; "Britain's Crusade Against the Mormons," *Millennial Star* 84:25 (June 22, 1922), 385-389; Andrew T. Jacobsen, "Messages from the Missions: Intended Evil Doing Unintended Good," *Improvement Era* 25:8 (June 1922), 744-745; "Passing Events," *Improvement Era* 25:8 (June 1922), 759; "Messages from the Missions: Progress a Result of Persecution," *Improvement Era* 25:10 (August 1922), 940-941; "Messages from the Missions: Birmingham Conference Reports Energetic Work," *Improvement Era* 26:2 (December 1922), 202-203; A. Walter Stevenson, "Messages from the Missions: A Nottingham Parson on the Rampage," *Improvement Era* 26:3 (January 1923), 290-291. For information about the film's restoration see Jeff Vice, "Talking pictures: 'Trapped' is a rare piece of anti-Mormon media," *Deseret News*, October 1, 2006, http://www.deseretnews.com/article/650194839/Trapped-is-a-rare-piece-of-anti-Mormon-media.html?pg=all (accessed October 1, 2006), and for the best recent analysis of the film see D'arc, "The Mormon as Vampire," 164-187.

344 "'A Puritan Conscience,'" *Moving Picture World*, January 2, 1915, 90, http://www.archive.org/stream/movingpicturewor23newy#page/90/mode/2up (accessed January 2, 2018); "A Puritan Conscience," *Motography*, January 9, 1915, 78, http://www.archive.org/stream/motography13elec#page/78/mode/2up (accessd January 2, 2018); Anthony Slide, *The New Historical Dictionary of the American Film Industry* (London: Routledge, 2013), 78.

345 Gifford, *The British Film Catalogue,* entry number 06008; Nelson, "A History of Latter-day Saint Screen Portrayals," 81128, 7.

346 Nelson, "A History of Latter-day Saint Screen Portrayals," 88; "Deadwood Dick," *Wikipedia*, https://en.wikipedia.org/wiki/Deadwood_Dick (accessed January 4, 2018); Buck Rainey, *Serials and Series: A World Filmography*, 1912-1956 (Jefferson, North Carolina: McFarland & Company, Inc., 1999), 10; Gifford, *The British Film Catalogue*, entry number 05743; Brian McFarlane, ed., *The Encyclopedia of British Film*, 4th ed. (Manchester: Manchester University Press, 2013), 687.

347 "Excuse Me," *Moving Picture World*, January 1, 1916, 138, http://www.archive.org/stream/movingpicturewor27newy#page/138/mode/2up (accessed January 2, 2018).

348 "Min Svigerinde fra Amerika," *Danish Film Institute*, http://www.dfi.dk/faktaomfilm/film/en/20922.aspx?id=20922 (accessed January 5, 2018).

349 "Han er Mormon," *Danish Film Institute*, http://www.dfi.dk/faktaomfilm/film/en/33791.aspx?id=33791 (accessed February 24, 2018).

350 Nelson, "A History of Latter-day Saint Screen Portrayals," 176-179; Edward Finney interview with Richard Nelson, December 18, 1973, Richard Alan Nelson Collection, L. Tom Perry Special Collections, Harold B. Lee Library, Brigham Young University, Box 2, Folder 5; Michael L. Simmons, "Hands Up," *Exhibitor's Trade Review*, January 23, 1926, 21, http://www.archive.org/stream/exhibitorstrade-00new#page/n497/mode/2up (accessed January 4, 2018); Sally Benson, "The Screen in Review," *Picture Play*, April 1926, 67, http://www.archive.org/stream/pictureplaymagaz24unse#page/n197/mode/2up (accessed January 4, 2018).

351 "Comments on the Films: General Film Company," *Moving Picture World*, July 29, 1916, 807, http://www.archive.org/stream/moviwor29chal#page/n903/mode/2up (accessed November 1, 2017), this article incorrectly gives the scout's name as Len Spillsbury; "Distinct Honor," *Ogden Standard-Examiner,* June 8, 1920, 6, https://chroniclingamerica.loc.gov/lccn/sn85058393/1920-06-08/ed-1/seq-6 (accessed March 7, 2018); "Some Short Reels: 'Towering Wonders of Utah'—Urban Popular Classics—Vitagraph," *Film Daily,* September 17, 1922, 16, http://www.archive.org/stream/filmdaily2122newy#page/n643/mode/2up (accessed November 1, 2017).

352 Joseph F. Smith, untitled address, *Conference Report*, April 1912, 10.

353 Charles W. Penrose, untitled address, *Conference Report*, April 1912, 16-17.

354 Heber J. Grant, untitled address, *Conference Report*, April 1912, 28.

355 David O. McKay, untitled address, *Conference Report*, April 1912, 53-54.

356 David O. McKay, "Editorial: 'Picture Show' Prodigals," *Millennial Star* 85:41 (October 11, 1923), 648-649.

357 "Rocky Mountain Moving Picture Company," *Moving Picture World*, August 29, 1908, 155, https://archive.org/stream/movingor03chal#page/n161/mode/2up (accessed February 25, 2018).

358 "Film Manufacturing Plant at Salt Lake," *Moving Picture World*, November 21,1908, 401, https://archive.org/stream/movingor03chal#page/n407/mode/2up (accessed February 25, 2018).

359 Journal History of the Church, June 30, 1910, 7-8, https://dcms.lds.org/de-livery/DeliveryManagerServlet?dps_pid=IE360124 (accessed February 25, 2018); see also "New Moving Picture Company Organized," *Salt Lake Tribune*, July 26, 1908, 24, https://chroniclingamerica.loc.gov/lccn/sn83045396/1908-07-26/ed-1/seq-24 (accessed February 25, 2018).

360 Koszarski, *An Evening's Entertainment*, 104.

361 "Revier Motion Picture Company" advertisement, *Moving Picture World*, October 8, 1910, 794, http://www.archive.org/stream/moviwor07chal#page/794/mode/2up (accessed February 26, 2018), please note this advertisement ran in various issues throughout the year.

362 "Manufacturers in Monthly Banquet," *Salt Lake Tribune*, February 11, 1910, 2, https://chroniclingamerica.loc.gov/lccn/sn83045396/1910-02-11/ed-1/seq-2 (accessed February 27, 2018); Nelson, "A History of Latter-day Saint Screen Portrayals," 71-72; D'arc, *When Hollywood Came to Town*, 264; "He's Sadder but Wiser Man," *Moving Picture World*, November 12, 1910, 1113, http://www.ar-chive.org/stream/moviwor07chal#page/1112/mode/2up (accessed February 26, 2018); "Harry Revier," *Internet Movie Database*, http://www.imdb.com/name/nm0720886/?ref_=nv_sr_1 (accessed February 26, 2018).

363 "Films to Picture Mormonism's Story," *Evening Standard,* January 27, 1912, 1, https://chroniclingamerica.loc.gov/lccn/sn85058397/1912-01-27/ed-1/seq-1 (accessed March 2, 2018); Nelson, "A History of Latter-day Saint Screen Portray-als," 69-70; "Mr William H. Harbeck," *Encyclopedia Titanica*, https://www.ency-clopedia-titanica.org/titanic-victim/william-harbeck.html (accessed March 3, 2018); John Lamoreau, "The Strange Mysteries of Movie Make William Harbeck," *Encyclopedia Titanica*, https://www.encyclopedia-titanica.org/the-strange-mys-teries-movie-maker-william-harbeck.html (accessed March 2, 2018).

364 Jim Tully, "A Thousand Dollars a Day," *Motion Picture Classic*, October 1923, 77, http://www.archive.org/stream/motion1724moti#page/n593/mode/2up (ac-cessed December 8, 2014).

365 Rudger Clawson, "The Stolen Temple Pictures," *Millennial Star* 73:40 (Octo-ber 5, 1911), 632.

366 Kent Walgren, "Inside the Salt Lake Temple: Gisbert Bossard's 1911 Photographs," *Dialogue: A Journal of Mormon Thought* 29:3 (Fall 1996), 9-51; Alexander, *Mormonism in Transition*, 242, 250; Brad Westwood, "Architectural Records," *Mormon Americana*, 393; "*The House of the Lord*," *Wikipedia*, https://en.wikipedia.org/wiki/The_House_of_the_Lord (accessed March 4, 2018); "Bossard Ousted from the Church," *Evening Standard*, October 4, 1911, 4, https://chroniclingamerica.loc.gov/lccn/sn85058397/1911-10-04/ed-1/seq-4 (accessed March 4, 2018); "Overflow Meeting Held in Chill Air," *Salt Lake Tribune*, October 6, 1913, 12, https://chroniclingamerica.loc.gov/lccn/sn83045396/1913-10-06/ed-1/seq-12 (accessed March 4, 2018). For coverage of the affair in the film industry press, including dueling advertisements between the two sets of photographs, see "Mormon Temple Pictures," *Moving Picture World*, October 28, 1911, 297, http://www.archive.org/stream/moviwor10chal#page/n301/mode/2up (accessed March 4, 2018); "Mormon Church Pictures" advertisement, *Moving Picture World*, October 28, 1911, 301, http://www.archive.org/stream/moviwor10chal#page/n305/mode/2up (accessed March 4, 2018); "Genuine Slides of the Mormon Temple," *Moving Picture World*, November 4, 1911, 387, http://www.archive.org/stream/moviwor10chal#page/n391/mode/2up (accessed March 4, 2018); "The Original and Only Genuine Mormon Temple Pictures," *Moving Picture World*, November 4, 1911, 418, http://www.archive.org/stream/moviwor10chal#page/n423/mode/2up (accessed March 4, 2018); "Warning" Levi Co., Inc. advertisement, *Moving Picture World*, November 11, 1911, 503, http://www.archive.org/stream/moviwor10chal#page/n507/mode/2up (accessed March 4, 2018); "Caught with the Goods," *Moving Picture World*, November 11, 1911, 504, http://www.archive.org/stream/moviwor10chal#page/n509/mode/2up (accessed March 4, 2018); "The Mormon Temple," *Graham Guardian*, January 17, 1913, 2, https://chroniclingamerica.loc.gov/lccn/sn95060914/1913-01-17/ed-1/seq-2 (accessed March 4, 2018). Cinematographer Arthur Powelson also claimed to have photographed inside the Salt Lake Temple: "Cameramen," *Motion Picture News Studio Directory*, October 21, 1916, 142, http://www.archive.org/stream/motionpicturestu-00moti#page/142/mode/2up (accessed March 4, 2018). For Anderson's work see Richard G. Oman and Robert O. Davis, *Images of Faith: Art of the Latter-day Saints* (Salt Lake City: Deseret Book Company, 1995), 67. For *Kawich's Gold Mine* see "A New Book," *Evening Standard*, February 10, 1913, 6, https://chroniclingamerica.loc.gov/lccn/sn85058397/1913-02-10/ed-1/seq-6 (accessed March 5, 2018).

367 It should be noted that the burning of houses at Haun's Mill was a fictional invention, perhaps conflated from other events in the Missouri War. Concerning the film's "feature" status, in Patrick Robertson, *Film Facts* (New York: Billboard Books, 2001), 9–14, 211, *One Hundred Years* is described as the sixth feature film made in the United States. For his list Robertson uses the Cinémathèque française's definition, "a commercially made film over one hour duration," and includes only those films that were shown in their entirety in a continual screening. Before the first film on his list, *Oliver Twist* (May 1912), at least two other pictures of sufficient length were produced in the United States but released serially in one-reel installments. Robertson also identifies *One Hundred Years* as one of the first three documentaries produced anywhere in the world. This of course is erroneous because, while historical, the film was definitely a scripted fictional production. Contrary to how the Cinémathèque française uses it in this context, the term "feature" originally had no correlation with length but, more logically, corresponded with the prominence of a film on a program that included multiple titles, although this sense of the word was beginning to change when *One Hundred Years* came out. Historian Richard Koszarski has written that the "use of the word 'feature' to describe the main item on a program, not simply a film of four or more reels, dated from the nickelodeon era and was already disappearing by 1915." Koszarski, *An Evening's Entertainment*, 64. Still, we see the *Deseret News* describe the roughly fifteen-minute *A Trip to the Moon* as a feature in 1906, and in 1907 the Salt Lake City paper *Goodwin's Weekly* stated that because of low quality, not length, the current films showing at the Orpheum theater "could hardly be counted a feature." "Dramatic," *Deseret Evening News,* February 10, 1906; "With the First Nighters," *Goodwin's Weekly,* March 2, 1907, 8, https://chroniclingamerica.loc.gov/lccn/2010218519/1907-03-02/ed-1/ seq-8 (accessed March 4, 2018). When *One Hundred Years* came out most of its newspaper advertisements described it as a feature film, but one anonymous reviewer put this in perspective when he wrote, "It is a pleasure to get away from the unusual number of mediocre or average every-day pictures that are touring the country as feature films, and which are usually long-drawn-out stories without heart interest of action that gives reason for the existence of the film." "Amusements," *Salt Lake Tribune*, July 10, 1913, 12, https://chroniclingamerica. loc.gov/lccn/sn83045396/1913-07-10/ed-1/seq-12 (accessed March 5, 2018). In the early 2000s the website *LDSFilm.com* utilized Robertson's description of the film as the country's sixth feature. "One Hundred Years of Mormonism: the first feature-length documentary ever made," *LDSFilm.com*, http://www.ldsfilm.com/ docu/HundredYears.html (accessed August 2, 2008).

368 "'One Hundred Years of Mormonism,'" *New York Clipper*, November 9, 1912, 4, http://www.archive.org/stream/clipper60-1912-11#page/n27/mode/2up (accessed March 5, 2018).

369 The most complete record of the film's contents, in its February 1913 version, is from "Amusements," *Salt Lake Tribune,* February 4, 1913, 9, https://chroniclingamerica.loc.gov/lccn/sn83045396/1913-02-04/ed-1/seq-9 (accessed March 5, 2018). Since the film is lost this is an invaluable resource:

"The story is divided into two parts, the first opening with the founder of Mormonism as a baby in his parents' home at Sharon, Windsor county, Vermont. Later he is seen working in the fields. The angel credited with having revealed to him the hiding place of the golden plates appears several times, guiding the first president of the church in the finding and translating of the plates.

"When the plates have been translated, Moroni is seen to gradually materialize from the vacant air, pick up the plates and fade with them into nothingness. The part of the angel is enacted by a lean and somewhat wiry man. When he gave Smith the urim and thummim, which enabled the young farmer to penetrate the hidden meaning of the inscriptions, the audience last night applauded knowingly.

"The scene in the cottage where the church was organized is enacted. Then comes a succession of viscissitudes and persecutions, given in spectacular and realistic detail. When baptism is attempted the Mormons are mobbed and Joseph

Smith is arrested for inciting the riot. They are driven from place to place. The burning of Mormon homes is shown. Finally, at Carthage, Mo. [sic], where the founder has been imprisoned, a mob surrounds the jail, which is inadequately protected, and Smith is murdered.

"The second part shows the advent of Brigham Young as president of the church. Preparations for the long journey across the plains are made. The Mormons dispose of their homes. One exchanges a house worth $3000 for a team of horses and a wagon. Somebody presents Brigham Young with a horse.

"The caravan is seen on the prairie and blazing the trail through thick brush and across treacherous streams and suffering the hardships which have been so frequently recounted. On the way the emigrant train meets a trapper, who advises President Young to take his people to Oregon. This causes a division in the ranks, but in the end the advice of the leader prevails.

"Young falls sick and has to be carried in a wagon. He continues to direct the train, however. When a view of Salt Lake valley, as observed by the van of the company from Emigration canyon, was given the audience, recognizing the familiar land, was profoundly impressed. The teams and emigrants are seen descending the mountain side. Brigham Young looks out over the flat and declares, 'This is the place.' The train moves into the valley and a camp is established.

"President Young selects the site for the temple, driving a staff into the ground to mark the spot. The city of Salt Lake has been started. The reel concludes with a few views of the modern city.

"The above is a concise account of what the pictures show. Great care in arranging faithful reproductions is manifest. The subject of polygamy is ignored entirely."

370 For primary sources regarding the film's production, see "Mormon Story to be Told by Film," *Salt Lake Tribune*, July 13, 1912, 14, https://chroniclingamerica. loc.gov/lccn/sn83045396/1912-07-13/ed-1/seq-14 (accessed March 5, 2018), reprinted in *Logan Republican*, July 16, 1912, https://chroniclingamerica.loc.gov/ lccn/sn85058246/1912-07-16/ed-1/seq-7 (accessed March 5, 2018); "Church History in Moving Pictures," *Iron County Record*, July 19, 1912, 1, https://chroniclingamerica.loc.gov/lccn/sn85058259/1912-07-19/ed-1/seq-1 (accessed March 5, 2018); "Mormons to Have Picture," *Moving Picture World*, July 27, 1912, 355, http://www.archive.org/stream/moviwor13chal#page/n357/mode/2up (accessed March 5, 2018); "State Right Buyers Get Busy and Wire" advertisement, *Moving Picture World*, July 27, 1912, 369, http://www.archive.org/stream/ moviwor13chal#page/n371/mode/2up (accessed March 5, 2018); "Mormon Pictures," *Motography*, August 3, 1912, 110, http://www.archive.org/stream/motography78elec#page/110/mode/2up (accessed March 5, 2018); "World's News Condensed," *Honolulu Star-Bulletin*, August 13, 1912, 7, https://chroniclingamerica.loc.gov/lccn/sn82014682/1912-08-13/ed-2/seq-7 (accessed March 5, 2018); "Taking of Mormon Films is Delayed," *Salt Lake Tribune*, September 18, 1912, 14, https://chroniclingamerica.loc.gov/lccn/sn83045396/1912-09-18/ed-1/seq-14 (accessed March 5, 2018), which reports that a camera was damaged while

filming in Emigration Canyon; "The Utah M. P. Co.," *New York Clipper*, November 2, 1912, 5, http://www.archive.org/stream/clipper60-1912-11#page/n3/mode/2up (accessed March 5, 2018); "Utah," *Motography*, November 9, 1912, 380, http://www.archive.org/stream/motography78elec#page/380/mode/2up (accessed March 5, 2018); "Doings at Los Angeles," *Moving Picture World*, January 25, 1913, 353, https://archive.org/stream/movingpicturewor15newy#page/352/mode/2up (accessed March 5, 2018); "To Picture Mormonism," *Variety*, January 31, 1913, 13, http://www.archive.org/stream/variety29-1913-01#page/n171/mode/2up (accessed March 5, 2018); "'100 Years of Mormonism,'" *Logan Republican*, February 6, 1913, 1, 8, https://chroniclingamerica.loc.gov/lccn/sn85058246/1913-02-06/ed-1/seq-8 (accessed March 5, 2018); Ernest A. Dench, "For the Photo-play Writer," *Cinema*, February 19, 1913, 39, http://www.archive.org/stream/cinenewgaz02cine#page/n721/mode/2up (accessed March 3, 2018); "Pictures of Cumorah Hill," *Logan Republican*, April 17, 1913, 1, https://chroniclingamerica.loc.gov/lccn/sn85058246/1913-04-17/ed-1/seq-1 (accessed March 5, 2018); Arthur Edwin Krows, "Motion Pictures—Not For Theatres," *Educational Screen*, January 1939, 14, http://www.archive.org/stream/educationalscree18chicrich#page/14/mode/2up (accessed March 5, 2018).

371 "Salt Lake Theatre: 100 Years of Mormonism" advertisement, *Salt Lake Tribune*, February 3, 1913, 7, https://chroniclingamerica.loc.gov/lccn/sn83045396/1913-02-03/ed-1/seq-7 (accessed March 5, 2018).

372 "'One Hundred Years of 'Mormonism,'" *Deseret Evening News*, July 5, 1913, section 2, p. 4, quoted in Nelson, "A History of Latter-day Saint Screen Portrayals," 77.

373 "Amusements," *Salt Lake Tribune*, July 7, 1913, 5, https://chroniclingamerica.loc.gov/lccn/sn83045396/1913-07-07/ed-1/seq-5 (accessed March 5, 2018).

374 Nelson, "A History of Latter-day Saint Screen Portrayals," 78; Cannon and Olmstead, "'Scandalous Film,'" 72-73, fn 57. For an example of a lecturer speaking as a film screened, see "Bert Levy to Speak," *Deseret Evening News*, February 22, 1907, 2, https://chroniclingamerica.loc.gov/lccn/sn83045555/1907-02-22/ed-1/seq-2 (accessed March 5, 2018). The practice was particularly popular in Japan, where its performers were known as *benshi* and it became a refined artform that lasted well into the twentieth century.

375 Levi Edgar Young, "'Mormonism' in Picture," *Young Woman's Journal* 24:2 (February 1913), 79-80.

376 "Century of 'Mormonism': Exhibition of Film Before Select Audience—President Smith's Commendation," *Deseret Evening News* February 3, 1913, Journal History of the Church, February 3, 1913, 1, https://dcms.lds.org/delivery/DeliveryManagerServlet?dps_pid=IE306369, Image 11 (accessed March 5, 2018).

377 Alexander, *Mormonism in Transition*, 250.

378 "'Mormonism' in Picture," *Deseret Evening News*, February 5, 1913, 4, quoted in Nelson, "A History of Latter-day Saint Screen Portrayals," 76.

379 Young, "'Mormonism' in Picture," 79-80.

380 "State Rights Selling Fast," *Motography*, June 14, 1913, 450.

381 Heath, *In the World: The Diaries of Reed Smoot,* 19.

382 "Amusements," *Salt Lake Tribune*, July 8, 1913, 7, https://chroniclingamerica.loc.gov/lccn/sn83045396/1913-07-08/ed-1/seq-7 (accessed March 5, 2018).

383 "'100 Years of Mormonism'" advertisement, *Moving Picture World*, November 9, 1912, 591, http://www.archive.org/stream/movinwor14chal#page/n595/mode/2up (accessed March 5, 2018).

384 "Motion Pictures to Tell Story of Mormonism: Big Sums Spent on Films for Propaganding the Faith," *San Francisco Call*, August 13, 1912, 3, https://chroniclingamerica.loc.gov/lccn/sn85066387/1912-08-13/ed-1/seq-3 (accessed March 5, 2018), reprinted in "Mormons Adopt 'Movies,'" *New York Tribune*, August 13, 1912, 7, https://chroniclingamerica.loc.gov/lccn/sn83030214/1912-08-13/ed-1/seq-7 (accessed March 5, 2018).

385 Tully, "A Thousand Dollars a Day," 77.

386 For primary sources regarding the film's distribution, see "One Hundred Years of Mormonism" legal notice, *Moving Picture World*, December 28, 1912, 1331, http://www.archive.org/stream/movinwor14chal#page/1330/mode/2up (accessed March 5, 2018); "Green Room Jottings: Little Whisperings from Everywhere in Playerdom," *Motion Picture Story Magazine*, January 1913, 156, http://www.archive.org/stream/motionpicturesto04moti#page/156/mode/2up (accessed March 5, 2018); "Joseph Smith the Mormon Prophet Tarred and Feathered" advertisement, *Logan Republican*, February 1, 1913, 4, https://chroniclingamerica.loc.gov/lccn/sn85058246/1913-02-01/ed-1/seq-4 (accessed March 5, 2018); "Amusements," *Salt Lake Tribune*, February 3, 1913, 7, https://chroniclingamerica.loc.gov/lccn/sn83045396/1913-02-03/ed-1/seq-7 (accessed March 5, 2018); "100 Years of Mormonism," *Logan Republican*, February 4, 1913, 8, https://chroniclingamerica.loc.gov/lccn/sn85058246/1913-02-04/ed-1/seq-8 (accessed March 5, 2018); "Translation of the 'Book of Mormon' One of the Scenes in the Motion Picture Film '100 Years of Mormonism,'" *Logan Republican,* February 6, 1913, 8, https://chroniclingamerica.loc.gov/lccn/sn85058246/1913-02-06/ed-1/seq-8 (accessed March 5, 2018); "'100 Years of Mormonism'" advertisement, *Logan Republican*, February 6, 1913, 4, https://chroniclingamerica.loc.gov/lccn/sn85058246/1913-02-06/ed-1/seq-4 (accessed March 5, 2018); "One Hundred Years of Mormonism: Sale Open Tomorrow," *Evening Standard*, February 14, 1913, 6, https://chroniclingamerica.loc.gov/lccn/sn85058397/1913-02-14/ed-1/seq-6 (accessed March 5, 2018); "Church Officials Sanction 100 Years of Mormonism," *Evening Standard,* February 15, 1913, 6, https://chroniclingamerica.loc.gov/lccn/sn85058397/1913-02-15/ed-1/seq-6 (accessed March 5, 2018), an advertisement for its engagement at the Orpheum Theatre in Ogden; "Orpheum Theatre: 100 Years of Mormonism" advertisement, *Evening Standard,* February 17, 1913, 9, https://chroniclingamerica.loc.gov/lccn/sn85058397/1913-02-17/ed-1/seq-9 (accessed March 5, 2018); "Orpheum Theatre: 100 Years of Mormonism" adver-

tisement, *Evening Standard*, February 18, 1913, 5, https://chroniclingamerica.
loc.gov/lccn/sn85058397/1913-02-18/ed-1/seq-5 (accessed March 5, 2018);
"Doings at Los Angeles," *Moving Picture World*, March 1, 1913, 875; "Mormon
Films Tonight," *Arizona Republican*, March 3, 1913, 3, https://chroniclingamerica.
loc.gov/lccn/sn84020558/1913-03-03/ed-1/seq-3 (accessed March 5, 2018);
"The Mormon Films," *Arizona Republican*, March 5, 1913, 8, https://chroniclin-
gamerica.loc.gov/lccn/sn84020558/1913-03-05/ed-1/seq-8 (accessed March
5, 2018); "Another Big Crowd," *Arizona Republican*, March 6, 1913, 8, https://
chroniclingamerica.loc.gov/lccn/sn84020558/1913-03-06/ed-1/seq-8 (accessed
March 5, 2018); "100 Years of Mormonism," *Graham Guardian*, March 14, 1913,
2, https://chroniclingamerica.loc.gov/lccn/sn95060914/1913-03-14/ed-1/seq-2
(accessed March 5, 2018); "Salt Lake Theatre: 100 Years of Mormonism" advertisement, *Salt Lake Tribune*, March 20, 1913, 11, https://chroniclingamerica.loc.
gov/lccn/sn83045396/1913-03-20/ed-1/seq-11 (accessed March 5, 2018); "100
Years of Mormonism" advertisement, *Eastern Utah Advocate*, April 10, 1913, 5,
https://chroniclingamerica.loc.gov/lccn/sn86091022/1913-04-10/ed-1/seq-
5 (accessed March 5, 2018); "100 Years of Mormonism, Return Engagement,"
Evening Standard, April 11, 1913, 6, https://chroniclingamerica.loc.gov/lccn/
sn85058397/1913-04-11/ed-1/seq-6 (accessed March 5, 2018); "Scene in '100
Years of Mormonism,'" *Evening Standard,* April 14, 1913, 6, https://chroniclin-
gamerica.loc.gov/lccn/sn85058397/1913-04-14/ed-1/seq-6 (accessed March
5, 2018); "Last time tonight in Ogden—'100 Years of Mormonism,' Orpheum,"
advertisement, *Evening Standard,* April 15, 1913, 6, https://chroniclingamerica.
loc.gov/lccn/sn85058397/1913-04-15/ed-1/seq-6 (accessed March 5, 2018);
"'100 Years of Mormonism,'" *New York Clipper*, June 14, 1913, 8, http://www.
archive.org/stream/clipper61-1913-06#page/n35/mode/2up (accessed March
5, 2018), for its Chicago screenings; "100 Years of Mormonism in Six Reels of
Realism," *Motography*, June 14, 1913, 11, http://www.archive.org/stream/mo-
tography09elec#page/n681/mode/2up (accessed March 5, 2018); "Colonial:
100 Years of Mormonism" advertisement, *Salt Lake Tribune*, July 3, 1913, 12,
https://chroniclingamerica.loc.gov/lccn/sn83045396/1913-07-03/ed-1/seq-
12 (accessed March 5, 2018); "States Rights Withdrawn," *Exhibitors' Times*, July
5, 1913, 36, http://www.archive.org/stream/exhibitorstimes01wmaj#page/36/
mode/2up (accessed March 5, 2018); "Colonial: 100 Years of Mormonism" advertisement, *Goodwin's Weekly*, July 5, 1913, 9, https://chroniclingamerica.loc.gov/
lccn/2010218519/1913-07-05/ed-1/seq-9 (accessed March 5, 2018); "Amusements," *Salt Lake Tribune,* July 9, 1913, 12, https://chroniclingamerica.loc.gov/
lccn/sn83045396/1913-07-09/ed-1/seq-12 (accessed March 5, 2018); "Ogden
Theater: 100 Years of Mormonism" advertisement, *Ogden Standard,* July 9, 1913,
10, https://chroniclingamerica.loc.gov/lccn/sn85058396/1913-07-09/ed-1/
seq-10 (accessed March 5, 2018), which includes the pitch, "Every Mormon and
Gentile Should See It"; "Amusements," *Salt Lake Tribune*, July 10, 1913; "At Ogden
Theater, '100 Years of Mormonism,' commencing tomorrow, Saturday matinee,
10c and 20c" advertisement, *Ogden Standard*, July 11, 1913, 7, https://chronicl-
ingamerica.loc.gov/lccn/sn85058396/1913-07-11/ed-1/seq-7 (accessed March
5, 2018); "States Rights Withdrawn," *Motography*, July 12, 1913, 28, http://www.
archive.org/stream/motography10elec#page/n43/mode/2up (accessed March
5, 2018); "Ogden Theater Tonight" advertisement, *Ogden Standard,* July 12, 1913,
13, https://chroniclingamerica.loc.gov/lccn/sn85058396/1913-07-12/ed-1/seq-

13 (accessed March 5, 2018); "Added Mormon Feature," *Variety*, August 29, 1913, 14, http://www.archive.org/stream/variety31-1913-08#page/n149/mode/2up (accessed March 5, 2018); "Feature Film Notes," *Moving Picture News*, September 13, 1913, 20, http://www.archive.org/stream/movingpicturenew81unse#page/n403/mode/2up (accessed March 5, 2018); "Mormon Church Plans to Win Converts," *Weekly Times-Record*, December 4, 1913, 9, https://chroniclingamerica.loc.gov/lccn/sn89074274/1913-12-04/ed-1/seq-9 (accessed March 5, 2018), which deals with the Canadian campaign; "'100 Years of Mormonism,' Globe, today only" advertisement, *Ogden Standard*, May 11, 1914, 5, https://chroniclingamerica.loc.gov/lccn/sn85058396/1914-05-11/ed-1/seq-5 (accessed March 5, 2018); "'100 Years of Mormonism' at Lyric Theater," *Logan Republican*, May 21, 1914, 1, https://chroniclingamerica.loc.gov/lccn/sn85058246/1914-05-21/ed-1/seq-1 (accessed March 5, 2018). "Doings at Los Angeles," *Moving Picture World*, April 26, 1913, 368, http://www.archive.org/stream/movingpicturewor16movi#page/368/mode/2up (accessed March 5, 2018) says that Ernest Shipman had already sold his firm's rights to the picture at that point, but this must be a mistake because he was involved with reshoots and selling of the picture throughout the subsequent summer.

387 Nelson, "A History of Latter-day Saint Screen Portrayals," 72.

388 Ibid., 80, emphasis in the original.

389 "See Their History in Motion Pictures," *Salt Lake Tribune*, March 18, 1913, Journal History of the Church, March 18, 1913, 3, https://dcms.lds.org/delivery/DeliveryManagerServlet?dps_pid=IE494113, Image 70 (accessed March 5, 2018); also in Nelson, "A History of Latter-day Saint Screen Portrayals," 78.

390 Nelson, "A History of Latter-day Saint Screen Portrayals," 72-81; Nelson, "Utah Filmmakers of the Silent Screen," 9-11; Nelson, "From Antagonism to Acceptance," 61-63; Nelson, "The History of Utah Film," 9-10; Jacobs, "The History of Motion Pictures," 5-9, 39-40; Phil Hall, "Classic film review: 'One Hundred Years of Mormonism' (1913)," *Byte Clay*, January 26, 2016, https://byteclay.com/classic-film-review-one-hundred-years-of-mormonism-1913 (accessed March 4, 2018).

391 "Doings at Los Angeles," *Moving Picture World*, January 25, 1913.

392 Jason Swensen, "Images preserve first filmmaking attempt," *Church News*, August 23, 2003, 6, http://www.ldschurchnewsarchive.com/articles/44224/Images-preserve-first-filmmaking-attempt.html (accessed May 12, 2008).

393 Anthon Johan Theodor Sorensen, "Highlights of My Life and Production of Motion Pictures of Book of Mormon, 1915," n.d., unpublished manuscript, Church History Library, The Church of Jesus Christ of Latter-day Saints, Salt Lake City, folder 1, p. 22.

394 Ibid., folder 2, p. 2 of Morton's letter to Sorensen, July 15, 1915.

395 Sorensen, "Highlights of My Life," in its entirety is the best source for the production of *The Story of the Book of Mormon*. See also "Book of Mormon to be Seen in Films," *Salt Lake Tribune*, December 21, 1913, second news section, p. 15,

https://chroniclingamerica.loc.gov/lccn/sn83045396/1913-12-21/ed-1/seq-15 (accessed March 6, 2018).

396 "Book of Mormon Films," *American Fork Citizen*, November 6, 1915, 3, https://chroniclingamerica.loc.gov/lccn/sn85058027/1915-11-06/ed-1/seq-3 (accessed March 6, 2018); "Week's Theatre Program," *Logan Republican*, January 29, 1916, 8, https://chroniclingamerica.loc.gov/lccn/sn85058246/1916-01-29/ed-1/seq-8 (accessed March 7, 2018); "Story of Book of Mormon at the Oak," *Logan Republican*, February 1, 1916, 5, https://chroniclingamerica.loc.gov/lccn/sn85058246/1916-02-01/ed-1/seq-5 (accessed March 6, 2018); "North Logan," *Logan Republican*, February 8, 1916, 2, https://chroniclingamerica.loc.gov/lccn/sn85058246/1916-02-08/ed-1/seq-2 (accessed March 6, 2018). For the images and text in the *Juvenile Instructor*, see William A. Morton, "The Prophet Lehi," Juvenile Instructor, January 1917, 46-48; William A. Morton, "Lehi Preaching Repentance," *Juvenile Instructor*, February 1917, 95-96; William A. Morton, "Lehi Relating his Dream to his Family," *Juvenile Instructor*, March 1917, 112, 158-159; William A. Morton, "The Sons of Lehi Casting Lots," *Juvenile Instructor*, April 1917, 168, 211-212; William A. Morton, "How the Brass Plates were Obtained," *Juvenile Instructor*, May 1917, 224, 271-272; William A. Morton, "Finding the Liahona," *Juvenile Instructor*, June 1917, 280, 320-321; William A. Morton, "Marriage of the Sons of Lehi," *Juvenile Instructor*, July 1917, 376-377; William A. Morton, "Nephi's Vision," *Juvenile Instructor*, August 1917, 429-431; William A. Morton, "Burial of Ishmael," *Juvenile Instructor*, September 1917, 492-493; William A. Morton, "The Rebellion on the Waters," *Juvenile Instructor*, October 1917, 542-544; William A. Morton, "Arrival in the Promised Land," *Juvenile Instructor*, November 1917, 605-606; William A. Morton, "The Separation," *Juvenile Instructor*, December 1917, 662-664. My thanks to Ardis Parshall for alerting me to this series of articles. See her article "Mormon Movies: Life of Nephi, 1913," *Keepapitchinin*, February 6, 2018, http://www.keepapitchinin.org/2018/02/06/mormon-movies-life-of-nephi-1913 (accessed March 20, 2018), which also contains many of the images from the *Juvenile Instructor*.

397 Sorensen, "Highlights of My Life," folder 1, p. 21.

398 Swensen, "Images preserve first filmmaking attempt," *Church News*.

399 Nelson, "Utah Filmmakers of the Silent Screen," 11-18; Nelson, "The History of Utah Film," 18; Nelson, "A History of Latter-day Saint Screen Portrayals," 71, 174; William Judkins Hewitt, "Carnival Conversation," *New York Clipper*, August 29, 1914, 20, http://www.archive.org/stream/clipper62-1914-08#page/n115/mode/2up (accessed March 6, 2018); "Picture Company is Incorporated," *Ogden Standard*, August 22, 1917, 6, https://chroniclingamerica.loc.gov/lccn/sn85058396/1917-08-22/ed-1/seq-6 (accessed March 7, 2018). For the Ogden Pictures Corporation, see "Weber Academy 'Junior Prom' at Berthana is Pretty Affair," *Ogden Standard*, May 3, 1917, 6, https://chroniclingamerica.loc.gov/lccn/sn85058396/1917-05-03/ed-1/seq-6 (accessed March 7, 2018); "Predicting Success for the Ogden Pictures," *Ogden Standard*, August 11, 1917, 16, https://chroniclingamerica.loc.gov/lccn/sn85058396/1917-08-11/ed-1/seq-20 (accessed March 7, 2018); "Auto Company Sues Ogden Pictures Corporation," *Ogden Standard*, August 29, 1917, 6, https://chroniclingamerica.loc.gov/lccn/

sn85058396/1917-08-29/ed-1/seq-6 (accessed March 7, 2018); "'Lust of the Ages,'" September 8, 1917, 27, http://www.archive.org/stream/exhibitorsherald05exhi#page/n525/mode/2up (accessed March 7, 2018); "Ogden Pictures Corp. Engages G. W. Beynon to Write Music Score for 'Lust of Ages' Film," *Exhibitors Herald*, September 8, 1917, 33, http://www.archive.org/stream/exhibitorsherald05exhi#page/n531/mode/2up (accessed March 7, 2018); "Big Corporation is to Produce Films," *Salt Lake Tribune*, March 4, 1917, Journal History of the Church, March 3, 1917, 7, https://dcms.lds.org/delivery/DeliveryManagerServlet?dps_pid=IE367719, Image 23; "Ogden Movies Are to Be Exhibited in All Parts of the World by Selznick," *Ogden Standard*, March 28, 1917, 7, https://chroniclingamerica.loc.gov/lccn/sn85058396/1917-03-28/ed-1/seq-7 (accessed March 7, 2018); "Lillian Walker Arrives and is Accompanied by an International Beauty," *Ogden Standard*, April 17, 1917, 6, https://chroniclingamerica.loc.gov/lccn/sn85058396/1917-04-17/ed-1/seq-6 (accessed March 7, 2018). For Utah Productions, see "Utah Firm's Second," *Variety*, May 2, 1928, 12, http://www.archive.org/stream/variety91-1928-05#page/n11/mode/2up (accessed March 11, 2018).

400 Wray, *On the Other Hand*, 23-24.

401 Powelson's name is occasionally spelled Powellson and Pawelson. J. C. Jessen, "In and Out of West Coast Studios," *Motion Picture News*, 2195, http://www.archive.org/stream/motionpicturenew132unse#page/2194/mode/2up (accessed March 7, 2018); "Editor's Table: The Centennial Celebration at Palmyra," *Improvement Era* 27:1 (November 1923), 74-75; Robert H. Malan, *B. H. Roberts: A Biography* (Salt Lake City: Deseret Book Company, 1966), 114-116; B. H. Roberts, *The Autobiography of B.H. Roberts* (Salt Lake City: Signature Books, 1990), 231-233; Truman G. Madsen, *Defender of the Faith: The B.H. Roberts Story* (Salt Lake City: Bookcraft, 1980), 320-322; "Primary Arranges Convention Dates: Special Programs Planned by 3 Mission Societies," *Church News*, March 17, 1934, 2. The Church History Library's collection of this footage is under the title "Vignettes from Eastern States Mission, circa 1920." Within a few years a desire to repeat the success of the 1923 conference led to the creation of an annual outdoor pageant on the slope of the Hill Cumorah, and today the Hill Cumorah Pageant is the largest and best-known of all Mormon pageantry.

402 "The Funeral of Bishop Hiram B. Clawson," *Millennial Star* 74:17 (April 25, 1912), 257-263, 267-268; "Passing Events: Hiram B. Clawson," *Improvement Era* 15:7 (May 1912), 666; "Hiram B. Clawson," *Wikipedia*, https://en.wikipedia.org/wiki/Hiram_B._Clawson (accessed November 13, 2014); Oman and Davis, *Images of Faith*, 15; Jacobs, "The History of Motion Pictures," 12-13. In May 1900 Shirl crashed his pony cart into a cyclist, destroying the bicycle and giving the rider minor injuries. "Bicyclist was Hurt," *Salt Lake Herald*, June 1, 1900, 3, https://chroniclingamerica.loc.gov/lccn/sn85058130/1900-06-01/ed-1/seq-3 (accessed March 9, 2018). Emily Partridge Young mentions Shirl and Chet several times in her personal history. Young, *Diary and Reminiscences*, https://archive.org/details/MS2845F0001. Regarding Shirl, she notes when she accompanied him and his mother on a trip to San Francisco (p. 82), when he drove her home from a family dinner in what she calls his donkey cart (p. 93), when he was set apart as president of the Twelfth Ward deacons' quorum (p. 111), and two other trips he made to San Francisco and Alberta, where his sister lived (p. 112-113,

116-117). Regarding Chet, she mentions his birth (p. 74), when he visited with his parents (p. 86), his baptism and confirmation (p. 97), when he was sent away to avoid catching his youngest brother Scott's scarlet fever (p. 112), and when she accompanied him "to camp" after watching some Rocky Mountain Rough Riders leave the city to go fight in the Spanish-American War (p. 113). Most insightful of young Chet's personality is this record from March 5, 1890, when he was seven and while she was helping the family settle into a new home (p. 87-88): "We had an execution this morning. It was only a rat. Last evening I espied in the back yard a rat trap. For the fun of it I set it not for a moment thinking to catch anything in it. This morning Chester came run[n]ing in from his play his eyes bunged out with excitement, 'Ma you know that thing out there well its got a rat or something in it.' And sure enough there was a big rat. Nobody dare touch it. So when I got ready I called Chester and [his younger sister] Josephine and we went into the cellar and turned some water in a tub and drowned it. Then Chester took it out in the back lands and buried it or threw it away. I dont know which and thats the execution we had."

403 John S. Tanner, "Shakespeare Among the Saints," *Journal of Mormon History* 32:1 (Spring 2006), 86; Ila Fisher Maughan, Pioneer Theatre in the Desert (Salt Lake City: Deseret Book Company, 1961), 8; Givens, *People of Paradox*, 150; Walker and Starr, "Shattering the Vase," 67; Jacobs, "The History of Motion Pictures," 12-13; "Minstrels at Fair," *Salt Lake Herald*, February 19, 1905, 8, https://chroniclingamerica.loc.gov/lccn/sn85058130/1905-02-19/ed-1/seq-8 (accessed March 8, 2018); Orestes Bean, *Corianton, an Aztec Romance: A Romantic Spectacular Drama, in Four Acts* (Salt Lake City: Salt Lake Theatre, 1902), 2, https://archive.org/stream/coriantonanaztec00beanrich#page/n5/mode/2up (accssed March 9, 2018); "Music and Drama," *Deseret Evening News*, August 2, 1902, part 2, page 11, https://chroniclingamerica.loc.gov/lccn/sn83045555/1902-08-02/ed-1/seq-11 (accessed March 9, 2018); "'Corianton' a Failure But May Go into Hands of Eastern Manager," *Salt Lake Herald*, October 10, 1902, 8, https://chroniclingamerica.loc.gov/lccn/sn85058130/1902-10-10/ed-1/seq-8 (accessed March 9, 2018).

404 For Shirl's early life, see "Farewell for Elder," *Salt Lake Herald*, November 22, 1905, 8, https://chroniclingamerica.loc.gov/lccn/sn85058130/1905-11-22/ed-1/seq-8 (accessed March 9, 2018); "From the Mission Field," *Millennial Star* 69:45 (Novmber 7, 1907), 717; "Salt Lakers in Gotham," *Deseret Evening News*, February 22, 1908, part 2, page 15, https://chroniclingamerica.loc.gov/lccn/sn83045555/1908-02-22/ed-1/seq-15 (accessed March 9, 2018); "Salt Lakers in New York," *Salt Lake Herald*, February 23, 1908, magazine section page 3, https://chroniclingamerica.loc.gov/lccn/sn85058130/1908-02-23/ed-1/seq-19 (accessed March 9, 2018); "Vaudeville Air is Getting Warm," *Deseret Evening News*, February 1, 1910, 7, https://chroniclingamerica.loc.gov/lccn/sn83045555/1910-02-01/ed-1/seq-7 (accessed March 9, 2018); "Salt Lake Music Lovers Hasten to Enroll on Subscription Lists for Grand Operatic Concert, September 7," *Salt Lake Tribune*, August 18, 1910, 4, https://chroniclingamerica.loc.gov/lccn/sn83045396/1910-08-18/ed-1/seq-4 (accessed March 9, 2018). For his marriage, see "Weddings and Engagements," *Salt Lake Tribune*, January 8, 1911, 8, https://chroniclingamerica.loc.gov/lccn/sn83045396/1911-01-08/ed-1/seq-8 (accessed March 9, 2018); "Society in Salt Lake," *Salt Lake Tribune*, February

8, 1911, 5, https://www.newspapers.com/image/76389404 (accessed March 9, 2018). For Chet, see "Society," *Salt Lake Tribune,* November 5, 1904, 5, https://chroniclingamerica.loc.gov/lccn/sn83045396/1904-11-05/ed-1/seq-5 (accessed March 9, 2018); Chester Y. Clawson Real Estate Invts. Fire Insurance, Rentals advertisement, *Salt Lake Herald-Republican*, August 15, 1909, section 2, page 14, https://chroniclingamerica.loc.gov/lccn/sn85058140/1909-08-15/ed-1/seq-14 (accessed March 9, 2018); "Society," *Salt Lake Herald-Republican*, May 26, 1910, 5, https://chroniclingamerica.loc.gov/lccn/sn85058140/1910-05-26/ed-1/seq-5 (accessed March 9, 2018); "Society," *Salt Lake Tribune*, June 17, 1910, 5, https://chroniclingamerica.loc.gov/lccn/sn83045396/1910-06-17/ed-1/seq-5 (accessed March 9, 2018); "Incorporations," *Salt Lake Herald-Republican*, July 3, 1910, section 2, https://chroniclingamerica.loc.gov/lccn/sn85058140/1910-07-03/ed-1/seq-17 (accessed March 9, 2018); "Personals," *Deseret Evening News*, July 27, 1910, 2, https://chroniclingamerica.loc.gov/lccn/sn83045555/1910-07-27/ed-1/seq-2 (accessed March 9, 2018); "Salt Lake Statistics: Births," *Salt Lake Tribune,* April 4, 1911, 5, https://chroniclingamerica.loc.gov/lccn/sn83045396/1911-04-04/ed-1/seq-5; "New Incorporations," *Salt Lake Tribune*, August 31, 1911, 3, https://chroniclingamerica.loc.gov/lccn/sn83045396/1911-08-31/ed-1/seq-3 (accessed March 9, 2018).

405 Heath, *In the World: The Diaries of Reed Smoot,* 120.

406 "Licensed Film Stories: Pathé," *Moving Picture World,* November 4, 1911, 408, http://www.archive.org/stream/moviwor10chal#page/n413/mode/2up (accessed December 30, 2017). There is some confusion in the actual article, which comes from the film industry press rather than a Mormon source. It identifies the Patriarch as "Henry Smith," indicating some confusion between Patriarch John Smith and President John Henry Smith. (The two men's fathers, Hyrum Smith and George Albert Smith, respectively, were cousins; their grandparents, Joseph Smith, Sr. and John Smith, were brothers.) But if the Patriarch was filmed with the First Presidency both men would have been included, along with President Joseph F. Smith and First Counselor Anthon Lund. Of course, Reed Smoot's diary indicates that he and other Church leaders were included as well.

407 Jacobs, "The History of Motion Pictures," 48-49, 52; "Roll of States: Utah," *Motography*, August 23, 1913.

408 Jacobs, "The History of Motion Pictures," 22.

409 Ibid., 13-14; Ardis Parshall, "'I Take Up My Pen': Bee Hive Film Co., 1914," *Keepapitchinin*, March 9, 2017, http://www.keepapitchinin.org/2017/03/09/i-take-up-my-pen-bee-hive-film-co-1914 (accessed March 19, 2018).

410 Jacobs, "The History of Motion Pictures," 14.

411 "Church Officials See Themselves on Movie Screen," *Salt Lake Telegram*, April 15, 1916, Richard Alan Nelson Collection, L. Tom Perry Special Collections, Harold B. Lee Library, Brigham Young University, box 2, folder 10, also quoted in Jacobs, "The History of Motion Pictures," 17.

412 "Church President as Picture Actor," *Salt Lake Tribune,* April 9, 1916, Journal History of the Church, April 9, 1916, 11, https://dcms.lds.org/delivery/Delivery-ManagerServlet?dps_pid=IE386420, Image 103 (accessed March 9, 2018).

413 "Church Officials See Themselves on Movie Screen," *Salt Lake Telegram,* April 15, 1916.

414 Heath, *In the World: The Diaries of Reed Smoot,* 332; Jacobs, "The History of Motion Pictures," 15-17.

415 David A. Smith to Joseph F. Smith, March 14, 1918, David A. Smith collection, Church History Library, The Church of Jesus Christ of Latter-day Saints, Salt Lake City, box 1, folder 4. My thanks to Ardis Parshall for both alerting me to this film and discovering and providing this correspondence.

416 Nelson, "Utah Filmmakers of the Silent Screen," 15.

417 "Pathé News, No. 50," *Film Daily,* June 18, 1919, [3?], http://www.archive.org/stream/filmdailyvolume778newy#page/923/mode/2up (accessed February 24, 2018); Ardis E. Parshall, "Lost Mormon Movie Masterpiece (1918)," *Keepapitchinin,* March 12, 2018, http://www.keepapitchinin.org/2018/03/12/lost-mormon-movie-masterpiece-1918 (accessed March 17, 2018). For more about how golf came to be an integral part of Smith's last years and other Church leaders' lives, see *Nauvoo Times,* October 10, 2012, http://www.nauvootimes.com/columns/james-b-allen/2012-10-10.html (accessed March 17, 2018).

418 Jacobs, "The History of Motion Pictures," 31-56. Jacobs includes the Church Historian's office's entire listings for the Clawsons' films at the time he wrote, 1967, and the Church History Library has listings of their holdings today. See also "Passing Events: The Boy Scout Caravan," *Improvement Era* 23:10 (August 1920), 947; Charles L. Ray, "Historic Pioneer Grounds," *Improvement Era* 24:9 (July 1921), 832-834; "Passing Events," *Improvement Era* 28:7 (May 1925), 708, and "Passing Events," *Improvement Era* 30:9 (July 1927), 844, on the Mormon Battalion Monument; "Video: BYU Track and Field 1927," *Church News,* March 25, 2011, http://www.ldschurchnews.com/articles/60673/Video-BYU-Track-and-Field-1927.html (accessed March 26, 2011).

419 J. M. Heslop, "1920 Film of Ward Activities," *Church News,* July 11, 1970, 15.

420 Harold H. Jensen, "A Providential Escape," *Improvement Era* 27 (November 1923), 62.

421 Heath, *In the World: The Diaries of Reed Smoot,* 512.

422 Donald G. Godfrey, Val E. Limburg, and Heber G. Wolsey, "KSL, Salt Lake City: At the Crossroads of the West," *Television in America: Local Station History from Across the Nation,* ed. Donald G. Godfrey and Michael D. Murray (Ames, Iowa: Iowa State University Press, 1997), 340.

423 Heber G. Wolsey, "The History of Radio Station KSL from 1922 to Television," (Ph.D. dissertation, Michigan State University, 1967), 12. Smith discussed all

the technological firsts the Church had been involved with. "And now, to cap the climax, we have the opportunity of talking over a wireless telephone, and having it broadcast to very many stations scattered at intervals anywhere from 500 to 1,000 miles away. I had the privilege once of sending the first wireless telegram that was ever received by President Joseph F. Smith, when I was out in the Atlantic Ocean, but I look upon this wireless telephone as the culmination of all the marvelous experiences to which the human family has thus far been heir...."

424 Fred C. Esplin, "The Church as Broadcaster," *Dialogue: A Journal of Mormon Thought* 10:3 (Spring 1977), 28-29; Pearl F. Jacobson, "Utah's First Radio Station," *Utah Historical Quarterly* 32:2 (1964), 130-142; Godfrey, Limburg, and Wolsey, "KSL, Salt Lake City," 339-340; Wolsey, "The History of Radio Station KSL from 1922 to Television," 7-12, 53-69, 72-80; "Editor's Table: Proclaiming the Gospel Through the Air," *Improvement Era* 25:8 (June 1922), 735-736.

425 Godfrey, Limburg, and Wolsey, "KSL, Salt Lake City," 341.

426 Ibid., 341; Wolsey, "The History of Radio Station KSL from 1922 to Television," 81-95; Sherry Baker, "Mormon Media History Timeline, 1827-2007," http://scholarsarchive.byu.edu/cgi/viewcontent.cgi?article=1958&context=facpub (accessed June 2, 2016).

427 Heber J. Grant, "Editors' Table," *Improvement Era* 28:1 (November 1924), 75.

428 Wolsey, "The History of Radio Station KSL from 1922 to Television," 66, 95; Sherry Baker, "Mormon Media History Timeline, 1827-2007," http://scholarsarchive.byu.edu/cgi/viewcontent.cgi?article=1958&context=facpub; "Lafount Urges Broadcasters to Adopt Liberal Policy for Political Candidates," *Broadcasting*, September 15, 1932, 12, http://www.archive.org/stream/broadcasting13unse#page/n779/mode/2up (accessed July 8, 2009), for FDR; "Mutual Work: Our Radio Hour," *Improvement Era* 32:5 (March 1929), 431; "We Pay Our Respects to—Arthur Burdette Church," *Broadcasting*, April 15, 1933, 21, http://www.archive.org/stream/broadcasting04unse#page/n261/mode/2up (accessed July 4, 2009); "We Pay Our Respects to---Elmer William Pratt," *Broadcasting*, June 1, 1933, 21, http://www.archive.org/stream/broadcasting04unse#page/n361/mode/2up (accessed July 6, 2009). See also Robert W. Donigan, *An Outline History of Broadcasting in the Church of Jesus Christ of Latter-day Saints, 1922-1963* (Provo: Brigham Young University, 1963); "Mormon Messages to Reach Ends of World, Smoot Says," *Radio Digest*, October 6, 1923, 8, http://www.archive.org/stream/radiodigest1923461923radi#page/8/mode/2up (accessed July 5, 2009); "Mormons Put Conference on Air for First Time," *Radio Digest*, November 10, 1923, 2, http://www.archive.org/stream/radio192317919231924radi#page/n99/mode/2up (accessed July 5, 2009); "KDYL to Broadcast Meet Direct from Mormon Church," *Radio Digest*, June 21, 1924, 6, http://www.archive.org/stream/radio192317919231924radi#page/n1073/mode/2up (accessed July 6, 2009), about a convention for disabled World War I veterans; "War Vets Hear Convention," *Radio Age*, July 1924, 14, http://www.archive.org/stream/radioage03unse#page/n363/mode/2up (accessed July 5, 2009); "Radiophone Broadcasting Stations," *Radio Digest*, August 9, 1924, 19, http://archive.org/stream/radi-19241101219241925radi#page/n113/mode/2up (accessed July 6, 2009), for

Notes - The First Wave: The New Frontier

KFOO; "Vast Throng Hears Great Conference," *Radio Digest*, October 25, 1924, 5, http://www.archive.org/stream/radi19241101219241925radi#page/n391/mode/2up (accessed July 5, 2009); Earl J. Glade, "Preaching the Gospel Through the Radio," *Improvement Era* 28:3 (January 1925), 242-245; "Passing Events," *Improvement Era* 28:3 (January 1925), 305; "Passing Events," *Improvement Era* 28:3 (January 1925), 307; "Passing Events," *Improvement Era* 28:3 (January 1925), 308; "Combination Talking Machine-Radio Outfits Prove Winners in Salt Lake City," *Talking Machine World,* February 15, 1925, 170, http://www.archive.org/stream/talkingmachinewo21bill#page/n417/mode/2up (accessed July 6, 2009); "Passing Events," *Improvement Era* 28:5 (March 1925), 493; "Talking Machine and Radio Business in Salt Lake Territory Is Satisfactory," *Talking Machine World*, March 15, 1925, 160, http://www.archive.org/stream/talkingmachinewo21bill#page/n633/mode/2up (accessed July 7, 2009); "Passing Events," *Improvement Era* 28:8 (June 1925), 799; "Passing Events: 'Movies' at home," *Improvement Era* 31:11 (September 1928), 983; "Mutual Work: Mutual Hour on the Radio," *Improvement Era* 32:8 (June 1929), 697-698; "Church Events: Tabernacle concerts to be broadcasted," *Improvement Era* 32:10 (August 1929), 875; "Mormon Choir and Organ," *What's on the Air,* August 1930, 43, http://www.archive.org/stream/whatsonair-01what#page/n481/mode/2up (accessed July 13, 2009).

429 "Committee to Perpetuate 1847 Pioneer History By Means of Moving Pictures: July 24 Celebration Plans Call for Undertaking Which Will Establish Record of Permanent Nature," *Deseret Evening News*, June 30, 1923, second section, p. 1, Richard Alan Nelson Collection, L. Tom Perry Special Collections, Harold B. Lee Library, Brigham Young University, box 2, folder 5.

430 "Pioneer Entrance Re-enacted," *Improvement Era* 26:11 (September 1923), 1048-1049.

431 Nelson, "The History of Utah Film," 26; Nelson, "A History of Latter-day Saint Screen Portrayals," 173; Jacobs, "The History of Motion Pictures," 21-22, 28-29.

432 A profile of Simpson in *Motion Picture Classic* magazine proved ironic given how often he would play Mormon characters. After noting his Scottish ancestry the author asks, "But how, then, account for the fact that in 'The Exodus' he is the only one who carries actual conviction of being a Mormon? He certainly isn't one. And he'd better not try to be while Mrs. Simpson has her health." Herbert Cruikshank, "Curth You, Jack Dalton!," *Motion Picture Classic*, April 1929, 94, http://www.archive.org/stream/motionpicturecla28moti#page/n381/mode/2up (accessed March 11, 2018). Simpson is probably best remembered today for playing Pa Joad in John Ford's *Grapes of Wrath* (1940).

433 "Over the Teacups," *Picture Play,* December 1928, 29, http://www.archive.org/stream/pictureplaymagaz29unse#page/n287/mode/2up (accessed March 11, 2018); "Utah's Own History Vividly Portrayed in 'All Faces West,'" *Salt Lake Tribune*, March 4, 1929, 12.

434 Louella O. Parsons, "Mormon History Now to be Shown on Movie Screen," *New York City American*, August 14, 1928.

435 Ibid. See also an untitled *Deseret News* notice, November 13, 1928, 6, in Richard Alan Nelson Collection, L. Tom Perry Special Collections, Harold B. Lee Library, Brigham Young University, box 2, folder 5.

436 Nelson, "The History of Utah Film," 34-35; "Marie Prevost's Lingerie," *Screenland*, December 1928, 76, http://www.archive.org/stream/screenland18unse#page/n169/mode/2up (accessed March 11, 2018).

437 Nelson, "A History of Latter-day Saint Screen Portrayals," 185.

438 "Utah-Made Picture at Victory Saturday," *Salt Lake Tribune,* March 1, 1929, 16; untitled *All Faces West* advertisement, *Salt Lake Tribune*, March 2, 1929, 18; "Utah Picture Holds Interest at Victory," *Deseret News*, March 4, 1929, 11. These indicates that organist Jewel Cox was accompanied by an orchestra for each screening; the vocal quartet consisted of James Haslam, Roy Utley, Harold Keddington, and Alexander P. Anderson.

439 "Utah-Made Film Draws Acclaim at the Victory," *Salt Lake Tribune*, March 3, 1929, 9, Richard Alan Nelson Collection, L. Tom Perry Special Collections, Harold B. Lee Library, Brigham Young University, box 2, folder 5.

440 Nelson, "The History of Utah Film," 24-31; Nelson, "A History of Latter-day Saint Screen Portrayals," 180-186; Nelson, "From Antagonism to Acceptance," 65-66; Nelson, "Utah Filmmakers of the Silent Screen," 19-23; "Mormon Film in Utah," *Variety*, April 4, 1928, 14, http://www.archive.org/stream/variety90-1928-04#page/n13/mode/2up (accessed March 11, 2018); "Studio in Salt Lake," *Variety*, May 16, 1928, 10, http://www.archive.org/stream/variety91-1928-05#page/n169/mode/2up (accessed March 11, 2018); "To Make Mormon Film," *Exhibitors Daily Review*, August 15, 1928, 4, http://www.archive.org/stream/exhibi01exhi#page/n157/mode/2up (accessed March 10, 2018); "Moomaw Starts Mormon Historic Picture," *Exhibitors Daily Review*, August 22, 1928, 4, http://www.archive.org/stream/exhibi01exhi#page/n187/mode/2up (accessed March 10, 2018); "Ill and Injured," *Variety*, September 19, 1928, 53, http://www.archive.org/stream/variety92-1928-09#page/n181/mode/2up (accessed March 11, 2018); Joe Blair, "Moomaw Raises Bankroll for Mormon Film," *Exhibitors Daily Review*, September 21, 1928, 6, http://www.archive.org/stream/exhibi01exhi#page/n295/mode/2up (accessed March 10, 2018); "FBO After Lyon," *Exhibitors Daily Review*, September 24, 1928, 4, http://www.archive.org/stream/exhibi01exhi#page/n303/mode/2up (accessed March 11, 2018); "Dick Grace Signed," *Exhibitors Daily Review*, November 16, 1928, 3, http://www.archive.org/stream/exhibi01exhi#page/n489/mode/2up (accessed March 11, 2018); "The Shadow Stage: All Faces West," *Photoplay*, April 1929, 113, http://www.archive.org/stream/photoplay3536movi#page/n535/mode/2up (accessed March 11, 2018); "Brief Reviews of Current Pictures," *Photoplay*, May 1929, 6, http://www.archive.org/stream/photoplay3536movi#page/n583/mode/2up (accessed March 11, 2018); "Head of Mormon Church Mixed Up In Film Failure," *Variety*, September 25, 1929, 6, http://www.archive.org/stream/variety96-1929-09#page/n237/mode/2up (access March 11, 2018).

441 "Trying to Sell Mormon Mob Scenes for Remake," *Variety*, September 17,

1930, 16, http://www.archive.org/stream/variety100-1930-09#page/n167/mode/2up (accessed March 11, 2018).

442 "'Call of the Rockies,'" *Film Daily*, July 12, 1931, 10, http://lantern.mediahist.org/catalog/filmdailyvolume55657newy_0096 (accessed March 11, 2018).

443 My thanks to Chris Beheim for providing much of the information about this film. His forthcoming research about Moomaw will undoubtedly provide even more details about the production and fate of *All Faces West*.

444 Roland Parry's papers are held at Weber State University Special Collections/Howell Library department in Ogden, Utah. Although his father was named Chauncey Parry, this is a different Chauncey Parry than the one who promoted film production in southern Utah.

445 "Motion Picture Producer Dies as Blasts Wreck Laboratory," *Salt Lake Tribune*, October 24, 1929, 1, Richard Alan Nelson Collection, L. Tom Perry Special Collections, Harold B. Lee Library, Brigham Young University, folder 20.

446 Bordwell *et al*, *The Classical Hollywood Cinema*, 116-117.

447 Jacobs, "The History of Motion Pictures," 47-48.

448 "Motion Picture Producer Dies as Blasts Wreck Laboratory," *Salt Lake Tribune*, 1-2; Jacobs, "The History of Motion Pictures," 22-28, 30; "Chester Young Clawson," Geni.com, https://www.geni.com/people/Chester-Clawson/6000000001915074890 (accessed January 7, 2018); handwritten note about the Clawson family donation to BYU in Richard Alan Nelson Collection folder 20. Information on the footage they shot inside the Salt Lake Theatre is in Walker and Starr, "Shattering the Vase," 85.

3 - The Second Wave: Home Cinema

01 "The American Religion: The Mormon Centenary and Utah," *Time*, April 7, 1930, http://www.4vf.net/the-american-religion-the-mormon-centenary-and-utah (accessed July 22, 2017).

02 "Financial Statement," *Conference Report*, April 1928, 4; "Financial and Statistical Report," *Conference Report*, April 1934, 4-5.

03 D. Michael Quinn, *The Mormon Hierarchy: Extensions of Power* (Salt Lake City: Signature Books in association with Smith Research Associates, 1997), 218-219.

04 David Kent Jacobs, "The History of Motion Pictures Produced by the Church of Jesus Christ of Latter-day Saints" (master's thesis, Brigham Young University Dept. of Dramatic Arts, 1967), 58.

05 Terry Lindvall, *Sanctuary Cinema: Origins of the Christian Film Industry* (New York: New York University Press, 2007), 172.

06 Ibid., 174.

07 Eugene England, "Mormon Literature: Progress and Prospects," *Mormon Americana: A Guide to Sources and Collections in the United States*, ed. David J. Whittaker (Provo: BYU Studies Monographs, 1995), 462.

08 Nephi Anderson, "Purpose in Fiction," *Improvement Era* 1:4 (February 1898), 271.

09 Leonard J. Arrington, *Great Basin Kingdom: An Economic History of the Latter-day Saints, 1830-1900*, New Edition (Urbana and Chicago: University of Illinois Press, 1958), 47.

10 Ibid., 26, 112-113; Quinn, *The Mormon Hierarchy: Extensions of Power*, 764-766; L. Dwight Israelsen, "United Orders," *Encyclopedia of Mormonism*, Vol. 4, ed. Daniel H. Ludlow (New York: Macmillan Publishing Company, 1992), 1493-1495.

11 Arrington, *Great Basin Kingdom*, 224.

12 Elsie Talmage Brandley, "Editorial: More Talk About the Talkies," *Improvement Era* 37:8 (August 1934), 479.

13 "Roscoe Dines, Speaks, Shakes Hands, Goes On," *Motion Picture News*, March 17, 1917, 1675, http://www.archive.org/stream/motionpicturenew152un-se#page/1674/mode/2up (accessed November 20, 2014).

14 "A Loathsome Incident," *Deseret News*, September 12, 1921, Journal History of the Church, September 12, 1921, 1, Church History Library, The Church of Jesus Christ of Latter-day Saints, Salt Lake City, https://dcms.lds.org/delivery/Delivery-ManagerServlet?dps_pid=IE306008 (accessed November 18, 2014). The author adds, "The world would be healthier and safer if some of these abhorrent per-verts (posing, many of them, as artists, and yet too disgusting to be called beasts without insulting the natural animal creation) were put out of the way." They should be grateful for life imprisonment, "unless, indeed, their crime is so pecu-liarly atrocious that an even more condign punishment should be meted out."

15 Heber J. Grant, "Telegram from Heber J. Grant to Sen R. Smoot," Richard Alan Nelson Collection, L. Tom Perry Special Collections, Harold B. Lee Library, Brigham Young University, box 2, folder 13; Richard Alan Nelson, "A History of Latter-day Saint Screen Portrayals in the Anti-Mormon Film Era, 1905-1936" (master's thesis, Brigham Young University Dept. of Communications, 1975), 131, footnote 20; "Passing Events," *Improvement Era* 25:8 (June 1922), 760; Quinn, *The Mormon Hierarchy: Extensions of Power*, 817; John Hatch, "Can 'Good Mormons' Watch R-Rated Movies?," *Sunstone* 126 (March 2003), 18, 22, footnotes 11 and 12; Gilbert King, "The Skinny on the Fatty Arbuckle Trial," *Smithsonian*, November 8, 2011, https://www.smithsonianmag.com/history/the-skinny-on-the-fatty-ar-buckle-trial-131228859 (accessed November 20, 2014). For a full history of the Arbuckle scandal, see David Yallop, *The Day the Laughter Stopped: The True Story of Fatty Arbuckle* (New York: St. Martin's Press, 1976). Historians have concluded that Rappe most likely suffered from peritonitis while others have suggested, more speculatively, that she was in San Francisco that week to have an abortion,

which was botched and resulted in the fatal lesion in her bladder.

16 "The Week in Review: Friday, December 18," *Exhibitor's Trade Review*, December 19, 1925, 6, http://www.archive.org/stream/exhibitorstrade00new#page/n197/mode/2up (accessed April 4, 2016).

17 "Business Men Favor Open Sunday in Logan," *Variety*, June 3, 1925, 27, http://www.archive.org/stream/variety79-1925-06#page/n23/mode/2up (accessed April 3, 2016).

18 Chad M. Orton, *More Faith Than Fear: The Los Angeles Stake Story* (Salt Lake City: Bookcraft, 1987), 122; "Anti-Censorship Stand Helps Salt Lake Mayor," *Film Daily*, November 9, 1931, 1, http://www.archive.org/stream/filmdailyvolume-55657newy#page/986/mode/2up (accessed March 2, 2018). For one example of the Mormon press praising the increasing restrictiveness of the Code, see "Lights and Shadows on the Screen," *Improvement Era* 36:2 (December 1932), 100.

19 Nelson, "A History of Latter-day Saint Screen Portrayals," 138, footnote 31. This quotation is from an April 13 letter Smoot wrote to Grant recounting his letter to Hays. See also D'arc, "Darryl F. Zanuck's *Brigham Young*," 9.

20 Production Code, reprinted in Jack Vizzard, *See No Evil: Life inside a Hollywood Censor* (New York: Simon and Schuster, 1970), 370.

21 Dennis Baron, "The First Amendment: III. Obscenity and censorship," *Department of English, University of Illinois*, http://www.english.illinois.edu/-people-/faculty/debaron/310/310_powerpoints/1AmendObscenity.pdf (accessed March 3, 2018).

22 Baron, "The First Amendment: III. Obscenity and censorship"; Tom Head, "Censorship in the United States," *ThoughtCo*, July 24, 2017, https://www.thoughtco.com/censorship-in-the-united-states-721221 (accessed March 5, 2018); "Motion Picture Production Code," *Wikipedia*, https://en.wikipedia.org/wiki/Motion_Picture_Production_Code (accessed March 8, 2018). For one thorough history of the Code see Leonard J. Leff and Jerold L. Simmons, *The Dame in the Kimono: Hollywood, Censorship, and the Production Code* (Lexington: University Press of Kentucky, 2001). Pages 1-56 discuss the Code's creation, and the remaining pages its application from 1934-1966. Part of the reason for the Code's piecemeal evolution was the additional pressure put on the MPPDA to reign in incalcitrant studios. For instance, in 1933 many conservative groups thought the new Roosevelt administration would be lenient toward motion pictures; the Catholic League of Decency even proposed creating its own rating system, with implied Catholic boycotts of pictures that didn't receive a proper rating. This prompted Hays to tighten studio heads' compliance with the Code to avoid this; by 1934 economic incentives and the tough measures of Hays's assistant Joe Breen finally got Hollywood studios to accept the Code's regulations. Though the Catholic, not Mormon, church had been one of the powerhouses behind the reformation, Mormon leaders were greatly in favor of the new measures.

23 Olga J. Martin, *Hollywood's Movie Commandments: A Handbook for Motion*

Picture Writers and Reviewers (New York: H. W. Wilson Company, 1937), 174, quoted in Nelson, "A History of Latter-day Saint Screen Portrayals," 197, and D'arc, "Darryl F. Zanuck's *Brigham Young*," 29, footnote 13.

24 Heber J. Grant, "Changing Attitudes Toward the Church," *Improvement Era* 39:10 (October 1936), 587-589; Richard J. Marshall, "Exhibitions and World's Fairs," *Encyclopedia of Mormonism*, Vol. 2, ed. Daniel H. Ludlow (New York: Macmillon Publishing Company, 1992), 479.

25 Nelson, "A History of Latter-day Saint Screen Portrayals," 194-195; "*Hell's Highway* (1932 film)," Wikipedia, https://en.wikipedia.org/wiki/Hell's_Highway_ (1932_film) (accessed October 3, 2017); "*The Man from Utah*," *Wikipedia*, https:// en.wikipedia.org/wiki/The_Man_from_Utah (accessed October 3, 2017); "*Trouble in Texas*," *Wikipedia*, https://en.wikipedia.org/wiki/Trouble_in_Texas (accessed October 3, 2017); "*The Utah Kid* (1944 film)," *Wikipedia*, https://en.wikipedia. org/wiki/The_Utah_Kid_(1944_film) (accessed October 3, 2017); "*The Utah Kid* (1930 film)," *Wikipedia*, https://en.wikipedia.org/wiki/The_Utah_Kid_(1930_film) (accessed October 3, 2017); "*The Utah Trail*," *Wikipedia*, https://en.wikipedia.org/ wiki/The_Utah_Trail (accessed October 3, 2017); David E. Jensen, "Matt Warner: Utah's Outlaw," *Utah Stories*, August 11, 2015, http://utahstories.com/2015/08/ matt-warner-utahs-outlaw (accessed March 20, 2018); "*The Heritage of the Desert* (film)," *Wikipedia*, https://en.wikipedia.org/wiki/The_Heritage_of_the_Desert_(film) (accessed October 2, 2017); *Heritage of the Desert* (1932 film)," *Wikipedia*, https://en.wikipedia.org/wiki/Heritage_of_the_Desert_(1932_film) (accessed October 3, 2017); "*Heritage of the Desert* (1939 film)," *Wikipedia*, https://en.wikipedia.org/wiki/Heritage_of_the_Desert_(1939_film) (accessed October 2, 2017); "*Riders of the Purple Sage* (1925 film)," *Wikipedia*, https://en.wikipedia.org/wiki/ Riders_of_the_Purple_Sage_(1925_film) (accessed October 3, 2017); "*Riders of the Purple Sage* (1941 film)," *Wikipedia*, https://en.wikipedia.org/wiki/Riders_of_the_Purple_Sage_(1941_film) (accessed October 2, 2017); "*The Rainbow Trail* (film)," *Wikipedia*, https://en.wikipedia.org/wiki/The_Rainbow_Trail_(film) (accessed October 3, 2017); "*Wild Horse Mesa*," *Wikipedia*, https://en.wikipedia. org/wiki/Wild_Horse_Mesa_(1925_film) (accessed October 2, 2017); "*Wild Horse Mesa* (1932 film)," *Wikipedia*, https://en.wikipedia.org/wiki/Wild_Horse_Mesa_ (1932_film) (accessed October 3, 2017); "*Wild Horse Mesa* (1947 film)," *Wikipedia*, https://en.wikipedia.org/wiki/Wild_Horse_Mesa_(1947_film) (accessed October 3, 2017); "*A Study in Scarlet* (1933 film)," *Wikipedia*, https://en.wikipedia.org/ wiki/A_Study_in_Scarlet_(1933_film) (accessed October 3, 2017); "*Utah* (film)," *Wikipedia*, https://en.wikipedia.org/wiki/Utah_(film) (accessed October 3, 2017); "*The Big Cat* (film)," *Wikipedia*, https://en.wikipedia.org/wiki/The_Big_Cat_(film) (accessed October 2, 2017); "*Salt Lake Raiders* (1950)," *Turner Classic Movies*, http://www.tcm.com/tcmdb/title/88948/Salt-Lake-Raiders (accessed March 30, 2018); "*The Hills of Utah*," *Internet Movie Database*, http://www.imdb.com/title/ tt0043641/?ref_=nv_sr_2 (accessed October 3, 2017); "*Utah Wagon Train* (1951)," *Turner Classic Movies*, http://www.tcm.com/tcmdb/title/94603/Utah-Wagon-Train (accessed October 3, 2017); "*49th Parallel* (film)," *Wikipedia*, https://en.wikipedia. org/wiki/49th_Parallel_(film) (accessed March 22, 2018). Many of these films came to my attention from material in the Richard Alan Nelson Collection, L. Tom Perry Special Collections, Harold B. Lee Library, Brigham Young University, such

as box 5, folder 18, which contains information about *Utah, Hills of Utah*, and
Utah Wagon Train. Interestingly, live theater underwent no equivalent process
as the Production Code in films, although interest in Mormonism was rather
diminished from previous decades. In 1933 an original play staged in Omaha
called *Brigham Young* earned a visit from both LDS and RLDS lawyers. The LDS
representatives were concerned it overdid "matter regarding trading of wives and
other polygamic practices," while the RLDS representatives objected that the
play implied Joseph Smith instigated polygamy, a claim that ran against the official church position. The play ran unchanged, however, and no legal action was
pursued by either church. "Mormons Check Up Play Dealing with Church," *Variety*,
March 28, 2018, 42, http://www.archive.org/stream/variety109-1933-03#page/
n209/mode/2up (accessed March 25, 2018); "'Brigham Young' Goes On Amid
Mormon Debate," *Variety*, April 4, 1933, 37, http://www.archive.org/stream/vari-
ety109-1933-04#page/n35/mode/2up (accessed March 25, 2018). In 1936 the
play *Moroni*, staged in Schenectady outside Albany, New York, depicted Joseph
Smith's life, with particular emphasis on a love affair with Sylvia Law, wife of
William Law; although this topic, relating to Smith's assassination, remains a
powder keg for faithful Mormons, the play evidently earned no official LDS or
RLDS response. "Moroni (Union College)," *Variety*, August 26, 1936, 82, http://
www.archive.org/stream/variety123-1936-08#page/n267/mode/2up (accessed
March 25, 2018).

26 "Irwin Making Series of Historical Pictures," *Film Daily*, July 19, 1929, http://
www.archive.org/stream/filmdaily4950newy#page/152/mode/2up (accessed
March 22, 2018); "Wally Van Opens Offices at Tec-Art," *Hollywood Filmograph*,
August 31, 1929, 32, http://www.archive.org/stream/hollywoodfilmogr91hol-
l#page/32/mode/2up (accessed March 22, 2018).

27 "Mormon Story Based on Brigham Young, Par Idea," *Variety*, April 4, 1933,
4, http://www.archive.org/stream/variety109-1933-04#page/n3/mode/2up
(accessed March 20, 2018). This article, which announces Paramount's project,
refers to a film that is probably *All Faces West* but could have been another
unreleased production: "Two years ago, a picture based on [Brigham] Young's life
was produced in Utah with capital raised in Salt Lake City. Production was never
released."

28 James V. D'arc, "Darryl F. Zanuck's *Brigham Young*: A Film in Context," *BYU
Studies* 29:1 (Winter 1989), 29, footnote 12. See Motion Picture Producers and
Distributors of America, Inc., Production Code Administration File, Academy of
Motion Picture Arts and Sciences Library, Beverly Hills, California.

29 May Mann, "Events in Mormon Pioneering Of Salt Lake Will Be Chronicled In
Hollywood Production," *Deseret Evening News*, December 26, 1936, 3.

30 "Picture Studio Plans Film On Utah Theme: Research in Progress For Produc-
tion, Director Discloses," *Salt Lake Tribune*, July 11, 1941, 17, Richard Alan Nelson
Collection, L. Tom Perry Special Collections, Harold B. Lee Library, Brigham Young
University, box 5, folder 18.

31 Nelson, "A History of Latter-day Saint Screen Portrayals," 198-205; Richard

Alan Nelson Collection, L. Tom Perry Special Collections, Harold B. Lee Library, Brigham Young University, box 2, folder 13 and 15, which includes some advertising material from the film's initial release; Richard Alan Nelson, untitled master's thesis draft, Richard Alan Nelson Collection, chapter 7, pages 7-11; "Polygamy," *Internet Movie Database*, http://www.imdb.com/title/tt0031475/?ref_=nm_ flmg_prd_11 (accessed March 2, 2018); Ken Driggs, "Twentieth-Century Polyamy and Fundamentalist Mormons in Southern Utah," *Dialogue: A Journal of Mormon Thought* 24:4 (Winter 1991), 45-48.

32 "Movietone's Mormon Organ," *Variety*, January 18, 1928, 54, http://www. archive.org/stream/variety89-1928-01#page/n301/mode/2up (accessed March 23, 2018).

33 "20 Vitaphone Shorts in the Cutting Room," *Film Daily*, February 16, 1935, 6, http://www.archive.org/stream/filmdaily67wids#page/n443/mode/2up (accessed March 26, 2018); "13 Vitaphone Shorts Set for March Release," *Film Daily*, February 25, 1935, 4, http://www.archive.org/stream/filmdaily67wids#page/ n487/mode/2up (accessed March 26, 2018); "'The Mormon Trail,'" *Film Daily*, March 28, 1935, 4, http://www.archive.org/stream/filmdaily67wids#page/ n803/mode/2up (accessed March 26, 2018); "'The Mormon Trail,'" *Motion Picture Daily*, April 10, 1935, 16, http://www.archive.org/stream/motionpicturedai37un-se_0#page/n93/mode/2up (accessed March 26, 2018); Scott Tiffany, ed., *City Saints: Mormons in the New York Metropolis* (New York: Nauvoo Books, 2004), 227; "Warner-Vitaphone," *Film Daily*, April 12, 1935, 27, http://www.archive.org/ stream/filmdail67wids#page/n129/mode/2up (accessed March 26, 2018); "Short Subjects," *National Board of Review Magazine*, May 1935, 19, http://www.archive. org/stream/nationalboardofr8910nati#page/n409/mode/2up (accessed March 26, 2018); Nelson, untitled master's thesis draft, chapter 7, page 5.

34 Ardis Parshall, "*The Miracle of Salt Lake*: A Mormon Movie You Probably Never Heard Of," *Keepapitchinin*, January 26, 2011, http://www.keepapitchinin. org/2011/01/26/the-miracle-of-salt-lake-a-mormon-movie-you-probably-never-heard-of (accessed May 2, 2012).

35 "Church History: 50 Years Ago," *Church News*, March 18, 1989, 2.

36 Parshall, "*The Miracle of Salt Lake*."

37 "The Church Moves On: Church Receives Historical Film," *Improvement Era* 42:6 (June 1939), 355; Nelson, "A History of Latter-day Saint Screen Portrayals," 195.

38 "Travel America: A Report on the Use of Films in Travel Promotion," *Business Screen* 3:6 (Summer 1941), 29, http://www.archive.org/stream/business1940s-creenmavol31941rich#page/216/mode/2up (accessed March 25, 2018).

39 "Visualizing the Rio Grande Route," *Business Screen Magazine*, December 1946, 23, http://www.archive.org/stream/business1944screen1946ma6an-d7rich#page/912/mode/2up (accessed March 26, 2018).

40 "Wings of the West!," *British Pathé*, https://www.britishpathe.com/video/

wings-of-the-west (accessed May 7, 2018).

41 "20th-Fox Sets Release Dates For 4 New 1943-44 Features," *Showmen's Trade Review*, August 21, 1943, 5, http://www.archive.org/stream/showmenstraderev3839lewi#page/n349/mode/2up (accessed March 26, 2018); "Short Subject Reviews: 'Mormon Trails,'" *Motion Picture Daily*, August 31, 1943, 11, http://www.archive.org/stream/motionpicturedai54unse#page/n447/mode/2up (accessed March 26, 2018); "Short Reviews: 'Mormon Trails,'" *Film Daily*, September 3, 1943, 6, http://www.archive.org/stream/filmdaily84wids#page/n511/mode/2up (accessed March 26, 2018); "Short Subject Reviews: Mormon Trails," *Showmen's Trade Review*, September 4, 1943, 50, http://www.archive.org/stream/showmenstraderev3839lewi#page/n497/mode/2up (accessed March 26, 2018), which gives it a mediocre review, calling the imagery eye candy and the narration perhaps too boisterous—"This subject won't cause any excitement whatever, but it makes a fine filler for a program overladen with action and heavy drama"; "Twentieth Century-Fox," *Motion Picture Herald*, November 27, 1943, 60, http://www.archive.org/stream/motionpictureher153unse#page/n359/mode/2up (accessed March 26, 2018), which indicates that it was playing in Ontario in November.

42 "Short Subject Reviews: 'Salt Lake Diversions,'" *Motion Picture Daily*, February 10, 1944, 10, http://www.archive.org/stream/motionpicturedai55unse#page/n381/mode/2up (accessed March 26, 2018); "City of Brigham Young," *Internet Movie Database*, http://www.imdb.com/title/tt0240418 (accessed March 26, 2018); "'Monumental Utah,'" Film Daily, September 22, 1944, 7, http://www.archive.org/stream/filmdaily86wids#page/n629/mode/2up (accessed March 26, 2018); "Recommended Short Subjects," *National Board of Review Magazine*, November 1944, 16, http://www.archive.org/stream/newmoviesnationa1920nati#page/n107/mode/2up (accessed March 26, 2018); J. Spencer Cornwall, *A Century of Singing: The Salt Lake Mormon Tabernacle Choir* (Salt Lake City: Deseret Book Company, 1958), 172.

43 Heber J. Grant, untitled address, *Conference Report*, October 1936, 3.

44 Matthew Bowman, *The Mormon People: The Making of an American Faith* (New York: Random House, 2012), 172.

45 "In the Newsreels," *Motion Picture Herald*, December 26, 1936, 89, http://www.archive.org/stream/motionpictureher125unse#page/88/mode/2up (accessed March 13, 2018).

46 Richard L. Evans, "'Time Marches On' with the Church Security Plan," *Improvement Era* 40:4 (April 1937), 214.

47 "Short Subject: 'March of Time—No. 6,'" *Motion Picture Daily*, January 21, 1937, 6, http://www.archive.org/stream/motionpicturedai41unse#page/n207/mode/2up (accessed March 26, 2018).

48 Evans, "'Time Marches On' with the Church Security Plan," 214-215; "Shorts: The March of Time," *Film Daily*, January 22, 1937, 5, http://www.archive.org/stream/filmdaily71wids#page/n235/mode/2up (accessed March 26, 2018);

"Short Subjects," *National Board of Review Magazine,* February 1937, 19, http://www.archive.org/stream/nationalboardofr1112nati#page/n189/mode/2up (accessed March 26, 2018); "*The March of Time*," *Wikipedia*, https://en.wikipedia.org/wiki/The_March_of_Time (accessed March 20, 2018); Jacobs, "The History of Motion Pictures," 66; Nelson, "A History of Latter-day Saint Screen Portrayals," 195-196; "9 March Of Time Mormonism Videos and B-Roll Footage," *Getty Images*, https://www.gettyimages.com/videos/march-of-time-mormonism?offlinecontent=include&phrase=march%20of%20time%20mormonism&sort=best#license (accessed March 14, 2018). Additional material on the film is in the Richard Alan Nelson Collection, box 2, folder 9.

49 Arch A. Mercey, "The Federal Film," *Educational Screen*, June 1939, 214, http://www.archive.org/stream/educationalscree18chicrich#page/214/mode/2up (accessed March 26, 2018); "A Checklist of Motion Pictures for Science Instruction," *See & Hear: The Journal of Audio-Visual Learning* 7:5 (1950), 39, http://www.archive.org/stream/seehear194850journaloneaucrich#page/38/mode/2up (accessed March 26, 2018); "Newsreel Synopses," *Showmen's Trade Review*, August 3, 1940, 22, http://www.archive.org/stream/showmenstraderev-3233lewi#page/n161/mode/2up (accessed March 26, 2018); "Utah – This Land of Ours," *Travel Film Archives*, http://www.travelfilmarchive.com/item.php?id=12191 (accessed May 26, 2018); Nelson, untitled master's thesis draft, chapter 9 page 9; Jacobs, "The History of Motion Pictures," 66-67; Nelson, "A History of Latter-day Saint Screen Portrayals," 195.

50 T. Edgar Player, "Your Page and Ours: Temple Used in Advertisement," *Improvement Era* 39:2 (February 1936), 128.

51 James V. D'arc, "The Saints on Celluloid: The Making of the Movie *Brigham Young*," *Sunstone* 1:4 (Fall 1976), 11.

52 Richard Paul to Dennis Rowley, Curator of Archives & Manuscripts, Brigham Young University, March 25, 1976, quoted in D'arc, "The Saints on Celluloid," 11.

53 D'arc, "The Saints on Celluloid," 12; D'arc, "Darryl F. Zanuck's *Brigham Young*," 30, footnote 20; "Bromfield Reports at 20th-Fox For Work on 'Brigham Young,'" *Showmen's Trade Review*, May 27, 1939, 35, http://www.archive.org/stream/showmenstraderev30lewi#page/n315/mode/2up (accessed March 30, 2018).

54 "The Church Moves On: Brigham Young Subject for Film Production," *Improvement Era* 42:6 (June 1939), 355. See also "War, Biography and History Form New Cycle of Films," *Motion Picture Daily*, June 5, 1939, 7, http://www.archive.org/stream/motionpicturedai45unse_0#page/n451/mode/2up (accessed March 30, 2018), which puts *Brigham Young* in the context of a wave of similar biopics at the time, including films on Thomas Edison, Alfred Nobel, and Abraham Lincoln; and "Fox Makes First Announcement of Product for 1940-41, Listing 52," *Motion Picture Herald*, April 13, 1940, 27, http://www.archive.org/stream/motionpictureher1381unse#page/26/mode/2up (accessed March 30, 2018).

55 Ralph Wilk, "Zanuck Again Wants Brown," *Film Daily*, August 8, 1939, 10, http://www.archive.org/stream/filmdaily76wids#page/n279/mode/2up (ac-

cessed March 29, 2018).

56 Arthur Schlesinger, Jr., "When the Movies Really Counted," *Show*, April 1973, 77, quoted in D'arc, "Darryl F. Zanuck's *Brigham Young*," 6.

57 "Film Epic Thrills Audiences," *Deseret News*, August 23, 1940, 6, quoted in D'arc, "Darryl F. Zanuck's *Brigham Young*," 5.

58 D'arc, "The Saints on Celluloid," 13; Grant's quotation comes from Thomas Brady, "Profits vs. Prestige," *New York Times*, July 28, 1940, section 9, page 3.

59 D'arc, "Darryl F. Zanuck's *Brigham Young*," 10-11.

60 Heber J. Grant to Charles Zimmerman, October 22, 1939, typescript, in Heber J. Grant, Journal, Church History Library, The Church of Jesus Christ of Latter-day Saints, Salt Lake City, 183, quoted in D'arc, "Darryl F. Zanuck's *Brigham Young*," 10.

61 Heber J. Grant to Kenneth Macgowan, August 30, 1939, quoted in D'arc, "The Saints on Celluloid," 13-14.

62 Orton, *More Faith Than Fear*, 112; "Okay Mormon Script," *Variety*, November 8, 1939, 2, http://www.archive.org/stream/variety136-1939-11#page/n49/mode/2up (accessed March 29, 2018).

63 "Tyrone Power Gets Love Scenes," *Deseret News*, August 22, 1940, 13.

64 James V. D'arc, "A Tale of Two Brighams," *Sunstone* 3:2 (January-February 1978), 34.

65 D'arc, "The Saints on Celluloid," 26.

66 "Little Makeup Needed for Star Of Picture 'Brigham Young,'" *Salt Lake Telegram*, August 8, 1940, 9, https://newspapers.lib.utah.edu/details?id=16847399&q=Little+Makeup+Needed+for+Star+&facet (accessed March 28, 2018), also in George D. Pyper Collection, Special Collections, J. Willard Marriott Library, University of Utah, box 81, folder 11. Most of Pyper's memorabilia from the shoot are in this folder.

67 Vincent Price to James D'arc, February 17, 1972, quoted in D'arc, "The Saints on Celluloid," 14.

68 Darryl F. Zanuck to Kenneth Macgowan, Memorandum, April 22, 1939, Fox Archives, quoted in D'arc, "Darryl F. Zanuck's *Brigham Young*," 8. Both *Alexander Graham Bell* and *Jesse James* were actual films released by Twentieth Century-Fox in 1939.

69 D'arc, "Darryl F. Zanuck's *Brigham Young*," 17; D'arc, "The Saints on Celluloid," 23. See also "10 Beauts for Brigham," *Variety*, July 17, 1940, 3, http://www.archive.org/stream/variety139-1940-07#page/n97/mode/2up (accessed March 30, 2018), which claims that footage of ten additional wives is being added for the film's roadshow release; while this apparently was mere advertising, it does list the ten actresses who must have been in the company pay roll for these oblique

roles.

70 Mary Astor, *My Story* (New York: Dell Publishing Company, 1960), 227, quoted in D'arc, "The Saints on Celluloid," 17. For the budget, see D'arc, "Darryl F. Zanuck's *Brigham Young*," 31, footnote 50. The high figure of $2.7 million is mentioned in a few sources, including Weston N. Nordgren, "'Brigham Young,'" Improvement Era 43:9 (September 1940), 532, and, most importantly, internal Twentieth Century-Fox production notes provided by Linda Lambert to Richard Nelson. Richard Alan Nelson Collection, L. Tom Perry Special Collections, Harold B. Lee Library, Brigham Young University.

71 Astor, *My Story*, 228, quoted in D'arc, "The Saints on Celluloid," 17; see also Mary Astor, *A Life on Film* (New York: Delacorte Press, 1967), 146-150.

72 "High L.D.S. Officials Preview *Brigham Young*," *Salt Lake Tribune*, August 14, 1940, 8. Quinn, *The Mormon Hierarchy: Extensions of Power*, 827 attributes an additional statement to Grant: "My eyes were full of tears of gratitude for the fine picture."

73 Jeff Breinholt, "Mormons and Intellectual Property," *Mormon Matters*, October 3, 2009, http://www.mormonmatters.org/mormons-and-intellectual-property (accessed March 30, 2018) gives the citation for Harris's legal actions as *Harris v. Twentieth Century Fox Film Corporation*, 35 F. Supp. 153 (S.D.N.Y. 1940) and *Harris v. Twentieth Century Fox Film Corp.*, 43 F. Supp. 119 (S.D.N.Y. 1942). For the film's dedication to Grant, see "The Church Moves On: Brigham Young Film Dedicated to Church," *Improvement Era* 43:10 (October 1940), 605.

74 D'arc, "The Saints on Celluloid," 20-21; Bill Brogdon, "'Brigham' Preems 7 S. L. Cinemas; 'Kit Carson' in 6 Denver Houses," *Variety*, August 28, 1940, 8, http://www.archive.org/stream/variety139-1940-08#page/n167/mode/2up (accessed March 30, 2018); "7 Houses For 'Brigham Young,'" *Showmen's Trade Review*, August 31, 1940, 13, http://www.archive.org/stream/showmenstraderev3233lewi#page/n303/mode/2up (accessed March 29, 2018). For more information on the premiere, see the George D. Pyper Collection, box 81, folder 11. A Twentieth Century-Fox Movietone newsreel on the premiere may also be seen on the DVD of *Brigham Young*.

75 D'arc, "The Saints on Celluloid," 21; D'arc, "Darryl F. Zanuck's *Brigham Young*," 17, 19. For more contemporary reviews, publicity, and commentary on the film, see Gladys Hall, "I Have Seven Wives!," *Modern Screen*, August 1940, 48-49, 67-68; Barbara Hayes, "We Cover the Studios," *Photoplay*, August 1940, 44, 72, http://www.archive.org/stream/photoplay52chic#page/n149/mode/2up (accessed March 30, 2018); "Reviews of New Films," *Film Daily*, August 27, 1940, 6, http://www.archive.org/stream/filmdaily78wids#page/n365/mode/2up (accessed March 30, 2018), which says it's "a stirring sage of the Mormon people" with "epic sweep" and a "vivid picturization" of early Mormon hardships; "Brigham Young," *Showmen's Trade Review*, August 31, 1940, 18, http://www.archive.org/stream/showmenstraderev3233lewi#page/n309/mode/2up (accessed March 30, 2018), which calls it "one of the finest outdoor pictures ever turned out by Hollywood" and "a sure winner with plenty of mass appeal for any type of audience"; "The

Notes - The Second Wave: Home Cinema

Problem of Sharing a Husband!," *Silver Screen*, September 1940, 26-27, 80, 82-84, http://www.archive.org/stream/silverscreen10unse_0#page/n283/mode/2up (accessed March 30, 2018); "Brigham Young: An STR Showmananalysis," *Showmen's Trade Review*, September 14, 1940, 18, http://www.archive.org/stream/showmenstraderev3233lewi#page/n395/mode/2up (accessed March 30, 2018); "Movie of the Week: *Brigham Young*," *Life*, September 23, 1940, 59, Richard Alan Nelson Collection, which calls the film "fatuous, dull and false," with a "tepid love story" and serious flaw in evading polygamy; "Brigham Young," *American Cinematographer*, October 1940, 472, http://www.archive.org/stream/american21asch#page/472/mode/2up (accessed March 30, 2018); "Screen and History," *National Board Review Magazine*, October 1940, 13, http://www.archive.org/stream/nationalboardofr1415nati#page/n377/mode/2up (accessed March 30, 2018); "The Film Estimates: Brigham Young," *Educational Screen*, October 1940, 358, http://www.archive.org/stream/educationalscree19chicrich#page/358/mode/2up (accessed March 30, 2018); Wolfe Kaufman, "Movie Reviews: Brigham Young," *Modern Screen*, November 1940, 14, http://www.archive.org/stream/modernscreen2021unse#page/n991/mode/2up (accessed March 30, 2018); "The Shadow Stage: Brigham Young," *Photoplay*, November 1940, 68, http://www.archive.org/stream/photoplay52chic#page/n447/mode/2up (accessed March 30, 2018), which opines "the doctrine of polygamy could and should have been honestly defended instead of being so obviously side-stepped"; "Miniature Reviews," *Hollywood*, January 1941, 17, http://www.archive.org/stream/hollywood-30fawc#page/n19/mode/2up (accessed March 30, 2018). For a sampling of the film's print advertisements, see "*Brigham Young* advertisement," *Modern Screen*, October 1940, 18, http://www.archive.org/stream/modernscreen2021unse#page/n905/mode/2up (accessed March 30, 2018).

76 "Zanuck Assails Attempt to Censor Films," *Motion Picture Daily*, Septemberr 29, 1941, 5, http://www.archive.org/stream/motionpicturedai50unse#page/n577/mode/2up (accessed March 30, 2018); D'arc, "Darryl F. Zanuck's *Brigham Young*," 19-20, 31, footnote 50; "H.O.s Litter L.A. and Biz Spotty; 'Brigham,' Tariff-Tilted, $26,000, Ditto 'Partners' with 'Divorcement,'" *Variety*, September 11, 1940, 8, http://www.archive.org/stream/variety139-1940-09#page/n63/mode/2up (accessed March 30, 2018); "Sheridan-Cagney Nice $6,000 in N.G. Memphis," *Variety*, September 25, 1940, 10, http://www.archive.org/stream/variety139-1940-09#page/n161/mode/2up (accessed March 30, 2018).

77 D'arc, "Darryl F. Zanuck's *Brigham Young*," 24-28.

78 Ibid., 26.

79 Bowman, *The Mormon People*, 184.

80 May Mann, "How a Mormon Girl, Laraine Day, Conquered Hollywood by Faith!," *Screenland*, January 1941, 20-21, 78-79, http://www.archive.org/stream/screenland42unse#page/n217/mode/2up (accessed April 5, 2018).

81 Untitled editorial, *Deseret News*, August 24, 1940, 4, quoted in D'arc, "The Saints on Celluloid," 21.

82 Fred Johnson, "A Mormon Eyes 'Brigham Young': S. F. Descendant Resents 'Vacillating' Hero," *San Francisco Bulletin*, October 9, 1940, quoted in D'arc, "The Saints on Celluloid," 22. For more on the development of Brigham Young's doubting characterization, see D'arc, "Darryl F. Zanuck's *Brigham Young*," 22-23.

83 Spencer W. Kimball, *Faith Precedes the Miracle* (Salt Lake City: Deseret Book Company, 1975), 29. See also Spencer W. Kimball, "The Gospel Vision of the Arts," *Ensign*, July 1977, 5, in which he predicts future cinematic masterpieces treating Brigham Young's story and says that only a faithful inspired Latter-day Saint could truly accomplish such a task.

84 Heber J. Grant, untitled address, *Conference Report*, October 1940, 96.

85 Carolyn Guss and Betty Stoops, "Evaluation of New Films: Driven Westward," *Educational Screen*, April 1949, 166, http://www.archive.org/stream/educationalscree27chicrich#page/166/mode/2up (accessed March 30, 2018); *Films for Classroom Use* (New York: Teaching Film Custodians, Inc., 1954), 34, http://www.archive.org/stream/filmsforclassroo00virgrich#page/34/mode/2up (accessed March 30, 2018).

86 James D'arc, "The Conversion of Hollywood's 'Brigham Young,'" *Ensign*, June 1973, https://www.lds.org/ensign/1973/06/portraits-in-miniature/the-conversion-of-hollywoods-brigham-young?lang=eng (accessed March 30, 2018); "Church News death: Dean Jagger," *Church News*, February 16, 1991, http://www.ldschurchnewsarchive.com/articles/21585/Church-News-death-Dean-Jagger.html. For more general sources on the film, see Linda Lambert's production notes, Richard Alan Nelson Collection; Nordgren, "'Brigham Young,'" 532-533, 547; Ardis E. Parshall, "'Brigham Young' (1940): 20th Century Fox Studio Publicity," *Keepapitchinin*, January 27, 2010, http://www.keepapitchinin.org/2010/01/27/"brigham-young"-1940-20th-century-fox-studio-publicity (accessed March 30, 2018); Kate John, "'I'm Glad I Wasn't Married 100 Years Ago' Says Tyrone Power," *Hollywood*, September 1940, 28-29, 38, http://www.archive.org/stream/hollywood29fawc#page/n581/mode/2up (accessed March 30, 2018); Chester James Myers, "Brigham Young as a Public Speaker," 44:6 (June 1941), 333, 377-378, which analyzes Jagger's courtroom speech from the film; Chris Hicks, "'Brigham Young': 20th Century Fox Finally Brings 1940 Fictionalized Mormon Epic – a Huge Hit Around these Parts – to Video," *Deseret News*, March 16, 1995, https://www.deseretnews.com/article/409792/BRIGHAM-YOUNG--20TH-CENTURY-FOX-FINALLY-BRINGS-1940-FICTIONALIZED-MORMON-EPIC----A-HUGE-HIT.html (accessed March 30, 2018); R. Scott Lloyd, "1940 motion picture was turning point," *Church News*, April 3, 1999, http://www.ldschurchnewsarchive.com/articles/35456/1940-motion-picture-was-turning-point.html. For information on the film's 2003 DVD release, see R. Scott Lloyd, "'Brigham Young' on special DVD," *Church News*, July 12, 2003, http://www.ldschurchnewsarchive.com/articles/44034/Brigham-Young-on-special-DVD.html; Chris Hicks, "'Brigham Young' DVD release is coup for viewers," *Deseret News*, July 18, 2003, https://www.deseretnews.com/article/997313/Brigham-Young-DVD-release-is-coup-for-viewers.html (accessed March 30, 2018); Carma Wadley, "Brigham Young: A Pioneering Film," *Deseret News*, July 18, 2003, https://www.deseretnews.com/article/997287/Brigham-Young-a-pioneering-film.html (accessed March 30, 2018).

87 "The Screen in Review; 'Madonna of the Seven Moons,' British Importation Starring Pyllis Calvert in Two Roles, Is New Bill at Winter Garden; 'Bad Bascomb,' Wherein Wallace Beery Meets With Margaret O'Brien's Simplicity, Comes for a Stay at Loew's Criterion," *New York Times*, May 23, 1946, http://movies2.nytimes.com/mem/movies/review.html?_r=2&title1=Bad%20Bascomb&title2=&reviewer=&pdate=19460523&v_id=84285&oref=slogin&oref=login (accessed May 22, 2006).

88 Ibid.

89 "Reviews of New Films: 'Bad Bascomb,'" *Film Daily*, February 8, 1946, 6, http://www.archive.org/stream/filmdaily89wids#page/n329/mode/2up (accessed March 30, 2018).

90 Nelson, untitled master's thesis draft, chapter 9, pages 3-4; "Metro Trade Show Feb. 4," *Film Daily*, January 22, 1946, 2, http://www.archive.org/stream/filmdaily89wids#page/n203/mode/2up (accessed March 30, 2018); "The Box Office Slant: Bad Bascomb," *Showmen's Trade Review,* February 9, 1946, 22, http://www.archive.org/stream/showmenstraderev4344lewi#page/n457/mode/2up (accessed March 30, 2018); "Five Pix Are Candidates For Metro 16th Block," *Film Daily*, February 20, 1946, 2, http://www.archive.org/stream/filmdaily89wids#page/n401/mode/2up (accessed March 30, 2018); "Metro's 'Anniversary 5' In Next Block of Films," *Film Daily,* March 4, 1946, 2, http://www.archive.org/stream/filmdaily89wids#page/n463/mode/2up (accessed March 30, 2018); "Bad Bascomb," *Modern Screen*, April 1946, 16, 18, http://www.archive.org/stream/modern-screen3233unse#page/n397/mode/2up (accessed March 30, 2018).

91 Patrick Ford, interview by James V. D'arc, April 25, 1979, L. Tom Perry Special Collections, Harold B. Lee Library, Brigham Young University, typescript p. 10. Ford identified *Young Mr. Lincoln* (1939) as his father's favorite "eastern."

92 Peter Bogdanovich, *John Ford* (Berkeley: University of California Press, 1978), 88.

93 For additional perspectives on the film's position in Ford's oeuvre, see Gaylyn Studlar and Matthew Bernstein, "Introduction," *John Ford Made Westerns*, ed. Gaylyn Studlar and Matthew Bernstein (Bloomington: Indiana University Press, 2001), 9; Barry Keith Grant, "John Ford and James Fennimore Cooper: The Two Rode Together," *John Ford Made Westerns*, 210; Charles J. Maland, "From Aesthete to Pappy: The Evolution of John Ford's Public Reputation," *John Ford Made Westerns*, 242; see also Nelson, "The History of Utah Film," 48.

94 Ford, interview by D'arc, 13-14.

95 Ibid., 6.

96 Joseph McBride, *Searching for John Ford: A Life* (New York: St. Martin's Press, 2001), 496.

97 Ford, interview by D'arc, 6.

98 McBride, *Searching for John Ford*, 497.

99 Ford, interview by D'arc, 7; see p. 6-10 for more on the crew's interactions with local Mormons.

100 Ibid., 14-15.

101 Charles Ramírez Berg, "The Margin as Center," *John Ford Made Westerns,* 79-82.

102 Peter Lehman, "How the West Wasn't Won: The Repression of Capitalism in John Ford's Westerns," *John Ford Made Westerns*, 132, 143, 144.

103 McBride, *Searching for John Ford*, 499.

104 Ibid., 497.

105 Ford, interview by D'arc, 33. See also Ford's entire interview with D'arc as well as Donald Dewar, interview by James V. D'arc, March 25, 1996, L. Tom Perry Special Collections, Harold B. Lee Library, Brigham Young University.

106 Nelson, untitled master's thesis draft, chapter 10, page 9. Chapter 10 beginning on page 8 contains the unedited manuscript of an interview Nelson conducted with Finney on December 18, 1973; see also chapter 7, page 4, and chapter 10, page 8-9. On page 8 Finney claims to have produced a film called *The Mormon Trail* at Grand National Films, but I haven't been able to correlate that with any known films by that title, including the 1920 western *The Mormon Trail* directed by Elliott Howe, the 1921 episode of the *Exploits of Battling Dick Hatton* serial *The Mormon Trail*, or the 1935 Warner Brothers "See America First" travelogue *The Mormon Trail*. See also "Edward Finney," *Wikipedia*, https://en.wikipedia.org/wiki/Edward_Finney (accessed March 31, 2018); "Grand National Films Inc.," *Wikipedia*, https://en.wikipedia.org/wiki/Grand_National_Films_Inc. (accessed March 31, 2018); Kevin Prusse, "Who is Leo J. Muir?," *Muir Elementary*, https://www.davis.k12.ut.us/domain/3003 (accessed March 30, 2018); Jack A. Nelson, "Newspapers, LDS," *Encyclopedia of Mormonism*, Vol. 3, ed. Daniel H. Ludlow (New York: Macmillon Publishing Company, 1992), 1011.

107 Nelson, untitled master's thesis draft, chapter 10, page 9; "The Church Moves On," *Improvement Era* 53:5 (May 1950), 358; Milton R. Hunter, "The 1950 Mormon Battalion Trek," *Improvement Era* 53:6 (June 1950), 478-479, 524-525; "The 1950 Mormon Battalion Trek," *Improvement Era* 53:7 (July 1950), 562-563.

108 Nelson, untitled master's thesis draft, chapter 10, page 10-11.

109 Ibid., chapter 10, page 10. See also Patricia King Hanson, ed., *American Film Institute Catalog of Motion Pictures Produced in the United States: Feature Films, 1941-1950, Film Entries M-Z* (Berkeley: University of California Press, 1999), 1610; "Los Angeles SUP Shows Films of Mormon Battalion Trek," *Church News*, May 14, 1950, 15; "*The Mormon Battalion* (1950)," *Film & History*, http://www.filmandhistory.org/documentary/war3/mormon.php (accessed November 3, 2016).

Notes - The Second Wave: Home Cinema

110 Gregory A. Prince and William Robert Wright, *David O. McKay and the Rise of Modern Mormonism* (Salt Lake City: University of Utah Press, 2005), 53-55; Quinn, *The Mormon Hierarchy: Extensions of Power*, 838.

111 Bowman, *The Mormon People,* 185.

112 J. Michael Hunter, "The Mormon Influence at Disney," *Mormons and Popular Culture: The Global Influence of an American Phenomenon*, Vol. 1, ed. J. Michael Hunter (Santa Barbara: Praeger Publishers, 2013), 48.

113 Prince and Wright, *David O. McKay and the Rise of Modern Mormonism,* 256-257; Orton, *More Faith Than Fear,* 90-91 (see p. 75-123 for a discussion of the stake while it remained under that name from 1927-1939); "New Lessons Mailed Out To Over 100,000: Sunday School Outline For 1934 Contains New Features," *Church News*, December 9, 1933, 1; "Mormons' Film Windfall," *Variety*, June 22, 1938, 4, http://www.archive.org/stream/variety130-1938-06#page/n173/mode/2up (accessed March 31, 2018); Edward O. Anderson, "The Los Angeles Temple," *Improvement Era* 56:4 (April 1953), 225; Quinn, *The Mormon Hierarchy: Extensions of Power*, 824; "The Church Moves On: California Sees More Stake Changes," *Improvement Era* 43:1 (January 1940), 30, about the division of the Hollywood Stake in 1939. For more information on the growth of the Church in California in this period see also Leo J. Muir, *A Century of Mormon Activities in California*, 2 vol. (Salt Lake City: Deseret New Press, 1952), (volume 1 is historical and volume 2 is biographical); Richard O. Cowan and William E. Homer, *California Saints: A 150-Year Legacy in the Golden State* (Provo: Religious Studies Center, Brigham Young University, 1996), and G. Byron Done, "The Participation of the Latter-day Saints in the Community Life of Los Angeles" (Ph.D. dissertation, University of Southern California, 1939).

114 "Bishop Macdonald Ties Knot," *Film Daily*, June 26, 1941, 6, http://www.archive.org/stream/filmdail79wids#page/n599/mode/2up (accessed March 31, 2018); "Wilford Marion Jonsson Merrill," *Find a Grave*, https://www.findagrave.com/memorial/60383575/wilford_marion-jonsson-merrill (accessed April 1, 2018); "RKO Pictures," *Wikipedia*, https://en.wikipedia.org/wiki/RKO_Pictures (accessed April 1, 2018); "Atlas Corporation," *Wikipedia*, https://en.wikipedia.org/wiki/Atlas_Corporation (accessed April 1, 2018); "Atlas Buys Block of R.K.O. from R.C.A.; Lehman Brothers Also Figure in Deal for Part of Controlling Interest," *New York Times,* October 12, 1935, https://www.nytimes.com/1935/10/12/archives/atlas-buys-block-of-rko-from-rca-lehman-brothers-also-figure-in.html (accessed April 1, 2018); "50 RKO Pictures Set Next Season," *Motion Picture Daily*, April 2, 1940, 1, 5, https://archive.org/stream/motionpicturedai47unse_0#page/n13/mode/2up (accessed April 1, 2018), this is one of many examples of Merrill being listed among RKO's officers at events and conferences, although his first name is frequently given as William, not the common Mormon name Wilford; "Wilford J. Merrill, Film Executive, 42; Vice President of RKO-Radio Had Served in World War," *New York Times*, April 11, 1941, 21, https://www.nytimes.com/1941/04/11/archives/wilford-j-merrill-film-executive-42-vice-president-of-rkoradio-had.html (accessed April 1, 2018); "An Overtaxed Heart Caused W. J. Merrill's Death; Mormon Family," *Variety*, April 16, 1941, 7, http://www.archive.org/stream/variety142-1941-04#page/n101/mode/2up (accessed April 1, 2018); Tim Gray,

"'Citizen Kane' 75th Anniversary and Orson Welles' Hell to Get the Film Released," *Variety*, May 1, 2016, http://variety.com/2016/film/awards/citizen-kane-75th-anniversary-orson-welles-history-hearst-1201750801 (accessed March 30, 2018).

115 "Wilford Marion Jonsson Merrill," *Find a Grave*, https://www.findagrave.com/memorial/60383575/wilford_marion-jonsson-merrill (accessed April 1, 2018); "RKO Pictures," *Wikipedia*, https://en.wikipedia.org/wiki/RKO_Pictures (accessed April 1, 2018); "Atlas Corporation," *Wikipedia*, https://en.wikipedia.org/wiki/Atlas_Corporation (accessed April 1, 2018); "Atlas Buys Block of R.K.O. from R.C.A.; Lehman Brothers Also Figure in Deal for Part of Controlling Interest," *New York Times*, October 12, 1935, https://www.nytimes.com/1935/10/12/archives/atlas-buys-block-of-rko-from-rca-lehman-brothers-also-figure-in.html (accessed April 1, 2018); "50 RKO Pictures Set Next Season," *Motion Picture Daily*, April 2, 1940, 1, 5, https://archive.org/stream/motionpicturedai47unse_0#page/n13/mode/2up (accessed April 1, 2018), this is one of many examples of Merrill being listed among RKO's officers at events and conferences, although his first name is frequently given as William, not the common Mormon name Wilford; "Wilford J. Merrill, Film Executive, 42; Vice President of RKO-Radio Had Served in World War," *New York Times*, April 11, 1941, 21, https://www.nytimes.com/1941/04/11/archives/wilford-j-merrill-film-executive-42-vice-president-of-rkoradio-had.html (accessed April 1, 2018); "An Overtaxed Heart Caused W. J. Merrill's Death; Mormon Family," *Variety*, April 16, 1941, 7, http://www.archive.org/stream/variety142-1941-04#page/n101/mode/2up (accessed April 1, 2018); Tim Gray, "'Citizen Kane' 75th Anniversary and Orson Welles' Hell to Get the Film Released," *Variety*, May 1, 2016, http://variety.com/2016/film/awards/citizen-kane-75th-anniversary-orson-welles-history-hearst-1201750801 (accessed March 30, 2018).

116 James V. D'arc, *When Hollywood Came to Town: A History of Moviemaking in Utah* (Layton, Utah: Gibbs Smith), 142; "Hugh R 'Denver' Brandon," *Billion Graves*, https://fi.billiongraves.com/grave/Hugh-R-Denver-Brandon/5244653 (accessed March 31, 2018).

117 LeGrand Baker, Kelly D. Christensen, Darren Bell, Thomas E. Patterson. "Rosel H. Hyde Biography," *Register of the Rosel H. Hyde Collection* (Provo: Wells Freedom Archives, Archives and Munscripts, Harold B. Lee Library, Brigham Young University, 1992), 8.

118 Ibid., 16.

119 Ibid., 5-16; Lee A. Daniels, "Rosel H. Hyde, 92, Chairman of F.C.C. Under 4 Presidents," *New York Times*, 1992, https://www.nytimes.com/1992/12/22/us/rosel-h-hyde-92-chairman-of-fcc-under-4-presidents.html (accessed April 1, 2018); "Rosel H. Hyde," *Wikipedia*, https://en.wikipedia.org/wiki/Rosel_H._Hyde (accessed April 1, 2018); Quinn, *The Mormon Hierarchy: Extensions of Power*, 820; "Nixon signs legislation banning cigarette ads on TV and radio," *This Day in History*, https://www.history.com/this-day-in-history/nixon-signs-legislation-banning-cigarette-ads-on-tv-and-radio (accessed April 2, 2018); "Merrill Post," *Broadcasting Telecasting*, October 13, 1952, 25, 48, http://www.archive.org/stream/broadcastingtele43unse_0#page/n133/mode/2up (accessed April 1, 2018); "Our Respects To: Eugene Hyde Merrill," *Broadcasting Telecasting*,

October 13, 1952, 60, 63, http://www.archive.org/stream/broadcastingtele43un-se_0#page/n169/mode/2up (accessed April 1, 2018); "Eugene H. Merrill (politician)," *Wikipedia*, https://en.wikipedia.org/wiki/Eugene_H._Merrill_(politician) (accessed April 1, 2018).

120 Gordon B. Hinckley, "Utah Mormon Girl Wins Fame in Film Capital," Church News, June 12, 1949, 10; "MCA Inc.," *Harvard Business School Baker Library Historical Collections*, https://www.library.hbs.edu/hc/lehman/company.html?company=mca_inc (accessed April 2, 2018).

121 "Chatter," *Variety*, August 5, 1936, 54, http://www.archive.org/stream/variety123-1936-08#page/n53/mode/2up (accessed April 4, 2018); Weston N. Nordgren, "Introducing Lionel Banks," *Improvement Era* 41:12 (December 1938), 708; Mann, "How a Mormon Girl, Laraine Day, Conquered Hollywood by Faith!"; "May Mann; Hollywood Columnist and Biographer," *Los Angeles Times*, April 26, 1995, http://articles.latimes.com/1995-04-26/news/mn-58998_1_biographer (accessed April 5, 2018); "May Mann," *Wikipedia*, https://en.wikipedia.org/wiki/May_Mann (accessed April 5, 2018).

122 Nordgren, "Introducing Lionel Banks," 708; "Lionel Banks," *Wikipedia*, https://en.wikipedia.org/wiki/Lionel_Banks (accessed April 4, 2018); "Lionel Banks," *Internet Movie Database*, http://www.imdb.com/name/nm0052206/?ref_=nmbio_bio_nm (accessed April 4, 2018).

123 Josie L. Bird Miller, interview, October 1989, Church History Library, The Church of Jesus Christ of Latter-day Saints, Salt Lake City.

124 Myrna Oliver, "Charles Lang; Won Oscar of 'A Farewell to Arms,'" *Los Angeles Times*, April 21, 1998, http://articles.latimes.com/1998/apr/21/local/me-41435 (accessed April 2, 2018); "Charles Bryant Lang, Cinematographer, 96," *New York Times*, May 4, 1998, https://www.nytimes.com/1998/05/04/arts/charles-bryant-lang-cinematographer-96.html (accessed April 2, 2018).

125 Hunter, "The Mormon Influence at Disney," 48-49, 52-53, 56; "Leigh Harline," *Wikipedia*, https://en.wikipedia.org/wiki/Leigh_Harline (accessed April 4, 2018); "Leigh Harline," *Internet Movie Database*, http://www.imdb.com/name/nm0363316/?ref_=nv_sr_1 (accessed April 4, 2018); Quinn, *The Mormon Hierarchy: Extensions of Power*, 828, 865. See Howard Swan, *Music in the Southwest: 1825-1950* (San Marino: Huntington Library, 1952) for more information about Mormon film composers in this period.

126 Hunter, "The Mormon Influence at Disney," 48, 55; Bob Thomas, *Disney's Art of Animation from Mickey Mouse to Beauty and the Beast* (New York: Hyperion, 1991), 11-13; "Les Clark," *Internet Movie Database*, http://www.imdb.com/name/nm0164203/?ref_=nv_sr_1 (accessed April 4, 2018); "Les Clark," *Wikipedia*, https://en.wikipedia.org/wiki/Les_Clark (accessed April 4, 2018).

127 Hunter, "The Mormon Influence at Disney," 46-48.

128 Wetzel O. Whitaker, *Looking Back: An Autobiography* (n.d., n.p.), 9-10. This is the most detailed account of how Judge acquired the name, including his

description of how Judge Nelson stood pumping their gas while holding a baby under his arm like a sack of potatoes. Initially Ferrin's taunts were accompanied by holding a pillow like it was the baby and pretending to work the gas pump with the other hand. It's also the only account that reveals this was initially upsetting to Judge, causing him to cry and hit Ferrin, although he soon came around and accepted the title.

129 Ibid., 35.

130 Ibid., 37.

131 Hunter, "The Mormon Influence at Disney," 50.

132 Mormon temple weddings are performed not just "for time," or for mortality, but "for time and all eternity," so that they are in force after death and resurrection. Joseph Smith described the authority to perform such marriages as the sealing power, which he received from the Biblical Elijah in 1836 (see D&C 110:13-16), and thus couples that are married in the temple are said to "be sealed"; children may also be sealed to parents and the thrust of Mormonism's genealogical interest is in vicariously sealing the living to all their ancestors in a continual chain (see D&C 128:8-11 and 132:7, 13-21). Sealings can only occur inside the temple, and thus whenever couples like the Whitakers are married elsewhere they may later go to a temple to be sealed.

133 Whitaker, *Looking Back*, 44.

134 Ibid., 15-45; Hunter, "The Mormon Influence at Disney," 49-50; "Judge Whitaker," *Internet Movie Database*, http://www.imdb.com/name/nm0924279/?ref_=nv_sr_1 (accessed April 4, 2018).

135 John Canemaker, *Walt Disney's Nine Old Men & the Art of Animation* (New York: Disney Editions, 2001), 56.

136 Ibid., 55-76; Hunter, "The Mormon Influence at Disney," 51-52, 54-56, 58; Thomas, *Disney's Art of Animation*, 176; Grayson Ponti, "Eric Larson," *50 Most Influential Disney Animators*, https://50mostinfluentialdisneyanimators.wordpress.com/2011/10/07/9-eric-larson (accessed April 5, 2018); Gordon B. Hinckley, "Skilled Artists Contribute—To Production of Welfare Films," Church News, November 10, 1948, 10.

137 Hunter, "The Mormon Influence at Disney," 54; see also p. 53.

138 "LDS Girl Is Disney 'Ambassador,'" *Church News*, July 9, 1966, 14.

139 See Hunter, "The Mormon Influence at Disney," in its entirety, p. 45-70.

140 J. H. Paul, "Has the Desert Failed to Blossom?," *Improvement Era* 34:5 (March 1931), 254.

141 J. Michael Hunter, "Profiles of Selected Mormon Actors," *Mormons and Popular Culture: The Global Influence of an American Phenomenon*, Vol. 1,

234-235; "Laraine Day," *Internet Movie Database*, http://www.imdb.com/name/nm0206478/?ref_=nv_sr_1 (accessed April 5, 2018); "Laraine Day," *Wikipedia*, https://en.wikipedia.org/wiki/Laraine_Day (accessed April 5, 2018); "As Hollywood Sees Laraine Day," *Improvement Era* 43:5 (May 1940), 263; "Melchizedek Priesthood: A Marvelous Girl," *The Improvement Era* 43:6 (June 1940), 360; James Hilton, "Mormon Maid: The Story of Fascinating Laraine Day," *Photoplay*, July 1940, 21, 76, http://www.archive.org/stream/photoplay52chic#page/n31/mode/2up (accessed April 5, 2018); Frederick James Smith, "Dawn of a New Day," *Silver Screen*, July 1940, 26-27, 64, 71, http://www.archive.org/stream/silverscreen10unse_0#page/n113/mode/2up (accessed April 5, 2018); Dennis Morteline, "Personal History of a Foreign Correspondent," *Hollywood*, August 1940, 34-36, 63, http://www.archive.org/stream/hollywood29fawc#page/n517/mode/2up (accessed April 5, 2018); John Crowin Burt, "She's An 'Oscar' Menace," *Hollywood*, January 1941, 21, 52-53, http://www.archive.org/stream/hollywood30fawc#page/n23/mode/2up (accessed April 5, 2018); "Exhibitors Nominate Stars of Tomorrow," *Motion Picture Herald*, August 9, 1941, 14-15, http://www.archive.org/stream/motionpictureher144unse#page/n513/mode/2up (accessed April 5, 2018); Marjorie Deen, "What's Cookin', America?," *Modern Screen,* September 1944, 98-99, http://www.archive.org/stream/modernscreen2829unse#page/n921/mode/2up (accessed April 5, 2018); Florabel Muir, "Suddenly it's love!," *Modern Screen*, April 1947, 12, 130, http://www.archive.org/stream/modernscreen3435unse#page/n399/mode/2up (accessed April 5, 2018); Ivan M. Lincoln, "Couple travels 'brick road' together," *Church News*, August 12, 1989, http://www.ldschurchnewsarchive.com/articles/18716/Couple-travels-brick-road-together.html (accessed April 5, 2018); untitled documents from the program *Postscript* by Alan Neuman of Mor-Film Fare Inc., Richard Alan Nelson Collection, L. Tom Perry Special Collections, Harold B. Lee Library, Brigham Young University, box 2, folder 6.

142 Rhonda Fleming, "I was a teen-age bride," *Modern Screen*, 80, http://www.archive.org/stream/modernscreen50unse#page/n755/mode/2up (accessed April 5, 2018).

143 Hunter, "Profiles of Selected Mormon Actors," 236; "John Crosthwaite Graham," *History.LDS.org*, https://history.lds.org/missionary/individual/john-c-graham-1839 (accessed April 5, 2018); "Rhonda Fleming," *Internet Movie Database*, http://www.imdb.com/name/nm0281766/?ref_=nv_sr_1 (accessed April 5, 2018); "Rhonda Fleming," *Wikipedia*, https://en.wikipedia.org/wiki/Rhonda_Fleming (accessed April 5, 2018); Fleming, "I was a teen-age bride," 58, 79-82; Maude Cheatham, "What It's Like Working With Bing Crosby," *Screenland*, 25, 56-57, http://www.archive.org/stream/screenland532unse#page/n113/mode/2up (accessed April 5, 2018); *Rhonda Fleming*, http://www.rhondafleming.com/home.html (accessed April 5, 2018).

144 Terry Moore, "Brighten the Corner," *Modern Screen*, May 1955, 79, http://www.archive.org/stream/modernscreen49unse#page/n421/mode/2up (accessed April 8, 2018).

145 Hunter, "Profiles of Selected Mormon Actors," 243-244; "Terry Moore," *Internet Movie Database*, http://www.imdb.com/name/nm0601930/?ref_=nv_sr_1 (accessed April 8, 2018); "Terry Moore (actress)," *Wikipedia*, https://en.wikipe-

dia.org/wiki/Terry_Moore_(actress) (accessed April 8, 2018); Kirtley Baskette, "Hollywood's Newest Sex Queen," *Modern Screen,* April 1953, 48-49, 88-91, http://www.archive.org/stream/modernscreen4647unse#page/n429/mode/2up (accessed April 8, 2018); Ben Maddox, "Terry's Technique for Dating," *Screenland plus TV-Land*, July 1953, 34-35, 60-62, http://www.archive.org/stream/screen-landplustv57unse#page/n465/mode/2up (accessed April 8, 2018); "The Inside Story," *Modern Screen*, January 1954, 4, http://www.archive.org/stream/modern-screen48unse#page/n111/mode/2up (accessed April 8, 2018); Louis Reid, "I Want to Live Like a Movie Star," *Screenland plus TV-Land*, February 1954, 34-35, 66-67, http://www.archive.org/stream/screenlandplustv58unse#page/n257/mode/2up (accessed April 8, 2018); "The Inside Story," *Modern Screen*, July 1954, 4, http://www.archive.org/stream/modernscreen48unse#page/n785/mode/2up (accessed April 8, 2018); Marva Peterson, "Terry Moore: can a glamour girl live happily at home with mama?," *Modern Screen*, July 1954, 44-46, 85-86, http://www.archive.org/stream/modernscreen48unse#page/n729/mode/2up (accessed April 8, 2018); "Don't Cry, Terry—Everybody's looking," *Modern Screen*, May 1955, http://www.archive.org/stream/modernscreen49unse#page/n767/mode/2up (accessed April 8, 2018); "What My Faith Means to Me: 8 stars tell of the presence of God in their lives," *Modern Screen*, December 1958, 34-35, 62, http://www.archive.org/stream/modernscreen52unse#page/n903/mode/2up (accessed April 8, 2018); Eunice Field, "East Gossip West," *TV Radio Mirror*, October 1962, 8-9, http://www.archive.org/stream/radiotvm00ma#page/8/mode/2up (accessed April 8, 2018); "Howard Hughes Kept Scores of Secrets, and Terry Moore Claims She Was One of Them," *People*, April 26, 1976, http://people.com/archive/howard-hughes-kept-scores-of-secrets-and-terry-moore-claims-she-was-one-of-them-vol-5-no-16 (accessed April 8, 2018); James Endrst, "Howard Hughes' widow clinging to the memories of the recluse," *Deseret News*, July 9, 2000, https://www.deseretnews.com/article/770295/Howard-Hughes-widow-clinging---to-the-memories-of-the-recluse.html (accessed April 8, 2018).

146 Jane Ardmore, "Bob Horton Fights for his Life," *TV Radio Mirror*, September 1962, 76, http://www.archive.org/stream/radiotvm00ma#page/n323/mode/2up (accessed April 9, 2018); "Robert Horton," *Internet Movie Database*, http://www.imdb.com/name/nm0395667/?ref_=nv_sr_1 (accessed April 9, 2018); "Robert Horton (actor)," *Wikipedia*, https://en.wikipedia.org/wiki/Robert_Horton_(actor) (accessed April 9, 2018).

147 Hunter, "Profiles of Selected Mormon Actors," 245; Ardis E. Parshall, "Moroni Olsen: Class Act," *Keepapitchinin*, July 26, 2009, http://www.keepapitchinin.org/2009/07/26/moroni-olsen-class-act (accessed April 5, 2018); "Moroni Olsen," *Internet Movie Database*, http://www.imdb.com/name/nm0647752/?ref_=nv_sr_1 (accessed April 5, 2018); "Moroni Olsen," *Wikipedia*, https://en.wikipedia.org/wiki/Moroni_Olsen (accessed April 5, 2018); "Lights and Shadows on the Screen," *Improvement Era* 38:11 (November 1935), 694, 719. For a full analysis of his life and career, see Crae James Wilson, "The Acting and Directing Career of Moroni Olsen," (Ph.D. dissertation, Brigham Young University, 1981). There is speculation that Olsen was a closeted homosexual and this was the cause of his bachelorhood, but no reliable sources have anything to say about it either way.

148 Hunter, "Profiles of Selected Mormon Actors," 252; "Leora Thatcher," *Utah*

History to Go, http://historytogo.utah.gov/people/utahns_of_achievement/leo-rathatcher.html (accessed April 5, 2018); "Leora Thatcher," *Internet Movie Database,* http://www.imdb.com/name/nm0857133/?ref_=nv_sr_1 (accessed April 5, 2018). See also Mavis Gay Gashler, "Three Mormon Actresses: Viola Gillette, Hazel Dawn, Leora Thatcher," (master's thesis, Brigham Young University, 1970).

149 "Frank Rasmussen: Actor, Director, Playwright, Teacher," *Brigham Young University High School,* http://www.byhigh.org/Alumni_P_to_T/Rasmussen/Frank. html (accessed April 5, 2018); "Frank Rasmussen," *Internet Movie Database,* http://www.imdb.com/name/nm0711325/?ref_=nv_sr_3 (accessed April 5, 2018). Like Olsen, Rasmussen was a lifelong bachelor.

150 Hunter, "Profiles of Selected Mormon Actors," 230; "Billy Barty," *Internet Movie Database,* http://www.imdb.com/name/nm0000863/?ref_=nv_sr_1 (accessed April 6, 2018); "Billy Barty," *Wikipedia,* https://en.wikipedia.org/wiki/Billy_Barty (accessed April 6, 2018); "Mormon Firsts," *LDS Living,* http://www.ldsliving. com/Mormon-Firsts/s/68718 (accessed April 8, 2018); *Little People of America,* http://www.lpaonline.org (accessed April 8, 2018).

151 Hunter, "Profiles of Selected Mormon Actors," 230, 241-242, 253-255; "Edwina Booth," *Internet Movie Database,* http://www.imdb.com/name/ nm0095693/?ref_=fn_al_nm_1 (accessed April 5, 2018); "Duel Takes Active Advantage of Local Interest In Player," *Motion Picture Herald,* August 15, 1931, 62, http://www.archive.org/stream/motionpictureher104unse#page/n835/ mode/2up (accessed April 5, 2018); "Robert Walker," *Internet Movie Database,* http://www.imdb.com/name/nm0908153/?ref_=fn_al_nm_2 (accessed April 5, 2018); "Robert Walker (actor, born 1918)," *Wikipedia,* https://en.wikipedia.org/ wiki/Robert_Walker_(actor,_born_1918) (accessed April 5, 2018); Kirtley Baskette, "Bob Walker," *Modern Screen,* February 1946, 32-35, 88-93, http://www. archive.org/stream/modernscreen3233unse#page/n39/mode/2up (accessed April 5, 2018); "Gordon Westcott," *Internet Movie Database,* http://www.imdb. com/name/nm0922503/?ref_=nv_sr_1 (accessed April 5, 2018); "Gordon Westcott," *Wikipedia,* https://en.wikipedia.org/wiki/Gordon_Westcott (accessed April 6, 2018); "Marie Windsor," *Internet Movie Database,* http://www.imdb. com/name/nm0934798/?ref_=nv_sr_1 (accessed April 6, 2018); "Marie Windsor," *Wikipedia,* https://en.wikipedia.org/wiki/Marie_Windsor (accessed April 6, 2018); "Jean Sullivan," *Internet Movie Database,* http://www.imdb.com/name/ nm0838130/?ref_=fn_al_nm_1 (accessed April 8, 2018); "Jean Sullivan," *Wikipedia,* https://en.wikipedia.org/wiki/Jean_Sullivan (accessed April 8, 2018); "Jean Sullivan, 79, Film Actress, Dancer and Museum Executive," *New York Times,* March 12, 2003, https://www.nytimes.com/2003/03/12/arts/jean-sullivan-79-film-ac-tress-dancer-and-museum-executive.html (accessed April 8, 2018); for more on Sullivan see the Richard Alan Nelson Collection, box 1, folder 4; "Haila Stoddard," *Internet Movie Database,* http://www.imdb.com/name/nm0831001/?ref_=nv_sr_1 (accessed April 8, 2018); "Haila Stoddard," *Wikipedia,* https://en.wikipedia. org/wiki/Haila_Stoddard (accessed April 8, 2018); Martin Cohen, "3 Jewels for Mother," *Radio TV Mirror,* November 1954, 50-51, 72-73, http://www.ar-chive.org/stream/radiotvm00macf#page/n509/mode/2up (accessed April 8, 2018); "Joi Lansing," *Internet Movie Database,* http://www.imdb.com/name/ nm0487103/?ref_=nv_sr_1 (accessed April 9, 2018); "Joi Lansing," *Wikipedia,*

https://en.wikipedia.org/wiki/Joi_Lansing (accessed April 9, 2018); "Information Booth," *Radio TV Mirror*, August 1957, 13, http://www.archive.org/stream/radiotvmir00mac#page/n121/mode/2up (accessed April 9, 2018); "Lenore Romney," *Wikipedia*, https://en.wikipedia.org/wiki/Lenore_Romney (accessed April 6, 2018).

152 "Casey Robinson," *Wikipedia*, https://en.wikipedia.org/wiki/Casey_Robinson (accessed April 9, 2018), which quotes a *New York Times* article that is no longer accessible.

153 "Casey Robinson," *Wikipedia*; "Casey Robinson," *Internet Movie Database*, http://www.imdb.com/name/nm0732452/?ref_=nv_sr_1 (accessed April 9, 2018); Tom Stempel, *Framework: A History of Screenwriting in the American Film*, third ed., (Syracuse: Syracuse University Press, 1988), 88-92. Robinson went by his middle name Casey; his first name was Kenneth.

154 "Sloan Nibley," *Internet Movie Database*, http://www.imdb.com/name/nm0629237/?ref_=nv_sr_1 (accessed April 10, 2018); "Sloan Nibley," *Wikipedia*, https://en.wikipedia.org/wiki/Sloan_Nibley (accessed April 10, 2018); "Christopher Nibley," *Internet Movie Database*, http://www.imdb.com/name/nm0629233/?ref_=nm_ov_bio_lk1 (accessed April 10, 2018).

155 "Joseph M. Newman," *Internet Movie Database*, http://www.imdb.com/name/nm0628149/?ref_=nv_sr_1 (accessed April 10, 2018); "Joseph M. Newman," *Wikipedia*, https://en.wikipedia.org/wiki/Joseph_M._Newman (accessed April 10, 2018); Ehsan Khoshbakht, "The Noir World of Joseph M. Newman," December 2, 2009, *Notes on cinematograph*, https://notesoncinematograph.blogspot.com/2009/12/noir-world-of-joseph-m-newman.html (accessed April 10, 2018)

156 D. B. Jones, "The Canadian Film Board Unit B," *New Challenges for Documentary*, ed. Alan Rosenthal (Berkeley: University of California Press, 1988), 133-147; Christopher E. Gittings, *Canadian National Cinema: Ideology, Difference, and Representation* (London: Routledge, 2002), 89-91; Jack C. Ellis and Betsy A. McLane, *A New History of Documentary Film* (Continuum: New York, 2005) 167, 245; Marc Glassman, "Remembering Colin Low (1926-2016): A Filmmaker of Vision," *POV Magazine*, http://povmagazine.com/articles/view/remembering-colin-low (accessed April 10, 2018); Etan Vlessing, "Colin Low, Canadian Imax Format Pioneer, Dies at 89," *Hollywood Reporter*, February 25, 2016, https://www.hollywoodreporter.com/news/colin-low-dead-canadian-imax-869703 (accessed April 14, 2018); "Colin Low," *Film Reference Library*, http://www.filmreferencelibrary.ca/index.asp?layid=46&csid1=43&navid=46 (accessed January 4, 2006); "Colin Low," *Northern Stars*, http://www.northernstars.ca/directorsal/low_colin.html (accessed January 4, 2006); "Colin Low," *National Film Board of Canada*, https://www.nfb.ca/directors/colin-low (accessed April 10, 2018); "Colin Low's Moving Pictures," *Montreal.com*, http://www.montreal.com/cgi/review.cgi?id=50, (accessed January 5, 2006); "Colin Low," *Internet Movie Database*, https://www.imdb.com/name/nm0522800/?ref_=nv_sr_1 (accessed April 10, 2018); "Colin Low (filmmaker)," *Wikipedia*, https://en.wikipedia.org/wiki/Colin_Low_(filmmaker) (accessed April 10, 2018); "Moving Picture," *The Photographic Historical Society of Canada*, http://www.phsc.ca/moving-picture.html, (accessed January 5, 2006); "Royalty and Canadian Film Producer," *Church News*, May 31, 1958, 2.

157 "Bar candy on the air," *Sponsor*, 56, http://www.archive.org/stream/sponsor51spon#page/n131/mode/2up (accessed April 10, 2018).

158 Nelson, "The History of Utah Film," 45; "People on the move," *Deseret News,* October 24, 1999, https://www.deseretnews.com/article/724195/People-on-the-move.html (accessed April 9, 2018); Jill Pellettieri, "Make It a Large for a Quarter More?: A short history of movie theater concession stands," *Slate*, http://www.slate.com/articles/news_and_politics/summer_movies/2007/06/make_it_a_large_for_a_quarter_more.html (accessed April 9, 2018).

159 Louella O. Parsons, "James Cruze to Do Mormon Production," *Pittsburgh Post-Gazette*, November 14, 1931, https://news.google.com/newspapers?nid=1129&dat=19311114&id=uLhRAAAAIBAJ&sjid=rWkDAAAAIBAJ&pg=3488,1678279&hl=en (accessed August 3, 2015).

160 "The trail and trails [sic] of the Mormon pioneers," *Mormon Bibliography, 1830-1930,* https://atom.lib.byu.edu/mormonbib/269 (accessed April 18, 2018); "Alleges Illegal Story Use In 'Big Trail,' Suing Fox," *Motion Picture Herald*, July 25, 1931, 53, http://www.archive.org/stream/motionpictureher104unse#page/n385/mode/2up (accessed April 18, 2018); "Producers Hauled by Writers Before Acad.," *Variety*, July 25, 1933, 4, http://www.archive.org/stream/variety111-1933-07#page/n203/mode/2up (accessed April 18, 2018); Marilyn Ann Moss, *"The Big Trail,"* *Library of Congress*, https://www.loc.gov/programs/static/national-film-preservation-board/documents/big_trail.pdf (accessed April 18, 2018); *Official Gazette of the United States Patent Office, Volume 292,* (Washington, D.C.: United States Patent Office, 1921), 256.

161 Plays became a very popular source for films with the coming of sound, but Broadway had actually been popular with Hollywood producers throughout the 1920s. For instance, the 1926 film version of *The Great Gatsby* was adapted from a 1925 play, not F. Scott Fitzgerald's novel from the same year. Richard Koszarski, *An Evening's Entertainment: The Age of the Silent Feature Pictures, 1915-1928* (Oakland: University of California Press, 1994), 106.

162 Richard H. Cracroft, "The Didactic Heresy as Orthodox Tool: B. H. Roberts as Writer of Home Literature," *Tending the Garden: Essays on Mormon Literature*, ed. Eugene England and Lavina Fielding Anderson (Salt Lake City: Signature Books, 1996), http://signaturebookslibrary.org/b-h-roberts-as-writer-of-home-literature (accessed March 2, 2018). See B. H. Roberts, "A Story of Zarahemla," *Contributor* 10:1 (November 1888), 94-101.

163 B. H. Roberts, "Corianton," *Contributor* 10:5 (March 1889), 171-176; 10:6 (April 1889), 206-210; 10:7 (May 1889), 245-248; 10:8 (June 1889), 286-290; 10:9 (July 1889), 324-330; Robert H. Malan, *B. H. Roberts: A Biography* (Salt Lake City: Deseret Book Company, 1966), 41; Truman G. Madsen, *Defender of the Faith: The B. H. Roberts Story* (Salt Lake City: Bookcraft, 1980), 296; Ardis E. Parshall, "'Corianton': Genealogy of a Mormon Phenomenon," *Keepapitchinin*, June 8, 2007, http://www.keepapitchinin.org/archives/corianton-genealogy-of-a-mormon-phenomenon (accessed June 15, 2007), also in *Times and Seasons*, June 8, 2007, http://timesandseasons.org/index.php/2007/06/corianton-genealogy-of-a-mor-

mon-phenomenon.

164 Parshall, "'Corianton': Genealogy of a Mormon Phenomenon," *Keepapitchinin*.

165 Madsen, *Defender of the Faith*, 297. In the *Improvement Era* actor and newspaperman S. A. Kenner wrote a review vigorously defending the play's liberties with the scriptural text, lauding it as a doctrinal and historical work more than for its dramatic merits. S. A. Kenner, "The Play 'Corianton,'" *Improvement Era* 5:12 (October 1902), 980-983.

166 Parshall, "'Corianton': Genealogy of a Mormon Phenomenon," *Keepapitchinin*.

167 Ibid.; Madsen, *Defender of the Faith*, 297; "'Corianton' a Failure But May Go into Hands of Eastern Manager," *Salt Lake Herald*, October 10, 1902, 8, https://chroniclingamerica.loc.gov/lccn/sn85058130/1902-10-10/ed-1/seq-8 (accessed August 2, 2015). "O U. Bean a Mormon," *Variety*, August 30, 1912, 12, http://www.archive.org/stream/variety27-1912-08#page/n169/mode/2up (accessed January 3, 2018) claims that the play had previously shown in London and it played in Philadelphia immediately before its New York premiere. For the original text of the play itself see Orestes U. Bean, *Corianton, an Aztec Romance: A Romantic Spectacular Drama, in Four Acts* (Salt Lake City: Salt Lake Theatre, 1902), https://archive.org/stream/coriantonanaztec00beanrich#page/n1/mode/2up (accessed April 3, 2011).

168 "Film to Be Made From Corianton: Great L.D.S. Choir Tabernacle Organ to Take Part," *Deseret News*, November 2, 1929, n.p., Richard Alan Nelson Collection, L. Tom Perry Special Collections, Harold B. Lee Library, Brigham Young University.

169 "Anthony C. Lund and Tracy Y. Cannon Sponsor New Movie Star!," *Deseret News*, Dec 21, 1929, "Amusement" section, page VII.

170 "Film to Be Made From Corianton," *Deseret News*, November 2, 1929.

171 "History of the Film Industry in Fort Lee," *Fort Lee Film Commission*, http://www.fortleefilm.org/history.html (accessed April 25, 2018); "World/Peerless & Metropolitan Studios," *Historical Marker Project*, https://www.historicalmarkerproject.com/markers/HM115E_world-peerless-metropolitan-studios_Fort-Lee-NJ.html (accessed April 25, 2018); "Increase in Activity Among Eastern Studios," *Film Daily*, October 26, 1930, 5, http://www.archive.org/stream/filmdailyvolume55354newy#page/1132/mode/2up (accessed April 25, 2018); "Mormon Feature Starting," *Film Daily*, October 31, 1930, 2, http://www.archive.org/stream/filmdailyvolume55354newy#page/1182/mode/2up (accessed April 25, 2018); "Mormon Picture Starts," *Film Daily*, November 2, 1930, 5, http://www.archive.org/stream/filmdailyvolume55354newy#page/1190/mode/2up (accessed April 25, 2018).

172 Untitled notice, *Deseret News*, December 14, 1929, section 3 page II c; Harry N. Blair, "Planning 'Ben Hur' Successor," *Film Daily*, November 9, 1930, 4, http://www.archive.org/stream/filmdailyvolume55354newy#page/1240/mode/2up (accessed April 25, 2018). Various coloring systems had been attempted since

the beginning of cinema in the 1890s, with a flourish of activity in the late '20s. At this point the Technicolor process, which would soon achieve industry hegemony, was not yet fully developed as it used two strips of film rather than its subsequent three-strip process. Walt Disney's animated short *Flowers and Trees* (1932) was the first film done entirely in the three-strip process, and the first live-action film that used it from beginning to end was the twenty-minute *La Cucaracha* in 1934, both well after *Corianton*'s development in 1930. John Belton, "Technology and Innovation," *The Oxford History of World Cinema*, ed. Geoffrey Nowell-Smith (Oxford: Oxford University Press, 1996), 260; Koszarski, *An Evening's Entertainment*, 128.

173 Noel A. Carmack, "'A Picturesque and Dramatic History': *George Reynolds's Story of the Book of Mormon*," *BYU Studies* 47:2 (2008), 127.

174 "Byron Parks to Film Mormons," *Film Daily*, September 10, 1930, 13, http://www.archive.org/stream/filmdailyvolume55354newy#page/738/mode/2up (accessed August 18, 2016).

175 "Anthony C. Lund and Tracy Y. Cannon Sponsor New Movie Star!," *Deseret News*, Dec 21, 1929.

176 Personal communication from Samuel Taylor to Richard Alan Nelson, December 11, 1973, Richard Alan Nelson papers, box 1 folder 2; Parshall, "'Corianton': Genealogy of a Mormon Phenomenon," *Keepapitchinin*; "Court Order Stops Sale of Stock by Corianton," *Film Daily*, May 20, 1930, 4, http://www.archive.org/stream/filmdailyvolume55152newy#page/1232/mode/2up (accessed March 30, 2018).

177 "Mormons Cool on Sect Film with Poor Sound," *Variety*, November 10, 1931, 4, http://www.archive.org/stream/variety104-1931-11#page/n67/mode/2up (accessed April 10, 2018). The audio quality of the restored digital version of the film, although it was restored, is of sufficient quality to indicate that the problem was indeed with the Playhouse Theater and not the film's recorded soundtrack.

178 Parshall, "'Corianton': Genealogy of a Mormon Phenomenon," *Times and Seasons*.

179 Eric Samuelsen, "Mormon Drama," *Mormons and Popular Culture: The Global Influence of an American Phenomenon*, Vol. 1, ed. J. Michael Hunter (Santa Barbara: Praeger Publishers, 2013), 152. For information on the 1933 Los Angeles production of *Corianton*, see "Mormon Spectacle Planned," *Variety*, May 2, 1933, 47, http://www.archive.org/stream/variety110-1933-05#page/n45/mode/2up (accessed January 2, 2017); "Spectacle Staying," *Variety*, June 20, 1933, 37, http://www.archive.org/stream/variety110-1933-06#page/n155/mode/2up (accessed January 2, 2017); "Mormon Show Set Back," *Variety*, June 27, 1933, 53, http://www.archive.org/stream/variety110-1933-06#page/n219/mode/2up (accessed January 2, 2017); "Low Cash Delays L.A.'s Mormon Spec," *Variety*, July 25, 1933, 52, http://www.archive.org/stream/variety111-1933-07#page/n251/mode/2up (accessed January 2, 2017); "Inside Stuff—Legit," *Variety*, September 5, 1933, 76, http://www.archive.org/stream/variety111-1933-09#page/n75/mode/2up

(accessed January 2, 2017).

180 Ibid.; Richard Alan Nelson Collection, box 2 folder 10.

181 My particular thanks to Kent Larson, James D'arc, and Ardis Parshall for their assistance with this material concerning *Corianton*. In particular much of the preceding draws from Parshall, "'Corianton': Genealogy of a Mormon Phenomenon," *Keepapitchinin*; Ardis E. Parshall, "*Corianton: A Story of Unholy Love*," *Keepapitchinin*, October 4, 2016, http://www.keepapitchinin.org/2016/10/04/corianton-a-story-of-unholy-love (accessed June 14, 2017); and Ardis E. Parshall, "Oh, You Bean!," *Keepapitchinin*, June 24, 2009, http://www.keepapitchinin.org/2009/06/24/oh-you-bean (accessed June 14, 2017). See also Nelson, "A History of Latter-day Saint Screen Portrayals," 187-190; Nelson, "The History of Utah Film," 31-33; Rory Swensen, "Corianton — An Unholy Review," *Times and Seasons*, September 20, 2009, http://timesandseasons.org/index.php/2009/09/corianton-an-unholy-review (accessed September 23, 2009); Michael De Groote, "1931 Mormon film about Corianton fuels laughter—but also offers some meat," *Deseret News*, March 11, 2010, http://www.deseretnews.com/article/700015499/1931-Mormon-film-about-Corianton-fuels-laughter-2-but-also-offers-some-meat.html?pg=all (accessed March 15, 2010); Andrew K. Steedman, correspondence with the Corianton Corporation, 1930-31, L. Tom Perry Special Collections, Harold B. Lee Library, Brigham Young University; Collection of Corianton film materials, L. Tom Perry Special Collections, Harold B. Lee Library, Brigham Young University. The BYU Special Collections also contains various broadside posters used to advertise the film.

182 "Early Settlement theme of Movie," *Kane County Standard*, May 12, 1939, quoted in D'arc, *When Hollywood Came to Town*, 119.

183 D'arc, *When Hollywood Came to Town*, 116-120. My thanks to D'arc for discussing details about this production with me.

184 "Sullivan Calvin 'Sully' Richardson," *The Orville Sutherland Cox Website*, http://oscox.org/richardson/sulliecrichardson.html (accessed April 28, 2018); "Register of the Sullivan Calvin Richardson Papers," *J. Willard Marriott Digital Library*, https://collections.lib.utah.edu/details?id=462968 (accessed April 28, 2018).

185 Sullivan C. Richardson, "Hole-in the-Rock," *Improvement Era* 43:1 (January 1940), 19-20.

186 Richardson, "Hole-in the-Rock," 18-21, 54-56; "The Richardson Pan-American Highway Expedition of 1941," *Geo-Mexico, the geography and dynamics of modern Mexico*, October 22, 2015, http://geo-mexico.com/?p=13322 (accessed March 27, 2018). A video of *Rough Road to Panama*, including the footage of the San Juan Expedition trail, is available online at "Rough Road to Panama," *Archive.org*, https://archive.org/details/rough_road_to_panama (accessed March 4, 2018).

187 William A. Wilson, "The Study of Mormon Folklore: An Uncertain Mirror for

Notes - The Second Wave: Home Cinema

Truth," *Dialogue: A Journal of Mormon Thought* 22:4 (Winter 1989), 108-109.

188 Barry Salt, *Film Style & Technology: History & Analysis*, 2nd ed. (Southampton, England: Starword, 1992), 205; "Classic Motion Picture Cameras," *Internet Encyclopedia of Cinematographers*, http://www.cinematographers.nl/CAMERAS1. html (accessed May 1, 2017); "Bolex," *Wikipedia*, https://en.wikipedia.org/wiki/ Bolex (accessed May 1, 2017).

189 Richard L. Evans, "Nauvoo 'Opera House' Acquired by Wilford C. Wood," *Improvement Era* 40:6 (June 1937), 356; Rosemary G. Palmer, "Nauvoo's Walking Tour," *Meridian Magazine*, July 14, 2011, https://ldsmag.com/article-1-8338 (accessed April 29, 2018); Rosemary G. Palmer, "Growing Up in Nauvoo," *Meridian Magazine*, December 22, 2009, https://ldsmag.com/article-1-5285 (accessed April 29, 2018).

190 LaMar C. Berrett, *An Annotated Catalog of Documentary-Type Materials in The Wilford C. Wood Collection* (Woods Cross, Utah: Wilford C. Wood Foundation, 1972) (pages 230-231 list Wood's film catalog); "Church receives historical films," *Church News*, January 7, 1978, 14; Julie A. Dockstader, "Foresight preserves historical legacy," *Church News*, June 1, 1991, http://www.ldschurchnewsarchive. com/articles/21644/Foresight-preserves-historical-legacy.html (accessed June 1, 2015); "Wilford C. Wood," *Wilford Wood Museum*, http://wilfordwoodmuseum. com/WilfordC.Wood.htm (accessed April 29, 2018); "Wilford C. Wood," *Mormon Wiki*, https://www.mormonwiki.com/Wilford_C._Wood (accessed April 29, 2018); Marba C. Josephson, "Church Acquires Nauvoo Temple Site," *Improvement Era* 40:4 (April 1937), 226-227; Michael De Groote, "Preserving the past: Wilford C. Wood pursued purchase of LDS Church history sites," *Deseret News*, June 11, 2009, https://www.deseretnews.com/article/705309776/Preserving-the-past-Wilford-C-Wood-pursued-purchase-of-LDS-Church-history-sites.html (accessed April 29, 2018); Quinn, *The Mormon Hierarchy: Extensions of Power*, 820, 826, 839.

191 Joseph Smith Peery, interview by Clinton D. Christensen, December 2001, Church History Library, The Church of Jesus Christ of Latter-day Saints, Salt Lake City, 6.

192 Ibid.

193 Lisle Chandler Updike Photographs 1901-1976, Arizona State University Library, Tempe, Arizona, http://www.azarchivesonline.org/xtf/view?docId=ead/ asu/updikephotos.xml (accessed May 2, 2018); Lisle Chandler Updike Historic sites footage, circa 1945, Church History Library, The Church of Jesus Christ of Latter-day Saints, Salt Lake City, https://eadview.lds.org/resource/public/collection/pdf/2518 (accessed May 2, 2018).

194 "Antoine R. Ivins," *Wikipedia*, https://en.wikipedia.org/wiki/Antoine_R._Ivins (accessed March 25, 2018); Anthony W. Ivins, "Mexico After the War," *Improvement Era* 21:8 (June 1918), 715-719. Other information about the motion picture footage shot by Ivins and many other people in this section is from the Church Library and Archives in Salt Lake City, whose holdings may be searched at https://history. lds.org/section/library?lang=eng. Information about the filmmakers and the con-

tent of their collections comes from the library catalog.

195 Jacobs, "The History of Motion Pictures," 73; "Death: LaMar Stevenson Williams," *Deseret News*, February 1, 1996, https://www.deseretnews.com/article/469029/DEATH-LAMAR-STEVENSON-WILLIAMS.html (accessed May 2, 2018); Jay Hildebrandt, "Historic home movies of 1940 Idaho Falls Temple cornerstone ceremony discovered," *Local News 8*, June 5, 2017, http://www.localnews8.com/news/idaho-falls/historic-home-movies-of-1940-idaho-falls-temple-cornerstone-ceremony-discovered/529395262 (accessed December 2, 2018).

196 "Catawba Indians," *University of South Carolina Moving Image Research Collections Digital Video Repository*, https://mirc.sc.edu/islandora/object/usc%3A54228 (accessed April 30, 2018); Jerry D. Lee, "A Study of the Influence of the Mormon Church on the Catawba Indians of South Carolina, 1882-1975," (master's thesis, Brigham Young University Dept. of History, 1976), 67; "Samuel Taylor Blue," *Wikipedia*, https://en.wikipedia.org/wiki/Samuel_Taylor_Blue (accessed May 1, 2018).

197 Rangi Parker and Emily W. Jensen, "*The Hui Tau*: Cultural Heart of the New Zealand Mission," *Pioneers in the Pacific*, ed. Grant Underwood (Provo: Religious Studies Center, Brigham Young University, 2005), 121-131.

198 Alfred G. Gunn, "Mission call sparked unusual love story," *Deseret News*, May 7, 2009, https://www.deseretnews.com/article/705301814/Mission-call-sparked-unusual-love-story.html (accessed September 2, 2012). The Church History Library also has additional film footage attributed to the Missionary Department itself for the years 1949-1958, with President McKay appearing in several of them.

199 Kuulei Bell, "A Servant of God: A Story of Jack Sing Kong," https://scholarsarchive.byu.edu/cgi/viewcontent.cgi?article=1138&context=mphs (accessed March 13, 2018).

200 Harvard S. Heath, ed., *In the World: The Diaries of Reed Smoot* (Salt Lake City: Signature Books in association with Smith Research Associates, 1997), 655.

201 George M. Easter, "New York Celebrates Coming of Elijah," *Church News*, May 16, 1936, 2.

202 Alton Morton Independent Film Collection, 1947-1968, Special Collections, J. Willard Marriott Library, University of Utah, http://archiveswest.orbiscascade.org/ark:/80444/xv53997/op=fstyle.aspx?t=i&q=0&f_names=Amateur+Cinema+League; "John Morton," *Geni.com*, https://www.geni.com/people/John-Morton/6000000026208345969 (accessed May 1, 2018); "Maria Watkins," *Geni.com*, https://www.geni.com/people/Maria-Watkins/6000000026205985642 (accessed May 2, 2018); "Filmmaker: Al Morton," *Amateur Cinema*, http://www.amateurcinema.org/index.php/filmmaker/458 (accessed May 2, 2018); "Filmmaker: Thelma Morton," *Amateur Cinema*, http://www.amateurcinema.org/index.php/filmmaker/thelma-morton (accessed May 2, 2018); "The Alton Watkins Morton Photograph Collection, 1930s-1960s," *Utah Department of Heritage and Arts* (cached), https://

Notes - The Second Wave: Home Cinema

webcache.googleusercontent.com/search?q=cache:_2fCCfsRtewJ:https://heritage.utah.gov/apps/history/findaids (accessed May 2, 2018); Al Morton, "Boy Scout Camp Filmed," *Movie Makers*, January 1945, 429, 442-444, http://www.archive.org/stream/moviemakers20amat#page/428/mode/2up (accessed November 1, 2017); Court Mann, "On the newest Reader's Digest cover, a bittersweet Utah story," *Daily Herald*, June 24, 2017 (accessed June 27, 2017).

203 "Filmmaker: Glen H. Turner," *Amateur Cinema*, http://www.amateurcinema.org/index.php/filmmaker/glen-h.-turner (accessed May 2, 2018).

204 "Utah Amateur Movie Club," *Amateur Cinema*, http://www.amateurcinema.org/index.php/club/utah-amateur-movie-club (accessed May 1, 2018); "Utah Cine Arts Club," *Amateur Cinema*, http://www.amateurcinema.org/index.php/club/utah-cine-arts-club (accessed May 1, 2018); "'Utah' Search Results," *Amateur Cinema*, http://www.amateurcinema.org/index.php/search/2e0b-42c35e67179f54ae47fb13e9d974/P0 (accessed May 2, 2018); "Filmmaker: L. Clyde Anderson," *Amateur Cinema*, http://www.amateurcinema.org/index.php/filmmaker/l.-clyde-anderson (accessed May 2, 2018); "Filmmaker: Mildred Greene," *Amateur Cinema*, http://www.amateurcinema.org/index.php/filmmaker/mildred-greene (accessed May 2, 2018); "Closeup—What amateurs are doing," *Movie Makers*, January 1932, 361, http://www.archive.org/stream/moviemakers07amat#page/360/mode/2up (accessed May 1, 2018).

205 "Angel Moroni takes flight to London Temple," *Church News*, December 19, 2008, http://www.ldschurchnewsarchive.com/articles/56309/Angel-Moroni-takes-flight-to-London-Temple.html (accessed July 1, 2014).

206 Truman Madsen, "B. H. Roberts and the Book of Mormon," *BYU Studies* 19:4 (Summer 1979), 8.

207 Heber J. Grant, untitled address, *Conference Report*, April 1930, 5.

208 "The Centennial Pageant," *Improvement Era* 33:7 (May 1930), 504.

209 *The Message of the Ages* program (Salt Lake City: Deseret News Press, 1930), George D. Pyper Collection, Special Collections, J. Willard Marriott Library, University of Utah, box 76, folder 1; see also B. H. Roberts, *A Comprehensive History of the Church of Jesus Christ of Latter-day Saints*, vol. 6 (Salt Lake City: Deseret News Press, 1930), 545. Mormons frequently spell the word "fullness," particularly in the context of "the dispensation of the fullness of times" in reference to our modern age, with only one "l," making it a form of Mormon vernacular that I have retained in direct quotes and the title of the radio series "The Fulness of Times."

210 Francis M. Gibbons, *George Albert Smith: Kind and Caring Christian, Prophet of God* (Deseret Book Company: Salt Lake City, 1990), 149; Quinn, *The Mormon Hierarchy: Extensions of Power*, 821; *The Message of the Ages* program; "The Centennial Pageant," *Improvement Era*, 460-461, 503-504; George D. Pyper, untitled address, *Conference Report*, April 1930, 167-169; George D. Pyper, "'The Message of the Ages,'" *Conference Report*, April 1930, 192-196; "Message of the Ages,"

Improvement Era 33:8 (June 1930), 551.

211 "Society Announcements: Hollywood Convention," *Journal of the Society of Motion Picture Engineers* 17:1 (July 1931), 152, http://www.archive.org/stream/journalofsociety17socirich#page/152/mode/2up (accessed March 24, 2018); "Musical Program at Photophone," *Film Daily*, July 15, 1931, 2, http://www.archive.org/stream/filmdailyvolume55657newy#page/118/mode/2up (accessed March 25, 2018); "Demonstration of RCA Sound Improvement," *Film Daily*, July 17, 1931, 2, http://www.archive.org/stream/filmdailyvolume55657newy#page/140/mode/2up (accessed March 25, 2018); William Stull, "Pathe Studio Uses New Photophone Portable Recorder," *American Cinematographer*, October 1931, 13, http://www.archive.org/stream/amri11asch#page/n477/mode/2up (accessed March 24, 2018).

212 Centennial News Bureau, James M. Kirkham Chairman, *How Centennial News was Circulated*, 1930, 112, George D. Pyper Collection, Special Collections, J. Willard Marriott Library, University of Utah, box 76, folder 7.

213 "Mormon Centennial" advertisement, *Film Daily*, May 1, 1930, 6-7, http://www.archive.org/stream/filmdailyvolume55152newy#page/1054/mode/2up (accessed June 13, 2015). See also Jacobs, "The History of Motion Pictures, 59, 67-68; Nelson, "A History of Latter-day Saint Screen Portrayals," 192-193, which indicates that, at least when he wrote in 1975, the Church History Library had a shrunken 35mm print of the film; Edwin M. Bradley, *The First Hollywood Sound Shorts, 1926-1931* (Jefferson, North Carolina: McFarland & Company, Inc., 2005), 281; "Salt Lake City," *Variety*, April 16, 1930, 86, http://www.archive.org/stream/variety98-1930-04#page/n245/mode/2up (accessed March 24, 2018); Phil M. Daly, "Along the Rialto," *Film Daily*, May 1, 1930, 9, http://www.archive.org/stream/filmdailyvolume55152newy#page/1056/mode/2up (accessed March 24, 2018).

214 "News from the Dailies About Hollywood," *Variety*, April 30, 1930, 25, http://www.archive.org/stream/variety98-1930-04#page/n353/mode/2up (accessed October 3, 2017).

215 Jacobs, "The History of Motion Pictures," 59.

216 "The Centennial Pageant," *Improvement Era*, 503-504.

217 Nelson, untitled master's thesis draft, chapter 7, page 1.

218 "Church Leaders Give Speech On Talking Film," *Church News*, October 22, 1932, 2.

219 Gordon B. Hinckley, "The Romance of a Celluloid Strip," *Church News*, May 2, 1936, 4; Anuli Akanegbu, "Vision of Learning: A History of Classroom Projectors," *EdTech*, https://edtechmagazine.com/k12/article/2013/02/vision-learning-history-classroom-projectors (accessed December 20, 2017); "History of Slide Projectors," *Ithaca College Visual Resources Collection*, https://www.ithaca.edu/hs/vrc/historyofprojectors (accessed December 19, 2017).

220 European Mission mission presidents' conference meeting minutes, Church

Notes - The Second Wave: Home Cinema

History Library, The Church of Jesus Christ of Latter-day Saints, Salt Lake City. My thanks to Ardis Parshall for providing me with both this information and the fact that near the end of his mission in New York City in 1927 B. H. Roberts assisted a missionary departing for Buenos Aires to procure a projector. It's unknown whether this was a filmstrip projector or magic lantern, however.

221 Jacobs, "The History of Motion Pictures," 60.

222 Richard O. Cowan, *The Church in the Twentieth Century* (Salt Lake City: Bookcraft, 1985), 162.

223 Jacobs, "The History of Motion Pictures," 61; "Historical chronology of The Church of Jesus Christ of Latter-day Saints," *Church News*, February 8, 2010, https://www.ldschurchnews.com/archive/2010-02-08/historical-chronology-of-the-church-of-jesus-christ-of-latter-day-saints-35088 (accessed March 14, 2017); Casey Paul Griffiths, "Joseph F. Merrill and the Transformation of Church Education," *A Firm Foundation: Church Organization and Administration*, ed. David J. Whittaker and Arnold K. Garr (Provo: Religious Studies Center, Brigham Young University, 2011), 377-402. Merrill also spent much of 1930-31 battling to save the Church's educational system from government interference, and his appointment as an apostle was also a reward for his successful service in that arena.

224 James Henry Moyle, *Mormon Democrat: The Religious and Political Memoirs of James Henry Moyle*, ed. Gene Sessions (Salt Lake City: Historical Department of the Church of Jesus Christ of Latter-day Saints, 1975), 300.

225 Gordon B. Hinckley, *James Henry Moyle: The Story of a Distinguished American and an Honored Churchman* (Salt Lake City: Deseret Book Company, 1951), 325.

226 Moyle, *Mormon Democrat*, 302.

227 Ibid., 302-309. Henry D. Moyle later donated a copy of this film to the Church Historian's Office.

228 Hinckley, *James Henry Moyle*, 325-329; Peery, interview by Clinton D. Christensen, 1-5; "James H. Moyle, Utah Leader, Dies," *Deseret News*, February 20, 1946, http://wiki.nycldshistory.com/w/1946-02-20-Deseret_News-James_H._Moyle,_Utah_Leader,_Dies (accessed August 3, 2017); Forace Green, "The Eastern States Mission," Improvement Era 36:9 (July 1933), 518-520.

229 "Enterprising Elder Uses Film Tour To Foster Interest in Book of Mormon," *Church News*, May 1, 1949, 15; "John Goddard (adventurer)," *Wikipedia*, https://en.wikipedia.org/wiki/John_Goddard_(adventurer) (accessed May 1, 2018); Tiffany Kelly, "'Real life Indiana Jones,' adventurer John Goddard dies at 88," *Los Angeles Times*, May 20, 2013, http://www.latimes.com/tn-vsl-0523-real-life-indiana-jones-adventurer-john-goddard-dies-at-88-story.html (accessed May 1, 2018).

230 Mark B. Garff, "The Danish Mission," *Improvement Era* 35:7 (May 1932), 401, 415.

231 "Lantern Slide Lectures Are Popular in Mission," *Church News*, March 23, 1935, 8; "Motion Pictures Of Early Israel To be Exhibited," *Church News*, April 28, 1934, 5.

232 George M. McCune, *Gordon B. Hinckley: Shoulder for the Lord* (Salt Lake City: Hawkes Publishing Inc., 1996), 193.

233 This is according to McCune, *Gordon B. Hinckley*, 196. According to Sheri Dew, *Go Forward with Faith: The Biography of Gordon B. Hinckley*, (Salt Lake City: Deseret Book Company, 1996), 61, Widtsoe was traveling on the continent at the time and Hinckley was received by British Mission President James H. Douglas instead. Widtsoe's enthusiasm for new media such as motion pictures was mentioned in Chapter 1 in connection with salvation history. In a statement from this time, just before being released as European Mission President, he wrote: "Tracting has been a valuable means of spreading gospel news. It has also been of real help in building young missionaries into spiritual maturity. Now, however, other helps must come. The radio, the phonograph, the motion picture have come to benefit humanity. The tracting age is approaching its end in missionary work as in most life concerns. The old cheaply-printed tract is left untouched; the present world wants its reading matter in brief, concise sentences, artistically printed. As we move over the earth with our message, we need more and more to use all of these devices, as they come along. I pleaded often that President Grant would make a record of a sermon, or part of one, so that the Europeans might have the inspiration that would come from his living voice. These things no doubt will come, for the Church of Christ is always progressing without violating the fundamentals of our faith." John A. Widtsoe, *In a Sunlit Land: The Autobiography of John A. Widtsoe* (Salt Lake City: Deseret News Press, 1952), 202-203.

234 McCune, *Gordon B. Hinckley*, 193-196; Dew, *Go Forward with Faith*, 66-72.

235 Dew, *Go Forward with Faith*, 77.

236 Alan K. Parrish, *John A. Widtsoe: A Biography* (Salt Lake City: Deseret Book Company, 2003), 519.

237 Heber J. Grant, untitled address, *Conference Report*, October 1930, 3.

238 Parrish, *John A. Widtsoe*, 520.

239 Ibid., 520.

240 Today the "film sermons" are held in the John A. Widtsoe Collection at the Church History Library, The Church of Jesus Christ of Latter-day Saints, Salt Lake City. For the Book of Mormon film, see Ora F. Pate, "Suggested Material for a Book of Mormon Lecture" and "Suggestions for Detailed Arrangement of Book of Mormon Film" in the Widtsoe Collection, as well as "Book of Mormon lecture material" in the David A. Smith Collection, Church History Library, The Church of Jesus Christ of Latter-day Saints, Salt Lake City, box 3 folder 5.

241 Parrish, *John A. Widtsoe*, 526; see p. 520-526.

Notes - The Second Wave: Home Cinema

242 Ibid., 526.

243 Ibid., 526.

244 Dew, *Go Forward with Faith*, 83-85; McCune, *Gordon B. Hinckley*, 208-209; Parrish, *John A. Widtsoe*, 526-527; Cowan, *The Church in the Twentieth Century*, 163.

245 Dew, *Go Forward with Faith*, 87.

246 Ibid., 88, 93, 102-103; Parrish, *John A. Widtsoe*, 527.

247 Dew, *Go Forward with Faith,* 89.

248 Ibid., 89-90.

249 Jacobs, "The History of Motion Pictures," 64.

250 Ibid., 63-65; Dew, *Go Forward with Faith*, 86-105; Parrish, *John A. Widtsoe*, 528; McCune, *Gordon B. Hinckley*, 225-226; Glynn Bennion, "New Ways Of Prose-lyting And The Reason Therefore," *Church News*, January 25, 1936, 1, 7; "Salt Lake Temple," *Improvement Era* 40:4 (April 1937), 233-238; "Film Strip Depicts Early Civilization," *Church News*, January 26, 1949, 4; "Stick of Joseph: Book of Mormon Film Released to Missions," *Church News*, October 24, 1951, 1, 3.

251 Hinckley, "The Romance of a Celluloid Strip," 4.

252 J. Shelby Arrigona, "Success with 'Visual Aid' in the California Mission," *Improvement Era* 41:7 (July 1938), 421. Similar success was reported in Philadelphia in 1944: L. Marsen Durham, "'The Philadelphia Story' New Style," *Improvement Era* 47:4 (April 1944), 212.

253 Joseph F. Merrill, "The Missionary and His Tools," *Improvement Era* 38:12 (December 1935), 730-731.

254 Quentin S. Hale, ""L.D.S. Leaders Show Films Aboard Ship," *Church News*, January 5, 1946, 8 (see p. 6 also); B. Grant Pugh, "Interned Italians Hear Mis-sionary: Church Music And Films Cheer Men In Detention Camp," *Church News*, December 13, 1941, 1, 7.

255 Dew, *Go Forward with Faith*, 99.

256 Ibid., 101 (see p. 94-95, 97-101); McCune, *Gordon B. Hinckley*, 222-224, 228; Heber G. Wolsey, "The History of Radio Station KSL from 1922 to Television," (Ph.D. dissertation, Michigan State University, 1967), 7, 10-11, 18-19; "Church Records Historical Dramas: Plays To Be Heard Over Radio," *Church News,* November 5, 1938, 1; "Mormon Test," *Broadcasting*, December 15, 1938, 71, http://www.archive.org/stream/broadcasting15unse#page/70/mode/2up (accessed November 2, 2016); "Radio Dramatizations Bring Many Comments," *Church News*, February 11, 1939, 2; Gordon B. Hinckley, "Dramatic Mormon History *On the Air*: Great Charac-ters of History Will Be Given Voice," *Church News*, October 4, 1941, 1-2.

257 Donald D. Glad, "A 'Mormon' Reading Room Inside and Out," *Improvement Era* 39:3 (March 1936), 166-167; Marba C. Josephson, "Progress in the Missions," *Improvement Era* 40:4 (April 1937), 218-221.

258 Marshall, "Exhibitions and World's Fairs," *Encyclopedia of Mormonism*, 479-480; Cowan, *The Church in the Twentieth Century*, 165-167; Quinn, *The Mormon Hierarchy: Extensions of Power*, 821; Dew, *Go Forward with Faith*, 95-97; McCune, *Gordon B. Hinckley*, 230; "The Church Moves On," *Improvement Era* 42:2 (February 1939), 97, 100; "Church Has Popular Exhibit At Exposition: Miniature Of Tabernacle Is Interesting Center," *Church News*, March 11, 1939, 7; Gordon B. Hinckley, "Church Contacts Over Million Persons Through Golden Gate Exposition Exhibit," *Church News*, December 2, 1939, 5; "The Church Moves On: Church Exhibit at Coast Fair Continues," *Improvement Era* 43:6 (June 1940), 351.

259 Jacobs, "The History of Motion Pictures," 65; "The Purpose And Values Of A Mission: A Missionary Dramatization: Presented by B.Y.U. Faculty Members and Students," *Church News*, February 5, 1938, 4.

260 "Missionaries Succeed With New Picture Story Of Mormonism," *Church News*, July 11, 1936, 1, 8.

261 Frank S. Wise, interview by Gordon Irving, December 1980-January 1981, James Moyle Oral History Program, Historical Department of The Church of Jesus Christ of Latter-day Saints, Church History Library, The Church of Jesus Christ of Latter-day Saints, Salt Lake City, 1-17, 21-22; Jacobs, "The History of Motion Pictures," 64-65, 69-70; "Technicolor Tells Utah Story," *Church News*, May 10, 1941, 7; "Photo Expert Helps Draft Color for Mission Service," *Church News*, June 21, 1941, 2; "Historic Highlights of Mormonism: New Lecture Compiled For Use Of Missionaries," *Church News*, January 24, 1942, 1, 4; "The Church Moves On: New Illustrated Lecture Released to Missionaries," *Improvement Era* 45:3 (March 1942), 158; "One Camera; Lots of Nerve," *Church News*, August 19, 1967, 11. In McCune, *Gordon B. Hinckley*, 226, he claims that the Radio, Publicity and Mission Literature Committee produced a 16mm travelogue called *Scenic Utah* in 1937, with a re-release in 1942. No other documentation on such a production has been found, however, although it's possible it may be referring to Wise's *Western Wonderlands*. Some sources have implied that *Western Wonderlands* is a motion picture, in fact, but in his interview with Gordon Irving Wise himself seems to indicate that it was a filmstrip or slideshow, which is how I have portrayed it here.

262 McCune, *Gordon B. Hinckley*, 233-243; Cowan, *The Church in the Twentieth Century*, 289-290.

263 "Movie Shorts Challenge Tobacco Advertisers," *Church News*, April 4, 1951, 9.

264 Parrish, *John A. Widtsoe*, 531. For additional information on this era and Hinckley's work in particular, see Matthew Porter Wilcox, "The Published Writings of Young Gordon B. Hinckley," *BYU Religious Education 2010 Student Symposium* (Provo: Religious Studies Center, Brigham Young University, 2010), 35-48; Rob Taber, "The Church Enters the Media Age: Joseph F. Merrill and Gordon B. Hinck-

ley," *Journal of Mormon History* 35:4 (Fall 2009), 218-232.

265 Juanita Brooks, "Whose Business is Recreation?," *Improvement Era* 41:10 (October 1938), 596-597; "The Church Moves On: Adams Ward Opens Recreation Center," *Improvement Era* 43:12 (December 1940), 734.

266 "Course of Study: Motion Pictures," *Improvement Era* 33-41:1 (November 1929), 78.

267 Jeremy Bonner, "State, Church and Moral Order: The Mormon Response to the New Deal, in Orem, Utah, 1933-40," *Journal of Mormon History* 28:2 (Fall 2002), 100.

268 Ibid., 101.

269 Wise, interview by Gordon Irving, 33.

270 Bonner, "State, Church and Moral Order," 81-103; Lorna Maycock and Ruth Peterson, "Recreation," *It Happened in Orem: A Bicentennial History of Orem, Utah* (Orem, Utah: City of Orem, 1978), 115-121. Church leaders then as now admonished members to avoid inappropriate activities such as watching movies on the Sabbath. In Salt Lake City in 1936 an MIA conference apparently focused on Sabbath observance enough to frighten local exhibitors that they were going to lose revenue. They watched the situation closely, but thankfully—for them—the Mormon youth seemed to disregard the counsel and continue patronizing theaters on Sundays. "Mormon Pan on Sundays Worries Utah Show Biz," *Variety*, July 29, 1936, 26, https://archive.org/stream/variety123-1936-07#page/n289/mode/2up (accessed May 23, 2018). For a contemporary opinion, see John A. Widtsoe, "Evidences and Reconciliations: Should We Go to Movies on Sunday?," *The Improvement Era* 43:8 (August 1940), 481, 511.

271 A. Hamer Reiser, oral history, interviews by William G. Hartley, 1974, James Moyle Oral History Program, Historical Department of The Church of Jesus Christ of Latter-day Saints, Church History Library, The Church of Jesus Christ of Latter-day Saints, Salt Lake City, 98; Wise, interview by Gordon Irving, 18.

272 David A. Smith, "Melchizedek Priesthood: The Talkie Goes to Church," *Improvement Era* 36:6 (April 1933), 359; "Mormon Club Houses as Theatres in Direct Opposition to Utah's Showmen," *Variety*, February 16, 1932, 1, https://archive.org/stream/variety105-1932-02#page/n111/mode/2up (accessed February 2, 2018).

273 Jacobs, "The History of Motion Pictures," 63 (see also p. 62); Reiser, interviews by William G. Hartley, 86-89; Smith, "Melchizedek Priesthood: The Talkie Goes to Church," 359. Mormons were sufficiently involved in film exhibition that in 1936 *Variety* reported that two Mormon "clans" in St. Johns, Arizona were feuding over audiences. "Ariz. Mormonites Use Theatres as Weapons in Feud," *Variety*, March 4, 1936, 43, https://archive.org/stream/variety121-1936-03#page/n41/mode/2up (accessed May 23, 2018).

274 Smith, "Melchizedek Priesthood: The Talkie Goes to Church," 359; "Church Tests Out Teaching By Films: Talking Pictures Will Be Used by Sunday Schools,"

Church News, July 2, 1932, 3.

275 "Free Circulating Library Ready for Sunday School Reference," *Church News*, July 23, 1932, 2; "Sunday Schools Plan Libraries For All Districts," *Church News*, October 8, 1932, 2; "Church Leaders Give Speech on Talking Film," *Church News*; "Film Projectors Made Available: Sunday School Union To Rent Apparatus Upon Request," *Church News*, November 12, 1932, 2; "Sunday School Notes: Films Available to Stake Boards," *Church News*, March 4, 1933, 3; "Visual Instruction In Sunday Schools To Be Emphasized: General Board Has Permanent Exhibit to Aid," *Church News*, September 9, 1933, 1; "Visual Teaching Exhibit Attracts Wide Atten-tion: Sunday School Union Display Open to Public Daily," *Church News,* November 25, 1933, 2; "New Lessons Mailed Out To Over 100,000: Sunday School Outline For 1934 Contains New Features," *Church News*, December 9, 1933, 1.

276 "Melchizedek Priesthood: The Sunday School Picture," *Improvement Era* 43:1 (January 1940), 38; "Melchizedek Priesthood: Report from Grant Stake," *Improvement Era* 43:10 (October 1940), 614; "Melchizedek Priesthood: Weber Stake Record," *Improvement Era* 43:12 (December 1940), 745; "'You Can Teach It Better With Pictures,'" *Church News*, January 10, 1951, 8; "Slide Films To Improve S.S. Teaching," *Church News*, July 11, 1951, 6; "Saviors on Mt. Zion: Sunday School Board Produces Third Film," *Church News*, July 25, 1951, 6. For more on the Sun-day School's use of filmstrips, see "Sunday School Faculty Meetings Improved: Bonneville Stake Superintendency Inaugurates Two-Point Program," *Church News*, March 10, 1945, 6; M. Lynn Bennion, "Teaching with Pictures," *Improvement Era* 50:3 (March 1947), 153; "Film Strips Prepared To Aid S.S. Teachers," *Church News*, February 7, 1951, 5.

277 Wise, interview by Gordon Irving, 23. See also A. Hamer Reiser, "...And So the Movies!," *Improvement Era* 51:6 (June 1948), 377, in which he says that the war trained them in the use of educational films.

278 Jack C. Ellis and Betsy A. McLane, *A New History of Documentary Film* (Con-tinuum: New York, 2005) 179.

279 Jacobs, "The History of Motion Pictures," 70-71; Reiser, interviews by William G. Hartley, 90; Wise, interview by Gordon Irving, 32-33; "Sound, Motion Picture Equipment Now Made Available," *Church News,* February 3, 1945, 3; Frank S. Wise, "The 'EYES' have it," *Improvement Era* 52:1 (January 1949), 20-21, 58; Clarence S. Barker, "Conference Talks To Be Recorded on Sound Film," *Church News*, April 9, 1950, 2; "Basic Equipment for Ward Movies / Now! Two Great Film-osounds," *Improvement Era* 56:3 (March 1953), 130-131; "Sound movies—teach fast, effectively!," *Improvement Era* 56:3 (March 1953), 131; "They learn faster, remember longer with sound movies!," *Improvement Era* 56:5 (May 1953), 339; "Now you can make low-cost sound movies," *Improvement Era* 56:8 (August 1953), 583; "Two Kinds of Bell & Howell Specialists to serve you and your motion picture program," *Improvement Era* 56:11 (November 1953), 843.

280 "Course of Study: Motion Pictures," *Improvement Era*, 76-80; "Motion Pictures," *Improvement Era* 33:8 (June 1930), 576-577, 582; "Community Ac-tivity Dept. Committee: Motion Pictures," *Improvement Era* 34:5 (March 1931),

293; "Community Activity Dept. Committee: Motion Pictures," *Improvement Era* 34:6 (April 1931), 348; "Community Activity Dept. Committee: Motion Pictures," *Improvement Era* 34:7 (May 1931), 419; "Motion Pictures," *Improvement Era* 35:5 (March 1932), 297-298; "Lights and Shadows on the Screen," *Improvement Era* 35:6 (April 1932), 350-351; Dalton Trumbo, "Glancing Through: Brief Summary of Magazine Articles: Frankenstein in Hollywood," *Improvement Era* 35:6 (April 1932), 353-354; "Let's Talk It Over," *Improvement Era* 35:6 (April 1932), 383; "Lights and Shadows on the Screen," *Improvement Era* 35:7 (May 1932), 420-421; "Motion Pictures," *Improvement Era* 35:8 (June 1932), 512; Walter P. Cottam, "Seeing Through a Glass Eye," *Improvement Era* 35:10 (August 1932), 596-597; "Lights and Shadows on the Screen," *Improvement Era* 35:12 (October 1932), 740-741; "Lights and Shadows on the Screen," *Improvement Era* 36:1 (November 1932), 40-41; "Let's Talk It Over: Movies Are Not All Bad," *Improvement Era* 36:1 (November 1932), 64; "Lights and Shadows on the Screen," *Improvement Era* 36:2 (December 1932), 100; "M Men-Gleaners," *Improvement Era* 36:3 (January 1933), 180; "Lights and Shadows on the Screen," *Improvement Era* 36:4 (February 1933), 231; W. Earl Lyman, "How to Make Good Pictures Indoors," *Improvement Era* 36:5 (March 1933), 281; "Lights and Shadows on the Screen," *Improvement Era* 36:5 (March 1933), 298; "Lights and Shadows on the Screen," *Improvement Era* 36:6 (April 1933), 358; "Lights and Shadows on the Screen," *Improvement Era* 36:8 (June 1933), 490, 496; "Lights and Shadows on the Screen," *Improvement Era* 36:13 (November 1933), 803-804; "Lights and Shadows on the Screen," *Improvement Era* 36:14 (December 1933), 862, 891-892; "Your Page and Ours," *Improvement Era* 36:14 (December 1933), 897 (inside back cover); "Lights and Shadows on the Screen," *Improvement Era* 37:2 (February 1934), 101; "Lights and Shadows on the Screen," *Improvement Era* 37:3 (March 1934), 168; "Lights and Shadows on the Screen," *Improvement Era* 37:4 (April 1934), 226; "Lights and Shadows on the Screen," *Improvement Era* 37:5 (May 1934), 290; Elsie Talmage Brandley, "Editorial: Moving Pictures—What About Them?," *Improvement Era* 37:6 (June 1934), 350-351; "Lights and Shadows on the Screen," *Improvement Era* 37:6 (June 1934), 360; "Lights and Shadows on the Screen," *Improvement Era* 37:7 (July 1934), 425; Elsie Talmage Brandley, "Editorial: More Talk About the Talkies," *Improvement Era* 37:8 (August 1934), 478-479; Your Page and Ours: Are We Working Toward Better Films?," *Improvement Era* 37:8 (August 1934), 512; "Lights and Shadows on the Screen," *Improvement Era* 37:9 (September 1934), 548; "Lights and Shadows on the Screen," *Improvement Era* 37:10 (October 1934), 610, 612; "Lights and Shadows on the Screen," *Improvement Era* 37:11 (November 1934), 674; "Lights and Shadows on the Screen," *Improvement Era* 37:12 (December 1934), 738; "Lights and Shadows on the Screen," *Improvement Era* 38:1 (January 1935), 34; "Lights and Shadows on the Screen," *Improvement Era* 38:2 (February 1935), 100; "Lights and Shadows on the Screen," *Improvement Era* 38:3 (March 1935), 157; "Lights and Shadows on the Screen," *Improvement Era* 38:5 (May 1935), 308; "Lights and Shadows on the Screen," *Improvement Era* 38:6 (June 1935), 370; "Lights and Shadows on the Screen," *Improvement Era* 38:8 (August 1935), 505; "Lights and Shadows on the Screen," *Improvement Era* 38:10 (October 1935), 622; "Lights and Shadows on the Screen," *Improvement Era* 38:11 (November 1935), 694, 719; "Lights and Shadows," *Improvement Era* 38:12 (December 1935), 760; Henry Maxfield, "He Made 'Em Like Spinach," *Improvement Era* 39:1 (January 1936), 26-27, 34, this is about the comic strip Popeye but exhibits the same characteristics of culture critique as the Era's film-related articles; "Screenings," Improvement Era 39:1 (January 1936), 36; "Screenings," *Improvement Era* 39:2 (February 1936), 104; "Screenings," *Improvement Era* 39:3 (March 1936), 168; Robert M. Hyatt, "The Movies are Rewriting History," *Improvement Era* 40:1 (January 1937), 30-31; "Ten Best Moving Pictures of 1936," *Improvement Era* 40:2 (February 1937), 120; Glynn Bennion, "Forty Years of Change," *Improvement Era* 40:11 (November 1937), 672-675, 726; "Homing: Here's How—Popular Screen Actress Advocates Milk for Beauty," *Improvement Era* 42:8 (August 1939), 485, on Bette Davis; Alice Pardoe West, "Beauty Builder a la Hollywood," *Improvement Era* 44:8 (August 1941), 464, 488; "Motion Pictures that Advertise Liquor," *Improvement Era* 45:7 (July 1942), 422-423.

281 "Church Council to Appraise Films," *Church News*, January 3, 1948, 4. The mainstream press, not inaccurately, characterized the Council as "a censorship board" which would control "what pictures can and cannot be shown." "Mormon Church Has New Censor Board," *Motion Picture Daily*, January 23, 1948, 8, https://archive.org/stream/motionpicturedai63unse#page/n113/mode/2up (accessed May 23, 2018).

282 "Church Film 'Screenings,'" *Church News*, May 30, 1948, 4.

283 Marba C. Josephson, "...And So the Movies!," *Improvement Era* 51:1 (January 1948), 31.

284 Marba C. Josephson, "...And So the Movies!: On Being True to Life," *Improvement Era* 51:3 (March 1948), 134.

285 Josephson, "...And So the Movies!," *Improvement Era* 51:1, 25, 31; Marba C. Josephson "...And So the Movies!: Humor," *Improvement Era* 51:2 (February 1948), 70-71; "The Church Moves On: L.D.S. Film Council," *Improvement Era* 51:2 (February 1948), 115; Josephson, "...And So the Movies!: On Being True to Life," 134, 164; Marba C. Josephson, "...And So the Movies!: Plot and Theme," *Improvement Era* 51:4 (April 1948), 198; "Film Council at Work—Group Catches Up On Screen Backlog," *Church News*, May 23, 1948, 4; "Church Film 'Screenings,'" *Church News*, May 30, 1948, 4; Reiser, "...And So the Movies!," *Improvement Era*, 51:6. In addition to Reiser and Hinckley the initial Council members were William E. Stoker, Robert Murray Stewart, J. LeRoy Linton, Willard R. Smith, Frank M. Openshaw, Mary Grant Judd, N. Blaine Winters, Lynn McKinlay, Gaylen S. Young, J. Holman Waters, Emily H. Bennett, George W. Ashton, and Wayne F. Richards. Josephson apparently wasn't actually on the committee, despite the close relationship between her work and theirs. For additional articles on Mormon thought on film in the Second Wave, see Franklin S. Harris, Jr., "Exploring the Universe," *Improvement Era* 43:4 (April 1940), 195, about high-speed cinematography; Edith Russell, "A Woman's Point of View," *Keepapitchinin*, June 18, 2017 (originally from the August 1945 Millennial Star), http://www.keepapitchinin.org/2017/06/18/edith-russell-associate-editor-15 (accessed May 2, 2018), in which she recommends seeing Laurence Olivier's Henry V (1944).

286 Wise, interview by Gordon Irving, 23.

Notes - The Second Wave: Home Cinema

287 Reiser, "...And So the Movies!," *Improvement Era* 51:6, 377.

288 "Film Screening Council Offers Projection Training Course," *Church News*, August 22, 1948, 12; "Church Council Sponsors Scouting Films," *Church News*, August 8, 1948, 12; "Unusual Story on Tithing Available on Film," *Church News*, September 1, 1948, 10; "Wheat Story Film Secured for Wards At Reduced Prices," *Church News*, October 27, 1948, 4.

289 Ernest L. Wilkinson and Leonard J. Arrington, ed., *Brigham Young University: The First One Hundred Years*, Vol. 3 (Provo: Brigham Young University Press, 1976), 656.

290 W. W. Henderson, "Church Schools and Seminaries: B.Y.U. Establishes Visual Instruction Service," *Improvement Era* 37:1 (January 1934), 40.

291 Wilkinson & Arrington, *Brigham Young University*, 657-658; "History of the Division of Instructional Services, no author, in the office of Darrel J. Monson, included in draft of 'A CITY ON A HILL (Auxiliary and Special Services)' first draft by R. E. Bennett, February 7, 1975," University Archives 566, box 122, folder 2, L. Tom Perry Special Collections, Harold B. Lee Library, Brigham Young University, 44; Reiser, interviews by William G. Hartley, 93-94, 99; Josephine Hoffman, "Brigham Young University Extends Service," *Educational Screen*, November 1933, 249, https://archive.org/stream/educationalscree12chicrich#page/248/mode/2up (accessed May 23, 2018); Ellsworth C. Dent, "Visual Instruction Meeting Well Attended," *Educational Screen*, November 1933, 253, https://archive.org/stream/educationalscree12chicrich#page/252/mode/2up (accessed May 23, 2018); "Visual Instruction Emphasized During Leadership Week," *Educational Screen*, February 1934, 43, http://www.archive.org/stream/educationalscree13chicrich#page/42/mode/2up (accessed May 23, 2018); "Do You Know About Off-Campus Services of the Church University?," *The Improvement Era* 43:10 (October 1940), 582.

292 "Parents to Hear Visual Ed Talk," *Daily Herald*, January 2, 1936, https://www.newspapers.com/newspage/14775530 (accessed May 2, 2018); "Harold B. Lee Library. Learning Resource Centers Dept.," *Harold B. Lee Library*, https://byuorg.lib.byu.edu/index.php/Harold_B._Lee_Library._Learning_Resource_Centers_Dept. (accessed March 13, 2017); Holly Heap, "Library opens new addition," *Daily Universe*, August 10, 1999, http://universe.byu.edu/1999/08/10/library-opens-new-addition (accessed March 13, 2017).

293 Mary Lynn Bahr, "Varsity Theatre Stops Editing," *BYU Magazine*, Winter 1998, 9; Eric D. Snider, "Varsity Theatre to stop editing movies," *Daily Universe*, July 31, 1998, http://universe.byu.edu/1998/07/31/varsity-theatre-to-stop-editing-movies (accessed March 13, 2017); Jeffrey P. Haney, "BYU closing movie theater for first time in 30 years," *Deseret News*, April 5, 2000, B4, or https://www.deseretnews.com/article/753251/BYU-closing-movie-theater-for-first-time-in-30-years.html (accessed May 23, 2018); "International Cinema," *Brigham Young University*, http://ic.byu.edu (accessed March 13, 2017).

294 Reiser resigned from Deseret Book in response to criticism that he wasn't fulfilling his mandate for the company but was merely attempting to milk a com-

fortable position for personal gain. He then spent some time in private business in Idaho before David McKay indicated his continued trust in him by calling him to preside over the British Mission. Reiser, interviews by William G. Hartley, 199.

295 Heath, *In the World: The Diaries of Reed Smoot*, 662. The specific day was September 26, 1927. Incidentally in 1932 one sales representative tried to convince Church officials to license *The King of Kings* for distribution among the wards, but evidently nothing came of this. "Chatter: Salt Lake City," *Variety*, June 7, 1932, 46, https://archive.org/stream/variety106-1932-06#page/n45/mode/2up (accessed March 10, 2018).

296 For *Citizen Kane* see David O. McKay, diary, December 1, 1941, David Oman McKay Papers, 1897-1983, Special Collections, J. Willard Marriott Library, University of Utah. My thanks to John P. Hatch for alerting me to this item. For *A Man Called Peter*, see David O. McKay, untitled address, *Conference Report*, April 1955, 3; "Plants 'Robin Hood' Archery Tournament," *Motion Picture Herald*, July 23, 1938, 67, http://www.archive.org/stream/motionpictureher132unse#page/n315/mode/2up (accessed April 30, 2018). See also Elder Richard R. Lyman's published endorsement of a film of the Oberammergau Passion Play, Richard R. Lyman, "'The Passion Play'—Movie," *Improvement Era* 35:9 (July 1932), 571, and future General Authority G. Homer Durham's essay on the film *The Searching Wind* (1946), G. Homer Durham, "These Times," *Improvement Era* 49:10 (October 1946), 617.

297 "To Show 'Union Pacific' In the Mormon Tabernacle," *Film Daily*, December 28, 1938, 7, http://www.archive.org/stream/filmdail74wids#page/n603/mode/2up (accessed May 1, 2018); Sam Shain, "Insider's Outlook," *Motion Picture Daily*, January 3, 1939, 2, http://www.archive.org/stream/motionpicturedai-45unse#page/n9/mode/2up (accessed May 1, 2018); "'U.P.' Preview First Pic in Mormon Temple," *Variety*, January 4, 1939, 6, http://www.archive.org/stream/variety133-1939-01#page/n5/mode/2up (accessed May 1, 2018); "Film in Tabernacle," *Motion Picture Herald*, January 14, 1939, 58, http://www.archive.org/stream/motionpictureher134unse#page/n171/mode/2up (accessed May 1, 2018); "Morning Railroad Fete Will Recall Pioneer Days, Wood Burner Will Pull into Station," *Salt Lake Tribune*, April 25, 1939, 9; "Omaha Relaxes from Strain Of 'Union Pacific' Opening," *Motion Picture Daily*, May 1, 1939, 1, http://www.archive.org/stream/motionpicturedai45unse_0#page/n207/mode/2up (accessed May 1, 2018); "The Church Moves On: Union Pacific Anniversary Recalls Utah Episode," *Improvement Era* 42:6 (June 1939), 355, 362, 383.

298 Wallace Stegner, *Mormon Country* (New York: Duell, Sloan and Pearce, 1942), 16-20.

299 Reiser, interviews by William G. Hartley, 109-110. On p. 98 he indicates that the Presiding Bishopric's Office under LeGrand Richards desired that each ward use their projection equipment at least once per month; part of the reason Deseret Book supplied so many titles was to accommodate this (artificial) demand, and it indicated to Reiser just how sorely missed films on Mormon topics were.

300 Jacobs, "The History of Motion Pictures," 72.

301 Wise, interview by Gordon Irving, 25.

302 Jacobs, "The History of Motion Pictures," 79.

303 Ibid., 81.

304 Wise, interview by Gordon Irving, 28.

305 Ibid., 31 (see p. 24-31); Jacobs, "The History of Motion Pictures," 79-81, 91-98, which gives an alphabetical listing of the speeches shot between 1941 and 1952; "Leaders Addresses Now on Film," *Church News*, February 12, 1950, 3; Barker, "Conference Talks To Be Recorded on Sound Film," *Church News*, April 9, 1950; "One Camera; Lots of Nerve," *Church News*, August 19, 1967, 11.

306 Jacobs, "The History of Motion Pictures," 73.

307 Reiser, interviews by William G. Hartley, 16; David O. McKay, "The Utah Centennial," *Improvement Era* 49:5 (May 1946), 272-273, 278.

308 Francis M. Gibbons, *George Albert Smith: Kind and Caring Christian, Prophet of God* (Salt Lake City: Deseret Book Company, 1990), 139.

309 Ibid., 314.

310 Wise, interview by Gordon Irving, 24.

311 Gibbons, *George Albert Smith*, 315.

312 Wise, interview by Gordon Irving, 38.

313 Ibid., 38; Gibbons, *George Albert Smith*, 139-147, 314-317; J. Stapley, "Mental Illness and George Albert Smith," *By Common Consent*, January 4, 2012, https://bycommonconsent.com/2012/01/04/mental-illness-and-george-albert-smith (accessed May 25, 2018); "Film Of Pioneer Trek Of Church President Made Ready," *Church News*, January 4, 1947, 5.

314 Wise, interview by Gordon Irving, 40; Reiser, "...And So the Movies!," *Improvement Era* 51:6. For the First Presidency's remarks and prayer at the dedication, along with a commendation from President Truman, see George Albert Smith, "'This Is The Place' Monument Dedication, *Improvement Era* 50:9 (September 1947), 570-571, 627.

315 Reiser, "...And So the Movies!," *Improvement Era* 51:6; Jacobs, "The History of Motion Pictures," 83, which gives the film's running time as fifteen minutes; Rock M. Kirkham, "Pioneer Centennial Scout Camp," Improvement Era 50:8 (August 1947), 230.

316 Jacobs, "The History of Motion Pictures," 84.

317 Reiser, interviews by William G. Hartley, 17.

318 Ibid., 17, 96-97; Wise, interview by Gordon Irving, 36-37; "The Church Moves

On: Tabernacle," *Improvement Era* 50:8 (August 1947), 531; "Centennial Days," *Improvement Era* 50:9 (September 1947), 575-577; Reiser, "...And So the Movies!," *Improvement Era* 51:6; "The Church Moves On: Temple Square Visitors," *Improvement Era* 51:2 (February 1948), 68. The Tabernacle received an interior and exterior repainting—the ceiling was done in blue—after *The Message of the Ages'* lights and stage were removed and the centennial festivities concluded.

319 Wendell J. Ashton, "Centennial Trek," *Improvement Era* 50:9 (September 1947), 682; see his entire record of the journey, *Improvement Era* 50:9 (September 1947), 578-580, 618-620; 50:10 (October 1947), 646-647, 682-686; Nelson, untitled master's thesis draft, chapter 9 page 9; Jacobs, "The History of Motion Pictures," 83-84, 97; "The Church Moves On: Sons of Utah Pioneers Auto Trek," *Improvement Era* 49:12 (December 1946), 808.

320 J. H. Whitaker, "Utah Films Interest Brazilians in Gospel," *Church News*, June 13, 1951, 12; Cornwall, *A Century of Singing*, 172-173; Jacobs, 83-84.

321 Quinn, *The Mormon Hierarchy: Extensions of Power*, 833 lists commemorative celebrations in Austria, Czechoslovakia, Denmark, Netherlands, West Germany, and Japan. "This Week in Church History," *Church News*, March 15, 1997, 2, https://www.ldschurchnews.com/archive/1997-03-15/this-week-in-church-history-11318 (accessed May 28, 2018); "Video: Days of 47 parade from 1947 in color," *LDS Living*, http://www.ldsliving.com/Video-Days-of-47-parade-from-1947-in-color/s/69590 (accessed December 1, 2016). This eight-minute video includes a compilation of apparently amateur 16mm footage for the most part taken on the parade route but including a few other scenes. Any existing soundtrack has been replaced with *The Nutcracker*. Nevertheless it is a wonderful online glimpse into the year 1947.

322 Nelson, "The History of Utah Film," 47.

323 Ibid., 46-47; D'arc, *When Hollywood Came to Town*, 74-83.

324 Kenneth S. Rothwell, *A History of Shakespeare on Screen: A Century of Film and Television* (Cambridge: Cambridge University Press, 1999), 73-78; "Estimates of Key City Grosses: Salt Lake City," *Motion Picture Daily*, June 4, 1947, 6, http://www.archive.org/stream/motionpicturedai61unse_0#page/n403/mode/2up (accessed May 24, 2018); "*Macbeth* (1948 film)," *Wikipedia*, https://en.wikipedia.org/wiki/Macbeth_(1948_film) (accessed May 24, 2018).

325 "Short Subjects: Preems," *Independent Exhibitors Film Bulletin*, August 4, 1947, 9, http://www.archive.org/stream/independ15film#page/n379/mode/2up (accessed May 26, 2018); "'Desert Fury' Star Meets Mormon Church President," *Showmen's Trade Review*, August 2, 1947, 9, http://www.archive.org/stream/showmenstraderev47lewi#page/n223/mode/2up (accessed May 26, 2018); "Estimates of Key City Grosses: Salt Lake City," *Motion Picture Daily*, June 4, 1947; "Kroehler Air-Expresses Theater Furniture," *Film Daily*, September 5, 1947, 2, http://www.archive.org/stream/filmdaily92wids#page/n421/mode/2up (accessed May 27, 2018).

326 Jacobs, "The History of Motion Pictures," 85.

327 "The Church Moves On," *Improvement Era* 52:9 (September 1949), 550; Geoffrey S. Nelson, "Would-be Saints: West Africa Before the 1978 Priesthood Revelation," *Mormon Press,* February 10, 2013, http://www.mormonpress.com/would_be_saints_west_africa_before_the_1978_priesthood_revelation (accessed May 24, 2018); "Death: LaMar Stevenson Williams," *Deseret News,* February 1, 1996; R. Scott Lloyd, "Youth Symphony and Chorus Look Back on 'Modest Dream,'" *Deseret News*, December 9, 1989, https://www.deseretnews.com/article/79400/YOUTH-SYMPHONY-AND-CHORUS-LOOK-BACK-ON-MODEST-DREAM.html (accessed May 24, 2018).

328 Jacobs, "The History of Motion Pictures," 75.

329 Wise, interview by Gordon Irving, 41.

330 Jacobs, "The History of Motion Pictures," 75.

331 Ibid., 75; Wise, interview by Gordon Irving, 25, 40-41; Cornwall, *A Century of Singing,* 173; "Film in Technicolor Takes All On Tour of Historic Temple Square," *Church News*, May 15, 1949, 5.

332 Reiser, "...And So the Movies!," *Improvement Era* 51:6.

333 Wise, interview by Gordon Irving, 39; Jacobs, "The History of Motion Pictures," 76-78.

334 Wolsey, "The History of Radio Station KSL," 10-11.

335 Cornwall, *A Century of Singing*, 223.

336 Heidi S. Swinton, *America's Choir: A Commemorative Portrait of the Mormon Tabernacle Choir* (Menomonee Falls, Wisconsin: Shadow Mountain and Mormon Tabernacle Choir, 2004), 101 (see also p. 101-112); Lloyd D. Newell, "Seventy-Five Years of the Mormon Tabernacle Choir's *Music and the Spoken Word*, 1929-2004: A History of the Broadcast of America's Choir," *Mormon Historical Studies* 5 (Spring 2004), 127-142; Cornwall, *A Century of Singing,* 224-230; Charles Jeffrey Calman, *The Mormon Tabernacle Choir* (New York: Harper & Row Publishers, 1979), 84-85, 87, 93, 97; William Mulder, "'Music and the Spoken Word' from Temple Square," *Improvement Era* 42:7 (July 1939), 396-397, 439-442; "As The Nation Listens: Response Comes From Thousands," *Church News*, March 29, 1941, 1-2.

337 Calman, *The Mormon Tabernacle Choir*, 93.

338 Cornwall, *A Century of Singing*, 174 (see also p. 170-173); Calman, *The Mormon Tabernacle Choir,* 93; Sherry Baker, "Mormon Media History Timeline, 1827-2007," http://contentdm.lib.byu.edu/cdm/ref/collection/IR/id/157 (accessed May 27, 2018), 46-47; "The Church Moves On: Choir Recordings Heard on Significant Experimental Program," *Improvement Era* 43:5 (May 1940), 286; "Right Off the Reel: Progress Report on Color TV," *Business Screen Magazine*, 15:3 (1954), 37, http://www.archive.org/stream/businessscreen1954mav15rich#page/n287/

mode/2up (accessed May 27, 2018); "Sound Masters Lights Mormon Tabernacle for Alcoa Short," *Business Screen Magazine*, 15:3 (1954), 47, http://www.archive. org/stream/businessscreen1954mav15rich#page/n449/mode/2up (accessed May 27, 2018). See It Now included a three-minute documentary that, even as late as 1954, caused the production company problems while trying to light the Tabernacle's massive domed interior.

339 Earl J. Glade, "To the Ends of the Western Hemisphere," *Improvement Era* 34:4 (February 1931), 223; see p. 222.

340 Quinn, *The Mormon Hierarchy: Extensions of Power*, 828; McCune, *Gordon B. Hinckley*, 220; Wolsey, "The History of Radio Station KSL, 22, 27 (for the stake conference broadcast); Cowan, *The Church in the Twentieth Century,* 165; Bruce L. Christensen, "Broadcasting," *Encyclopedia of Mormonism*, Vol. 1, 232-234; "The New KSL Is Ready!: 50,000 Watts of Power," *Improvement Era* 35:12 (October 1932), 767; "Your Page and Ours: A Good Team—*Improvement Era* and Radio," *Improvement Era* 36:5 (March 1933), 320; "Editorial: President Grant Addresses the Nations," *Improvement Era* 38:6 (June 1935), 367; "First American-European Broadcast of the Church, with the First Presidency Speaking," *Improvement Era* 39:5 (May 1936), 270-273; "Equipment," *Broadcasting and Broadcasting Yearbook 1938,* May 1, 1938, 79, http://www.archive.org/stream/broadcastingbroa14un-se#page/78/mode/2up (accessed May 26, 2018); "The Church Moves On: Church History on Farm and Home Hour," *Improvement Era* 43:2 (February 1940), 95; Albert L. Zobell, Jr., "Radio and the Gospel Message," *Improvement Era* 50:4 (April 1947), 205, 255.

341 Fred C. Esplin, "The Church as Broadcaster," *Dialogue: A Journal of Mormon Thought* 10:3 (Spring 1977), 30; see the entire essay, p. 25-45, for an excellent history and overview of Church broadcasting efforts.

342 Wolsey, "The History of Radio Station KSL," 127.

343 Ibid., 128.

344 Ibid., 127; Donald G. Godfrey, Val E. Limburg, and Heber G. Wolsey, "KSL, Salt Lake City: At the Crossroads of the West," *Television in America: Local Station History from Across the Nation*, ed. Donald G. Godfrey and Michael D. Murray (Ames, Iowa: Iowa State University Press, 1997), 342; Quinn, *The Mormon Hierarchy: Extensions of Power,* 827; Jack C. Ellis and Betsy A. McLane, *A New History of Documentary Film* (Continuum: New York, 2005) 180.

345 Gustive O. Larson, "Mormon Missionaries on Sweden's Television Screen," *Improvement Era* 42:2 (February 1939), 90, 118; "The Church Moves On," *Improvement Era* 63:5 (May 1960), 294; Douglas H. Parker, "Eastern States Mission Centennial Chorus," *Improvement Era* 51:1 (January 1948), 16, 46.

346 Albert L. Zobell, Jr., "The Conference Story," *Improvement Era* 51:5 (May 1948), 264.

347 "First Experiment in Television Thrills Conference Crowds," *Church News*, April 10, 1948, 3.

348 George Albert Smith, opening remarks and untitled address, *Conference Report* (April 1948), 10-11. Page 1 of the *Conference Report* says, "Television equipment had been installed in the Assembly Hall, thus enabling those who gathered in that building to see as well as hear the speakers and those who had furnished music." This announcement is repeated in the October *Report*, although by April 1949 it is amplified with: "Large numbers of others who could not be accommodated in either of these buildings listened to the services by means of amplifying equipment upon the grounds" This apparently refers to audio only.

349 "First Experiment in Television Thrills Conference Crowds," *Church News*.

350 Wolsey, "The History of Radio Station KSL," 128-129; Godfrey, Limburg, & Wolsey, "KSL, Salt Lake City," 343; Arch Madsen, "KSL Radio," *Encyclopedia of Mormonism*, Vol. 2, 800; "Telecast Sessions Make New History," *Church News*, October 9, 1949, 12-13; "Scott Clawson," *Salt Lake Tribune*, September 8, 2010, http://www.legacy.com/obituaries/saltlaketribune/obituary.aspx?pid=145162599 (accessed May 9, 2018).

351 David O. McKay, "Plea for Living the Gospel Expressed," *Improvement Era* 56:12 (December 1953), 978; "The Church Moves On," *Improvement Era* 64:6 (June 1961), 368.

352 "The Church Moves On," *Improvement Era* 60:6 (June 1957), 376.

353 Wolsey, "The History of Radio Station KSL," 32; Quinn, *The Mormon Hierarchy: Extensions of Power*, 849, 855; Wise, interview by Gordon Irving, 30.

354 Randy Astle, "The Eyes of Babes: A Historical Survey of LDS Children's Media," *Irreantum: A Review of Mormon Literature & Film* 9:1 (2007), 101, 103-104. Taylor's "We Listen to the Radio" column began appearing at least before 1945, including the following. Miriam Taylor, "We Listen to the Radio: Television Today and Tomorrow," *Children's Friend*, March 1946, 123; Miriam Taylor, "We Listen to the Radio," *Children's Friend*, July 1946, 298-299; Miriam Taylor, "We Listen to the Radio," *Children's Friend*, March 1948, 119; Miriam Taylor, "We Listen to the Radio," *Children's Friend*, June 1948, 253; Miriam T. Meads, "Radio and Television," *Children's Friend*, July 1949, 297; "Children's Friend of the Air," *Church News*, May 23, 1951, 9; "Primary Children Enjoy Skit on TV," *Church News*, October 18, 1952, 5; "'Junior Council' Birthday: Primary T-V Show Completes Fifth Year," *Church News*, May 23, 1953, 5; "Junior Council Television: Primary Program Has Sixth Birthday," *Church News*, June 26, 1954, 8; Olive Milner, "Primary Television," *Children's Friend*, May 1956, 209; "Orchard Ward Presents TV Show," *Church News*, December 8, 1956, 5; Olive Milner, "Junior Council," *Children's Friend*, June 1958, 25; Olive Milner, "Children's Friend Television," *Children's Friend*, September 1958, 33.

355 "The Church Moves On," *Improvement Era* 53:6 (June 1950), 464.

356 Prince and Wright, *David O. McKay and the Rise of Modern Mormonism*, 124. In addition, Bowman, *The Mormon People*, 190 adds: "By 1962, 330 television stations worldwide regularly broadcast the choir's weekly Sunday morning devotional service. By the same year, the church's broadcasting company, KSL, had gained

affiliates nationwide; in April 1962 fifty-two stations carried the church's General Conference from coast to coast."

357 J. Reuben Clark, Jr., untitled address, *Conference Report*, October 1949, 194.

358 Godfrey, Limburg, & Wolsey, "KSL, Salt Lake City," 344-345.

359 "The 'Show-Me Boys' move into tv," *Sponsor*, December 6, 1958, 31, http://www.archive.org/stream/sponsor58sponno3#page/n1195/mode/2up (accessed May 27, 2018). Robert W. Donigan, *An Outline History of Broadcasting in the Church of Jesus Christ of Latter-day Saints 1922-1963* (Provo: Brigham Young University, 1963); Robert W. Donigan, "A Descriptive Analysis of the Effectiveness of Broadcasting by The Church of Jesus Christ of Latter-day Saints in the Northern States Mission Area," (master's thesis, Brigham Young University Dept. of Communication, 1964); Don Gale and Jeff Winget, *Eyewitness to 50 Years: KSL Television 1949 to 1999* (Salt Lake City: KSL Television, 1999; Herbert F. Murray, "A Half Century of Broadcasting," Ensign (August 1972), 48-51; and Heber G. Wolsey, "Religious Broadcasting by the LDS (Mormon) Church," (master's thesis, Northwestern University, 1949).

360 W. Eugene Manning, "The History of Broadcasting Education at Brigham Young University to 1962," (master's thesis, Brigham Young University Dept. of Communications, April 1973), 17-19, 29-38, 41-59, 83-91; Carl F. Eyring, "When Space Talks and Sings," *Improvement Era* 25:7 (May 1922), 628-633; "The Purpose And Values Of A Mission: A Missionary Dramatization: Presented by B.Y.U. Faculty Members and Students," *Church News*, February 5, 1938, 4. It's possible that Lester Card, coming from Cardston in Canada, was related to Lester Park, one of whose daughters married into the Card family, but I have thus far been unable to establish a connection.

361 Wise, "The 'EYES' have it," *Improvement Era*, 21; "The Church Moves On: Salt Lake Wards See Defense Film," *Improvement Era* 45:7 (July 1942), 457; "Sunday School Faculty Meetings Improved," *Church News*, March 10, 1945, 6.

362 Wetzel O. Whitaker, "Interview, 1985," by Thomas Cheney, July 30, 1985, L. Tom Perry Special Collections, Harold B. Lee Library, Brigham Young University, 3.

363 Ibid., 5.

364 Whitaker, *Looking Back*, 49.

365 Whitaker, "Interview, 1985," 6; Wetzel O. Whitaker, "Pioneering with Film: A History of Church and Brigham Young University Films," unpublished manuscript, n.d. (est. 1983), L. Tom Perry Special Collections, Harold B. Lee Library, Brigham Young University, 6; Jacobs, "The History of Motion Pictures," 86-88.

366 Whitaker, "Pioneering with Film," 6.

367 Ibid., 7; see also Whitaker, "Interview, 1985," 8; Whitaker, *Looking Back*, 51.

368 Jacobs, "The History of Motion Pictures," 90. This is from a transcript of a lecture Whitaker gave in Salt Lake City, January 22, 1966, and I have corrected the mistakes and punctuation.

369 Joseph Lundstrom, "Welfare Films Completed: Hollywood Professional Artists Produce Two Unusual Church Films," *Church News,* April 3, 1949, 11.

370 Jacobs, "The History of Motion Pictures," 91.

371 Whitaker, *Looking Back*, 52; see also Whitaker, "Pioneering with Film," 6-9; Whitaker, "Interview, 1985," 8; Jacobs, "The History of Motion Pictures," 86-91, 94; Gordon B. Hinckley, "Skilled Artists Contribute—To Production of Welfare Films," *Church News*, November 10, 1948, 10; "Second Welfare Film—Previewed By General Committee," *Church News*, November 10, 1948, 4; "The Church Moves On: Church Welfare Films," *Improvement Era* 51:12 (December 1948), 780; Lundstrom, "Welfare Films Completed," *Church News*, 11-12; "The Church Moves On," *Improvement Era* 52:10 (October 1949), 616.

372 "Leaders Addresses Now on Film," *Church News,* February 12, 1950; Barker, "Conference Talks To Be Recorded on Sound Film," *Church News*, April 9, 1950.

373 Quinn, *The Mormon Hierarchy: Extensions of Power*, 772.

374 Emily W. Jensen, "History behind the first non-English temple ceremony translation," *Deseret News*, June 26, 2013, https://www.deseretnews.com/article/865582222/History-behind-the-first-non-English-temple-ceremony-translation.html?pg=all (accessed May 18, 2018).

375 Prince and Wright, *David O. McKay and the Rise of Modern Mormonism*, 261.

376 Ibid., 261.

377 Ibid., 262.

378 First Presidency Letterpress Copybooks, 1877-1949, Vol. 75, July 22-Dec. 27, 1927, David John Buerger Collection, Special Collections, J. Willard Marriott Library, University of Utah, box 23 folder 25.

379 Martha Sonntag Bradley, "'The Church and Colonel Saunders': Mormon Standard Plan Architecture," (master's thesis, Brigham Young University Dept. of History, 1981), 43.

380 Ibid., 43-44.

381 Dew, *Go Forward with Faith*, 179.

382 Shaun D. Stahle, "Intensity to serve developed during missionary struggles," *Church News*, June 13, 1998, https://www.ldschurchnews.com/archive/1998-06-13/intensity-to-serve-developed-during-missionary-struggles-14191 (accessed May 28, 2018).

383 Dew, *Go Forward with Faith*, 180.

384 Ibid., 181.

385 Prince and Wright, *David O. McKay and the Rise of Modern Mormonism*, 261-263; Dew, *Go Forward with Faith*, 176-193, 289, 479-480; Richard O. Cowan, *Temples to Dot the Earth* (Salt Lake City: Bookcraft, 1989), 158-160; John C. Thomas, "To Take the Temples to the People," *Out of Obscurity: The LDS Church in the Twentieth Century* (Salt Lake City: Deseret Book Company, 2000), 328-329; David John Buerger, *The Mysteries of Godliness: A History of Mormon Temple Worship* (San Francisco: Smith Research Associates, 1994), 166-167; McCune, *Gordon B. Hinckley*, 7, 295-298, 300; Wise, interview by Gordon Irving, 52-53, 91, 94; Marba C. Josephson, "A Temple is Risen to Our Lord," *Improvement Era* 58:9 (September 1955), 624-626, 684-687; "The Church Moves On," *Improvement Era* 58:11 (November 1955), 853; "Church News: Obituary [Winnifred Bowers]," *Deseret News*, March 15, 1999, https://www.ldschurchnews.com/archive/1999-03-13/church-news-obituary-15295 (accessed May 28, 2018), which indicates that she was a member of Hinckley's committee; Shaun D. Stahle, "Swiss Temple: Dedication a bold act of faith," *Church News*, September 17, 2005, http://www.ldschurchnewsarchive.com/articles/47832/Swiss-Temple-Dedication-a-bold-act-of-faith.html (accessed May 28, 2018).

386 Prince and Wright, *David O. McKay and the Rise of Modern Mormonism*, 268. In this case, the Salt Lake Temple has never used a film presentation. The Ogden Temple was built in 1972, with no changes made beforehand to the Logan Temple. Overcrowding remained an issue in Logan, and it was renovated with a filmed endowment added, and rededicated in 1979. "Logan Temple: Interior, Renovation, and Restoration," *Historic LDS Architecture*, July 30, 2015, http://ldspioneerarchitecture.blogspot.com/2015/07/logan-temple-interior-renovation-and.html (accessed December 2, 2015).

387 Quinn, *The Mormon Hierarchy: Extensions of Power*, 849.

388 Buerger, *The Mysteries of Godliness*, 167.

389 For instance, see Tad Walch, "LDS Church begins using another new temple film," *Deseret News*, January 15, 2014, http://www.deseretnews.com/article/865594237/LDS-Church-begins-using-another-new-temple-film.html (accessed February 2, 2014); Tad Walch, "LDS Church begins using a 3rd new temple film," *Deseret News*, July 15, 2014, https://www.deseretnews.com/article/865606973/LDS-Church-begins-using-a-3rd-new-temple-film.html (accessed July 15, 2014).

390 Whitaker, "Pioneering with Film," 10.

391 Ibid., 10.

392 Ernest L. Wilkinson and W. Cleon Skousen, *Brigham Young University: A School of Destiny* (Provo: Brigham Young University Press, 1976), 703.

393 Whitaker, "Pioneering with Film," 10.

394 Ibid., 10-11; Jacobs, ""The History of Motion Pictures," 101-107; Wilkinson

Notes - The Second Wave: Home Cinema

and Skousen, *Brigham Young University*, 703-704; Wilkinson & Arrington, *Brigham Young University*, Vol. 4, 381; Whitaker, "Interview, 1985," by Thomas Cheney, 9-10.

395   Wise, interview by Gordon Irving, 42-44.

396   Reiser, interviews by William G. Hartley, 95.

INDEX

20th Century Vikings, 328

26 Men (television series, 1957-59), 308

42nd Street (1933), 267

49th Parallel (1941), 244

101 Dalmatians (1961), 292, 296

127 Hours (2010), 130, 139

195 Dresses (2011), 100

711 Ocean Drive (1950), 308

2001: A Space Odyssey (1968), 131, 312

A/S Fotorama, 162

Aardman Animations, 296

Abandoned (1949), 308

ABC, 278, 417

Abilene, TX, 334

Above Rubies (1932), 117

Absent-Minded Professor, The (1961), 33

Abundant Life, The, 365

Académie Julian, Paris, 48-49, 78

Academy Awards, 2, 4, 114, 119, 256, 259, 272, 291-293, 308, 310

Academy of Motion Picture Arts and Sciences, 115, 316

Academy of Music, Philadelphia, 127

Accomplishments of the Mormon People, 365

Acord, Art, 122

Acres, Birt, 67, 69

Across the Continent; or, From the Atlantic to the Pacific (painting), 43

Adam, 14, 45

Adam-ondi-Ahman, MO, 331, 400

Adams Ward, Hollywood Stake, 374

Adams, Amy, 2-3

Adams, Ansel, 38

Adams, Bob, 425

Adams, Emily C., 383

Adams, John Quincy (theologian), 158

Adams, LeeAnne Hill, 38

Adams, Maude, 3, 35

Adams, Merle "Cowhide", 135

Adler, Max, 155

Adventure South, 328

Adventures of Deadwood Dick, The (1915), 188

Adventures of Kit Carson, The (television series, 1951-55), 308

Adventures of Robin Hood, The (1938), 390

Adventures on the Colorado (1947), 343

Aesop, 428

Affleck, Casey, 4

African Queen, The (1951), 388

After Earth (2013), 139

Agee, James, 385

Agents of S.H.I.E.L.D. (television series, 2013-), 308

Aladdin (play, 1885), 36

Alaska, 193, 223-224

Alaska-Yukon-Pacific Exposition (1909), 108

Alberta, 18, 200, 209, 309, 316, 430

Alberta Temple, see Cardson, Alberta Temple

Alexander, Sarah, 123

Alexander, Thomas, 61

Alfred Hitchcock Hour, The (television

series, 1962-65), 309

Alfred Hitchcock Presents (television series, 1955-65), 301, 303

Alhambra theater chain, 168

Alhambra Theater, Ogden, 85, 168

Alice films (1923-27), 291

Alice in Wonderland (1951), 295, 428

All About Eve (1950), 257

Allen, Harold, 38

All Faces West (1929), 223-229, 245, 259, 314-315, 319, 325, 347, 350, 441

All Faces West (stage musical), 302

Alps, 431

Amarillo, TX, 170

Amateur Cinema League, 342

Ambrose and Walrus franchise, 121

Ameche, Don, 257, 261

American Academy of Dramatic Arts, 304

American Art-Union, 44

American Ballet Theatre, 305

American Civil War, 18, 63, 68, 78, 182, 190

American Film Company, 125

American Film Manufacturing Company, see Flying A

American Fork, UT, 55, 205

American Laboratory Theatre, 306

American Photoplay Weekly, 88

American Society of Cinematographers, 125

American theater, Park City, 86

American Theater, Salt Lake City, 83-84, 87, 90, 157

Amsterdam, Netherlands, 165, 366

Amy, Dustin, 31

Ancient American Landscapes, 365

Andersen, Valdemar, 189

Anderson, Broncho Billy, 124

Anderson, Edward (architect), 30

Anderson, Edward (MIA leader), 107

Anderson, Edward O., 431-432

Anderson, George Edward, 37, 51, 195

Anderson, L. Clyde, 344

Anderson, Nephi, 33, 60

Anderson, Paul Thomas, 4

Anderson, Scott S., 37

Anderson, Travis, 5

Anderson, W. R., 344

Andreasen, Juel LeRoy, 339

Andreasen, McKay, 339

Angel and the Beehive, The, 61

Angel Moroni Monument, 32, 207, 337, 360

Angel Moroni statue, 49, 55

Angell, Truman, 29, 208

Angels of Darkness, 174

Ann Arbor, MI, 335

Anna Christie (1930), 258

Anna Karenina (1935), 258

Annex Cafeteria company, 209

Apostasy, The, 365

Appeal to the Great Spirit, 31

Apperly, Ida Adair, 118

Apple Dumpling Gang, The (1975), 4

Arabian Nights (1942), 135

Arbuckle, Fatty, 112, 119, 124, 242

Arcade Fire, 27

Arches National Park, 139

Ardern, Jacinda, 20

Ardmore, OK, 170

Argentina, 19, 340

Argosy Pictures Corporation, 139, 275, 277, 279

Arizona, 16, 76, 85, 109, 114, 119, 131, 133, 137, 192, 198

Arizona Days (1937), 279

Arkansas, 17

Arlington (Los Angeles) Ward, 289

Arliss, George, 107, 113

Armat, Thomas, 76

Armitage, William, 39, 44

Arnheim, Rudolf, 305

Arrington, James, 36

Arrington, Leonard, 64

Arrowhead Motion Picture Company, 206

Art Institute of Chicago, 293

Artemus Ward: His Panorama, 155

Ashby, Hal, 3

Ashton, Marvin J., 250, 376, 394

Ashton, Wendell J.,373, 404

Ashurst, Henry, 242

Asper, Frank, 251

Asphalt Jungle, The (television version, 1961), 309

Assembly Hall, Salt Lake City, 56-58, 213, 418-419

Association of Film Commissioners International, 140

Astaire, Fred, 235

Astle, Neil L., 30

Astor, Mary, 4, 262, 264-267

Atkinson, Laura Erekson, 32

Atkisson de Moura, Valerie, 32

Atlanta, GA, 30-31

Atlantic City, NJ, 156

Atlas Corporation, 284-285

Auburn Theological Seminary, 158

Auckland, New Zealand, 347

Audio-Visual Committee of the National Council for Social Studies, 270

Audiovisual Department, see LDS Church Audiovisual Department

Augusta, GA, 193

Auricon, 330, 394-395, 399-400

Auschwitz, 267

Austin Powers in Gold Member (2002), 131

Australia, 95, 157, 166, 181, 186, 200

Autry, Gene, 244

Autumn Leaves (1956), 113

Avard, Sampson, 152

Aviator, The (2004), 301

Ayres, Lew, 301

Baber, Zonia, 55

Bacchae, The, 24

Bachman-Turner Overdrive, 27

Bachman, Randy, 27

Back Stage (1919), 124

Back to the Future Part III (1990), 131

Bad Bascomb (1946), 184, 224, 228, 256, 270-272, 278, 326, 389

Bad Man, The (1941), 299

Bad Man of Brimstone, The (1937), 134

Badger, Clarence, 189

BAFTA awards, 310

Baird, John Logie, 128

Baker, Elna, 34

Baker, Joseph, 388

Bakersfield, CA, 287

Baldwin, Jim, 420

Ballantyne, Richard, 380

Ballard, M. Russell, i-ii, 69

Ballard, Martha J., 316

Ballard, Melvin, 107, 215, 220

Ballo, Domenico, 26

Baltimore, MD, 55, 157

Bamberger, Simon, 181

Bambi (1942), 296

Band Concert, The (1935), 290

Banff School of Fine Arts, 309

Bangs, David C., 58

Banks, Lionel, 288

Banvard, John, 41

Baptists, 14, 106, 236

Barber, Phyllis, 34

Barker, The (1928), 119

Barlow, John, 247

Barlow, Reginald, 321

Barney, Matthew, 4

Barnum & Bailey Circus, 113

Barnum, P. T., 35, 88

Barrie, James, 3

Barrymore family, 35

Index

Barrymore, Lionel, 300

Bartholdi, Frédéric, 49

Barty, Billy, 303

Basel, Switzerland, 434

Basic Instinct (1992), 248

Bates, Kathy, 4

Battle at Apache Pass, The (1952), 139

Battle of Crooked River, 152

Battle of Midway, The (1942), 273

Battle of San Pietro, The (1945), 414

Battle of the Big Blue River, 1833, 42

Battleship Potemkin (1925), 73

Battlestar Galactica franchise, 3

Bazin, André, 385

Beach, Leroy, 297

Beale, Joseph Boggs, 52

Bean, Orestes Utah, 37, 209, 318-320, 322, 324-325, 328

Bean, Zoan E. Houtz, 324

Bear River Migratory Bird Refuge, 404

Bear River Mountains, UT, 339

Beard, George, 38-39

Beatie, Ross, 223

Beaty Brothers, 78

Beautiful Britain, 365

Beaver, UT, 119, 128, 291

Beck, Glenn, 21

Beck, Martin, 80

Beck, Wayne M., 338

Bednar, David A., 69

Bee Hive Film Company, 211

Beery, Noah, 184

Beery, Wallace, 184, 270

Beesley, Ebenezer, 26

Beethoven, Ludwig van, 409

Before Columbus, 365-366

Beijing, China, 131

Beira, Mozambique, 171

Belfast, Ireland, 59

Belgium, 266

Bell & Howell Company, 381-382, 386,

392, 395

Bell Telephone Laboratories, 126

Bellah, James Warner, 138

Bellamann, Henry, 306

Bells of Coronado (1950), 307

Bells of San Angelo (1947), 307

Ben Lomond Mountain, 93

Ben-Hur (1925), 320

Ben-Hur (magic lantern presentation), 52, 58

Benedict, Sadie, 59

Benin, 20

Benjamin Franklin Institute, Philadelphia, 128

Bennett, Constance, 113

Bennett, John C., 152, 158

Benning, James, 4

Bennion, Milton, 377

Bennion, Samuel O., 362-363

Benson, Ezra Taft, 19, 27, 186, 336, 395

Berg, Charles Ramirez, 277

Bergman, Ingmar, 389

Bergman, Ingrid, 300, 307

Berkeley Ward, 339

Berkeley, CA, 339

Berlin, Germany, 67, 128, 199, 357, 367

Bern Switzerland Temple, 46, 432-433, 436-437

Bern, Switzerland, 432, 434, 436

Bernhardt, Sarah, 97

Berton, Pierre, 310

Bess, Oliver C., 285

Bessie Baine; or, The Mormon's Victim, 154

Best Two Years of My Life, The (play), 37

Best Two Years, The (2003), 37

Between Heaven and Hell (1956), 300

Beverly Hillbillies, The (television series, 1962-71), 306

Beverly Hills, CA, 287-288, 299, 302

Bible, 115, 150, 307, 356

Big Cat, The (1949), 244

Big Heart (1914), 206

Big Parade, The (1925), 118

Big Trail, The (1930), 314

bigamy, see polygamy

Bigler, Erin Boley. 307

Billy the Kid (1941), 138

Billy Barty's Big Top (television series, 1963-67), 304

Bingham, George Caleb, 44

Bingham Canyon copper mine, 348

Biograph, 75, 81, 124, 142-144, 148

Bioscope, see International Bioscope Company

Bioskop (camera), 67

Bird, Brad, 296

Birmingham, England, 165, 186

Birth of a Nation, The (1915), 78, 87, 177-179, 187, 201

Birth of Mormonism, The, 158

Birth of Mormonism in Picture, The (book, 1909), 38, 195

Bison Life Motion Pictures, 172

Black and Tan (1929), 125

Black Dragons (1942), 115

Black Ey'd Susan (play, 1829), 36

Black Narcissus (1947), 235

Black Satchel, The (1951), 344

Blackmail (1929), 226

Black, Dustin Lance, 3

Blackfoot, ID, 128

Blackham, Deniece, 108

Blair, George Elias, 317

Blake, William, 1

Blanchard, E. L., 36

Blanding, UT, 273-274, 327

Blaney, Charles E., 156

block teaching, see home teaching

blogs, blogging, 34

Blom, August, 163

Blood and Sand (1941), 260

Blood Arrow (1958), 228

blood atonement, 153-155, 159

Blood of a Poet, The (1930), 343

Blood, Harry, 391

Blood, Henry, 265

Blue (1968), 139

Blue Is the Warmest Color (2013), 248

Blue, Monte, 326

Blue, Samuel Taylor, 336

Bluff, UT, 273, 289

Bluth, Don, 3, 299

Boadicea: The Mormon Wife, 154

Bogdanovich, Peter, 120, 274

Boggs, Francis, 171

Boggs, Lilburn, 15

Bohn, Jacob Johannes Martinus, 39

Bolex, 329-330

Bombardment of Vera Cruz, The (painting), 41

Bonaparte, Napoleon, 55

Bond, Ward, 4, 276-280

Bonneville Stake, 424

Book of Commandments, 331

Book of Mormon, The, i, 2-3, 14-15, 19, 36, 44-45, 59, 72, 83, 86, 123, 148, 152, 195-197, 202-205, 208-209, 211-212, 222, 253, 276, 303, 317-319, 321-322, 326-327, 333, 335, 347, 348, 356, 360, 364, 367-368, 370-372

Book of Mormon, The (2011 play), 21

Book of Nature (book, 1300s), 40

Booth, Edwina, 304

Booth, Ezra, 152

Boots and Saddles Pictures, 279

Border River (1954), 139

Borglum, Gutzon, 23, 31

Borglum, Solon, 31

Borzage, Frank, 4, 178, 290

Bosen, Mae, 123

Bossard, Gisbert, 194

Bosworth, Hobart, 196

Boston Herald, 74

Index

Boston Music Hall, 31

Boston, MA, 31, 268

Boud, Joseph E., 224

Bournemouth, England, 370

Bountiful, UT, 54, 281, 343

Bowen, Albert, 335, 364

Bowers, Winnifred, 433

Bowman, John, 241

Bowman, Matthew, 141, 283

Bowman, Pat, 32

Box Elder County, UT, 292

Boy Scouts of America, 102, 378, 387, 389

Boyle, Danny, 4

Brady, Matthew, 37

Bradys Among the Mormons; or, Secret Work in Salt Lake City, The, 154

Braginton, James, 176

Brandley, Elsie Talmage, 239, 383

Brandon, Hugh "Denver", 285

Brass Choir, The, 378

Brazil, 10, 19, 20, 166, 171, 340, 407

Brazilian cinema, 10

Breen, Joseph, 239, 241, 245, 282

Brent, Evelyn, 185

Brentwood Country Club, Santa Monica, 214

Brickey, Joseph, 39

Bridger, Jim, 72, 265

Brigham City, UT, 85, 294, 302, 308

Brigham Young (1940), 183, 190, 196-200, 224, 229

Brigham Young, 15-17, 26-27, 32, 35, 45-46, 55, 68, 98-99, 112, 114, 116, 130, 133, 153, 158, 167, 188, 200, 208-209, 213, 218, 225, 230

Brigham Young Academy, see Brigham Young University

Brigham Young College, Logan, 302

Brigham Young Monument, 210, 340

Brigham Young University, 4, 24, 28, 32, 38, 55, 60, 64, 90, 120, 126, 128-129, 209, 215-216, 231, 307, 326, 338, 341-342, 345, 364, 388-391, 398, 409, 423-425, 430, 435

Brigham Young University Bureau of Visual Instruction, 386-387

Brigham Young University College of Fine Arts and Communications, 388, 422

Brigham Young University Extension Division, 386-387

Brigham Young University Harold B. Lee Library, 386

Brigham Young University International Cinema, 5, 388-389

Brigham Young University Learning Resource Centers Department, 388

Brigham Young University Physics Department, 126, 422

Brigham Young University Radio Club, 423

Brigham Young University Theatre & Media Arts Department, 422

Brigham Young University -Idaho, 64

Brigham Young University Art Caravan, 38

Brigham Young University Ballroom Dance Company, 28

Brigham Young University Motion Picture Archive, 120

Brigham Young University Motion Picture Department, 8, 231, 389, 391, 398, 409, 438-441

Brigham Young University Motion Picture Studio, see Brigham Young University Motion Picture Department

Brigham Young University Museum of Art, 24, 390

Brigham's Destroying Angel, 155

Bringhurst, Samuel E., 431

Bringing Up Baby (1938), 285

Bristol, England, 165

British Empire Exhibition (1924-25), 117

British Film Institute, 175, 272

British Incorporated Pictures, 117

British Mission, 337, 360, 377, 389

British Parliament, 152

British Pathé, 252

Broadcasting Hall of Fame, 413

Brocka, Lino, 3

Broken Arrow (1996), 131

Bromfield, Louis, 258-259, 267

Bronson, J. Scott, 36

Brontë, Charlotte, 149-150

Brooklyn Branch/Ward, 249, 342

Brooks, Joanna, 5, 34

Brooks, Juanita, 282

Brossard, Edgar, 341

Brown, Clarence, 258

Brown, Hugh B., 337

Brown, Sally, 336

Brussells, Belgium, 140

Bryce Canyon National Park, 131, 134, 216, 254-255, 328, 341, 348, 372

Buch, Frederik, 189

Buchanan, James, 17

Buddhists, Buddhism, 448

Buenos Aires, Argentina, 199, 266

Buffalo Bill, see Cody, William Frederick "Buffalo Bill"

Buffalo, NY, 156, 180, 416

Bungalow theater, Salt Lake City, 82

Bunker, Bryan L., 418

Bunny Welden's Greenwich Village Dancers, 321, 323

Burbank, CA, 294, 434

Burgess, Edward A., 344

Bureau of Information, 109, 405-406, 418

Burnett, Frances Hodgson, 114

Burns, Ken, 310

Burns, William J., 203

Burton, Gideon, iii, 4

Burton, Harold, 30, 438

Bush, Pauline, 170

Bushman, Richard L., iii, 2

Butch Cassidy and the Sundance Kid (1969), 71, 131

Butte, MT, 91

Buzz Lightyear (fictional character), 3

By Common Consent (blog), 34

BYU Broadcasting, 129, 423-425

BYUtv, 422

Cabanne, Christy, 121

Cabrini, Frances Xavier, 284

Cadet Rousselle (1947), 309

Cagney, James, 120

Caine, John T., 35

Caineville (1953), 343

Calamity Jane (1949), 135

Calder, David, 26

Calder's Park (fairground), 54

Caldwell County, MO, 15

Calgary Institute of Technology, 309

Calgary, Alberta, 309

California, 30, 58-59, 91, 109-113, 123-124, 131-132, 135-137, 149, 166, 169, 175, 178, 180, 193, 195, 204, 207, 223, 228, 244, 262-265, 267-268, 279, 281, 283, 285, 288, 290, 292, 298-301, 303, 305, 308-309, 339, 342, 345, 366, 369, 373, 390, 398, 406-407, 418, 422, 425, 435, 438

California Gold Rush, 16

California Intermountain News, 279

California Mission, 103

California-Pacific International Exposition in San Diego (1935-36), 369

Call of the Canyons (1947), 343

Call of the Rockies, see *All Faces West* (1929)

Callis, Charles, 335, 365

Caméflex, 330

camera obscura, 40, 51-54, 60, 77

Campbell, Robert, 39

Camping with the Troop (1948), 386

Index

Canada, 18, 20, 30, 119, 169, 181, 187, 200, 244, 248, 311, 313, 370, 416, 420

Canada Carries On (1940-59), 309

Canada, polygamous colonies, 18, 119

Canadian Pacific Railway, 193

Cannes Film Festival, 310

Cannibal Capers (1930), 292

Cannon, George Q., 32, 47, 142, 184, 382

Cannon, Georgius Young, 30

Cannon, John Q., 142

Cannon, Marsena, 37

Cannon, Sylvester Q., 215, 356, 379

Cannon, Zina, 103

Can't Help Singing (1944), 134

Canyonlands National Park, 131, 139

Capitol Theatre, Salt Lake City, 35, 79, 91, 392, 409

Capitol Records, 434

Capra, Frank, 262, 384, 424

Caprice of the Mountains (1916), 123

Captain Blood (1935), 306

Captain Fury (1939), 384

Card, Lester, 423

Card, Orson Scott, 33, 83

Cardston, Alberta, 18, 119, 200, 209, 311-312, 432

Cardston, Alberta Temple, 437

Careless, George, 26

Carew, Ora, 125

Carewe, Edwin, 133

Carey, Harry, Jr., 274

Carey, Harry, Sr., 304

Carl Dudley Productions, 255

Carlson, Don A., 416

Carlyle, Pat, 247-248

Carlyne, Dolores, 245

Carman, Richard, 344

Carnegie Hall, 3, 127

Carnival in Costa Rica (1947), 407

Carolyn Dorfman Dance Company, 28

Carpenter, George E., 28, 87-88, 93, 96

Carradine, John, 262

Cars (2006), 138

Carson City (1952), 307

Carter, Charles W., 37

Carthage Jail, 42, 334, 336, 402

Carthage, IL, 16, 334, 405

cartoons, newspaper, 145-148, 295

Cartwright, Randy, 296

Casablanca (1942), 235, 268, 307

Casino theater, Salt Lake City, 81, 86

Casler, Herman, 67, 74

Casper, WY, 399

Castle Dale, UT, 285

Castle Gate, UT, 214

Catawba Native American tribe, 336

Catholic League of Decency, 383

Cat's Meow, The (2001), 120

Catholics, Catholicism, see Roman Catholics or Orthodox Catholics

Cave, George, 371

CBS Corporation, 3, 256, 414, 416, 419, 422

Cedar Breaks National Monument, 132-133, 346

Cedar City, UT, 131-134, 137

censorship, 8, 24, 98, 107, 169, 179, 241-244, 385

Centennial Scout Camp (1947), 401

Central Congregational Sunday School, 52

Central Pacific Mission, 338

Centre Theater, Salt Lake City, 391

Cézanne, Paul, 48

Challenge for Change film series, 311

Chamberlain, Bonnie, 326

Chamberlain, Guy, 134

Champ, The (1931), 270

Chamorro (language), 19

Chaney, Lon, 114, 119

Chaplin, Charlie, 97, 122

Chapu, Henri, 49

Charles P. Madsen & Co., 92-93

Charles R. Savage Company, 205

Charlie's Angels (television series, 1976-81), 304

Charlotte, SC, 336

Cheddar Gorge, England, 175

Cheechakos, The (1923), 223-224

Chekhov, Anton, 36

Chen Kaige, 10

Chesterfield, England, 164

Cheyenne Autumn (1964), 138

Chicago Board of Censors, 180

Chicago World's Fair (1932), 127

Chicago World's Fair, see World's Columbian Exposition in Chicago, 1893

Chicago, IL, 39, 44, 61, 80, 82, 84, 85, 91, 92, 124, 126, 133, 157, 170, 180, 199, 225, 227, 244, 254, 268, 295, 328, 361, 383, 405, 424

Chichen Itza, Mexico, 357-358

Chichicastenango, Guatemala, 358

Chihuahua, Mexico, 237, 327

Child and the Beast, The (1915), 206

Child Bride of Short Creek (1981), 247

Child's Life of Our Savior, A, 202

Children of God (book, 1939), 33, 261-262

Children's Friend, 102, 419-420

"Children's Friend of the Air", 419-420

Chile, 19, 330

China, 10, 19-20, 41, 51, 339-340

Chinese cinema, 10

Choate, Francis B., 75

Choir's Rehearsing for Easter (television show, 1954), 414

"*Christ on the Mount of Olives*", 409

Christ's Appearance to the Nephites (painting), 44

Christensen, C. C. A., 39-44, 47-48, 72

Christensen, J. A., 59

Christensen, P. A., 34

Christians, Christianity, ii, 62, 69, 159, 242

Christie, Al, 119

Church academies, see Church Educational System

Church Administration Building, 340, 393

Church archive, see Church History Library

Church Ball (2006), 102

Church Building Committee, 29-30, 342, 433

Church Educational System, 54, 64

Church film distribution, 59, 379

Church General Welfare Committee, 425

Church Historian, 51, 109, 203-204, 216, 246, 281, 356

Church History Library, 201, 205, 207, 210, 214, 231, 335-338, 341, 345, 348, 402, 406, 413

Church History Museum, 39, 43

Church Hour, 221, 367

Church in Action (1970-85), 231, 411

Church Information Service, 372

Church Missionary Committee, 372

Church News, 30, 367, 386, 398, 402, 403, 418

Church of England, 118

"*Church of the Air*", 367, 411, 414-415, 420

Church Radio, Publicity, and Mission Literature Committee, 234, 237, 364, 369-370, 372-374, 377, 386, 411, 415

Church schools, see Church Educational System

Church Welfare in Action (1948), 425-427, 438, 441

Church Welfare Plan, The, 365

Church Welfare Program, 19, 254-255, 340, 365, 378, 411, 424-428, 437-440

Church welfare program, see welfare program

"*Church's Attitude, The*", 368

Index

Church, Arthur Burdette, 222

Churchill, Frank, 290

Churchill, Winston, 158

cigarettes and tobacco, 78, 105, 128-129, 238, 286-287, 343, 373, 402, 411, 429, 439, 441

Cinderella (1950), 292, 294-296, 428

cinématographe (camera), 67

Citizen Kane (1941), 285, 390, 406

Citizen Saint (1947), 284

City Hall, Los Angeles, 280

City of Brigham Young (1944), 253, 413

City of Gold (1957), 309-311

City Slickers II: The Search for Curly's Gold (1993), 139

Civil War, see American Civil War

Civilization (1916), 125

Clark, J. Reuben, 125, 129, 235, 249, 257, 262, 336-338, 342-343, 359, 362, 392, 395, 403, 422, 423

Clark, James, 291

Clark, Les, 291-292, 295

Clawson Film Co., 213, 234

Clawson, Chester "Chet", 35, 38, 71, 107, 113, 125, 190, 192, 203, 207, 208-219, 220, 222-223, 229-231, 233, 234, 236-238, 319, 328-329, 335, 340, 345, 359, 363, 373, 393, 397, 400, 410, 411, 441

Clawson, Elliot J., 113-114

Clawson, Emily Augusta Young, 208

Clawson, Gertrude Romney, 209

Clawson, Hiram B., 35, 66, 71-73, 125, 208, 230

Clawson, John, 47

Clawson, John Willard, 302

Clawson, Lawrence Dallin "Dal", 125, 321

Clawson, Margaret, 125

Clawson, Rudger, 104, 113, 125, 161, 164-165, 168, 202, 208, 211, 215, 218, 361-362

Clawson, Scott, 418

Clawson, Shirley Young "Shirl", 35, 38, 71-73, 107, 113, 124-125, 190, 192, 202-203, 207, 208-219, 220, 222-223, 229-231, 233-234, 236-238, 317-319, 328-329, 335, 340, 345, 359, 363, 373, 393, 397, 400, 410, 411, 418, 441

Clawson, Scott, 418

Clawson, Stanley, 125

Clay County, MO, 15, 334

Clay, Andrew Dice, 4

Clay, H. M., 75

Clayton, Marguerite, 124

Clayton, William, 45

Clegg, Rue L., 406

Clements, Ron, 296

Cleopatra (1934), 114

Cleveland, Grover, 65

Cleveland, OH, 15, 180, 295

Cleveland, UT

Clifton, UT, 95

Clinton, DeWitt, 28

Clock, The (1945)

Cloninger, Ralph

Clooney, George, 98

Cluff, Benjamin, 138

Coalville, UT, 76

Cocteau, Jean, 343

Cody, William Frederick "Buffalo Bill", 90, 156, 302

Coe, Al, 425

Colbert Report (television series, 2005-14), 21

Colbert, Stephen, 4, 21

Cold War, 278

Colgate Theatre (television series, 1949), 305

Colonia Díaz, Mexico, 327, 335

Colonial Theatre, Salt Lake City, 199, 318

color film, 137, 235, 285, 327, 387

Colorado, 115, 131, 137, 139, 140, 156, 180, 252, 327, 372, 399

Colorado City, AZ, 247

Colorado River, 327

Columbia Broadcasting Company, 357

Columbia Broadcasting System, see CBS Corporation

Columbia Pictures, 293, 300

Columbia University, 126, 360

Columbus, OH, 106

Colvig, Pinto, 428

Colvin, William G., 197

Comancheros, The (1961), 139

Come Back, Little Sheba (1952), 300

"Come, Come Ye Saints", 229

Commerce, IL, see Nauvoo, IL

Compson, Betty, 112, 118-119, 240, 314

CONDER/dance, 28

Confederate States of America, 189

Congo, see Democratic Republic of the Congo

Congregationalists, Congregationalism, 52-53, 81, 106, 234

Congress, see United States Congress

Conklin, Chester, 121

Connecticut Yankee in King Arthur's Court, A (1949), 300

Connell, Robert M., 251

Conqueror, The (1956), 131

Constitution Hall, Washington, D.C., 127

Contributor, 315

Cooper, Gary, 114, 133-134, 245

Cooper, Merian C., 120, 273-276, 300, 336

Cooperative Retrenchment Associations, 99

Cop, The (1930), 114

Cope, John, 220

Copenhagen, Denmark, 39, 163-164

Corianton (1931), 37, 206, 237, 259, 313-328, 333, 346, 348, 352, 413, 441

Corianton (play, 1902), 60, 122, 209

Corianton Corporation, 319, 322-323

Corliss, Richard, 307

Cornell University, 306

Cornwall, Allen, 253

Cornwall, J. Spencer, 253, 290, 413

Coronet magazine, 136

Corral (1954), 310

Correlation, 30, 373

Cort, John, 78

Cosmopolitan, 158,

Cotton, Joseph, 287

Cougarettes, 28,

Council Bluffs, IA, 400

Council House, Salt Lake City, 208

Council of Fifty, 65

Count of Monte Cristo, The (1934), 125

Cover Girl (1944), 298

Covered Wagon, The (1923), 112, 194, 245

Covington, Niki, 32

Cowboy in Manhattan (1943), 384

Cowdery, Oliver, 14-15, 152

Cowley, Matthew, 335, 338, 424

Cowley, Matthias, 145

Cowley, WY, 108

Cox, A. M., 84

Cozy Theater, Duchesne, 323

Cozy theater, Ogden, 185, 323

Cracroft, Richard, 151

Creedon, Dick, 295

crickets, 16, 134, 253-255, 262-264, 269, 410

Crimean War, 37

Crockwell, James, 38

Crosby, Bing, 289, 384

Crowther, Bosley, 265, 385

Crowther, Norman, 179

Cruise on the Minnie-Lee (1960), 344

Cruze, James, 3, 111-113, 119, 123, 193-194, 240, 245, 314

Cruze, May, see Bosen, Mae

Cuba, 20, 142

Index

Cuernavaca, Mexico, 341

Cukor, George, 308

Culmer, Henry Lavender Adolphus, 39

Cummings, Horace C., 202

Cunard, Grace, 175

Currier & Ives, 44

Curse of the Cat People, The (1944), 124

Cutler, Doral, 342

Curtiz, Michael, 139, 307

Czech cinema, 10

Czech Republic, 20

Czechoslovak Mission, 337

Czechoslovakia, 11, 337, 355, 367

D'arc, James V., 120, 130, 261, 265-266, 324-326

Daddy Long Legs (1955), 300

Daguerre, Louis, 37

daguerreotypes, daguerreotypy, 37

Dahnken, Fred, 84

Dallas, TX, 157, 277

Dallin, Cyrus, 31, 47, 49, 55, 125

Dalys, Augustin, 36

Damstedt, George, 338

Damon and Pythias (play, ca. 1564), 35

Dancing with the Stars (television series, 2005-), 28

Dangerfield, Rodney, 4

Dangerous Crossing (1953), 308

Daniel Boone (television series, 1964-70)

Danieldsen, Anna, 204

Daniels Theater, Salt Lake City, 82

Danish Film Institute, 164, 189

Danish Mission, 345

Danish-Norwegian Mission, 109

Danite Chief, The, 154

Danites, 152-159, 166, 170-171, 176-177, 188, 235

Danites in the High Sierras (play), 154-155, 170

Dark Victory (1939), 306

Darnell, Linda, 260-262, 265

Darwell, Jane, 4, 260, 274

Daughters of Utah Pioneers, 222, 279

Daveline, Adam, 37

Daveline, Andrea, 37

David Copperfield (1935), 308

Davis, Bette, 306

Davis, Donald, 425

Dawn, Hazel, 122

Day in the Country, A (1930), 344

Day-Time Wife (1939), 260

Day, Elias, 298

Day, Laraine, 268, 288, 298

Daynes, Joseph J., 26

Days of Glory (1944), 307

Dazzy Shows His Album, 380

de Azevedo, Lex, 27

de Havilland, Olivia, 134

de Jong, Gerrit, Jr., 422

Deadwood Coach, The (1924), 132, 183

Deadwood Dick (1922), 188

Deadwood Dick (1940), 188

Deadwood Dick and the Mormons (1915), 188

Deadwood Dick Spoils Brigham Young (1915), 188

Deadwood, SD, 188

Dean, Julia, 124

Death Valley Days (television series, 1952-70), 308

Defence of Sevastopol (1911), 196

Degas, Edgar, 32, 48

Deja, Andreas, 296

Del Rio, Dolores, 133

Delaware, 319

DeLong, Lisa, 40

Delta Theatre, Delta, 86

Delta, UT, 86

DeLuxe Feature Film Exchange, 92

DeMille, Cecil B., 114, 116, 124, 134,

177-178, 245-246, 365, 390-391

Demme, Jonathan, 4

Democratic Party, 17, 63, 65, 66, 215, 279, 356

Democratic Republic of the Congo, 19

Demos, Bill, 433

Denmark, 20, 39, 109, 111, 158, 161-164, 166, 169, 189, 266, 340, 359

Dent, Ellsworth, 386-387, 396, 422

Denver and Rio Grande Western Railroad, 251-252, 372, 399

Denver, CO, 81, 84, 96, 123, 266, 293, 305, 318, 325, 403, 422, 424

Derr, E. B., 246

Deseret Book Company, 204, 359, 373-374, 380-386, 392-393, 396, 399-401, 404, 407-408, 410, 428, 441

Deseret Dramatic Association, 35, 209

Deseret Dramatic Association orchestra, 26

Deseret Film Productions, 213, 234, 335-336, 385, 393, 396-397, 400-401, 403, 407, 409-411, 424-425, 437

Deseret Gymnasium, 105

Deseret Museum, 57

Deseret News, 57, 69, 73, 76, 104, 117, 123, 124, 142, 153, 168, 198, 214, 220, 222-223, 227, 240, 245, 265, 268, 288, 295, 318-321, 340, 354, 362, 393

Deseret News Building, Salt Lake City, 214, 340, 393

Deseret Sunday School Union, see Sunday School

Deseret Theater Company, 83

Desert Empire (1938), 251-252

Desert Fury (1947), 407

Desert Mesa (1935), 244

Desperadoes, The (1943), 135

Despicable Me franchise, 3

Detroit, MI, 84, 180, 250, 327-328, 405

Detroit News, 328

Devil's Passkey, The (1920), 125

Dewey, John, 100

Dewey, Simon, 39

Diablo Rides, El (1939), 134

Dialogue: A Journal of Mormon Thought, 2,

Diamond, Ed, 217

Diamondville, WY, 76

Diary of a Sergeant (1945), 308

Dibble, Philo, 42-45, 52-53, 58, 331

DiCaprio, Leonardo, 301

Dickens, Charles, 239

Dickson, William K. L., 67, 69

Dionysus, 24

Disney, Roy, 291

Disney, Walt, 250, 285, 290-291, 293, 296-297, 425, 427-439

Disneyland, 297, 438

Disraeli (1921), 107-108, 113

Dixie Junior College, 374

Dixon, Denver, 134, 326

Dmytryk, Edward, 139

Docks of New York, The (1928), 119

Doctor Dolittle (1967), 5, 72

Doctrine and Covenants, 220, 331

Dodge (Fiat Chrysler car brand), 405

Don't Go Near the Water (1957), 388

Donald Duck (fictional character), 292, 294-295

Donald Gets Drafted (1942), 295

Donlevy, Brian, 262

Doomed Dozen; or, Dolores, the Danite's Daughter, The, 154

Dougall, Lily, 156

Douglas, Stephen A., 155

Dove, Billie, 298

Down Pioneer Trails, 365, 401

Downey, ID, 286, 300

Doyle, Arthur Conan, 3, 117, 154, 159, 174

Dr. Kildare franchise, 298

Dr. Strangelove (1964), 389

Dr. X (1932), 120

Index

Dream of a Racetrack Fiend, The (1906), 89

Dream of a Rarebit Fiend, The (1906), 80

Dresden, Germany, 243, 369

Drew, Donna, 123

Drifters (1929), 73, 218, 250

Driggs, Howard R., 342

Driven Westward (1948), 270

Driver Harris Wire Company, 92

Dru, Joanne, 274

Drums Along the Mohawk (1939), 137, 258

Dude Rancher, The (1934), 135

Dumb and Dumber (1994), 131

Du Mont Television Network, 417

Duchesne, UT, 323

Duchess and the Dirtwater Fox, The (1976), 228

DuckTales (television series, 1987-90), 304

Dumbo (1941), 296

Dunning, George, 309

Durbin, Deanna, 134

Durham, G. Homer, 359

Dutcher, Richard, 7, 284

DVD, 9, 278, 313, 380

Dwan, Allan, 170

Dynamic Kernels Institute, 386

Dynamiter, The, 155

Eagle Gate (statue), 31, 208, 249

Eagle Plume: The White Avenger: A Tale of the Mormon Trail, 154

Earle, John, 140

East Asia, 266

East Canyon, UT, 223

East Central States Mission, 345

East Germany, 431

East Side Kids franchise, 115

East Side of Heaven (1939), 384

Eastern Arizona College, 64

Eastern States Exposition (1930),

Eastern States Mission, 168, 179, 207, 333, 336, 356

Eastman Kodak Company, 3, 329-330, 342, 387

Eastman School of Music, 127

Eastman, George, 67

Easy Rider (1969), 131, 138

Eccles, Parlay, 110

Echo Canyon, UT, 222

Eckhart, Aaron, 3

Éclair, 330

Eden Park (fairground), 54

Edison Company (Thomas A. Edison, Inc.), 160,

Edison, Thomas A., 55, 67, 69, 71, 73-76, 89, 105, 126, 148, 160, 193, 320

Edmunds Act (1882), 18

Edmunds-Tucker Act (1887), 18, 53, 145, 152

Edouarde, Carl, 321

Education Film and Service Corporation, 104, 210

Educational Screen, 386

Edward, Lizzie Thomas, 59

Egan, Howard, 153

Egypt, 57, 131, 347

Egyptian, The (1954), 307

Egyptian Theater, Ogden, 85

Egyptian theater, Park City, 86

Eiffel Tower, 49

Eiger Sanction, The (1975), 138

Eighty-sixth Annual Conference of the Church of Jesus Christ of Latter-day Saints, The (1916), 213

Eisenhower, Dwight D., 286

Eisenstein, Sergei, 235, 250

Eisner, Michael, 297

El Camino, CA, 345

Elden, Eric, 321

Electric Theater, Salt Lake City, 80-81

Electric Theatre, Ogden, 89

Electrical Research Products,

Electrical Research Products Inc., 229, 378, 381

electricity, electrification, 49, 58, 66, 69, 128, 133

Electrick Children (2013), 247

Elite Theater, Salt Lake City, 81

Elko, NV, 95, 264

Ellaye Motion Picture Company, 195-197, 199, 212

Ellington, Duke, 125

Ellison, Homer E., 84, 93

Ellsworth, German E., 331

Elsaesser, Thomas, 11

Elvis and the Colonel (book) 288

Emergency Committee to Save the Jewish People of Europe, 267

Emigration Canyon, UT, 196, 222, 398

Emigration Canyon (monument), 31, 251

Emperor Jones, The (1933), 125

Empire (television series, 1962-63), 301

Empire Marketing Board of the UK, 218

Empire State Building, 3, 49

Empire Strikes Back, The (1980), 1

Empire Theater, Salt Lake City, 81, 84

Empire Theater, London, 250

Empress Theater, see Paramount-Empress Theater, Salt Lake CityEnabling Act of 1894, 66

Encyclopedia Britannica, 382

endowment ceremony, 44, 46, 204, 372-373, 395, 411, 428-436

endowment ceremony, film version, 234, 372-373, 395, 411, 428-436, 439, 441

Endowment House, Salt Lake City, 45

Engholm, Harry, 174

England, 31, 60, 67, 118, 150, 154, 158-159, 161, 164-165, 168, 172-173, 185-188, 209, 218, 250, 254, 266, 278, 282, 355, 360, 363-371, 401, 431, 435

England, Eugene, 32, 34, 236

Englewood, NJ, 125

Ensign magazine, 96

Ensign Camera Co., 370

Ensign Stake Twentieth Ward, 216

Enterprise Productions, 406

Ephraim, UT, 244

Episode of Early Mormon Days, An (1911), 166-167, 170, 210

Equal Rights Amendment, 19

Equitable Motion Pictures Corporation, 176

ERA, see Equal Rights Amendment

Ericksen, Ephraim Edward, 61, 383

Erickson, Hilda Anderson, 71

Erie Canal, 14

Erie, PN, 334

Escape from Polygamy (2013), 247

Escape in the Desert (1945), 305

Ecstasy (1933), 248

Essanay Film Manufacturing Co., 124

Estes Park, CO, 242

Eunice Goodrich Vaudeville Co., 76

Euripedes, 24

Europe, 10, 15-16, 18-20, 26, 29, 36, 41, 49-51, 54, 56, 61-62, 67, 73, 116, 122, 144, 152, 158-162, 164, 166, 170, 176, 183-184, 186, 193, 199, 266, 267, 272, 284, 297, 309, 338-339, 354, 356, 359-361, 365, 370, 372, 387, 415, 430-432

European Film Commissions Network, 140

Evans, C. Richard, 417

Evans, David, 337

Evans, Edwin, 48

Evans, Fred, 187

Evans, John Henry, 195

Evans, Paul, 432-433, 435

Evans, Richard L., 254, 403, 412

Evans, Will, 187

Evarts, Hal, 314

Eve's Leaves (1926), 113

Evening Dispatch, 53

Everlasting Hills, 365

Index

Everson, George, 128

Everybody Comes to Rick's, 307

Everybody's Magazine, 158

Excuse Me (1915), 188-189

Exhibitors Trade Review, 108

Exile, The (1931), 320

Exploits of Battling Dick Hatton, The (1921), 184

Expo '67, Montreal, 310-311

Exposition Universelle, 1889, 48

Extinct (television series, 2017), 422

Eyring, Carl F., 370, 387, 422

Ezra the Mormon, 158

Facebook, 69

Facing East (play, 2007), 37

Factor, Max, Jr., 383

Fairbanks, Avard T., 32, 345, 369

Fairbanks, Douglas, 96, 107, 237

Fairbanks, J. Leo, 32

Fairbanks, John B., 38

"Faith in Action", 372

Faith of an Observer: Conversations with Hugh Nibley (1985), 231

Fallon, John, 52

"Family Hour, The", 419

Family Theatre, Salt Lake City, 80

Famous Adventures of Mr. Magoo (1964-65), 308

Famous Players Film Company, 94, 122, 175

Famous Players-Lasky Corporation, 94, 114, 175, 187

Fanchon & Marco, Inc., 95

Fantasia (1940), 296, 434, 439

Far West, MO, 15, 399,

Farber, Manny, 385

Farmington, UT, 54, 217, 332

Farnsworth Television and Radio Corporation, 129

Farnsworth, Pem, 3, 128, 416

Farnsworth, Philo T., 127-129, 285, 415-416

Farnum, William, 182

Faroe Islands, 109

Fascinating Salt Lake City, 365

Father Noah's Ark (1933), 290

Fassbinder, Rainer Werner, 11

Faucett Publications syndicate, 288

Fauré, Gabriel, 414

Faust, James E., 345

Faye, Alice, 257

Fayette, NY, 15, 335, 372

Fazenda, Louise, 173

Federal Communications Commission, see United States Federal Communications Commission

Federal Radio Commission, see United States Federal Radio Commission

Federal Reserve System, 100

Feminist Mormon Housewives (blog), 34

Fennemore, James, 37

Ferguson, Otis, 385

Ferron, UT, 378

Ferry, Joan, 188

Feud on the Range (1939), 134

Fidelity Picture Plays Syndicate, 184

Fielding, Romaine, 114

Fifty Shades of Grey (2015), 3

Fighting Shepherdess, The (1920), 184

Fighting the Fire Bomb (1942), 424

Fillmore, UT, 303

Film Daily, 94, 321, 350

filmstrips, 5, 6, 64, 143, 234-236, 330, 333-334, 340, 352-356, 358, 360, 362-374, 376-380, 386-390, 401, 403, 405, 412, 422, 424, 432, 437

Finland, 56, 338

Finney, Edward, 279-282, 313, 328

Firefly, The (1937), 308

First Fam'lies of the Sierras, 155

First National Film Company (UK), 117

First National Pictures, 95, 121, 132

First Presidency, 20, 47, 59, 60, 103,

105, 107, 141, 145, 164, 166, 184, 192, 202-203, 210, 240, 253, 265, 307, 318, 333, 335, 341, 357-363, 375, 377-378, 383, 389, 396, 419, 431, 433

First Vision, 14, 43, 48, 197, 347, 409

Fischer, Margarita, 176

Fisher, Vardis, 33, 257-259, 266

Fitzhamon, Lewin, 161

FitzPatrick, James A., 252

Fitzpatrick, John, 415

Five Continents Exchange and Sales Company, 199

Flagstaff, AZ, 85, 182

Flaherty, Robert, 216, 218, 255, 336

Flame of Life, The (1923), 114

Flaming Gorge, WY, 339

Flamingo Film Company, 187

Flanagan, Alma, 86

Fleischer, Dave, 404

Fleischer, Max, 404

Fleming, Rhonda, 299-300

Flesh and the Devil (1926), 118

Fletcher, Harvey, 126-127, 413-415

Flight to Hong Kong (1956), 308

Flint, MI, 294

Floating Gardens of Xochimilco, 341

Flockhart, Calista, 4

Florence, NE, 398

Florence, Max, 81-82, 92-95, 158, 194

Flower of the Mormon City, The (Mormonbyens Blomst, 1911), 161, 164-167, 170-171

Flying A, 170

Flynn, Errol, 289, 306, 390

Foch, Nina, 289

Fogo Island Communications Experiment, 311

Foley, Jack, 251

Folkersen, Le Roy Ronald, 338

Folsom, William H., 29

Fonda, Henry, 137-138, 267, 287

Fonda, Peter, 138

Fontaine, Anne, 389

Footloose (1984), 131

Ford International Weekly, 107

Ford Motor Company, 328

Ford Television Theatre, The (television series, 1952-57), 299

Ford, Francis, 175

Ford, Glenn, 300

Ford, Harriet, 176

Ford, James J. 206

Ford, John, 4, 113, 137-139, 175, 258-260, 272-278

Ford, Patrick, 273-274

Ford, Thomas, 16

Fordham, Elijah, 30

Foreign Correspondent (1940), 298

Forest Dale Ward, 204

Forgotten Empires, 365-366

Forrest Gump (1994), 131

Fort Apache (1948), 138, 273

Fort Bridger, WY, 400, 404

Fort Douglas, UT, 207, 401

Fort Laramie, WY, 399

Fort Lauderdale Branch, 340

Fort Lauderdale, FL, 193, 340

Fort Lee, NJ, 320

Fort Missoula, MT, 367

Fort Moore, CA, 279, 380

Fort Ord, CA, 339

Fort Russell, WY, 142

Foster, Lucian R., 37

Fotorama, see A/S Fotorama

Fountain Green Theatre, 108

Fountain Green Ward, 375

Four Horsemen of the Apocolypse, The (1921), 115, 125

Fox, see Twentieth Century-Fox

Fox Movietone News, 249

Fox, Alexander, 37

Fox, Esther Vida, 209

Fox, F. Wilken, 386

Index

Fox, William, 123, 182-183, 249, 256, 390

Foy, Eddie, 35

France, 10, 11, 48, 54, 67, 109, 116, 122, 164, 167, 174, 187, 266-267

Free Public School Act (1890), 64

Freece, Hans Peter, 161, 169, 184

French cinema, 10

French Polynesia, 19

French, Charles, 190

Friedman Enterprises, Inc., 180

Friedman, Benjamin, 180

Friend, 419-420

Friendly, Fred, 414

From Plowboy to Prophet: Being a Short History of Joseph Smith, for Children

From the Manger to the Cross (1912), 104, 191

Frontier Guardian, 27

Frost, Alice, 320

Frozen River (1929), 113

Fugitive, The (1947), 273

Fuller, William, 51-52

Fuller's Hill Pleasure Gardens (fairground), 51-52

Fullmer, Nathan O., 220

"*Fulness of Times, The*", 368, 412, 415

Fun and Fancy Free (1947), 295

Fundamentalist Church of Jesus Christ of Latter-day Saints, ii, 4, 18, 247

fundraising, Church or ward, 5-6, 55, 103, 107, 192, 204, 374-376, 382, 398

Furthman, Charles, 314

Gable, Clark, 136, 288

Gadsden Purchase, 279

Gaffney, Lillian, 247-248

Gage, Harvey, 245

Gagin-Melton Agency, 287

Gagin, Mildred, 287, 373

Galaxy Quest (1999), 131

Gambling with Souls (1936), 247

Gance, Abel, 389

Gangs of New York (1938), 112

Garbo, Greta, 118, 258, 287

Garden City, KS, 123

Gardens of Versailles, 41

Gardiner, B. Clifford, 128

Gardner, Ava, 304

Gardner, Blythe M., 337

Gardner, Florinda, 314

Garff, Mark, 340, 432

Garfield County, UT, 131

Garland, Judy, 270, 304

Garner, Julia, 4

Garrett, Grant, 271

Gärtner, Heinrich, 189

Gates, Harvey H., 114

Gates, Susa Young, 33, 114, 419

Gateway to Hollywood, 299

Gattfredson, Floyd, 292

Gauguin, Paul, 48

Gaumont, Léon, 193

gay rights, see LGBTQ rights, issues, films

Geary, Edward, 34

Geertsen, Norman, 423

Gem Theatre, Salt Lake City, 80

Genealogical Society of Utah, 102, 359

General Authorities at Christmastime (1945), 340, 432

general conference, 5, 26, 86, 106, 129, 143, 147, 191, 194, 198, 203, 205, 210, 213-214, 218, 221-222, 233, 253, 269, 336, 339, 346, 361-362, 371-372, 382, 390, 393, 396, 399, 409, 414, 416, 418, 420-421, 429

general conference, broadcasting of on radio and television, 221-222, 372, 393, 399, 409, 416, 418, 420, 429

general conference, filming of, 213-214, 218, 339

General Features syndicate, 288

General Federation of Women's Clubs,

383

General Film Company, 92-93

General Post Office of the UK, 218

Geneva (fairground), 54

Geneva Steel plant, Orem, UT, 339

Gentleman's Agreement (1947), 257

George Albert Smith-In Memoriam (1951), 411

George VI, 337

George Washington Bridge, 320

George Washington University, 286, 306

German cinema, 11

German-Austrian Mission, 337

Germany, 11, 20, 39, 67, 90-91, 109, 131, 136, 152, 158, 161, 189, 244, 266, 268, 298, 337-338, 347, 381, 388, 422, 431, 433, 435

Geronimo: An American Legend (1993), 139

Get Smart (television series, 1965-70), 303

Getty Images, 254

Ghana, 345, 408

Giant Joshua, The (book, 1942), 33

Gilbert, Guy, 85

Gilbert, John, 118-119

Gilbert, Walter, 118

Giles, John D., 332, 400

Giles, John Davis, 370

Gilman, Ada, 156

Girl from Utah, The, 157, 177

Girl of the Golden West, The (1938), 87

Givens, Terryl, 23, 43, 48, 61, 154, 158

Glade, Earl J., 221

Glasgow, Scotland, 58-59

Glen Canyon, UT, 273

Glendale Center Theater, 427

Glendale, CA, 297, 300, 373

Glenwood Park (fairground), 77

Glover, Aaron, 345

Glover, Crispin, 4

Glynne, Agnes, 175

Go West, Young Man (1918), 121

God, 13-14, 16, 24, 36, 46-47, 68-69, 72, 129, 138, 150, 237, 251, 262, 264, 267, 269, 316, 355, 429

God Is My Landlord (1948), 386

God's Army (2000), 201, 314, 329

Goddard, John M., 358-359

Godless Girl, The (1929), 226

Godsoe, Harold, 319

Gold Diggers of 1933 (1933), 303

gold rush, see California Gold Rush or Klondike Gold Rush

Gold Rush, The (1925), 121

golden plates, 14, 49, 68, 198

Golden Gate International Exposition (1939)

Golden State Moving Picture Company, 199

Goldwater, Barry, 334

Goldwyn, Samuel, 177, 285

Gone with the Wind (1939), 118, 235, 263

Good Earth, The (1937), 249

Goodyear Blimp, 265

Goosson, Stephen, 288

Gordon, William F., 312

Gordon-Levitt, Joseph, 4

Gorham, Christopher, 4

Gorin, Igor, 229, 302

Gosling, Ryan, 3

Gospel Primer, The, 202

Goss, Joe, 85

Gotham (television series, 2014-), 284

Goulding, Harry, 137

Goupil & Cie, 44

Grable, Betty, 289

Grace, Dick, 225

Graduate, The (1967), 72

Graham, Effie, 299

Graham, John Crosthwaite, 299

Graham, Winifred, 158-159, 184

Grain of Dust, The (1918), 206

Index

Grammy Awards, 127

Grand Café, Paris, 67

Grand Canyon, 96, 132-133, 157, 182, 280, 326, 344

Grand Canyon Voyage (1951), 343

Grand County, UT, 139-140

Grand Historical Panorama of the Antediluvian World (painting), 41

Grand National Films, 279

Grand Opera House, Salt Lake City, 66, 78, 143

Grand Staircase-Escalante National Monument, 133, 273

Grand Theater, Salt Lake City, 84, 89

Granite Flats (television series, 2013-15), 422

Granite High School, 102

Granite Stake, 102-103, 105, 355

Grant, Cary, 113

Grant, Cliff W., 156

Grant, Heber J., 48, 129, 132, 182-183, 191, 215-217, 220, 222-223, 233, 235, 239-243, 247, 249, 251-254, 258-261, 264-265, 268-269, 283, 301, 315, 332, 337, 341, 345-346, 348, 350-352, 356, 361, 363-364, 375, 370, 390-391, 397, 414-415, 427, 431, 441

Grant, Jedediah, 153

Grant, Ulysses, 249

Grantsville, UT, 341

Grapes of Wrath, The (1940), 71, 257, 258, 260, 266

Grass (1925), 56, 218

Grasshopper and the Ants, The (1934), 290, 428

Grauman's Chinese Theatre, Los Angeles, 265

Grauman's Metropolitan Theatre, California, 91, 265

Great Accommodation, 61, 65, 101, 381

Great Adventures of Wild Bill Hickok, The (1939), 135

Great Basin Kingdom (book, 1958), 64

Great Britain, 109, 165, 359, 370

Great Depression, 19, 87, 95, 97, 148, 233-234, 236, 238, 245, 248, 250-256, 283, 289-291, 293, 298, 309, 312-313, 315, 319, 321, 324-325, 333-334, 342, 352, 363, 374-376, 392

Great Falls, MT, 305

Great Island Holding Company, 284

Great Northern Films, 162, 169

Great Northern Special Feature Film Company, see Great Northern Films

Great Rupert, The (1950), 300

Green River Expedition (1950), 343

Great Salt Lake, 16, 51, 77, 112, 215, 253, 264, 344, 404

Great Train Robbery, The (1903), 79

Greatest Story Ever Told, The (1965), 131, 139

Greed (1924), 115, 125

Green Grass of Wyoming (1948), 135

Green Slime, The (1968), 301

Greenaway, Peter, 4

Greene Christmas, A (1939), 344

Greene, Graham, 273

Greene, Matthew, 37

Greene, Mildred, 344

Grey, Zane, 10, 137, 157-158, 181-183, 244, 258

Grierson, John, 218, 309

Griffin, Eleanor, 257

Griffith, D. W., 72, 78, 97, 106, 177, 235

Griffith, Raymond, 190

Grilikhes, Michael, 299

Grimsby, England, 186

Groveland, ID, 335

Grow, Henry, 29

Guangdong, China, 339

Guaraní (language), 20

Guatemala, 358

Guess Who, 27

Gulf States Mission, 345

Gulliver's Travels Among the Lilliputians

and the Giants (1902), 79

Gunfight at the O.K. Corral (1957), 300

Gunnison, UT, 86, 431

Gypsy Baron, The, 290

Haag, Herman, 48

Hadlock, Neil, 32

Hafen, John, 47-48, 212

Haight, Isaac, 282

Hal Roach Studios, 373, 384

Hale, Karl, 32

Hale, Nathan, 32, 36, 427

Hale, Ruth, 36

Hale's Tours and Scenes of the World, 160

Hales, Wayne, 370, 387

Hallstrom, Angela, 33

Halverson, A. Reed, 338

Hamblin, Fay, 135-136

Hamblin, Ina, 136-137

Hamblin, Jacob, 135, 326

Hamilton, New Zealand Temple, 433, 435

Hamlet (ca. 1600), 36

Hammerstein, Oscar, 318

Hammond Hall, Salt Lake City, 53

Hancock, Levi, 42

Handcart Ensemble, 37

Handcart Pioneer Monument (statue), 32, 405

handcarts, 16, 43, 140, 172-173, 246, 252, 275, 347, 349, 400, 409

Hands Up! (1926), 189, 229

Hanks, Ephraim, 153

Hansen, Harold I., 433

Hansen, Louise, 36-37

Hansen, Ramm, 341

Hansen, Valdemar, 189

Harbeck, William H., 193

Harding, Warren G., 132, 221, 239-240

Hardy, Nicole, 34

Hardy, Ralph, 370-371

Harline, Leigh, 290-291

Harmon, W. Glenn, 339

Harms, Gus, 95

Harper Prize, 258

Harper, Olive, 157

Harris, Ed, 4

Harris, Eleanor, 257, 264, 267

Harris, Franklin S., 388, 422

Harris, Martin, 331, 334

Harris, Trent, 3

Harrison, Benjamin, 65

Harrison, NJ, 92

Harry Lauder and Julian Eltinge vaude-ville company, 78

Hart, Charles H., 215

Hartley, William G., 397

Harvard University, 284

Harwood, James T., 47

Hatch, Nathan, 68

Hathaway, Anne, 4

Hathaway, Henry, 4, 134, 244, 258, 262-266, 313, 376, 410

Hatton, UT, 289

Havana, Cuba, 141-142

Hawaii, 18, 28, 109, 220, 335, 337-339, 341-342, 430

Hawaii Temple, see Laie Hawaii Temple

Hawaiian Punch (2013), 12

Hawks, Howard, 235

Haworth, Joseph, 317

Haws, Karl N., 340

Hawthorne Ward, 378

Hawthorne, Nathaniel, 384

Hayes, Rutherford B., 62

Hays Code, see Production Code

Hays Production Code, see Production Code

Hays, Will H., 239

Hayward-Deverish Agency, 287

HBO, 254

Index

He Is a Mormon (*Han er Mormon*, 1922), 189

He Who Gets Slapped (1924), 118, 249

Head, Edith, 289

Headless Horseman, The (1922), 107

Hearst, William Randolph, 120, 240, 285

Heavenly Father, see God

Heavenly Mother, see God

Heber City, UT, 292

Hedengren, Mark, 38

Heigl, Katherine, 3

Heise Hot Springs, ID, 225

Helena, MT, 123, 318

Hell's Highway (1932), 243

Helsengreen, Gunnar, 166

Hemingway, Ernest, 33, 307

Henefer, UT, 400, 404

Henn, Mark, 296

Henry, Prince of Prussia, 78

Hepburn, Audrey, 289

Hepburn, Katharine, 298, 304

Hepworth Manufacturing Company, 161

Hepworth Studios, 370

Her Gilded Age (1922), 88

Herbie Fully Loaded (2005), 308

Here Comes Trouble (1948), 119

Heritage of the Desert, The (1924), 183, 244

Heritage of the Desert, The (1932), 244

Heritage of the Desert, The (1939), 244

Heroes (television series, 2006-10), 308

Hess, Riley, 344

Heston, Charlton, 4

Hickman, William, 153, 155

Hicks, Michael, 25-26

High Noon (1952), 276

High School Musical franchise, 131

Hill Cumorah, 14, 207, 331-332, 334-336, 339, 345-347, 358, 433

Hill Cumorah Monument, see Angel

Moroni Monument (statue)

Hill Cumorah Pageant, 345-346, 433

Hill, Dwayne, 409

Hill, Napoleon, 321, 323

Hill, Walter, 139

Hiller & Wilk, 179-181

Hills of Utah, The (1951), 244

Hinckley, Ada, 361

Hinckley, Alonzo A., 359, 364

Hinckley, Bryant S., 103, 359-360, 363, 383

Hinckley, Gordon B., 219, 234, 236, 238, 330, 354, 357, 359, 364, 370, 373, 389, 401, 408, 411, 413, 432, 434, 441

Hinckley, Ramona, 365

Hindus, Hinduism, 58

Hiram, OH, 331

His Girl Friday (1940), 71, 289

His Hour (1924), 118

Historic Highlights of Mormonism, 365, 371

History of the Church of Jesus Christ of Latter-day Saints in Film, The, 356, 379

Hitchcock, Alfred, 4, 226, 298, 300-304, 309, 385

Hitler, Adolf, 294, 371

Hobbs, Forrest, 419

Hodkinson, William W., 93-95

Hoglund, Albin, 426, 428, 439

Hoffman, Dustin, 4

Hoffman, Philip Seymour, 4

Hole in the Rock formation, 273, 327-328

Hole, William, 204

Hollywood Citizen-News, 278

Hollywood Reporter, 278

Hollywood Stake, 110, 241, 274, 283

Hollywood Walk of Fame, 119, 299, 304

Holmes, Burton, 52

Holmes, Katie, 4

Holmes, Sherlock (fictional character), 3, 154, 174-176, 187

Holocaust, the, 267

Holy Bible, see Bible

Holy Ghost, the, 2, 426

Home Cinema movement, 8, 236-238, 313, 315, 328-329, 345, 400, 405, 407, 429, 440-441

Home Dramatic Club, 35

Home Industry movement, 33, 48, 98, 237-238

Home Literature movement, 33, 36, 236-237, 315, 317, 347, 407, 419

Home Teachers, The (2004), 103

home teaching, 103

Homestead Resort, Midway, 438

Hong Kong cinema, 10

Hong Kong, China, 19

Hoover, Herbert, 132, 255, 339

Hopper, Dennis, 138

Horton, Bob, 345

Horton, Robert, 301

Hotel Alexandria, Los Angeles, 280

Hotel Utah, Salt Lake City, 193, 340, 378

House of Lies, The (1916), 117

House of Rothschild, The (1934), 267

House of Seven Gables, The (1940), 384

House of Shame, The (unmade), 184

House of the Lord, The, 194-195, 207, 373

House of the Lord, The (filmstrip), 365

House Un-American Activities Committee, 113, 275, 299

Housing Problems (1935), 219

Houston Ballet, 28

Houston, Sam, 302

How Green Was My Valley (1941), 257

How Near to the Angels (1956), 100

How the West Was Won (1963), 130

Howe Danceworks, 28

Howe, Eber, 152

Howe, Elliott, 184

Howe, Lyman H., 52

Howe, Susan, 33, 37

Howells, Adele Cannon, 420

Howells, David P., 95

Hub Theatre, Cowley, 108

Huey, Dewey, and Louie (fictional characters), 292

Hughes, David, 31

Hughes, Howard, 273, 275, 278, 301

Hughes, Rupert, 246

Hulk (2003), 131

Hull, England, 165, 186

Human Jungle, The (1954), 308

Humanology Film Producing Company, 176

Hunchback, The (play, 1832), 36

Hunchback of Notre Dame, The (1939), 285

Hunt, George W. P., 242

Hunt, Helen, 4

Hunter, Howard W., 26-27

Huntington Park Ward, 294

Huntington, Elfie, 38

Hurlbut, Philastus, 152, 158

Huston, John, 414

Hutchinson, S. W., 192

Hyde Park, UT, 95

Hyde, George Osmond, 186

Hyde, Orson, 287

Hyde, Rosel H., 285-287, 417

hymns, hymnody, 5, 22, 25, 29, 34, 53, 87, 332, 372, 405, 430

Hypocrites (1915), 125

I Am a Polygamist, 247, 248

I Cover the Waterfront (1933), 112-113

I Walked a Crooked Trail (1950), 344

I Wonder Who's Kissing Her Now (1947), 284

"*I Wonder Who's Kissng Her Now*" (song), 284

I'm a Mormon (webseries, 2011-), 218

Ibsen, Henrik, 36

Index

Ice Station Zebra (1968), 5

Iceland, 109

Ickes, Harold, 406

Idaho, 16, 64-65, 76, 85-87, 95, 104, 168, 179-180, 197, 200, 205, 224, 229, 261, 286, 291-292, 300, 304, 321, 335, 342, 355, 396, 410, 430

Idaho Falls, ID, 127, 225, 335

Idaho Falls, Idaho Temple, 332, 335-336

Idiot Witness (play), 35

Idle Class, The (1921), 121

Illinois, 15-16, 131, 151, 153-154, 157, 249, 267, 332, 399, 404

Imagine Dragons, 27

IMAX, 3, 311-312

Imperial Russian Ballet Company, 115-116

Improvement Era, 74, 96, 101, 107, 110, 115, 217, 340, 351, 362, 366, 376-377, 383, 384, 417

In Old Chicago (1938), 257

In the Labyrinth (1967), 310

In the Service of God (2003), 103

In the Top of the Mountains, 365

Ince, Thomas, 72, 118, 120, 125, 173

Indepdence Day (1996), 131

Independence Hall, 30, 53

Independence Rock, WY, 398

Independence, KS, 93

Independence, MO, 196, 222, 333, 399, 475

India, 58

Indiana Jones and the Last Crusade (1989), 130, 140

Indonesia, 40

Industrial Revolution, 49, 71

influenza pandemic of 1918, 90, 105, 123

Informer, The (1935), 273

Ingram, Rex, 115, 125

Innocents, The (2016), 389

Inspiration Pictures, 133

Instagram, 69, 329

Institute of Human Relations, 242

institutes, see Church Educational System

Intercollegiate Broadcasting System, 423

Interdenominational Council of Women, 161

Intermountain Theatres Association, 110, 265

International Bioscope Company, 79

Internet, 6, 9, 23, 34, 219

Iowa, 16, 26, 131, 225, 400

Ipswich, England, 165

Iraq, 20, 131

Ireland, 43, 131, 161, 355

Iron County, UT, 131

Iron Horse, The (1924)

Irwin, William R., 245

Isis Theater Company, 92

Isis Theatre, Salt Lake City 81, 82

Isleworth, England, 175

Israel, 131

It's a Wonderful Life (1946), 302, 384

It's Love I'm After (1937), 306

It's the Ward Teachers (1956), 103

Italian cinema, 11

Italy, 11, 54, 131

Ithaca, NY, 193

Ivens, Joris, 343

Ivins, Anthony W., 215, 233, 335

Ivins, Antoine R., 335-336

Ives, Burl, 136

Jack the Giant Kiler (1962), 125

Jack and Jill in Songland, 379

Jackie Gleason Show, The (television series, 1952-59), 305

Jackson County, MO, 15

Jackson Hole, WY, 272

Jacksonville, FL, 142

Jacobs, David, 201, 231

Jagger, Dean, 4, 261, 263, 265, 268, 270

James, Jesse, 261-262

Jane Eyre, 149-150

Japan, 20, 41, 79, 337-339, 381

jazz, 26-28, 105

Jazz Singer, The (1927), 226, 288, 319

Jeffers, William M., 390

Jefferson, Samuel, 44

Jenkins, Ab, 139, 265

Jenkins, Charles Francis, 76, 128

Jennings, DeWitt C., 124,132

Jennings, W. L., 80

Jensen, A. B., 76

Jensen, Julie, 36

Jenson, Andrew, 109, 165, 203-204, 353

Jenson, Harold, 217

Jepperson, Samuel Hans, 39

Jeppson, Joseph, 109

Jerome, ID, 157

Jerrold, Douglas, 36

Jersey City, NJ, 84

Jesse Lasky Feature Play Company, 94

Jesus Christ, 13, 14, 201, 204, 246, 347, 355, 370, 379, 415, 341

Jevne, Jack, 113

Jewel Theatre, Santaquin, 86

Jews, Judaism, 21, 81, 95, 111, 152, 241, 266-268, 294, 303, 320

Johansen, Franz, 32

John Carter (2012), 130, 139

Johnny Apollo (1940), 258

Johnny Lingo (1969), 404

Johns Hopkins University, 55

Johnson, Ben, 274, 277

Johnson, Charles Ellis, 38

Johnson, Claudell, 416

Johnson, Eva, 81, 89

Johnson, Ezekiel, 327

Johnson, Gladys, 224

Johnson, John, 331

Johnson, Lyman, 152

Johnson, Nephi, 326

Johnson, Raymond, 224

Jolly Boatman, The (painting), 44

Jolson, Al, 35, 158

Jonasson, Frank, 122

Jones, Jennifer, 304

Jones, John Wesley, 41

Jones, Kumen, 327

Jones, Sidney, 157

Jones, Spike, 304

Jordan River, UT, 197

Joseph F. Smith (1999), 231

Joseph in the Land of Egypt (1914), 112

Joseph Smith-An American Prophet, 360, 366

Joseph Smith Preaching to the Indians (painting), 44

Josephson, Marba C., 384

Josseph Smith's Own Story, 369

Juarez Academy, 64

Judge Roy Bean (television series, 1956-57), 308

Jungle Book, The (1967), 296

Junior Council (television series, 1948-1960), 420

Jura Mountains, Switzerland, 431

Juvenile Instructor (periodical), 34, 44, 101, 204-205, 380, 419

Kalem Film Company, 104, 122

Kalaupapa Branch, 339

Kanab Area Motion Picture Association, see Kanab Movieland, Inc.

Kanab Kid, The, see Feud on the Range (1939)

Kanab Movieland, Inc., 140

Kanab Pictures, Inc., 285

Kanab, UT, 133-140, 285, 289, 325-326, 397

Kanarraville, UT, 86

Kanosh, UT, 289

Index

Kansas City, MO, 15, 222, 318, 399

Karlstejn Castle, Czechoslovakia, 337

Kathleen Mavoureen (1906), 80

Katzenberg, Jeffrey, 297

Kauffman, Ruth, 176

Kawich's Gold Mine, 195

KBYU radio and television, 422, 423

KDYL radio, television, 416-417, 419-420

Keane, Glen, 296

Keaton, Buster, 124, 235, 279

Keene, Tom, 246

Keep Your Powder Dry (1945), 298

Kelleher, Helen, 60

Keller, Arthur C., 127

Kelley, Edgar Stillman, 321

Kelly, Grace, 276

Kelly, Harry A., 195-196

Kemper, Charles, 630

Kendis, J. D., 247

Kennedy, John F., 286

Kent, Sidney, 257-258

Kentucky, 142

Kentucky Moonshine (1938), 331

Kenyon, Doris, 113

Kern, Jerome, 157

Kerrigan, J. Warren, 123, 170

Keystone Kops, 73

Keystone Studios, 120-121, 189

KFOO radio, 222

KFPT radio, 221

KHJ radio, 295

Kickapoos vaudeville company, 76

Kid, The (1920), 97

Kigali, Rwanda, 140

Killers, 27,

Killing, The (1956), 305

Kimball, Camilla, 404

Kimball, Edward, 90-91, 221, 341, 379, 412

Kimball, Heber C., 38, 115-116, 153

Kimball, J. Golden, 214

Kimball, Spencer W., 1, 2, 1, 26, 269, 341, 388, 408

Kinema theater, Salt Lake City, 87

kinescopes, 418-420

kinetoscope, 67, 74-81, 92, 103

King Features syndicate, 288, 292

King Kong (1933), 3, 120, 273, 300

King of Kings, The (1927), 365, 390

King Sisters, 27

King's Row (1942), 306

King's Row (book), 306

Kirkham, James M., 349

Kirkham, Reuben, 39, 43

Kirtland Safety Society, 332

Kirtland Temple, 29, 45, 195, 332, 334-335, 342

Kirtland, OH, 15, 45, 331, 334

Kiss, The (sculpture), 24

Kit Carson (1940), 138

Klappkir, R. H., 81

Kleinman, Bertha, 347

Klondike (television series, 1960-61), 306

Klondike Gold Rush, 121, 310

Knaphus, Torlief, 32, 341, 358, 405

Knight, Gladys, 27

Knight, Walter, 231

Knott's Berry Farm, 280

Knowles, James Sheridan, 36

Knox, Harley E., 280

Knox, John, 302

Koch, Howard W., 136

Kodachrome film stock, 342, 344m 371

Kodak, see Eastman Kodak Company

Koenig, Wolf, 310

Kong, Jack Sing, 339

Korean War, 301

KOVO radio, 423

Koyaanisqatsi (1982), 138

Kroitor, Roman, 310-311

KSL Players, 302

KSL Radio, 221, 367, 371, 395, 404, 406, 411, 415-417

KSL-TV, 352, 362, 373, 393, 411-412, 414-422, 432

KTVT television station, 420

Ku Klux Klan, 177

Kubrick, Stanley, 305, 310, 389

Kurtz, Gary, 1

KZN radio, 220-222, 412, 422

L. Clyde Anderson Film Laboratory, 344

L.A. Story (1991), 308

La Plante, William, 227

La Verkin, UT, 86

LaBute, Neil, 3, 36

Lady and the Tramp (1955), 296

Lady Chatterley's Lover, 242

Lady of the Tropics (1939), 308

Lady on a Train (1945), 384

Laemmle Film Service, 84

Lagoon (fairground), 54

Laie Hawaii Temple, 18, 335, 337, 342, 458

Laie, HI, 18, 335, 387, 342

Lake Powell, 132, 274, 328

Lake, Veronica, 406

Lamarr, Hedy, 248, 289

Lamb, Harold, 246

Lambart, Evelyn, 309

Lambourne, Alfred, 39, 43

Lamorisse, Albert, 344

Lamour, Dorothy, 289

Lancashire, England, 117, 360

Lancaster, Burt, 407

Landmarks of Church History, 365

Lane, Agnes Rose, 317

Lang, Charles B., Jr., 289

Lang, Fritz, 135, 300, 307

Lang, Gertrude, 289

Lange, Dorothea, 38

Lange, Jessica, 4

Lansing, Joi, 305

Large Format Cinema Association, 311

Larger Than Life (1996), 139

Lark, UT, 119

Larsen, Holger M., 359

Larsen, Lance, 33

Larsen, Loren "Dude", 285

Larsmo, Finland, 338

Larson, Clinton F., 33, 36

Larson, Eric, 295-297, 425-426, 428

Larson, Gertrude, 295

Larson, Gustive O., 109, 353

Larson, Melissa Leilani, 37

Larson, Peter, 295

Larson, Virginia B., 416

Las Vegas, NV, 16

Lasky, Jesse, 94

Lasseter, John, 296

Last of the Mohicans, The (1932), 304

Latin America, 19-20, 354

Latter-day Saint Leaders: Past and Present (1948), 73, 209, 231, 410, 440

Latter-day Saint Leadership, 365

Latter-day Saint Temples, 365, 371

Latter-day Saint University, 221-222

Latter-day Saints High School, 288, 359

Latter-day Saints: A Study of the Mormons in the Light of Economic Conditions, The, 176

Lauer, Robert, 37

Laurel and Hardy, 113, 344

Lauritzen, Lau, Sr., 189

Law of Success, The, 321

Law, Craig J., 38

Lawrence, D. H., 242

LDS Business College, 64

LDS Church Audiovisual Department, 201, 220

LDS Church Historical Department, 333

LDS Film Council, 383-386, 419

Index

LDS Publicity Bureau, 362

Le Brandt, Joseph, 157

Leatherneck, The (1930), 114

Lee, Harold B., 253, 335, 424, 438, 444

Lee, J. Bracken, 280

Lee, John D., 156, 282

Lee, Robert E., 304

Lee, Rowland V., 125

Lee, Russell, 38

Legally Blonde 2 (2003), 131, 349

Legends (1985), 303

Lego Movie, The (2014), 138

Lehi Banner, 79

Lehi, UT, 57

Lehman Brothers, 284

Leigh, Lisle, 123

Leo I (Pope), 302

Leonard, Robert Z., 178

Leone, Sergio, 138

Leroux, Gaston, 114

Les Misérables (1917), 162

Lessons from the Life of Nephi (book, 1891), 44-45

Lettermen, 27

Levi Company, 194

Lewis, Bernell, 137

Lewis, Bert, 290

Lewis, George Edward, 224-225

Lewis, John, 425

Lewis, William S., 30

LGBTQ rights, issues, films, 20

Liahona College, Tonga, 338

Liberty Park, Salt Lake City, 210, 223

Liberal Party, 63

Liberia, 20

Liberty Jail, 72, 152, 331-332

Liberty Theater Company, 88

Liberty Theater, Logan, 85

Liberty Theater, Salt Lake City, 81, 88-89

Life magazine, 136

Life Among the Saints in Hawkes Bay, New Zealand (1938-48), 338

Life of Jesus of Nazareth Portrayed in Colours, The, 204

Life of an American Fireman (1903), 79

Life of Nephi, The, see *Story of the Book of Mormon, The* (1915)

Lincoln, Abraham, 155, 249

Lindbergh, Charles, 214

Linder, Max144

Lindvall, Terry, 22

Linn, William Alexander, 158

Lion House, Salt Lake City, 213-214, 265

Lipman, William, 241

Little Cottonwood Canyon, UT, 332

Little Foxes, The (1941), 285

Little Girl (1955), 344

Little House on the Prairie (television series, 1974-83), 304

Little Lord Fauntleroy (1921), 107

Little Mermaid, The (1989), 297

Little People of America, 304

Little Red Riding Hood (ca. 1903), 79

Little Women (1949), 270

Liverpool, England, 165, 175, 299

Lives of a Bengal Lancer (1935), 114, 258

Living Scriptures, 231

Lloyd, Frank, 182

Lloyd, Harold, 88, 283-284

Locket, The (1946), 299

Logan Tabernacle, 339

Logan Temple, 29, 46, 195, 215, 339, 435

Logan, UT, 47, 76, 85, 116, 118, 205, 241, 284, 302-303, 305-306, 308, 318, 339, 397, 436

Logan, Charles, 157

London, England, v. 3, 40, 54, 115-117, 122, 149, 157, 164-165, 174-175, 181, 184-185, 199, 218, 244-245, 360, 305, 337, 340, 345, 359-361, 365, 370, 431,

435

Londema, Albert "Al", 344

London, Jack, 116

Lone Pine, CA, 264

Lone Ranger (fictional character), 235

Lone Ranger, The (2013), 131, 139, 235

Lone Ranger, The (television series, 1949-57), 301

Long Beach Players' Guild, 298

Long Beach, CA, 291, 293, 298

Long Island, NY, 284, 372

Longest Day, The (1962), 257

Lord of the Rings, The (1978), 304

Lord's Way, The (1948), 425-428, 438

Lorentz, Pare, 250

Los Angeles Chamber of Commerce, 167-168

Los Angeles Mission, 287

Los Angeles Stake, 241, 289

Los Angeles Times, 265, 278

Los Angeles, CA, 5-6, 28, 38, 72, 84, 93, 95, 110-111, 113-114, 116, 120-121, 123, 125, 128-129, 133, 137, 140, 142, 167, 182, 193, 196-197, 199, 201, 203-204, 211, 222, 245, 263, 265, 268, 274-275, 279-28, 283-284, 287-293, 295, 297, 300-301, 304-305, 308, 322, 324, 330, 340, 342, 328, 358, 368, 390, 407, 425, 430, 431

Lost Generation of Mormon authors, 10, 33, 257

Louis Marcus Enterprises, 95

Louis, Harold, 299

Louisiana Story (1948), 216, 255

Love (1927), 118

Love Story of a Mormon, The, 158, 184

Love, Kennedy (2017), 34

Love's Sorrow (1910), 193

Low, Colin, 3, 309-311

Low, Stephen, 312

Loxley, D. A., 271

Lubin Manufacturing Company, 112

Lubitsch, Ernst, 113-114, 308

Lucas, George, 2

Lumet, Sidney, 284

Lùmiere, Auguste, 67, 69, 71, 216-217

Lùmiere, Louis, 67, 69, 71, 216-21

Luna theater, Salt Lake City, 82

Lund, A. William, 204

Lund, Anthon H., 215

Lund, Anthony C., 321

Lundahl, Ezra Christian, 336

Lure of the Wasteland (1939), 134

Luske, Ham, 295, 296

Lust of the Ages, The (1917), 206

Lutherans, Lutheranism, 106, 161

Lütscher, Hans, 435

Lux Video Theatre (television series, 1950-57), 299

Luxembourg, 266

Lyceum theater, Ogden, 85

Lyceum Theatre, Salt Lake City, 76

Lyman, Francis M., 215

Lyman, Richard R., 215

Lynchburg, SC, 256

Lyne, Thomas A., 35, 208

Lyon, Ben, 224-228

Lyon, T. Edgar, 366

Lyric theater, Logan, 85

Lyric theater, Price, 86

Lyric Theatre, Salt Lake City, 80

M.E.L.D. Danceworks, 28

M'Liss (1918), 124

Mabey, Charles, 183, 211

Mabey, Rendell N., 345

Macbeth (1948), 406-407

Macbeth (1606), 36, 406-307

MacDonald, Julia A., 317

Macdonald, Karl, 284

Macgowan, Kenneth, 259, 262

MacGregor, Norval, 196-198, 201

MacGyver (television series, 1985-92),

Index

139

Mack Swain Theatre Company, 120

MacKnight, J. A., 55

MacMurray, Fred, 135

Macy's department store, 421

Madame La Presidente (1916), 117

Madsen, Arch, 423

Madsen, Charles P., 91-92

magic lantern, 40, 42, 43, 53-59, 76-78, 98, 103-104, 106, 109, 126, 158, 161, 194, 201, 205, 219, 234, 317, 354, 356, 358, 373, 386, 387, 402-403, 417

Magnavox Theatre, The (television series, 1950), 303

Magnusson, George E., 337

Maillol, Aristide, 31

Main, Marjorie, 272

Maine, 273, 357

Maine (ship), 141

Majestic Park (fairground), 54

Major, William Warner, 39

Make Mine Music (1946)

Malad, ID, 95, 304

Malemute Kid, The (unmade), 225

Malone, UT, 203

Malta, ID, 87

Man Called Peter, A (1955), 390

Man Called Shenandoah, A (television series, 1965-66), 301

Man from Red Gulch, The (1925), 114

Man from Utah, The (1934)

Man of Aran (1934), 216

Man on Watch, The (1915), 123

Man Who Played God, The (1922), 113

Man Who Would Be King, The (1975), 131

Man with a Movie Camera (1929), 73

Man with My Face, The (1951), 33

Man with My Face, The (book, 1948), 33

Man's Search for Happiness (1964), 6, 138

Managua, Nicaragua, 30

Manchester Ward (Los Angeles), 342

Manchester, England, 60, 218

Manet, Edouard, 48

Manhattan Opera House, New York City, 318

Manhattan, New York, NY, 6, 28, 148, 199, 285, 317-318, 320

Manifesto (1890), 18, 48, 62-63, 65, 143-145, 150, 155, 258

Manitoba, 359

Manley, R. G. Harwood, 337

Mann, May, 268, 288

Mansfield, Jayne, 288

Manti Temple, 29, 32, 46-47, 195, 347, 436

Manti, UT, 29, 32, 46-47, 195, 347, 436

Maori, 337-339, 433

March of Time, The (1935-51), 254-255, 427

Marcus, Louis, 88, 91, 93, 95, 241

Maready, Josh, 38

Marines Come Through, The (1938), 303

Mark of Zorro, The (1940), 260

Mark Strand Theatre, New York City, 84

Marlo Theater, Salt Lake City, 265

Maroon 5, 27

Marriage or Death (1912), 167, 171-172, 210

Married to a Mormon (1922), 117, 173, 184-185, 191, 218, 282

Marryat, Frederick, 153-154, 159

Mars Attacks! (1996), 308

Marshall, Donald R., 33, 388

Marshall, Garry, 4

Marshall, Milton, 370, 387

Martin Dentler GmbH, 189

Martin handcart company, 17

Martin, Edward, 37, 172

Marty, Martin E., 155

Marx Brothers, 249

Mary Poppins (1964), 296

Marysvale, UT, 305

Mason, Rupert, 117

Massachusetts, 52, 62, 131, 176, 357

Massasoit, 31

Master Films, 184

Masters of the Universe (1987), 303

Mathis, June, 115-116, 123

Matinee Theater (television series, 1955-58), 301

Mattson, Joseph L., 416

Maudsley, Sutcliffe, 39

Maui, HI, 405

Mauna Loa volcano, HI, 339

Mauss, Armand, 61

Maverick (1994), 130

Maw, Herbert, 376, 397, 400, 404

Max Florence Film Exchange, 92

May Cody, or Lost and Won, 156

Maybey, Charles R., 183

Mayer, Louis B., 118, 125, 184

Mayor's Office of Film, Theatre & Broadcasting, New York City, 140

Maytime (1937), 308

McAllister, Stanley, 357

McBride, Joseph, 275, 278

McClellan, John Jasper "J. J." Jr., 26, 90-91, 209, 213, 221

McClure's, 158

McCoy, Violet, 80

McCrea, Joel, 406

McCutcheon, Wallace, 144

McDowall, Roddy, 135

McElwee, Ross, 4

McKay, David O., 60, 129, 186, 191, 215, 235, 254-255, 282-283, 302, 332, 335, 337-342, 344, 356, 360-361, 363, 372, 375, 377-379, 383, 389, 390, 396-397, 404, 418, 420-421, 428-432, 435, 437, 440-441

McKay, Edward Riggs, 341

McKay, Emma, 341

McKay, James Gunn, 353

McKay, Lottie, 341

McKay, Thomas E., 108, 161

McKinley, William, 78, 104

McKinley, William, depicted on film, 78, 104

McLaren, Norman, 309

McMurrin, Joseph, 215

McNaughton, Jon, 40

McPherson, Harry, 288

Meakin, Charles, 122

Measure of a Man (1962), 100

Medea, 302

Medford, MA, 176

Meet Me in St. Louis (1944), 270

Meet the Mormons (2014), 219

Mehesy theater, Salt Lake City, 81

Méliès, George, 79

Melbourne, Australia, 181

Mendelssohn, Felix, 89, 90

Melody Time (1948)

Memphis, TN, 266

Men of the Fighting Lady (1954), 301

Merchant of Venice, The (1914), 125

"*Mercury Theatre on the Air, The*", 367

Merrill, Elna, 284

Merrill, Eugene Hyde, 287

Merrill, Joseph F., 355

Merrill, Kieth, 284

Merrill, Marriner W., 284, 355

Merrill, Wilford J., 284, 355

Merry Widow, The (1925), 118

Merry Widow, The (1934), 308

Mersch, Mary, 182

Mertens and Price Radio Feature Service, 368

Merthyr Tydfil, Wales, 359

Mesa, AZ, 119, 197, 280, 347

Message of the Ages, The, 249, 315, 346, 351-352, 394, 402, 409, 413, 440-441

Methodist Episcopal Centenary, 106

Methodists, Methodism, 14, 104, 106, 234

Index

Metro Pictures Corporation, see MGM

Metro-Goldwyn-Mayer, see MGM

Metropolitan Pictures, 134

Metropolitan Sound Studios, 320, 350, 352

Mexican Mission, 335

Mexican-American War (1846-48), 17, 119

Mexico, 16-20, 38, 42, 64, 116, 121-122, 131, 181, 237, 242, 255, 279-280, 327, 335, 341, 358, 399

Mexico City, Mexico, 335, 341, 358, 399

Mexico, polygamous colonies, 17-18, 237, 327

Meyer, Stephenie, 21, 33

MGM, 95, 114-115, 118, 125, 133, 245, 249, 251-252, 258, 270, 272, 289, 291, 298, 301, 304, 306-308

MIA, see Mutual Improvement Association

Michigan, 90, 294, 306, 356, 362

Mickey McGuire franchise, 303

Mickey Mouse (fictional character), 290-292

Mickey's Grand Opera (1936), 290

Mickey's Pals (1927), 303

Middle East, 20

Midgley, J. George, 38

Midgley, Stanley, 344

Midgleys film exhibition company, 81, 84, 92

Midnight Madness (1928), 113

Midsummer Night's Dream (1937), 344

Midway, UT, 438

Mighty Joe Young (1949), 300

Mike, Jim, 327

Milford, UT, 203, 240

Millennial Star, 165, 360

Miller, David, 138

Miller, Frank, 184

Miller, Joaquin (Cincinnatus Heine), 154

Miller, Josie L. Bird, 289

Miller, Mox E., 227

Miller, Orrin P., 215

Millikan, Robert, 126

Million Dollar Mystery, The (1914), 112

Million Ways to Die in the West, A (2014), 138

Mills, Howard S., 84

Millsboro, PA, 303

Milner, Olive, 419-420

Milton, John, 315

Milwaukee, WI, 369

Minnesota, 351

Minor, Charles, 81

Minor, William, 81

Mintz, Charles, 291, 293-294

Miracle Man, The (1919), 119

Miracle of the Gulls, 16, 134, 229, 248-252, 255, 257, 262, 264, 269, 344, 398, 409-410

Miracle of Salt Lake, The (1938), 249, 251, 255-256

Mission: Impossible II (2000), 131

Mission Home, Salt Lake City, 360

Mission Publicity Committee, see LDS Publicity Bureau

missionaries, missionary work, Missionary Department, 3, 6, 17, 19-20, 48, 57, 59-60, 78, 109, 114, 150, 152, 158, 161, 164-165, 169-172, 179, 183-186, 191, 201-203, 207, 212, 218-219, 233-234, 243, 250, 287, 303-304, 330, 333, 335-341, 345-346, 353-373, 401-402, 404-405, 408, 411, 416, 418, 433-434, 437, 439

Missionary Training Center, Provo, 360

Mississippi, 15, 41, 51, 336, 423

Mississippi River, 263

Missouri, 15-16, 28, 35, 37, 42, 124, 131, 133, 151-154, 196, 222, 256, 267, 331-334, 356, 399-400

Missouri Legend, 261

Missouri River, 35

Mitton, Samuel LeRoy, 339

Mix, Tom, 132, 183, 244

Moab Chamber of Commerce, 139

Moab Film Commission, 140

Moab Movie Committee, 139

Moab to Monument Valley Film Commission, 140

Moab, UT, 130, 139-140, 274, 275

Moana (1926), 73, 216, 218

Moby Dick (1930), 288

MOD Theatre Company, 37

Modern Mormon Men (blog), 34

Molokai, HI, 339

Monet, Claude, 48

Monogram, 134, 243, 279, 325-326

Monks, Martha, 150

Monson, Thomas S., 20

Monroe, Marilyn, 288

Monsieur Violet: His Travels and Adventures among the Snake Indians, 153

Montana, 65, 91, 305, 359

Monson, Walter, 179

Monument to Balzac (sculpture), 24

Monument Valley, 137-140, 273

Monterey, CA, 339

Montgomery Ward, Inc., 293

Montgomery, George, 244

Monticello, UT, 273

Montreal, Quebec, 199, 309-311

Monumental Utah (1944), 253, 413

Moody, Milton W., 345

Moonrise (1948), 288

Moore, Samuel D., Jr., 356

Moore, Terry, 300

Moomaw, Lewis H., 223-245

Moon, Arthur Morse, 123

Moore, Tom, 121

Morality for Youth (1982), 100

Moreau, Gustave, 48

Morgan, UT, 95

Mormon architecture, 22, 28-30, 382

Mormon Battalion, 17, 27, 42, 149, 215, 279-282, 369, 403

Mormon Battalion, The (1950), 256, 280-282, 313, 328, 441

Mormon Conquest, The (1935), 134, 325-326

Mormon Conquest, The (1939), 313, 441

Mormon Country, 391

Mormon cricket, see crickets

Mormon Cricket, The (1939)

Mormon dance, 22

Mormon drama, 60

Mormon Historic Sites Foundation, 331

Mormon literature, 4, 9-11, 32, 34, 155-156

Mormon Literature & Creative Arts Database, 9

Mormon Maid, A (1917), 147, 157, 160, 178-181, 185, 187, 189-190, 196, 200, 222, 241-242, 259

Mormon Moment, ca. 2012, 21

Mormon music, 22, 25-26

Mormon painting, 22

Mormon Panorama (painting), 40, 43

Mormon Peril, The, see Trapped by the Mormons (1922)

Mormon photography, 22

Mormon Prophet, The, 156

Mormon Queen, The, 156

Mormon sculpture, 22

Mormon Senator, The, 157

Mormon Tabernacle Choir, 3, 25, 127, 2221, 290, 400, 413-414

Mormon theater, see Mormon drama

Mormon Trail, 38, 228, 244, 332

Mormon Trail, The (1920), 184

Mormon Trail, The (1935), 249

Mormon Trails (1943), 252-253

Mormon Uncle, The (Der Mormonenonkel, 1920), 173, 189

Mormon visual art, see Mormon painting

Mormon War (1838), 15

Index

Mormon Wife, The, 154, 156

Mormon Wives, 154

Mormon Youth Symphony and Chorus, 166, 170

Mormon, The (1912), 157, 166

Mormon, The (play staged in Chicago), 157

Mormon's Troubles, The, 156

Mormoness: The Trials of Mary Maverick, The, 154

Mormonism in Transition (book, 1996), 61

Mormonism Unvailed, 162

Mormons Celebrate Centenary (1930), 255, 349, 413

Mormons, The (play staged in Baltimore), 156

Moroni Olsen Players, 302-303

Morosco Theatre, New York City, 116

Morosco, Oliver, 114, 116-117, 201

Morosco, Walter, 116

Morosco, Walter, Jr., 117

Morrill Act (1862), 18

Morris Sign Company, 293

Morris, Errol, 4

Morris, George Q., 401

Morrow, Dwight, 341

Morton, Alton "Al", 342

Morton, Thelma, 342

Morton, William A., 59-60, 106, 201-205

Moscow Art Theatre, 305

Most Dangerous Game, The (1932), 120

Moth and the Flame, 27

Mother Knows Best (1928), 249

Mother Stories from the Book of Mormon, 202

Motion Picture Alliance for the Preservation of American Ideals, 299

Motion Picture Association of America, 140, 239-241

Motion Picture Daily, 254

Motion Picture Distributing and Sales Company, 168, 170

Motion Picture News, 1123, 178-179, 267

Motion Picture Patents Company, 94, 193

Motion Picture Producers and Distributors of America, see Motion Picture Association of America

Motion Picture Production Code, see Production Code

Motion Picture Story, 88

Motley Vision, A (blog), 34

Motography, 178

Mount Rushmore, 23, 31

Mount Timpanogos, UT, 344

Mountain Meadows Massacre, 17, 130, 153-156, 166-168, 171, 282-283

Mountain Meadows Massacre, The (1912), 166-168

Mountain Meadows Massacre, The (book), 282

Moving Picture World, 90, 166, 200

Moving Pictures (2000), 311

Moyle, Henry D., 341, 358, 438

Moyle, James H., 333, 356-358, 360-361

Moyle, John Rowe, 358

Mr. Smith Goes to Washington (1939), 289

Mt. Pleasant, UT, 102

Much Ado About Nothing, 301

Muir, Leo J., 279, 281

murals, mural painting, 45-48, 60, 432, 436

Murder, She Wrote (television series, 1984-96), 399

Murdock Resort (fairground), 54

Murnau, F. W., 120, 249, 326

Murphy, Henry Castle Hadlock, 337

Murray Opera House, 66

Murray, Mae, 178

Murray, UT, 196

Murrow, Edward R., 414

Museum of Fine Arts, Boston, 31

Music and the Spoken Word, 90, 221, 243, 254, 352, 412-413, 418

Music Corporation of America, 287

music in silent films, 90, 290, 342

Musker, John, 296

Muslims, Islam, 20, 40, 58, 152

Mutiny on the Bounty (1935), 124, 249, 383

mutoscope, 67, 74-75, 86, 142-143, 146

Mutual Hour, 222

Mutual Improvement Association, 57-58, 101, 103, 105, 113, 288, 320, 391

My Darling Clementine (1946), 137

My Friend Flicka (1943), 135

My Sister-in-Law from America (*Min Svigerinde fra Amerika*, 1917), 189

My Son, My Son! (1940), 298

My Turn on Earth (play, 1977), 27

Myer, Peter, 32

Mystery of the Wax Museum, The (1933), 120

NAACP, 100

Naish, J. Carrol, 271

Nanook of the North (1922), 56, 73, 216, 218

Napoléon (1927), 389

Napoleon Dynamite (2004), 3

NASA, 310

Nation, Carrie, depicted on film, 78

National Anti-Mormon League, 179, 180

National Board of Review of Motion Pictures, 168-171, 179

National Film Act of 1939 (Canada), 309

National Film Board of Canada, 309

National Geographic, 136, 328

National Lampoon's Vacation (1983),138

National Museum of American History, 31

National Park Service, 132, 327, 341

National Park Transportation and Camping Company, 132

National Reform Association, 180

National Theatre Supply Company, 95

Native Americans, 40, 152, 172, 206, 271, 277, 282, 321, 334, 336, 338, 343, 398

NATO, 187

Natural Born Killers (1994), 3

Natural Bridges Monument, 327

Nauvoo Brass Band, 26

Nauvoo Dramatic Company, 35

Nauvoo Legion, 331

Nauvoo Legion bands, 26

Nauvoo Opera House, Nauvoo, 331, 375

Nauvoo Restoration, Inc., 331

Nauvoo Temple, 29-31, 37, 45-47, 49, 195, 369

Nauvoo Tinners Association, 31

Nauvoo, IL, 15-16, 22, 26-31, 35, 37-42, 45, 151, 153, 192, 196, 208, 257, 262-263, 280, 331-332, 334, 347, 356, 375, 398-399, 403-404, 429

Navajo Native American tribe, 276-277, 326

Nazi Party, Nazis, 266-268, 337

Nazimova, Alla, 116

NBC, 221, 278, 291, 301, 412, 414

Nebraska, 16, 27, 30, 41, 131, 215, 391, 398-399

Neff, David, 224

Negri, Pola, 88

Nelson, England, 360

Nelson, Lowry, 388

Nelson, Richard Alan, 77, 79, 178, 180, 247, 282, 352

Neon Trees, 27

Nephi, UT, 85

Neslen, Clarence, 183, 216, 220, 231

Netherlands, 66, 158, 165, 266, 307, 345, 401

Index

Neuhausen, Carl M., 80

Nevada, 16, 95, 109, 131, 263-264, 304

Nevada (1927), 133

Neville, John T., 246

New Batman Adventures, The (television series, 1997-99), 304

New Brunswick, 157

New Deal, 19, 250, 253

New England, 22, 24, 31, 58, 180, 191

New Grand Theatre, Salt Lake City, 80

New Harmony, UT, 86

New Hollywood cinema, 10

New Jersey, 38, 92, 125, 167, 178, 193, 320, 322

New Mexico, 334

New Orleans, LA, 156

New Royal Cinema, Pontypool, 359

New Testament, 370, 379, 387

New Theatre, New York City, 90

"New Witness for Christ, A", 368, 372

New York Dramatic Mirror, 114

New York Times, 21, 156, 179, 265, 270, 318

New York Herald-Tribune, 288

New York Motion Picture Company, 172

New York Stake, 126, 284

New York University, 342

New York World, 147, 306

New York World's Fair (1939), 128, 369

New York, New York Stake, 126, 284

New York, NY, 20, 23, 28, 31, 37, 39, 44, 49, 50, 72, 84, 90, 93, 95, 97, 110, 114, 115, 116, 120, 122, 123, 126, 128, 140, 142, 153, 163, 168, 169, 170, 178, 179, 187, 193, 194, 199, 207, 252, 261, 265, 266, 270, 283, 284, 285, 288, 298, 299, 301, 302, 304, 305, 306, 307, 317, 318, 320, 322, 332, 333, 336, 341, 342, 349, 356, 357, 358, 361, 369, 397, 407, 421

New Zealand, 20, 95, 157, 181, 337-339

New Zealand Temple, see Hamilton, New Zealand Temple

Newcastle District, 360

Newfoundland and Labrador, 311

Newhouse Theatre, Salt Lake City, 90

Newhouse, Samuel, 90

Newman, Alfred, 264

Newman, E. M., 249

Newman, Joseph M., 308

Newman, Paul, 4

Newsweek, 21, 265

Newton, John, 22

Niagara Falls, 332, 337

Nibley, Agnes Sloan, 307

Nibley, Alexander, 307

Nibley, Charles W., 192, 213-215, 231, 301, 431

Nibley, Christopher, 307

Nibley, Hugh, 231

Nibley, Margaret, 215

Nibley, Preston, 215, 400

Nibley, Sloan, 307

Nicaragua, 30, 358

Nichols, Mike, 4

Nichols, Red, 27

Nickelodeon theater, Salt Lake City, 80

nickelodeons, 79-84, 209

Nielsen, Renee Johnson, 338

Nielsen, Thayle, 338

Nigeria, 345, 408

Night at the Opera, A (1935)

Night Mail (1936), 219

Nineteenth Century Club, Provo, 74

Nixon, Richard, 287, 299

Nobel Prize in Physics, 126

Noble, Wendell, 425

Nocturne (1946), 291

Nolan, H. T., 95-96

Nordgren, Weston N., 437-438

Nordisk Films Company, 162-164, 166, 189

North America, 2, 18-19, 41, 162, 166, 187, 278, 310, 414, 430

North Carolina, 31, 356

North Central States Mission, 358

North Dakota, 65, 359

North Hollywood, CA, 294, 425

North Salt Lake, UT, 3331

North, Wilfred, 319

Northwestern States Mission, 314, 362, 367

Norton, Etta, 270

Norway, 39, 59, 109, 164, 266

Norwich, England, 60, 165, 186

Notable Feature Film Company, 88, 95

Notorious (1946), 302, 385

Nova Scotia, 157

Novelty Advertising Company, 55

Now, Voyager (1942), 306

NTSC video standard, 3, 286

Nugent, Frank, 274, 278

Nuttall, L. John, 122, 197

Nuttall, William T., 197

Nutting, John D., 53

Nye, Ephraim H., 103

O'Brien, George, 244, 326

O'Brien, Margaret, 4, 270, 326

O'Conner, Flannery, 25

O'Hara, Maureen, 285

O'Higgins, Harvery, 176

Oahu Stake, 341

Oahu, HI,, 18, 114, 341

Oak theater, Logan, 85,205

Oakland Temple, 339, 436

Oakland, CA, 84, 339, 436

Obama, Barack, 21

Oberammergau, Germany, 347

October Byways (1935), 344

Odyssey Dance Theatre, 28

Off the Beaten Path (ca. 1946), 356

Ogden Feature Film Company, 206

Ogden Pictures Corporation, 206, 315

Ogden Stake, 108

Ogden Standard, 93

Ogden Temple, 339, 436

Ogden, UT, 17, 54, 74, 76-77, 81-82, 84-85, 89-90, 92-94, 96, 112, 119, 122-124, 143, 193, 206, 226, 261, 291, 302, 305, 318, 344, 390-391, 422, 433-436

Ohio, 15, 106, 181, 184, 331-332, 356

Oklahoma, 131, 170, 349

Old Bowery, Salt Lake City, 35, 209

Old Ironsides (1926), 112, 123

Old Mill, The (1937), 290

Old North Church, Boston, 31

Old Testament, see Bible

Old Town, San Diego, 280

Oldham, England, 60

Oldroyd, John, 108

Oliver Morosco Photoplay Company, 116, 125

Olivier, Laurence, 261

Olsen, Edward Arenholt, 302

Olsen, Greg, 39

Olsen, Martha Magdaline Hoversholst, 302

Olsen, Moroni, 301-303

Olsen, Ole, 162

Olson, E. LeRoy, 416

Omaha, NE, 16, 95, 209, 266, 273, 318, 391

Oman, Richard, 40, 43

OMNIMAX, 311

On the Old Spanish Trail (1947), 307

On the Way Home (1992), 100

On with the Dance (1920), 87

Once I Was a Beehive (2015), 12

Once Upon a time in the West (1968), 130, 138

One Hundred Wives,

One Hundred Years of Mormonism (1913), 34, 43, 72, 83, 130, 194-196, 199-202, 206-207, 211-212, 222-223, 227, 314, 373

One Hundred Years of Mormonism (book), 195

Index

One Summer Day (1949), 344

...One Third of a Nation... (1939), 284

One Touch of Venus (1948), 304

online video, 6, 34, 219

Open Stories Foundation, see Mormon Stories

Opera House, Brigham City, 85

Opera House, Logan, 85

Oracle theater, Ogden, 85

Orchard Ward (Bountiful), 342

Orchestra at Temple Square, 408

Oregon, 93, 109, 112, 223-224, 307, 398

Oregon Short Line Railroad, 209

Oregon Trail, 112, 398

Orem, UT, 375-376, 438

Orlob, Harold, 284, 318

Orpheum theater, Ogden, 85

Orpheum Theater, Salt Lake City, 80-82, 84, 86, 89, 95

Orthodox Catholics, Orthodox Catholicism, 20

Ortiz Rubio, Pascual, 255

Orton, Erik, 36

Oscars, see Academy Awards

Osmond family, 3, 27

Osmond, Donny, 3

Osmond, Joe, 409, 433

Osmond, Marie, 3

Oswiecim, Poland, 267

Othello (1603), 36

Otis Brothers and Company, 49

Ottawa, Ontario, 311

Otterstrom, Charles, 425

Ottinger, George M., 39

Otto, Henry, 206

Ouelessebougou, Mali, 20

Ouspenskaya, Maria, 305

Out of the Dust, 324

Out of the Past (1947), 300

Outlaw Josey Wales, The (1976), 135

Overland Feature Film Company, 206

Overland with Kit Carson (1939), 135

Oz, Frank, 1

Ozu, Yasujiro, 235

pageants, 35, 233, 249, 280, 302, 339, 342, 346-350, 352, 358, 373, 377, 403-404, 433

Paiute Native Americans, 17, 133

Palme d'Or, 310

Palmyra, NY, 14, 50-51, 207, 219, 332, 334, 337, 359

Palo Alto Company, 112

Pan-American Highway, 328

Panguitch, UT, 85

Panic of 1893, 64

Panoptikon Theater, Copenhagen, 164

panorama painting, 40-45, 47-48, 52-53, 58-59, 72, 80, 98, 198

Panoramic View of the Hudson River (painting), 41

Pantoscope of California, Nebraska, Utah, and the Mormons (painting), 41

Paramount News, 254

Paramount Pictures Corporation, 93-95, 133, 136-137, 177, 180, 246, 255, 257-258, 284, 289, 306, 390

Paramount Svenska Journalen, 255

Paramount Theatre, Salt Lake City, 390

Paramount Theatre, San Francisco, 265

Paramount-Empress theater, Salt Lake City, 87-88, 90, 93-35, 190

Pardoe, T. Earl, 422-423

Paris Art Mission, missionaries, 48, 60, 212

Paris, France, 23, 31-32, 47-48, 71, 91, 193, 199, 307

Paris, KY, 142

Parisian Princess, A (play), 80

Park City, UT, 86, 178

Park Theatre, New York City, 178

Park, Allen, 192, 323

Park, Byron, 321

Park, D. Lester, 83, 184, 166, 206, 313, 315, 318, 321, 324

Park, Lester, see Park, D. Lester

Park, Walter, 192-193

Parker, George, 108

Parker, Mary-Louise, 4

Parker, Rangi, 339

Parker, Tom, 288

Parker, Trey, 4

Parkinson, Harry B., 185

Parley's Canyon, UT, 223

Parowan, UT, 85

Parowan Gap, 134

Parry, Chuancey, 131-136, 183

Parry, Gronway, 131-134, 136-137, 183

Parry, John, 26

Parry, Louise, 135

Parry, Roland, 226, 229, 302

Parry, Whitney, 131, 137

Parshall, Ardis, 250, 316

Parson, Del, 39

Parsons, Louella, 265

Partridge, Edward, 25, 208

Partridge, Emily, 208

Pasadena Playhouse, 302-304

Pathé Frères, 167, 190, 209, 214

Pathé News, Pathé Sound News

Patriarch, The (sculpture), 31

Patriot, The (1930), 114

Patrol Method, The (1948), 386

Paul, Aaron, 4

Paul, Fred, 175, 188

Paul, J. H., 298

Paul, Robert W., 67, 69

Paulo, Harry, 175

Paxton, Bill, 4

Pay Day (1922), 121

Payson Enterprise, 44

Payson, UT, 44

Peace on Earth, 370, 379

Peach, Kenneth, 425

Pearl and the Beard, 27

Pearl Harbor, 246, 268, 367, 397

Pearson, Carol Lynn, 36

Pearson, George, 174-175

Pearson, Winifred, 175

Pearson's, 158

Peck, Gregory, 300, 307

Peculiarities (2006), 37

Peek-a-Boo Canyon, UT, 326

Peer Gynt (1915), 117

Peery, Harmon W., 92

Peery, Joseph Smith, 333, 335, 341, 352, 358

Penguin Group, 34

Penn, Sean, 4

Pennington, Theo, 321

Pennsylvania, 39, 303, 318, 331, 334, 356, 357

Pennsylvania Station, New York City, 318

Penrose, Charles W., 166, 190, 204, 214

People of Paradox, 23

People's Institute settlement house, 168

People's Party, 63

Peoria, IL,, 157

Perilous Ride, A (1911), 160

Perkins, "Bishop", 273-274-276

Perkins+Will, 30

Perley, Frank, 318

Perry, Anne, 10

Perschon, William F., 434

Pershing, John J., 190

Personal (1904), 144

Peru, 19-20

Peter Gunn (television series, 1958-61), 303

Peter Pan (1953), 295, 428

Peter Pan (fictional character), 3, 296, 428

Petersen, Mark E., 393, 424

Peterson, Levi S., 33

Index

Peterson, Pearl W., 431

Peyton Place (1957), 300

Pfeiffer, Walt, 293

Phantom of the Opera, The (1925), 114

Phelps, William W., 25, 32, 46, 152, 430

phenakistoscope, 50

Philadelphia Orchestra, 127

Philadelphia Story, The (1940), 71

Philadelphia Temple, 30

Philadelphia, PA, 35, 58, 93, 128-129, 157, 192

Philippines, 19-20, 181

Phillips Company, 416

Philo T. Farnsworth Society, 129

Phoenix, AZ, 334-335

phonograph, gramophone, 60, 69, 74, 87, 89, 109, 266, 346, 353

Photoplay, 96, 124

Photoplay theater, Salt Lake City, 81-82

Physioc, Joseph, 320

Pickering, Frank, 44

Pickford, Mary, 97, 108, 124, 161

Picture Play, 224-225

Picture Story of Mormonism, A, 370

Pidgin, Charles Felton, 184

Pilgrim, The (1923), 121

Pilgrim's Progress, The (magic lantern presentation), 52

Pink Lady, The (play), 122

Pinocchio (1940), 71, 291, 296

Pinterest, 34, 69

Pioneer Day, 48, 199, 210, 215, 220, 255, 309, 339, 342, 397-398

Pioneer Film Corporation, 223-224, 226

Pioneer Sesquicentennial (1997), 21

Pioneer Stake, 253

Pioneer Trails (1947), 401, 440-441

pioneers, 5, 17, 21-23, 26-27, 29, 31, 33, 37, 42-43, 48-49, 58, 61, 64-66, 71-73, 83, 85-86, 109, 119, 122, 126-127, 131, 139-140, 149, 172-174, 194, 196-202, 207, 210, 215, 220, 222-229, 236, 239, 244-246, 248-249, 252, 255-259, 264, 268-269, 272-276, 285, 288, 291, 298-299, 309, 311, 326-328, 341, 347, 365, 397, 399, 403-404, 406, 419

Pioneers in Petticoats (1969), 100

Pips, the, 127

Pissarro, Camille, 48

Pitt, William, 26

Pittsburgh, PA, 79, 93, 184, 266

Pixar Animation Studios, 296

Pizarro, or Virgins of the Sun (play, 1799), 35, 208

Plainsman, The (1936), 114, 248

Plainsman, The (1966), 130

Plan of Salvation, 13

Plan-B Theatre Company, 37

Planet of the Apes (1968), 131, 135

Planet of the Apes (2001), 131

Plant Growth, 378-379

Platte River, 399

Playboy, 301

Player, William W., 30

Playhouse Theater, Salt Lake City, 322-323

Plow that Broke the Plains, The (1937), 250

Plummer, Louise, 33

plural marriage, see polygamy

Plymouth Rock, 31

Plymouth, England, 360

Pocatello, ID, 85, 95

Pohnpeian (language), 19

Poelman, Stuart L., 345

Poland, 19, 267, 371

Pollyanna (1920), 107

Polaroid film, 335

Polygamy (1936), 247-248

Polygamy (play), 178

polygamy, 16-18, 53, 62-65, 101, 116, 119, 129, 143-151, 155-159, 162, 167-168, 170, 174, 177-178, 184-188, 190, 196, 225, 228, 235, 241-243, 245, 247-

248, 257, 259, 262, 271, 276, 306, 309, 318, 335, 342, 361

Polynesia, 28

Polynesian Cultural Center, 28

Pomarede, Leon, 41

Pompeii, Italy, 56-57

Pontypool, Wales, 359

Pony Express (1953), 130

Pony Express, The (1925), 112

Pope, Hyrum, 30

Popular Science, 74

Porter, Edwin S., 79-80

Portland, OR, 113, 266, 307

Portugal, 19

Post No Bills (1906), 11

Post, Charles "Buddy", 124

Powell, Michael, 235

Powelson, Arthur, 207

Power and the Glory, The, 273

Power of the Mormons, The (unmade), 184

Power, Tyrone, 4, 257-258, 260

Prague, Czechoslovakia, 337, 369

Pratt, Lorus, 48

Pratt, Parley P., 25, 32, 160

Pratt, Rey L., 215

praxinoscope, 50

Preminger, Otto, 4

Presbyterians, Presbyterianism, 52, 106, 241

Presiding Bishopric, 231, 319, 333-334, 342, 354, 356, 376, 379, 381-382, 389, 410, 415, 438

Presidio Park, San Diego, 280

Presley, Elvis, 288

Pressburger, Emeric, 235, 244

Preston, England, 360

Preston, ID, 95, 380

Prevost, Marie, 224-228

Price, Harrison Theodore, 337

Price, UT, 86

Price, Vincent, 4, 260-262

Pride of the Market, The (play), 35

priesthood, 2, 14-15, 19, 48, 65, 99, 145, 214, 331, 342, 345, 351, 371-372, 391, 401, 408, 411, 427, 439

priesthood, ban for black members, 19

Primary children's organization, 102, 105, 351, 411, 419-420

Princess Theater, Provo, 85

Princess theater, Salt Lake City, 81

printing press, 16, 68, 412

Prisoners of Love (1921), 119

Proctor, Richard A., 55

Prodigal Son (sculpture), 316

Production Code, 236, 238-2441, 245-248, 256, 260, 262, 271, 283, 307, 314, 389

Progressive Era, 69, 97-98, 100-101, 103, 168, 210, 234, 237, 376, 380

Progressive Film Exchange, 92-93

Prohibition, 101, 206, 243

Promised Valley Playhouse, see Orpheum Theater, Salt Lake City

Promontory Point, UT, 391

Prophet, The (sculpture), 31

Prophet's Prey (2015), 247

Protestants, Protestantism, 20, 25-26, 52, 62, 99, 101, 158-159

Proud Rebel, The (1958), 134

Providence, RI, 266

Provo City Center Temple, 19

Provo City Hall, 32

Provo Free Reading Room, 55

Provo Temple, 436

Psilander, Vlademar, 162-163

Psychological and Ethical Aspects of Mormon Group Life, The (book, 1922), 61

Public Health Cigarette Smoking Act, 287

Public Works Administration, 376

Puccini, Giacomo, 90

Index

Puck, 155

Pueblo, CO, 399

Pugh, Ralph J. , 117

Punch and Judy shows, 54

Puriri, Ra, 338

Puritan Conscience, A (1915), 173, 187

"*Purposes and Values of a Mission, The*", 370, 422

Pyper, George D., 78, 104-105, 216, 224, 227-228, 259, 261, 332-333, 347, 402

Queen Christina (1933), 118

Quichua (language), 19

Quincy, IL, 399

Quinney, Joseph, Jr., 362

Quo Vadis (magic lantern presentation), 52

Quorum of the Twelve Apostles, 15, 63, 145, 192, 194, 208, 210, 218, 253, 358, 360, 372, 389, 431

Racing Luck (1948), 115

radio, 8, 23, 69, 87, 110, 127-129, 219-222, 224, 234-237, 254, 284-287, 290, 295, 299, 302-303, 319, 330, 333, 346, 357, 361-362, 364, 367-374, 377, 385-386, 391-392, 395, 404-406, 408, 411-423, 437-438

Radio Club of Salt Lake, 222

Radio Service Corporation, 415

Radio, Publicity, and Mission Literature Committee, see Church Radio, Publicity, and Mission Literature Committee

Rafferty, Frances, 272

Raid, anti-polygamy legislation, 18, 47, 54, 181, 316

Rain (1929), 343

Rain Man (1988), 4

Rainbow Bridge National Monument, 137, 255, 327

Rainbow Trail (1948), 344

Rainbow Trail, The (1918), 182, 187

Rainbow Trail, The (1932), 326

Rainbow Trail, The (book), 181

Rains Came, The (1939), 258

Rambova, Natacha, 115-116, 124

Ramona (1926), 132

Rampton, Calvin, 135, 140

Ramrod (1947), 406

Ramsay, Ralph, 31

Rand theater chain, Salt Lake City, 82, 84

Rand, Harry R., 81-82, 92

Rand, Walter, 82

Randolf, Anders, 224-225

Randolph, UT, 95

Rankin, McKee, 170

Rankin, William, 257

Rappe, Virginia, 240

Rarotonga, Cook Islands, 345

Rasmussen, Frank, 303

Ratcatcher, The (magic lantern presentation), 54

Rath, Franz, 90

ratings, 388-389

Rational Faiths (blog), 34

RCA, 128, 323, 348, 378

Reader's Digest, 376

Reagan, Ronald, 299

Real Reels, 88

Realart Pictures Corporation, 289

Rebel without a Cause (1955), 388

Reckless Rosie (1929), 122

Reconstruction, 18, 63, 177

Red Balloon, The (1956), 344

Red Canyon (1949), 135

Red Shoes, The (1948), 235

Red Skies of Montana (1952), 308

Red Theatorium, Salt Lake City, 80-81

Reed, Harry, 139

Reformation of 1856-57, 153

Reggio, Godfrey, 138

Reichenbach, Henry M., 67

Reid, Harry, 21

Reid, Rose Marie, 24

Reid, Wallace, 112

Reiser, A. Hamer, 234, 282, 350-352, 359, 374, 376-385, 387, 389, 392-393, 396-399, 401-403, 408, 410, 413, 424, 430, 440

Reitz, Edgar, 4

Relief Society, 29, 99, 105, 204, 253, 317, 340, 342, 351

Relief Society Building, Salt Lake City, 340

Reno, NV, 304

Renoir, Auguste, 48

Renoir, Jean, 235

Reorganized Church of Jesus Christ of Latter-day Saints, ii, 202, 248, 332

Republic Pictures, 244, 276, 279, 307, 406-407

Republican Party, 17, 21, 63-65, 144, 155, 190, 239, 241, 255, 286

Rescuers Down Under, The (1990), 304

Return of October, The (1948), 300

Revere, Paul, 31

Revier Motion Picture Company, 193

Revier, Harry, 193, 206, 225

Rex Film Exchange, 92

Rex theater, Ogden, 85, 90

Rex theater, Salt Lake City, see Bungalow theater, Salt Lake City

Rey, Alvino, 27

Reykjavik, Iceland, 109

Reynolds v. United States (1879), 18, 44

Reynolds, Dan, 27

Reynolds, Debbie, 289

Reynolds, George, 44, 320, 370

Reynolds, Lynn, 132

Reynolds, Scott, 37

Rhode Island, 349

Rhodes, Cecil, 337

Rhys, Jean, 150

Ricalton, James, 51

Rice, Henry Grantland, 255

Rich, Ben E., 168

Rich, Charles C., 149, 298

Richard III (ca. 1593), 35

Richard Loraine, 157

Richards, George W., 215

Richards, Harriet, 47

Richards, LeGrande, 283, 342, 262, 381, 385, 389

Richards, Melvin R., 345

Richards, Stephen L., 105-106, 215-216, 361, 364-365, 372, 377, 401

Richards, Wayne, 410

Richards, Willard, 37, 302

Richardson, F. H., 96

Richardson, Sullivan C., 327-328, 403-404

Richey, Walter, 93

Richfield, UT, 120-121, 316, 322-323

Richmond, UT, 284

Ricks College, see Brigham Young University-Idaho

Riddell, R. J., 80

Riders of the Frontier (1939), 279

Riders of the Purple Sage (1912 book), 10, 157

Riders of the Purple Sage (1918), 181, 187, 222, 244

Riders of the Purple Sage (1925), 183, 244

Riders of the Purple Sage (1931), 326

Riess, Jana, 34

Rigby, ID, 127

Rigdon, Sidney, 152

Riggs, Frank, 32

Rigolot, Albert-Gabriel, 48

Riley, I. Woodbridge, 158

Rin Tin Tin (fictional character), 113

Rio Conchos (1964), 139

Rio Grande (1950), 139

Rip Van Winkle (1903), 79

Riptide (1934), 308

Riskin, Robert, 120

Index

Rite of Spring, The, 434

River, The (1938), 250

Riverside Memorial Chapel, New York City, 285

Riverside, CA, 124

RKO Pictures, 273, 275, 278, 284-285, 291, 298-299, 355, 383, 427

road shows, 35, 102, 375

Road to Panama (1946), 328

Robe, The (1953), 127

Robert Hall Clothes, 421

Robert Montgomery Presents (television series, 1950-57), 303

Roberts, B. H., 51, 101, 144, 156, 207, 215, 219, 242, 315-318, 323, 337, 345-346, 357

Robin Hood (1922), 107

Robin Hood (1938), 390

Robin Hood (1973), 296

Robinson Crusoe (1903), 79

Robinson, Casey, 306

Robinson, Edward, 120

Rochester, NY, 127, 180

rock and roll, 28

Rockville, UT, 86

Rockwell, Orrin Porter, 153, 262-263

Rocky Mountain Moving Picture Company, 192

Rocky Mountain Riders Jacksonville (1898), 142

Rocky Mountain Riders Rough Riding (1898), 142

Rocky Mountain Riders, see Rough Riders

Rocky Mountains, 16, 110, 142, 205

Rodin, Auguste, 24, 31, 49

Roelsgaard, Jenny, 166

Rogell, Albert, 133

Rogers, Ginger, 235, 285

Rogers, H. L., 56

Rogers, Jean, 263

Rogers, Roy, 244, 307

Rogers, Thomas F., 36

Rogers, Will, 107, 136

Roll Wagons Roll (1940), 326

Roman Catholics, Roman Catholicism, 20, 58, 115, 124, 178, 241, 254, 273, 284, 295, 349, 367, 383, 398

Romance of Mormonism, The (unmade), 193

Romance of the Utah Pioneers, The (1913), 172-173, 193

Romance of Transportation in Canada, The (1952), 310-311

Rome, Italy, 19, 56, 199

Romero, Cesar, 265

Romney, George S., 362

Romney, George W. 306, 362

Romney, Gertrude, 209

Romney, Lenore, 306

Romney, Marion G., 186, 362

Romney, Mitt, 21, 306

Romney, Orson Douglas, 211

Rooney, Mickey, 303

Roosevelt, Franklin Delano, 222, 356, 375, 414

Roosevelt, Theodore, 100, 131, 142, 148, 222, 286, 293, 356-357, 375, 414

Roosevelt, UT, 287, 298

Rose, Ernest D., 338

Rosher, Charles, 178

Rosson, Richard, 124

Rotary Club, 87, 378

Rough Riders, 142-143

Rough Riders and Army Mules (1898), 142

Rough Riding (1898), 142

Roughing It, 155

Roughly Speaking (1945), 305

Roxy Theatre, New York City, 265

Royal Academy of Art, Copenhagen, 39

Royal Baking Powder Company, 284

Royall, Paul F., 400, 409

Rubber River (1946), 328

Rubens, Paul, 157

Rudd, Clive, 340

Rudd, Farrest, 340

Rudd, Paul, 4

Rugged Road to Cape Horn (1947), 328

Ruling Passion, The (1922), 113

Run, Cougar, Run (1972), 139

Russell, Isaac, 169

Russell, Keri, 3

Russell, Lillian, 35

Russia, 30, 56-57, 196, 294, 297, 338, 427

Russo-Japanese War (1904-05), 79

Rwanda Film Commission, 140

Sacagawea, 399

Sacred Grove, 14, 331, 334, 349

Safford, AZ, 197

Sahara (1919), 87

Said, Edward, 159

Saint Helena, 55

Salia, Peter, 248

Saint John the Baptist Preaching (sculpture), 24

Saito, Yuki, 3

Sal of Singapore (1930), 114

Salt Lake City Band, 26

Salt Lake City Company of Rocky Mountain Riders (1898)

Salt Lake City Stock Company, 123

Salt Lake City, UT, 4-5, 16-18, 20-21, 28, 30-31, 35, 37, 43, 46-47, 49-51, 53-55, 58, 64, 66, 68, 71, 74, 76-77, 79-93, 95-97, 99, 102, 104, 111, 113-115, 118-125, 128-131, 139, 143, 148, 157, 160, 163-164, 179, 184, 190, 192-193, 198-199, 201, 203-208, 214-217, 220, 223-226, 251-255, 257-258, 262-265, 279-281, 288-290, 292, 302-305, 312, 314-315, 317-319, 322, 325-326, 330, 332, 334-336, 338, 340-342, 344, 346-348, 350, 352, 354, 356-357, 359-361, 365, 372, 376, 378, 380, 387, 391, 397, 399-400, 402-406, 413, 422, 424-426, 428, 437-438

Salt Lake City, Utah, and its Surroundings (1912), 160

Salt Lake Commercial Club, 167-169

Salt Lake Diversions (1944), 252-253

Salt Lake Eighteenth Ward, 103, 191

Salt Lake Eleventh Ward, 121

Salt Lake Fifteenth Ward, 56

Salt Lake Film Society, 85

Salt Lake Fourteenth Ward, 56

Salt Lake Fourth Ward, 58

Salt Lake Herald, 56, 57, 73-74, 86, 92, 114, 145

Salt Lake Herald-Republican, 104

Salt Lake High School, 124

Salt Lake Opera Company, 90

Salt Lake Raiders (1950), 244

Salt Lake Seventeenth Ward, 57

Salt Lake Sixteenth Ward, 57

Salt Lake Tabernacle, 27, 29, 31, 58, 116, 249, 369

Salt Lake Telegram, 213

Salt Lake Telegraph, 119, 206

Salt Lake Temple, 23, 29, 44, 46-48, 60, 66, 84, 121, 138, 158, 163, 194-195, 204, 208, 217, 249, 340, 357-358, 365, 413, 429, 432-433, 435

Salt Lake Theatre, 35-36, 43, 55, 58, 71, 78, 87, 97, 104, 124, 197, 208-209, 230, 318, 331, 347

Salt Lake Trail (1926), 184

Salt Lake Tribune, 77, 104, 142, 145, 194, 201, 213, 226, 229, 318, 437

Salt Lake Twelfth Ward, 208

Salt Lake Twentieth Ward, 56, 59

Salt Lake Twenty-fourth Ward, 114

Salt Lake Twenty-second Ward, 57

Salt Lake Valley, 16-17, 26, 149, 198, 200, 208, 220, 262, 279, 326, 349, 380, 397, 404, 417

Salt Palace, Salt Lake City, 54, 79

Saltair Pavilion 77-78, 214, 251

Index

Sam T. Jack's Theatre, Chicago, 157

Samaké, Niankoro Yeah, 20

Samoa, 19, 218, 433

Sampson, O. T., 192

Samuel Goldwyn Company, 285

Samuelsen, Eric, 36-37, 324

Samuelson Films, 174-175, 188

Samuelson, George B., 174-175, 188

San Bernardino, CA, 18, 280

San Diego, CA, 243, 279-281, 304, 369, 398

San Fernando Stake, 295

San Francisco (1936), 308

San Francisco Chronicle, 114

San Francisco Examiner, 114

San Francisco, CA, 16, 39, 63, 81, 93, 115-116, 121, 128-129, 142, 167, 197, 240, 252, 265-266, 268, 290, 305, 369

San Juan County, Utah, 140

Sanders, James, 344

Sandlot, The (1993), 131

Sandow the strongman, 74

Santa Barbara, CA, 340

Santa Clause, The (1994), 308

Santa Monica Second Ward, 270

Santa Monica, CA, 6, 136, 214-215, 270, 283

Santaquin, UT, 86

São Paulo, Brazil, 338

Saratoga (fairground), 54

Saratov Approach, The (2013), 12

Sarave, C. K., 57

Sarnoff, David, 128

Sarris, Andrew, 272

Sarver, Charles, 178

Saskatchewan, 359

Satan, 46

Satchwa General Amusement Enterprises Company, 206

satellites, satellite broadcasts, 3, 9, 69, 219, 286, 372, 386

Saturday Evening Post, 136, 328

Saturday's Warrior (2016), 12

Saturday's Warrior (play, 1974), 27

Saunders, John Monk, 120

Savage, Charles R., 37, 56, 194, 205, 207

Savage, Ralph, 194

Scandinavia, 201

Scaramouche (1923), 125

SCERA, 375-376, 388

Schafer, George, 285

Schenck, Joseph, 257

Schmidt, Aage, 166

Schmidt, Helmut, 11

Schneider, C. F., 79

Schoedsack, Ernest, 300

School of the Prophets, 237

Schramm, F. C., 183

Schreiner, Alexander, 91

Schubert, Franz, 90

Science Fiction Theatre (television series, 1955-57), 308

Scientologists, Scientology, 21

sciopticon, see magic lantern,

Scorsese, Martin, 301

Scotland, 20, 109, 131, 360, 407

Scott, Lizabeth, 407

Scott, Ridley, 139

Scottsbluff, NE, 399

Scout in the Forest, The (1948), 386

Scout Trail to Citizenship, The (1948), 386

Scoville, Kenneth, 227

Scowcroft, Albert, 84, 93, 206

Screen Actors Guild, 305

Screen Gems, 294

Screenland, 268, 288

Scriabin, Alexander, 127

seagulls, 18, 134, 246, 253, 255, 257, 262, 264, 269, 344, 398, 410

Sealed (unmade), 246

Sealed Women, 184

Search for Tomorrow (television series,

1951-86), 303

Searchers, The (1956), 138

Seattle, WA, 108, 113, 193, 266, 302, 348, 418

Seberg, Jean, 4

Second Great Awakening, 14, 68

Second International Hygiene Exposition in Dresden (1930), 368

Second Manifesto, 143, 145

Second Ward, Liberty Stake (Salt Lake City), 342

Secret Garden, The (1949), 270

Secret Storm, The (television series, 1954-68), 303

Security National Pictures, 134, 325

See It Now (television series, 1951-58)

Seitz, George B., 138

Selig Polyscope Company, 170

Selig-Tribune, 190

Selznick, David, 300

seminaries, see Church Educational System

Sennett, Mack, 120-121

September Dawn (2007), 283

Sermon, Wayne, 27

Serpent of the Nile (1953), 300

Seurat, Georges, 48

Seventh Seal, The (1957), 389

Seventy, see Quorums of the Seventy

Sevigny, Chloë, 4

Seville (1992), 311

Seyfried, Amanda, 4

Seymour, Jane, 4

Shakers, 14

Shakespeare, William, 22, 48, 112, 134, 315, 317, 406-407

Shanghaied (1912), 162

Sharon Stake, 375-376

Sharon, VT, 333-334

Sharp, Ida, 340

Sharp, Ivor, 417

Sharp, June Bennion, 337, 340

Sharp, Marianne Clark, 340

Sharp, Thomas, 152

Sharpsteen, Ben, 293

Shaw, Joseph, 432-433, 435

She Stoops to Conquer (play, 1773), 36

She Wore a Yellow Ribbon (1949), 138, 273

SHeDAISY, 27

Sheffield, England, 172

Shepherd of the Hills, The (1926), 132

Shepherd of the Hills, The (1941), 376

Sherman, Harry, 246

Shipler, James, 38

Shipley, W. E., 82

Shipman, Ernest, 198, 200-201

Shipman, Nell, 196, 196

Short Creek, AZ, 247

Short, B. F., 104

Short, C. A., 184

Shubert Theatre, see Lyric Theatre, Salt Lake City

Shumway, Leonard "Lee", 122

Siggurd, UT, 292

Sight and Sound, 272

Sign of the Cross, The (1932), 114

Sign of the Pagan (1954)

Signac, Paul, 48

Signal Productions, Inc., 373

Sillitoe, Linda, 33

Sills, Carlton T., 251

Silly Symphonies, 290, 292, 295, 427

Simi Valley, CA, 309

Simmons, Grant, 425

Simon, S. Sylvan, 270

Simpson, Homer (fictional character), 4

Simpson, Russell, 4, 224, 272, 274

Simpsons, The (television series, 1989-), 4

Sims, Harry A., 81

Singin' in the Rain (1952), 306

Index

Sirk, Douglas, 302

Sisson, Vera, 123

Sjöström, Victor, 249

Skladanowsky, Maximillian, 67

Skousen, W. Cleon, 425, 438

Sky Trooper (1942), 295

Skyscraper (1930), 114

Skywalker, Luke (fictional character), 1-2

Slaves in Bondage (1937), 247

Sleeping Beauty (1959), 296

Slover, Tim, 36

Small One, The (1978), 297

Smart Money (1931), 120

Smith, Alvin, 334

Smith, Andrew, 32

Smith, David A., 214-215, 319, 333-334m 352-356, 359, 361-363, 377, 389

Smith, Dennis, 32

Smith, E. Wesley, 215

Smith, Edna L. 215

Smith, Emma, 25, 29, 331-332

Smith, George Albert, 215, 220, 280-282, 331-332, 335, 340, 347, 396-401, 404, 407, 411, 415, 417-418, 428, 440-441

Smith, George Henry, 215

Smith, Hyrum, 16, 26, 29, 42-43, 72, 331-332, 399-400

Smith, Hyrum G., 215

Smith, Hyrum J.

Smith, Hyrum Mack, 215

Smith, John, 215

Smith, John Henry, 210, 215, 397

Smith, John Rowson, 41

Smith, Joseph F., 47, 63, 72, 77, 91, 143-148, 166, 171, 191-192, 194, 197-198, 203, 210-217, 231

Smith, Joseph, Jr., i, 14-16, 22-23, 25, 27-30, 32, 35, 39, 42-46, 49, 51, 60, 64, 66, 68, 98, 100, 116, 141, 152, 156, 158, 167, 195, 197-198, 202, 207-208, 218, 220, 251, 258, 260-262, 267, 330-331,

342, 347, 367, 369, 375, 399-400, 402, 409

Smith, Joseph, Jr., portrayed on film, 197-198, 202, 207, 218

Smith, Julina L., 215

Smith, Paul, 290

Smith, Robert, 44

Smith, Win, 292

Smith, Yeardley, 4

Smithfield, UT, 95

Smoke Signal (1955), 139

Smoky (1946), 135

Smoot-Hawley Tariff of 1930, , 148

Smoot, Harlow, 341

Smoot, Reed, 110, 117, 143-145, 148, 156, 168, 183, 190, 200, 210, 214-215, 240-241, 244, 249, 258, 341, 356, 390

Smoot, Zella, 341

Snake River, 225

Snedaker, R. Lloyd, 30

Snow White and the Seven Dwarfs (1937), 235, 290, 292, 294, 296, 302

Snow, Clifford G., 339

Snow, Eliza R., 25

Snow, Erastus, 335

Snowball Express (1972), 4

Snows of Kilimanjaro, The (1952), 307

Snowville, UT, 292

So You Think You Can Dance (television series, 2005-), 28

Social Advisory Committee, 105-106, 375, 383, 386

Social Hall, Salt Lake City, 35

Society of Motion Picture Engineers, 348

Soderbergh, Steven, 4

Soffe, Beth, 382

Sokolowsky, Brian, 206

Solomon's temple, Biblical building, 29

Somerset, England, 175

Song Car-Tunes films, 404

Song of Ceylon, The (1934), 250

Song of Love (1947), 304

Song of the Gringo (1936), 279

Sonne, Alma, 335

Sons of Perdition (2010), 247

Sons of Utah Pioneers, 279-280, 369, 403

Sorbo, Kevin, 4

Sorensen, Anton J. T., 201

Sorensen, Virginia, 33

Souls of Mettle (unmade), 245

sound films, 74, 126-127, 226, 290, 314, 319-320, 352, 377-378, 393, 410, 431

Soup to Nuts (1930), 122

Sousa, John Philip, 58

South Africa, 157, 171, 181, 183-184, 186, 294, 337, 368

South African Mission, 337, 340

South Carolina, 208, 256, 336

South Dakota, 65, 131, 188, 359

South Davis Stake, 332

South of Monterrey (1946), 328

Southern States Mission, 362

Southey, Trevor, 32

Southport, England, 175

Soviet Union, see Russia

Sowards, Anne, 34

Spanish Fork, UT, 42

Spanish-American War, 141, 155

Special Aids to Teaching and Making Lessons Live, 380

Spellbound (1945), 300

Spielberg, Steven, 140

Spike Jones Show, The (television series, 1954), 304

Spilsbury, Lem, 190

Spoilers of the Plains (1951), 307

Spokane, WA, 91, 104

Sprague, Leslie Willis, 71

Springdale, UT, 86

Springfield, MA, 357

Springville Museum of Art, 343

Springville, UT, 343, 387

Spry, William, 168-169, 192

Spy Killer, The (1969), 301

St. George Temple, 29, 46-47, 195, 435

St. George, UT, 131, 134, 247, 285, 305, 335, 343, 374

St. Johns, AZ, 334

St. Louis Stake, 284

St. Louis Times, 293

St. Louis World's Fair (1904), 79

St. Louis, MO, 41, 79

St. Paul, MN, 124

St. Petersburg, Russia, 199

Stagecoach (1939), 137, 258, 273, 277

Staiger, Janet, 229

Stallings, A. L., 315

Stallings, G., 323

Stallion Canyon (1948), 285

Standard Oil Company, 255

Stanford University, 114, 136

Stanford University Press, 136

Stanton, Bette L., 140

Stanton, Harry Dean, 4

Stapley, Delbert, 282, 335

Star theater, Price, 86

Star Theatre, Jerome, 86

Star Trek (2009), 131

Star Wars (1977), 1-2

Star Wars franchise, 1-2

Star Wars: Clone Wars (2003), 2

Starling, Robert, 201, 206

State Hall, San Diego, 280

Statue of Liberty, The, 49

Steamboat Willie (1928), 291, 292

Stebar, Jeff, 30

Stegner, Wallace, 391

Stephens, Evan, 26

Stephenson, Morris C., 89

stereo, 3, 127, 414

stereo view, see stereoscope

stereograph, see stereoscope

Index

stereophonic sound, see stereo

stereopticon, see magic lantern

stereoscope, 50

Sternberg, Josef von, 119

Steve Allen Show, The (television series), 305

Stevens, Robert Stringham, 337

Stevenson, Robert Louis, 115

Stewart, Anita, 125

Stewart, Douglas, 36

Stewart, Mahonri, 37

Stick of Joseph, The, 365

Stockholm, Sweden, 255, 338, 416

Stockholms-Tidningen, 416

Stockwell, Samuel B., 41

Stoddard, Haila, 305

Stoddard, John, 52

Stokowski, Leopold, 127, 413

Stone Mountain, GA, 31

Story of Alexander Graham Bell, The (1939), 262

Story of the Book of Mormon, The (1915), 59, 72, 83, 201-202, 204-205, 209, 211-212, 325

Story of the Book of Mormon, The (book, 1888), 44-45, 207, 212, 320, 370

Story of the Mormons, 158

"*Story Princess, The*", 419

"*Story Telling Time*", 419

Strand Theatre, see Mark Strand Theatre, New York City

Strangers on a Train (1951), 304

Strauss, Johann, 290

Strebel, George Lofstrom, 38

Streep, Meryl, 4

Strindberg, August, 36

Stroheim, Erich von, 125

Strong, Maude, 89

Studio Theatre, Salt Lake City, 252, 264

Study in Scarlet, A (1887 book), 3, 154, 174

Study in Scarlet, A (1933), 244

Study in Scarlet, A (France, 1915), 173-176, 187

Study in Scarlet, A (UK, 1914), 173-176, 187-188, 273

Study in Scarlet, A (USA, 1914), 173-174, 176, 187

Study in Skarlit, A (1915), 173, 175, 187

Study of Infant Behavior, The, 379

Stunt Man, The (1927), 122

Sugarhouse Park, Salt Lake City, 404

Sullivan, Dan, 43

Sullivan, Jean, 305

Summer Olympics (1936), 128

Summers, Don, 275, 297

Sun Also Rises, The (1957), 257

Sun Shines Bright, The (1953), 273

Sundance Film Festival, 2, 86, 140

Sunday Evening on Temple Square, 221, 408

Sunday School, 6, 25, 56-57, 59-60, 103-105, 109, 165, 195, 197, 202, 205, 216, 259, 280, 334, 351-353, 359, 370, 374, 376, 379-381, 386-387, 410, 424, 428

Sunderland, England, 165

Sunrise (1927), 120, 249, 326

Superman (fictional character), 235

Supreme Court, see United States

Surrey, England, 115, 345, 430

Susquehanna River, 32, 331

Sutter's Gold (1936), 112

Swain, Cora King, 121

Swain, Mack, 121, 190

Swanson, Connie Jean, 297

Swanson, William H. "Billy", 82-83, 92, 95, 168-170

Sweden, 152, 161, 184, 215, 290, 297, 338, 368, 405, 416

Swedish Mission, 338

Swindle, Liz Lemon, 39

Swiss Temple, see Bern Switzerland Temple

Swiss-Austrian Mission, 431, 434

Switzerland, 337, 431-432, 434-435

Sydney, Australia, 181, 307

Sylvan Glen (fairground), 54

Symons, Charles W., 37

synchronized sound, see sound films

Syncopation (1929), 125

Syndicate Exchange, Inc., 227

Syracuse, NY, 180

Syria, 20

Systematic Program for Teaching the Gospel, The, 365

Tabernacle Choir, see Mormon Tabernacle Choir

Tabernacle, Biblical building, 29

Tabernacle, see Salt Lake Tabernacle

Tabernacle organ, 31, 116, 249, 251, 331, 379, 403-404, 406, 413-414, 417,

Tacoma, WA, 113

Tahiti, 337

Taiwan, 19

Tale of Two Cities, A (1917), 182

Talk of the Town, The (1942), 289

Talmage, James E., 55-60, 101, 107, 109, 143, 184, 194, 198, 202, 207, 215, 222, 357

Taming of the Shrew, The, 113, 208

Tapp, Irene, 344

Tapp, Orland Lavell "O. L.", 344

Tartakovsky, Genndy, 2

Tarzan, the Ape Man (1959), 308

Taylor, Alma, 161, 370

Taylor, Elizabeth, 289

Taylor, John, 18, 218, 331

Taylor, John W., 145

Taylor, Miriam, 419

Taylor, Samuel W., 33

Taylor, Zack, 38

Taza, the Son of Cochise (1954), 139

Te Puea Herangi, 337

Teaching Film Custodians, Inc., 270

Teasdel, Mary, 47

Tec-Art Studios, 245

Technicolor, 134, 137, 235, 252-253, 277, 289, 300, 320, 350-351, 371, 386

Teddington, England, 184

Teichert, Minerva, 39

telegraph, 68, 85, 221, 240,

television, 3, 6, 8-9, 11, 21, 23, 28, 94, 110, 122, 127-129, 131, 134-135, 137, 139, 219, 247, 254-255, 278, 283-287, 291, 299-306, 308-309, 313, 319, 324, 372-374, 380, 389, 393, 409, 411, 413-423, 429, 437-438

Telford, John, 38

Tempe, AZ, 28

Temple Block, see Temple Square

temple endowment, see endowment ceremony

Temple Square, 32, 35, 39, 54, 56, 58, 79, 87, 108-109, 122, 209, 213, 221-222, 229, 251-252, 332, 335, 339-340, 358, 368-369, 380, 390, 403-405, 408-409, 412, 417, 433

Temple Square (1949), 408-410, 413

Temple, Shirley, 270

temples, art in, 45-49

Ten Commandments, The (1923), 320

Ten Commandments, The (1956), 289

Ten Who Dared (1960), 139

Ten Women for One Husband (1905), 144

Tennessee, 340

Tennessee Valley Authority, 250

Tenting Tonight on the Old Camp Ground (1943), 244

Terrible Frost, The, 209

Tess of the Storm Country (1922), 107

Texas, 109, 131, 170, 334, 369

Thanhouser Film Corporation, 112, 123

That Lass o' Lowrie's, 114

Thatcher, George, Jr., 318

Index

Thatcher, Leora, 302-303

Thatcher, Moses, 302, 318

Thaumatrope, 50

Thayer, Douglas, 33

Theater Candy Distributing Company, 312-313

Thelma and Louise (1991), 131, 139

Theobald, J. A., 139, 274

They Call Me Trinity (1970), 190

They Won't Forget (1937), 303

Think and Grow Rich, 321

Thiriot, Richard Vernon, 340, 344

Thirtieth International Eucharist Conference, 349

This Is Cinerama (1952), 414

This Is the Place (1947), 403-405

This Is the Place Monument, 31, 251, 397-398, 400-401

This Island Earth (1955), 308

Thomas, Charles J., 26

Thomas, Lowell, 252, 414

Thompson, Beckie, 419-420

Thompson, Kristin, 71

Thompson, Marshall, 272

Three Caballeros, The (1944), 295

Three Little Pigs, The (1933), 250-251

Three Musketeers, The (1921), 107-108

Three Musketeers, The (1935), 302

Three Stooges, 5, 122

Three Stooges Meet Hercules, The (1962), 5

Three Witnesses Monument, 215-216

Through Death Valley, or the Mormon Peril, 157, 164

Through the Breakers (1928), 120

Thunder Town (1946), 244

Thurman, Mary, 120-121

Thurman, Victor, 121

Tian Zhuangzhuang, 10

Tiffany and Company, 49

Tilly and the Fire Engines (1911), 161

Tilly and the Mormon Missionary (1911), 161, 173, 370

Tilly's Party (1911), 161

Timbuktu (1959), 125

Time magazine, 28, 233, 263

Time, Inc., 254, 427

Times and Seasons (blog), 34

Times and Seasons (periodical), 331

Times Square, New York City, 84, 157, 318

Tiomkin, Dmitri, 414

Titanic, 172, 193

Tithing, 65, 68, 172, 233, 238, 254, 374, 386

Toast of New York, The (1937), 303

Tobin, Maurice, 90

Todd, Thelma, 134

Tolstoy, Leo, 13

Tonga, 19-20, 38, 338

Tongues of Men, The (1915), 117

Tony Awards, 3, 134

Topper (1937), 113

Toronto, Wallace Felt, 337

Torrey, Jay L., 141-142

Touch of Evil (1958), 306

Touched by an Angel (television series, 1994-2003), 131

Toulouse-Lautrec, Henri de, 48

Toumanova, Tamara, 307

Tourneur, Jacques, 125

Tower Theater, Salt Lake City, 85

Towering Wonders of Utah (1922), 190

Toy Story franchise, 3

Tracy, Spencer, 136, 261

Trader Horn (1931), 304

Tragedy of Thompson Dunbar, A Tale of Salt Lake City, The, 155

Trail and Trials of the Mormon Pioneers (unmade), 314-315

Trailer in the Pines (1959), 343

transcontinental railroad, 17, 33, 43, 50, 53, 72, 98, 130, 237, 390-391

Transformers: Age of Extinction (2014), 138

Transitions (1986), 311

Trapped by the Mormons (1922), 117, 160-161, 173, 184-187, 191, 218, 250, 282

Trapped by the Mormons (2005), 185

Trapped in Tia Juana (1932), 304

Trapper John, M.D. (television series, 1979-86), 304

Trek: The Movie (2018), 279

Trent & Wilson, 81, 83, 92

Trial of Billy Jack, The (1974), 138

Trial of Joan of Arc, The, 302

Triangle Film Corporation, 92, 121

Tribute to Faith (1947), 401

Trip Through the Emerald Isle, A, 43

Trip to Salt Lake City, A (1905), 144, 146-149, 160, 173 189

Trip to the Moon, A (1902), 79

Trip to Utah, A (1907), 160

Tripplehorn, Jeanne, 4

Trotti, Lamar, 258-260, 267

Trouble in Texas (1937), 243, 279

Truman, Harry S., 286-287, 339, 406

Trumbo, Isaac, 66

Tu Books, 34

Tuacahn Center for the Arts, 134

Tullidge, Edward William, 36

Tullidge, John, 26, 39

Tumblr, 34

Tunisia, 349

Turner, Glen H., 343-344

Tuttle, S. Adella, 74, 79

Twain, Mark, 151, 155

Twelve Apostles, see Quorum of the Twelve Apostles

Twelve O'Clock High (1949), 257

Twentieth Century-Fox, 71, 84, 92, 118, 132-134, 181-183, 236, 244, 246, 249, 252, 256-260, 265-266, 270, 273, 284, 288, 291, 307, 314, 326, 328, 427

Twenty-ninth Ward, Riverside Stake, 341-342

Twilight franchise, 3, 33

Twilight in the Sierras (1950), 307

Twilight Zone, The (television series, 1959-64), 309

Twin Falls, ID, 291

Twitter, 69

Tyler, Parker, 385

U.S. Grant Hotel, San Diego, 280

Uchtdorf, Dieter F., 20

Udall, Brady, 33

Uintah Mountains, UT, 323, 342

Ukraine, 19

Uncertain Glory (1944), 305

Uncle Moses (1932), 320

Uncle Tom's Cabin (1903), 79

Uncle Tom's Cabin (book), 154

Under the Gaslight, 36

Undercurrent (1946), 298

Underwood & Underwood, 50-51

Union and Central Pacific Railroad, see Union Pacific Railroad

Union Pacific (1939), 71, 134, 390-391

Union Pacific Railroad, 74-75, 86, 132, 390-391, 393

Unitarians, Unitarianism, 52

United Artists, 97, 125, 137

United Kingdom, 19, 109, 164, 184, 244, 250, 371

United Order, economic communalism, 64-65, 237

United Productions of America, 308

United Services Organizations, 305

United States Air Force, 306, 358

United States Army, 141-143, 206, 224, 246, 279, 295, 339-340, 372, 381, 414-415

United States Army Signal Corps, 372

United States Army Special Services

Index

radio network, 414

United States Capitol Building, 32, 145

United States Civil Service Commission, 286

United States Coast Guard, 301

United States Congress, 21, 65-66, 132, 141, 144-145, 148, 157, 168, 208, 242, 318, 356, 375

United States Department of Agriculture, 255

United States Department of the Interior, 132, 406

United States Federal Communications Commission,

286-287, 416-417

United States Federal Radio Commission, 286

United States House of Representatives, 144, 318

United States Library of Congress, 146

United States National Park Service, 132, 327, 341

United States Naval Academy, 128

United States Navy, 273, 302, 307, 424

United States of America, 15-21, 30, 40, 54-55, 62, 64, 66-68, 78-79, 92, 96, 98-99, 106, 110, 121, 141, 145, 148, 154, 158-160, 163, 166-167, 171, 173-174, 176, 180, 187, 193, 200, 213, 220, 222, 234-235, 241-242, 245, 250, 254, 266, 273, 279, 287, 294, 303, 320, 334, 341, 346, 356, 358, 367-368, 371-372, 381-382, 414-416, 419, 424, 430, 432

United States Office of Civilian Defense, 424

United States Office of Public Buildings and Public Parks,

286

United States Patent Office, 129

United States Senate, 144-145, 148, 168, 242, 356, 375

United States Supreme Court, 18, 44, 291

United States War Production Board, 312

Universal Studios, 82, 92, 113-114, 119, 122-125, 134, 175, 211, 245, 251, 257, 298

Universal Weekly, 114

Universe (1960), 309-311

University of California, Los Angeles, 281, 300-301, 305, 407

University of Chicago, 126

University of Kansas, 386

University of Miami, 301

University of Southern California, 288

University of Utah, 24, 51, 55, 106-107, 120, 125, 131, 136, 288, 290, 295, 302-303, 306, 345, 355, 360, 376

Unusual Pictures, 247

Up for Murder (1931), 251

Updike, Lisle Chandler, 334-335

Uprising of the Utes, The (1910), 160

Urge Within, The (1928), 206

Urrutia, Benjamin, 2

Urry, Francis L., 404

Uruguay, 20, 345, 408

USO, see United Services Organizations

USS Saginaw Bay, 367

USSR, see Russia

Utah, 16-20, 23, 26-27, 30-31, 33, 35, 37-40, 42-45, 47, 50-53, 55, 58-60, 63-68, 71-79, 81-83, 86, 88-89, 91-99, 104, 106, 108-112, 114-115, 117-118, 121-124, 127, 129-137, 139-143, 145-147, 153, 162, 164, 166-168, 171-172, 174-175, 179-185, 188, 190, 192-203, 205-209, 211, 214, 216-218, 224-226, 229, 236, 240-241, 243-245, 247-249, 251-253, 255-256, 263, 265, 271, 273-274, 279-281, 284-286, 288-290, 295, 298-301, 303, 305-306, 309, 312-313, 315-316, 318, 321, 323-328, 331-333, 335-336, 338-339, 341-344, 356, 359, 360, 367, 369-371, 373, 375, 376, 378, 396-398, 400, 402, 404-407, 414-416, 420, 430-431, 435, 441

Utah (1906 play), 157

Utah (1945), 244

Utah (unmade), 246

Utah Amateur Movie Club, 342-344

Utah Capitol Building, 225, 340, 348-349, 351

Utah Centennial celebration, 396-408

Utah Centennial Commission, 397, 405

Utah Cine Arts Club, 342-344

Utah Copper Company, 251

Utah Department of Publicity & Industrial Development, 139, 405-406

Utah Film Commission, 140

Utah Genealogical and Historical Magazine, 102

Utah Kid, The (1930), 243-244

Utah Kid, The (1944), 243

Utah Lake, 54, 339, 344

Utah Manufacturers' Association, 192

Utah Motion Picture Company, 192

Utah Moving Picture Company, 195-196, 198, 201

Utah Parks Company, 132-133

Utah Pioneer Trails and Landmarks Association, 398-399

Utah Productions, 206

Utah Radio Products Company, 224

Utah Savings and Trust Building, Salt Lake City, 209

Utah Shakespeare Festival, 134

Utah State Agricultural College, see Utah State University

Utah State Fair, 86, 252

Utah State National Bank, 233

Utah State Parks and Recreation Commission, 376

Utah State Tourist and Publicity Council, 343

Utah State University, 284

Utah Symphony Orchestra, 229

Utah Territorial Legislature, 64

Utah theater, Ogden, 85

Utah Theatre Company, 206

Utah Theatre, Salt Lake City, 205, 265, 390, 406

Utah Trail (1938), 244, 279

Utah Trail, The (1942), 343

Utah Trails and Landmarks Association, 332

Utah Valley, UT, 85, 205, 343, 387

Utah Wagon Train (1951), 244

Utah War, 17, 246

Utah-The Rainbow Land (1949), 255

Utah-Grand Canyon Transportation Company, 132

Utah, statehood, 18, 52, 63, 65-66, 141, 208

Utah: The Center of Scenic America (1950), 255

Ute Native American tribe, 111, 160, 327

Uxmal, Mexico, 357

Vaasa, Finland, 338

Valentino, Rudolph, 115-116, 118, 387

Valley of the Dolls (1967), 72

Valley of Triumph (1947), 404-405, 409, 413, 441

Vampire Bat, The (1933), 120

Van Dyke, W. S., 308

Van Gogh, Vincent, 48

Van Sickle, Selah, 45

Van Voorhis, Westbrook, 254

Vandercook & Co., 44

Vanishing American, The (1925), 137-138

Vanishing Private, The (1942), 295

Variety, 78, 80, 87, 96-97, 177, 185, 245, 249, 350

Varney, Arthur, 206

Varsity Theatre, Brigham Young University, 388-389

Vaudeville, 76-78, 80, 85-86, 89, 93, 97, 103, 108, 119, 121, 312, 421

Venice Film Festival, 310

Index

Venice Theater, Nephi, 85

Vermilion Cliffs National Monument, 326

Vermont, 14, 334, 356, 375

Victim of the Mormons, A (Mormonens Offer, 1911), 72, 147, 160-171, 191, 195-196, 241

Victory Theater, Salt Lake City, 226

video games, 3, 138

Vidor, Charles, 298

Vidor, King, 118, 124, 270

Vietnam War, 19

Viking Corporation, 403

Villa Theatre, Salt Lake City, 80

Villa, Pancho, 190, 270, 327

Vineyard, UT, 339

Virgin of Stamboul, The (1920), 87

virtual reality, 23

visitors' centers, 9, 108-109, 372, 405, 441

Vitagraph, 89, 190, 320

Vitascope, 74-76

Voight, Jon, 4

von der Esch, Leigh, 140

W. & J. Sloane, 284

Wackiest Ship in the Army, The (1960), 388

Wadsworth, Glass & Co., 55

Wagner, Richard, 90, 317

Wagon Master (1950), 139, 228, 236, 248, 256, 271-278, 281, 298, 325, 389, 441

Wagon Train (television series, 1957-65), 278, 301, 308

Wales, 122, 359-360

Walk in the Sun, A (1945), 301

Walker Brothers' Grand Opera House, Salt Lake City, 66

Walker, Ann Agatha, 150

Walker, Lillian, 206

Walker, Paul, 3

Walker, Robert, 304

Walsh, Raoul, 305, 314

Walt Disney Company, 2-3, 5, 139, 285, 290-298, 411, 423-425, 427-428, 434, 439

Walter, John, 344

Walton-on-Thames, England, 370

Walton, Ivan R., 339

Walton, Rick, 33-34

Waltons, The (television series, 1971-81), 303-304

Wanderer, The, 157

War of the Worlds, 367

ward movie night, see Church film distribution

ward teaching, see home teaching

Ward, Artemus, 151, 155

Ward, J. H., 56-57

Ward, Thomas, 39

Warhol, Andy, 25

Warlock (1959), 130, 139, 159

Warner Brothers, 249, 282-284, 305-307, 427

Warner, George, 89

Warner, Matt, 244

Warren, Earl, 280

Warrens of Virginia, The (1915), 124

Wasatch Mountains, 94, 292

Washington state, 65

Washington Branch, 341

Washington, D.C., 62-63, 127, 142, 145, 148, 207, 240, 287, 337, 357, 390,

Washington, D.C. Temple, 343, 436

Washington, George, 58, 65, 302

Washington, Ned, 291

Water Wheel (1958), 343

Waters of Lodore (1951), 343

Waters, John, 133

Watkins, Arthur V., 375-376

Watson's Cozy Corner, New York, 157

Watts, Isaac, 25

Way Out West (1937), 113

Wayne, John, 4, 243, 273, 277, 376,
Wayne, Willard, see Wertz, Alfred W.
Weber College Singers, 229
Weber State University, 64, 229, 302, 422
Weber, Lois, 125
Wedding March, The (1928), 120
Weekend Cruise (1950), 344
Weeks, William, 29-30
Weggeland, Danquart A., 39
Weight, F. Harmon, 113
Weihe, Willard, 89-91
welfare program, see Church Welfare Program, Committee
Welker, Roy A., 365-366
Welles, Orson, 235, 285, 367, 406-407
Wells, Daniel H., 121
Wells, Emmeline B., 33
Wells, Frank, 297
Wells, John, 215
Wells, Rulon S., 215
Wembley Central Film Studios, 117
Wembley National Studios, 117
Wendover, UT, 340
Wertz, Alfred W., 124
West German cinema, see German cinema
West Germany, 11, 431
West of Zanzibar (1928), 114
West Orange, NJ, 320
West, Mae, 248, 289
West, Paul, 178
Westbound Stage (1939), 134, 326
Westcott, Gordon, 304-305
Westcott, Helen, 305
Western Electric Company, 126, 378
Western Realty & Investment company, 209
Western States Mission, 362
Western Union, 93
Western Union (1940), 135

Western Wonderlands (1939), 370-371
Westinghouse Desilu Playhouse (television series, 1958-60), 308
Westward by Prairie Schooner, 270
"What of the Mormons?", 372
When George Hops (1928), 122
When the Clouds Roll By (1919), 107
Where Nothing Is Long Ago, 33
Where the Buffalo Roam (1938), 279
Where the Saints Have Trod (1947), 219, 397-401, 409, 413, 440
While the City Sleeps (1956), 300, 307
Whipple, Maurine, 33
Whistler, James Abbott McNeill, 48
Whitaker, Arnold, 327-328
Whitaker, Doris, 293, 426
Whitaker, Ferrin, 292-293
Whitaker, J. H., 405
Whitaker, Scott, 138, 293-294, 297, 425, 427-428
Whitaker, Wetzel "Judge", 8, 40-41, 138, 231, 284, 292-295, 297, 373, 389, 411, 424-428, 438-439, 441
White Line Fever (1975), 138
White Slave Girl, The (1907), 162
White Slave Trade, The (1910), 162-163
White Slave Trade's Final Victim, The (1911), 163
White, Andrew D., 13
White, Chrissie, 161
White, Essie, 139
White, George, 139-140, 274
Whiteman, Paul, 27, 120
Whitley, Thomas Farr, 38
Whitman, Stacy, 34
Whitmer, David, 152, 334
Whitmer, John, 152
Whitmer, Peter, 335, 372
Whitney, CA, 345
Whitney, Newel K., 331
Whitney, Orson F., 33, 48, 186, 215, 315-316, 347, 356

Index

Why We Fight film series, 424, 427

Whytock, Grant, 125

Wide Sargasso Sea, 150

Wide Wide World (television series, 1955-58), 414

Widtsoe, John A., 69, 101, 215, 259-260, 337, 360-364, 374, 437

Wife No. 19, or The Story of a Life in Bondage, 155

Wilcoxon, Henry, 245-246

Wild Horse Mesa (1925), 244

Wild Horse Mesa (1932), 244

Wild Horse Mesa (1947), 244

Wild Huntress, The, 154

Wild Oranges (1924), 124

Wild Water and Bouncing Boats (1957), 343

Wildfire (television series, 1986), 304

Wiles-Barre, PN, 357

Wilford C. Wood Museum, 331

Wilkins, Roy, 89

Wilkinson, Ernest L., 388, 437-439

Willard, Fred, 4

Willard, UT, 217

William Morris Circuit, 90

William Tell Overture, 290

Williams, Clarissa S., 215

Williams, LaMar S., 219, 330, 335-336, 396, 399-403, 405, 408-410, 425

Williams, Terry Tempest, 34

Willie handcart company, 16-17, 400

Willkie, Wendell, 255

Willoughby, Louis, 185

Willow (1988), 303

Wilshire Ward, Hollywood Stake, 427

Wilson, Carey, 249-250

Wilson, Don, 251

Wilson, G. H., 85

Wilson, Mellwood, 89

Wilson, Patrick, 4

Wilson, William A., 329

Wilson, Woodrow, 214, 241, 356-357

Windows of Heaven (1963), 386, 404

Winds of the Pampas (1928), 206

Windsor, Marie, 305

Wings of the West! (1940), 252

Winslet, Kate, 4

Winter Camping (1948), 386

Winter Olympics (2002), 21

Winter Quarters, NE, 16, 27, 32, 42, 216, 331-332, 399

Winters, Rebecca, 399

Winters, Shelley, 289

Wirthlin, Joseph L., 438-439

Wisconsin, 359

Wise, Frank S., 5, 219, 231, 235, 238, 282, 333, 335-336, 340, 370-372, 376-377, 381-382, 385, 389, 392-397, 399-405, 407-411, 417-419, 424-425, 428, 432-434, 440

Withers, Jane, 265

Wizard of Oz, The (1939), 235, 351

Woman of Affairs (1928), 118

women's suffrage, franchise, 18

Wonder Man (1945), 113

Wood, Daniel, 330, 356

Wood, Wilford C., 330-333, 335-336, 356, 375, 398

Woodbury, Ellen, 296,

Woodruff, Elias S., 220

Woodruff, Wilford, 18, 47, 60, 62-63, 141-145, 258

Woods Cross, UT, 279, 330

Woolley, Gordon R., 338

Woolley, James, 257

Woolley, Lorin, 247

Woolley, Taylor, 30

Word of Wisdom, 243, 299, 343, 360, 368, 370, 379-380, 383

Works Progress Administration, 376

World at Your Door, The (unmade), 229

World Film Corp., 95

World War I, 33, 105, 113, 118, 122, 174,

176, 215, 222, 257, 302

World War II, 18-19, 233, 255, 272, 284, 287, 307, 338-339, 346, 358, 367, 372, 376, 381, 392, 413, 419, 424

World's Columbian Exposition in Chicago (1893), 60-61, 108, 143, 242, 368

World's Fastest Indian, The (2005), 130

Worth Scouting For (1945), 343

Wrangell, Basil, 249

Wray, Fay, 3, 119-120, 206-207

Wren, Christopher, 29

Wright, Frank Lloyd, 29-30

Wright, Katherine, 207

Wright, Norma Jean, 425

Wylie, William W., 132

Wyoming, 39, 65, 76, 104, 108, 131, 142, 168, 272, 339, 370, 398-400

Xochicalco, Mexico, 358

Yankee Girl, The (1915), 117

Yearling, The (1946), 407

Yellowstone National Park, 53, 340-341

Yoda (fictional character), 1-2

York, England, 165, 186

Yosemite National Park, 340

You Are on Indian Land (1969), 311

You Can Teach It Better With Pictures, 380

You Can't Take It with You (1938), 289

Young Dr. Malone (television series, 1958), 303

Young Ladies Mutual Improvement Association, see
Mutual Improvement Association

Young Men's Mutual Improvement Association, see
Mutual Improvement Association

Young Rajah, The (1922), 115

Young Woman's Journal, 68

Young Women's program, see Mutual Improvement Association

Young, "Pop", 76

Young, Ann Elza, 155

Young, Brigham, 15-17, 26-27, 32, 35-36, 45-46, 58, 68, 98-99, 112, 114-116, 123, 129, 133, 153-157, 200, 208-209, 213, 218, 224, 229-230, 237-238, 245, 251-253, 257-258, 260-262, 265, 268-270, 282, 302, 331, 343, 349, 393, 404, 429-430

Young, Brigham, portrayed on film, 167, 174, 176, 188, 190, 196, 223, 228, 245-246, 260-261, 267-269

Young, Brigham S., 317

Young, Brigham, Jr., 141, 317

Young, Bryant S., 204

Young, Frank, 196

Young, George Cannon, 347

Young, Harold, 284

Young, J. H., Mrs., 79

Young, Joseph Don Carlos, 30, 341, 347

Young, Levi Edgar, 68, 104, 108, 197-199, 202, 210, 215, 224

Young, Mahonri, 31, 251, 341, 345, 397-398

Young, Margaret Blair, 33

Young, Mary Ann, 260, 262

Young, Richard W., 224

Young, Seymour B., 215

Young, Waldemar, 114

YouTube, 69, 329

Yucatán, Mexico, 357-358

Yukon, 193

Yuma, AZ, 280

Zanuck, Darryl F., 257-268

ZCMI, 204, 208, 238, 340, 421, 422

Zhang Yimou, 10

Ziegfeld Follies, 122

Zielinski, Kathy, 296

Ziemer, Charles, 93

Zimbabwe, 337

Zion Canyon/National Park, 131-132,

Index

215, 252-253, 326, 344, 370, 406

Zion, MO, 15, 28, 100

Zion, theological concept, 18, 22, 66, 68, 72, 141, 212, 220, 236, 392

Zion's Camp, 332

Zion's Savings Bank and Trust Company, 237

Zoetrope, 40, 50

Zudora (1914), 112

Zukor, Adolph, 94, 106, 177

Zulu (language), 19

Zuni Native American tribe, 334

Zworykin, Vladimir, 128